THE RESURRECTION

OF THE SON OF GOD

"The most monumental defense of the Easter heritage in decades.... *The Resurrection of the Son of God* marches through a clearly organized case that confronts every major doubt about Easter, ancient and modern."

Richard N. Ostling, Associated Press

CHRISTIAN ORIGINS AND THE QUESTION OF GOD

Volume Three

THE **RESURRECTION**

OF THE **SON OF GOD**

N. T. Wright

FORTRESS PRESS
Minneapolis

THE RESURRECTION OF THE SON OF GOD
Christian Origins and the Question of God, vol. 3

First North American edition published 2003 by Fortress Press.

Scripture quotations, unless otherwise noted, are either the author's own or from the New Revised Standard Version of the Bible, copyright © 1989 by the Division of Christian Education of the National Council of Churches in the U.S.A., and are used by permission.

Excerpts from John Updike's "Seven Stanzas at Easter," *Telephone Poles and Other Poems* (New York: Alfred A. Knopf), are quoted by permission of the author.

Cover graphic: Titian. Averoldi Polyptych. Brescia. Santi Nazzaro e Celso.

The Library of Congress has catalogued this series as follows:

Wright, N. T. (Nicholas Thomas)
    Christian Origins and the Question of God / N. T. Wright — 1st Fortress Press ed.
        p. cm.
    Includes bibliographical references and indexes.
    Contents: v. 1 The New Testament and the people of God — v. 2 Jesus and the victory of God.
    ISBN 0-8006-2681-8 (v. 1: alk. paper)
            0-8006-2682-6 (v. 2: pbk.)
            0-8006-3089-0 (v. 2: hardcover)
    1. God—Biblical teaching. 2. God—History of doctrines—Early Church ca 30–600. 3. Bible. N.T.—Theology. 4. Christianity—Origin. 1. Title.
    BS2398.W75 1992
    225.6—dc20   92-19348

ISBN 0-8006-2679-6 (paperback); 0-8006-3615-5 (hardcover)

The paper used in this publication meets the minimum requirements of American National Standard for Information Sciences — Permanence of Paper for Printed Library Materials, ANSI Z329.48-1984.

Manufactured in Canada
09

for Oliver O'Donovan and Rowan Williams

CONTENTS

PREFACE

I

This book started life as the final chapter of *Jesus and the Victory of God* (1996), the second volume in the series *Christian Origins and the Question of God*, of which the first volume is *The New Testament and the People of God* (1992). The present work now forms the third volume in the series. This is a departure from the original plan, and since people often ask me what is going on some explanation may be appreciated.

A few months before I finished work on *Jesus and the Victory of God* (hereafter *JVG*), Simon Kingston of SPCK came to see me to say that, since the covers for the book had already been printed, I had an absolute maximum number of pages available, and what did I propose to do? Had the work run its intended course, with the material in what is now the present book compressed (as I had foolishly thought I could compress it) into seventy pages or so, *JVG* would have been at least 800 pages long, and would have burst out of its own new covers, not a sight a middle-aged scholar wishes to see.

As providence would have it, I was at the same time turning over in my mind the choice of topic for the Shaffer Lectures at Yale Divinity School, which I was due to give in the Fall of 1996, shortly after the publication date for *JVG*. The topic was supposed to be something to do with Jesus. I had puzzled over how I might either compress material from the big book which would just have been published, or try to lecture on some aspect of Jesus I had not covered in the book (which I had hoped would be reasonably exhaustive; certainly I did not intend to leave out three lectures' worth of original material). The two problems solved each other: miss out the resurrection chapter from *JVG*, lecture on the resurrection in Yale, and turn the three lectures into a small book to join the present series, in between *JVG* and the originally projected third volume on Paul, which would now become Volume IV. (This had the unexpected result that some reviewers of *JVG* accused me of not being interested in, or not believing in, Jesus' resurrection. I trust that this accusation may now be laid gently to rest.)

The Shaffer lectures were exciting, for me at any rate. My hosts at Yale were warm in their hospitality to my wife and myself, and encouraging in their response, on top of the honour they had shown me by their invitation. But it was clear that each lecture needed expanding considerably. So, to help me towards what I still hoped would be a short book, I frequently chose the same topic when lecturing elsewhere in the next three years: the Drumwright Lectures at South-Western Theological Seminary in Fort Worth, Texas, the Bishop's Lectures at Winchester, the Hoon-Bullock Lectures at Trinity University in San Antonio, Texas, the DuBose Lectures at the University of the South in Sewanee, Tennessee, the Kenneth W. Clark Lectures at Duke Divinity School, Durham, North Carolina, and the Sprunt Lectures in Union Seminary, Richmond, Virginia. (The Sewanee version was published in the *Sewanee Theological Review* 41.2, 1998, 107–56; I have published other lectures and essays on the subject from time to time, details of which are in the Bibliography.) I gave similar lectures to the Princeton Theological Seminary Summer School at St Andrews; and I compressed the argument into a single lecture for various establishments, including St Michael's Seminary, Baltimore, the Pontifical Gregorian University in Rome, and Truett Seminary, Baylor University, Waco, Texas. I have grateful memories of all these institutions. Their hospitality was uniformly magnificent.

But the highlight, enabling me to lay out the material in much more detail and giving me space and time to ferret around and fill in lots of gaps, came when I was appointed to the MacDonald Visiting Chair at Harvard Divinity School for the Fall Semester of 1999. Suddenly, instead of three or four lectures, I had the chance to give more than twenty on the topic, to a large, intelligent and, in the best sense, critical student audience. Of course, I emerged from each lecture realizing that the material still deserved much more expansion. My initial dream of writing up this book as I went along (and my initial expectation that it would be a *small* book) was unrealizable. But I was able to lay the foundation for the present work far more deeply than before, in a wonderfully congenial setting. I am extremely grateful to my colleagues and friends in Harvard, and to Al MacDonald, the founder of the Chair, whose personal support and enthusiasm for my work has been a great encouragement. Thus, though the book has changed its shape considerably since late 1999, the seeds sown in Yale bore fruit in Harvard, fruit which in this book is brought at last to harvest. I trust my friends in both august establishments will not object to finding themselves thus associated with one another.

II

The book has reached its present length partly because, as I have worked over the material and read as much as I could of the voluminous secondary literature, it has seemed to me that all kinds of misconceptions about both the key ideas and the key texts have over the years become widely accepted. As with certain types of garden weed, there are occasions when the only thing to be done is to dig deeper to get right under the roots. In particular, it has become accepted within much New Testament scholarship that the earliest Christians did not think of Jesus as having been bodily raised from the dead; Paul is regularly cited as the chief witness for what people routinely call a more 'spiritual' point of view. This is so misleading (scholars do not like to say that their colleagues are plain wrong, but 'misleading' is of course our code for the same thing) and yet so widespread that it has taken quite a lot of digging to uproot the weed, and quite a lot of careful sowing to plant the seeds of what, I hope, is the historically grounded alternative. Readers may be glad that I have not had space to highlight more than a few examples here and there of what I take to be misleading views both of Judaism and of the New Testament. I have preferred to expound the primary sources, and to let them shape the book, rather than to offer a lengthy 'state of the question' and to allow that to dominate the horizon. (The first part of *Jesus and the Victory of God* provides a general background to the discussion.)

Just as the book could have grown considerably if I had entered into debate with, or even simply cited, all the writers from whom I have learned, whether in agreement or disagreement, it could easily have doubled in length if I had explored all the interesting-looking secondary roads that lead off this particular highway. There are lots of side-issues that get a cursory mention, if that. Those who continue to work on the Turin Shroud, for instance, may be disappointed to find no further mention of it here.[1] I am aware that I have annotated some discussions much more fully than others, and that in some cases a bare statement of my own view has had to stand in for the detailed debate with colleagues and friends that should ideally have taken place. This is so particularly in Part II, on Paul, for which I hope to make amends, to some extent at least, in the next volume in the series. My main concern here has been to lay out the large-scale argument which seems to me in urgent need of clear statement. I envisage the present book, unlike either of its predecessors, as essentially a simple monograph with a single line of thought, of which I provide an advance map in the first chapter. The shape of the argument is hardly novel, but the particular point of entry, namely, the study of the way in which 'resurrection', denied by pagans but affirmed by a good many Jews, was

[1] See e.g. Whanger and Whanger 1998.

both reaffirmed and redefined by the early Christians, has not, I think, been followed like this before. Nor has a similar range of material, some of it inaccessible to many readers, been made available in this way. I hope the book will contribute to the clarity of future discussions as well as to historical understanding and responsible faith.

Several introductory matters about style and indeed content are dealt with in the prefaces to *The New Testament and the People of God* (hereafter *NTPG*) and *JVG*. One fresh comment is called forth by questions I sometimes receive. I refer to the non-Jewish and non-Christian inhabitants of the ancient world as 'pagans' for the same reason as most ancient historians do: not intending it as in any way a term of abuse, but finding it the most convenient way to designate a large number of otherwise disparate peoples. The term is of course etic rather than emic (i.e. it was not, in our period at any rate, a term used by anyone to describe *themselves*, but reflects rather the perspective of others, in this case Jews and Christians, on the people in question). It has here a purely heuristic value.

Despite the anxiety of some, I have continued for the most part to write 'god' with a small 'g'. This is not an irreverence. It is to remind myself, as well as the reader, that in the first century, as increasingly in the twenty-first, the question is not whether we believe in 'God' (with it being assumed that we all know who or what that word refers to), but rather to wonder which god, out of the many available candidates, we might be talking about. When first-century Jews, and early Christians, spoke of 'the god who raises the dead', they were implicitly making a case that this god, the creator god, the covenant god of Israel, was in fact God, the one and only being to whom the word appropriately refers. Most of their contemporaries did not see it like that; not for nothing were the early Christians known as 'atheists'.[2] Even New Testament scholars, seeing the word 'God', can easily be tricked into making unwarranted assumptions about the identity of the being thus referred to – precisely the sort of assumptions that an investigation like the present one is meant to challenge. However, when I lay out the views of the early Christians, and quote from their writings, I shall often use the capital to indicate that the authors were making just this point, that the god they worshipped and invoked was in fact God. In the concluding chapters I shall begin to use the capital myself, as I did at the equivalent points in *JVG*, for reasons that I hope will become apparent. I hope this is not too confusing. The alternative is to adopt the standard usage and thus fail, for most readers most of the time, to alert them to the most important question which underlies this entire series.

One other vital matter must be mentioned at this point, since space has precluded fuller treatment in the body of the text.[3] I constantly run into

---

[2] cf. e.g. *Mt. Pol.* 9.2.
[3] I have expanded this point somewhat in 'In Grateful Dialogue' 261f. See e.g. below, 109, 253f.

loose talk about a 'literal' resurrection as opposed to a 'metaphorical' one. I know what people mean when they say that, but those words are unhelpful ways of saying it. The terms 'literal' and 'metaphorical' refer, properly, to *the ways words refer to things*, not to the things to which the words refer. For the latter task, the appropriate words might be 'concrete' and 'abstract'. The phrase 'Plato's theory of forms' *literally* refers to an *abstract* entity (in fact, a doubly abstract one). The phrase 'the greasy spoon' refers *metaphorically*, and perhaps also metonymically, to a *concrete* entity, namely the cheap restaurant down the road. The fact that the language is being used literally or metaphorically tells us nothing, in and of itself, about the sort of entities it is referring to.

When ancient Jews, pagans and Christians used the word 'sleep' to denote death, they were using a metaphor to refer to a concrete state of affairs. We sometimes use the same language the other way round: a heavy sleeper is 'dead to the world'. Sometimes, as in Ezekiel 37, Jewish writers used 'resurrection' language as a metaphor for concrete political events, in that case the return of the Jews from exile in Babylon. The metaphor enabled the prophet to *denote* the concrete event while *connoting* the idea of a great act of new creation, a new Genesis. As we shall see, the Christians developed their own fresh metaphorical usages, which likewise referred to concrete states of affairs. But most of the time those Jews and pagans who spoke of resurrection, whether they were affirming it (as the Pharisees did) or denying it (as the Sadducees did, along with the entire world of greco-roman paganism), used the word to refer to a hypothetical concrete event that might take place in the future, namely the coming-to-life in a full and bodily sense of those presently dead. Though the words they used (e.g. *anastasis* in Greek) had broader meaning (*anastasis* basically denotes the act of making something or someone stand or rise up, or of doing so oneself), they acquired the specially focused meaning of this 'rising' from the dead. Thus the normal meaning of this language was to refer, literally, to a concrete state of affairs. One of the main questions of this book is whether the early Christians, who were in so many ways cheerful and eager innovators, used the language of resurrection like that as well.

III

I am grateful to the many family members, friends, colleagues and lecture-audiences who have discussed this topic with me over the years. I have learnt much from many and hope to continue to do so. I am especially grateful to my beloved wife and children for their encouragement and support, not least to my son Dr Julian Wright for taking time from his own historical research to read right through the text and make dozens of helpful comments. One of the most extraordinary modes of encouragement came out of the blue through the invitation to write the libretto for Paul Spicer's *Easter Oratorio*, based on John 20 and 21. The work received its first performance at the Lichfield Festival in July 2000, and has since then been performed on both sides of the Atlantic, as well as being broadcast in part on BBC radio. Paul and I have both written about this experience in *Sounding the Depths*, edited by Jeremy Begbie (London: SCM Press, 2002). Working with Paul made me think about the resurrection from several new angles, and I cannot now read the Johannine Easter stories without thinking of his music all the time, and without an enormous sense of gratitude and privilege.

Having explained the delay in *JVG* by reference to a move of house and job, I find myself doing so again; our move to Westminster in 1999–2000 took time and energy, and inevitably slowed things down. That they have now speeded up again is due not least to the support of my new colleagues, particularly the Dean of Westminster, Dr Wesley Carr, and my fellow Canons; and also the cheerful assistance, in matters great and small, of the Canons' Secretary, Miss Avril Bottoms. On the technical side, Steve Siebert and the manufacturers of *Nota Bene* software are again to be congratulated on the magnificent product which has helped so many scholars to produce their own camera-ready copy, even for a work of this complexity. I am very grateful to several friends and colleagues who have read some or all of the manuscript and helped me to avoid mistakes; they are not, of course, to be blamed for those that remain. In particular, I thank Professors Joel Marcus, Paul House, Gordon McConville and Scott Hafemann; Drs John Day, Jason König, and Andrew Goddard; and several members of various faculties at Baylor University, Waco, Texas, notably Professors Stephen Evans, David Garland, Carey Newman, Roger Olson, Mikeal Parsons and Charles Talbert, each of whom provided searching critique and detailed comment as the book neared completion. Professor Morna Hooker generously lent me her own copy of a newly-published work so I could take note of it at the last minute. The many mistakes which remain are, of course, all my own work.

Pride of place in acknowledgment, though, goes this time to my publishers, SPCK, themselves. Having challenged me to take on a substantial programme of writing, they have provided excellent support, not only in the editorial department, but particularly in the shape of a research assistant. Dr Nicholas Perrin, himself a published scholar, has filled that role with tireless good cheer for the last two years, putting his own wide-ranging expertise at my disposal, ferreting out sources ancient and modern, providing a one-man equivalent of a university common room where I could try out ideas and get instant quality feedback, and functioning in general as helper, adviser, critic and friend. Working with him on an almost daily basis has been an intellectual and personal delight.

The dedication reflects a long-standing double debt of friendship and scholarship. I met Oliver O'Donovan (in a Hebrew class) on my first day in Oxford; his wise friendship, scholarly example and profound theological and philosophical understanding have been an inspiration ever since. I got to know Rowan Williams when we both returned to Oxford in 1986. Our shared teaching, and the many layers of friendship which surrounded it, are among my happiest memories of that time. Oliver and Rowan have themselves, of course, written distinguished books on the resurrection, and that alone would have justified my offering them this token of affection and respect. But when, on the day I wrote the final section of this book, it was announced that Rowan was to become the new Archbishop of Canterbury, that sense of justification turned to compulsion. Congratulations to him, and gratitude to them both.

N. T. Wright

Westminster Abbey

Part One

Setting the Scene

ἄνσχεο, μηδ' ἀλίαστον ὀδύρεο σὸν κατὰ θυμόν·
οὐ γάρ τι πρήξεις ἀκαχήμενος υἷος ἑοῖο,
οὐδέ μιν ἀνστήσεις, πρὶν καὶ κακὸν ἄλλο πάθῃσθα.

Bear up, and don't give way to angry grief;
Nothing will come of sorrowing for your son,
Nor will you raise him up before you die.

Homer, The Iliad, 24.549–51

אִם יָמוּת גֶּבֶר הֲיִחְיֶה

If mortals die, shall they live again?

Job 14.14

Chapter One

THE TARGET AND THE ARROWS

1. Introduction: The Target

The pilgrim who visits the Church of the Holy Sepulchre in Jerusalem faces several puzzles. Is this after all the place where Jesus of Nazareth was crucified and buried? Why is it inside the city walls, not outside as one had supposed? How does the present building relate to the original site? How did the place come to be so different from what the New Testament leads us to expect (a garden with a tomb in it, close to a hill called Golgotha)? And, even supposing this is roughly the right place, is this the right *spot*? Is this rocky outcrop, now enclosed within an upstairs chapel, actually the top of Golgotha? Is this marble slab really where the dead Jesus was laid? Is this highly ornate shrine really the site of the tomb? And – a different sort of question, but a pressing one for many visitors – why are different groups of Christians still squabbling about who owns the place? These puzzles, though, do not noticeably affect the appeal of the place. Despite archaeological, historical and ecclesiastical squabbles, the church retains its evocative and spiritual power. Pilgrims still flock to it in their hundreds of thousands.[1]

Some of them still question whether it all really happened. Did Jesus of Nazareth, they ask, really rise from the dead? Whether or not they realize it, they join a different throng on a different pilgrimage: the jostling, over-heated crowd of historians investigating the strange reports of events at the tomb of Jesus on the third day following his execution. Here they are confronted with a similar set of problems. The story of Easter, like the church at its supposed location, has been demolished and reconstructed again and again over the years. The tantalizing narratives in the gospels are as puzzling to the reader as the building is to the visitor. How do they fit together, if at all? What precisely happened? Which school of thought today, if any, is telling the story truly? Many have despaired of discovering what, if anything, happened on the third day after Jesus' crucifixion. Yet, despite perplexity and scepticism, billions of Christians around the world regularly repeat the

[1] For the details, see Murphy-O'Connor 1998 [1980]; Walker 1999.

original confession of Easter faith: on the third day after his execution, Jesus rose again.

So what did happen on Easter morning? This historical question, which is the central theme of the present book, is closely related to the question of why Christianity began, and why it took the shape it did.[2] This in turn is the fourth of five questions I set out in *Jesus and the Victory of God*, which proposed answers to the first three (where does Jesus belong within Judaism? what were Jesus' aims? and why did Jesus die?). (I hope to address the fifth question, why the gospels are what they are, in a subsequent volume.) The question of Christian origins is inevitably a question about Jesus himself as well as about the early church. Whatever else the early Christians said about themselves, they regularly explained their own existence and characteristic activities by speaking of Jesus.

It is remarkable but true that in order to determine what happened on one particular day nearly two thousand years ago we find ourselves obliged to call and cross-examine a wide variety of witnesses, some of whom are simultaneously being questioned by advocates of other answers to the question. The debate has frequently been bedevilled by oversimplifications, and to avoid this we shall have to set things out reasonably fully. Even so, there is no space for a full-scale history of research on the subject. I have chosen certain conversation partners, and regret that there was no room for more. My impression from reading the literature is that the primary sources themselves are not well enough known, or carefully enough studied. This book seeks to remedy that, without always noting the scholars who either agree or disagree.[3]

---

[2] See *JVG* 109–12.

[3] Substantial bibliographies on the resurrection, in addition to those in other works mentioned here, are available in e.g. Wissman, Stemberger, Hoffman et al. 1979; Alves 1989, 519–37; Ghiberti and Borgonovo 1993; Evans 2001, 526–9. A full-scale bibliography by G. Habermas is, I understand, due to be produced shortly. There have been several recent symposia on the resurrection: e.g. Avis 1993a; Barton and Stanton 1994; D'Costa 1996; Davis, Kendall and O'Collins 1997; Longenecker 1998; Porter, Hayes and Tombs 1999; Avemarie and Lichtenberger 2001; Mainville and Marguerat 2001; Bieringer et al. 2002. Cf. too *Ex Auditu* 1993. The major monographs with which I have been in implicit dialogue throughout include Evans 1970; Perkins 1984; Carnley 1987; Riley 1995; Wedderburn 1999; and, in rather different categories, Barr 1992; Lüdemann 1994 and Crossan 1998. (On Lüdemann see now Rese 2002.) Older works, notably Moule 1968; Marxsen 1970 [1968]; Fuller 1971, are presupposed (often with as much disagreement as agreement), but there has been little space for detailed interaction, any more than with recent continental scholarship, e.g. Oberlinner 1986; Müller 1998; Pesch 1999. On Marxsen and Fuller, see the useful critique in Alston 1997. I acknowledge a debt, too, to Gerald O'Collins, whose many works on the resurrection (e.g. 1973; 1987; 1988; 1993; 1995 ch. 4) have continued to stimulate, even where, again, I maintain some disagreements. I also here salute C. F. D. Moule, the opening remarks of whose 1967 monograph seem as relevant as ever. To the logical shape of his argument, though not its substance or in every respect its conclusions, I accord the sincerest form of flattery (cf. too Moule and Cupitt 1972).

As the overall title of the project indicates, and as Part I of the first volume explained, my intention is to write both about the historical beginnings of Christianity and about the question of god. I am, of course, aware that for over two hundred years scholars have laboured to keep history and theology, or history and faith, at arm's length from one another. There is a good intention behind this move: each of these disciplines has its own proper shape and logic, and cannot simply be turned into a branch of the other. Yet here of all places – with Christian origins in general, and the resurrection in particular – they are inevitably intertwined. Not to recognize this, in fact, is often to decide tacitly in favour of a particular type of theology, perhaps a form of Deism, whose absentee-landlord god keeps clear of historical involvement. Preserving this position by appeal to divine 'transcendence' is a way of restating the problem, not of settling it.[4] The mirror-image of this is the assumption of a rank supernaturalism whose miracle-working god routinely bypasses historical causation. Elsewhere on the map are various forms of pantheism, panentheism and process theology in which 'god' is part of, or closely related to, the space-time world and the historical process. To recognize the link between history and theology, therefore, is not to decide questions of history or theology in advance, but to give notice of the necessary many-sidedness of the topic.

This is near the heart of the multiple disagreements I find between myself and one of the major writers on the subject in the last twenty years, Archbishop Peter Carnley.[5] There seems to be an implicit argument in his work (and in that of some others) according to which (a) historical-critical scholarship has thoroughly deconstructed the events of the first Easter but (b) anyone attempting to engage with this scholarship on its own terms is told that to do so is to cut the resurrection down to size, to reduce it to a merely mundane level. Historical work, it seems, is fine, necessary even, as long as it comes up with sceptical results, but dangerous and damaging – to genuine faith! – if it tries to do anything else.[6] Heads I lose; tails you win. While not wishing to embrace the older historical-critical methods uncritically, we must insist that the appeal to history still matters and can still be made, without prejudging theological questions at this stage. We can be content neither with 'an apologetic colonizing of historical study' nor with 'a theologically dictated indifference to history'.[7] I agree with Carnley (345,

---

[4] See Via 2002, 83, 87, 91.

[5] Carnley 1987, esp. ch. 2. Coakley 2002 ch. 8 takes Carnley as her starting-point, and never, to my mind, sees the deep flaws in his position.

[6] A different though related position has been detected in Barth: 'claiming historical reality for the resurrection and yet denying historians the right to pronounce on the matter' (O'Collins 1973, 90, 99; see Coakley 2002, 134f.). There is, sadly, no space in this work to discuss Barth's contribution to the subject; a good way in is via Torrance 1976, another extremely valuable work which cannot here find more than an occasional mention.

[7] Williams 2000, 194.

365) that we must not be lured into a one-sided preoccupation with the attempt to establish factual propositions about Jesus; but he uses that warning as a way of allowing demonstrably spurious historical reconstructions to remain unchallenged. As Moule insisted, taking history seriously does not constitute a vote for liberal Protestantism.[8] Nor did the question of 'what actually happened' only begin to be felt important with John Locke.[9]

For much of the present investigation, the 'question of god' introduces itself in the form: what did the early Christians believe about the god of whom they spoke? What account of this god's being and action did they give in their earliest days, and how did this express and undergird their reasons for continuing to exist as a group at all, after the death of their leader? In other words, for Parts II, III and IV we shall be concerned with the historical reconstruction of what the early Christians believed about themselves, about Jesus and about their god. It will become clear that they believed in the god of the Israelite patriarchs and prophets, who had made promises in the past and had now, surprisingly but powerfully, fulfilled them in and through Jesus. Only in the final part must we open up the far harder issue: in reaching historical conclusions about what happened at Easter, we cannot avoid the question of the historian's own worldview and theology. Here, once again, not to do so is usually tacitly to decide in favour of a particular worldview, often that of post-Enlightenment scepticism.

The shape of the book is thus determined by the two main sub-questions into which the principal question divides: what did the early Christians think had happened to Jesus, and what can we say about the plausibility of those beliefs? The first of these is the subject of Parts II, III and IV, and the second is addressed in Part V. The two obviously overlap, since part of the reason for the conclusion of Part V is the striking beliefs discovered in Parts II–IV, and the difficulty of accounting for those beliefs except on the hypothesis that they were true. But in theory the questions are separable. It is perfectly possible for a scholar to conclude (a) that the early Christians thought Jesus had been bodily raised and (b) that they were wrong.[10] Many

---

[8] Moule 1967, 78. See too 79: 'the alternatives are not either mere history coupled with a rationalistic estimate of Jesus . . . or commitment to a preached but unauthenticated Lord.' The Christian creed, he says, 'is not a series of assertions made in a vacuum', but relates inescapably to an event, which is itself 'particular, yet transcendental'. My only quarrel with that is the 'yet', which seems to me to concede too much to the Enlightenment's split-level worldview (see *NTPG* Part II).

[9] As Coakley 2002, ch. 8 seems to imply. I fully agree with Coakley that the resurrection raises questions of a renewed epistemology as well as of a renewed ontology, but she seems to me to collapse the latter into the former, implying that 'seeing the risen Jesus' is a coded way of speaking about a Christian view of the world, ignoring the sharp distinction in all the early writers between the meetings with the risen Jesus during the short period after his resurrection and subsequent Christian experience.

[10] It would of course be logically possible for someone to conclude (a) that the early Christians did not think Jesus had been bodily raised and (b) that in fact he had been. I

have taken that view. It is incumbent on anyone who does, however, to provide an alternative account of why (a) came to be the case; and one of the interesting features of the history of research is the range of quite different answers that continue to be given to that question.

As the present book, and the research leading to it, have grown over the last few years, I have become conscious that there is at the moment a broadly dominant paradigm for understanding Jesus' resurrection, a paradigm which, despite numerous dissenting voices, is widely accepted in the worlds both of scholarship and of many mainline churches. Though my approach throughout the book will be positive and expository, it is worth noting from the outset that I intend to challenge this dominant paradigm in each of its main constituent parts. In general terms, this view holds the following: (1) that the Jewish context provides only a fuzzy setting, in which 'resurrection' could mean a variety of different things; (2) that the earliest Christian writer, Paul, did not believe in *bodily* resurrection, but held a 'more spiritual' view; (3) that the earliest Christians believed, not in Jesus' bodily resurrection, but in his exaltation/ascension/glorification, in his 'going to heaven' in some kind of special capacity, and that they came to use 'resurrection' language initially to denote that belief and only subsequently to speak of an empty tomb or of 'seeing' the risen Jesus; (4) that the resurrection stories in the gospels are late inventions designed to bolster up this second-stage belief; (5) that such 'seeings' of Jesus as may have taken place are best understood in terms of Paul's conversion experience, which itself is to be explained as a 'religious' experience, internal to the subject rather than involving the seeing of any external reality, and that the early Christians underwent some kind of fantasy or hallucination; (6) that whatever happened to Jesus' body (opinions differ as to whether it was even buried in the first place), it was not 'resuscitated', and was certainly not 'raised from the dead' in the sense that the gospel stories, read at face value, seem to require.[11] Of course, different elements in this package are stressed differently by different scholars; but the picture will be familiar to anyone who has even dabbled in the subject, or who has listened to a few mainstream Easter sermons, or indeed funeral sermons, in recent decades. The negative burden of the present book is that there are excellent, well-founded and secure historical arguments against each of these positions.

---

know of no one, scholar or otherwise, who has taken this view. More importantly, it is vital not to collapse one's own view of what 'must have' happened, or what 'could' or even 'should' have happened, into pseudo-historical statements of what the early Christians *claimed had* happened. On this, see O'Collins 1995, 89f.

[11] As Davis 1997, 132–4 notes, it is easier to find scholars declaring that Jesus was not 'resuscitated' than to find a single writer who says that he was. The denial of 'resuscitation' is frequently used as the thin end of a wedge towards the denial of 'resurrection' itself, which as we shall see is a non sequitur.

The positive thrust, naturally, is to establish (1) a different view of the Jewish context and materials, (2) a fresh understanding of Paul and (3) all the other early Christians, and (4) a new reading of the gospel stories; and to argue (5) that the *only* possible reason why early Christianity began and took the shape it did is that the tomb really was empty and that people really did meet Jesus, alive again, and (6) that, though admitting it involves accepting a challenge at the level of worldview itself, the best historical explanation for all these phenomena is that Jesus was indeed bodily raised from the dead. (The numbering of these arguments corresponds to the Parts of the present volume, except that (5) and (6) correspond to the two chapters (18 and 19) of Part V.)

Debate has focused on a dozen or so key points within these topics. Just as day trippers to the English Lake District make for the main towns (Windermere, Ambleside, Keswick) and remain within a few miles of them, so those who write articles and monographs on the resurrection come back, again and again, to the same key points (Jewish ideas about life after death, Paul's 'spiritual body', the empty tomb, the 'sightings' of Jesus, and so on). The day tripper, however, does not get the best out of the Lakes; does not, perhaps, really understand the area at all. In this book I propose to head for the hills and the narrow country lanes as well as the more populated areas. As an obvious example (but it is remarkable how many seem to ignore it), to write about Paul's view of the resurrection without mentioning 2 Corinthians 5 or Romans 8 – which many have done – is like saying you 'know' the Lake District when you have never climbed Scafell Pike or Helvellyn (England's highest mountains). One of the reasons this book is longer than I expected is that I was determined to include all the evidence.

Two preliminary subjects, both themselves controversial, must be examined before we can get to the heart of the question. First, what sort of historical task are we undertaking in talking about the resurrection at all? This introductory chapter attempts to clear the necessary ground on this point. Without it, some readers would object that I was begging the question of whether it is even possible to write historically about the resurrection.

Second, how did people in Jesus' day, both Gentiles and Jews, think and speak about the dead and their future destiny? In particular, what if anything did the word 'resurrection' (*anastasis* and its cognates, and the verb *egeiro* and its cognates, in Greek, and *qum* and its cognates in Hebrew) mean within that spectrum of belief?[12] Chapters 2 and 3 address this question, clarifying in particular – a vital move, as we shall see – what the early Christians meant, and were heard to mean, when they spoke and wrote about

---

[12] The Latin *resurrectio* seems to be a Christian coinage; the earliest refs. noted in LS 1585 are Tert. *Res.* 1 and Aug. *City of God* 22.28, and then the Vulgate of the gospels. The standard articles in *TDNT* etc. are presupposed in what follows. See too the recent study of O'Donnell 1999.

Jesus' resurrection. As George Caird once pointed out, when a speaker declares 'I'm mad about my flat' it helps to know whether they are American (in which case they are angry about their puncture) or British (in which case they are enthusiastic about their living quarters).[13] When the early Christians said 'The Messiah was raised from the dead on the third day', what might they have been heard to be saying? This may seem obvious to some readers, but it was by no means obvious, according to the evangelists, when Jesus said similar things to his followers, and a glance at contemporary literature will show that it remains far from obvious to many scholars today.[14] As well as the question of *meaning* (what did this kind of talk mean at the time?) we must consider the question of *derivation*: what, if anything, did the Christian shaping of ideas and language about Easter owe to the wider context, both Jewish and non-Jewish? Chapter 2 examines the non-Jewish world of the first century with these two questions in mind; chapters 3 and 4, developing the brief discussion in the first volume of this series, the Jewish world.[15]

Let me then spell out somewhat more fully the brief, almost formulaic account given a moment ago of how the argument develops from there. I shall come at the main question of Parts II–IV by asking: granted the wide range of views about life after death in general and resurrection in particular, what did the early Christians believe on these topics, and how can we account for their beliefs? We shall discover that, although the early Christians remained, in one sense, within the Jewish spectrum of opinion, their views on the subject had clarified and indeed crystallized to a degree unparalleled elsewhere in Judaism. The explanation they gave, for this and much besides, was the equally unparalleled claim that Jesus of Nazareth had himself been bodily raised from the dead. Parts II, III and IV will show that this belief about resurrection in general, and about Jesus in particular, presses the historian to account for such a sudden and dramatic mutation from within the Jewish worldview.

In exploring these issues, I shall follow a non-traditional route. Most discussions have begun with the resurrection stories contained in the final chapters of the four canonical gospels, and moved outwards from there. Since those chapters are among the most difficult parts of the material before us, and since they were by common consent written down later than our primary literary witness, namely Paul, I propose to leave them until last, preparing the way by looking at Paul himself (Part II) and the other early Christian writers, both canonical and non-canonical (Part III). Despite what is sometimes suggested, we shall discover substantial unanimity on the basic point: virtually all the early Christians for whom we have solid evidence

[13] Caird 1997 [1980], 50.
[14] cf. Mk. 9.9f.; Lk. 18.34.
[15] cf. *NTPG* 320–34.

affirmed that Jesus of Nazareth had been bodily raised from the dead. When they said 'he was raised on the third day', they meant this literally. Only when we have seen how strong this case is can we do justice to the resurrection stories in the gospels, which will occupy us in Part IV.

Part V will then close in on the question: what can historians in the twenty-first century say about Easter on the basis of the historical evidence? I shall argue that far and away the best explanation of the early Christian mutation within Jewish resurrection-belief is that two things had happened. First, Jesus' tomb was found to be empty. Second, several people, including at least one, and perhaps more, who had not previously been followers of Jesus, claimed to have seen him alive in a way for which the readily available language of ghosts, spirits and the like was inappropriate, and for which their previous beliefs about life after death, and resurrection in particular, had not prepared them. Take away either of these historical conclusions, and the belief of the early church becomes itself inexplicable.

The further question then is, why was the tomb empty, and what account can be given of the sightings of the apparently risen Jesus? I shall argue that the best *historical* explanation is the one which inevitably raises all kinds of *theological* questions: the tomb was indeed empty, and Jesus was indeed seen alive, because he was truly raised from the dead.

Proposing that Jesus of Nazareth was raised from the dead was just as controversial nineteen hundred years ago as it is today. The discovery that dead people stayed dead was not first made by the philosophers of the Enlightenment. The historian who wishes to make such a proposal is therefore compelled to challenge a basic and fundamental assumption – not only, as is sometimes suggested, the position of eighteenth-century scepticism, or of the 'scientific worldview' as opposed to a 'pre-scientific worldview', but also of almost all ancient and modern peoples outside the Jewish and Christian traditions.[16] I shall advance both historical and theological arguments in favour of making this quite drastic move, drawing as I do so on the early Christian theological reflections which followed from the belief in Jesus' resurrection – the reflections which, from very early indeed, came to the conclusion that the resurrection demonstrated that Jesus was God's son, and that, equally importantly, the one true God was now to be known most truly as the father of Jesus. The circle of the book will thus be complete.

Before we can even take aim at the targets, however, we must ask: is such a task even possible?

---

[16] Against e.g. Avis 1993b, who implies that this is mainly a modern problem.

2. The Arrows

(i) Shooting at the Sun

There was once a king who commanded his archers to shoot at the sun. His strongest bowmen, using their finest equipment, tried all day; but their arrows fell short, and the sun continued unaffected on its course. All night the archers polished and refeathered their arrows, and the next day they tried again, with renewed zeal; but still their efforts were in vain. The king became angry, and uttered dark threats. On the third day the youngest archer, with the smallest bow, came at noon to where the king sat before a pond in his garden. There was the sun, a golden ball reflected in the still water. With a single shot the lad pierced it at its heart. The sun splintered into a thousand glittering fragments.

All the arrows of history cannot reach God. There may, of course, be some meanings of the word 'god' that would allow such a being to be set up like a target in a shooting-gallery, for historians to take pot-shots at. The more serious a pantheist someone is, the more likely they will be to suppose that in studying the course of events within the natural world they are studying their god. But the god of Jewish tradition, the god of Christian faith, and indeed the god of Muslim devotion (whether these be three or one does not presently concern us) are simply not that kind of god. The transcendence of the god(s) of Judaism, Christianity and Islam provides the theological equivalent of the force of gravity. The arrows of history are doomed to fall short.

And yet. Deep within both Jewish and Christian tradition there lies a rumour that an image, a reflection, of the one true god has appeared within the gravitational field of history. This rumour, running from Genesis through the Wisdom tradition, and then into Jewish beliefs about Torah on the one hand and Christian beliefs about Jesus on the other, may yet offer a way for the circle to be squared, for the cake to be both eaten and possessed, for the transcendence of this god to come within bowshot.

> This commandment is not in heaven, that you should say, 'Who will go up to heaven for us, and get it for us so that we may hear it and observe it?' Neither is it beyond the sea, that you should say, 'Who will cross to the other side of the sea for us, and get it for us so that we may hear it and observe it?' No, the word is very near to you; it is in your mouth and in your heart for you to observe.[17]

And what Moses said of Torah, Paul said of Jesus, with reference not least to his resurrection.[18]

These reflections set the context for us to consider what history can and

---

[17] Dt. 30.12–14.
[18] Rom. 10.6–10; cf. Wright, *Romans*, 658–66 (with ref. also to the use of the passage in contemporary Jewish writings).

cannot say about what happened at Easter. Some have supposed that by offering historical 'proofs' of the Easter event they have thereby proved, in some modern, quasi-scientific sense, not only the existence of the Christian god but also the validity of the Christian message.[19] Turning their arrows into space-rockets, they have forgotten Icarus and have set out boldly towards the sun. Others, remembering the force of gravity, have declared the whole enterprise pointless, and actually worse than pointless. If we claim to have hit the target, have we not reduced God to an idol? Thus, as in the previous volume, we find ourselves at the intersection of history and theology, which in the early twenty-first century means that we are still wrestling with the ghosts of our Enlightenment past. These questions, powerful and complex already when we talk about Jesus himself, become all the more pressing when we attempt to speak of the resurrection. What then are we trying to do in this book?

(ii) Resurrection and History

(a) The Senses of 'History'

It has frequently been argued, indeed insisted upon, that, whatever we mean by the resurrection of Jesus, it is not accessible to historical investigation. Some have even suggested that it is not to be thought of in any meaningful sense as 'an event within history' at all. The archers cannot see the target properly; some doubt if it even exists. Over against this, I shall argue that the resurrection of Jesus, whatever it was, can and must be seen as at least a historical *problem*.

What, though, do we mean by 'historical'?[20] 'History' and its cognates have been used, within debates about Jesus and the resurrection, in at least five significantly different ways.

First, there is history as *event*. If we say something is 'historical' in this sense, it happened, whether or not we can know or prove that it happened. The death of the last pterodactyl is in that sense a *historical* event, even though no human witnessed it or wrote about it at the time, and we are very unlikely ever to discover when and where it took place. Similarly, we use the word 'historical' of persons or things, to indicate simply and solely that they existed.[21]

---

[19] An example taken almost at random from popular Christian writing: McDowell 1981.

[20] For fuller details, cf. *NTPG* ch. 4; and Wright, 'Dialogue', 245–52.

[21] Contemporary English usage is confused at this point, with 'historical' often being used where, properly, 'historic' is meant; see below. Thus a sign on the A446, south of Lichfield, points to 'The Historical Cock Inn', though no one has ever, so far as I know, denied its existence or supposed that it only appeared to the eye of faith.

Second, there is history as *significant event*. Not all events are significant; history, it is often assumed, consists of the ones that are. The adjective that tends to go with this is 'historic'; 'a historic event' is not simply an event that took place, but one whose occurrence carried momentous consequences. Likewise, a 'historic' person, building or object is one perceived to have had particular significance, not merely existence. Rudolf Bultmann, himself arguably a historic figure within the discipline of New Testament studies, famously used the adjective *geschichtlich* to convey this sense, over against *historisch* (sense 1).

Third, there is history as *provable event*. To say that something is 'historical' in this sense is to say not only that it happened but that we can demonstrate that it happened, on the analogy of mathematics or the so-called hard sciences. This is somewhat more controversial. To say 'x may have happened, but we can't prove it, so it isn't really *historical*' may not be self-contradictory, but is clearly operating with a more restricted sense of 'history' than some of the others.

Fourth, and quite different from the previous three, there is history as *writing-about-events-in-the-past*. To say that something is 'historical' in this sense is to say that it was written about, or perhaps could in principle have been written about. (This might even include 'historical' novels.) A variant on this, though an important one, is *oral history*; at a time when many regarded the spoken word as carrying more authority than the written, history as *speaking-about-events-in-the-past* is not to be sneezed at.[22]

Fifth and finally, a combination of (3) and (4) is often found precisely in discussions of Jesus: history as *what modern historians can say* about a topic. By 'modern' I mean 'post-Enlightenment', the period in which people have imagined some kind of analogy, even correlation, between history and the hard sciences. In this sense, 'historical' means not only that which can be demonstrated and written, but that which can be demonstrated and written *within the post-Enlightenment worldview*. This is what people have often had in mind when they have rejected 'the historical Jesus' (which hereby, of course, comes to mean 'the Jesus that fits the Procrustean bed of a reductionist worldview') in favour of 'the Christ of faith'.[23]

Confusion between these senses has of course bedevilled this very debate about the so-called 'historical Jesus', the phrase being used by some to mean Jesus as he actually was (sense 1), by others to mean what was significant about Jesus (sense 2), by others to mean that which we can prove about

---

[22] Plato *Phaedr.* 274c—275a, has Socrates warning against substituting written documents for oral traditions: people will stop using their memories, he says. See too Xen. *Symp.* 3.5; Diog. Laert. 7.54–6. In the early church, Papias is famous for having declared that he preferred living witnesses (Eus. *HE* 3.39.2–4).

[23] A good example is provided by Nineham 1965, 16, discussed by Wedderburn 1999, 9: 'historical' events are those which are 'fully and exclusively human and entirely confined within the limits of this world'.

Jesus, as opposed to that which we must either doubt or take on faith alone (sense 3); by others again to mean what people have written about Jesus (sense 4). Those who, as I mentioned, have taken the phrase in sense 5 have often rejected the Jesus not only of that sense but, apparently, of the previous four as well.[24] *Jesus and the Victory of God* constitutes, in part, a response to this position. But we must now face one very specific, particular and in some senses peculiar case of the problem. In what sense, if any, can Jesus' resurrection be spoken of as 'historical'?

Ever since the time of Paul, people have tried to write about Jesus' resurrection (whatever they meant by that). The question, of course, rebounds: were they thereby writing about an event in the past? Were they writing 'history'? Or was it all actually the projection of their own faith-experience? When they said 'Jesus was raised from the dead on the third day', were they intending to make some kind of historical claim about Jesus, or did they themselves know that this was a metaphor for their own remarkable new religious experience, the rise of their faith, and so on? This pushes us back to sense 1, which is the question at stake throughout much of this book: was the resurrection something that actually happened, and if so what precisely *was* it that happened? We do not seem to have had much polemic against 'the historical resurrection' in the same way that there has been angry rejection of 'the historical Jesus'.[25]

There is no problem about predicating sense 2 of Jesus' resurrection. Virtually everyone will agree that whatever-it-was-that-happened was extremely significant. Indeed, some recent writers agree that it was very significant while continuing to argue that we cannot know what 'it' is. There are enormous problems about sense 3: it all depends on what you mean by 'proof', and we shall return to that question in due course. Sense 4 is unproblematic: the 'event' has been written about, even if it was all made up. But it is sense 5 that has caused the real headache: what can historians in today's world say on the subject? Unless we keep these distinctions clear in our minds as we proceed, we shall not just have enormous problems; we shall go round in ever-decreasing circles.

Is it, then, possible to speak of the resurrection of Jesus as an event within history? In his rightly famous book *The Historical Jesus*, J. D. Crossan says, of the Quest for Jesus as a whole, that there were some scholars who said it couldn't be done, and some who said it shouldn't be done; and that there were some who said the former when they meant the latter.[26] This is equally true, if not more so, when it comes to the resurrection. Since I believe we can and must discuss the resurrection as a historical problem, it is important that we address these questions head on. There are six objections;

[24] cf. e.g. Johnson 1995; 1999.
[25] cf. *JVG* 109–12; and e.g. Johnson, as prev. note.
[26] Crossan 1991, xxvii. For Crossan's account of the resurrection, see below.

I shall divide them into two broad groups, beginning with those who say that such historical study of the resurrection *cannot* be undertaken, and going on to those who suggest that it *should not* be. The parable of the archers and the sun applies more to the latter than to the former group. A little modification of the parable will give us a double picture. Those who think we *cannot* study the resurrection historically suppose either that there is no target at all or that, if there is, the archers cannot see it. Those who think we *should not* study the resurrection historically suppose that the target lies outside the gravitational range of their arrows. The first group of objectors, assuming the target to be an ordinary terrestrial one, protest that the archers cannot aim at something they cannot see; the second declare that no arrow can reach ever the sun, so that the quest is doomed, and guilty of a kind of hubris, from the very start.

(b) No Access?

The first objection to treating the resurrection historically is made often enough, and is associated in the scholarship of the last generation with Willi Marxsen in particular.[27] Marxsen denies that we have any access, as historians, to the resurrection itself. There may be a target somewhere, but we can't see it and so can't shoot at it. All we have, apparently, is access to the beliefs of the early disciples. No sources, except the late and unreliable so-called *Gospel of Peter*, purport to describe Jesus' coming out of the tomb; even that strange text does not describe the moment of his first awakening and shaking off the grave-clothes.[28] Therefore, says Marxsen, we should not speak of the resurrection itself as 'historical'. A remarkable number of subsequent scholars have followed him in this assertion.[29]

This proposal appears to be cautious and scientific. It is, however, neither of these things. It involves a rash dismissal of an important question, and a misunderstanding of how science, including scientific historiography, actually works. It says, in fact, both too little and too much.

Too little: in standard positivistic fashion it appears to suggest that we can only regard as 'historical' that to which we have direct access (in the sense of 'first-hand witness accounts' or near equivalent). But, as all real historians know, that is not in fact how history works. Positivism is, if anything, even less appropriate in historiography than in other areas. Again and again the historian has to conclude, even if only to avoid total silence, that certain events took place to which we have no direct access but which are

---

[27] Marxsen 1970 [1968] ch. 1; Marxsen 1968.

[28] Crossan thinks the *Gospel of Peter*, or at least this part of it, is early, but would still not say, of course, that it is in any sense historically reliable; see below, 592–6.

[29] See the various discussions in e.g. Moule 1968; Evans 1970, 170–83.

the necessary postulates of that to which we do have access. Scientists, not least physicists, make this sort of move all the time; indeed, this is precisely how scientific advances happen.[30] Ruling out as historical that to which we do not have direct access is actually a way of not doing history at all.

As a result, this view also says too much. On its own epistemology, it ought not even to claim access to the disciples' faith. Even the texts themselves do not give us direct access to this faith in the way that Marxsen and others seem to regard as necessary. All we have in this case are texts; and, though Marxsen did not address this question, the same relentless suspicion, applied in regular postmodern fashion, might lead some to question whether we even have those. If, in other words, you want to be a no-holds-barred historical positivist, only accepting as historical that to which you have (in this sense) direct access, you have a long and stony road ahead of you. Few if any actual practising historians travel by this route.

This is a classic case of failing to distinguish between the different senses of 'history'. Marxsen recognizes that nobody, at least so far as we know, *wrote* about the actual transition of Jesus from death to life (sense 4 above), deduces from this that nothing can be *proved* about the event (sense 3), and constantly writes as if this means that *we as 'modern historians'* can say nothing about it (sense 5), or indeed about what 'it' in this sense might even be, whether or not we could say anything sensible about it (sense 1). At the same time, he wants to suggest that whatever happened or didn't happen, it was obviously *significant* (sense 2), because otherwise the early church would never have come into being. This is, to say the least, highly misleading. Marxsen's whole position will be steadily outflanked as we proceed.

(c) No Analogy?

The second objection is associated, famously, with Ernst Troeltsch. He argued that we can only speak or write as historians about things which have some analogy in our own experience; resurrections do not occur in our experience; therefore we cannot, as historians, speak of the resurrection.[31] We haven't ever hit at a target like this before, so there's no point shooting at

---

[30] Polkinghorne 1994, ch. 2, esp. 31f. So, for that matter, do textual critics: Professor Alden Smith of Baylor University points out to me that the great C18 classicist Richard Bentley made exactly this sort of move in restoring the digamma (an archaic Greek letter) to certain passages in Homer whose metre would otherwise remain deficient. Via 2002, 82 is right to say that history moves from fragmentary evidence to full-blown reconstruction, but wrong to imply that this takes place in a kind of neutral zone free from all theological or religious presuppositions.

[31] Troeltsch 1912–25, 2.732. Coakley 1993, 112 n. 14 suggests that if Pannenberg had used Troeltsch's more mature work on analogy (3.190f.) he would have found Troeltsch less vulnerable to the criticism he advances (see below).

this one now. This does not necessarily mean that it did not in some sense occur ('history' sense 1) or that people have written things purporting to be about it (sense 4); only that it is illegitimate to try to write about it as history today (sense 5), let alone to try to prove it (sense 3). This is sometimes understood as a nuanced restatement of Hume's famous objection to miracles in general.[32] But I think it is, in principle at least, more subtle than that: Jesus' resurrection might have occurred, but we simply cannot say anything about it.

Pannenberg, equally famously, has proposed an answer to Troeltsch on this point. He suggests that the ultimate verification of the resurrection of Jesus Christ (sense 3) will eventually be provided through the final resurrection of those in Christ, which will constitute the required analogy. There will, in other words, come a time when we shall all shoot at the target and not miss. This, in effect, concedes Troeltsch's point, but pleads for a stay of verdict pending eschatological verification.[33] But I wonder if Pannenberg has not given too much away here?

At the comparatively trivial level, we can easily conceive of an event in which something quite new occurs. We did not have to wait for the second space flight before being able to talk, as historians, about the first one. True, space flight might be thought to have partial analogies in the flight of aeroplanes, not to say birds (or even arrows). But part of the point of the resurrection, within the Jewish worldview, was (as we shall see) that it would be in line with, though going significantly beyond, the great liberating acts of God on behalf of Israel in the past – not to mention the partial analogies with the resuscitations of people in the Old Testament, and indeed with remarkable healings.[34] There were partial anticipations and analogies, even though the event itself was significantly new.

It is important to note what would follow if we took Troeltsch's point seriously: we would be able to say nothing about the rise of the early church as a whole.[35] Never before had there been a movement which began as a quasi-messianic group within Judaism and was transformed into the sort of movement which Christianity quickly became. Nor has any similar phenomenon ever occurred again. (The common post-Enlightenment perception of Christianity as simply 'a religion' masks the huge differences, at the point of origin, between this movement and, say, the rise of Islam or of Buddhism.) Both pagan and Jewish observers of this new movement found it highly anomalous: it was not like a club, not even like a religion (no sacrifices, no

---

[32] cf. Hume 1975 [1777] section x, with the famous line: 'no testimony is sufficient to establish a miracle, unless the testimony be of such a kind, that its falsehood would be more miraculous, than the fact, which it endeavours to establish.'

[33] Pannenberg 1970 [1963] ch. 2; 1991–8 [1988–93], 2.343–63; 1996. See the incisive discussion in Coakley 1993, with other bibliography at 112 n. 6; Coakley 2002, 132–5.

[34] See Wedderburn 1999, 19.

[35] cf. *NTPG* Part IV; and below, Part III, esp. ch. 11.

images, no oracles, no garlanded priests), certainly not like a racially based cult. How, in Troeltsch's scheme, might we speak of such a thing, which had not been seen before and has never been seen since? Only at best by partial analogy, by saying both what it was like and what it was not like. To squash the movement into already existing categories, or to deny its existence on the grounds that it was unprecedented, would be the work, not of a historian, but of a Procrustean philosopher.

The rise of the early church thus constitutes in itself a counter-example to Troeltsch's general point. If we are to speak truly about the early church, we must describe something for which there was no precedent and of which there remains no subsequent example. In addition, as we shall see, the early church by its very existence forces upon us the question which we, as historians, must ask: what precisely happened after Jesus' crucifixion that caused early Christianity to come into being? Ironically, then, it is precisely the uniqueness of the rise of the early church that forces us to say: never mind analogies, what happened?[36]

(d) No Real Evidence?

The third objection to treating the resurrection of Jesus as a historical event is more varied. Here I draw together various disparate aspects of recent research and writing on the subject. The basic point is that the apparent evidence for the resurrection (i.e. the gospel accounts and the testimony of Paul) can be explained away. I shall return to some of these discussions later; here I want simply to clear another potential 'Road Closed' sign out of the way.

There have been two different, though related, 'Road Closed' signs under this heading. The first, common throughout post-Bultmannian New Testament studies, has been the attempt to analyze the material according to its hypothetical tradition-history. What naive readers think of as a target at which to aim the arrow of history is in fact a trick of light and shade, somewhere between the observer and what appears to be a target, which has created instead nothing more than a target-shaped mirage.

It has proved difficult to subject the resurrection stories to form-critical analysis, though this has not stopped intrepid souls from making the attempt.[37] But the range of suggestions about which group in the early church wanted to add which pebble to the growing pile of stones in the tradition, and then about what the different evangelists or their sources intended to convey to their readers in their turn, has grown enormous of late, as one

---

[36] On the question of analogy see now O'Collins 1999, in debate with Carnley 1997 in particular.
[37] See below, 596f.

can see from the bewildering range surveyed by Gerd Lüdemann.[38] And the problem with all such theories is that they are themselves based on nothing more than elaborate guesswork. We simply do not know very much about the early church, and certainly not enough to make the kind of guesses that are on offer in this area. When traditio-historical study (the examination of hypothetical stages by which the written gospels came into existence) builds castles in the air, the ordinary historian need not feel a second-class citizen for refusing to rent space in them.[39]

The second way of explaining away the evidence, notable especially in the work of Crossan, is to apply to the texts a ruthless hermeneutic of suspicion.[40] This too results in a form of tradition-history. Now, however, instead of offering suggestions as to which theological or pastoral point the tradition might be making, we are offered political ones: power-plays in which the accreditation of different apostles or would-be apostles is fought out on the battleground of (fictitious) resurrection narratives. Crossan declares that the resurrection narratives trivialize Christianity, turning it away from its origins as an aphoristic alternative-lifestyle movement and into a collection of power-seeking factions. What looks like a target is the cunning work of power-brokers trying to get people to shoot arrows in the wrong direction.

What is more, Crossan traces the origins of resurrection stories themselves to an educated, middle-class scribal movement which developed away from the pure, early peasant roots of Jesus himself, and of the early 'Q' people, into a more bourgeois and establishment-minded organization. The resurrection narratives are thus declared worthless as history: they are projected politics, and the politics (what is more) of the wrong sort of people, the wicked educated scribes instead of the noble virtuous peasants.

With Lüdemann and Crossan, and the dozens of scholars who offer similar accounts, it would of course be easy to offer a kind of *ad hominem* rebuttal. Lüdemann himself stands within a highly developed tradition-history, in which the post-Bultmannian world has gone on adding hypothetical stones to a pile which itself originated in guesswork. Crossan himself uses his historical hypotheses, sometimes in a none-too-subtle manner, as scribal political ploys against groups in today's church and society – often non-scribal groups! – that he regards as dangerous.[41] In his own terms, quoted earlier, it looks as though Crossan is saying it can't be done when he means that it shouldn't be.

---

[38] cf. esp. Lüdemann 1994.

[39] It is important to distinguish between different types of tradition-criticism: cf. Wright, 'Doing Justice to Jesus', 360–65.

[40] cf. e.g. Crossan 1991, 395–416; 1998, 550–73.

[41] See particularly Crossan 1995, an angry polemic against the work of Raymond Brown in particular.

Such replies do not, of course, advance the argument. But they alert us to a phenomenon not sufficiently remarked upon. A hermeneutic of suspicion in one area is routinely balanced by a hermeneutic of credulity in another.[42] Neither Lüdemann's alternative scenario of Easter, in which Peter and Paul experience fantasies brought on by grief and guilt respectively, nor Crossan's, in which a group of scribal Christians begin, years after the crucifixion, to study the scriptures and to speculate about Jesus' fate, is based on any evidence whatsoever. Those who feel the force of Marxsen's doubts over evidence for Jesus' resurrection ought to be even more anxious about these reconstructions. In particular, the common traditio-historical scenarios owe a good deal more to nineteenth- and twentieth-century theories about how early Christians 'must' have preached and lived than to any sustained attempt to reconstruct the worldviews and mindsets of actual communities in the first century.[43] The suggestions on offer as to what the evangelists, their sources and earlier redactors or handers-on of tradition were wanting to convey to their communities are usually remarkably trite, and have more in common with the piety of post-reformation (and often post-Enlightenment) Europe than with early Judaism or Christianity. When all is said and done, the historian is still bound to address the question: how did Christianity actually start, and why did it take the shape it did? Despite their ingenuity, the very different solutions of Lüdemann and Crossan are not, as we shall see, capable of answering that question in terms which make sense within actual first-century history. This objection to the study of Easter as a historical phenomenon, like the first two, will not hold water. Those who say the target cannot be seen do not seem to be looking in the right direction.

(iii) Resurrection in History and Theology

(a) No Other Starting-Point?

This brings me to the second set of arguments which might preclude such historical study: those which say not that it can't be done but that it shouldn't be. These objections are more overtly theological in character. The

---

[42] cf. Caird 1997 [1980], 60f., speaking of 'those sceptics who find that they cannot believe the biblical account of the trial, death and resurrection of Jesus and undertake to tell us instead "what actually happened"': 'Anyone who takes [such conceits] seriously is more credulous than the most naive believer in the biblical text.' He concludes: 'We can respect the genuine agnostic who is content to live in doubt because he considers the evidence inadequate for belief, but not the spurious agnostic who prefers fantasy to evidence.' See too Williams 2002, 2: 'It is remarkable how complacent some "deconstructive" histories are about the status of the history that they deploy themselves.'

[43] Not that some such serious attempts are not made; cf. e.g. Nodet and Taylor 1998; Theissen 1999.

target, say the objectors, is not just difficult to see or to shoot at; it is in principle unreachable.

We begin with the argument which I find in various writers, and trace back to Hans Frei among others.[44] If I have understood Frei, he was arguing that we should not try to investigate the resurrection historically because the resurrection is itself the ground of a Christian epistemology. Everything that Christians know, they know because of the resurrection and for no other reason. There can therefore be no other starting-point, no neutral ground on which one might stand, from which one might observe the resurrection itself. Even to try to find one constitutes a kind of epistemological blasphemy. You must not try to shoot arrows *at* this target, because the only appropriate place *from* which to shoot at anything is where the target itself is standing.

This, in my view, simply begs the question. There is no reason in principle why the question, what precisely happened at Easter, cannot be raised by any historian of any persuasion. Even if some Christians might wish to rule it off limits, they have (presumably) no a priori right to tell other historians, whether Muslims, Jews, Hindus, Buddhists, New Agers, gnostics, agnostics, or anyone else, what they may and may not study. It might of course be the case that, in the last analysis, what Christians mean by the resurrection of Jesus would turn out to be so large and all-embracing a fact, or concept, that it would, if accepted, illuminate all other areas of thought and practice.[45] But we cannot decide that question in advance. Certainly it is not true that what most twentieth-century New Testament scholars have thought 'happened at Easter' is incapable of being researched historically. Bultmann thought that what happened at Easter was the rise of Christian faith, and he wrote quite a lot of history (sense 4) about it. Lüdemann thinks that Peter and Paul had major internal, psychologically explicable experiences, and has written quite a lot of history (also sense 4) about them. And so on.

Frei's proposal, in the last analysis, is always in danger of describing a closed epistemological circle, a fideism from within which everything can be seen clearly but which remains necessarily opaque to those outside. However much this happens to accord with that branch of contemporary literary theory in which the discovery of extra-textual reality is ruled out from the start, and however much this also accords, whether by coincidence or the happy confluence of different streams of thought in Yale University at a certain period, with an insistence on the biblical canon as the epistemological starting-point for Christian reflection (and with a sense of despair over the present state of historical biblical scholarship), this position seems to me

---

[44] cf. e.g. Frei 1993 chs. 2, 8 and 9; in a larger context, Frei 1975.

[45] In the same way, a determined solipsism (the belief that the five senses tell one nothing about an external world, but only about oneself) will, if accepted, radically undermine other epistemologies, and the symbolic universes that depend on them.

profoundly untrue to the worldview of the early Christians. Even if it were true that a fully Christian epistemology would want to begin all its knowing with Jesus, confessed as the crucified and risen Messiah, that does not mean that there is no access to Jesus and his death and resurrection in the public world. Peter did not need to appeal to Christian writings when reminding the crowd of what they already knew about Jesus.[46]

A further obvious point could be made, on the analogy of other well-known arguments. (Think, for instance, of the standard reply to the logical positivists' principle that we can only count as 'knowledge' that which could in principle be falsified: how might that principle itself be falsified?) If Frei were right, how could we *know* that the resurrection was the only valid epistemological starting-point? If the answer is, because only that will work, how do we respond to those who say that other starting-points work just as well?

Another analogy may help here. Ed Sanders, in his well-known reading of Paul, argues that Paul did not start off with a problem and then discover that Jesus was the solution; he discovered Jesus, found him to be God's solution, and then figured out that there must have been some kind of problem.[47] This can be shown to be, not exactly mistaken, but misleading. There was an earlier stage involved as well: Paul's thought moved *from* his Jewish perception of 'the plight' *to* the solution offered in Christ *and thence to a fresh analysis of the problem*.[48] The 'problem' he eventually described was a rethought version of the 'problem' he had before he began. He moved from an initial epistemological starting-point to (what he came to see as) fresh knowledge; then, reflecting on what had happened, concluded that there was actually a better starting-point from which he could see things clearly.

In the same way, I suggest, historical knowledge about the resurrection, of a sort that can be discussed without presupposing Christian faith, cannot be ruled out a priori, even if the resurrection, if acknowledged, would then turn out to offer a differently grounded epistemology. Some such movement takes place in the story of Thomas in John 20. He begins by insisting on the sense of touch as the only foolproof epistemology. He is confronted by the risen Jesus. He then discovers that visibility is enough (he abandons his intention of touching), only to be told 'blessed are those who have not seen, and yet believe'. His original epistemology led him in the right direction, even though, when faced with the risen Jesus, he abandoned it in favour of a better one, and was pointed towards a better one still.[49]

I suspect that we are faced here with one of the long-range outworkings of Barth's rejection of natural theology, and of the various counter-proposals

---

[46] Ac. 2.22; cf. Lk. 24.18–20; Ac. 10.36–9.

[47] Sanders 1977; 1983; 1991.

[48] Wright, *Climax*; Thielman 1989.

[49] See below, chs. 17, 18. I think this may be a way of getting at what Frei was after, for instance, 1993 ch. 9, without leaving so many issues so disarmingly open-ended.

that have been and can be made to his position.[50] (Equally, one still meets the proposal that one should not engage in historical study of Jesus for fear of turning one's faith into a work.[51]) New Testament scholars have long avoided grasping nettles in this area, and I am not going to pursue the point further at this stage. I simply suggest that Frei's objection, though offering important reminders at one level, should not prevent us from continuing to investigate the resurrection from a historical point of view. As Moule put it at the conclusion of his important little monograph:

> A Gospel which cares only for the apostolic proclamation and denies that it either can or should be tested for its historical antecedents, is really only a thinly veiled gnosticism or docetism and, however much it may continue to move by a borrowed momentum, will prove ultimately to be no Gospel.[52]

Or, if you prefer: all earthly activity takes place within the sun's gravitational field; but this doesn't mean that we cannot act within the earth's own gravity. Or that the historical arrow can never reach the sun's true image.

(b) Resurrection and Christology

This brings us to the second more theological objection. One of the reasons Frei and others have taken the line they have is because, in a good deal of Christian theology, the resurrection has been seen as the demonstration of Jesus' divinity. Some, indeed, may understand the title of the present book in that sense. This is where the parable of the king's archers comes fully into its own.

Resurrection and incarnation are often muddled up. Theologians often speak of the resurrection as if it directly and necessarily connotes Jesus' divinity, and indeed as though it connotes little else besides. The objection to a historical investigation of the resurrection is then obvious: the arrows will simply not reach the sun. You cannot mount a historical argument and end up proving 'god', or proving that Jesus was the incarnation of the One True God.[53] The historian ought not even to attempt to pronounce on a topic

---

[50] A recent study on Barth and the resurrection is that of Davie 1998. On the relation between Barth and Frei, see e.g. Frei 1993 ch. 6, esp. (on this point) 173 (admiring Barth for affirming that both the possibility and the need for the factual event of 'incarnate Reconciliation', and hence also for faith in its saving power, 'are . . . to be explained solely from the event itself'); and, more generally, Demson 1997. The relation between this point and the senses in which Frei admitted a continuing need for some level of 'natural theology' (e.g. 1993, 210) raises issues too complex to deal with here.

[51] Barclay 1996a, 28 reports this view, without saying whether he agrees with it.

[52] Moule 1967, 80f.

[53] Thus e.g. Schlosser 2001, 159: one cannot pronounce on the reality of the resurrection, because that would be to pronounce on the reality of the transcendent, which is beyond historical enquiry.

which would lead so directly to the question of whether this god was in Christ. Even Pannenberg, who of course does think we can speak historically of the resurrection, seems to me to go too far in the direction of a direct link between resurrection and incarnational Christology.[54]

Part of the problem here – and to this we shall return – lies in the confusion that still occurs about the meaning of Messiahship.[55] To say that Jesus is 'the Christ' is, in first-century terms, to say first and foremost that he is Israel's Messiah, not to say that he is the incarnate Logos, the second person of the Trinity, the only-begotten son of the father. Even the phrase 'son of god', during Jesus' ministry and in very early Christianity, does not mean what it came to mean in later theology, though already by the time of Paul a widening of its meaning can be observed.[56] But even when we have reminded ourselves of all this it is still not the case that resurrection necessarily entails Messiahship. If one of the two brigands crucified alongside Jesus had been found to be alive three days later, or if one of the Maccabaean martyrs (who were reported to have died with the promise of resurrection on their lips) had been raised from the dead a few days afterwards, it would have delighted their families and astonished their friends; a large hole would have been made in the second-Temple Jewish expectation, not to mention non-Jewish worldviews; but no one would have concluded that such a person was the Messiah, far less that he (or she, for at least one notable Maccabaean martyr was a woman) was in any sense an incarnate divine being.[57]

We can make a similar point in relation to Paul's argument in 1 Corinthians 15, that all Christians will be raised as Jesus was raised. This does not turn all Christians into Messiahs; nor does it mean that they will thereby share (let alone that they already share!) the unique divine sonship which, in the same letter (15.28; cf. 8.6), Paul attributes to Jesus. Already in Paul, in fact, we see the clear distinction between resurrection (a newly embodied life after death) and exaltation or enthronement, a distinction which some scholars have suggested only enters the tradition with Luke.[58] Resurrection does not of itself connote cosmic Lordship, or divinity. This brings us to the important point: the theological conclusions that the early Christians drew from the resurrection of Jesus had far more to do with what they knew of Jesus prior to his crucifixion, and with what they knew of the crucifixion itself, and with what they believed about Israel's god and his purposes for Israel and the world, than with the bare fact (granted we could ever speak of

[54] Pannenberg 1991–8 [1988–93], 2.343–63. This forms part of a long chapter dealing with 'The Deity of Jesus Christ'. The same problem recurs in e.g. Koperski 2002.

[55] cf. *NTPG* 307–20; *JVG* ch. 11; and below, chs. 11, 18.

[56] cf. e.g. Gal. 2.20; Rom. 1.3f.; 8.3, 32; and Wright, *Climax*, ch. 2. See below, ch. 19.

[57] This point can be seen to good advantage in the remarkable thesis of Lapide 1983 [1977]: Jesus was indeed bodily raised from the dead, but this proves not that he was Messiah but that he was a crucial part of the god-given preparation for the Messiah.

[58] See below, Part II.

such a thing) of the resurrection itself. For the moment we may simply note that whatever we think about Jesus' divinity, that cannot have been, in the first century, the primary meaning of his resurrection – even if, as we shall see, the train of thought which began with belief in Jesus' resurrection led the early Christians towards such a belief.

The converse is also important. Let us suppose for a moment that the disciples had become convinced, on other grounds, that Jesus of Nazareth was indeed the Messiah. (A contemporary analogy suggests itself: the Hasidic Jews of the Lubavitcher movement believe that their Rebbe was indeed the Messiah, and they do not regard his death in 1994 as evidence to the contrary.[59]) This would not have led the early disciples to say that he had been raised from the dead. A change in the meaning of 'Messiah', yes (since nobody in the first century supposed that the Messiah would die at the hands of the pagans); but not an assertion of his resurrection. No second-Temple Jewish texts speak of the Messiah being raised from the dead. Nobody would have thought of saying, 'I believe that so-and-so really was the Messiah; therefore he must have been raised from the dead.'

If this is true of Jesus' Messiahship, it is certainly true *a fortiori* of any suggestion of his 'divinity'. For the disciples to become convinced, on other grounds, that Jesus was divine would not of itself have led them to say that he had been raised from the dead. Nothing in Jewish beliefs about the Jewish god, and certainly nothing in non-Jewish beliefs about non-Jewish gods, would suggest to devotees that they should predicate resurrection of their object of worship. Some sort of new life beyond the grave, quite possibly; resurrection, certainly not.[60]

We should not, then, be put off the historical investigation by theological coyness.[61] We must keep our nerve. It should be perfectly possible for historians to study the reports of, and beliefs about, Jesus' resurrection, just as one should be able to study reports, however startling, of the re-embodiment of any other second-Temple Jew, without supposing that by so doing we are necessarily committed to boldly going where no historian has ever gone

---

[59] cf. the recent discussion of Marcus 2001.

[60] On dying and rising gods in oriental cults, and similar phenomena, see ch. 2 below.

[61] Nor by the kind of dismissive comments we find in Carnley 1987, 26–8, 85–7, where he implies that the concern to bring rigorous historical study to bear on the Easter events (he has 'fundamentalist writers and ultra-conservative popularizers of the Easter faith' in mind) is to show that one has 'no present knowing of the raised Christ', resulting in 'the projected hostility of the believer's own "shadow side" of repressed doubt' against the wicked historical critics who point out discrepancies in the narratives, etc. Attempted psychoanalysis of one's opponents, and making slurs against their personal spirituality, is hardly either scholarly or helpful. One stage worse is Wedderburn's scornful attack (1999, 128) on those who pride themselves on a 'strong' faith as 'some sort of virility symbol, or as a form of self-assertion'. Would he say that of Abraham's faith – even granted its specific content! – in Rom. 4.19–22?

before.[62] What we make of our findings is another question altogether. We cannot, by short-circuiting the theological issue, escape the challenge of history. Reminding the archers about gravity should not put them off their task.

(c) Resurrection and Eschatology

The final problem is a broader version of the question of resurrection and Christology. It has commonly been said that the resurrection is of necessity an *eschatological* event, and that since, once again, the historian is not equipped to study eschatology, he or she should keep at a safe distance.[63] Just because the sun's heat and light may suddenly penetrate the thick clouds, that doesn't mean you can shoot at the sun itself. Sometimes, indeed, this is elided into the former objection, since it is sometimes supposed, in a muddled sort of post-Bultmannianism, that talk of 'eschatology' means, more or less, talk of God breaking into history, and that talk of God breaking into history means talk of Christology. But if we are to use words with any historically rooted meaning we must be much more precise.

There are at least ten meanings of the word 'eschatology' currently being employed within the guild of New Testament Studies.[64] If we are to keep as strictly as possible to meanings that relate to particular phenomena within the world of second-Temple Judaism, what we ought to mean as historians if we spoke of the resurrection as an eschatological event would be that it was the sort of event that second-Temple Jews would see in terms of the apocalyptic climax of their own history. But saying that an event would be read in those terms by those people would certainly not rule out the study of the same event by historians today. After all, the successful Maccabaean revolt was understood eschatologically by (at least) the author of 1 Maccabees, but nobody has therefore suggested that we should not examine the event as historians.[65] The fall of Jerusalem in the sixth century BC, and the similar and equally catastrophic events of the first century AD, were understood 'eschatologically' by a good many people then and subsequently (this was,

---

[62] Pinnock 1993, 9 insists that 'one cannot make the resurrection a historical construct and expect people to be transformed by it.' What matters is preaching, witness and the Spirit. While not ultimately dissenting from this, it is quite clear that many people have succeeded in convincing others that, as a matter of history, the resurrection did *not* happen, and have thereby transformed people in a variety of ways. What people believe about what has actually happened is often an extremely powerful element in human transformation. The moment when Elizabeth Bennet learns what actually happened between Darcy and Wickham is, arguably, the turning-point of *Pride and Prejudice* (see, on this point, Marcus 1989).

[63] cf. e.g. Barclay 1996a, 14. For Schillebeeckx's use of 'eschatological' in this sense see ch. 18 below (701–6).

[64] cf. Caird 1997 [1980], ch. 13; *JVG* chs. 2, 3, 6, esp. 207–9.

[65] cf. especially the language of 1 Macc. 14.4–15.

after all, 'the day of YHWH'), but nobody suggests that we therefore cannot investigate or understand those events historically. The tragic poetry of Jeremiah does not bar us from studying the events of 597 and 587 BC. We are not kept from writing history about AD 70 by the apocalyptic nature of the visions in 4 Ezra, and the conviction that an eschatological event had taken place.

It could of course be objected that, if one concluded that the resurrection of Jesus had in fact taken place, it would be necessary to understand it eschatologically, that is, to commit oneself to a worldview in which the god of Israel acted climactically at certain points, including particularly this one. But this is misleading. It arises from the effect of perspective. Those who have written about Jesus and the resurrection in the last two centuries have done so, for the most part, from within either a Christian, a semi-Christian or a sub-Christian worldview, within which such a connection appears very natural. (It is possible, of course, to go so far in the direction of deJudaizing the word 'eschatological' that it simply means 'miraculous'; the objection then collapses into a restatement of Troeltsch, or even Hume.) But within either an ancient pagan worldview or a contemporary non-Christian world-view no such conclusion would be reached. Those Romans who supposed that a 'Nero redivivus' was alive and kicking certainly had no thoughts of interpreting this phenomenon within the worldview of second-Temple Jewish eschatology.[66] Those in our own world (in New Age movements, for instance) who suppose that all human beings are going to be 'recycled' sooner or later are often bitterly opposed to a Jewish or Christian view of reality, not least the Christian claim that Jesus himself was, uniquely, raised at Easter. Once again, even if we were to accept the bodily resurrection of Jesus, the decision to interpret that event as connoting anything beyond an exceedingly puzzling and unexpected turn of events *depends to begin with at least on the worldview within which we come to it.* Why 'to begin with at least'? Because some events seem to have the power to challenge world-views and generate either new mutations within them or complete trans-formations; and of such events the resurrection of Jesus, according to the early Christians, was the most obvious. The reason why the early Christians interpreted the resurrection eschatologically was that they were second-Temple Jews who had been either part of, or spectators of, a would-be eschatological movement focused on Jesus himself. They then came to reshape their worldview around the resurrection as the new central point. But that takes us too far towards our later discussions.

This summary of several complex arguments has not, I fear, done full justice either to the positions I have opposed or to the possible counter-arguments. To some readers, I will have skated over the key issues; to others, I may have fallen into the traditional theologians' trap of giving

---

[66] On Nero-myths, see 68 below.

incomprehensible answers to questions nobody was asking. But I hope it is sufficient to show that several reasons frequently advanced for not considering the resurrection as a historical problem are not in themselves cogent. We are left with the positive conclusion: at the end of the day the historian can and must ask why Christianity began, and why it took the shape it did. Since the universal early Christian answer to that question had to do with Jesus and the resurrection, the historian is forced to ask further questions: (a) what the early Christians meant by that, (b) whether and in what sense we could say that they were right, and (c) whether we have any alternative proposals that will stand up to scrutiny. The historian cannot, then, be debarred from asking whether or not it is true that Jesus was raised from the dead.

3. The Historical Starting-Point

What, then, is our target, and what arrows can we use to shoot at it?

Our target is to investigate the claim of the earliest Christians, that Jesus of Nazareth was raised from the dead. In order to be sure we are aiming at that target, it is important to locate their claim where it belongs, within the worldview and language of second-Temple Judaism. In addition, since this (still recognizably Jewish) claim was quickly advanced within the wider non-Jewish world of the first century, it is important also to map out where the claim belonged within that larger universe of discourse.

This triple mapping operation will be undertaken in reverse, beginning with the pagan worldview, moving inwards to the Jewish, and thence to early Christianity. It is not a question of describing the entire worldview in each case. That would take many volumes for each segment. We shall focus on those aspects that concern life after death in general and resurrection in particular. It will become clear – and this is among the first major conclusions of our historical study – that the early Christian worldview is, at this point at least, best understood as a startling, fresh mutation within second-Temple Judaism. This then raises the question: what caused this mutation?

Among the more striking aspects of the mutation is the fact that nowhere within Judaism, let alone paganism, is a sustained claim advanced that resurrection has actually happened to a particular individual.[67] Since this claim has huge effects in other areas of the early Christian worldview, these too must be examined. How, in particular, do we explain the early Christian

---

[67] One or two possible exceptions will be noted in the proper place: e.g. Euripides' tale of Alcestis, and Herod Antipas' reported comment about Jesus as a resurrected John the Baptist (below, 65–8, 412). The suggestion of Frei 1993, 47, that the early Christian claim was 'not all unique' on the grounds that 'Gods were raised from the dead in liberal numbers in the ancient world', thus providing 'a very large number of candidates for the same unproved miraculous occurrence', represents a remarkable misunderstanding of the historical situation: see further below, 80f.

claim that the crucified Jesus was indeed Israel's Messiah? How do we explain the belief that 'god's kingdom' though in some senses still future, has become, in a new way, a present reality? Like the mutation within the meaning of 'resurrection', these features point towards the central question: what happened at Easter? This is the subject of Part V.

I described and defended my preferred historical method in Part II of *The New Testament and the People of God*, and exemplified it in Parts III and IV of that work, and in Parts II and III of *Jesus and the Victory of God*. This method recognizes that all knowledge of the past, as indeed of everything else, is mediated not only through sources but also through the perceptions, and hence also the personalities, of the knowers. There is no such thing as detached objectivity. (To say, therefore, that we can investigate other historical claims in a neutral or objective fashion, but that with the resurrection an element of subjectivity inevitably creeps in, is to ignore the fact that all historical work consists of a dialogue between the historian, in community with other historians, and the source materials; and that at every point the historians' own worldview-perspectives are inevitably involved.) But this does not mean that all knowledge collapses into *mere* subjectivity. There are ways of moving towards fair and true statements about the past.

Among these is the attempt to plot the worldview of a particular community by studying, not just its ideas (which are often only accessible to us through the writings of an intellectual elite), but the praxis, stories and symbols which constitute the other bottom-line elements of a worldview.[68] It might be possible in principle to structure the following investigation along those lines, studying each element in turn (as I did in *Jesus and the Victory of God* Part II), but this would involve a substantial amount of overlap and repetition. The line I have taken draws on all these as need arises, but within a different structure. The central parts of the book are mostly concerned with one particular question, that of beliefs about life after death in general and about what happened to Jesus after his death in particular. But these beliefs are surrounded, at least implicitly, with praxis, stories and symbols which we shall draw on from time to time: burial habits, characteristic stories about life after death, and the symbols associated with death and what lies beyond. Thus, rather than simply attempting an explanation of the rise of the early church in terms of ideas and beliefs alone ('people who believe/think X will, under certain circumstances, modify that belief/idea in such and such a way', and so on), we should look as well for wider explanations ('people who live within the following controlling story-world will, if confronted by certain events, retell their story in the following ways'; 'when people whose lives are ordered around the following symbols are confronted by certain events they will re-order their lives, and those symbols, in the following ways'; and 'if people who habitually behave in the following fashion are

---

[68] cf. *NTPG* 122–6.

confronted by certain events, they will alter their behaviour in the following ways'). We wish we knew more about early Christian praxis, stories and symbols; but we know enough to see where help may be found. We must broaden the investigation to include the communities that actually existed within the first-century world, as opposed to those communities that, projected back by modern scholarship, reflect simply the dogma and piety (or, indeed, the impiety) of our own times. These communities – pluriform first-century paganism, Judaism and Christianity – provide our best access to the questions of what the Christian claim meant and how we today can assess it.

Sketching these large entities is of course complex. As is now widely agreed, there are only first-century Judaisms and Christianities, and for that matter paganisms; it is not so frequently noted that there must be something singular in each case of which these pluralities are variant forms.[69] Equally, despite those who have tried to keep them apart, very early Christianity should itself properly be seen as a sub-branch of first-century Judaism.[70] Studying these two closely related movements is the place to start. These are the initial targets at which the historical arrows are to be aimed.

The point of this obvious suggestion is its negative corollary. Many studies of the resurrection have begun by examining the accounts of the Easter experiences in Paul and the gospels, subjecting those accounts to detailed traditio-historical analysis. This puts the cart before the horse. Such analysis is always speculative; until we know what resurrection meant in that world, we are unlikely to get it right. This is not just a matter of seeing the big picture ahead of the little details, though that is important too; it is about knowing what we are talking about before we begin to talk about it.[71]

Here we need some working definitions. 'Death' and its cognates regularly denote: (a) the event of a particular death – of a person, animal, plant or whatever; (b) the state of being dead that results from that initial event; and (c) the phenomenon of death in general, in the abstract, or as a personification ('Death shall be no more').[72] The loose phrase 'life after death' can thus denote: (a) the state (whatever it is) that immediately follows *the event of bodily death*; or (b) the state (if there is one) that follows *a period of being bodily dead*; or, conceivably – though this is not found frequently – (c) the state of affairs after death in the abstract has been abolished.[73] When people speak of 'life after death' they usually mean (a), the life that follows

---

[69] cf. *NTPG* 147 n. 1.

[70] cf. Neusner 1991, discussed in *NTPG* 471–3.

[71] I am reminded of what the British Prime Minister John Major said about his opponent Neil Kinnock. When Mr Kinnock began to speak, declared Major, he never knew what he was going to say, and thus not unnaturally never knew when he had finished saying it.

[72] *OED* lists two primary meanings: 'the act or fact of dying' (subdivided into 'of an individual' and 'in the abstract'), and 'the state of being dead'. The quotation is from John Donne's 'Holy Sonnets' no. 6. Cf. too e.g. Barr 1992, 33–5.

[73] As e.g. in 1 Cor. 15.26; Rev. 20.14; 21.4.

immediately after bodily death. People often assume, in fact, that this is among the primary things that Christians believe and that atheists deny.

Sense (a) is not what 'resurrection' meant in the first century. Here there is no difference between pagans, Jews and Christians. They all understood the Greek word *anastasis* and its cognates, and the other related terms we shall meet, to mean (b): new life after a period of being dead. Pagans denied this possibility; some Jews affirmed it as a long-term future hope; virtually all Christians claimed that it had happened to Jesus and would happen to them in the future. All of them were speaking of a new life *after* 'life after death' in the popular sense, a fresh living embodiment *following* a period of death-as-a-state (during which one might or might not be 'alive' in some other, non-bodily fashion). Nobody (except the Christians, in respect of Jesus) thought that this had already happened, even in isolated cases.

Thus, when the ancients spoke of resurrection, whether denying it or affirming it, they were telling a two-step story. Resurrection itself would be preceded (and was preceded even in the case of Jesus) by an interim period of death-as-a-state. Where we find a single-step story – death-as-event being followed at once by a final state, for instance of disembodied bliss – the texts are not talking about resurrection. Resurrection involves a definite *content* (some sort of re-embodiment) and a definite *narrative shape* (a two-step story, not a single-step one). This meaning is constant throughout the ancient world, until we come to a new coinage in the second century.[74]

The meaning of 'resurrection' as 'life *after* "life after death"' cannot be overemphasized, not least because much modern writing continues to use 'resurrection' as a virtual synonym for 'life after death' in the popular sense.[75] It has sometimes been proposed that this usage was current even for the first century, but the evidence is simply not there.[76] If we are to engage in history, rather than projecting the accidents of (some) contemporary usage on to the remote past, it is vital to keep these distinctions in mind.

The place to start, then, is the turbulent world of first-century paganism. Without looking ahead to the answer supplied by Acts 17, we must ask: what would someone in Ephesus, Athens or Rome have understood Paul to be talking about when he announced to them that the Messiah had been raised from the dead? And what reaction would their existing framework of beliefs suggest to them?

---

[74] For the latter, see 534–51.

[75] This confusion is present in Marcus 2001, 397. Some within the Lubavitcher messianic movement have apparently used 'resurrection' language in relation to their Rebbe (who died in 1994) as a way (Marcus suggests, following Dale Allison) of 'speaking of a dead person being alive'. What seems to be happening, rather, is that some have picked up a misunderstood Christian term and used it in a sense that goes against their own ancient literature. Another example, almost at random, is the essay of Wiles 1974, 125–46.

[76] See e.g. the remarkably imprecise, arm-waving remarks of Goulder 2000, 95.

Chapter Two

SHADOWS, SOULS AND WHERE THEY GO:
LIFE BEYOND DEATH IN ANCIENT PAGANISM

1. Introduction

In so far as the ancient non-Jewish world had a Bible, its Old Testament was Homer. And in so far as Homer has anything to say about resurrection, he is quite blunt: it doesn't happen.

The classic statement is that of Achilles as he addresses the grief-stricken Priam, mourning his son Hector whom Achilles has killed:

> You must endure, and not be broken-hearted. Lamenting for your son will do no good at all. You will be dead yourself before you bring him back to life.[1]

Nor, declares Hector's mother, could Achilles raise up his dead companion Patroclus, despite dragging her son round his body.[2]

The tradition is maintained unbroken through the hallowed Athenian dramatists. Here, from Aeschylus' *Eumenides*, is Apollo, speaking at the foundation of the Athenian high court, the Areopagus:

> Once a man has died, and the dust has soaked up his blood, there is no resurrection.[3]

So too Electra, mourning her father Agamemnon, is reminded by the Chorus that one cannot call him back (the word used is *anstaseis*, 'resurrect' him) from Hades, either by weeping or by lamentation.[4] Similarly, Herodotus

---

[1] *Il.* 24.549–51 (tr. Rieu). The last sentence, literally translated, is even more emphatic: 'you will not resurrect him [*oude min ansteseis*] before you suffer a further evil.'

[2] *Il.* 24.756. Achilles' mocking prophecy that the Trojans he has slain 'will rise up from the murky darkness' (21.56) is simply a way of expressing astonishment that Lycaon has escaped from slavery in Lemnos; he proceeds to kill him in order, he says, to see whether he will also return from the underworld (21.61f.), which of course he does not.

[3] Aesch. *Eumen.* 647f. The key final phrase is *outis est' anastasis*.

[4] Soph. *El.* 137–9. Cf. too, similarly, Aesch. *Ag.* 565–9, 1019–24, 1360f.; Eurip. *Helen* 1285–7; cp. Aristot. *De Anima* 1.406b.3–5. Aristoph. *Ecclesiaz.* 1073 fantasizes about a

recounts the tale of Cambyses, son of Cyrus, who, warned by a dream, had his brother Smerdis killed on suspicion of plotting against him. A plot is nevertheless discovered, with a different Smerdis at its head. Cambyses rebukes Prexaspes, the servant charged with the killing, for failing in his duty, and receives this reply:

> Master, it isn't true! Your brother Smerdis has not risen up against you . . . I myself did what you ordered me, and buried him with my own hands. So now, if dead men rise up [*ei men nun hoi tethneotes anesteasi*], you may believe, if you will, that Astyages the Mede may rise up against you; but if things continue the way they do, you may be sure that you will never have anything untoward to fear from Smerdis.[5]

'If dead men rise up': but Prexaspes and Cambyses, like everyone else, know they don't.[6] This basic tenet of human existence and experience is accepted as axiomatic throughout the ancient world; once people have gone by the road of death, they do not return. When the ancient classical world spoke of (and denied) resurrection, there should be no controversy about what the word and its cognates referred to: it was a coming back again into something like the same sort of life that humans presently experience. 'Resurrection' was not one way of describing what death consisted of. It was a way of describing something everyone knew did not happen: the idea that death could be reversed, undone, could (as it were) work backwards.

Not even in myth was it permitted. When Apollo tries to bring a child back from the dead, Zeus punishes both of them with a thunderbolt.[7] Virgil allows that some 'sons of the gods', specially beloved by Jupiter, have been lifted up to the heavens (*ad aethera*); but for the rest, though the door into the underworld stands open for anyone to enter, retracing one's steps to the world above is impossible.[8] What is this crazy idea, asks Pliny, that life is renewed by death? Everyone knows that such talk is nonsense.[9]

This stern denial of any way back from the dead was far from being a mere poets' fancy or scholars' scepticism. Street-level wisdom took exactly the same view. 'What's it like down there?' a man asks his departed friend. 'Very dark,' replies the dead friend. 'Is there any way back up?' 'It's a

---

witch 'risen up' (*anestekuia*) from among 'the majority' (i.e. the dead), but this is dismissed as 'scoffing' (1074).

[5] Hdt. 3.62.3f. The passage plays off 'rise up' as resurrection against 'rise up' as rebellion. Astyages, Cyrus' grandfather, ruled Media 594–559 BC, dying more than thirty years before the present incident.

[6] cf. Eurip. *Madn. Hercl.* 719; Herod. *Mim.* 1.41–4 (a ref. I owe to Michael C. Sloan).

[7] Pindar *Pyth.* 3.1–60; the key passage is 3.55–7, which speaks of bringing back from death one who is its lawful prey.

[8] *Aen.* 6.127–31.

[9] Pliny (the Elder) *NH* 7.55.190, towards the end of a section cataloguing, and ridiculing, various standard beliefs about life after death. Here he refers particularly to Democritus, on whom see below.

lie!'[10] Everybody knew that dead people did not return.[11] 'Resurrection in the flesh appeared a startling, distasteful idea, at odds with everything that passed for wisdom among the educated.'[12]

Many went further (at all levels of culture), and effectively denied the dead any real existence whatever. 'I wasn't, I was, I am not, I don't care': this epitaph was so well known that it was often reduced on tombstones to its initial letters, in Latin as well as Greek.[13] The only real immortality, many decided, was fame.[14] 'A name and a beautiful image' was the most one could hope for.[15] Several philosophers and writers throughout the Classical period and world declared that the dead were, basically, non-existent.[16] This was the position of the Epicureans in particular: for them, the soul was made of extremely fine particles of matter, and was therefore dissolved, along with the other matter of the human being, at physical death.[17] Though in other ways Epicurus and Lucretius were dependent on Democritus, they made a point of distancing themselves from his supposed views on this point (the idea that, because the atoms of soul and body have come together by chance, there is always the possibility that, after being scattered in death, they might be brought together again).[18] Even Socrates, in whose mouth

---

[10] Callimachos *Epigrams* 15.3f. There were, however, compensations: in Hades, you could buy a large ox for a single copper coin (15.6).

[11] cf., emphatically, Bowersock 1994, 102f., citing also the article on Resurrection in *RAC* (Oepke).

[12] MacMullen 1984, 12.

[13] Beard, North and Price 1998, 2.236, with further refs.; Klauck 2000, 80. Some examples miss out the second stage.

[14] *Il.* 9.413 (Achilles); Polybius *Hist.* 6.53.9–54.3.

[15] Burkert 1985 [1977], 197 (referring in particular, as typical of this attitude, to a statue with inscription from Merenda in Attica: details in Burkert 427 n. 29).

[16] In Sall. *Cat.* 51.20, Julius Caesar, speaking as *pontifex maximus*, declares that 'death puts an end to all mortal ills and leaves no room either for sorrow or for joy.' When Dido finds love for Aeneas stirring within her, she wrestles with her duty to her own late husband, and invokes a curse on herself that if she forgets him ('May the Almighty Father hurl me with his bolt to the shades – the pale shades and abysmal night in Erebus'). Her sister Anna then tells her that 'dust and buried shades' will pay no attention to her mourning (*Aen.* 4.25–7, 34).

[17] cf. e.g. Lucretius *De Rer. Nat.* 3.31–42, 526–47, 1045–52, 1071–5. In 3.978–97 he insists that the mythical torments of Tantalus, Tityus and Sisyphus are descriptions of present rather than future life. For Epicurus himself see e.g. Diog. Laert. 10.124–7, 139 ('Death is nothing to us', echoed in Lucret. *De Re Nat.* 3.830), 143. See also e.g. Eurip. *Helen* 1421. Other refs. in Riley 1995, 37f.

[18] For Epicurus' critique, cf. Cic. *Tusc. Disp.* 1.34.82; see the discussions in e.g. Bailey 1964, 226 (Epicurus called Democritus 'Lerocritus', i.e. 'nonsense'), 353, 363, 403f.; Guthrie 1962–81, 2.386–9, 434–8. It remains an open question (for Cicero, as for modern writers) whether Epicurus, and other writers like Pliny (see above), were thus misrepresenting Democritus' main point (that it was difficult to tell the precise moment of death, because, for instance, hair and nails can continue to grow after apparent death), or whether Democritus really did believe in the possibility of the reassembling of atoms. That is the proposal Lucretius dismisses at 3.847–53: even if, he says, time (*aetas*) shall gather

Plato elsewhere places such a rich view of the state of the soul after death, admits that one possible theory of what happens is 'dreamless sleep'.[19] Thus, although as we shall see most people took a less severe position, for many in the ancient world there was no life at all beyond the grave.

The immediate conclusion is clear. Christianity was born into a world where its central claim was known to be false. Many believed that the dead were non-existent; outside Judaism, nobody believed in resurrection.

This has recently been questioned by Stanley Porter.[20] He claims that, while there is little Jewish evidence regarding physical or bodily resurrection, 'the same cannot be said for what is found in Greek and Roman religion', where 'there is a shockingly strong tradition of contemplation of the soul's destiny in the afterlife, along with examples of bodily resurrection.'[21] However, all he has succeeded in showing is that (a) many in the ancient Greek world believed in some kind of survival after death; (b) this was developed into various theories of the soul's immortality; (c) that the mystery cults provided specialized variations on this ('even if', as Porter notes damagingly, 'bodily resurrection is not a part of it');[22] and (d) that Euripides' *Alcestis* has a remarkable story of Hercules rescuing the heroine and restoring her to life, a tale which is referred to once by Plato and once by Aeschylus. Points (a), (b) and (c) are all well known, not 'shocking' at all, and have nothing to do with resurrection – indeed, they are precisely ways of *not* predicating it. We shall discuss the *Alcestis* presently. This can hardly be said to constitute a 'tradition of resurrection'; indeed, it indicates a uniform and universal tradition within which resurrection is known *not* to happen, except in one dreamlike moment of poetic imagination. By contrast, as we shall see in the next two chapters, the Jewish evidence, though by no means unanimous, is solid and impressive.

One might think that this was all we needed to know for our purposes, but things are seldom that simple. We have neither need nor space for a full survey of ancient attitudes to death and beliefs about an afterlife. Whole books have been written on single aspects of these complex and fascinating topics, and in much of what follows I concur with mainstream opinions.[23] Brief restatement of the basic points, though, is necessary, for two reasons.

---

together our matter (*materia*) after death, that would be irrelevant, since there would be no continuity between the earlier person and the new one. Unless Democritus' lost treatise *Concerning Those in Hades* turns up, the matter may well remain unresolved. I am grateful to Christopher Kirwan and Jane Day for advice on this fascinating corner of the subject.

[19] Plato *Apol.* 40c–41c. See too Callim. *Epigr.* 11, preferring to speak of 'sleep' rather than 'death' in the case of good people.

[20] Porter 1999a.

[21] Porter 1999a, 69.

[22] Porter 1999a, 77.

[23] Clear, brief, recent treatments of the whole subject include Klauck 2000 [1995/6], 68–80; Baslez 2001; also (from one particular angle) Zeller 2002. The older classic works on the subject include Rohde 1925 [1897]; Cumont 1923, 1949.

First, our earliest witness to Christian belief in the resurrection of Jesus, and to Christian views on the resurrection of all God's people, is Paul; and Paul, though he remained here and elsewhere very Jewish in his thinking, saw himself primarily as the apostle to the pagan world.[24] It is therefore vital to understand the context into which one of the most central features of his proclamation was addressed. Indeed, this point could be widened: the first-century Judaism within which Christianity was born was itself located within, and (despite some efforts) not hermetically sealed against, the wider world of ancient paganism.

Second, in some recent writing on the origin of Christian belief in Jesus' resurrection it has been suggested that we should look for parallels to, and perhaps even derivations from, certain aspects of pagan belief. Jesus' followers, say the gospels, ate and drank with him after his death; so, say some, did the ancients with their late lamented friends.[25] The disciples saw Jesus apparently alive again; so, claim some, did many of the ancients with the recently deceased.[26] Jesus' followers, after his death, used the language of resurrection to express their belief about where he was now; so, say some, did other peoples with their revered dead.[27] The gospel stories of what happened at Easter feature puzzled friends discovering an empty tomb; exactly what, according to some, we find in many ancient writings, not least the novels that emerged in hellenistic literature at the time.[28] The Christians believed that one would be given a new body at some stage after death; this corresponds, suggest some, to the quite frequent ancient belief in the transmigration of souls. Jesus' followers believed that he had been exalted to a state of heavenly supremacy; so, say some, did many of the ancients believe about their heroes.[29] The early church worshipped the Jesus who had died and been raised; so, say some, did many pagans with their dying and rising gods.[30] It might seem premature to comment on these matters at this stage of the book, and we shall indeed refer back to this chapter at various later stages; but since it can be shown on good historical grounds that these suggested parallels and derivations are figments of the (modern) imagination, it may be as well to deal with them in this early chapter in order to clear the ground for our more central subject-matter. In any case, the question in the first instance is not whether the existence of such beliefs offers parallels to early Christian beliefs about Jesus or about the Christian resurrection hope;

---

[24] On the non-polemical, merely descriptive, use of 'pagan' here and elsewhere, cf. Preface, xvii. For Paul's self-understanding as the apostle to the *ethne*, i.e. the pagan or non-Jewish nations, cf. e.g. Rom. 1.5; 11.13.

[25] Riley 1995, 67, and his ch. 1 *passim*, followed by e.g. Crossan 1998, xiv; see below.

[26] e.g. Crossan 2000, 103; and esp. Lüdemann 1994, 1995.

[27] Davies 1999; see below.

[28] Corley 2002, 129–32. For discussion, see below, section 3 (v).

[29] A. Y. Collins 1993, followed by e.g. Patterson 1998; see below.

[30] So, curiously, Frei 1993, 47; see, further, below, 80f.

the key question is, do they constitute exceptions to the rule laid down by Homer, Aeschylus and Sophocles?[31]

The historian must, of course, pay attention, not least in a topic like this, to a range of phenomena far beyond explicit statements of belief in literary sources, or even in popular-level inscriptions. As I said in the first chapter, and have argued elsewhere, we must deal not only with explicit answers to explicit *questions* but with *praxis* (that which people do habitually, characteristically and usually unreflectively), *symbol* (cultural phenomena, including objects and institutions, in which, not least by association with praxis and story, the worldview comes to visible and tangible expression), and *story* (the narratives, great and small, whether intended as factual or fictitious, which encode the worldview).[32] We shall draw on all four elements – praxis, symbol, story and questions – in analysing the worldview at this point, not least the aims, intentions and beliefs, in relation to the phenomenon of death, of the early Christians' non-Jewish contemporaries.

A further word about each of these will clear the way for briefer subsequent reference. The characteristic *praxis* in question consists, obviously, of funeral customs and practices; less obviously, but equally importantly, of post-funeral rituals and practices, continued often for years after a death. Frustratingly, scholars have found it impossible to correlate the quite drastic changes of burial-praxis – from inhumation to cremation, for instance, or vice versa – with any obvious change in belief or worldview.[33] Equally frustratingly, a good deal that must have gone on, precisely because it was taken for granted, is not described in literature, inscriptions or artwork such as vase paintings (a key source for ancient praxis). Burial of the dead was not a particularly 'religious' event, in the sense that it did not involve the gods directly;[34] however, it is often implied that liturgical rites did take place, though we do not know much about what they were.[35] When we do have descriptions of such rites, they are often those for a royal or aristocratic

---

[31] It hardly needs to be said that, though like all good historians I write *sine ira et studio* (Tac. *Ann.* 1.1; I intend the same irony), the present arguments fall within the wider hermeneutical spiral of which this book is but one part. I am no more a neutral fly-on-the-wall observer than those with whom I disagree; but this does not in principle affect the status or value of historical arguments (cf. *NTPG* Part II, and above, ch. 1).

[32] cf. *NTPG* 122–6.

[33] cf. e.g. Burkert 1985, 190–94; Toynbee 1971 ch. 2; Ferguson 1987, 191–7, with bibliog.

[34] Price 1999, 100.

[35] See esp. Toynbee 1971 ch. 3; Garland 1985, xi, 30f., 36; and, among primary sources, e.g. *Il.* 23.43–54, 114–53, 161–225 (making a barrow, shaving one's head, lighting the pyre, sundry drink-offerings and animal sacrifices); 23.236–61 (quenching the pyre with wine, removing the bones, placing them in an urn, and burying them in the barrow); and the close parallels to all the above in 24.777–804; Soph. *Antig.* 429–31 (triple offering to the dead), 876–82 (funeral hymn), 900–02 (libations on graves); Virgil *Aen.* 3.62–8; 6.212–35.

funeral, and hence – though some similarities may be assumed – should not be taken as typical.[36] One would not learn very much about day-to-day British funeral practice from watching the funerals of the royal family.

The relevant *symbols* include funeral monuments, often with inscriptions and carvings indicating the sort of existence the dead were believed to possess. Objects are often buried with the dead, such as the coin placed in the mouth with which the deceased was to pay Charon, the ferryman in charge of passage across the underworld's river Styx.[37]

The *stories* about the dead range from the spectacular scenes in Homer, through Plato's myths of the afterlife, to the entertaining fantasies of the hellenistic novels. Of course, the demands of the genre in each case mean that the historian will be careful not to assume that all readers took them as statements of the writer's actual belief, let alone as statements of literal truth, and certainly not as prescriptive statements of what ought to be believed. Many of the texts we shall look at are explicit about their own fictional status. But they are, again, a vital part of the web of evidence to be studied.[38]

Within the context created by these three elements, we may understand, and try to correlate, the answers given to the implicit worldview *questions* in relation to the dead: who are they, where are they, what (if anything) is wrong, what (if anything) is the solution, and what time (if anything) is it in the sequence of relevant events? Though there is, as we shall now see, quite a range of answers to these questions given within the world of late antiquity, they fall along a comprehensible spectrum and, as we have already seen, exclude certain answers throughout. Lots of things could happen to the dead in the beliefs of pagan antiquity, but resurrection was not among the available options. To test this we must lay out the spectrum, in order then to ask whether there are signs of further beliefs about the dead which might anticipate, even in tangential ways, the Christian beliefs about Jesus.

2. Shadows, Souls or Potential Gods?

(i) Introduction

In this section I shall describe, in the manner already indicated, the range of options for belief about the dead that were available in the classical world of

---

[36] e.g. Polybius *Hist.* 6.53f.; Dio Cassius 75.4.2–5.5 (texts in Beard, North and Price 1998, 226–8).

[37] See e.g. Burkert 1985, 190–4; Toynbee 1971, 43–61; Garland 1985, ch. 3. For Charon's fare, see (among dozens of examples) Juv. *Sat.* 3.265–7; 8.97.

[38] The two great Homeric scenes are the appearance of Patroclus to Achilles (*Il.* 23.62–107) and Odysseus' visit to the underworld (*Od.* 10.487—11.332). For Plato's Myth of Er, cf. *Rep.* 10.614b—621d (the close of the work; see below, 78f.). On the hellenistic novels, see section 3 (v) below.

late antiquity – roughly two or three hundred years either side of the time of Jesus.[39] There is, again, neither need nor space to treat in full the parallel phenomena from ancient Egypt, Canaan, Mesopotamia and Persia; they will appear from time to time, but the unique aspects of each – for instance, the practice of mummification in Egypt – can be left aside as not impinging on the world of thought we are studying.[40] Our survey in this section moves from the bleak world depicted by Homer, through various pictures in which the dead, though disembodied, seem to lead an otherwise fairly normal existence, and on to more apparently exciting possibilities.

(ii) Witless Shadows in a Murky World?

The two Homeric narratives that left deep imprints on the greco-roman imagination throughout the period are worth looking at closely. They offer not only a wealth of detail which is then picked up by later writers and, at a popular level, in epitaphs and funeral practices; they convey a mood which may safely be seen as the basic assumption, the working point from which other views diverged.[41]

The first is the scene in the *Iliad* where Achilles is confronted with the shade of his recently killed bosom friend, Patroclus. The moment is critical for the entire plot of the epic, which is all about the wrath of Achilles: it explains his return to the fray after his long sulk. Once he is fighting again, Troy's defeat is assured, though he will himself die in the process.

Patroclus, whom Achilles has sent into battle, has been killed by Euphorbus and Hector. There is a struggle over his corpse, which is eventually recovered and brought back to the Greek camp.[42] Achilles and his comrades wash Patroclus' body, but do not yet bury it. Instead, for several books of the poem, Achilles goes off at last to fight, driven by his frantic grief (18.22–125), and finally killing Hector himself (22.247–366). Only then does he return to the task of mourning the now avenged Patroclus.

He addresses the dead man as now resident in Hades (23.19), telling him of his vengeance, and he makes preparation for the funeral on the morrow. That night, however, as he slept,

> There came to him the spirit of hapless Patroclus, in all things like his very self, in stature and fair eyes and in voice, and in like raiment was he clad withal; and he stood

---

[39] On this whole section, see the recent and helpful summary of Bolt 1998.

[40] For a brief and helpful survey of ancient oriental beliefs and practices, see Yamauchi 1998. A fairly full account, with some tendentious features, is Davies 1999, Part I. Davies addresses the question of the relevance of these worlds to that of first-century Judaism and Christianity in his ch. 4, which I shall discuss below.

[41] On this whole topic, and for more detail, see e.g. Garland 1985, ch. 3.

[42] *Il.* 16.805–63; 17 *passim*; cf. 18.231–8.

above Achilles' head and spake to him, saying: 'Thou sleepest, and hast forgotten me, Achilles. Not in my life wast thou unmindful of me, but now in my death! Bury me with all speed, that I pass within the gates of Hades. Afar do the spirits keep me aloof, the phantoms of men that have done with toils, neither suffer they me to join myself to them beyond the River, but vainly I wander through the wide-gated house of Hades. And give me thy hand, I pitifully entreat thee, for never more again shall I come back from out of Hades, when once ye have given me my due of fire . . .[43]

In response, Achilles seeks to embrace his old friend:

Achilles held out his arms to clasp the spirit, but in vain. It vanished like a wisp of smoke and went gibbering underground. Achilles leapt up in amazement. He beat his hands together and in his desolation cried: 'Ah then, it is true that something of us does survive even in the Halls of Hades, but with no intellect at all, only the ghost and semblance of a man; for all night long the ghost of poor Patroclus (and it looked exactly like him) has been standing at my side, weeping and wailing, and telling me of all the things I ought to do.'[44]

Achilles then arises from his sleep, and completes the elaborate funeral (23.108–261).

The passage is full of interest for our purposes, quite apart from its dramatic significance within the unfolding climax of Homer's great work, and its influence on Virgil, the greatest poet of the Augustan age.[45] Achilles, it seems, has nurtured doubts as to whether the dead have any existence at all; but now this ghostly vision has settled the matter, though hardly in a pleasing manner. Who is Patroclus now? A ghost or spirit (*psyche*), a phantom or semblance (*eidolon*). Where is he? On his way to Hades (wandering, but apparently restless, in 'the wide-gated house of Hades'), but unable to cross the river Styx and find his proper place of rest until the appropriate funeral has been held.[46] (The counterpoint to the drama is that Achilles is at the same time forcibly retaining the unburied corpse of Hector, whose eventual funeral closes the epic.[47]) What's wrong? Patroclus is no longer properly human, just a gibbering and witless phantom. What's the solution? There is none. He can be helped on his way to Hades, but he will not find a full or enriching existence there, and he will certainly not return. The drama proceeds on its way, but Patroclus is gone for good, and Achilles himself will soon be joining him both in their shared grave (23.82–92) and in gloomy Hades.

---

[43] *Il.* 23.65–76 (tr. Murray).

[44] *Il.* 23.99–107 (tr. Rieu).

[45] Virgil *Aen.* 6.756–885, where Aeneas' visit to his father Anchises in the underworld includes a similar scene of attempted embraces. Achilles' nocturnal trial has become proverbial by this period: Juvenal (*Sat.* 3.278–80) can use it as a simile for a drunkard's sleepless night, even though, in the original, Achilles is indeed sleeping.

[46] 'The wide-gated house of Hades' is the area owned by the god Hades, not 'Hades' as a place (Patroclus is not yet there). On Hades see the material in Bremmer 2002, 136 n. 33.

[47] *Il.* 24.777–804.

The second Homeric account of the underworld is put in the mouth of Odysseus, relating how he and his companions escaped from Circe's island. Circe allows him to go home, but first he must make another journey, to the house of Hades and Persephone (Hades is the name not only of the place but of its king; Persephone is his wife).[48] There he must summon the ghost of the blind Theban seer, Teiresias; he alone, she says, can still think clearly, while the other ghosts 'flit about like shadows'.[49] The thought of this journey fills even the redoubtable Odysseus with gloom, but Circe tells him both where to go and what to do when he gets there: he must dig a pit, pour drink-offerings, invoke the shades with the promise of sacrifices. So the company sets off.[50] Having arrived at the land of perpetual night – it is surprisingly easy to get there, it seems, given a good wind – Odysseus does what he is told. Attracted by the blood of the sacrifices, though they are not allowed near it until Teiresias has appeared, each ghost (*psyche*) in turn appears and holds a conversation with the hero, beginning with his most recently deceased comrade, Elpenor, who, like Patroclus with Achilles, requests a proper burial.[51] Then comes Odysseus' mother Anticleia, and then Teiresias himself. Why, asks the seer, has the hero come to this place?

> Why have you left the light of the sun and come here to behold the dead and the place where there is no joy?[52]

Odysseus allows him to drink the sacrificial blood, whereupon the seer prophesies what will happen to Odysseus and his companions. Teiresias then departs, having told the wanderer how the other ghosts may come to recognize him and speak with him: they too must drink the sacrificial blood (11.146–8). So, beginning with his mother, Odysseus converses with the shades.[53]

Anticleia enquires how her son has come 'beneath the murky darkness', and tells him what has happened at Ithaca in his absence. Like Achilles with Patroclus, Odysseus attempts to embrace her:

> Three times I sprang toward her, and my will said, 'Clasp her,' and three times she flitted from my arms like a shadow or a dream.[54]

[48] See Burkert 1985, 195f. for the background.

[49] *Od.* 10.487–95.

[50] *Od.* 10.496–574.

[51] *Od.* 11.51–83; Elpenor's funeral takes place in 12.8–15.

[52] *Od.* 11.93f.

[53] To suggest, on the basis of this scene, coupled with the pouring of libations to the dead and so forth (see below), that the ancient world in general believed that ghosts 'could eat' (Riley 1995, 47f.; cf. 67) strains credulity. Riley says this point is 'missed by some New Testament scholars'; I think it is Riley who has missed the point.

[54] *Od.* 11.206–08.

He complains to her: since he has come to the house of Hades, why may they not embrace? Is it really her, or only 'some phantom' (*ti eidolon*)?[55] This, she replies, is how it is with mortals after death:

> For the sinews no longer hold the flesh and the bones together, but the strong force of blazing fire destroys these, as soon as the spirit [*thymos*] leaves the white bones, and the ghost [*psyche*], like a dream, flutters off and is gone.[56]

With that, the tension relaxes, and Odysseus relates how the shades of other women, the wives and daughters of chieftains, came to him and, drinking the blood, told their varied tales.[57] His hearers persuade him to go on, and to tell how he met his old comrades, Agamemnon, Achilles and the rest; of them only Ajax refuses to speak to him, still angry at having lost the contest for the arms of Achilles.[58] Achilles' response to Odysseus reveals clearly its view of the afterlife ('Hades, where dwell the unheeding dead, the phantoms [*eidola*] of men outworn').[59] The living hero tries to console the dead one by telling him that, as he was honoured like a god during his lifetime, so he now rules mightily in his new location. Achilles, weeping, will have none of it:

> Never try to reconcile me to death, glorious Odysseus. I should choose, so I might live on earth, to serve as the hireling of another, some landless man with hardly enough to live on, rather than to be lord over all the dead that have perished.[60]

Hades, clearly, is not fit for human habitation.[61] Odysseus does, however, bring Achilles some comfort: his warlike son Neoptolemus is making a great name for himself on earth (Achilles, we note, has not heard this until now). The comfort is small; the ghosts who come to speak to Odysseus are sorrowful, or angry, or both. That, it seems, is the way things are in Hades.[62]

Then come figures of a different sort. The poet cannot resist the opportunity to include vignettes which, though they heighten the sense of wonder

---

[55] *Od.* 11.210–14.

[56] *Od.* 11.219–22; cf. Virgil *Aen.* 6.697–702 (Aeneas' failed attempt to embrace the 'form' (*imago*) of his father Anchises). It is typical of the extraordinary claims of Riley 1995 that he suggests that passages like these stand behind the post-Easter scenes in Luke and John in which the risen Jesus offers himself to be touched by the disciples (53).

[57] *Od.* 11.225–332.

[58] *Od.* 11.385–567.

[59] *Od.* 11.475f.

[60] *Od.* 11.488–91.

[61] cf. too Hesiod *Works* 152–5.

[62] Riley, with scenes like this in text after text, can still find it possible to say that 'the dead were in the main conceived of as were the living: resting and waking, conversing with both the living and other dead, eating and drinking, and carrying on post-mortem much as they had in life.' The fact that examples of each of the above activities can be supplied from Homer and so on is irrelevant; the whole which Riley has created is considerably greater than the sum of the parts he has collected.

and mystery, relax the tension of the overall plot. Minos is there, giving judgment over the other dead (so they have lawsuits there, it seems), and Orion with a herd of wild beasts; they seem to be in quite good shape.[63] But then appear three very different characters: Tityus, who had raped Zeus' consort Leto, and is now tortured by pecking vultures; Tantalus, unable to reach the water below him or the fruit above; and Sisyphus, forever pushing his stone up a hill.[64] These seem to be stock figures who add little to our knowledge of the fate, or location, of ordinary folk after death. But finally, and not without some apparent contradiction, Odysseus meets the phantom (*eidolon*) of Hercules. The real Hercules, he explains, is feasting with the immortal gods, married to Hebe, the daughter of Zeus and Hera; but this does not prevent his shade living in the house of Hades.[65]

Odysseus is tempted to remain and meet other heroes of old; but before he can do so

the myriad tribes of the dead came thronging up with an eerie cry, and pale fear seized me, that august Persephone might send upon me out of the house of Hades the head of the Gorgon, that terrible monster.[66]

That is enough for him. He and his companions escape.

Who then are the dead, for Homer and the subsequent centuries that read him devoutly? They are shades (*skiai*), ghosts (*psychai*), phantoms (*eidola*). They are in no way fully human beings, though they may look like them; the appearance is deceptive, since one cannot grasp them physically.[67] The Latin word *Manes* conjures up the same sort of world, with similar variations.[68]

---

[63] *Od.* 11.568–75. On the role of Minos in the underworld, see below.

[64] *Od.* 11.576–600. The question of whether this passage is a later interpolation, as some have thought, need not concern us. On this, and on the punishment of only some in the underworld, cf. Burkert 1985, 197, with other refs.; Garland 1985, 60–66, tracing the theme of judgment of the wicked through the Homeric hymns, through the Mysteries (see below) and the mocking of Aristophanes (*Frogs* 139–64, where Hercules advises Dionysus how to get to Hades and what he will find there), to the great judgment scene at the end of Plato's *Gorgias* (523a—527a). See further below.

[65] *Od.* 11.601–27. On the translation of Hercules to the upper world see below.

[66] *Od.* 11.632–5. Odysseus is perhaps afraid he will be trapped and unable to escape.

[67] In *Aen.* 6.290–94 Aeneas, in his visit to the underworld, is only prevented from attacking the monstrous forms he meets by his companion Achates reminding him that 'these were but faint, bodiless lives, flitting under a hollow semblance of form'. When he meets the Greek heroes, they see 'the arms and the man' (an echo, of course, of 1.1) and try to raise a shout in fear – but all they can manage is a faint noise, which mocks their open mouths (6.489–93). This is important to remember in view of Virgil's occasional use of *corpora*, normally translated 'bodies', for the shadowy residents of the lower world (against e.g. Riley 1995, 55f.), and his indication that the shades can still bear the marks of the wounds they received (e.g. Dido: 6.450f.; cf. too Aesch. *Eumen.* 103; Ovid *Met.* 10.48–9, and (again in Virgil) Hector, Sychaeus, Eriphyle and Deiphobus (*Aen.* 1.355; 2.270–86; 6.445f., 494–7)). See Riley 1995, 50f.

[68] e.g. *Aen.* 4.427; Juv. *Sat.* 2.154.

Where are they? They are in Hades, under the eponymous rule of the under-world's god and his dread wife. What's wrong? They are sorry both to be where they are and at much that happened in their previous human exis-tence. They are sad at their present subhuman state. In some cases they are tormented, as punishment for particularly heinous crimes (though we are not told, interestingly, the crimes of Tantalus and Sisyphus). There may be some who have a shadowy alter ego in a better place; we shall come to Hercules presently. But for most of them, including those who have been great and good in their former life, Hades holds no comforts, no prospects, but only a profound sense of loss.[69] With the single exception (invented for dramatic purposes?) of Teiresias, they have lost their wits and much else besides. They remain essentially subhuman and without hope.

This sense of gloom, of a place at best dreary and monotonous, at worst of terror,[70] is reinforced throughout both ancient literature and what we know, from inscriptions, artefacts and reported customs, of the attitudes and beliefs of ordinary non-literate people. Although the dead could be referred to as 'blessed', 'fortunate' (because no longer suffering the pains of the present life) and 'excellent', these epithets seem to have more to do with the respect due to the dead from the living than with their actual present condi-tion.[71]

One feature of these descriptions is of particular interest. Prior to the developed philosophical reflection that flowered in Plato, the 'soul' (*psyche*) was not seen as a glorious immortal being that would enjoy life away from the body. Indeed, the 'soul' is something other than the person's true 'self'. The *Iliad* opens with this very distinction, with Achilles hailed as the one whose wrath

> sent down to Hades many valiant souls of warriors, and made the men themselves (*autous de*) to be the spoil for dogs and birds of every kind.[72]

We should not suppose that the Platonic revolution (on which see below) did more than offer an alternative viewpoint. The Homeric tradition, and the many other writings and popular beliefs that flowed from it and echoed it, remained powerful well into the early Christian period.[73] If Agamemnon,

---

[69] See Price 1999, 101.

[70] For the latter, see Polyb. *Hist.* 6.56.6–15, praising the Romans for reminding people of the terrors of Hades and so encouraging good behaviour in the present life. This conflicts with Plato's moral stance: see below.

[71] For the tradition of speaking words of respect and hope at funerals, see MacMullen 1984, 11, with notes; for the general point, Garland 1985, 8–10. The unknowability of the world beyond emerges in e.g. Eurip. *Hippol.* 186–92.

[72] *Il.* 1.3–5.

[73] The fact that Juvenal can grumble about women comparing Homer and Virgil at din-ner parties is indicative of the continuing prominence of the epic tradition (*Sat.* 6.437; cf. 7.36–9). The description of souls beyond the grave given by Plutarch in *De Ser. Num.*

Achilles, Ajax and the rest were in miserable Hades, what hope was there for anyone else?

(iii) Disembodied but Otherwise Fairly Normal?

Some at least cherished the hope that despite the gloomy Homeric picture there would after all be elements of normal life. We have already seen that Minos would preside over court cases, which, though not the most pleasant of prospects (except for lawyers, who are not mentioned as taking part), indicates some minimal continuity at least between activities in the sunlit world and those beneath. But here the symbolic praxis of burial customs comes into play.

In many ancient cultures, and on into much later times, it has been common to bury, along with the deceased, the kind of household goods one might be supposed to need. Adornments, charms, toiletries and the like are common. The wealthy might find themselves accompanied by slaughtered animals and slaves, and sometimes even wives, to keep them company and attend to their wants in the next world.[74] Throughout the ancient world all kinds of objects might be buried with the corpse; at Malton in Yorkshire an infant's tomb was found containing a miniature jet bear, presumably a toy.[75] The more elaborate physical preservation involved in mummification was accompanied, in ancient Egypt, by tombs that were, in effect, surrogate homes, containing all that one might require for a fairly full life.[76]

The stories that were told of the dead frequently involved a life similar to the present one – albeit with not much to do, no hunter-gathering or similar tasks, and hence more time to gossip and mope. Many believed that they would meet old friends again.[77] Already in Pindar the Homeric gloom has chinks of light: riding, gaming, gymnastics and especially drinking-parties feature in writing, painting and other decorations illustrating the life of the dead in the subsequent classical period. We should not try to reconcile this picture of a fairly normal life with the Homeric one; nobody was looking for consistency in these matters, and though it is possible that the illustrations in question were really designed to evoke memories of the deceased's happier

---

Vindic. 563f—567f, though influenced by later philosophical beliefs, clearly owes a good deal to the Homeric background.

[74] See e.g. Burkert 1985, 192; Garland 1985, 25–8.

[75] *Antiquaries Journal* 28 (1948), 173–4, pl. 25a. Curiously, the day I drafted this section (7 June 2000), the London *Times* printed a letter from the current Vicar of Malton recounting how two couples who spent all their time playing bridge had asked to reserve grave spaces in a foursome. If ancient children can go on playing with toys in the Yorkshire underworld, why should not modern adults go on playing bridge?

[76] Davies 1999, 30–33. Cf. Riley 1995, 53f. But would the ancients have been surprised to discover that the toys, dice and other playthings had not in fact been touched?

[77] e.g. Antiphanes (C4 BC) *Aphrodisias* (frag. in Kock (ed.), *Stobaeus*, 124–7).

hours, it may well be that, as in our own world, all kinds of contradictory beliefs swirled around cheerfully alongside one another in popular culture.[78] Certainly, though, Socrates envisaged conversing with the famous dead as something to look forward to in the life to come. There is even evidence that people supposed marriage and sexual activity might be possible.[79] We should, however, remind ourselves that most of the written evidence comes from poetry and other writing clearly not intended as literal description. There is little evidence that anyone except very tough-minded philosophers ever took these suggestions so seriously as to face death, their own or that of another, with real equanimity. Even those who appear to do so, and who indeed seem rather to relish this last opportunity to hold centre stage and make a telling, witty political point may well simply be playing out the last moves in a complex game of honour, as with the suicides of Cato, Scipio and others.[80]

One possible exception is the world of Egypt. Though this is not strictly relevant to our subject – the burial customs of ancient Egypt were not practised in Palestine or the areas in which most early Christian evidence is found, and the Osiris cult was in something of a decline in the first half of the first century – one recent study of Egyptian customs has argued strongly that the dead were thought of as continuing into a still very complete life.[81] Despite the opinion of Augustine, according to Jon Davies, that the practice of mummification indicated a belief in resurrection, death in ancient Egypt provided 'more of an opportunity for fulfilment, rather than [being] experienced as a negation requiring a rebirth, a resurrection'.[82] Ancient Egypt did not look forward to any future cataclysm or End Time; after death, people continued in a many-sided form of life, the only hazard being the possibility of a second death. The Egyptian *Books of the Dead* were concerned with 'going out into the day', the new day in which the deceased hoped to be identified with Osiris, the god of the dead, husband and brother of Isis.[83]

---

[78] See Garland 1985, 69–72.

[79] Socrates: Plato *Apol.* 40c–41c; *Rep.* 2.363c–e; 6.498d (see below). Marriage and sex: Garland 1985, 159, with several refs.; Riley 1995, 54.

[80] Cato: Dio 43.12.1; Scipio ('*Imperator se bene habet*' – 'the general is doing just fine, thank you'): Sen. *Ep.* 24.9f.; cf. Val. Max. 3.2.13. See the shrewd discussion in Plass 1995, 89–91. The whole book provides much food for thought on our topic.

[81] Davies 1999, ch. 1. Subsequent page refs. are to this work. For the proposal (which gets revived every few decades) that the Osiris cult is the true background for Paul's view of the resurrection, cf. Bostock 2001. For the decline in the Osiris cult in the early C1, see Fraser 1972, 1.272f.

[82] Davies 28. For Augustine on Egypt (though without a specific statement of belief in resurrection), see *City of God* 8.26f.

[83] Whom Davies 31 confusingly describes as 'goddess of resurrection, of fertility, of the moon'. See below. On Isis, Osiris etc. cf. Koester 1982a, 183–91, rightly denying (190) that Osiris was held to have risen from the dead; and see the forthcoming article on Osiris and 1 Cor. 15 by Dr Nicholas Perrin.

Davies then, strangely, declares that the Egyptians

> were essentially ritual optimists, believing fervently in the 'resurrection' of the dead as an individualized, embodied self, with the whole purpose and point of the funeral rite being to rejoin the *ba* (soul) with the body. Cremation was abhorrent, reserved for evil-doers who would thereby be rendered totally non-existent. The point of the funeral was to accomplish the 'going out into the day', the new life with Osiris and as Osiris, in the delights of eternity.[84]

There is a problem with this description, and it is crucial to our investigation. Davies is right to say, in the earlier passage, that 'resurrection' is an inappropriate word for Egyptian belief. The word denotes, as he sees, a further re-embodiment, a return to a this-worldly life, after a period in which the dead person is *not* alive in this way. Mummification and its other attendant practices, however, imply that the person still is 'alive' in some bodily sense, despite appearances.[85] The passage just quoted, however, muddles exactly this point, using 'resurrection' to mean, not a coming back into bodily life, but the continuing existence in a mummified and hence, in that sense, 'bodily' state after death. There were, Davies later declares, 'no boundaries between these worlds [of the living and the dead]':

> There was no eschatology, no apocalypse, no collective cataclysm, because there was no crisis. Death was life.[86]

That picture makes sense as an account of an Egyptian worldview. What does not belong here is the word 'resurrection'. To use it at all in this setting simply creates confusion. When the Greek-speaking ancient world spoke of *anastasis* and its equivalents, as we saw at the start of this chapter, they did not mean that the existence into which the dead passed immediately was a continuing bodily one, but that, at some point after bodily death, there would be a new embodiment, a coming back into a this-worldly sort of life.

Having clarified that, we can leave Egypt and its mummies as one extreme example of the phenomenon observed in this section. Despite widespread fear of gloomy Hades, some practices, pictures and stories indicated the hope for a continuing life not too different from the present one.

(iv) Souls Released from Prison?

If Homer functioned as the Old Testament for the Hellenistic world – which by the first century included the entire Middle East – its New Testament was

---

[84] Davies 34f.

[85] See Yamauchi 1998, 25–8. The fact that Egyptian beliefs include some kind of apparent physicality for the departed does not mean that the mummies themselves were expected to come to life in a new way thereafter.

[86] Davies 39.

unquestionably Plato.[87] The relationship between the older poet and the newer philosopher is fascinating and complex, worth pondering both in itself and in its many partial analogies to that between the ancient Jewish scriptures and the early Christian writings. And at no point is Plato's newness more striking than in what he has to say about death and its aftermath.

So radical is his perspective, in fact, that – like an Athenian Marcion! – he proposes cutting out of Homer the very scenes which express the poet's view of life after death. He takes his censor's scissors to *Iliad* 23 and *Odyssey* 11; the tales of Achilles and Patroclus, and of Odysseus' journeys in the underworld, will, he thinks, do the young no good.[88] How will we ever get people to be good citizens, he asks, to serve in the army, to do their duty to their friends, if their view of the future life is conditioned by epic pictures of gibbering ghosts in a gloomy underworld? Instead, the young must be taught the true philosophical view: death is not something to regret, but something to be welcomed. It is the moment when, and the means by which, the immortal soul is set free from the prison-house of the physical body.[89]

Plato (and before him Socrates; we cannot here discuss the Socrates of history and the philosopher of Platonic faith) was working at a time when a certain amount of development in the same direction was already noticeable in wider culture. Vase-paintings from roughly 500 BC show the soul as a small human creature (a 'homunculus', as it is often called) hovering above the body of a dead warrior.[90] Pindar, writing in the early sixth century, had already suggested that the soul was immortal.[91] Pythagoras is sometimes credited with the vital development of the idea.[92] But it was Plato who brought these beliefs to their classic expression.

Here is the central difference between Homer and Plato. Instead of the 'self' being the physical body, lying dead on the ground, while the 'soul' flies away to what is at best a half-life, now the 'self', the true person, is precisely the soul, while it is the corpse that is the ghost.[93] At the risk of oversimplifying what is inevitably a complex matter, we may suggest that Plato

---

[87] Homer is generally reckoned to have lived in the C8 BC; Plato certainly lived in the late C5 and early C4.

[88] *Rep.* 3.386–7.

[89] Classic statements: e.g. *Phaedo* 80–85; *Phaedrus* 250c (the soul is imprisoned like the oyster in its shell); *Cratylus* 400c (the famous *soma/sema* pun, 'body/tomb', cf. too *Gorgias* 493a); 403e–f. Substantially the same view is found in later Roman thought, e.g. M. Aurelius *To Himself* 3.7.

[90] cf. M. Halm-Tisserant, *Ktema*, 1992 (1988), 233–44.

[91] Pindar *Ol.* 2.56–80; *Frag. Dirg.* 131 (96). See Burkert 1985, 298f. and notes.

[92] cf. Bremmer 2002, ch. 2.

[93] *Laws* 12.959b–c: the word for 'ghost' here, denoting the corpse rather than the disembodied soul, is *eidolon*, which in Homer and elsewhere usually means much what 'ghost' means in modern English. The most famous statement is in *Phaedo* 115c–d: 'you can bury me,' says Socrates to his friends, 'if I don't slip through your fingers!' Clearly 'I' for Socrates meant the soul, not the body.

has radically modified three central and interlocking concepts: the soul, Hades itself, and the fate of the dead. A word about each, and an explanation for the revolution, is in order.

For Plato, the soul is the non-material aspect of a human being, and is the aspect that really matters. Bodily life is full of delusion and danger; the soul is to be cultivated in the present both for its own sake and because its future happiness will depend upon such cultivation. The soul, being immortal, existed before the body, and will continue to exist after the body is gone.[94] Since for many Greeks 'the immortals' were the gods, there is always the suggestion, at least by implication, that human souls are in some way divine.

Because the soul is this sort of thing, it not only survives the death of the body but is delighted to do so. If it had known earlier where its real interests lay it would have been longing for this very moment. It will now flourish in a new way, released from the prison that had hitherto enslaved it. Its new environment will be just what it should have wanted.[95] Popular opinion would attempt to bring the dead back if that were possible, but this would be a mistake.[96] Death is frequently defined precisely in terms of the separation of soul and body, seen as something to be desired.[97]

Hades, in other words, is not a place of gloom, but (in principle at least) of delight. It is not terrifying, as so many ordinary people believe, but offers a range of pleasing activities – of which philosophical discourse may be among the chief, not surprisingly since attention to such matters is the best way, during the present time, of preparing the soul for its future. The reason people do not return from Hades is that life is so good there; they want to stay, rather than to return to the world of space, time and matter.[98] Plato suggests that the word 'Hades' itself is derived, in terms both of etymology and basic meaning, either from the word for 'unseen', or from the word for 'knowledge'.[99]

What happens to souls in Hades – at least, to souls who go there to begin with – is then far more interesting than anything envisaged in Homer. Judgment is passed according to the person's previous behaviour: we see here the philosophical roots of those judgment scenes that became so familiar in the

---

[94] On all of this, see e.g. *Phaedo* 80–82; *Phaedrus* 245c—247c; *Meno* 81a–e.

[95] cf. e.g. *Apol.* 41c; *Cratyl.* 403f. In *Phaedo* 68a–b Socrates speaks of lovers of wisdom gladly following their beloved into the next world where wisdom will be possessed fully and truly.

[96] e.g. *Crito* 48c. At 68d, Plato's Socrates admits that everyone other than philosophers sees death as a great evil.

[97] e.g. *Phaedo* 64c; 67d; 106e; 107d–e; *Gorg.* 524b. Cf. Ferguson 1987, 195. Celsus (in Or., *C. Cels.*, 5.14) quotes Heraclitus as disparaging physical bodies, which 'ought to be thrown away as worse than dung'.

[98] *Cratyl.* 403d.

[99] 'Unseen': *Phaedo* 80d, *Gorg.* 493b; 'knowledge', rather than 'unseen': *Cratyl.* 404b, though cf. 403a, where fear of Hades is given as the reason why people refer instead to Pluto as god of the underworld.

Platonized Christianity (or was it Christianized Platonism?) of the Middle Ages. Three judges are appointed, one each from Europe and Asia and one (Minos, conveniently from Crete, poised as it were between the two continents) as the judge of appeal. At last, after all the botched earthly attempts at justice, truth will out and judgment will be just; the virtuous will find themselves sent to the Islands of the Blessed, and the wicked will be put in Tartarus.[100] From here it is a short step to the view of Cicero and others, that virtuous souls go to join the stars.[101] Plato needs to be careful here, since he wants simultaneously to deny the normal gloomy view of the entire underworld (hence the censorship mentioned earlier) and to develop a strong theology of post-mortem punishment for the wicked. His way round this dilemma, clearly, is to emphasize the blessings that await the virtuous – not just the philosophers, but those who exhibit courage in battle and sundry other civic virtues.[102] And the central point is important: judgment, even when negative, is emphatically a good thing, because it brings truth and justice to bear at last on the world of humans.[103]

Plato frequently hints at a future for souls *after* their immediate post-mortem existence; some will return into other bodies. I shall discuss this theory of transmigration presently. For the moment we may simply note the probable reasons why Plato developed these views, and the ways in which

---

[100] Classic statements: *Phaedo* 63b; 69d–e; 113d—114c; *Gorg.* 522d–526d. (The Isles of the Blessed are first mentioned in Hesiod *Works* 166–73.) Cf too *Laws* 10.904d–905d; *Rep.* 2.363c–e. According to *Symp.* 179d–e, Achilles is sent directly to the Isles of the Blessed, because he was ready to die, whereas Orpheus was refused Eurydice because he tried to cheat death and was not ready to put love ahead of continuing bodily life. Homer, of course, knows of the Isles of the Blessed, but virtually nobody goes there (Menelaus alone, it seems, in *Od.* 4.561–9; rather more in Hesiod *Works* 168–73). The earliest statement of real post-mortem punishment seems to be the *Hymn to Demeter* 480f., on which see discussion in Garland 1985, 61, 156. On post-mortem judgment in Pindar and Euripides, cf. Garland 157, with refs. Minos continues his role in Virgil *Aen.* 6.432; Aeneas in the underworld comes to the place where roads part, one to Elysium and the other to Tartarus (6.540–43, launching a fearsome description of the latter and then a blissful account of the former). The Isles of the Blessed feature in Lucian's fanciful tale *A True Story* (the title is heavily ironic, as Lucian himself points out at the beginning, 1.4). Despite claims to the contrary, even in Lucian's description the dead are intangible, without flesh; their only attributes are shape and form – though he does then go on to describe their very 'human' lifestyle in some detail. They are naked souls moving about, like shadows though upright and not dark (2.12). Riley 1995, 56–8, tries implausibly to suggest that the impalpability of these souls is a survival from an earlier theory, and that Lucian really believes that they have a more substantial bodily life; it seems to me that he misses the point, that Lucian is making a joke about the 'True Story' being so thoroughly unreliable and inconsistent.

[101] e.g. *De Rep.* 6.13–16. See the survey of Latin views in Perkins 1984, 56–63; and see below, 110–12, for a discussion of 'astral immortality'.

[102] For Socrates' readiness to plead a defence before the judges of the next world, cf. *Crito* 54b.

[103] Annihilation would let the wicked off the hook: *Phaedo* 107c–d.

his ideas were developed in subsequent centuries, through to the first and beyond.

There were at least three influences that steered Plato towards his view of the soul and life after death. To begin with, it is a natural outworking of his larger ontology: according to the theory of Forms, the world of space, time and matter is of secondary ontological significance, and the unseen world of Forms, or Ideas, is primary. Applied to human beings, this obviously privileges the soul over the body, and encourages people to regard the nurture of the soul as more important than the pleasures and pains of bodily existence. In addition, Plato's hopes for a better society in the present world were expressed in various political proposals. Some of these were only, perhaps, semi-serious; but at the heart of it all was the conviction that things went badly in human society when people lived only on the bodily level, without regard to the soul, and that the way to improve this was to teach people to value their souls, both for the sake of a better world in the present and because of the prospect of glorious immortality, at least for those who lived the right sort of life here and now. Thirdly, the irresistible combination of teaching and example offered by Socrates, as reported in the dialogues that lead up to his death (the *Apology*, the *Crito* and the *Phaedo*), offer the strongest support, in terms of personal loyalty, for these views. One would have to be a very determined and hard-hearted materialist not to be affected by Socrates' discourse on the soul, and on the life to come, when he himself was to drink the hemlock by the close of day. Thus the death, as much as the teaching, of the most famous philosopher of all time clearly did much both to contextualize and to reinforce the new view of the soul, and of life after death.

By no means everybody in the ancient world read Plato. He continued to influence philosophical discourse, of course, as he has done on and off ever since. But popular culture, even when it did not know him at first hand, continued to be affected by his work in several directions, of which two are worth noting right away.

Already in Socrates' time the mystery religions had begun to flourish, offering (so it seemed) a comparable benefit to philosophical wisdom but without the hard intellectual work. Beginning with the Orphic cult, but fanning out much more widely, these religions (if that is indeed the right term for them) offered the initiate access to a world of private spiritual experience in the present time which would continue into the world beyond death.[104] Socrates knows about them; Aristophanes makes fun of them; they were popular in Rome.[105] They offered what in post-Enlightenment terms would appear a more overtly *religious* approach to human possibility in this world,

---

[104] The basic work remains Burkert 1987; cf. too Burkert 1985, ch. 6; Koester 1982a, 176–83; Meyer 1999 [1987]; Bolt 1998, 75–7.
[105] Socrates: *Phaedo* 69b–c; Aristoph.: *Frogs* 353–71; Rome: e.g. Juv. *Sat.* 6.524–41.

and happiness in the next: instead of the dry, refined world of philosophical discourse, they offered satisfaction for the emotions, as the reborn soul experienced bliss here and hereafter. Although, therefore, Plato himself does not advocate this route, his positive view of the soul undoubtedly helped to create a climate in which such views and practices could flourish.

A further development, whose origins are obscure and controversial, was gnosticism.[106] Many lines of Platonic thought led straight in this direction. The immortal (and perhaps even divine) soul is imprisoned in the unsuitable body, forgetting its origin in the process.[107] During the present life those with this spark may have the fact revealed to them; as a result, they become possessed of a 'knowledge' (*gnosis*) which sets them apart from other mortals, and are assured of a continuing blissful existence thereafter, with death becoming more or less irrelevant. Though Plato himself did not go in this direction – he did not, for example, limit the divine spark to certain persons only – one can again see how his ideas prepared the way.

Who were the dead, for Plato? They were souls who had been released from their temporary embodiment. Where were they? In Hades, but a very different Hades, and for many a much pleasanter one, than the Homeric version. What was wrong? Nothing: this was a far better place and condition for them to be. Of course, wicked souls were being punished, but that, though unpleasant for them, was not a bad thing, since it represented the triumph of justice at last. No further 'solution' was necessary – though transmigration remained a possibility (see below).

Plato did not sweep the board of subsequent opinion at either a popular or an intellectual level. Socrates' own followers were clearly unable to sustain the master's cheerfulness about his departure into the next world; if even they, with his own example, teaching and specific exhortation, could not refrain from inconsolable grief, it was perhaps unwise to suppose that anyone else would manage it either.[108] In any case, other conflicting ideas were on offer as well. We glanced at Democritus and Epicureanism earlier; Stoic philosophers continued to debate such matters.[109] Plato's ideas on the soul (and much else besides) were, in addition, severely modified by his equally influential pupil Aristotle. He took the view that the soul was the subtance, or the species-form, of the living thing; this represents a turning away from

---

[106] See the brief account in *NTPG* 155f.; and below, 534–51. Dating the origins of this movement is part of the controversy; it is certainly in existence by the middle of the second century AD, and some would argue considerably earlier.

[107] On the soul's forgetfulness of its origin, cf. e.g. *Meno* 81a–d; *Phaedo* 76c–d.

[108] *Phaedo* 116d; 117c–e.

[109] For the Epicurean position, cf. e.g. Epicur. *Ep. ad Men.* 124b–127a; Plut. *Non Posse Suav.* 1103d; 1105a (the whole discussion in Plutarch is an interesting survey of different views); Diog. Laert. 10.139; and above, 34f. On Stoic debates see Diog. Laert. 7.156f.: the Stoics, he says, regard the soul as the breath of life, and hence that it is physical (a *soma*); Cleanthes holds that all souls continue to exist until the general conflagration, whereas Chrysippus says that only the souls of the wise do so.

the lively Platonic view of the soul as a more or less independent, and superior, entity to the body. Aristotle did allow, however, that 'the highest aspect of reason might be immortal and divine'.[110] These exceptions do not, however, damage the general rule, followed with innumerable variations over the succeeding centuries: in Greek philosophy, care for and cure of the soul became a central preoccupation.[111] And – this is, after all, the point for our present enquiry – neither in Plato nor in the major alternatives just mentioned do we find any suggestion that resurrection, the return to bodily life of the dead person, was either desirable or possible.

It is hard to overestimate the importance of Homer and Plato for the later, and wider, world into which, all unexpected, there burst the phenomenon we know as Christianity. Epictetus, one of our best witnesses to what was pondered and believed at a fairly popular level towards the end of the first century AD, draws freely on both, coming to different conclusions from Plato about Achilles' mourning for Patroclus, but emphasizing that Homer wrote to teach subsequent generations about the danger of even the greatest of heroes making the wrong kind of judgments.[112] The example and teaching of Socrates, particularly in his death and his attitude to it, is continually present behind Epictetus' tireless insistence on the irrelevance of death: 'And now, with Socrates dead, the memory of him is not less useful to us, but rather more, than the things he did and said during his lifetime.'[113] It is, indeed, one of Epictetus' great themes, that death is inevitable and therefore irrelevant: one should learn not to be troubled by death, either one's own or that of someone near and dear. Did we think we were immortal?[114]

Epictetus is not, though, simply expounding a philosopher's doctrine for its own sake. His teaching is designed to liberate people from fear of tyrants with their sharp swords and other threats. The terrors of death are just a sham, frightening us the way children are scared of a grimacing but empty mask.[115] Death is simply the separation of soul from body, with the physical matter returning whence it came.[116] Death is a change from what we are now to something else, something different from what the world now needs.[117] As Socrates stressed at his death, the real 'me' is not the corpse that will be buried (or not, as the case may be: remarkably, Epictetus professes not to

---

[110] C. J. Rowe in *OCD* 1428 s.v. 'soul'.

[111] Arist. *De An.*; cf. e.g. Nussbaum and Rorty 1992; Brunschwig and Nussbaum 1993. On the importance of the cure of souls, cf. e.g. Epictetus *Disc.* 2.12.20–25; *Frag.* 32.

[112] Epict. *Disc.* 1.11.31; 4.10.31, 36. The refs. that follow are to this work.

[113] 4.1.169; cf. 4.1.123, 159–69. Cf. too 2.1.26. For Socrates during his last days writing a hymn of praise to Apollo and Artemis, cf. Diog. Laert. 2.42.

[114] e.g. 1.1.21–32; 1.27.7–10; and frequently. Cf. too Marcus Aurelius *To Himself* 12.35f.

[115] 2.1.13–20.

[116] 3.10.13–16; 4.7.15.

[117] 3.24.92–4; the passage, unfortunately, is obscure.

care about burial) but that which presently employs the limbs and organs.[118]
A human being is 'a little soul carrying around a corpse'. Nature taught you
to love the body in the first place, and when Nature tells you it's time to let
it go, you shouldn't complain.[119] Epictetus' whole aim is that one should
learn to be happy, or at least not unhappy, in this world. His adaptation of
the whole Greek tradition within a popular-level Stoicism is gritty, dogged,
and lacks the leisured flavour of Plato's portrait of Socrates; but, apart from
some specific Stoic details, we may suppose that Plato, and perhaps Socrates
himself, would have been pleased with this much later dissemination of their
point of view.

The similar testimony of Seneca, from a different social and cultural
background, is itself evidence that such views were not confined to one cultural stream but made their way widely in the greco-roman world. For
Seneca, the immortal human soul has come from beyond this world – from
among the stars, in fact – and will make its way back there. Though one
might hold that it simply disappeared, it is more likely that it will go to be
with the gods.[120] Death is either the end of everything, in which case there is
nothing to be alarmed about, or it is a process of change, in which case,
since the change is bound to be for the better, one should be glad.[121] The
soul, in fact, is at present kept as a prisoner within the body, which is both a
weight and a penance to it.[122] One should not, then, fear death; it is the birthday of one's eternity.[123] As long as one ceases to hope, one may also cease
to fear.[124] Once again, though the thought has developed somewhat, we are
still clearly within the broad stream of Platonism, carrying Cicero and others
along with it.[125] And if death is to be welcomed, it follows that an early
death is a good thing, despite popular opinion. 'Those whom the gods love
die young'; few who quoted this at the death of Princess Diana will have
realized that it goes back to the fourth-century BC poet Menander, with
echoes in other ancient plays.[126]

[118] 4.7.31f.

[119] *Frag.* 26 (in Marcus Aurelius 4.41); *Frag.* 23.

[120] Seneca, *Ep. Mor.* 71.16; 79.12; 102.21–3; 120.17–19. Otherwise unattributed refs. in
what follows are to the same work.

[121] 65.24.

[122] *Pondus ac poena*: 65.16–22.

[123] 102.25–8. Seneca agrees with Epictetus that for the corpse to be unburied is not
something to worry about: 92.30.

[124] *Ep. ad Lucilium* 5.7–9.

[125] cf. *Tusc. Disp.* etc. (Riley 1995, 39f.).

[126] Menander *Dis Exapaton* frag. 4; cf. Soph. *Oed. Col.* 1225–8; Eurip. *Hippol.* frag.
449; Cic. *Tusc. Disp.* 1.48; Diog. Laert. 10.126; Plut. *Letter to Apollonius* 108e—109d;
115b–e, part of a long and interesting discussion about death being not so bad after all.
Plutarch cites several other writers and says (115e) he could cite several more, 'but there is
no need to go on at length'. Quite so.

Of course, if philosophers like Seneca or Epictetus needed to go on like this about not fearing death, that is itself evidence that most of their readers were not yet inclined to such a robust philosophical view. They witness, indeed, to both sides: the obvious popular view of death as a catastrophe, and the by now standard philosophers' view of death (however differently nuanced here and there) as the release of the soul from its bodily prison. The grief of Achilles and the calm of Socrates confront one another, half a millennium and more on, as the two positions between which the greco-roman world oscillated. As will already be obvious, neither bore any resemblance to the belief and message of the early church.

(v) Becoming a God (or at least a Star)?

'Oh dear,' the Emperor Vespasian is reported to have said on his death-bed, 'I think I'm becoming a god.'[127] He was neither the first nor the last to think such thoughts, though perhaps the only one to put it so memorably. From early Greek writings onwards we find hints that some mortals at least would not just find their souls going to the Isles of the Blessed; they would actually join the Immortals themselves, the greco-roman pantheon. When it became first possible and then fashionable for Roman emperors to see their predecessors as divine – and for less reserved subjects to accord the same honour to the living emperor – the idea was hardly new, but rather a fresh mutation within a long line of speculation.[128]

In the earlier Greek world, a careful distinction had been made between gods and heroes, and between gods and ancestors.[129] Indeed, dead heroes were in some respects thought to be nearer at hand than the gods, which is one reason at least why, as we shall see presently, feasts were held at their tombs.[130] However, within the world of mythology there were certain exceptions to the rule. The principal one was Hercules, who after his proverbial labours was admitted not just to the bliss of a righteous Platonic soul but actually to the company of the gods themselves.[131] Other less well-known heroes were sometimes accorded similar status, among whom we should mention Dionysus (the god most frequently represented in ancient art), the heavenly twins Castor and Pollux, and the healing god Asclepius.[132] Within

[127] Suet. *Vesp.* 23.

[128] On the divinization of emperors, see e.g. Bowersock 1982; Price 1984; Zanker 1988; Klauck 2000, ch. 4.

[129] See Burkert 1985, 203–05.

[130] So Burkert 207.

[131] Alluded to in e.g. Juv. *Sat.* 11.60–64, along with Aeneas. See Burkert 1985, 198f., 208–11. On Hercules being simultaneously in Hades and with the immortals see above.

[132] Burkert 1985, 212–15. The divinization, or near-divinization, of mortals occurs in Homer also: e.g. Ganymede, the beautiful son of Tros (*Il.* 20.230–35); his relative Tithonius

the Roman world, similar mythological founding heroes (Aeneas, Romulus and perhaps Latinus, the mythical king of the Latins) may have managed to break the normal taboo against humans becoming divine, though even in these cases things are not straightforward. They may simply have been identified with already existing gods.[133]

The possibility that a human being could become a god developed from these mythological beginnings (many later worshippers of Dionysus, for instance, may never have realized that he had started off as a mortal) to the divinization of hellenistic rulers, particularly notable in the case of Alexander the Great (356–323 BC). At least as early as 331 (in his mid-twenties, in other words) he had begun to represent himself as a son of Zeus, and to put himself alongside Hercules, expecting apotheosis (divinization) after his death.[134] Encouraged by the quasi-worship of his Persian and Egyptian subjects (for whom such attitudes were simply good manners), he requested actual worship in Greece and Macedonia. His subjects there were not so eager to comply, but after his early death his cult was quickly established and, though imitated by his less well-known successors, outlasted them all, and provided both a model and an inspiration for the Roman imperial cult four centuries later.[135]

By the early Christian period similar beliefs were widespread throughout the Roman world.[136] Tiberius, who became emperor in AD 14 upon the death of Augustus, lost no time in having his adoptive father declared divine, as Augustus himself had done with Julius Caesar. Though for the first century of the empire (roughly 31 BC to AD 70) living emperors were not allowed divine honours in Rome itself, the iconography on Augustus' early coins shows the way the wind was blowing: already before 31 BC, i.e. while still engaged in civil war with Antony, Octavian (as he then was) had himself described as 'son of the divine Caesar', and displayed in the guise of Neptune, holding symbols of universal power and standing with one foot on a globe.[137] By the time of the New Testament the emperors were routinely worshipped as divine, in the eastern parts of the empire at least, during their lifetime.[138]

---

seems to have been regarded similarly as having been elevated to be the spouse of the goddess Dawn (*Il.* 11.1; cf. 19.1f.). Cf. too Cleitos in *Od.* 15.248–52.

[133] See Beard, North and Price 1998, 1.31.

[134] cf. e.g. Arrian *Anabasis* 3.3.2; 4.10.6f.; 7.29.3; Aelian, *Hist. Misc.* 2.19; cf. 5.12. Alexander's father, Philip of Macedon, had already begun to move in this direction (Diod. Sic. 16.92.5; 19.95.1; cf. Welles's note in vol. 8, 101 of the Loeb edn.).

[135] For the establishment of the cult, cf. e.g. Diod. Sic. 18.60f.; for Athenian worship of Demetrius Poliorcetes (late C4/early C5 BC) cf. e.g. Plut. *Demetr.* 10.3f.; 12.2f.; 13.1. On the influence of the Alexander-myth in Rome see esp. Gruen 1998.

[136] Bolt 1998, 71f., with refs. See now esp. Collins 1999, 249–51.

[137] Beard, North and Price 1998, 2.224f.

[138] See esp. Price 1984. Vell. Pat. 2.107.2 has Tiberius being regarded as divine even before becoming Emperor, after Augustus had made him his heir.

The expectation of divinization, and the normal process by which it was accorded, were well established in the early empire. Witnesses were made to swear that they had seen the soul of the late emperor ascending to heaven, a theme made famous by Augustus' interpretation of the comet which appeared at the time of Julius Caesar's death.[139] The system was already sufficiently established to be lampooned by Seneca on the death of Claudius and the accession of Seneca's own pupil Nero in AD 54.[140] So useful was the emperor's divinity to the Roman empire and its stability that the practice continued through successive centuries. A detailed description of apotheosis is given by Cassius Dio, himself an eyewitness of the funeral rites of the Emperor Pertinax in AD 193.[141] We smile wryly when Eusebius, a pious tear in his eye, describes the coin that was struck after the death of his beloved Constantine, representing the emperor as a charioteer, drawn by four horses, being received up into heaven.[142]

In one or two isolated cases, when a mortal was taken to be with the immortals, at least in mythology, his or her body was supposed to be taken away along with the soul.[143] But the normal supposition seems to have been that apotheosis, or the taking of the soul to the land of the immortal gods, was completely consistent with the dissolution, often the burning, of the physical body. Thus in Apollodorus' account of Hercules' ascent to heaven, Hercules mounts his own funeral pyre, and while it is burning is wafted to heaven by a peal of thunder.[144] The graves of heroes played an important part in their post-mortem cult; nobody supposed such graves were empty.[145]

It was not only heroes and emperors who, in some accounts, could go to live with the gods. The virtuous, the philosophers (they were, after all, making up the rules at this point) might attain to the stars as well.

[139] For Julius Caesar's divinity cf. e.g. Val. Max., *Memorable Doings and Sayings* 1.6.13; 1.8.8, where '*divus Iulius*' appears to Cassius before the battle of Philippi, saying that the conspirator had not actually killed him, since his divinity could not be extinguished. For the comet see e.g. the altar of the Lares (c. 7 BC), now in the Vatican Museum (Zanker 1988, 222).

[140] Seneca, *Apoc.*

[141] Dio Cassius 75.4.2—5.5. On this occasion an eagle flew up from the pyre, affording evidence of Pertinax's becoming immortal; cp. Titus' Arch (still in the Forum in Rome).

[142] Euseb. *Life of Const.* 4.73.

[143] So Rohde 1925, 57; see Collins 1993, 125f. On Romulus, see below, section 3.vi.

[144] Apollodorus *The Library* 2.7.7; cf. Diod. Sic. 4.38.5. This may be the source of the legend reported by Theophilus, *Autocl.* 1.13. The suggestion that because thereafter Hercules marries Hebe, Hera's daughter, and has children, therefore he is embodied in the afterlife (Collins 1993, 126; cf. Riley 1995, 54) is a category mistake: he has entered the realm of mythology, where the gods from Zeus and Cronus downwards engage in marrying, begetting and so on, without anyone, particularly after Plato, supposing that they were in any ordinary sense embodied. In Seneca, *Herc. Oet.* 1940–43, 1963, 1976, 1977–8, Hercules is divine, among the stars.

[145] See Burkert 1985, 205f. For the suggestion that the heroes had been taken out of their tombs and carried to heaven, see Collins (discussed above).

This latter theme (often under the label 'astral immortality') has been important in the study of ancient Jewish as well as pagan beliefs, and we must briefly set out its main features. The idea that after death humans (or some of them – it can be thought of as a reward for special virtue) actually *become* stars goes back behind the Socratic period to Pythagorean philosophy and Orphic religion, and is found also in Babylonian and Egyptian sources.[146] It is already found in the fifth-century playwright Aristophanes, and finds classic early expression in Plato's *Timaeus*.[147]

Having explained to Socrates how the creator of the world made everything out of the four elements (earth, fire, water and air), Timaeus describes how this creator speaks to the gods – themselves created beings – and gives them instructions as to how to make the human race and what will happen to them.[148] These humans will have an immortal part, the soul, as well as mortal bodies. And so it happens:

> Into the cup in which he had previously mingled the soul of the universe he poured the remains of the elements, and mingled them in much the same manner . . . and having made it he divided the whole mixture into souls equal in number to the stars and assigned each soul to a star, and having there placed them as in a chariot he showed them the nature of the universe and declared to them the laws of destiny, according to which their first birth would be one and the same for all.[149]

The souls are thus to be implanted into human bodies, which are of two kinds – male, the superior one, and female, the inferior.[150] Their main task is to master the feelings and desires which the bodies will produce – pleasure, pain, fear, anger and so on. Upon their success or otherwise will then depend their fate:

> He who lived well during his appointed time was to return and dwell in his native star, and there he would have a blessed and congenial existence. But if he failed in attaining this, at the second birth he would pass into a woman, and if, when in that state of being, he did not desist from evil, he would continually be changed into some brute who resembled him in the evil nature which he had acquired.[151]

Even here, we note, Plato does not say that the virtuous souls *become* stars, merely that the individual stars are their homes, to which they will return – unless they fail the moral test, in which case they will return to one body or another, according to the theory of transmigration.[152] But the idea of the soul going off to where the stars are, and in some way almost being identified

[146] See e.g. West 1971, 188; for an early Egyptian origin, cf. Kákosy 1969.
[147] Aristoph. *Peace* 832–7. For an earlier survey of the material cf. Cumont 1923, ch. 3.
[148] *Tim.* 29d—38b; 41a–d. Refs. in subsequent notes are to the same work.
[149] 41d–e. Tr. Jowett in Hamilton and Cairns 1961, 1170f.
[150] 41e—42a.
[151] 42b–c.
[152] See below, section 3. vii.

with the stars, became popular across the hellenistic world.[153]

This belief found a further classic expression in a work written about a hundred years before the time of Paul. The epilogue of Cicero's *De Republica* consists of a reported dream: the dreamer is the second-century BC Scipio Aemilianus, and in the dream he meets his famous father and grandfather.[154] His grandfather addresses him first, and tells him that all those who have been good statesmen will go to heaven, which is after all where they came from in the first place:

> All those who have protected or assisted the fatherland, or increased its greatness, have a special place reserved for them in heaven, where they may enjoy perpetual happiness . . . It is from heaven that the rulers and preservers of the cities come, and it is to heaven that they eventually return.[155]

The younger Scipio, in his dream, is frightened, and he asks the old man whether he and the rest of them are really still alive:

> 'Yes they are,' he replied, 'and freed from their chains, from that prison-house – the body; for what you call life is in fact death.'[156]

The dreamer's own father then appears, and he asks him why, if the present life is really death, and the life beyond is the true life, he cannot come and join him there at once. His father answers that he has been placed in the present cosmos, which is the 'temple' of the universal god (Cicero is here not far from a Stoic pantheism), for a purpose, and must not abandon it until given permission:

> The human race was generated on purpose to inhabit the globe called earth, that you can see in the middle of this 'temple', and they were provided with souls from those eternal fires called stars and constellations . . . So you and all the righteous must allow your soul to stay in the body's custody . . . or else you will be evading the duty laid on humans by god . . . . Cultivate justice and piety, qualities we owe to parents and kinsmen, but even more to the fatherland. That is the life that leads to heaven and to the company of those who have lived out their lives, been released from their bodies and now dwell in the area you can see there, which you Romans (following the Greeks) call the Milky Way; for there was a splendid circle of light shining out amongst all the other fires.[157]

We notice that, as in Plato, by no means everyone gets to be a star. And the way in which Cicero has shamelessly slanted Plato's doctrine towards an

---

[153] Full details and discussion in Cumont 1949, 142–288; other details in Hengel 1974, 1.197f., 2.131. A typical epitaph reads, 'I have become an evening star, among the gods' (tr. in Lattimore 1942, 35).

[154] Cic. *De Rep.* 6.13–16; tr. taken from Beard, North and Price 1998, 2.220f. (where further relevant secondary lit. is cited). Refs. in subsequent notes are to this work.

[155] 6.13.

[156] 6.14.

[157] 6.15f.

encouragement to good statesmanship makes us wonder how many of his readers took him absolutely seriously on the question of qualifications for stardom. But clearly he is drawing on, and giving attractive expression to, a much more widely held theory.

The basis of the theory, from Plato to Cicero, is obviously that stars and souls are made of the same kind of material. There was considerable philosophical debate down the years as to what exactly this material was (which of the elements it contained, in what proportion, and so on), but there was no sense that souls and stars were quite different sorts of things.[158] They were, so to speak, made for each other. Thus the Stoics, for instance, believed that the soul was a particularly specialized sort of 'body', made of a fire-like substance – exactly the sort of thing that would be at home in, or on, or even as, a star.[159]

The vexed question of whether these ideas influenced Jewish and Christian writers and thinkers must be addressed in its proper place. For now we may sum up by asking: in these special cases, who were the dead? They were humans who, through quite extraordinary lives, had shown themselves either worthy of translation to divine status or perhaps to have been all along a divine being in disguise. Where were they? In the heavenly home of the immortal gods; perhaps among the stars.

They had not, however, been raised from the dead. Cicero is quite clear, and completely in the mainstream of greco-roman thought: the body is a prison-house. A necessary one for the moment; but nobody in their right mind, having got rid of it, would want it or something like it back again. At no point in the spectrum of options about life after death did the ancient pagan world envisage that the denials of Homer, Aeschylus and the rest would be overthrown. Resurrection was not an option. Those who followed Plato or Cicero did not want a body again; those who followed Homer knew they would not get one. The embargo remained.

3. Further Life from Within the World of the Dead?

(i) Introduction

The claim just made must now be tested against seven counter-claims which have made their way into recent discussions of death and resurrection, not least that of Jesus of Nazareth. At several points in the praxis, the symbols, the stories and the theories of the ancient non-Jewish world, various scholars have found evidence that the dead were regarded as in some sense 'alive', and have suggested that this anticipates and parallels the claims made by the

---

[158] cf. Martin 1995, 118.
[159] Details in Hengel 1974, 2.133 n. 595.

early Christians about Jesus. Final comment on these proposals is of course impossible until we have reviewed the early Christian writings themselves; but a preliminary survey of these options is important at this stage.[160] As I said before, these proposals are for the moment to be measured, not against the beliefs of the early Christians, but against the emphatic statements set out at the head of this chapter. The question must be: would Homer, Aeschylus, Sophocles, and those who read them and used the same language over the succeeding centuries, have recognized any of these as constituting exceptions to their striking and specific denial of 'resurrection'?

(ii) Eating with the Dead

The list of possible exceptions to the rule that there is no resurrection begins with the widespread and well-attested practice of eating and drinking with the dead. Designed to honour, and perhaps humour, the dead person, a wide range of such practices has been noted, going back very early.[161] From the time of the funeral itself, and at regular intervals thereafter, including specific festivals, relatives and friends of the deceased would gather for a meal at the tomb.[162] Sometimes a place would be laid for the dead person. Drink might be poured down a tube into the grave. Sometimes food would actually be cooked on site, in purpose-built ovens.[163]

Part of the purpose, it seems, was to affirm tribal or familial continuity and solidarity.[164] The specific practices seem to imply, as do grave-goods and, in Egypt, mummification and its attendant practices, that the dead are still in need of physical things that the living can supply:

> The cult of the dead seems to presuppose that the deceased is present and active at the place of burial, in the grave beneath the earth. The dead drink the pourings and indeed the blood – they are invited to come to the banquet, to the satiation with blood; as the libations seep into the earth, so the dead will send good things up above.[165]

It is on this basis that remarkable claims have recently been made that such settings form the context within which to understand the early Christian

---

[160] Johnston 1999, sadly, came to my attention too late for use in this study.

[161] Full details in e.g. Burkert 1985, 191–4; Garland 1985, ch. 7 (summary, 120); Ferguson 1987, 191–2; Klauck 2000, 75–9, with recent bibliog.

[162] On the festivals, cf. Beard, North and Price 1998, 1.31, 50; 2.104f., 122.

[163] Beard, North and Price 1998, 2.105.

[164] Burkert 1985, 191.

[165] Burkert 194f., citing Aristophanes *Frags.* 488.13f., and comparing Rohde 1.243–5; Wiesner 1938, 209f. According to Artemidorus (*Dreams* 5.82) the party was said to have been 'given by the deceased because of the honours paid to him by his fellows'; Garland 1985, 39 overinterprets this to say that the dead person 'was believed to be present in the capacity of host'.

stories about Jesus eating and drinking with his followers some time after his death.[166]

Whatever we say about that – and we shall come to it much later – it is clear at once that nothing done at tombs or said about such practices comes remotely near to challenging Homer and the tragedians. These practices do not imply that which the word *anastasis* and its cognates referred to, namely, that the person who died is now, after a period of being dead, alive again within the present world. Indeed, another interpretation of the practices in question is that they were designed precisely to clarify the new position of the dead. The point of doing these things was to ensure that the dead were well and truly sent on their way to the next world, rather than returning to haunt this one.[167] Furthermore, it appears that at least some meals at the tomb were put there only for the dead, with the living being prohibited from partaking, serving to confirm the new status of the dead person; that is why the appropriate emotion for participants in such practices was grief.[168] Had anything approaching resurrection been even momentarily imagined or supposed, one might expect first surprise and then, except of course for hard-nosed Platonic philosophers, delight. Nothing of the kind is found. The post-funeral practices were widespread and well known throughout the ancient world, the very world that denied that resurrection could ever take place.

(iii) Spirits, Souls and Ghosts

Necromancy – communication with the departed – likewise has a long and variegated history. Most cultures, and most historical periods, offer stories of the living establishing contact with the departed, or indeed the departed taking the initiative and appearing unbidden to the living. From Patroclus' appearance to Achilles onwards, ancient literature is replete with such incidents. Some of the classic encounters between the living and the departed are in dreams: not only Achilles with Patroclus, but, in a famous scene already noted, Scipio with his grandfather.[169] Sometimes the dead seem to be summoned back for such visitations by the mourning relatives, especially women.[170] Alternatively the mourners are taken, by a kind of translation, to

---

[166] See particularly Riley 1995, 44–7, 67; followed by Crossan 1998, xiv. Riley, 53, sees that the Homeric souls are very different from the risen body of Jesus in Luke and John, but does not let this get in the way of the extraordinary theory he tries to propose.

[167] So Garland 1985, 39f.

[168] Garland 38–41; 110–15; 104–10.

[169] Cicero *De Rep.* 6.9–26; cf. Riley 1995, 39–40. See above, 59f.

[170] e.g. Hercules, called up by his mother Alcmena: Seneca *Herc. Oet.* 1863–1976; though we should note that Hercules insists in this passage that he is not in Hades, but among the stars.

be with the dead, albeit not in the underworld but in heaven.[171] The dead, in such scenes, sometimes have wisdom to offer the living about the realities of which they are now aware; sometimes they come to guide, or to warn, at a particular moment of crisis. A memorable scene in Herodotus involves the Spartan King Demaratus (c. 515–491 BC), whose parentage had been questioned (he was supposed to be the son of the former king Ariston). His mother explains that 'a phantom resembling [Ariston]' visited her early in the marriage and made her pregnant; diviners confirmed that the phantom visitor was the hero Astrabacus.[172] Even the Old Testament, where such contact was anathema, furnishes one classic example.[173]

Sometimes contact would be made through a living person, i.e. what we might loosely call a medium. In these circumstances it was difficult to tell quite what one was in touch with. Was it a god, an angel, a daemon, a soul, or what? Usually in ancient stories of this kind the apparition would claim to be divine; only rarely would it identify itself as a human soul.[174]

Of particular use to the living, it was thought, were dead heroes. They retained something of their old power, and could be summoned for advice and help in battle.[175] Aeschylus' *Persians* has a visitation from Darius; in Aristophanes, a whole chorus of heroes makes an appearance to warn the living of what they, the heroes, can still do.[176]

It might be objected that these are all literary figments, reflecting perhaps a popular belief or superstition but not giving real indications of things that ordinary people in the greco-roman world would expect to encounter on a regular basis. One would not expect Shakespeare's plays to provide straightforward evidence of the sort of things that ordinary residents of Stratford-on-Avon expected to happen in their daily lives. However, the hellenistic novels give plenty of evidence that people were aware of hauntings, appearances, and so forth, and had both a fairly well-developed view of what they were about and quite a full vocabulary to describe them. In Chariton's novel, the eponymous heroine Callirhoe, who has been buried alive, hears a robber breaking into the tomb, and wonders if it is 'some deity' (*tis daimon*) coming for her; the robber, finding her alive, returns the compliment.[177] Callirhoe then dreams of her lover Chaereas: in an echo of the scene between Achilles and Patroclus (further evidence of the huge

---

[171] e.g. Ovid *Met.* 14.829–51; *Fasti* 3.507–16.

[172] Hdt. 6.69.1–4. The word for 'phantom' here is *phasma*.

[173] Samuel appearing to Saul: 1 Sam. 28. For details, and also of the OT prohibitions, see below, 93f.

[174] On this, cf. Dodds 1990 (1965), 53–5, with ancient refs.

[175] Burkert 1985, 207.

[176] Aesch. *Pers.* 759–86 and the sequence that follows; Aristoph. *Frags.* 58: see Burkert 1985, 207f., 431 n. 55. Cf. too Hdt. 8.36–9 (two gigantic soldiers, heroes of old, defend Delphi from the Persians).

[177] Chariton *Call.* 1.9.3f. Refs. in the next two notes are to this work.

influence of the Homeric background) she tries to embrace him but without success. He is, however, still alive, despite a second dream of him in chains which Callirhoe assumes must mean that he is dead.[178] Throughout the plot various characters wonder whether they have seen a ghost (*eidolon*), or whether the person they see is actually alive.[179]

Ordinary people in the greco-roman world clearly thought that from time to time one might see ghosts, spirits or visions of dead people. It was even possible to precipitate such encounters oneself.[180] But we should not make the mistake of supposing that this had anything to do with resurrection.[181] No such experiences would have persuaded anyone in that world that the total denial of resurrection in Homer and the tragedians had been broken. These visions and visitations were not cases of people ceasing to be dead and resuming something like normal life, but precisely of the dead remaining dead and being encountered as visitors from the world of the dead, who have not and will not resume anything like the kind of life they had before. This is the vital distinction that must be maintained if we are to understand the ancient pagans in their own terms, never mind Judaism or Christianity.

(iv) Returning from the Underworld

There are of course occasional tales, all from the world of mythology and recognized by the ancients as such, about those who attempt to leave the underworld.[182] Sisyphus tells his wife not to bury him properly, and as a result is not allowed to pass on into Hades, but instead returns. His triumph, however, is short-lived, and his eventual existence in the underworld is all the worse.[183] Orpheus attempts to rescue his beloved Eurydice, but fails to keep the condition imposed by Hades; he looks back as he is leading her out, and she is lost for ever.[184] The first Greek to be killed at Troy, Protesilaus, became legendary in this respect: his wife was so distraught that the gods were persuaded to let him return from Hades for a day (in some versions, for three hours), after which, on his going again, she committed suicide (in some versions, this follows her becoming obsessive about an image of her late husband, which her father then burns).[185] The tale is developed in

---

[178] 2.9.6; 3.6.4; he is, in fact, captured and sold as a slave.

[179] e.g. 5.9.4. On the issues raised by the novel see below, 68–76.

[180] A famous account in the classical world is Heliodorus *Aethiopica* 6.14f.

[181] So, rightly, Bowersock 1994, 101f. The story of Astrabacus (63 above) is cited by Riley (1995, 54, 58) as evidence that the dead could be touched; but the story, which even in Herodotus appears as quite literally an old wife's tale, hardly warrants this conclusion.

[182] On this, see Vermeule 1979, 211 n. 1.

[183] For the tale, cf. Alcaeus *Fr.* 38; Pherecydes of Athens *Fr.* 119.

[184] Virgil *Georg.* 4.453–525; Ovid *Met.* 10.1—11.84; cf. Eurip. *Alcest.* 357–62.

[185] *Il.* 2.698–702; Hdt. 9.116–20; Catull. 68.73–130; Ovid *Her.* 13; cf. Hyg. *Fab.* 103.

Philostratus' *Heroikos*, where Protesilaus appears to people much later, putting them straight about the stories in Homer.[186] In Chariton's famous novel, Dionysius thinks Chaereas, apparently returned from the dead, is a sort of Protesilaus.[187] In the second century AD, Aelius Aristides suggests that Protesilaus now 'associates with the living'.[188] He even becomes, in his new-found life, a metaphor for sexual rejuvenation.[189] Other tales exist too: Hercules, whom we shall soon meet yet again in another connection, is spoken of as having come back from the depths of Hades.[190] Hyginus, in his *Fabellae*, lists sixteen people who were allowed special permission to come back from the world below.[191]

The most famous of all such stories is probably Plato's Myth of Er, with which his greatest dialogue reaches its conclusion.[192] The main point of the story is to teach the doctrine of transmigration of souls, which we shall discuss presently (section (vii) below). But the interesting thing at this stage is what is said about Er himself. In the tale, Er is a soldier who has been killed in battle, but whose body is still uncorrupted ten days later. On the twelfth day, on his funeral pyre, he revives and tells what he has seen during his underworld sojourn. Er himself is not allowed to join the other souls and drink from the River of Forgetfulness, but instead must return to tell his tale.

Plato clearly regarded this story simply as a convenient vehicle for the doctrine he wished to propound; if we wished to put the experience of Er into a category, we might say he had had a 'near-death experience'. He only seemed to have died, but in fact had not.[193] But this is not the point of the story, which belongs alongside Aesop's fables; it is told not as though it were literally true, but for the wisdom that it can convey.

The other story to be discussed in this connection is the myth of Alcestis. In the legend, Alcestis is the wife of Admetus, king of Pherae (Thessaly), to

---

[186] See Bowersock 1994, 111–13: the text is at Philostr. *Her.* 135f. Cf. Anderson 1986, ch. 13.

[187] *Call.* 5.10.1.

[188] *Orat.* 3.365.

[189] Petronius *Sat.* 129.1.

[190] Eurip. *Madn. Hercl.* 606–21. See further below.

[191] Hyg. *Fab.* 251. There is some doubt over which Hyginus this is: the best-known writer of this name (*ODCC* lists four of them) lived in the late C1 BC, but the *Fabellae* or *Fabulae* is probably from the C2 AD. Remarkable healings, bringing people back immediately after death like the resuscitations performed by Elijah and Elisha in the Old Testament and Jesus, Peter and Paul in the new, come in a different category: they mostly concern the heroic Asclepius, the 'blameless physician' of the *Iliad* (4.405; 11.518), son of Apollo and subsequently a much-favoured god of healing.

[192] *Rep.* 10.614d–621d.

[193] This is the explanation offered by Pliny the Elder (7.51f.) for such reported experiences (including that of a woman supposedly dead for seven days, 7.52.175). Such tales were known to Celsus, the C2 pagan critic of Christianity; and Theophilus (*Autocl.* 1.13), perhaps a little too enthusiastically, cites stories of this kind about Hercules and Asclepius. See below, 506–8.

whom Apollo has been enslaved as a punishment. In return for Admetus' hospitality, Apollo tricks the Fates into granting him (Admetus) the privilege of escaping death on condition that someone else should die in his place. The only volunteer is Alcestis herself, his beloved wife. After her death and burial, she is brought back to Admetus, either by Persephone or, in the better-known version, by Hercules, who fights physically with Death (*Thanatos*, a character in the play), beats him, rescues Alcestis and restores her to Admetus. Interestingly, in Euripides' play, the revived Alcestis does not speak. When asked about this, Hercules explains that she is still consecrated to the gods below, and that it will take three days to purify her.[194]

The tale, best known through Euripides, shares some of its features with Shakespeare's *A Winter's Tale*, and has recently been cited as the main evidence that 'a tradition of resurrection' existed in the Greek world.[195] The myth was known in various versions. Aeschylus alludes to it at one point in the *Eumenides*,[196] and it is discussed briefly in Plato's *Symposium*, where it is coupled, as one might have anticipated, with the story of Orpheus and Eurydice.[197] It appears in art through to the Roman period, with Hercules pictured as leading a hooded Alcestis out of the tomb.[198]

---

[194] *Alcest.* 1144–6. In another version, Persephone sends Alcestis back: see e.g. Apollodorus *Library* 1.9.15; Hyg. *Fab.* 51.

[195] Porter 1999a, 80. Most of Porter's article simply demonstrates, what no one would deny, that there was a large tradition of varied speculation about 'life after death'. The Alcestis legend (already clearly part of the Hercules legend) is his one example of actual return to bodily life, going against the grain of all other classical literature.

[196] Aesch. *Eumen.* 723f. (hard on the heels of the key denial of resurrection quoted at the start of this chapter): the chorus reminds Apollo of the time when, in the house of Pheres (Admetus' father), he moved the Fates to make mortals free of death. This reference, though, (*pace* Porter 79f.) seems to be not to Alcestis' being freed from death (that was not the work of Apollo persuading the Fates, but of Hercules fighting Death) so much as to Apollo finding a way to let Admetus himself avoid death.

[197] Pl. *Symp.* 179b–d. Phaedrus, the speaker, concludes that Alcestis' self-sacrificing love was what made the difference between her fate and that of Orpheus and Eurydice (the parallel is not exact, since the failure to bring Eurydice back is due to a lack of love, not on her part, but on that of Orpheus). Alcestis, says Phaedrus, has been granted a privilege given to very few, that of the soul returning from Hades (*ex Haidou aneinai palin ten psychen*); he names no other instances (179c). Phaedrus goes on (179e—180b) to cite as another parallel Achilles being sent to the Isles of the Blessed because he determined to avenge his lover Patroclus, even though he knew it would cost him his own life. This too, of course, is not a parallel to the Alcestis story. Perhaps by that stage of the symposium the wine was taking its toll on clear thought.

[198] One example among many is displayed in Boardman 1993, 318 (plate 316). This is the more interesting in that it is found in the Via Latina Catacomb in Rome, set in parallel with biblical scenes 'which impart a Christian message of salvation' (Boardman 319). Was this Hercules scene, perhaps, the model for the subsequent regular iconographic tradition of depicting Jesus leading Adam and Eve out of the underworld? On this, see further Grabar 1968, 15, fig. 35; Weitzmann 1979, 242f. no. 219; other details and refs. in *LIMC* s.v.

The Alcestis story is fascinating, but scarcely provides evidence of an actual belief in resurrection. Alcestis does indeed return from the dead to bodily life. She will presumably die again, like Lazarus in John's gospel, but even so her return is remarkable enough, being the only such tale we have from the entire ancient world. However, as we have seen, intelligent pagans contemporary with early Christianity knew about such stories, and dismissed them as mythic fictions. Celsus 'knew the old myths of returning from the Underworld, but he was perfectly capable of distinguishing these from the actual resurrection in the body'.[199] A fifth-century Athenian audience would not have thought of the story as in any way realistic. A tale in which Apollo and Death appear on stage as speaking characters, in which Hercules arrives as a guest and displays his extraordinary powers, is hardly good evidence for what ordinary people believed happened in everyday life. One might as well invoke the *Ring* cycle as evidence of marital and family customs among the nineteenth-century German bourgeoisie. No burial customs invoke Alcestis as a patron or model. No prayers are offered that Hercules may do for others what he did for her. No further stories are told which build on or develop the theme; the closest near-parallel seems to be the legend that Hercules had rescued Theseus after the latter (who had modelled himself on Hercules) had been imprisoned in the underworld during an (unsuccessful) expedition to rescue Persephone.[200] Alcestis may have come back (in the ancient legend), but she was the exception in the light of which the prevailing rule stands out the more clearly.

Thus, though the story, and similar tales of heroes and legendary figures from long ago, continued to be known throughout the classical period, they never became popular reference points as did the great Homeric scenes of Achilles and Odysseus.[201] No tombstones suggest that maybe this corpse

---

[199] Bowersock 1994, 117f., citing Origen *C. Cels.* 2.55 (see below, 523). In the passage, Celsus cites Zamolxis, whom we have already met, and also Pythagoras (cf. Diog. Laert. 8.41, citing Hermippus), and the Egyptian Rhampsinitus (Hdt. 2.122), who played dice in Hades with Demeter and returned with a golden napkin she had given him. It is important to note that Rhampsinitus, like Theseus (see below), is not said to have died; and it is equally important to note that Celsus does *not* mention Alcestis, as he should have done had there been a 'tradition' about her. For Pliny, see above, 33, 65.

[200] cf. e.g. Apollodorus *Library* 2.5.12. See too Diod. Sic. 4.26.1; Eurip. *Madn. Hercl.* 619–21. Several other refs. are given in the Loeb edn. of Apollodorus, vol. 1, 235. Theseus (king of Athens; already a legendary figure by the time of Homer) had not, it seems, actually died in the process, so the story, like that of Rhampsinitus, is not a true parallel; further bibliog. in *ODCC* s.v. For Theseus imitating Hercules, cf. Plut. *Thes.* 6.6; 8.1; 9.1; recognized as 'another Hercules', 29.3. Plutarch's account of Theseus includes the interesting point (29.5) that Hercules had initiated the custom of allowing enemies to take back their dead, and thus 'was the first to give back the dead'. Perhaps this was where the legends began; alternatively, perhaps this is Plutarch's later demythologization of them, as seems to have been the case in his version of the rescue story (35.1f.).

[201] The only reference to Alcestis in the Virgil corpus is the (probably spurious) *Culex* 262–4, where Alcestis, now properly dead and in the underworld, is free from all care as a

will be one of the lucky ones (would they, in any case, have thought coming back such a lucky thing?). One Alcestis, with a small scatter of subsequent allusions, scarcely makes a 'tradition'.[202] It certainly made no dent in the ruling assumption from Homer to Hadrian and beyond. Life after death, yes; various possibilities open to souls in Hades and beyond, yes; actual resurrection, no.

A curious footnote to this section. After Nero's death, his popularity in the East, and among his old soldiers, gave rise to the double myth of a 'Nero redux' and a 'Nero redivivus'. Either he had not really died (few people ever saw his corpse or his burial), and was in hiding, perhaps in Parthia, and would return at the head of an army to reclaim the throne; or, while he had really died, he would come back to life.[203] No fewer than three lyre-playing impostors appeared claiming to be the late emperor, and attracted followers; impersonating recently departed leaders (such as Alexander the Great) was by no means unknown in the ancient world.[204] Confusion at the time between the two versions of the rumour makes it impossible for us at this distance to regard the idea of a revived Nero as more than a remarkable oddity – an exception, if indeed it is that, that again proves the normal rule.[205]

What is perhaps most interesting about the whole episode is that it occurred at exactly the moment when, it seems, the motif of cheating death was beginning to make its appearance in works of romantic fiction.

(v) Cheating Death: The *Scheintod* Motif in Novels

We have already met the eponymous heroine of Chariton's novel *Callirhoe*. We must now explore the twist of plot which brought her to our attention.[206]

---

reward for her great deed. Juvenal's only reference (6.652) is the grumpy comment that the wives of his own day would cheerfully sacrifice their husbands, if only to save a lap-dog.

[202] Porter 80 suggests that this 'tradition' was 'to various extents continued in later thinkers', without suggesting any other than Plato (not much later than Euripides) and Aeschylus (earlier). Plato and Aesch. themselves, as we have seen, are quite clear that bodily resurrection does not in fact occur; and the Aesch. ref. (*Eumen.* 723f.) refers, not to the rescue of Alcestis as Porter (79f.) suggests, but (as the material he cites makes clear) to Apollo's action in persuading the Fates to allow Admetus, her husband, to be spared his natural death if someone would die in his place.

[203] Primary sources include: Tac. *Hist.* 2.8f.; Suet. *Nero* 57; Dio Chrys. *Orat.* 21.9f.; Dio Cass. 64.9; Lucian *Adv. Ind.* 20. Juvenal refers to Domitian as 'Nero' (*Sat.* 4.38); this is not intended as a compliment. The popular belief is reflected in Jewish and Christian works: cf. e.g. *Sib. Or.* 3.63–74; 4.138f.; *Asc. Isa.* 4.1–14; Rev. 13.3; 17.8, 11; Commod. *Instr.* 41.7. The best recent summary of the evidence, with full bibliog., is Aune 1997–8, 737–40. Cf. too Bauckham 1998a, 382f.

[204] cf. Aune 1997–8, 740.

[205] On Nero, see further Warmington 1969.

[206] Tr. Goold, LCL. Cf. too Reardon 1989, 17–124, with notes and bibliography.

The Greek and Latin novel seems to have been a new genre in exactly the New Testament period. Some date Chariton's writing as early as the first century BC, and some as late as the early second century AD, but the majority reckon that it belongs in the middle or the second half of the first century AD. Most of the other novelists are clearly later.[207] The storylines include regular features of romance: boy meeting girl (or sometimes boy), dangerous journeys to exotic places, young love thwarted and rediscovered, low-life realism and sexual intrigue, and particularly – hence our current interest – something that looks like death, but turns out not to be. This 'apparent death' (*Scheintod* is the technical term) appears again and again in *Callirhoe*, which we mentioned above in another connection, and variously thereafter in other novels. A brief survey will show what is involved.

Callirhoe, set in Syracuse, opens with a wedding and a funeral. The young man Chaereas marries the beautiful heroine; but rejected suitors trick him into thinking her unfaithful, and in anger he kicks her and seems to have killed her. She is buried in a wonderful tomb with costly funeral gifts, which attract the attention of grave-robbers. Callirhoe is not, however, dead, but only in a deep swoon, and wakes up in the grave just as the robbers are breaking into it. At first they think she is a ghost (*daimon tis*), and she thinks they are, too; but the chief robber, realizing the truth, decides to steal the girl as well as the gold. They make off, via Greece, to Miletus.

Meanwhile, back in Syracuse, Chaereas goes to the tomb and finds it empty. The scene is so interesting that we must set it out in full:

> Hurrying in the dark, the tomb robbers had been careless in shutting the tomb. Chaereas waited for dawn to visit the tomb, ostensibly to bring wreaths and libations, but really in order to kill himself . . . When he arrived, he discovered that the stones had been moved and that the entrance was wide open. He was astonished at the sight and seized by a fearful bewilderment at what had happened. Rumor swiftly brought the shocking news to Syracuse, and everyone hastened to the tomb, but no one ventured to go inside until Hermocrates gave the order. The man sent in gave a full and true account. It seemed unbelievable that not even the corpse was lying there. Then Chaereas himself decided to go in, eager to see Callirhoe once more even though she was dead, but on searching the tomb he could find nothing. Many others entered incredulously after him. All were baffled, and one of those inside said, 'The funeral offerings have been stolen! This is the work of tomb robbers. But where is the corpse?'
> Many different speculations were entertained by the crowd. But Chaereas, looking up to heaven, stretched forth his hands and said, 'Which of the gods has become my rival and carried off Callirhoe and now keeps her with him, against her will but compelled by a mightier fate? Is this then why she died suddenly, that she might not succumb to disease? So did Dionysus once steal Ariadne from Theseus and Zeus Semele from Actaeon.[208] Or can it be that I had a goddess as my wife and did not know it, and

---

[207] On the Greek novel, see Reardon 1991; Bowersock 1994. Nb. Bowersock 22: 'The beginning of the massive proliferation of fiction can be assigned pretty clearly to the reign of the emperor Nero' (i.e. AD 54–68).

[208] Ariadne and Semele were mortals who were thus deified; this, according to Reardon 1989, 53 n. 1, is the point of the double allusion, in which the usual stories of Theseus

she was above our human lot? But, even so, she should not have disappeared from the world so quickly or for such a reason. Thetis, too, was a goddess, but she remained with Peleus and bore him a son, while I have been deserted at the very peak of my love . . .[209]

As the plot thickens, the exiled Callirhoe prays in despair to Aphrodite, listing the extraordinary things that she has suffered:

I have suffered enough: I have died, I have been resurrected [*tethneka, anezeka*], I have been kidnapped and taken into exile; I have been sold and made a slave.[210]

Later, it is Chaereas' turn to cheat death. So convinced are Callirhoe and her new companions that he is dead that they build a tomb to his honour, in accordance with ancient Greek custom.[211] Chaereas meanwhile has a second escape, this time narrowly missing being crucified.[212] But when one Mithradates claims that Chaereas is alive, Dionysius, an Ionian nobleman who has now married Callirhoe, accuses him of wanting to have her himself. 'When he wishes to commit adultery', declares Dionysius, 'he brings the dead to life!'[213] Mithradates succeeds in producing Chaereas, and the original pair greet one another in joy. When they are again separated, Callirhoe begins to have doubts:

Have you really seen Chaereas? Was that my Chaereas, or is this too an illusion [*e kai touto peplanemai*: literally, 'or am I deceived in this too']? Perhaps Mithradates conjured up a ghost [*eidolon*] for the trial. They say there are magicians [*magoi*] among the Persians . . .[214]

Dionysius is angry with Chaereas, calling him a sort of Protesilaus, coming back from the dead, and is determined to retain Callirhoe and prevent the original pair being reunited.[215] Chaereas decides to hang himself (he is again, of course, thwarted), but in his would-be final speech he calls on Callirhoe to visit his grave:

When I am gone, pay a visit to my corpse and, if you can, weep over it. For me this will be better than immortality. As you bend over the tombstone, say, even if your husband and child are looking on, 'Now, Chaereas, you are really gone. Now you are dead. At the king's tribunal I would have chosen you.' I shall hear you, wife, perhaps even believe you. You will raise my standing with the gods below.

---

abandoning Ariadne, and of Semele being killed by Zeus' thunderbolt, have been modified.
[209] *Call.* 3.3.1–6 (tr. Goold). Refs. in what follows are to this work.
[210] 3.8.9.
[211] 4.1.3.
[212] 4.3.5f. This, alongside other mentions of crucifixion in the ancient world (e.g. Juv. *Sat.* 6.219–23) show how frequent this ghastly death had become, and how casually it was inflicted by those with the power to do so.
[213] 5.6.10 (*anistesi tous nekrous*).
[214] 5.9.4.
[215] 5.10.1. On Protesilaus, see above.

Even if in Hades' halls men forget the departed,
yet shall I even there remember you, my dear.[216]

Eventually, as the genre demands, the original lovers are reunited, and sail home to Syracuse. Callirhoe's father, embracing her, and echoing her own earlier question, asks,

Are you alive, child, or am I deceived in this, too?

And the heroine replies,

Yes, father, I am, and really so now that I have seen you.[217]

The full tale is told; the couple, of course, live happily ever after.

The story, and the key assumptions behind the twists in the plot, are full of interest for our study of the world into which Christianity was born. We should be quite clear, to begin with, that even in the cheerfully fictitious story no actual resurrection ever occurs, and nobody supposes it actually can. Everybody, though, knows what it would mean if it did: it would mean that someone who was truly dead had truly come back into the world of the living. It would not have been a metaphorical manner of speaking about the blissful life that the dead might be having hereafter, perhaps enjoying some kind of status among the *daimones* down below in Hades. No: the language of 'resurrection' denotes renewed bodily life among the living. It is specifically not compatible with the translation of a soul to be with the immortals. This, as we saw, is one of the options Chaereas considers in the early scene: Callirhoe's disappearance may, he thinks, mean she was a goddess already, or that a god has taken her to be with him. Either way she will not be coming back into the world of living humans; when she does just that, it means of course that she has not been 'translated' in this fashion, that she is not after all a goddess.[218] Behind the plot, once more, stands Homer: the scene between Achilles and Patroclus, adapted to suit the new setting, is just one of many such references throughout the story.

What is particularly striking, of course, is the story of the empty tomb, with a mourner going at dawn, finding the stones moved away, the rumour spreading quickly, and people eventually going in and finding the tomb empty. Whatever other parallels there may or may not be between pagan literature and the New Testament, one cannot mistake this one. What are we to make of it?

[216] 5.10.8f., quoting (and adapting) *Il.* 22.389 (Achilles on Patroclus).
[217] 8.6.8. The Greek for the father's question is *zes, teknon, e kai touto peplanemai*; and the response is *zo, pater, nun alethos, hoti se tetheamai*. To be alive truly, *alethos*, here clearly means to have a solid, this-worldly, embodied existence.
[218] On the 'translation' option, see below. Bowersock 1994, 106 is wrong by his own reckoning when he says that Chaereas infers 'a divine resurrection'.

As we shall see when studying the resurrection narratives in detail, it is virtually certain that the evangelists, or whoever first told the story of Jesus' empty tomb, were not borrowing the motif from Chariton, who claims to be writing in Aphrodisias, a city in Caria roughly halfway between Ephesus and Colosse. Even supposing the novel to have been written earlier than the middle of the first century AD, the likelihood of such borrowing must be adjudged remote in the extreme.[219] For Mark (or anyone else) to invent such a story about Jesus on the basis of a plot-twist in a romantic novel is patently absurd. However, it is by no means impossible, as Bowersock has recently suggested, that borrowing may have taken place in the opposite direction. If we suppose that strange, wild rumours of a real empty tomb were going around the ancient world in the middle of the first century, it is perfectly plausible to suppose that writers of fiction – in a very different genre to that of the gospels! – would have picked it up and developed it within their own narrative worlds.[220]

The motif is not without ancient roots. In *The Incredible Things Beyond Thule* by Antonius Diogenes, sadly preserved only in small fragments and in summaries by the ninth-century Christian writer Photius and others, allusion is made to Herodotus' tale of one Salmoxis (sometimes spelled Samolxis, and sometimes with an initial Z), who had died several hundred years earlier, only to be raised from death and regarded as a god.[221] Herodotus gives two variations on the Salmoxis story, in the context of describing the Getae, a northern Greek tribe who supposedly believe that they never die. In the first, Salmoxis is a local god, to whom people go when they die; the living can make intercession to him by giving instructions to a messenger and then ritually killing him. In the second, he is a native of Samos who, having told his lavishly entertained guests that neither he nor they would ever die, constructs an underground chamber, disappears into it for four years, and then re-emerges as though from the dead.

Herodotus, as often, suspends judgment on the story.[222] Within Antonius Diogenes' tale, a different though related motif makes its appearance within a highly convoluted plot: two travellers are condemned to die each day and

---

[219] Corley 2002, 130 seems to conflate the *Scheintod* motif with the stories of heroes being 'translated', and suggests that this combined context is the best one to understand Mark's account of the empty tomb, which is, she says, 'a fictional anti-translation or deification story'.

[220] See esp. Bowersock 1994, 119, 121–43.

[221] Hdt. 4.93–6. For text and full details, see Stephens and Winkler 1995, 101–57. The Photius ref. is to *Bibliotheca* cod. 166, referred to by the page numbers of Bekker's edn., 109a6—112a12; here at 110a16.

[222] For other ancient refs. to Salmoxis, regarding him as a cheat and associating him with Pythagoras, cf. Hellanicus *Fr.* 73; Strabo 7.3.5. From this it appears that it is misleading to say (Bowersock 1994, 100) that Herodotus has Salmoxis die, be resurrected and then be treated as a god. In the one story, he dies and becomes a god; in the other, he fakes both death and resurrection.

to be revived the following night. Once again apparent death and burial is followed by emergence from the tomb.[223] Deathlike trances are inflicted and removed. In one fragment, Myrto, a dead family servant, gives a message to her mistress to warn her against a similar fate.[224]

Variations on the theme continue to appear in romances from the same period, i.e. roughly AD 50–250. Xenophon of Ephesus has a tale, not unlike that of Callirhoe's untimely burial, in which the heroine, Anthia, attempts to commit suicide by poisoning herself, is taken for dead, and buried – only to wake up from drugged sleep, to be stolen by grave-robbers, taken away and sold into slavery.[225] In order to attain originality within the *Scheintod* motif, ever more fantastic tricks had to be devised: Achilles Tatius (late second century AD) has his heroine Leucippe apparently sacrificed, her entrails extracted and eaten in a cannibalistic feast, and her body placed in a coffin – only for her to come to life again and show that her death had been a trick, using a sword with a retractable blade and an animal's skin, full of entrails, as a false stomach.[226] Leucippe is then, apparently, decapitated at sea, only to emerge once again.[227] This time her fiancé Clitophon is persuaded to get engaged to another, one Melite, but postpones the consummation of their marriage; Melite, at the banquet which follows, comments, 'How unique! This is rather like the ceremony for people whose bodies can't be found. I've heard of a tomb without a tenant, but not of a bridal bed without a bride.'[228] Finally Clitophon is informed, wrongly as it turns out, that Leucippe has been killed, only for her to reappear yet once more.[229] Clearly such writers assumed that their audiences could not get enough of the theme of cheating death. It even shows up in theatrical performances (one thinks again of *A Winter's Tale*); in one celebrated instance, it involves, on stage, the apparent death, and later revival, of a dog.[230]

Among the Latin novels one in particular stands out: the *Metamorphoses*, also known as *The Golden Ass*, by the second-century AD African writer Apuleius.[231] This work, too long and involved for easy summary, turns again

[223] Photius 110a41—110b11 (Stephens and Winkler 1995, 125).

[224] The frag. is *PSI* 1177, ll. 6–9: text and discussion in Stephens and Winkler 1995, 148–53.

[225] Xen. Eph. *An Ephesian Tale* 3.5–9 (Reardon 1989, 150–53).

[226] Achill. Tat. 3.15–21 (Reardon 1989, 216–19). Refs. in the next three notes are to this work.

[227] 5.7; 5.19.

[228] 5.14. The apparent reference is to the sort of 'funeral' for the absent dead envisaged in Chariton, *Call.* 4.1.3 (see above), though the reader might perhaps be expected to hear an allusion to tales of tombs that once were occupied but are now empty.

[229] 7.1–15.

[230] Plutarch *De Soll. Anim.* 973e—974a (full of admiration for the dog that played the part to perfection, in the presence of the aged Emperor Vespasian); cf. Winkler 1980, 173–5; Bowersock 1994, 113f.

[231] See the recent translation and introduction of Kenney 1998.

and again on the themes of communication with the dead, necromancy, and visits to the underworld; on the transformation of the hero Lucius into an ass (with his family and friends thinking him dead); and on his restoration to human life again, in a sort of life-after-death, a symbolic rebirth. In this work, the religious context which some have suspected behind the *Scheintod* motif in the hellenistic novels is quite explicit: Apuleius is clearly drawing on the mystery religions, particularly Isis-worship. The book incorporates a retelling of the old myth of Cupid and Psyche, which itself involves descent and re-ascent to and from the underworld.[232] Smaller-scale versions of such stories are provided from time to time as well.[233]

A final group of stories must be considered here, though they begin to encroach upon our next two categories. Philostratus' lengthy *Life of Apollonius of Tyana* (Apollonius was a first-century AD sage), is in some ways like the hellenistic romances: it involves travel and danger, exotic places and unusual people. Apollonius, however, is not a love-struck teenager, but a philosopher and mystic, who believes in reincarnation, including his own, and is capable of working miracles. At one point, in Rome, he raises to life, with a touch and a whisper, a girl who has died in the hour of her wedding; the scene is reminiscent of Luke 7.11–17, where Jesus raises a widow's son in the village of Nain. Philostratus comments:

> whether [Apollonius] detected some spark of life in her, which those who were nursing her had not noticed, – for it is said that although it was raining at the time, a vapour went up from her face – or whether life was really extinct, and he restored it by the warmth of his touch, is a mysterious problem which neither I myself nor those who were present could decide.[234]

This was presumably a regular ancient attitude: if something like this happens, one should assume that either death has been wrongly diagnosed (as with Callirhoe) or that some kind of primitive kiss-of-life technique has been effective.

After the death of Apollonius (about which Philostratus does not have exact information; he reports various sources as locating the event in different places) the story was told of his assumption into heaven – by now, as we shall presently see, quite a regular feature not only for emperors but for

---

[232] *Golden Ass* 4.28—6.24.

[233] e.g. *Golden Ass* 2.28–30, where a corpse is briefly allowed back from the underworld to accuse its wife of murder; 10.11–12, where a boy who appears to be dead, but is in fact only drugged, rises from his coffin. On this, see Bowersock 1994, 108f.

[234] *Apoll.* 4.45 (tr. Conybeare in Loeb edn.). The story opens with the statement, not that the girl had actually died (as the tr. implies), but that *tethnanai edokei*, 'she seemed to have died'. Bowersock 1994, 101 is wrong to say that before the mid-first century AD there is no parallel for such stories: he had overlooked the raising of children by Elijah (1 Kgs. 17.17–24) and Elisha (2 Kgs. 4.18–37). On Apollonius and similar stories see also Habermas 1989, 172f.; the article contains useful brief discussion of other ancient narratives as well.

others with some claim, within the pagan worldview, to be immortal.[235]
Having taught the immortality of the soul during his life, Apollonius continued to do so after his death; he appeared in a dream-vision to a young
man who had prayed to him (having previously grumbled that Apollonius 'is
so utterly dead that he will not appear to me . . . nor give me any reason to
consider him immortal'), and spoke lines of which the sentiments, though
perhaps not the expression, would have gladdened Socrates himself:

> The soul is immortal, and 'tis no possession of thine own, but of Providence;
> And after the body is wasted away, like a swift horse freed from its traces,
> It lightly leaps forward and mingles itself with the light air,
> Loathing the spell of harsh and painful servitude which it has endured.
> But for thee, what use is there in this? Some day when thou art no more thou shalt
> believe it.
> So why, as long as thou art among living beings, does thou explore these mysteries?[236]

Apollonius, then, lives on, but not in a body, which is just as well so far as
he and his biographer are concerned. Nothing here challenges the combined
worldview of Homer and Plato.

There are other similar tales; a good example (deserving more space than
we can give it here) is Lucian's satirical story about Peregrinus. They add
extra decoration to this larger picture, without disturbing its main lines.[237]

The truly striking thing about all these apparent deaths, and their strange
reversals or overcomings, is how they suddenly proliferate in the literature
of the middle or late first century AD onwards. It would be daring to suggest
that this is the result of the early Christian story of Jesus making its way into
the wider greco-roman world; such a proposal could hardly be elaborated at
this stage of our investigation. Equally, it is difficult to give a definite explanation for the famous Greek inscription, from the same period, found near
Nazareth: the emperor (unnamed, but almost certainly Claudius) issues an
edict warning of penalties for breaking open or violating tombs.[238] But it is
even more difficult to suggest that the early Christian stories about Jesus
were copied or adapted from these greco-roman sources. As we shall see
when we study the gospels themselves, they are simply not that kind of
thing. When, two centuries after Jesus, the educated pagan Celsus took it
upon himself to controvert the gospel stories of the resurrection, he, like
some more recent sceptics, could place them within this wider setting; but

---

[235] *Apoll.* 8.30.
[236] 8.31.
[237] On Lucian *Pereg.* see Bowersock 1994, 115f., and esp. König 2003. See too
Plutarch *De Ser. Num. Vindic.* 563b–e, describing the 'near-death experience' of a character
called Aridaeus, who recounts his experiences (563e–567f), and is finally snatched back to
find himself alive, but about to be buried as though dead (568a).
[238] See Barrett 1987 [1956], 14f., with refs. to secondary discussions; and see below,
708f. The Greek is presumed to be translated from a Latin original.

he knew that they were claiming something more.[239] Nobody in the pagan world of Jesus' day and thereafter actually claimed that somebody had been truly dead and had then come to be truly, and bodily, alive once more.

(vi) Translated to Be With the Gods

Apollonius, according to Philostratus, was immortal; so indeed are we all, according to the long Platonic tradition. But from Homer to the late classical period, as we saw, some of the dead were thought to have been transferred or translated to a place of special bliss and honour. Do these stories provide in any way exceptions to the general rule in the classical world that dead people do not rise?

The answer is a clear negative. In no case do the stories of deification or translation affirm that which Homer and the others deny.

Some of the stories, to be sure, exhibit interesting features. Livy tells how Romulus, the supposed co-founder of Rome, was sitting on his throne on the Campus Martius, when suddenly a storm blew up and a cloud enveloped him; when the cloud dispersed, the throne was empty. Those present began to hail him as a god or the son of a god; some suggested that he had been torn to pieces by jealous senators; and a shrewd man called Julius Proculus quickly told the Assembly that Romulus had appeared to him, had told him that Rome would become the capital of the world, and had again been taken up into the sky.[240] The story may have a basis in earlier legend, but when Livy tells it he cannot but be aware of the divinization of Julius Caesar, and the likely subsequent apotheosis of his (Livy's) friend Augustus. Herodotus, never one to pass up a good story, tells the tale of one Aristeas, who fell down dead in a fuller's shop, was seen alive walking outside the town, and was missing from the shop when the fuller returned. He reappeared elsewhere seven years later, wrote a poem, and vanished again. In a further twist, his ghost appeared and instructed the people of Marmora to erect an altar to Apollo, and a statue of himself beside it; this they duly did, having consulted the oracle at Delphi. Aristeas, in other words, had joined the immortal gods, at least at a junior level.[241] Similar stories are told about Cleomedes, who disappeared from a chest, and about Hercules himself disappearing off his own funeral pyre.[242] Interestingly, when Josephus presents the stories of Elijah, Enoch and Moses, he does so in the language of this hellenistic tradition, declaring that they had not died, but had been taken up

---

[239] On Celsus, see below, 518–26.

[240] Livy 1.16.2f.

[241] Hdt. 4.14f.

[242] Pausanias 2.9.7; Diod. Sicul. 4.38.5. Hercules, we should note, ascended precisely because his mortal nature had been burned away so that his immortal part could join the gods: so Lucian *Hermotimus* 7.

alive to immortality.[243] This, as we shall see, is typical of Josephus' presentation of Jewish tradition in Greek dress.[244] Interestingly, Plutarch pours scorn on incidents like the assumption of Romulus, not just because such things don't happen but because nobody in their right mind would want them to. Why would anyone want an earthly body in a future life?[245]

The important thing to stress is that nobody in the ancient world took these stories as evidence of *resurrection*.[246] It is in any case a category mistake to lump stories of apotheosis with the romantic *Scheintod* motif, as Kathleen Corley does; it is equally mistaken to suppose, as does Adela Yarbro Collins, that translation or apotheosis is equivalent to resurrection.[247] When a hero such as Hyacinthos or Asclepius died and was buried, and was then believed to have been translated to heaven, this is not the resurrection which Homer, Aeschylus and others denied, nor yet the 'resurrection' that seemed to have taken place following a *Scheintod*.[248] The novels may be of interest as evidence for a new wave of speculation about death and its aftermath, but they shed no light on the early Christian belief in, and stories about, the resurrection of Jesus.

(vii) Transmigration of Souls

There was one belief, held quite widely by philosophers at least, according to which the dead did indeed return to some kind of this-worldly and bodily existence. This was the theory of *metempsychosis*, the transmigration or reincarnation of souls. This was what Celsus thought was at the basis of the Christian theory of resurrection.[249]

---

[243] See Collins 1993, 127, citing Tabor 1989 and an unpublished piece by C. Begg.

[244] On the possible parallel to this in *Pseudo-Phocylides* 97–104 (Collins 1993, 127f.), see below, 141.

[245] Plut. *Romulus* 28.4–8, mentioning other stories of other disappearing, and supposedly divinized, bodies.

[246] Contra e.g. L. H. Martin 1987, 121, following J. Z. Smith.

[247] Corley 2002, 129–31; Collins 1993, 123–8, 137–8. At crucial points Collins follows the line of Rohde 1923, which seems to me clearly mistaken.

[248] On the idea that Jesus' followers saw him as a hero, resulting in ceremonies at his tomb, and generating stories about his resurrection, see below, 701f. Cf. Perkins 1984, 93f., 109f. (with literature), 119. For Asclepius cf. e.g. Luc. *Salt.* 45; Paus. 2.26.5.

[249] Or. *C. Cels* 7.32. On *metempsychosis*, cf. e.g. Diod. Sic. 10.6.1–3 (including the story of Pythagoras recognizing the shield he had carried in a former life). What seems to be a vivid though macabre example is provided in *Aen.* 3.19–68: Polydorus, Priam's youngest son, has been killed and buried, and turned into a clump of trees, which ooze black blood when Aeneas tries to uproot them. A happier example is when Pythagoras, seeing someone beating a puppy, told him to stop; he recognized by its voice that the soul was that of a friend of his (Price 1999, 122, quoting Xenophanes frag. 7a). *Metempsychosis* ('transmigration') is of course to be distinguished from *metamorphosis*, which simply means 'transformation'. See Bremmer 2002, 11–15.

The classic statement of this is found in Plato, who developed the idea from the work of the sixth-century Pythagoras; but belief in transmigration was also fostered in the Orphic cult, and continued among philosophers and cult practitioners thereafter, though without ever gaining much popular adherence.[250] Properly speaking, the theory exists in at least two distinct forms, one holding that the soul passes into another body immediately upon death, the other that the soul waits for a longer or shorter period before entering another body. This distinction does not affect our present discussion.

Plato's fullest statements are in the Myth of Er which closes the *Republic*, and in the *Phaedrus*, but other references are scattered widely throughout his extant writings.[251] His basic scheme is reasonably straightforward: after death, the souls of all humans wait for a period – whether for nine years, as in the Pindar fragment quoted in the *Meno*, or for a thousand, as in the Myth of Er – whereupon they are given the choice of what sort of creatures they will become in their next existence. In the Er story, Orpheus becomes a swan, Ajax a lion, Agamemnon an eagle, and so on.[252] Odysseus, who seems to have learnt more than most others from his previous life, chooses to be 'an ordinary citizen who minded his own business'.[253] The souls then proceed through the Plain of Oblivion, drink of the River of Forgetfulness, and so pass into their next existence, unaware of who they have been, or even that they have been anything at all. Since for Plato, as for the Hindu and Buddhist schemes of the same type, return to embodied existence means that the soul is once more entering a kind of prison, the ultimate aim is not simply to choose the right type of existence for one's next life, but to escape the cycle altogether.[254] We are here not far from one version at least of Hindu and other doctrines of *karma*.[255]

How, then, do we know about all this? Partly, in the myths, because one or two have returned to tell us; but also for a more philosophically satisfying reason. When we learn things in the present life, we sometimes have the sense that we are recalling things we have dimly known before. The best

---

[250] See e.g. Burkert 1985, 199, 298–301; Price 1999, 122f. For Pythagoras himself see Diog. Laert. 8.31; cf. Plut. *De Ser. Num. Vindic.* 564a–c. For the effect of this on ordinary grieving etc., see e.g. Plut. *Consolatio ad Uxorem* 611e–f. For restriction of belief in transmigration to philosophical circles cf. Garland 1985, 62f.

[251] *Rep.* 10.614b—621d; *Phaedr.* 245b—249d; cf. *Phaedo* 80c—82c, 84a–b; *Gorg.* 523a—526d; *Meno* 81b–d (quoting a fragment of Pindar (133) to good effect).

[252] *Rep.* 10.620a–b.

[253] *Rep.* 10.620c–d.

[254] e.g. *Phaedr.* 249a–d: if the soul chooses the philosophical life three times, it regains its wings and can speed away. Such a person 'will be rebuked by the ignorant multitude as being out of his wits, for they know not that he is possessed by a deity' (*pros to theio gignomenos*) (tr. Hackforth in Hamilton and Cairns 1961, 496).

[255] On *karma*, cf. O'Flaherty 1980; Neufeldt 1986.

explanation for this, according to Plato, is that we have known them in a previous life.[256]

This belief in transmigration seems to have been embraced in circles where Pythagorean or Platonic influence is unlikely: thus Caesar reports it as the belief of the Gallic Druids.[257] Among the other evidence for its continuance through to the New Testament period are some inscribed gold leaves from Thurii in southern Italy, which promise the bearer passage into the next world in terms which are at least compatible with transmigration.[258] But Pythagoreanism was regarded by some within the Roman world as a threat to the established order and religion, and does not seem to have been widely popular.[259]

Transmigration must be distinguished carefully from two other beliefs. The Stoics believed that at the end of the present age everything would be dissolved in fire, and the whole order of the universe would come round again just as before. This *palingenesia*, birth-over-again, is clearly not the same as *metempsychosis*, transmigration, which involves the movement and change of individual souls until, if they find the right path, they can cease to be reincarnated and live for ever in the immortal state.[260] Similarly, we should distinguish carefully between transmigration and resurrection. It is precisely part of the Pythagorean (and Platonic) theory that the souls in question do not come back as the creatures, the persons, they once were; and certainly there is no question of continuity between the earlier physical body and the new one, which as we shall see was central to early Christian belief.

In any case, to come back at all is clearly to have failed in the soul's ultimate destination. It is to return to jail. For believers in resurrection, by contrast – that is, many Jews and virtually all early Christians – the new embodied life is to be looked forward to and celebrated.[261] It is not part of a cyclic movement, round and round between life and death. As some Jews glimpsed, and as the early Christians emphasized, it is a matter of going through death and out into a newly embodied life beyond. Transmigration offered a far more interesting prospect for the future life than the gloomy world of Homeric Hades. But Homer's basic rule remained in force. Nobody was allowed to return from Hades and resume the life they once had.

---

[256] e.g. *Meno* 81c–d.

[257] Caes. *Gall. War* 6.14.5; though cf. Diod. Sic. 5.28.6, where such a link is postulated.

[258] Burkert 1985, 299; Price 1999, 123.

[259] For the C2 BC Roman burning of Pythagorean texts cf. Pliny *NH* 13.84–6.

[260] Though cf. Servius, commenting (as part of an interesting wider discussion) on Virg. *Aen.* 3.68: for Pythagoras what mattered was *palingenesia* rather than *metempsychosis*. The roots of this misunderstanding are too deep for us to dig for them further at this point.

[261] On Josephus' ambiguous language see 175–81 below. On possible exceptions among some C2 Christians, cf. 534–51 below.

(viii) Dying and Rising Gods

The final category to be examined here for possible non-Jewish hints of resurrection is the world of oriental religion in which was celebrated the death and rebirth of various deities. This is a vast area in itself, and fortunately we do not need to stay long on it.

From very early times, in Egypt and elsewhere, some of the major religions centred their symbols, stories and praxis on the cycles of nature, and on the gods and goddesses who were believed to enact, or to have enacted, these cycles in themselves. Thus there emerged, gradually and with far too many variations even to list, the well-known dying and rising gods and goddesses of the ancient near east.[262] The roll-call is impressive, conjuring up centuries of customs that developed, intertwined, combined, separated out again and recombined, and that gave shape and meaning to the lives of millions over a wide geographical area: Adonis, Attis, Isis and Osiris, Dionysus, Demeter and Persephone, corn-kings and corn-mothers in profusion; and, away to the wild north, Balder the beautiful, son of the great god Odin. Migration and conquest, the mix of cultures and the dissemination of ideas, ensured that by the time of the early Christians these (with the exception of the last) were familiar throughout the known world.

At the heart of the cults was the ritual re-enactment of the death and rebirth of the god, coupled with sundry fertility rites. The productivity of the soil, and of the tribe or nation, was at stake; by getting in touch with the mysterious forces that underlay the natural world, by sympathetic and symbolic re-enactment of them, one might hope to guarantee both crops and offspring. The myth which accompanied these rituals was indeed the story of resurrection, of new life the other side of death.

Did this in any way form an exception to the rule laid down in the ancient world? Did any worshipper in these cults, from Egypt to Norway, at any time in antiquity, think that actual human beings, having died, actually came back to life? Of course not.[263] These multifarious and sophisticated cults enacted the god's death and resurrection as a *metaphor*, whose concrete referent was the cycle of seed-time and harvest, of human reproduction and fertility. Sometimes, as in Egypt, the myths and rituals included funerary practices: the aspiration of the dead was to become united with Osiris. But the new life they might thereby experience was not a return to the life of the present world. Nobody actually expected the mummies to get up, walk about

---

[262] The classic account is Frazer 1911–15 (abridged version, 1956 [1922]).

[263] Porter 1999a, 74–7, having begun by suggesting that the mystery religions included the notion of resurrection, rightly concludes (77) that 'bodily resurrection is not a part' of such cults and their beliefs. The best-known recent attempt to locate early Christianity within the world of 'dying and rising gods' is that of Smith 1990; see the shrewd criticisms of Bremmer 2002, 52–5 (a fresh version of Bremmer 1996, 104–07), suggesting that the cults of e.g. Attis and Mithras show evidence of influence from Christianity itself.

and resume normal living; nobody in that world would have wanted such a thing, either. That which Homer and others meant by resurrection was not affirmed by the devotees of Osiris or their cousins elsewhere.

We can go further, anticipating our later arguments. The Jewish world into which Christianity was born was influenced in many ways by the wider greco-roman world. Hellenistic ideas and practices had made inroads since at least the time of Alexander the Great. But, remarkably enough, there is no sign of dying and rising gods and goddesses within the Jewish world. Ezekiel had charged Jerusalem women with taking part in the Tammuz-cult, but we do not find such practices in the second-Temple period.[264] As we shall see, when Jews spoke of resurrection it was not something that they expected would happen to their god YHWH. Nor was it something that would happen to them again and again; it would be a single, unrepeatable event.

Likewise, when the Christians spoke of the resurrection of Jesus they did not suppose it was something that happened every year, with the sowing of seed and the harvesting of crops. They could use the image of sowing and harvesting to talk about it; they could celebrate Jesus' death by breaking bread; but to confuse this with the world of the dying and rising gods would be a serious mistake.[265] The early Christians did not engage in the relevant praxis; they only tangentially employed the same symbols (bread, we should note, is not the same thing as corn); and they told a very different story from those of Adonis, Attis and the rest. Their answers to the worldview questions were radically different. And the set of beliefs and aims that were generated from within their worldview were simply not on the same map. It is of course quite possible that, when people in the wider world heard what the early Christians were saying, they attempted to fit the strange message into the worldview of cults they already knew. But the evidence suggests that they were more likely to be puzzled, or to mock. When Paul preached in Athens, nobody said, 'Ah, yes, a new version of Osiris and such like.' The Homeric assumption remained in force. Whatever the gods – or the crops – might do, humans did not rise again from the dead.

4. Conclusion: The One-Way Street

The road to the underworld ran only one way. Throughout the ancient world, from its 'bible' of Homer and Plato, through its practices (funerals, memorial feasts), its stories (plays, novels, legends), its symbols (graves, amulets,

---

[264] Ezek. 8.14. On Tammuz (a Mesopotamian deity known in many sources and traditions) see e.g. Handy 1992.

[265] It used to be suggested, following the impact of Frazer's work, that Christian belief in Jesus' resurrection, and some facets of early Christian practice, were an offshoot from, or at least heavily influenced by, the oriental cults; but this view is not usually advanced in scholarship today. For a basic-level refutation, cf. McKenzie 1997.

grave-goods) and its grand theories, we can trace a good deal of variety about the road to Hades, and about what one might find upon arrival. As with all one-way streets, there is bound to be someone who attempts to drive in the opposite direction. One hears of a Protesilaus, an Alcestis or a Nero *redivivus*, once or twice in a thousand years. But the road was well policed. Would-be traffic violators (Sisyphus, Eurydice and the like) were turned back or punished. And even they only occurred in what everybody knew to be myth.

We can, then, answer the worldview questions in relation to the dead. Who were the dead thought to be, in the ancient pagan world? They were beings that had once been embodied human beings, but were now souls, shades or *eidola*. Where were they? Most likely in Hades; possibly in the Isles of the Blessed, or Tartarus; just conceivably, reincarnated into a different body altogether. They might occasionally appear to living mortals; they might still be located somewhere in the vicinity of their tombs; but they were basically in a different world. What was wrong? Nothing, for a good Platonist, or a Stoic like Epictetus; the soul was well rid of its body – a sentiment echoed by many non-philosophers in a world without modern medicine, and often without much justice. Almost everything, for most people: some kind of life might continue after death, but it was unlikely to be as rich and satisfying as the present one could be, at least in theory. Death was felt as a grievous loss both to the dying and to the bereaved, and rare indeed were those (Socrates, Seneca perhaps) who could overcome such feelings. What's the solution? If embodiment or re-embodiment is seen as a problem, the eventual solution will be to escape it altogether. But if death, the separation of soul and body, is seen as the problem – as it obviously was by the vast majority of people, as witnessed by tomb inscriptions and funeral rites throughout the ancient world – there was no solution. Death was all-powerful. One could neither escape it in the first place nor break its power once it had come. The ancient world was thus divided into those who said that resurrection couldn't happen, though they might have wanted it to, and those who said they didn't want it to happen, knowing that it couldn't anyway.

It is important to stress this because of the frequent misunderstandings one meets on the point, caused, I suspect, not least by the loose usage of the word 'resurrection' in contemporary western discussions.[266] This brings us back to the point we emphasized at the close of the first chapter. We cannot stress too strongly that from Homer onwards the language of 'resurrection' was not used to denote 'life after death' in general, or any of the phenomena supposed to occur within such a life. The great majority of the ancients believed in life after death; many of them developed, as we have seen, complex and fascinating beliefs about it and practices in relation to it; but, other

---

[266] e.g. Porter 1999a, 68, discussed above (34f.).

than within Judaism and Christianity, they did not believe in resurrection. 'Resurrection' denoted a new embodied life which would *follow* whatever 'life after death' there might be. 'Resurrection' was, by definition, not the existence into which someone might (or might not) go immediately upon death; it was not a disembodied 'heavenly' life; it was a further stage, out beyond all that. It was not a redescription or redefinition of death. It was death's reversal.

The multiple significance of all this will not be missed. To anticipate our later arguments, we may highlight three issues in particular.

1. When the early Christians spoke of Jesus being raised from the dead, the natural meaning of that statement, throughout the ancient world, was the claim that something had happened to Jesus which had happened to nobody else. A great many things supposedly happened to the dead, but resurrection did not.[267] The pagan world assumed it was impossible; the Jewish world believed it would happen eventually, but knew perfectly well that it had not done so yet. Jew and non-Jew alike heard the early Christians to be saying that it had happened to Jesus. They did not suppose the Christians were merely asserting that Jesus' soul had attained some kind of heavenly bliss or special status. They did not think Jesus' disciples were merely describing, with gross hyperbole, their regular feasts at his tomb.[268]

2. The early Christian belief that Jesus was in some sense divine cannot have been the cause of the belief in his resurrection. Apart from old tales like Livy's story of Romulus, those who became divine mostly had graves, either known and cherished or assumed, unless of course they had been burnt on a funeral pyre. Divinization did not require resurrection; it regularly happened without it. It involved the soul, not the body.

3. Within second-century Christianity, as we shall see in chapter 11, a few writers used the language of 'resurrection' to denote, not what the entire ancient world, both pagan and Jewish, had meant by it up to that point, that is, some kind of a return to bodily and this-worldly life, but rather something which was well known as a concept but for which this language had never before been used, namely, a state of blissful disembodied immortality.[269] They thus took a key term in Judaism and Christianity, which referred to something hardly anyone believed in, and used it to denote something a great many people believed in. 'Resurrection' (*anastasis* and its cognates) was not in use elsewhere in the ancient world as a description of non-bodily

---

[267] The belief in the uniqueness of Jesus' resurrection is not, then, a modern fundamentalist invention, as is suggested by Crossan 1998, xviii. The whole introductory section of Crossan's book (xiii–xx), and the first chapter of Riley 1995 upon which Crossan leans, is challenged at its root by the present chapter. Evans 1970, 27, seems to me 180 degrees wide of the mark when he says that the doctrine of resurrection was, among Jewish ideas, 'the most eminently exportable' to the greco-roman world. See e.g. Zeller 2002, 19.

[268] On the significance of such events as the raising of Lazarus see below, 443f.

[269] See e.g. Riley 1995, 58–68; and below, ch. 11.

life after death. It did not denote the passage of the soul into the life beyond or below, or even the migration of the soul into a different body. Those within the second-century Christian world who used 'resurrection' in this way were, therefore, innovating, describing something that Plato and others believed in but using language which Plato and others used for something they did *not* believe in. The point for the moment is this: such usage is only explicable as a subsequent mutation from within an earlier Christianity that asserted resurrection in the normal sense (return to bodily life). It was a variation that attempted to retain Christian language about Jesus, and about the future destiny of Christians, while filling it with non-Christian, and for that matter non-Jewish, content. If this mutation had been the norm, and belief in bodily resurrection the odd variant, why would anyone have invented the latter? And would not Celsus have pointed all this out?

The task of the present chapter has been largely negative. But also necessary: if the claims of the early Christians are to be understood, they must be allowed to appear three-dimensionally within the world where they were proclaimed. For this, it has been important first to live within that world for a while, to sense its flavours and moods as well as its worldviews, beliefs, hopes and aims. Having done that, and having eliminated some misunderstandings which have obscured the subject for some time, we must now move into a world which, though located within wider greco-roman society, and penetrated by it in numerous ways, regarded itself with good reason as essentially different: that of first-century Judaism. And to understand that world we must first familiarize ourselves with the pictures of death, and life beyond it, in the Jewish scriptures themselves.

Chapter Three

TIME TO WAKE UP (1):
DEATH AND BEYOND IN THE OLD TESTAMENT

1. Introduction

'The Messiah', declared Paul, 'was raised on the third day in accordance with the scriptures.'[1] What the early Christians said about the resurrection of Jesus was consciously rooted from the start within the worldview of second-Temple Judaism, shaped not least by the Jewish Bible. Granted what we have just seen about pagan expectations, this was the only place where the story had any chance of making itself at home. 'Resurrection' is not part of the pagan hope. If the idea belongs anywhere, it is within the world of Judaism.[2]

It is all the more surprising, then, to discover that, within the Bible itself, the hope of resurrection makes rare appearances, so rare that some have considered them marginal.[3] Though later exegesis, both Jewish and Christian, became skilled at discovering covert allusions which earlier readers had not seen – a skill shared, according to the gospels, by Jesus himself – there is general agreement that for much of the Old Testament the idea of resurrection is, to put it at its strongest, deeply asleep, only to be woken by echoes from later times and texts.[4]

---

[1] 1 Cor 15.4; see below, 319–22.

[2] On other possible locations (e.g. Zoroastrianism) see below. There is no serious suggestion that the first disciples were influenced, in their talk of resurrection, by anything other than Jewish beliefs.

[3] See e.g. the treatment in von Rad 1962–5, 1.407f., 2.350; Brueggemann 1997, 483f. ('only at the edge of the Old Testament').

[4] The literature is immense. See e.g. Tromp 1969; Greenspoon 1981; Spronk 1986; Krieg 1988; Barr 1992; Ollenburger 1993; J. J. Collins 1993, 394–8; Segal 1997; Grappe 2001; Mettinger 2001; Johnston 2002. Older studies that still have considerable value include Martin-Achard 1960. The massive work of Puech 1993 is not only about the Essenes, as its title might imply; its substantial first volume covers the OT, second-Temple Judaism, and the NT and early Fathers as well.

This is often presented not simply as a surprise but as a problem, at least for Christians and Jews today who want to remain loyal both to the Old Testament and to their own specific sources of belief (the New Testament on the one hand and the rabbis on the other). It seems ironic that most of the clearest statements of what was to become the mainstream viewpoint are to be found, not in scripture itself, but in post-biblical (i.e. second-Temple and rabbinic) texts which never attained canonical status. Many Christians have adopted some kind of theory of progressive revelation, according to which the earlier parts of the Old Testament held little or no belief in life after death, some of the more mature parts began to affirm a life beyond the grave, though without being very specific, and then, right at the end of the Old Testament period, some writers began to proclaim the quite different and radically new belief in bodily resurrection. This is routinely seen as a kind of crescendo, beginning with the near-silence, as it were, of the grave itself, and moving towards the fully orchestrated statement of the theme which will dominate the New Testament. We shake our heads, it is implied, more in sorrow than in disloyalty at the large tracts of early Israelite faith and life which seem to contribute little to the belief which became central to early Christianity.

Studies and surveys of ancient Israelite beliefs about life after death have thus tended to plot three distinct types or phases. In the early period, there was little or no hope for a life of joy or bliss after death: Sheol swallowed up the dead, kept them in gloomy darkness, and never let them out again. At some point (nobody knows when; dating of developments in such matters is notoriously difficult) some pious Israelites came to regard the love and power of YHWH as so strong that the relationship they enjoyed with him in the present could not be broken even by death. Then, again at an uncertain point, a quite new idea came forth: the dead would be raised.

Three positions thus emerge: absence of hope beyond death; hope for blissful life after death; hope for new bodily life *after* 'life after death'. Very different they seem.

Though this analysis is broadly accurate, I intend to challenge the regular interpretation of it. There are important links between the apparently different positions. It is of course true that the third position, explicit belief in resurrection, is only one of several strands in the range of biblical beliefs about death and what happens afterwards, and that this belief developed markedly in the post-biblical period. In particular, the third, though clearly cutting across the first in certain ways, joins the first in affirming the goodness and vital importance of the present created order, which is to be renewed by YHWH, not abandoned. For both, the substance of hope lies within creation, not beyond it. Generations of Christian exegetes, convinced that 'life after death' (whether embodied or disembodied) is what true faith and hope are all about, have regarded it as strange that the Old Testament should have so little to say on the subject. In fact, however, an interest in 'life after death' for its own sake was characteristic of various pagan worldviews (that of Egypt, for instance), not of ancient Israel; and when belief in resurrection eventually appeared, it is best understood, as I shall argue below, not as a strange foreign import but as a re-expression of the ancient Israelite worldview under new and different circumstances. It is sown in the same soil as the beliefs of the Patriarchs; seed and soil, indeed, are important clues to the continuity, as well as the discontinuity, between (for instance) Genesis and Daniel.

The present chapter and the following one seek to do for the Jewish world what the previous one did for the pagan world of late antiquity: to plot the spectrum of beliefs about life after (the event of) death, and particularly about resurrection (i.e. a further life after an interim state of being dead), held by Jews in the time of Jesus and the early church. Since, as we have already noted, much of the Old Testament is not particularly concerned with life after death at all, still less with resurrection, we must be careful to locate this discussion within its own larger world, that of the wider hope and expectation of the ancient Israelites. These are the questions we must now put to the relevant material (mostly texts, with some archaeological data).[5] Our eventual focus (in chapter 4) must be on the beliefs held in the first century AD, as seen not only in the new texts that were produced within second-Temple Judaism but in the way the Old Testament itself was being read in that period (at Qumran, for instance, or by the Septuagint). The present chapter will prepare for this by examining the key biblical passages which form the basis of all subsequent varieties of Judaism.

2. Asleep with the Ancestors

(i) Next to Nothingness

A casual reader of many parts of the Old Testament could be forgiven for thinking that ancient Israelite belief about life after death was not very different from that of Homer:

> In death there is no remembrance of you;
> in Sheol who can give you praise?[6]

> The dead do not praise YHWH, nor do any that go down into silence.[7]

---

[5] On burial customs in the early period the work of Wiesner 1938 is still valuable; and see below, 90f.
[6] Ps. 6.5.
[7] Ps. 115.17.

Dust you are, and to dust you shall return.[8]

What profit is there in my death, if I go down to the Pit?
Will the dust praise you? Will it tell of your faithfulness?[9]

My soul is full of troubles, and my life draws near to Sheol.
I am counted among those who go down to the Pit;
I am like those who have no help,
like those forsaken among the dead, like the slain that lie in the grave,
like those you remember no more, for they are cut off from your hand.
You have put me in the depths of the Pit, in the regions dark and deep.
Your wrath lies heavy upon me, and you overwhelm me with all your waves . . .
Do you work wonders for the dead? Do the shades rise up to praise you?
Is your steadfast love declared in the grave, or your faithfulness in Abaddon?
Are your wonders known in the darkness,
Or your saving help in the land of forgetfulness?[10]

In the noontide of my days I must depart;
I am consigned to the gates of Sheol for the rest of my years.
I said, I shall not see YHWH in the land of the living;
I shall look upon mortals no more among the inhabitants of the world . . .
For Sheol cannot thank you, death cannot praise you;
those who go down to the Pit cannot hope for your faithfulness.
The living, the living, they thank you, as I do this day;
fathers make known to children your faithfulness.[11]

We must all die; we are like water spilled on the ground, which cannot be gathered up.[12]

The living know that they will die, but the dead know nothing; they have no more reward, and even the memory of them is lost. Their love and their hate and their envy have already perished; never again will they have any share in all that happens under the sun . . .
   Whatever your hand finds to do, do with your might; for there is no work or thought or knowledge or wisdom in Sheol, to which you are going.[13]

Now [sc. if I had died at birth] I would be lying down and quiet;
I would be asleep; then I would be at rest, with kings and counsellors of the earth . . .
There the wicked cease from troubling, and there the weary are at rest.
There the prisoners are at ease together; they do not hear the voice of the taskmaster.
The small and the great are there, and the slaves are free from their masters.[14]

Sheol, Abaddon, the Pit, the grave. The dark, deep regions, the land of forgetfulness. These almost interchangeable terms denote a place of gloom

[8] Gen. 3.19.
[9] Ps. 30.9; cf. the same terminology in e.g. Ps. 16.10.
[10] Ps. 88.3–7, 10–12.
[11] Isa 38.10f., 18f.
[12] 2 Sam. 14.14.
[13] Eccles. 9.5f., 10.
[14] Job 3.13f., 17–19.

and despair, a place where one can no longer enjoy life, and where the presence of YHWH himself is withdrawn.[15] It is a wilderness: a place of dust to which creatures made of dust have returned.[16] Those who have gone there are 'the dead'; they are 'shades', *rephaim*,[17] and they are 'asleep'.[18] As in Homer, there is no suggestion that they are enjoying themselves; it is a dark and gloomy world. Nothing much happens there. It is not another form of real life, an alternative world where things continue as normal.

The most lively biblical scene of continuing activity in Sheol merely confirms this. Isaiah 14 offers a splendid depiction of the king of Babylon arriving in the underworld to join the erstwhile noble shades who are there already. In a passage worthy of Homer, he is grimly informed that things are very different down here:

> Sheol beneath is stirred up to meet you when you come;
> it rouses the shades to greet you, all who were leaders of the earth;
> it raises from their thrones all who were kings of the nations.
> All of them will speak and say to you:
> 'You too have become as weak as we! You have become like us!'
> Your pomp is brought down to Sheol, and the sound of your harps;
> maggots are the bed beneath you, and worms are your covering.[19]

Allowing for poetic licence, this indicates a minimal human activity of recognition; but the greeting is made in order to inform the newly arrived monarch that his power counts for nothing in this miserable world. Indeed, he is even worse off than the others, because he was not even buried in his own land. Thus, while

> All the kings of the nations lie in glory, each in his own tomb . . .
> You are cast out, away from your grave, like loathsome carrion;
> clothed with the dead, those pierced by the sword,
> who go down to the stones of the Pit, like a corpse trampled underfoot.[20]

If there are different degrees within Sheol, they are degrees of misery and degradation. The passage reveals something else: a fluidity of thought between Sheol as a mythical abode of the shades on the one hand and the physical reality of the grave – stones, worms, maggots and all – on the other.

---

[15] On the meaning of the words see e.g. Martin-Achard 1960, 36–46; Tromp 1969; Sawyer 1973; Barr 1992, 28–36; Day 1996, 231f.; Jarick 1999; Johnston 2002, ch. 3.

[16] cf. Dan. 12.2.

[17] cf. e.g. the repeated warnings against the adulteress in Prov. 2.18; 5.5; 7.27; 9.18 ('he knows not that the dead [*rephaim*, 'the shades'] are there; that her guests are in the depths of Sheol'). So also e.g. Ps. 88.10; Isa. 14.9; 26.14, 19, etc. On the key terms see esp. Johnston 2002, ch. 6.

[18] Again, Dan. 12.2. They are 'flimsy creatures, mere carbon-copies of living beings in the eternal filing systems of the underworld' (Caird 1966, 253).

[19] Isa. 14.9–11.

[20] Isa. 14.18f.

It would be wrong to give the impression that the early Israelites were particularly gloomy about all this. Only a world which had already begun to hope for something more interesting and enjoyable after death would find this vision unusual or depressing. Their minds, and their hopes, were on other things. When Jacob declares that losing another son 'would bring down my grey hairs with sorrow to Sheol', he does not mean that such a tragedy will result in him going to Sheol rather than somewhere else, but that his passage there will be accompanied by sorrow rather than by contentment at a long and worthwhile life.[21] The description of his eventual death does not mention Sheol, but rather says that he 'was gathered to his people'; there is no reason, though, to suppose that his descendants thought he was anywhere other than in Sheol. The tension remains between that belief and the implicit hope, on a different level altogether, contained in the instructions that his body be taken back to the family burial place.[22] The same hope underlies Joseph's command that his bones be eventually taken back to the promised land.[23]

This combination of themes is taken up and repeated in what becomes the regular formula for dying kings. David 'slept with his ancestors, and was buried in the city of David', which is the more interesting since his ancestors were not buried there. 'Sleeping with one's ancestors', in other words, was not simply a way of saying that one was buried in the same grave or cave, but that one had gone to the world of the dead, there to be reunited with one's forebears.[24] The minimal sort of 'life' that the shades had in Sheol, or in the grave, approximated more to sleep than to anything else known by the living. They might be momentarily aroused from their comatose state by an especially distinguished newcomer, as in Isaiah 14, or (as we shall see) by a necromancer; but their normal condition was to be asleep. They were not completely non-existent, but to all intents and purposes they were, so to speak, next to nothing.[25]

This conclusion, though it seems so clear in the texts, has sometimes been challenged on the basis of the archaeological evidence of ancient Hebrew burials and their attendant customs. Eric Meyers, in particular, has argued that the ancient and widespread practice of secondary burials (collecting and storing the bones after the flesh has decomposed) reflects a

---

[21] Gen. 42.38 (cf. 37.35; 44.29, 31).

[22] Gen. 49.29–33. For a (controversial) way of combining the two ideas see below on burial customs.

[23] Gen. 50.24–6; cf. Ex. 13.19; Josh. 24.32.

[24] 1 Kgs. 2.10; cf. 1.21; 2 Sam. 7.12. For the repeated formula cf. 1 Kgs. 11.43; 14.20, 31; 15.8; 16.28; 22.40, 50; 2 Kgs. 8.24; 10.35; 12.21; 13.13; 14.16, 20, 29; 15.7, 22, 38; 16.20; 20.21; 21.18; 24.6. The few exceptions (e.g. Josiah in 2 Kgs. 23.30) are probably not significant.

[25] On the question of whether Sheol's inhabitants know things or not, and of whether YHWH has power over Sheol see Day 1996, 233f., and other literature there.

belief in a continuing *nephesh*, enabling the bones to provide 'at least a shadow of their strength in life', with the mortal remains constituting 'the very essence of that person in death'.[26] Many ancient Israelite tombs show evidence of grave-goods, apparently providing for the needs of the dead.[27] Thus being 'gathered to one's fathers', or, in the case of Qumran (so Meyers suggests) to one's brethren, meant that one's bones would be stored along with theirs.[28] This, coupled with the suggestion of some other scholars that there was a reasonably widespread cult of the dead in ancient Israel, as in the ancient non-Jewish world, has caused some to question whether the picture of life after death was really as shadowy as the biblical texts indicate. Have they, perhaps, deliberately covered over a more popular belief with an 'orthodox' statement of the next-to-nothing existence of the dead, perhaps to discourage interest in and association with the dead?[29]

The latter proposal seems to be ruled out on closer inspection. The evidence simply does not support it. And it is important to heed the warning of an eminent archaeologist, himself a student of the same phenomena: 'any analysed rite or custom lends itself to more than one interpretation.'[30] The practice of secondary burial can itself be interpreted in various ways; its sudden reintroduction in the middle of the second-Temple period is often (though still controversially) linked with the rise of resurrection belief, as we shall see in the next chapter.[31] Earlier statements proposing that ancient Israelites thought of the dead as dangerous and hostile are without foundation.[32] And various scholars have pointed out that, while grave-goods and the provision of food and drink can be interpreted as helping the newly deceased to pass on to the underworld, once that process was complete there was no need for further provision. The dead had gone and were not part of the ongoing life of the people in the way that they were, and are, in many other cultures.[33]

Death itself was sad, and tinged with evil. It was not seen, in the canonical Old Testament, as a happy release, an escape of the soul from the prison-house of the body. This, of course, is the corollary of the Israelite belief in the goodness and god-givenness of life in this world. Hence the robust if stern wisdom of Ecclesiastes: since this is the way things are, your best course is to enjoy life to the full.[34]

---

[26] Meyers 1970, 15, 26. See too Meyers's larger study (1971).

[27] Details conveniently available, with further bibliog., in e.g. Bloch-Smith 1992.

[28] Meyers 1970, 22.

[29] e.g. Lewis 1989. See the full discussion in Johnston 2002, ch. 8.

[30] Rahmani 1981/2, 172. The whole four-part article is very significant.

[31] See e.g. Hachlili 1992, 793; Rahmani 1981/2, 175f. In some later rabbinic thought, the decomposition of the flesh was associated with atoning for sins, leaving the bones ready for resurrection to new life (see e.g. Rahmani 175).

[32] For details and refutation see e.g. Rahmani 1981/2, 234.

[33] See e.g. Cooley 1983, 52; Johnston 2002, 61f.

[34] Eccles. 2.24; 3.12f., 22; 5.18–20; 6.3–6; 8.15; 9.7–10; 11.9f.; 12.1–8.

Around this point we meet a tension, well known and full of theological import, between death as the natural ending of all mortal life and death as the punishment for sin. This tension runs back (assuming the point of view of a first-century reader) to Genesis 2.17, 3.3, and 3.22: eating from the tree of knowledge will result in death, but even after the first pair have done so there remains the possibility that they might eat from the tree of life and so live for ever. We may note the especially pregnant point that if the promised punishment for eating the forbidden fruit was death, the *actual*, or at least immediate, punishment was banishment from the garden. Since, however, the point of banishment was so that they could not eat from the tree of life and thus live for ever (3.22–4), the two amount more closely to the same thing than it might appear at first sight.

This complex issue has been suggestively discussed by James Barr as part of his argument that, despite the too-much-protesting statements of Cullmann and others, the Bible does indeed concern itself with human immortality.[35] Barr is surely right to stress that the Genesis story as it now stands indicates that humans were not created immortal, but had (and lost) the chance to gain unending life. For his discussion to be taken forward, however, it is vital to distinguish at least four senses of immortality: (a) ongoing physical life without any form of death ever occurring; (b) the innate possession of an immortal part of one's being, e.g. the soul (which is itself in need of further multiple definition), which will survive bodily death; (c) the gift from elsewhere, e.g. from Israel's god, to certain human beings, of an ongoing life, not itself innate in the human make-up, which could then provide the human continuity, across an interim period, between the present bodily life and the future resurrection; (d) a way of describing resurrection itself. The first, it seems, is what Adam and Eve might have gained in Genesis 3; the second is the position of Plato; the third emerges, as we shall see later, in second-Temple writings such as the Wisdom of Solomon; the fourth is emphasized by Paul.[36] Barr, however, never draws such distinctions with any clarity. His proof that the Bible is indeed concerned with 'immortality' thus fails to hit all the relevant nails squarely on the head.

It is not difficult to see what expulsion from the garden would have meant (not only to readers, but to editors of the Pentateuch) during and after the exile in Babylon, especially in the light of the promises and warnings of the great Deuteronomic covenant. Moses held out to the people life and death, blessings and curses, and urged them to choose life – which meant, quite specifically, living in the promised land as opposed to being sent into the disgrace of exile.[37] But already in Deuteronomy there was the promise that even exile would not be final: repentance would bring restoration and

---

[35] Barr 1992, ch. 1.
[36] 1 Cor. 15.53.
[37] Dt. 30.19f. with 28.1–14, 15–68; 29.14–28. See e.g. Lohfink 1990.

the renewal both of the covenant and of human hearts.[38] This explicit link of life with the land and death with exile, coupled with the promise of restoration the other side of exile, is one of the forgotten roots of the fully developed hope of ancient Israel. The dead might be asleep; they might be almost nothing at all; but hope lived on within the covenant and promise of YHWH.

(ii) Disturbing the Dead

The regular forbidding of making contact with the dead is normally taken as good evidence that many in ancient Israel tried to do so.[39] It would be extraordinary if they had not. Ancestor-cults were widespread in the ancient world, as they still are in many places today.[40] Most human societies have been aware that one might be able to get in touch with those who had gone before, and that there might be some advantage to be gained by doing so, whether to ward off any malign influence, to gain insight into things outside normal human knowing, or simply to re-establish contact with departed loved ones. Such practices were common among the Canaanites whom the Israelites were to dispossess, and were high on the list of the things that the covenant people were to renounce.

The principal scene which illustrates the point is the meeting between Saul and the dead Samuel.[41] Saul himself, as part of his royal reforms, had forbidden necromancy, banishing the mediums and wizards through whom contact could be established. But when he faced a military crisis, and YHWH remained silent in response to his prayers, Saul himself, in disguise, sought out a medium (his servants apparently had little trouble in finding one, despite the ban), and at his instruction she called up Samuel. The multiple theological and emotional layers of the story are remarkable – it was, after all, Samuel who had pronounced divine judgment on Saul for earlier disobedience[42] – but for our purposes the point is what happened next. As the medium called up Samuel, she was given superhuman knowledge, recognizing Saul through his disguise (v. 12). Saul reassured her, and she continued, seeing an *elohim* coming up out of the ground (v. 14). *Elohim* normally means 'god' or 'gods'; this usage presumably reflects Canaanite belief in the

---

[38] Dt. 30.1–10.

[39] So e.g. Ex. 22.18; Lev. 19.31; 20.6, 27; Dt. 18.11; 1 Sam. 28 *passim*; Isa. 8.19. Cf. Lewis 1989, 171–81; Eichrodt 1961–7, 1.216–23; Cavallin 1974, 24 n. 5; Martin-Achard 1960, 24–31; Riley 1995, 13–15, on which see below. Schmidt 1994, however, argues powerfully that necromancy was introduced late into Israel, being kept at bay until the late monarchy at the earliest.

[40] cf. Barley 1997, ch. 4. For ancient Israel cf. esp. Schmidt 1994.

[41] 1 Sam. 28.3–25.

[42] 1 Sam. 15.13–31.

divinity of the dead, surviving here as a kind of linguistic fossil.[43] Here it seems to mean 'a spirit', 'a being from the world of the gods'. It is indeed Samuel, angry at being disturbed (v. 15); he really does know the future (he had already warned Saul of divine judgment, but he now knows precisely when it will arrive); but it is not good news. YHWH is taking away from the rebellious king his kingdom, victory and life itself:

> Moreover, YHWH will give Israel, together with you, into the hands of the Philistines; and tomorrow you and your sons shall be with me. YHWH will also give the army of Israel into the hands of the Philistines.[44]

While the scene plays its own part within the dramatic build-up towards the climax of the book, in Saul's death and David's imminent accession, it also served as an awful warning for its readers. Necromancy might be possible, but it was both forbidden and dangerous. Doubtless people would continue to advocate it, as Isaiah mockingly said:

> Now if people say to you, 'Consult the ghosts and the familiar spirits that chirp and mutter; should not a people consult their *elohim*, the dead on behalf of the living, for teaching and instruction?' Surely, those who speak like this will have no dawn! They will pass through the land, greatly distressed and hungry . . . they will see only distress and darkness, the gloom of anguish, and they will be thrust into thick darkness.[45]

But it will only bring ruin. The living god is the only source of true life, wisdom and instruction, and he will give it to those who truly seek him. The dead are to remain undisturbed in their long sleep.

(iii) The Unexplained Exceptions

Two figures, and perhaps a third, stand out from this story. They appear to escape the common lot of mortals, and find their way by a different route to a different destination.[46]

Genesis 5 offers a genealogy of the antediluvian patriarchs, with the common refrain 'and he died', echoing the judgment of Genesis 3.[47] Into this list breaks Enoch, son of Jared, father of Methuselah. Enoch, says the writer, 'walked with God; then he was no more, because God took him' (verse 24). This simple, unadorned statement, at first sight merely a gently euphemistic way of marking the passing of a devout man, gave rise to enormous later

---

[43] I owe this point to Dr John Day.

[44] 1 Sam. 28.19.

[45] Isa. 8.19–22 (cf. too 19.3). The passage is textually and linguistically complex, but the overall meaning seems clear: cf. e.g. Motyer 1993, 96–8; Childs 2001, 69–77.

[46] On this cf. Day 1996, 237–40; Johnston 2002, 199f.

[47] Gen. 5.5, 8, 11, 14, 17, 20, 27, 31.

speculation. What had happened to Enoch? Where was he? Had he escaped death? To Enoch, as a result, were attributed later books of secret revelation and wisdom.[48]

Along with Enoch goes Elijah, who went up to heaven in a whirlwind, snatched away by the heavenly horsemen and chariots.[49] Even Elisha, who inherited a double portion of Elijah's spirit, was not granted that favour. It is perhaps because of his unusual departure – the text stresses that his body was not to be found – that later tradition envisages him returning again before the final day of YHWH arrives.[50] Elijah, too, became the putative author of apocalyptic writings, and speculation about his coming was clearly an important feature of first-century expectation.[51]

Thirdly, the fate of Moses himself was shrouded in uncertainty. Deuteronomy states clearly enough that Moses died in the land of Moab having looked into the promised land from Mount Nebo, and that he was buried in a valley opposite Beth-peor, but that nobody knows the precise location of his grave.[52] This was presumably aimed at preventing his tomb from becoming a place of pilgrimage. But the uncertain location of both his death and his burial opened the door to a different sequence of possibilities. Eventually some came to believe that he, like Elijah, had not actually died in the normal way, but had been taken up to heaven.[53]

None of these three was held up as a model for what a pious or devout Israelite might expect to happen again. Nobody suggested that if someone lived an exceptionally holy life, or accomplished some great deed, they might be similarly treated. No explanation is given as to why Enoch and Elijah were given a favour – if favour it was – denied to such great figures as Abraham, Joseph or Samuel. No account is available of what sort of existence they had gone to (a question of particular relevance, one might think, to later developments about the resurrection), or, in particular, of the kind of heavenly world in which Elijah could still possess his body. They remain the unexplained exceptions to the otherwise universal rule.

---

[48] For helpful surveys of this lively tradition cf. VanderKam 1984, 1995.

[49] 2 Kgs. 2.1–18. Cf. Martin-Achard 1960, 65–72.

[50] 2 Kgs. 2.16–18; cf. Mal. 4.5; Sir. 48.9f.

[51] e.g. Mk. 9.11–13; cf. *JVG* 167f. and other refs. there. Greenspoon 1981, 316f. adds to the discussion Elijah's taunting of Baal in 1 Kgs. 18.27: maybe, he says, Baal is asleep and needs waking up. If this is an allusion to Baal as a dying and rising god, Elijah would be heard to be saying (whether by his audience or that of 1 Kgs. is immaterial for our present purposes) that YHWH is not like that: YHWH is the sort of god who has dominion over the natural world.

[52] Dt. 34.5f.

[53] See e.g. Goldin 1987; Barr 1992, 15f.; Ginzberg 1998, 3.471–81. For the very interesting interpretation of all this by Josephus see Tabor 1989. The 'tomb of Moses' at Nabi Musa in the Judaean wilderness is, of course, a late invention (see Murphy-O'Connor 1998 [1980], 369f.): built in 1269 as a shrine from which one could look across the Dead Sea to Mount Nebo, tradition transformed it into his actual tomb.

Equally, the one or two miraculous resuscitations of the dead attributed to Elijah and Elisha are not particularly relevant to the study of Israelite beliefs about death and life beyond.[54] The people concerned would die again. Our main interest in these stories – apart from their anticipation of stories about Jesus – is their implicit assumptions about death. The life-force (*nephesh*, always difficult to translate) departs from the child and then returns when Elijah revives him. Elisha's servant tells him that the child has not 'woken up'.[55] This language anticipates some of the key ideas that are used in connection with resurrection itself.

(iv) The Land of No Return

'The undiscover'd country, from whose bourn/ No traveller returns.' Thus Shakespeare's Hamlet, musing on death – all the more remarkably in a play written from within Christendom.[56] But the sentiment is an accurate description of the regular Old Testament belief about the fate of the dead: death is a one-way street, on which those behind can follow but those ahead cannot turn back.[57] Humans are here today, gone tomorrow, and seen no more.[58] The book of Job contains the most emphatic statements on the subject:

Remember that my life is a breath; my eye will never again see good.
The eye that beholds me will see me no more;
while your eyes are upon me, I shall be gone.
As the cloud fades and vanishes, so those who go down to Sheol do not come up;
they return no more to their houses, nor do their places know them any more.[59]

A mortal, born of woman, few of days and full of trouble,
comes up like a flower and withers, flees like a shadow and does not last . . .
For there is hope for a tree, if it is cut down,
that it will sprout again, and that its shoots will not cease.
Though its root grows old in the earth, and its stump dies in the ground,
yet at the scent of water it will bud, and put forth branches like a young plant.
But mortals die, and are laid low;
humans expire, and where are they?
As waters fail from a lake, and a river wastes away and dries up,
so mortals lie down and do not rise again;
until the heavens are no more, they will not awake or be roused out of their sleep.

[54] 1 Kgs. 17.17–24; 2 Kgs. 4.18–37; 13.21. Cf. Cavallin 1974, 25 n. 17.

[55] 1 Kgs. 17.21f.; 2 Kgs. 4.31.

[56] *Hamlet* 3.1.79f.

[57] So e.g. David on the death of Bathsheba's first child by him: 2 Sam. 12.23: 'Can I bring him back again? I shall go to him, but he will not return to me.'

[58] e.g. Ps. 39.4, 12f.

[59] Job 7.7–10. I do not see here the note of 'calm resignation' which Eichrodt claims to find in v. 9, nor in his other examples of 2 Sam. 12.23 and Ps. 89.49 (Eichrodt 1961–7, 2.500 n.5).

Oh that you would hide me in Sheol,
that you would conceal me until your wrath is past,
that you would appoint me a set time, and remember me!
If mortals die, will they live again?[60]

The last question, clearly, expects the answer 'no', which is reinforced elsewhere in Job, and echoed in (among other places) Jeremiah.[61] Within the book, part of the point is Job's insistence that YHWH must give judgment in his favour during this life. The dead have no future; so God's judgment must take place here and now. This, perhaps, is the point of the book's controversial ending (42.10–17), though we cannot discuss this here.

The passage in Job often thought an exception to this rule is almost certainly not. The older translations show why it was thought an exception; the more recent, why it is now doubted:

I know that my redeemer liveth,
and that he shall stand at the latter day upon the earth:
and though, after my skin, worms destroy this body,
yet in my flesh shall I see God:
whom I shall see for myself,
and mine eyes shall behold, and not another. (AV)

In my heart I know that my vindicator lives
and that he will rise last to speak in court;
and I shall discern my witness standing at my side
and see my defending counsel, even God himself,
whom I shall see with my own eyes,
I myself and no other. (NEB)

I know that I have a living Defender
and that he will rise up last, on the dust of the earth.
After my awakening, he will set me close to him,
and from my flesh I shall look on God.
He whom I shall see will take my part:
my eyes will be gazing on no stranger. (NJB)

For I know that my Redeemer lives,
and that at the last he will stand upon the earth;
and after my skin has been thus destroyed,
then in my flesh I shall see God,
whom I shall see on my side,
and my eyes shall behold, and not another. (NRSV)[62]

---

[60] Job 14.1f., 7–14.

[61] Job 16.22; Jer. 51.39, 57 ('they shall sleep a perpetual sleep and never wake'; though this, as a specific judgment on Babylon and its officials, may conceivably imply that without this judgment there might after all have been a time of awakening?). The much-controverted Job 19.25–7 is discussed immediately below. Job 29.18 is almost certainly not a reference to the self-revivifying phoenix; cf. Day 1996, 252.

[62] Job 19.25–7.

Though the New Revised Standard Version thus returns, in a measure, to the tradition of the Authorized (King James) Version, the others reveal just how problematic this is; and the marginal notes in most modern translations admit that nobody quite knows exactly what the crucial passages mean (for instance, the NRSV points out that for 'in my flesh' we could read 'without my flesh', which would of course change the meaning completely). Most scholars agree that, difficult though the passage is to translate, it is still more difficult to suppose that, in the teeth of the other passages explored above, it suddenly holds out a hope for a bodily life beyond the grave.[63] It is true that the response to Job's speech in chapter 19 is that of Zophar in chapter 20, in which the traditional view is strongly reaffirmed as though by way of rebuke ('they will perish for ever like their own dung . . . they will fly away like a dream, and not be found; they will be chased away like a vision of the night . . .'[64]). This could have some oblique retrospective bearing on the supposed meaning of chapter 19. But even if this were to shift the balance back a small way towards the traditional understanding, it would hardly be enough to force us, through all the translation problems and against the run of the rest of the book, to insist that this little passage forms an exception to the otherwise complete view of death offered by Job.

Ecclesiastes, too, insists that death is the end, and there is no return. Though nobody can be sure what precisely happens at death, as far as we can tell humans are in this respect no different from beasts:

> The fate of humans and the fate of animals is the same; as one dies, so dies the other. They all have the same breath, and humans have no advantage over the animals; for all is vanity. All go to one place; all are from the dust, and all turn to dust again. Who knows whether the human spirit [or: 'breath', *ruach*] goes upward and the spirit of animals goes downward to the earth?[65]

No: to die is to be forgotten for good.[66] Death means that the body returns to the dust, and the breath to God who gave it; meaning not that an immortal part of the person goes to live with God, but that the God who breathed

---

[63] So e.g. Martin-Achard 1960, 166–75; Day 1996, 251f.; Johnston 2002, 209–14. Hartley 1988, 296f. suggests that, though the passage probably does not itself refer explicitly to resurrection, it was 'built on the same logic' that eventually led to the early Christian viewpoint. Those who still maintain that the passage envisages a post-mortem vindication include e.g. Osborne 2000, 932; Fyall 2002, 51, 64 suggests, in a careful and sensitive argument, that Job makes a 'leap of faith' to a 'life beyond physical decay'. For older bibliography see Horst 1960, 277.

[64] Job 20.7f.

[65] Eccles. 3.19–21. The meaning of the final rhetorical question seems to be that the same breath of life, God's breath, is in the nostrils of both humans and beasts, not that there is a specific theory about human spirits going to a place of blessedness – and even if there was such a theory, this verse would be challenging it with straightforward agnosticism.

[66] So Eccles. 2.16, on which see e.g. Bream 1974.

life's breath into human nostrils in the first place will simply withdraw it into his own possession.[67]

(v) The Nature and Ground of Hope

When Walther Zimmerli wrote his short, clear monograph, *Man and his Hope in the Old Testament*, the question of life beyond the grave was not only not the main issue; it hardly rated a discussion.[68] This is a reminder that our present question was simply not faced head on by the majority of the Old Testament writers. They took for granted the picture we have sketched above, and got on with other things. The hope of the biblical writers, which was strong and constant, focused not upon the fate of humans after death, but on the fate of Israel and her promised land. The nation and land of the present world were far more important than what happened to an individual beyond the grave.

The hope of the nation was thus first and foremost that the people, the seed of Abraham, Isaac and Jacob, would multiply and flourish. Even in the story of the Fall there is hope in childbearing.[69] Children, and then grandchildren, are God's great blessing, and to live long enough to see them is one of the finest things to hope for.[70] It is a sign of Joseph's great blessedness that he was able to see and hold his own great-grandchildren.[71] Conversely, to remain childless is a sign of great misery (people today in Europe and America, with all kinds of other aspirations, often regard the ancient stigma of childlessness as quaint and small-minded, but in a world where children are the centre of one's future hope it makes a lot of sense). To see one's children die or be killed was perhaps the greatest possible personal disaster.[72] To perpetuate not only the nation but one's individual family line was thus a sacred responsibility, requiring special customs and laws to safeguard it.[73] Such beliefs and practices are hardly unique to ancient Israel, but they became all the more important through their association with the promises made to Abraham and his heirs, and through the events that had formed Israel into a people with a distinct sense of vocation and mission in the world. To the devout Israelite, the continuance of the family line was not simply a matter of keeping a name alive. It was part of the way in which

---

[67] Eccles. 12.7; cf. Ps. 104.29 – though the next verse of the psalm opens a new possibility, on which see below.

[68] Zimmerli 1971 [1968].

[69] Gen. 3.16, 20; see Zimmerli 1971 [1968], 47f.

[70] Pss. 128; 129.

[71] Gen. 50.23.

[72] e.g. Ruth 1.20f.; 2 Kgs. 25.7. Cp. also 1 Sam. 4.17f.; Lk. 1.25.

[73] cf. Gen. 38.6–11, 26; Dt. 25.5–10; Ruth 1.11–13; 3.9–13; 4.1–17. On the Levirate law cf. Cavallin 1974, 25; Martin-Achard 1960, 22f.; and below, 420–23.

God's promises, for Israel and perhaps even for the whole world, would be fulfilled. Hence the importance, particularly in the post-exilic period when the nation was gathering itself together again, of those genealogies which seem so bafflingly unreligious to late modernity, and of the prophetic insistence on the 'holy seed'.[74]

Along with the family went the land. God had promised to give the land of the Canaanites to Abraham's family, and this remained the patriarchal hope up to the eventual conquest.[75] This explains, of course, why the narrator attaches great significance to Abraham's purchase of a field containing a cave for use as a burial place (Genesis 23: the story of the purchase takes up the entire chapter). There Abraham buries Sarah, and is then buried himself; they are later joined by Isaac and Rebekah, by Leah, and finally by Jacob himself.[76] The point of all this was not to engage in any kind of post-mortem reunion, but to make certain the promise of God, which was not at this stage for an individual life beyond the grave but for the family's possession of the promised land.

This is, of course, why the great prophetic promises, constituting the major hope of Israel throughout the period, focus on the peace and prosperity of the land, and of the nation within it. Deuteronomy, with the promised land in sight, expands the initial vision of Exodus (a land flowing with milk and honey) to embrace all kinds of agriculture.[77] If one can see nation and land flourishing, one can go to the grave in peace.

As some biblical writers focused the hope of the nation more on the royal family, so the hope of the land became focused on Jerusalem. The two went together, of course, as from the time of David Jerusalem was the royal city, and from Solomon's day the site also of YHWH's Temple. The prosperity of king, city and Temple are thus not a separate hope to that of the nation and the land, but rather its quintessence, its sharp point. From this root grow the lavish hopes expressed in the Zion-oracles and the songs of royal blessing and victory, drawing on the older theology and re-expressing it as a promise and hope of prosperity for Israel and, wider, for the whole world:

In days to come,
the mountain of YHWH's house
shall be established as the highest of the mountains,
and shall be raised above the hills;

---

[74] e.g. 1 Chron. 1—9; Ezra 2.1–63 (nb. vv. 62f., where absence of genealogical information calls into question a would-be part of the priestly clan); 8.1–14; Neh. 7.5–65. On the 'holy seed' cf. Ezra 9.1f.; Mal. 2.15; cp. Isa. 6.13.

[75] e.g. Gen. 12.7, and often thereafter; Ex. 3.8, 17, and frequently throughout the story. Cf. Zimmerli 1971 [1968], 49–53.

[76] Gen. 23.19; 25.9; 35.29; 47.30; 49.29–32; 50.13. Cf. Zimmerli 1971 [1968], 63f.

[77] Ex. 3.8; 13.5; 33.3; cp. e.g. Lev. 20.24; Num. 13.27; Dt. 26.9, 15; cf. Jer. 11.5; 32.22; Ezek. 20.6. For the expansion of the vision cf. e.g. Dt. 6.10f.; 8.7–10; 11.10–15; 26.1–11; and esp. 28.1–14.

all the nations shall stream to it.
Many peoples shall come and say,
'Come, let us go up to the mountain of YHWH,
to the house of the God of Jacob;
that he may teach us his ways,
and that we may walk in his paths.'
For out of Zion shall go forth instruction,
and the word of YHWH from Jerusalem.
He shall judge between the nations,
and shall arbitrate for many peoples;
they shall beat their swords into ploughshares,
and their spears into pruninghooks;
nation shall not lift up sword against nation,
neither shall they learn war any more.[78]

A shoot shall come out from the stump of Jesse,
and a branch shall grow out of his roots.
The spirit of YHWH shall rest upon him:
the spirit of wisdom and understanding,
the spirit of counsel and might,
the spirit of knowledge and of the fear of YHWH.
His delight shall be in the fear of YHWH . . .
The wolf shall live with the lamb,
the leopard shall lie down with the kid;
the calf and the lion and the fatling together,
and a little child shall lead them . . .
They will not hurt or destroy on all my holy mountain;
for the earth shall be full of the glory of YHWH as the waters cover the sea.[79]

Here is my servant, whom I uphold,
my chosen, in whom my soul delights;
I have put my spirit upon him;
he will bring forth justice to the nations . . .
He will not grow faint or be crushed until he has established justice in the earth;
and the coastlands wait for his teaching.[80]

The spirit of YHWH is upon me, because YHWH has anointed me;
he has sent me to bring good news to the oppressed, to bind up the brokenhearted,
to proclaim liberty to the captives, and release to the prisoners . . .
They will be called oaks of righteousness,
the planting of YHWH, to display his glory.
They shall build up the ancient ruins, they shall raise up the former devastations;
they shall repair the ruined cities, the devastations of many generations . . .
For as the earth brings forth its shoots,
and as a garden causes what is sown in it to spring up,
so the sovereign God YHWH will cause righteousness and praise

[78] Isa. 2.2–4; cp. Mic. 4.1–3, adding in v. 4 the promise that all will sit in peace under their vines and fig-trees.
[79] Isa. 11.1–9. The promise of a new and non-violent creation is expanded in 65.17–25.
[80] Isa. 42.1, 4.

to spring up before all the nations.[81]

Give the king your justice, O God,
and your righteousness to the king's son.
May he judge your people with righteousness,
and your poor with justice.
May the mountains yield prosperity for the people,
and the hills, in righteousness.
May he defend the cause of the poor of the people,
give deliverance to the needy, and crush the oppressor . . .
May he have dominion from sea to sea,
and from the River to the ends of the earth . . .
For he delivers the needy when they call,
the poor and those who have no helper.[82]

Once and for all I have sworn by my holiness; I will not lie to David.
his line shall continue for ever, and his throne endure before me like the sun.
It shall be established for ever like the moon, an enduring witness in the skies.[83]

These and similar promises are of course well known, much studied and beyond our present enquiry. But they must be recalled here in case any impression be given that the absence, for most ancient Israelites, of any statement of human life beyond the grave meant that they were without a living and vibrant hope. At the heart of that hope was the knowledge that YHWH, the God of Israel, was the creator of the world; that he was faithful to the covenant with Israel, and beyond that with the whole world; and that, as such, he would be true to his word both to Israel and to the whole creation. How this would be worked out, what role a future ideal king might have in it, what place there would be for Jerusalem within it, and at what time the promises would eventually be fulfilled – all this remained to be seen, and I have written about it elsewhere.[84] Some of the prophets preached about a 'day of YHWH' when threats as well as promises would be carried out.[85] It is true that, as we shall see, at some points within this tradition a new word was spoken, promising life beyond the grave. But for the vast majority in ancient Israel the great and solid hope, built upon the character of the creator and covenant god, was for YHWH's blessing of justice, prosperity and peace upon the nation and land, and eventually upon the whole earth. Patriarchs, prophets, kings and ordinary Israelites would indeed lie down to sleep with their ancestors. YHWH's purposes, however, would go forwards, and would be fulfilled in their time.

[81] Isa. 61.1, 3f., 11. Note the way in which agricultural imagery and promise are mixed together.
[82] Ps. 72.1–4, 8, 12.
[83] Ps. 89.35–7.
[84] e.g. *NTPG* ch. 10; *JVG* 481–6.
[85] Isa. 13.6, 9; Jer. 46.10; Ezek. 30.2, 3; Joel 1.15; 2.1, 11, 31; 3.14; Obad. 15; Zeph. 1.14, 15; Zech. 14.1.

Such was the foundational hope of ancient Israel. It is important now, in moving to examine what appear to be developments within various biblical traditions, to appreciate that these developments are also built on this foundation, however much they disagree in what appear to us as significant details.

3. And Afterwards?

(i) Introduction

The constant love of YHWH was never merely a theological dogma to the ancient Israelites. In many parts of their literature, and supremely the Psalms, we find evidence that they knew this love in vivid personal experience. It was this personal experience, rather than any theory about innate immortality, that gave rise to the suggestion that, despite the widespread denials of such a thing, YHWH's faithfulness would after all be known not only in this life but in a life beyond the grave.

It is impossible now to tell when this idea first made its appearance. We must resist the temptation to postulate a steady chronological development, starting with the picture described above, continuing into the dawnings of a hope for something beyond death, and finally ending with resurrection. The latter belief does indeed seem to be a late arrival in its explicit form; but it would be a mistake to think that it grew out of a sort of firming-up, or making more concrete, of the gentle probe into 'afterwards' that we shall now describe. It is by no means always the case that ideas develop in a regular or unilinear fashion. In any case, what seems to contemporary western minds as a natural or logical progression may well bear no relation to what actually happened in other times and cultures. It would in any case be a mistake to suppose that belief in resurrection was, as it were, a further development beyond the beliefs we shall now examine. In all sorts of ways it is, on the contrary, a kind of reaffirmation of, or new outgrowth from, the earlier position. But to make this clear we must examine the texts themselves.

(ii) Delivered from Sheol?

There are some passages which appear, at least on one reading, to offer hope that YHWH will deliver people from Sheol. The problem with these passages is to know whether this refers to a deliverance that lies *beyond* Sheol – i.e. that YHWH will snatch the dead person out of Sheol, either taking them, after death, to some other, more attractive, post-mortem existence, or rescuing them after a short stay – or whether it simply refers to deliverance from death, i.e. prolonging life to a good old age rather than being cut off in one's prime.

The best-known of these passages is Psalm 16:

> I have kept YHWH before me; because he is at my right hand, I shall not be moved.
> Therefore my heart is glad, and my soul rejoices; my body also rests secure.
> For you do not give me up to Sheol, or let your faithful one see the Pit.
> You show me the path of life; in your presence there is fullness of joy;
> in your right hand are pleasures for evermore.[86]

There is legitimate doubt over whether this refers to escaping death or passing through it to a life beyond,[87] but there is no question of the basis of the hope. It is YHWH himself, the one the Psalmist embraces as his sovereign one (verse 2), his portion and cup (verse 5), the one who gives him counsel in the secret places of his heart (verse 7).

The same question can be raised in connection with Psalm 22. The Psalmist is clearly in deep trouble, physical danger, and distress: 'you lay me', he says, 'in the dust of death' (verse 15). Nevertheless, he prays that God will save his life, and, in a famous reversal of fortunes, the closing verses of the Psalm give thanks that God has done just that (verses 22–31). As part of this thanksgiving, the Psalm celebrates the fact that everyone will eventually submit to God, even the dead:

> To him shall all the proud of the earth bow down;
> before him shall bow all who go down to the dust,
> and he who cannot keep himself alive.[88]

The main hope, though, seems to be that of rescue from violent death, rather than a deliverance the other side of the grave. The Psalm ends with a re-affirmation of the traditional hope of Israel, for the coming 'seed' who will give God thanks (verses 30–31).[89]

This affirmation of continuing life, rather than of resurrection itself, is presumably what is intended by Psalm 104 as well:

> When you hide your face, they [animals and sea creatures] are dismayed;
> when you take away their breath, they die, and return to the dust.

---

[86] Ps. 16.8–11.

[87] See Eichrodt 1961–7, 2.524; von Rad 1962–5, 1.405; Martin-Achard 1960, 149–53; Johnston 2002, 201f. Cp. Ps. 86.13, where 'you have delivered my soul from the depths of Sheol' is clearly not a statement that the writer has already been literally raised from the dead. On the thesis of Dahood 1965/6, postulating a post-mortem hope in several Psalms see e.g. Day 1996, 234f.; Lacocque 1979, 236–8.

[88] Ps. 22.29.

[89] Eichrodt 1961–7, 2.511 is perhaps going too far when he says that this Psalm expresses 'the idea of the return of the dead to living fellowship with God'. Strictly, the Psalm is about the *almost* dead. This does not, of course, preclude its being read in subsequent Judaism in connection with hopes for beyond the grave.

When you send out your breath [or 'spirit'] they are created;
and you renew the face of the ground.[90]

The question of how this might be read in the later second-Temple period is
again a separate issue, to which we shall return in the next chapter.

The same questions are raised by an equally famous passage from Job.
God, declares Elihu, opens mortal ears to hear his warnings,

that he may turn them aside from their deeds, and keep them from pride,
to spare their souls from the Pit, their lives from traversing the River.

Then, when they draw near to that fate,

Their souls draw near the Pit, and their lives to those who bring death.
Then, if there should be for one of them an angel,
a mediator, one of a thousand, one who declares a person upright,
and he is gracious to that person, and says,
'Deliver him from going down into the Pit; I have found a ransom;
let his flesh become fresh with youth;
let him return to the days of his youthful vigour.'
Then he prays to God, and is accepted by him,
he comes into his presence with joy . . .
That person sings to others and says,
'. . . He has redeemed my soul from going down to the Pit,
and my life shall see the light.'
God indeed does all these things . . .
to bring back their souls from the Pit,
so that they may see the light of life.[91]

This appears to be less ambiguous than Psalm 16, and, in keeping with the
rest of Job, it is best to see it as referring to rescue from an early, untimely
death, rather than to a rescue which happens afterwards. However, both
these passages could well have been read within post-biblical Judaism in the
sense of a post-mortem rescue. While it is true, as we shall see presently,
that the original meaning of passages like these may be uncertain, it is also
true that the uncertainty could easily be removed in later translation and
comment.

(iii) Glory after Suffering?

Something more definite can be said about Psalm 73 at least.[92] One of the
classic biblical complaints about the apparent injustices of life (the wicked
and arrogant always seem to get away with it), this Psalm takes its place

---

[90] Ps. 104.29f.
[91] Job 33.15–30.
[92] See Day 1996, 255f.; Johnston 2002, 204–06, with other literature.

alongside the book of Job itself. It offers, though, a different sort of answer. For a start, when the Psalmist goes into God's sanctuary, he realizes that the wicked will indeed be condemned, though how and when this will happen remains unclear:

> Truly you set them in slippery places; you make them fall to ruin.
> How they are destroyed in a moment,
> swept away utterly by terrors!
> They are like a dream when one awakes; on awaking you despise their phantoms.[93]

But that is not all. The Psalmist himself discovers that he is grasped by a love that will not let him go, a power that even death, and the dissolution of the body, cannot thwart:

> Nevertheless I am continually with you; hold my right hand.
> You guide me with your counsel, and afterward you will receive me to glory.
> Whom have I in heaven but you?
> And there is nothing on earth that I desire other than you.
> My flesh and my heart may fail,
> but God is the strength of my heart and my portion for ever . . .
> For me it is good to be near God;
> I have made the Lord YHWH my refuge, to tell of all your works.[94]

It seems clear that 'and afterward' ($w^e achar$) in verse 24 refers, not to an event that will take place later on within the present life, but to a state which will obtain after the present life of being guided by God's counsel. This is confirmed by verse 26, where, with echoes of Isaiah 40.6–8, human frailty and even death are met by the unshakeable strength of God himself. Unfortunately the crucial word *kabod*, translated here as 'to glory' – crucial because it would be good to know what exactly the Psalmist thought lay ahead – could equally well be translated, with NRSV, as 'with honour'. We are left with a tantalizing glimpse of a life beyond the grave, a life in which (as the logic of the Psalm demands) wrongs will be put to right, and God's justice will be perceived; a life in which those who have known God's love in the present will discover that this love is stronger than death itself, and will 'receive' them to a status of honour or glory.[95]

This same verb, 'receive', occurs also in Psalm 49.15.[96] The whole Psalm is a sobering meditation on the mortality of all human life: no better than the

---

[93] Ps. 73.18–20.

[94] Ps. 73.23–7. The word for 'receive' in v. 24 could be translated 'take'; it is the same word as is used of God's 'taking' of Enoch in Gen. 5.24 (see Barr 1992, 33).

[95] On Ps. 73 see Eichrodt 1961–7, 2.520f.; Martin-Achard 1960, 158–65; Brueggemann 1997, 481. There is nothing at all said here about 'resurrection', despite e.g. Osborne 2000, 932, who appears to be using the word simply as a synonym for 'life after death'. Ps. 17.15 is in some ways close to 73.26. On these points cf. section 4 below.

[96] See Day 1996, 253–5, with other literature.

beasts, humans will all come to the grave at last, and all their pomp and posturing in the present will be of no avail:

> Their graves are their homes forever, their dwelling places to all generations . . .
> They will go to the company of their ancestors, who will never again see the light.[97]

What follows depends on the contrast between the foolish, who will go to Sheol and remain there, leaving their worldly fame and fortune behind, and the Psalmist himself, who expects a different sort of future. This inner logic of the Psalm means that we would be wrong to place it in the earlier category, of being rescued from an untimely death; instead, we seem to be confronted, as in Psalm 73, with at least a glimmer of assurance of God's ransoming power being stronger than death itself. Otherwise the Psalm's only affirmation would be that the wise and righteous have a short stay of execution, but that they will in good time follow the foolish to Sheol. No:

> Like sheep they are appointed for Sheol; Death shall be their shepherd;
> straight to the grave they descend, and their form shall waste away;
> Sheol shall be their home.
> But God will ransom my soul from the power of Sheol, for he will receive me.[98]

If this is the correct understanding, many later worshippers might see the point even where, as in Psalm 16, historical exegesis might question it.[99]

These three Psalms stand out.[100] By contrast, in Psalms 34 and 37, the reward of the righteous is firmly this-worldly. The anguished entreaties of Psalm 88, one of the bleakest of all, ask their awful questions without, it seems, any hope of a positive answer.[101] Psalm 16 in its way, and Psalms 73 and 49 in theirs, are alone among the biblical texts in hinting at a future of which the rest of the ancient Israelite scriptures remain ignorant.

(iv) The Basis of Future Hope

Where we find a glimmer of hope like this, it is based not on anything in the human make-up (e.g. an 'immortal soul'), but on YHWH and him alone.

---

[97] Ps. 49.11, 19.

[98] Ps. 49.14f.

[99] On Ps. 49 cf. von Rad 1962–5, 1.406; Martin-Achard 1960, 153–8; Day 1996, 253f. It seems unlikely that the Psalmist has in mind the kind of unusual bypassing of death represented by Enoch and Elijah (above, 94f.), though the idea of God intervening to prevent someone going to Sheol or the grave is of course compatible with such a phenomenon.

[100] We should perhaps also add Ps. 116 to the inventory as well in the light of Paul's use of it in 2 Cor. 4 (below, 363f.). Johnston 2002, 207–09, adds four passages from Prov.: 12.28; 14.32; 15.24; 23.14. Whatever the original meanings, such passages might have been later read as referring to a post-mortem future.

[101] See above, 88f.

Indeed, YHWH is the substance of the hope, not merely the ground: he himself is the 'portion', i.e. the inheritance, of the righteous, devout Israelite.[102] At the same time, it is his power alone that can make alive, as some ancient prayers have it.[103] 'With you is the fountain of life,' sang the Psalmist; 'in your light we see light.'[104] When this strong faith in YHWH as the creator, the life-giver, the God of ultimate justice met the apparent contradiction of the injustices and sufferings of life, at that point there was, as we have seen, a chance of fresh belief springing up. Not that the sufferings of Israel always evoked this response. Psalm 88, and the book of Job, are evidence to the contrary. Ecclesiastes, who sometimes seems to cast himself as the Eeyore of the Old Testament, would simply shrug his shoulders and tell you to make the best of what you had. But if YHWH was the inheritance of his people, and if his love and faithfulness were as strong as Israel's traditions made out, then there was no ultimate bar to seeing death itself as a beaten foe. That, of course, was what several key texts went on to do, and we must now examine them head on.

4. Awakening the Sleepers

(i) Introduction

Nobody doubts that the Old Testament speaks of the resurrection of the dead, but nobody can agree on what it means, where the idea came from, or how it relates to the other things the scriptures say about the dead. But since the Jewish world of Jesus' and Paul's day looked back to these texts as the principal sources for their widespread belief in resurrection, we must take care at least to examine the relevant texts and know how they work. Is resurrection here an innovation, bursting upon an unready Israelite world? In which case, where did it come from? Or is it, rather, the climax of the ancient Jewish hope?

It is important once more to be clear on the key topic before we go any further.[105] The texts we shall consider, however we understand their detailed nuances, are not speaking about a new *construal of* life after death, but about something that will happen *after* whatever 'life after death' may involve. Resurrection is not just another way of talking about Sheol, or about what happens, as in Psalm 73, 'afterwards', that is, after the *event* of bodily death. It speaks of something that will happen, if it does, after that again. Resurrection means bodily life *after* 'life after death', or, if you prefer, bodily life

---

[102] So e.g. Brueggemann 1997, 419.

[103] Dt. 32.39; 1 Sam. 2.6: 'YHWH kills and makes alive.' See too Ps. 104.29f., quoted at 104f. above.

[104] Ps. 36.9.

[105] See above, 30–32.

after the *state* of 'death'. That is why it is very misleading – and foreign to all the relevant texts – to speak, as does one recent writer, of 'resurrection to heaven'.[106] Resurrection is what did *not* happen to Enoch or Elijah. According to the texts, it is what *will* happen to people who are at present dead, not what *has already* happened to them. If this point is grasped, a good deal becomes clear; if forgotten, confusion is bound to follow.

The text which became central for much later Jewish thought on this subject is Daniel 12.2–3. Though it is almost certainly the latest of the relevant passages, there are three good reasons for starting with it. First, it is the clearest: virtually all scholars agree that it does indeed speak of bodily resurrection, and mean this in a concrete sense. Second, it draws on several of the other, probably older, relevant texts, showing us one way in which they were being read in the second century BC. Third, conversely, it seems to have acted as a lens through which the earlier material was seen by subsequent writers. To read Daniel 12 is thus to stand on the bridge between the Bible and the Judaism of Jesus' day, looking both backwards and forwards, and watching the passage of ideas that went to and fro between them.

(ii) Daniel 12: The Sleepers Wake, the Wise Shine

We begin with the central passage, Daniel 12.2–3:

> [2]Many of those who sleep in the dust of the earth shall awake, some to everlasting life, and some to shame and everlasting contempt. [3]Those who are wise shall shine like the brightness of the sky, and those who lead many to righteousness, like the stars for ever and ever.

There is little doubt that this refers to concrete, bodily resurrection.[107] The metaphor of 'sleep' for death was, as we have seen, already widespread; sleeping in the dust of the earth (literally, 'the earth of dust' or 'the land of dust') was a clear biblical way of referring to the dead.[108] It was therefore

---

[106] Davies 1999, 93.

[107] See e.g. Day 1996, 240f.; Cavallin 1974, 26f. says that the sub-text behind Daniel 12, Isa. 26.19, refers to a corpse (Heb: *nebelati*). Collins 1993, 391f. says there is 'virtually unanimous agreement among modern scholars that Daniel is referring to the actual resurrection of individuals from the dead'. For the concrete/abstract distinction as opposed to the literal/metaphorical one see above, xvii–xviii, and below, 253f.: in this case, the passage uses the *metaphor* of sleep and waking to denote the *concrete event* of resurrection.

[108] For 'sleep' = 'death': 2 Kgs. 4.31; 13.21; Job 3.13; 14.12; Ps. 13.3; Jer. 51.39, 57; Nah. 3.18; 'dust' as the destination of the dead: Gen. 3.19; Job 10.9; 34.15; Ps. 104.29; Eccles. 3.20; 12.7; Isa. 26.19. NRSV translates the obscure first clause of Ps. 22.29 as 'to him, indeed, shall all who sleep in the earth bow down', in parallel to the next clause, 'before him shall bow all who go down to the dust'. See McAlpine 1987, 117–53, showing that the metaphor of sleep for death is very ancient, found in Mesopotamian and Egyptian sources as well.

natural to continue the metaphor by using 'awake' to denote bodily resurrection – not a different sort of sleep, but its abolition. This is not, of itself, an 'otherworldly' idea, but a very much 'this-worldly' one.[109]

Those who awake are 'many', but not, it appears, all.[110] The passage is not attempting to offer a global theory of the ultimate destination of the whole human race, but simply to affirm that, in a renewed bodily life, God will give everlasting life to some and everlasting contempt to others. In the context (see below) there can be little doubt who these persons are: they are the righteous who have suffered martyrdom on the one hand, and their torturers and murderers on the other. The rest – the great majority of humans, and indeed of Israelites – are simply not mentioned.

Verse 3 offers two parallel similes to describe the final state of the resurrected righteous (or, just conceivably, of a sub-set of them). They are denoted as 'the wise', *hammaskilim*, and as 'those who turn many to righteousness', or perhaps 'those who justify many', an allusion to Isaiah 53.11 (see below). They will, says the verse, 'shine like the brightness of the sky', and 'like the stars for ever and ever'. This has led some to suggest that their final state is actually to *become* stars, in some kind of 'astral immortality'. Such a reading has become accepted quite widely, and influential on other readings of Jewish and early Christian texts.[111] There are, however, serious problems with this interpretation, and the matter is sufficiently important to warrant a brief excursus.

To begin with the present text itself. It is not clear how metaphorical the passage intends to be: a short poetic statement, echoing an earlier scriptural passage, and itself located within a climactic vision of the future, can scarcely be treated as a precise or exact description.[112] The two clauses are similes: the passage predicts that the righteous will be *like* stars, not that they will *turn into* stars, nor even that they will be *located among* them.[113] Moreover, if the second clause were to mean that the *maskilim* would become actual stars, the parallelism with the first clause ('shine like the brightness of the sky') would force the meaning there that 'the wise' would *become* the sky itself, which is clearly out of the question. Two other strong considerations

---

[109] So Eichrodt 1961–7, 2.514. Eichrodt suggests (513) that the present statement is so brief because by the time Daniel 12 was written the idea was well known; this is supported by the usage of the (earlier) Aramaic Enoch. See too Kellermann 1989, 69.

[110] Day 1996, 240f.; Collins 1993, 392.

[111] So e.g. Hengel 1974, 196f.; Lacoque 1979, 244f.; Cohen 1987, 91; Perkins 1994, 38; Martin 1995, 118. For the subject see 55–60 above. Hengel 1974, 196 even suggests that Isa. 26.19 (the peculiar phrase 'dew of light') refers to an 'astral component', but it is certainly preferable to take it in the sense either that light will shine on the risen ones (so Seitz 1993, 195) or that there will be a miraculous dew, composed of light, which will be the means whereby the shades in Sheol are restored to bodily life (so Kaiser 1973, 218).

[112] So Goldingay 1989, 308; the earlier passage is of course Isa. 52.13 and 53.11.

[113] See Collins 1993, 394. Collins traces hellenistic influence at this point, but stresses the distinction: 'The wise in Daniel are not said to become stars but to shine like them.'

must be borne in mind as well: first, that there is no hint whatever of the kind of supporting or surrounding cosmology which we find in Plato, Cicero or other expressions of the classic 'astral immortality'; second, that the sequence of thought in verses 2 and 3 presents a *two-stage* future, quite unlike what we find in the *Timaeus*, Scipio's dream, or in the various epitaphs where 'astral immortality' found popular expression. In all of those, the point was that the soul departed immediately upon death, to rejoin its proper place among the stars. Here, by contrast, 'the wise' are at present dead, 'asleep', and will 'wake up' at some point still in the future. That is when they will 'shine like the sky, and like the stars'. The structure of the belief, the surrounding cosmology, and the actual exegesis all prevent us from linking Daniel 12.3 with the line of thought from Plato (and perhaps elsewhere) to Cicero and beyond.

Nor do the Jewish parallels regularly adduced serve to strengthen the case. There are some similar passages, of course, as one might expect in such a variegated phenomenon as the wide world of Judaism within its hellenistic environment. Perhaps the most striking is 4 Maccabees 17.5, where the martyred mother is addressed in glowing and certainly 'astral' terms:

> The moon in heaven, with the stars, does not stand so august as you, who, after lighting the way of your star-like seven sons to piety, stand in honour before God and are firmly set in heaven with them.

Certainly any reader in the hellenistic world would know what to make of that.[114] We should not be so sanguine, though, about some of the other references that are sometimes put forward on this point.[115] There are three or four passages which seem at least to borrow the idea (though still transplanting it into a Jewish cosmology): the *Testament of Moses* offers a good example, as does *2 Baruch*.[116] There are even, it seems, a couple of possible examples at

---

[114] 4 Macc. 9.22 speaks of the oldest son, during his torture, 'as though transformed by fire into immortality'; here, it seems, the theology of 2 Macc. has itself been transformed by Plato into Hellenism. See the discussion in the following chapter.

[115] e.g. Wis. 3.7, on which see ch. 4 below; *Ps.-Phil.* 19.4; 51.5; *Ps. Sol.* 3.12 (not every mention of 'light' in relation to the future world can be made to mean that the righteous *become* light!). In *Sib. Or.* 4.189 the resurrected ones will *see* the light of the sun. 4 Ezr. 7.97, 125a are deliberate echoes of Dan. 12.3, and it is clear that what is intended is simile, not identification ('their face will shine like the light of the sun, and they will be like the light of the stars' – once again, the parallel of the clauses rules out identification of the resurrected with the heavenly bodies themselves); in *2 En.* 66.7 the righteous will shine seven times more brightly than the sun, which again explicitly rules out identification.

[116] *T. Mos.* 10.9: 'God will raise you to the heights; yes, he will fix you firmly in the heaven of the stars, in the place of their habitations'; Priest (in Charlesworth 1983, 933) warns that it remains problematical whether this should be understood literally or metaphorically. *2 Bar.* 51.10, in a passage to which we shall return, declares that 'they will live in the heights of that world and they will be like the angels and be equal to the stars'. We note, though, that they will be *like* angels, and *equal to* stars; not identical. There is one Jewish tombstone from the diaspora (from Corycus in Cilicia) which seems to indicate an

Qumran.[117] The best-known source of possible parallels for an 'astral' interpretation is *1 Enoch*; but even there caution is advisable with most of the references that are often cited.[118] The doctrine of resurrection itself tells against it, since it envisages a two-stage future (first being dead, then, later, being raised), not a single step into a shining immortality. The only passage that seems either to suggest that the righteous *become* stars, or to move towards a world more like that of the *Timaeus*, are *1 Enoch* 58.3 ('the righteous shall be in the light of the sun, and the elect in the light of eternal life which has no end, and the days of the life of the holy ones cannot be numbered' – set in a chapter which is all about the coming world that will be full of light) and 108.11–14 (immediately before the close of the book):

> So now I shall summon their spirits if they are born of light, and change those who are born in darkness . . . I shall bring them out into the bright light, those who have loved my holy name, and seat them each one by one upon the throne of his honour; and they shall be resplendent for ages that cannot be numbered . . . the righteous ones shall be resplendent.

Here, as in Plato or Cicero, the spirits come from light and go back to light. Granted the composite nature of *1 Enoch*, however, it is impossible to cite the book as a whole as a representative of the 'astral' view; indeed, granted that there were several previous opportunities to say this kind of thing, and that these were not taken, we might suggest that at the very least the multiple authors, and the eventual redactor, were not eager to press such a point. Thus, though several texts play with the idea of 'light' in general, and many refer directly to Daniel, it is hard to make a case that 'astral immortality' had taken root in ancient Judaism as it clearly had in ancient paganism.

We return from this important digression to the meaning of Daniel 12 itself. The similes in verse 3 indicate, not so much that the righteous and the wise will be shining and twinkling like stars, but that in the resurrection they will be leaders and rulers in God's new creation. The imagery, set in the biblical context which is surely the primary world from which to understand the author's meaning, suggests a *royal* connotation: it is kings who are spoken of as stars or celestial beings.[119] God-given kings and rulers are to provide

---

'astral' belief (*CIJ* 2.788). The scarcity of such references indicates, if anything, a firm Jewish mindset against the idea.

[117] 1QS 4.8 ('a crown of glory and a garment of majesty in unending light'); 1QM 17.7 ('with everlasting light will he lighten with joy the children of Israel'); but these, clearly, can scarcely be used in the service of a full-blown 'astral' theory.

[118] cf. *1 En.* 39.7; 50.1; 62.15 (this is clearly a glorious bodily resurrection, not a matter of becoming a star); 80.1, 6f.; 86.3f. (the stars used as images in visions); 92.4 (walking in eternal light); 100.10 (sun, moon and stars witnessing against sinners). The frequently cited 104.2 is simply a quote from Dan. 12.3 ('you shall shine like the lights of heaven'), and like Dan. itself says nothing about the righteous *becoming* stars.

[119] e.g. Num. 24.17; 1 Sam. 29.9; 2 Sam. 14.17, 20; Isa. 9.6 [MT 5]. So Goldingay 1989, 308.

light to the world as the stars in the firmament were made, according to Genesis 1, to give light to the earth.[120] This appears to be, in line with other ideas in Daniel, a kind of democratization of earlier royal traditions: it belongs with the idea that 'the saints of the Most High' will receive the kingdom (7.18, 22, 27). By looking at the stars, commentators have missed the real point: the righteous, the wise, will not so much be transformed into beings of light, as set in authority over the world. Daniel 12.3 adds to 12.2, then, the sense that the resurrection is not simply a resuscitation in which the dead will return to life much as they knew it before. They will be raised to a state of glory in the world for which the best parallel or comparison is the status of stars, moon and sun within the created order.

Where does this remarkable passage belong historically? Does that help us to explain why it comes out with this remarkable idea at this late stage in the growth of biblical tradition? The immediate context of the passage is martyrdom: the martyrdom which occurred during the crisis of the 160s (see 1 and 2 Maccabees), and, in particular, the martyrdom of faithful Israelites under the persecution of Antiochus Epiphanes.[121] Daniel 11.31 speaks of Antiochus' desecration of the Jerusalem Temple, and his setting up of the 'abomination of desolation' mentioned already in 9.27. Verses 32–5 of chapter 11 describe what happens next, as some Judaeans compromise with the pagan invader and others stand firm and suffer for it, some of them being killed. Verses 36–45 then describes the final boasting and sudden fall of Antiochus, the earlier verses (36–9) staying close to what we know as actual events, and the later ones (40–45) diverging – at the point, we assume, where the writer's own time is to be located. But what matters is that at the time of Antiochus' fall, a time of unprecedented anguish for Israel (12.1), the angelic prince Michael will arise to fight on their behalf and deliver them. This is the context for the prediction of resurrection. The remainder of the passage and indeed of the book (12.4–13) contains final revelations (if they can be called that; they have, notoriously, seemed to tease as much as to reveal) about the timing of the forthcoming events, and a last promise to Daniel himself (v. 13) that, after his own 'rest', he will join the *maskilim* and rise (the word *ta'amod* here means 'stand up') for his reward at the end of the days. The 'resurrection' envisaged here is not a state upon which the righteous enter immediately upon death, but is a further event, following an intermediate period.

The prediction of resurrection is not an isolated piece of speculation about the ultimate fate of humans, or even Judaeans, in general, but a specific promise addressed to a specific situation. Israel's god will reverse the actions of the wicked pagans, and raise the martyrs, and the teachers who

---

[120] Gen. 1.14–18. Cf. too Wis. 3.7f., on which see below, 162–75.

[121] On the specific historical referent of Dan. 10—12 cf. e.g. Goldingay 1989, 289, 292–306. See further *NTPG* 157–9, and other literature there.

kept Israel on course, to a glorious life. Simultaneously, he will raise their persecutors to a new existence: instead of remaining in the decent obscurity of Sheol or 'the dust', they will face perpetual public obloquy. The whole scene, in fact, carries with it elements of the lawcourt, in which YHWH as the righteous judge puts wrongs to right, punishing the wicked and vindicating the righteous.[122] Michael, the angel or 'prince' who is Israel's specific protector, will be YHWH's agent in bringing this judgment to pass.[123]

Once we grasp this larger picture we can see that it, in turn, belongs closely with the still larger vision of the book of Daniel as a whole. Again and again the book tells of pagan rulers attacking YHWH's people, trying to make them conform to new pagan ways, boasting arrogantly against the true god and his people, and of the faithful and wise Israelites holding on, retaining their loyalty and integrity, and being vindicated in the end as their god acts dramatically to rescue them and condemn or overthrow their oppressors.[124] In particular, 11.31–5 and 12.1–3, the key passages here, are anticipated frequently in the earlier parts of the book, and, together with chapters 10—12 as a whole, are clearly intended to draw out fuller significance from what has been said before. This encourages us to see the prediction of resurrection as the final and most explicit promise in a much longer line, which begins with the setting up of the divine kingdom over against all pagan kingdoms (2.35, 44–5), and continues through the exaltation and vindication of the son of man (representing the people of the saints of the most high (7.13–14, 18, 27)), including frequent narratives of deliverance from death (hinted at in 1.10; explicit in 2.13; plotted throughout chapters 3 and 6).[125] Daniel's prayer in chapter 9, questioning the meaning of Jeremiah's prophecy of a seventy-year exile, receives the answer that the exile will in fact last seventy times seven years, i.e. 490 years, coming to its climax in the setting up of the abomination of desolation, the cutting off of an anointed prince, and final judgment on the oppressor (9.2, 24–7).[126] Chapters 10—12 then spell all this out in more detail. This is how Israel's long exile will reach its climax, how the arrogant pagans will be judged, how the righteous will be delivered.

---

[122] So e.g. Nickelsburg 1972, 23, 27; Goldingay 1989, 302.

[123] For Michael cf. Dan. 10.13, 21; *T. Dan.* 6.2; Jude 9; Rev. 12.7.

[124] Thus: ch. 1 (the king's rich food); ch. 2 (the king's dream); ch. 3 (the king's statue, and the fiery furnace); ch. 4 (the king's dream and madness); ch. 5 (the king's banquet and the writing on the wall); ch. 6 (the king's edict, and the lions' den); ch. 7 (the beasts and the 'son of man'); ch. 8 (the ram, the goat and their horns); ch. 9 (Daniel's prayer, and the warning of the coming abomination).

[125] Goldingay 1989, 283f. gives details of the links between Dan. 10—12 and the earlier sections of the book, particularly chs. 7—9.

[126] This prophecy, with related passages, was used as the basis of intense chronological speculation about the date of the coming redemption, and the coming Messiah. See *NTPG* 208, 312–14, and esp. Beckwith 1980, 1981, now reprinted in Beckwith 1996.

Chapters 10—12, then, and particularly the passage at the end of chapter 11 and the start of chapter 12, provide a different lens through which to view the same events as those spoken of in 2.31–45 and 7.2–27. The stone cut from the mountain that smashed the multi-metalled statue and became a mountain in turn; the 'one like a son of man' who is exalted over the beasts; the suffering *maskilim* being raised to shine like the stars, while their persecutors receive everlasting contempt; these are essentially the same. Any second-Temple Jew who pondered the book would find in 12.2–3 not a new and outlandish idea, unanticipated and unforeseen, but the crown of all that had gone before.

This would be all the more so for a reader whose ears were open to the biblical overtones of the text. Appropriately, considering the exilic theme of the whole book (the fictive setting is of course Babylon, and the historical setting is that of the 'continuing exile' of 9.24, under various pagan rulers climaxing in the Syria of Antiochus), the most obvious biblical precursors are those which themselves speak of exile and restoration.[127] We note, for instance, the echo of Jeremiah 30.7 in 12.2: the time of unprecedented anguish is that spoken of by the earlier prophet, not long after he had repeated his promise about a seventy-year exile which Daniel has now reinterpreted.[128] And the warning of anguish to come is part of a larger prophecy of return, rebuilding, peace and security. The pagan yoke will be broken, and the Israelite monarchy restored.[129]

(iii) The Servant and the Dust-Dwellers: Isaiah

The main source for Daniel's ideas and images in 12.2–3 is undoubtedly Isaiah. Before looking at the most obvious passage, we note first the close links with Isaiah 52—3.[130] The *maskilim* seem to be a plural version of the 'servant', who in 52.13 'deals prudently' (*yaskil*). They are those 'who justify many', as does the servant in 53.11. The 'shining' of the righteous in Daniel 12.3 may possibly echo the 'light' which, in some early versions, features in Isaiah 53.11.[131] And of course the entire theme – those who remain faithful to YHWH despite torture and death, and who are then vindicated – fits exactly the scenario with which Isaiah 40—55 reaches its great climax.

---

[127] On the theme of continuing exile, which continues to be misunderstood in some quarters cf. *JVG* xviif.; and, in further explanation, Wright 'Dialogue', 252–61.

[128] Jer. 25.12; 29.10.

[129] Jer. 30.3, 8–11.

[130] On this combination cf. further *JVG* 584–91, with other refs. there. Another allusion to Isa. is the reference to the abhorrence or contempt suffered by the resurrected wicked in Dan. 12.2 (echoing Isa. 66.24).

[131] Cavallin 1972/3, 51. The versions in question include three Qumran MSS and the LXX. Other details in Goldingay 284; Day 1996, 242f.

If the servant-figure in Isaiah was in the first place a personification of the nation, or of the righteous few within it, what we have here is not exactly a democratization of the servant-concept, as is sometimes said, but a repluralization.[132] The suffering *maskilim* are now the bearers of the promise of exile and restoration; Isaiah's vision is coming true in them.[133] This coheres, of course, with the theme of the book of Daniel as a whole.

But does Isaiah 53 itself speak of the servant dying and rising again? There is no explicit mention of resurrection itself, and only an oblique statement of what will happen to the servant after his death (53.11). But it is clear that the servant (a) dies and is buried (53.7–9), and (b) emerges in triumph, however densely expressed (53.10–12).[134] What matters most for our purposes, however, is that Daniel provides evidence that some people were already reading Isaiah this way; and so, it was argued some time ago, does the form of the Isaiah text as we have it in Qumran.[135] The result of all this for the meaning of the central passage should not be missed. Though Daniel 12.2–3 speaks clearly of bodily resurrection for individuals, this is not something other than God's long-promised act of vindication for the exiled nation. The either/or that has tended to drive a wedge between different interpretations of key passages (*either* 'individual resurrection' *or* 'national restoration') must be exposed as fallacious. In Daniel 12, the resurrection of God's people (at least in the persons of the martyrs, seen as representing the nation) is the form that national restoration takes. This is the real end of the deepest exile of all.

Behind Daniel 12, though, stands also the most obvious 'resurrection' passage in Isaiah. Isaiah 24—7 offers a scene not just of national crisis but of cosmic judgment, through which God's people will be rescued and the dead will be raised.[136] Few doubt that this passage was strongly present to the writer of Daniel 12.2–3:

Your dead shall live, their corpses shall rise.
O dwellers in the dust, awake and sing for joy!
For your dew is a radiant dew,
and the earth will give birth to those long dead.[137]

---

[132] cf. e.g. Nickelsburg 1972, 24f.; Day 1996, 242f.

[133] Childs summarizes the message of Isa. 49—55 as follows: 'God intervenes to end the exile and to usher in his eschatological reign' (2001, 410).

[134] See the judicious assessment of Childs 2001, 419. On the possibility of a similar, though cryptic, sequence of thought in Zech. 12—13 cf. Eichrodt 1961–7, 2.508 n. 1. One can trace a similar sequence in e.g. Ps. 22, where the Psalmist is 'laid in the dust of death' in v. 15, and then rescued in vv. 22–31.

[135] See Sawyer 1973, 233f.

[136] The dating of the passage is still controverted. The only thing we can be sure of is that to postulate a developmental scheme in which mention of a bodily resurrection is sufficient to earn a text a late date simply begs the question.

[137] Isa. 26.19.

The context is a vivid prayer of loyalty to YHWH in the midst of fierce and continuing persecution by pagans. Other lords have ruled over Israel, 'but we acknowledge your name alone'.[138] Pagans, and those who follow their ways, have no future beyond death to look forward to:

> The dead do not live, shades do not rise –
> because you have punished and destroyed them,
> and wiped out all memory of them.[139]

But those who seek YHWH in distress find themselves in pangs like a woman giving birth; and when birth comes it turns out to be the new birth of the dead themselves (26.16–19). The original Hebrew refers literally to bodily resurrection, and this is certainly how the verse is taken in the LXX and at Qumran.[140] It is still possible, of course, that here resurrection is, as we shall see in Ezekiel, a metaphor for national restoration; but the wider passage, in which God's renewal of the whole cosmos is in hand, opens the way for us to propose that the reference to resurrection is intended to denote actual concrete events.[141]

All is based upon the sovereign justice of YHWH himself, who will bring to light the wickedness done on earth (26.20–21).[142] His power alone can do this: in the previous chapter, preparing the way for the climax in chapter 26, we find this statement of both national and personal restoration:

> On this mountain YHWH of hosts will make for all peoples
> a feast of rich food, a feast of well-aged wines,
> of rich food filled with marrow, of well-aged wines strained clear.
> And he will destroy on this mountain the shroud that is cast over all peoples,
> the sheet that is spread over all nations; he will swallow up death for ever.
> Then the sovereign one, YHWH, will wipe away the tears from all faces,
> and the disgrace of his people he will take away from all the earth,
> for YHWH has spoken . . .
> For the hand of YHWH will rest on this mountain.[143]

This image of the eschatological banquet draws together the divine promise to the individual, to Israel, and to creation itself. We should separate out

---

[138] Isa. 26.13.

[139] Isa. 26.14.

[140] See Cavallin 1974, 106; Motyer 1993, 218f. For Isa. 26.19 as an anticipation of 52.1f. ('Awake, awake . . . shake yourself from the dust . . .') cf. Nickelsburg 1971, 18; cp. Puech 1993, 42–4. On 'dew' as part of a larger theme in which God's rain bringing forth fruit from the ground is parallel to resurrection cf. Hos. 6.1–3, and below on the rabbis. (See too above on Dan. 12.3.)

[141] Day 1996 points out that 27.8, with its reference to the exile, nudges the verse in the direction of 'return from exile' on the lines of Ezek. 37.

[142] For the note of YHWH's justice underneath the whole passage cf. Nickelsburg 1971, 18; for YHWH's glory, Eichrodt 1961–7, 2.510.

[143] Isa. 25.6–8, 10.

these levels neither in our own reading of Isaiah, nor in our assessment of how the book would have been read in the second-Temple period.[144]

(iv) On the Third Day: Hosea

Behind these remarkable passages in Isaiah, offering arguably the earliest Old Testament references to bodily life the other side of death, we find two passages in Hosea, firmly located chronologically in the eighth century BC. John Day has argued impressively that Isaiah 26.19 is dependent on Hosea 13.14:

> Shall I ransom them from the power of Sheol?
> Shall I redeem them from Death?
> O Death, where are [or: I will be] your plagues?
> O Sheol, where is [or: I will be] your destruction?
> Compassion is hidden from my eyes.[145]

The original Hebrew text is almost certainly denying that YHWH will redeem Israel from Sheol and Death. However, the LXX and other ancient versions, and also the New Testament, take the passage in a positive sense, and there is no reason why the author of Isaiah 26.19 should not have read it thus as well.[146] The evidence that he did so is cumulative but overwhelming: no fewer than eight features of text and context can be paralleled.[147] Behind Hosea 13, in turn, there stands the (equally ambiguous) Hosea 6:

> Come, let us return to YHWH;
> for it is he who has torn, and he will heal us;
> he has struck down, and he will bind us up.
> After two days he will revive us;
> on the third day he will raise us up, that we may live before him.[148]

From a later perspective, this appears as it stands as a prayer of faith in the life-giving, restorative power of YHWH. However, in its original context it almost certainly was intended as a description of a prayer that the prophet regarded as inadequate. It indicated a failure to repent at a deep level, a simplistic hope that maybe YHWH could be bought off.[149] Once again,

---

[144] cf. Childs 2001, 191f. Thus, though Day is right (1996, 243f.) to see here a strong note of exile and return, this does not preclude a reference also to bodily resurrection.

[145] Day 1980; 1996, 244f.

[146] In the NT see esp. 1 Cor. 15.54f.

[147] Day 1980; 1996; 1997.

[148] Hos. 6.1f. Day 1996, 246f. (and 1997, 126f.) shows clearly that this passage does indeed refer to death, not merely to sickness as some have suggested.

[149] cf. e.g. Eichrodt 1961–7, 2.504f.; Martin-Achard 1960, 86–93; Zimmerli 1971 [1968], 91f. Martin-Achard 86 takes Hos. 6 as indicative of personal resurrection, as do Andersen and Freedman 1980, 420f., against e.g. Wolff 1974.

though, it is entirely possible that later readers, including later biblical writers, would have taken it in a more positive sense. When read in this sense, the passage has a claim to be the earliest explicit statement that YHWH will give his people a new bodily life the other side of death. It appears to have influenced Daniel 12, perhaps via Isaiah. We shall have more to say in a moment on the origin of Hosea's ideas, or those of the people whose prayer he was reporting.

(v) Dry Bones and God's Breath: Ezekiel

There is one remaining major text, whose relation with those just discussed is problematic, but whose importance for subsequent thought can hardly be denied. Ezekiel 37 is perhaps the most famous of all 'resurrection' passages in the Old Testament; it is the most obviously allegorical or metaphorical; it does not appear to have influenced, or to have been influenced by, either Isaiah or Daniel; yet the parallels of overall thought are remarkable.

Once again, of course, the context is the exile. For the Temple-centred Ezekiel, one of Israel's main problems was impurity; cleansing from that impurity formed a key part of his promise of restoration (36.16–32). This is set among sustained oracles about the restoration of the land itself, with its people, its buildings, its agriculture, its flocks and its herds (36.1–15, 33–8). The overall aim of the prophecy at this stage of the book was to point to a renewal of Israel's national life in which the Davidic monarchy would be restored, the nation would be reconstituted, and (ultimately) a new Temple would be built.[150] But uncleanness remained at the heart of the problem.

Of all the unclean objects an observant Jew might encounter, unburied corpses or bones would come near the top of the list. That is the state, metaphorically, to which Israel has been reduced. God, declares Ezekiel, will deal with this in an act of new creation:

> The hand of YHWH came upon me, and he brought me out by the spirit of YHWH and set me down in the middle of a valley; it was full of bones. He led me all around them; there were very many lying in the valley, and they were very dry. He said to me, 'Son of man, can these bones live?' I answered, 'O sovereign YHWH, you know.' Then he said to me, 'Prophesy to these bones, and say to them: "O dry bones, hear the word of YHWH. Thus says the sovereign YHWH to these bones: I will cause breath to enter you, and you shall live. I will lay sinews on you, and will cause flesh to come upon you, and cover you with skin, and put breath in you, and you shall live; and you shall know that I am YHWH."'
>
> So I prophesied as I had been commanded; and as I prophesied, suddenly there was a noise, a rattling, and the bones came together, bone to its bone. I looked, and there were sinews on them, and flesh had come upon them, and skin had covered them; but there was no breath in them. Then he said to me, 'Prophesy to the breath,

---

[150] Ezek. 34.1–31; 37.15–28.

prophesy, mortal, and say to the breath: "Thus says the sovereign YHWH: Come from the four winds, O breath, and breathe upon these slain, that they may live."' I prophesied as he commanded me, and the breath came into them, and they lived, and stood on their feet, a vast multitude.

Then he said to me, 'Son of man, these bones are the whole house of Israel. They say, "Our bones are dried up, and our hope is lost; we are cut off completely." Therefore prophesy, and say to them, "Thus says the sovereign YHWH: I am going to open your graves, and bring you up from your graves, O my people; and I will bring you back to the land of Israel. And you shall know that I am YHWH, when I open your graves, and bring you up from your graves, O my people. I will put my spirit within you, and you shall live, and I will place you on your own soil; then you shall know that I, YHWH, have spoken and will act, says YHWH."'[151]

Both the content of the vision and the immediate conclusion that the prophet draws from it mark out this passage as an intentional and sustained metaphor.[152] Ezekiel is no more envisaging actual bodily resurrection than he envisaged, when writing chapter 34, that Israel consisted of sheep rather than people. This is further confirmed by the surface contradiction between the vision itself and the application. In the vision (verses 1–10) the bones are lying unburied on the surface of the ground, as in a battlefield rather than a graveyard;[153] but in the application (verses 11–14) God promises to open Israel's graves and bring up the dead. There should not, then, be any question but that the original purpose was to provide a highly charged and vivid metaphor of the way in which unclean Israel would be cleansed, exiled Israel restored to the land, and scattered Israel regathered, by a powerful and covenant-renewing act of new creation. It is possible that the roots of the image are found in the promises of return from exile in Deuteronomy, where covenant renewal is a matter of new, god-given life in place of death, but this may simply be a distant echo.[154] The echoes of Genesis 1—2 are not far from the surface, particularly in the promise of the breath/spirit – YHWH's own breath/spirit, it turns out – which will make them once again a living people.[155] This is not a mere resuscitation, like the miracles performed by Elijah and Elisha. The fleshless bones can only be brought to life by a new and unprecedented act of the creator god.[156]

The undoubted allegorical character of this passage did not stop it being seen, from at least the early rabbinic period, as a prediction of literal resur-

---

[151] Ezek. 37.1–14. The Hebrew word for 'breath', 'wind' and 'spirit' throughout is *ruach*.

[152] For discussion of the passage cf. Martin-Achard 1960, 93–102; Eichrodt 1970, 505–11; Stemberger 1972, 283; Koenig 1983.

[153] So Martin-Achard 1960, 95.

[154] cf. Dt. 30.1—10, which is certainly echoed in Ezek. 34—6; and cp. also Dt. 30.15–20; 32.39–43.

[155] Ezek. 37.8–10, 14; cf. Gen. 2.7 (though a different word, *nishmath* rather than *ruach*, is used there for 'breath', translated by the LXX as *pnoe* rather than *pneuma* as in Ezek.).

[156] So Martin-Achard 1960, 95.

rection. Evidence for this is found in textual marginalia from early manuscripts, and in the remarkable paintings found at Dura-Europos.[157] But it is
only in such subsequent use that we can detect anything like a confluence
between Ezekiel 37 and the stream of thought that runs (mostly underground) from Hosea, through Isaiah, to Daniel.[158] None of those other texts
mentions, let alone highlights, the main focus of Ezekiel's vision, namely
bones; and Ezekiel lacks the regular language of sleepers waking, of dwellers in the dust, or of the resurrected shining with a new glory. What all
these texts refer to in one way or another, though, was the common hope of
Israel: that YHWH would restore her fortunes at last, liberate her from pagan
dominion, and resettle her in justice and peace, even if it took a great act of
new creation to accomplish it. This is where the solid hope of the earlier
period (hope for nation, family and land) joins up with the emerging belief
in the creator's faithfulness even beyond the grave. This coming together of
(what seem to us) different strands of thought demands closer investigation.

(vi) Resurrection and the Hope of Israel

What place, within the wider context of Israel's faith and life, can we give to
these varied expressions of a hope for new life beyond 'life after death'?
Where did the idea come from, and how does it relate to the other types of
hope (and the explicit statements of a lack of hope for post-mortem life) in
the rest of the Old Testament? Here there are two related points to be made,
the first about the relation of this hope to the mainstream Old Testament
expectation, and the second to do with origin and derivation.

It would be easy, and wrong, to see the hope for resurrection as a new
and extraneous element, something which has come into ancient Israelite
thinking by a backdoor or roundabout route. Each of the passages we have
studied is set in the context of the continuing affirmation of the Jewish hope
for restoration, for liberation from exile, persecution and suffering. Sometimes, as in the case of Ezekiel, this metaphorical character is clear throughout the passage. Sometimes, as in Daniel, actual bodily resurrection is
likewise clearly intended. Elsewhere, as in the Isaiah passages, there is room
for genuine uncertainty as to where the balance lies. But however concrete
the reference in any of the passages, there is no doubt that even in such cases
the overarching context is that of the hope of the nation for national restoration and resettlement in the land. In other words, *this is not a move away
from the hope which characterized all of ancient Israel, but a reaffirmation*

---

[157] Riesenfeld 1948; Cavallin 1974, 110 n. 28; Martin-Achard 1960, 93 n. 1 with other
refs.
[158] According to Martin-Achard 1960, 100f., the creation-stories are the basis for the
Ezekiel passage.

of it. It is a reaffirmation, indeed, in a way which the hope simply for a blessed but non-bodily personal life after death (as perhaps witnessed by Psalm 73 and one or two other passages) would not be. This resurrection hope is not like that of ancient Egypt, where life after death was thought of as a continuation of normal life by other means.[159] Such an idea would have been seen by ancient Israel as a denial of the hope for nation, family and land to thrive and flourish.

What we have, in fact, in these passages can best be seen in these terms: hope for bodily resurrection *is what sometimes happens when the hope of ancient Israel meets a new challenge*, which might include the threat of judgment, as in Hosea and Isaiah 24—7, and, more specifically, the fact of exile, as (in different ways) in Ezekiel 37 and Isaiah 53. Daniel 12 is best seen, in line with chapter 9, as reflecting an awareness of *extended and continuing* exile, focused now in suffering and martyrdom. Of course, exile and indeed martyrdom does not necessarily have this effect, otherwise we would find resurrection ideas in (for instance) Jeremiah and 1 Maccabees as well as in Ezekiel, Daniel and 2 Maccabees.[160] But where a strong sense of exile as divine punishment for rebellion, disloyalty and idolatry was present (one wonders whether the story in Genesis 3, of Adam and Eve being expelled from the garden, was read in this period as a paradigm of Israel's expulsion from the promised land, but direct evidence for this connection is lacking), then it was but a short step for that expulsion to be seen as 'death',[161] life in exile to be seen as the strange half-life lived after that death, and return from exile to be seen as life beyond that again, newly embodied life, i.e. resurrection. That seems to be precisely the route taken by both Ezekiel and Daniel, the latter drawing on Isaiah and perhaps Hosea. Thus, though the promise of resurrection contradicts head on the view so frequently stated in the material we surveyed earlier in which all hope beyond the grave was ruled out, it forms an equally strong reaffirmation of the hope which ancient Israel did indeed hold: hope for renewal of national life, in the land, life as the gift of YHWH the creator god.

This latter point, indeed, needs to be highlighted. Echoes of the Genesis creation narratives lurk in the shadows of these passages: it is from the dust that YHWH creates humans, breathing into them his own breath, and when he takes it away again they return to dust once more.[162] The fresh gift of his breath will then bring the dust to life.[163] The promise of resurrection is thus firmly linked to creation itself, which was the basis of the normal ancient Israelite celebration of life in the present, bodily life in YHWH's good land.

[159] See above, 45–7; and Davies 1999, ch. 1.

[160] For the latter see section 4 (iii) of the following chapter.

[161] cf. Dt. 30.15–20 in the context of the ch. as a whole.

[162] Gen. 2.7; 3.19; Ps. 104.29; see Johnston 2002, 238f. Dust becomes a regular image in connection with death: e.g. Ps. 7.5; 22.15, 29; 30.9; 119.25.

[163] Ps. 104.29; cf. Isa. 26.19; Dan. 12.2; also 1 Sam. 2.8; Ps. 113.7.

This robust affirmation of the goodness of life in YHWH's world and land is what is called into question when Israel sins and faces punishment in the form of national catastrophe. We should not be surprised, then, when at that point it is to the language of creation itself that the prophets turn for help. Just as in Genesis 3 death is linked to expulsion from the garden, so in the fullest biblical statements of hope we discover a creative fluidity between the restoration of Israel to the land and the new bodily creation of human beings after the state of death.

This movement of thought is what we see in earlier writings such as Hosea. Under pressure, and in trouble, the nation begins to use the language of a new life after 'life after death', and this turns into the celebratory out-burst of Isaiah 26. We might suggest that the likely turning-point in the sequence – the moment when somebody really begins to think in terms of human beings themselves actually dying and actually being given a newly embodied life at some point thereafter – is to be found in Isaiah's servant passages. That is where, supremely, the hope for the nation and land becomes focused on an individual, or at least what looks like an individual; even if this is a literary code for the nation as a whole, or for a group within the nations, there are signs in the text itself, as well as in subsequent inter-pretation, that at least some of the 'servant' passages in Isaiah may have an individual, representing the nation, in mind.[164] That is where, we might also suggest, the belief that Israel's god will restore the nation after exile breaks through into the belief – albeit not yet expressed very clearly – that he will restore the nation's *representative* after death. The earlier national hope thus transmutes, but perfectly comprehensibly, into the hope that Israel's god will do for a human being what Israel always hoped he would do for the nation as a whole. From there we can perceive a more obvious straight line to Daniel 12, where the nation's representative has become plural. The experi-ence of suffering, persecution and martyrdom had, so the writer believed, brought the exile to a new and appalling climax. The suffering righteous ones had found themselves enacting, corporately, the role of Isaiah's ser-vant.

Two preliminary conclusions follow from this, which we can set out in terms of the relations between the three positions presented in this chapter:

[164] The identity of the 'servant' is of course controversial. The portrait begins (42.1–9) with royal features echoing Isa. 11.1–10, with the servant as the strange messenger of YHWH; at this point the servant appears to be the nation itself, rebellious though it is (42.22–5; 44.1f., 21f., 26; 45.4). But the servant also stands over against, and is given a ministry to, the nation (49.1–6; 50.10), and at one point at least (48.20) appears to consist of the exiles in Babylon, who have borne the weight of suffering on behalf of the whole people. 49.5 and 50.4–10 could refer to the prophet himself. But, read in the context of chs. 40—55 as a whole, the key passage (52.13—53.12) towers above all of this from a literary as well as a theological point of view, with its portrait of the servant as one at whom faith-ful Israel itself looks on in horror, awe and ultimately gratitude. Among recent discussions see e.g Williamson 1998, ch. 4; Balzer 2001, 124–8.

(a) the dead are 'asleep with the ancestors'; (b) the dead may be 'received' by YHWH into some continuing life; and (c) some at least of the dead can hope for resurrection *after* any such 'life after death'.

First, (c) is not so much a development out of (b), as is sometimes suggested; it is, rather, a radical development from within (a) itself. The resurrection hope does not deny, as (b) seems at least to deny, that at death people go to Sheol, to the dust, to the grave. Nor does it affirm, as (b) seems at least to affirm, that a non-bodily post-mortem existence, in the presence and love of YHWH, is the final good for which one might hope. It does not deny that the dead are now 'asleep'. It simply affirms – against, admittedly, the clear denials in several statements of (a) – that YHWH will do something new for them *after* that. The same theological and devotional belief that seems to have generated (b) can be seen also under (c) – the belief, that is, not that humans are innately immortal, but that YHWH's love and creative power are so strong that even death cannot break them. However, (c) (resurrection in the future) is a quite different sort of thing from (b) (happy disembodied life after death), and is closer in all sorts of ways, in theology and in practical effect, to (a) itself (in which the only future hope is that of the nation, not the individual).[165]

Second, the meanings of 'bodily resurrection for dead humans' and 'national restoration for exiled/suffering Israel' are so closely intertwined that it does not matter that we cannot always tell which is meant, or even if a distinction is possible, in relation to particular passages; that is part of the point. The intertwining adds to the robustness of the emerging belief. The idea of resurrection was not an odd 'apocalyptic' invention, intruding into an otherwise easy progression towards a spiritual (in the sense of 'non-bodily') hope.[166]

If this account of the origin of resurrection belief in ancient Israel is anywhere near the mark, it outflanks the two other accounts that have often been given. Each is, in any case, subject to damaging criticism in its own right.

The first account, which remains popular in some quarters despite being regularly refuted, attempts to trace the emergence of Israelite belief in resurrection to ancient Zoroastrianism, pointing out that the belief seems to have emerged in Israel around the time, or shortly thereafter, that Israel was exiled in the parts of the world – Babylon, then Persia – where Zoroastrianism was the official religion of the Persian empire.[167] This proposal has been

---

[165] Barr 1992, 22, seems to me to come close to this.

[166] As e.g. von Rad (1962–5, 1.390) seems to imply. This is perhaps related to von Rad's admission that 'our own theological outlook' is innately suspicious of the 'unspiritual and external' side of Yahwism (1.279).

[167] On Zoroastrianism cf. e.g. Boyce 1975–91; 1992; McDannell and Lang 2001 [1988], 12–14; Nigosian 1993, with the comments of Hengel 1974, 1.196; 2.130f.; Griffiths 1999, 1047f.; and the brief account by Davies 1999, ch. 2. The main surviving texts are

debated for well over a century, hampered not least by our radical uncertainty (because of the lateness of the primary sources) as to what ancient Zoroastrianism actually consisted of.[168] John Day has pointed out that since Daniel, the main biblical exponent of the doctrine, is clearly echoing not only Isaiah but also Hosea, this takes the stream of thought back behind any likely influence from Persia; and that, when Ezekiel speaks of the dead being raised from their graves, this cannot be related to Zoroastrianism, since the Persians exposed, rather than buried, their dead.[169] We may add that the thrust of resurrection, emerging around the time of the exile and being re-emphasized in the second century BC, was upon Israel's status as the unique chosen people of the one creator god. To express this by borrowing a key idea from the very people who were causing the problem – like a prisoner of war trying to escape by putting on the hated uniform of the oppressing forces! – does no justice to the much subtler process of reflection, devotion and vision that seems to have taken place. Indeed, the very understatedness of the idea in Isaiah 53 strongly implies otherwise. The only way the Zoroastrian hypothesis could make any sense would be for resurrection to be seen as an odd, extraneous addition to Israelite faith – as it is, for instance, when a now discredited idea of 'apocalyptic' prevails, in which that mood or movement is seen as dualistic in the same sense that, according to most analysts, Zoroastrianism was.[170] But the emerging Israelite belief in resurrection was not dualistic. It was a development, albeit a startling one, whose roots lay deep within ancient Israel itself. It grew directly from the emphasis on the goodness of creation, on YHWH as the god who both kills and makes alive, and on the future of nation and land.[171]

---

from the C9 AD (principally *Bundahishn* 30); knowledge of the early period is largely from writers such as Theopompus (C4 BC), as reported by Plutarch *De Isid.* 47; Diog. Laert. 1.9 (prologue); Aeneas of Gaza *De Animali Immortalite* 77. Hengel (as cited earlier in this note), in company with some others, suggests that the line of probable influence runs from Jewish and Christian conceptions to the more developed Iranian ones.

[168] See the previous note. For a discussion of older debates etc. cf. Martin-Achard 1960, 186–9; Greenspoon 1981, 259–61; Bremmer 1996, 96–8. Day 1996, 241n. lists proponents of the Zoroastrian hypothesis, from W. Bousset in the early C20 to Cohn 1993. Opponents include Eichrodt 1961–7, 1.516f.; Lacocque 1979 [1976], 243; Barr 1985; Goldingay 1989, 286, 318, with further refs.; J. J. Collins 1993, 396 ('although Persian influence on the Jewish belief was accepted as obvious by an earlier generation of scholars, the popularity of this view has waned considerably. There is no evidence of Persian motifs in such crucial Jewish passages as Daniel 12 and *1 Enoch* 22. At most, the metaphorical use of resurrection for the restoration of the Jewish nation after the Exile (Ezekiel 37; Isaiah 26) may have been prompted indirectly by acquaintance with the Persian belief.' The echoes of Gen. 2—3 in the latter two passages, however, casts some doubt on even that concession); Day himself (1996, 240–42); Bremmer 1996, 99–101; Johnston 2002, 234–6.

[169] Day 1996, 241f. The latter point is, though, an admission that Ezekiel's vision itself, with the bones scattered in the valley, corresponds to Persian practice.

[170] On 'apocalyptic' and 'dualism' see *NTPG* ch. 10.

[171] See further Eichrodt 1961–7, 2.516f. These remarks apply also to the suggestion that

What then of the alternative hypothesis, espoused by Day and others: that the first hints of resurrection (in Hosea, particularly) were derived by a process of imitation from the dying and rising deity (Baal) of Canaanite mythology?[172] This proposal, which resurfaces from time to time in the guise of similar speculations about the origin of Christian belief in Jesus' resurrection, has some initial plausibility in relation to Hosea, since the cults he opposed certainly included religions of this type. Hosea 6.1–2 ('he has torn, that he may heal . . . after two days he will revive us; on the third day he will raise us up, that we may live before him') can indeed be read as the kind of prayer the prophet might ascribe to Baal-worshippers who are now invoking YHWH (insincerely), and who are themselves borrowing the language of new life after death from their surrounding culture. That would explain why he seems to reject such a prayer as useless. According to Day, Hosea is ironically suggesting (as in 13.1) that Israel deserves to die for worshipping Baal, in which case repentance would mean resurrection.[173] But even if he is correct, it is hard to see this as more than one starting-point from which subsequent traditions, under different circumstances, made their own way forwards, through the fleeting references in Hosea, through the varied passages in Isaiah, and finally to Daniel.[174]

In particular, the hypothesis of Canaanite origins hardly explains either Daniel 12, or the two Isaiah passages which it employs, or Ezekiel 37. In addition, there is no reason to think that the dying and rising of Canaanite gods was a concept ever applied to Canaanites themselves, either nationally or individually. Furthermore, it was axiomatic to Yahwism that YHWH was not like those deities, specifically in that he did not die and rise. He was not a vegetation god, part of a fertility-cult; he was sovereign over creation, not

---

resurrection developed in Judaism as a result of borrowing from the hellenistic language of reincarnation (e.g. Glasson 1961 1f., 5f., 30; Mason 1991, 170). This is not to say that the *language* of reincarnation could not be used by Greek-speaking Jewish writers to *describe* resurrection belief; this is what we find in at least one passage of Josephus (below, 178).

[172] Day 1996, 245–8; 1997. For older debates see Martin-Achard 1960, 195–205; see too Xella 1995; Mettinger 2001.

[173] Day 1996, 245–7.

[174] I do not find help in Day's suggestion (1996, 247) that 'mythological imagery was first demythologized' (i.e. by referring Baal-cult language to the nation of Israel) 'and subsequently remythologized' (i.e. by referring national-restoration language to the resurrection of the individual). Dan. 12.2 is not remythologizing, going back to the world of dying and rising gods and their cult, but proposing a concrete solution to a pressing problem, viz. the deaths of the martyrs. Nor do I think that 1 Cor. 15.36f. and Jn. 12.24 (Day 248) are traces of an earlier, and not quite forgotten, connection of resurrection with nature-cults. Imagery drawn from the world of creation is not the same thing as long-distance borrowing from ancient cults. Day's suggestion, however, that the post-exilic situation, with its attention to the problem of suffering and theodicy, contributed materially to the development of earlier hints into a full-blown proposal (private correspondence, June 2000), seems to me fair enough.

a part of it.[175] This, indeed, may help to explain why Jewish thinkers came to a belief in resurrection only very late, when the main opponent to traditional belief was not a local vegetation-cult, but the power of Babylon and, later, Syria.[176] We may make a similar point to the earlier one about the unlikeliness of Zoroastrian borrowings: if Israel's exile had come about through compromise with the pagan gods and their nature-religions, it is hardly likely that the prophets who predicted that the exile would be undone, and the covenant renewed, would borrow a central image from those religions to develop their theme. The safest conclusion we can draw is that the belief in resurrection we find in Daniel 12.2–3 is the surprising but comprehensible result of the bringing together of two other beliefs: (a) Israel's ancient belief that her god, YHWH, was the creator god, and that human life reflecting his image meant bodily life in this world, not disembodied post-mortem existence; and (b) the new belief that Israel's exile was to be seen as the punishment for sin, and the belief that exile reached a kind of climax in the fate of the martyrs. YHWH's answer to his people's exile would be, metaphorically, life from the dead (Isaiah 26, Ezekiel 37); YHWH's answer to his people's martyrdom would be, literally, life from the dead (Daniel 12). This was a bold step indeed, but it was the last step in a comprehensible line of thought going back to the earliest roots of Israelite belief.

5. Conclusion

The constant factor, throughout the types of belief we have surveyed, is Israel's god himself. The vision of YHWH's creation and covenant; his promises and his faithfulness to them; his purposes for Israel, not least his gift of the land; his power over all opposing forces, including finally death itself; his love for the world, for his human creatures, for Israel in particular, and especially for those who served him and followed in his way; his justice, because of which evil would eventually be condemned and righteousness upheld – this vision of the creator and covenant god underlies the ancient belief in the national and territorial hope, the emerging belief that the relationship with YHWH would be unbreakable even by death, and the eventual belief that YHWH would raise the dead. The biblical language of resurrection ('standing up', 'awakening' etc.), when it emerges, is simple and direct; the belief, though infrequent, is clear. It involves, not a *reconstrual* of life after death, but the *reversal* of death itself. It is not about discovering that Sheol is not such a bad place after all. It is not a way of saying that the dust will

---

[175] So Martin-Achard 1960, 202; Johnston 2002, 237. Yamauchi 1965, 290 finds that in relation to the mythological embodiments of these gods (Tammuz, Adonis, etc.) clear, pre-Christian evidence for the resurrection of these gods is said to be lacking. There is nothing like bodily resurrection, either. See, more recently, Mettinger 2001, 70.

[176] So Martin-Achard 1960, 203, following Baumgartner.

learn to be happy as dust. The language of awakening is not a new, exciting way of talking about sleep. It is a way of saying that a time will come when sleepers will sleep no more. Creation itself, celebrated throughout the Hebrew scriptures, will be reaffirmed, remade.

The national element in this hope is never abandoned. The promise remains. But out of that promise there has grown something new, which, once grown, will not (as we shall see) wither away: the belief in resurrection, not just as an image for the restoration of nation and land but as a literal prediction of one element in that restoration; not simply metaphor, but also metonymy. It is that double function that we shall now explore as we trace the meaning of 'resurrection', within the broader context of continuing thought about life after death, through the turbulent world of second-Temple Judaism.

Chapter Four

TIME TO WAKE UP (2):
HOPE BEYOND DEATH IN POST-BIBLICAL JUDAISM

1. Introduction: The Spectrum

Jews, it used to be said, believed in resurrection, while Greeks believed in
immortality. Like most half-truths, this one is as misleading as it is informative, if not more so. If the Bible offers a spectrum of belief about life after
death, the second-Temple period provides something more like an artist's
palette: dozens of options, with different ways of describing similar positions and similar ways of describing different ones. The more texts and
tombstones we study, the more there seem to be. Almost any position one
can imagine on the subject appears to have been espoused by some Jews
somewhere in the period between the Maccabaean crisis and the writing of
the Mishnah, roughly 200 BC to AD 200.[1]

And yet. The old half-truth had got hold of something which is in itself
quite remarkable. As we have seen, the Bible mostly denies or at least
ignores the possibility of a future life, with only a few texts coming out
strongly for a different view; but in the second-Temple period the position is
more or less reversed. The evidence suggests that by the time of Jesus,
roughly in the middle of the period we are now examining, most Jews either
believed in some form of resurrection or at least knew that it was standard
teaching. Comparatively few remained sceptical. Some held to a kind of
middle position – not exactly that of Psalm 73, but not too far off from it
either – in which a blessed, albeit disembodied, immortality awaited the

---

[1] Some older surveys of this material carried an agenda according to which it was
important to show all forms of second-Temple Judaism to be either a declining away from
biblical standards or a failure to anticipate early Christianity (cf. e.g. Eichrodt 1961–7,
2.526–9). This is methodologically misleading. New post-biblical situations called forth
new expressions; and the early Christians were all second-Temple Jews, who certainly did
not read the Bible 'straight', in the sense of a reading unmediated by their own culture. The
short survey of some recent scholarship in Barr 1992, 1–4, itself of course mediated by
Barr's own ideas, indicates the kind of minefield into which these discussions lead.

righteous after their death. But there is widespread evidence that the belief which burst into full flower in Daniel 12 had become standard. That text, indeed, seems to stand behind a good deal of the later development.

In approaching this many-coloured palette of beliefs, we must remind ourselves once more that the words 'resurrection' and 'immortality' have become used far too loosely, often as though they were equal and opposite, so that one might swap them to and fro as alternatives within the same sort of sentence or paragraph. The reality is more complex. Those who believed in resurrection believed also that the dead, who would be raised in the future but had not been yet, were alive somewhere, somehow, in an interim state. Whether we call this state 'immortality', or find another word to indicate a continuing though disembodied existence, is itself a delicate question. The word 'immortality' is often taken to imply, not just that the humans in question happen to be in some sense still alive after their deaths, but that there always was within them, as for Plato, an immortal element, perhaps the soul, which is incapable of dying. But this, as we saw earlier, is not the view of those biblical writers who, it seems, came to believe that their relationship with YHWH would continue after their death. Such continuation was based solely on YHWH's character (as the loving, powerful creator), not on anything innate within human beings. Thus all who believed in 'resurrection' believed in some sense in the continuing existence, after death, of those who would be raised, as did those who believed simply in the immortality of the soul; but how they described that continuing existence, and what they based it on, could vary significantly. Furthermore, those who believed in 'resurrection', as we have seen in relation to the biblical material, did not conceive of that final goal as simply a parallel option to those who believed in a permanently disembodied future state. It was not that some believed in a continuing disembodied life and others believed in a continuing embodied one. Resurrection, we must again insist, meant life *after* 'life after death': a two-stage future hope, as opposed to the single-stage expectation of those who believed in a non-bodily future life.

Since the expectations of second-Temple Jews form the grid of meaning within which the early Christians' use of resurrection-language must be plotted (however much it burst the boundaries, it was those boundaries, rather than some other ones, that it was bursting), we must focus particular attention on what exactly they meant by 'resurrection' itself.[2] We shall discover that the concept is quite specific in some respects and quite vague in others. It clearly refers to a newly embodied existence; it is never a way of talking about ghosts, phantoms or spirits. Yet what precisely the resurrection will be like – how Daniel 12.2–3 will work out in practice, if you like – remains imprecise. Will it, for instance, be some kind of resuscitation into a

---

[2] For the present chapter, see, in addition to the works already referred to at the start of ch. 3, Stemberger 1972; Bauckham 1998a, 1998b.

life barely different from the present one, except more pleasant? Or will it involve a kind of transformation? On this point there is no precision; and this imprecision is itself a matter of considerable interest as we approach the study of early Christianity.

In order to locate the meanings of 'resurrection' within the larger picture, it is important again to examine the full range of views on the whole subject of life after death. At one point at least we can be precise and certain. The Sadducees, who were the ruling elite of Judaea, including the high priestly family, denied that there would be a future life. This denial remains important in the literature of both early Christianity and rabbinic Judaism, and we must begin our survey here.

2. No Future Life, or None to Speak of: The Sadducees

The three best sources for the beliefs, positive and negative, of the Sadducees are the New Testament, Josephus and the rabbis.[3] None of them was neutral in reporting the Sadducees. The New Testament, not surprisingly, sees their rejection of resurrection as their main characteristic. Josephus (who, as an aristocrat, may have been closer to them than he cares to let on) describes them as though they were really a hellenistic philosophical school. The rabbis speak mostly of their attitude to purity. This is all we have to go on. After AD 70 there were no Sadducees left to answer back or put the record straight. But from the sources' fairly solid agreement on the point it is clear that we are on the right track. Basically, the Sadducees denied resurrection; it seems more than likely that they followed a quite strict interpretation of the Old Testament, and denied any significant future life at all. But, as will become apparent, the contemporary instinct to see the Sadducees as the radicals, because they denied the resurrection, is 180 degrees wide of the mark. They denied it because they were the conservatives.

Matthew, Mark and Luke all report the Sadducees' question to Jesus, designed (as were similar questions reported by the rabbis) to make fun of the idea of resurrection and so to disprove it by a *reductio ad absurdum*. The three synoptists simply state, by way of introduction, that the Sadducees 'say there is no resurrection'; and the question they ask shows well enough the line of argument they present. Just imagine a particular case, they say, and you will see how absurd resurrection is.[4]

---

[3] On the Sadducees cf. *NTPG* 209–13; and e.g. Meyer in *TDNT* 7.35–54; Le Moyne 1972; Schwankl 1987, 332–8; Saldarini 1988, ch. 13; Sanders 1992, ch. 15; Porton 1992, 2000; Puech 1993, 202–12; Stemberger 1999 (with full bibliog.); Juhász 2002, 112–4. We have no documents that we can be sure are written by Sadducees themselves. Porton 1992, 892 points out that when Josephus three times describes the belief of the Sadducees (*War* 2.162; *Ant.* 13.293; 18.16f.), no single belief appears in all of the lists.

[4] Mt. 22.23/ Mk. 12.18/ Lk. 20.27. The passages will be discussed below, ch. 9, 415–29.

Less well known perhaps, but equally important, is Luke's comment in Acts as Paul faces a hearing before the Jewish council. Paul, he says, realizing that some council members were Sadducees and some Pharisees, declares that what is at stake in his case is resurrection itself, on which (he says) he sides firmly with the Pharisees. This precipitates an argument between the two factions, and the court breaks up in disorder. Luke's description is interesting, though tricky, and we must look at it carefully because it provides important evidence not only for the Sadducees but also for the Pharisees:

> [7]As he said this, a row flared up between the Pharisees and the Sadducees, and the gathering was split down the middle. [8](The Sadducees say that there is no resurrection – neither angel, nor spirit – but the Pharisees confess them both.) [9]There was a great uproar, and some of the scribes from the Pharisaic party rose up and became belligerent. 'We find nothing wrong with this man,' they said. 'Supposing a spirit or an angel spoke to him?'[5]

The scene is thoroughly believable; and we must remember, of course, that the Luke who is writing this, and making sidelong explanatory comments, is the same Luke who describes Jesus' own resurrection in considerable detail in the final chapter of his gospel. The crucial phrase comes in the strange sentence in brackets in verse 8. Many translations flatten it out: NRSV, for example, writes, 'the Sadducees say that there is no resurrection, or angel, or spirit; but the Pharisees acknowledge all three.' There are three problems with this. First, if that was what Luke intended to say, he went about it a very strange way, using 'neither . . . nor' with 'angel' and 'spirit', followed by a word which means 'both', as of two, not 'all three'.[6] The Pharisees' response, interestingly, confirms this, and helps to elucidate matters, by highlighting not the resurrection itself but the either/or of angel and spirit. Second, there is no other evidence that the Sadducees denied the existence of angels and spirits; since they claimed to base their views on the Pentateuch, in which angels make frequent appearances and spirits are far from unknown (not least the spirit of YHWH, though that is perhaps not relevant

---

[5] Ac. 23.7–9. On the passage see recently Kilgallen 1986; Schwankl 1987, 332–8; Daube 1990; Viviano and Taylor 1992. See too below, 454.

[6] BDAG 55 suggests 'all' as a possible meaning of *amphotera*, the word in question; but since the NT evidence offered consists of the present passage and the strange passage in 19.16, with very few classical parallels, it is better to take it as meaning 'both' if possible. LSJ cite only Ac. 19.16 and a single papyrus as evidence of the meaning 'all', whereas not only is the meaning 'both' normal, frequent and widespread, but compounds from the word always have a sense of duality (e.g. *amphoterakis*, 'in both ways', or *amphoterekes*, 'two-edged'). Stemberger's suggestion (in Wissman, Stemberger, Hoffman et al. 1979, 441) that angels/spirits must be taken as a hendiadys, so that 'both' means resurrection on the one hand and angels/spirits on the other, is very hard to square with the 'neither . . . nor' of the text, and the 'spirit or angel' of v. 9.

here), it is very unlikely that they did in fact deny their existence.[7] Third, Luke is very clear both in his gospel and in Acts that the resurrection of Jesus himself did *not* involve Jesus becoming, or even becoming like, an angel or a spirit.[8] Thus, though attempts have been made to say that 'neither angel nor spirit' refers to different interpretations of the resurrection – resurrection life seen as angelic or spiritual – it is far more likely that Luke meant something else.[9]

The most likely interpretation – and a very revealing one it is – is that those who held to belief in resurrection in this period, that is, the Pharisees, had also developed regular ways of describing the intermediate state.[10] In that world, nobody supposed the dead were *already* raised; resurrection, as we have seen, describes new bodily life *after* a present mode of 'life after death'.[11] So: where and what are the dead now? To this, we may surmise (and verse 9 will demonstrate it further), the Pharisees gave the answer: they are at present like angels, or spirits. They are presently disembodied; in the future, they will receive their new embodiment. What the Sadducees denied, then, was on the one hand the resurrection, and on the other hand the two current accounts of the intermediate state. They did not deny the existence of angels or spirits, but they denied that the dead were in a state that could be so described.[12]

The Pharisees' retort is then spot on. They do not suppose for a moment that Paul has actually been a witness of the resurrection itself; that is out of the question as far as they are concerned. 'The resurrection', from their point of view, will take place at a future date when all the righteous dead are raised to share God's new world. But they wonder – in the heat of the argument, and without knowing very much of Paul's developed views – whether he may perhaps have had a visitation from someone who, though not yet bodily raised, is presently in the intermediate state between death and resurrection, and whose existence in that state, and communication with the living from that state, provides evidence (they would say) that they *will* be

---

[7] Though that is the view of the C4 AD Epiphanius, *Panarion* 14 – presumably dependent on the present passage.

[8] cf. e.g. Lk. 24.37–9; and see below, chs. 8 and 9, on Lk. and Ac.

[9] Lk. 24.37–9. The view I am opposing is that taken by e.g. Viviano and Taylor 1992.

[10] In this I follow Daube 1990, who is supported by Fletcher-Louis 1997, 57–61. Fletcher-Louis is wrong, however, to suggest that Daube's position was anticipated by Stroumsa 1981; Stroumsa, agreeing that the angel and spirit are something different from the resurrection, interprets them as the Pharisaic beliefs in a special angel and spirit associated with messianic expectation.

[11] Daube 1990, 493: 'the span between death and resurrection, which, in widespread belief, a good person spends in the realm or mode of an angel or spirit'.

[12] It is of course also possible, amid the variegated speculations of the times, that they would also deny what is asserted in e.g. *2 Bar.* 51.10, that the righteous will be 'like angels'. Here, though, as in Mk. 12.25 and par., it is not stated that the righteous *become* angels, merely that they are *like* them; cf. 421f. below.

raised in the future.[13] (This, as we shall see, is similar to the argument Jesus uses when he is himself in debate with the Sadducees.) While not, therefore, giving any credence to Paul's actual claim, that Jesus was already raised from the dead (they may not even have been aware that that was the centre of Paul's message), they are quite prepared to allow that he may have had a meeting with an 'angelic' or 'spiritual' being, to be identified as the post-death but pre-resurrection state of someone or other. Paul is thus, from their point of view, potentially at least on the side of the angels.

An interesting parallel to this text is found in an earlier passage in Acts 12, where Luke gives an unexpected display of talent in comic writing. Peter has just been miraculously released from prison by an angel, the night before Herod Agrippa was intending to have him executed. A group of Christians is meeting in the house of Mary, Mark's mother, to pray for him. Peter comes to the house and knocks at the door, and a maid called Rhoda goes to answer it:

> [14]When she recognized Peter's voice, from sheer joy she didn't open the door, but ran in and announced that Peter was standing outside the door. [15]'You're mad,' they said to her. But she insisted it was indeed the case. 'It's his angel!' they said. [16]Peter continued knocking; they opened the door, saw him, and were amazed.[14]

The key phrase is in verse 15: 'It's his angel.' The praying Christians – a wonderful example of faith in answered prayer – believed that Peter must have been executed in the prison. They, like most societies ancient and modern, knew well enough that grieving friends and relatives sometimes receive what seems like a personal visit, vision or apparition in which the recently deceased appears for a few moments, perhaps says something, and then disappears again. This is perfectly compatible with them going off (in this case) to the prison, requesting the body, and burying it in the normal way. 'It's his angel', in other words, does not mean, 'He has been raised from the dead.' It is a way of referring to the intermediate 'angelic' state in which the person will now remain, with his body dead and buried, until the resurrection. And it is this intermediate state, in whatever form it is described, that the Sadducees seem to have denied, along with the doctrine of resurrection itself.

The New Testament account of the Sadducees is backed up in this respect by Josephus. The Sadducees, he says, will have nothing to do with 'the persistence of the soul after death, penalties in the underworld, and rewards'.[15] More specifically, 'the Sadducees hold that the soul perishes along with the

---

[13] Daube 1990, 495 speaks of the Pharisees wondering whether Paul had been converted 'not by Jesus resurrected but by Jesus on leave as, or represented by, an angel or spirit'.

[14] Ac. 12.14–16.

[15] *War* 2.165. Josephus' picture of the Sadducees here is not far removed from his sketch of the Epicureans in *Ant.* 10.278 (see below on mSanh 10.1); similarly, he aligns the Pharisees with the Stoics, and the Essenes with the Pythagoreans, in an attempt to make the Jewish sects seem to his audience like hellenistic philosophical schools.

body.'[16] This, as will be apparent, is closely in line with Luke's account: the Sadducees not only deny the resurrection, but also rule out any post-mortem existence that might lead to it.

The Mishnah and Talmud are equally clear:

> The Sadducees asked Rabban Gamaliel whence it could be proved that the Holy One, blessed be He, makes the dead alive again. He said to them: From the Law, the Prophets, and the Writings. But they would not accept this.[17]

> All Israelites have a share in the world to come . . . And these are they that have no share in the world to come: he that says that there is no resurrection of the dead prescribed in the Law; and he that says that the Law is not from Heaven; and an Epicurean.[18]

Some texts of the Mishnah omit the phrase 'prescribed in the Law'; this makes the ban all the more general – denial of resurrection, not just denying that it is taught in Torah – but probably misses the point of the original debate, in which the Sadducees held the resurrection to be a recent innovation, not taught in the Five Books of Moses. The controversy was reflected in a liturgical change:

> At the close of every Benediction in the Temple they used to say, 'For everlasting' [lit.: 'from the age']; but after the heretics had taught corruptly and said that there is but one age, it was ordained that they should say, 'from everlasting to everlasting' [lit.: 'from the age to the age'].[19]

The point here is that the Sadducees are accused of teaching that there is no 'age to come' or 'world to come'; the same Hebrew word, *'olam*, means both 'world' and 'age'. The Pharisees believed strongly in 'the age/world to come', in which present wrongs would be righted. Without that, they held, one would simply work for rewards and compensations in the present life –

---

[16] *Ant.* 18.16. On the Josephus passages cf. *NTPG* 211f., 325, and below, 177f.

[17] bSanh. 90b. The Gamaliel in question is presumably the Gamaliel of Ac. 5.34; the debate in question is therefore roughly contemporary with Jesus and Paul. (The fact that the source may have stylized it does not mean it is not thoroughly credible in exactly that period.)

[18] mSanh. 10.1. 'Epicurean' may be an abusive way of referring to the Sadducees as licentious, an accusation which probably combines memories of the Sadducees' wealthy lifestyle and their known denial of any future life in which retribution could be made (cf. mAb. 1.7). On this passage see Urbach 1987 [1975, 1979], 652, and the notes (991f.) on mBer. 5.2; mSot. 9.15. The Sadducees are not named in this passage, but there is no question that it is they who are in mind; the absence of the label enables the text to refer to anyone who might revive such a point of view.

[19] mBer. 9.5. Some MSS read 'Sadducees' instead of 'heretics' (so Danby note in loc., citing *JQR* 6, 1915, 314); this is certainly the intended meaning. Cf. Le Moyne 1972, 97–9. The Sadducees thus unwittingly precipitated a liturgical change which remains a feature of many prayers, Christian as well as Jewish, to the present day.

a doctrine which would have suited the Sadducees very well, and would have suited anti-Sadducean polemic even better.

The closest we come to statements from the Sadducees themselves, or to one whom they might regard as a spiritual ancestor, is the Wisdom of Jesus ben Sirach ('Ecclesiasticus'). From what we know of them, the Sadducees would certainly have approved of Sirach's attitude to death and what might lie beyond:

> Give, and take, and indulge yourself,
> because in Hades one cannot look for luxury.
> All living beings become old like a garment,
> for the decree from of old is, 'You must die!'[20]

> Who will sing praises to the Most High in Hades
> in place of the living who give thanks?
> From the dead, as from one who does not exist, thanksgiving has ceased;
> those who are alive and well sing the Lord's praises.[21]

> Do not forget, there is no coming back;
> you do the dead no good [by excessive mourning], and you injure yourself.
> Remember his fate, for yours is like it;
> yesterday it was his, and today it is yours.
> When the dead is at rest, let his remembrance rest too,
> and be comforted for him when his spirit has departed.[22]

> This is the Lord's decree for all flesh;
> why then should you reject the will of the Most High?
> Whether life lasts for ten years or a hundred or a thousand,
> there are no questions asked in Hades.[23]

There is one passage in Sirach where it looks for a moment as though the prospect of post-mortem judgment is being brought to bear on moral behaviour:

> It is easy for the Lord on the day of death
> to reward individuals according to their conduct.
> An hour's misery makes one forget past delights,
> and at the close of one's life one's deeds are revealed.[24]

But the next verse indicates that the reward in question is simply that of good or bad reputation:

---

[20] Sir. 14.16f.

[21] Sir. 17.27f. Cf. Riley 1995, 11.

[22] Sir. 38.21–3.

[23] Sir. 41.4. On the scribal additions to and reinterpretations of Sir., and their possible relevance for our present question see Puech 1990 (on 48.11); 1993, 74–6; Gilbert 1999, 275–81.

[24] Sir. 11.26f.

Call no one happy before his death;
by how he ends, a person becomes known.[25]

It is this reputation, and the hope contained in the new generation, that offers such hope as is to be found in the present life:

Like abundant leaves on a spreading tree
that sheds some and puts forth others,
so are the generations of flesh and blood:
one dies and another is born.
Every work decays and ceases to exist,
and the one who made it will pass away with it.[26]

There is hope here of a kind, but it is not the kind that the Pharisees were offering.

Why, we may ask, did the Sadducees hold out against the doctrine of resurrection? It is noticeable that aristocrats down the years, and across many cultures, have taken what steps they could to ensure that the comfort and luxury they have enjoyed in the present life will continue into the future one. Certainly this was so in ancient Egypt and many other societies. Sometimes slaves would be killed, perhaps even wives, to provide appropriate household members for the deceased in the life beyond. Likewise, powerful groups have sometimes advocated a strong post-mortem hope as a way of stopping the poor and powerless grumbling about their lot in the present life. And, where 'resurrection' has become an official dogma within a powerful system, it has had the capacity to become simply another instrument to keep the ordinary people in line. It goes against such sociological assumptions to see first-century Jewish aristocrats staunchly denying any future life. Their own supposed explanation – that the doctrine was not to be found in the foundational texts of scripture, namely the Pentateuch – is as we have seen *prima facie* true; there is nothing remotely like Daniel 12.2–3, Isaiah 26.19 or Ezekiel 37.1–14 to be found either in the Pentateuch or in the whole of the 'Former Prophets' (the historical books from Joshua to Kings). But by the first century, as we shall see, the discovery of 'resurrection' texts even in the Torah itself had become a regular occupation of the Pharisees, as it was to become, in a measure, of the Christians also. Why were the Sadducees committed to resisting this?

One possibility is that they were afraid of the wrong kind of interest in the dead. Granted the widespread pagan practices we looked at earlier in this section, it is not to be wondered at if Jewish leaders would regard the cult of the dead as dangerous and unsavoury. They may well have seen belief in resurrection, with its attendant beliefs in angelic and spiritual intermediate

---

[25] Sir. 11.28 – echoing, of course, the well-known maxim of Solon (cf. Hdt. 1.32.7).
[26] Sir. 14.18f.

states, as half way to spiritualism or necromancy. But this does not, I think, get to the heart of it.

The real problem was that resurrection was from the beginning a revolutionary doctrine.[27] For Daniel 12, resurrection belief went with dogged resistance and martyrdom. For Isaiah and Ezekiel, it was about YHWH restoring the fortunes of his people. It had to do with the coming new age, when the life-giving god would act once more to turn everything upside down – or perhaps, as they might have said, right way up. It was the sort of belief that encouraged young hotheads to attack Roman symbols placed on the Temple, and that, indeed, led the first-century Jews into the most disastrous war they had experienced.[28] It was not simply, even, that they thought such beliefs might lead the nation into a clash with Rome, though that will certainly have been the case.[29] It was that they realized that such beliefs threatened their own position. People who believe that their god is about to make a new world, and that those who die in loyalty to him in the meantime will rise again to share gloriously in it, are far more likely to lose respect for a wealthy aristocracy than people who think that this life, this world and this age are the only ones there ever will be.[30]

We should note carefully the difference, at this point, between the promise of 'heaven', seen as a post-mortem comfort offered by the wealthy and powerful to the poor and powerless, on the one hand, and resurrection on the other. Resurrection is precisely concerned with the present world and its renewal, not with escaping the present world and going somewhere else; and, in its early Jewish forms right through to its developed Christian forms, it was always concerned with divine judgment, with the creator god acting within history to put right that which is wrong. Only if we misunderstand what resurrection actually involved can we line it up with the kind of 'pie in the sky' promises which earned the scorn of many twentieth-century social reformers.[31]

It is possible that, since the Sadducees were the spiritual and probably the physical descendants of the priest/king dynasty of the Hasmonean period, they may have retained a memory of the book of Daniel, and the doctrine of resurrection, as being in favour with those who wanted to subvert them in that earlier period. Significantly, Jesus' discussion with the Sadducees is set

---

[27] Segal 1997 eventually sees this point (113) in relation to the rabbis, having apparently missed it (106f.) in relation to the Sadducees.

[28] cf. *NTPG* 172, 176–81, 190–97.

[29] So Martin-Achard 1960, 226, following the C19 scholar F. Schwally.

[30] So e.g. Stemberger in Wissman, Stemberger, Hoffman et al. 1979, 442, stressing that the conservatism of the Sadducees and the priests in general was religious in nature.

[31] The 'pie in the sky' jibe originated with the American labour leader and songwriter Joe Hill (Joel Hägglund, 1879–1915), in a bitterly satirical song called 'Preacher and the Slave,': 'You will eat, bye and bye,/ in that glorious land above the sky,/ Work and pray, live on hay,/ You'll get pie in the sky when you die' (from his 'Songs of the Workers' (1911)).

by the synoptic evangelists among a string of other discussions and parables all of which in some way or other highlight the revolutionary nature of what Jesus had just done in the Temple.[32]

If the Sadducees were the main proponents of the view which, claiming considerable biblical support, denied any significant future life, they were not, it seems, the only people who took that line.[33] Three writings from the final centuries BC indicate a similar position, and we have no reason to suppose that they were specifically Sadducean. In strong contrast to the book which now follows it, 1 Maccabees holds out no hope for a future life, but only for a glorious memory among those who come after.[34] Tobit, a book which has more than most to say about death, has nothing whatever to say about what comes afterwards, except when, in the final prayer, it echoes Deuteronomy's statement about Israel's god leading people down to Hades and bringing them up from the abyss – which seems, in context, to be a prediction of the eagerly awaited return from exile.[35] Apart from that, the only advice seems to be to avoid death at all costs, in particular by giving alms.[36] And 1 Baruch, like Sirach, repeats the regular Old Testament warning: those in Hades, whose spirit has been taken from their bodies, will not ascribe glory or justice to YHWH.[37] This may be an argument from silence; but when a context cries out for something to be said, when a culture provides the possibility to say something, and when a text refuses that possibility, the argument is not as weak as is sometimes supposed.

We should hardly be surprised that this view persisted quite strongly throughout the period up to AD 70. (We may suspect that many Jews held it after that time as well, though with the disappearance of the Sadducees, and the dominance of the post-Pharisaic rabbis, such people have left us no trace except perhaps the odd tombstone.) It was, after all, consonant with the natural meaning of much of the biblical text. As we have seen, it can also be explained in terms of the political dynamics of the time. Resurrection, depending as it did on a strong belief in the justice and sovereign power of the good creator god, was always bound to be a revolutionary doctrine. But before we can examine this further we must look at the second major option

---

[32] See *JVG* 493–510; and below, 415–29.

[33] I leave to one side the interesting, but for our purposes irrelevant, position of the Samaritans, some or all of whom seem to have denied the resurrection: cf. Isser 1999, 580–88. For a funerary inscription from Mount Scopus which seems to deny the resurrection cf. Cross 1983; Williams 1999, 75–93.

[34] 1 Macc. 2.49–70.

[35] Tob. 13.2, 5; cf. Dt. 32.39; 30.3.

[36] Tob. 4.10; 12.9; 14.10f.

[37] Bar. 2.17. In context this is part of a prayer, not just for the individual to be spared death, but for Israel, already in exile, to be spared the full 'death' of remaining in exile for ever. Baruch thus prays for the same end as Ezek. 37, but, instead of seeing Israel already 'dead' and needing resurrection, sees the nation as *almost* dead and, like the Psalmist in Ps. 16 (above, 104), prays to be spared this fate, even at the eleventh hour.

for Jews at this period. There might after all be a life beyond death which did not involve a new this-worldly existence. A blessed but disembodied post-mortem life seemed to some to have the best of both worlds, Jew and Greek alike.

3. Blessed (and Disembodied) Immortality

By the time of Jesus and Paul, Judaism had found itself for over two centuries at the centre of swirling cultural and political winds. The conquests of Alexander the Great in the fourth century, and of Antiochus in the second, together with all the social and cultural changes they brought, challenged devotion, faith and understanding as much as they did political structures.[38] Here the historian may be tempted to oversimplify, not least because some of our key texts do so as well, seeing Judaism divided into those who kept the true faith and those who capitulated to Hellenism, as much in their thinking as in their compromised politics. Yet even those who resisted assimilation did so, in our period, from within what was inescapably hellenistic Judaism; by the time of the first century AD all the many varieties of Judaism were to a lesser or greater extent hellenistic, including those anchored firmly in the soil and cult of Palestine.

There is still, however, a distinction between being forced to drink polluted water and bottling it up for sale – or, to put it from the other point of view, between gratefully accepting and profiting from the god-given wisdom of the wider world and stubbornly clinging to outmoded concepts. Many Jews, we may suspect, were only dimly aware of these great cultural questions and their tell-tale everyday signs, which the historian can pick out with the advantage not only of hindsight but of the random process of selection known as 'the vagaries of history'. Thus from our very limited evidence, and our distant perspective, it appears to us that there were some Jews in this period who rejected the Sadducees' denial, believing that there was indeed a future life beyond death, but who equally rejected the increasingly popular belief in resurrection. Instead, they postulated, and celebrated, a future blissful life for the righteous, in which souls, disencumbered of their attendant physical bodies, would enjoy a perfect life for ever.

For such thoughts to be thinkable, the step had to be taken, more explicitly than anywhere in the Old Testament, to describe how the soul or spirit would leave the physical body at death and be capable, not just of going to Sheol, but of further more dynamic experiences.[39] There are several

---

[38] For a brief account of the period cf. *NTPG* ch. 6.

[39] We cannot here go into more detail on the multiple problems caused by the regular LXX translation of *nephesh* as *psyche*, for instance in Ps. 16 [LXX 15].10, 'you will not leave my *nephesh/psyche* in Sheol', where the Hebrew seems to designate the whole life, while

signs of this move in the second-Temple period. 'The soul lives on after death,' declares *Pseudo-Phocylides*:

> For the souls remain unharmed among the deceased.
> For the spirit is a loan of God to mortals, and his image.
> For we have a body out of earth,
> and when afterward we are resolved again into earth we are but dust;
> and then the air has received our spirit . . .
> All alike are corpses, but God rules over the souls.
> Hades is our common eternal home and fatherland,
> a common place for all, poor and kings.
> We humans live not a long time but for a season.
> But our soul is immortal and lives ageless forever.[40]

However, a couple of lines earlier the same text declares, confusingly to our ears:

> It is not good to dissolve the human frame;
> for we hope that the remains of the departed
> will soon come to the light again out of the earth;
> and afterward they will become gods.[41]

So, too, the *Testament of Abraham* (which is later, and may reflect Christian influence) declares that Abraham will be taken after his death to Paradise,

> where there are the tents of my righteous ones and [where] the mansions of my holy ones, Isaac and Jacob, are in his bosom, where there is no toil, no grief, no moaning, but peace and exultation and endless life.[42]

A further example of this new perspective on the make-up and destiny of human beings is found in the Ethiopic book of Enoch. Though there are suggestive echoes of Daniel 12.2–3 later on in the same passage, here at least we seem to be moving in a decidedly hellenistic direction, in which the immortal soul passes out of the body and on to either bliss or torment:

> All good things, and joy and honour are prepared for and written down for the souls of those who died in righteousness . . . The spirits of those who died in righteousness shall live and rejoice; their spirits shall not perish, nor their memorial from before the face of the Great One unto all the generations of the world . . . Woe unto you sinners who are dead! . . . You yourselves know that they will bring your [other MSS: their] souls down to Sheol; and they shall experience evil and great tribulation . . .

---

the Greek, read within post-Platonic hellenistic culture, would push the reader in the direction of a body/soul dualism.

[40] *Ps.-Phoc.* 105–15 (tr. van der Horst in Charlesworth 1985, 578). The work is hard to date but probably from the first centuries BC or AD.

[41] *Ps.-Phoc.* 102–04. See the next section below.

[42] *T. Abr.* [rec. A] 20.14 (tr. Sanders in Charlesworth 1983, 895). Cf. *NTPG* 331 n. 168. On the use of 'Abraham's bosom' in Lk. 16.22f. see below, 438.

> Your souls shall enter into the great judgment; it shall be a great judgment in all the generations of the world.[43]

In the same way Hillel (first century BC) was supposed to have spoken of the soul as being a guest in the house of life;[44] and Johanan ben Zakkai (late first century AD) was said to have wept at the end of his life because he feared the judge who had power to assign people either to the Garden of Eden or to Gehenna.[45] We must assume, from everything else we know of the Pharisaic tradition (see below), that these great sages believed in eventual resurrection; here they seem to have been employing new concepts of a body/soul dualism to explain what happened between bodily death and the final state of blessedness. So too 4 Ezra, which seems clearly to teach eventual resurrection, speaks explicitly of the spirit or soul leaving the 'corruptible vessel', i.e. the mortal body, with wicked souls condemned to wander about in torments, and righteous souls entering into a joyful rest in anticipation of final glory.[46] The idea of a soul separable from the body, with different theories as to what might happen to it thereafter, was widespread in the varied Judaisms of the turn of the eras.[47] Several funerary inscriptions bear witness to this kind of belief.[48]

This offered one way, though by no means the only one, of coming to terms with persecution and suffering. Though, as we shall see, 2 Maccabees used the story of the persecutions under Antiochus to teach a definitely bodily resurrection, the later 4 Maccabees went in the other direction, insisting that though the body could be harmed and killed, the soul could not.[49] This means that one can cheerfully give up one's body; the true gift of God is the soul, which cannot be taken away. Thus, in a passage with interesting resonances for those who know the New Testament, 4 Maccabees urges:

> Let us with all our hearts consecrate ourselves to God, who gave us our lives, and let us use our bodies as a bulwark for the law. Let us not fear him who thinks he is killing us, for great is the struggle of the soul and the danger of eternal torment lying before those who transgress the commandment of God. Therefore let us put on the full armour of self-control, which is divine reason. For if we so die, Abraham and Isaac and Jacob will welcome us, and all the fathers will praise us.[50]

The body is thus demeaned; it must be overcome by the rational faculty of

---

[43] *1 En.* 103.3–8; for the fuller picture in this passage see below, 156f.

[44] Lev. R. 34.3 (on 25.25).

[45] bBer. 28b.

[46] 4 Ez. 7.75, 78–80, 88, 95; see below, 160.

[47] For a summary see e.g. Dihle in *TDNT* 9.633–5.

[48] See Williams 1999, 90f.

[49] 4 Macc. 10.4 (not all MSS contain this verse). On the apparent parallel with Mt. 10.28/Lk. 12.4f. see below, 431.

[50] 4 Macc. 13.13–17.

the soul.[51] Those who give their lives for God share the immortality of the patriarchs:

> They believe that they, like our patriarchs Abraham and Isaac and Jacob, do not die to God, but live to God . . .
> They knew also that those who die for the sake of God live to God, as do Abraham and Isaac and Jacob and all the patriarchs.[52]

The book ends with a confident statement of the same theme:

> But the sons of Abraham with their victorious mother are gathered together into the chorus of the fathers, and have received pure and immortal souls from God, to whom be glory forever and ever. Amen.[53]

Assuming, as we must, that the writer knew and was using 2 Maccabees, we may state confidently that for this book at least there was a conscious redactional decision to delete all mention of bodily resurrection and substitute a version of the doctrine of the immortal soul, or at least of souls that could become immortal through the pursuit of wisdom. The critical point for our investigation is that, whereas in 2 Maccabees there is a two-stage expectation (a period of waiting following the martyr's death, and then bodily resurrection at some future date), here, quite clearly, there is only one stage: the martyrs go, immediately upon death, into the blissful immortality already enjoyed by Abraham, Isaac and Jacob. This is not just, then, what we shall find in some passages of Josephus, namely, a 'translation' of resurrection belief into the language of pagan philosophy; it looks as though the author intends not merely to communicate a strange idea to an uncomprehending audience, but actually to change the idea itself.[54]

It is possible that we should see a similar move made in a (controverted) passage in *Jubilees* (written around the middle of the second century BC). The writer describes how people will eventually return to the study and practice of the commandments, and how life will flourish and wickedness be abolished. Without, it seems, a cataclysmic break, the world, or at least Israel, will live in peace and rejoicing, with no Satan, no evil one to destroy (23.27–9). Then, the passage goes on:

---

[51] 4 Macc. 3.18; 6.7; 10.19f.

[52] 4 Macc. 7.19; 16.25; cf. 9.22; 14.5; 16.13; 17.12. On the apparent parallel between 'live to God' here and Jesus' words in Lk. 20.38 see below, 252, 425; and cp. Rom. 6.10; 14.8f.; Gal. 2.19. Grappe 2001, 60–71 makes 'live to God' a main aspect of one part of his discussion.

[53] 4 Macc. 18.23f.

[54] Barr 1992, 54 is right to see 4 Macc. as offering solace for the persecuted, but (in view not least of 2 Macc.) surely wrong to imply that the teaching of the immortality of the soul functioned in this way on a wider basis. For a 'translation' of resurrection to disembodied immortality in a pagan description of Jewish belief cf. Tac. *Hist.* 5.5. Hengel 1989 [1961], 270 shows that Tacitus connects this belief with martyrdom.

the LORD will heal his servants,
and they will rise up and see great peace.
And they will drive out their enemies,
and the righteous ones will see and give praise,
and rejoice forever and ever with joy;
and they will see all of their judgments and all of their curses among their enemies.
And their bones will rest in the earth,
and their spirits will increase joy,
and they will know that the LORD is an executor of judgment;
but he will show mercy to hundreds and thousands,
to all who love him.[55]

According to the translator, the last verse five lines of the extract can be taken in two quite different ways. It can denote spirits who remain conscious and blissful in a disembodied post-mortem state; or it can indicate, with poetic hyperbole, the righteous dying happy because they know that God will vindicate them at a later date. The earlier lines, especially 'they will rise up and see great peace', suggest that the latter is perhaps to be preferred: in other words, that 'they will rise up' is a definite prediction of a future resurrection, while 'their bones will rest . . . and their spirits will increase joy' refers to the time in between their death and resurrection. This seems to me the probable interpretation. Nevertheless, *Jubilees* is often cited as a representative of the 'disembodied immortality' position; if this is correct, so that 'bones resting in the earth and spirits increasing joy' refers to the final state of those concerned, we would have to say that 'they will rise up' in the previous verse is the only occurrence in the relevant literature of something that looks like resurrection language being used to denote something other than new bodily existence.[56]

The great first-century exponent of a thoroughgoing hellenistic viewpoint is of course the Alexandrian philosopher Philo. His subtle and fascinating writings contain much food for thought, on this point and many others. But since it is beyond controversy that he taught the immortality of the soul rather than the resurrection of the dead, his place in our present survey can be limited to a brief statement rather than the full study he deserves.[57]

Philo was a highly trained philosopher, as well as a cultured and respected senior figure within the social and political world of Alexandrian Jewry. He drew in a sophisticated way not only on Plato and Aristotle, and their successors in subsequent hellenistic philosophy, but on the Stoic and Neopythagorean writers as well. But he remained deeply Jewish, opposing any attempt to get away from the specificity, and physicality, of Jewish

---

[55] *Jub.* 23.30f. (tr. Wintermute in Charlesworth 1985, 102).

[56] The translation in Sparks 1984, 77 (that of Charles, rev. Rabin) has 'they shall be exalted and prosper greatly', an apparent allusion to Isa. 52.13.

[57] On Philo see the recent surveys, with thorough bibliographies, by Borgen 1984; Morris 1987; Dillon 1996 [1977], 139–83; Barclay 1996b, 158–80; Mondésert 1999.

observances and expectations.[58] It is this remarkable cocktail of influences which, shaken together in the cosmopolitan world of Alexandria and its Jewish community, produced the powerful brew of Philo's thought on many topics, not least the nature and destiny of human beings.

Here his thought is unambiguously dualistic. The soul is immortal – or, strictly, the soul is divided into various parts, one of which is immortal.[59] The body is a prison in which the spirit is confined, that spirit which has been breathed by God into humankind. Indeed, the body is a tomb or coffin for the soul; the *soma/sema* (body/tomb) pun of standard Platonic exposition emerges in Philo too.[60] There are even hints in Philo of an idea popular in the Platonism of the time, that the present world is really the Hades referred to by the Greek poets.[61] One's main calling in the present life is therefore, with God's help, to energize the soul or spirit towards the vision of God. From this, all that remains for completeness is to be finally rescued from the body, so that the soul can return to its original non-bodily condition. This is God's reward for those who, during their embodied phase, have remained pure from sensual defilement.[62] Those who follow the patriarchs down this road will, after death, become equal to the angels; the immortal soul does not, after all, die, but merely departs. Like Abraham, called to leave his country and go to another one, the soul leaves its present habitation and sets off for the heavenly realms, the 'mother city'.[63]

Philo anticipated by nearly two centuries the labours of Alexandrian Christian thinkers like Clement and Origen, who were also concerned to bring together the insights of their faith with the intellectual culture around them. They used him a good deal, and the story of subsequent Christian wrestling with some of these problems is thus indebted, for good and ill, to this remarkable, indeed unique, Jewish thinker.[64] But for our purposes he stands as the clearest first-century Jewish exponent of the view which did *not* come to dominate the horizon. There is no place in his thinking, any more than there was in that of Plato himself, for the resurrection of the body.

---

[58] Observances: *Migr.* 89–93. Expectations (return to Jerusalem and the Holy Land in the eschatological age): *Praem.* 165; cf. *Mos.* 2.44. On Philo's awareness of treading a fine line between pure philosophical contemplation and his own necessary political work see particularly Goodenough 1967 [1938].

[59] *Quaes. Gen.* 3.11 (see Dillon 1996 [1977], 177). For the possibility that Philo, like (probably) Wis. and 4 Macc., saw the soul as *potentially* immortal, becoming so only through the pursuit of wisdom see e.g. *Quaes. Gen.* 1.16; *Op.* 154; *Conf.* 149.

[60] Prison: *Ebr.* 26 (101); *Leg.* 3.14 (42); *Migr.* 2 (9). Spirit or soul from God: *Deter.* 22 (80); *Opif.* 46 (134f.); *Spec.* 1.295; 4.24 (123). Tomb: *Migr.* 3 (16). Body as *sema*: *Leg.* 1.33 (108).

[61] *Heres* 45, 78; *Somn.* 1.151, 2.133. See Dillon 1996 [1977], 178.

[62] cf. *Abr.* 44 (258); *Leg.* 1.33 (108) (quoted in Morris 1987, 888 n. 83).

[63] Equal to angels: *Sac.* 5; soul departing: *Heres* 276; soul leaving body: *Heres* 68–70; mother city (*metropolis*): *Quaes. Gen.* 3.11.

[64] cf. esp. Chadwick 1966.

Those familiar with discussions of the immortality of the soul in second-Temple Judaism may at this point feel that they are missing an absent friend. Where, they will say, is the Wisdom of Solomon? Surely it belongs in this category? Is it not, also, the work of an Alexandrian Jew who believed in the immortality of the soul rather than the resurrection of the body? The answer is not as obvious as is usually supposed. But to address this properly we must turn to our main category. From several angles at once we are confronted with overwhelming evidence that the small seed of Daniel 12.2–3, and the other Old Testament passages we looked at earlier, had grown into a large shrub. Changing the metaphor, resurrection was in the air. Since this was the air the early Christians were breathing when they said what they believed had happened to Jesus, it is vital that we analyse it carefully.

4. Resurrection in Second-Temple Judaism

(i) Introduction

Judaism was never a religion of speculation or private devotion only. It was rooted in daily, weekly and annual observances and worship. At the heart of that worship, open to all Jews whether or not they could get to the Temple with any regularity, was the life of prayer. And the central prayers, in the first century as in the twenty-first, were and are the *Shema Israel* ('Hear, O Israel . . .') and the *Tefillah*, the 'prayer' of all prayers, also known as the *Shemoneh Esre* or 'Eighteen Benedictions'.

The second of these Benedictions is quite explicit: Israel's god is the Lord who gives life to the dead:

> You are mighty, humbling the proud; strong, judging the ruthless; you live for evermore, and raise the dead; you make the wind to return and the dew to fall; you nourish the living, and bring the dead to life; you bring forth salvation for us in the blinking of an eye. Blessed are you, O Lord, who bring the dead to life.[65]

This prayer, with all its overtones and echoes, is presupposed in all subsequent rabbinic Judaism.[66] It is thus, as we shall see, woven into the daily

---

[65] Singer 1962, 46f. (my summary and translation). This text follows the Palestinian recension of the Talmud; the Babylonian version is somewhat longer. mBer. 4.1—5.5 gives regulations about the saying of this prayer; 5.2 specifies the prayer about resurrection. The Talmud (bBer. 33a) comments that the resurrection is mentioned in connection with the coming of rain because rainfall means life to the world just as the resurrection does. See too 4Q521 fr. 7 and 5, 2.6 (below, 186f.).

[66] cf. bBer. 60b. Full details in S-B 4.1.208–49. We may assume that in the first century this prayer would have been controversial, and may well have been confined to the (admittedly quite wide) circles influenced by Pharisaic teaching. In other words, we should not imagine that the Sadducees might have had to say it, through clenched teeth, during the Temple liturgy.

and weekly life and thought of mainstream Jews from at least the second century of the common era. Some funerary inscriptions from this period bear witness to this.[67]

But the resurrection was not simply a doctrine of the Pharisees and their putative successors, the rabbis. All the evidence suggests that, with the few exceptions noted already, it was widely believed by most Jews around the turn of the common era. It is important that we now review this material quite carefully, since both the popularity of the doctrine, and what precisely was meant by it, are crucial to our subsequent investigation.

(ii) Resurrection in the Bible: The More Greek the Better

Along with prayer there went of course the regular reading of scripture. Without going into too much detail, we can state what seems at first a remarkable paradox, at least for those who had supposed that 'resurrection' was a Hebrew or Jewish notion and 'immortality' a Greek one: that as the Bible was translated into Greek (in Egypt, in the third century BC) the notion of resurrection became, it seems, much clearer, so that many passages which might have been at most ambiguous became clear, and some which seemed to have nothing to do with resurrection might suddenly give a hint, or more than a hint, in that direction.[68]

It is impossible to tell, at this remove, what overtones different Jewish readers of the Greek Old Testament might have heard in the different words. What is more, it is quite impossible, at this stage of our knowledge of early text-forms, to be sure in any given case that when we compare even the best modern editions of the Hebrew and Greek Bibles we are in touch with either the Hebrew that the original LXX translators used or the Greek that they first wrote. In many cases it is quite possible that the LXX gives us access to an earlier Hebrew form, though in many others the LXX seems to represent a sharp move away from the original. However, with these notes of caution, certain things stand out.

First, the passages which already speak unambiguously of bodily resurrection come through loud and clear; there is no attempt to soften them. Daniel 12.2–3, 13, and the relevant passages in 2 Maccabees (e.g. 7.9, 14; 12.44) all use what became the standard 'resurrection' language, namely the Greek verbs *anistemi* and *egeiro* and their cognates. We find the same with Isaiah 26, both in the verse that denies resurrection (14) and the verse that affirms it (19). They both emerge clearly in the Greek: 26.14 declares that

---

[67] See Williams 1999, 91.

[68] Brief introductions to the study of the LXX, indicating the complexity of the problems in this area, can be found in Schürer 3.474–93 (Goodman); Peters 1992. There is a whole research project waiting to be undertaken on the question of resurrection in the LXX.

the dead will not see life (*hoi nekroi zoen ou me idosin*), and that 'the doctors' will not rise (*oude iatroi ou me anastesosin*).[69] In its turn, 26.19 insists that the dead will be raised (*anastesontai hoi nekroi*), and that those in the tombs will be aroused (*egerthesontai hoi en tois mnemeiois*). Similarly, the passage in Hosea (6.2) that some think (whatever its original meaning) provided a key influence for both Isaiah and Daniel, is also explicit in the Greek: on the third day we shall be raised and live in his presence (*anastesometha kai zesometha enopion autou*). No second-Temple reader would have doubted that this referred to bodily resurrection.

Cavallin lists other passages where, despite the lack of actual reference in the original, the translators may have intended to refer to resurrection. These include Deuteronomy 32.39, Psalms 1.5 and 21.30 (22.29).[70] In addition, he notes the striking way in which the LXX has reversed the sense of Job 14.14; instead of a blank denial of a future life ('if a man die, shall he live again?'), the LXX declares boldly, 'If a man dies, he shall live' (*ean apothane anthropos, zesetai*). In the same way, the deeply obscure passage Job 19.26a ('after my skin has been thus destroyed') has been turned around: God 'will resurrect my skin' (*anastesai to derma mou*). Finally, the LXX adds a postscript to the book. After 42.17, where Job dies, an old man and full of days, it adds (42.17a LXX): 'It is written of him that he will rise again with those whom the Lord will raise' (*gegraptai de auton palin anastesesthai meth' hon ho kyrios anistesin*). Clearly, whoever drafted the translation of LXX Job had no doubt both of the bodily resurrection and of the propriety of making sure the biblical text affirmed it.[71]

A similar point emerges from the LXX of Hosea 13.14. The Hebrew text asks, 'Shall I ransom them from the power of Sheol? Shall I redeem them from Death?' and expects the answer 'No'. The LXX, however, has turned this into a positive statement: I shall rescue them from the hand of Hades, and I shall redeem them from Death (*ek cheiros Hadou rhusomai autous kai ek thanatou lutrosomai autous*). Someone who read the text in this way might well then hear overtones of resurrection in the next chapter as well: 'I will be like the dew to Israel . . . they shall blossom as the vine . . .'[72]

In the light of this, we may cautiously suggest some other passages in which similar influence might be present. Of course, most occurrences of *anistemi* and *egeiro* are simply regular ways of saying that someone got up, whether from sitting or lying, or 'arose' in the sense of 'there arose a mighty king in Israel'.[73] But *anastasis* is the word for 'resurrection' in 2 Maccabees

---

[69] *iatroi* ('doctors') here, as in Ps. 88.10 [LXX 87.11], appears to be the result of the LXX translators assuming that *rephaim* ('shades') was derived from *rapha'* ('heal'). On this point see Johnston 2002, 129f.

[70] Cavallin 1974, 103f. Cf. too e.g. Dt. 18.15 (see below, 453).

[71] On this cf. e.g. Grappe 2001, 51.

[72] Hos. 14.5–7 (LXX 6–8).

[73] One of the rare instances of the noun *anastasis* comes into this category (Lam. 3.63);

7.14 and 12.43, and two of its other three occurrences are interesting in their own way.[74] The word *anastaseos* ('of the resurrection') has been added to the title of Psalm 65 (MT 66), and though some (including the editor in Rahlfs's edition) have seen this as a very early Christian addition, indicating the use of this psalm in Easter liturgies, a case can be made, in the light of verse 9 ('you hold my soul in life'), for the title reflecting a pre-Christian Jewish insight.[75] In Zephaniah 3.8, YHWH instructs his people to wait for him, for the day when he arises as a witness, gathering the nations for judgment. In the LXX this comes out as the summons to wait 'for the day of my resurrection (*eis hemeran anastaseos mou*) for witness'. This could simply mean 'the day when I arise' in the same sense as the Hebrew. But the close connection in Jewish and Christian thought between resurrection and judgment may indicate that the translator was thinking of the day when the god-given gift of resurrection would bring the world to judgment at last. Certainly – this is a different point, but one that hovers on the edge of a discussion like this – a Christian, reading the Bible in Greek as most of them did, might well have made the connection, and might have gone even further, to guess at a hidden christological message.

That possibility (of an early Christian reading in support of a christological belief) may cautiously be explored in relation to a few of the prophecies of a coming king. God promises to David that he will 'raise up' his seed after him, the one of whom it is said, 'I will be his father, and he will be my son': any early Christian reading 2 Samuel 7.12, *kai anasteso to sperma sou*, would have had no difficulty identifying who the *sperma* was.[76] So too the various messianic promises in Jeremiah and Ezekiel could easily have been taken, and were perhaps intended by their LXX translator(s) to be taken, as indicating the resurrection through which God's leader(s) would 'arise' in the age to come. God will 'raise up' shepherds, and especially a righteous Branch, to rule over Israel and the world.[77] 'I will raise up one shepherd over them, my servant David,' declares YHWH: *kai anasteso ep' autous poimena hena, ton doulon mou Dauid.*[78] We should be wary of reading too much into verses like this; equally, we should be just as wary of reading too little. Who can tell, at this remove, what overtones second-Temple Jews and first-generation Christians might not have detected?

Likewise, the language of some of the psalms may be taken in a more explicit way as a prayer for resurrection. Psalm 40.11 (41.10 MT) prays:

---

cf. Ps. 138 (139).2, where *egersis* simply means 'my getting up' as opposed to 'my lying down'.

[74] The third is Dan. 11.20, where despite the eschatological context an 'ordinary' meaning seems to be intended.

[75] See Cavallin 1974, 104, citing Volz.

[76] LXX 2 Kgds. 7.12; cf. too 2 Chron. 7.18.

[77] Jer. 23.4, 5; cf. 37 (30 LXX).9.

[78] Ezek. 34.23 cf. v. 29.

'Lord, be gracious to me; raise me up (*anasteson me*), that I may repay them.' Psalm 138 (139 MT).18b declares that, when the Psalmist has tried to count the vast range of God's thoughts, he will 'come to the end', or perhaps 'awake', and find himself still with God. In the LXX this has become a more explicit pointer towards a future life: *exegerthen*, 'I will be raised up' (the same verb that is used in the Theodotion version of Daniel 12.2). There may well be more hints in the same direction; these are, I suggest, straws in the wind.

The evidence of the Septuagint, then, is worth pondering, especially when we consider what, granted certain regular scholarly assumptions, we *might* have thought we were going to find. After all, here is a Hebrew text being translated into Greek – in Egypt, most likely. We might have expected that every reference to resurrection would have been flattened out into something more Platonic (as happened, for instance, between 2 Maccabees and 4 Maccabees). We might have expected that the translators would have introduced suggestions of either the Ben-Sirach point of view (forget about a life after death, concentrate on getting this one straight) or that of Philo (strive to attain disembodied bliss hereafter). They do not. All the indications are that those who translated the Septuagint, and those who read it thereafter (i.e. most Jews, in both Palestine and the Diaspora), would have understood the key Old Testament passages in terms of a more definite 'resurrection' sense than the Hebrew would necessarily warrant, and might very likely have heard overtones of 'resurrection' in many places where the Hebrew would not have suggested it. When, in this context, we find stories about those who suffered and died in loyalty to God and his law, we should not be surprised to hear that they spoke boldly about the newly embodied hope that would await them in the future.

One such story is that of the Maccabaean martyrs, as related in 2 Maccabees.

(iii) New Life for the Martyrs: 2 Maccabees

The second book of Maccabees begins where Daniel left off, with the promise of new bodily life, at some future date, for those who had died horrible deaths out of loyalty to Israel's god and the law. This book provides far and away the clearest picture of the promise of resurrection anywhere in the period.[79]

---

[79] Cf. *NTPG* 323f.; a certain amount of repetition of the material presented there is inevitable in what follows. Kellermann 1979, 81 and elsewhere tried to argue for a view of 'resurrection' in 2 Macc. as 'going to a heavenly life', which seems to me a complete misreading of the texts (though followed by Schwankl 1987, 250–57); 'heaven' is never mentioned as the place where the resurrections will take place. It is remarkable that Perkins 1984, 44 can claim that the only explicit reference to resurrection in 2 Macc. is at 7.11: see

The context is that of pagan persecution. The Syrian tyrant Antiochus Epiphanes, as part of his drive to bring Judaism into line with his imperial ambitions, is attempting to make loyal Jews disobey their god-given laws (specifically, the prohibition on eating pork), under pain of torture and death. The story focuses on a mother and her seven sons, who refuse to eat the unclean food, and are tortured one by one. As they go to their various gruesome deaths, several of them make specific promises to their torturers about the form that their divine vindication will take:

> You accursed wretch, [said the second brother,] you dismiss us from this present life, but the King of the universe will raise us up to an everlasting renewal of life, because we have died for his laws.[80]

> [The third brother] put out his tongue and courageously stretched forth his hands, and said nobly, 'I got these from Heaven, and because of his laws I disdain them, and from him I hope to get them back again.'[81]

> When he was near death, [the fourth brother] said, 'One cannot but choose to die at the hands of mortals and to cherish the hope God gives of being raised again by him. But for you there will be no resurrection to life!'[82]

> [The mother] encouraged each of them in the language of their ancestors. Filled with a noble spirit, she . . . said to them, 'I do not know how you came into being in my womb. It was not I who gave you life and breath, nor I who set in order the elements within each of you. Therefore the Creator of the world, who shaped the beginning of humankind and devised the origin of all things, will in his mercy give life and breath back to you again, since you now forget yourselves for the sake of his laws.'[83]

> [The mother spoke secretly to the youngest son:] 'I beg you, my child, to look at the heaven and the earth and see everything that is in them, and recognize that God did not make them out of things that existed. And in the same way the human race came into being. Do not fear this butcher, but prove worthy of your brothers. Accept death, so that in God's mercy I may get you back again along with your brothers.'[84]

> [The youngest son said,] 'You . . . will not escape the hands of God. For we are suffering because of our own sins. And if our living Lord is angry for a little while, to rebuke and discipline us, he will again be reconciled with his own servants . . . For our brothers after enduring a brief suffering have drunk of everflowing life, under God's covenant; but you, by the judgment of God, will receive just punishment for your arrogance. I, like my brothers, give up body and life for the laws of our ancestors, appealing to God to show mercy soon to our nation and by trials and

---

below. On Jason of Cyrene (the supposed original author of the (now edited) material in 2 Macc.) and the setting of his beliefs cf. Hengel 1974, 1.95–7.

[80] 2 Macc. 7.9.

[81] 2 Macc. 7.11.

[82] 2 Macc. 7.14; note the variation from Dan. 12.2, where the wicked are also raised in order to be judged.

[83] 2 Macc. 7.21–3.

[84] 2 Macc. 7.28f.

plagues to make you confess that he alone is God, and through me and my brothers to bring to an end the wrath of the Almighty that has justly fallen on our whole nation.'[85]

This remarkable chapter draws together the strands we observed in Daniel 12. The martyrs' suffering is redemptive for the nation; there seems to be an element of Isaiah 53 in the final flourish of the youngest brother. Their loyalty will be rewarded, and the torturers' brutality punished, by the god of justice. The new life they will receive, which is seen in very 'bodily' terms, is the gift of the creator god who made them and all the world in the first place. And the resurrection they await is not the same as the 'everflowing life' they have already drunk.[86] It is still awaited. The writer of 2 Maccabees did not suppose that the brothers and the mother had already been given their hands, tongues and whole bodies back again. Their resurrection would surely happen, but it certainly had not happened yet. It is simply nonsense to describe this belief, as does one recent writer, as 'a resolute view of death as resurrection'.[87] Resurrection is never a redescription of death, but always its overthrow and reversal.

A similar incident, if anything more grisly yet, occurs in 2 Maccabees 14. A Jew called Razis, one of the elders in Jerusalem, was about to be arrested by Nicanor as a leading loyalist. When he found himself surrounded, he fell on his own sword, rather than suffer the outrages of the soldiers:

> But in the heat of the struggle he did not hit exactly, and the crowd was now rushing in through the doors. He courageously ran up on the wall, and bravely threw himself down into the crowd. But as they quickly drew back, a space opened and he fell in the middle of the empty space. Still alive and aflame with anger, he rose, and though his blood gushed forth and his wounds were severe he ran through the crowd; and standing upon a steep rock, with his blood now completely drained from him, he tore out his entrails, took them in both hands and hurled them at the crowd, calling upon the Lord of life and spirit to give them back to him again.[88]

This tale has the same underlying point: the creator god, the one who gives 'life and spirit', or perhaps 'life and breath' (the reference is surely to Genesis 2, as in Ezekiel 37) will perform a mighty act of new creation, in which the martyrs will be given new bodies.

The one final mention of resurrection in 2 Maccabees is less dramatic but equally interesting. Judas Maccabaeus and his companions discover that those who had died in the battle against Gorgias' troops had been wearing idolatrous tokens under their robes. This, Judas and the others concluded, was the reason they had been killed. Judas's response was to praise the

---

[85] 2 Macc. 7.31–3, 36–8.

[86] The translation 'drunk' presumes, with most editors, an original text of *pepokasin* for the LXX *peptokasin*.

[87] Davies 1999, 122.

[88] 2 Macc. 14.43–6.

righteous judge for bringing this to light; to pray that the sin might be blotted out; and to take up a collection so that a sin offering could be made in Jerusalem. In doing this, comments the writer, Judas 'acted very well and honourably, taking account of the resurrection':

> For if he were not expecting that those who had fallen would rise again, it would have been superfluous and foolish to pray for the dead. But if he was looking to the splendid reward that is laid up for those who fall asleep in godliness, it was a holy and pious thought. Therefore he made atonement for the dead, so that they might be delivered from their sin.[89]

This passage has, of course, been a happy hunting-ground for later theologians wondering about the validity or otherwise of praying for the dead, and has also been invoked as a possible background for Paul's comment about people being baptized on behalf of the dead.[90] But for our present purposes the point is, again, that the resurrection had not yet taken place, but Judas and his companions believed that it would in the future. The secret idolaters were now, after their deaths, in some kind of intermediate state; they needed to be forgiven their sin, so that when the resurrection happened they would be able to join with the martyrs and all the righteous. Resurrection belief, throughout 2 Maccabees, means new bodily life, a life which comes after the 'life after death' that dead people currently experience.[91] And the whole book is introduced with the reported prayer, from the time of Nehemiah, that God would gather the scattered people of Israel, punish the Gentiles for their arrogance and oppression, and plant his people in the holy place.[92] Resurrection, in other words, is both the personal hope of the righteous individual and the national hope for faithful Israel.

(iv) Judgment and Life in God's New World: Resurrection and Apocalyptic

The contemporary enthusiasm for apocalyptic has produced almost as much confusion as the preceding distaste for it. Studies of the material from every conceivable angle abound, and the dawn of the third Christian millennium has added extra fuel to a fire of interest, even obsession, that was already burning brightly.[93] And in the middle of the texts and their subject-matter we find frequent reference to the purposes of Israel's god for his people after their death. In keeping with the genre and style of apocalyptic writing, these references are often cryptic; but again and again the hope they express, as

---

[89] 2 Macc. 12.44f.

[90] 1 Cor. 15.29; see below, 338f.

[91] Porter 1999a, 59f. attempts, unsuccessfully in my view, to minimize the force of 2 Macc.

[92] 2 Macc. 1.24–9.

[93] On apocalyptic see *NTPG* ch. 10; recently, Rowland 1999.

we might expect from the spiritual heirs of Daniel and Ezekiel, is not for a permanently disembodied immortality but for a resurrection at some time still in the future.

We begin with the longest and most convoluted of these works: the Ethiopic book of Enoch (known as *1 Enoch*).[94] The book, which is a composite work, dated variously during the last two centuries or so BC (with some parts possibly later still), opens with a great judgment scene. God will come forth from his dwelling; the earth shall be rent asunder; all will be judged, including the righteous:

> But for the righteous he will make peace, and he will keep safe the chosen, and mercy will be upon them. They will all belong to God, and will prosper and be blessed, and the light of God will shine upon them.[95]

Though this does not mention resurrection as such, it clearly envisages (as do several subsequent passages) that the righteous dead are at the moment still awaiting this final judgment, and that when it comes it will effect a change of state for them with a new dimension of blessing.[96] This is spelled out in 5.7, which predicts that 'to the elect there shall be light, joy, and peace, and they shall inherit the earth'. This vision of future blessing for the righteous, and the whole world, is elaborated further in 10.17—11.2; it is both a very much this-worldly time of prosperity and one from which all injustice and wickedness have been banished. It is hard to imagine such a state without the fresh mighty act of God which the book predicts. When we reach chapter 25, the vision of the tree of life introduces the idea of a this-worldly paradise. The angel declares to Enoch:

> 'As for this fragrant tree, not a single human being has the authority to touch it until the great judgment, when he shall take vengeance on all and conclude everything forever. This is for the righteous and the pious. And the elect will be presented with its fruit for life. He will plant it in the direction of the northeast, upon the holy place, in the direction of the house of the Lord, the Eternal King. Then they shall be glad and rejoice in gladness, and they shall enter into the holy place; its fragrance shall penetrate their bones, long life will they live on earth, such as your fathers lived in their days.'
>
> At that moment [Enoch now comments], I blessed the God of Glory, the Eternal King, for he has prepared such things for the righteous people, as he had created them and given it to them.[97]

---

[94] Trs. are taken either from Knibb (in Sparks 1984) or Isaac (in Charlesworth 1983).

[95] *1 En*. 1.8 (Knibb).

[96] cf. e.g. *1 En*. 22.1–14. Unfortunately the image in this passage, of the storehouses where the souls of the dead are kept until the day of judgment, focuses almost exclusively on the wicked rather than the righteous, so we cannot tell what fate the writer envisages for the latter. However, it is clear that the future life is regarded as having two stages: the time of waiting and the time of final judgment. Schürer 2.541 (Cave) takes the passage to refer to resurrection, though suggesting that this 'does not accord with the bulk of chs. 1—36'.

[97] *1 En*. 25.4–7 (Isaac).

The vision of the new Jerusalem (chapters 26—7) has the same emphasis on a future this-worldly state of blessedness. This is not quite so explicit in the description of the home of the righteous in the next (and most likely independent) section of the book, the 'Similitudes' (chapters 37—71); in chapter 39 the holy ones dwell with the angels, in a special dwelling place 'underneath the wings of the Lord of the Spirits'.[98] In chapter 51, however, there is an explicit description of the future resurrection, set within the promise for all creation to be renewed:

> In those days the earth will return that which has been entrusted to it, and Sheol will return that which has been entrusted to it, that which it has received, and destruction will return what it owes. And he will choose the righteous and holy from among them, for the day has come near that they must be saved . . . And in those days the mountains will leap like rams, and the hills will skip like lambs satisfied with milk, and all will become angels in heaven. Their faces will shine with joy [or: like kids satiated with milk. And the faces of all the angels in heaven shall glow with joy], for in those days the Chosen One will have risen; and the earth will rejoice, and the righteous will dwell upon it, and the chosen will go and walk upon it.[99]

Here there is no doubt: this is resurrection, linked somehow to the rising of the mysterious 'Chosen One'. This much-discussed figure, also called 'the son of man', will sit on a glorious throne, in a judgment scene reminiscent of Daniel 12 and Isaiah 52—3:[100]

> The righteous and elect ones shall be saved on that day; and from thenceforth they shall never see the faces of the sinners and the oppressors. The Lord of the Spirits will abide over them; they shall eat and rest and rise with that Son of Man forever and ever. The righteous and elect ones shall rise from the earth and shall cease being of downcast face. They shall wear the garments of glory . . .[101]

The next section of the book (chapters 72—82) concerns the secrets of the heavenly luminaries. The subsequent division (chapters 83—90), 'The Dream Visions', has Enoch telling his son, Methuselah, his visions of the future, providing a swift and symbolic overview of the history of Israel from his own day to the time of the Maccabaean crisis. Following prophetic precedent (e.g. Ezekiel 34), he sees the people of Israel as sheep and lambs, harried by vultures and other birds of prey, but defended and eventually rescued by 'the Lord of the sheep'. At that time (in other words, after the events of 167–164 BC), the sheep, including those who have died, are

---

[98] *1 En.* 39.5, 7 (Isaac).

[99] *1 En.* 51.1f., 4f. (Knibb; alternative tr., Isaac). This is the only passage in *1 En.* recognized by Schwankl 1987 as certainly speaking of resurrection (188f.); he supposes it to be an addition by a final redactor. Ironically it is one of the rare passages in the literature we are surveying which speaks of people actually *becoming* angels.

[100] So Nickelsburg 1972, 77.

[101] *1 En.* 62.13–15 (Isaac). Cf. too 62.3. We cannot here go into the question of the meaning of 'son of man' in this and similar passages.

regathered and brought to the house of the Lord of the sheep (90.33). This is the prelude to the messianic kingdom.

The book's final section (chapters 91—107) sets out the 'two ways' of the righteous and sinner (a familiar theme in works as otherwise distinct as the Qumran Community Rule and the *Didache*). Like the larger book of which it now forms part, it opens with a great scene of judgment, in which, among many other things, 'The righteous will rise from sleep, and wisdom will rise and will be given to them.'[102] Other similar descriptions follow, more florid than theologically precise,[103] and, as before, more concerned with the vivid judgment awaiting sinners. But the message remains the same: the present time is a period of waiting, in which both the living and the already dead await a still-future judgment. In that context, the righteous dead, whose souls are in Sheol, are told not to be anxious.[104] The sinners will suppose that they have celebrated a triumph over them (102.6–11); but God has prepared wonderful things for them:

> The spirits of those who died in righteousness shall live and rejoice; their spirits shall not perish; nor their memorial from before the face of the Great One unto all the generations of the world.[105]

More specifically, with clear echoes of Daniel 12,

> In heaven the angels will remember you for good before the glory of the Great One; and your names shall be written before the glory of the Great One. Be hopeful, because formerly you have pined away through evil and toil. But now you shall shine like the lights of heaven, and you shall be seen; and the windows of heaven shall be opened for you. Your cry shall be heard. Cry for judgment, and it shall appear for you . . . Be hopeful, and do not abandon your hope, because there shall be a fire for you; are about to be making a great rejoicing like the angels of heaven.[106]

The book ends with a final judgment scene, in which the righteous are transformed as well as revivified:

> And now I will call the spirits of the good who are of the generation of light, and I will transform those who were born in darkness, who in the flesh were not recompensed with honour, as was fitting to their faith. And I will bring out into shining light those who love my holy name, and I will set each one on the throne of his honour. And they will shine for times without number, for righteousness is the judgment of God, for with the faithful he will keep faith in the dwelling of upright paths.

---

[102] *1 En.* 91.10 (Knibb).

[103] e.g. *1 En.* 96.1–3.

[104] *1 En.* 102.4f.

[105] *1 En.* 103.4 (Isaac). Schürer 2.541 (Cave) quotes this passage as possible evidence of belief in ultimate disembodied immortality rather than resurrection (see too e.g. Barr 1992, 52); but, though this book more than most can surely admit of inconsistencies, the surrounding chapters do seem to teach bodily resurrection, and the passage should almost certainly be read this way.

[106] *1 En.* 104.1–4 (Isaac).

And they will see those who were born in darkness thrown into darkness, while the righteous shine. And the sinners will cry out as they see them shining, but they themselves will go where days and times have been written down for them.[107]

Thus, though again the imagery does not always permit precision, it is quite clear that those who have died, both righteous and wicked, are presently awaiting a future day when their fate will become not only permanent but also public and visible. They have not, in other words, passed at death into a permanent state of either blessedness or woe; the wider context from chapter 91 onwards, particularly chapter 102, suggests that after their period of waiting they will indeed rise again to a newly embodied life. This may after all be the intention of the passage in *Pseudo-Phocylides* we examined earlier.[108] Though there is no reason to suppose that *1 Enoch*, with all its varied parts, contains a single doctrine on this topic, as a whole it supports something like the view of resurrection we find in Daniel and 2 Maccabees, and also shows the various ways in which something like this could be said, not least ways which could include the transformation, as well as revivification, of the righteous dead (thus making a distinction between the righteous, who are raised to be transformed, and the wicked, who are raised to be judged).

Other shorter apocalypses make their distinct contribution.[109] The *Testament of Moses* speaks of Israel being exalted to the heights, and fixed firmly in the starry heaven, from where they will look on God's judgment of those who have oppressed them.[110] This seems clearly dependent both on Daniel 12.3 (the righteous shining like stars) and on Isaiah 52.13 (the servant being exalted).[111] Scholars are divided as to whether this designates an otherworldly salvation or whether it is drawing on extravagant biblical metaphors to explain the significance of a this-worldly redemption, i.e. resurrection. In my judgment, the allusion to Daniel 12, whose teaching is after all clear on the subject of bodily resurrection, settles the issue in favour of the latter.[112]

The *Apocalypse of Moses* is clearer.[113] When Adam dies, God sends the archangel Michael to tell Seth not to attempt to revive him. Oil from the tree of mercy will be given at the end of times, when

---

[107] *1 En.* 108.11–15 (Knibb).

[108] *Ps.-Phoc.* 102–15; see above, 141. This is urged by Puech 1993, 158–62; cf. Gilbert 1999, 287–90, reminding us, wisely, that 'le poète peut se contenter d'allusions!' (290).

[109] On *Jubilees*, which should perhaps belong here see above, 143.

[110] *T. Mos.* 10.8–10. (The work used to be known as the *Assumption of Moses*, through identification with another work of that name, now almost certainly lost.)

[111] So Nickelsburg 1972, 28f.

[112] Other-worldly: e.g. Laperrousaz 1970; Rowley 1963. Biblical metaphor: Priest 1977, 1983. We should not, of course, press these texts for an overall 'consistent' pattern; *Test. Abr.*, for instance, which speaks simply of immortality, also draws on Dan. 12.

[113] This traditional title for the book is misleading; it is a variant on the *Life of Adam and Eve*. See Schürer 3.757 (Vermes, Goodman); Johnson in Charlesworth 1985, 259n. The book's date is unknown, but a time between 100 BC and AD 100 is probable.

all flesh from Adam up to that great day shall be raised, such as shall be the holy people; then to them shall be given every joy of Paradise and God shall be in their midst.[114]

Seth will witness Adam's soul making 'its fearful upward journey' (13.6), but this will not be the end of the matter. God calls to Adam's dead body, and says:

I told you that you are dust and to dust you shall return. Now I promise to you the resurrection; I shall raise you on the last day in the resurrection with every man of your seed.[115]

When, in her turn, Eve dies, and the book comes to an end, Michael tells Seth how to conduct burials – and incidentally reveals a standard way in which, in this period, belief in the soul leaving the body at death and belief in the future resurrection were combined:

Thus you shall prepare for burial each man who dies until the day of resurrection. And do not mourn more than six days; on the seventh day rest and be glad in it, for on that day both God and we angels rejoice in the migration from the earth of a righteous soul.[116]

A further statement of a similar position, from roughly the same period, is found in *Sibylline Oracles* 4.179–92:

But when everything is already dusty ashes,
and God puts to sleep the unspeakable fire, even as he kindled it,
God himself will again fashion the bones and ashes of men
and he will raise up mortals again as they were before.
And then there will be a judgment over which God himself will preside,
judging the world again.
As many as sinned by impiety, these will a mound of earth cover,
and broad Tartarus and the repulsive recesses of Gehenna.
But as many as are pious, they will live on earth again
when God gives spirit and life and favor
to these pious ones. Then they will all see themselves
beholding the delightful and pleasant light of the sun.
Oh most blessed, whatever man will live to that time.[117]

What all these otherwise quite varied statements have in common is the placing of resurrection within a judgment scene. In other words, this belief is

---

[114] *Ap. Ad. Ev.* 13.3f. Tr. Johnson in Charlesworth 1985.

[115] *Ap. Ad. Ev.* 41.2f.

[116] *Ap. Ad. Ev.* 43.2f.; cf. too 13.1–6. The parallel conclusion of the *Life of Adam and Eve* has Michael command Seth not to mourn longer than six days, 'because the seventh day is a sign of the resurrection, the rest of the coming age, and on the seventh day the LORD rested from all his works' (51).

[117] Tr. Collins in Charlesworth 1983, 389. Collins 1974 is prepared to date the fourth book to around 300 BC.

not a general statement about the likely ultimate destination of human beings, but arises, as with Daniel and 2 Maccabees, in the context of God's judgment on the wicked and his vindication of the righteous.

The same is true for the *Testaments of the Twelve Patriarchs* (which may well include Christian interpolations, but cannot be ruled out as evidence for pre- and non-Christian Judaism). The *Testament of Levi* predicts the coming of a new priest, to replace the wicked ones upon whom judgment has fallen, and declares that 'his star shall rise in heaven like a king', and that he 'will shine forth like the sun in the earth', bringing peace and joy to earth and heaven.[118] The *Testament of Judah* also envisages the coming of a Messiah, after whose saving work Abraham, Isaac and Jacob will be resurrected to life, with the twelve patriarchs themselves acting as chiefs in Israel. At that time

> those who died in sorrow shall be raised in joy;
> and those who died in poverty for the Lord's sake shall be made rich;
> those who died on account of the Lord shall be wakened to life.[119]

In the same way, Zebulun tells his children not to grieve because he is dying. He will rise again amongst them as a leader among their sons, and will be glad in the midst of his tribe, while fire will rain down on the wicked.[120] Finally, Benjamin, the youngest brother, gives similar testimony to his children:

> Then you will see Enoch and Seth and Abraham and Isaac and Jacob being raised up at the right hand in great joy. Then shall we also be raised, each of us over our tribe, and we shall prostrate ourselves before the heavenly king. Then all shall be changed, some destined for glory, others for dishonor, for the Lord first judges Israel for the wrong she has committed and then he shall do the same for all the nations.[121]

An allusion to Daniel is again likely, this time because of the double resurrection, both to glory and to shame. Throughout these writings, resurrection is God's way of firmly setting the world, and Israel, to rights after the long years of earthly injustice and the even longer years in which the righteous have waited, after death, for final vindication.

This longing for judgment and vindication, plentifully evident during the period between the Maccabaean crisis and AD 70 when most of the above texts were taking shape, was renewed in the period immediately after the disaster of 70, when the bright hope of revolution, of the kingdom of God coming on earth as in heaven, was snuffed out by the ruthless might of Rome. Two apocalypses from this period, perhaps not surprisingly, turn to

---

[118] *T. Lev.* 18.3f. Tr. Kee in Charlesworth 1983, 794.
[119] *T. Jud.* 25.4. The motif of 'wakening' is probably an allusion to Dan. 12.2.
[120] *T. Zeb.* 10.1–3.
[121] *T. Benj.* 10.6–9.

the promise of resurrection in their longing for the covenant god to act at last.

Fourth Ezra consists of a series of vivid visions, with interpretations, concerning the destruction and rebuilding of Jerusalem.[122] The first vision issues in a discussion between 'Ezra' and the angel Uriel, in which Ezra is rebuked for impatience; the angel points out that 'the souls of the righteous in their chambers' are not being impatient about how long they have to wait for their reward. The chambers of souls in Hades, Uriel explains, are like the womb of a pregnant woman. As the birthpangs make the woman eager to give birth, so these chambers are eager to give back that which has been committed to them.[123] The same belief about the future of those currently dead underlies various passages in the second vision also.[124]

The third vision gives rise to the prediction of the coming messianic age, when the messianic son of god will be revealed and celebrate his kingdom for four hundred years. After this he will die, and the world will return to a primordial silence. Then, after seven days,

> the world, which is not yet awake, shall be roused, and that which is corruptible shall perish. And the earth shall give up those who are asleep in it; and the chambers shall give up the souls which have been committed to them.[125]

Then shall follow a great judgment scene, in which 'the nations that have been raised from the dead' will be addressed by the Most High, who will reveal to them the delights of paradise on the one hand and the torments of hell on the other.[126] There follows a description of the state of the dead before the final judgment, in which one of the delights of the faithful is that it will be shown to them 'how their face is to shine like the sun, and how they are to be made like the light of the stars, being incorruptible from then on' – yet another allusion to Daniel 12.[127] At the moment, they are resting, watched over by angels, awaiting the glory of the last days.[128] In those days, 'death itself will be gone, hell will have fled, corruption will be forgotten, sorrows will have passed away, and the treasure of immortality will be made manifest'.[129] All this occurs, in context, within the vision of an entire new world order, in which Israel's wrongs will be righted, evil will be punished,

---

[122] On the book and its varied nomenclature cf. Metzger in Charlesworth 1983, 516–23 (including (516) a useful chart of books named after Ezra). Parts of the book, notably chs. 1—2 and 15—16, are later Christian additions, so the ref. to resurrection in e.g. 2.16 can be discounted from the present survey. Cf. Harrington 2002.

[123] 4 Ezra 4.35, 42.

[124] cf. 4 Ezra 5.41f.

[125] 4 Ezra 7.28–32. The echoes of Dan. 12.2 should again be noted.

[126] 4 Ezra 7.36f.

[127] 4 Ezra 7.97.

[128] 4 Ezra 7.95.

[129] 4 Ezra 7.53f.

Jerusalem will be rebuilt, and Israel's god, the creator, will be seen to be righteous.

The final apocalypse to be considered here is the Syriac Apocalypse of Baruch, known as *2 Baruch* to distinguish it from the book of the same name found in the Apocrypha. Here too we find visions of judgment on the nations and the rebuilding of Jerusalem after the cataclysm of AD 70. In the middle of this, the angel speaking to 'Baruch' promises that

> it will happen after these things when the time of the appearance of the anointed One has been fulfilled and he returns with glory, that then all who sleep in hope of him will rise. And it will happen at that time that those treasuries will be opened in which the number of the souls of the righteous were kept, and they will go out and the multitudes of the souls will appear together, in one assemblage, of one mind.[130]

At that time, 'dust will be called, and told, "Give back that which does not belong to you and raise up all that you have kept until its own time"' (42.8). Once again, the context is that of judgment:

> For the earth will surely give back the dead at that time; it receives them now in order to keep them, not changing anything in their form. But as it has received them so it will give them back. And as I have delivered them to it so it will raise them. For then it will be necessary to show those who live that the dead are living again, and that those who went away have come back. And it will be that when they have recognized each other, those who know each other at this moment, then my judgment will be strong, and those things which have been spoken of before will come.[131]

At that time, those who are condemned will see that the people they have been lording it over will be changed into a more glorious form, into the glory (in fact) of the angels; while they, the damned, will be changed into 'startling visions and horrible shapes' (51.5). This gives rise to a remarkable passage about the new forms the righteous will take:

> They will live in the heights of that world and they will be like the angels and will be equal to the stars. And they will be changed into any shape which they wished, from beauty to loveliness, and from light to the splendor of glory. For the extents of Paradise will be spread out for them, and to them will be shown the beauty of the majesty of the living beings under the throne, as well as all the hosts of the angels . . . and the excellence of the righteous will then be greater than that of the angels.[132]

This passage has sometimes been appealed to in support of the idea of an 'immaterial' resurrection (and hence as a possible antecedent of Paul's 'spiritual body' in 1 Corinthians 15) but this will not do.[133] The immediately

---

[130] *2 Bar.* 30.1f. (tr. Klijn in Charlesworth 1983, 631). See again Harrington 2002.
[131] *2 Bar.* 50.2–4.
[132] *2 Bar.* 51.8–12.
[133] See e.g. Carnley 1987, 231, quoting Kirsopp Lake.

previous chapters in *2 Baruch* make it clear that this is indeed 'resurrection'. Some kind of radical transformation is obviously envisaged, but this passage hardly indicates that the shift in question is from a material existence to a non-material one. The careful distinction between the righteous and the angels in 51.12 should also be noted. The text is noteworthy, though, as providing the only clear anticipation of what we do find in the New Testament: the sense that resurrection will involve some kind of life-enhancing transformation.[134]

Finally, though it is not an apocalypse, we may add to this section the *Psalms of Solomon*, a work most likely from the first century BC, and showing strong traces of a revolutionary Pharisaism. 'The destruction of the sinner is forever,' declares the Psalmist,

> and he will not be remembered when God visits the righteous. This is the share of sinners forever, but those who fear the Lord shall rise up to eternal life, and their life shall be in the Lord's light, and it shall never end.[135]

Other passages, though not so explicit, hint at the same theme – and, once more, set it within a fierce longing for divine judgment on the enemies of Israel, and vindication for the righteous.[136]

Resurrection thus belongs clearly within one regular apocalyptic construal of the future that Israel's god has in store. Judgment must fall, because the wicked have been getting away with violence and oppression for far too long; when it does, bringing with it a great change in the entire cosmic order, then those who have died, whose souls are resting patiently, will be raised to new life. Many of these apocalypses, as we have seen, allude to Daniel 12 in making the point. And all of them, in doing so, hold together what we have seen so closely interwoven in the key biblical texts: the hope of Israel for liberation from pagan oppression, and the hope of the righteous individual for a newly embodied, and probably significantly transformed, existence.

(v) Resurrection as the Vindication of the Suffering Wise: The Wisdom of Solomon

The old assumption that Greeks believed in immortality while Jews believed in resurrection is not merely historically inaccurate; it is conceptually muddled. And where concepts are muddled, texts are misread. Nowhere is this so

---

[134] See below on Phil. 3.20f.; 1 Cor. 15.35–58; and the summary at the end of ch. 10.

[135] *Ps. Sol.* 3.11f.; tr. R. B. Wright in Charlesworth 1985, 655. There is no warrant for saying (Perkins 1984, 52) that this 'could refer simply to the soul'. This passage will be important in discussing Wis. 3.1–8 (below, 162–75).

[136] e.g. *Ps. Sol.* 13.11; 14.10; cf. Cavallin 1974, 57–60. Cf. too Day 1996, 240.

evident as in the treatment of a central and important book which may well be from more or less exactly the same period as very early Christianity, namely the Wisdom of Solomon.[137] There are signs that Paul knew Wisdom, alluding to it, and perhaps in oblique dialogue with it, at several points in Romans.[138] This is not to say that the early Christians relied on Wisdom as a major source of ideas. But studying the way in which the book actually works is an object lesson in understanding first-century texts. This should help us later on.

Wisdom clearly teaches the immortality of the soul; therefore, it has regularly been assumed, it cannot simultaneously teach the resurrection of the body. That assumption remains widespread in current scholarship.[139] It has often been challenged, more often in fact than one might suppose from reading some scholars. In earlier times, Thomas Aquinas insisted that Wisdom believed in resurrection; in more recent times, the massive scholarship of Émile Puech has been brought to bear at the same point.[140] Yet the assumption persists, and cannot, it seems, be rooted out simply by detailed suggestions about some of the particular texts involved. A further assumption may be involved here: the quite erroneous idea that 'wisdom' and 'apocalyptic'

---

[137] For the dating of Wis. see e.g. Winston 1979, 20–25, urging a date under Gaius (i.e. AD 37–41). Others are more cautious (e.g. Collins 1998, 179), but still place the book somewhere between the mid-first century BC and the mid-first century AD. Behind most modern understandings of Wis. there stands the seminal work of Larcher (1969, 1983).

[138] e.g. Rom. 1.18–32 with Wis. 13.1–19; 14.8–31; Rom. 2.4 with Wis. 12.10; Rom. 9.14–23 with Wis. 12.12–22; Rom. 9.20f. with Wis. 15.7; Rom. 13.1–7 with Wis. 6.3. On all this see Wright, *Romans*, ad loc.

[139] e.g. Reese 1970, 109f.; Schürer 3.572 (Vermes); Collins 1998, 183–6; Gillman 1997, 108–12; Grabbe 1997, 52; VanderKam 2001, 125. Grabbe 53 sees that 'immortality' and 'resurrection' are not in fact antithetical, but does not develop this or see what this insight does to the reading of ch. 3 in particular. Boismard 1999 [1995], 77 is at least shameless about his *a priori* assumptions: 'We think this hypothesis [of resurrection in Wis.] is excluded for the following reason: according to Platonic theory, a resurrection of the body was unthinkable.' He then, tellingly, has to claim that 5.16b–23 and 3.7–9 are interpolations, 'erratic fragment[s] inserted into the text of Wisdom at a later date', and from a different hand (78f.). This kind of surgery tells its own story. Horbury 2001 suggests that the book offers a 'doctrine of immortality' as the confirmation of God's righteousness (650), teaching a 'spiritual rather than carnal' revival of the righteous in 3.7, even though he sees (651, 656) that in other ways the thought of the book is close to that of 2 Macc., and that 'immortality' and 'resurrection' can easily coexist, as in 1 Cor. 15.53f. and *Ps.-Phoc.* 102–15.

[140] Aquinas, *Summa Contra Gentiles* 4.86; Puech 1993, 92–8, 306. Other supporters of this position are listed in Pfeiffer 1949, 339; Beauchamp 1964; Larcher 1969, 321–7; Cavallin 1974, 133 n. 4; to which should now be added, e.g. Gilbert 1999, 282–7. It is simply not true, as Collins 1978, 188 n. 39 asserts, that Larcher (or any of the others here) proposed that Wis. teaches resurrection 'because of an unsubstantiated assumption that such was standard Jewish belief'; actual arguments have been repeatedly offered. It is, on the contrary, all too frequent that scholars have *denied* the possibility of resurrection in this text because of an unsubstantiated assumption that any mention of an immortal soul means Platonism.

are precise and discrete categories, and that no thinker or writer of the period could belong to both at the same time.[141]

The argument for a different understanding of Wisdom must be made at three levels. First, we must look briefly at the concepts involved. Then (the bulk of the argument) we must examine the underlying story-line of the book. Finally, and briefly once more, we must investigate the wider context within which the book seems to be set.

The first of these should by now be straightforward. The concepts 'resurrection' and 'immortality' are not in themselves antithetical.[142] Of course, if the word 'immortality' is used as a shorthand for wholesale Platonism, then resurrection is out of the question. Scholars have often allowed themselves to forget that Platonic 'immortality' (in which a pre-existent immortal soul comes to live for a while in a mortal body, from which it is happily released at death) is not the only meaning of the word 'immortality' itself. By itself, the word simply means 'a state in which death is not possible'; unless one adopts a Platonic position ahead of time, this cannot of itself be limited to disembodied states. Resurrection, in fact, is one *form* or type of 'immortality'; that is what Paul is saying in 1 Corinthians 15.53–4. He is not 'combining' two disparate beliefs; he is simply describing resurrection itself, a new bodily life in which there can be no more death.[143] Likewise, any Jew who believed in resurrection, from Daniel to the Pharisees and beyond, naturally believed also in an intermediate state in which some kind of personal identity was guaranteed between physical death and the physical re-embodiment of resurrection. This, too, is a form of 'immortality'. Unless we were to suppose that 'resurrection' denoted some kind of newly embodied existence into which one went immediately upon death – and there is no evidence that any Jews of this period believed in such a thing – it is clear that some kind of ongoing existence is assumed. Granted how the word 'immortality' has been used, it may be a misleading label to use for this intermediate state; but in so far as that state involves some kind of personal identity which has not been removed by bodily death the term is not inappropriate.[144]

This kind of continuing state is exactly what is in view in Wisdom 3.1–4, a passage which itself enjoys an ongoing life (in the form of anthems and readings at funerals and memorial services) in the Christian church, long after the rest of the book has been laid to rest, to be nibbled at by the worms and moles of scholarship. It is a consoling passage, and by itself it seems to teach the non-bodily final destiny we meet in Philo and elsewhere:

[141] cf. e.g. Gaventa 1987, 139. On this point see esp. *JVG* 210–14; and Wright, 'Jesus'.

[142] On the logic of 'resurrection' language, and the place of 'immortality' within it, see above, 92.

[143] On 1 Cor. 15 see ch. 7, below.

[144] Cohen 1987, 92 rightly speaks of immortality as a 'close ally' of bodily resurrection. Barr 1992, 105 is right to say that immortality is invoked in support of resurrection; though this obviously does not apply to e.g. 4 Macc.

[1]But the souls of the righteous are in god's hand,
and no torture will ever touch them.
[2]To the eyes of those without understanding, they appeared to have died,
and their departure was thought to be evil,
[3]and their journey away from us to be their ruin;
but they are in peace.
[4]For even though they seemed in human eyes to be punished,
their hope is full of immortality.

This is a warm and moving account of the present state of the righteous after death. The picture of the souls being in god's hand has connections with many other Jewish texts, both biblical and from the writer's own day.[145]

But this passage cannot so easily be lifted out of its context. Its context is a *story*, a story in which these verses are one moment in a sequence. Unfortunately, many readers of the book, treating it as a philosophical discourse about 'wisdom', organized into separate 'topics', have ignored this narrative, producing 'analyses' which carefully put asunder what the writer was equally careful to join together, or simply treating the text as a ragbag of isolated sayings on detached topics.[146] What has then happened is that, spotting the word 'immortality' here and there, and assuming the disjunction noted above, scholars have concluded that the text cannot teach anything else.

The narrative offered in chapters 1—5, within which we must highlight the smaller, and focal, story of 1.16—3.10, is about the actions and respective fates of the 'righteous' and the 'wicked'. It is told, ostensibly, as a warning to the rulers of the earth (1.1; 6.1–11, 21, 24), and this setting may be more than simply a fictitious framework for more general teaching. The story is put into the mouth of Solomon, the wise king of old. He understood wisdom, and his kingdom was established; the book is urging the world's present rulers to do the same. Chapter 6 thus draws together the lesson of chapters 1—5, leading in to the central section of the book, the praise and commendation of Wisdom herself (chapters 7—9). This in turn introduces a retelling of the story of Israel from Adam to the Exodus (chapters 10—19), to which we shall return.

The story told in chapters 1—5 is a classic Jewish narrative of how the wicked are triumphing at present and of how the divine judgment will overtake them in the future. It describes the wicked mulling over the way of the world, and coming to the conclusion that, since death is the end of everything, they may as well live for the moment (1.16—2.9). What is more, they

---

[145] cf. e.g. Dt. 33.3; Philo *Abr.* 258; *Quaes. Gen.* 1.85f.; 3.11; 1.16; *Her.* 280; *Fug.* 97; Sifre Num. 139, quoting 1 Sam. 25.29, as do many Jewish tombstones of the period (see Winston 1979, 125). See too below on Wis. 5.16.

[146] e.g. Winston 1979, 78; Collins 1998, 182, following Kolarcik 1991 (see below). Nickelsburg 1972, 48–92 (see esp. 48 n. 1) divides the material into distinct segments, which ensure that the overall narrative sequence is never considered. It is particularly remarkable that he considers the section 2.21—3.9 as among the 'editorial comments that do not advance the action' in the story of the persecuted and vindicated righteous man.

observe the righteous man, and resent his presence and his witness to a different way of life; whereupon they plot against him (there is a fluidity here between a singular 'righteous man' and 'righteous people' in the plural). The righteous man claims to be the child of the creator; well, they think, let's put this to the test. Let's torture and kill him, and see what will become of him then. He claims that there will be a 'visitation', some kind of future event which will prove him right.[147] They do not believe this for a moment; they have made a compact with death itself (1.16), despite the fact that, as the writer insists, death is a mere intruder into the creator's beautiful and wholesome creation (1.12–15). 'God did not make death,' declares the writer (1.13).[148]

Already the historian will be forming hypotheses. Who are these wicked people? Are they Sadducees, seen from a Pharisaic point of view – rich, powerful aristocrats, persecuting the poor? Are they Epicurean philosophers, or even some variety of atheist?[149] Or are they, as seems likely to me, simply Gentiles seen from a Jewish point of view, perhaps more particularly from the viewpoint of a Jewish community feeling itself under threat or attack? The rhetoric of the 'wicked' in 1.16—2.20 is easily comprehensible as a Jewish summary of many of the viewpoints we have outlined in chapter 2 above; and the contemptuous description of the 'righteous', put into the mouth of the 'wicked' in 2.12–20, is exactly the sort of thing that Jews would have understood as pagan critique of them, not least in a place like Alexandria in the first century.[150] In particular, the challenge they offer to the 'righteous man' is that they will put to the test his claim to be god's child. This forms an important sub-theme of the entire book, and eventually emerges as the point of the Exodus, in which the creator god reveals before the pagan Egyptians that Israel really is his firstborn son.[151]

The writer pauses, at the end of the speech of the 'wicked', to reflect on their ignorance of the way the world actually is, and of the purposes of the creator. Death never was the creator's intention; therefore, he implies, death will not have the last word. The creator has made us for incorruption (*aphtharsia*, an important word for Paul as well), making us in the image of

---

[147] Wis. 2.20. The connection of this 'visitation' (*episkope*) with that in 3.7 is completely obscured in most translations.

[148] This does not mean that death is seen as somehow less than real (as suggested by e.g. Collins 1978, 186, 191; Barr 1992, 129f.). For Wis., *bodily* death is real and matters, just as bodily life is real, and matters, too. The point being made is that, despite bodily death, Israel's god has a surprise gift up his sleeve: a blissful temporary rest, with the hope of final – and, as I shall argue below, bodily – immortality, i.e. resurrection.

[149] See e.g. Gilbert 1999, 309, following Larcher; Grabbe 1997, 50. As we saw above (134), Josephus likens the Sadducees to Epicureans.

[150] For political tension in Alexandria see again Goodenough 1967 [1938].

[151] Wis. 2.13, 16, 18; 5.5; 18.13; cf. also 14.3. This is another narrative link that most scholars seem to ignore.

his own eternity.[152] This brings the writer to the point where he can disclose what is in fact the case. The righteous, though they may have been killed by the wicked, have not, as the wicked suppose, disappeared for ever. At present they are at peace, in the hand of god, away from all possibility of torment. This has brought us back to the famous passage quoted above (3.1–4), which continues with a reflection on how Israel's god tests the righteous like gold in a furnace, and accepts their suffering and death as a sacrificial burnt offering (3.5–6). But the writer is not content with drawing attention to the present state of the 'righteous'. He wants his readers to focus on what is going to happen next.

This is where, in my judgment, the most serious misreadings of the text have occurred.[153] Wisdom 3.1–10 offers a *two-stage* description of what happens after the death of the 'righteous': a *story* in which the present existence 'in the hand of god' is merely the prelude to what is about to happen:

> [7]And at the time of their visitation they will shine forth,
> and run about like sparks in the stubble.
> [8]They will judge nations, and rule over peoples,
> and the Lord will be their king for ever.
> [9]Those who trust in him will understand truth,
> and those who are loyal and faithful will remain with him in love;
> for his grace and mercy are upon his chosen ones.[154]
> [10]But the ungodly will receive their reward according to their own reasonings,
> because they disregarded the righteous, and rebelled against the Lord.[155]

It should be clear that verses 7–10 are describing a *further* event which *follows upon* the state described in verses 1–4.[156] The passage is not simply a second, parallel description, a reinterpretation.[157] After all, the 'souls' in

---

[152] Wis. 2.23. Some MSS, by dropping a single letter, read 'nature' for 'eternity'.

[153] e.g. Kellermann 1979, 102–04, who, despite the theme of his whole book, only actually discusses Wis. 3.1–6.

[154] Some MSS add an extra line, as in 4.15: 'and he watches over his elect'.

[155] Many texts and translations insert a paragraph break between vv. 9 and 10. This would not affect the present argument; though it does seem to me that v. 10 goes naturally with what precedes, completing the judgment scene. 3.11—4.15 then offers an extended meditation on the lives of the wicked, before 4.16 takes up the story once more.

[156] So, rightly, e.g. Nickelsburg 1972, 89; Cavallin 1974, 127f., though neither of them discerns what this second stage consists of. The correct conclusion is drawn by Larcher 1969, 322f., citing F. Focke: the present state of passive peace (vv. 1–4) 'n'est pas encore la béatitude définitive'. Boismard 1999 [1995], viii recognizes the two-stage sequence, but says that 'the souls of the righteous are led to God after sojourning in Hades for a period of time'. How being 'in the hand of God' can (a) be equated with Hades and (b) designate a location *from which* one is 'led to God' is, I confess, baffling.

[157] Against e.g. Kolarcik 1991, 82–5. Kolarcik manages to avoid discussing the meaning of v. 8, and (42) runs together vv. 7a and 9b to make it look as if the writer is simply saying that, in this blessed immortal state, the righteous 'will shine forth as sparks flashing in stubble, and they will remain with God in love'. The writer is not merely contrasting 'appearance' (vv. 2–3a) with 'reality' (vv. 7–9), but present with future.

verse 4 still have a '*hope* full of immortality'; this implies that they have not yet fully attained to it. The mainstream reading of the passage has not, in fact, taken seriously enough the writer's own polemic against death itself (1.12–16; 2.23–4), based firmly on the typical Jewish belief in the goodness of the created world (1.14), a point which is reiterated at the end of the book when creation itself comes to the aid of the Israelites as they escape from Egypt.[158] There is always the danger that commentators will agree with the wicked in making an alliance with death – a position adopted unwittingly, it seems, by Alan Segal, when, intending to summarize 3.1–4, he says that there is here 'no obvious end of time with a judgment' (there would have been, had he continued a few verses further) and, tellingly, that 'there is no remedy for death, in that no one returns from it.'[159] That, of course, is what, according to the writer, the *wicked* have been saying (2.1–5); the present passage is written, not to support that point of view, but to refute it. Clearly, if exegesis stands the text on its head like this, something has gone badly wrong. Segal declares that the work 'uses a Greek notion of immortality in describing the more traditionally Jewish notion of resurrection for martyrs'.[160] I shall now argue that the work does describe resurrection, and that any Greek borrowing (which after all pervades all Judaism throughout the period) is held firmly within this essentially Jewish notion. 'Immortality' is pressed into service, in fact, to enable the picture of resurrection to attain clarity.

To return for a moment to the picture of the righteous, with their souls safe in the hand of the creator god (3.1–4). They seemed to the unrighteous to have died, says the writer; the sinners, after all, have declared their belief that death is the end of everything (2.1–5), and this contrast between appearance and reality is noted elsewhere in both pagan and Jewish writings.[161] The reality, though, is that the righteous have come through a time of fierce testing, through which their god has regarded them as a sacrificial offering.[162] Now they are at peace. Their hope is for immortality, a deathless life to which they look forward.[163] Though there are some puzzles here, the author clearly believes, as a general point, that the soul is not naturally immortal, but can attain immortality through obtaining wisdom.[164]

---

[158] cf. Wis. 16.17–29; 19.6–12, 18–21. This point is rightly emphasized by Beauchamp 1964.

[159] Segal 1997, 103.

[160] Segal, ibid.

[161] e.g. Plato *Phaedo* 106e, 114c, 115d; *1 En.* 102.6f.

[162] The same word, *holokautoma*, is used of Isaac in 4 Macc. 18.11.

[163] 'Soul at peace' was a frequent inscription on Jewish tombstones of the period; see Winston 1979, 126f. for details.

[164] See Wis. 4.1; 8.13, 17; 15.3; and cf. Philo *Quaes. Gen.* 1.16; *Op.* 154; *Conf.* 149. There are perhaps some potential parallels here between the role of Wisdom in the present book and that of faith, or even of Christ, in the NT, not least in Paul (I am grateful to Dr Andrew Goddard for raising this point).

The end of the story, though, only now comes into view. Verses 7–10 describe a further event: the *future* status of the righteous.[165] We must take this step by step; the case is not cumulative, since the logic of the entire passage hinges on this reading, but the details add considerable weight to the narrative structure.

'The time of their visitation' (v. 7) clearly refers to an event still in the future.[166] Within the book, 'visitation' (*episkope*) is a regular word for a day of judgment on which the creator will condemn the wicked and vindicate the righteous. This is the moment which the righteous had spoken of, causing the wicked to mock, and to put them to the test (2.20). It is referred to again a few verses after the present passage (3.13), and then once more in the immediate setting (4.15)[167] and twice later in the book (14.11; 19.15). On each occasion it refers to a divine 'visitation' through which justice will be done, whether positively or negatively. The word is frequent in the LXX, with the same range of meaning;[168] the New Testament offers two examples of the word in this sense, both striking.[169] When evildoers, especially idolators, act boastfully and wickedly, there will eventually be a 'visitation' in which God will put things to rights. In the present context, the point is that verse 7 cannot be *reinterpreting* the events of verses 1–4 from another point of view. It must be adding a new point: that, after a time of rest, something new will happen to the righteous.

But what is this 'something new'? They will 'shine forth', declares the writer, 'and run like sparks through the stubble'. This, too, cannot be assimilated to 3.1–4. It is not simply suggesting that, in their post-mortem state, the souls of the righteous have become like stars. It is not a reference to 'astral immortality'.[170] As in Daniel 12.3, what is described here is not the state upon which the righteous enter immediately after death. Rather, it is the glorious, prestigious new condition in which they will reappear upon the earth, ruling and judging the nations. The word for 'they will shine forth' (*analampsousin*) is very close to the Theodotion version of Daniel 12.3 (*eklampsousin*), and the image is similar to passages in *1 Enoch* where resurrection is certainly in view.[171] The rare Greek verb *analampo* does indeed mean 'shine forth', and can be used of the shining of the sun; but it is also used metaphorically to mean 'flame up', as of envy, or 'blaze up' with

[165] So, rightly, e.g. Puech 1993, 97; against e.g. Kolarcik 1991, 42, 84f.

[166] So Cavallin 1974, 127f.; Grappe 2001, 65.

[167] The same phrase also occurs in the longer reading at Wis. 3.9 (see above).

[168] e.g. Gen. 50.24f.; Ex. 3.16; 4.31; Num. 16.29; Isa. 10.3; 23.17; 29.6; Sir. 16.18; 23.24. Of particular interest is Jer. 6.15, and esp. 10.15f., where the phrase is identical to the one in our present passage.

[169] Lk. 19.44; 1 Pet. 2.12. Cf. the cognate verb in Lk. 1.68, 78; 7.16; Ac. 15.14.

[170] Despite many writers, e.g. Reese 1970, 79; Martin 1995, 274 n. 57; Grabbe 1997, 56, following Dupont-Sommer 1949. On 'astral immortality' see above (57–60; 110–12).

[171] e.g. *1 En.* 38.4; 39.7; 62.13–16; 104.2; 108.12–14. See too 4 Ezra 7.97; 2 *Bar.* 51.10.

enthusiasm. In one interesting passage, Plutarch uses it of Brutus 'reviving,' 'coming to himself'.[172] This, I suggest, is something like the required sense here. The righteous, whose souls are presently in the hands of their maker, have not yet attained the ultimate goal. At the time of their 'visitation' they will 'revive', and attain the same kind of glory as the 'wise' in Daniel 12.2–3 (which, as most agree, stands closely behind Wisdom 2—3); in other words, they will be set in authority over the created order. This is at once confirmed in the following verses. Indeed, the coherence of the whole sequence of thought, read this way, provides a strong argument in its favour.

'Running like sparks through the stubble' does not evoke some kind of astral or celestial bliss or glory, but rather speaks of judgment, as in Isaiah 5.24 and Obadiah 18.[173] The image thus prepares us for the next verse, in which the righteous will judge nations and rule over peoples, taking on the role marked out for the eschatological people of YHWH in (for instance) Daniel 7.22, Sirach 4.15 and 1QpHab 5.4. The whole point is that this is *not* happening at the moment, i.e. in the time described in 3.1–4; at the moment, the righteous seem to be lost and gone, and the wicked are celebrating their disappearance; but they will return as the masters of the world. This is more or less the same image that we find in the royal Psalms such as 72 and 89.19–37, and in such prophetic passages as Isaiah 11.1–10. We are thus not surprised when, at the equivalent point in the larger narrative, the righteous are given kingly crowns and diadems (Wisdom 5.15). This is familiar ground, not least from the Danielic picture of the suffering 'saints of the most high' who receive the kingdom and judge the nations.

We are, in fact, in the middle of what we might call 'kingdom-of-god' theology, in the classic apocalyptic mode.[174] If Wisdom 3.8b had not referred explicitly to Israel's god becoming king, we might have been tempted to use the phrase ourselves as a summary of the drift of the whole passage. 'The Lord will be their king', or 'the Lord will reign over them as king', for ever. This sends us back once again to a long biblical tradition in which YHWH's coming kingdom will mean, very explicitly, the overthrow of the wicked, especially the pagan nations, and the vindication of the righteous, which normally means Israel.[175] The reign of YHWH will be universal, and universally effective for justice against evildoers and vindication of the

---

[172] Plut. *Brut.* 15; cf. 2.694f. Other refs. in LSJ s.v.

[173] See Reese 1970, 79, with other refs. Cf. too Joel 2.5; Nah. 1.10. In the Obad. passage the Jews are the fire and the Edomites the stubble.

[174] On 'apocalyptic' (a slippery word, but still perhaps just useful here) see *NTPG* 280–99, including discussion of Daniel. See too *JVG* frequently, esp. 95–7, 207–14, and (on the relation between 'wisdom' and 'apocalyptic') 311–16.

[175] e.g. Ex. 15.18, very similar in wording to Wis. 3.8b (all the more significant in view of the major Exodus-motif in the final section of the book); Ps. 10.16; 29.10; 146.10; Jer. 10.10; Lam. 5.19; and esp. Dan. 4.34; 6.26. Each of these passages could be explored in more detail, and the point would emerge all the more clearly.

righteous. That is what the present passage is about, as verse 10 makes abundantly clear.

This means that 3.9 cannot simply refer to the blissful state, abiding in God's loving presence, which has already been referred to in 3.1 and 3.3. It is a new moment in the story, especially if the longer reading of v. 9 is accepted.[176] The entire sequence of thought is in fact spelling out, making more precise, what we find again and again in the book of Daniel, reaching its climactic statements in chapter 7 and in 12.1–3. The links between Wisdom 2—3 and Daniel have often been noted, but this lesson has seldom been drawn out as it should have been; similarly, the links to Isaiah 53 should by now not only be clear, as many have suggested, but should be allowed their full weight.[177] The present passage does not mention the word 'resurrection' – perhaps because the author really does want to address an audience which will include pagans, and he knows full well that 'resurrection' denotes something that all pagans firmly deny.[178] But that it teaches the same as Daniel does about the ultimate fate of God's people there should now be no doubt.

When the judgment scene reappears in 4.16—5.23, after the 'aside' about the behaviour of the wicked and the righteous (3.11—4.15), we have once more a clear sense of being on the ground marked out by Daniel and the later apocalyptic writers. The wicked, who are at present mocking the righteous, both living and departed, will have to face the consequences of their deeds and words. The righteous, whom they thought dead and gone, will confront them once more, since they will 'stand with great confidence' in the presence of their oppressors; the word 'stand' (*stesetai*) does not by itself indicate resurrection, but it is closely cognate with the word that would have done (*anastasis*), and since the point is that formerly dead people are now, surprisingly, confronting and judging the wicked, it is safe to say that resurrection is what is meant.[179] The scene is linked with the earlier one not least by the puzzlement of the wicked at discovering that the righteous really are the children of the creator god.[180] The wicked then turn out to be insubstantial, like wind or smoke; they have embraced the pagan way, and the

---

[176] Against e.g. Kolarcik 1991, 42.

[177] See esp. e.g. Nickelsburg 1972, 61–6 (on Isa.); 62–86 (on Dan.); Cavallin 1974, 127, with other refs. in 133 n. 8; also e.g. Winston 1979, 146 on the parallels with, and influence of, Isa.

[178] See Puech 1993, 96f.

[179] Cavallin 1974, 129 agrees that for the righteous man to be 'standing', and to be visible, does seem to demand that he has a body, but denies that this language can be 'forced to prove' that the author believed in bodily resurrection. By itself maybe not; in the context of chs. 1—5 as a whole, it may well do.

[180] Wis. 5.5; cf. 2.13, 16, 18. The final appearance of this theme in 18.13, echoing Ex. 4.22f., 12.31, indicates that 'god's children' here means 'Israel', not 'angels', as is sometimes suggested (e.g. Cavallin 1974, 129, 134 n. 17; Winston 1979, 147).

pagan fate has come upon them.[181] The righteous, meanwhile, are rewarded with crowns and diadems, because YHWH will do what he promised in Isaiah 59.17–18, namely, putting on his armour and winning the decisive victory. Interestingly, creation itself will join in the battle on the side of righteousness (5.20), as it will in the retold Exodus narrative later in the book. There is no suggestion that all this is what is 'really' going on while the souls of the righteous are in God's hand, out of sight; on the contrary, the logic of the entire narrative, in which the wicked (having thought they had seen the last of the righteous) are confronted with them back again, insists that it is a further stage, a new moment of decisive judgment, a 'visitation' from God.

What then of the other passages, further on in the book, which assert the immortality of the soul, and perhaps a more Platonic view of the body? It does appear that in chapters 8 and 9 the author, meditating on Wisdom and urging his readers to seek her, does use expressions that have more in common with Philo than with the biblical tradition. Wisdom 8.13 speaks of Wisdom conferring immortality. In 8.19–20 the writer (speaking in the mouth of Solomon) speaks of a good soul falling to his lot, and then at once corrects himself: 'or rather, being good, I entered an undefiled body'. Some have supposed that this was an allusion to the theory of transmigration.[182] Others have suggested that the writer over-corrected, and did not intend verse 20 to be taken strictly as it sounds.[183] Certainly the mention of an 'undefiled' body sits uncomfortably alongside 9.15, which states that 'a perishable body weighs down the soul, and this earthy tent burdens the thoughtful mind' – a sentence which readers of Paul will find interestingly familiar from 2 Corinthians 4.16—5.5.[184] But the main contrast does not seem to be the Platonic one between an immortal soul and a dispensable body; rather, the problem – as with Paul – is that the present body is 'perishable', doomed to die. To complain about such a body is not to long for a disembodied existence, but rather for a body worthy of the inner life that is already there. If we take seriously what was said about death in the first three chapters, it should be clear that, unless the writer has changed his mind quite drastically, death, which for a Platonist would be a good thing to be warmly welcomed, freeing one from the nuisance and evil of a material body, is to be regarded as an enemy, an intruder into God's good world. Wisdom 8 and 9, however, no doubt in implicit dialogue with the same world of thought as Philo, has certainly used expressions which by themselves could be taken in various different ways. This is not true, though, of 16.13, which picks up the biblical emphasis that YHWH is the one who truly has the power of life and death; he

---

[181] Wis. 5.9–14.

[182] See Grabbe 1997, 55.

[183] Winston 1979, 25f., following Larcher. Cf. de Boer 1988, 59, pointing out that the book's anthropology is in any case not consistently articulated.

[184] For a possible Platonic parallel cf. *Phaedo* 66b, 81c; for other comparative material cf. Winston 1979, 207, to which add Hor. *Sat.* 2.2.77–9. On 2 Cor. 4—5 see ch. 7, below.

brings mortals down to the gates of Hades and back again.[185] This is again a different point, but emphasizes the strong Jewish belief in YHWH as the Lord of creation.

The book reaches its denouement in the great retelling of the Exodus in chapters 16—19. Here at last we see where it has all been going, what the scenes between the wicked and the righteous were pointing towards. The Egyptians hold the Israelites in their power (17.2), but the plagues come upon them, while for the Israelites there is light and protection (18.1–4). This corresponds, more or less, to 3.1–4 within chapters 1—5. And this, too, is but the prelude to the final scene, when Israel's god judges the Egyptians and rescues the Israelites, bringing death on the former but not on the latter (18.5–13). It is this that makes the Egyptians declare that Israel really is god's child after all (18.13).[186] Meanwhile, the created world, which is not a gloomy, evil place, as in Platonism, but is the good creation of the good creator, as in 1.14, fights on Israel's side. It renews itself, behaving in unexpected ways, and enables the liberation of YHWH's people to take place despite all the forces ranged against them.[187]

Finally, we must enquire about the implicit setting of this remarkable book. Though certainty is impossible, I agree with Winston and others who have urged that it be read as a coded message both to Israel and her potential or actual persecutors in a time of danger and distress. The god who acted at the Exodus to rescue Israel from the pagan Egyptians can and will do so again. Death, the greatest weapon of the tyrant, is an intruder in the creator's world, and YHWH has it in his power to overcome it and not only restore the righteous to life but install them as rulers, judges and kings.

It may not be possible at this remove, and without new evidence, to decide whether the implied opponents, from the 'wicked' in the early chapters to the Egyptians in the closing scenes, are the pagan Egyptians of the writer's day (assuming for the sake of argument that he lives in Egypt, possibly in Alexandria), or the Romans, or simply the pagan world in general.[188] But we should not screen out the political dimension from the book, which after all announces right at the start its intention of addressing the world's rulers (1.1), and returns to the theme when introducing the central section (6.1–11). Just as scholars have recently been rediscovering the political implications of Paul's writings, so now it may be time to read Wisdom not simply as a philosophical treatise but as a coded warning to would-be pagan

---

[185] Cf. Dt. 32.39; 1 Sam. 2.6.

[186] See above on this theme in Wis. 2.13, 16, 18; 5.5.

[187] cf. Wis. 16.17–29; 19.6–12, 18–21.

[188] The possibility of a coded attack on imperial Rome, more specifically the celebrated *pax Romana*, is increased by Wis. 14.22, where the pagans, who 'live in great strife due to ignorance', 'call such great evils peace'. This reminds us of the wry comment Tacitus puts into the mouth of the Briton Calgacus: 'They make a wilderness, and call it "peace"' (*Agr.* 30.6). See *NTPG* 154.

oppressors of the Jews, and as a coded encouragement to Jewish readers, urging them to stand firm and trust their god for eventual vindication.[189] If we think of the Maccabaean crisis, and the very different ways it was used in subsequent writing; of the Roman takeover in 63 BC, and the reflection of that in various works; of the turbulent events in Palestine, Egypt and elsewhere in the first half of the first century AD; and of the awful catastrophe of AD 70 itself – then it will not be difficult to imagine situations in which the book would be read, and read eagerly, not as a cool, detached essay about how to gain immortality through the pursuit of Wisdom, but as an exciting and dramatic call to courage and perhaps even resistance. And, once disciplined historical imagination has got that far, it is only a short step to suppose that this was what the writer intended.

We can, then, confirm and strengthen the proposal of Puech, Gilbert and others. The Wisdom of Solomon certainly does teach 'immortality', but it is (a) an immortality which is *attained* through wisdom, not innate in a preexistent soul (leaving 8.19–20 as a remaining puzzle, but not allowing it to veto what the rest of the work, in form and shape as well as content, actually says); and (b), probably more important, an immortality which would ultimately consist not in a disembodied soul but in a renewed bodily life, when at last the soul is given a body to match it (9.15). The time when 'the souls of the righteous are in god's hand' (3.1) is simply the temporary period of rest during which they are looked after, like Daniel going to his 'rest', or the souls under the altar in Revelation, until the time when they, like him, rise for their reward, and indeed for their rule over the world.[190] There is no 'tension' here between two different doctrines.[191] To suggest such a thing is simply to fail to see how the story works, and how those who believe in a final resurrection necessarily also believe in an intermediate time when those to be raised in the future are kept alive not by an innate immortality but by the power and love of Israel's god.[192] Exactly this sequence, in not

---

[189] On Paul see e.g. Horsley 1997; 2000. On Wis. see the remarks of Winston 1979, 24 n. 35. Collins 1998, 179 is right to say that the book cannot be read as a 'veiled historical commentary', in other words that we cannot mirror-read a precise situation from it. The possibility of a strong political intention remains open. See again the parallel with Philo drawn out by Goodenough 1967 [1938].

[190] Dan. 12.13; Rev. 6.9–11.

[191] Cavallin 1974, 128 suggests that 'the two types of eschatology are apparently only juxtaposed without very much reflection on the tension between them', citing also Larcher 1969, 316ff. With respect, we suggest that the lack of reflection is more properly predicated of the scholarly tradition (that of mainstream biblical scholarship for many years) in which such a suggestion could be made. To be fair, the remaining puzzles of 8.19f. and 9.15 have as it were thrown dust in the eyes of those reading 3.1–10; but there is no inconsistency in chs. 1—5. Nickelsburg 1972, 87–90 seems to me to make unduly heavy weather of the whole question.

[192] Cavallin's summary (1974, 132f.), though correct to say that resurrection is not mentioned, seems to me tendentious, and to avoid the whole thrust of the narrative involved. The text of Wis. 3.7–9 is scarcely represented adequately by his statement that 'after death

dissimilar language to that of chapter 3, is what we find in the near-contemporary *Pseudo-Philo* (see below).

This in turn leads to a reflection on how the full picture emerged within Judaism. It is unlikely that a quasi-Platonic belief in continuing disembodied existence after death could lead to a belief in resurrection, as Barr suggests; such a move would be cutting off the branch it had just begun to sit on.[193] Rather, it seems probable that the emerging belief in resurrection (grounded, as we have seen, in the same belief in YHWH as creator as characterized ancient Israel) precipitated further reflection on the continuing identity of the people of YHWH in between bodily death and resurrection. For that task, hellenistic language about the soul lay ready to hand. It was capable of being imported without necessarily bringing all its latent Platonic baggage with it.

Like the martyrs in 2 Maccabees, the 'righteous' described in chapters 2—5 are faithful Jews who hold fast to their god in the face of torture and death, and are finally declared to be truly his children through the resurrection, the great event for which the Exodus from Egypt was the prototype. The resonances set up by this theme are of enormous importance not only for understanding second-Temple Judaism in general, but for grasping the heart of its extraordinary mutation, early Christianity.

(vi) Resurrection, in Other Words: Josephus

The statements of Josephus (c. AD 37–100) on the resurrection have frequently been discussed, and are not controversial in the way that the Wisdom of Solomon has been. It will be sufficient here to set out the key passages and draw the relevant conclusions.[194] We begin with passages in which Josephus, so far as we can tell, intends to express his own beliefs.

In the early days of the Jewish revolt against Rome, Josephus, as a young army commander, found himself involved in the fall of Jotapata.[195] Those

---

the righteous will be glorified and transformed into the glory of angels, enjoying a life in close fellowship with God and sharing his rule' (133); that sounds as though the righteous have simply (in the later, slipshod way of putting it), 'gone to heaven', which is hardly consonant with their ruling over nations and peoples in the kingdom of god. Cavallin's own statement (133) that the writer is working with 'traditional Jewish apocalyptic ideas about a final universal judgment' is a pointer in the right direction, but the implications have not been followed through.

[193] See Barr 1992, 54–6.

[194] We here follow the line of *NTPG* 324–7, noting some more works that have come to hand since that was written: e.g. Mason 1991, 156–70, 297–308; Puech 1993, 213–15. On Josephus' interesting and relevant understanding of the 'ascension' of Elijah, Elisha and Moses see Tabor 1989.

[195] *War* 3.316–39. Josephus gives the exact date: the new moon of Panemus in the thirteenth year of Nero's reign, i.e. 20 July, AD 67 (3.339).

with him urge him to commit suicide rather than surrender to the Romans.[196] He, however, argues vehemently that suicide is a crime. We receive our life from the creator god, and his gifts ought not to be scorned.[197] Surely you know, he says,

> that people who depart from this life in accordance with nature's law, thus repaying what god had lent them, when the giver wants to claim it back again, win everlasting fame. Their houses and families are secure. Their souls remain without blemish, and obedient, and receive the most holy place in heaven. From there, when the ages come round again [*ek peritropes aionon*], they come back again to live instead in holy bodies. But when people lay hands upon themselves in a fit of madness, the darker regions of Hades receive their souls; and god, their father, pays back their descendants for the arrogant acts of their parents.[198]

A very similar picture, again expounded by Josephus as his own belief, is found in *Against Apion*. People who live in accordance with the Jewish law, he boasts, do not do so for silver or gold, or for public marks of acclamation. No:

> Every person, trusting in the evidence of their own conscience, on the basis of the lawgiver's prophecies and the strong faithfulness of god, is persuaded that if they observe the laws and, if necessary, are prepared to die for them, god has given them a renewed existence [*genesthai te palin*], and to receive a new life out of the renewal [*ek peritropes*].[199]

In the first of these passages we have a clear two-stage personal eschatology, just as I have argued in relation to Wisdom 3. First, the souls go to heaven. Then they return, to live in a new kind of body, a holy one. By the phrase 'when the ages come round again', literally 'out of the turning around of the ages', Josephus does not, I take it, mean to refer either to transmigration in the strict, Platonic sense, nor to the Stoic doctrine of the world being consumed by fire and everything beginning all over again, but to 'the age to come' in the normal rabbinic sense.[200] Though this has been shortened in the second passage to 'out of the renewal' or 'out of the turning around', we should not doubt that the same two-age doctrine is what he has in mind. In

---

[196] *War* 3.355–60.

[197] *War* 3.371. Translations of Josephus are my own except where noted.

[198] *War* 3.374f.

[199] *Ap.* 2.217f.

[200] Against the suggestion of e.g. Harvey 1982, 150f., followed by Carnley 1987, 53; and cf. e.g. Barr 1992, 133 n. 32. Harvey complains that scholars have 'shouted down' the Pythagorean implications of Josephus' language in their eagerness to find orthodox rabbinic doctrine here, albeit reinterpreted to be intelligible to Greek readers. The problem with this is (a) that there is plenty of evidence, in Josephus and elsewhere, that he and others did 'translate' Jewish ideas into Greek ones (e.g. his description of Jewish parties as philosophical schools), and (b) that Josephus elsewhere speaks more explicitly of resurrection itself. See too Sanders 1992, 301, warning against pressing Josephus' language too hard.

the second passage, too, Josephus makes the strong claim that belief in resurrection is supported not only by conscience and the faithfulness of God, but by 'the lawgiver's prophecies'. As we have seen in the rabbis, and shall see in the New Testament, the question of whether the resurrection was prophesied by Moses himself was at the heart of at least some first-century debate on the subject. Josephus is here adopting a clear-cut Pharisaic position, both on the content of the belief and on its biblical basis. And, as with the Wisdom of Solomon, a belief in resurrection entails, of course, a belief in some sort of continuity between the person who dies and the person who will receive a new body in God's new age; and this continuity is provided easily enough by a belief in the immortality of the soul. Josephus certainly believed in this, and it stands in no tension, for reasons already given, with resurrection.[201]

When, however, Josephus is describing the official positions of the 'schools' or 'philosophies', he does his best to make them correspond to the three major schools of greco-roman thought, the Stoic, the Epicurean and the Pythagorean.[202] He aligns the Epicureans with the Sadducees, and the Pythagoreans with the Essenes, which means that he wants to be able, for his apologetic reasons, to describe the Pharisaic belief in terms similar to the Stoics. Thus he declares that the Pharisees attribute everything to Fate and to the deity, while humans have the task of co-operating with Fate.[203] When it comes to the soul and the future life,

> [the Pharisees] hold that every soul is immortal, but that only the souls of the virtuous pass on into another body, while those of the wicked are punished with an everlasting vengeance.[204]

Meanwhile the Sadducees, he says, want nothing to do with any of these ideas.[205] This again could conceivably mean transmigration or reincarnation, as some indeed have suggested.[206] But in the context of the earlier passages we are safe in concluding that Josephus is *referring to* the doctrine of bodily resurrection, even though using language which by itself would be capable of connoting other views – understandable enough when seeking to communicate with non-Jews, whose age-old disbelief in resurrection Josephus

---

[201] For an incidental mention of his belief in the soul's immortality cf. *Ant.* 17.354.

[202] Why he does not follow Cicero's distinctions (*De Nat. Deor.*), and include the Academics instead of the Pythagoreans, is not clear, at least not to me.

[203] *War* 2.162. As is often pointed out, 'fate' here is a term with which pagan readers would be familiar, though Jewish thinkers might more naturally have referred to 'providence'.

[204] *War* 2.163. Segal 1997, 108 rightly comments that this does not mean metempsychosis or reincarnation, but the gift of a different kind of body: 'like Paul, [Josephus] sees a new incorruptible flesh'. This, Segal suggests, may be close to the beliefs found in *1 En.*

[205] *War* 2.165.

[206] e.g. Thackeray in Loeb edn. 386 n.; Schürer 2.543 n. 103 (Cave).

would know well enough. It was not part of his purpose, at this point at least, to make the leading Jewish sect look ridiculous to his readers.[207]

This tendency, to make the Pharisees appear like a hellenistic philosophical school, is visible again in the equivalent passage in the *Antiquities*:

> They believe that souls have immortal power, and that there are rewards and punishments under the earth for those who have done well or badly in their life. Evil souls receive eternal imprisonment, while virtuous ones have an easy route to a new life.[208]

Feldman, in his note in the Loeb edition, is right to point out that the doctrine Josephus is describing is unmistakably the Pharisaic belief in resurrection, not (as some have suggested), reincarnation or transmigration.[209] That, in describing this belief, he uses language which would remind pagan hearers of those views is quite another thing.[210] The word for 'to a new life', literally 'to a living again', is *anabioun*, cognate with *anabiosis* in 2 Maccabees 7.9, which certainly refers to the resurrection.[211] However, the idea of rewards and punishments 'under the earth', *hypo chthonos*, is clearly an accommodation to pagan thought-forms, since Josephus earlier said that the righteous go first to heaven and thence to a new life. The main thrust, though – the underlying story-line – remains, as in 2 Maccabees and Wisdom 3, a *two-stage* personal journey for the righteous at least: first, they go to the place of the dead; then (in this case by an 'easy passage'), they come into a new mode of life.

This is the view which we should assume lies behind the teaching of the sages on risking death for Israel's god and the Torah. Josephus describes the learned doctors, obviously Pharisees, egging on the young men to pull down the eagle which Herod had set up at the Temple gate.[212] Even if this is risky, they say,

> it is a noble deed to die for the law of your country, for the souls of those who come to such an end attain immortality, and an everlasting sense of bliss.[213]

---

[207] This undermines the suggestion of Porter 1999a, 54–7, that Josephus indicates that 'traditional Greek thought of the afterlife is the dominant motif,' even among the Pharisees.

[208] *Ant.* 18.14.

[209] Loeb 13 n., against Thackeray. Mason 1991, 156–70 argues that resurrection is a peculiar, Jewish, non-dualistic form of 'reincarnation', and in a sense this is of course correct. But the distinctions between 'resurrection' and 'reincarnation' are as important as the similarities, and the regular and popular meaning of the latter idea, in both the ancient and the modern world, tends to focus on those differences (a cyclic view of personal and cosmic history, the undesirability of the soul's being embodied, and so on), making it unhelpful, in my view, to elide the two beliefs.

[210] This is the strong point of Mason's argument (see previous note).

[211] So Feldman, loc. cit.

[212] For the incident cf. *NTPG* 172.

[213] *War* 1.650. The young men repeat this lesson when Herod asks them why they did the deed (1.653).

As in Wisdom, we note, such people *attain* immortality; they do not, so it seems, possess it automatically, as in Plato. The longer version of the same incident in the *Antiquities* adds a few more elements:

> Those who are about to die in order to preserve and safeguard their ancestral way of life regard the virtue they acquire in death far more profitable than the pleasure of going on living. For, since they gain eternal fame and glory for themselves, they will be praised by those alive at the moment, and will leave the continuing memorial of their lives to subsequent generations. Moreover (said the teachers), even people who live lives free of danger cannot escape the chance of death. Those who strive for virtue, then, do well to accept their fate with praise and honour when they depart this life. For death comes much more easily to those who risk danger for an upright cause; and, at the same time, they win for their children, and their surviving male and female relatives, whoever they may be, the benefit of the renown they have won.[214]

If this was all we had to go on, we would never suppose Josephus was thinking about resurrection; but from all we know of the incident concerned, and the virtual certainty that the 'doctors' in question were Pharisees, we cannot doubt that the actual speeches were far more reminiscent of the mother's words to the seven sons in 2 Maccabees, rather than, as here, the sort of thing Greek or Roman teachers might say to people who were about to act, and probably die, in a noble cause.

That is, in fact, what is going on. Throughout his work, Josephus is trying to explain to his audience that the mainstream Jewish teachers, the 'schools', were really philosophers, and that it was a different group, the 'fourth philosophy', who were to blame for the disasters that had befallen his countrymen. They were the revolutionaries, the brigands, the wild and lawless men who pulled down the national life into the vortex of their own crazy dreams.[215] Since, on his own showing, a large number of his fellow Jews were caught up in this movement, he has his work cut out to narrow down the field and find a small group to name and shame in this way, but he does his best.

We should not be surprised, then, that when the arch-ringleader of the revolutionaries, Eleazar, the leader of the Sicarii on Masada, makes his last great speech, Josephus puts into his mouth quite different views from those set out above. Josephus himself had stayed within the bounds of Judaism; Eleazar will appear as a pagan philosopher. Josephus had spoken strongly against suicide; Eleazar will advocate it:

> Life, not death, is man's misfortune. For it is death which gives liberty to the soul and permits it to depart to its own pure abode, there to be free from all calamity; but so long as it is imprisoned in a mortal body and tainted with all its miseries, it is, in

---

[214] *Ant.* 17.152–4. Here, too, the culprits repeat their lessons under interrogation (17.158f.).
[215] On these movements see *NTPG* 170–81, 185–203.

sober truth, dead, for association with what is mortal ill befits that which is divine. True, the soul possesses great capacity, even while incarcerated in the body . . . But it is not until, freed from the weight that drags it down to earth and clings about it, the soul is restored to its proper sphere, that it enjoys a blessed energy and a power untrammelled on every side, remaining, like God himself, invisible to human eyes. For even while in the body it is withdrawn from view: unperceived it comes and unseen it again departs, itself of a nature one and incorruptible, but a cause of change to the body. For whatever the soul has touched lives and flourishes, whatever it abandons withers and dies; so abundant is her wealth of immortality.[216]

And Eleazar goes on to speak of death in terms of sleep – not to make the point, as in Daniel and the New Testament, that those who sleep may wake again to a new day,[217] but to celebrate the fact, widely recognized in paganism, that during sleep humans become independent, with new powers of travel, knowledge of the future, and intercourse with divine beings.[218] Even if we do not go all the way with Morton Smith's caustic description of this speech as 'Josephus' last insult to his dead opponents', we can certainly agree that it sounds a lot less like a hard-line revolutionary Jewish leader and a lot more like a pagan philosopher.[219] Josephus is managing simultaneously to distance himself from the revolutionaries and to portray them, too, in their final hours, in a manner that might after all have some appeal to a Roman audience, despite all the trouble they had caused. They were not good Jews; he wants to make that clear; but they may command some respect nevertheless – from their fellow pagans![220]

Josephus, then, is important in three ways for our present purposes. First, his own views, as reported in the first two passages quoted, are significant: he was a highly educated first-century Jew, and we should suppose him typical of many. And the view he espouses is clear. It is a *two-age cosmic eschatology*, consisting of 'the present age' and 'the age to come', coupled with a *two-stage personal eschatology*, in which the righteous soul lives in heaven with Israel's god after death until, in the age to come, it receives a new body. 'Resurrection', while it denotes this final event, connotes not simply this eventual bodily 'life after death' as opposed to a non-bodily one; it connotes the process whereby that end is achieved, namely, an initial stage of disembodied rest with Israel's god followed by some kind of re-embodiment. This re-embodiment, Josephus says, will be into a holy and renewed body – perhaps the closest that we come in non-Christian Judaism to the picture of transformed embodiment we find in Christianity. What is

---

[216] *War* 7.343–8 (tr. Thackeray). The opening lines quoted here are reminiscent of a fragment from Euripides (*Frag.* 634, ed. Dindorf): see Thackeray's note in Loeb 3.605. The final line is an echo of Soph. *Trach.* 235 (Thackeray 603).

[217] Dan. 12.2; 1 Cor. 15.20, 51; 1 Thess. 4.13–15.

[218] *War* 7.349f., and the note in *NTPG* 327 n. 145.

[219] Smith 1999, 560.

[220] So, rightly, Segal 1997, 109.

more, this new life has been promised by the Bible, by Moses himself; and the promise is underwritten by the creator's own power.

Second, Josephus' description of the Pharisees' belief is important, when we 'decode' his statements and place them alongside what we know of the Pharisees from elsewhere, not least from the subsequent rabbinic writings. As we would have deduced from passages like Acts 23, the Pharisees shared the view of 2 Maccabees and such books as *1 Enoch* and 4 Ezra.

Third, Josephus is a good example of the phenomenon I argued for in the Wisdom of Solomon, namely, the way in which the *idea* of resurrection can be present even when the word is not. He does not use 'resurrection', either for his own view or when describing that of the Pharisees; I have suggested that this may be because the word was regularly used in the ancient world to describe something that all sensible pagans (Josephus' target audience) believed could not, did not, and never would happen. He did not want them to mock either him or those Jewish 'schools' of thought he was anxious to commend. That is why his description of the Pharisees' viewpoint sounds from time to time more like some version of transmigration, a variant on a known pagan possibility, rather than a shocking Jewish innovation.

It is important for understanding early Christian language, and the fresh shaping it received, that we grasp the double point, stated in a preliminary way at the end of chapter 1 and now exemplified by a good many texts. (a) Belief in resurrection is characterized, not necessarily by the presence of the word, but by a two-age cosmic and personal eschatology ending with a new embodiment. Where that story is being told, we have resurrection. (b) The word 'resurrection' and its cognates, in Hebrew or Greek, is never used to denote something other than this position. The belief can occur without the word, but never the other way round. 'Resurrection' is never a way of re-describing death itself, or of 'coming to terms' with it as though it were not after all particularly significant. (Nor, strictly, does it refer to the first stage of the process, but always the second, which brings the first with it as its necessary preliminary.) It is always a way of reaffirming, as does Wisdom 1—3, the goodness of the world, the nature of death as an evil intrusion into it, and the creator's promise to overcome death by the gift of new bodily life.

(vii) Resurrection at Qumran?

Learning to 'decode' Josephus comes in handy when we address the question of whether the Essenes believed in resurrection.[221] Josephus indicates

---

[221] On the Essenes see the sketch in *NTPG* 203–09; the relevant literature of the last decade is of course enormous. I assume, with most scholars, that the scrolls found at Qumran broadly at least represent Essene teaching. Nothing in my overall argument hinges on the still-disputed questions of dating, the development of the sect's ideas, etc. The present

that they do not; but Hippolytus, writing in the early third century, says they do (or at least did). The natural reaction to this – that Hippolytus was writing much later, and that Josephus claims to have himself spent time with the sect – should be restrained, precisely because of Josephus' strategy of presenting the Jewish groups as philosophical 'schools', with his description of the Essenes matching the Pythagoreans in various ways.[222] The task of the historian is then to compare these two non-Essene sources with one another, and with the writings from Qumran. The first part of this is easier than the second, and may be done briefly as follows.[223]

We begin with Josephus. After his description of the Essenes' suffering and martyrdom during the revolt against Rome, he explains their cheerful bravery thus:

> For it is a fixed belief of theirs that the body is corruptible and its constituent matter impermanent, but that the soul is immortal and imperishable. Emanating from the finest ether, these souls become entangled, as it were, in the prison-house of the body, to which they are dragged down by a sort of natural spell; but when once they are released from the bonds of the flesh, then, as though liberated from a long servitude, they rejoice and are borne aloft. Sharing the belief of the sons of Greece, they maintain that for virtuous souls there is reserved an abode beyond the ocean, a place which is not oppressed by rain or snow or heat, but is refreshed by the ever gentle breath of the west wind coming in from the ocean; while they relegate base souls to a murky and tempestuous dungeon, big with never-ending punishments.
>
> The Greeks, I imagine, had the same conception when they set apart the isles of the blessed for their brave men, whom they call heroes and demigods, and the region of the impious for the souls of the wicked down in Hades, where, as their mythologists tell, persons such as Sisyphus, Tantalus, Ixion, and Tityus are undergoing punishment. Their aim was first to establish the doctrine of the immortality of the soul, and secondly to promote virtue and to deter from vice; for the good are made better in their lifetime by the hope of a reward after death, and the passions of the wicked are restrained by the fear that, even though they escape detection while alive, they will undergo never-ending punishment after their decease.
>
> Such are the theological views of the Essenes concerning the soul, whereby they irresistibly attract all who have once tasted their philosophy.[224]

The Essenes 'attract all', do they? All, it seems, except Josephus himself, since he says that he followed the discipline of the sect for a while before moving on – though as he claims to have done the same with the Pharisees and Sadducees, and then to have spent three years with the ascetic Bannus,

---

section was completed before the important article of Lichtenberger 2001 came to hand.

[222] We may leave out of consideration Philo's account of the 'Therapeutae' (*De Vita Contempl.* 13), where he says that the sect, in their longing for the immortal and blessed life, regard themselves as having already ended their mortal lives, and therefore abandon their property to their kinsfolk. Philo's account of the Essenes (*Quod Omn.* 75–91) omits any mention of their beliefs about a future life.

[223] See now the major treatment of Puech 1993, 703–69. Puech is carefully criticized by Bremmer 2002, 43–7.

[224] *War* 2.154–8 (tr. Thackeray).

all before the age of nineteen, we may doubt whether he knew quite as much about it all as he likes to make out.[225] The flourish at the end of the paragraph, together with the double mention of 'the Greeks', and the frequent allusions to classical works and beliefs such as we studied in chapter 2, indicate well enough what he is doing: he is projecting on to the comfortably blank screen of the Essenes (blank so far as his readers are concerned) the beliefs of post-Platonic Hellenism, not least those handed down by the Pythagoreans. But any student of the Dead Sea Scrolls, reading this account, would be forced to come to the conclusion that either the Essenes did not write the Scrolls after all, or that the documents dealing with the topics Josephus mentions have yet to come to light (perhaps they are still in a basement cupboard in Jerusalem or Harvard?), or that Josephus was making it all up in the service of a quite different agenda. Since the last suggestion is the one most commonly adopted, that opens the way for a reconsideration not only of Hippolytus' evidence but also, of course, for a closer examination of the Scrolls themselves.

In fact, there are two indications within Josephus' own accounts that he, too, knew of a different Essene viewpoint. In the passage immediately prior to the one quoted at length above, he says something which could reflect a view more like that of 2 Maccabees:

Smiling in their agonies and mildly deriding their tormentors, they cheerfully resigned their souls, confident that they would receive them back again.[226]

The final phrase reads *hos palin komioumenoi*, 'as those about to receive them again'. This is the same verb, in a similar phrase, as we find twice in the famous passage in 2 Maccabees 7. The third brother declares that he got his tongue and hands from God, and hopes to get them back again from him (*tauta palin elpizo komisasthai*). The mother urges the youngest son willingly to accept death, so that in God's mercy she may get him back again (*komisomai se*) along with his brothers.[227] The way Josephus has put it, it looks as though the Essene martyrs are saying the same thing the other way round: they are happy to have their souls taken away, because they believe that they will receive them back again. This implies, totally against the grain of the following section, that the individual consists primarily of the body, which will be deprived of its animating soul for a while but will then receive it back again. My guess – it can only be that – is that Josephus was here echoing, whether consciously or otherwise, the language either of 2 Maccabees or of similar martyrological texts now lost to us, and is providing evidence, albeit oblique, that the Essenes did in fact face death at the hands of

---

[225] *Life* 9–11.

[226] *War* 2.153 (tr. Thackeray). This passage sometimes goes unnoticed in secondary discussions where one might have thought it important, e.g. Nickelsburg 1972, 167–9.

[227] 2 Macc. 7.11, 29.

the Romans with a very similar belief to that with which the seven brothers faced death at the hands of Antiochus Epiphanes.[228]

This may perhaps be strengthened by the second hint, though here again certainty is impossible. It is usual to refer to the brief account of Essene belief in the *Antiquities* as if it simply repeated what was said at more length in the *War*, but there is a hint of something else besides. In Feldman's translation, the passage reads:

> [The Essenes] regard the soul as immortal and believe that they ought to strive especially to draw near to righteousness.[229]

But the final phrase has always been recognised as problematic.[230] It reads *perimacheton hegoumenoi tou dikaiou ten prosodon*, literally 'considering the *prosodos* of righteousness to be worth fighting for'. The word *prosodos* certainly can mean 'approach', but it can also mean 'payment', 'return on investment', and does so in some classical philosophical texts.[231] Several interpreters have taken it in this sense, so that the sentence means 'they believe that the future rewards of righteousness are worth striving for' – which looks like a way of referring not simply to a blissful disembodied immortality, though that would still be possible, but to a more solid 'reward' in the sense of resurrection. Feldman has to work hard, in a long note, to explain why he has translated it in the other sense, especially since it would be more natural, in Greek, to say *prosodon pros to dikaion* if one meant 'to draw near to righteousness'. Feldman relies, in fact, rather heavily on the assumed beliefs of the Essenes as reconstructed in the early days of Scrolls scholarship.[232] Since this question should now be regarded as at least open (see below), the balance of probability in my judgment tilts towards regarding this phrase as indicating an Essene belief in future post-mortem rewards. Once again, we should not be beguiled into the old antithesis of 'immortality' versus 'resurrection'; for a future resurrection to happen, there needs to be continuity between the present life and the future one, and, as in the Wisdom of Solomon, one obvious way of describing this continuity is by using the language of the 'soul'. I suggest, therefore, that despite Josephus'

---

[228] See too *War* 2.151 (a few sentences earlier than the passage just quoted), where Josephus says, somewhat puzzlingly, that the Essenes prefer death, if it arrives with honour, to immortality. 'Immortality' here seems to mean 'continuing life'. On both passages see Puech 1993, 709, who raises the question whether they point to a more mainstream view of resurrection, without concluding that they necessarily do so.

[229] *Ant.* 18.18.

[230] See Feldman's full note in the Loeb edn. ad loc. Nickelsburg 1972, 169 fails to discuss this phrase, leaving the impression that an affirmation of the soul's immortality settles other issues.

[231] e.g. Plato *Laws* 8.847a.

[232] Feldman in Loeb 9, 15n, quoting Strugnell 1958. Puech 1993, 707 says that the idea of drawing near to righteousness and that of the reward for it are inseparable, which seems to me dubious.

'official' account in *War* Book 2 of a thoroughly hellenized Essene belief in a future disembodied bliss, even he may include tell-tale hints of a different view.

That different view might well, then, be the one set out by Hippolytus:

> Now the doctrine of the resurrection has also derived support among them; for they acknowledge both that the flesh will rise again, and that it will be immortal, in the same manner as the soul is already imperishable. And they maintain that the soul, when separated in the present life, [departs] into one place, which is well ventilated and lightsome, where, they say, it rests until judgment. And this locality the Greeks were acquainted with by hearsay, and called it 'Isles of the Blessed.' And there are other tenets of these which many of the Greeks have appropriated, and thus have from time to time formed their own opinions . . . Now they affirm that there will be both a judgment and a conflagration of the universe, and that the wicked will be eternally punished.[233]

Hippolytus, of course, is no more 'neutral' than Josephus. His own agenda, in this passage and elsewhere, is to suggest that everything worthwhile that was believed by the Greeks had been learned from the Jews in the first place. Thus, whereas Josephus is treating the Essenes as a Greek philosophical school, Hippolytus is treating them as a source of Greek wisdom. He seems to be simultaneously aware of Josephus' account (Josephus was after all read more by Christians than by Jews in Hippolytus' day) but firmly correcting it: the 'Isles of the Blessed' are a *temporary* resting-place where the immortal soul waits to receive its newly immortal body.[234] The notion of 'immortal flesh' only sounds strange to ears accustomed to the siren voices that insist on a strict disjunction between immortality and resurrection;[235] Paul speaks of the dead being 'raised incorruptible', and Hippolytus was of course roughly contemporary with Tertullian, who insisted strongly on 'the resurrection of the flesh'.[236] All in all, it seems preferable to conclude, with Puech, that Hippolytus reflects the true state of affairs here at least more accurately than Josephus, whether or not he has introduced various errors on the way.[237]

I conclude that the external evidence about the Essenes, reading between the lines of the two main sources, points firmly in the direction that they

---

[233] Hippol. *Ref.* 9.27.1–3. As with Josephus' description in *War* Book 2, this is prefixed (9.26.3b–4) by a statement of the Essenes' fearless attitude to death, though without including at that point any suggestion of their future hope.

[234] Or perhaps, as some have argued (Smith 1958), Josephus and Hippolytus are drawing on a common source or sources. Guesses as to what these two very different writers are likely to have done may not get us very far. Hippolytus might not have wanted to alter a heretical source to make it look more orthodox, but this could simply mean that he got the material in its present form from a source. See Black 1964 [1954]; Nickelsburg 1972, 167f.

[235] Nickelsburg 1972, 168.

[236] 1 Cor. 15.52. On Tertullian see 510–13, below. See too the criticisms of Nickelsburg in Puech 1993, 716–18.

[237] Puech 1993, 760–62, after a long, careful discussion; *pace* Bremmer 2002, 45f.

believed (like the Pharisees, and like the author of Wisdom) in the righteous at least having souls that survived bodily death. At the same time, the evidence points, less firmly but with a definite possibility, towards a belief in a new bodily life the other side of a period of temporary disembodiment; in other words, to a two-stage personal eschatology. We must now test this against the evidence of the Scrolls themselves.

All students of the Scrolls, and of the question of life after death in second-Temple Judaism, are massively indebted to Émile Puech, whose two-volume work on Essene beliefs about the future will remain a standard text for a long time to come.[238] Though disagreements will persist, we are safe in concluding that if any of the existing Qumran texts carry any scent of resurrection, Puech will have sniffed it out and brought it to light. We need not, therefore, repeat his exhaustive survey of all possible evidence, and can simply focus on the three key texts upon which his case principally rests.[239]

The best known of these is the striking prediction in 4Q521:

> The heavens and the earth will listen to his Messiah, and none therein will stray from the commandments of the holy ones. Seekers of the Lord, strengthen yourselves in his service! All you hopeful in your heart, will you not find the Lord in this? For the Lord will consider the pious and call the righteous by name. Over the poor his spirit will hover and will renew the faithful with his power. And he will glorify the pious on the throne of the eternal kingdom. He who liberates the captives, restores sight to the blind, straightens the crooked. And for ever I will cleave to the hopeful and in his mercy . . . And the fruit will not be delayed for anyone. And the Lord will perform marvellous acts such as have never been, as he said; for he will heal the wounded *and will make the dead live*, he will bring good news to the poor, he will lead . . . and enrich the hungry . . .
>
> . . . see all the Lord has made: the earth and all that is in it, the seas and all they contain, and all the reservoirs of waters and torrents . . . those who do what is good before the Lord . . . like these, the accursed. And they shall be for death . . . *he who gives life to the dead of his people*. We shall give thanks and announce to you . . . of the Lord, who . . . [240]

This tantalizingly fragmentary text speaks of the work of the coming Messiah, and does so in language not dissimilar to Matthew 11.2–6/Luke 7.18–23, with obvious echoes of biblical prophecies.[241] The prediction that

---

[238] Puech 1993.

[239] In addition to the evidence from the burial places of Khirbet Qumran and Ain el-Ghuweir; see Puech 1993, 693–702; Lichtenberger 2001, 88–90.

[240] 4Q521 frag. 2 col. 2.1–13; frags. 7 and 5 col. 2.1–7. Tr. Vermes 391f.; GM 1045–7 (conflated and slightly adapted). Italics added for purposes of subsequent reference (see below).

[241] On the synoptic passages cf. *JVG* 494–7; 530–33. For other bibliography see GM 1044f. Collins 1995, 117–22 argues that the Messiah in question is prophetic, rather than either priestly or royal, and that his action in raising the dead belongs with the stories about, and speculations concerning, Elijah and others.

the Messiah will make the dead live (line 12 of fragment 2, italicized in the first extract) does not seem to be a prophecy of eventual resurrection in the sense intended by Daniel 12, but rather of the sort of actions performed by Elijah and Elisha – and, according to the gospels, by Jesus – in bringing back into the present life some who had just died: a dramatic extension of 'healing', in fact. However, the italicized phrase in the second extract reads much more like the standard prayer formula noted above from the *Shemoneh Esre*: God is praised as the life-giver, the one who will raise the dead.[242]

The second pieces of evidence are found in the Hymns:

> Then at the time of judgment
> > the sword of God shall hasten,
> and all the sons of his truth shall awake
> > to overthrow wickedness;
> all the sons of iniquity shall be no more . . .[243]
> . . . Hoist a banner,
> > O you who lie in the dust!
> O bodies gnawed by works,
> > raise up an ensign for [the destruction of wickedness]!
> [The sinful shall] be destroyed
> > in the battles against the ungodly.[244]

> For the sake of thy glory
> > thou hast purified man of sin
> that he may be made holy for thee,
> > with no abominable uncleanness
> > and no guilty wickedness;
> that he may be one with the children of thy truth
> > and partake of the lot of thy holy ones;
> that bodies gnawed by worms may be raised from the dust
> > to the counsel of thy truth,
> and that the perverse spirit may be lifted
> > to the understanding which comes from thee;
> that he may stand before thee
> > with the everlasting host
> > and with thy spirits of holiness,
> to be renewed together with all the living
> > and to rejoice together with them that know.[245]

It is not clear from the context whether these passages are to be taken metaphorically, as a vivid way of speaking of the coming victory over evil, or literally, as denoting the concrete event of bodily resurrection. But other passages in the earlier poem which speak of the Community as a tree putting

---

[242] Frags. 7 and 5, 2.6. On the prayer formula see above, 146f.

[243] 1QH 14.29f. (earlier edns., 6.29f.). Sanders 1992, 302 sees this as clear evidence of resurrection hope (though curiously not mentioning the subsequent passages below).

[244] 1QH 14.34f. (earlier edns., 6.34f.); tr. Vermes 274; cf. GM 176f.

[245] 1QH 19.10–14 (earlier edns. 11.10–14); tr. Vermes 288; cf. GM 188f.

down deep roots, growing its branches as an everlasting plantation, covering the world with its shade, watered by the streams of Eden, and so forth, do suggest that here we have an exalted vision of the age to come within which is found a prediction of the dust-dwellers rising to newly embodied life, echoing Daniel 12.2 and perhaps also Job 19.26.[246] The idea of the sons of truth awakening and judging the wicked is close to the picture we observed in Wisdom 3.7–8, which in turn sends us to the Aramaic Apocalypse in which God's people, or perhaps God's Messiah, will exercise a kingdom 'like the sparks of a vision'.[247] And the second poem we have quoted begins (after the normal opening lacuna) with praise to God because of what he does with 'dust'.[248] These do seem to be straws in the wind, indicating that, if the question came up (not that it seems to have done very often), some at least of the Qumran Community would have agreed with the Pharisees rather than the Sadducees on the question of resurrection.[249] However, even if this is so, it is a matter of note that despite the considerable volume of finds the belief in question rates so little mention.

The final passages which may point in the same direction are in the so-called Pseudo-Ezekiel (4Q 385, 385c, 386, 391). The key passage, emerging variously from these fragments, develops the picture of resurrection from Ezekiel 37 as a prophecy of how the true Israelites will be rewarded in the future for their loyalty to YHWH:

> I have seen many in Israel, O Lord, who love your name and walk on the paths of justice. When will these things happen? And how will they be rewarded for their loyalty? And YHWH said to me: I will make the children of Israel see and they will know that I am YHWH. And he said, Son of man, prophesy over the bones, and say, May a bone connect with its bone . . . [the text continues, following Ezekiel 37] . . . and they will live, and a large crowd of men will rise and bless YHWH of hosts who caused them to live.[250]

Here there seems to be no question: Ezekiel 37 is being seen, not simply as a metaphor for the return from exile, but as a prophecy of actual resurrection. This is, so far as I know, the earliest post-biblical text to take Ezekiel in this way, anticipating the usage of some of the later rabbis.

It remains the case, of course, that the great majority of the finds from Qumran say nothing whatever about the future fate of the dead, and this

---

[246] See 1QH 14[4].14–18. Vermes 1997, 88 appears to sit on the fence on this question; in the light of our earlier discussions, it will not do to suggest that where we find mention of post-mortem immortality this rules out ultimate resurrection.

[247] 4Q246 2.1f. (Vermes 577; GM 494f.). The text is clearly rooted in Daniel.

[248] 1QH 19[11].3.

[249] Against e.g. Collins 1995, 133 (suggesting that the only clear refs. are 4Q521 and 4Q385). For earlier debates about the interpretation of these passages see e.g. Nickelsburg 1972, 150f.

[250] 4Q385 frag. 2.2–9 (GM 768f.); see too 4Q386 frag. 1.1–10 (GM 774f.); 4Q388 frag. 8.4–7 (GM 778f.).

must indicate that the question was not a point of contention for the sect as it was for the Pharisees and Sadducees. The Essenes are anxious to rule out all sorts of other Jewish opinions, legal rulings and so on, but they never argue either against those who insist on belief in resurrection or against those who deny it. Where the belief appears, it emerges not so much as a topic of controversy, marking the writer out against opponents, but as the natural outgrowth of a belief in the sovereignty of YHWH over all evil, death included. To that extent I agree with Puech: the Essenes' future hope was an extension, beyond death and into the future world, of their present religious experience.[251]

At the same time, it is important to stress that for Qumran the vision of the age to come, and the life of the blessed within it, was far more splendid than simply a return to something more or less like the present world. 'All the glory of Adam' would belong to the redeemed.[252] No theory is developed as to what precisely is involved or how it will be accomplished. The main concerns of the sect lie with present purity rather than future destiny.

(viii) Pseudo-Philo, *Biblical Antiquities*

The *Biblical Antiquities* of the so-called Pseudo-Philo are preserved in Latin, but almost certainly go back, through a Greek text which the Latin translator has used, to a Hebrew original.[253] The work places considerable emphasis on what happens after death, and articulates as full a doctrine of two-stage post-mortem existence as we find in any of these sources.

After death, the souls of the righteous are at peace:

> At the end the lot of each one of you will be life eternal, for you and your seed, and I will take your souls and store them in peace until the time allotted the world be complete. And I will restore you to your fathers and your fathers to you, and they will know through you that I have not chosen you in vain.[254]

If this was all we had, we would perhaps expect readers to conclude that the righteous enjoy a blessed disembodied life in perpetuity – just as people conclude from reading Wisdom 3.1–5 out of context. But the mention of the 'time allotted the world' alerts us to the fact that this is only the first stage of

---

[251] Puech 1993, 792.

[252] 1QS 4.23; CD 3.20; 1QH 4.15 (earlier edns., 17.15); 4Q171 3.1f. (where the text speaks of all the 'inheritance' of Adam).

[253] See Harrington in Charlesworth 1985, 297–303 (and cp. Harrington 2002); Nickelsburg 1984, 107–10. The author gets his title because the work was transmitted together with the genuine works of the Alexandrian philosopher. The work is sometimes abbreviated as *LAB* for its Latin title, *Liber Antiquitatum Biblicarum*.

[254] *LAB* 23.13. 28.10 speaks of the righteous being in 'repose', or 'sleeping with their fathers'; 51.5 speaks of the just 'going to sleep' and so being freed.

a two-stage procedure. The writer has plenty more to say about this moment and its results:

> But when the years appointed for the world have been fulfilled, then the light will cease and the darkness will fade away. And I will bring the dead to life and raise up those who are sleeping from the earth. And hell will pay back its debt, and the place of perdition will return its deposit so that I may render to each according to his works and according to the fruits of his own devices, until I judge between soul and flesh. And the world will cease, and death will be abolished, and hell will shut its mouth. And the earth will not be without progeny or sterile for those inhabiting it; and no one who has been pardoned by me will be tainted. And there will be another earth and another heaven, an everlasting dwelling place.[255]

The sequence is even more explicit in a later passage:

> I will take you from here and glorify you with your fathers, and I will give you rest in your slumber and bury you in peace . . . And I will raise up you and your fathers from the land of Egypt in which you sleep and you will come together and dwell in the immortal dwelling place that is not subject to time. But this heaven will be before me like a fleeting cloud and passing like yesterday. And when the time draws near to visit the world, I will command the years and order the times and they will be shortened, and the stars will hasten and the light of the sun will hurry to fall and the light of the moon will not remain; for I will hurry to raise up you who are sleeping in order that all who can live may dwell in the place of sanctification I showed you.[256]

First, a blissful rest, asleep in glory with the 'fathers', in a 'heaven' which will itself be only temporary; then a new existence, a new heaven and earth, a place of final sanctification. And, as so often in Jewish and early Christian texts, part of the point is appropriate judgment. Resurrection is the divine way of setting all wrongs to right.[257] There is no question where this author stands on our central topic – or how close he is to some of the central early Christian texts, not least the book of Revelation.

(ix) Pharisees, Rabbis and Targumim

If the Pharisees were the most popular of the Jewish parties and pressure groups at the turn of the eras, the events of AD 70 left their heirs and successors, the rabbis, with the field to themselves.[258] The beliefs and practices they developed in the century or so before the compilation of the Mishnah

---

[255] *LAB* 3.10. For YHWH's future 'remembering the world' cf. 48.1.

[256] *LAB* 19.12f.

[257] cf. e.g. *LAB* 25.7.

[258] On Pharisees and rabbis see *NTPG* 181–203; Cavallin 1974, 171–92; Puech 1993, 213–42; Segal 1997, 113–25. With most writers of today I assume a reasonably high degree of continuity across the AD 70 watershed.

(roughly AD 200) and the two Talmuds (roughly AD 400) were rooted in earlier thought and life, though they were of course developed to meet new situations and debates. The two crises of AD 70 and 135 brought major changes, as the rabbis adjusted to living in a world where social and political revolution against pagan overlordship had become unthinkable – where crushing defeat of two large and popular revolts had forced a change from a kingdom-focus to a Torah-focus, from (more or less) politics to piety.[259] There are signs that this had an effect on what was already a widespread and strongly held belief in resurrection.[260]

We begin with the earlier period, from the time of the Maccabaean crisis and thereafter. The exchanges between Pharisees and Sadducees which form the backdrop for the debates reported in the early Christian writings, and for the 'philosophical' descriptions in Josephus, certainly reflect positions that had been taken up well before the turn of the eras.[261] The liturgical traditions in which God is praised as the one who gives life to the dead certainly date from this early time. Segal speaks of the 'innumerable' references to the resurrection which are found dotted through the Jewish prayer book.[262] The second benediction in the *Amidah*, the *Shemoneh Esre*, is only one among many; at random, I turn up the concluding service from the liturgy for the Day of Atonement, and find, 'Thou art also faithful to revive the dead. Blessed art thou, O Lord, who revivest the dead.'[263] We might also note the morning prayer found in the Babylonian Talmud *Berakoth* 60b, which ends by praising God for 'restoring souls to dead corpses', where the word for 'soul', *neshamah*, is not an immortal part of the human being, but is the breath which returns to God upon death and which is then given back to bring about resurrection.[264] Returning to the *Amidah*, the second benediction is mentioned in the Mishnah, which interprets it in terms of 'the power of rain'; the Talmud later explains this as drawing a parallel between the way rain brings life to the world and resurrection brings life to the dead.[265] Nobody, I think, doubts that these prayers, or something like them, take us back to the liturgical life of the late second-Temple period, and hence to the thinking, believing and debating of the period even earlier than that.

[259] See the remark of Rabbi Nehunya ben ha-Kanah quoted in mAb. 3.5 (discussed in *NTPG* 199).
[260] Many relevant passages are conveniently noted in SB 3.473–83.
[261] For the NT evidence cf. esp. Ac. 23.6–9, discussed above, 191, and below, 454; and the writings of Paul, discussed in Part II below. For Josephus see above, 175–81.
[262] Segal 1997, 123.
[263] de Sola 1963, 184. The Hebrew for 'to revive the dead' is *lehahyoth methim*; the phrase 'who revivest the dead' is *mehayyeh hammethim*. On the dating of the second benediction of the *Amidah* see Cavallin 1973, 177f.
[264] cf. Gen. 2.7, and the sequence of thought in Ps. 104.29f. (though the word there is *ruach*). Cp. Cavallin 1973, 178.
[265] mBer. 5.2; bBer. 33a. Cf. mTaan. 1.1f., where rain is to be prayed for only at the appropriate times of the year.

Further evidence of this is found in the debates reported from the second century BC, following the dictum of Antigonus of Soko, the first rabbi to be named in the great list in *Aboth*.[266] 'You should not', he declared, 'be like slaves serving the master for the sake of receiving a gift, but like slaves serving the master without any prospect of receiving a gift.' According to a later tradition, preserved in a double form, two of Antigonus' pupils, Zadok and Boethos, debated what this might mean, and concluded that it ruled out all doctrines of a future life, especially the idea of a resurrection in which rewards might be given. They became, according to this tradition, the founders of the Sadducees and the Boethians respectively, both denying the future world and the resurrection. This incident, preserved (of course) in rabbinic tradition, indicates what the Pharisees thought they were up against. It also provides a telling illustration of the comparative novelty of resurrection belief; Zadok and Boethos reasoned that if resurrection had been a mainstream teaching from earlier days, Antigonus could not have spoken thus.[267]

This leads us to the major rabbinic statements of the doctrine of resurrection from the Mishnaic period (AD 70–200). The best known is a warning: those who do not believe in the age to come, and more specifically in the resurrection, will forfeit it:

> All Israelites have a share in the world to come, for it is written, *The people also shall be all righteous, they shall inherit the land for ever; the branch of my planting, the work of my hands that I may be glorified*. And these are the ones who have no share in the world to come: he that says that there is no resurrection of the dead [prescribed in the Law], and he that says the Law is not from Heaven, and an Epicurean. Rabbi Akiba says: Also he that reads the heretical books, or that utters charms over a wound . . . Abba Saul says: Also he that pronounces the Name with its proper letters.[268]

The phrase 'prescribed in the Law' is missing from several important manuscripts, and probably reflects one strand of debate; clearly there is quite a difference between denying the resurrection altogether and denying that it is taught in the Five Books of Moses (though in practice the same people probably did both).[269] Since, however, the section goes on to note the additions of Akiba (early second century) and Saul (mid-second century), we can be sure that the basic list – denial of resurrection, of the god-givenness of Torah, and of moral and spiritual values altogether – is from at least the middle of the first century and probably earlier than that. As Urbach says,

---

[266] mAb. 1.3. For Antigonus, and the location of Soko see Schürer 2.360 (Doubles).

[267] See *Aboth de R. Nathan* 5, in recensions A and B.

[268] mSanh. 10.1. The italicized prooftext is from Isa. 60.21. 'Epicurean' refers, not to the pagan philosophy of that name, but to one who behaves licentiously and thinks sceptically. The Talmud wryly comments (bSanh. 90a) that God always rewards measure for measure.

[269] For the details see Urbach 1987, 991 n. 11.

the mention of resurrection in this passage indicates, not the beginning of this belief, but 'the struggle for its acceptance against its opponents'.[270] Subsequent passages in the same Mishnah tractate presuppose that the life of the world to come will involve resurrection. Thus, for instance, we find a discussion of whether the men of Sodom and the wilderness generation will 'stand' in the judgment, and Eliezer's telling quotation of 1 Samuel 2.6 to prove that the company of Korah, who went down alive into Sheol, will be brought back again: 'The Lord kills and makes alive, he brings down to Sheol and brings up.'[271]

The other well-known Mishnaic passage may be a later addition, not being found even in some of the early printed versions:

> Rabbi Phineas b. Jair says: Heedfulness leads to cleanliness, and cleanliness leads to purity, and purity leads to abstinence, and abstinence leads to holiness, and holiness leads to humility, and humility leads to the shunning of sin, and the shunning of sin leads to saintliness, and saintliness leads to the Holy Spirit, and the Holy Spirit leads to the resurrection of the dead. And the resurrection of the dead shall come through Elijah of blessed memory.[272]

The passage, though extremely stylized,[273] introduces two points of interest for the student of Jewish and Christian thought on the resurrection: the agency of the Holy Spirit in the resurrection, and the activity of Elijah, promised in Malachi 4.5, in bringing about the age to come and thereby also the resurrection of the dead.[274] For our purposes, though, it is enough to note that the resurrection is assumed to be the ultimate prize, the reward for a life of holiness and Torah-observance. There is no indication of any serious dissent from this judgment in Pharisaic and rabbinic thought during the final century BC or the early centuries AD.[275]

The same conclusion may be affirmed, albeit cautiously, from the evidence of practices of the time in relation to death. David Daube has catalogued the ways in which, during the two centuries spanning the turn of the eras, the Pharisees effected far-reaching changes in the methods used to

---

[270] Urbach 1987, 653.

[271] mSanh. 10.3. Eliezer (ben Hyrcanus) taught in the late C1 AD. Insistence on future judgment was a characteristic of a much earlier teacher, Nittai the Arbelite (C1/2 BC) (mAb. 1.7).

[272] mSot. 9.15. For the textual point cf. Urbach 1987, 992 n. 11.

[273] For a similar sequence cf. 2 Pet. 1.5–7.

[274] For Elijah bringing resurrection cf. also Cant. R. on Song 1.1. Other refs. in Moore 1927–30, 2.272.

[275] It is thus puzzling when Barr (1992, 45) describes the rabbinic view as 'a rather vague and fluid combination of resurrection of the body and immortality of the soul'. True, by the time of Maimonides and Spinoza all sorts of things had had time to get vague and fluid; but with the rabbis we are on the solid ground of (a) an ultimate bodily resurrection and hence (b) an intermediate state which ensures continuity between the present and the ultimate future.

execute those guilty of capital offences. Stoning was moderated; burning was to be done by forcing burning liquid down the throat; strangling was by a particular method; all was in aid of leaving the bone structure intact. The body was important, and its most durable parts, the bones, were to be rescued from destruction. Cremation was avoided for the same reason.[276] In the same way, secondary burial, involving the careful preserving, folding and storage of the entire skeleton, was widely practised in the period.[277] While this may have been partly due to actual or perceived shortage of space, there is every reason to suppose that belief in the importance of the bones for future resurrection played a significant part.[278] In the same way, the evident desire on the part of Diaspora Jews to be buried in Palestine is a pointer to the belief that the resurrection of the dead would take place there.[279] This appears, too, in the remarkable theory that was developed, according to which the bones of Jews buried outside the Holy Land would roll through underground tunnels in order to arrive there for the resurrection.[280] This seems to be, among other things, a novel way of combining the metaphorical meaning of Ezekiel 37 (return from exile) with a literal reading (bodily resurrection).

Before we move into the later rabbinic discussions, which are revealing in themselves, it is worth pausing to note the shape of the belief that is implied throughout this survey. The resurrection of the dead, though confidently expected, has not yet occurred. The dead, righteous and wicked alike, are still dead. There is room for doubt over whether all of them will in the end be raised; one of the greatest areas of disagreement among both rabbis and Christians is whether all the dead will be raised (with the wicked being raised in order to face their judgment) or whether only the righteous will be raised at all. But there can be no room for doubt that those who believed in the future resurrection believed also that the dead were alive in some intermediate state, place or manner. The language of souls being stored away in cupboards, or dwelling in a temporary Paradise, is as we saw developed in one or two writings of this period; there seems to have been no precision

---

[276] Daube 1956, 303–08.

[277] bSem. 49a. In mMo. Kat. 1.5 the gathering together of one's parents' bones is permitted on the days in the middle of a festival week, since (the Mishnah explains) doing this is an occasion of rejoicing, not of mourning – which can only mean that the bones are being collected and stored in anticipation of the resurrection. Further details in Meyers 1970, 1971; Figueras 1974; 1983; Rahmani 1981–2. Figueras's work is full of fascinating details about the decoration of ossuaries, which though important would take us too far afield at present.

[278] See Park 2000, 170–72; with Meyers 1970; Puech 1993, 190f., 220.

[279] cf. bKetub. 111a; bBer. 18b; jKetub. 12.3; Gen. Rab. 96.5; Pesiq. Rab. 1.6. I owe these references to Park 2000, 172 (see further, behind him, Meyers 1970; Fischer 1978; van der Horst 1992; and Puech 1993).

[280] cf. e.g. jKil. 32c; jKet. 35b; Targ. Cant. 8.5; cf. Moore 2.380 n.; Cavallin 1974, 192 n. 15.

about the exact terminology to be employed, but clearly some kind of inter-mediate state was as popular a belief as resurrection itself. And – a point that could have saved scholars a lot of trouble – this does not imply anything peculiar in terms of combining 'resurrection' and 'immortality', of putting together supposedly 'Jewish' and 'Greek' ideas. This is still a hangover from the old half-truth with which the previous chapter opened. Part of the Pharisaic belief in future bodily resurrection is the belief that some sort of continuing personal identity, however hard it may be to describe, is neces-sary if the person being raised at the last day is after all to be identical with the person who has died. If that is not the case, the whole theological rationale for resurrection, namely, the reward of justice in the future life, collapses in ruins. The fact that both the major Pharisaic schools maintained some version of the intermediate state is indicated well enough by their debate as to whether, in the case of those who were neither extremely virtuous nor extremely wicked, this state would be pleasant or unpleasant.[281]

The justice of the creator god is, in fact, one of the central tenets that underlie the later rabbinic discussions of the resurrection. These focus on three questions: how will YHWH accomplish it? what will the body be like (clothed or naked; the same or changed)? and, particularly, which texts in the Bible predict it?[282]

The question of how YHWH will accomplish resurrection is the subject of a fascinating debate between the Pharisaic/rabbinic schools of Hillel and Shammai, reported in Genesis Rabbah 14.5 and Leviticus Rabbah 14.9.[283] The two schools are debating whether YHWH will make the new body by starting with skin and flesh and firming them up until finally sinews and bones are formed (the opinion of the Hillelites), or whether YHWH will start with the bones (the opinion of the Shammaites) and work outwards from there. The Shammaites, of course, claim Ezekiel 37 on their side, interpret-ing that passage as the LXX had perhaps already done.[284] The Hillelites,

---

[281] Tos. Sanh. 13.3; bRosh ha-Sh. 16b—17a; see Moore 1927–30, 2.318, 390f. The Shammaites, not surprisingly, envisaged a kind of purgatory for such people; the Hillelites reckoned that YHWH would tip the scales in favour of mercy at that point. An interesting sideline on this discussion is provided by the tale of Yohanan ben Zakkai on his deathbed, unsure as to whether he is bound for Paradise or Gehenna (bBer. 28b; Aboth de R. Nathan 25).

[282] Many of the rabbinic texts relevant to this enquiry are collected in SB 1.885–97.

[283] Both works reached their final form no earlier than around AD 400, though probably incorporating older material. Lev. R. shows signs of dependence on Gen. R. See Strack and Stemberger 1991 [1982], 300–08; 313–17. On the Hillel/Shammai schools and debates cf. *NTPG* 164, 183f., 194–201.

[284] See 147–50 above on LXX; and Cavallin 1974, 107. Another tradition envisages an almond-shaped bone, the tip of the coccyx, being able to resist all attempts to crush, break, burn or otherwise dispose of it, and so being available as the starting-point for the yet-to-be-formed resurrection body: Gen. R. 28.3; Lev. R. 18 (thereby providing an ingenious exegesis of Eccles. 12.5, 'the almond tree blossoms').

more tenuously perhaps, claim Job 10.10, reading the passage firmly in the future tense ('You will pour me out like milk and curdle me like cheese; you will clothe me with skin and flesh, and knit me together with bones and sinews').

It is impossible to tell at what period the debate is supposed to have taken place, and it is by no means clear what subtexts, if any, we should listen for in the usual areas of politics or purity. The main difference on the surface seems to be that whereas the Shammaites insist on physical continuity between the previous body and the future one, the Hillelites allow that God will make a totally new creation – since the skin and flesh will of course have corrupted completely – and thus make space for the classic problems experienced by most people who have tried to think through, let alone explain to anyone else, what precisely bodily resurrection entails. What, one is asked, will happen to people who are burnt to ashes and then scattered far and wide? What about those who are dismembered so that their bones now lie hundreds of miles apart? It is not implausible to suppose that the Hillelites, though not weakening the basic Pharisaic emphasis on the bodiliness, the physicality, of the final product, are allowing for the difficult cases to which, as they can perhaps see, the Shammaite position is exposed. But the point for our purposes is precisely that there is no weakening of the emphasis on the eventual physicality of the resurrection body. There is no warrant for saying, as one commentator does, that the Hillelite point of view may be interpreted to be 'less literalistic and more "spiritual" than the Shammaite position'.[285]

Other aspects of the question 'how' are discussed in the famous passage from the Babylonian Talmud tractate Sanhedrin, 90a—92b. Several parallels or analogies are cited from the natural world to show that, though surprising, the creation of the resurrection body is not to be deemed inconceivable. A brief (no doubt fictitious) dialogue between the Roman emperor and the daughter of Gamaliel II (late first century) is used as a showcase for one such point. The emperor asks how dust can come to life, and Gamaliel's daughter replies with a counter-question: there are two potters in town, one making pots from water and one from clay; which is superior? The one who makes them from water, replies the emperor. Well, replies the girl, when God creates humans from water, how much the more can he do so from clay.[286] This story is followed by another analogy: if flesh and blood can break and repair a piece of glass, how much more can the Holy One repair the flesh and blood that was created by his spirit in the first place.[287] The examples then tail off a bit, citing the appearance of moles out of the earth, and of snails which suddenly appear after rain.[288]

---

[285] Cavallin 1974, 173.
[286] bSanh. 90b—91a.
[287] ibid.
[288] ibid. 91a.

More significant for the reader of the New Testament is the illustration that appears quite often: the resurrection of the body is like the corn rising from the seed. This is regularly employed, as Paul uses it in 1 Corinthians 15, to answer the question: what sort of body will it be? Will it be the same or different? Will it come naked or clothed? A further dialogue is staged, this time between Rabbi Meir (a disciple of Akiba, i.e. mid-second century) and Queen Cleopatra (standing here for a devout enquirer). Meir's answer is that, as the seed of wheat is sown naked but appears clothed, so the resurrection body will be all the more clothed because it was already clothed when buried.[289] The bodies will, though, be recognizable, to the extent that (in one account) those who have suffered wounds or deformities will, to begin with, retain them in order that they can be identified. Once that is done, however, they will be healed.[290]

The final question, again with implications for the student of early Christianity, is the biblical support that the Pharisees, and then the rabbis, were able to claim. Nobody doubted that Daniel 12 spoke of bodily resurrection; by the first century some at least were reading Ezekiel in that way, though with metaphorical overtones of return from exile still audible as well. But the key question which the Sadducees pressed on the Pharisees (and, it appears, on Jesus), was: can you find resurrection in the Torah itself, in the narrower sense of the Five Books of Moses?[291]

The answer was an emphatic 'Yes – once you know what you are looking for.' The main Talmudic discussion (Sanhedrin 90—92) offers plenty of examples. Gamaliel II (late first century) is cited as using Deuteronomy 31.16, where YHWH promises Moses that he will sleep with his fathers and will rise.[292] The Sadducees object that it is not Moses who will 'rise' in this text, but the people who will 'rise up' to do evil, which to us at this remove seems reasonable; but the same text is used by Gamaliel's contemporary Joshua ben Hananiah and, a century later, by Simeon ben Yohai.[293] In the same passage, Gamaliel rehearses texts from the prophets and writings as well (Isaiah 26, an obvious passage; Song of Songs 7.10, less obvious to us, but speaking of people whose lips move during sleep, which some rabbis interpreted to refer to the lips of a dead teacher moving silently in the tomb when someone quotes his sayings).[294] But Gamaliel then returns to Deuteronomy, this time to 11.9: since YHWH swore to the patriarchs that he would

---

[289] bSanh. 90b; cf. too Pirqe de R. Eliezer 33.245; Gen. R. 95.1.

[290] Eccles. R. 1.4.

[291] On this question cf. Moore 1927–30, 2.381–4; Cavallin 1974, 179f.; Segal 1997, 121–3.

[292] On the potential confusion between the two Gamaliels, and the possibility that this story concerns the one claimed as his teacher by Paul in Acts (22.3) see Cavallin 1974, 185; Neusner 1971, 1.341f.

[293] bSanh. 90b.

[294] cf. bYeb. 97a; bBer. 31b.

give the land to *them,* not merely to their descendants, the oath could only be fulfilled by their being raised from the dead.[295] A slightly different kind of argument is the use of Numbers 18.28 ('you shall give YHWH's portion to Aaron the priest') to indicate that Aaron will be alive again in the future and will receive the offering from the Israelites.[296] Other passages from the Five Books that were employed include Numbers 15.31 (the remaining guilt of the offender will be accountable in the world to come); Deuteronomy 32.39 (YHWH declares, 'I kill and I make alive; I wound and I heal'); and Deuteronomy 33.6 ('may Reuben live, and not die out').

Among the more ingenious of the exegeses from other parts of scripture we find Psalm 50.4, where God 'calls to the heavens above, and to the earth, that he may judge his people'. The soul of the deceased, says the commentator, is presently in heaven, and the body on earth, and for the purposes of judgment God will summon both to come back together.[297] This is later in origin, but it well exemplifies the kind of reading that was employed from the Pharisaic period onwards. Exactly the same concern for the rejoining of soul and body for the purposes of judgment is found in the parable of Rabbi Judah in Sanhedrin 91a–b, where the human being is likened to two men working together (a lame man sitting on a blind man's shoulders in order to steal figs). Neither could have managed it without the other, just as the soul and the body by themselves cannot act responsibly; but God will bring them together again, and judge them as a unity.

The Targums, though again very difficult to date, give some final tell-tale indications of where the emphasis lay in mainstream rabbinic teaching from the late second-Temple period through to the Amoraic period (the time between Mishnah and Talmud).[298] The Targumists fastened on to the biblical statements about YHWH 'killing and making alive', and interpreted them consistently with a clear 'resurrection' meaning.[299] The famous line in 1 Samuel 25.29 ('The life of my lord shall be bound in the bundle of the living under the care of YHWH your God; but the lives of your enemies he shall sling out as from the hollow of a sling'), the first part of which is found in various funerary inscriptions from this period, is interpreted in the Targum in terms of the soul of the departed being kept in the 'treasury' (*gnz,* as in 'genizah') of the life of the age to come. In other words, the souls of the

---

[295] bSanh. 90b. Other teachers in the same passage say that Gamaliel quoted Deut. 4.4 ('those of you who held fast to YHWH your God are all alive today'). Ex. 6.4 is also quoted to the same effect.

[296] bSanh. 90b; the saying is ascribed to Johanan (mid-second century). The argument is reminiscent of Heb. 7.9, where Levi pays tithes to Melchizedek before he (or even his grandfather Isaac) has been conceived.

[297] Midr. Tann. on Deut 32.2; other refs. in Moore 1927–30, 2.383f.

[298] Fuller surveys in Cavallin 1974, 186–92; Puech 1993, 223–42.

[299] TgJ. II on Deut. 32.39; TgJon. on 1 Sam. 2.6; TgJon. on Isa. 26.19 (the passage above all used by Gamaliel II in bSanh. 90b).

righteous are looked after in an intermediate state and/or place until the time of the resurrection, while the souls of the wicked are dispatched to Gehenna or somewhere equally unpleasant.[300] In one case the Targum – like Paul in two separate passages – speaks of the trumpet which will sound to wake the dead.[301] The last mentioned is one of various passages which explicitly link the resurrection of the dead with the return from exile.

One of the more striking Targumic interpretations of a 'resurrection' passage is that of Hosea 6.2. Where the Masoretic text has 'After two days he will revive us; on the third day he will raise us up, and we shall live in his presence', the Targum has 'He will revive us for the days of consolation which are to come; on the day of the resurrection of the dead he will raise us and we shall live in his presence'. This is one of several Jewish texts, from the Bible through to the second-Temple period and beyond, which speak of the 'third day' as the time when Israel's god will accomplish his work of salvation and/or resurrection.[302]

A further twist is provided where the LXX and Targum make independent but parallel adjustments to the biblical text. In Psalm 1.5, where the Masoretic text declares that the ungodly will not be able to 'stand' in the judgment, the LXX declares that they will not 'rise again', *ouk anastesontai*; the Targum, meanwhile, interprets this as 'shall not be justified'. The parallel of resurrection and justification points to a world of thought which readers of Paul will readily understand.

Finally, one of the most blatant denials of resurrection to be found in the Old Testament, that in Job 14.12–14, has been altered in the Targum, as in the LXX, so that it only denies the future life of the wicked, leaving the way clear for a resurrection of the righteous – which may indeed be mentioned in the Targum on Job 19.25–6, though this passage, like its Masoretic original, is obscure.[303] As with the main rabbinic writings themselves, so with the Targumim; there is no question but that they insist, again and again, on interpreting scripture in the direction of bodily resurrection.

The rabbinic explanations of the resurrection, and biblical proofs for it, show extremely clearly what was and what was not meant by resurrection throughout this period. Resurrection, the 'making alive of the dead', was not simply about 'life after death'; it was about a new, embodied life *after* 'life after death'. Nobody supposed that the patriarchs, Moses, Reuben or anyone else had yet been given this resurrection life. The point of demonstrating

---

[300] TgJon. on 1 Sam. 25.29; see too Cavallin 1974, 191 n. 2. For the funerary inscriptions which quote this text cf. Park 2000, 150–54.

[301] Tg. Jon. on Isa. 27.12f.; cf. 1 Cor. 15.52; 1 Thess. 4.16. Cf. too *Ps. Sol.* 11.1f.; *Apoc. Abr.* 31.1; 4 Ezra 6.23.

[302] cf. Gen. 22.4; 42.18; Ex. 15.22; 19.16; Jos. 2.16; 2 Kgs. 20.5; Jon. 2.1, 11; Esther 4.16; 5.1; Gen. R. 56.1; 91.7; Est. R. 9.2; Midr. Pss. 22.5. Cf. McArthur 1971.

[303] See 148 above on the LXX reading here.

that there were promises yet outstanding to the patriarchs was that God must be capable of fulfilling them in the world yet to come.

Nor was this 'making alive' anything to do with the present religious experience of Israel. All the wonderful literature of Jewish meditation, prayer and mysticism, all the powerful sense of the presence and help of Israel's god – none of this was taken to mean that the resurrection *had* occurred; simply that it *would* do so, because this god was both the creator and the judge. When the Sages of the Herodian period and afterwards saw it as one of their chief tasks to instruct the people about the resurrection of the dead, it was this future bodily renewal that they had in mind.[304] And in offering that instruction the teachers seem to have developed, in line with other writings that affirm ultimate resurrection, various ways of talking about an intermediate state, which, though they may sometimes use the language of the 'soul', seem more or less innocent of any developed Platonic idea of the soul as an (or the) immortal element of all human beings. Souls that wait in cupboards until the resurrection – or even souls that remain 'in the hand of God' during that period – are not the same kind of thing as the pre-existent beings of Plato's *Phaedrus* and elsewhere. By the time that early Christianity burst upon an unsuspecting world, both Jewish and Greek, the Jewish belief in bodily resurrection had made its way into the consciousness, not least the Greek-speaking Bible-reading consciousness, of Jews both in Palestine and in the Diaspora. When the New Testament writers spoke of resurrection, both their own and that of Jesus, this is the grid of language-use within which they must have assumed their words made sense.

5. Resurrection in Ancient Judaism: Conclusion

There is much more that could be said (the reader may be surprised to learn) on the after-death beliefs of ancient Judaism. The New Testament, indeed, provides plenty more material which should properly be classified here, and we shall survey it in due course. The conclusion we can now draw ought not to be particularly controversial, though it may seem so to many who have written about Jesus' resurrection with scant attention to the complete Jewish

---

[304] See Urbach 1987, 660; cf. too 628. I confess to complete puzzlement about Finkelstein's claim (1962 [1938], 158f.) that as the Pharisees became more sophisticated they accepted the Greek philosophical doctrine of immortal souls, which rendered belief in bodily resurrection superfluous and unnecessary. Since Finkelstein gives no evidence for this claim, we must regard it as, at most, an attempt (like that of Josephus in the first century!) to make the Pharisees more palatable to a certain type of modern audience. As we have seen all along, belief in future resurrection *entails* some kind of post-mortem continuity, for which the word 'soul' can sometimes be used, but this does not of itself mean that the ontological basis of present or future human existence has been radically altered.

context – despite the fact that it provides the setting within which the early disciples' use of the relevant language must be understood.[305]

There was a wide spectrum of belief in second-Temple Judaism regarding the fate of the dead, both in the short and the long term. By no means all Jews believed in a coming resurrection. Other views were known and (until the disappearance of the Sadducees and the post-70 ascendancy of the rabbis) taught. But there was a strong strand of resurrection belief, growing out of various biblical passages, called forth by the new circumstances of post-exilic Judaism, and expressed in a wide range of texts emanating from right across the second-Temple period and through into the rabbis.[306]

We begin by reaffirming the preliminary definition with which we began. 'Resurrection', with the various words that were used for it and the various stories that were told about it, was never simply a way of speaking about 'life after death'.[307] It was one particular story that was told about the dead: a story in which the *present* state of those who had died would be replaced by a *future* state in which they would be alive once more. As we noted at the end of chapter 1, 'resurrection' was a life *after* 'life after death', the second of two stages in the post-mortem programme. Resurrection was, more specifically, not the *redefinition* or *redescription* of death, a way of giving a positive interpretation to the fact that the breath and blood of a human body had ceased to function, leading quickly to corruption and decay, but the *reversal* or *undoing* or *defeat* of death, restoring to some kind of bodily life those who had already passed through that first stage. It belonged with a strong doctrine of Israel's god as the good creator of the physical world. It was the affirmation of that which the pagan world denied, as we discovered throughout chapter 2.

We can see this clearly enough if we reflect for a moment on the main metaphorical meaning that 'resurrection' possessed in the Old Testament

---

[305] This is particularly so in the case of Carnley 1987. Even Wedderburn (1999) seems content not to draw upon his massive history-of-religions learning for this particular topic. Indeed, the main purpose which the Pharisaic background seems to serve for him (e.g. 117, 119, 144, 147) is to enable him to say, in effect, 'Well, you would expect an ex-Pharisee like Paul to think like that, wouldn't you?', and to add (120f.) that if resurrection meant anything like what it means in 2 Maccabees, one would be better off without it. When he says, two-thirds of the way through the book (147), that 'for the first century . . . "resurrection" usually meant that something was raised up to life again and that something was a body,' we are left wondering, not only what the word 'usually' is doing, but also why this point was not made clear, and allowed to influence the discussion, a good deal sooner.

[306] It is extraordinary, in view of the last fifty pages or so, to find Porter 1999a, 67f. declaring that 'there is only a faint hint of the concept of a bodily resurrection to be found' in this period.

[307] This is the heart of the problem with the language of e.g. Carnley 1997, 38 about 'the heavenly existence of the raised Christ'. Phrases like that are bound to be heard (and were presumably intended to be heard) as implying that to say 'Jesus was raised from the dead' is a special way of saying 'Jesus went to heaven when he died'. This is based on e.g. Carnley 1987, 74f., 246.

and some subsequent readings. Ezekiel's dramatic picture of dry bones coming together, being clothed with skin and flesh, and finally being animated by breath, was a rich allegory for the return of Israel from exile. If no 'return' of any sort had ever happened, one can just about imagine somebody proposing a reinterpretation: what Ezekiel had in mind, they might say, was that you should learn to feel good about your exile, to discover the life-giving presence of YHWH within Babylon instead. But one cannot imagine too many readers of Ezekiel being taken in by this sort of thing. The point of the whole story, they would say, was that they would return to their land. If that hadn't happened, the prophecy remained unfulfilled.

This metaphorical meaning of 'resurrection', then, retained a concrete referent. We must not allow current usage to mislead us into supposing that 'metaphorical' means 'abstract'.[308] Ezekiel, and possibly the original author of Isaiah 26, intended to speak of the literal and concrete return from exile, using the metaphor of corpses coming to new bodily life. They were telling the story of an actual people and an actual land – and an actual god, YHWH, the creator, whose covenant with Israel was so unbreakable, so powerful, that he would act in a new way to restore what had been lost in the exile, namely land, Temple and national life. YHWH was the god of justice, and would not for ever leave Israel to suffer oppression at the hands of the pagans. We can see how this belief sustained the national hope even when, after the geographical 'return', Israel remained under foreign domination through the period of the second Temple. 'Resurrection', at this metaphorical level, was always a revolutionary doctrine because, by means of the metaphor of the revivifying of corpses, it spoke of the concrete hope of national freedom. The twin doctrines of creation and justice sustained the national hope and, so to speak, kept the metaphor of resurrection alive.

But increasingly, from at least the third century BC (as witnessed by the LXX), the metaphor itself came to life in a new way, precisely (so it seems) through reflection on the suffering of those who withstood the pagans in the hope of national redemption. The book of Daniel bears witness to the emerging, not as we saw of a totally new idea, but of the reaffirmation in a new form of the ancient Israelite belief in the goodness and god-givenness of the created world and of bodily human life within it. By the time 2 Maccabees was written the metaphor has become literal, having now the concrete referent of re-embodiment – getting back hands, tongues, entire bodies – without losing the larger concrete referent of national restoration. Josephus' description of the Pharisees as a philosophical school may make it look as though their belief in resurrection was simply about 'what happens to people after they die', and indeed his language on the subject is so imprecise that at some points it sounds as though he is simply talking about reincarnation, an

---

[308] See my remarks on literal/metaphorical and concrete/abstract in Wright 'In Grateful Dialogue' 261f.

endless sequence of the soul returning to another body, and then another, and another. Even this makes it clear that he is at least talking about bodies, not simply disembodied souls or spirits. The other writers who (we have argued) speak, however obliquely, about the same basic belief (Wisdom, the Scrolls), are likewise talking about the new world which Israel's god will make, and the newly embodied human beings – i.e. the righteous – who will inhabit it. This is reflected in the popular-level belief which could generate a remark such as that ascribed to Herod Antipas in the gospels.[309] Whatever else he believed about life after death, when he suggested that Jesus might be John the Baptist risen from the dead, he did not suppose that Jesus was a ghost.

This widespread belief in the future resurrection naturally generated a belief in an intermediate state. There were different ways of expressing this: it could even sometimes look fleetingly like a hellenistic, perhaps Platonic, theory of a continuing soul, without (as has often been suggested) strain or contradiction. 'Resurrection' entails some kind of belief in continuing post-mortem existence; this need not mean a belief that all humans have an immortal soul in the Platonic sense, since the belief in YHWH as creator which is necessary for belief in resurrection is also a sufficient explanation for the dead being held in some kind of continuing existence, by divine power rather than in virtue of something inalienable in their own being.

As with our survey of pagan views, we can therefore put to this range of material the worldview questions, slanting them towards the fate of the dead within the belief of the mainstream belief in resurrection. Who or what are they? They are, at present, souls, spirits or angel-like beings, held in that state of being not because they were naturally immortal but by the creative power of YHWH. Where are they? They are in the hand of the creator god; or in paradise; or in some kind of Sheol, understood now not as a final but as a temporary resting-place. What's wrong? They are not yet re-embodied, not least because their god has not completed his purposes for the world and Israel. What's the solution? Ultimate re-embodiment, which will be caused by YHWH's power and spirit. What time is it? It is still 'the present age'; the 'age to come' has not yet begun (except, in the case of the Essenes, in the sense of a secretly inaugurated eschatology). This contrasts, of course, not only with the pagan views surveyed in the previous chapter, but with the two other main Jewish options, that of the Sadducees and that of Philo and the others in that category. These worldview questions have their analogue in the stories that we have examined, from the biblical narratives of Ezekiel, Daniel and the others to the stories told by the rabbis, with sundry other key narratives like 2 Maccabees 7 somewhere in between. And they went with equivalent praxis and symbol: from burial customs to the fomenting of revolution, belief in resurrection influenced and energized many concrete aspects

---

[309] Mk. 6.14–16 and pars.; cf. 412 below.

of first-century Jewish life. Resurrection was not a strange belief added on to the outside of first-century Judaism. Except for the Sadducees and those who insisted on a final disembodied state, resurrection had been woven into the very fabric of first-century Jewish praying, living, hoping and acting.

Resurrection, therefore, seems to possess two basic meanings in the second-Temple period, with considerable fluidity between them. In each case the referent is concrete: restoration of Israel ('resurrection' as metaphorical, denoting socio-political events and investing them with the significance that this will be an act of new creation, of covenant restoration); of human bodies ('resurrection' as literal, denoting actual re-embodiment). Nothing in the entire Jewish context warrants the suggestion that the discussion in 1 Corinthians 15 was about 'resurrection *in heaven*',[310] or that the Jewish literature of the period 'speaks both of a resurrection of the body and a resurrection of the spirit without the body'.[311] Some Jews speak of eternal disembodied bliss, but this is not described as 'resurrection'; when 'resurrection' is spoken of, it is the second stage in post-mortem life, not the instant destiny upon death. Nothing here, either, would prepare us for the use of 'resurrection' to mean 'that after his crucifixion . . . Jesus entered into the powerful life of God' or 'the passage of the human Jesus into the power of God'.[312] Despite the protestations of some, 'resurrection' was not used to describe the exaltation of Enoch or Elijah.[313] 'Resurrection' in its literal sense belongs at one point on the much larger spectrum of Jewish beliefs about life after death; in its political, metaphorical sense it belongs on a spectrum of views about the future which YHWH was promising to Israel. Both senses generated and sustained nationalist revolution. The hope that YHWH would restore Israel provided the goal; the hope that he would restore human bodies (especially of those who died in the cause) removed the fear that might have undermined zeal. No wonder the aristocratic Sadducees rejected resurrection. Anyone who used the normal words for 'resurrection' within second-Temple Judaism would have been heard to be speaking within this strictly limited range of meaning.

Talk of resurrection, though, remained unspecific about details. The large-scale prophetic pictures of a renewed Israel in a renewed creation were never worked out in details about precise forms of government, in the socio-political equivalents of Ezekiel's astonishingly detailed picture of the rebuilt Temple. The many references to resurrection never describe exactly what the risen body will be like: Daniel declares that the righteous will shine like stars, the Wisdom of Solomon that they will shine forth and run like sparks

---

[310] Harvey 1994, 74 (italics original).

[311] Avis 1993b, 6. See, correctly, Brown 1973, 70: the NT refs. to Jesus' resurrection cannot be ambiguous as to whether they mean bodily resurrection, because 'there was no other kind of resurrection'.

[312] Johnson 1995, 134, 136.

[313] Against e.g. Lohfink 1980.

through the stubble, but the texts that drew on these and similar ideas do not allow us to be clear as to whether this was meant literally (human beings shining like torches) or whether this was an image for world rulership, like the promises of David's kingdom being like the sun and the moon.[314] Nowhere do the pre-70 texts discuss how the body will be like, or unlike, the present one. Though by the time of Jesus it appears that most Jews believed in resurrection, there was no clarity as to what precisely it would look like or what sort of continuity and discontinuity there would be with present existence. This, as we shall see, is one of the striking contrasts between mainstream Jewish belief and the virtually uniform early Christian hope.

Of course, the rabbis do discuss, as we have seen, the questions of *what* and *how*: will the new bodies be clothed or unclothed? will there be sexual relations in the world to come? will God start with the bones, as in Ezekiel, or with the skin, as in Job? and so forth. It might be tempting to suggest that these questions assume more significance only after the two great disasters of AD 70 and 135 – only, in other words, when the dream of political and social independence has disappeared. But this would not be strictly true. Unless we are to adopt an extremely sceptical approach to the traditions about Gamaliel II, for instance, we have to say that these questions were already alive in the first century, however much they may have been emphasized more in the later period. And, as we shall see, they are important for the early Christian movement as well.[315] But it remains the case that resurrection, in the world of second-Temple Judaism, was about *the restoration of Israel* on the one hand and *the newly embodied life of all YHWH's people* on the other, with close connections between the two; and that it was thought of as the great event that YHWH would accomplish at the very end of 'the present age', the event which would constitute the 'age to come', *ha'olam haba*. All of this was concentrated, for many Jews, in the stories of the righteous martyrs, those who had suffered and died for YHWH and Torah. Because YHWH was the creator, and because he was the god of justice, the martyrs would be raised, and Israel as a whole would be vindicated.

But nobody imagined that any individuals had already been raised, or would be raised in advance of the great last day. There are no traditions about prophets being raised to new bodily life; the closest we come to that is Elijah, who had gone bodily to heaven and would return to herald the new age. There are no traditions about a Messiah being raised to life: most Jews of this period hoped for resurrection, many Jews of this period hoped for a Messiah, but nobody put those two hopes together until the early Christians did so.[316] It may be obvious, but it needs saying: however exalted Abraham,

---

[314] Ps. 72.5; 89.36f.

[315] See particularly Jesus' discussion with the Sadducees (below, 415–29).

[316] Except in the sense that the resurrection would occur in the Messiah's time, or through his work; e.g. *Test. 12 Patr.* (above, 159). This calls into question Barr's suggestion (1992, 109) about people expecting a religious leader to come alive again after death.

Isaac and Jacob may have been in Jewish thought, nobody imagined they had been raised from the dead. However important Moses, David, Elijah and the prophets may have been, nobody claimed that they were alive again in the 'resurrection' sense. The martyrs were honoured, venerated even; but nobody said they had been raised from the dead. The world of Judaism had generated, from its rich scriptural origins, a rich variety of beliefs about what happened, and would happen, to the dead. But it was quite unprepared for the new mutation that sprang up, like a totally unexpected plant, within the already well-stocked garden.

Part Two

Resurrection in Paul

One short sleepe past, wee wake eternally,
And death shall be no more; death, thou shalt die.

John Donne, *Holy Sonnets*

Chapter Five

RESURRECTION IN PAUL
(OUTSIDE THE CORINTHIAN CORRESPONDENCE)

1. Introduction: The Early Christian Hope

One of the most striking features of the early Christian movement is its virtual unanimity about the future hope. We might have expected that the first Christians would quickly have developed a spectrum of beliefs about life after death, corresponding to the spectrums we have observed in the Judaism from within which Christianity emerged and the paganism into which it went as a missionary movement; but they did not.

This observation forms the hinge upon which turns one of the central arguments of the present book. This can be expressed in the form of a question. Granted that the early Christians drew freely on Jewish traditions, and engaged energetically with the pagan world of ideas, how does it happen that we find virtually no spectrum of belief about life after death, but instead an almost universal affirmation of that which pagans said could not happen, and that which one stream (albeit the dominant one) of Judaism insisted would happen, namely resurrection? Let us be quite clear at this point: we shall see that when the early Christians said 'resurrection' they meant it in the sense it bore both in paganism (which denied it) and in Judaism (an influential part of which affirmed it). 'Resurrection' did not mean that someone possessed 'a heavenly and exalted status'; when predicated of Jesus, it did not mean his 'perceived presence' in the ongoing church. Nor, if we are thinking historically, could it have meant 'the passage of the human Jesus into the power of God'. It meant bodily resurrection; and that is what the early Christians affirmed.[1] There is nothing in the early Christian view of the promised future which corresponds to the pagan views we have studied;

---

[1] Against Carnley 1987, 7f., who seems in the introduction to his book to be already abandoning a historical understanding of the key terms; also Johnson 1995, 136. Johnson, like Carnley, repeatedly downgrades the real historical question ('the effort to reduce the resurrection experience to just another historical event' (139); 'not simply a resuscitation of Jesus' body but his entry into God's own life' (142), etc.).

nothing at all which corresponds to the denials of the Sadducees; virtually no hint of the 'disembodied bliss' view of some Jewish sources; no Sheol, no 'isles of the blessed', no 'shining like stars', but a constant affirmation of newly embodied life. As Christopher Evans put it a generation ago, 'there emerged in Christianity a precise, confident and articulate faith in which resurrection has moved from the circumference to the centre'.[2]

This alone demands historical explanation. But there is more. There are substantial mutations from within the 'resurrection' stream of Judaism. In particular, the historian must account for the fact that, with early Christianity thus being so clearly a 'resurrection' movement in the Jewish sense, the well-established metaphorical meaning of 'resurrection' – the restoration of Israel in a concrete socio-political sense – is almost entirely absent, and a different set of metaphorical meanings emerge instead. How does it come about, in other words, that early Christianity located its life-after-death beliefs so firmly at the 'resurrection' end of the Jewish spectrum, while simultaneously giving the word a metaphorical meaning significantly different from, though in long-range continuity with, the meaning it had within Judaism? How do we account for both the strong similarity between Christianity and Judaism (there is no sign, in early Christian resurrection belief, of anything remotely like a move in a pagan direction) and the equally clear dissimilarities?

The shape of the remainder of this book is determined by these questions, and by the two-layered answer we shall give them. In Parts II and III, we shall examine the early Christian movement with two ancillary questions in mind: what did the early Christians believe about life after death? and what metaphorical meanings did 'resurrection' have, and how did they relate to the metaphorical meanings current in Judaism? We shall discover that early Christianity was a 'resurrection' movement through and through, and that, indeed, it stated much more precisely what exactly 'resurrection' involved (it meant going through death and out into a new kind of bodily existence beyond, and it was happening in two stages, with Jesus first and everyone else later); second, that though the literal 'resurrection' of which the early Christians spoke remained firmly in the future, it coloured and gave shape to present Christian living as well. In the final chapter of Part III we shall widen the scope by asking two other questions which reinforce the central one: why did early Christianity take the shape it did, and why, in particular, did the early Christians believe that the crucified Jesus of Nazareth was the Messiah?

Throughout Parts II and III, and on into Part IV, we shall examine the reasons the early Christians themselves gave for their beliefs about life after death, for their fresh metaphorical usage of 'resurrection', and for the shape of their own movement and their view of Jesus. Their answer – this may

---

[2] Evans 1970, 40.

seem obvious, but it must be spelled out – was that their future hope for ultimate bodily resurrection and the various ways in which that hope had been made more precise, their redefinition of the metaphorical meanings of 'resurrection', and their sense of who they themselves were and who Jesus was, were based on their firm belief that Jesus of Nazareth had himself been raised from the dead. This will enable us to clarify more precisely what exactly the early Christians meant when they used this language. What can we say, as historians, about what they thought had happened at Easter?

This leads to Part IV, in which we shall turn to the accounts of the first Easter in the canonical gospels. These have been treated, almost routinely within much post-Enlightenment scholarship, as mere back-projections of later Christian belief, with only the shakiest claim to historical veracity. We shall discover that this position, fashionable though it has been, creates enormous historical problems which disappear when the accounts are treated as, at least in principle, descriptions of what the first Christians believed had actually happened on the first Easter day. The accounts, in fact, make sense not as the final product of a development of theological and exegetical reflection within the early church, but as something like the source from which that development emerged. They are not the leaves on the branches of early Christianity. They look very like the trunk from which the branches themselves sprang, even though the writings in which we meet them are to be dated towards the end of the first generation, or even later.

This will lead us, in Part V, to stand back and ask what, if anything, the contemporary reader – the historian, the student of worldviews, the theologian – can say by way of comment on this early Christian belief. If the first Christians really did believe that Jesus had been raised bodily from the dead, what can *we* say about their belief? Have we an alternative explanation for the rise of the early church, and particularly for its reaffirmation, development and modification of the Jewish resurrection belief? If not, what must we say, as historians, about Easter itself?

The sources do not, of course, lay the matter out in so orderly a fashion. They weave together, in many rich patterns, the questions of their own future hope on the one hand and the resurrection of Jesus himself on the other. This is so particularly in the case of our earliest and most detailed source, the apostle Paul. (We leave until Part IV the question of whether the gospel accounts go back to oral traditions as early as Paul; he, certainly, is our earliest *written* source.) As usual, Paul mocks our attempts to tidy everything into neat bundles. He frequently speaks in a single passage, sometimes (one suspects) in a single breath, about the resurrection of Christians, about Jesus' death and resurrection, about the present life which grows out of the latter and anticipates the former, and about various other vital topics (justification, say, or the Jewish law). It would be both artificial and unbearably repetitive if we were to parcel out his thought into separate sections; one would meet the same passages, and often the same verses, over and over again in category after category. For this reason, and also because the contribution of Paul to the entire discussion has often itself been controversial, it seems best to devote this Part of the book to his writings, and by working through them with an eye to the central questions of Parts III and IV: what was the early Christian hope? what meanings did 'resurrection' carry? what answers would the early Christians have given to the worldview-questions, framed in relation to the dead, that we put to ancient paganism and Judaism? what, in particular, did the early Christians think had happened to Jesus after his death? Part II thus takes us once around the circle of questions which will occupy us in Parts II and III, focusing on our earliest evidence.

This investigation of Paul must itself be seriously curtailed. Most aspects of Paul's thought link up with most other aspects in a wonderfully complex web of ideas, biblical echoes, implicit narratives and practical instructions. The resurrection (of Christians, and of Jesus) is central in much of this, and to follow through all the ramifications of what Paul says would entail writing detailed commentaries on many sections of many letters, and engaging in discussion with a whole world of monographs and articles. Here, to keep length under control, I must refer to detailed discussions elsewhere; much of the material in the present and following chapter is uncontroversial, and is included principally to set the context, in a way which is usually not done in treatments of the resurrection, for the harder questions raised in 1 Corinthians 15 and 2 Corinthians 4 and 5.[3] Among the many debates into which there is no room to enter is the vexed question of which of the 'Pauline' letters were actually written by Paul himself. My main arguments rest firmly on the letters commonly regarded as authentic, namely, Romans, the two Corinthian letters, Galatians, Philippians, Philemon and 1 Thessalonians. Ephesians and Colossians are important but not foundational (and their contribution remains significant even if they are held to be by someone writing later within a 'Pauline' tradition); 2 Thessalonians offers little help on our topic, so the question of its authenticity does not impinge. The Pastoral Epistles have some significant points to add, and we shall discuss them in a separate section at the end of the present chapter.

Pragmatic reasons suggest a particular path through the material. The two letters to Corinth are full of interest for our topic, both because 1 Corinthians 15, Paul's major statement on our subject, is complex and controversial, and because many scholars have argued that a significant development took place in Paul's thought between the two letters, particularly between 1 Corinthians 15 and 2 Corinthians 4 and 5.[4] It will be as well, therefore, first to survey the material in the other letters, and then to come to the Corinthian

---

[3] See particularly Wright, *Climax*; *Romans*; and the fourth projected volume in the present series. I assume the many standard commentaries on the individual letters.

[4] On development hypotheses see recently Longenecker 1998.

correspondence with some idea of the range and force of Paul's thinking in this area. Nothing much hinges on the order in which we take the other letters, and I shall examine them in what I believe (controversially, of course) to be something like their historical sequence: the Thessalonian letters and Galatians first, followed by the Prison Letters, and ending with Romans. Then will come the appended note on the Pastorals.

Within the framework already outlined, there are three particular questions to put to these rich and dense texts, and indeed to all the other early Christian texts (which we shall examine in Part III). (1) Where does Paul's belief about the ultimate Christian hope belong on the spectrum of possibilities in the ancient world? This question subdivides into four: (1a) Granted that he spoke frequently of this hope in terms of resurrection, what did he mean by that? (1b) Did he, like various Jewish thinkers, develop ways of speaking about an intermediate state between death and eventual resurrection? (1c) How did he handle questions of continuity and discontinuity between the present life and the ultimate future one? (1d) How does the resurrection function within his larger picture of the future which the true god had promised? (2) In what ways did Paul use 'resurrection' and similar language and ideas metaphorically? What has happened, in his writings, to the Jewish metaphorical use, denoting the restoration of Israel? (3) What does he say about Jesus' own resurrection, and what precisely does he mean by it? This investigation is the more urgent in that, as we shall see, a serious misreading of Paul on the crucial point has become so widespread in secondary and indeed popular discussions as to be almost taken for granted. It is commonly asserted, often indeed simply assumed, that Paul held what in the modern sense is called a 'spiritual' view of the resurrection, that is, one for which a body, and an empty tomb, would be irrelevant. This whole Part of the book is designed not least to argue conclusively against this idea, and in particular against a disastrous mistranslation in 1 Corinthians 15 which has given it wide currency.[5]

2. 1 and 2 Thessalonians

1 Thessalonians, by common consent, dates from around AD 49/50, shortly after Paul's brief visit to Thessalonica on his first journey in Greece.[6] A letter of pastoral rather than polemical character, much of its value for our present enquiry lies in what Paul takes for granted and refers to in simple

---

[5] Examples from one or two recent symposia: Avis 1993b, 6; Badham 1993, 30–33. Cf. too e.g. Wedderburn 1999, 111, 118f., arguing in a similar direction to that of Robinson 1982; Borg 1999, 123. On 1 Cor. 15.42–9 see 347–56 below. An older, still useful, work on the meaning of the resurrection for Paul is Stanley 1961.

[6] See Ac. 17.1–8.

summaries. There is, however, one passage of central relevance, which needs close and careful attention.

Paul's opening summary of the Thessalonians' initial faith focuses on how they came to believe in the true and living God as opposed to the idols of paganism (1.9). Then, in a hint of what is to come towards the end of the letter, he summarizes what his gospel has to say about Jesus:

> . . . and to wait for God's son from heaven, whom he raised from the dead: Jesus, who delivers us from the coming wrath.[7]

Jesus' resurrection; his present location in heaven; his future return, and his deliverance of his people from wrath: these are commonplace in Paul's developed thinking, and here we see that they were central from very early on in his writing, and capable of succinct summary. So, too, in the next chapter, he can indicate the future Christian hope with one word we have already met in Galatians and another which will become a major theme, to be explored more fully elsewhere: you must, he says, walk worthy of the God who calls you 'into his own kingdom and glory'.[8] Here, as in Galatians 5.21, the 'kingdom of God' is the future state.

But how will that future arrive? This is what concerns Paul in a major passage for our purposes, namely 4.13—5.11:

> [13]We don't want you to be ignorant, my dear family, about those who have fallen asleep, so that you don't grieve like others, those who have no hope. [14]If, you see, we believe that Jesus died and rose again, in the same way God will, with Jesus, bring those who have fallen asleep through him. [15]For this is what we must tell you by the word of the lord: we who are left alive until the royal presence of the lord will not precede those who have fallen asleep. [16]For the lord himself will come down from heaven with a shout of command, with the voice of an archangel, and with God's trumpet. The Messiah's dead will rise first; [17]then we who are left alive will be snatched up, along with them, on the clouds, to meet the lord in the air. In this way, we shall always be with the lord. [18]So comfort each other with these words.
>
> [5.1]But when it comes to times and seasons, my dear family, you don't need me to write to you. [2]You yourselves know very well that the day of the lord comes like a thief in the night. [3]When people say 'peace and security', then sudden destruction will come on them, like labour-pains on a pregnant woman, and they won't be able to escape. [4]But you, my dear family, are not in the darkness, for the day to overtake you like a thief. [5]For you are all children of light, children of the day. We are not of the night or of darkness. [6]So, then, let's not fall asleep, as the others do, but let's stay awake and keep watch.
>
> [7]People who sleep, you see, sleep at night. People who get drunk get drunk at night. [8]But we are of the day: so let's keep watch, putting on the breastplate of faith and love, and the hope of salvation for a helmet. [9]For God has not appointed us to wrath, but to possess salvation, through our lord, Jesus the Messiah. [10]He died for us

---

[7] 1 Thess. 1.10. Note that in quotations from and summaries of Paul's thinking I use the capital 'G' for God, reflecting his own point of view.

[8] 1 Thess. 2.12.

so that, whether we wake or sleep, we shall always live with him. [11]Therefore comfort one another, and build each other up, just as you are doing.

This is a spectacular text, addressing a particular pastoral problem (what happens to those who die before the lord returns?), and exhibiting several of Paul's key beliefs about the resurrection. Unfortunately it is also a highly contentious passage, being used with astonishing literalness in popular fundamentalism and critical scholarship alike to suggest that Paul envisaged Christians flying around in mid-air on clouds. The multiple apocalyptic resonances of the passage on the one hand, and its glorious mixed metaphors on the other, make this interpretation highly unlikely. Fortunately, the rest of the passage is reasonably clear, and contributes substantially to our investigation on all fronts.[9] We may take our questions in order, beginning with the overall topic: (1) Where does Paul come on the spectrum of ancient views about life beyond the grave?

(1a) What does Paul mean by 'resurrection'? In this passage he clearly indicates that those who have already died will, at some future date, be raised from the dead 'in the same way' (*houtos*, 4.14). Jesus' resurrection will be the model for that of his people. Those currently dead will rise up (*anastesontai*, 4.16), and so possess 'salvation' rather than being the objects of 'wrath' (5.9). The words Paul uses, the nature of his argument, and the underlying story-line, all make it crystal clear that he belongs, at this point, right in the middle of second-Temple Jewish beliefs about resurrection. Take Jesus out of this picture, and what is being asserted – the future resurrection to salvation from wrath, for those presently dead who belong to the people of the one god – is familiar from our study of Judaism: it is the position of the Pharisees. Whatever other beliefs Paul revised following his conversion, resurrection remained constant. This means that we are bound to see resurrection as *bodily*, not only because of the terminology (there is no evidence that the *anastasis* root meant anything other than bodily resurrection, either in the paganism that denied it or the Pharisaic Judaism that affirmed it), not only because of the obviously Jewish context, but also because of the narrative logic. Resurrection is something new, something the dead do *not* presently enjoy; it will be life *after* 'life after death'.

The close parallel between 4.16–17 and 1 Corinthians 15.51–2, which we shall explore later, suggests that 'being snatched up on the clouds to meet the lord in the air' is functionally equivalent, in Paul's mind, to being 'changed' so that one's body is no longer corruptible, but now of the same type as the lord's own risen body.[10] Again, we should not be misled by the metaphor of going up on a cloud. The picture evokes Daniel 7.13, which uses this image to speak of the *vindication* of the covenant people after their suffering. It is, in other words, another way of saying what Paul said in

---

[9] On the central question cf., in addition to the commentaries, Plevnik 1984.
[10] See too Phil. 3.20f., on which see below, 223–33.

Galatians 5.5: the people who belong to the one God will be vindicated. That vindication will consist, for those already dead, in their resurrection; for those still alive, in their transformation so that their body is no longer of the corruptible sort. This will mean 'salvation' (as opposed to 'wrath' as in 1 Thessalonians 5.9), in the sense of rescue from death itself.

(1b) What does Paul have to say about an intermediate state? Like other second-Temple Jews who believed in resurrection, Paul is left with an interval between bodily death and bodily resurrection, and this passage provides his fullest description of it. To begin with, he uses the regular image of falling asleep for death, enabling him to speak of people who are currently asleep but who will one day wake up again, and to do so with echoes of Daniel 12.2, which as we saw was one of the primary biblical passages on the subject.[11] Three times, in 4.13, 14 and 15, Paul uses this language, employing it also in a different sense in 5.6–10 (see below). This has led some interpreters to speak of 'the sleep of the soul', a time of unconscious post-mortem existence prior to the reawakening of resurrection.[12] But this is almost certainly misleading – another case of people picking up a vivid Pauline metaphor and running down the street waving it about. For a start, though Paul can refer to the 'soul' (*psyche*) among other anthropological terms, it is noticeable that he does not employ this term when referring to the intermediate state – unlike, say, the Wisdom of Solomon, and indeed Revelation.[13] In fact, if we were speaking strictly, we should say that it is the *body* that 'sleeps' between death and resurrection; but in all probability Paul is using the language of sleeping and waking simply as a way of contrasting a stage of temporary inactivity, not necessarily unconsciousness, with a subsequent one of renewed activity.[14] The other references to the presently dead in this passage refer to them as 'the dead in the Messiah' (4.16), and as people who, though having fallen asleep, continue (and will continue) to 'live with him' (5.10), to be 'with Jesus' (4.14), or 'with the lord' (4.17). That is the paradox and tension inherent in belonging to the risen Messiah on the one hand and being bodily dead, and not yet raised, on the other.

(1c) What signs are there of continuity and discontinuity between the present life and that final resurrection state? In 5.4–8, Paul states boldly that Christians are already 'children of light, of the day'. When he speaks of not falling asleep, but of staying awake, he is not envisaging someone staying up later and later into the night, but of someone getting up very early, while it is still dark before dawn. This, he insists, is the present condition of Christian believers. When the day dawns – the biblical 'day of the lord', now

---

[11] See also Jn. 11.11–13; Ac. 7.60.

[12] This was a major topic of controversy among the C16 reformers. See e.g. Tavard 2000 on the question in Calvin; Juhász 2002, on the controversy between Tyndale and Joye.

[13] For *psyche* cf. 1 Thess. 5.23. Paul's other uses will be discussed below (340–56).

[14] Had Paul supposed this state to be unconscious, I do not think he would have written 2 Cor. 5.8 or Phil. 1.23, on which see below, 226, 367, 369.

reinterpreted as 'the day of the lord Jesus' – those who are already up and awake will not be startled by it. As in Galatians, this has a strong ethical implication: it is important to be conducting oneself as though it were already daytime. The passage thus offers an *inaugurated eschatology* in which Paul draws on the (Genesis-based) imagery of night and day to say that Christians are *already*, as it were, 'resurrection people'. Their bodies still need to be transformed, but in terms of the resurrection-related imagery of sleeping and waking they are already 'awake', and must stay that way.

(1d) How does resurrection in this passage function within Paul's larger picture? Initially, as an incentive to the right sort of grief (4.13): not the kind of grief that overtakes people without hope, people in the pagan world the Thessalonians knew so well. There is nothing unchristian about grief, and Paul can refer to grief, including his own, as a Christian phenomenon need-ing no apology.[15] This is, in fact, as close as we come in early Christian lit-erature to the theme much beloved of preachers at funerals, namely the promise of a reunion beyond the grave with Christians already dead. Noth-ing is said, one way or the other, about such a reunion taking place before the resurrection itself; but the pastoral logic of the passage insists that an eventual reunion is what the creator God has in mind, and will accomplish at the time of Jesus' return.

Equally important is the picture of heaven and earth, and of their eventual joining, which Paul draws on in his much-misunderstood language about the lord descending, believers going up on the clouds, and meeting the lord 'in the air'. The language of this passage is a rich blend of two things in particu-lar.[16] First, there is Daniel 7, already referred to, from which we get the idea of being taken up on the clouds; here this refers, obviously, to believers rather than to Jesus. Second, there is the language, well known in the pagan world, of an emperor or other dignitary making a state visit to a city or pro-vince – or even, when the emperor had been elsewhere, his return to Rome. In fact, the Greek word *parousia*, which has become a technical term for the literalistic construct of an early Christian hope involving the end of the space-time world, with Jesus 'coming down' in a 'second coming' and believers flying upwards to meet him, is drawn, not from the Bible at all, but from the world of pagan usage, where it was almost a technical term for this kind of imperial 'visitation'. Properly, *parousia* means 'presence' as oppo-sed to 'absence'; Paul can use it in that way of himself, without implying that he is going to be flying downwards on a cloud;[17] but the point here is that the 'meeting' – another almost technical term in the Greek – refers, not to a meeting after which all the participants stay in the meeting-place, but to

---

[15] 1 Cor. 7.5–13; Phil 2.27 – not to mention the personal agonies of 2 Cor.

[16] There are no doubt other allusions as well, e.g. to Jacob's ladder (Gen. 28.10–17; cf. Jn. 1.51).

[17] e.g. Phil. 2.12.

a meeting outside the city, after which the civic leaders escort the dignitary back into the city itself. This passage thus belongs very closely with 3.13, and with Philippians 3.20–21, pointing towards the larger picture of 1 Corinthians 15.20–28 and Romans 8.12–30, indicating not that believers will be taken away from the earth, leaving it to its fate, but that – in the language of apocalyptic imagery, not in literal spatial reality – they will 'meet' the lord as he comes from heaven (1.10) and surround him as he comes to inaugurate God's final transformative, judging-and-saving reign on earth as in heaven.[18]

(2) What has happened to the metaphorical usage of 'resurrection' in second-Temple Judaism, referring to God's deliverance of Israel from oppression and exile and investing that event with the meaning of new creation? It has disappeared, and has been replaced by an equivalent metaphorical construct, in which language relating to resurrection (sleeping and waking, as in Daniel 12.2) is re-employed to denote the transformation of life which comes about through the preaching of the gospel, the 'word' which has done its work in the community (2.13) and must now have its full effect of producing holy and generous lives.[19] Through this metaphor, Paul is able both to draw on an inaugurated eschatology to reinforce his moral teaching (you already *are* this sort of people, so make sure you live out your real identity), and to invest that theological and moral teaching with the overtone that says: what Israel longed for, both resurrection and restoration, is already coming true in your lives in Christ, empowered by the Spirit.

(3) What, finally, does this passage have to say about the resurrection of Jesus himself? It is the presupposition of the whole argument, as the brief credal formula in 4.14 indicates; 4.14 is, in fact, a succinct summary of virtually the whole of 1 Corinthians 15. The fact that Paul carefully models the resurrection of presently dead Christians on the resurrection of Jesus himself ('in the same way', 4.14) indicates, since he is fairly explicit about certain aspects of the Christians' resurrection, what he believed to be true about the Messiah. For Paul, the resurrection of Jesus was not something that happened immediately upon his death, an exaltation which was virtually synonymous with death itself (death 'seen as' resurrection, or something of the kind). There is no indication, in other words, that Paul meant by 'rose again' (*aneste*) in 4.14 anything other than what that word would have meant to an ancient pagan or to a reader of the Septuagint. As far as Paul was concerned, resurrection, for Jesus as for Christians, was a new life *after* a period of 'life after death', not a new state into which he had slipped at bodily death, leaving his body to be buried as irrelevant. He does not say that Jesus had been 'asleep' between his death and his resurrection, but he implies that there must have been a period between the two events. And,

---

[18] On the counter-imperial overtones of the whole passage see Wright, 'Caesar'.

[19] 1 Thess. 4.1–12; note the emphasis on sanctification in 5.23.

since the language he uses about the death and resurrection of believers is soaked in the language of various biblical passages, both the Genesis account of the creation of night and day and Daniel's prediction of sleepers awakening, we have a strong sense that, for Paul, the resurrection of Jesus was the sharp, shocking fulfilment of the hope of Israel, inaugurating a new, unexpected period of history in which those called by the gospel would live as children of the day, waiting for dawn to break at last.

Little is added to this picture in 2 Thessalonians, though the picture of the 'day of the lord' is considerably expanded in 2.1–12. But the two verses which follow that passage, which are actually a functional equivalent to Paul's great summary of his argument in Romans 8.29–30, indicate again what we saw in 1 Thessalonians 2.12: Paul can describe the final goal of the Christian as that of sharing the glory of the lord Jesus, the Messiah (2 Thessalonians 2.14). This 'glory' is set in parallel with the 'salvation' spoken of in verse 13, which presumably is the same thing as the 'salvation' in 1 Thessalonians 5.9. We are beginning to build up a picture of the multiple ways Paul could describe the ultimate goal of the Christian. The clue to it all is that in the death and resurrection of Jesus the creator God has defeated the power of death, so that the life of his new world, the new creation, the dawning new day, is already anticipated in the lives of those who have been grasped by the word of the gospel, and will be completed at the return of the Messiah. At that time the dead will be raised and the living transformed, so that all his people, rescued ('saved') from ultimate corruption, will share the glory he already enjoys.

3. Galatians

Resurrection is not a main theme in Galatians, but neither the overall argument nor the detail is comprehensible without it. Paul's opening rhetorical flourish indicates that the covenant God has already mounted a rescue operation 'to deliver us from the present evil age'; Paul was clearly thinking within the eschatological categories of the Pharisees and rabbis. Something had happened, he believed, because of which the 'age to come' had broken in to 'the present age'.[20] The very first verse of the letter indicates what this 'something' was: 'God the father . . . raised [Jesus the Messiah] from the dead.'[21] Paul thus associates the breaking-in of the coming age with the twin events of Jesus' death and resurrection, seeing the former as his self-giving 'for our sins', in fulfilment of the overall divine purpose.

It is, in fact, inconceivable (as we shall see in chapter 12) that the death of a messianic pretender could by itself give rise to the notion that the 'age

[20] Gal. 1.4f.
[21] Gal. 1.1, the only explicit mention of resurrection in the letter.

to come' had already broken in, and that people could even now be delivered from 'the present evil age'. As frequently, we have to supply a reference to the resurrection (hinted at here in the opening verse) to make sense of each reference to the cross, drawing on other passages in which Paul makes the fuller picture clear.[22] Galatians 1.4–5 thus already addresses questions 1(d), 2 and 3. The death and resurrection of Jesus are the inauguration of the promised new age; and this 'age to come' is the long-awaited time of deliverance. The Jewish metaphorical meaning (resurrection as the rescue and restoration of Israel after exile and oppression) is retained but transformed: the divine rescue operation through Jesus is for all people, and delivers Jew and Gentile alike from the present evil age.

This points to the dramatic passage at the end of chapter 2, where Paul describes how he confronted Peter in Antioch. The heart of his argument is that he, Paul, has 'died' and now 'lives' in a new way:

> [19]For through the law I died to the law, so that I might live to God. I have been crucified with the Messiah; [20]nevertheless I am alive – but it isn't me, it's the Messiah who lives in me; and the life I now live in the flesh, I live by faith in the son of God who loved me and gave himself for me.

Scholars have long debated whether Paul, speaking of his own 'death' and 'coming alive again', was referring to his conversion (including baptism), or whether he was looking behind that to the death and resurrection of Jesus himself.[23] The answer is probably that both are in view, and that here we have an example of the Jewish metaphorical usage: 'resurrection' as the rescue of Israel from oppression and exile, coming true in a new way in the person of Paul himself, in a transformation which is rooted in the events of Jesus' own death and resurrection and which results in Paul's bearing of a new identity, no longer defined by his 'fleshly' existence. This new identity is the point of the paragraph, in which Paul is arguing strenuously (by means of reporting to the Galatians the argument he had used to Peter during the confrontation in Antioch) that the old solidarities of the 'flesh', meaning here particularly ethnic identity, had become irrelevant in defining the people of the covenant god.[24] All, Jew and Gentile alike, now belonged at the same table; the symbolic differentiation between them had been done away with, and their sole badge of identity was now *pistis Iesou Christou*, the faithfulness of Jesus the Messiah.[25]

---

[22] See esp. e.g. 1 Cor 15.17: 'if the Messiah is not raised . . . you are still in your sins'. In other words, without the resurrection the great deliverance has not yet occurred; but Paul's whole worldview is based on the belief that it has.

[23] See e.g. Martyn 1997a, 255–60. On Paul's conversion, and the significance of Gal. 1.13–17, see ch. 8 below.

[24] On the Pauline meanings of 'flesh' see e.g. Wright, *Romans*, 417f.

[25] On *pistis Christou* here and elsewhere see e.g. Hays 2002 [1983]; Hooker 1989; Dunn 1991 (reprinted and updated in Hays 2002 [1983], 249–71), with other bibliog. there.

Paul is here speaking of dying and rising in a metaphorical sense. He has not actually died physically, or been raised physically. But the referent of the metaphor remains a concrete reality, namely his identity as a renewed human being and his table-fellowship with all those who have similarly 'died and been raised'. The reason he can speak in this way is once more because of the concrete events of Jesus' death and, still unstated but powerfully present, his resurrection. The new life that is given the other side of this 'death' can be described (a) as 'living to God' and (b) as possessing, within, the life of the Messiah. Both of these are quasi-technical terms which we shall meet again as we make our way through Paul.

The transformed fulfilment of the Jewish hope is one of Paul's main subjects in Galatians 3. He describes in verses 10–14 how the promise to Abraham, that the whole world would be blessed 'in him', had apparently got stuck when Israel fell victim to the curse of the law. But Israel's God has acted through the Messiah, who bore the law's curse on Israel's behalf, so that 'the blessing of Abraham might come on the Gentiles in the Messiah, Jesus – and that we (Jewish Christians, in other words) might receive the promise of the Spirit through faith'.[26] The implicit narrative underlying this passage is that of Israel's subjugation and the divine rescue – in other words, that for which the picture of 'resurrection' had been used in various Jewish texts; and the reason why Paul can declare that the promises have been fulfilled is, obviously, the death and resurrection of Jesus.[27] The promises have not, however, been fulfilled in the way that most Jews, including Paul himself, had expected or wanted. That is why there is such a huge problem facing the early Christians, the problem to which Galatians is part of Paul's answer. His way of addressing the matter demonstrates that he has taken the existing metaphorical meaning and has allowed it to be redefined by the events he believed to have taken place concerning Jesus.

One of the most crucial passages in the whole letter is 4.1–7. Once again, Paul does not here mention resurrection explicitly; instead, he tells a story in which 'resurrection' overtones are powerfully present. In describing the way in which Israel's God sets the slaves free from their bondage and makes them his own children, Paul draws, as in Romans 8, on the well-known Jewish story of the exodus.[28] Through the work of the son, the one God has broken the power of the slavemaster; through the work of the Spirit, the same God assures his people of their own status as his children and heirs.[29]

---

[26] Gal. 3.14. On this passage see Wright, *Climax*, ch. 7.

[27] The same sequence of thought can be observed in 3.22, which reads, following the line of the Greek rather than of polished English: Israel's god, through 'scripture', shut up everything under sin, so that the promise could be given to those who believe, on the basis of the faithfulness of the Messiah, Jesus. As frequently in 2 Cor. (see below), such juxtaposition of negative and positive embodies the pattern of death and resurrection.

[28] See Keesmaat 1999, chs. 2–4; Wright, *Romans*, 510–12.

[29] Jesus' sonship and resurrection are linked in Rom. 1.3f. (below, 572, 723–6).

In Romans 8, the same story is developed with an explicit focus on resurrection. Even without this parallel, we only have to place Galatians 4 alongside 1 Corinthians 15.20–28 to see that substantially the same ideas are involved.

So far in Galatians, then, Paul has drawn on the underlying (and usually unstated) idea of resurrection to inform and direct his particular concern. World-changing events have occurred; Paul himself has become a different person through them; the promises have been fulfilled in a different way from Israel's (and his own) previous expectation. In the next passage, he refers to the personal and still-future hope, again without mentioning resurrection explicitly, but speaking instead of final 'vindication', attaining the status of 'righteous' in the ultimate divine lawcourt: 'for we, by the Spirit, and on the basis of faith, eagerly await the hope of righteousness'.[30] Similar passages elsewhere in Paul, not least in Romans 8, suggest that Paul could easily have written *elpida anastaseos*, 'the hope of resurrection', in place of *elpida dikaiosunes*, 'the hope of righteousness'. He has chosen to speak of the *status* Christians will possess at the last day, rather than the *state* they will be in, because of the specific argument of Galatians. The proximity of thought between the two highlights something important for Paul, which will emerge later: the conceptual link, at various stages in his thought, between resurrection and 'justification', past, present and future.

The future, and its effect on the present, is in view towards the end of Galatians 5, where Paul warns that people who behave in certain ways 'will not inherit the kingdom of God' (5.14). Though he can speak of this kingdom as present,[31] he more often sees it as future, using the phrase to denote the ultimate future seen as the time when, because the creator's writ runs fully and without exception, nothing that spoils or defaces the creation, and in particular the creatures that bear the divine image, will be allowed any further space.[32] Paul's main contrast in this passage is between the 'flesh' and the 'spirit', seen as the two spheres of life, character and behaviour in which a human being can live. His thought, as often, moves at a rapid pace, and leaves much to be understood by implication; but it is clear that those who, in his terms, 'walk according to the Spirit' will 'inherit God's kingdom'. This is, then, another way of describing the ultimate future for the covenant people, using language which any first-century Pharisee would have lined up at once with the hope of resurrection. And the immediate implication of this future hope is that the present life in the power of the Spirit is the guarantee of the future inheritance – a point which Paul amply reinforces elsewhere.

He develops this in chapter 6, using a different image. Where before he had spoken of 'walking', he now thinks in terms of 'sowing and reaping':

---

[30] 5.5.
[31] e.g. Rom. 14.17; 1 Cor. 4.20. See below, 566–8.
[32] cf. e.g. 1 Cor. 6.9f.; cp. 15.50; Eph. 5.5.

[7]Don't be deceived; God is not mocked. People reap whatever they sow. [8]If you sow to your flesh, from the flesh you will reap a harvest of corruption; but if you sow to the Spirit, from the spirit you will reap eternal life. [9]So let's not grow weary of doing what is right; for in due time we shall reap, if we don't lose heart.

Several points emerge here which fit exactly into some of Paul's developed expressions of the future hope, and which indicate that, even when writing rapid polemic, he still gives evidence of the detailed belief about the future which we see him expound more carefully elsewhere. He describes the future goal in terms of reaping the harvest from plants sown earlier. This is not exactly the same use of the 'seed' metaphor which we find in 1 Corinthians 15.35–8, 42–4, but it is not far removed (and it shows, incidentally, how flexible Paul is in the subtle variations he can make within the same metaphor); there he uses 'sowing' as an image of 'dying' (as in John 12.24), whereas here he simply thinks of behaviour and its long-term results. This, too, is how he envisages the continuity between the present life and the life to come: not because certain types of behaviour in the present establish a claim on the covenant God, but because behaviour is an indication of which of the two spheres one belongs in, 'flesh' or 'Spirit'. While 'flesh' is, for Paul, always corruptible, decaying and often rebellious as well, the 'Spirit', when it refers as here to the divine Spirit, is always, in his usage, the gift of the one God in the present, through which the future inheritance is assured.

We observe, too, that Paul can denote the final goal – the same, we presume, as 'righteousness' in 5.5 and 'God's kingdom' in 5.21 – with the phrase 'eternal life'. We shall meet this phrase in Romans, where I shall argue that it does not mean, as it is so often taken to mean, 'continuing life in disembodied bliss', but rather 'life in the "age to come" for which Israel longs'.[33] In our present passage it corresponds to 1.4: the covenant God has rescued us from 'the present evil age', and those who now 'sow to the Spirit' will, in place of that present age, inherit 'the age to come'. Finally, the exhortation to continue in well-doing without growing tired corresponds closely to 1 Corinthians 15.58. For Paul, in these very different letters, the thought of the future inheritance (however he describes it) is never an incentive to shrug one's shoulders and wait passively for the final divine rescue operation, but always to be doing in the present those things which properly anticipate, and hence lead to, the future inheritance itself. As in the first letter to Corinth, this speaks powerfully about the *continuity* between the present and final state of Christian existence.

This picture is confirmed by Galatians 6.14–16, where Paul declares that the one thing that matters is neither circumcision nor uncircumcision, but new creation. It is precisely the appeal to the one God as creator which underlies the mainstream Jewish hope for resurrection; and in this final,

---

[33] Rom. 2.7; 5.21; 6.22, 23. Elsewhere in the wider Pauline corpus the phrase is only found in 1 Tim. 1.16; 6.12; Tit. 1.2; 3.7. It is frequent in John; see 441 below.

dense passage we see how once more Paul's thought about the death and resurrection of Jesus has reshaped both his vision of the renewed world and his understanding of what it means to live in the present in the light of that future:

> [14]God forbid that I should boast, except in the cross of our lord Jesus the Messiah, through whom the world has been crucified to me, and I to the world; [15]for neither circumcision nor uncircumcision is anything, but only new creation. [16]And as many as walk by this rule, peace be upon them and mercy, even upon the Israel of God.

Note, here, the threefold sequence which shows how Paul's mind works, even when drawing together the threads of a hasty, dense and polemical letter. First, the sequence of 'cross – new creation' has all the marks of resurrection upon it, and moreover resurrection seen precisely as new *creation*. The resonances with 2 Corinthians 5.17 are important; so too are the echoes of the various Jewish sources which speak of Israel's God renewing his world in a great new creative act. As we shall see later, Paul keeps Genesis 1 and 2 in the back of his mind at all times, and regularly (but particularly in 1 Corinthians 15) sees the final act of redemption not as a *rescue from* creation but as the *renewal of* creation. This places him firmly on the Jewish map of eschatological hope; and, as in 2.19–20, Paul understands the events of Jesus' death and resurrection to mean that the world is a different place, and that he is a different person in relation to it. The result, again, is that the distinction between Jew and non-Jew ceases to have any relevance. Those who 'walk by this rule' (the rule of 'no ethnic barriers, but rather new creation') will have the 'peace and mercy' that Israel's God promised to his people. The biblical echoes summon up the picture not just of 'peace and mercy' in the present time, but of Israel's long-term hope for ultimate salvation, for the new world in which the covenant people will dwell free and secure.[34]

Thus, though Galatians does not mention the resurrection explicitly, there are many points at which it is so close to the surface that we can see it just below the waterline, supporting those other aspects of Paul's thought which protrude more obviously because he needs them for his 'above-the-surface' argument. The resurrection of Jesus, part of the divine plan to usher in 'the age to come' in place of 'the present age', is the beginning of the creator's 'new creation', and gives retrospective meaning to Jesus' death, enabling it to be seen as the divine act of redemption, dealing with the curse of the law, setting the slaves free, and exhibiting, indeed, the love of Jesus himself (2.20).

What has happened, in Galatians, to the metaphorical meaning of 'resurrection' in second-Temple Judaism, according to which Israel was to be set free from pagan oppression? Paul seems to have developed it in a new

[34] cf. Pss. 125.5; 128.6.

way. He speaks of a different slavery, and a different freedom: the bondage of humankind under the 'elements of the world', and of Israel under the law, on the one hand, and the present life of the Christian, led by the Spirit, already part of the new creation, free from the law and the powers of the world, on the other (4.1–11). It is a life of faith (2.20), a life lived 'to God' (2.19); a life in which ethnic boundary-markers, especially circumcision, are no longer necessary or relevant, because new creation has begun, and all those who believe the gospel belong to the single family which the one true God promised to Abraham (3.28–9), and must order their common life accordingly. The Christian hopes eagerly for the future moment when 'righteousness' will finally be accorded, for the full and final coming of the kingdom; present life in the Spirit is a genuine anticipation of this 'age-to-come' life. This is significantly different from anything we find in second-Temple Judaism outside early Christianity (though it has some analogies at Qumran, precisely because there too we find an inaugurated eschatology); but it is only explicable as a mutation from within the worldview of the second-Temple Jews. It is remarkably well developed in Paul's mind, whenever we date Galatians (but especially if we place it early, as I am inclined to do). Precisely because resurrection and new creation is not the main topic of the letter, it is all the more striking that, every time Paul comes near the subject, what he says about it falls into the pattern which his other writings so firmly articulate.

4. Philippians

With the letter to Philippi we reach something of a climax in Paul's reference to, and use of, the resurrection. (There is still no agreement on which prison Paul was in when writing this letter; I incline towards Ephesus, thus placing the letter between the first and second letters to Corinth, though the arguments on this point are not without their difficulties. Nothing for our present purpose hinges on this, since I am not proposing a developmental scheme.) This letter offers a hint, stronger than anywhere else except 2 Corinthians, that Paul is facing the serious possibility of his own imminent death; so we should not be surprised to find here as well some of his clearest statements about the Christian hope beyond death. These are set within a more overtly counter-imperial theology than we have seen up to now: Jesus is lord and saviour, and by strong implication, easily audible to residents in a Roman colony, Caesar is not.[35] The integration of an explicit resurrection-based theology with a politically subversive gospel has not been sufficiently remarked upon, and we shall note it further as we proceed.

---

[35] See Wright, 'Paul's Gospel'.

The tight thematic integration of Jesus' story with that of believers is one of the main themes of the letter, and the parallels and other links between 2.6–11 and 3.20–21 must be explored in more detail presently. But Paul's opening statements, too, are full of interest for our topic. In his initial thanksgiving he affirms that the God who 'began a good work in you' will 'bring it to completion until the day of the Messiah, Jesus'. As in 1 Thessalonians, Paul envisages the preaching of the gospel as the vehicle of the Spirit, effecting a radical change of heart and life. The point here is *continuity* (question 1c): Paul believes that what this God has already done in the present life through gospel and Spirit is the guarantee of the final salvation which he will describe more fully in 3.20–21.

This leads him to some extended reflections on his own situation, in which he thinks through the issues that face him, and which indeed are out of his control: will he die, presumably through being condemned to death by the Roman authorities, or will he live and continue his apostolic work? He turns the matter this way and that, revealing almost casually the way in which he looks at death in the most telling of cases, namely his own:[36]

> [1.18b]Well, but I shall go on celebrating, [19]because I know that this will result in my deliverance, through your prayers and the continued working of the Spirit of Jesus the Messiah, [20]in accordance with my eager expectation and hope, that I won't be ashamed in any way, but that with all boldness, as always and so now, the Messiah will be honoured in my body, whether by life or by death.
>
> [21]To me, you see, living means the Messiah, and death means gain. [22]If it is to be living in the flesh, that means fruitful work for me; so I don't know which to choose. [23]I am pulled hard by both at once: I badly want to make my departure and be with the Messiah; that would be better by far. [24]But to stay on in the flesh is more necessary for your sake. [25]Since I'm convinced of this, I know that I shall remain, and continue on with all of you, for your benefit and the joy of your faith, [26]so that your celebration may abound in me in the Messiah, Jesus, through my coming to you again.

If this was the only passage of Paul, or even of Philippians, which addressed the question of what happens to Christians after they die, we could be forgiven for thinking that Paul held a one-stage view of life after death: Christians depart and go to be with the Messiah (verse 23). We know from the other letters that this was not his position; but, more importantly, we know from Philippians itself that he believed in a two-stage view: final resurrection will follow 'life after death' (3.20–21). What we have here, therefore, is a reinforcement of what we saw in 1 Thessalonians 4: between death and resurrection, Christians are 'with the Messiah'. Paul describes this in such glowing terms ('better by far') that it is impossible to suppose that he envisaged it as an unconscious state. He looks forward to being personally present with the one who loved him and whose love will not let him go.[37]

[36] Phil. 1.18b–26.
[37] See Gal. 2.20; Rom. 8.35–9.

This is the clearest answer we ever get from Paul to question 1b, the question of an intermediate state. He does not speak of 'going to heaven', though he would presumably have given that as the present location of the Messiah. His present life is defined in terms of the Messiah, and his future one will be as well (1.20–21).

We note, too, that as in Galatians 2.20 Paul describes the present life as living 'in the flesh'. He does not here give this phrase the negative *moral* connotation it sometimes acquires elsewhere (e.g. in Romans 8.9). Rather, it carries negative *ontological* connotations: the flesh is weak and corruptible, and will one day die. He does not in this passage give an equivalent anthropological term (such as 'soul' or 'spirit') to denote the sort of entity he will be after his death and before his resurrection. It is, again, enough to know that during that period he will be 'with the Messiah'.

Paul's initial appeal to the Philippian Christians, in 1.27–30, is that they will live worthy of the gospel in their public, even civic, life (1.27). He returns to this theme in 2.12–18. They will, of course, meet opposition, and face persecution, as they are already doing. But their cheerful refusal to be cowed will be a sign to their opponents that they (the opponents) are on the broad road to destruction, while those who belong to the Messiah, Jesus, are assured of *soteria*, not here necessarily 'deliverance' in the sense of escaping persecution or even martyrdom, but a deeper 'salvation' which nothing in the imperial system can either rival or harm. Putting this together with the rest of the epistle, we can be confident that Paul understands this 'salvation' to consist in rescue from death, not by avoiding it, nor by regarding it as an irrelevant transition to a better life, but by the overcoming of death in bodily resurrection (3.20–21).

With the famous passage 2.6–11 we meet a particular problem: that Paul here speaks, not of Jesus' death and resurrection, but of his death and *exaltation*.[38] It has often been suggested that these were more or less synonymous for the earliest Christians, and that it was only later, with Luke's two-part work, that a distinction was made between the resurrection and 'ascension'.[39] This is at best a half truth, and, so to speak, the wrong half. John, often cited as a representative of the view in which resurrection and ascension mean the same thing, has the risen Jesus declare that he has 'not yet ascended';[40] and Paul is well able to tell a fuller story, in which both resurrection and exaltation have a sequential and differentiated place.[41] What is more, the way Paul develops the present passage in chapter 3 indicates, as

---

[38] cf. Wright, *Climax*, ch. 4; for the political dimension, Wright, 'Paul's Gospel'. On 'exaltation rather than resurrection' cf. Reumann 2002, 410–13, 418–22.

[39] Robinson 1982 established a trend now routinely followed: e.g. Evans 1970, 138f.; more extreme in Riley 1995, 106.

[40] Jn. 20.17. See below, 666f., 673f.

[41] e.g. Rom. 8.34, etc. On this point cf. Rowland 1993, 77.

we shall see, that resurrection was very much in his mind. Why then did he not highlight it here?

One way of getting round the difficulty is to suggest that the poem is written by someone else, and that Paul is simply quoting it. This, too, has been advanced as a reason for supposing that the earliest Christians told a story about Jesus' death and exaltation rather than resurrection. I regard this as not only unprovable but unlikely. The poem is carefully constructed, and dovetails so well, at so many levels, with chapter 3 that I find it much easier to suppose that Paul wrote it himself for this purpose, or at the very least that it was written by someone he knew and trusted and that he quoted it here because it said what he wanted to say both in chapter 2 itself and as the basis for chapter 3. A much better answer, I believe, and one which fits well with the thrust of the letter as a whole, is that Paul was consciously modelling the poem, and its portrait of Jesus, not simply on Adam and Israel, as I argued in an earlier work, but also more specifically on Caesar (or rather, perhaps, on the whole tradition of arrogant emperors going back at least to Alexander the Great, with the Roman emperors as the current embodiments of the type). Jesus succeeded where Adam failed; he completed the task assigned to Israel; and he is the reality of which Caesar is the parody. As has recently been argued, the poem follows quite closely the narrative sequence of imperial propaganda, and thereby stresses the point for which the Paul of Acts was accused: of saying that there is 'another king, namely Jesus'.[42] He, not Caesar, is the world's true lord.[43]

Part of the point, of course, is that the one thing Roman emperors did *not* claim was that they or anyone else had been raised from the dead. Exalted to heaven, yes; resurrected, no. The counter-imperial theme is then reinforced in the following verses, where Paul urges his readers to work out in practice what *their* type of salvation means, as opposed to the sort that Caesar offered (2.12–13).[44] And – a tell-tale hint and a very important one – those who learn how to be Jesus' people in Caesar's empire will 'shine like lights in the world'. This is a deliberate echo of Daniel 12.3, indicating that Paul, here as elsewhere, had thought through the *present* life and vocation of Christians in terms of a resurrection life which had already, in one sense, begun, even though it was to be completed in the bodily resurrection itself.[45]

The pen-portraits of Timothy and Epaphroditus provide an unexpected interlude at the end of chapter 2, and offer one bright spotlight on Paul's

---

[42] Ac. 17.7. Cf. Oakes 2001, ch. 5, and other material discussed there.

[43] Nero was described as *ho tou pantos kosmou kyrios*; cf. Oakes 2001, 149.

[44] This understanding seems to me preferable to supposing that Paul is here talking about 'working' in the sense of the normal faith-and-works debates.

[45] cf. Phil. 3.10f., 20f. We might comment in addition that the poem's central point – that Jesus was 'obedient unto death, even the death of the cross' – places the stress on humiliation, which is then reversed by exaltation; but it also strongly implies that death is itself to be defeated or reversed, which of course means resurrection.

attitude to death. Epaphroditus was the messenger through whom the Philippian church had sent money to the imprisoned apostle. He then fell sick and was near to death, but recovered; and Paul's comment on this (2.27) is that 'God had mercy on him, and not only on him but also on me, so that I would not have one sorrow on top of another.' This is a long way from the Stoic portrait of 'the Christian facing death' that the later church has often presented, and it indicates more clearly what Paul means when he commands the Thessalonians not to grieve like those without hope: not that they should not grieve, but that their grief, however deep, should be of the hopeful variety.[46]

This brings us to chapter 3 (more specifically, 3.2—4.1; 3.1 is an introduction whose problems need not detain us here), where the resurrection, in several different senses, plays a vital part. As we have suggested, the whole passage is closely modelled on 2.6–11, and indeed on 1.27—2.18; this is important for interpreting the references to 'resurrection' throughout. As often with Paul, it will help to begin at the end, to understand the climax to which he is aiming. The end, in fact, is itself one of Paul's clearest statements of what he believes about all the topics we are presently considering.

Paul introduces the crucial passage by warning against those who are 'enemies of the Messiah's cross', who are opposed, in other words, to the message set out in 2.6–8. They are heading, he says, for destruction; their belly has become their God, and they set their minds on the things of the earth.[47] But, he continues in 3.20–21,

> [20]our citizenship is in heaven; and it is from there that we eagerly await the Saviour, the lord, Jesus the Messiah. [21]He will transform the body of our humiliation to be conformed to the body of his glory, according to the power which gives him the ability to put all things in subjection to himself.

And this leaves Paul with a strong and clear conclusion (4.1):

> Therefore, my beloved family, whom I long for, my joy and my crown – stand firm in the lord in this way, my beloved ones.[48]

The most important point to get clear from the start is the nature of citizenship. Countless readers have assumed that what Paul means in 3.20 is that, being 'citizens of heaven', Christians look forward to the time when they will return and live there for ever.[49] Verse 21 has thus been read – despite what it actually says! – as an affirmation of this point. This basically assimilates Paul to Philo, who says clearly that true wisdom lies in not regarding the present world as anything other than a temporary abode, and keeping

---

[46] 1 Thess 4.13; see above, 217.

[47] Phil. 3.18–19.

[48] For this as the conclusion, cp. 1 Cor. 15.58.

[49] A good example is Richard 1995 on 1 Thess. 4.16f.

one's sights on heaven, from whence we came and whither we must return.[50] But this is precisely what Paul does *not* say. Philo, expounding the wickedness of those who settled at Babel and built the tower there, makes a clear distinction between temporary sojourners and 'colonists'. Temporary settlers, for whom Abraham sets the pattern, know that they are only in this body for a while, and act accordingly. But colonists (like the Babel-builders) take up permanent residence in their new abode, which stands in Philo's allegory for those who settle down all too comfortably in the present body.[51] Paul and Philo are not complete opposites here, but very nearly. Paul agrees with Philo that the important thing is to be a citizen of heaven, but he draws the opposite conclusion from it. Paul knew, the Philippians knew, and surely even Philo knew, that Roman citizenship (the obvious model behind this imagery) created neither an expectation that one would make the city one's eventual home nor an entitlement to do so. The point about citizenship is a point about status and allegiance, not about place of residence. Indeed, the colonists of Philippi a century before Paul's day had been placed there precisely because nobody wanted them back in Rome, or even in Italy: there was too much overcrowding, unemployment and shortage of food in Rome as it was. Those who were granted Roman citizenship in non-colonial cities such as Alexandria, Philo's home, would certainly not interpret that as a standing invitation to retire to Rome in due course. The logic of colonies and citizenship works the other way round, as Philo himself saw when he urged that one should see oneself as a temporarily displaced heaven-person rather than a colonist: the Roman citizens whose forebears had originally colonized Philippi were there to stay. Their task was to live in the colony by the rules of the mother city, not to yearn to go home again.[52] What they might need from time to time was not a trip back to Rome, but for the emperor to come *from* Rome to deliver them from any local difficulties they might be having.

That is the model Paul is drawing on, and it is operating here on at least two levels. First, it functions powerfully at the *anthropological* level. For Paul, there is no sense that any human being (other than Jesus) existed prior to conception, no sense of a soul trapped temporarily in a body from which it hopes to be released, able to go back home whence it came. That idea comes from Pythagoras and Plato, not from the Hebrew Bible.[53] The punchline of Paul's statement – and the heart of our present concern with this passage – is that the body will be *transformed*, not abandoned. This is one of his clearest answers to the question, what did he mean by resurrection? Here he means that in the new world which the creator God will make through the all-encompassing authority of the Messiah, his people will be given renewed

---

[50] Philo, *Conf.* 77f. On Philo see 144f. above.

[51] *Conf.* 77–82.

[52] Cf. Cic. *De Leg.* 2.2.5; Oakes 2001, 138.

[53] cf. Wis. 8.19f. (above, 172); and cf. e.g. Hierocles 3.2.

bodies. Those who are presently alive (the ones he is referring to here) will be transformed; we assume, filling in the gaps from the parallel passages in 1 Thessalonians and 1 Corinthians, that those who have died will be raised into bodies that have been similarly renewed and transformed. More specifically, the transformation will be from 'humiliation' to 'glory'; in the parallel passage in 1 Corinthians 15.43, 49, 52 the emphasis is on the contrast of 'corruptible' and 'incorruptible'. The two are different aspects of the same thing: the most 'humiliating' thing about the present body is that it is corruptible, bound for death. As in Romans 8.29, the Christian is promised that he or she will be 'conformed to the image of God's son'. The present body is not a prison from which to escape; what it needs is transformation.

What lies underneath this? A theology of creation very different from that of Philo. The final phrase of verse 21 echoes Psalm 8.6, just as in 1 Corinthians 15.27–8; the Messiah here is the truly human being, the fulfilment of God's purpose in creation, now set in authority over the rest of the created order. There is no need to escape from the created order; the Messiah is its lord. Nor is there any need to escape from earth to heaven; instead, the Messiah will come from heaven to earth, to rescue his people not by snatching them away from earth but by transforming their bodies.[54] Paul does not here develop the wider context for this, that of the transforming renewal of creation itself; but when he does just that in Romans 8 he merely fills in the details of the present lightning sketch rather than adding anything that alters its shape and content. It is because of this *continuity* between the present and the future that the practical conclusion of Paul's argument here, exactly as in 1 Corinthians 15.58, is focused not on waiting for a different life altogether but on 'standing firm in the lord' (4.1).

Second, this functions very differently at the *political* level, and this is closely intertwined with resurrection itself. Though, as Goodenough showed sixty years ago, Philo too was capable of serious and sustained political critique of Rome, not only explicitly in the *Legatio* and *Ad Flaccum* but in a coded form,[55] for him the goal of the process was always to escape from the present world order entirely, whatever intermediate tasks might occupy him meanwhile. For Paul there is much more sense of confrontation. The return of Jesus from heaven to earth, the *parousia*, was formulated, probably by Paul himself as the earliest Christian thinker known to us, in conscious opposition to the *parousia* of Caesar. The idea of the emperor coming from the mother city to rescue the beleaguered colony had explicit resonances in

---

[54] For the revelation 'from heaven' see e.g. Rom. 1.18; 1 Thess. 4.16; 2 Thess. 1.7. Among the OT background echoes we should note Ps. 57.3 [56.4 LXX]; the entire psalm is significant, not least its insistence on God's sovereignty and glory over earth as well as heaven (vv. 5, 11). The whole new-creation theme tells strongly against Robinson 1982, 7, who leaps from Phil. 3.21 to a declaration that Paul 'visualized the resurrected Christ as a heavenly body, luminous'.

[55] Goodenough 1967 [1938] chs. 1–3.

the Philippians' own experience.[56] The christological titles Paul uses here for Jesus (saviour, lord, Messiah) are blatantly counter-imperial, with the word 'saviour' in particular, used here for the only time in the normally accepted Pauline letters, echoing around the Mediterranean world with the claims of Caesar.[57] And the all-embracing claim of verse 21, echoing Psalm 8.6, and thereby reminding us of 1 Corinthians 15.25–8, positively shouts that it is Jesus, not Caesar, who holds power over all things, and who will exercise that power in transforming the present 'body of humiliation' so that it corresponds to the 'body of his glory'. This corresponds, of course, to 2.6–11, where Jesus himself accepted humiliation and death and now is exalted and glorified.

The underlying story on which Paul is here drawing concerns the fulfilment of the creator's plan for the world. The aim had been, all along, as in Genesis 1, that this should be put into operation through the agency of the image-bearing human race. Paul sees this plan fulfilled in Jesus, and now to be completed through Jesus' people sharing his glory, reflecting God's image in the same way. The Adam-Christology which was partly responsible for Paul's formulation in 2.6–8 now comes full circle.[58] God's plan for the world is thus, in Paul's mind, the reality of which Caesar's dream of world domination is the parody. And the 'power' of which he speaks explains more fully what he meant in 1 Thessalonians 1.5 and 2.13, and what he will say in Romans 1.16: the gospel is God's *power*, because when Jesus is announced as lord his rule is extended, pointing forwards to the day when, by the power which raised him from the dead, God completes the task of bringing the whole creation to life and order, defeating death itself, the tyrant's final weapon.

These verses at the end of Philippians 3 give us a vantage point from which much of Paul's thought on resurrection can be surveyed. Running through our questions, we note the following.

(1a) Paul looks for the still-embodied future of the true people of the one God. Those presently alive will be transformed; by implication, those already dead will be raised to a new kind of bodily life. The key contrast here between 'humiliation' and 'glory', which is cognate with similar contrasts in 1 Corinthians 15, does not speak of a future in which believers will shine like stars (Paul has already used that as a metaphor for the *present* life of the church), but of the future rule over the world which believers will share with the Messiah, in contrast to their present state of subjugation.

---

[56] See above, 214–18, on 1 Thess. 4. For the imperial rescue from the Thracians see Collart 1937, 249–51.

[57] See Oakes 2001, 139f., quoting an inscription from Ephesus dated to 4 BC, referring to Augustus as 'the God made manifest [*epiphanes*], offspring of Ares and Aphrodite, and saviour [*soter*] of human life'. For Claudius as *soter kai euergetes* see Oakes 140. *Soter* is found frequently in the Pastorals: 2 Tim. 1.10; Tit. 1.4; 2.11, 13; 3.6.

[58] See Wright, *Climax*, 57–62.

Since the resurrection of those already dead is implied rather than being his main focus, he does not here mention any kind of intermediate state (1b); he has, of course, already done that in chapter 1.

(1c) He emphasizes the continuity between the present world and the future one. The body is transformed, not abandoned, and the present Christian task is to stand firm.

(1d) The future resurrection of believers fits in to his larger story of the power of the creator God transforming the whole world through the rule of his image-bearing son.

There is here no suggestion of a metaphorical meaning of 'resurrection' (question 2), but, as we shall see, the earlier part of Philippians 3, working towards this conclusion, contains just such a thing. And all is based, most significantly (question 3), on what Paul believes was and is true of Jesus. Where did Paul arrive at his belief in the future transformation of believers from humiliation to glory, if not from what he believed about Jesus himself? And does this not imply a belief that Jesus' body, too, was transformed, not abandoned? Here we see, in other words, the answer to the puzzle about exaltation and resurrection in 2.6–11. The poem was formulated to make a specific contrast with the rhetorical claims of Caesar, and hence did not highlight resurrection; but the present passage, drawing out its significance a stage further, makes it clear that the exaltation of Jesus involved, not the abandonment of his body to corruption, but its transformation from the humiliation of death to the glory of resurrection.

The deeply Jewish nature of all this is seen not least in the political implications, making more explicit what we glimpsed in 1 Thessalonians 4 and 5. The resurrection and exaltation of Jesus proclaim and install him as the world's true lord and saviour; in other words, according to Paul's gospel it is because of the resurrection that Jesus is lord and Caesar is not. The future resurrection and glorification of Jesus' followers will vindicate them as the true people of the one true God, despite their present suffering and humiliation, and herald the victory of the gospel over the powers of the world through the final act of new creation. As in Pharisaic belief, resurrection challenges the powers of the world, as no other theology or spirituality can do, with the news of the kingdom of the creator and covenant God.

The earlier part of Philippians 3 can now be seen in its proper light. In verses 2–14 Paul tells his own story, offering it as a model in verses 15–16 and then, in verse 17, urging his readers to imitate him. This sets the context for the passage just studied; the two stand in close correlation. Paul's own story, set out here more fully than elsewhere in his writings, consists of two halves: his life as a Pharisee, and his life in the Messiah. We should not read this as pronouncing a negative judgment on the world of Judaism as a whole, since what Paul claims to have gained in his new life are precisely the Messiah and resurrection, the great twin hopes that as a Pharisee he had cherished.[59] There is a strong note of fulfilment as well as of renunciation; what he has renounced is his status 'according to the flesh' (verse 4) and 'under the law' (verse 6). The story of the Messiah's own humiliation and vindication, told in 2.6–11, is now acted out in the life-story of those who are 'in him' (verses 7–14).

There are many fascinating aspects of this description of the Christian's life and status which are not relevant to our enquiry. But it is striking that at the centre stands the claim, 'I count everything as loss because of the surpassing worth of knowing the Messiah, Jesus as my lord.' At the heart of Paul's vision of the renewed-Jewish, or fulfilled-Jewish, life is the Messiah, described in terms which, echoing 2.10–11, provide the reason why Paul cannot say that 'Caesar is lord', and which look forward to the climax of the argument in verses 19–21. And this is filled in by the promise of resurrection (3.8–11):

> . . . so that I may gain the Messiah, [9]and that I may be found in him, not having a status of 'righteousness' of my own, based on the law, but that which is through the faithfulness of the Messiah, the righteous status from God which is upon faithfulness, [10]which means knowing him and the power of his resurrection and the companionship of his sufferings, becoming conformed to his death, [11]if somehow I may attain to the resurrection of the dead.

Out of this dense juxtaposition of almost all of Paul's soteriological language and categories – justification, faith, being 'in the Messiah', knowing the Messiah, suffering and resurrection – we here draw the main point for our current purposes: for Paul, the resurrection is primarily a future event, corresponding to the resurrection of Jesus himself, but that its power is already made known in the present life, even in the midst of suffering and death. The small chiasm in verses 10–11 (resurrection, suffering: death, resurrection) links this statement backwards to 2.6–11 and forwards to 3.19–21. The Messiah took the *morphe doulou*, the 'form of a servant', in 2.7; so Paul will be 'conformed' (*summorphizomenos*) to the Messiah's death through his present suffering and potential martyrdom. When the Messiah returns from heaven, however, the body of present humiliation will be 'conformed' (*summorphon*) to his glorious body. Verse 10 is clear: those who are 'in the Messiah', who through their faith and his faithfulness have the status of 'righteous' in the present (verse 9), already know the power of his resurrection even in the midst of present suffering, and they look forward eagerly (verse 11) to the final resurrection. The language of 'power' (*dynamis*) remains important here, another link to 3.21 and the political meaning of resurrection. Paul believes that God's power, unleashed in Jesus' resurrection and awaiting its full unveiling when Jesus returns, is already

---

[59] For the hope of resurrection as central to Judaism, seen from Paul's point of view, we may compare Ac. 23.6; 24.15, 21; 26.5–8, on which see 451–7 below.

available through the gospel for all who believe, who 'know the Messiah'. 'Resurrection' is, for him, part of present Christian experience, however paradoxical this may be in the midst of suffering.

Paul remains emphatic, however, that the primary meaning of 'resurrection' is future. Eschatology is inaugurated, but not complete (3.12–14):

> [12]Not that I have already obtained this, or am already completed; but I press on to make it my own, for the reason that the Messiah, Jesus, has made me his own. [13]My dear family, I don't reckon that I have made it my own, but I do this one thing: I forget what is behind, and strain forward for what lies ahead, [14]and press on towards the finishing-post, for the prize of God's upward call in the Messiah Jesus.

The 'upward call' is not, in the light of 3.19–21, to be interpreted as a call which summons people to leave 'earth' for ever and live instead in 'heaven'. That which lies ahead is ultimately the life of the resurrection, not of a state of bliss which leaves the body behind. And this resurrection life remains in the future for the presently living as well as the presently dead; there can be no sense of a super-spirituality in which resurrection life in all its fullness is already possessed by the Christian.[60]

I have argued elsewhere that this whole section, telling Paul's story based on that of the Messiah himself in order to hold it up as a model for the Philippians to imitate, is a coded call to those living under imperial rule to celebrate the unique lordship of Jesus the Messiah, being prepared to sit loose to the privileges of empire as Paul was prepared to sit loose to his status as a Pharisee.[61] I find further confirmation of this, beyond what I set out there, in the model provided by Philo in his coded attack on the Roman government in Egypt.[62] Paul moves in 3.18–19 from the rejection of his former status under Pharisaism to a general warning against pagan society and its manner of life. In the light of this, his summons to his readers both to set themselves the same standard that he does (3.15–16) and especially to imitate him (3.17) must be seen as part of his overall aim: that Christians should live in the present as members, already, of the world that is yet to be. This new-age reality was inaugurated at Easter, and will be completed, through the powerful return of Jesus, in and through the final resurrection of all his people. The future resurrection thus provides and undergirds the present status, the present political stance, and the present ethical life of Christians. Moreover, this future resurrection is of course based foursquare on the resurrection of the Messiah, Jesus himself, which tells us a good deal about how Paul saw that event. The continuity of the present Christian life (lived 'in the power of his resurrection') with the future resurrection itself shows that for Paul there was continuity as well as discontinuity between the Jesus

---

[60] Some were suggesting this, it seems, by the time of 2 Tim. 2.18; see below, 267–70.
[61] Wright, 'Paul's Gospel'.
[62] Especially in *Som.* 2; see Goodenough 1967 [1938] ch. 2.

who died and the Jesus who rose, and that this continuity was not a matter of spirit or soul, but of body.

5. Ephesians and Colossians

Most scholars still regard the two central 'prison epistles' as deutero-Pauline, the work of an imitator rather than the apostle himself. I belong to the recalcitrant minority, not least because the reading of the other letters to which I have come over the years suggests that the differences between them and these two are less significant than is often suggested, and in some cases are actually non-existent.

The resurrection itself highlights the point. It is frequently stated, and often simply assumed, that Ephesians and Colossians differ significantly from the rest of Paul's writings precisely in this, that whereas elsewhere the resurrection of believers is still in the future, these letters see it as a present reality: 'if you were raised with the Messiah, seek the things that are above', as Colossians 3.1 puts it. But, though it is true that both these letters do indeed emphasize the present state and situation of the church rather than the future, in both there are clear signs that the writer – to whom I shall refer as 'Paul', cheerfully begging the question of authorship – was well aware of the future dimension, and had not collapsed the tension of inaugurated eschatology into a spirituality in which the End had already arrived, full and entire, in the present.

This is so already in Ephesians 1.14, where the image of 'inheritance', already seen in Galatians 3 and 4 in terms of the promises made to Abraham, emerges again in the language about the Spirit as the 'guarantee of our inheritance until we gain possession of it', *arrabon tes kleronomias hemon eis apolytrosin tes peripoieseos*. As in Galatians 4.7, the gift of the divine Spirit provides the sure knowledge of the future 'inheritance', which is assured but not yet possessed.[63] Clearly Paul sees both continuity and discontinuity between present Christian experience and final Christian hope; there is still an 'inheritance', which speaks of this future hope not now in terms of the Christian's own *state of being*, but of *possession and responsibility*. Those who 'inherit' the age to come will do so after the manner of Israelites 'inheriting' the promised land. Ephesians 1.3–14 is, among other things, a retelling of the exodus story.

This leads Paul to a celebration, in prayer, of the present position of the church as it awaits this full inheritance (1.15–23). The key to this is a retelling of the story of Jesus, emphasizing the divine power that was at work in him to raise him from the dead and (as a separate event) to sit him at the right hand of the sovereign God in the heavenly places, putting all things

---

[63] See too Eph. 1.18; 4.30; and below, 257–9, 304, on Rom. 8.12–17; 2 Cor. 1.22; 5.5.

under his feet; we note once more the use of Psalm 8.6 to indicate the present rule of the Messiah over the whole world, fulfilling the divine intention for the human race. The power which did all this, says Paul, is at work on our behalf (1.19). As in Philippians 3.10, the future hope is anticipated in present reality.

Having told the story of the sovereign God and of Jesus as an exodus-narrative (1.3–14) and as the story of this God's victory in the Messiah over all the powers of the world (1.20–23), Paul now tells the story of how humankind has been brought from universal death to life in the Messiah (2.1–10, focused on 2.5–6). The present state of those in the Messiah is that they have already been 'raised with the Messiah' and seated with him in the heavenly places; what is true of the Messiah in 1.20–23, in other words, is true of those who are 'in him'. This is part of the central Pauline answer to our second question, concerning the metaphorical uses of 'resurrection' in early Christianity: 'resurrection' here refers, not to the restoration of Israel, to a 'return' from exile or oppression, as in Ezekiel 37, but to the restoration of humankind that has been effected through the gospel, the 'return' from the exile of sin and death. Without downplaying the future hope of actual resurrection itself, the fact that the church lives in the interval between the Messiah's resurrection and its own ultimate new life means that the metaphorical use of 'resurrection' language can be adapted to denote the concrete Christian living described in 2.10: 'we are God's workmanship, created in the Messiah Jesus for good works, which God planned beforehand for us to walk in them.'

This enables Paul to sketch the larger picture of the coming together of the whole human race in the Messiah (2.11–22), for which again the resurrection of Jesus is the strongly implicit foundation. The covenant God has abolished, he says, the enmity between Jew and Gentile in the Messiah's flesh (2.14, 16), so that he might create a single new humanity in him. This looks on to 4.13, where the notion of 'mature humanity', growing up in all things into the Messiah, again resonates with other Pauline passages in which the point of the resurrection is the reaffirmation of the divine plan for the human race. Resurrected humanity, it seems, is humanity reaching its full goal.

This metaphorical use – resurrection in the present as the ground of Christian living – is strongly emphasized in 5.14, where, in a passage full of echoes of 1 Thessalonians 5.1–10, Paul quotes what appears to be an early Christian song or poem:

Awake, you sleeper!
Rise up from the dead!
The Messiah will shine on you.

As with Philippians 2.12–16, the darkness of the present world is contrasted with the light of the creator's new day, a light which Christians, along with the Messiah, must already shine. And, as in Philippians, this echoes the promise of Daniel 12.3, but brings it into the present rather than saving it for the future – without in any way implying an over-realized eschatology. Final resurrection remains in the future (the 'inheritance' still to come, as in 1.14 and 5.5); but those on their way to it must shine like lights even in the present time. As the final chapter of Ephesians makes clear, Christians still have a battle to fight (6.10–20); the enemies are not yet finally defeated; but the eschatology that has been inaugurated in the resurrection of Jesus means that victory is assured.

Colossians also speaks of the future hope still to be realized as well as the present metaphorical resurrection life of believers. The introductory thanksgiving emphasizes 'the hope which is stored up for you in the heavens' (1.5), which, as we shall see with other similar phrases, does not mean that Christians must leave 'earth' and go to 'heaven' in order to make this hope their own, but that 'heaven' is where the divine purposes for the future are stored up, waiting to be brought to birth in the new reality, the new age in which heaven and earth will be joined in a fresh way. This comes to the fore in the central passage, 3.1–4:

> [1]So then, if you were raised with the Messiah, seek the things that are above, where the Messiah is seated at God's right hand. [2]Think about the things that are above, not about the things on the earth. [3]For you died, and your life has been hidden with the Messiah in God. [4]When the Messiah appears – he is your life! – then you too will appear with him in glory.

The 'appearing' of the Messiah, and the 'appearing' of believers with him, is a fresh way of referring to the same event that Paul described in Philippians 3.20–21, and indeed this passage has several other echoes of that chapter. Despite popular impressions, Paul is just as happy to speak of the time when Jesus will 'appear' as he is to refer to his 'arrival' or 'second coming'. And the language of 'appearing', not least in its double usage here, indicates well enough what is going on: heaven and earth are at present opaque to one another, but the day will come when the reality at present hidden in the heavenly places – the reality of the Messiah, reigning in glory, and of his people, presently 'with him' – will be revealed. This, we may confidently say, is the moment of resurrection itself, the moment when the future hope comes to full realization. The present status of Christians, on the basis of baptism, is that they have already died with the Messiah and been raised with him, as 2.13 makes clear: 'You were buried with him in baptism, in which you were also raised with him through faith in the power of the God who raised him from the dead.' Those who were 'dead' both in their sins and in their Gentile status, excluded from the covenant people, have been 'made alive' with the Messiah, their transgressions being forgiven (2.13). In the Jewish thought where 'resurrection' was used metaphorically for 'return from exile', one central part of that hope was that Israel's sins would finally be forgiven.[64] Throughout this sequence of thought, the *present* metaphorical 'resurrection' of Christians, replacing the metaphorical usage in some Jewish texts, denotes their status 'in the Messiah' who has himself been concretely raised from the dead; and it takes its meaning from the fact that it anticipates their *future* literal 'resurrection', their eventual sharing of the Messiah's glory. In the meantime, as in Philippians 3.14, 18–19, they are to set their minds on things above, not on the things of the earth.[65]

The basis of this sequence of thought is the unveiling of the Messiah as the image of the creator God, the 'firstborn' both of creation and then of the new creation. Colossians 1.15–20, a spectacular early Christian poem, places Jesus' resurrection (1.18) in parallel with the creation of the world (1.15), seeing it as the ground and origin of what the creator has now accomplished and is now implementing, namely the reconciliation of all things to him.[66] The very shape of the poem insists that Jesus' resurrection, as a one-off event, is an act not of the abolition of the original creation but of its fulfilment: the same Messiah and lord is the one through whom all things were made in the first place, the one in whom all things cohere, the one in and through whom all things are now brought into a new relationship with the creator God and with one another. This passage has, of course, considerable implications both for Pauline cosmology (the whole cosmos is good, God-given, and, despite the rebellion of the powers within it, it has been reconciled to its maker) and politics (all the power structures of the world were created in, through and for the Messiah, verse 16).

The personal result is displayed on either side of the poem, and in both cases the story of Jesus' resurrection undergirds the narrative that is told. The creator God has qualified his people to share in the inheritance of the saints in light, by delivering them from the kingdom of darkness and transferring them into the kingdom of his son, in whom they have redemption, the forgiveness of sins (1.12–14); Jesus' death and resurrection, in other words, function as the moment of the new exodus, of the 'return' from the long exile of sin and death, of the overthrow of all the powers that enslaved the world, and those who now belong to the Messiah share the benefits of all this. Likewise, as in Ephesians 2, those who were estranged from, and hostile to, the one true God, have been reconciled by Jesus' death, and must now stand firm on 'the hope of the gospel' which has been announced to every creature under heaven. This can only mean that with the resurrection itself a shock wave has gone through the entire cosmos: the new creation has been born, and must now be implemented.[67]

---

[64] See *JVG* 268–71.

[65] This world of thought is many a mile away from the 'left wing of the Pauline school' invented by Robinson 1982, 19 as an anticipation of gnostic thought.

[66] On the poetry and theology of the passage see Wright, *Climax*, ch. 5.

[67] See Wright, *Colossians*, 76f., 84f.

The result of all this, for basic Christian living, is a new lifestyle in which the divine intention for the human race is at last fulfilled. This means, in 3.5–11, no immorality, no anger and evil talk, and no distinctions of race or class. But for our purposes the key element, reflecting one of Paul's central themes in Romans and the Corinthian correspondence, is the contrast between old and new humanity (3.9–10). The former has been done away with in baptism's modelling of the death of the Messiah; the latter has been created in baptism's modelling of his resurrection:

> . . . seeing that you have put off the old humanity (*ton palaion anthropon*) with its deeds, and have put on the new one, which is being renewed into knowledge in accordance with the image of the creator.[68]

This belongs exactly in the network of ideas we have been discovering, not least in Philippians 3, and which we will see developed in Paul's major statements elsewhere. The point of the resurrection, so far as Paul is concerned, is the reaffirmation of creation, not its denial. Already, before the final disclosure in which the Messiah's people will 'appear with him in glory' (3.4), this new creation, human beings remade in God's image, must be seen in the common life of the church.

In these respects at least, therefore, Ephesians and Colossians are not out of line with the treatment of resurrection in the other Pauline letters, either the ones studied so far or those we shall come to presently. In both, the resurrection of Jesus himself is the historical event through which the creator's plan to rescue the world from sin and death has been decisively inaugurated, following the death whereby sin was itself dealt with. In both, the inheritance of the Messiah's people lies still in the future. Yet, in both, the present life of Christians is already, metaphorically, one of 'resurrection', not now referring, as in second-Temple Judaism, to the restoration of ethnic Israel, but rather to forgiveness of sins and a new pattern of behaviour. When it comes to the meanings of resurrection, these letters belong where they are at the heart of the Pauline corpus.

6. Philemon

Before we turn to Romans, and then to the Corinthian letters, we may note, almost as an interlude, the way in which resurrection functions by implication within the argument of the short letter to Philemon. In urging Philemon to take back the runaway slave Onesimus, Paul draws on the language of redemption he has employed in Galatians 4.1–7, and will use again in

---

[68] For the baptismal overtones cf. 2.12f.; the theme of new creation links the passage back to 1.18–20, 23.

Romans 8.12–17, with echoes in both passages of God's 'redemption' of Israel from slavery in Egypt:

> Perhaps this was why he was separated from you for a while, that you might have him back for ever – no longer as a slave, but as much more than a slave, a beloved brother, beloved to me, and how much more to you, both in the flesh and in the lord![69]

The logic of the surrounding verses fills in the details of Paul's implicit narrative. Paul is bound to Onesimus with bonds of love; in sending him back he is 'sending his very heart' (verse 12). Yet Paul is also bound in ties of fellowship and mutual love and obligation with Philemon (verses 17–20). He can therefore appeal to Philemon to accept Onesimus as he would accept Paul himself. If Onesimus owes him anything, Philemon is to put it down on Paul's account. This combination of representation and substitution has a familiar ring to anyone at home in Paul's varied accounts of the cross; what we are seeing is the lived-out gospel of the death of Jesus.[70] Once we realize that, we should be able to see, as well, the lived-out gospel of the resurrection. Onesimus is to be a slave no longer, but a brother of Philemon, because both are redeemed children of the one true God.

7. Romans

(i) Introduction

Romans is suffused with resurrection. Squeeze this letter at any point, and resurrection spills out; hold it up to the light, and you can see Easter sparkling all the way through. If Romans had not been hailed as the great epistle of justification by faith, it might easily have come to be known as the chief letter of resurrection (not, of course, that the two are unrelated); the Corinthian letters would be strong contenders for such a title, but Romans would give them a good run for their money. Romans offers plenty of answers to all our main questions, while supplying a massive framework of thought – it is, after all, one of the intellectual masterworks of the ancient world – within which to locate them. We shall have to be careful, in what follows, not to pursue its many lines of thought too far, so as to keep this treatment within the bounds of a subsection of a chapter.[71]

---

[69] Philem. 15f.
[70] See Wright, *God's Worth*, ch. 6.
[71] For many more details see Wright, *Climax*, chs. 2, 10—13; *Romans*.

(ii) Romans 1—4

We begin where Paul begins, with a passage which many readers have leap-frogged in their eagerness to get to what exegetical tradition has declared to be the main theme, stated in 1.16–17. In that passage, Paul announces that the gospel is God's power to salvation for all who believe, Jew and Greek alike, because in it God's righteousness is revealed from faith to faith. Very well, exegetes have declared: this letter is about the gospel, that is, justification by faith, and the salvation which results. I have argued elsewhere that this is a severe truncation of Paul's meaning in these verses alone; but the main fault of this exegetical move is that it ignores what Paul says right at the start of the letter, by way of a summary of 'the gospel', which forms part of his own self-introduction (1.3–5):

> [God's gospel] . . . concerning his Son, who was descended from the seed of David according to the flesh, and marked out as Son of God in power according to the Spirit of holiness by the resurrection of the dead, Jesus the Messiah our lord, through whom we have received grace and apostleship to bring about the obedience of faith among all the nations for the sake of his name . . .

When Paul says 'the gospel', then, he does not mean 'justification by faith', though of course justification is the immediate result of the gospel. The 'good news' Paul has in mind is the proclamation of Jesus, the Davidic Messiah of Israel, as the risen lord of the world. This short passage, which has often been allowed to fall off the front of the letter, is in fact intended as every bit as much a thematic introduction as 1.16–17. The Messiahship of Jesus, with all that follows from it, is central to the whole letter, as we can see in Paul's subsequent christological summaries, both at the conclusion of several arguments and at the introduction to the crucial section chapters 9—11.[72]

The point about this for our purposes is that Jesus is seen as who he is, with all the significance Paul will attach to this identification, because of his resurrection. Many were descended from David's seed according to the flesh; James the brother of the lord could have made that claim, as could the various blood relatives of Jesus who are known in the early church.[73] But only one Davidic descendant had been raised from the dead. This, Paul declares, marks him out as the 'son' of Israel's God: that is, the Messiah.[74]

---

[72] cf. Rom e.g. 4.24f.; 5.11, 21; 6.11, 23; 7.24; 8.39; 9.5, on all of which see Wright, *Romans*, ad loc. In ch. 12 below I argue against the idea that *Christos* has become for Paul simply a proper name.

[73] See below, 554–63.

[74] For the 'messianic' meaning of 'son of God' at this point see Wright, *Romans*, 416–19. Paul builds in other meanings to this phrase in, e.g. 5.10 and 8.3; but these, though rich and dense, have not left behind the home base of 'Messiah', which is indicated here not least by the reference to David and by the 'royal' overtones of his worldwide rule in 1. 5.

Place this claim in its second-Temple context, and it becomes apparent that Paul cannot possibly have meant that Jesus of Nazareth, after his execution by the Romans, had been exalted to a place of honour, like the martyrs, awaiting resurrection; or that his soul was in the hand of God, as Wisdom 3.1 puts it of the recently dead righteous ones. Nor is he talking about an apotheosis like that of the Roman emperors, whose souls were borne aloft, in popular belief and iconography, on a comet (as in the case of Julius Caesar), or by an eagle (as in the carving on Titus' Arch).[75] That would have constituted him as a divine being, with his heir and successor as his 'son', like a new emperor becoming 'son of God' by divinizing his predecessor. No. Paul's point is this: that the resurrection has declared Jesus of Nazareth, descended from David, truly to be the Messiah, 'son of God' in that sense. This carried, once more, enormous political significance in a world where Caesar was the son of a god and the lord of the world; the resurrection has marked Jesus out as the true world ruler, the one of whom Caesar is a mere parody. We are here – at the start of a letter to Rome itself! – on the same page as Philippians 2.6–11 and 3.19–21. This is a Jewish message about a king of the Jews, designed (as Josephus knew such messages were designed) to challenge the pretensions of pagan empire.[76] That is one of the reasons why Paul notes that the 'marking out' of Jesus was 'in power'; as we have seen, when Paul thinks of Easter he regularly thinks of divine power, and when he thinks of power he is thinking about the challenge which divine power offers those in the present world who suppose they have a monopoly on it. This is good Pharisaic theology, refocused around Jesus. The resurrection always was a highly political doctrine, and with the totally unexpected event of Jesus' own resurrection the powers of the world have been confronted with a new reality, the Jewish hope come to life, the vindication of the 'son of man' after his suffering at the hands of the beasts. This was not an isolated, freak occurrence. This was, in embryo, 'the resurrection of the dead', of *all* the dead.[77]

Why then did Paul imagine that the resurrection constituted Jesus as Messiah, as 'son of God' in that sense? As we saw in reviewing the extensive second-Temple literature on resurrection, at no point did anyone envisage a Messiah who would die a shameful death, let alone be raised from the dead. So deafening is the silence on the subject that we might conclude that, if someone else had been found to be thoroughly alive again after being thoroughly dead, people might have concluded that the world was a very strange place; they might have wondered if such a person was a great prophet, perhaps even Elijah; but there is no reason to suppose they would at

---

[75] See above, 57.

[76] Jos. *War* 3.399–408; 6.312–15; discussed in *NTPG* 304, 312f.

[77] The collective implication of Jesus' resurrection are hinted at in Paul's phrase *ex anastaseos nekron*, literally 'from the resurrection of the dead ones' (1.4). There is a link from here to the 'firstfruits' image in 1 Cor. 15.20.

once say that he was the Messiah. The Psalms and prophetic texts upon which the early Christians drew to make the connection between Messiahship and resurrection – which we see in Acts 2, for instance, as well as the present passage – were not, as far as we know, read like that at the time.[78]

But nor, we must add, would anyone have supposed, three minutes, three days or three weeks after the death of Jesus of Nazareth, that he was in fact the Messiah. Anybody who knew anything about messiahs knew that a messiah who had been crucified by the pagans was a failed messiah, a sham. I have argued in detail elsewhere that Jesus of Nazareth did do and say things during his lifetime which indicated to his closest followers at least, and in the end to some kind of a Jewish court, that he really did believe himself to be Messiah.[79] But nobody, not even his closest friends and associates, would have dreamed of saying that he really was the Messiah despite it all, unless something else had happened, after his violent and shameful death, to make them think such a thing.

Thus neither Jesus' life, deeds and teachings on the one hand, nor his resurrection on the other, could *by themselves* have had the effect of making people say at once, 'He really was and is the Messiah.' But put them together – which is what the early Christians did, including Paul immediately upon his conversion – and the result is clear. A would-be messianic life would be an insufficient condition for such a result; even resurrection by itself would likewise be insufficient; but both remain necessary conditions for the claim to be made. Put them together, however, and they become sufficient.[80] The resurrection of the person who had done and said these things, and who had been put to death as a messianic pretender, said it all. Israel's God, the creator, had reversed the verdict of the court, in reversing the death sentence it carried out. Jesus really was the king of the Jews; and, if he was the Messiah, he really was the lord of the world, as the psalms had long ago insisted.[81] The event precipitated the exegesis: once early Christians had glimpsed the idea that a would-be Messiah, a descendant of David, had been put to death as a messianic pretender but had been raised from the dead, it was not long before the Septuagintal language about Israel's God 'raising up' David's seed after him, to sit on his throne, would come into its own.

To repeat the point: nothing short of resurrection, in the sense carried by that word in both ancient paganism and second-Temple Judaism, could possibly have had this effect. We can be more precise still. Nothing short of the firm belief that resurrection had occurred in this one case could have produced this result. We must hold over until Part V the question of what we

---

[78] See the speculations attributed to Herod, and to Galilean Jews in general, in Mk. 6.14–16 (discussed below, 411–14). The present point is developed further in ch. 12.

[79] See *JVG* ch. 11.

[80] On necessary and sufficient conditions see below, ch. 18.

[81] Pss. 2.7–9; 72; 89.19–37; cf. the portrait of Solomon in 1 Kgs. 10.14–29 (which belongs quite closely with Ps. 72).

can say as historians about this belief; but we cannot reasonably doubt that Paul (or whoever wrote 1.3–4, if as some have suggested he was quoting an earlier source) intended by this statement to refer to an event involving the body of Jesus acquiring new life after having been thoroughly dead. There is no other available referent imaginable within Paul's world, other than bodily resurrection, which (a) could be described with the language he uses here and which (b) would have had the effect of him, or anyone else, saying of a dead man that he was after all the Messiah, the anointed one of Israel's God. The bodily resurrection of Jesus is the foundation of this letter, the heart of the gospel of Jesus' Lordship, the centre of Paul's implicit critique of Caesar, and the source of his doctrines of justification and salvation. Paul will return to the same point in 15.12, precisely when he is rounding off the main theological argument of the letter. Only when we see this link, which we shall explore below, will we grasp the centrality of Jesus as the resurrected Messiah in Paul's thought in general and in Romans in particular.

As frequently elsewhere, Paul indicates that the resurrection was accomplished by the Holy Spirit. This is one of many elements in this packed opening statement which Paul will draw on in his climactic exposition in chapter 8.

The first major section of the letter (1.18—3.20) concerns the revelation of God's justice against all human evil. After the opening scene (1.18–32), Paul sketches a brief picture of the final judgment, in which, as in much Jewish thought, the Messiah himself will be the judge.[82] This scene, full of stock elements, contains a rich description (2.6–11) of the final state of those who are saved, as well as of those who are not:

> [6] [God] will give to every person according to their deeds. [7]To those who, according to patience in good works, seek for glory and honour and incorruptibility, he will give the life of the age to come; but to those who are contentious and do not obey the truth, but obey unrighteousness, there will be wrath and rage. [9]There will be suffering and distress for every human soul (*psyche*) who performs evil, Jew first and also, equally, Greek; [10]but glory and honour and peace for everyone who performs good, Jew first and also, equally, Greek. [11]For God shows no partiality.

Many expositors have marginalized this passage as though Paul did not really mean it, or was only holding out a hypothetical possibility which he would then deny; but this is unnecessary. This is the *final* judgment scene, and there is no need to 'protect' Paul from speaking of the 'good works' which people perform during their lifetime, in accordance with which this final judgment will be given.[83] And, albeit in summary form, Paul sets out clearly his vision of the future for the true people of Israel's God. They will

---

[82] Ps. 2.7–9; *Ps. Sol.* 17—18; Ac. 17.31. When Paul says in 1.32 that 'those who do such things deserve to die', he is setting up this part of his argument for the answer which comes, with the defeat of death, later in the letter (see below).

[83] See Wright, 'Law'; *Romans*, 440–43; and e.g. Gathercole 2002.

inherit 'the life of the age to come', or, as *zoe aionios* is normally translated, 'eternal life'; and this will be because, through a life of patience in well-doing, they have been 'seeking for glory (*doxa*) and honour (*time*) and incorruptibility (*aphtharsia*)'. The last term is often translated 'immortality', and overlaps in meaning with that word (normally *athanasia*, 'deathless-ness'); strictly, however, *aphtharsia* means 'non-decaying', 'unable to be corrupted'. Clearly Paul did not think that this quality was already possessed by human beings during the present life; and since the two terms are so close in their regular referent, it is safe to say that he did not regard immortality, either, as an automatic possession of human beings.[84] When Paul repeats the list in verse 10 he substitutes 'peace' for 'incorruptibility', not because he intends to deny that his God will give the latter gift, but because this too is among the blessings of the age to come which, anticipated in the present (compare 5.1), will be part of the coming reward. While, then, Paul does not mention the resurrection specifically, the fact that *aphtharsia* is part of the list of blessings of the new age indicates clearly enough that he envisages it; and putting 'honour and peace' beside 'glory' indicates, as we shall see more fully in due course, that by 'glory', here and elsewhere, he does not mean so much a luminous or light-giving quality, but a position of esteem, responsibility and perhaps authority.

The next main section of Romans (3.21—4.25) explains how 'God's righteousness' – that is, God's faithfulness to the covenant with Abraham – has been unveiled in the gospel events concerning Jesus. His death and resurrection are God's way of doing what he always said he would do (giving Abraham a Jew-plus-Gentile family), while simultaneously dealing with the universal sin that looked as if it might thwart this purpose. Romans 4 expounds Genesis 15, the chapter where the promise was made and the covenant established, and demonstrates that this chapter always envisaged that Abraham and his family would be marked out by faith – not works, not circumcision, not possession of Torah, but the faith which humankind as a whole had refused (1.18–32): faith in God the life-giver, who 'gives life to the dead and calls non-existent things into existence'.[85] This faith is evidenced by the fact that he believed in the divine power to give him a child even when he and his wife Sarah were 'as good as dead' because they were long past child-bearing age:

> [4.19]He did not weaken in faith as he considered his own body, which was already dead (*nenekromenon*, 'having been put to death') because he was a hundred years old, and the deadness (*nekrosin*) of Sarah, the mother. [20] He did not waver in unbelief at God's promise, but grew powerful in faith, and gave God glory, [21]being fully convinced that [God] had the power to do what he had promised. [22]That is why his faith was 'reckoned to him as righteousness'.

---

[84] cf. 1 Tim 6.16 (see below, 269).
[85] Rom. 4.17. The last phrase is literally 'calls not-being things as being'.

The whole point of this faith, it seems, is that it gains its own power from reflecting on the power and promise of the creator God; and, as we have seen elsewhere, this 'power' is what Paul associates in particular with the resurrection. It was refusal to give glory to the creator, and to recognize his power, that paved the way for idolatry and the consequent corruption, dishonouring, degrading and death of humankind in the first place.[86] Part of Paul's purpose here is to indicate the way in which faith in the true God, and in his life-giving power, is the sign that humankind is being restored. There can be no doubt, from this passage, that Paul envisages the resurrection of Jesus as bodily. Anything less than that would simply not fit the parallel with Abraham and his 'resurrection faith'. It would not take a special, unique act of divine power to translate Jesus' soul into a glorious heavenly existence.

The conception and birth of Isaac is therefore an anticipation of Jesus' resurrection, and Christian faith thus claims its share in the Abrahamic promise of Genesis 15:

> [23]But it was not written for his sake alone that 'it was reckoned to him'. [24]It was also on account of us, to whom it will also be reckoned – to us who believe in the one who raised Jesus our lord from the dead, [25]who was handed over because of our trespasses, and raised because of our justification.

The final pregnant phrases are at first sight obvious in meaning, but become denser and more difficult on closer inspection. Much paper and ink has been used up in wrestling with the question of whether Paul really intends the two 'because of' clauses (*dia* plus accusative in each instance) to be exactly parallel, and, if not, why he has written it like that. The earlier part of the passage is reasonably clear, especially in the light of 10.9, where believing that the creator raised Jesus from the dead is, along with confessing him as lord, the criterion for justification and salvation. Abraham believed in the God who gives life where there is only death; so, Paul says, do we Christians, and thus, since we share Abraham's faith, we share his justification. But is the final verse anything more than an imprecise rhetorical flourish?

Yes, it is. In several other passages Paul draws together statements about Jesus' death and statements about his resurrection, and the same subtle imbalance is present in each. This is particularly so in the dense and complex 'as . . . so . . . ' clauses of 5.12–21.[87] And there is no real problem in seeing *dia* with the accusative meaning 'because of' in relation to an antecedent cause on the one hand (he was given up *because of* our sins) and an intended result on the other (he was raised *because of* [God's plan for] our

---

[86] Rom. 1.18–32, esp. 1.20f.; more details in Wright, *Romans*, 432–6.
[87] I owe this point to a paper given by Professor Morna Hooker, now published as Hooker 2002.

justification). The real question is, in what way is Jesus' resurrection some-how specially instrumental in securing justification?

Paul can, of course, speak equally well of Jesus' death having this func-tion (as for instance in 5.9). But reflection on 1.3–4, which I have already suggested was designed as a proleptic statement of much of the epistle's theology, indicates a way forward. Jesus' resurrection was the divine *vindication* of him as Messiah, 'son of God' in that sense, the representative of Israel and thence of the world.[88] Similarly, God's 'justification' of all believers refers to his declaration that they are in the right, that their sins are now forgiven. We may compare the train of thought in 1 Corinthians 15.17: if the Messiah is not raised, your faith is futile and you are still in your sins. The resurrection demonstrates that the cross was not just another messy liq-uidation of a would-be but misguided Messiah; it was the saving act of God.[89] God's raising of Jesus from the dead was therefore the act in which justification – the vindication of all God's people 'in Christ' – was contained in a nutshell (see below on 5.18). Chapter 4 thus not only shows that for Paul the resurrection of Jesus was a life-giving event, overcoming death itself by the sheer power of the creator God; it was part of the larger story in which the covenant God was demonstrating his faithfulness by vindicating all those who believe in him, as he promised to Abraham. Moreover, the passage explains, again quite densely, that this vindication is appropriate, because unlike those in chapter 1 who worship idols and so degrade their humanness, those who believe in the life-giving God are themselves being remade as genuinely human beings. They are, as Colossians 3 puts it, being renewed in knowledge after the image of the creator.

(iii) Romans 5—8

Romans 5—8 is the most majestic set piece Paul ever wrote. Carefully struc-tured in sequential arguments, each with its own initial statement, develop-ment, and christological climax, it argues in a long arch, from the opening assertion that those who are justified by faith have peace with the true God and rejoice in the hope of his glory (evoking 2.6–11), to the final conclusion (8.31–9) in which this is again the central theme, now stated with the force of a QED. At every point, in the large structure and in the smaller argu-ments, the death and resurrection of Jesus and the gift of the Spirit play key roles. And from at least chapter 6 through to chapter 8 Paul is deliberately echoing a story which, as we have already seen, was often just below the surface in his writing: the exodus.[90] Our present task, as well as to avoid

---

[88] See Wright, *Climax*, ch. 2.

[89] cp. too 1 Cor 15.56f., where the resurrection is the answer to the problem of death, sin and the law.

[90] More details in Wright, 'Exodus'; *Romans* 508–14.

being distracted by the multiplicity of themes, is to focus on the meaning of the resurrection throughout, not least in the magnificent chapter 8, where most of the major themes of the letter, and of Paul's theology as a whole, are gathered up in powerful celebration.

The overarching theme itself exhibits the shape of Paul's picture of resurrection. As he declares in the succinct summary, those whom God justified, them he also glorified (8.30); in other words (as Ephesians puts it), those who are 'in Christ' are already seated with the Messiah in the heavenly places. Already they stand on resurrection ground (6.6–14). And the opening of the section, unfolding step by step from the initial statement in 5.1–2, makes the same point in its shape as well as its content: suffering produces hope, and hope does not make us ashamed (compare Philippians 1.20), because love for God has been poured out in our hearts through the Holy Spirit who has been given to us.[91] The powerful resurrection of Jesus constitutes the sphere within which Christians now live, already justified and reconciled to God, and now looking forward to final rescue from wrath (which is functionally equivalent to being given 'glory, honour, incorruption and peace' as in 2.7, 10), in other words, to the life of the age to come (5.21, reflecting 2.7). Thus:

> [9]How much more, then, since we are now justified by his blood, shall we be saved through him from wrath. [10]For if when we were enemies we were reconciled to God by the death of his son, how much more, now that we are reconciled, shall we be saved in his life.

'In his life': this, clearly, is the resurrection life of the Messiah, the new life that follows his sacrificial death. This is what Paul will expound more fully in Romans 6 and 8.

The next paragraph, 5.12–21, is as notorious among scholars for its compactness as it is among struggling students working out how Paul can write Greek sentences, as in verse 18, without subject, verb or object. Yet it is here, not least in verse 18 itself, for all its Tacitean density, that we find something very near the heart of Paul's understanding of the effects of Jesus' death and resurrection. Sin has spread through all humanity, bringing universal death; the true God has dealt with the problem, in fulfilment of the covenant promises, through the one man Jesus the Messiah, for the benefit of all, Jew and Gentile alike. The paragraph (like several passages already studied) depends for its force on Paul's underlying theology of what human beings are in the divine intention and purpose; the tragedy of Adam is not just that he introduced sin and hence death into the world, but that humans were made to be the creator's wise agents over creation, and if they worship and serve the creature rather than the creator this purpose goes unfulfilled. When summing up the same train of thought in 8.29, Paul puts it like this:

---

[91] Rom. 5.3–5. For details see Wright, *Romans* 516f.

we were, he says, 'predestined to be conformed to the image of God's son, that he might be the firstborn among a large family of siblings'. So here, in verse 17, we may be surprised to read that the result of God's grace in the gospel is that those who receive the gift will themselves 'reign in life as kings (*basileusousin*).' This is what human beings were made for. It is also what Caesar thinks he can do without reference to the one true God; but he will discover his mistake.

Paul states his principal thesis in verse 18:[92] 'So then, as through one trespass – to all people – unto condemnation, in the same way also through one act of righteousness – to all people – unto the justification of life!' Paul splashes his verbal paint on to the canvas in huge dollops, and does not stop to touch it up. We are left to add the smaller details: the 'act of righteousness' appears to be a way of referring to Jesus' obedient death, indicating that it balances and indeed outweighs Adam's trespass, and 'the justification of life' appears to refer to the resurrection as God's act of vindication, not only of Jesus himself but, proleptically, of all those who are 'in him'. Paul can therefore explain in the next verse that it is through the 'obedience' of the one man (now seeing Jesus' death and resurrection as a single act) that the many are given the status of 'righteous' (verse 19). He then introduces the darker note of the law and its effects, which will take him all of chapter 7 to work through; but his assertion that God has dealt with this problem too leads him to the final statement of the chapter (5.21), which in turn will serve as a quarry from which subsequent arguments can be drawn:

> . . . so that, just as sin reigned in death, so also grace might also reign through righteousness to the life of the coming age (*eis zoen aionion*) through Jesus the Messiah our lord.

'Grace' here is obviously a shorthand for 'the true God, acting freely and generously'; 'righteousness', though sometimes wrongly translated 'justification', clearly means that God is acting in and through his own faithfulness to the covenant, the covenant which was always intended to deal with sin and death; and the result is that all those who benefit from this action (Paul does not spell this out here but it has been present throughout the paragraph) will inherit *zoe aionios*, 'eternal life', or, as I have suggested as a preferable translation for readers soaked in Platonic imagination, 'the life of the age to come', that of which the Pharisees and rabbis spoke so eagerly, and which for them meant one thing only: resurrection. The resurrection is thus the creator's answer not only to sin but to its consequences.

Part of the point of this sharp and dramatic paragraph for our purposes is to highlight the fact that Paul here draws together his thinking about the death and resurrection of Jesus in terms of their constituting the single act of divine grace and power through which the entail of human sin and death is

---

[92] For the shape of the paragraph cf. Wright, *Romans*, 523–5.

broken. This is what he will now explore in the coming chapters. And he begins right away, in chapter 6, by drawing out the implications of 5.21 in terms, first of the *status* of the baptized, then in terms of their *behaviour*. In both, the resurrection of the Messiah leads, through the identification of the believer with him in baptism, to personal 'resurrection', both literally in the future and metaphorically in the present.[93]

This is where the now traditional scholars' disjunction between Romans and the other 'principal letters' on the one hand, and Ephesians and Colossians on the other, is I believe mistaken.[94] Granted, Paul does not use exactly the same terminology here as we find there; but that is true of almost all parallels and near-parallels between any passages in his various letters. But the questions he asks, and the answers he gives, only make sense if he is affirming a *present* 'resurrection' life for the Christian as well as a *future* one.

The first question in chapter 6, despite popular impressions to the contrary, is about status, not behaviour. 'Shall we continue in sin' treats 'sin' as a place where one might go on living, not as an activity one might continue to perform. The question depends for its force on Paul's insistence on the grace of God reaching down 'while we were still sinners' (5.8). Do we then, he asks, have to remain as 'sinners' for God's grace to reach us there? Is that to be our continuing status? Shall we stay as we are?

Certainly not, he replies. Something has happened to bring us out from that place, that state, that status. Baptism means identification with the Messiah; what is true of him becomes true of those who are baptized; and the Messiah died to sin, once, as a completed action, and was then raised to new life. We 'died to sin', Paul says, with the Messiah. Where, then, is the baptized person now? In a kind of limbo, or intermediate state, after death but before resurrection?

In a sense, yes, and this is not insignificant; but in a sense, no. This is very important for our overall argument, and must be unpacked further.

In a sense, yes. Paul is very clear that there is a still-future resurrection yet to come. The future tenses in 6.5 and 8 ('if we were planted together with him in the likeness of his death, *we shall be* also [in the likeness] of his resurrection'; if we died with the Messiah, we believe that we *shall* also live with him) are disputed; they may be real futures, that is, predicting a final resurrection, or they may be logical.[95] Whatever we decide about that, 6.23 envisages the eventual gift of the 'life of the age to come', *zoe aionios*, which in 2.7 Paul declared was the divine gift, at the final judgment, to those

---

[93] For very different metaphorical uses of 'resurrection' language for present experience see below, 534–51. A recent study of resurrection and ethics in Paul is Lohse 2002.

[94] See 236–40 above.

[95] An example of a logical future: '*if* you have locked the door, we *shall* be safe'. If the condition is satisfied, we *are already* safe; the only actual futurity consists in our discovering whether or not you did lock the door.

who persisted patiently in well-doing. And in 8.10–11 (see below), and the long paragraph to which it leads (8.12–30), there is no question: however much inaugurated eschatology there is, however much 'now', there is a massive 'not yet' as well. The resurrection, in its literal meaning and with its concrete referent, has not yet happened, except to Jesus himself. From that point of view, the Christian who has 'died with Christ' in baptism is indeed in a kind of intermediate state; and it is interesting that Paul can use, of such a person, a phrase which was used precisely for the intermediate state by some Jews who believed in bodily resurrection. Those who have died are now 'alive to God'.[96]

This must, however, be immediately qualified. Paul uses the same language of Jesus himself in 6.10, and he does not suppose that Jesus is in any kind of intermediate state. Perhaps the best account of the passage is this: Paul is aware that he is borrowing, and adapting, language from his native Judaism (in which nobody expected the Messiah to be raised in advance of anyone else), in order to describe the new situation in which, he believed, exactly that had happened. If there is a sense in which those who have died with Christ in baptism are, until their eventual resurrection, in a kind of intermediate state, there is a sense, too, and a more important one, in which they are not. Paul does not believe that those who have died with Christ are in some kind of neutral territory, half way between death and life. His argument about status in verses 2–11, and his arguments about behaviour in verses 12–14 and 15–23, depend for their force throughout on his belief that in baptism the Christian not only dies with the Messiah *but rises as well*. 'Reckon yourselves as well to be dead indeed to sin, and alive to God in the Messiah, Jesus' (verse 11). When Paul says 'reckon', he does not mean that the act of 'reckoning' something creates a new entity (even if he did, that would still mean that the Christian who had thus 'reckoned' was already alive the other side of death); the language of 'reckoning' is that of adding up a sum, a column of figures. When I add up the money in my bank account, that does not create the money; life is not, alas, that easy. It merely informs me of the amount that is already there. When I have completed the 'reckoning', I have not brought about a new state of affairs in the real world outside my mind; the only new state of affairs is that my mind is now aware of the way things actually are.

So it is here. When Paul says in verse 4 that 'as the Messiah was raised from the dead through the father's glory, so also we are to walk in newness of life', he is not asking of Christians something that, being still 'dead', they are unable to perform. That is the strong argument for seeing the future tenses of verses 5 and 8 as logical, not temporal. And when the argument for status, whose conclusion is verse 11 (the Messiah died and was raised; you are in the Messiah; therefore you must reckon that you have died and been

---

[96] Rom. 6.11; cf. 4 Macc. 7.19; 16.25; and 425 below (on Lk. 20.38).

raised) gives way to the argument for behaviour in verses 12–14, there can be no doubt. 'Yield yourselves to God as people alive from the dead (*hosei ek nekron zontas*), and your members as weapons of righteousness to God' (verse 13). If the *hosei* simply meant 'as if', implying 'which is not, of course, the case', Paul would be perpetrating an cruel tease. Telling someone to yield themselves to God, and their members as weapons of righteousness, when they are not in any sense 'alive from the dead', is like telling someone to leap from a high building 'as if you had wings' when they do not.

Paul's strong ethical argument, then, is not simply that there are two ways to live, and that one must choose between them; it is that the baptized have changed their ground, and must learn to behave according to the territory they now find themselves in, like someone moving to a new country and having to learn the appropriate language. This is the force of 6.15–23, which continues the 'exodus' theme – the story of how the slaves get to freedom by coming through the water of the Red Sea – by speaking of the former slavery to sin and the new condition in which, having been set free from sin, the baptized must live in the appropriate manner. Paul will later warn against behaviour that would be equivalent to the children of Israel wanting to go back to Egypt (8.12–17); but at the moment he simply rubs the point in, that his readers are no longer slaves to sin, and must not behave as if they were. Even here, therefore, where the argument is more focused on behaviour, we find that underlying status and ultimate destination are what matters. The underlying status of the baptized is that they have been set free from sin. Their ultimate destination, the divine free gift (as in 5.21), is the life of the age to come, *zoe aionios*.

So far, Paul's argument has hinged on the central and decisive events of Jesus' death and resurrection, and on the ways in which they create a new world of freedom from sin, which leads those who enter it to the literal and concrete future resurrection itself, the life of the age to come, by way of the metaphorical, though still concrete, 'resurrection' of a radical change in behaviour. This is the fullest example of something we have increasingly observed: that the metaphorical 'resurrection' in second-Temple Judaism, whose concrete referent was the return from exile, the connotation of which was release from sin (in Isaiah, Jeremiah and Ezekiel in particular), has been replaced in Paul by the equally metaphorical 'resurrection' of the new life of the baptized believer, whose concrete referent is the communal and personal new life in which the shackles of sin have been broken. This is not, then, an arbitrary reuse of 'resurrection' as a metaphor. It is dependent upon the literal use in relation both to Jesus and to the future resurrection of believers, just as the metaphorical use within Jewish texts could be combined with a literal use in relation to the eventual resurrection of the righteous, and sometimes the wicked as well. Resurrection, when it was metaphor, was usually metonymy as well; and so it was with Paul. This is not, then, as has some-times been supposed, the start of a move away from the literal meaning, towards something which will call itself 'resurrection' but which in fact belongs in a different worldview entirely, such as we find in the later gnostic writings.[97] Paul's metaphorical use is a new development from within the frame of reference provided by second-Temple Judaism, a development occasioned by the events concerning the Messiah and by Paul's interpretation of what those events meant for those 'in him' both in the present and the future.

From this point, however, Paul moves into a different phase within the overarching argument of chapters 5—8. He has spoken frequently, in one-line remarks within other arguments, about the place of the Jewish law within the overall divine plan. He now turns to address the question directly; and, in doing so, he gives a different colouring to what he says about 'life', the life which the law could not give, and the life which God will give by the Spirit. This is not simply an attempt to deal with a problem ('what am I saying about the law?'), though no doubt it is that as well. It is his way of explaining further what he means by speaking of the gift of God as 'eternal life' (6.23), of 'grace reigning through righteousness to eternal life' (5.21). It is his way, within the continuing new-exodus narrative, of speaking of what happens when YHWH's people arrive at Sinai; only now, finding that Torah has become part of the problem instead of part of the solution, they must learn that the Messiah and the Spirit have done 'what the Torah could not do.'[98] 7.1—8.11 forms a single section; the argument runs on to its triumphant climax in 8.11. At the same time, 8.1–11 is the start of the argument which continues, in one of Paul's greatest passages, to the end of the chapter. But to understand those crucial eleven verses, with their rich exposition of resurrection, we must pass through the dark tunnel of chapter 7.

In 7.4 Paul sums up his argument in a typically dense and pregnant sentence:

> Even so, my dear family, you too died to the law through the body of the Messiah, so that you might belong to another, to the one who was raised from the dead, so that we might bear fruit for God.

The basis for this is the evocation, in verses 1–3, of the Adam/Christ contrast of 5.12–21, seen in the light of its development in 6.3–11. Paul envisages someone who is 'under the law', that is, a Jew or proselyte who has lived under the regime of the Jewish Torah, as being bound by the law to the Adam-solidarity, just as a married woman is bound by the law to her husband. But when the husband dies – in Paul's developed picture, when the 'old human being' of 6.6 dies with the Messiah – then the 'you', the woman

[97] See e.g. Robinson 1982; see below, ch. 11.
[98] On Rom. 7 see Wright, *Romans*, 549–72.

in the illustration, is free to marry again; and the Messiah now appears on the other side of the picture, as in the double statements of 4.25, 5.9–10 and 6.3–4, 10, this time in the guise of the new bridegroom. Belonging to him enables 'you', like Abraham and Sarah despite their old age, to 'bear fruit'. The resurrection of Jesus as the new bridegroom has opened new possibilities not previously available, which Paul then describes in 7.5–6 in the language which elsewhere we associate with the renewal of the covenant: we now serve, he says (echoing 6.15–23) not in the 'oldness of the letter' but in the 'newness of the Spirit'.[99] Once again, the literal resurrection of Jesus sets the context for the metaphorical resurrection of believers as the anticipation of their own literal resurrection, which Paul will shortly describe. And, just in case there is any doubt, we note that both the literal and the metaphorical meanings have concrete referents, the literal referring to bodily resurrection and the metaphorical referring to practical holiness and service.

This prepares the way for Paul's intricate and complex exposition of what happened when the Torah arrived on Sinai, and when Israel continued to try to live under it, knowing it to be God's law, holy and just and good. The law did indeed promise life, life as Deuteronomy had made clear (and as many second-Temple Jewish texts agreed).[100] But those who embraced Torah found that from the moment of its arrival it highlighted the ways in which Israel was breaking it, and was thus recapitulating the sin of Adam (compare 5.12, 20); and those who continued to live under it – seen now with Paul's Christian hindsight – discovered that the more they tried, the more the Torah condemned them. They were, after all, in Adam, and the Torah could not help becoming as it were a shadowy parody of itself (7.22–3), reminding Adamic Israel of its own sin and death. It could not give the life it promised, not because there was anything wrong with it in itself, but because, as we might say, the material it had to work with was not of the right sort. As in Galatians 3.10–14, Paul analyses the problem in terms of a promise of God which has become stuck at the point of Israel's rebellion. Here, as there, he solves the problem in terms of the death of the Messiah and the gift of the Spirit.

'There is therefore now no condemnation for those in the Messiah, Jesus': Romans 8.1 has become one of Paul's most famous sentences, not least through being set to music by J. S. Bach in his motet *Jesu, Meine Freude*. The 'condemnation' in question is the Adamic condemnation spoken of in 5.12–21, which in turn looks back to the condemnation of sin in 1.18—3.20. The reason this condemnation is taken away for those 'in the Messiah' is given in verses 2–11, with constant reference to the resurrection:

---

[99] cf. 2 Cor. 3, where the 'new covenant' theme is developed more explicitly; in Rom., cf. 2.25–9.

[100] Deut. 30.15–20; Sir. 17.11; 45.5; Bar. 4.1; *Ps. Sol.* 14.2.

God has done what the Torah could not do, condemning sin in the flesh of the Messiah, as the representative of all his people, and by his Spirit giving life, in the present in terms of a new orientation and mindset (8.5–8), in the ultimate future in terms of bodily resurrection. This is Paul's clearest statement of what he understands by the future resurrection of the Messiah's people:

> [9]But you are not in the flesh, you are in the Spirit, if the Spirit of God dwells in you. [10]If the Messiah is in you, though the body is dead because of sin, the Spirit is life because of righteousness. [11]If the Spirit of him who raised Jesus from the dead dwells in you, he who raised the Messiah from the dead will give life to your mortal bodies also, through his Spirit who dwells in you.

There can be no question but that Paul means by this that (a) the present body, the body that will die because of its innate mortality and corruptibility, is the body that will be raised, (b) this is in exact parallel to what happened to Jesus himself, and (c) there is a causal connection between the two. These are the most important conclusions to be drawn for our present purposes.[101] But there are two other things to note as well.

First, the one who accomplishes the resurrection, both of Jesus and of believers, is the living God himself, as Paul regularly insists; but the means by which he will accomplish it is the Spirit. The Spirit, here as throughout Paul's thought, is the *present* guarantee of the *future* inheritance, and of the body which will be appropriate for that new world; this strand has run right through the Pauline material we have so far studied, and remains important in the Corinthian letters as well.

Second, however, the language of the 'indwelling' of the Spirit belongs, within second-Temple Jewish thought, with the 'indwelling' of the Shekinah in the Temple, the 'tabernacling' presence of YHWH in the midst of Israel. The suggestion, then, that the Spirit is the one through whom the body will be raised belongs with Paul's 'new Temple' theology, in Ephesians 2.11–21 and, more especially, in 1 Corinthians 3.16–17 and 6.19–20. The major resonances which Paul sets up, within his Jewish world, when he speaks of the resurrection of the Messiah and of all those who belong to him, are the rebuilding of the Temple (which cannot be done, of course, as long as Israel remains exiled in Babylon) and the strange but complete fulfilling of Torah.

Once again, in the process, those who live 'in the Messiah', in the interval between his resurrection and their own, stand on resurrection ground. They 'set their mind on the Spirit', rather than on the flesh, just as Paul gave

---

[101] The now standard assertions that Paul did not believe in bodily resurrection usually ignore Rom. 8 (e.g. it is hardly mentioned in Avis 1993a, an exception being Rowland 1993, 83). Perkins 1984, 270, suggests strangely that the 'making alive' in 8.11 has to do with a present aliveness which becomes the basis of ethics. The language surely works the other way around, as in 1 Cor. 6 (see below, ch. 6): *because* the body will be raised in the future, *therefore* it is important how it behaves in the present.

similar commands to the Philippians and the Colossians.[102] As a result, they enjoy 'life and peace' in the present as well as the future. This is where Paul makes the sharpest of his anthropological distinctions, pressing some of his key technical terms harder than he does anywhere else: 'you are not in the flesh, but in the Spirit'. He had earlier spoken of himself as being 'in the flesh', though not determined by it;[103] now, to insist on the radical break that has taken place in baptism (6.2–23), he insists that the Christian is no longer 'in Adam', no longer 'in the flesh'. The Christian still clearly possesses 'flesh', as we see when Paul warns against living 'according to the flesh' in 8.12–14. But Paul increasingly focuses his argument on the 'body', the body which at present is corruptible and doomed to death – and whose 'deeds' can still be aligned with the 'flesh' in 8.13 – and yet which will be given new life, resurrection life, by the Spirit of the living God.

The remaining major argument of chapter 8 runs from verse 12 to verse 30, coming back at the end to the point where Paul began in 5.1–11: those who are justified by faith are assured of 'glory', sharing indeed the glory of the one true God (5.2), or, as he now puts it, being co-glorified with the Messiah (8.17). That last verse is the fulcrum around which these nineteen verses turn, with verses 12–16 leading up to it, verses 18–27 explaining it, and verses 28–30 summing up and drawing the conclusion.

Here, as in Philippians and elsewhere, the final resurrected state of the justified is described as 'glory'. By this Paul seems to mean, not luminosity (there is nothing particularly godly, after all, in shining like a star), but the dignity, worth, honour and status that the Messiah's people will enjoy, sharing that of the Messiah himself, whose 'glory' is now that he is the world's true lord. As Paul said in 5.17, those who are his will share his kingly reign. This corresponds to the meaning of the request put by James and John to Jesus in Mark 10.37: they ask to sit at Jesus' right and left in his 'glory'. They do not imagine that they, or he, will be shining like torches; and indeed Matthew's version of the saying (20.21) has 'in your kingdom'. That is the point here: those who patiently walk through the present wilderness, being led by the Christian equivalent of the pillar of cloud and fire, in other words, by the Spirit, will eventually receive the 'inheritance'. Romans 8.12–17, in other words, is another part of the Pauline retelling of the exodus story, the part that follows from the crossing of the Red Sea and the arrival at Sinai. The Messiah's people must suffer with him, as Paul insisted in Philippians 3.10–11, in order to be glorified. The parallel indicates well enough that 'glory' is at least in part a synonym for 'resurrection'.

But only in part. It is true that, as in Philippians 3.20–21, 'glory' here is a *characteristic* of the risen body; but, again as in that passage, it is here also a *function* of it. The risen body will be 'glorious' in that it will no longer be

---

[102] Phil. 4. 8f.; Col. 3.2.
[103] Gal. 2.20; cf. 2 Cor. 10.3.

subject to decay and death. But those who are raised will also enjoy 'glory' in the sense of new responsibilities within the new creation. This leads the eye towards the 'inheritance', the theme we met in Galatians 3 and 4 and Ephesians 1 and which now forms the main theme of verses 18–25. This part of Paul's larger picture of the world to come, the promised new age, focuses not so much on what sort of bodies those 'in Christ' will have in the resurrection, but on the sphere over which they will exercise their rule.

Verses 18–24 insist that the sphere in question is the whole renewed cosmos – and, indeed, that the cosmos will be renewed precisely through the agency of those who are thus raised from the dead to share the 'glory', that is, the kingly rule, of the Messiah.[104] Paul is more precise in verse 21 than some of his translators: the creation itself, he says, will be set free from its bondage to decay 'unto the freedom of the glory of the children of God'. He does not mean, I think, that creation will share the glory; that is not his point. Creation will enjoy the freedom which comes when God's children are glorified – in other words, the liberation which will result from the sovereign rule, under the overlordship of Jesus the Messiah, of all those who are given new, resurrection life by the Spirit. The marginalization of this part of Romans 8 in much exegesis down the years has robbed Christian imagination of this extraordinary picture of the future; only by restoring it to its rightful place – which is, after all, in Paul's build-up to the climax of the central section of his most important letter! – can we understand the larger picture within which his vision of resurrection makes sense. It is a picture in which the corruption and futility of creation itself, created good but doomed to decay, is seen as a kind of slavery, so that creation, too, needs to experience its exodus, its liberation. And God's people, indwelt by the Spirit, find that they themselves, being in their own mortal bodies part of this same creation, groan in labour-pains as they await the birth of God's new world. The Spirit is, once again, the gift that indicates what the future holds, here seen in terms of the 'first-fruits' metaphor, the first sheaf of harvest offered as a sign of the larger crop still to come.[105] The Spirit thus again provides an inauguration of the eschatological fulfilment, even in the present time; Paul here sees this in terms of prayer (8.26–7), as the church anticipates, in inarticulate groanings, the glory that is to come when God's people are set in authority over the world.

Paul sums up the whole argument in 8.28–30. Here, once more, the status of Jesus as the true divine image, and of Jesus' people as being renewed in that image (and thus taking their rightful place as the creator's wise agents, bringing his order to creation) comes to the fore, as in Philippians 3.20–21

---

[104] This passage calls into question the suggestion of Longenecker 1998, 201 that there seems to be a reduction in apocalyptic imagery and expressions as we move into the later letters.

[105] For the 'first-fruits' metaphor cf. Rom. 11.16; 16.5 (and the commentary on those passages in Wright, *Romans*, 683f., 762); 1 Cor. 15.20, 23; 16.15; 2 Thess. 2.13.

and Colossians 3.10. This is so important that Paul even interrupts his own sequence of climactic verbs to bring it in at the appropriate moment. When he speaks of 'predestination' here he does not refer to an arbitrary decree; he means the creator's provision of image-bearing humans to bring to his creation order, justice, renewal and above all freedom from the slavery of decay. And, turning the argument back to the human beings who have been its main subject, Paul repeats in six words what he said in 5.1–2 in thirty-eight: *hous de edikaiosen, toutous kai edoxasen*, 'those whom he justified, them he also glorified'. Justification flows from the death and resurrection of Jesus; those who are justified already share his glory in the proleptic sense indicated in Ephesians, and will share it fully when their present bodies are transformed, as in Philippians 3.20–21, to be like that of Jesus himself. The metaphorical present looks on to the literal future.

The line of thought which runs from Jesus' death and resurrection to that of his people is then celebrated in the final paragraph of Romans 8 (verses 31–9). Rhetorical questions enquire whether anything can now come between the Messiah's people and final salvation, and each time Paul answers in terms of what God has already done in the Messiah. Central to this is verse 34, emphasizing that Jesus' resurrection is the cornerstone of the Christian hope:

> Who is there to condemn? It is the Messiah, Jesus, who has died – yes, rather, who was raised, who is also at God's right hand, who also intercedes for us![106]

The present suffering, persecution and martyrdom of God's people is as nothing in the light of the love God has poured out through the Messiah. Paul is persuaded (8.38–9) that

> neither death nor life, nor angels nor rulers, nor things present nor things to come, nor powers, nor height nor depth nor any other creature, will have power to separate us from God's love in the Messiah, Jesus our lord.

And the most fundamental reason why he is convinced of this is that death itself, heading this list of potential enemies, has been defeated. Not redefined; not understood in a different light; defeated. That is one of the most central points in the whole of Romans, and it undergirds Paul's belief in both the love and the power of the creator and covenant God.[107]

---

[106] On the punctuation, a vexed problem throughout the paragraph, see Wright, *Romans* 612f.

[107] Most translations render *dynesetai* in the last line simply as 'will be able', but part of the point is the contrast between the *dynamis* of God (1.4, 16, 20; 4.16), seen most particularly in the resurrection of Jesus and the gospel which announces it, and all the *dynameis* of the world.

(iv) Romans 9—11

After the repeated emphasis on Jesus the Messiah and his death and resurrection in the letter so far, chapters 9—11 are rightly felt as a contrast, but it is important not to press this point beyond Paul's obvious rhetorical intention, namely to bring the reader up short with the shock of personal grief following hard on the heels of the exalted conclusion of chapter 8. Chapters 9—11 are in fact closely and carefully integrated with the rest of the letter. The older attempts to prise the section away as a separate treatment of a different topic, and the more recent attempts to suggest that Jesus Christ plays no role in the argument, leaving the way clear for a 'salvation' for Israel which owes nothing to him, are without exegetical or theological foundation.[108]

In fact, the whole argument – a lengthy retelling of the story of Israel, from Abraham to Paul's own day, highlighting various features which draw out the point he wants to make – comes to its head in the middle of chapter 10, where the resurrection of Jesus as Messiah is the centrepiece, the focus of faith, and the climax of the long covenant history of God and Israel. *Telos gar nomou Christos*, declares Paul in 10.4: the Messiah is the goal of Torah, the place where the whole story was heading, the point at which the divine faithfulness to the promises is finally unveiled. Israel had been languishing in the 'exile' of which Moses and the prophets had warned, longing for the time when her God would rescue her. One of the central passages of both warning and promise, drawn on both by later biblical writers and at least two important post-biblical sources, was Deuteronomy 27—30. This passage details, first, the blessings that will follow from covenant obedience; then the curses that will result from covenant disobedience, the final and most devastating of which is exile itself; and then, in chapter 30, the promise that if, in exile, Israel returns to YHWH with all her heart and soul, YHWH will gather her again and enable her to love him from the heart. At that time, Torah itself, which would up to that point prove difficult or impossible for Israel to keep, will come near to them; they will not need to go up to heaven for it, or across the deep sea, because it will be 'on their lips and in their hearts', so that they may keep it.

When we place Paul alongside other second-Temple readings of this passage, the meaning of Romans 10.4–13 becomes clear; and the resurrection of Jesus is at the middle of it all.[109] The book of Baruch interpreted Deuteronomy 30 in terms of God's Wisdom; that was what Israel needed if she was to escape from exile. The Qumran letter known as 4QMMT interpreted the

---

[108] On these questions see Wright, *Romans*, 620–26. The best example of the former mistake is C. H. Dodd (Dodd 1959 [1932], 161–3); of the latter, Krister Stendahl (Stendahl 1976 ch. 1; Stendahl 1995).

[109] Details in Wright, *Romans*, 655–66. Vos 2002, 303–10, sees this as part of the 'shadow side' of Paul's resurrection-gospel.

chapter in terms of the particular rules of Torah the sect was anxious to see followed in the Temple. In both cases it was assumed that the covenant renewal promised in Deuteronomy 30 was on the point of happening, perhaps had already begun to happen. Paul agrees, but for a very different reason; he sees that the covenant has been renewed in and through the Messiah. As in many other passages he predicates of the Messiah things that other second-Temple Jews had said of Wisdom or Torah, so here he rereads Deuteronomy 30.11–14, as a focal point of the chapter about covenant renewal, in order to say: this passage is coming true *whenever people believe the gospel of Jesus the risen Messiah and lord!* The passage is admittedly dense, but if approached in this light it falls into place:

> [4]The Messiah is the goal of Torah with a view to righteousness for all who believe. [5]For Moses writes, concerning the righteousness of Torah, that 'The one who does them shall live in them' [Leviticus 18.5]; [6]but the righteousness of faith says [Deuteronomy 30.12–14], 'Do not say in your heart, "Who will go up to heaven?",' that is, to bring the Messiah down; [7]'or "Who will go down into the abyss?",' that is, to bring the Messiah up from the dead. [8]But what does it say? 'The word is near you, on your lips and in your heart,' that is, the word of faith, the word which we proclaim; [9]because, if you confess with your mouth 'Jesus is lord', and believe in your heart that God raised him from the dead, you will be saved. [10]For with the heart one believes unto righteousness, and with the mouth one makes confession unto salvation.

The basic confession of Christian faith ('Jesus is lord'), and the fundamental belief upon which it is based (that the creator God raised him from the dead), are the signs, when they occur, that covenant renewal has taken place, and that those who exhibit this faith are its true members and beneficiaries – even if, being born Gentiles, they have never been part of the ethnic family of Israel. Paul here draws together several threads in the letter and in his wider thought (within Romans, a line can be traced from 2.25–9, through 3.27–30 and 8.4–8, all the way to the present passage), and proposes the covenant renewal that has taken place in the Messiah as the basis for the Gentile mission upon which he himself is engaged (10.12–18). For him, clearly, the resurrection of Jesus is the covenant-renewing moment; and belief in that event, as the decisive act of Israel's God, is the defining characteristic of those who belong to this renewed covenant, just as with Abraham in 4.18–22. And the point for our present investigation is this: the only possible meaning we can assign to Paul's claim about the resurrection as the covenant-renewing event, and about belief in it as the covenant-defining badge, is that he was referring to the bodily raising of Jesus from the dead. Not only is that what 'raising from the dead' meant, in both paganism and Judaism. No other meaning (that Jesus was now 'in heaven' as a disembodied spirit, for instance, however exalted a status he might be assigned) remotely fits the logic of this paragraph. Many other patriarchs, heroes and righteous men and women were already resting in a place of honour after their death, according to much Jewish belief; if Jesus had simply joined their number, it is impossible to envisage Paul saying what he here does about the significance of his resurrection.

There is one other occurrence of resurrection terminology in Romans 9—11, and it echoes but transforms the metaphorical uses current in Judaism. In 11.1–10 Paul explains that there is at the present time a 'remnant' of ethnic Jews who, like himself, have believed in Jesus as the risen Messiah and lord, while the others, not believing, have been 'hardened'. Well then, he asks in 11.11, is this the end of the matter? Can any more Jews be saved? His answer is an emphatic yes; and to explain this he describes the 'trespass' and 'diminution' of ethnic Israel in language which echoes what he had said, both about Adam and about the Messiah, in chapter 5: 'if their trespass means riches for the world, and their diminution means riches for the Gentiles, how much more will their full inclusion mean?' (11.12).[110]

He then looks his Gentile readers in the face. I am the apostle to you Gentiles, he says (11.13); and I make a big fuss of this task to which I've been assigned, because, in line with what Deuteronomy said about Israel being made jealous by non-Jewish people coming in to share their privileges, my aim is to make my fellow Jews jealous, and so save some of them (11.13–14). Actually, the word he uses for 'my fellow Jews' is, more literally, 'my flesh', in other words 'my kinsmen according to the flesh', as in 9.3; but the idea of making the 'flesh' jealous, and so saving it, presents to his mind the entire sweep of what he had already said in Romans 5—8 about what God does with the 'flesh', about the ultimate importance of no longer being 'in the flesh', defined by flesh, but of being in the Spirit and thereby being given resurrection life. This enables him to speak of the restoration of ethnic Jews to membership in the renewed covenant, using the metaphorical language traceable at least as far back as Ezekiel 37:

> For if their casting away means reconciliation for the world, what will their receiving back again be if not life from the dead?[111]

Many have argued that *zoe ek nekron* here means literal resurrection, suggesting that the restoration of Jews to membership will come all in a rush on the last day, when they will all be raised to life. I am persuaded, however, that Paul does indeed mean it metaphorically, and that what he has in mind, here and throughout the passage, is ethnic Jews abandoning their unbelief in the gospel (11.22) and coming to membership in the polemically redefined 'all Israel'.[112] But our only present concern with this question is in so far as

---

[110] On the parallels with earlier passages see Wright, *Romans* 681.
[111] Rom. 11.15.
[112] Rom. 11.26; see Wright, *Romans*, 688-93.

it enables us to decide what precisely 11.15 means; and it seems to me highly probable that Paul here, for the only time in all early Christian writings, uses the language of resurrection to speak of the restoration of Israel to full covenant membership, much as Ezekiel had done. The meaning is still, of course, reworked around Paul's basic Christian paradigm; there is no hint of a geographical 'return', as in the prophet. But this passage suggests that the resurrection of the Messiah was at the heart of Paul's understanding of the Messiah's people 'according to the flesh', and that he was able, in the light of that resurrection, to reuse ancient imagery to fresh purpose.

(v) Romans 12—16

The final section of Romans is considerably more important than many commentators have implied, and contains some further significant references to the resurrection. The framework for the whole argument is set by 12.1–2, which establishes the eschatological perspective of the overlap between the present age and the age to come. Christians, here as elsewhere, are urged to live according to the coming age which has already broken in, and they are to do so by the renewal of the mind:

> 12.1I appeal to you therefore, my dear family, through the mercies of God, to present your bodies as a living sacrifice, holy and acceptable to God; this is your reasonable worship. 2Do not be conformed to this present age, but be transformed by the renewal of your minds, so that you may discover in practice what is the will of God, what is good and acceptable and perfect.

Reading this passage in the light of Galatians 1.4, Philippians 3.20–21, Colossians 3.1–11, and the earlier parts of Romans, four points emerge which relate to our present enquiry. First, we note the contrast of the present age (which Galatians describes as 'evil') with the new world that is now breaking in; Paul does not refer to it specifically as 'the age to come', but his language here and in 13.11–14 indicates that he is working with this two-age scheme, and that he believes that the 'age to come' has already begun with the resurrection of Jesus.

Second, we should therefore not be surprised that when he refers to Christian obedience he speaks not of the 'flesh', but of the 'body'. As has often been noted, the 'body', *soma*, is the transition point in his anthropology. It will still die, because it remains corruptible (8.10); it can still even sin, though this is now neither necessary nor desirable (6.12–14; 8.12–14); but it will be raised, and this makes it appropriate as the locus of present Christian worship and service. This is perhaps the place to note, uncontroversially, that like most of Paul's anthropological terms 'body' is holistic in content. Whereas 'flesh' refers to the entire human being seen as corruptible and heading for death, with the frequent further overtones of 'rebellious' and 'sinful', 'body' refers to the entire human being, much as our modern word 'person' might do, seen as present within the good world of creation, within space and time, and called to live there in joyful obedience.[113] It is possible that we should see 12.5, too, in this light; Paul identified ethnic Jews as 'the Messiah's people according to the flesh' in 9.5, and here, in a similarly programmatic statement for the material still to come, he speaks of the multiplicity of Christians as forming 'one body in the Messiah'. This does not mean that the church is 'the resurrection body of the Messiah' without remainder, as used sometimes to be said by those eager to combine a denial of Jesus' bodily resurrection with a high ecclesiology.[114] Rather, the church, composed of Jew and Gentile alike, is as it were the resurrection version, the new-covenant version, of the ethnic solidarity of Israel. And for that the appropriate language is not 'flesh', but 'body'.

Third, when Paul speaks of being 'conformed' (*syschematizesthe*) and 'transformed' (*metamorphousthe*) in verse 2, he uses similar language to what we find in Philippians 3.21, where he promises that Jesus will 'transform' (*metaschematisei*) the present body to be like his glorious body. There, however, he was referring to the future event of resurrection itself (or, more precisely, the transformation of those still alive at the time); here he speaks of something that must happen in the present time. This too, it seems, is a piece of inaugurated eschatology, similar to that which we saw in Romans 6; and it applies specifically to the mind. That was where the human race had gone wrong (1.18–25); that was where its renewal would have to begin. Body and mind together, then, must live according to the new age, the period that has now begun with Jesus.

Fourth, this 'transformation' of the mind corresponds quite closely to what Paul said in Colossians 3.10: the 'new human' is being renewed in knowledge according to the creator's image. Paul has already said that the divine aim was to create renewed humans who would be conformed to the image of his son (8.29); now we see something of what that will mean in practice. Paul is allowing part of his cluster of 'resurrection' language to make its way forwards from Jesus' resurrection, and backwards from the promise of eventual bodily resurrection, into a foundational statement of what it means to live as truly human beings within the new age.

This eschatological introduction to the section introduces a sequence of thought which circles around and returns to the same point in 13.11–14.[115] This adds little to what we have already seen, but is particularly interesting for its echoes of 1 Thessalonians 5.1–11, with its imagery of the night which is passing away and the day which is already dawning. Christians belong to

---

[113] cf. e.g. Gundry 1976.
[114] e.g. Robinson 1952.
[115] For the structure of Romans 12—13 see Wright, *Romans*, 700–03.

the day, says Paul once more, and they need to behave in daytime manner rather than night-time – and here, too, we find the same mixed metaphor, of requiring the appropriate 'weapons' (13.12). Like Romans 6, this passage depends for its appeal on the belief that the Christian already stands on resurrection ground. Only so does it make sense to issue a command not to make provision for 'the flesh' (13.14). As in Ephesians 4.24 and Colossians 3.10, so here Paul urges his readers to 'put on' the new humanity, which is the Messiah himself, the risen lord Jesus.

The long argument of 14.1—15.13 is the centre of the section, and the theological conclusion of the letter as a whole. Paul is urging Christians from different social and particularly ethnic backgrounds to find ways of coming together, particularly of worshipping together, while respecting one another's consciences on matters over which they disagree. This is not a merely pragmatic argument, but is based on the central gospel events, as chapter 14 explains:

> [7]We none of us live to ourselves, and we none of us die to ourselves. [8]For if we live, we live to the lord, and if we die, we die to the lord. So then, whether we live or whether we die, we belong to the lord. [9]For this was why the Messiah died and lived, so that he might be lord of both dead and living.
> [10]You there, why do you judge your brother? Or you – why do you despise your brother? For we must all be presented before the judgment seat of God,[116] [11]for it is written, 'As I live, says the lord, to me every knee shall bow, and every tongue shall make confession to God.' [12]So then, each of us will give an account of ourselves to God.

Just when most expositors thought they were safely away from dense theology and into 'practice' or 'ethics', Paul writes a stunning little section like this, full of echoes of key passages in the other letters, not least Philippians 2.10–11, where he declares that every knee shall bow and every tongue confess that Jesus is lord. The universality of Jesus' Lordship is emphasized here; in fact, part of Paul's point in the section has been to use the word *kyrios*, 'lord', both in its full christological sense, as here, and in its metaphorical sense as 'master' in relation to servant or slave (see verse 4). That verse is itself significant in terms of 'resurrection' language: 'What do you mean by judging someone else's household servant? He stands or falls before his own master; and he will stand, for the master has the power to make him stand.' The language of 'standing', cognate with 'standing up', *anastasis*, and the emphasis that the master/lord has the *power* to 'make him stand', should almost certainly be taken as at least a sidelong reference to resurrection. At the last judgment, all must give an account of themselves, and the lord will 'make to stand', in other words, raise from the dead, not

---

[116] Several MSS read 'of the Messiah', but this is almost certainly an assimilation to 2 Cor 5.10, and to the normal Jewish expectation that the Messiah would judge the world (cf. Rom. 2.16; Ac. 17.31).

those who have kept to a certain cultural code, however venerable, but those who have lived as his faithful servants.

This passage, then, holds together a clear statement of Jesus' own death and resurrection with a statement (verse 8), similar to that in Philippians 1.18–26, and particularly 1.21, of the Christian's position, belonging to the lord whether in life or in death. The fact that Jesus is lord of both dead and living (verse 9) is the basis for the final judgment; when Paul quotes Isaiah 49.18 in verse 11, the opening words, 'as I live, says the lord', pick up the theme of the Messiah's resurrection, and he is now, as lord of dead and living alike, in the right position to summon all the living and departed to judgment. The eschatological framework enables the ecumenical project between culturally divergent Christian groups to move forwards on the basis of the gospel itself.

The final 'resurrection' passage in the letter comes, significantly, as Paul is drawing together the threads of his entire argument. He began with a statement of the gospel in which Jesus, as the Davidic Messiah, has been marked out as such by the living God in the resurrection. He closes his long argument for the unity of the church across traditional Jew-and-Gentile boundaries with a quotation from Isaiah 11.10, choosing to go with the Septuagint version in which the point becomes clear:

> There shall be a root of Jesse,
>   One who rises to rule the nations;
> In him shall the nations hope.

This verse (15.12) thus completes the huge circle that began with 1.3–5. The Davidic Messiah has been marked out by the resurrection as truly Messiah, the lord and judge of all.[117] Paul's mission has been precisely to bring about the obedience of faith among all the nations for the sake of his name. Now he grounds the appeal for unity in the gospel once more, adding only a concluding blessing (15.13) which points to hope, hope in the power of the Holy Spirit – which to the reader of Romans can only mean one thing, namely, hope for the resurrection itself. For Paul, the resurrection of Jesus of Nazareth is the heart of the gospel (not to the exclusion of the cross, of course, but not least as the event which gives the cross its meaning); it is the object of faith, the ground of justification, the basis for obedient Christian living, the motivation for unity, and, not least, the challenge to the principalities and powers.[118] It is the event that declares that there is 'another king', and summons human beings to allegiance, and thereby to a different way of life, in fulfilment of the Jewish scriptures and in expectation of the

---

[117] It was only when completing this book that I discovered where I had first met this exegesis of 15.12: in Torrance 1976, 30.

[118] On the integration of Rom. 13.1–7 with this theme see Wright, *Romans*, 715–23.

final new world which began at Easter and which will be completed when the night is finally gone and the day has fully dawned.

Once again, there can be no question that when Paul speaks of resurrection in all these ways it is the bodily resurrection of Jesus he has in mind. His multiple metaphorical uses of the idea highlight, rather than diminish, the literal usage. They are in any case consistent developments from within the ancient Jewish picture, where resurrection was used as an image for national restoration and forgiveness as well as referring literally to the new bodily life in store for God's people. But when Paul wants to ground his argument in bedrock, it is to the literal, bodily resurrection that he returns.

8. Interlude: The Pastoral Epistles

Debates about the Pastoral Epistles and their authorship will no doubt continue, and I do not wish to add to them here. I simply want to note, within this discussion of resurrection in the Pauline corpus, the contribution that they make to the overall picture of early Christianity. (It would be just as arbitrary to exclude them from a 'Pauline' section as to include them, since even if, as most scholars have supposed, they are not by Paul himself, they are clearly by someone, or more than one person, who thought they should belong closely with his work and thought.) Our question has to do with early Christian traditions about resurrection, not with plotting the contours of Paul's theology, and that of his hypothetical followers, for its own sake. In fact, the rather slight reference to resurrection, though not unprecedented in the commonly accepted Pauline letters, is one of the reasons why the question of authorship has remained open for so long.

The Pastorals do not have much to say about the Christian hope. The clearest passage is the warning in 2 Timothy 2 about two men who appear to be teaching something at variance with the rest:

> [16]Avoid godless chatter, which leads people into further impiety; [17]their talk will eat its way like gangrene. In this category are Hymenaeus and Philetus; [18]they have swerved away from the truth by saying that the resurrection has already happened. They are upsetting the faith of some. [19]But God's firm foundation stands, and this is its seal: 'The lord knows those who are his,' and 'everyone who names the lord's name must depart from unrighteousness.'

The best explanation of what Hymenaeus and Philetus were teaching is that they were pioneering a view which, as we shall see, was to become popular in other circles in due course, according to which 'the resurrection' was now to be interpreted, not in terms of a future bodily hope after death, but purely and simply in terms of a spiritual experience which could be enjoyed during the present life. Certain people had had this experience; they were already, in this new metaphorical sense, 'raised from the dead'. It is not clear whether the two were encouraging others to have this experience as well, or whether the point of their teaching was that if one was not already among those favoured in this way there was now no hope. One way or another, they were drawing people away from what was being seen as mainstream Christian hope.

What is especially interesting is the answer the writer provides in verse 19, in the form of two biblical quotations. Numbers 16.5 ('YHWH knows those who are his!') comes from the chapter which describes the rebellion of Korah, and particularly of Dathan and Abiram, the sons of Eliab (a grandson of Reuben). The phrase quoted here is Moses' comment when faced with rebellion; YHWH will show whether Moses and Aaron have arrogated to themselves their positions of leadership, or whether they hold them in virtue of God's appointment. The further specific rebellion of Dathan and Abiram is to deny that the hope of a land flowing with milk and honey will ever come true.[119] On the next day, the answer comes: Korah, Dathan, Abiram and their families are separated from the rest of the Israelites, and Moses declares that if they go on to die a natural death, then YHWH has not sent him, but that if YHWH creates something new, namely, an instant death in which the ground opens up and swallows them so that they go down alive into Sheol, then it will be clear that the rebels are the ones who have despised YHWH. And so it happens.[120]

There are many resonances between this story and the situation that seems to be addressed in 2 Timothy 2. Hymenaeus and Philetus may be seen as rebels, challenging the authority of the appointed leaders of the church, though this is not said specifically. What they are doing, more particularly, is challenging the future hope, as Dathan and Abiram challenged the promise of the land. And whereas the promise of resurrection is that God will do a new thing, out beyond what anyone could have expected, the punishment of Dathan and Abiram consisted of God doing a new thing in terms of judgment, different to what had happened to anyone else before. How much of all this was in the writer's mind is of course impossible to say; it seems to me highly likely that some of it was. The upshot is not unlike the rabbis' retort to the Sadducees: if you don't believe in resurrection, you won't share it. The writer of 2 Timothy is warning that God will make it clear, in a future act of judgment, who belongs to him and who does not; in other words, which is the true teaching and which is not.

The second biblical quotation is less clear ('Let those who name the name of the lord depart from iniquity'). It appears to be a combination of two passages: Sirach 17.26 ('return to the Most High and turn away from

---

[119] Num. 16.12–14. This story was woven into Israelite tradition at other points: cf. Ps. 106.16–18.
[120] Num. 16.26–33.

iniquity'[121]), and Isaiah 26.13 ('O YHWH our God, other lords besides you have ruled over us, but we name your name alone'[122]). Both passages are about what happens after death. Sirach, of course, believes that nothing happens: the next two verses declare that nobody sings praise to the Most High in Hades, and that thanksgiving ceases once people are dead. Is the writer of 2 Timothy aware of this, and perhaps warning Hymenaeus and Philetus of the fate in store if they say the resurrection is already past? The likelihood of this is increased by the context of Isaiah 26.13: there, the verse immediately following insists that those who are punished by YHWH have no chance of a future life, while verse 19, famously, proclaims: 'Your dead shall live, their corpses shall rise!'[123] Second Timothy 2.19 appears to draw together in, dare we say, an almost Pauline density passages which, taken together, declare that Hymenaeus and Philetus are indeed wrong, and that the future judgment and resurrection which they deny will be the final evidence against them.

The Pastorals' only other significant mention of the life beyond the grave is the repeated reference to 'immortality'. In 1 Timothy 6.16, the writer declares that Jesus the Messiah is the true king (the passage is replete with echoes of imperial rhetoric, and cannot but be seen as subversive; but that is a topic for another time): he is the only potentate, king of kings and lord of lords, and 'he alone has immortality', dwelling in unapproachable light. This appears to indicate that, contrary to the general hellenistic view in which all humans naturally possess an immortal soul, Jesus is the only one who has gone through death and into a world where death has no more power over him. This, of course, corresponds closely to the picture we find in Paul. At the same time, Jesus himself has, according to 2 Timothy 1.10, 'abolished death, and brought life and incorruption to light through the gospel'. Thus the denial that anyone else has immortality as their own possession is balanced by the affirmation that death has been defeated and a new life beyond has been opened up through the work of Jesus. Nobody else has yet attained it, but it is there for the asking. This, too, belongs closely with Paul.

Here, too, 'resurrection' language can be used to denote present Christian living. As in the synoptic tradition, which is surely the origin of this next passage from 2 Timothy 2, the challenge of the gospel can be phrased in terms of passing through death to life:

[11]The saying is sure:
If we die with him, we shall live with him;
[12]if we are patient, we shall reign with him;
if we deny him, he will deny us;
[13]if we are faithless, he remains faithful –
for he cannot deny himself.

---

[121] cf. too Job 36.10.
[122] cf. too Lev. 24.16; Sir. 23.10 (on invoking the name of the lord).
[123] See 116–8 above.

As in Romans 6, it is open to question whether 'we shall live' is a strictly temporal future, or whether it is logical, referring to a 'life' which already begins here and now. The parallel with the next clause ('we shall reign with him'[124]) implies that it remains in the future. The gospel tradition of passages such as Mark 8.34–8 and parallels is here given a mnemonic form, in the service of the gospel itself. This is dependent, like Mark 8, on the confession of Jesus as Messiah which immediately precedes in 2 Timothy 2:

> [8]Remember Jesus the Messiah, risen from the dead, of the seed of David, according to my gospel, [9]in which I suffer, including wearing chains like a criminal; but God's word is not chained.

This is as close as any other New Testament text comes to a direct echo of Romans 1.3–4, in which Jesus' Davidic Messiahship and divine sonship (which here amounts to the same thing) are affirmed, on the basis of his resurrection, as the core of the gospel. The tradition in Mark 8 and parallels was itself, of course, closely joined with Peter's confession of Jesus as Messiah (8.29). The whole passage (2.8–13), when put back together, seems to build on that sequence of thought: Jesus as Messiah, followed by the challenge to suffering, to confessing him rather than denying him. Now, however, Jesus' Messiahship is confirmed by his own resurrection, which reinforces the challenge to die with him in order to live with him. This in turn prepares the way for the warning about the teaching of Hymenaeus and Philetus in verses 16–19.

This leaves the puzzling little poem in 1 Timothy 3.16. Loosely attached to its present context (detailed instructions about the behaviour expected of office-holders in the church), it bursts in with a compact statement of Jesus' story:

> He was manifested in flesh,
> > he was justified in the Spirit,
> He was seen (*ophthe*) by angels,
> > he was announced among the nations,
> He was believed in the world,
> > he was taken up in glory.

Though we might be surprised at there being no explicit mention of the resurrection in such a formulaic statement, it is clearly some kind of a poem or hymn rather than a creed (it does not mention the cross, either), and should not be pressed for details of matters about which it does not speak. However, two points of interest remain for our purposes. It is likely that 'he was justified' (*edikaiothe*) is an oblique way of referring to the resurrection: Jesus was 'vindicated' by the living God – not least as Messiah – after being condemned and killed. We have already noted the subtle and important links

---

[124] Corresponding to Rom. 5.17; cf. too 1 Cor. 4.8, though that is heavy with irony.

between resurrection and justification.[125] The phrase 'in the Spirit' will then refer to the *agency* of the Spirit in his resurrection, as regularly in Paul, not to a supposed 'non-bodily' sphere in which this 'justification' takes place.[126] The mention of Jesus' being 'seen by', or 'appearing to', angels (*ophthe angelois*) is unique; nowhere else is there a mention of the angels seeing the risen, or for that matter the ascended, Jesus, though we should assume that first-century Christians took this for granted. And the final line of the poem (if that is what it is) certainly implies that Jesus' being 'taken up in glory' is a separate event to those described in the first two lines – though not presumably chronologically after all the other events spoken of, since the proclamation to the nations and the belief of the world follow, rather than precede, the ascension in all early Christian schemes that mention it.

The Pastoral Letters thus offer a few small vignettes of early Christian belief both in the future resurrection of Christians and in the bodily resurrection of Jesus himself, and in the link between them. Apart from the last passage, which remains opaque, they fit closely into the matrix of thought we have already studied. The comparative lack of mention of resurrection does at least raise a query over their supposed link with Paul; but what is said, though sometimes put in a different way to what we find elsewhere in Paul, is not obviously theologically distinct from the main letters.[127]

9. Paul (outside the Corinthian Correspondence): Conclusion

There are five concluding points to be made from this Pauline survey.

First, Paul clearly held a richly variegated, but fluently integrated, understanding of resurrection, on which he could draw for different purposes at different times. It comprised basically three 'moments', which remain constant, and in the same mutual relation, throughout the writings we have studied: (1) the bodily resurrection of Jesus the Messiah himself, as the powerful act of the creator God; (2) the future bodily resurrection of those who belong to the Messiah (with the transformation of those still alive at the time so that they share the same quality of new, incorruptible bodily life); and (3) the anticipation of the second, on the basis of the first, in terms of present Christian living, to which 'resurrection' language applies as a powerful metaphor in line with the metaphorical usage available, alongside the literal

---

[125] On e.g. Rom. 4.24f. see above, 247f.

[126] Against e.g. Harvey 1994, 74: 'The place where we are justified is in heaven: by being united with [Christ] in his resurrection we share his justification, which was in the spiritual (not bodily) realm.' This seems to me to put the cart thoroughly before the horse. The resurrection is the basis of justification, not vice versa; and, as we have seen, the resurrection is always bodily (and occurs through the work of the Spirit). For the phrase cf. 1 Cor. 6.11: 'you were justified . . . in the Spirit of our God'.

[127] On resurrection in the Pastorals and the main Paulines cf. R. F. Collins 2002.

use, in Judaism. In terms of the Jewish spectrum of belief, there can be no question: Paul is a firm believer in bodily resurrection. He stands with his fellow Jews against the massed ranks of pagans; with his fellow Pharisees against other Jews.

We observe him, too, cautiously sketching ways of referring to an intermediate state, and developing new language for it derived from his own Christian belief. Those who die go to be 'with the Messiah', or they are 'asleep in the Messiah'. He probably intended 'sleep' metaphorically, without a suggestion of unconsciousness. And all is set within a larger picture, articulated most fully in Romans 8, of the entire new world that God is going to make, and of how this will be accomplished. These are the answers Paul gives to the questions we raised at the start of this chapter.

Paul seldom presents this complete picture all at once. The closest we have seen so far is undoubtedly in Romans. But the multiple and varied occurrences of 'resurrection' language elsewhere in his writings all fit comfortably within this framework.

Second, the only visible development (as opposed to the differences of emphasis necessary for different situations) over the course of the writings we have studied is the change from Paul's early conviction, that he would be among those still alive when the Messiah returned, to his later suspicion that he would probably die before this happened. This comes out most clearly, as we shall see, in 2 Corinthians, but it is already present as a question in Philippians 1, and nothing in Romans indicates that Paul expects to be among those who escape death itself.[128] In particular, though the emphasis of Ephesians and Colossians is of course different to that of the other letters, just as the emphases of 1 Thessalonians, Philippians and Romans are all very different from one another, there is no reason to suppose, on this subject at least, that a great gulf is fixed between those two prison letters and the rest of the corpus.

Third, Paul's views on resurrection remain rooted firmly in Judaism – which is hardly surprising, because no pagans known to us ever imagined that resurrection could or would really take place, let alone offered any developed framework of thought on the subject. But within his Jewish context Paul developed the notion in no fewer than seven striking new ways.

(1) He believed himself to be living at a new stage in the eschatological timetable: the 'age to come' had already begun, precisely with the Messiah's resurrection. Other Jewish groups (notably Qumran) were capable of articulating an inaugurated eschatology, but, again not surprisingly, they never gave it this particular starting-point. Nobody supposed that the Teacher of Righteousness had been bodily raised from the dead.[129]

---

[128] Longenecker 1998 offers a recent alternative proposal concerning development..

[129] For a possible challenge to this (which so far, it seems, has not been taken seriously by other scholars) cf. Wise 1999.

(2) Paul's articulation of what resurrection actually *meant,* for Jesus, for believers in the future, and in the metaphorical use for believers in the present, is noticeably sharper and more focused than anything we find in Judaism. Resurrection has a concrete referent (that is, it means bodies, whether in final resurrection or present Christian obedience); but it always means *transformation*, going through the process of death and out into a new kind of life beyond, rather than simply returning to exactly the same sort of life, as had happened in the scriptures with the people raised to life by Elijah and Elisha, and as the writer of 2 Maccabees seems to have envisaged.

(3) At the same time, we observe a subtle rethinking from within the Jewish setting. The best-known biblical passage predicting bodily resurrection, Daniel 12.2–3, while continuing to supply some language and imagery, is modified; neither the risen Jesus nor the risen believers (as they will be in the future) are said to shine like stars, but Paul does use exactly that image to describe present Christian witness in the dark world, the 'present evil age'. He uses it, in other words, similarly to the way he uses (and transforms) the Jewish metaphorical language in which 'resurrection' denoted 'return from exile/forgiveness of sins', while connoting 'a new act of grace by the creator and covenant God'.

(4) Paul, like those Jews (particularly his former Pharisaic colleagues and their rabbinic successors) who believed in resurrection, based his thinking firmly on the power of the creator God; though he constantly grounds this, when referring to the resurrection (future and present) of believers, in the resurrection of Jesus as well. And, once more like Ezekiel, he sees the 'breath' or 'spirit' of the creator God as the personal agent of resurrection; this is itself, of course, an echo of Genesis 2.7, and in fact the Genesis narrative, and its summary in Psalm 8.4–6, is clearly part of the substructure of his thinking on the whole subject. Again, he is here in line with Jewish thought but has made it much more precise. One obvious way of accounting for this is precisely because he believed the Messiah to have been raised from the dead, so that the 'son of man' text in Psalm 8.4, which some have suggested had already been applied to the Messiah, indicated to him that the Messiah was hereby the truly human being, the one whose resurrection constituted him as the lord of all creation.

(5) Again from within the Jewish world of resurrection-thought, Paul developed new linguistic tools to articulate the fresh position to which he had come. His crucial distinction between 'flesh' (*sarx*) and 'body' (*soma*) enabled him to establish both continuity and discontinuity between the present embodied existence and the future embodied existence. His use of 'glory' as a technical term, not so much for visible luminosity as for honour, prestige and fresh responsibility within God's new world, draws on Jewish texts, but goes far beyond anything we studied earlier.

(6) Paul's belief in the resurrection of Jesus, and in the consequent resurrection of those who belong to him, enables him to develop a new version of

the widespread Jewish doctrine of final judgment. This judgment has itself been divided chronologically into two, with 'condemnation' happening, in one sense, already at the cross (Romans 8.3), so that there is now 'no condemnation for those who belong to the Messiah, Jesus' (8.1). The two-stage resurrection is thus, especially in Romans, the framework for Paul's central doctrine of justification by faith, based on the accomplishment of Jesus and anticipating the verdict of the last day.

(7) Perhaps the most striking development from within the Jewish tradition is the sheer volume and frequent recurrence of resurrection in Paul's thought – a conclusion which our next chapters, on 1 and 2 Corinthians, will reinforce dramatically. Even among those Jewish writings which speak of, and indeed celebrate, resurrection, at no point do we find this belief woven into the fabric of anyone's thought, informing and undergirding one topic after another, in the way it is in Paul. This phenomenon itself demands historical explanation.

In all these ways, Paul kept both feet firmly on the soil of his own Jewish tradition, while making significant developments and modifications, not at all in the direction of a paganization of the concepts and beliefs, but by rethinking them in the light of the Messiah.

Fourth, Paul's entire worldview, which we have not studied in this book but which I have written about elsewhere, remained, in the same way, solidly grounded in Judaism but dramatically rethought around Jesus, and particularly around his resurrection.[130]

(1) The controlling narratives upon which he regularly drew included creation and exodus, the foundation stories within any Jewish worldview. Paul employed them, however, to speak of the new creation, and the new exodus, which were accomplished through Jesus' death and new life. He understood the larger story of Israel, from Abraham to the exile and beyond, as coming to a shocking but satisfying completion in Jesus as the crucified and risen Messiah.

(2) The different aspects of his apostolic praxis – the Gentile mission, prayer, the vocation to suffering, his collection from Gentile churches to help the impoverished Jewish ones – all grow out of a Jewish, indeed Pharisaic, worldview, but have again been reordered, turned inside out one might say, by the events of the gospel, particularly the resurrection. It is only because Paul believes that God's new age has arrived that he believes it is time for the Gentiles to hear the good news; and there is no question why he thinks such a dramatic shift in the eschatological timetable has occurred. It can only be because he believes that Jesus has been raised from the dead.

(3) The symbols of his work, and of the communities he founded, include his own proclamation of the gospel, and the encoded narrative of baptism

---

[130] On the analysis of worldviews see *NTPG* esp. 122–6. For a sketch of Paul's worldview see e.g. Wright, 'Paul and Caesar'.

(Galatians 3, Colossians 2, Romans 6). These, too, are very closely tied to the death and the bodily resurrection of Jesus.

(4) The answers Paul would give to the worldview questions are easily tabulated:

(i) Who are we? We are 'in the Messiah', identified solely by our confession and faith in him as the risen lord; we are the new-covenant people, the Torah-fulfilling people, the worldwide family promised to Abraham by the one true God.

(ii) Where are we? In the good creation of the good God; creation is still groaning in travail, awaiting its own liberation from decay, but is already under the lordship of the risen and ascended Messiah.

(iii) What's wrong? The world, and we ourselves, are not yet redeemed as we shall be. Most people in the world, pagans and Jews alike, remain ignorant of what Israel's God has done in Jesus the Messiah. In particular, the present world rulers (Caesar and the rest, and the dark 'spiritual' powers that stand behind them) are at best a parody, and at worst a monstrous and blasphemous distortion, of the true justice and peace the one God intends for his world. Because sin still has idolatrous humankind in its grip, death still acts as a tyrant.

(iv) What's the solution? In the long term, the creator's great act of new creation, through which the cosmos itself will be liberated, true justice and peace will triumph over all enemies, all the righteous will be raised from the dead, and believers alive at the time will be transformed. In the short term, the gospel must be announced to the world, doing its own powerful work of challenging, transforming, healing and rescuing, and thus creating 'resurrection' people in the metaphorical sense.

(v) What time is it? The 'age to come' has been inaugurated, but the 'present age' still continues. We live between resurrection and resurrection, that of Jesus and that of ourselves; between the victory over death at Easter and the final victory when Jesus 'appears' again. This now/not yet tension runs right through Paul's vision of the Christian life, undergirding his view of (for instance) suffering and prayer.

Paul's worldview thus shows at every point *both* that he remained rooted in Judaism, drawing his basic inspiration and categories from that rich stock, *and* that he consistently developed them, specifically around and because of the resurrection of Jesus and the conclusions he drew from that event. This leads to our fifth and final point.

The fifth point raises the urgent historical question. If Paul was indeed drawing so thoroughly upon the Jewish beliefs and hopes about resurrection, what could have caused him to speak of it in this way? He knew that 'the resurrection' as envisaged in the prophets and in later Jewish traditions had simply not happened. Abraham, Isaac, Jacob and the rest had not been raised to new bodily life; nor, in the metaphorical sense of 'resurrection', had Israel been liberated from her present position of oppression, enslavement and 'exile'. So why did Paul say the resurrection *had* occurred, and say so not just as one odd statement out of the blue, but as the very cornerstone of his proclamation, the reason for believing that Jesus was the Messiah, the reason for redrawing and revising his entire worldview?

Paul's own answer is of course obvious: he said it because he believed it. When he spoke of Jesus' resurrection, this was not a coded way for saying that he personally had had a dramatic new spiritual experience, or that he had glimpsed a new pathway of spiritual or psychological development. Nor was it a way of saying something like, 'The one God loves us even more than we thought.' It was a way of referring to something Paul believed had actually happened. What is more, the developments in his view of what 'resurrection' meant, developments from within the Jewish view but going to places where no Jew had gone before, indicate that he thought he knew something more about what resurrection was, something for which his tradition had not prepared him. Resurrection was now happening in two stages (first Jesus, then all his people); resurrection as a metaphor meant, not the restoration of Israel (though that comes in alongside in Romans 11), but the moral restoration of human beings; resurrection meant, not the victory of Israel over her enemies, but the Gentile mission in which all would be equal on the basis of faith; resurrection was not resuscitation, but transformation into a non-corruptible body. And the only explanation for these modifications is that they originated in what Paul believed had happened to Jesus himself.

This initial survey of Paul, leaving aside for the moment the two letters where some of the more contentious exegetical battles have taken place, is hugely important not only for our understanding of Paul but also, because he is our earliest witness, for our understanding of early Christianity as a whole. We must not, of course, make the mistake of thinking that Paul spoke for all other early Christians. He gives plenty of indications that this was not so. But however much he criticizes other teachers, however much he develops his own thought in his own way, he hardly ever has cause to disagree with anyone on the basic point that the Messiah had been raised from the dead.

All of which brings us at last to the correspondence Paul had with his beloved, muddled, infuriating – and, for our purposes, very informative – church in Corinth.

Chapter Six

RESURRECTION IN CORINTH (1):
INTRODUCTION

1. Introduction: The Problem

The resurrection – that of Jesus, and that of Jesus' people – dominates the Corinthian correspondence. Discussion of such a central topic inevitably becomes tangled in all kinds of other issues, some of which (the identification of parties and opponents in Corinth, for instance, and the question of whether 2 Corinthians is a single letter or a combination of two or more) are as complex and unresolved today as they were when critical scholarship first began to investigate them. Whole books have been written on 1 Corinthians 15 alone, and recent massive monographs and commentaries on the correspondence and matters relating to it all clamour for attention. The scope of the present project precludes the kind of detailed discussion one would ideally hope for. What must be tackled, though, is the question of the relationship between the two central passages, 1 Corinthians 15 and 2 Corinthians 4.7—5.10. Again and again it is said that a radical change took place between the first of these and the second; that Paul moved from a more or less typically Jewish view of resurrection in the first passage to a much more hellenistic, even Platonic, view in the second.[1]

These sections are not straightforward even in their own terms. First Corinthians 15 provides a long argument, one of the most sustained Pauline treatments of any topic, in the course of which Paul develops several images, and uses several technical terms, which are not found elsewhere. Some of these, particularly the phrase 'spiritual body' (*soma pneumatikon*) in 15.44–6, have become major storm centres in their own right, and at times it seems as though the entire worldview of an interpreter will hinge on how we understand, perhaps even translate, this single phrase. Chapters 4 and 5

---

[1] e.g. recently, Boismard 1999 [1995]. Boismard places these two sections in the two different main halves of his book, listing the first under 'the resurrection of the dead' and the second under 'the immortality of the soul'.

of 2 Corinthians likewise use language Paul does not employ elsewhere, some of which has regularly been controversial; all agree it is often misunderstood, but there is no agreement on which interpretation is to be preferred.

In order to provide as sure a route as possible to a historically justifiable understanding, we shall proceed as follows. First, in the present chapter, I shall look at the two letters more broadly, deliberately omitting the key sections. It will appear that 1 Corinthians 15 is not a detached treatment of the subject, stuck on near the end of the letter either because it was simply the last topic in a long line or because (as some have suggested, bizarrely in my view) early Christians tended to put 'eschatological' subjects towards the end of their writings.[2] On the contrary; the regular references to resurrection and cognate ideas throughout the letter strongly suggest that Paul regarded this topic as one of the keys to everything else he wanted to say, and had deliberately been saving it for the end, not because it was about 'the end' in that sense but because it was the unifying theme of this particular letter. Likewise, 2 Corinthians 4.7—5.10 is obviously far from being a detached discussion of death and resurrection as one topic among others. It comes at the heart of a longer section about the paradoxical nature of Paul's apostleship, which is itself the principal subject of the whole letter as we now have it. What Paul says here about suffering and death on the one hand, and future and present resurrection on the other, inform and enrich the entire work.

Because these passages are central to their respective letters, it might have seemed more appropriate to deal with them first. But because they are so controversial, it is preferable to approach them step by step by reading the other parts of each letter, with the question: what is Paul saying here about the resurrection, not least in relation to the questions we listed at the start of the previous chapter and have attempted to answer in relation to the rest of the Pauline corpus? If we can clear the ground in this way, the assault on the central passages in the two letters, and the relation between them, may then be more straightforward. That will be our task in the chapter that follows.

2. Resurrection in 1 Corinthians (apart from Chapter 15)

(i) Introduction

A glance through 1 Corinthians is like a stroll down a busy street. All of human life is there: squabbles and lawsuits, sex and shopping, rich and poor, worship and work, wisdom and folly, politics and religion. Some of the people we meet are puffed up with their own importance; others are being

---

[2] See e.g. Lüdemann 1994, 33, citing Mk. 13; 1 Thess. 4 and 5; *Did.* 16; *Barn.* 21.

squeezed to the edges of society. It is, in fact, like a stroll through the main streets, and the forum, of ancient Corinth itself.

The letter introduces us, in swift succession, to several topics of Christian discourse any one of which could generate many volumes of learned and complex discussion. The unity of the church; the wisdom of God; the nature of knowledge; the practice of holiness, not least in relation to sex; monotheism and idolatry; apostolic freedom and authority; sacramental faith and practice; spiritual gifts and their use. It is remarkable that this letter, though one of Paul's longest, is not twice as long as it is.

What place, within such a swirling catalogue of human life and Christian reflection, should be given to chapter 15 and the topic of the resurrection? Is this chapter just another in the list of puzzles presented to Paul by the Corinthians, whether by letter or in person? If so, this would be strange, in that it would be the only topic in the letter discussed in the abstract, as purely a *belief*, without immediate reference to practical matters in the church.[3] However central belief in the resurrection was, this still seems unlikely. Rather, we should expect to find a more organic connection between the topic of the resurrection – both Jesus' resurrection and that of his people – and the other topics covered in the letter.

A major proposal was made some years ago to address this: that the Corinthians held some form of over-realized eschatology, and were inclined to believe that they were already 'raised' in all the senses they ever needed to be.[4] This was then advanced to explain such passages as 4.8 ('Already you're filled! Already you're rich! Without us, you are kings!'), and several other parts of the text. Chapter 15 was written, according to this theory, to put the record straight, and to argue at length for a *future* resurrection which would show up the present posturing of the super-spiritual Corinthians as so much 'puffed-up' boasting. (Being 'puffed up' is a major theme of this letter; the word *physioo* occurs six times here, and only once in the rest of the New Testament.[5])

Despite the advocacy of A. C. Thiselton, the greatest contemporary commentator on 1 Corinthians, this theory is now increasingly abandoned. Many scholars have come round to the view argued by Richard Hays that the problem at Corinth was not too much eschatology but not nearly enough.[6] The Corinthians were attempting to produce a mixture of Christianity and paganism; their 'puffed-up' posturing came not from believing that a Jewish-style eschatology had already brought them to God's final future, but from putting together their beliefs about themselves as Christians with ideas

---

[3] We may discount the practical asides in 1 Cor. 15.29–34; these show no signs of being the main reason for the writing of the chapter.

[4] See esp. Thiselton 1978.

[5] 1 Cor. 4.6, 18, 19; 5.2; 8.1; 13.4. The other appearance is Col 2.18. Cf. too *physiosis* in 2 Cor. 12.20.

[6] Hays 1999.

from pagan philosophy, not least the kind of popular-level Stoicism which taught that all who truly understand the world and themselves are kings. Paul urgently wanted to teach them to think of themselves, corporately, individually and cosmically, in a more thoroughly Jewish fashion, in terms of the great Jewish stories of God, Israel and the world. Within this, he also had to address questions which emerged from the social and cultural tensions in a city like Corinth. Attempts to 'map' these tensions by plotting them on the grid of rich and poor on the one hand, and on various philosophical positions on the other, have not been notably successful.[7] There are too many variables, at least at the present stage of research, and it is too easy for contemporary social concerns to be read back into history. This does not excuse us, however, from remaining alert to the socio-cultural dimensions of all the issues Paul tackles.

The best way to work through these problems is to take the walk down the busy street, to move swiftly through the bustling chapters of the letter, and to see for ourselves the various elements that point forward towards the great chapter on resurrection.

(ii) 1 Corinthians 1—4: God's Wisdom, God's Power, God's Future

The introductory prayer of thanksgiving (1.4–9), as so often a good indicator of what is in Paul's mind, already locates the Corinthians in the now/not yet grid of characteristic Pauline eschatology. On the one hand, they are indeed 'enriched in every way' in the Messiah, not least in speech and knowledge (verse 5); but at the same time they are still 'eagerly awaiting the revelation of our lord Jesus the Messiah' (verse 7), the one who will strengthen them to keep them firm and blameless on 'the day of our lord Jesus the Messiah'. There is no question that they have already 'arrived'. The language of 'eager expectation' and 'the day of the lord' are of course familiar to us from our earlier survey of Paul.

Paul then introduces (1.10–17) the topic that will occupy him through to chapter 4: the problem of personality cults within the church ('I am of Paul', 'I am of Apollos', 'I am of Cephas', 'I am of Christ'). There is no agreement as to whether these divisions fell along specific theological or ethnic lines, and that is not how Paul addresses the question. The problem seems to have to do with 'wisdom'; there are some who are teaching a particular kind of wisdom, and whether rightly or wrongly they are claiming the backing of a particular leader in doing so. This wisdom is what enables some of them at least to feel that they have attained a superior level to ordinary people, perhaps to other Christians.

---

[7] The best of such attempts seems to me that of Winter 2001.

Paul's way of dealing with this, as with many things, is to go back to the foundation of the gospel, and in this case he highlights in particular the message about the Messiah's cross. God, he declares, has turned the world upside down, confounding expectations, making the wise look foolish and the powerful weak by means of his own 'foolishness' and 'weakness' which were embodied in the cross of the Messiah. This, he declares, is where the divine power truly resides. We should not suppose that Paul is here deliberately omitting mention of the resurrection. As we shall see in 15.3–4, cross and resurrection featured together at the heart of his message. But what the Corinthians needed to hear at the moment was the cross, the cross as the moment when the true god became weak and so overcame the powers of the world.

In the middle of it all is Paul's analysis, upon which the Corinthians' own status as Christians depended, of how their 'call' came about: the true god chose them and called them even when they were neither wise nor powerful nor noble (1.26–7), because that is his way; he is the god who chooses and calls 'the things that are not, so that he might abolish the things that are'. Our minds jump to the similar language in Romans 4.17, where this characteristic of the true god – again invoked to prevent human boasting – is tied closely with the divine power to give life to the dead. All that the Corinthians need, not just wisdom, but everything else too, they have in the Messiah. That is why, when Paul first visited them (2.1–5), he did not attempt to teach anything sophisticated, in case they thought the point of the gospel was to give them intellectual or cultural pretensions. In fact, it is designed as a showcase for the divine power; all human power, therefore, needs to be removed from the picture. That is the first lesson they need to learn.

They need to understand in particular that through the events of Jesus' death and resurrection there has burst upon the cosmos a new world order which, like the unveiling of a mystery, confronts the powers of the present world with the news that their time is up. Paul introduces here once more the Jewish idea of the two ages, the present age and the age to come, and he declares that 'the rulers of the present age' are doomed to perish, whereas the wisdom which belongs to the age to come, the wisdom now available in the gospel, will provide all that a mature Christian could want (2.6–8). There are things yet to be revealed, things which belong to the future when God's new age is fully revealed; at the moment they are only accessible through the Spirit. The 'wisdom' which the gospel unveils, the 'understanding' which Paul is eager to teach those who are mature enough for it, is about things which have only just begun to break upon the world; it is not a new way of organizing the concepts and wisdom-teaching of the present world. And, just as elsewhere we have seen that the Spirit is the one who brings God's future into the present, the 'guarantee' or 'first-fruits' of what is still to come, so here the Spirit is the one who makes known in the present the secrets of the future (2.9–13).

Who then is able to receive such teaching, such wisdom? The mature (*teleioi*, 2.6); the 'spiritual' (*pneumatikoi*, 2.13). This leads Paul to the fundamental contrast between two different types of people, a contrast which points all the way ahead to the central contrast between the two different types of 'body' in chapter 15: the 'spiritual' and the 'soulish', the *pneumatikos* and the *psychikos*. (I translate *psychikos* as 'soulish' because it is derived from *psyche*, 'soul', and though both the noun and the adjective became technical terms of hellenistic anthropology they retained a close link.) There is a third category as well, but we had better stop and ponder these two, set out at the end of chapter 2, before we go further:

> [14]The soulish person does not receive the things of God's Spirit; for they are folly to such people, and they cannot know them because they are to be discerned spiritually. [15]The spiritual person calls everything to account, but is not called to account by anyone. [16]For 'who has known the mind of the lord, so as to instruct him?' But we have the mind of the Messiah.

The context for the distinction has already been established: the overlap of the 'two ages' (2.6–8). The 'soulish' person, it seems, is one whose life is determined by the 'present age', animated merely by the ordinary 'soul' (*psyche*) that everyone has.[8] The Spirit is the gift of the creator god, coming from the future where the divine plan for the complete new age is already secure (having been made secure, as we shall learn, through the resurrection of Jesus the Messiah); and the Spirit is breaking into 'the present age' which still rumbles on, unaware that the future has decisively invaded it. The 'spiritual' person is the one in whose heart and mind the living god has worked by the Spirit so that he or she understands the strange new truths of the strange new age, and can see into the mystery, the wisdom, which Paul longs to impart. The contrast is sharpened in verse 16: Isaiah 40.13 declares that nobody in the present age could guess what YHWH had in mind, but Paul responds that those whose minds are illuminated by the gospel know 'the mind of the Messiah'. This, by implication, refers to the divine plans, laid up in the Messiah, already unveiled in the gospel but still to be implemented.

The distinction between *psyche* and *pneuma*, then, cannot simply be read off the surface of a lexicon of ancient Greek (still less, for that matter, in terms of what the words 'soul' and 'spirit' mean to an average reader in the modern western world). Paul is defining his terms as he goes along, and the critical grid of definition is the eschatological one. The *psyche* is not to be

---

[8] The translation 'unspiritual' for *psychikos* in e.g. NRSV is misleading. Paul is defining people here not in terms of what they are not, but in terms of what they are. This is cognate with the later struggles of the RSV/NRSV on the word; see below.

thought of as the Platonic immortal soul, the 'real' part of an otherwise unfortunately 'material' human being, the part that will last, will gloriously survive the longed-for death of the corruptible body, and will then fly free to the Isles of the Blessed or wherever.[9] Rather, by *psyche* here Paul basically means what the Hebrew *nephesh* regularly meant: the whole human being *seen from the point of view of one's inner life*, that mixture of feeling, understanding, imagination, thought and emotion which are in fact bound up with the life of the body and mind but which are neither in themselves obviously physical effects nor necessarily the result, or the cause, of mental processes. Just as, for Paul, *soma* is the whole person seen in terms of public, space-time presence, and *sarx* is the whole person seen in terms of corruptibility and perhaps rebellion, so *psyche* is the whole person seen in terms of, and from the perspective of, what we loosely call the 'inner' life. And Paul's point is that this person, this *psychikos*, 'soulish', person, still belongs in the present age, deaf to the music of the age to come. Here (2.11) and elsewhere Paul can use the word *pneuma* to refer to the human 'spirit', by which he seems to mean almost what he sometimes means by *kardia*, 'heart', the very centre of the personality and the point where one stands on the threshhold of encounter with the true god. But when he describes someone as 'spiritual' (*pneumatikos*) he does not simply mean that they are more in touch with their own 'spirit' than the 'soulish' person is, but that the Spirit of the living god has opened their hearts and minds to receive, and be changed by, truth and power from the age to come.

This has now set the terms for the topic Paul wishes to address in particular, the personality cults he described briefly in 1.10–13. The attitudes the Corinthians have adopted reveal that they are not simply *psychikoi* as opposed to *pneumatikoi*; they are 'fleshly', *sarkinoi* or perhaps *sarkikoi*. Here is a sub-puzzle within Paul's language; strictly, the Greek forms ending in *-nos* refer to *the material of which something is composed*, while the forms ending in *-kos* are either ethical or functional, and refer to *the sphere within which it belongs* or *the power which animates it*.[10] There are good reasons to suppose that this distinction (which is in any case a subtle one) was not regularly observed in Paul's day; among these reasons is the fact that almost every occurrence of either word in Paul has manuscript evidence for scribes changing it to the other one.[11] Though a case can be made for Paul's preserving the distinction in at least some instances, the present passage, which switches (in the best manuscripts) from *sarkinos* in 3.1 to *sarkikos* (twice) in 3.3, provides a clear enough indication that the terms are virtually identical in his mind.

[9] See above, ch. 2, e.g. 50.
[10] See ch. 7 below, 347–56, on 1 Cor. 15.42–9.
[11] See the evidence set out in BDAG 914, and esp. Parsons 1988. The use of the key terms in 1 Cor. 15 will be discussed in the next chapter.

Having set that puzzle aside, we can proceed to the main one: are there then three different types of people, the *pneumatikoi*, the *psychikoi* and the *sarkikoi*? I think not.[12] The 'soulish' and the 'fleshly' are both what Paul describes as 'ordinary human' people, people simply living in the present age and by its values, as opposed to those who are living by the inbreaking age to come. *Psychikos* describes such people in terms of their being animated by ordinary human life; *sarkikos* describes the same people in terms of 'flesh', *sarx*, which does not simply mean 'physical substance', as so often in contemporary English, but rather, as always in Paul, corruptible physicality on the one hand and rebellious creation on the other, the two often being elided. Paul's basic charge against the Corinthians is that as long as they are squabbling over personalities and different teachers they are showing all too clearly that they are not only not *pneumatikoi*; they are positively fleshly, corruptible and rebellious human beings, with no smell of the divine future about them at all. The fundamental contrast of the present age and the future one, and the kind of human existence and behaviour that belong to each, is of the utmost importance in understanding chapter 15. So is a clear understanding of the language Paul uses to describe the whole situation.

After his opening rebuke (3.1–4), Paul proceeds to describe how his work and that of Apollos fit together in the plan and calling of the true god (3.5–9). The Corinthians need to think in terms not of personalities, but of the overall divine project, how it is going forward, and how different gifts contribute to that. The builder cannot claim credit over the architect because the builder produces a house while all the architect produces is drawings. Paul seems to be responding to the charge that his teaching had been very basic, whereas Apollos' had been more intellectually stimulating. That, he says, is what you should expect when one person lays a foundation (which then remains out of sight and mind) and someone else builds an exciting building on top of it. But the critical point again has to do with eschatology. Founder and builder alike must recognize that there is coming a day (Paul has already mentioned it, we recall, in 1.8) when the work of building will be judged (3.10–15). On that day, some work will be burnt up, while other work will last. The image of fire sweeping through a great building, with some parts going up in smoke and other parts remaining solid, enables Paul to speak vividly of continuity and discontinuity between the present age and the age to come:

---

[12] The closest we might get to a clear differentiation, in my judgment, is that offered by Schweizer in *TDNT* 9.663: the unbeliever is *psychikos*, i.e. merely living an ordinary human life, whereas a Christian who is 'making no progress' or is 'exclusively set on what is earthly' is *sarkikos*. This is possible, but it is not clear to me that Paul uses the terms with that precision.

¹²Now if anyone builds on the foundation with gold, silver, precious stones, wood, hay, straw – ¹³each one's work will become obvious, because the day will disclose it, since it will be revealed in fire; and the fire will test everyone's work, to see what sort it is. ¹⁴If someone's work, that they have built, stands the test, they will receive a reward. ¹⁵But if someone's work is burned up, they will suffer loss. They themselves will be saved, though, but only in such a way as through a fire.

This is, clearly, a fairly similar picture to the one sketched in some of Paul's other great judgment scenes, such as those in 2 Thessalonians 2 and Romans 2. The idea of a coming day of worldwide judgment is of course familiar from passages like Romans 14.10 and 2 Corinthians 5.10. But nowhere else do we have such a strong sense of the continuity, across the moment of fiery judgment, between the work done in the present and the new world that the creator god intends to make. Well-built houses, says Paul, will *last*; they will, in other words, be part of the coming world the creator intends. Good, faithful apostolic work, whether in foundation-laying or in building, will last; that is what matters, not the apparent brilliance or dullness of the teaching involved. Once again, Paul is longing for the Corinthians to understand themselves, the church and the work of their teachers within an eschatological narrative, a story which runs from the present age to the age to come, with church and apostle alike poised in the tense overlap between the two.

This continuity gives specific focus to several aspects of 1 Corinthians, leading in the end to what would otherwise be a non sequitur at the end of chapter 15: because of the *future* resurrection, get on with your work in the *present* (15.58)! Paul believes that with the resurrection of the Messiah the new world has already begun; that the Spirit comes from that future into the present, to shape, prepare and enable people and churches for that future; and the work done in the power of the Spirit in the present will therefore last into the future. This is none other than the pattern of resurrection as we have seen it articulated throughout the other letters.

The point is made sharper in 3.16–17 by Paul's invoking of the Temple-image: you (plural) are the Temple of the true god, and his Spirit dwells in you, as the Shekinah dwelt in the Jerusalem Temple. The Temple, of course, is therefore holy. If anyone destroys it – as, by implication, factional bickering and personality-cults are destroying it, pulling down the fabric of the community's life – they face the threat of being themselves destroyed in the divine judgment. But, behind this threat, we should also hear a promise, to which we have alluded in discussing Romans 8.1–11: the gospel-project is (from one point of view) about building the new Temple, the long-awaited eschatological dwelling-place for the divine name among all the nations, and this project will be completed precisely through the resurrection. The chapter then closes with another contrast between the wisdom of the present age and the glories of the world to come, which already belong to Christians because they belong to the Messiah (3.18–23).

Chapter 4 rounds off the discussion of wisdom and of personalities, once again placing the question within the context of eschatological judgment (4.1–5). You are judging me, Paul implies, but the only judgment that counts is the one that will come on the last day, and I am happy to face that. What the Corinthians need is a strong dose, in other words, of what Paul will set out in 15.20–28: the coming day when the kingdom of the Messiah will be complete, when all that opposes the true god has been defeated, when this god is seen at last to be God, when he is 'all in all'. If they learn to see Paul and Apollos (and no doubt others as well) in this light, they will realize that their posturing, their puffing-up of themselves, are simply a way of reinforcing their standing within the present age, while Paul's apostolic labours and the hardships he endures are a sign that he is living at the point where the two ages, the present and the future, overlap and grind together like millstones. His appeal in 4.8–13 is thus making more or less the same point as the interlude (verses 29–34) in the middle of chapter 15.[13] Meanwhile (4.14–21), Paul's own threatened return to Corinth will provide a sudden bit of realized eschatology: apostolic judgment, anticipating the final Day. God's kingdom depends, he says, not on talk but on power (4.20), and when Paul speaks of power he regularly has the resurrection (or sometimes the cross, as in chapter 1) in mind.

The long opening section of the letter (nearly as long as Philippians or Colossians in their entirety) is thus shot through with Paul's desire to teach the Corinthians to think eschatologically; more specifically, to get them to understand the present time not simply as a moment to preen and pride themselves on how clever they are, or how the new teaching they have received will distinguish them socially or culturally, but as the moment at which the new age is breaking in to the present evil age, and in which therefore what they need is not merely human wisdom but the wisdom from above. They need, in short, to be *pneumatikoi* rather than *psychikoi*, still less *sarkinoi* or *sarkikoi*: they need to be energized by the divine Spirit so that they live in the present age in the light, and by the standards, of the age to come. We should not be surprised that a letter which opens with this argument should close with a full-scale treatment of the resurrection, or that its key language about the resurrection body will focus on the distinction between the *soma psychikon* and the *soma pneumatikon*.

(iii) 1 Corinthians 5—6: Sex, Lawyers and Judgment

Paul now turns to the next set of specific issues that have been raised by the people from Corinth who have come to see him in Ephesus. There is a case of incest in the church, a man living with his stepmother; and Christians are

---

[13] See below, 338–40.

going to law against one another before the regular pagan courts. Both of these fill Paul with horror and dismay; have the Corinthians taken leave of their senses? What they need to understand once more is the reality of divine judgment. They need to bring that future judgment into the present, exercising discipline over those whose lives display the features of pagan, or in this case worse than pagan, immorality. (Presumably the person guilty of incest, and the church as a whole looking on, had assumed that all normal social mores could be suspended now that they were Christians.) Paul's response is not difficult to analyse. Christians must not compromise with the present world; they must live in the light of the future one. He thus sketches out the Christian version of a Jewish eschatological framework.

This involves judgment: the future judgment at 'the day of the lord' (5.5, 13a), and the judgment that the community itself must exercise in disciplining the offender (5.3–5). They must use Paul's own apostolic authority to implement this judgment, and must banish the man from Christian fellowship (this is presumably what is meant by 'delivering to the satan' in verse 5) so that his 'flesh' may be 'destroyed' and his 'spirit' may be 'saved'. This does not mean simply that Paul envisages the man dying physically and then enjoying a non-physical salvation, as a hasty and anachronistic reading might suggest. It sets *present* judgment by the community in relation to *future* judgment on the day of the lord, and employs the 'flesh/spirit' contrast to sum up quickly the difference between the corruptible and rebellious human nature and the God-given life which, Paul assumes, the man does indeed possess, even though he is not letting it work through to his behaviour. If what ought to be the final judgment can be brought forward into the present, there will be a chance of the offender then coming to repentance and so, instead, being rescued. There are echoes of 3.12–15 here too; a judgment is coming in which the work of some people will be burnt up, though they themselves may still be saved.

The heart of Paul's analysis and critique, though, is what we might call 'messianic Judaism', in other words, the Jewish-style controlling story, redefined through Jesus the Messiah; this is the story the Corinthians ought to be telling themselves about who they are and how their lives should be shaped. Becoming Christians does not simply free them from the constraints of their previous lives in order to leave them in a moral, or even narratival, vacuum. It weaves them into a new grand narrative, which Paul describes as explicitly *paschal*: the Messiah, as our true Passover lamb, has been sacrificed, and we must celebrate this feast, not by behaving in a pagan fashion, but with the moral standards for which the 'unleavened bread' of a Passover celebration provides a good (though otherwise unexplained) metaphor. Chapter 5 ends with another warning that the church must judge members who are behaving in ways that are inconsistent with the gospel. Thus far Paul has not explained the basis for the standards of verses 9–11, but from the other letters it is clear that he is thinking of the renewal of humanity in Christ, a renewal which these practices would jeopardize.

Judgment is once again at issue in chapter 6, this time because the church is committing a theological solecism: going to law before unbelievers. Once again Paul's response is that they have not been thinking in terms of the Christian eschatological hope, in other words, the Jewish apocalyptic hope reshaped around Jesus the Messiah. Do you not know, he says (most readers today will reply 'No!') that the saints will judge the world, and that we are to judge angels (6.2–3)? This remarkable statement is based on Paul's vivid awareness of texts like Daniel 7, in which 'the people of the saints of the Most High' are given authority to execute judgment over the beasts, and to rule the nations. He would have been quick to insist that Jesus himself was the ultimate judge, but he assumes a basic early Christian theology in which this judgment is *shared* with all Jesus' people. Once again he draws conclusions about the *present* from what will be true in the *future*: this is how things *will* be, so this is how they *must now* be. Learn to think in terms of the world that is to be, he is saying, and of the people you will be within it, and then you will see clearly who you must be in the present time. If you do that, you will see that there can be no place for Christians to go to law with one another in front of non-Christian courts. Paul does not suggest that every single Christian will be capable of exercising a judicial role in the present, but he assumes that within even a small community, such as we assume the Corinthian church to have been, there will be some who are 'wise enough' to exercise this function. At all events, the eschatological reality (that God's people will share in bringing his judgment to the world) must be brought forward into the present. If, for whatever reason, that is not possible, it would be better to suffer wrong than to turn that reality on its head and have secular courts sitting in judgment on Christians.

Paul then returns to the wider issue of Christian morality, particularly sexual behaviour, and within that more specifically to prostitution (6.9–20). What counts here, he says, is 'inheriting the kingdom of God' (verse 9, 10). Paul does not often use this phrase, but when he does it mostly refers (not indeed to a place where the righteous go when they die, but) to the final 'kingdom' that will come when the Messiah has finished his work of bringing all the enemies of the true god and his good creation into subjection (15.24–8). The two references here look on to that passage, and also to 15.50 ('flesh and blood cannot inherit the kingdom of God'), where Paul advances essentially the same argument as here: 'corruptible things cannot inherit incorruptible'; 'God will destroy both stomach and food' (15.50b; 6.13b).[14]

---

[14] cf. too Gal. 5.21; Eph. 5.5. Paul can refer to God's kingdom as a present reality, as in e.g. Rom. 14.17; 1 Cor. 4.20; Col. 1.13; 4.11; other 'future' refs. include 1 Thess. 2.12; 2 Thess. 1.5; 2 Tim. 4.1; 4.18.

In particular, the argument of 6.12–20 depends on Paul's belief that what is done with the present body matters precisely because it is to be raised.[15] The continuity between the present body and the future resurrection body is what gives weight to the present ethical imperative:

> [13b]The body is not meant for immorality but for the lord, and the lord for the body. [14]God both raised the lord, and will also raise us through his power. [15]Do you not know that your bodies are members of the Messiah? Shall I therefore take the Messiah's members and make them members of a prostitute? Certainly not! [16]Or don't you know that anyone who joins himself to a prostitute becomes one body? For scripture says 'the two shall become one flesh'. [17]But the one who joins himself to the lord becomes one spirit [with him].

Verse 14 is the key. The emphasis of the Greek, hard to bring out in English, is as crucial here as in chapter 15: the 'both . . . and . . .' joins together the resurrection of Jesus and that of believers, both of them accomplished (as usual in Paul) by the divine power (*dynamis*). Clearly Paul assumes that the body – the same body which can be abused in immoral behaviour – is meant 'for the lord'; this refers, it seems, (a) to the eventual union with the Messiah, anticipated in baptism, which will take place in the resurrection, and also (b) to the service to the Messiah which is supposed to take place (as in Romans 6.12–14; 12.1–2) during the present time. Indeed, Romans 6.13 and 19 provide a close parallel to the idea of the 'members': they are parts of the body which can be used for the wrong purpose, or can be used in the service of the Messiah. In particular, Paul suggests, on the basis of Genesis 2.24, that union with a prostitute is inappropriate because it links one's 'members' with part of the pagan culture.

Bewilderingly at this point, granted all that has been said above about his anthropological terms, Paul first declares that sex with a prostitute results in becoming 'one *body*', on the basis of a scriptural text that speaks of being 'one *flesh*', and then parries the suggestion of behaving in this way by saying that Christians become one *spirit* with the Messiah. As in 5.5, there seems to be an underlying flesh/spirit antithesis in Paul's mind, which explains the rhetorical force of the last contrast. And the fact that he has said in verse 13 that the body and the lord are meant for one another – in a setting where 'body' clearly means the same body which could be used for sexual immorality – shows that he is not thinking, when he says 'one spirit' (verse 17), of a relationship which a Platonically minded reader would envisage as 'purely spiritual'. We may compare 7.34, where Paul can speak of the call to be holy 'in body and spirit'. He would never say 'in flesh'; the only way 'flesh' (in his terminology) can be holy is by being put to death.

Paul's train of thought may be explained as follows. When writing verse 16a (sex with a prostitute means becoming 'one body'), he was still thinking

---

[15] This is O'Donovan's point (1986, 13–15): 'Christian ethics depends upon the resurrection of Jesus Christ from the dead.' See the discussion of continuity in Thrall 2002.

of what he had been saying in verses 13b–15, where the body and the members were the main subject. Then, having proved his point with the Genesis quotation which spoke of 'flesh', he naturally looked for the main antithesis which 'flesh' would suggest, and so wrote 'spirit'. This has produced some surface-level jostling of anthropological language, precisely because he wants to speak about the continuity between the present physical body, the self-same body which is abused if allowed to indulge in sexual immorality, and the future body which is meant for the lord, and to show the wrongness of such abuse by means of the contrast of 'flesh' and 'spirit'. The continuity between the present bodily life and the future bodily resurrection means that what Christians presently do with their bodies matters, matters eschatologically. There is that about the body which will be destroyed (verse 13a): in the non-corruptible future world, food and the stomach are presumably irrelevant. So, for that matter (since food and stomach point metaphorically here to sexual behaviour and sexual organs[16]) will human reproduction be irrelevant.[17] Paul is again treading a fine line here, since he wants to say simultaneously *both* that the creator will destroy the bits of the body which are being touted by some in Corinth as theirs to do what they like with, *and* that there is bodily continuity between the present person, behaving this way or that, and the person who will be raised to new bodily life. It might be possible to say that 'God will destroy' is a warning about destructive judgment for those who go this route, and who will therefore not experience the resurrection to life; but this is not strictly necessary for his argument to work, since 'body', as we have said before, refers to the whole person seen from the point of view of space, time and matter. The central point, which is then powerfully reinforced by chapter 15, is that the future resurrection, based and modelled on the past resurrection of Jesus, means that present bodily behaviour matters in the future kingdom.[18]

The close of the chapter returns to the Temple-image (6.18–20), this time in an individual sense (the 'your' is plural, but the sense is clearly to be applied to each Christian individually). The body is a Temple of the Holy Spirit; you were bought with a price, so glorify God in your body. This again looks on to the future for which the Spirit is the guarantee: God has purchased the whole person, presumably in the 'redemption' which took place through the Messiah's death.[19] God intends to make good that purchase in the future, and this will come about as the body, already in the present, becomes a place where the living God is glorified, so that the promised glory of the final resurrection will be the appropriate consummation of what is already true in the present.

---

[16] cf. e.g. Hays 1997, 103.

[17] cf. the discussion between Jesus and the Sadducees (below, ch. 9).

[18] So, rightly, Perkins 1984, 268f.

[19] cf. 1 Cor. 7.23; Gal. 4.5.

(iv) 1 Corinthians 7: Marriage

It might be supposed that Paul's argument in 6.16 proved too much. What will happen to the eschatological union with the Messiah when husband and wife become 'one flesh'? If such a question had crossed Paul's mind, he would probably have answered that the point about prostitution is that it is part and parcel of the culture of paganism. Many pagan temples kept prostitutes on the staff as part of the cult, and conversely many prostitutes would hang around pagan temples as a place where likely customers, at the end of a drunken meal, would be ready for their services.

In any case, the next chapter, the first to address the concerns about which the church had written to him (7.1), deals directly with matters to do with marriage. Most of the argument does not concern us, though if there were space for wider reflection it would be interesting to ponder the fact that to allow, let alone to advocate, celibacy under some conditions at least represented a radical break with Judaism, which may well itself be related to Paul's eschatological beliefs, based of course on the resurrection of Jesus (and perhaps also on his teaching and example). Only at one point in the chapter does Paul suddenly invoke what has seemed to many an eschatological timetable, speaking of the present time as *synestalmenos*, 'constrained' (7.29). It is a time, he says, in which people should live as though they were not involved with the world, because everything is due for radical change; those who are married should live as if they were not, those who mourn or celebrate as if they were not doing so, and so on – 'for the form of this world is passing away' (*paragei gar to schema tou kosmou toutou*) (7.29–31). This has regularly been seen as an indication that Paul envisaged the second coming of the Messiah very soon, so soon that there was no point in giving oneself to the ordinary concerns of life.

This view has, though, received stiff challenges in the last generation, not least from historians who have studied Corinth in the mid-50s. It seems far more likely that Paul was referring to the present time as a time of great famine and hardship throughout the Aegean world, when, according to the records, many suffered greatly. That is what he means by the present time being 'a time of great distress'.[20] However, to say that 'the form of this world is passing away' does have the ring of 2.6 about it (the rulers of this world being doomed to perish). Behind the present distress, the immediate constraining circumstances in which it is better not to engage in new domestic projects, Paul sees the larger truth: the present world, with all its natural life (including marriage and reproduction), is due to be replaced by the new world which has already begun through Jesus and his resurrection.

[20] Winter 2001, 216–25.

(v) 1 Corinthians 8—10: Idols, Food, Monotheism and Apostolic Freedom

The next subject raised by the Corinthians is that of meat offered to idols – in other words, almost all meat on sale in a city like Corinth where idol temples doubled as butchers' shops and restaurants.[21] The three chapters devoted to this topic contain a middle section that looks irrelevant but turns out to contain a point which will prove to be crucial in the final argument. Thus: chapter 8 sets up the problem, and provides a basic rule of thumb to be going on with; chapter 9 appears to be about something else, namely Paul's practice as an apostle, but turns out to be about the 'freedom' to which he is entitled, but which he regularly renounces for the sake of the gospel; and chapter 10 then draws the moral, applying the example of chapter 9 to the question of chapter 8. The way to address the problem of food offered to idols is to recognize where you belong in the eschatological narrative, the Jewish story of the creator's good world and of how it has been redeemed by the Messiah. Through that story you must learn how to regulate your apparent rights and freedoms with the overarching responsibilities that are yours because of who and what you are in the Messiah.

At each point Paul makes use of arguments relevant to our present topic. At the heart of the question he faces in chapter 8 is the challenge posed for Jewish-style monotheism by the world of pagan polytheism. Faced with full-scale, ubiquitous idolatry, in which (so it must sometimes have seemed) every part of the physical universe had been divinized, worshipped, invoked and served – with, from the Jewish point of view, devastatingly dehumanizing results – it would have been easy for a Jew with a tender conscience to retreat from the world altogether into a 'safe' sphere beyond the reach of contamination. If that meant eating no meat at all, in the absence of a kosher butcher, and in a city where an innocent-looking market stall would contain meat that had all been offered in sacrifice to some god or other, that was the route many Jews would take. And, since Christianity was essentially a kind of Judaism (and must always have seemed so to pagan eyes), worshipping the one true god, ignoring pagan temples, and so forth, it was natural that within the Christian community there would be those who would be inclined to retreat in just that way – not simply those who were themselves from a Jewish background, but also those ex-pagans who, sickened by their own environment and perhaps their own past, had embraced with relief a religion of holiness, purity and hope. Equally, there would be many Christians, like Paul himself, who would take a robust view of the created order and have no scruples of conscience about eating anything at all. How should the church cope with this?

---

[21] On 1 Cor. 8.1–6 in particular see Wright, *Climax*, ch. 6. For the context and social situation see Horsley 1998; Winter 2001.

Underneath Paul's nuanced answer lies, as I have hinted, his basic creational monotheism. It might be much 'safer' to retreat from the world; but it would imply that the one true god was not after all the creator of the present world, or equally that he was not intending to claim it as his own in a great act of new creation. Paul refuses to lapse into such dualism, which has so often been the shadow side of ordinary paganism. That is why, in 10.26, he quotes Psalm 24.1: the earth belongs to the lord, with all its fullness. But, as in Romans 14, his long pastoral experience tells him that not all consciences become re-educated at the same pace, and that it is far better to live with apparent anomaly than to force someone to act against their own conscience.[22] Respect for one another's consciences, and the consequent readiness to limit one's own freedoms and rights, are therefore the rules that 'strong' Christians must always be ready to follow; that is the conclusion from both 8.7–13 and 10.23—11.1. At the same time, Paul insists that Christians should never go into an idol temple itself (10.14–22). However, creational monotheism is the overall guiding light (10.25–6, 30), and it is precisely this that undergirds the theology of resurrection in chapter 15. The present created order is good, and – however much easier it might be to make moral judgments if things were otherwise – the creator intends to reaffirm it.

On the way to this conclusion, Paul insists in chapter 9 that as an apostle (one who has seen the risen lord, we note in 9.1, as opposed to almost all other Christians, who had not; see 15.5–11) he has certain rights which he has chosen not to use, at least in Corinth, so that the progress of the gospel may not be hindered. His basic reason for going into all this, as we noted, was to offer his own example of giving up rights for the sake of the gospel and one's fellow Christians; but, en route, he reveals some interesting points for our present purposes. He speaks in 9.11 of having sown *ta pneumatika*, spiritual things, and of it being quite appropriate, as a kind of *a fortiori* argument, that he should in principle reap *ta sarkika*, fleshly things. What he means here, as in Romans 15.27, is that rewards in cash or kind for preaching the gospel are thoroughly appropriate. More significantly, in the final paragraph of the chapter (9.24–7), he speaks of the difference between the perishable crown that an athlete covets when training and the imperishable one that he, Paul himself, is working towards – which is exactly the contrast he employs again in 15.42, 53 and 54. To this end, just as in 6.12–20, the body must be disciplined. Thus:

> [25]Everyone who competes in the games exercises self-control in all things. They do it so as to obtain a perishable crown, but we an imperishable. [26]So then, I do not run without a goal; I do not box like someone punching thin air; [27]I punish my body and bring it into slavery, in case, having heralded [the gospel] to others, I myself should be disqualified.

---

[22] See Wright, *Romans*, 730–43, where the differences as well as the similarities between that context and the present one are clarified.

The goal Paul has in view is clearly the resurrection. Elsewhere, when he speaks of obtaining a 'crown', it is more usually his churches, in their standing firm for the gospel; but the metaphor works just as well in this guise.[23] His goal is the newly embodied life promised in the resurrection. Bodily discipline in the present – saying 'No' even to some things to which one might have a right – is a necessary part of the way to that goal.

The opening of chapter 10 is one of Paul's classic retellings of the story of Israel, designed to explain to his mostly ex-pagan hearers the narrative world they ought to be living in. The people of Israel had been rescued from Egypt at Passover. They were wandering through the wilderness on their way to receive their inheritance. Paul sets this story both in parallel and in sequence with the story he believes the church to be living in. In parallel: the original Passover experience has been recapitulated in the messianic events of Jesus' death and resurrection (5.7); the Christian baptism and eucharist recapitulate the crossing of the Red Sea and the miraculous wilderness feedings (which he describes as *pneumatikos*, 'spiritual' food and 'spiritual' drink); Christians are bound to be tempted as the Israelites were tempted, but they must succeed where the Israelites failed. In sequence: the original exodus was an earlier moment in the story of which Jesus the Messiah was and is the climax, and the church the current product; the Israelites were God's people 'according to the flesh' (10.18, obscured in many translations), but the new community is now a worldwide family composed of people from many origins, and must now live out their new identity before the watching world of Jews and Greeks alike (10.32).

None of this has direct bearing on chapter 15, except in this broad but important sense: Paul is here in the same world of thought as he was in Romans 8, where, in another retelling of the exodus story, the 'inheritance' was the whole redeemed creation. His attempt to teach the Corinthians to think of themselves within the narrative of creation and covenant, promise and fulfilment, exodus, wilderness and inheritance, is part of the same strategy we see in chapter 15. He wants them to tell the story of the creator and the world in a thoroughly Jewish way, albeit now with Jesus in the middle of it, and to locate themselves accurately on that map.

(vi) 1 Corinthians 11—14: Worship and Love

The next problem concerns the eucharist. Paul addressed this question in the same way he had addressed the others: by telling the story again in such a way as to show them where they belonged within it (11.17–34). The main difficulty seems to have been the accentuation (instead of the abolition) of

---

[23] cf. Phil. 4.1; 1 Thess. 2.19; 2 Tim. 2.5; 4.8.

social divisions when celebrating the lord's meal.[24] Paul retells the narrative of institution, emphasizing that the cup signifies 'the new covenant' in the Messiah's blood. This is where the exodus story of the previous chapter opens up more explicitly, in narrative sequence: the Jew/Gentile church formed around the Messiah and his death and resurrection is the beneficiary of the long-awaited 'new covenant'. And this covenant, like so much in Paul, partakes of the now/not-yet eschatological tension: 'as often as you eat this bread and drink this cup, you announce the lord's death until he comes' (11.26). The eucharist is thus another bridge between past, present and future; the central actions of the meal look back to the crucifixion and on to the day of Jesus' return, as in 15.23–4. The church's worship, Paul is saying, must constantly have in mind the time-frame within which it is set, otherwise it will collapse into mere social posturing.

The theme of the body, often vital in this letter, comes into its own in chapter 12 with one of Paul's greatest metaphors. When he develops his picture of the church as the body of the Messiah, he seems to be aware that this is not a metaphor chosen at random. As he says at several points elsewhere in his letters, and will emphasize particularly in chapter 15, what the creator god has accomplished in and through Jesus is the renewal of the human race, that for which humankind was made in the first place. What better image, then, to use for its corporate life than that of a human body, with limbs and organs working as they were meant to do? The present unity of the church is important not least because it will thereby anticipate the perfect harmony of the resurrection world, when members of the *soma Christou*, the Messiah's body, who have each exercised their *pneumatika*, spiritual gifts, are finally raised to life, to be given the *soma pneumatikon* (15.44–6), the entire body energized and animated by the divine Spirit.

Paul introduces the chapter – another topic, it seems, which the Corinthians had raised – with the key term *pneumatikos*, now used as a noun, 'spiritual things'. The meaning here is clearly 'spiritual gifts', though he simply says *pneumatika*, without a separate word for 'gifts'.[25] Here is the irony of 1 Corinthians: that the church had all the 'spiritual things' anyone could want, and yet were themselves in danger of failing to be genuinely *pneumatikoi*, as chapters 2 and 3 warned. These 'spiritual gifts', however, are not of the same order as the quality and character he was there commending; tongues, prophecy and the like will not be needed in the age to come (13.8–10), even though they may serve in the present time as messengers from the future world the creator has in mind. Nevertheless, the basis of the church's unity – the fact that it is the same Spirit, the same lord,

---

[24] cf. e.g. Thiselton 2000, 848–53.

[25] The regular term 'spiritual gifts' in theological discussion comes from the word *charismata* (1 Cor. 12.4, 9, 28, 30, 31; also 1 Cor. 1.7; Rom. 12.6). Paul uses this word in different senses in 1 Cor. 7.7, and in Rom. 1.11; 5.15f.; 6.23; 11.29.

the same god 'who works all in all' (12.6) – looks on once more to chapter 15, where the end of the whole story is that this god, the creator and lord of history and the world, will eventually be 'all in all' (15.28).

In between the long and involved chapters 12 and 14, like the slow movement in a concerto, stands the short and deeply poetic chapter 13. So often read at weddings, it has not often been heard as what it is, namely, a poem about the now/not-yet tension of Christian living, and the way in which love, *agape*, is not so much a virtue to be worked at, though it is surely that as well, as the ultimate bridge, in terms of human character, from present Christian living into the future kingdom. Many things do not last; love does:

> [8]Love never fails; but if there are prophecies, they will be abolished; if there are tongues, they will fall silent; if there is knowledge, it will be abolished. [9]For we know only partially, and we prophesy only partially; [10]but when the complete has arrived, the partial will be abolished.
> [11]When I was a child, I spoke like a child, I thought like a child, I reasoned like a child; but when I grew up, I did away with childish things. [12]For in the present time we are looking at puzzling reflections in a mirror, but then we shall see face to face; in the present time I know partially, but then I shall know in the same way that I am also known. [13]So now these three things last: faith, hope and love; but the greatest of these is love.

Love is what will hold the church together when various pressures threaten to pull the Messiah's body apart – when those with different gifts, or enthusiasm for a particular teacher, or a sense of their own rights and a disregard for other people's conscience, or a failure to recognize those of different social standing as equal at the lord's table, seem to want to go their own way. This chapter has a claim, alongside chapter 15, to be considered the real heart of the letter. If the church can only grasp this, it will solve at least half the problems Paul has been grappling with. And yet even this exquisite chapter looks forward, particularly in the section just quoted, to the final discussion, which will concern the resurrection, the new world that God will make, *and the continuity between the resurrection life and life here and now.* The point of 13.8–13 is that the church must be working *in the present* on the things that will last *into God's future.* Faith, hope and love will do this; prophecy, tongues and knowledge, so highly prized in Corinth, will not. They are merely signposts to the future; when you arrive, you no longer need signposts. Love, however, is not just a signpost. It is a foretaste of the ultimate reality. Love is not merely the Christian duty; it is the Christian destiny. To hold the Corinthian church together, Paul needs to teach them love; but to teach them love he needs to teach them eschatology.[26] All the lines of the letter, therefore, are now pointing towards chapter 15.

---

[26] cf. O'Donovan 1986, ch. 12; e.g. 246: 'love, the form of the moral life, is grouped, not with the spiritual gifts, which have their own intelligibility, but with faith and hope which depend for intelligibility upon the end of history.'

The long argument for order and discipline in worship (chapter 14) stands under this rubric as well. This, too, is ultimately a new-creation theology, for 'God is not a god of disorder, but of peace' (14.33).

The final chapter of the letter adds its own small hints: 16.2 instructs the church to use the first day of the week as the time to set aside money for the collection. Already by the mid-50s Sunday, the lord's day,[27] was being kept by the church as the day for worship and the transaction of the church's business, and the obvious significance of this will be explored later. The standard exhortation of 16.13–14 ('keep watch, stand firm in the faith, be courageous, be strong; let everything you do be done in love') draws together typical themes from eschatological exhortation, appropriate for those who, as in 1 Thessalonians 5.1–11 or Romans 13.11–14, find themselves living as day-people while the night passes away. And the final greetings of the letter contain the invocation which, for all its opaque linguistic history, places the emphasis where Paul knew it had to be placed when he faced a church all too inclined to live in the present, to collapse eschatology back into pagan philosophy, to live for themselves rather than for their coming lord: 'Maranatha! Our lord, come!' (16.22). Paul has lost no opportunity, throughout the letter, to stress to the Corinthians the vital importance of living in the present on the basis not only of the past events of the gospel but also of the future events which those past events guarantee. The resurrection of Jesus the Messiah, and the consequent resurrection of all his people on the day of his coming (15.23), are the themes which make sense of everything else he has been saying. We should not only not be surprised that 1 Corinthians 15 is what it is and where it is. We should also have a good idea, when we come to read it for itself, what sort of things Paul is likely to be saying in it.

3. Resurrection in 2 Corinthians (apart from 4.7—5.11)

(i) Introduction

The mood has changed. Reading the opening verses of 2 Corinthians straight after the earlier letter, we find ourselves like people revisiting a house the morning after a cheerful, boisterous family gathering, and discovering the atmosphere sombre, leaden and gloomy. Something has gone terribly wrong.

Paul is, of course, looking us in the eye and speaking of comfort and new life. That is the sort of person he is:

> [3]Blessed be the God and father of our lord Jesus, the Messiah – the father of all mercies and the God of all comfort! [4]He comforts us in all our suffering, so that we may have power to comfort those who are undergoing any kind of suffering, with the

[27] Rev. 1.10; cf. Ac. 20.7. See below, 579, 594.

comfort with which we ourselves are comforted by God. ⁵Just as the afflictions of
the Messiah are multiplied for us, you see, so our comfort is also multiplied through
the Messiah. ⁶If we suffer, it is for your comfort and salvation; if we are comforted,
it is for your comfort, which is at work as you undergo with patience the same sufferings that we are suffering. ⁷Our hope is firm on your behalf, knowing that as you
have shared our sufferings, so also you will share our comfort.

But his tone of voice, even his style of writing, indicates, before he so much
as mentions what has happened, that in the comparatively short interval
between the letters – a year or two at most – something has happened which
has changed him, and that he and the Corinthians have been through something that has changed their relationship. In both cases the changes have left
them, like the wedding guest in *The Ancient Mariner*, sadder and wiser. In
both cases the anchor that Paul has held on to, of which he will now speak,
is the resurrection.

The second letter to the Corinthians, like the earlier letter, is in a sense all
about resurrection. But Paul is now going to draw on the central gospel
events to mount a very different argument to meet a very different situation.
What precisely that situation was remains, tantalizingly, just out of reach of
scholarly enquiry.²⁸ Hypotheses dance before our eyes like mirages, but
when we walk up to them to test them against the texts, they melt away. The
letter has been divided up (different segments perhaps reflect different
moods, as Paul receives various messages from Corinth); or it has been put
back together again, with its shifts of mood and voice being after all little
different from, say, the transition between Romans 8 and Romans 9. Even
when in great pain, Paul remains a master of rhetoric.

Two things, however, may be said at a general level. The first is that Paul
has suffered enormously in Ephesus, in ways that Acts only hints at (the riot
in Acts 19 was probably only the surface noise; the story was written up, it
seems, to stress that the local magistrates decided there was no reason for
uproar, but it hides the deepest things Paul actually underwent). Paul does
not say what precisely had happened, but he tells the Corinthians the effect
that it had on him (in a deliberate and completely justifiable plea for personal sympathy): he was so utterly overwhelmed, beyond any capacity to
cope, that he despaired of life itself (1.8). He felt as though he had received
the sentence of death in himself (1.9). This language – internalizing a death-
sentence – sounds close to what we might call a nervous breakdown, and
certainly indicates severe depression. It was brought on, it seems, by the
combination of two things. First, Paul went through severe physical suffering, almost certainly imprisonment (there is no concrete evidence of an
Ephesian imprisonment, but this hypothesis at least seems less of a mirage
the closer we get to it) and quite possibly torture and deprivation of food or

²⁸ See the recent full treatment in Thrall 1994–2000, 49–77.

sleep. Second, he was plunged into despair over the steep decline in his relationship with the Corinthian church itself.

This is the second general thing that must be said: that after writing 1 Corinthians, with its strict instructions in chapter 5 about discipline, including the command to expel at least one person from the church, Paul paid a surprise visit to Corinth, and discovered that (from his point of view) things were not as they should be. (We may assume that he went by sea across the Aegean; from Ephesus to Corinth was a short and much-travelled route, a hellenic maritime corridor roughly equivalent in frequency of travel to the flight path from New York to Chicago, or the rail link between London and Birmingham. Going by land, as he was doing when writing 2 Corinthians, was roughly four times as far, and considerably more dangerous.) Paul then, it seems, wrote a 'painful letter' of rebuke, which grieved the church; this is the point at which the hypotheses become murky, with no agreement as to whether the 'painful letter' is 1 Corinthians itself, or part of it, or whether it is a letter now lost, or whether it is part of what we now call 2 Corinthians (e.g. all or part of chapters 10—12). Fortunately, we do not need to decide these matters in order to get to the topic of our present concern.

The relationship between Paul and Corinth was not just deteriorating because of sorrow or anger caused by a visit and a letter. It was also going wrong because of teachers who had come to Corinth and were leading the church in a different direction, socially, culturally, intellectually and spiritually. Again, hypotheses have been multiplied as to the identity of these teachers, without any agreement. The point for our purposes is simple: they had poured scorn on Paul, giving the impression that he was of little significance, and should even be required, should he wish to make another visit, to come equipped with letters of recommendation from one of the other churches, so that they could be sure of his credentials. Had Paul been on top form, physically and mentally, when hearing of this, he might have dealt with it with the epistolary equivalent of a wave of the hand. Coming when it did, in the middle of his suffering in Ephesus, the news of this rebellion, and of the teachers who were fostering it, was the last torpedo that finally sank the ship. That was how it had been for Paul. That, too, became the point at which he discovered that the gospel of the resurrection was, once more, his only and ultimate comfort.

The role of the resurrection in 2 Corinthians, beginning with the opening *berakah* quoted above, is therefore subtly different from its role in 1 Corinthians. There, Paul drew on it freely to undergird his practical instructions, returning again and again to the point that because there was bodily continuity between the present life and the life of the world to come, it was vital to live consciously within the story-line that went through death and on to resurrection. It was equally vital whether one was dealing with sexual morality as in chapter 6, or with love as in chapter 13. The creator god raised the lord, and will also raise us, so glorify this god in your body; 'spiritual gifts' will be abolished, but love will go on from the present age into the age to come. But in much of 2 Corinthians his point, though closely related, is significantly different. Paul has not stopped looking to the future. Far from it. But now, instead of looking to the future and seeing the present as the appropriate preparation for it, he is looking to the future and discovering that it works its way back into the present in ways he had not previously explored, giving hope and strength when neither seemed available by any other means. In both letters, what matters is the continuity between future Christian hope and present Christian experience. But whereas in 1 Corinthians the movement is primarily towards the future, straining towards the resurrection and discovering what needs to be done in the present to anticipate it, in 2 Corinthians the movement is primarily towards the present, discovering in the powerful resurrection of Jesus and the promised resurrection for all his people the secret of facing suffering and pain here and now.

(ii) 2 Corinthians 1—2: Suffering and Comfort

This movement of thought from the resurrection of Jesus to the present situation emerges in the opening passage, already quoted. The rhythm of suffering and comfort, emphasized almost obsessively here, is explicitly echoing the gospel rhythm of the Messiah's death and resurrection. This becomes even clearer when Paul continues:

> [8]We do not want you to be ignorant, my dear family, about the suffering we experienced in Asia [i.e. in Ephesus]. We were overwhelmed, above measure and beyond our power to bear it. As a result, we despaired of life itself. [9]Actually, we even found the sentence of death within ourselves; but this was so that we would not trust in ourselves, but in the God who raises the dead. [10]He rescued us from so great a death, yes, and he will rescue us. We have set our hope on him that he will rescue us again. [11]You too can join in helping us by your prayers, so that, just as many people will be praying for us, so many also will give thanks on our behalf.

Trusting in 'the God who raises the dead'; this echoes, of course, not only good Pharisaic theology, embodied in the Eighteen Benedictions,[29] but also Paul's usage elsewhere, most explicitly in Romans 4.17.[30] Here, however, Paul is not saying, 'so I decided I would be happy to die, knowing that God would raise me up hereafter'. Rather, with Psalm 16.10, he declares that God would rescue him *from* death. (We may cautiously suggest that this is what happens when Paul looks *back* at the situation which in Philippians 1.18–26 was still in prospect.[31])

---

[29] See above, 146f.
[30] cf. too Heb. 11.19.
[31] See above, 226f.

It is important to spell out the logic of what he is saying, because in 2 Corinthians all this is controversial. (a) He believes, as a good Pharisaic Jew, that the creator God raises the dead, in the normal sense. (b) He believes this all the more strongly because he believes that God has already done it in the case of Jesus. (c) He believes that he is living between Jesus' resurrection and his own future resurrection. (d) He therefore claims, and discovers in practice, that God's power to raise the dead is at work in the present time, one of its results being that God can and sometimes does rescue his people from what had seemed imminent and certain death. This is inaugurated eschatology in the service of urgent pastoral need.

In both the passages already quoted, there is another feature which we must note, because it will be important in the central passage 4.7—5.10. Throughout this letter, but particularly in the first six chapters, Paul speaks of his own sufferings and comfort, his own 'death' and 'life', as being bound up with the suffering and comfort of the Corinthian church. As in Colossians 1.24, he seems to see himself in some kind of organic relationship to the church as a whole, and particularly the churches he has founded; not just that he is their founding apostle, their original teacher, nor yet that he has built up a complex and now fraught relationship with them in person and by letter. Somehow, in what Morna Hooker has referred to as a process of 'interchange', something of the give-and-take of suffering and glory which occurs between the Messiah and the church also occurs between the apostle and the church.[32] We have glimpsed this in miniature in the letter to Philemon, as Paul brings Philemon and Onesimus together in his own person, insisting on taking upon himself any pain or blame that there may still be in the relationship. Now, as part of his strategy to join the Corinthian church back to himself in bonds of mutual love and gratitude, Paul loses no opportunity of pointing out to them not only how much he has been suffering, but also the fact that this suffering has been, strangely, on their behalf. The underlying appeal of the letter is: this is what I have been through, and it has all been for you!

The basis of his confidence is, as usual, the story in which he believes himself to be living. This story is rooted in the Old Testament promises; it looks ahead to God's future in the resurrection; and it emphasizes that the Spirit, given in the present, is the guarantee of that future:

> [1.20]In [the Messiah], all God's promises find their 'Yes'. That is why, through him, we utter the Amen to God, to his glory, on your account. [21]The one who establishes us with you into the Messiah, the anointed one, and who has anointed us too, is God, [22]who has also put his seal upon us, giving the down payment of the Spirit in our hearts.

[32] See the studies collected in Hooker 1990.

The close parallels elsewhere in Paul to this idea of the Spirit as the 'down payment' or 'guarantee' of what is to come, in contexts where the resurrection is clearly in mind, leave us in no doubt that the same is true here.[33] And this mention of the Spirit in the hearts of believers lays some of the groundwork for the central argument of chapter 3.

Once Paul has come to see his own extraordinary suffering and rescue as an outworking in the present of the creator's power to raise the dead, it does not take him long to realize that he is therefore, in himself, a walking symbol of the gospel:

> 2.14Thanks be to God! He always leads us in triumph in the Messiah, and through us makes the fragrance of the knowledge of him apparent in every place. 15We are the aroma of the Messiah to God, you see, among those who are being saved and those who are being lost: 16to the latter, an aroma from death and towards death, and to the former an aroma from life and towards life.

The fact of who Paul is, of what he has suffered, and of his being alive to tell the tale of the God who raises the dead, is itself a sign both to the church and to the world of the gospel of the Messiah. It is indeed an *embodiment* of the Messiah, so that Paul is, as it were, a sweet-smelling, Messiah-smelling sacrifice to his God (verse 15), a sacrifice whose aroma, like that of the sacrifices in a triumphal procession, reminds the prisoners of the fate that awaits them, and the victors of their celebration. The message in both cases is one of death and life: the god who raises the dead is making known his gospel of death and life in the (metaphorical) dying and rising of the apostle.

(iii) 2 Corinthians 3.1—6.13: the Apostolic Apologia

This leads Paul to his major explanation – an apologia, we should perhaps call it – for his life, work and style of apostleship. The main exposition of this theme runs from 3.1 to 6.13, though Paul returns to the subject again in the closing chapters of the letter (assuming for the moment that they were written in this sequence). The central passage of this section, 4.7—5.10, is the part we are reserving for fuller treatment in the next chapter (this may seem odd in terms of sustained exegesis, but the debates about Paul's views on the resurrection demand that we approach it this way). But we must get a sense at this stage of the way the overall argument runs, so that we can move in towards that central passage with a clear idea of what Paul at least thinks he is talking about.

Paul's apostolic apologia has a sharp polemical edge, because the Corinthians (or some of them at least) have put him on the spot. They want him to produce letters of recommendation or accreditation; they are ashamed of

---

[33] cf. Rom. 8.23; Eph. 1.14; and, below, 2 Cor. 5.5.

his suffering (if he really was an emissary of the true god, surely he should not be subject to such indignities?). They have questioned whether his style of life and work, his bold and blunt way of speaking, are really what they should want or expect. They may be implying that his mode of apostleship is out of line with their view of the Christian God and of the gospel, though Paul suspects that the real problem is that his person, style and message does not fit with their view of their own social status and prestige. Anyway, he sets himself the task of explaining who he is and what he does.

The narrative he chooses to carry his apologia is the story of the covenant: the covenant made with Moses, and renewed through the Messiah, thereby accomplishing 'what the Torah could not do' (Romans 8.3). I do not think Paul chose this narrative because his opponents had already made a fuss of Moses, though that is possible; Paul's mind returns to the exodus so frequently, in so many different letters and contexts, that we do not need to suggest that anybody else forced him to talk about it here as well.[34] Part of the point of covenant renewal is that this was God's intended way of renewing creation itself; this is the larger framework of thought within which Paul is operating. His apostolic ministry may look bizarre, even offensive, when lined up against the cultural expectations of Corinth, and perhaps against the theological schemes of his shadowy opponents. But once the Corinthians learn to tell the story of new covenant and new creation, of the way in which all the promises find their 'yes' in the Messiah (1.20), they will see that Paul's style of life and work is not just a pointer to what the true God is doing, but is actually an embodiment of it. That is the overall point of the entire section.

The opening passage (3.1—4.6), launching this grand narrative, insists that Paul's gospel ministry really is a ministry of 'glory', even though, as Paul is well aware, it does not look like it.[35] Like an art expert leading a beginner round a gallery, Paul is taking the risky route of explaining why something is splendid, when the cynic is always able to respond that it doesn't look that way to him. Paul begins by protesting that he scarcely needs to bring letters of recommendation with him, since they themselves, the Christians in Corinth, constitute such a letter, written not with pen and ink but by the Spirit in human hearts (3.1–3). This enables him to open up the main theme: when the Spirit writes in people's hearts, this can only mean that Jeremiah 31 and Ezekiel 36 are being fulfilled. The God who established the original covenant is now renewing it, as he had always promised (3.4–6).

This results in a great transition, with sharp contrasts between old and new. No longer will the covenant people be marked out by possession of the stone tablets of the Torah. A new mode of operation has been introduced,

[34] See esp. Hafemann 1995.
[35] On this passage see Wright, *Climax*, ch. 9; Matera 2002, 390–92.

and it has been the peculiar glory of Paul's work to be the one through whom it has taken effect. When this point is understood it becomes apparent that Paul's ministry truly is a ministry of 'glory'; not (despite what the Corinthians might have hoped) that Paul's face shines like that of Moses had done, but because there is a kind of 'glory', a more important kind, which has to do with the life-giving work of the Spirit. The Spirit, by anticipating and guaranteeing the final resurrection (1.22), gives resurrection life in the present, in the same sense as we have seen in several other letters, not to the exclusion or replacement of the future resurrection but precisely as its down payment. Like the critic explaining why a painting is beautiful to someone who had not realized that it was, Paul explains that his ministry has 'glory' even though it does not look like it. His argument is that his ministry is consistently superior to that of Moses, which obviously had glory. His ministry, after all, involves life rather than death, justification rather than condemnation, permanence rather than transitoriness (3.7–11).[36]

This explains why Paul uses such boldness (*parrhesia*) (3.12). Moses' audience was hard-hearted, and could not understand what was being said. Paul's audience – the Corinthians themselves, in fact – have had the Spirit at work in their hearts, so that they should be able to understand. Paul here echoes something of what he had said in 1 Corinthians 2 and 3, and this constitutes a challenge to his readers: if they are truly *pneumatikoi*, they should be able to understand and appreciate the message he delivers with such holy and blunt frankness. The result, as in several other passages already studied, is that by the Spirit's work in the present something of the future glory is anticipated, so that as Christians look at one another, and as in particular the apostle and his congregation face one another, what they see in each other's faces is reflected glory, the glory of the lord, of Jesus the Messiah, produced by the Spirit (3.18). How then can he not be bold, frank and direct? Why then should he need to use sophisticated but perhaps obfuscatory speech?

In fact, Paul's work must take this course, because it is indeed the work of new creation (4.1–6). The god who said 'let light shine out of darkness' – in other words, the Genesis god, God the creator – has shone in our hearts, he says, to give 'the light of the knowledge of God's glory in the face of Jesus the Messiah' (4.6). Not everyone can see this glory, because 'the god of this world' has blinded their minds, placing them in the same category as the Israelites to whom Moses was speaking (4.4). But that does not mean there is anything wrong with Paul's gospel, or his manner of proclaiming it. It does not mean he has anything to be ashamed of on that account (4.1–3).

The opening part of this central section, then, stakes out the ground of new covenant and new creation – substantially the same ground, in fact, that Paul was to return to more fully in Romans 7 and 8. That parallel (as well as

---

[36] To understand what is going on in Paul's mind here, we need of course to add the discussions of the law in Rom. and Gal.

the other 'new creation' references such as Galatians 6.15) means that we are not surprised when, in the third part of this section (5.11—6.13) Paul speaks in so many words of the 'new creation' that comes about through the reconciling work of the gospel (5.17). All this comes about because of the gospel itself:

> ¹⁴For the love of the Messiah puts us under constraint, since we have settled it in our minds that one died for all, therefore all died. ¹⁵And he died for all [Paul here echoes Galatians 2.19–20] so that those who live might live no longer for themselves, but for his sake who died and was raised for them.

Here again we find the death and resurrection of the Messiah as the basis of the argument, revealing both love and power; and the new life of believers in the present is seen as a sharing in the risen life of the Messiah and as an anticipation of what is still to come. On this basis, human standards of judging one another, not least of assessing people's ministry, cease to have any relevance.[37] New creation is what matters, and new creation is what the gospel offers in the Messiah, through the work of reconciliation which was accomplished in him and is now applied through the apostolic ministry (which is still, of course, Paul's main subject here). Again and again Paul moves to and fro between the Messiah's death and resurrection, between his saving death and the new life of the covenant people. This is the narrative within which everything Paul does makes sense.

The climax comes in 5.21: 'God made the Messiah to be sin for us, though he knew no sin, so that in him we might become, might embody, God's righteousness, God's covenant faithfulness' (*hina hemeis genometha dikaiosune theou en auto*). This phrase has routinely been understood in terms of the righteous status which the covenant god reckons or 'imputes' to believers, but this interpretation then regularly leaves the verse dangling off the edge of the argument.[38] Every other time Paul uses the phrase *dikaiosune theou* he refers, not to the status which believers have *from* this god (*ek theou*, as in Philippians 3.9), but to God's own righteousness, God's faithfulness to the covenant, the faithfulness through which the new creation is brought to birth. Since Paul's whole argument from 3.1 to 6.13 is about the way in which his apostolic ministry embodies that covenant faithfulness, and implements that new creation, this reading stitches the verse far more tightly and satisfactorily into the rest of the passage than the usual alternatives. Furthermore – and this is the point of going into this detail here – it also indicates, by the very shape of Paul's statement, that this is once again a way of talking about *the experience of 'resurrection' in the present*, within

---

[37] Paul is here echoing 1 Cor. 4.1–5. He is not, as used often to be suggested, making a comment about 'not knowing people according to the flesh' or 'not knowing Christ according to the flesh' in the sense of refusing to have anything to do with history.

[38] I have made this argument briefly in Wright, 'Becoming the Righteousness'.

Paul's experience of apostolic work, covenant work. The Messiah died, and we live; the Messiah died, and reconciliation happens; the Messiah died, and we embody and implement the covenant faithfulness of the covenant God. These are all ways of exploring the meaning of verse 15b: the Messiah died and rose again for us.

The closing paragraph of the section (6.1–13) increases the rhetorical volume; Paul was well aware, here and supremely in chapter 11, of the ironic value of saying 'I am not using rhetoric' and then using it for all it was worth. He insists – this has been his point all along – that the day of salvation has come forward from the future into the present (6.2): 'Now is the acceptable time, Now is the day of salvation!' In this present time, with resurrection life paradoxically available in the midst of suffering and sorrow, the lifestyle and work of the apostle is bound to reflect the tension between the old age which is passing away and the new one which is dawning. The pattern of the Messiah's death and resurrection is worked out, lived out, acted out in the work of the apostle, the work that has so puzzled the Corinthians:

> 6.8We are treated as deceivers, and yet are true; 9as unknown, and yet we are well known; as dying, and look! we are alive; as punished but not killed, 10as sorrowful, yet always celebrating, as poor, yet bringing riches to many, as having nothing yet possessing everything.

The final flourish, echoing 1 Corinthians 3.21–3 ('all things are yours . . .'), looks on once more to the new creation in which the covenant people will inherit the world (Romans 4.13). The 'dying and living' in the middle of the sequence look back, of course, to what Paul had said in chapters 1 and 2. The whole passage, like the larger argument of which it forms the final and decisive part, constitutes a meditation on the death and resurrection of the Messiah, on the way in which that is embodied and lived out in the apostle, and the way in which this apostolic ministry, so far from being a cause for shame for the church, ought to be their glory. This fits exactly with several other Pauline passages, notably Philippians 2.17–18, Colossians 1.24 and Ephesians 3.13. Even supposing the latter passage was written by an imitator, it sums up exactly what Paul is now saying to the Corinthians: 'I ask you not to lose heart over what I am suffering for you; it is your glory!' This is what happens when the past resurrection of the Messiah and the future resurrection of his people meet in the middle in the present ministry of the apostle. This is what inaugurated eschatology looks like and feels like in the streets and the prison cells of Ephesus. And this long argument about apostolic ministry, held in tension between past and future, squashed between the present age and the age to come, is the setting for the all-important passage 4.7—5.10, to which we shall return in the next chapter.

(iv) 2 Corinthians 6.14—9.15: Fragments?

The following segments of the letter offer the best reason for supposing that the document as we have it is composed of fragments. The mood changes drastically, from a short and specific warning against mixed marriages with unbelievers (6.14—7.1) to a further appeal coupled with news of Paul's travels (7.2–16, which links up with 2.13), and two chapters (8 and 9) of extremely careful and delicate instructions about the collection which Paul hopes to find ready for him when he arrives.[39] Sorting all these out is no part of our present purpose. All we need to do is to highlight the points at which Paul's resurrection-theology emerges in the various arguments.

The appeal of 7.2–16, not surprisingly, returns to the same theme as chapter 2, this time reflecting on the effect of the letter Paul had sent earlier. He is glad, not because the letter made them sad, but because the sadness was the kind that leads on to salvation and life, as opposed to the kind that leads to death (7.9–10). This is how the pattern of apostolic suffering and the church's comfort works its way out (1.6); this is how one can see that the message which warns some of death speaks to others of life (2.15–16).

The two chapters on the collection, remarkable for Paul writing thirty-nine verses about money without mentioning the word, are couched initially as an appeal about 'grace' – the grace which the living God has given to the Macedonian churches (where Paul has been, and perhaps still is, at this point in writing the letter, on his way by land around northern Greece), resulting in outstanding generosity. Once again, the pattern he has been exploring throughout the letter provides the framework for what he wants to say:

> During a severe and testing time of suffering, the abundance of their joy and the weight of their poverty overflowed into the wealth of their generosity . . .
> . . . For you know the grace of our lord Jesus the Messiah, that though he was rich he became poor for your sakes, so that you might become rich through his poverty.[40]

This is the same pattern of 'interchange' we observed earlier: the Messiah and the churches, the churches and one another, poverty and riches, death and life. And the underlying principle of this interchange is, once more, the death and resurrection of the Messiah, and of his people.

(v) 2 Corinthians 10—13: Weakness and Power

The final section of the letter returns to the apostolic apologia, and pursues the theme with all the rhetorical stops pulled out. They want Paul to boast of

---

[39] cp. 1 Cor. 16.1–4. On these fragments and their analysis see e.g. Thrall 1994–2000, 3–49.
[40] 2 Cor. 8.2, 9.

his achievements, do they? They want up-to-date recommendations of all that he has done, of his spiritual experiences, his heroic achievements for the gospel? Very well, he will boast; he will play the fool, if that is really what they want; but *he will boast of all the wrong things*. Paul lists, as though they were civic appointments, honours and triumphs, the multiple 'achievements' of his apostleship, knowing them to be the very things that were making the Corinthians ashamed of him: beatings, imprisonments, stoning, shipwrecks, constant danger, deprivation, anxiety (11.21–9). His crowning achievement is a wonderful parody of the *corona muralis*, the highest Roman military honour, gained through being the first besieger to climb over the wall of a city. When he, Paul, was himself under threat in Damascus, he was the first one over the wall – let down in a basket and running away (11.30–33).[41]

So too with spiritual experiences (12.1–10). Paul has had visions and revelations, but he is not permitted to disclose their contents, with one exception: the time when he prayed especially hard to be released from a particular 'thorn in the flesh', and was given the answer 'No'. Here we find, at the climax of this superbly written, heavily ironic and (one suspects) powerfully persuasive rhetoric, the same pattern of the Messiah's death and resurrection, and the recognition that the way to the latter was always going to be through the former:

> [8]Three times I begged the lord about this, that he would take it away from me. [9]And he said to me, 'My grace is sufficient for you, for my power is completed in weakness.' I will therefore all the more gladly boast of my weaknesses, so that the power of the Messiah may take up residence upon me. [10]So, then, I am well pleased in weaknesses, in insults, in difficulties, in persecutions and disasters, on behalf of the Messiah; for whenever I am weak, then I am powerful.

The phrase Paul uses at the end of verse 9 employs an extremely rare Greek word, *episkenoo*, which I have translated 'take up residence upon'. The root word *skene* means 'tent' or 'tabernacle', and its only occurrences in the New Testament happen to be in this letter (5.1, 4), in the passage we have reserved for later study. There may be a hint here, perhaps more than a hint, of the same Temple-theology that Paul evokes in Romans 8.5–11, speaking of the Spirit's 'indwelling' which results in the resurrection.[42] The triple emphasis on power – the lord's power completed in weakness, the Messiah's power taking up residence upon Paul, the power which belongs to Paul himself when he is weak – all fits with Paul's regular reference to the

---

[41] See Judge 1968, 47. It is remarkable that recent commentators (e.g. Furnish 1984, 542; Thrall 1994–2000, 765), though noting Judge's case, have neither picked up the rhetorical point, nor spotted one of the strengths of Judge's case: the *corona muralis* had to be claimed on oath, thus explaining Paul's solemn invocation in 2 Cor. 11.31.

[42] cf. too, of course, Jn. 1.14: 'the Word became flesh and "tabernacled" (*eskenosen*) in our midst', where the Temple-related overtones ought not to be disputed.

power of the living God: it is how the resurrection is accomplished. Verse 10 sums up not only all of 11.21—12.9, but, in a measure, the entire epistle: the weakness of the apostle, seen to good effect in all the extraordinary things he has to suffer, is the very point at which he is being identified with the Messiah, and hence the very point also at which the Messiah's resurrection power comes into the present apostolic life and work, anticipating, by the Spirit, the resurrection which still awaits him.

The last reference in the letter makes this more explicit still. Paul warns that, in his imminent third visit, he will not be lenient,

> 13.3since you seem to want proof that the Messiah is speaking in me. He is not weak towards you – no, he is powerful in your midst! 4For he was crucified in [literally 'by' or 'from'] weakness, but he lives by [or 'from'] the power of God. So we too are weak in him, but we shall live with him by [or 'from'] the power of God towards you.

Here we are back where we were earlier in this letter, and also in the sections of 1 Corinthians where Paul was speaking of discipline (especially 4.14–21; 5.4). The Messiah's crucifixion and resurrection provide the pattern for apostolic ministry in general, and apostolic discipline of recalcitrant churches in particular. And the point all through, as in 1 Corinthians 4.20, is that the kingdom of the true God does not consist in talk but in power – the divine power by which Jesus himself was raised, the power by which all God's people will be raised, the power which, linking those past and future events, enables the apostle in the present to be simultaneously weak and powerful. That is the primary lesson Paul wants to teach the church in Corinth, and he will shortly be with them not merely to explain it further in words but to embody it in his own person. From what we know of the sequel (Romans was written from the area of Corinth, not long after 2 Corinthians), it looks as though his appeal, and visit, had the effect he had hoped.

4. Conclusion: Resurrection at Corinth

For all their remarkable differences, not least in style and language, 1 and 2 Corinthians converge in what they say about the resurrection. As with our survey of the other Pauline letters, we may remark not only on the frequency of reference to resurrection, by contrast with those Jewish sources which themselves want to affirm it, but on the way it has already, within twenty-five years of Jesus' public career, woven its way into the very fabric of Paul's thinking, so that it emerges all over the place not as one topic among others, to be dealt with and then left behind, but as part of the structure of everything else. In both letters the death and resurrection of Jesus, the latter as the result of the power of the living God, are fundamental. In both letters the future resurrection of the apostle and all the covenant people, as part of the new creation, are either explicit or assumed. In both letters the life that is lived in between Jesus' resurrection in the past and that of believers in the future is radically determined by these two events, building on the earlier one and anticipating the later.

In 2 Corinthians, in particular, we have seen how the story of resurrection, of God's creative power at work in the midst of suffering, becomes the key to Paul's strange and (to some churches) shocking style of life and work. At every turn he is drawing on the controlling narrative of the Messiah's death and resurrection. It is almost as though it had been burned into his consciousness. That, in fact, is more or less what he says in 1.3–11.

These two letters, omitting for the moment their most important sections, have returned the same answer to our questions as the rest of the Pauline corpus:

(1) In terms of the ancient spectrums of belief about life after death, Paul is with the Jews against the pagans, and with the Pharisees (and the majority of other Jews) against the Sadducees and against any who looked for a disembodied immortality.

(1a) He saw the Spirit in the present as the guarantee of the resurrection to come, in which believers would have new bodies.

(1b) These letters say nothing much about an intermediate state, but offer nothing to contradict the view we gleaned from the others.

(1c) The continuity and discontinuity between the present Christian life and the future resurrection life is all-important, though in subtly different ways, in both the Corinthian letters. It is the point on which many of his arguments in the first letter rest, and the point which enables him, in the second letter, to interpret his apostolic ministry as one of paradoxical glory.

(1d) Several times he hints at the larger picture (new covenant, new creation) within which what he says about resurrection makes sense.

(2) He develops substantially the 'present' meaning of resurrection in both letters, making sustained and subtle metaphorical use of the concept, to denote aspects of present (concrete) Christian living and apostolic work while connoting their rootedness in the (concrete) resurrection of Jesus and their goal in the future (concrete) resurrection of believers, to the last of which the language continues to apply literally.

(3) Paul seldom addresses, in the passages we have studied here, the question of what precisely happened at Easter, of what Jesus' own resurrection actually consisted in. However, since he uses Jesus' resurrection again and again as the model both for the ultimate future, and for the present anticipation of that future, we can conclude that, as far as he was concerned, Jesus' resurrection consisted in a new bodily life which was more than a mere resuscitation. It was a life in which the corruptibility of the flesh had been left behind; a life in which Jesus would now be equally at home in both dimensions of the good creation, in 'heaven' and 'earth'.

We have surveyed in these two chapters all of Paul's references to the resurrection, except for the two key passages which have, over the years, caused so much controversy. We should now be able to approach them in the hope of finding the way through the problems and out to a fresh and firm conclusion the other side.

Chapter Seven

RESURRECTION IN CORINTH (2):
THE KEY PASSAGES

1. 1 Corinthians 15

(i) Introduction

We have now established the context within which we can approach the two central 'resurrection' passages in the Corinthian correspondence with a good hope of understanding them. Chapter 15 of 1 Corinthians 15 and chapters 4 and 5 of 2 Corinthians both contain significant problems of their own, which must be examined carefully; and the relationship between them (particularly, the question as to whether Paul's ideas developed and changed) can only be assessed when that has been done. We therefore take them in sequence.

First Corinthians 15 is a carefully composed whole, with a balancing introduction and conclusion (**A** and **a** below), two lengthy main arguments (**B** and **b**), each in two parts (**B1** and **B2**, **b1** and **b2**), with a short middle section (**C**) in a different tempo. The balance can be seen in the following outline, including the similarity of the word-count in the matching sections:[1]

    A 15.1–11 (161 words): introduction: Paul's gospel, and his own role
      B 15.12–28 (246 words): the question and the basic answer
          [**B1** 15.12–19 (111 words); **B2** 15.20–28 (135 words)]
                C 15.29–34 (81 words): practical interlude
      b 15.35–49 (214 words): what sort of body?
          [**b1** 15.35–41 (110 words); **b2** 15.42–9 (104 words)]
    a 15.50–58 (148 words): conclusion: the mystery revealed

I am not suggesting that the argument presents an exact chiasm in terms of content (e.g. that sections B/b discuss precisely the same themes); rather that

---

[1] The precise count of words depends of course on textual variants, but what matters here is rough equivalence of scale, not exact numbers.

Paul seems to have envisaged the argument as a complete whole, laying it out step by step, not simply improvising his way through a random selection of things he wished to say.[2] We have already seen that the letter as a whole leads the eye up to this chapter, demanding that something now be said about the continuity between the present life and the one believers are promised in the coming age. Now we discover what Paul had in mind all along.

The argument is, in fact, an exposition of the future resurrection of all those who belong to the Messiah, set out as an argument about new creation. Genesis 1—3 forms a subtext for the whole chapter, and even when Paul appears to be merely offering illustrations of his point these, too, are drawn from the creation stories (see on 15.35–41). Having warned against taking the B/b sections as too closely parallel, we nevertheless note that in both B2 (15.20–28) and b2 (15.42–9) the place of Adam, and the reversal and undoing of Adam's fall and its results, is central. In B2 Paul quotes, as we have seen him do elsewhere in related passages, from Psalm 8.7, with its evocation of the creation story, and in b2 he concludes triumphantly, as does the account of creation in Genesis 1, with humans bearing the 'image' – though now the image they bear, as in Romans 8.29, is the image of the truly human being, the Messiah. Section b2 is in fact the final nub of the argument, the place where Paul reaches his most detailed explanation of the continuity (and discontinuity) between the present body and the future body, and he establishes the link between this argument and B2 precisely by means of the Adam-reference. B2 itself takes the form of a small apocalyptic account of the coming of God's kingdom, establishing God's rule over the world and defeating all the enemies of his kingdom, much as Daniel 7, itself drawing on the creation account in Genesis 2, in which the human race was set in authority over the beasts, envisages YHWH's kingdom as a new creation. And in the concluding passage of b2 Paul draws into the discussion the most fundamental aspect of creation, heaven and earth, as in Genesis 1.1, showing how the new creation represents, at last, the Jewish dream of the kingdom, embodied in the new humanity that, as in Philippians 3.20–21, comes 'from heaven'. The two key moments in the argument, B2 (15.20–28) and b2 (15.42–9) thus possess a measure of thematic as well as formal parallelism.

Genesis 1—3 is thus not only a frequent point of allusion, but provides some of the key structural markers in the argument. Even in its own terms, there can be no doubt that Paul intends this entire chapter to be an exposition of the renewal of creation, and the renewal of humankind as its focal point. When we place it alongside the various Jewish expositions of a similar theology on the one hand, and Paul's own briefer statements studied earlier, it should be beyond argument that this chapter belongs with them both. In terms of the spectrum of beliefs in the ancient world, this passage is specifically Jewish rather than pagan; within Judaism, it is a classic example of

[2] See Mitchell 1991.

resurrection-theology, based on the twin beliefs in the creator god and his justice.[3] Within this framework of thought, death is an intruder, a violator of the creator's good world. The creator's answer to death cannot be to reach some kind of agreement or compromise. Death must be, and in the Messiah has been and will be, defeated (15.26).[4] Anything other than some kind of bodily resurrection, therefore, is simply unthinkable, not only at the level of the meaning of individual verses and phrases but at the level of the chapter's argument as a whole. 'Resurrection' does not refer to some part or aspect of the human being *not* dying but instead going on into a continuing life in a new mode; it refers to something that *does* die and is then given a *new* life.[5] This distinction, so often ignored in both popular and scholarly treatments of the topic, and of this chapter, is vital. Before we examine some of the ways in which Paul goes beyond anything that had been said in Judaism before, we must be quite clear that in outline and basic theology (i.e. the view of the true god presupposed throughout) he stands rock-solid within the worldview of Pharisaic (i.e. at this period mainstream) Judaism.

The overall structure and logic of the chapter thus confirms what we would have guessed from the direction in which the rest of the letter points: that this is intended by Paul as a long argument in favour of a future *bodily* resurrection.[6] As we saw in the previous chapter, Paul repeatedly indicates earlier in the letter that Christian behaviour in the present life is predicated upon continuity between this life and the future one. It would be surprising if now, addressing the issue head on at last, he were to undermine what he had said all along. There was, in any case, no indication in Judaism either before or after Paul that 'resurrection' could mean anything other than 'bodily'; if Paul was going to argue for something so oxymoronic as a '*non-bodily resurrection*' he would have done better not to structure his argument in such a way as to give the appearance of articulating a Pharisaic, indeed biblical, worldview in which the goodness of the present creation is reaffirmed in the age to come. Since that is the kind of argument he has composed, at the conclusion of a letter which constantly points this way, no question should remain. When Paul said 'resurrection', he meant 'bodily resurrection'.

In any case, as Dale Martin has importantly reminded us, we should not assume that the ontological dualism between what modern westerners since

---

[3] See e.g. Wis. 13.1–9 (pagan ignorance of the creator); cf. esp. 1 Cor. 15.34.

[4] See the fine exposition of this theme in de Boer 1988 ch. 4.

[5] Interestingly, Paul only mentions the 'soul' once, and then in relation to the first Adam (1 Cor. 15.45), where the word means, more or less, 'being' or 'living creature', with no hint of immortality.

[6] Against e.g. Harvey 1994, 74f., who claims that 'the most obvious sense of "Jesus was raised on the third day" was that he had been exalted into heaven.' The language itself simply cannot mean that; the entire argument of the chapter, the letter, and of Paul's writing as a whole (chs. 5 and 6 above) tells conclusively against this suggestion.

Descartes at least think of as 'physical' and 'spiritual', or 'material' and 'non-material', would have meant very much to Paul's audiences. Most pagan philosophers of the period who believed in the existence of souls would have thought that they, like the body, were composed of material, albeit in finer particles.[7]

But we can go further. Had Paul been concerned about a non-bodily survival of death, his argument would be unnecessary, since many people in a city like Corinth believed in that anyway. None of it, indeed, would make sense: neither in outline nor in detail does 1 Corinthians 15 resemble an argument for the immortality of the soul. The whole point is that, at some future moment beyond death, the creator god will perform an act of new creation which will correspond to, and be derived from, that already performed in the case of Jesus (verses 20–28). What matters for our purposes in the present book is the ground of Paul's argument, since unlike him we are not presupposing Jesus' resurrection and building on it a theology of Christian hope, but examining his theology of Christian hope in order to understand more precisely what he thought had happened to Jesus. The ground of his argument is the resurrection of Jesus himself (15.3–11), which is appealed to as the event through which 'the resurrection of the dead' has burst in upon the surprised world, and on the basis of which the future resurrection of those 'in the Messiah' is guaranteed (15.20–28, 45–9). The final body of the redeemed will correspond to that of the Last Man, the Messiah (verse 49). For our purposes, the more Paul says about the future resurrection, the more we can fill in the blanks of what he might have said about Easter itself. However much Paul develops and in some respects modifies the basic Jewish account of resurrection, it is still resurrection he is talking about.

The developments and modifications are basically threefold: they concern the *when*, the *what* and the *who* of resurrection. Still at the level of overall argument, they stand out strikingly. Section B (verses 12–28) addresses the timing of the resurrection: contrary to Jewish expectation, he argues that 'the resurrection of the dead', as an event, is to happen in two stages – *first* the Messiah, and *later* all those who belong to him. This also highlights the personal focus: instead of resurrection being simply for all the righteous, for 'all Israel' in some sense, it is first and foremost for Israel's representative in person, and thence for all those, whether Israelite or not, who belong to him. Section b (verses 35–49) addresses the *what*, i.e. the type of body envisaged: going beyond any previous Jewish expositions of the topic, Paul argues that resurrection is not merely a resuscitation into the same kind of

---

[7] Martin 1995, 115–17; 127–9; the whole chapter is important in its corrective to popular assumptions, though Martin's eventual solution does not, I think, do justice to the wider theology and exegesis with which Paul so carefully frames his account of the resurrection body. See too e.g. Galen, *Natural Faculties*, 1.12.27f.

body, but is rather a going on, out the other side of death and whatever lies immediately beyond, into a new, transformed embodiment. All these points need more detailed discussion, of course, but it is important that we see them, in an introductory bird's-eye glimpse, as modifications *from within* of the Jewish, more specifically the Pharisaic, worldview. They are new ways of emphasizing and reinforcing the Jewish view of God as creator and justice-bringer, rather than subtle abandonments of that worldview and theology. Nor do we have to seek far to discover the causes of these developments and modifications; they are predicated, obviously, on what Paul believed happened to Jesus at Easter. Jesus' resurrection remains, throughout, the prototype and model for the future resurrection. This enables us to work back quite precisely to what Paul meant when he said that the Messiah had himself been raised from the dead.

The aim of chapter 15 is to answer the challenge of verse 12: some of the Corinthian Christians had been saying that there was no resurrection of the dead. This must mean that they were denying a future bodily resurrection, and the strong probability is that they were doing so on the standard pagan grounds, as set out in chapter 2, that everybody knew dead people didn't and couldn't come back to bodily life. Even if they believed, like the two teachers mentioned in 2 Timothy 2.17–18, that 'the resurrection' as a whole had already occurred, in other words, that 'the resurrection' referred to some kind of spiritual experience or event, they would still be denying that there would be a future bodily resurrection. (The proto-gnostic belief is thus shown up already as what it really was and is, namely, a form of paganism rather than of Judaism.)[8] If the denial were to be sustained, clearly, much of Paul's previous argument would be undercut, depending as it does on the promise of resurrection. This is why Paul opens the chapter with a restatement of the fundamental Christian gospel, highlighting particularly the fact of Jesus' own resurrection, which will be the basis for both the initial argument in B1 (verses 12–19) and the developed argument of B2 (verses 20–28). An event has occurred which has changed the shape of the creator's history with the world.

The argument of chapter 15, then, runs as follows: what the creator god did for Jesus is both the *model* and the *means* of what he will do for all Jesus' people. As an aid to clarity in what follows, we may offer an overview of the whole chapter:

---

[8] The deniers were denying 'resurrection'. Had they held something like the view of the *Letter to Rheginos* (see below, ch. 11), they would have used the word 'resurrection' to refer to a present spiritual experience; but they did not deny that experience, but rather affirmed it. What is being denied in v. 12 is the resurrection of the *dead*. Likewise, if what the deniers were wanting to affirm was an ultimate non-physical 'spiritual' bliss, this still makes it clear that they were denying future bodily resurrection. That, therefore, must be what Paul is arguing for throughout the chapter.

A. The gospel is anchored in the resurrection of Jesus (verses 1–11).

B1. But if this did not happen then the gospel, with all its benefits, is null and void (verses 12–19).

B2. Jesus' resurrection is the beginning of 'the resurrection of the dead', the final eschatological event, which has now split into two; the risen Jesus is the 'first-fruits', both the initial, prototypical *example*, and also the *means* of the subsequent resurrection of his people, because it is through his status and office as the truly human being, the Messiah, that death and all other enemies of the creator's project are to be defeated (verses 20–28).

C. Paul then quickly mentions (verses 29–34) what would follow if the resurrection were *not* true after all: the central nerve of Christian living would be cut.

b. He then moves (verses 35–49) to the *what* of resurrection, which is based at several points on B2: the risen Jesus is the model for what resurrected humanity will consist of, and also, through the Spirit, the agent of its accomplishment.

a. He concludes triumphantly (verses 50–58) with a description of the future moment of resurrection, emphasizing the incorruptibility of the new body, and hence the character of the event as *victory* over death. He closes with both praise (verse 57) and exhortation (verse 58).

Keeping our eyes on the horizon provided by this overview should enable us to avoid motion sickness in the choppy exegetical waters through which we must now sail.

(ii) 1 Corinthians 15.1–11

The introduction is formal, solemn, complex and controversial. It stands as a fifth witness to the original Easter events, alongside the accounts in the four gospels, and is thus of extraordinary importance for our present study. Bultmann, famously, criticized Paul for citing witnesses to Jesus' resurrection, as though he considered it an actual event, instead of being merely a graphic, 'mythological' way of referring to the conviction of the early Christians that Jesus' death had been a good thing, not a bad thing.[9] The inauthenticity of an entire stream of twentieth-century New Testament scholarship is thus laid bare; if Paul really allowed himself, in so serious and sober an introduction to a carefully crafted chapter expressing the central point that underlay an entire letter, to say something as drastically misleading as Bultmann imagined, he is hardly a thinker worth wrestling with in the first place. But in fact Bultmann was simply wrong: the resurrection of Jesus was a real event as

---

[9] See Bultmann in Bartsch 1962–4, 1.38–41, 83.

far as Paul was concerned, and it underlay the future real event of the resurrection of all God's people.[10]

All this emerges at every point in verses 1–11. Paul refers to the resurrection of Jesus as an event for which there were witnesses – a large, though finite number, comprising at least 500 who had seen Jesus. Some of these witnesses had already died, and no more would be added to their number, because the sightings of the risen Jesus had a temporal end; when he, Paul, saw Jesus, that was the last in the sequence (verse 8).

This reference to seeing the risen Jesus cannot therefore, in Paul's mind at least, have anything to do with regular and normal, or even extraordinary, 'Christian experience', with ongoing visions and revelations or a 'spiritual' sense of the presence of Jesus. As is clear from 1 Corinthians 9.1, this 'seeing' was something which constituted people as 'apostles', the one-off witnesses to a one-off event. The Corinthians had had every kind of spiritual experience imaginable, as the previous chapters have made clear; but they had not seen the risen Jesus, nor did either they or Paul expect that they would do so.[11]

The introduction to the introduction (15.1–3a) sets out in solemn fashion the fact that Paul's gospel, which hinges on Jesus' resurrection, was the one he himself 'received' in the tradition of the very early church, and that it is this gospel alone which gives shape to Christian living and value to Christian hope:

> [1]So I must remind you, my dear family, of the gospel which I announced to you – which you also received, in which you stand firm, [2]through which you are also saved, if you hold fast to the word by which I announced it to you, unless indeed you believed in vain. [3]For I handed on to you at the start what I also received . . .

This ties in closely with the conclusion of the introduction (15.11):

> [11]So, then, whether it was I or whether it was they, that is the way we announced it, and that is the way you believed.

Paul is at pains to stress that this gospel, though announced by him, was not peculiar to him. The Corinthians, after all, had had visits from numerous other apostles and teachers, Cephas and Apollos being probably only two of many. Had Paul said something significantly different from the others, on this point above all, they would have noticed. He is quite capable of emphasizing something he wants to say on his own authority, in contradistinction

---

[10] Bultmann has been followed by many: a recent example is Patterson 1998, 218, who states that Paul was wrong to use 'appearance' stories to reinforce resurrection belief, since that implied that something had happened, whereas in fact all that happened was the coming to faith of the early church.

[11] See esp. Kendall and O'Collins 1992. Coakley 2002, ch. 8 never allows for this distinction.

to other Christian teachers; but in this case it is important to him (and to our investigation as well) that he knew, and that he knew the Corinthians knew, that in what he was about to say he was standing on exactly the same ground as all the other apostles.

Paul does not here undermine what he had said in Galatians 1 about the independence of his gospel.[12] The *content* – that Jesus had been raised from the dead, and the basic truths that followed from that – he had, it is true, received independently of anyone else, on the road to Damascus. But the *form*, this way of putting it, this manner of telling the story, was apparently passed on *to* him (verse 3), and passed on *by* him to his churches.[13] This is the kind of foundation-story with which a community is not at liberty to tamper. It was probably formulated within the first two or three years after Easter itself, since it was already in formulaic form when Paul 'received' it.[14] We are here in touch with the earliest Christian tradition, with something that was being said two decades or more before Paul wrote this letter.

The question of how much of verses 3b–8 constituted the core of this tradition need not concern us. It is quite possible that the whole passage was common tradition, with the final word being 'to Paul' instead of 'to me', and that Paul has added phrases like 'most of whom are still alive, though some have fallen asleep'. It is also possible that the traditional formula ended with verse 5 (the mention of the Twelve) and that Paul added verses 6–8;[15] or that Paul has combined two or more different traditions.[16] This does not affect the basic point to be made, either by Paul or by ourselves.[17] What counts is that the heart of the formula is something Paul knows the Corinthians will have heard from everyone else as well as himself, and that he can appeal to it as unalterable Christian bedrock.

The formula is dense and important, and we take it step by step, beginning with verses 3b–4:

> [3] . . . that the Messiah died for our sins in accordance with the scriptures, [4] and that he was buried, and that he has been raised on the third day in accordance with the scriptures . . .

It is important, first, that Jesus is designated in this formula as 'Messiah', *Christos*. Precisely because this is such an early formulation there is no chance that this word could have been a proper name without connotation, and every reason to suppose that the early Christians intended it to have its

---

[12] See Gal. 1.11.

[13] *paredoka* and *parelabon* (v. 3, the latter echoing *parelabete* in v. 1) are technical terms for the receiving and handing on of tradition.

[14] So Hays 1997, 255.

[15] So Hays 1997, 257.

[16] So e.g. Patterson 1998, 216f.

[17] I find the lengthy traditio-historical analysis of Lüdemann 1994, 33–109 almost entirely worthless.

royal designation. Paul himself mounts an explicitly 'messianic' argument in verses 20–28, complete with biblical proof-texts about the coming Messiah and with a statement of his worldwide kingly rule.[18] The evidence suggests that this is rooted in the earliest Christian conviction, expressed here in the formula. It is because Jesus is Messiah that his death represents the turning-point in which the present evil age is left behind and those who belong to Jesus are rescued from it; what Paul says in Galatians 1.4, that the Messiah 'gave himself for our sins to deliver us from the present evil age', is of the greatest relevance here, indicating that the dealing with sins which Paul has in mind is part of, is indeed the key focal point of, the great eschatological turning-point in the divine purpose. The turning-point in question is focused on those who now benefit from it, i.e. 'us': the Messiah died *for our sins*. Paul does not mention 'sins' again in the chapter except at verse 17 (and 'sin' at verse 56), but those occurrences are crucial: they reveal part of the point of the entire exposition. Without the resurrection, there is no reason to suppose that Jesus' crucifixion dealt with sins, or with sin. But, with the resurrection, the divine victory over sin(s), and hence over death, is assured.

The idea of God's dealing with sins once and for all is rooted, within second-Temple Jewish tradition, in the complex of thought for which 'return from exile', 'covenant renewal', and indeed 'resurrection' (in the metaphorical sense we find in Ezekiel 37), are all appropriate metonyms and/or metaphors.[19] The transition from 'the present evil age' to the incipient 'age to come', by means of sins being dealt with, is exactly (for instance) what is promised in those well-known, central and frequently cited passages Isaiah 40.1–11, Jeremiah 31.31–4, and Ezekiel 36.22–32. It is also the central subject of the great prayer in Daniel 9, which is simultaneously a prayer both for forgiveness of sins and for return from exile. Since the whole chapter, as we have seen, belongs so firmly in the tradition of Jewish restoration theology, this is without a doubt the right context within which to interpret such a reference.

This indicates, before we go any further, the primary meaning of 'in accordance with the scriptures'. Paul is not proof-texting; he does not envisage one or two, or even half a dozen, isolated passages about a death for sinners. He is referring to the entire biblical narrative as the story which has reached its climax in the Messiah, and has now given rise to the new phase of the same story, the phase in which the age to come has broken in, with its central characteristic being (seen from one point of view) rescue from sins, and (from another point of view) rescue from death, i.e. resurrection. We may again compare verses 56–7. There are of course several scriptural passages which point in this direction, including some of the Psalms

---

[18] For details see below, 553–63, 726–30.
[19] See *JVG passim* esp. e.g. 202–09.

and several parts of Isaiah 40—55; but Paul is primarily concerned with the entire sweep of biblical narrative.[20]

The mention of Jesus' burial (verse 4a) can only have attained such a significant place in a brief and summary traditional narrative if it was regarded as important in itself. Much debate has circled around this point, but the most likely reason for its mention is twofold: first, to certify that Jesus was really and truly dead (something the gospel accounts take care of in their own way, as we shall see); second, to indicate that when Paul speaks of resurrection in the next phrase it is to be assumed, as anyone telling or hearing a story of someone being raised from the dead would assume in either the pagan or the Jewish world, that this referred to the body being raised to new life, leaving an empty tomb behind it. The fact that the empty tomb itself, so prominent in the gospel accounts, does not appear to be specifically mentioned in this passage, is not significant; the mention here of 'buried, then raised' no more needs to be amplified in that way than one would need to amplify the statement 'I walked down the street' with the qualification 'on my feet'. The discovery of the empty tomb in the gospel accounts is of course significant because it was (in all the stories) the first thing that alerted Jesus' followers to the fact that something extraordinary had happened; but when the story was telescoped into a compact formula it was not the principal point. The best hypothesis for why 'that he was buried' came to be part of this brief tradition is simply that the phrase summarized very succinctly that entire moment in the Easter narratives.[21]

'He has been raised on the third day according to the scriptures.' The verb is actually perfect, not (as most translations imply) aorist ('he was raised', matching 'died', 'was buried' and 'was seen'); the Greek perfect tense indicates the ongoing result of a one-off event, in this case the permanent result that Jesus is now the risen Messiah and lord (see verses 20–28).[22] The verb, like the others here, is passive, indicating divine action; Paul regularly sees the resurrection of Jesus as a great act of the creator himself.[23] Like the scriptural narrative invoked as the world of meaning for 'the Messiah died for our sins', the qualifying phrase here looks back to the scriptural narrative as a whole, not simply to a handful of proof-texts. And the point Paul has in mind within that longer scriptural narrative is the point at which YHWH forgives Israel's sins, ushering in the new age, renewing the covenant, restoring creation – and raising his people from the dead. Ezekiel 37 is

---

[20] See *NTPG* 241–3; and e.g. Wright, *Romans*, 632–70 on Rom. 9.6—10.21.

[21] Hays 1997, 256: neither Paul nor any other early Christian could have conceived of a 'resurrection from the dead' which left a body in the tomb. See too Fee 1987, 725, with bibliog. (n. 61); and now esp. Hengel 2001, with plentiful recent German bibliography. Hengel's substantial paper should silence the suggestion that the argument is advanced 'somewhat desperately' (Wedderburn 1999, 87).

[22] So Hays 1997, 257.

[23] cf. e.g. Rom. 4.24f.; 6.4, 9; 1 Cor. 15.15. Cf. esp. Hofius 2002.

important here, but so, too, most would agree, is Hosea 6.2.[24] Whatever its original meaning, the signs are that by Paul's day this passage was being read in terms both of resurrection itself 'after three days', and of the restoration of Israel after sin. Paul seems to intend both of these meanings, and indeed they belong closely with each other.

The phrase 'after three days', looking back mainly to Hosea 6.2, is frequently referred to in rabbinic mentions of the resurrection.[25] This does not mean that Paul or anyone else in early Christianity supposed that it was a purely metaphorical statement, a vivid way of saying 'the biblical hope has been fulfilled'. In fact, the mention of any time-lag at all between Jesus' death and his resurrection is a further strong indication of what is meant by the latter: not only was Jesus' resurrection in principle a dateable event for the early Christians, but it was always something that took place, not immediately upon his death, but a short interval thereafter. If by Jesus' 'resurrection' the early church had meant that they believed he had attained a new state of glory with God, a special kind of non-bodily post-mortem existence, it is difficult to see why there should have been any interval at all; why should he have had to wait? If, however, the early church knew from the first that something dramatic had happened on the third day (counting inclusively) after the Friday when Jesus died, then not only the appeal to Hosea 6.2 and the wider tradition thereby represented, but also the shift represented by the Christian use of Sunday as 'the lord's day', is fully explained.[26]

In the tradition, then, firm, universal and early, we find unambiguous evidence that the earliest Christians believed both that Jesus had been bodily raised and that this event fulfilled the scriptural stories. These were perceived as stories not simply about a Messiah, emerging out of the blue, but about Israel, about the doing away with Israel's time of desolation, about the coming of the new age that would reverse the effects of the present evil age. Paul could appeal, in the mid-50s, to this entire tradition as something which all early Christians knew well.

But it is not enough for Paul, or the early tradition, simply to declare that the Messiah was in fact raised. Witnesses must come forward:

> [5]and that he was seen by/appeared to Cephas, then the Twelve, [6]then he was seen by/appeared to more than five hundred members of the family at one time, of whom most remain alive to this present day, though some have fallen asleep. [7]Then he was seen by/appeared to James, then by all the apostles.

---

[24] See above, 118f.

[25] Details in McArthur 1971. Other biblical 'third day' passages (listed in e.g. *Midrash Rabbah* on Gen. 22.4) include Gen. 42.18; Ex. 19.16; Josh. 2.16; Jonah 2.1; Ezra 8.32. On the question of whether 'according to the scriptures' goes with 'raised', or with 'after three days' see e.g. Thiselton 2000, 1196, with other literature.

[26] On Sunday see below, 579f.

As this carefully ambiguous translation shows, the verb *ophthe,* occurring three times here, and then again with reference to Paul in verse 8, can in principle be translated either way. Some, wanting to stress the 'visionary' nature of the appearances, and hence to insert the thin end of a wedge with which to force a 'non-objective' understanding of Easter, have emphasized the meaning 'appeared', and the parallel uses in which the subject is a non-bodily 'apparition', rather than someone or something within the normal space-time universe. The fact that it is followed in each case by a dative indicates that 'appeared to' may be marginally preferable. However, the verb is passive, and its normal meaning would be 'was seen by'.[27]

The use of *ophthe* is in fact quite varied, as a glance at the LXX concordance will show. The word occurs 85 times, of which a little over half refer either to YHWH, or YHWH's glory, or an angel of YHWH, appearing to people.[28] The remaining 39 occurrences refer to people appearing before YHWH in the sense of presenting themselves in the Temple;[29] or to objects being seen by people in a straightforward, non-visionary sense;[30] and to people 'appearing', in a non-visionary and unsurprising way, before someone else.[31] The classical background does not give much more help; the passive of the verb is not found in Homer, and the usage elsewhere more or less mirrors what we have seen in the LXX. It is in fact impossible to build a theory of what people thought Jesus' resurrection appearances consisted of (i.e. whether they were 'objective', 'subjective' or whatever – these terms themselves, with their many philosophical overtones, are not particularly helpful) on this word alone. The word is quite consistent with people having non-objective 'visions'; it is equally consistent with them seeing someone in the ordinary course of human affairs. Its meaning in the present context – both its meaning for Paul, and its meaning in the tradition he quotes – must be judged on wider criteria than linguistic usage alone.[32]

---

[27] How, in the light of the present passage, Perkins 1984, 137 can claim that 'the early traditions of resurrection . . . are auditory and not visionary,' I simply do not understand.

[28] e.g. Gen. 12.7; 17.1; 18.1; Ex. 3.2; 6.3; 16.10; Ps. 83 [MT 84].7; Isa. 40.5; 60.2. The total of all such occurrences is 46. See Newman 1992, 190–92. This is not sufficient, though, for Newman to claim that this language by itself is an indication that Paul defines his Christophany 'as a revelation of eschatological Glory'.

[29] Thus: Ex. 24.11; Deut. 16.16 (twice); 31.11; 1 Kgds. [MT Sam.] 1.22; Ps. 41 [MT 42].2; 62 [63].2; Sir. 32[35].4; Isa 1.12.

[30] Thus: Gen. 1.9; Lev. 13.14, 51; Deut. 16.4; Jdg. 5.8; 2 Kgds. [MT Sam.] 22.16; 3 Kgds. [1 Kgs.] 10.12; 4 Kgds. [2 Kgs.] 22.20; 2 Chron. 9.11 (= 3 Kgds. [1 Kgs.] 10.12); Ps. 16 [MT 17].15; Song 2.12; Jer. 13.26.

[31] Thus: Gen. 46.29 (Joseph appears, i.e. presents himself, to Jacob); Ex. 10.28 (Moses appearing before Pharaoh); 2 Kgds. [Sam.] 17.17 (Jonathan and Ahimaaz could not risk being seen); 3 Kgds. [1 Kgs.] 3.16 (two harlots appearing before Solomon); 18.1 (Elijah being told to 'appear', i.e. present himself, to Ahab); 18.2, 15; 4 Kgds. [2 Kgs.] 14.8, 11 (two kings looking each other in the fact) (paralleled in 2 Chron. 25.17, 21); Sir. 39.4 (the wise man appears before rulers); Dan. [Th] 1.13; 1 Macc. 4.6, 19; 6.43; 9.27.

[32] On the whole topic of 'seeing' the risen Jesus see the important essay of Davis 1997.

The list of witnesses, despite the anguished protests of Bultmann and his followers, is a clear indication that Paul does not suppose Jesus' resurrection to be a metaphorization of an experience of the disciples, or of some 'ineffable truth beyond history'.[33] What is more, 'the great variety in times and places of the appearances makes it difficult to hold all the reports of appearances to be legendary.'[34]

The mention of 'Cephas' accords with Paul's normal way of referring to Peter, though it almost certainly here belongs to the pre-Pauline tradition which he is quoting.[35] An early, personal appearance to him is mentioned in Luke, where he is named as 'Simon'.[36]

The appearance to 'the Twelve' is the more significant in that the gospel traditions make it clear that one of the Twelve, i.e. Judas Iscariot, was already dead by the time of the discovery of the empty tomb and the start of the appearances. In Matthew 28.16, Luke 24.9, 33 and the longer ending of Mark (16.14), they are referred to as 'the eleven', and in Acts 1.12–26 the eleven are listed and provision is made to appoint someone to replace Judas. It is difficult to know how much weight, and in what direction, to place on this reference. It could mean that the present tradition represents an early telling of the story which the gospel accounts have made more precise; or that the gospel accounts have preserved the early sense of loss over Judas, and that, by the time the tradition had solidified into the form before us here, not least once a replacement had been appointed (Acts 1.15–26), the story was being told in terms of 'the Twelve', as part of the reflection on the theological significance of the Twelve within early Christianity. Nothing much hinges on this for our present purposes, but we shall return to the point when examining the gospel accounts.

Attempts have sometimes been made to line up the appearance to the 500 with Luke's account of Pentecost.[37] This is not only unnecessary, but virtually impossible: a classic case of critical scholarship treating two incidents as variations on a single one, the equal and opposite syndrome to the scholarly penchant for 'discovering' two or more separate sources or 'original incidents' hidden within a single narrative. The suggestion does as

---

[33] So, rightly, Hays 1997, 257.

[34] Stuhlmacher 1993, 49. Stuhlmacher then backs off (50) from the implication, saying that the statements are confessional 'and not descriptive of an objective fact', justifying this not historically but in terms of the needs of a contemporary apologetic. Granted that there is such a thing as false 'objectification', that does not mean there is not also an opposite danger – of collapsing everything into subjectivity. Faced with these alternatives, 1 Cor. 15 looks as though it is more concerned to avoid the latter.

[35] cf. 1 Cor. 1.12; 3.22; 9.5; Gal. 1.18; 2.9, 11, 14.

[36] Lk. 24.34.

[37] This is advanced by e.g. Gilmour 1961, 1962; cautiously opposed by e.g. Sleeper 1965; swept aside as not generally accepted by Thiselton 2000, 1206. Gilmour 1961, 248f. traces the proposal back to C. H. Weisse in 1838, followed by Pfleiderer in 1887 and von Dobschütz in 1903, and by many others since then.

much violence to Luke's account of Pentecost as it does to Paul's account of a resurrection appearance which he expressly distinguishes from other types of Christian experience. Experience of the Spirit and seeing the risen Jesus are never, in early Christian writings, assimilated to one another.[38] (If they were, why should we not claim that the Pentecost-experience was 'in fact' a seeing of, and meeting with, the bodily resurrected Jesus? It is revealing that those who have suggested that 'experience of the Spirit', 'seeing the risen Jesus', 'acclaiming Jesus as the exalted one', and 'the beginnings of Christian community' are all 'really' different ways of talking about the same thing never dream of making that move.) It is far more likely that the appearance to the 500 was an occasion like that reported in Matthew 28.16–20 (though Matthew only mentions the eleven there). The crucial note here, at the end of verse 6, makes it clear why Paul (and/or the tradition he is quoting) is referring to the 500: though some are now dead, most are still alive, and – the strong implication – they could be interrogated for their own accounts of what they saw and knew. The whole thrust of the paragraph is about evidence, about witnesses being called, about something that actually happened for which eyewitnesses could and would vouch. Paul would hardly call eyewitnesses for an experience which continued unabated, not least in Corinth itself.

The appearance to James (this clearly refers to the brother of Jesus, not to either of the members of the Twelve who had that name) is especially interesting in that it is not mentioned in the gospel accounts, except for one much later text which may be dependent on our present passage.[39] It is of course common knowledge that James, the brother of Jesus, became the central leader in Jerusalem in the mid-century, while Peter and Paul and others were travelling around the world. Since he had probably not been a disciple of Jesus during the latter's public career, it is difficult to account for his centrality and unrivalled leadership unless he was himself known to have seen the risen Jesus.[40]

The mention of 'all the apostles', without being more specific, cannot be further glossed, except to say that Paul (or the tradition) seems to have thought that there were considerably more than 500 who had seen Jesus alive after his death; otherwise verse 7b seems otiose. Since an 'apostle' was, for him, one who had seen the risen Jesus, this seems to be a way of

---

[38] See Fee 1987, 730 n. 84. Contra e.g. Patterson 1998, 227–37, who argues that large groups do not see visions, therefore the Twelve did not, nor did a group of 500; what happened was a collective ecstatic experience, like glossolalia. The obvious responses are: (a) the Corinthians had glossolalia in plenty, but Paul knows they have not seen the risen Jesus; (b) if, as Patterson allows (237), the group in question did think of it as an 'appearance' of Jesus, this undermines his original premise, and reopens the question.

[39] *Gosp. Hebr.* (Jerome *De Vir. Ill.* 2).

[40] On James see *NTPG* 353f.; and e.g. Painter 1997; Chilton and Neusner 2001. On the significance of James in relation to Jesus' Messiahship see below, 560f.

saying, not that there was a last large-scale appearance to a sub-group of those already mentioned, but that there was an appearance to a larger group than the Twelve or perhaps even the 500.

The list of witnesses in verses 5–7 is impressive but, to the minds of readers of the gospels, interestingly incomplete. The two on the road to Emmaus are perhaps taken care of under 'all the apostles', though it seems as if the present list is designed to be in some kind of chronological order ('then . . . then . . . then . . . last of all'), and Luke presents their story earlier than the others (except for Simon/Cephas). More important, the list Paul quotes here, which by his day is traditional, makes no mention of the women who feature with such remarkable prominence in all four gospel accounts. How is this to be accounted for? Do we, as so many have done down the years, simply accuse Paul of being anti-women, and leave it at that?[41]

Recent scholarship has settled on what is far and away the most likely solution historically, one which explains the present passage and highlights the real shock in the gospel accounts. It is notorious that women were not regarded as reliable witnesses in the ancient world.[42] They could not be expunged from the gospel accounts; their story of finding the tomb remained a primary datum, which we shall discuss later.[43] But when, in the very early years, the Easter story was being told both for the benefit of members of the church itself and in its witness to outsiders, and especially when it was 'handed on' to new converts in the wider world, the pressure to omit mention of the women in a brief formal statement must have been enormous.[44] That this does not imply that Paul does not regard women as 'apostles', i.e. as witnesses to the resurrection, is clear from Romans 16.7.[45]

This brings us to Paul's reference to himself:

[8]Last of all, as to the one born at the wrong time, he also appeared to/was seen by me. [9]For I am the least of the apostles; I do not deserve to be called an apostle, because I persecuted God's church. [10]But it is by God's grace that I am what I am; and his grace towards me was not in vain. On the contrary: I worked harder than all of them – yet it was not me, but God's grace that was with me.

'Last of all': as we have already seen, Paul did not regard these 'sightings' or 'appearances' as part of normal ongoing Christian experience. When he saw Jesus, he was only just in time; the appearances were more or less at an

---

[41] e.g. Schüssler Fiorenza 1993, 78.

[42] See the careful survey in Bauckham 2002, 268–77, citing e.g. Jos. *Ant.* 2.219, though arguing that the key point in some of the Jewish material is not so much the unreliability of the women as the fact that men preferred to think of themselves as the mediators of divine revelation.

[43] Below, 607–9.

[44] So e.g. Carnley 1987, 141; Bovon 1995, 147–50; and cf. Hengel 1963; Benoit 1960.

[45] See Wright, *Romans*, 762. Bauckham 2002, 165–86 proposes that 'Junia' in this text is to be identified with the 'Joanna' in Lk. 8.3; 24.10.

end, and none had occurred after his own. (Had this not been known to be the case throughout the early church, Paul could scarcely have made this claim when writing to the Corinthians, who, in addition to their own rich variety of Christian experience, had heard several teachers who were independent of Paul.) This differentiation of Paul's seeing of Jesus from every subsequent type of vision, spiritual revelation and experience, including his own (see, for instance, 2 Corinthians 12.1–5[46]), and this placing of it not with such multiple later events but with the 'seeings' of Cephas, James and the rest, indicates not merely Paul's insistence on his own apostolic authority (that he was on a par with the other apostles) but also his sense, which he must have known would not be challenged even by those who wished to resist other aspects of his teaching, that he had seen what the other apostles had seen, namely Jesus himself, personally present.

Paul is aware, however, that the 'seeing' of Jesus that had been granted to him, though belonging in the sequence of the other primitive and non-repeatable 'seeings', was nevertheless peculiar within the sequence. He indicates this peculiarity with the little phrase *hosperei to ektromati*, which I have translated 'as to the one born at the wrong time'.

An *ektroma*, properly, is an untimely birth, due either to miscarriage or, more normally, abortion.[47] The word could be used as a term of abuse, and carried connotations of ugliness.[48] There are two important questions about what Paul says here. First, why has he described his seeing of Jesus, which took place *after* the other 'seeings' had come to an end, with a word that describes something happening too *early*? Second, why has he inserted the definite article, 'as to *the* one untimely born'?

Paul clearly cannot intend all the possible overtones of the word. An aborted or miscarried foetus would not normally live, but the event had brought him to life in a whole new way. However, the sense of something that happens too soon, too early, might be right, not for his place within the sequence of 'seeings', but for his own process of getting ready to be born – or rather, of his *not* being ready to be born. Place him for a moment in parallel with the other apostles, and the point becomes clear. The others had had a process of gestation, knowing Jesus, keeping company with him, watching, listening, praying, even helping during his public ministry. Paul had had none of this: he was a zealous young right-wing Torah student, ready for anything, including violence, that might hasten the kingdom of God and, with it, Israel's victory over pagans without and traitors within. The other apostles were not exactly ready to think in terms of Jesus' crucifixion and resurrection, but at least this was the Jesus they knew. Paul was not even on

[46] For the erroneous idea that this passage describes Paul's conversion see below, ch. 8.
[47] See LSJ ad loc.
[48] For ugliness cf. e.g. Num 12.12; cf LXX Job 3.16; Eccl. 6.3; Philo *Leg. All.* 1.76. See further Schneider in *TDNT* 2.465–7; Nickelsburg 1986; Thiselton 2000, 1208–10.

the map; in terms of the process of gestation and birth, he was many months from being ready to emerge into the light of a new day in which YHWH and Israel had been redefined around a crucified Messiah.[49]

This may be part of the reason why Paul used the image of an untimely birth. He was, as it were, ripped from the womb in a traumatic way, blinded by the sudden light like an infant whose organs had not yet developed sufficiently to cope with the demands of the outside world. Paul gives here, I suggest, a hint that he knows his 'seeing' of Jesus was indeed a little different from those of the others. The blinding light, the drama of it, as reported by Acts, may be stylized.[50] But the Luke who wrote Acts is the same Luke who also describes the road to Emmaus and the other 'ordinary', non-dazzling post-resurrection 'appearances'. And Paul explains the difference between himself and the others not in terms of his seeing of Jesus being a different sort of 'seeing', but in terms of his own personal unreadiness for such an experience. It took an emergency operation, he may be saying, to bring him into the list of witnesses to Jesus' resurrection; his 'seeing' of Jesus was the same as theirs in terms of the Jesus they saw, but it was radically different in terms of his own experience, being ripped from the womb of zealous Judaism, to come face to dazzling face with the crucified and risen lord.

The definite article (*the* untimely birth) remains a puzzle, and addressing it may help to gain more clarity here. It implies that Paul has in mind a particular example of an *ektroma*, a stillborn child. He could conceivably be echoing Job 3.16, where the phrase *hosper ektroma* occurs: Job is wishing that he could have been like a stillborn child who never sees the light. This would mean that Paul was alluding, not to the process of his 'birth' as such, but to the condition he was in immediately before it: he was like someone as good as dead, unable to see anything, but all that was changed in a fresh act of life-giving grace. The other possible allusion is to Numbers 12.12, where Moses prays that Miriam, who has opposed him and been punished with leprosy, should not remain leprous, 'like one equal to a dead person, like a stillborn infant (*hosei ektroma*) that comes forth from its mother's womb with its flesh half consumed'. This may offer more illumination.[51] The context is of Miriam and Aaron challenging Moses' leadership (Numbers 12.1–9). YHWH summons all three, and declares that he speaks with Moses face to face, and that Moses 'sees the form of YHWH' (the LXX has 'sees the glory of the Lord', probably to avoid speaking of someone actually seeing YHWH). If Paul is alluding to this story he is doing so in order to align himself with Miriam, and the early church with Moses, the ones who have seen the lord face to face. *Hosperei to ektromati*, again, would then allude, not so

---

[49] For this explanation cf. too Rowland 1982, 376.

[50] See below, ch. 8.

[51] I owe this suggestion (as indeed much else) to Dr Nicholas Perrin.

much to his experience of being 'born', as to the state he was in as a result of his persecution of those who had rightly claimed to have seen the lord. This makes án excellent link with what now follows, and – though as usual Paul's multiple imagery should not be pressed too far – it allows him to speak in biblical terms both of his opposition to the new covenant people on their wilderness wandering and of the divine forgiveness which had healed him of that condition.[52] Paul had been 'like *the* untimely birth [in the story]', until the forgiving grace of the covenant god caught up with him as well.[53] This is of course unprovable, but it at least opens up possibilities.

This explanation fits well with verses 9–10, which otherwise seem unnecessary. Introduced with *gar*, 'for', they explain something in verse 8, and the best candidate is the phrase 'as to the one untimely born'. Paul's earlier persecutions mean that he, unlike the others, does not deserve the title of 'apostle'; but he reinforces the fact that he bears this title none the less by referring to his tireless hard work. This, too, he says, is the result of the particular grace (personal commission, with the sense of divine power overcoming human undeserving) given to him.[54] Paul embodies in himself the transforming power of the age to come which has burst into the present age with the resurrection of Jesus. These two verses continue to keep him lined up alongside the other apostles, some of whom were themselves known to the Corinthians; but his point in verse 11, which has been the strength of the whole paragraph, is that the gospel he and they all preached was the same. Paul, Cephas, James and everyone else announced that the Messiah had died and been raised.

What they must have meant by this, for the present paragraph to work, is the sense that those words would naturally have borne in both the pagan and the Jewish worlds of the day: that, following bodily death and burial, the Messiah had been bodily raised from the dead. If Paul and the others had intended to refer to anything other than this, the talk of 'seeings' would be irrelevant; the idea that they occurred for a while and then no more would be incomprehensible; and the idea that with this event the new age had broken in to the present age would be unimaginable.

(iii) 1 Corinthians 15.12–28

(a) Introduction

Paul now faces the main challenge that has been reported to him (probably by his visitors, not through a letter) on this whole topic, the challenge that he

[52] cf. too 1 Tim. 1.15f.

[53] The only other occurrence of *ektroma* in the LXX is in Eccl. 6.3, which does not appear to be relevant here.

[54] cf. Rom. 1.5; 12.3, 6; 15.15; 1 Cor. 3.10; Gal. 2.9; Eph. 3.2, 7f.; Col. 1.25.

understands to be cognate with several of the main problems he has dealt with in the letter so far: some in the church have been saying that there is no such thing as resurrection of the dead (15.12). As already indicated (316 above), I regard it as highly probable that this refers, not to people who believe that 'the resurrection' has already in some sense happened to all the righteous, but to people who, on the normal grounds common to pagan antiquity and post-Enlightenment modernity, deny that any such thing can happen.[55] What is in mind here, clearly, is the future resurrection of God's people, not the past resurrection of Jesus. Paul shows in verses 13–15 that denying the future resurrection entails denying that of Jesus, and that this in turn falsifies the gospel proclamation itself.

This argument indicates what is, and is not, involved in the reported denial. It is to controvert this denial, and so to ground more securely the thrust of the whole letter, that Paul has designed the argument of verses 12–49, together with its final flourish in verses 50–58. The present section (B in our schema) is the first major section of this argument, subdividing (B1 and B2) into verses 12–19 and 20–28. In the first of these, Paul uses brief, rapid-fire *reductio ad absurdum* arguments to show what would follow from the denial. In the second, he unpacks the counter-affirmation, beginning with the Messiah's own resurrection (which had not been specifically denied) and showing how the resurrection of all the Messiah's people (which had been) follows from it.

Once more, there can be no question, granted the normal meaning of the words Paul uses, that what he has in mind is bodily resurrection. If we were to take the paragraph out of its context, it would be logically possible to understand it in terms of 'resurrection' meaning 'non-bodily survival of death'; but this is simply not possible historically or lexicographically. *Egeiro* and *anastasis* were words in regular use to denote something specifically distinguished from non-bodily survival, namely, a return to bodily life. There is no evidence to suggest that these words were capable of denoting a non-bodily survival after death.[56] Nor is there any reason to suppose that many in Corinth would have taken a hard line like the Sadducees, and a few

---

[55] So, rightly, Hays 1997, 252f.; Martin 1995, 106; cf., differently, Vos 1999; Delobel 2002. 2 Tim. 2.18 is not parallel (see above, 267–9). For the pagan context see above, ch. 2.

[56] Kellermann 1979, 65 suggests that the author of 2 Macc. 7 used *anistemi* to mean non-bodily ascension to God; but the vv. in question (9, 14) both speak of the future bodily resurrection. Schwankl 1987, 257 n. 47 supports this contention as follows: Philo, *Cher.* 115, describes the post-mortal progress of the soul to God with the verb *metanastesetai*. However, *metanastasis* and its cognates never had any overtones of 'resurrection'; the word-group simply means 'migration' (e.g. Xen. *Mem.* 3.5.12; Polyb. 3.5.5; other refs. in LSJ s.vv. *metanastasis, metanistemi*). Schwankl also cites a grave inscription of Antipater of Sidon (c. 170–100 BC), calling the post-mortal ascent of the soul an *anastasis* (*Anthologia Graeca* 7.748; text in Hengel 1974, 197); but the original inscription reads *astesin*, and even if the proposed emendation of this to *anstasin* be accepted this is hardly a firm base from which to overturn the otherwise universal usage.

pagan philosophers, and denied any form of future life at all. There is, however, plenty of reason to suppose that it would be quite natural for recently converted ex-pagans to doubt, and even to deny, a future bodily resurrection. Their entire culture was used to denying such a possibility; the multiple varieties of pagan worldview and theology offered nothing that would generate such a belief; common-sense observation of what happened to dead bodies, such as we find in the anti-Christian writings of subsequent centuries as well as in the modern period, militates against holding such a hope. But Paul sees that at this point no compromise is possible. You may be allowed to eat meat offered to idols, but you cannot deny the future bodily resurrection and claim that denial as an allowable Christian option.

In verses 12–19 he argues quickly, to establish some kind of bridgehead in their thinking, that such a denial produces radical inconsistencies at the heart of Christian identity. This will enable him to get into his stride and explain extensively how the worldview of new creation, new covenant and new age actually functions, and the place of the future resurrection within it (verses 20–28).

(b) 1 Corinthians 15.12–19

This rapid paragraph takes the shape of a spiral, in which the same argument occurs twice in quick succession. After the opening announcement of the theme ('If the Messiah is proclaimed as having been raised from the dead, how can some of you say that there is no resurrection of the dead?'[57]), Paul demonstrates, in very similar terms, that denying the future resurrection would entail the denial of the Messiah's resurrection, which in turn would undermine Christian faith:

> [13]If there is no resurrection of the dead, then nor was the Messiah raised; [14]and if the Messiah is not raised, our proclamation and your faith are both empty . . . [16]If the dead are not raised, then nor was the Messiah raised; [17]and if the Messiah is not raised, your faith is futile, and you are still in your sins.

These two are linked by verse 15, which draws from verses 12b–14 the further corollary that the apostles have been telling lies about the true god in saying that he raised the Messiah – because he did not do so if it is true that the dead are not raised. This indicates the real substratum of the argument: Paul's doctrine of God, which is the Jewish, more specifically Pharisaic, belief that the creator is the one who raises the dead.[58]

---

[57] Should it perhaps be translated, 'if the Messiah is announced (or: if [Jesus] is announced as Messiah) *because* he was raised from the dead . . .'? If so, this would be a close parallel with Rom. 1.4.

[58] See above, chs. 3 and 4. Fee 1987, 743 n. 24 points out that this verse only makes its point if Paul thinks of the resurrection of Jesus as a definite event.

The basic argument, then, is a *reductio ad absurdum*, showing that those who deny the future resurrection are cutting off the branch they are sitting on. Verse 14 takes this at one level: if the resurrection does not happen, the apostles have been talking empty nonsense, and those who believed them have believed empty nonsense.[59] Verse 17 takes this one degree further: their faith is not only 'empty', but 'futile', *mataia*, a waste of time; and the crucial point is not just that they are believing rubbish about the resurrection, and about Jesus, but that *the new age in which sins are left behind has not after all been inaugurated*. The foundation of the gospel, mentioned by Paul in the introduction to Galatians (1.4), has not after all been laid. For Paul, the point of the resurrection is not simply that the creator god has done something remarkable for one solitary individual (as people today sometimes imagine is the supposed thrust of the Easter proclamation), but that, in and through the resurrection, 'the present evil age' has been invaded by the 'age to come', the time of restoration, return, covenant renewal, and forgiveness. An event has occurred as a result of which the world is a different place, and human beings have the new possibility to become a different kind of people.

As we saw, this belief was embedded in the pregnant gospel formula in verses 3b–4. The logic of it is simple, granted the close link throughout scripture between sin and death: if God has overcome death in the resurrection of Jesus, then the power of sin is broken; but if he hasn't, it isn't. This generates the two-age eschatology which Paul will shortly expound in verses 20–28.

The last two verses of the subsection look ahead to verses 29–34. Denial of the resurrection, of believers and of the Messiah, would have two drastic consequences, both of which would undermine what Paul sees as ordinary Christian faith. On the one hand, Christians who have already died have 'perished'; in other words, they will not have a future life in any form worth the name (see verse 29). Verse 18 assumes that there are people who have already 'fallen asleep in the Messiah',[60] and that the doubters have raised questions about their future. On the other hand, those who at present suffer and struggle for the gospel are the most-to-be-pitied members of the human race, since they are undergoing the present hardships for the sake of a future which is not going to happen (see verses 30–34). These verses give a further sharp indication that what is at stake is indeed bodily resurrection. Paul simply does not rate a prospect of future disembodied bliss anywhere on the scale of worthwhile goals; he would not classify non-bodily survival of death as 'salvation', presumably since it would mean that one was *not*

---

[59] Hays 1997, 260: the emphasis on the futility of a non-resurrection position goes with the warning about believing 'in vain' in v. 2, and the similar emphasis in vv. 10, 32, 58.

[60] As in 15.6; 1 Thess. 4.13–18; only in the latter passage he was trying to alleviate anxiety about them, whereas here he is trying to stir it up (so Hays 1997, 261).

rescued, 'saved', from death itself, the irreversible corruption and destruction of the good, god-given human body. To remain dead, even 'asleep in the Messiah', without the prospect of resurrection, would therefore mean that one had 'perished'. For there to be no resurrection would mean that Christian faith and life, including suffering, would be 'for this life only'.

(c) 1 Corinthians 15.20–28

It would still be open, of course, for anyone in Corinth or elsewhere to look at verses 12–19, agree with the logic, and draw the conclusion that Christianity as a whole was indeed based on a mistake, and was empty, futile and without hope. But Paul will not of course leave it there. The second half of section (B2) lays out Paul's classic statement of the larger picture of resurrection, that of Jesus and that of all those who belong to him as Messiah. This is the point above all where Paul is trying to teach the Corinthians to think eschatologically, within the Jewish categories of 'apocalyptic' – not of an 'imminent expectation' of the end of the world, but of the way in which the future has already burst into the present, so that the present time is characterized by a mixture of fulfilment and expectation, of 'now' and 'not yet', pointing towards a future in which what happened at the first Easter will be implemented fully and the true God will be all in all.[61] This passage offers a rethought kingdom-of-God scenario, after the manner of many such pictures in second-Temple Judaism, with the victory of this God over all enemies as the subject, and the resurrection and rule of the Messiah as the key redefining elements.[62]

Paul never loses sight of the main question he is addressing, and nor should we. He is arguing for the certainty of the future bodily resurrection of all the Messiah's people. The present passage sketches the framework within which this belief not only makes sense (not least in terms of the timing: first the Messiah, later all the Messiah's people) but follows inescapably. The basic point is made, as often with Paul, in the opening verse of the sequence (in this case, verse 20): the Messiah has been raised from the dead as the *aparche*, the 'first-fruits', the first sheaf of the harvest which guarantees that there will be more to come.[63] This is explained as follows:

> [21]For since through a human came death, through a human came also the resurrection of the dead; [22]for as in Adam all die, so also in the Messiah shall all be made alive.

---

[61] On this whole theme cf. e.g. Lincoln 1981.

[62] For kingdom-expectation in the period cf. *NTPG* 302–07; *JVG* 202–09.

[63] cf. Rom. 8.23; 11.16; 16.5; 2 Thess. 2.13.

The future resurrection is guaranteed, in other words, by Jesus' status as the truly human being, the one who fully bears the divine image. Paul only mentions this theme at the very end of his main argument, in verse 49, but by holding it in mind throughout (as we often have to do with Paul) we can see where he is going. It is because humankind was created with the purpose of bringing the creator's order to the world that now, because Jesus is the truly human one, he is invested with the task of bringing the creator's *rescuing* new order to the world. This theme is closely correlated with the installation of Jesus, at the same time, as Messiah: his resurrection has already revealed him as the world's true lord, and he will rule, as the scriptures said the Messiah would, until he has conquered all the enemies of the creator god, that is, all the powers of the world (supremely of course death itself) that raise themselves against the good creation and the fulfilment of the creator's purposes for it. Thus, by asserting in verses 21–2 that Jesus is the true human and the Messiah, Paul explains both *that* his resurrection is the beginning of a larger harvest and *how* that harvest will be accomplished.

This passage is, indeed, all about new creation as the fulfilment and redemption of the old. Paul develops it, and the parallel argument in the second half of the chapter, not least by means of reflection upon some of the classic biblical texts which speak of the original creation and of humankind as the creator's image-bearing steward over it. The stories of creation and fall, as told in Genesis 1.26–8 and 3.17–19, lie below the surface throughout, and the later parts of the chapter will allude frequently to the same passages. The great Psalm which speaks of humankind's vocation to rule the creation as the creator's vicegerent (Psalm 8), is explicitly quoted in verse 27, where it is closely aligned with the messianic Psalm 110 and with the multiple echoes of Daniel.[64] This is not a mere 'appeal to scripture', as though Paul were mounting an argument about something else and needed to drag in a few proof-texts;[65] he is thinking his way through a theology of creation and of humankind, and the biblical allusions indicate the narrative of which the resurrection of Jesus now forms the climax, helping the story to its intended goal. Just as, when Israel failed to be the light-bearing people for the world, the covenant God did not rewrite the vocation but rather sent the Messiah to act in Israel's place (that is the argument of Romans 2.17—4.25, and indeed lies behind much of Romans 5—8 and 9—11), so now the failure of humankind ('Adam') to be the creator's wise, image-bearing steward over creation has not led the creator to rewrite the vocation, but rather to send the Messiah as the truly human being. The purpose is that in his renewed, resurrected human life he can be and do, for humankind and all creation, what neither humankind nor creation could do for themselves. That is the theology of the

---

[64] Note the close parallels with Phil. 3.20f. Cf. too 1 Pet 3.19–22; and the use of Ps. 8 in Heb. 2.5–9.

[65] Against e.g. Perkins 1984, 221. On Paul's use of scripture here see Lambrecht 1982.

true God, of humankind and of creation which, rooted at every point in the Old Testament, is reaffirmed in this treatment of the resurrection of those who belong to the Messiah. And this takes its place within the larger picture of Easter as the critical first step in the plan and purpose of this God to be, through the Messiah's victory, 'all in all' (verse 28). When, within a theology of new creation such as this passage manifestly offers (the reaffirmation of the old creation and the liberation of it from everything that spoils, defaces and kills it), we find 'resurrection' as the central theme, this clearly refers, should there be any lingering doubt, to the resurrection of the body.

The way is now open to the heart of the argument, which is about the appropriate order within which all this will happen – both the chronological *sequence* and the ontological or even metaphysical *hierarchy* through which the world is brought 'to order'.[66] Paul describes this 'ordering' by means of an extended exposition of Psalm 8.7, where the key verb ('God has *put all things in order* under his feet') is repeated and exploited to build a theology of new creation as the fulfilment of the intention for the old. Within this, he has woven the theme of kingship, of messianic rule, from Psalm 110 and Daniel, in order to emphasize that the future bodily resurrection of all the Messiah's people is guaranteed because Jesus fulfils the roles through which, according to the promises, the world is to be brought under the saving rule of its creator God. The focal point of this saving kingdom is the defeat and abolition of death itself (verse 26). And the defeat and abolition of death must of course mean new life, new bodily life, resurrection life.

We may set out this dense argument as follows, with bracketed comments indicating the themes, biblical allusions and echoes which give it its depth and power:

> [23]But each in their own *order* [*en to idio tagmati*]: the Messiah as the first-fruits, then, at his royal appearing [*parousia*], those who belong to the Messiah. [24]Then comes the end, when he hands over the kingdom to God the father, when he has abolished all rule and all authority and power. [25]For he must reign until he has 'put all his enemies under his feet'. [26]The last enemy to be destroyed is death. [27]For 'he [i.e. God] has put everything in *order* (*hypetaxen*, cognate with *tagma* in verse 23] under his feet.' But when it says that 'everything is *put in order* [*hypotetaktai*]', it is obvious that it makes an exception for the one who *put everything in order* [*hypotaxantos*] under him. [28]When he *puts everything in order* [*hypotage*] under him, then the Son himself will be *placed in order* [*hypotagesetai*] under the one who *placed everything in order* [*hypotaxanti*] under him, so that God may be all in all.

We should note, first, the primary biblical echoes. In the Theodotion version of Daniel 2.44, Israel's God will 'raise up a kingdom' (*anastesei ho theos basileian*); in Daniel 7.14, and particularly 7.27, the saints of the Most High receive the everlasting kingdom. The first of these resonates with verse 24,

---

[66] Though *tagma* principally means 'order' in terms of hierarchy, military rank etc., it can also refer to a stage in a sequence; see BDAG 987f., with other refs.

the second with verse 25. The idea of putting all the Messiah's enemies under his feet comes, of course, from Psalm 110.1, which is frequently used messianically in early Christianity.[67] Finally, Psalm 8.7 comes to dominate the argument completely, with Paul getting from it the idea of the divinely intended order in which humankind plays an intermediate role between creator and creation.

The human task and the messianic task thus dovetail together: the Messiah, the true Human One, will rule the world in obedience to God.[68] This task is carried out during the present age by Jesus, constituted as Messiah in virtue of his resurrection. The task involves activity for which in biblical and apocalyptic literature the imagery of battle and victory is standard, and the military overtones of the word *tagma* in verse 23 (drawing up soldiers in 'order' or 'array' for battle) may well be intentional.[69] The flurry of occurrences of this word, or rather its various cognates, in verses 27–8, dependent on Psalm 8.7, indicates that from the beginning of the paragraph Paul had intended to work towards this point, and that he saw the fulfilment of Psalm 8.7 precisely in terms of the Messiah's metaphorically 'military' victory over all the creator's enemies, the 'rulers, authorities and powers', both human and suprahuman, that threaten the good creation.[70] This is where the allusions to Psalm 110 and to Daniel make their point, fitting in well with the overall second-Temple Jewish viewpoint on the coming establishment of God's kingdom. The result is the establishment of a final, stable 'order' in which the creator and covenant god is over the Messiah, and the Messiah is over the world – with the Messiah, in other words, taking precisely the position marked out in Genesis 1 and 2 for the human race, and in Daniel 7 for 'the people of the saints of the Most High': under the creator, over the world, reflecting the divine image into the world in terms of bringing the creator's victorious, wise, rescuing order to the world that would otherwise be subject to the destructive rule of death and all the powers that lead to it.[71] This god will be seen to be God, and will in the end be 'all in all'.[72]

The heart and centre of it all, then, is the defeat of death in the future, based on the proleptic defeat inflicted in the resurrection of Jesus himself; or, to put it another way, it is the final completion of the 'age to come', which was inaugurated, in the midst of the 'present evil age', through the Messiah's death and resurrection. This is the moment when the events spoken of in verses 3–4 are finally worked out. And this, clearly, is the

---

[67] cf. *JVG* 507–09.

[68] Pss. 2; 72; 89.

[69] Hays 1997, 264.

[70] The same root occurs, perhaps itself dependent on Ps. 8.7, in Dan. 7.27 LXX: all authorities 'will be subject to him', *hypotagesontai auto*.

[71] On death as a 'power' see e.g. Rom. 8.36–8; 1 Cor 3.22.

[72] cf. Eph 1.22; Col. 3.11 (of the Messiah). 'All in all' is a Pauline idiosyncrasy (Fee 1987, 759). For the final sequence, compare 1 Cor. 3.22f.

moment when, at Jesus' royal appearing (*parousia*), all those who belong to him are themselves raised bodily from the dead.[73] Verse 23 makes it clear (not that Paul or any of his readers would have doubted it) that the Christian dead have *not* yet been raised; wherever they are at the moment, their resurrection has not taken place.

The statement about the *parousia* in verse 23 corresponds closely to what is said in 1 Thessalonians 4.14–18 (where the developed and highly metaphorical picture of the future is, as here, based on the fundamental gospel events of Jesus' own death and resurrection, noted formulaically in 4.14), and also in Philippians 3.20–21, which in turn is based on the gospel events set out in 2.6–11. Though the *parousia* is not mentioned specifically when Paul recapitulates the present chapter in verses 50–58, the reference to the final raising of the dead in verse 52 picks up what is said in verse 23, and the 'victory' spoken of in verse 57 is another way of summarizing the effect of the whole present paragraph. Thus, though our present passage is one of Paul's more dense and allusive pieces of writing, its main lines stand out clearly, and we can reconstruct them with a fair degree of certainty both through the network of biblical allusions and through what we know from his other writings on similar topics, and the larger context in the present letter. The whole argument establishes, with rock-solid theology and considerable rhetorical power, the point that the resurrection of Jesus the Messiah is the starting-point and means whereby the creator, in completing the work of rescuing and renewing the original creation, will raise all the Messiah's people to new bodily life.[74]

We should not ignore the political overtones in this, another letter to a Roman colony. The whole paragraph is about the Messiah through whose 'kingdom' (*basileia*) the one true God will overthrow all other authorities and rulers. 'Resurrection', as in Pharisaic thought, belongs firmly within kingdom-of-god theology; and every first-century Jew knew that kingdom-of-God theology carried inescapable political meaning. The present 'ordering' (*tagma*) of society places Caesar at the top, his agents in the middle, and ordinary people at the bottom; the creator's new ordering will have himself at the top, the Messiah – and his people, as in 6.2 and elsewhere! – in the middle, and the world as a whole underneath, not however exploited and oppressed but rescued and restored, given the freedom which comes with the wise rule of the creator, his Messiah, and his image-bearing subjects. This

---

[73] The question of whether there is a *further* moment at which *all* the dead are raised (the question, in other words, of whether *eita* at the start of v. 24 refers to a further 'then' that follows the resurrection of the Messiah's people in v. 23b, and if so, as seems likely, whether at this subsequent moment a further resurrection of all who have *not* belonged to the Messiah's people is envisaged) does not need to be settled for the purposes of our argument. See BDAG 988.

[74] See Fee 1987, 747, with e.g. McCaughey 1974. It should be noted that in v. 28 Jesus is spoken of as the divine 'son', with resonances of Psalm 2.7, 12 and Rom. 1.3f.

passage thus belongs with Romans 8, Philippians 2.6–11 and 3.20–21 as, simultaneously, a classic exposition of the creator God's plans to rescue the creation, and a coded but powerful reminder to the young church, living in Caesar's world, that Jesus was lord and that at his name every knee would bow.

(iv) 1 Corinthians 15.29–34

The next paragraph is short: something of an interlude, a brief respite from dense and involved argumentation.[75] Jerky writing; short sentences; swift subject-changes; a quotation from pagan poetry. The flavour is both *ad hoc* and *ad hominem*, a quick, improvised, scattergun approach to make sure the listener is still awake.[76] Four different subjects in five verses, with resurrection the thread that links them all; four small windows, each affording a glimpse of the continuity between the present life and the future one. Underneath is the logic which sustained verses 12–19: if the denial of the resurrection were to be upheld, think what that would actually mean for Christian symbolic practice, for Paul's own apostolic lifestyle, for the Christian ethic. Think, and be ashamed, he says, at the ignorance of the true god which the denial implies.[77]

The first topic remains controversial (verse 29). Paul assumes that people were being 'baptized on behalf of the dead', and declares that this practice can only have a point if the dead are to be raised. There is no agreement on what this 'baptism on behalf of the dead' was, there being no other reference to it in early Christianity. A case has recently been made for interpreting it simply as people seeking baptism (and hence joining the church) because a Christian relative or friend has recently died and they want to be sure of being reunited with them in the life to come.[78] That seems possible, but equally possible, I think, is the more traditional reading, that some people who had come to Christian faith in Corinth had died before being baptized, and that other Christians had undergone baptism on their behalf, completing vicariously in their own persons the unfinished sacramental initiation of the dead.[79] If we go with the majority interpretation, Paul is saying that the dead are still in some sense alive, but not yet raised, and the symbolic dying and rising with the Messiah which is portrayed in baptism can be claimed on their behalf, looking ahead to the resurrection which is still to come. If the other proposal is adopted, the argument still holds, though the practice of

[75] For the sudden change of style cp. e.g. Gal. 4.12–19.

[76] See Fee 1987, 62.

[77] On the passage see Winter 2001, 96–105.

[78] Thiselton 2000, 1240–49.

[79] See the lengthy discussion in Fee 1987, 763–7. Some have detected here echoes of the sacrifices on behalf of the dead in 2 Macc. 12.43–5 (above, 152f.).

seeking baptism in order to be sure of being reunited with dead friends or relatives would of course be equally compatible, at that level, with various different theories of what happened after death.

Paul then develops in verses 30–32a the thought he mentioned briefly in verse 19, alluding also to the mention of his apostolic labours in verse 10: what is the point of undergoing so much suffering, persecution, hard work and ill treatment if there is no coming resurrection?

> [30]Why do we undergo danger every hour? [31]I die every day – I swear it by the pride I take in you, my dear family, in the Messiah, Jesus our lord! [32]If it was for ordinary human reasons that I fought with wild animals at Ephesus, what profit is that to me?

Again, there are exegetical problems that do not concern us.[80] What matters is once more the *continuity* which Paul sees between the present life and the resurrection life, and the fact that the future life thus gives meaning to what would otherwise be meaningless.

The second half of verse 32 applies the same continuity to the question of Christian ethics, just as Paul did in chapters 5 and 6. He thinks into the logic of the denial of resurrection hope, echoing Isaiah 22.13 and following the argument of 'the wicked' in Wisdom 2.5–11: if there is no future life, why then, the present is to be enjoyed to the full.

> [32b]If the dead are not raised, 'Let us eat and drink, for tomorrow we die.' [33]Do not be deceived: 'Bad company destroys good habits.'

The context of Isaiah 22 is one of judgment: Israel had forgotten her God (22.11), and would not listen to his call to repentance (22.12), but instead went ahead with festivities (22.13a), saying, 'Let us eat and drink, for tomorrow we die' (22.13b). Israel's sins were thus not forgiven (22.14). Paul, having already warned that if the resurrection is not true 'you are still in your sins' (verse 18), seems to refer to this whole sequence of thought, as we see in the the sharp warning and exhortation that immediately follow.

It was not only careless ancient Israelites, of course, who could think like that, as the parallel in Wisdom shows. This attitude was popularly ascribed to the Epicurean school of philosophy.[81] Even the pagan poets know, says Paul as he quotes Menander's play *Thaïs* to the effect that living among people who are careless of the future will eat away at good moral habits.[82] Though Paul awakens many echoes both in the Bible and in the popular thought of the time, his main point is the same as earlier in the letter: the resurrection is the ultimate grounding of Christian moral effort.[83]

---

[80] For details see the commentaries.

[81] See Malherbe 1968; Thiselton 2000, 1251f.

[82] Menander, *Thaïs*, frag. 218. The phrase was probably a popular epigram; for other refs., see Thiselton 2000, 1254 n. 249.

[83] cf. 2 Pet. 2—3 (so Fee 1987, 775).

This leads naturally into the closing appeal of verse 34: sober up, think rightly, stop sinning! Some, Paul declares – presumably the 'some' in verse 34 are the same as the 'some' in verse 12, not a different group, and not outsiders – have no knowledge of the true god. The church should be ashamed of itself for allowing such a situation to develop. Jews often declared that Gentiles did not know the true God,[84] but this seems to be more specifically a charge that the people concerned do not know the power of this God to raise the dead.[85] A true knowledge would show what this God is capable of doing, and also that he is the judge who will call everyone to account. This charge goes closely with previous references to the creator God in the letter,[86] and indeed with the entire argument of the preceding chapters, not least 5 and 6. Get your thinking straightened out, Paul seems to be saying, instead of muddling along in the theological equivalent of a drunken stupor.[87] Recognize who the true God really is, and everything will become clear.

The brief interlude over, Paul resumes his large-scale task. He did not, presumably, suppose that verses 29–34 would by themselves win over any doubters; the task of this passage is rather to put down a few markers to remind his audience of various things that would follow if the views of the doubters were to become widespread. Though, as we have said, some parts of the passage might by themselves be compatible with a non-bodily view of post-mortem existence, the probable meaning of verse 29, and particularly the parallels between the ethical appeal and earlier parts of the letter where the resurrection is emphasized, rule this option out. Paul's way is now clear to address the hardest problem he faces. If the dead are indeed to be raised, how will this occur? What sort of a body will they have?

(v) 1 Corinthians 15.35–49

(a) Introduction

The key to understanding the next fifteen verses is to realize that they, like verses 20–28, are built on the foundation of Genesis 1 and 2. This, too, is part of Paul's theology of new creation. Its climax comes in the last verse (49), where Paul gives the final answer to his opening question: what sort of body will the dead receive when they are raised? They will bear – *we* shall bear, says Paul – the image of the man who is 'from heaven', that is, the

---

[84] cf. Martin 1995, 275 n. 79; and in Paul cf. Rom. 1.18–23 (see above, 245–7, 264).

[85] cf. Mk. 12.24b and pars.; Rom. 4.20f. See too the various second-century writers, for whom this was a regular theme (below, ch. 11).

[86] 1 Cor. 1.5; 8.1–6; 13.2, 8; see Wedderburn 1999, 233 n. 17.

[87] *eknepsate*, a *hapax legomenon* in the NT, comes from *eknepho*, 'become sober'.

'final Adam', the Messiah.[88] That question and answer is not only the critical thing to bear in mind throughout the passage; it also supplies the main thrust of our own reading of this passage, studying what Paul says about the future body which Christians will have to see, from this, what he believes about the resurrection body of Jesus himself.

A glance through Genesis 1—2 reveals how many of its major themes are alluded to in Paul's present argument. The creator God made the heavens and the earth, and filled both with his creatures; Paul mentions these two categories in verse 40, and uses a discussion of them to distinguish the first Adam from the final one. The powerful divine wind, or spirit, moved over the waters, and the divine breath or spirit also animated Adam and Eve; the life-giving activity of both the creator and Jesus is seen by Paul in terms of the *pneuma*, the spirit, wind or breath (verses 44–6). The creator made the lights in heaven, which Paul mentions in verse 41. He created plants bearing fruit containing seed, so that more plants could be produced; Paul makes this a major theme in verses 36–8, and then draws on the language of 'sowing' in verses 42–4. The creator made every kind of bird, animal and fish; Paul brings them, too, into his argument (verses 39–40). At the climax of Genesis 1, the creator made human beings in his own image, to have dominion over the rest of creation, and in Genesis 2 he entrusted Adam in particular with responsibility for naming the animals; for Paul, too, the climax of the story is the recreation of humankind through the life-giving activity of the final Adam, whose image will be borne by all who belong to him. This is indeed a deliberate and careful theology of new Genesis, of creation renewed.

Within this, Paul is mounting a step-by-step argument so that by the time we get to verse 49 we can see the full meaning of what he is saying. He will not say, right out, 'the new body will be like that of Jesus', though that, as in Philippians 3.21, is where he intends to arrive. He argues first for discontinuity within continuity: the plant is not the same thing as the seed, and yet is derived from it by the creator's power (verses 36–8). There are in any case different types of physicality throughout creation, each with its own special properties and dignity (verses 39–41). This constitutes the first subsection of his argument (b1 in our schema); Paul is setting up categories from the created order to provide a template of understanding for the new creation, to which he then turns. The new, resurrected body will be in continuity and discontinuity with the present one, not least because the present one is 'corruptible' whereas the new one will be 'incorruptible' (as he will emphasize in the final paragraph of the chapter). This will be because the new body will be brought into being, and held in incorruptible being, by the Spirit of the creator God, as a result of the life-giving work of the final Adam.

---

[88] Paul's phrase is *ho eschatos Adam* (v. 45), often translated 'last Adam', but Paul's point is not that there are plenty of 'Adams' of whom the Messiah happens to be the last one, but that he is the goal, the ultimate point. For this 'final' seems somewhat better.

For our purposes virtually every aspect of this is crucial.

(1) There should be no doubt that Paul is arguing for a *bodily* resurrection; we will deal below with the major misreading of this section which has often been used to challenge this, and to propose that the body is composed of glorious light rather than anything physical, and to interpret *soma pneumatikon* in verses 44–6 to mean 'spiritual, i.e. non-physical, body'.

(2) But Paul is also arguing for a bodily resurrection very different from a mere resuscitation. A seed does not come to life by being dug up, brushed down and restored to its pristine seediness. Having created hermeneutical space to talk about different types of bodies, by listing the many different types in the original creation, Paul exploits this to differentiate in several respects between the present body and the future one. This is a striking innovation within the Jewish traditions of resurrection discussions, though it obviously remains within the Jewish world of thought, and has not wandered off to link itself to pagan speculations with mere surface borrowing from Jewish tradition.

(3) The Messiah, as the final Adam, the start of the renewed human race (compare Colossians 1.18b), is not only the model for the new type of humanity. He possesses the authority to bring it into being. The power through which he exercises that authority is, as we should by now expect, the Spirit.

These three points tell us a good deal about what Paul thought had happened to Jesus. They also indicate, by their many innovations within Jewish tradition, that whatever else we say about this passage it is not simply an application to believers, or by extension to Jesus himself, of existing Jewish theological and exegetical explorations. It belongs firmly within the world of Judaism, but no Jewish writing had said anything quite like this before. Paul clearly believes that something has happened because of which new construals of well-known texts and themes are now appropriate.

We are now ready to plunge into the detail of the two subsections.

(b) 1 Corinthians 15.35–41

Paul's sharp reaction to the initial question ('Fool!', verse 36) makes best sense if we assume that he takes the question to be posed, like the Sadducees' question in the gospel, not as a genuine enquiry but as a dismissive put-down. 'How are the dead raised?', in other words, probably implies 'We all know it's impossible!'; 'In what sort of body will they come back?' implies 'I can't imagine any sort of body that would do that!' The word 'how' itself can carry this overtone: 'How can you say that the dead are raised?'[89]

---

[89] See BDAG 901, quoting e.g. Mt. 12.26 par. As Fee says (1987, 779), these questions

The two questions seem to focus on different points, not simply to be two ways of raising the same one.[90] The English word 'how' can slide easily from 'by what agency' to 'in what manner'. The meaning of 'How do I look?' will vary depending on whether the speaker is struggling to see through a telescope or emerging anxiously from a dressing-room. Though the Greek *pos* can carry several shades of meaning, and can point to a second question which simply elucidates the first,[91] the most natural way of reading the first question is not 'How, that is, in what appearance or type of body, are the dead raised?', but 'By what agency or power can this extraordinary thing happen?' Certainly the passage that follows answers this question as well as the one about the type of body. In the present subsection Paul prepares his answer to the first question by saying that, in the case of a planted seed, the creator 'gives it a body' (verse 38); in the following subsection he applies this specifically in terms of the Messiah's authority and the power of the Spirit (verses 44–6). In the present subsection he prepares the ground for his answer to the second one by insisting that there are many different types of body, and that it is possible for there to be continuity as well as discontinuity between different types. It looks as though he is giving a two-stage answer to two questions: 'How is it done?' and 'What sort of a thing will it be?' We may note – a rather obvious point, but perhaps it needs to be stressed – that he would scarcely have needed to go to all this trouble if what he meant was that the resurrection 'body' was not in some sense 'physical', if after all he had been talking about a non-embodied soul or spirit.[92]

Paul now glances quickly through different aspects of the present created order, beginning with seeds and plants, describing the process of sowing, germination and new life in language carefully chosen to serve as a model for what he is going to say. He does not, of course, suppose that the resurrection body will grow out of the present body, after burial, in the same way that an oak grows from a planted acorn. His point is that the creator's power 'gives life' to the seed that has 'died' (verse 36):

> [36]Fool! What you sow is not brought to life unless it dies. [37]And, when you sow something, you do not sow the body that is to be, but a naked husk, perhaps of

---

embody the kind of philosophical objections that must have lain behind the denial of the resurrection in v. 12. On the question of how well Paul understood the Corinthians' views see Perkins 1984, 300f., 324; Conzelmann 1975 [1969], 261–3; Martin 1995, 104–36. I have taken the view that their objection was not particularly complicated, since it expressed the more or less universal view of pagan antiquity, and that this is what Paul is addressing.

[90] Against Hays 1997, 269f.

[91] See LSJ s.v.: e.g. Eurip. *Hel.* 1543 ('How, by what ship, did you come?'); cp. Plato *Tim.* 22b.

[92] It is worth noting that Paul, having spoken largely of 'the dead' (*hoi nekroi*) up to this point in the chapter, here switches to speak of 'bodies' when thinking of that which is to be raised. 'The dead', for him, are not simply 'souls' (so, rightly, Fee 1987, 775).

wheat or some other grain. [38]But God gives it a body in accordance with his wishes, giving each of the seeds its own body.

In verse 36 the crucial verb should not be translated 'come to life', as in NRSV; it is passive, indicating divine action.[93] This is the point of verse 38, beginning the answer to the question 'how'. The basic image speaks of continuity (the corn growing from the seed), but Paul here stresses the discontinuity: seed and plant are not identical.[94] You do not sow a cauliflower, nor do you serve cauliflower-seed with roast beef. Paul is careful to describe the present body, the 'seed', as 'naked': it is not yet 'clothed' as one day it will be. When given its new *soma* it will no longer be 'naked'. This links with 2 Corinthians 5.3–4; behind both passages stands the nakedness of the first humans in Genesis 2 (the passage which, quoted in verse 45, reveals itself as having been in Paul's mind for some while).[95] The emphasis of verse 38 is then on the new body not only as the work of the sovereign God, but as a *gift*; Paul wants to stress that resurrection is a work of grace.

His initial implied answer to the question of verse 35, then, is this: resurrection will come about through the creator's agency; and the sort of body that it will involve is like the fully clothed version of something which at present is 'naked'.

Having established the seed-and-plant principle as a partial analogy for resurrection, Paul begins a different train of thought in verse 39. There are different types of 'body' or 'flesh', each with its own dignity and worth:

[39]Not all flesh is the same kind of flesh, but there is one sort for humans, another sort for animals, another for birds, and another for fish. [40]There are physical objects in the heavens, and there are physical objects on the earth; but the proper 'glory' of the heavenly ones is one kind of thing, and that of the earthly ones is another kind of thing. [41]The 'glory' of the sun is one kind of thing, the 'glory' of the moon is another, and the 'glory' of the stars is different again – for one star differs from another in 'glory'.

Paul's main purpose here is to establish that there are different kinds of physicality, each of which has its own proper characteristics. It is possible that he has Daniel 12.2–3 in mind, but if so he seems to be modifying it importantly as he goes along, since what he does *not* go on to say is that the newly embodied resurrected ones become like stars (still less does he suggest, of course, that they actually *become* stars).[96] The distinction between

---

[93] For the image cf. Jn. 12.24 (see below, 444f.).

[94] This is the first time the word *soma*, body, has occurred in this chapter. In the background, of course, is not only 6.13–20 but 12.12–27 (see above, ch. 6).

[95] On 2 Cor. 5 see below, 364–70.

[96] Hays 1997, 271 suggests Dan. 12 in the background; though this is likely, Paul does not seem to me to be emphasizing it. Boismard 1999 [1995], 40 declares that 'an earthly being is buried in the earth and a completely different being will rise, comparable to the stars shining in the sky.'

'heavenly' and 'earthly' bodies in verse 40 anticipates that of verses 47–9; though it is important that, whereas here the word he uses for 'earthly' is *epigeios*, 'upon-the-earth-ly', a word principally of *location* rather than *composition*, the word in verses 47–9 is *choikos*, 'earthy', a word describing physical composition.[97] Subtle changes like this are important in a carefully argued passage, as any politician or speech-writer, never mind philosopher or theologian, will tell you. Paul is careful not to imply that the *analogies* he is offering in the present subsection are actually *analyses* of how the resurrection itself will be. He is here setting up a network of metaphor and simile, not metonymy.

That the 'glory' of the different creatures does not primarily refer to luminosity, though in several cases it includes that, is clear from verse 40b, where physical objects in the heavens (i.e. in the sky) have one kind of glory, and those on the earth have another. Objects on earth do not shine as do the sun, moon and stars; but they still have their own proper 'glory'. Here 'glory' seems to mean 'honour', 'reputation', 'proper dignity'.[98] As we saw in discussing 2 Corinthians 3, the word remains multivalent even in a passage where some of its uses seem to refer more or less directly to 'shining'; Paul's other uses in the present letter do not have anything to do with luminosity.[99] It is of course the proper dignity, reputation and honour of the sun that it should shine brightly, and of stars that they should twinkle in their own appropriate manner, one differing from another (as Paul says) in its own particular way. The implicit contrast, as he makes clear in verse 43, is not between 'glory' (= 'luminosity, brightness') and 'darkness' (i.e. not shining), but between 'glory' (= the splendour proper to this object being fully what it is) and 'dishonour' or 'shame'.[100] Just because it is part of the 'glory' of a star that it shines, that does not mean that everything else must

---

[97] Cf. LSJ s.v. For *epigeios* as indicating location in the NT cf. e.g. Phil. 2.10; this can of course carry negative overtones, and be contrasted with the heavenly world, as in e.g. Phil. 3.19; cf. Col. 3.2. Dahl 1962, 113–16 seems to me to elide *epigeios* with *choikos*, making it mean 'corruptible', rather than observing Paul's distinction. *Choikos* is an extremely rare word formed from *chous*, 'soil' or 'dust'; Paul presumably has in mind Gen. 2.7, where this is the material from which God forms human beings (though LXX uses *ge*, earth, where one might have expected *chous* in Gen. 3.19; but cf. Ps. 103 [MT 104].29; Eccles. 3.20; 12.7; 1 Macc. 2.63, and perhaps also Ps. 21.16 [MT 22.15], where 'the dust of death', *chous thanatou*, seems to be a vivid way of referring to the grave).

[98] Fee 1987, 782: 'each is adapted to its own peculiar existence'.

[99] See 1 Cor. 2.7f.; 10.31; 11.7, 15.

[100] See e.g. Phil. 3.21, where 'glory' is contrasted with *atimia*, 'dishonour', and *tapeinosis*, 'humiliation'. In a vast range of ancient literature the regular meaning of *doxa* is 'good repute, honour', as opposed to shame and humiliation: see LSJ s.v. Indeed LSJ only list 'external appearance' as a meaning for the word in relation to a few biblical instances, e.g. Ex. 16.10. Perkins's comment (1984, 305) that the word changes its meaning after v. 42 from 'the brightness of heavenly bodies' to 'honour' misses the point. Boismard 1999 [1995], 45, says that the new body will be 'as if transformed into light (glory)'. This, I suggest, is precisely what Paul is *not* saying.

have 'glory' of that sort. It is no shame to a dog that it does not shine, or to a star that it does not bark.

Paul does not, then, think of 'heavenly bodies' as 'spiritual beings clothed with light'.[101] He is not buying in to the cosmology of the *Timaeus*; indeed, the way the entire chapter is built around Genesis 1 and 2 indicates that he is consciously choosing to construct a cosmology, and within that a future hope, from the most central of Jewish sources. The sun, moon and stars are objects in a different part of the universe, possessing their own properties, which happen to include shining. If Paul is aware of a shift in meaning between 'heavenly' as meaning 'the location of sun, moon and stars', as in the present passage, and 'heavenly' as he uses it in verse 48–9, he does not indicate it, but leaves his readers to make the transition through his move, in what now follows, from metaphor and simile to explicit description. Just as the seed/plant analogy remains important, though Paul does not suppose that resurrection bodies grow from corpses as cherry-trees do from cherry-stones, so the earthly body/heavenly body distinction remains important, though Paul does not suppose that resurrection means becoming a star – or, indeed, a sun or a moon.

There is thus no suggestion in this passage that he is intending to explain the resurrection body within the framework of 'astral immortality'. As we saw when discussing Daniel 12 and Wisdom 3, this concept will in any case not work for those Jewish texts that, like Paul here, see the future beyond death in *two* steps or stages. Nor does Paul suppose that there is a 'soul' which corresponds, in its material make-up, to the stars; if that had been his intention, he would hardly have spoken in verses 44–6 of the *present* body as the 'soulish' one, the *soma psychikon*. Nor is the problem he faces the same as the one Plato and Cicero dealt with in their exposition of 'astral immortality'. They were eager to escape the prison-house of the body; but for Paul the problem was not the body itself, but sin and death which had taken up residence in it, producing corruption, dishonour and weakness. Being human is good; being an embodied human is good; what is bad is being a rebellious human, a decaying human, a human dishonoured through bodily sin and bodily death. What Paul desires, to take his terminology at face value, is not to let the soul fly free to a supposed astral home, but to stop the 'soul', the *psyche*, from being the animating principle for the body. Precisely because the soul is *not*, for him, the immortal fiery substance it is for Plato, he sees that the true solution to the human plight is to *replace* the 'soul' as the animating principle of the body with the 'spirit' – or rather, the Spirit. And that takes us into the next section.

---

[101] Despite the suggestion of BDAG 388, citing Wendland. More recently cf. Martin 1995, 117–20.

(c) 1 Corinthians 15.42–9

'So it is with the resurrection of the dead.' This is Paul's main conclusion, drawing the argument together into a dense statement of how the new, resurrection body will differ from the present one, and of how this will be accomplished.[102] Paul continues with the language of sowing and harvesting, knowing it here to be metaphorical:[103]

> [42b]It is sown in corruption, it is raised in incorruption; [43]it is sown in dishonour, it is raised in glory; it is sown in weakness, it is raised in power; [44]it is sown as a *soma psychikon*, it is raised as a *soma pneumatikon*.

These four contrasts are mutually explanatory. The first is the main thing Paul wishes to stress at the level of the *nature* of the new body;[104] the last, as the sequel will show, is the point which explains *how* it is all achieved. Part of the problem of verse 44 is how to translate the key terms in that final phrase, which is why I have left them for the moment in Greek.

In the concluding section of the chapter, Paul will stress the distinction between a body which is corruptible, i.e. which can and will decay, die and ultimately disintegrate altogether, and a body of which none of this is true (verses 50b, 52b, 53, 54). This contrast of corruption/incorruption, it seems, is not just one in a list of differences between the present body and the future one, but remains implicit underneath the rest of the argument, not least between the present humanity in its *choikos* ('earthy') state, ready to return to dust, and the new type of humanity which will be provided in the new creation. The fundamental leap of imagination that Paul is asking the puzzled Corinthians to make is to a body which cannot and will not decay or die: something permanent, established, not transient or temporary.

Within this framework, verse 43 draws attention to two other features which the new body will have as a result: honour instead of shame, power instead of weakness. These are closely related. Earlier in the letter (6.2–3) he spoke of the future life as one in which the Messiah's people, at present insignificant and powerless, would be in a position of ruling or judging. As in Philippians 3.20–21, the new body will have both a status (see above on 'glory', *doxa*) and a capability of which the present body knows nothing. The sense, arising from the previous paragraph, is of human beings becoming what they were made to be, attaining at last their proper *doxa* instead of the shameful, dishonouring status and character they presently know. There are echoes here of Paul's earlier statements (1.25–31) about the 'weakness'

---

[102] For *houtos kai*, the introductory formula, see 1 Cor. 2.11; 12.12; 14.9, 12; Gal. 4.3; Rom. 6.11. Perkins 1984, 304 suggests that when we compare this passage with Rom. 5.12–21 it looks as though Paul is here on foreign territory. This seems precarious, to say the least.

[103] For the metaphor cf. e.g. Jn. 12.24; Rom. 6.5.

[104] Augustine (*Enchir.* 91) already saw this as the key point; see Torrance 1976, 75.

and 'power' of God; in the new world, the power of the creator, at present paradoxical and visible only to the eye of faith, will be manifest in the new bodies of his people.

The fourth and final contrast is the one that has caused the most problems in exegesis and interpretation. Paul phrases it slightly differently to the other three. Instead of the body being sown 'in' corruption, dishonour and weakness, and raised 'in' incorruption, glory and power,[105] it is now sown 'as' a *soma psychikon* and raised 'as' a *soma pneumatikon*. In fact, in English as in Paul's Greek, there is no need even for the 'as': it is sown a *soma psychikon*, it is raised a *soma pneumatikon*.

But what do these two phrases mean?[106] Here the ghost – or perhaps the *psyche* – of Plato must be chuckling at the quiet triumph achieved in so many English translations. The King James version made the two phrases 'a natural body' and 'a spiritual body', and while this appears a reasonable approximation it opened the door to the Revised Standard Version, and its widely used successor the New Revised Standard Version, which brazenly made them 'a physical body' and 'a spiritual body'.[107] The New English Bible, interestingly, made the first phrase 'an animal body', but its successor, the Revised English Bible, has followed the RSV into Plato's ugly ditch. So has the Contemporary English Version. It is safe to say that not only those who read the RSV, NRSV and REB, but quite a few who read other versions as well, assume at this point that Paul is describing the new, resurrection body as something which, to put it bluntly, is non-physical – something which you could not touch, could not see with ordinary eyesight, something which, if raised to life, would leave no empty tomb behind it. And though Paul is here of course talking about the resurrection bodies of Christians, not of Jesus himself, it is widely and correctly recognized that his picture of the Christian resurrection body is modelled closely on what he thinks was and is true of Jesus.[108]

The problem with the explicit contrast of 'physical' and 'spiritual', and with the word 'spiritual' itself when heard by most modern western persons in contrast also with words like 'natural' or 'animal', is that it sends highly misleading messages. As we saw earlier, the ancient philosophers made distinctions between different kinds of substance, but they did not draw the line

---

[105] 'In' here appears to mean 'in a state of'.

[106] Thiselton 2000, 1276–81, has an excellent extended note on the subject; his critique of Martin is important, as are his comments on the older 'non-physical' misreading of *pneumatikon* (e.g. Scroggs 1966, 66). Among older work cf. e.g. Clavier 1964.

[107] Knox, Phillips and NIV follow KJV, which was in turn following Tyndale. Few in the C16 or early C17, before the implicit dualisms of the modern world, would have supposed that by 'spiritual' here one should assume 'non-physical'.

[108] A classic example of the misreading that has become common is in Carnley 1987, 233: Paul more likely thought of the raised Christ 'in terms of a glorified "spiritual body" than the "yet to be glorified" mundane, visible, and tangible body envisaged by Luke and John'.

in the same place that modern western thought has done, between 'physical' and 'non-physical'. As a result, contemporary readers are liable to be thrown in quite the wrong direction: to the contrast between the world that science can observe and the world that it cannot, the division between the world of space, time and matter on the one hand and a very different, 'spiritual' world on the other hand, which according to the mainstream post-Enlightenment worldview do not intersect with one another. It evokes, that is, the Deist picture of a remote, detached God, and of a private 'spirituality' removed from public or political events; or, as one of the offshoots of such a position, the division between 'natural' and 'supernatural', with all its attendant philosophical problems.[109] (The Living Bible, though adding other elements of paraphrase, has 'natural' and 'supernatural' at this point.[110]) This multifaceted disjunction is simply untrue to ancient thought in general and to Paul's thought in particular.

At the same time, however, it would be wrong to think that the ancients, at either a popular or a sophisticated level, had no distinction corresponding to our material/non-material. If the soul was made of something, it was a totally different sort of something. Not that that means, of course, that Paul would think of the soul in the same way as did the tradition which embraced both Plato and the Stoics, which envisaged the soul going off eventually to join the stars.[111] In particular, such an analysis, every bit as much as the more common one, fails to get to grips with the precise words he uses, and what he himself has already indicated about the way he uses them.

We have, in fact, already met the key terms, in contexts where it should be quite clear what Paul means – and does not mean – by them. The two sorts of 'body', the present corruptible one and the future non-corruptible one, are, respectively, *psychikon* and *pneumatikon*; the first word is derived from *psyche*, frequently translated 'soul', and the second from *pneuma*, normally translated 'spirit'. In 1 Corinthians 2.14–15, the *psychikos* person does not receive the things of the spirit, because they are spiritually discerned, while the *pneumatikos* person discerns everything.[112] There is, of course, no question there of 'physical' and 'spiritual' as appropriate translations. Nor would those words, with the connotations they normally have today, be appropriate at 3.1, where Paul declares that he could not consider

---

[109] On which see *JVG* 186–8, with the continuing dialogue represented fleetingly by C. S. Evans 1999 and my response ('In Grateful Dialogue', 248–50). On Héring's proposal of 'supernatural' as opposed to 'immaterial' see Fee 1987, 786.

[110] Not unlike the German ecumenical translation of 1981 ('ein irdischer Leib . . . ein überirdischer Leib').

[111] cf. Martin 1995, 126–9. See, rightly, Dunn 1998, 60.

[112] The same contrast is made in Jude 19, where similar comments apply. In Jas. 3.15 wicked thoughts and behaviour are described as evidence of a wisdom that is 'earthbound' (*epigeios*), *psychikos* and demonic, in contrast to the wisdom that is 'from above' (*anothen*); this is quite a similar contrast to that which Paul is making here. These are the only NT occurrences of the term outside 1 Cor. 2 and 15.

the Corinthians as *pneumatikoi*, but merely as *sarkinoi* or perhaps *sark-ikoi*.[113] The words clearly refer to matters quite other than whether the people concerned are 'physical'; clearly they are, and the question is rather to do with whether they are indwelt, guided and made wise by the creator's Spirit, or whether they are living at the level of life common to all human-kind (*psychikos*), or whether indeed they are living at the level of life com-mon to all corruptible creation (*sarkinos*). So, too, when Paul discusses *pneumatika* in chapter 12, these 'spiritual gifts' are certainly not 'spiritual' in the sense of 'non-physical', but involve in most cases the operation of the Spirit precisely on aspects of one's physicality, whether through gifts of inspired speech, healing or whatever.[114] They are things which, though oper-ating within the human body and life, enable that body and life to do things which would otherwise be impossible. The same is true of many other uses of the word, in this letter and elsewhere in the New Testament.[115]

In fact, within the shadowlands of meaning and usage between ancient Hebrew thought and the highly influential Greek language, the word *psyche* and its cognates were able by this period to move to and fro over a wide range of meaning. This would be so not least for minds soaked in the Sep-tuagint. The range would lie between a minimal meaning of 'soul' as opp-osed to body – according to which, if one wanted to say 'non-physical', one would use *psychikos*, not *pneumatikos*, which shows how misleading the regular translations are! – and a maximal meaning corresponding broadly to our word 'life', or even (without the pantheist overtones) 'life-force': that is, the sense of aliveness, operating through breath and blood, energy and pur-pose, which is common to humankind.[116] That Paul has this maximal usage in mind seems evident from his explanatory quotation of Genesis 2.7 in verse 45, on which see below. Thus far, the *psychikos/pneumatikos* contrast of verses 44–6 would have to be characterized as 'ordinary human life' con-trasted with 'a life indwelt by the Spirit of God'. If there had been any varia-tion away from this, its effect would almost certainly have been to make

---

[113] See above, 283f.

[114] In any case, as Martin has pointed out, even within the post-Plato world there was no concept of absolute non-physicality such as many post-Enlightenment thinkers have read into Paul at this point; the Stoics believed that the soul itself was made up of a substance. See above, 348f.

[115] e.g. 1 Cor. 10.3f. ('spiritual' food and drink in the wilderness; Paul did not suppose this was 'non-physical'); 14.37 (those who consider themselves 'spiritual' are presumably not imagining themselves 'non-physical' – and this is close, within the letter, to our present passage); Gal. 6.1; Eph. 5.19/Col. 3.16; 1 Pet. 2.5 (a 'spiritual house' and 'spiritual sacrifices', where the point is not 'non-physical', but 'indwelt/energized by the Spirit').

[116] See *TDNT* 9.608–66 (Schweizer). In Arist. *Eth.* 1117b28, *psychikos* is opposed to *somatikos*, 'bodily', contrasting purer with grosser forms of pleasure; Plutarch *De Comm. Not.* 1084e speaks of the *pneuma psychikon*, the 'breath of life'. The cognate verb *psychoo* can likewise mean 'to give a psychical (as opposed to physical) character to physical sensations' (LSJ 2028, citing Plot. 4.4.28).

psyche less 'physical', not more; it would certainly be an extremely strange word to use, within either early Christian, second-Temple Jewish, or late-antique pagan usage if what one wanted to label was the 'physical' *as opposed to the non-physical*. Ironically enough, the modern form of Platonism which has crept into contemporary readings of 1 Corinthians 15 forbids forcing a cognate of *psyche*, which for so many people in the ancient world meant 'soul' instead of 'body', into meaning something that would have seemed to them more or less the opposite.[117] Had Paul wanted in any way to produce the kind of contrast suggested to a modern reader by 'physical' and 'spiritual', not only would *pneumatikos* have been an unhelpful word to have used for the latter idea, but *psychikos* would have been exactly the wrong word to use for the former.[118] In fact, if Paul had wanted to find a word for 'non-physical', *psychikos* (which could literally be translated as 'soulish') would itself have been a possible option.[119] If anything, if a reader of first-century Greek came upon a phrase containing the word *psychikos*, contrasted with anything else, he or she might well expect that, if there was a physical/non-physical contrast in the offing, *psychikos* would refer to the non-physical side, and whatever was being contrasted with it would be seen as more firmly bodily, more substantial.

There is one other factor to be be taken into account which tells strongly in the same direction. Though it is dangerous to generalize in so widespread and pluriform a language as Koine Greek, it is generally true (as we saw above in connection with 1 Corinthians 2) that adjectives formed with the ending *-ikos* have ethical or functional meanings rather than referring to the material or substance of which something is composed.[120] Had Paul wanted

---

[117] For the normal understanding see e.g. Plato, *Cratylus* 399e—400e.

[118] BDAG 1100 is therefore very misleading to include, as an extra definition of the word, 'a physical body', citing only v. 44, and, for its use as a noun, '*the physical* in contrast to *to pneumatikon*', quoting only v. 46, with Iren. *Haer.* 1.5.1, where, in the context of a description of Valentinian beliefs about three different orders of being, the word for 'material' is *to hylikon*, and *to psychikon* is used for 'animal', the middle term in the sequence. The contrast in question is not between (in our sense) 'physical' and 'non-physical', but has to do with quality, not substance. (See too Iren. 3.5.1.)

[119] cf. e.g. Ptol. *Apotel.* 3.14.1; Jos. *War* 1.430, describing Herod's remarkable gifts 'of soul and body', with *psychikos* used for the first; and e.g. 4 Macc. 1.32, where desires (*epithymiai*) are divided into *psychikai* on the one hand and *somatikai* on the other, sensibly translated by NRSV as 'mental' and 'physical'. All these and more are quoted by BDAG, but then ignored for the purposes of 1 Cor. 15. Overall, *psychikos* seems in any case to refer to a *quality*, without emphasizing materiality or non-materiality, though it is a quality which was frequently ascribed to what today would be thought of as non-material entities.

[120] Adjectives of 'material' tend to form in *-inos* (Moulton 1980–76, 2.359); those which end in *-ikos* indicate what something is 'like', giving an ethical or dynamic relation as opposed to a material one (Moulton 2.378, quoting Plummer on 1 Cor. 3.1). Robertson and Plummer 1914 [1911], 372 take this more or less for granted: 'Evidently, *psychikon* does not mean that the body is made of *psyche*, consists entirely of *psyche*: and *pneumatikon* does not mean it is made and consists entirely of *pneuma*. The adjectives

to contrast 'a body composed of *psyche*' with 'a body composed of *pneuma*' (even supposing that that would have made any sense), he might have chosen different adjectives; granted that neither *psychinos* nor *pneumatinos* is found in extant literature, Paul was perfectly capable of coining a few helpful words here and there. In any case, the classical usage of *pneumatikos* well illustrates the meaning that seems to be in Paul's mind. Aristotle speaks of wombs that are 'swollen with air', *hysterai pneumatikai*,[121] and Vitruvius (first century BC) speaks of a machine 'moved by wind', *pneumatikon organon*.[122] The adjective describes, not what something is *composed of*, but what it is *animated by*.[123] It is the difference between speaking of a ship made of steel or wood on the one hand and a ship driven by steam or wind on the other. The only major translation I know that attempts to come to terms with this is that of the Jerusalem Bible: 'when it is sown it embodies the soul, when it is raised it embodies the spirit. If the soul has its own embodiment, so does the spirit have its own embodiment.'[124]

We should by now be coming out of the jungle of misinterpretations and into something of a clearing; but before we can get much further we need to note no less than three other things which seem to be going on in this passage, and which have almost certainly helped to determine the way Paul has put his point.

The first is the way the Corinthians seem to have regarded themselves. It is likely that they used the word *pneumatikos* of themselves, imagining themselves to have developed beyond earlier categories, not least the one described as *psychikos*. Other people were 'merely human', living on the ordinary level, but they, especially with all their *pneumatika* gifts, were living on a different level entirely. Paul has already stuck a pin into this over-inflated balloon (2.14—3.4), and found it to contain, not *pneuma*, but a combination of *psyche* and *sarx* (a lot of hot air, in fact). Now he approaches the same question from a different angle: their very 'super-spiritual' boast has led them to imagine that there can be no such thing as a resurrection of the *body* – such an 'unspiritual' idea! But if they only knew who the real God was, and what he intended to do precisely through the work of his *pneuma*, they would see that the destination of the genuine *pneumatikos* was to be raised to new bodily life. The *psychikos* life, the ordinary human one, is what you have at the moment, even though you are indwelt by the Spirit

---

mean "congenital with," "formed to be the organ of.'" See too Conzelmann 1975 [1969], 283, quoting Bachmann and Kümmel: '*soma pneumatikon* is not simply a body consisting of *pneuma*, but one *determined* by pneuma' (my ital.); Witherington 1995, 308f. On 1 Cor. 2 see 282–4 above.

[121] *Hist. Anim.* 584b22.

[122] Vitr. 10.1.1.

[123] Not even, as Fee 1987, 786, the sphere in which it now operates, though this is no doubt true as well.

[124] See Hays 1997, 272. Unfortunately, the NJB has reverted to 'natural' and 'spiritual'.

of the living God; but that same Spirit will give life to your mortal bodies also. That, as in Romans 8.9–11, is the somewhat *ad hominem* argument underlying this passage.

The second theme which may be lurking in the undergrowth is a determination on Paul's part to rule out any suggestion of one particular interpretation of his key text, Genesis 1 and 2, which we know to have been current at the time and which may have been held by some within the Corinthian church.[125] In Philo's allegorical exegesis of Genesis, the first man, in Genesis 1, was 'heavenly' (*ouranios*), while the man created from the dust of the earth in Genesis 2 was 'earthy' (*geinos*).[126] The 'heavenly' man, according to Philo, was not physical, and hence not corruptible; those attributes belong to the second man. This reading of Genesis suggests that the real destiny of humankind is to leave the created order, the world of space, time and matter, entirely, and to make one's way back to the primal state of humanity, the 'first man', in whose existence of pure mind and spirit the physical universe is no longer relevant.

To this rich mixture of Jewish tradition and Greek philosophy Paul can have only one answer, and it is very germane to his point: when Genesis 2 speaks of the creator making Adam as a living *psyche*, this was not a secondary form of humanity, but its primary form. What humans now need is not to get away from, or back behind, such an existence, but rather to go on to the promised state of the final Adam, in which this physical body will not be abandoned, but will be given new animation by the creator's own Spirit. Paul does not believe in a return to a primal state, but in a redemption from the sin and death which has corrupted the primal state, in order that a way forward be found into the new creation which, though always in the mind of the creator, has never yet existed. And the 'heavenly man' is not one who, unsullied by the world of creation, remains in a purely non-physical state; he is the lord who will come from heaven (verses 47–9, corresponding closely to Philippians 3.20–21). He will enable other humans, not to escape from the physical world back to an original 'image of God', but to go on to bear, in the newly resurrected body, the 'image of the man from heaven'. The importance of this will unfold as we proceed.

The third element which Paul is carefully weaving in to his exposition, by contrast, is his own new-creation reading of Genesis which, as we saw, overarches the whole chapter. He has had the first two chapters of Genesis in mind throughout, and he now proceeds to draw on them both. Verse 44b

---

[125] This remains controversial: Hays 1997, 273 is inclined to think a reference likely, while Fee 1987, 791 disputes it.

[126] The latter adjective well illustrates the point made earlier about words ending in *-nos* being to do with physical composition. The passage is *Alleg.* 1.31f.; we should note that Philo precisely does *not* refer to the physical, 'earthy' human being as *psychikos*, and that when in the same passage he speaks of the *psyche* he is referring, naturally enough, to the soul, which in our modern sense is 'non-physical'.

provides his firm basic statement, his initial answer to the question, 'What sort of body will the dead have when they are raised?' They will have a *soma pneumatikon*, a body animated by, enlivened by, the Spirit of the true God, exactly as Paul has said more extensively in several other passages.[127] This helps to provide a satisfactory explanation for why he has homed in on this unique phrase at this point in the chapter. It is the most elegant way he can find of saying both that the new body is the *result* of the Spirit's work (answering 'how does it come to be?') and that it is the appropriate *vessel for* the Spirit's life (answering 'what sort of a thing is it?').

In fact, this is the first point in which *pneuma* has been mentioned in the whole chapter, because it is at last the point where Paul is giving his answer both to 'what sort of body will it be?' and also 'how will God do it?' If there is a *soma psychikon*, he declares – to which the answer is, of course there is: that is the normal sort of human *soma*, a body animated by the ordinary breath of life – then there is also a *soma pneumatikon*, a body animated by the Spirit of the living God, even though only one example of such a body has so far appeared. That is the point to which he is now building up, explaining that the unique, prototypical image-bearing body of Jesus is to be the model for the new bodies that Jesus' people will have. But he intends to get there not just by saying that the creator will accomplish this through the Spirit, but by the route he had already proposed in verses 20–28: Jesus himself, the Messiah who is already ruling the world under the father, and will finally hand it over to the father once all enemies have been overthrown, is the one who himself gives the Spirit which brings people to that new bodily life in which they will share his own new image-bearingness.[128] The earlier Adam-narrative in verses 20–28, made explicit in verse 22 but implicit throughout, establishes the fixed point to which Paul can now return. In that Adam-narrative, after all, the way was barred to the tree of life (Genesis 3.22–4); now, at last, the way has been thrown open.

Thus, if Genesis 2.7 spoke of the creator breathing into Adam's nostrils his breath of life, the *pnoe zoes*, making him a *psyche zosa*, Paul will now speak, in parallel and sequence, of the creator's new act of creation in and through the Messiah and his resurrection. Verse 45b depends on verses 20–28 in a number of ways; Paul is not simply inserting Jesus into the argument of Genesis without prior warrant. The Messiah has been raised, the first-fruits of those who slept; through him comes the resurrection of the dead (verses 20–21); thus, as in Adam all die, so in the Messiah shall all be

---

[127] e.g. Rom. 8.9–11. For background cf. Job 33.4; Ps. 104.30; Ezek. 36.27; 37.9f., 14.

[128] Lincoln 1981, 43 says that this argument is neither *a fortiori* nor inferred, but typological, based on inference from Gen. 2.7. My reading is that it is in fact based partly on vv. 20–28, expressed in the light of the reading of Gen. 2 which Paul is about to offer. This is not typological (two events related in pattern but not particularly in narrative sequence), but narratival: Gen. 2.7 begins a story which, in the light of vv. 20–28, and the analogies of vv. 35–41, Paul is now in a position to complete.

made alive. Very well: he is then the new type of humanity, and can be placed alongside the Adam of Genesis 2, with the differences brought to the surface. He is not just a *soma pneumatikon* in his own right, so to speak, the first example of the large number of such beings the creator intends to make through resurrection, but he is also the one *through* whom the creator will accomplish this – because he is the one who, as 'life-giving Spirit', will perform the work of raising the dead.[129] Genesis 2.7 is thus not so much a proof-text, more a part of the larger story which the Christian, looking at Jesus' resurrection, can now tell; and the good news which emerges from this is that Jesus has pioneered the way into the long-awaited future, the new age which the creator has planned (verse 46). The *pneumatikos* state is not simply an original idea in the mind of the creator, from which the human race fell sadly away; this model of humanity is the future reality, the reality which will swallow up and replace merely *psychikos* life.

Thus Paul develops the Adam–Messiah contrast, placing the discussions and assertions of the previous twelve verses within a larger narrative, the narrative of creation and new creation, of earth and heaven. As in Philippians 3.20–21 and other passages studied above, the 'second man' (who appears, for Paul, to be functionally identical to the 'final Adam') comes *from* heaven; this place of origin, the motion from it to earth (the final 'appearing' or 'coming' of Jesus, not his first appearing in incarnation), and above all the character of 'heaven' as the creator's own sphere, where Jesus is currently ruling, is then indicated by *epouranios*, 'heavenly', in verses 48–9.

The point is not, in other words, that the new humanity will exist in a place called 'heaven'. Rather, it will originate there, where Jesus himself currently is in his own risen and life-giving body; and it will transform the life of those who are presently located on earth and earthy in character (*ek ges choikos*, verse 47). The whole argument runs in the opposite direction not only to Philo but to all kinds of Platonism ancient and modern. The point is not to escape from earth and find oneself at last in heaven, but to let the present 'heavenly' life change the present earthly reality. Heaven and earth, after all, are the twin partners in the creation which, at the heart of the passage Paul has in mind throughout this chapter, the creator had declared to be 'very good'.[130]

---

[129] Note the fluidity, at exactly the same stage of the argument, between Christ and Spirit in Rom. 8.9–11; 2 Cor. 3.17f. Not that Paul makes Jesus and the Spirit identical (so, correctly, Fee 1987, 790 n. 15).

[130] Gen. 1.31; cf. 1.1; 2.1–4. This raises the question as to what is really driving Carnley (1987, 313) to say things like: 'Even the presence of a humanly generated "team spirit" is, after all, apprehended by the senses and it may be that something less material than a resuscitated corpse might also be apprehended by the deliverances of sense perception in the case of the Easter Jesus.' This sounds as though what Carnley wants to find is that the first disciples really did see a ghost. Or perhaps that they were aware of a new team spirit.

With that in mind, there is no sense that when Paul refers to the redeemed as 'the heavenly ones' (verse 48) he is thinking of them as astral bodies, stars, the kind of 'pneumatic bodies' postulated by various scholars over the years.[131] Verses 36–41 were illustrative, rather than part of his substantive point. Rather, in a climax reminiscent of Romans 8.29 (itself at the climax of a section which began with the Adam–Christ contrast in 5.12–21), of 2 Corinthians 3.17—4.6 (part of Paul's argument from new covenant to new creation, based in 3.1–6 on the life-giving work of the Spirit), and of Colossians 3.10 (based on the earlier poem about Christ as the image and firstborn of the creator God), Paul looks all the way back to the creation of humans in the divine image in Genesis 1.26–8, and all the way on to the ultimate future, when all those 'in the Messiah' will be 'renewed in knowledge after the image of the creator', will be 'conformed to the image of the son of God, so that he might be the firstborn of a large family'. The last verse of the section takes the bald statement of verse 44b ('if there is a soul-filled body, there is also a spirit-filled body') and applies it to 'us': just as 'we' have borne the image of the earthy man (Adam's image passed on to his descendants, as in Genesis 5.3), so 'we' shall bear the image of the man whose life shares the life of heaven.[132] The verb used for 'bear' (*phoreo*) is often used for the wearing of clothes; as in Ephesians and Colossians we found the language of putting off the set of clothes belonging to the former humanity, and putting on those belonging to the new one, so here, and as we shall see in 2 Corinthians 5, Paul speaks of present and future in terms of 'wearing' one model of human existence or the other one.

Not until this point, in the present chapter, has he spoken of the present location of Jesus, as he does for instance in Colossians 3.1–4. Now that he does so, we find the same integration between his view of Jesus as bodily risen from the dead (verses 12–28) and presently active in heaven as we did in Romans 8.34. Paul has completed his basic answer to the doubters of verse 12, and the questioners of verse 35; all that remains is to tell the story one more time, celebrating the victory of the creator God over all that destroys and corrupts the good creation.

(vi) 1 Corinthians 15.50–58

The final paragraph has the sustained excitement of a celebration. It adds no fresh arguments to those already advanced, but it explores more fully what it all means, not least for a group of people Paul has not mentioned up to now, namely, those who will find themselves still alive at the moment when Jesus reappears and the dead are raised. Paul, as we saw, takes it for granted in

---

[131] Most recently Martin 1995, 123–7.
[132] On the variant reading 'let us bear' see Hays 1997, 273f.; Fee 1987, 787 n. 5.

this passage that he will himself be one of that number. That perspective changes in 2 Corinthians and Philippians, but the underlying theology and eschatology do not.

The central emphasis of the paragraph is on the transformation that will be required for those presently alive if they are to be part of the kingdom.[133] This alone, closely parallel to Philippians 3.21, should have been enough to indicate what Paul's view of the resurrection was: people still alive when the kingdom finally arrives will not lose their bodies, but have them changed from their present state to the one required for God's future. As before, however, a few words have been seized upon to suggest that Paul holds a different view, involving the loss of physicality in the new life. Since the verse in question is the one which opens the paragraph, it may be as well to see what the thrust of the rest of it is before returning to the passage in question.

The main feature of God's new world will be, as Paul said in verse 26, that death itself will have been defeated. Victory is assured, because that which caused death from the beginning, namely sin, has been dealt with (verses 56–7).[134] And the central force of the paragraph is therefore that, as the dead are raised 'incorruptible' (verse 52), so 'we' – that is, we who are left alive – will be 'changed' (*allagesometha*):

> [52b]The trumpet shall sound; the dead shall be raised incorruptible; and we shall be changed. [53]For this corruptible [body] must clothe itself with incorruptibility; and this mortal [body] must clothe itself with immortality. [54]When this corruptible [body] has clothed itself with incorruptibility, and this mortal [body] has clothed itself with immortality, then shall come to pass the word that is written:
> Death is swallowed up into victory.
> [55]Where is your victory, death?
> Where is your sting, death?

The solemn repetition of virtually the same sentence in verses 53 and 54 is extremely rare for Paul, who (unlike some of us) seldom uses three sentences if he can get away with one. Clearly this is a point he wants to underline, to rub in as hard as he can, to stress against the doubters and the questioners, to make it clear to all the Christians in Corinth that the body is meant for the lord, and the lord for the body (6.13), and that the lord in whose own person death had been defeated would one day implement that defeat on behalf of all his people. They will not lose their bodies; nor will they be found 'naked' (verse 37).[135] They will 'put on a new suit of clothes', will be given a new

---

[133] cf. *2 Bar.* 51.10; see above, 161f.

[134] On the sin/death link, going all the way back in Jewish thought to Gen. 3, see e.g. Rom. 5.12–21; and, in the present passage, v. 17. As in Rom. 5.20, Paul slips in (v. 56) a cryptic remark about the way the law gave sin its power – a comment which he explains in Rom. 7.7–25 (whose closing outburst of thanksgiving (7.25a) is closely parallel to v. 57 in the present passage).

[135] See Perkins 1984, 307; this is an implicit rejection once more of Philo's worldview, as in e.g. *Gig.* 53–7; *Ebr.* 99–101; *Fug.* 58–64. See Horsley 1998, 224f.

type of physicality, whose primary characteristic, the first in the list in verses 42–4, is that it cannot wear out, cannot corrupt, cannot die.

This is what 'must' happen if those presently alive are to inherit the new creation. The final body will need to be 'incorruptible', 'immortal'. These words have different shading ('incorruptible' implies that no part can wear out or decay, 'immortal' that the body cannot die), but the two were near-synonyms in Paul's world.[136] However, a case was made nearly half a century ago for Paul intending 'the corruptible' here to refer to those already dead, and 'the mortal' to those still alive, giving verse 52 a double focus ('the dead' will be raised, and 'we' – that is, we who are left alive – will be changed).[137] This is important for understanding verse 50 (below).

Putting the two together brings Paul to the position where he can pick up a couple of lines from Isaiah and Hosea and turn them into a taunt song against Death. The whole chapter has been, not about coming to terms with Death, but with its defeat; and here, like a warrior triumphing over a fallen enemy, Paul mocks the power that has now become powerless.[138]

Thus, he declares, the creator God 'gives us the victory' (verse 57), just as this same God, faced with a naked seed buried in the earth, 'gives it a body' (verse 38). This is another part of the answer to the question 'how' in verse 35. God as creator and life-giver has been the main subject of the whole chapter; Paul takes this view of the living God for granted in many passages, mentioning it explicitly when he needs to do so (as in Romans 4, for example). This is, clearly, a theology in which the present physical body is not to be abandoned, nor yet to be affirmed as it stands, but is to be trans-formed, changed from present humiliation to new glory (Philippians 3.21), from present corruption and mortality to new incorruption and immortality. This is indeed the defeat of death, not a compromise in which death is allowed to have the body while some other aspect of the human being (the soul? the spirit?) goes marching on.

This should make it clear what is, and what is not, meant by the often controversial opening words of the paragraph:

> [50]This is what I mean, brothers and sisters: 'flesh and blood' cannot inherit God's kingdom, nor can corruption inherit incorruption. [51]Look! I am telling you a mystery. We shall not all sleep, but we shall all be changed – [52]in a moment, in the blink of an eye, at the last trumpet.

---

[136] So Fee 1987, 802 n. 31; see the use of the terms in e.g. Plutarch, *De soll. anim.* 960b; Philo *Op.* 119; Wis. 9.11–15.

[137] Jeremias 1955–6. See also Gillman 1982.

[138] On Paul's use of these texts see Hays 1997, 275f.; Tomson 2002. The MT of the Hos. text (13.14) speaks of judgment on Israel, but the LXX has turned it already into the promise of redemption; Paul takes this a step further again. The Isa. text (25.8) comes, of course, from one of the central OT promises of new life beyond the grave; however it was originally intended, Paul's reading of it was consistent with other second-Temple exegesis. For rabbinic use of it see e.g. mMoed Kat. 3.9 (so Fee, 1987, 803 n. 35).

Verses 51–2a fit easily into the line of thought we have been looking at. Paul describes the scene of the last day, in language reminiscent of 1 Thessalonians 4.16–17, the imagery being drawn from standard Jewish pictures.[139] This is a 'mystery', a vision of God's eschatological future, and an insight into how the creator will bring about a world in which his writ runs so completely that death itself is done away with. This will take a great act of new creation, as much for those still alive as for those already dead. That is exactly what Paul affirms.

Why then does he say 'flesh and blood cannot inherit God's kingdom'? Ever since the second century (and increasingly in scholarship during the twentieth) doubters have used this clause to question whether Paul really believed in the resurrection of the *body*. In fact, the second half of verse 50 already explains, in Hebraic parallelism with the first half, more or less what he means, as Paul's regular use of 'flesh' would itself indicate: 'flesh and blood' is a way of referring to ordinary, corruptible, decaying human existence. It does not simply mean, as it has so often been taken to mean, 'physical humanity' in the normal modern sense, but 'the present physical humanity (as opposed to the future one), which is subject to decay and death'.[140] The referent of the phrase is not the presently dead but the presently living, who need not to be raised but to be changed; and this brings us back to the dual focus of verses 53 and 54. Both categories of humans need to acquire the new, transformed type of body.[141]

The final verse of the chapter could be felt as an anticlimax, but only if we had allowed ourselves to forget the multiple ways in which this extensive discussion of resurrection was linked to the rest of the letter. A casual reading of Paul, assimilating his thought to popular piety, might have expected him to end such a chapter by saying, 'Therefore, brothers and sisters, look forward eagerly to the hope that is set before you!' Instead, he redirects their gaze to the present time, to the tasks awaiting attention and the call to be 'steadfast and immovable' in them. The point of it all has been that, despite the discontinuity between the present mode of corruptible physicality and the future world of non-corruptible physicality, there is an underlying continuity between present bodily life and future bodily life, and that this gives meaning and direction to present Christian living.[142] 'In the lord your

---

[139] e.g. the eschatological trumpet: details in Fee 1987, 801 n. 26.

[140] Perkins 1984, 306; Fee 1987, 799; Martin 1995, 127f.; Thiselton 2000, 1291f.

[141] We may note at this point that those who will be 'changed', here and in Phil. 3.21, will thus, it seems, pass directly from the present bodily life to the future bodily life, without any intermediate state. This is the exception, necessitated by the unique eschatological moment, to the otherwise universal truth, that belief in final resurrection involves a two-step progression (first into an intermediate state, then to new embodiment).

[142] This point is missed by e.g. Wedderburn 1999, 146, who caricatures Paul's view (and subsequent Christian views) in terms (169) of living a life which is '[simply] a preparation for another one beyond death and the grave'. That may be how some jaded Christians have put it; but what Paul describes is new creation bursting in to the present world.

labour' – your work for God's kingdom in the present – 'is not in vain.' If the Messiah had not been raised, Paul's proclamation and the Corinthians' faith would have been 'in vain'; but the Messiah, the lord, was indeed raised; and proclamation, faith and continuing labour are thereby rescued from 'vanity', from futility. What is done 'in the lord' in the present will last into God's future. That is the severely practical message which emerges from this, the prince of early Christian resurrection discussions.

(vii) 1 Corinthians 15: Conclusion

We saw in our previous chapter the many ways in which 1 Corinthians as a whole builds up to this long discussion. The fact of the future bodily resurrection, and the continuity between the present state and the future one, undergirds a great deal of the letter.

This emphasis, not least its rootedness in the creation-theology which marks Paul out as a good Pharisaic Jew, shows very clearly that Paul's view of the future life of the Messiah's people belongs at the Pharisaic end of the Jewish spectrum of belief, over against both non-Pharisaic Judaism (e.g. that of the Sadducees) and the entire pagan spectrum. This passage adds little to what he has said elsewhere about an intermediate state; he assumes that the Christian dead are awaiting final resurrection. Nor does it develop the metaphorical uses of 'resurrection', in relation to present Christian living, which we have observed elsewhere. Rather, it provides the central exposition of resurrection itself, which gives meaning and shape to those other questions.

What Paul has now added to his other statements, quite dramatically, is a detailed account, unprecedented in the Judaism of the time, both of the two-stage rising of the dead (the Messiah first, then his people when he returns), and of the mode of *dis*continuity (focused on the corruption/incorruption distinction and on the two types of humanity with the Spirit as the agent of the new one). Nor does Paul leave us in any doubt as to where these innovations come from. He believes in the two-stage resurrection because, against all expectations, the Messiah has been raised in advance of everyone else. And he believes in the discontinuity between the present body and the future one, as well as the continuity, because of what he believes happened to Jesus at his own resurrection. 'We shall bear the image of the man from heaven' (verse 49); 'he will change our humiliated body to be like his glorious body' (Philippians 3.21). Paul not only believed *that* Jesus had been bodily raised from the dead; he believed he knew *how* it was done, both in the sense of where the power came from (the Spirit of the creator God), and in the sense that he knew what the difference was (corruptibility and non-corruptibility) between the body which died on the cross and the body which rose.

It only takes the smallest step of logic, in fact, to work back from this chapter to a fairly complete view of what Paul thought had happened to

Jesus. His body had not been abandoned in the tomb. Nor had it merely been resuscitated, coming back into a more or less identical life, to face death again at some point in the future. It had been transformed, changed, in an act of new creation through which it was no longer corruptible. 'The Messiah, once raised from the dead, will never die again; death has no more dominion over him.' Paul wrote that in Romans (6.9); but we could equally well have deduced it from the present chapter.

There remains one task in this survey of Paul's view of the resurrection. He seems to have been very clear on the topic when he wrote his first letter to Corinth. Had he changed his mind by the time he wrote the second one?

2. 2 Corinthians 4.7—5.10

(i) Introduction

We have already looked at the sweep of thought through 2 Corinthians as a whole, and have seen the remarkable way in which the death and resurrection of Jesus form so much of the backbone of what Paul says. We have seen in particular how the section that runs from 3.1 to 6.13 forms a sustained apologia for Paul's apostolic ministry, grounded in the death and resurrection of Jesus and energized – and glorified, despite present appearances! – by the Spirit of the living God. We now return to the central passage in that section, to see the contribution it makes to its own context, the way in which it relates to what Paul says in 1 Corinthians, and the ways in which it fills in the larger picture of Paul's thought which we have built up. In particular, we must examine the central section of 2 Corinthians in the light of the proposal, regularly advanced over many years, that it represents a serious change from 1 Corinthians, which can be summarized as a move away from a Jewish-style eschatology, involving the resurrection of the body, towards a more hellenistic model.[143]

The main thrust of the passage is to insist on seeing the present in the light of the future. The present is full of suffering, especially for the apostle; but he sees it as organically connected to the future in which there is resurrection (4.14), glory (4.17), a new body (5.1), and judgment (5.10). This path of suffering is thus the embodiment of the covenant-renewing death of the Messiah, and itself carries, remarkably, something of the same significance; and it is also the beginning of, and the signpost to, the renewal of creation which follows from covenant renewal (5.17). This line of thought is necessarily different to that in 1 Corinthians, but I shall argue that Paul is drawing on exactly the same underlying ideas. He has changed his perspective, in that he now speaks openly of his own death as likely to occur before

---

[143] The most recent exponent of this is Boismard 1999 [1995].

the final resurrection (5.1–10); he draws on different aspects of his controlling narrative about present and future, since he is making different points; but he has not changed the narrative, or the theology, itself.

The passage can be divided up in various ways, since there are several turns and twists which could be seen as paragraph markers. Nothing much hinges on this. But I find the line of thought comes clearest when we take the passage in three segments: 4.7–15; 4.16—5.5; and 5.6–10. The first describes Paul's sufferings, and explains them as the making present of the dying and rising of Jesus; the second relates this entire experience to the future promise of the resurrection body; and the third reflects back on the present, explaining why, in the light of this future, it is appropriate to have confidence, and to work at pleasing the lord. This then leads in to the further explanation of the nature of apostolic ministry in 5.11—6.13, which we have already noted.

(ii) 2 Corinthians 4.7–15

The first of these paragraphs gives details of the sufferings of which Paul has become so aware, and of which the Corinthians, perhaps, have become so ashamed. Paul has been speaking of the power and glory of the living God, shining in the face of Jesus the Messiah; now he explains that, so far from this giving the apostle the right to stride through the world trailing clouds of glory, it actually means the opposite:

> [7]We have this treasure in earthenware pots, so that the surpassing nature of the power may belong to God, not to us. [8]We are troubled in every way, but not overwhelmed; we are at a loss, but not in despair; [9]we are persecuted but not abandoned; we are knocked down, but not destroyed. [10]We are always carrying the death of Jesus in the body, so that the life of Jesus may be manifest in our body. [11]For we who are alive are always being given over to death through Jesus, so that the life of Jesus may also be manifest in our mortal flesh. [12]Thus death is at work in us – but life in you.

This belongs naturally with 1 Corinthians 4, where Paul contrasts his hard and demanding apostolic work with the apparently easy life of the Corinthians. The picture has developed further, because of what Paul has suffered in the meantime; and this enables him to argue not only that there is an explanation for his strange style of ministry, but that it is in fact the necessary embodiment of the gospel, of the death and new life of Jesus. This is one of the most vivid of Paul's 'present resurrection' passages, declaring not only (as some later thinkers would put it) that resurrection in the present meant a new kind of spiritual life, but that the life of Jesus should be manifest 'in our body' (verse 10), and even 'in our mortal flesh' (verse 11)! Even the part of present humanity which remains mortal, and which will decay, die and rot, is to be suffused in the present with the signs of resurrection, the life which the risen Jesus already has and which his people will one day enjoy. This is Paul's vivid explanation of the 'not overwhelmed . . . not in despair . . . not abandoned . . . not destroyed' sequence in verses 8–9. He is himself a walking visual aid of the gospel of Jesus. As a result – the twist in the tail – it is not just that the life of Jesus is visible in his body: it is that, through the principle of interchange between apostle and church, as he draws the suffering on to himself, the church itself experiences life (verse 10).[144]

Paul now widens the picture with what at first sight appears a cryptic reference to the Psalms, but which, when explored, turns out to shed a flood of light on his thinking. We have, he says (4.13), the same spirit of faith as the one who wrote 'I believed, and therefore I spoke'. The quotation is from Psalm 116.10, which in the LXX is numbered as the first verse of Psalm 115; but there is good reason to suppose that, whether or not Paul was used to that division of the Psalms (the MT corresponds to the English versions at this point), he had the whole of Psalm 116 (114 and 115 in LXX) in mind.

The Psalm is a grateful love-song to YHWH. Israel's God has heard the poet's prayer, and won his eternal loyalty; more particularly, he answered him when 'the snares of death encompassed me, and the pangs of Sheol laid hold on me'. Paul has been through the same experience, and wants to say, with the Psalmist,

> Return, then, my soul, to your rest;
> for YHWH has dealt favourably with you.
> For you have rescued my soul from death,
> my eyes from tears, and my feet from stumbling.[145]

The next verse in the MT declares, as in most English versions, 'I will walk before YHWH in the land of the living'; but the LXX interprets 'walk', not unreasonably granted regular Hebrew usage, in terms of behaviour: 'I will be well-pleasing before the Lord', *euaresteso enantion kyriou*. Paul, as we shall see, echoes exactly this later in the passage (5.9). The Psalm seems to have been in his mind throughout, not only in this part of chapter 4.

The Psalm then continues (in the LXX, the new Psalm begins) with the verse Paul quotes. The point of quoting 'I believed, and so I spoke' is not simply that Paul is declaring that, when he preaches, he speaks out of genuine faith, but rather that the Psalmist 'believed, and spoke' when he was greatly afflicted (116.10), when he might have despaired of all human help (116.11). That is where Paul had been, as we know from chapters 1 and 2; now he joins the Psalmist (116.12–19) in praising YHWH for deliverance from death and calling out praise from others:

---

[144] cf. Eph. 3.13; Col 1.24.
[145] Ps. 116.7f. (LXX 114.7f.).

4.14for we know that the one who raised the lord Jesus will raise us with Jesus and present us with you. 15For all this is for your sake, so that the grace which overflows through the multitude of thanksgiving may abound to the glory of God.

The close parallel between verse 14 and passages such as 1 Corinthians 6.14, not to mention 1 Corinthians 15 in its entirety and such other clear statements as Romans 8.11, should have given pause to those scholars who have tried to assert that Paul here has left behind the Jewish doctrine of bodily resurrection and substituted something else instead. And the point of it all – the drawing in detail on the Psalm, the clear affirmation of resurrection – is that by sharing in the Psalmist's journey, from the snares of death to the joy of rescue, Paul is going through, in advance, the process of dying and rising which Jesus has already gone through. Thus, just as the church rejoices and praises God for the events of the gospel themselves, so they must celebrate with more and more thanksgivings when they see the same pattern working out in the lives of his people, not least his apostle. The apostolic sufferings, in other words, are not only not something to be ashamed of. They are a paradoxical revelation of glory, and are themselves an occasion for rejoicing and gratitude.

The Psalm has another secret to reveal, and so has Paul. In Psalm 116.15, after declaring that he will praise YHWH and pay his vows to him for deliverance, the poet says, 'Costly in the sight of YHWH is the death of his holy ones.'[146] Paul will not say that death is a good thing; it is still, for him, the final enemy (1 Corinthians 15.26). But even if it should occur, God is greater than death, and will perform on a large scale that rescue for which Jesus' resurrection is the model and present apostolic experience the foretaste. That is the point to which he will now give attention. In terms of our overall questions, 4.7–15 should leave us in no doubt that Paul still expects bodily resurrection, modelled on that of Jesus; and that this future resurrection is anticipated in the present, not merely as a metaphor for a kind of spirituality but in the to-and-fro which he must experience between suffering and death on the one hand and life and joy on the other.

(iii) 2 Corinthians 4.16—5.5

These conclusions, contrary to repeated scholarly assertions, are reinforced, not undermined, by the passage now before us.[147] Paul is continuing to

---

[146] Most translations render the first word as 'precious'; but cf. JB, 'The death of the devout costs Yahweh dear,' modified in NJB to 'Costly in Yahweh's sight is the death of his faithful.' The Hebrew *yaqar* means 'precious, prized, costly', reflected in LXX *timios*, which has a similar range. This leaves it open in theory as to whether the Psalmist means that YHWH welcomes the death of his faithful ones or regrets it; but the logic of the Psalm suggests the latter (see Weiser 1962, 720; Mays 1994, 370).

[147] Thrall 1994–2000, 398–400 carefully assesses various 'development' hypotheses.

explain why he is not downcast in the midst of his sufferings – and, by implication, why the Corinthians ought not to be ashamed of him because of them.[148] His reason is that, as in Romans 8.17, present suffering is the path to future resurrection. The covenant God is at work by his Spirit to prepare the apostle for, and ultimately to accomplish, the new existence which he is promised. At the moment he must keep the eyes of heart, mind and faith on the promise, and on the unseen future reality to which it points.

Paul's description of this unseen reality, and of its relation to the present life, introduces some terms which have caused exegetes problems, giving rise to the suggestion that he has here changed his views:

> [16]So we do not lose heart; but rather, even if our outer humanity is being destroyed, our inner humanity is being renewed day by day. [17]For our small and temporary suffering is accomplishing for us an eternal and incomparable weight of glory, [18]since we do not look at the things that can be seen, but at the things which cannot. For the things which are seen are temporary, but the things that are unseen are eternal.

So: the inner person rather than the outer, and the unseen realities rather than the seen! And then, in the next chapter, the present body being destroyed, and, instead, an eternal house, not made with hands, in the heavens (5.1)! This is what has enticed some readers into the view that Paul has shifted his ground from a Jewish eschatology to a Platonic cosmology.[149] But not only is this in itself highly unlikely (we would have to postulate that he then quickly shifted back again in time to write Romans not many months afterwards; and we would also have to postulate significant internal muddles in the present letter); it is exegetically unwarranted. It is always vital to read the whole argument and to understand technical language in terms of it, and this passage is no exception. The rest of the section, with some explanatory notes, will help to make this clear:

> [5.1]For we know that if the earthly house of our dwelling [literally, our earthly house of tent] is dissolved, we have a building from God, a house not made with hands, eternal, in the heavens. [2]For in this [present dwelling] we also groan, longing to put on, on top of it, our dwelling from heaven, [3]if thus also, putting it off [several good MSS read 'putting it on'], we shall not be found naked. [4]For we who are in [this] tent groan, being weighed down, not because we want to be unclothed but because we want to be more fully clothed [the same verb, in the passive, as 'put on on top' in verse 2], so that what is mortal may be swallowed up by life. [5]The one who worked this thing in us in preparation [literally, 'who accomplished us for this thing'] is God, who gives us the guarantee of the Spirit.

[148] Nb. the link of v. 16 with 4.1 (*ouk egkakoumen*, 'we do not lose heart').

[149] Most recently and blatantly, Boismard 1999 [1995], e.g. 82, explaining that Paul has discovered that his Greek-educated readers are 'allergic to any notion of resurrection' and so now 'adopts the theme of immortality and leaves aside that of resurrection' – not merely tactically, however (that would not suit Boismard's own agenda, which is to advocate abandoning the idea of bodily resurrection and to promote disembodied immortality in its place) but 'due to a profound theological reason'.

This is admittedly dense, and the problems of text and translation, noted in this extract, make it more so. But when we put the passage together, and read it in the light of the many interlinked passages elsewhere in Paul, it should be clear that he is finding fresh ways of exploring and explaining the same picture rather than changing to a new one. One good way in to the passage is to explore some of the obvious parallels in other Pauline expositions of similar themes.

In 4.17 he speaks of an eternal and incomparable weight of glory. One natural passage to set alongside this is Romans 8.17 ('. . . provided that we suffer with the Messiah in order also to be glorified with him'), which draws together the thought of the much larger unit, chapters 5—8. The theme of suffering and glory is flagged up in opening and closing summaries (5.2; 8.30), and expounded extensively (8.18–25). The latter passage also speaks, as does our present one, of hoping for something we do not yet see (8.24–5), and in the same context Paul frequently refers to the work of the Spirit in preparing us for it (Romans 5.5; 8.9–11, 13, 16f., 23). The idea of the Spirit as a guarantee of the future hope (*arrabon*, 2 Corinthians 5.5), the present gift whereby the living God is already secretly accomplishing the future salvation in advance within the believer, picks up the same theme in 2 Corinthians 1.22 and Ephesians 1.14; 4.30.[150]

The contrast between that which is seen and that which is not (4.18a) could by itself, of course, come straight from Plato, and might imply a dualism in which physicality, present and future, was downgraded in favour of a non-physical world and human existence.[151] But this ontological dualism is questioned in the second half of verse 18, and disproved entirely in 5.1–5. Verse 18b indicates that the contrast is actually an eschatological one: 'eternal', again, could be read platonically, but the following passage indicates that it has to do, as usual in Paul, with 'the age to come', over against the present evil age in which the apostle lives, whose evidences are visible all around. These things are only for a time, he says; the age to come will last. This contrast then opens up the regular distinction, with which we are now familiar from 1 Corinthians, between the present *corruptible* body and the future *incorruptible* one. Verse 4 makes it clear that this is what Paul has

[150] Note the link of *katergazetai*, 'accomplishing', in 2 Cor. 4.17, with *katergasamenos*, 'who accomplished', in 5.5. The frequent translation 'prepare' is adequate enough, provided one remembers that it means 'prepare' as in 'prepare a meal', not simply 'prepare' as in 'give advance information about something'. The root of *katergazomai* is after all *ergon*, 'work': the point is that the living God is already *doing* something, even though it remains often and largely out of sight. Moule 1966, 118 acknowledges that the sense he gives to the passage (that Paul envisages first being unclothed, and then being reclothed) requires that he take this verb in the sense of 'designed', 'created'.

[151] On dualisms and dualities see *NTPG* 252–6, 257–9. For the question in relation to 2 Cor. 4 and 1 Cor. 15 the article of Moule 1966 is still important, even though I remain unpersuaded by his main proposal; cf. too Thrall 2002, 292–300.

in mind when, in a clear echo of 1 Corinthians 15.54 (itself quoting Isaiah 25.8) he declares that what is 'mortal' will be 'swallowed up' by life.

This parallel with the chapter we have just been studying opens the way to a true understanding of the contrast in 5.1–4 between the present body and the future one. This corruptible, mortal body, he emphasized in 1 Corinthians 15.53–4, must 'put on' (*endusasthai*) incorruption, immortality. Here he says that we who are in the present body are longing to 'put on over the top' (*ependusasthai*) the new body, the new 'dwelling' (5.2, 4). In the analogy in 1 Corinthians 15.37, he spoke of the seed as being 'naked' when planted, but given a new body by God; so here (5.3) he speaks of the longing of present human beings not to be found 'naked', but to be more fully clothed. The language of 'nakedness', as is well known, could be used in the wider hellenistic world to refer to the soul when divested of the body.[152] Verse 4 may be read as declaring that Paul would prefer to go straight to the transformed body, as in the 'changing' language of 1 Corinthians 15.51–2 and Philippians 3.21, rather than divesting himself of his present body and then undergoing a period of waiting for the eventual resurrection. Granted, in Philippians 1.23 he speaks of departing and being with the Messiah, and in our present passage he speaks of being 'at home with the lord' if he were to die (5.8–9). This is about as explicit as he gets on the question of an 'intermediate state'; clearly he believes that people in such a state will be happy and content. But, precisely because Paul is still thinking in a very Jewish manner, his preference is for the final state, in which one will be given a new body to be put on over the top of the present one, clothing the Messiah's people in a new kind of physicality whose main characteristic is incorruption. Thus, though Moule is no doubt right that Paul can envisage here the possibility of 'exchange' (losing one body, getting another one) rather than 'addition', as in 1 Corinthians 15, we should not lose sight of the fact that even if such an 'exchange' were to take place the new body would be *more than* the present one: more substantial, more solid, more what a human being was made to be, as a result of the preparatory work that is already being accomplished through the Spirit.[153]

Why then does Paul speak of the new body as being 'in the heavens'? Does this not mean that he thinks of Christians simply 'going to heaven' after their death? No. This is one of the passages which have supplied later tradition with the materials for an unwarranted platonizing of Christian hope. As with Philippians 3.20–21, and indeed 1 Corinthians 15.47–9, the temptation of the tradition has been to drive a steamroller through what Paul actually says, clearing his careful words out of the way to make room for a

---

[152] e.g. Plato *Gorg.* 524d; *Crat.* 403b Philo *Virt.* 76; *Leg. All.* 2.57, 59. This potential meaning may be partly responsible for the textual problems of the verse, as different scribes read it with different expectations.

[153] See Moule 1966, 123.

different worldview in which the aim of Christian faith is 'to go to heaven when you die'. The tradition has always found it difficult to incorporate 'resurrection', in any Jewish or early Christian sense, into that scenario, which is perhaps why orthodox Christianity has found it hard to respond to the attacks of secular modernity at this point. 'Heaven' for Paul, here as elsewhere, is not so much where people go after they die – he remains remarkably silent on that, with the possible exception of Colossians 3.3–4 – but *the place where the divinely intended future for the world is kept safely in store*, against the day when, like new props being brought out from the wings and onto stage, it will come to birth in the renewed world, 'on earth as in heaven'. If I assure my guests that there is champagne for them in the fridge I am not suggesting that we all need to get into the fridge if we are to have the party. The future body, the non-corruptible (and hence 'eternal') 'house', is at present 'in the heavens' as opposed to 'on earth' (*epigeios*) (5.1); but it will not stay there.[154] For us to put it on on top of our present 'house' (clothes, bodies, houses, temples and tents; why mix two metaphors if four or five will do?) will require that it be brought *from* heaven (5.2).[155] This is a key passage not only for understanding Paul but for grasping similar language elsewhere in the New Testament.

With all this in mind, we can return to 4.16–18 with some hope of seeing what foundations Paul is laying for this fuller statement of ultimate resurrection hope. The contrast between the 'inner human being' and 'outer human being', the one increasingly worn out and decaying, the other being renewed, is not a prelude to a disembodied bliss in which an 'inner' life or soul eventually and thankfully escapes embodiment. Nor is the mention of 'being weighed down' in 5.4 an indication of that worldview, despite the obvious parallel with Wisdom 9.15.[156] Paul's other mentions of the 'inner human being' show that he can use the phrase in various ways; no conclusions about a radical change of philosophical perspective can be built on it, especially in the light of the entire passage and letter.[157]

The central segment of the central passage of this resurrection-centred letter, then, does not depart from the picture we have seen throughout Paul. He looks forward to eventual bodily resurrection, to a new body which will have left behind the decay and corruption of the present one, and which will function in relation to present life like a new and larger suit of clothes to be put on over the existing ones. The way to this future, exactly as in Romans and elsewhere, is by suffering and the Spirit. And the present life which

[154] cf. Col. 1.5 with 3.1–4; and see too 1 Pet. 1.4 (below, 465–7).

[155] Paul's language of 'tent' in 5.1f. should perhaps awaken overtones of the Temple and its rebuilding, as in the resurrection passage in Rom. 8.5–11.

[156] cf. 172–4 above.

[157] e.g. Rom. 7.22, where it denotes the inner life of the non-Christian Jew. Cf. too Eph. 3.16, which is closely cognate with our present passage; and the similar language about the renewal of new life in Col. 3.10.

anticipates this future, and which can use the language of future resurrection metaphorically to refer to its present state, is one of 'renewal' (4.16), of 'preparation' in the full sense indicated above, and of a faith and hope which can see where ordinary sight cannot. This is a full statement, not simply of the same Christian hope that Paul has articulated elsewhere, but also of the reason why the Corinthians should not be ashamed of Paul's sufferings, but should rather rejoice, both for him and for themselves, that the life of the age to come is already secure and assured, and is already breaking in, however paradoxically, into the present time of struggle and sorrow. It also, of course, carries forward the major theological theme which underpins this particular point, namely, the argument from new covenant to new creation. Paul, the minister of the new covenant, discovers the means of that covenant (the death and resurrection of Jesus) being worked out in his own life in the present. He knows that this is because the new creation, whose central feature is bodily resurrection, is being 'prepared'; and that he is part of it.

This opens the way for the final section of this vital passage.

(iv) 2 Corinthians 5.6–10

Paul has come round a corner in his argument, and is now looking to the future with his head held high. In 4.1 and 4.16 he denied that he was losing heart; here in 5.6 he exclaims that he is courageous and confident.[158] The reason for this, as in the closely cognate Philippians 1.18–26, is that there are only two options as he looks at the future, and he is content with both of them. Either he will die, or he will go on living for a while at least. Death (the dissolution of the present body) is not to be welcomed for its own sake, but it may be welcomed for its immediate result, namely, 'living away from the body and living at home with the lord' (5.8), since in the present body one is inevitably 'living at home in the body and living away from the lord' (5.6). That is why (5.7) the Christian life is one of faith, not sight, as Paul keeps emphasizing and as, we may suppose, he was eager for the Corinthians to understand. Together with the Philippians passage, this is as close as Paul ever comes to an account of the intermediate state between death and resurrection.

His eyes are not, however, on that state for its own sake, but on what follows for someone who has lived his life on the basis of Psalm 116, understood through the lens of the gospel events concerning Jesus. 'Whether we are at home or away from home', he says, 'we make it our aim to please him'; to 'walk pleasingly before the Lord,' as the Psalm has it, 'in the land

---

[158] *tharreo* occurs only here, and in 7.16; 10.1, in Paul; elsewhere in the NT only at Heb. 13.6.

of the living'.[159] This answers the question that might otherwise arise with Paul's talk of being 'away from the body'; there is nothing inherently wrong with being 'in the body', nothing gnostic or dualistic about Paul's desire to be 'at home with the lord'. The present body is the locus of present service and holiness; and the end of the final journey is the new body, the dwelling-place at present in heaven. All this looks on both to the final statement of hope in verse 10 and to that which follows immediately after: Paul lives his life, and engages in his apostolic work, not on the basis of what people in the surrounding culture might expect, but on the basis of what will please the lord. And this 'pleasing' has a day of reckoning in mind:

> [10]for we must all appear before the judgment seat of the Messiah, so that each may receive a recompense according to what has been done through the body, whether good or bad.

Paul refers to this future judgment sufficiently frequently for us to suppose that this was a fixed point in all his thinking, and he is always clear that on that day God's judgment will take account not simply of the state of one's heart and mind but of the deeds done in the *body*.[160] Indeed, throughout much of the Jewish literature we surveyed in chapters 3 and 4, and much of the early Christian writings we shall study in Part III, there is a close connection between the future judgment and the future resurrection. Here, as in 1 Corinthians, we find once more the continuity between present and future life seen in terms of the body.[161] This is the ultimate future expectation and hope that drives Paul's concern to live appropriately, and to exhibit the signs of an apostle, not least suffering and hope – whether the church, let alone the world, wants and understands it or not.[162] This passage now flows seamlessly into 5.11—6.13, concluding the discussion of new covenant and new creation, and the nature of apostleship as embodying both.

(v) Conclusion

We have seen no reason to suggest that Paul changed his mind between 1 and 2 Corinthians. As we have said, he changed his *perspective*, recognizing now that there was a good chance of his own death before the new age arrived in its complete form. He therefore articulated in a fresh way both what that would mean for him in the future (this is why we find brief hints of, and questions about, an intermediate state here, but not in the earlier letter) and what it means for his present work, whose character the church has

---

[159] Ps. 116 [114].9; see above.
[160] 2 Cor. 5.10; cf. Rom. 2.1–16; 14.10; Eph. 6.8; and e.g. Ac. 10.42; 17.31.
[161] cf. 1 Cor. 6.12–20 etc.
[162] cf. 2 Cor. 12.12.

challenged (this is why we find more emphasis on the present life, and its metaphorical death-and-resurrection character, than in 1 Corinthians). But there is no change of underlying story or theology.[163]

The necessary angle of approach here to the topic of the Christian's future hope has meant that there is less explicit reference to the death and resurrection of Jesus. But 4.14 states the link between Easter and Christian hope so clearly that it may be legitimate, as we did in 1 Corinthians 15, to probe a little further and enquire whether, through the study of 4.16—5.5 in particular, we can glimpse something more of what Paul believed had happened to Jesus. Did Paul, perhaps, believe that Jesus' new body, his incorruptible Easter body, had been all along waiting 'in the heavens' for him to 'put on over the top of' his present one? Certainly we may assume that he believed, with the Peter of Acts 2.24–36, that Jesus' body was not corrupted after death. Even on Holy Saturday Jesus had not become, if that is the right way to take 5.3, 'naked', with his physical body corrupted and his soul or spirit returning, without the body, to the father. (Paul appears innocent of the speculations about what Jesus was doing between his death and resurrection which we see in their early stages in 1 Peter 3.19.) The obvious link beween 5.4–5 and Romans 8.9–11 encourages us to press the point home: Paul probably believed that, at Easter, Jesus' 'mortal body' was 'swallowed up by life', a new bodily life in continuity but thus also discontinuity (immortality instead of mortality) with the previous one. And, as in Romans 2.16 and Acts 17.31, it is this resurrection of Jesus, in advance of everyone else, that qualifies him to be the judge of all, to sit on the *bema*, the judgment seat, and to bring God's justice to the world. Though we have not explored all the possible political overtones of Paul's resurrection language in 2 Corinthians, we should not ignore the fact that, for Paul and probably for most early Christians, it was precisely the resurrection of Jesus which declared that he was lord, saviour and judge, and that Caesar was not.[164]

The present life, caught between the present age and the age to come, held in tension between the past resurrection of Jesus and the future resurrection promised to all his people, is thus itself appropriately spoken of with the *metaphor* of resurrection, as in 4.10–12. As with the other passages we studied in chapter 5, this does not mean that Paul was using the word in a way foreign to the metaphorical usage within Judaism. It was precisely what he thought was meant, in the present time, by the restoration of God's people. Metaphorical and literal uses, both (it should be noted) with concrete referents, reinforce one another, and point to the rich but consistent worldview which Paul developed and did his best both to teach and to embody.

---

[163] So, rightly and emphatically, Matera 2002 (esp. the conclusion, 405).
[164] cf. too, of course, Phil. 3.20f.

3. Conclusion: Resurrection in Paul

This concludes our study of the key passages in Paul's letters. Understanding him must be near the heart of any understanding of early Christianity; certainly, getting to know where he stands on the question of death and resurrection, and more specifically of the death and resurrection of Jesus, is at the heart of discovering what the early Christians believed on these subjects. We may briefly summarize our findings.[165]

When we place Paul on the spectrum of beliefs outlined in chapters 2—4 above, he clearly belongs on the Jewish map rather than the pagan one, despite the efforts that scholars sometimes make to get him to change his mind. Within the Jewish spectrum, he belongs, with most Jews of his day, at the same place as the Pharisees, many writers of apocalypses, and others whom we studied in chapter 4 above. He believed, that is, in the future bodily resurrection of all the true people of the true God, and he cautiously explored, here and there, ways of referring to the intermediate state which was the necessary corollary of such a belief. He believed that Israel's God, being both the creator of the world and the God of justice, would accomplish this resurrection by his Spirit, who was already at work in the Messiah's people.

At the same time, Paul believed two things which are only comprehensible as mutations within the Jewish worldview, not as combinations of a Jewish eschatology with something else. First, he believed that 'the resurrection' had divided, as a historical moment, into two: the resurrection of the Messiah in the first place, and then, at his 'parousia', of all his people. Second, he believed, and articulated in considerable detail, that the resurrection would not only be bodily (the idea of a non-bodily resurrection would have been as much an oxymoron to him as it would to both Jews and pagans of his day; whether you believed in resurrection or not, the word meant bodies), but that it would also involve *transformation*. The present body is corruptible, decaying and subject to death; but death, which spits in the face of the good creator God, cannot have the last word.[166] The creator will therefore make a new world, and new bodies, proper to the new age. From one

---

[165] I regard as a strange curiosity the summaries by Boismard (1999 [1995], ix, 48) of his hypothetical development-scheme: first Paul thinks of an eschatological reign on earth (1 Thess.), then he gives this up and thinks the resurrection will take place in the sky, at the parousia (1 Cor.), then he comes to believe in a Platonic scheme whereby the resurrection has happened already and will become apparent, in heaven, immediately upon death (2 Cor.), and finally, 'at the end of his life', he placed 'our beatific vision in God' (Col.)! Where, one wonders, does Rom. 8 fit in this scheme?

[166] See de Boer 1988, 183f.: physical demise, for Paul, has been shown up as 'a terrible offense, the annihilation of the human person by an alien, inimical power'. The summary of Paul's view in Lüdemann 1994, 177 offers an example of the all-too-common view which our analysis rules out completely: that, according to Paul, 'Jesus entered God's presence directly at the moment of his death', and 'was exalted directly from the cross to God'.

point of view the new world, and the new bodies, are the redeemed, remade versions of the old ones; that is the emphasis of Romans 8. From another point of view the new world, and the new bodies, are 'stored up in heaven'. We should not play these off against one another; the latter phrase means, among other things, that they are safe in the mind, plan and intention of the creator God. Though Paul does not refer to the tree of life in Genesis 3, his controlling narrative is constantly pointing to the way in which the creator finally brings his human, image-bearing creatures, and indeed the entire cosmos, through the impasse of the fall, of the thorns and thistles and the whirling, flashing sword, to taste at last the gift of life in all its fullness, a new bodily life in a new world where the rule of heaven is brought at last to earth.

Furthermore, Paul frequently used the language of resurrection, in a metaphorical way, to denote the concrete, bodily events of Christian living, especially baptism and holiness; and also, on at least one occasion, to denote the renewal of the 'inner human being'. This, I have suggested, was a development of the metaphorical (and also metonymic) use of resurrection language within Judaism to denote the coming restoration of Israel, the great 'return from exile', the time spoken of in Ezekiel 37 and perhaps other passages.[167] This was not a 'spiritualization' of the idea of resurrection. Nor was it, as has often been suggested, a move away from Paul's now/not-yet tension and towards a more fully realized eschatology. Still less was it a move towards the later gnostic use of 'resurrection' language to denote a spiritual experience understood within an ontologically dualistic worldview.[168] It was, rather, a way of bringing to articulation the experience and belief of Jesus' earliest followers: that the Christian life belonged within a historical narrative which began with Jesus' resurrection and ended with the resurrection of all believers, and that the divine Spirit who accomplished the first would accomplish the second, and was even now at work to anticipate and guarantee that final event.

The question any historian must ask, discovering such a nest of intricate ideas, at once so Jewish and so unlike anything any Jew had said before, is obvious: what caused these developments-from-within, these newly articulated resurrection-beliefs? Paul himself would have answered: it was Jesus' own resurrection.[169] 'The resurrection', as envisaged by Jews of his day, had not happened; nor had the national restoration for which 'resurrection' could function both as metaphor and as metonym. However vivid the spiritual experience of Paul or other early Christians, there is no reason to suppose

---

[167] See 119–23 above.

[168] See below, ch. 11.

[169] Carnley 1987, 249f. states: 'Paul's own exposition of the nature of faith and hope is regularly traced back, not to an experience or vision of the bodily Jesus of some kind, but to the continuing presence of the Spirit of Christ.' He offers no grounds for this; nor, in the light of the last three chapters, could he have done so.

that they would have articulated their beliefs and hopes in anything like this way unless they really did believe that Jesus had been 'raised from the dead' in the sense that everybody in the ancient world would have understood, that is, bodily. Nor is there any explanation for why Paul developed his view of the future resurrection body in the way he did, except for the one that would have been obvious to him: that the Messiah's own resurrection body was certainly the same and curiously different, alive with a new kind of life. And since the call to holiness of life on the one hand, and suffering and persecution on the other, were major themes in Jewish literature, but in neither case was 'resurrection' language used metaphorically as a way of understanding or explaining them, we must draw the same conclusion about Paul's new-minted metaphorical language for the Christian life and experience.

At the same time, we may note that it was out of that call to holiness, suffering and persecution that there arose, in Daniel and elsewhere, the first clear articulations of resurrection hope. It was in embracing this vision that Jesus took the road which led to his own death and (so Paul believed) his own resurrection. This in turn shaped Paul's own understanding of holiness, suffering and persecution. That, one might say, is what the Corinthian correspondence is all about.

Paul's many and varied statements about future and present resurrection thus pose a historical question to which the only satisfactory answer, for him and for the historian, is his firm and sharply delineated belief in a past event, the resurrection of Jesus of Nazareth. How he arrived at this belief must be the subject of the next chapter.

Chapter Eight

WHEN PAUL SAW JESUS

1. Introduction

People who know little else about Paul know that he had a dramatic conversion. The phrase 'Damascus Road' has entered popular usage as a metaphor for a place, or even a moment, of sudden illumination and transformation, of discovering that one is on the wrong course and being turned around to follow a different one.

What is more, a surprising number of people with only limited biblical knowledge have a clear mental picture of what they think happened on the road to Damascus. Paul was riding along on horseback when a blinding light suddenly appeared, knocking him off the horse and onto the ground. In fact, like the ox, ass and camel of a thousand nativity scenes, Paul's horse belongs to later artistic imagination, not to the original texts. The incident, as we shall see, is described (at least) three times in Paul's own writings and three times in Acts, and at no point do we catch sight of a hoofprint, or even hear a faint whinny. The current perception owes a great deal to Michelangelo's fresco in the Pauline Chapel at the Vatican, to Caravaggio's stunning painting in the church of Santa Maria del Popolo, also in Rome, and to other similar works.[1] These in turn reflect earlier models. When the tourist guides tell us it is no longer customary to learn Bible stories from pictures, the popular conception of Paul's conversion gives us good reason to disagree.

A similar phenomenon, involving not horses but the way people talk about 'visions', has afflicted scholarly accounts of Paul's conversion. We are told repeatedly that what happened to Paul was that he had an intense spiritual experience; that this involved him 'seeing', not with ordinary eyesight but with the inner eye of the heart, a 'Jesus' who was not physically present, but who was a being of light (whatever that is). It was this experience of 'luminosity', it is said, which precipitated his conversion, and which

---

[1] e.g. those of Bruegel (1567, in Vienna) and Solimena (1689, in Naples).

influenced his subsequent theology.[2] 'From Paul,' writes Pheme Perkins, 'we may presume that [his basic vision] is a spiritual experience that carried with it the conviction of a revelatory encounter with God.'[3] And from this is regularly drawn the conclusion: if this was Paul's experience (and his texts are our earliest evidence), then this was probably what the other early disciples experienced as well. Reports of different kinds of 'seeing', as for instance in Luke and John, are therefore later attempts to turn a primary 'spiritual' vision into a more solid 'eyewitness' mode.[4]

Common though this interpretation is, it is as much a figment of the imagination as Caravaggio's splendid horse. What seems to have happened is that mainstream critical scholarship has forgotten its much-trumpeted principle of reading Paul's own letters as primary evidence and the accounts in Acts as secondary.[5] The spectacular picture of the Damascus Road event, related no fewer than three times in Acts, has coloured the imagination of those who have read the brief and perfunctory mentions in Paul himself; it has been wrongly aligned with one passage in particular (2 Corinthians 4.6) which is about something else; and this imaginative reading has distracted attention from what Luke was trying to do through telling the story in that way (or 'in those ways', since the three accounts differ). All this should prevent us from taking it as decisive evidence for a non-bodily 'seeing' of Jesus. To make this case we must look at the evidence piece by piece.

As we do so, we should note that the event has been discussed in recent years from two other points of view as well, neither of which is of central concern to us here. First, there has been considerable debate as to whether 'conversion' is the best term for it, since Paul was not, in our modern sense, 'changing religions', but receiving, so he believed, a fuller revelation from the god he had always worshipped. It has also been stressed, however (rightly in my view), that there are definite elements of 'conversion' in what happened to him.[6] I shall use this word in what follows, mindful that it can

---

[2] The classic statement of this in modern scholarship is Robinson 1982, 7–17. Robinson jumps from an unwarranted inference from 1 Cor. 15 and Phil. 3, via a glance at Acts and Rev. 1.13–16, to the conclusion (10) that Paul had an 'uninhibited luminous visualization of the resurrection', and that therefore all early experiences of it were 'luminous, the experience of a blinding light'. Robinson then admits, damagingly one might suppose, that when the hypothetical reaction to this set in – when, in other words, Matthew, Luke and John wrote their resurrection accounts – they were composing them against the 'foil' of 'this reduction of resurrection appearances to religious experiences' (11).

[3] Perkins 1984, 94.

[4] Two examples among many: Carnley 1987, 238f.; de Jonge 2002. A brief, clear answer to this line of thought is given by Davis 1997, 138f. A detailed discussion of the nature of 'visions' in this connection is provided by Schlosser 2001.

[5] On ancient parallels to the Acts/Paul relationship see Hillard, Nobbs and Winter 1993; for the relationship itself cf. Hemer 1989 ch. 6.

[6] Stendahl 1976, 7–23 argues for 'call' rather than 'conversion'; Segal 1990, 14–17, for elements of 'conversion' remaining appropriate. Cf. too e.g. Barrett 1994, 442: 'if such radical changes [as Paul's new attitude to the law, and his new mode of activity] do not amount

be problematic but also that repeated periphrases become tedious and cumbersome. (I shall also refer to the event in terms of 'the road to Damascus', conscious that Paul does not, strictly speaking, mention this location, but aware too that in his first telling of the story he says that he went immediately to Arabia 'and returned again to Damascus', implying both that that was where it happened and that his readers would have known about it.[7])

Second, most studies of Paul's conversion have highlighted the relationship between what happened to him on the road to Damascus and the shape and content of his subsequent theology. Although this is of concern to us in one particular aspect, namely what he believed about Jesus' resurrection, the larger questions can be bracketed for our purposes.[8]

A word at the start about epistemology.[9] Discussions of Paul's conversion over the last two centuries have repeatedly returned to the question of whether what happened was an 'objective' or a 'subjective' experience; that is, whether Paul saw and heard something or someone who was 'really there' in the public domain, or whether what happened to him was an 'internal' experience without any correlate in external reality.[10] This has regularly been aligned with different views of the resurrection itself, and we must do our best to avoid circularity. But it is worth noticing that the 'modernist' conception of 'religion', within which framework a good deal of critical scholarship has been pursued, has thought a priori of 'religious experience', including all reported experience of revelations from another world (e.g. 'heaven'), as of necessity 'internal'. That is part of the classic post-Enlightenment paradigm in which, following eighteenth-century Deism, anything to do with 'God' or 'religion' was removed by definition from contact with the world of space, time and matter. Thus, whenever someone constrained by this worldview comes upon a report of a heavenly vision, they are bound to classify it as 'internal'. That is all it can be – for them. But first-century Jews would not have seen things like that. For them, 'heaven' as God's sphere was every bit as real, and every bit as external to their own reality, their own hearts, minds and feelings, as the world of 'earth'. It is all very well for us to tell them, two thousand years later, what was 'really' going on. We need, perhaps, to be a bit more sure of our own ground before we patronizingly impose our etic view, squelching what would emerge from a more historical, a more emic, understanding.[11]

In addition, the opposition between objective and subjective is drastically

---

to conversion it is hard to know what would do so'; see also Dunn 1996, 119f.; Ashton 2000, 75–8.

[7] Gal. 1.17 (see below).

[8] See e.g. Longenecker 1997; and recently e.g. Kim 2002.

[9] cf. *NTPG* Part II.

[10] Ashton 2000, 80 traces this formulation of the problem back to F. C. Baur.

[11] See Rowland 1982, 378.

over-simple.[12] When an ambulance goes by in the street, wailing its siren, the fact that I can feel the noise in the centre of my skull does not mean that this is the only place it exists. When my eyes hurt in the dazzling sun, this is not because the sun doesn't exist, but because it does. There are of course states of consciousness which appear to be related to an external reality but which are produced simply by psychological or physiological processes. Dreams can do this to you, and so can drugs. But it would be arbitrary, and historically without warrant, to assume ahead of time that any claim about remarkable happenings in the external world, whether earthly or heavenly, which produce remarkable consequences in those who report them, can be reduced to terms of the state of consciousness of the person concerned. This would be to give Bishop Berkeley and his epistemology a late victory to which, frankly, he was never entitled in the first place – just as to insist that any statement about 'heavenly' or divine realities must be reduced to a statement about the person who claims to experience them is to throw up one's hands and give in to Feuerbach.[13] When, therefore, Paul speaks of seeing or hearing something which has a profound effect on him, this cannot of itself be allowed to mean that he was simply having a 'religious experience' without any objective correlate.[14] All experience is interpreted experience, but not all experience can be reduced to terms of the interpretation. This is not to decide issues in advance. It is, rather, an attempt precisely to prevent that being done by the linguistic frameworks conveniently supplied, on an insider-dealing basis, by the now widely questioned worldview of the Enlightenment.

We begin, as good historical method insists, with Paul's own accounts: with, that is, three passages where he clearly refers to the moment when he met and saw Jesus.

2. Paul's Own Accounts

(i) Galatians 1.11–17

Each time Paul mentions what happened to him on the road to Damascus he does so not for its own sake but to make a specific point, a different one in each case. In Galatians 1, the first of the three accounts, he is arguing passionately, presumably against accusations he had faced, that he had not

---

[12] This discussion is aimed in part at the long legacy of Bultmann's hermeneutic; see *NTPG* Part II.

[13] For a brief, clear account of Berkeley see e.g. Warnock 1995, with other bib. On Feuerbach cf. e.g. Wartofsky 1977.

[14] cf. e.g. Patterson 1998, 226f., n. 26: we may not be able to psychoanalyse Paul, but this does not mean that his experience 'was not deeply affected by his own subjectivity. His experience could in no wise be considered an "objective" event.'

received his gospel from the 'pillar' apostles such as Peter, James and John, but had received it directly as a commission from Jesus himself. Twice he describes this moment as a 'revelation' (*apokalypsis*):

> [11]For I want you to know, my brothers and sisters, that the gospel proclamation which was proclaimed by me was not according to human beings. [12]For I neither received it from human beings, nor was I taught it, but [it happened] through a revelation of Jesus the Messiah (*di' apokalypseos Iesou Christou*) . . . [Paul then describes his early life as a zealous Jew.] . . . [15]But when it pleased the God who separated me from my mother's womb, and called me through his grace, [16]to reveal his son in me (*apokalypsai ton huion autou en emoi*), so that I might proclaim the good news of him among the Gentiles, at once I did not confer with flesh and blood, [17]nor did I go up to Jerusalem to those who were apostles before me, but I went away to Arabia, and afterwards returned to Damascus.

Six points about this complex little passage need to be made for our present argument.[15] First, the rhetorical needs of Paul's argument lead him naturally to stress the difference between the 'revelation' he received and the possibility that he had 'received' his gospel from ordinary human sources, some way down a chain of tradition, in such a manner that the Galatians could then appeal over his head to the original source. This is why he chooses the *apokalypsis* root to make the point: this was an 'unveiling' of the truth itself, indeed, of Jesus himself, not a secondary handing on.[16] The word carries the overtones of the sudden uncovering of something previously concealed, in particular of something hidden in God's sphere of reality ('heaven'), something which would not normally be visible in the human sphere ('earth'), but which could become so under special circumstances.[17] Elsewhere in Paul this word-group has an eschatological force: something which one might expect to become manifest on the last day has been 'revealed' ahead of time.[18] Since these are the particular emphases Paul wants to draw out here, we cannot deduce anything from this word about the exact type of experience (ordinary seeing, or 'seeing' in the heart).

Second, Paul refers to his conversion/call in terms reminiscent of the call of the prophets.[19] There are echoes here of two classic prophets: Isaiah 49.1, 5 ('YHWH has called me from the womb, from the belly of my mother he has named me'. . . 'YHWH formed me in the womb to be his servant')[20] and

---

[15] In addition to the commentaries see e.g. Newman 1992, 196–207.

[16] The phrase could mean, by itself, either 'a revelation which came from Jesus' or 'a revelation whose content was Jesus'; v. 16 indicates that Paul means the latter (so e.g. Hays 2000, 211). Cf. too 1.1: Paul received his commission 'through Jesus the Messiah and God the Father who raised him from the dead' – the last clause being a key part of the whole picture.

[17] See Rowland 1982, 376f.

[18] cf. e.g. Rom. 1.18 with 2.5; 1 Cor 1.7; 2 Thess. 1.7 with the present passage. See too Newman 1992: the eschatological glory has been revealed in advance (see below).

[19] Baird 1985, 657; Sandnes 1991; Newman 1992, 204–07.

[20] cf. too Isa. 44.2.

Jeremiah 1.5 ('before I formed you in the womb I knew you, and appointed you a prophet to the nations'). This is one of two important parallels between Paul's own account, brief though it is, and Luke's fuller one, in which as we shall see Luke is at pains to describe what happened to Paul in the biblical terms appropriate for a (possibly inaugural) prophetic vision.

Third, this passage is a partial parallel to 1 Corinthians 15.3–11, which we studied in the previous chapter and to which we shall shortly return. Paul is making the point that Jesus the Messiah has been revealed to him, as well as to the other apostles who might otherwise have been thought primary.

Fourth, the crucial revelation was of 'the son of god'. This is the second important parallel with the accounts in Acts, where Paul's opening addresses to the Damascus synagogues have this as their central point: that Jesus is 'son of god' (9.20). There, as here and in Romans 1.3–4, the primary meaning of 'son of god' is not 'the second person of the Trinity' but 'Israel's Messiah'.

Fifth, the key phrase in verse 16 can be understood in two ways: as emphasizing either god's revelation of his son *to* Paul, or his revelation of his son *through* Paul. The Greek 'in' (*en*) could mean either, or perhaps both, but the next clause indicates the main thing Paul wants to say: that the divine purpose was for Paul to preach the gospel among the Gentile nations. Paul does not elsewhere speak of god's son dwelling in him as the means of his evangelistic mission.[21] But he sees his own life as a reflection of the life of Jesus, and as such to be imitated by the young church;[22] and in various passages, including an important one in the next chapter, he describes his own coming to Christian faith as a paradigm of what happens to people through the gospel.[23] If this is the emphasis of the passage, it seems that Paul is here referring primarily to god revealing Jesus *through* him, though this requires that first Jesus be revealed *to* him. This combination rules out the suggestion which is sometimes made, that the word 'in' points to a merely 'internal' revelation, a 'spiritual experience' *as opposed to* an outward seeing.[24]

Sixth, a comparison of this passage with Romans 1.3–4 and 1 Corinthians 15.1–4 reminds us that when Paul here talks about 'the gospel' he does not

[21] Gal. 2.20f. and Col. 1.28f. are the closest he comes.

[22] e.g. 1 Cor. 11.1.

[23] Gal. 2.19f.; cf. too e.g. 1 Tim. 1.16, where it is said that Jesus the Messiah intended to show his patience 'in Paul', as the chief or first example to subsequent believers.

[24] Longenecker 1990, 32 speaks of 'the inward reality of Christian experience'; Thrall 1994, 317, of Paul's experience containing 'an inward element', which is undoubtedly true, but not the point.; Patterson 1998, 223f. speaks of it as an 'inner' experience. Ashton 2000, 83 believes that this verse states unambiguously that Paul 'experienced the revelation . . . as happening somehow inside himself'. Ashton suggests that to translate 'to me' needs 'a lot of strenuous philological wriggling', but Martyn 1997a, 158 makes the case for 'to' with not a wriggle in sight. So does Rowland 1982, 376, citing those very non-wriggling grammarians, Blass-Debrunner and Moule.

mean 'justification by faith' or 'the inclusion of the Gentiles'. He means 'Jesus, the Messiah, is risen from the dead and is the lord of the world.'[25] Since we have a clear idea from both Romans and 1 Corinthians of what Paul meant by this kind of statement, the best way of taking Galatians 1.12 and 16 is to insist that when Paul spoke of the revelation of Jesus the Messiah, of God's son, he was taking it for granted that in and through this revelation he had become convinced that Jesus had been raised from the dead in the sense explained by those other two letters.

Galatians thus presents us, in this short passage, with some clear indications of how Paul interpreted what had happened to him on the road to Damascus. It does not help very much, though, with the question of what precisely it was that happened. But it points us forward to the two texts that do, both of them in 1 Corinthians.

(ii) 1 Corinthians 9.1

Within the larger argument of 1 Corinthians 8.1—11.1, concerning food offered to idols, Paul offers his own life as an example.[26] Not that he describes his own eating habits; we still know frustratingly little about them. Rather, he describes his own tactical use, and in this case non-use, of his freedom and rights as an apostle. He has the right to travel with a wife; he has the right to be paid for his work; but he has decided not to make use of these rights, for certain strategic reasons – including, perhaps, so as not to become enmeshed in the complex patron/client relationships that would otherwise be set up.[27]

The first two verses of chapter 9 introduce this illustrative sub-theme in typically trenchant fashion:

> [1]Am I not free? Am I not an apostle? Have I not seen Jesus our Lord? Are you not my work in the Lord? [2]If to others I am not an apostle, I certainly am to you; for you are the seal of my apostleship in the Lord.

As far as Paul was concerned, an 'apostle' was someone who had seen the risen lord; but the proof of apostleship came in the fruitfulness of the apostolic ministry.[28] Paul takes it for granted that apostleship bestows a freedom of sorts, and he mentions this first because this is the point he is going to develop. But for us the critical connection is between the second and third questions. He is an apostle because he has seen Jesus the lord.[29] He is one of

---

[25] See Wright, 'Gospel and Theology', and Wright, *Romans*, 415f.

[26] The passage is discussed briefly above, 292–4.

[27] For the detail of this see Thiselton 2000, 661–3.

[28] On apostleship see Thiselton 2000, 666–74, with copious refs. to other literature.

[29] Fee 1987, 395 n. 14 emphasizes that 'Jesus our Lord' is almost a technical term for the risen Christ.

those, a finite and limited number, who saw Jesus and remained marked for ever by the fact of having done so (that is the significance of the perfect tense of *heoraka*, 'I have seen': the perfect draws attention to the present and continuing significance of a one-off past event).[30] This is not a way of speaking that Paul has been drawn into by adopting, despite his own better judgment, 'the Christian practice of referring to such revelatory experiences as "seeing" the Lord'.[31] He wants to make this point because he believes it to be true, and the truth of it matters for his argument.

The combination of this verse with 15.8–11 (see below) makes it clear that Paul intends a 'seeing' which is something quite different from the manifold spiritual experiences, the 'seeings' with the eye of the heart, which many Christians in most periods of history have experienced. The Corinthians had had all kinds of spiritual experiences, for which indeed Paul congratulates them in 1.4–7; but they had not had this experience. Paul, too, has had many spiritual experiences as his life and work have progressed, but he is not here referring to something that might occur again. This was, for him, a one-off, initiatory 'seeing', which constituted him as an apostle but would not be repeated. The resurrection appearances of Jesus came to a stop. His was the last; almost, in fact, too late.

The word *heoraka*, 'I have seen', is a normal word for ordinary sight. It does not imply that this was a subjective 'vision' or a private revelation; part of the point of it, as Newman stresses, is that it was a real seeing, not a 'vision' such as anyone in the church might have.[32] The same is emphatically true of the other text from 1 Corinthians.

(iii) 1 Corinthians 15.8–11

We have already looked at this passage in our previous chapter, and here simply need to draw the point out a little more firmly. Paul is giving a list of people who have seen the risen Jesus, and who can be produced by the church as witnesses who could in principle be interrogated. After listing the appearances to Cephas, the Twelve, to more than 500 at once, and to James, he says,

> Last of all, as to the one untimely born, he appeared also to me.[33]

Nothing much can be made either way of the verb *ophthe*, 'he appeared'. As I argued earlier, this could be used for either a private vision or a public, and very ordinary and matter of fact, 'appearance' of somebody. But four factors

---

[30] Thiselton 2000, 668.
[31] Patterson 1998, 224. See, correctly, Newman 1992, 186.
[32] Newman 1992, 186.
[33] On 'untimely born' see above, 327–9.

tell strongly in favour of Paul's intention to refer to a real 'seeing' with his ordinary eyes, rather than a non-physical 'seeing' in the sense of a private or internal 'experience'.

First, the proximity of 9.1 means that we should assume here what is clear there, that Paul intends to refer to a 'seeing' which was on a par with normal human 'seeing'. It may have been more, but was not less. It was not simply a private experience.

Second, 'last of all' makes it clear that, as far as Paul at least is concerned, his 'seeing' of the risen Jesus was part of a sequence that came to an end. It was not part of an ongoing set of spiritual experiences that either he or anyone else were having, or were likely to have. It was of a different order.

Third, it is noteworthy that 15.1–11 as a whole clearly speaks of a *public event* for which there is *evidence* in the form of *witnesses* who *saw something and can be interrogated*. As we saw earlier, those who have wished to say that the risen Christ was not that kind of being, that the resurrection was not that sort of event, that it did not have that kind of evidence, and that any witnesses would simply be speaking of their own inner conviction and experience rather than the evidence of their eyes, have had to say that Paul has here undermined the point he really should have been making. The best example of this, giving hereby a sign of a hermeneutic that is about to walk blindfold over a cliff, is Rudolf Bultmann.[34]

Fourth, and in support of this, the rest of chapter 15 does not (as we have seen) speak of that interesting oxymoron, a non-bodily 'resurrection'. Nor does it speak of the risen body of Jesus as being made of light. Indeed, as we have observed at various points, and shall see particularly when examining the gospel accounts, it is the non-luminosity of Jesus' risen body that is striking (granted Daniel 12.3), not the luminosity, which is seldom mentioned in the New Testament (Jesus' body is not itself described as luminous in the accounts of Paul's conversion, but his appearance on the Damascus Road was accompanied by a blinding flash of light; the vision of Revelation 1.14–17 comes in a very different category) or in the fathers of the first two centuries. The very close connection between Paul's view of what happened to Jesus and his view of what will happen to all Christians, and the robustly 'bodily' account of the latter given throughout 1 Corinthians 15, present an unanswerable case for the fact that when Paul spoke of Jesus 'appearing' in verse 8 he did not mean that Jesus appeared in his (Paul's) heart or mind, but to his bodily eyes and sight, as a real human being, truly and bodily raised from the dead. Paul knows there was something different about his 'seeing' of Jesus from that of the others in the list. He was out of time; the appearances had all but come to a stop; but he was granted this not least as a sign of grace (15.10).

[34] See Bultmann in Bartsch 1962–4, 1.38f., 41, 83.

These passages are the only ones in which Paul writes of his 'conversion' or 'call'. There are, however, two others sometimes cited in this connection, not least in order to counteract the kind of argument I am advancing, and to argue instead for a non-bodily, luminous, 'internal' kind of 'seeing' – in other words (to use the regular problematic language), for a 'subjective' experience without a correlate in external reality. These are therefore highlighted here out of a larger number which give a 'before-and-after' account of Paul's life, or which mention Paul's primal commission from Jesus, but which tell us little or nothing about our particular question.[35]

(iv) 2 Corinthians 4.6

We have already looked at 2 Corinthians 3 and 4 in the previous two chapters, and can now draw on that treatment to highlight 4.5–6:

> [5]For we do not proclaim ourselves, but Jesus the Messiah as Lord, and ourselves as your servants through Jesus. [6]For it is the God who said 'Let light shine out of darkness' who has shone in our hearts, for the illumination of the knowledge of the glory of God in the face of Jesus the Messiah.

The 'shining' and the 'illumination' here must be read in the context of 3.1—4.6 as a whole, where two things become clear.

First, this is an experience which Paul assumes all Christians share. The first person plural here is not simply a polite version of 'I'; it reflects Paul's actual argument throughout the section, which is that every single Christian, not least those in Corinth, has had the new covenant written on his or her heart (3.3), so that Christian fellowship, not least the relation of the apostle to the church, is a matter of all Christians looking at one another and seeing the reflected glory of the one who, by the Spirit, lives in each (3.18).[36] This context (often ignored in discussion of Paul's conversion in relation to this passage) makes it clear that he is not speaking of his own unique experience, but of something which is common to all Christians; and that he is not talking about an initial experience of conversion or call, but of something which remains, in principle, a constant element in the experience of Christians.[37]

[35] e.g. Rom. 10.2–4; 1 Cor. 9.16f.; 2 Cor. 3.16; 5.16; Gal. 2.19f.; Phil. 3.4–12; Eph. 3.1–13; Col. 1. 23–9. Cf. too the formula about 'the grace given to me' in Rom. 1.5; 12.3; 15.15; 1 Cor. 1.4; 3.10; Gal. 2.9; Eph. 3.2, 7; Col. 1.25. On this see Kim 1984 [1981], 3–31; Newman 1992, 164–7.

[36] The theme of the 'heart' is prominent throughout the argument (2 Cor. 3.2, 3, 15; 4.6), strongly inclining us to read this reference in the light of the preceding ones. Thrall 1994, 316f. sees the plural 'hearts' as an objection to the 'conversion' reading of this text, but does not allow it its full force.

[37] So, rightly, Furnish 1984, 250f.; Murphy-O'Connor 1996, 78 n. 20. See too e.g. Dunn 1990, 93–7, against Kim 1984, who built a good deal on 2 Cor. 4.4–6 being an account of Paul's conversion in order to claim that Paul then perceived Jesus as divine. Kim

This is reinforced by the parallel between verse 6 and the preceding verse 4, where Paul declares that the god of this world has blinded the minds of the unbelievers, to keep them from seeing the light (*photismon*) of the gospel of the glory of Christ, who is the 'image of God'. Paul does not imagine that every time the gospel is preached, people see the lord in the same way that he did on the road to Damascus. What he is speaking of here is not, in fact, a literal 'seeing' at all, but a matter of the *mind* being able to grasp the fresh truth of the gospel, as in 3.14.

This leads to the second key point. The 'shining', the luminosity of which Paul here speaks, is not a visible luminosity, nor yet a brightness which is obvious even at the level of 'inner' experience. It is an illumination which is perceived by faith. That is why Paul has to *argue* in chapter 3 that the revelation of the new covenant in Christ is *in fact* glorious – because the Corinthians were disposed to doubt it. One does not stand outside at noon on a cloudless day and produce a long argument, working up from first principles, to prove that the sun is shining. Kim and others, affirming the external reality of the Jesus whom Paul saw at his conversion, distort this passage, which is about the inner eye of mind and heart, by trying to make it refer to the same event; just as Patterson and others, denying the external reality of the Jesus Paul 'saw' at his conversion, distort the passages where Paul describes that event by similarly linking them with the present one. Paul in 1 Corinthians declares that he saw Jesus; Acts, as we shall see, speaks (among other things) of a light that dazzled people's eyes, not their hearts. 2 Corinthians 4.6 speaks of neither.[38]

2002, 165–213 has presented an updated account of his view, in debate with various scholars including the present writer. I am not unhappy with his view that 2 Cor. 4.1–6 provides crucial insights into Paul's understanding of who Jesus was (though I think Kim has missed out some key moves that Paul makes), but I remain unpersuaded, for reasons given in the text, that this passage refers either explicitly or implicitly to Paul's conversion. Kim is followed by e.g. Thrall 1994, 1.316–18; Ashton 2000, 84–6, who do not seem to me to have reckoned with Furnish's arguments, or those advanced here. Newman 1992 is right, if overly polysyllabic, to say that 'Glory functions in Paul's convictional world in sociomorphic portrayal of transference, and in Paul's physiomorphic description of Christian progress,' but this tells, if anything, against the present passage referring specifically to the Damascus Road Christophany. If it did, how could Paul have generalized from his experience – granted his placing of his seeing of Jesus at the end of a one-off sequence in 1 Cor. 15.8 – to the experience he and the Corinthians all shared?

[38] cf. e.g. Patterson 1998, 226. We cannot know, he says, why Paul concluded that it was in fact Jesus who had appeared to him in an internal experience. 'All we can say is that on that day, for whatever reason, Paul came to the realization that Jesus had been right about God, that God had shone through in his life and ministry, and that the continuing work of his followers was indeed the work of God. And so he changed his mind'. So Paul's 'seeing' of Jesus has become first an internal spiritual experience and then an internal mental argument, a 'realization'. Paul never mentions anything about Jesus being right about God, and so forth, just as Patterson never mentions most of the things Paul himself says about the resurrection.

This brings out, in fact, the full force of verse 5. If Paul was preaching about his own inner 'experience' of some kind of spiritual illumination, which he then connected with Jesus, verse 5 would be disingenuous. He *would* be 'proclaiming himself', saying, in effect, 'I have had this experience; would you not like to have it as well?' That may be the way of some preachers, in the first century or the twenty-first, but it was not what Paul was about. Instead, he is speaking of Jesus, pointing away from himself and to the one who, having been raised from the dead, is now heralded and acclaimed as lord. To be sure, Paul believes that the Jesus who is now known through the new-covenant ministry of the Spirit in the heart is the same Jesus who died and was raised, the same Jesus who appeared to him on the road to Damascus. But he is not referring to this event here. His mention of Jesus' 'face' links this passage, not to a recognition of Jesus at the moment of conversion/call, but to the discussion of 'faces', both veiled and unveiled, in 3.12–18. The language of Genesis 1 ('let light shine out of darkness') is, as we saw earlier, part of Paul's theme of the new creation which emerges through the fulfilment of the new covenant (see 5.17). All this is something that is true, and goes on being true, of all Christians, not something that is true of a single experience of an apostle.

We shall have more to say presently about the relation of this passage to the early development and formation of Paul's view of Jesus. But for the moment we turn to the other passage sometimes cited in connection with Paul's experience of conversion or call.

(v) 2 Corinthians 12.1–4

The other passage is the highly ironic description of one particular vision in 2 Corinthians 12. Paul is 'boasting', with his tongue very firmly in his cheek, of all the things he can be proud of – or rather, in fact, of all the things which show how weak he is. The Corinthians have forced him to produce some kind of statement of his qualifications, a kind of *curriculum vitae* or indeed *cursus honorum*, and so eventually he does – but it is a list of all the wrong things.[39]

In this passage he turns to 'visions and revelations'. The Corinthians do not want to know about his original seeing of Jesus. He has already told them about that, both in person and by letter. What they want is an up-to-date account of his wonderful spiritual experiences, the more recent the better.[40] If Paul is a true apostle, surely he will be able to regale them with splendid tales of heavenly journeys, of revelations of secret wisdom, of

---

[39] See above, 307–09.

[40] I infer this from Paul's emphasizing, ironically as it seems to me, that the experience he relates took place fourteen years earlier.

glimpses of glory far beyond mortal eyes. Well, he declares, he will and he won't: he will only boast, once more, of the things that show his weaknesses (11.30; 12.9–10). So, although he makes it clear that he has had ecstatic experiences of a particularly remarkable kind, the main thing he wants to emphasize is the 'thorn in the flesh' which accompanied them, and which could not be shifted even by prayer (12.7–9).

The particular ecstatic experience to which he refers in 12.1–4 took place, it seems, around the year 40 (assuming a date in the mid-50s for 2 Corinthians):

> [1]I must boast; it's no use, but I will go on to visions and revelations of the Lord. [2]I know a man in Christ who, fourteen years ago – whether in the body or out of the body I do not know, God knows – who was snatched up to the third heaven. [3]And I know that this man – whether in the body or out of the body I do not know, God knows – [4]that this man was snatched up to paradise, and heard words that cannot be spoken, which no human being is allowed to utter.

It seems clear from later in the passage that Paul is talking about himself, though he uses this deliberately detached manner to distance himself from the possibility of spiritual pride at such experiences. It is also obvious, that this cannot be a reference to his Damascus Road experience; it is chronologically far too late, and belongs in a different category.[41] The language overlaps with descriptions of that event, as it is bound to do: when 'the heavens are opened', so that the realities of the heavenly dimension are suddenly visible to mortal eyes, the language of 'revelation' (*apokalypsis*) is the natural one to use. 'Vision' (*optasia*) is likewise a general word for something which is seen in a way which one would not normally expect; the same word is used in Acts 26.19 for Paul's 'vision' of Jesus. But the description of being 'caught up to heaven' is quite unlike anything either in Paul's own references to the Damascus Road event or in the accounts in Acts.[42]

Paul has already, as we have seen, categorized his own 'seeing' of Jesus as a different kind of thing from his subsequent experiences. The present passage was not, of course, written to address the kind of question we are asking here. He has taken no trouble to spell out the things we would like him to. But when we put together his own statements, both about what happened to him to change him from a zealous persecutor to a loyal disciple of Jesus, and about the ongoing nature of Christian experience with its settled state of 'glory' on the one hand (2 Corinthians 3 and 4) and its occasional extraordinary moments of spiritual elevation on the other (2 Corinthians 12), we should be clear that the two are, from his point of view, distinct.[43]

---

[41] So e.g. Sampley 2000, 163; Künneth 1965 [1951], 84.

[42] cf. Barrett 1973, 308: Paul did not regard the Damascus Road experience as a 'vision'; 'he then saw Jesus our Lord objectively.'

[43] On the passage see further Rowland 1982, 379–86.

It is still, of course, open to anyone to say that Paul has misdescribed one side or other of this non-balancing equation, and that in fact we, as historians, can detect that the Damascus Road experience was really the same sort of thing as the other experiences to which he alludes. But notice what happens if we do this. By making that kind of move, we admit that Paul is aware of certain specific, early, unrepeatable and defining experiences of 'seeing the risen Jesus', which the original apostles had had, and that he intends, by such misdescription, to place himself on a level with them. We admit, in other words, that the early 'seeings' of Jesus were not like the later ecstatic experiences – which was the point at issue in the first place. Since, then, there is nothing to be gained by a sceptical probing of Paul at this point, it is better to conclude that he knew what he was talking about (it is, after all, a bold critic who can tell someone else what they 'really' experienced, especially at such a distance of time and culture), and that when he distinguished his one-off, initial 'seeing' of Jesus from his subsequent Christian experiences, both 'normal' and abnormal, he knew what he was talking about. Part of the proof of this is the assumption we must surely make, as we said before about 1 Corinthians 15.1–11, that Paul must have known the Corinthians would not challenge him on this point. He had seen the risen Jesus; they hadn't; and they knew it as well as he did. That is the main point at issue.

3. Paul's Conversion/Call in Acts

It is notorious both that Luke tells the story of Paul's Damascus Road experience no fewer than three times, and that the accounts do not match one another in all respects. Sometimes the mismatch is a matter of detail; but sometimes, as in the question of what precisely Paul's companions saw and heard, there are real differences, best explained by Luke's following the hellenistic convention of style according to which variation in a narrative lends interest. Equally, the remarkable repetition of the story tells us quite a bit about Luke's motives.[44] Whether or not Acts was written specifically to vindicate Paul himself, it seems clear that not only the fact of Paul's conversion but the manner of it was intended to be seen as powerful testimony to the truth of the Christian faith, and powerful support for its legitimacy within the Roman empire.

This, I suggest, is what has been uppermost in the mind of the author as he has, clearly, developed and adapted a traditional story of what happened to Paul in the light of other traditional motifs. This is crucial: not that Luke has invented a story from whole cloth, or radically falsified one which

---

[44] See Alexander 2001, 1058: 'functional redundancy is an indicator of rhetorical importance.' See too e.g. Witherington 1998, 311–13.

already existed, but that he has highlighted and foregrounded elements in the story to serve particular purposes, not least to evoke memories and associations of other narratives. Let us be clear from the start: I shall argue that these factors, together with the normal priority given to Paul's own accounts over those in Acts (where they appear to disagree), prevent us from using Acts as a template, still less as a Procrustean bed, on which to fit, and perhaps to falsify, what Paul himself says in his letters.

To see this clearly, we need first to set out the three versions in sequence:

9.3As Paul was going along and getting near to Damascus, suddenly a light from heaven flashed around him. 4He fell to the ground and heard a voice saying to him, 'Saul, Saul, why are you persecuting me?' 5'Who are you, Lord?' he asked. 'I am Jesus,' came the reply, 'the one you are persecuting. 6But get up and go into the city, and it will be told you what you must do'. 7The men who were travelling with him stood speechless, hearing a voice but seeing nobody. 8Saul got up from the ground, but when he opened his eyes he saw nothing. So they led him by the hand and brought him to Damascus. 9And he went for three days without seeing, and neither ate nor drank.

22.6As I was going along and getting near to Damascus, suddenly about midday a strong light from heaven shone all around me. 7I fell to the ground, and heard a voice saying to me, 'Saul, Saul, why are you persecuting me?' 8I replied, 'Who are you, Lord?' and he said to me, 'I am Jesus the Nazarene, whom you are persecuting.' 9Now the people who were with me saw the light, but did not hear the voice of the one who was speaking to me. 10So I said, 'What shall I do, Lord?' And the Lord said to me, 'Get up and go into Damascus, and there it will be told you about everything that is set out for you to do.' 11And as I was unable to see, because of the glory of that light, I was led by the hand by my companions and came to Damascus.

26.12As I was going to Damascus with authority and commission from the chief priests, 13at midday on the road, O King, a light from heaven, brighter than the sun, shone around me and my travelling companions. 14We all fell to the ground, and I heard a voice saying to me in the Hebrew tongue, 'Saul, Saul, why are you persecuting me? It is hard for you to kick against the goad.' 15I said, 'Who are you, Lord?' and the Lord said, 'I am Jesus, whom you are persecuting. 16But get up and stand on your feet; for this is why I appeared (*ophthen*) to you, to appoint you as a servant and witness of what you have seen of me and of what you will see of me . . . 19So, King Agrippa, I was not disobedient to the heavenly vision (*optasia*) . . .

The parallels and divergencies between these three are obvious and interesting, but are not strictly part of our present purpose.[45] It is clear that none of these accounts has been written in order to support what Paul says in 1 Corinthians 9.1 or 15.8; none of them, that is, say directly what Paul there makes central, that he actually saw Jesus himself. This point is, however, clear from Acts 9.17, where Ananias speaks of Jesus having 'appeared (*ophtheis*) to you', and 9.27, where Barnabas explains how Saul had seen

---

[45] The parallels are set out in detailed synoptic form by e.g. Barrett 1994, 439f.; Witherington 1998, 305–07.

(*eiden*) the lord on the road.[46] In 26.16 Jesus speaks of having appeared to Paul, with the same verb as is repeated in 1 Corinthians 15, but speaks also of future seeings as well as the one that has just taken place. (One such subsequent vision of Jesus is described in 22.17–21.) As with Luke's 'flesh and bones' language in Luke 24.39, producing a surface tension with Paul's denial of 'flesh and blood entering the kingdom' in 1 Corinthians 15.50, the most we can say is that Luke was not concerned either to imitate Paul's language or to pursue his agendas. He clearly believes that Paul did see Jesus; the accounts cannot be played off directly against 1 Corinthians 9 and 15; but he finds no need to emphasize that fact, or the manner of its occurring. What he has added, dramatically, is that Paul's seeing of Jesus was accompanied by dazzling light. He never says, however, that Jesus appeared to Paul either as the source of that light or as a being of light.

The main differences between the accounts are easily explained in terms of the audience Luke envisages for each occasion. The first time, Luke is himself telling the story to his own readers; the second and third times, he is enabling his readers to 'listen in' as Paul retells it to two somewhat different audiences.[47] On the first occasion, Luke is introducing Paul and explaining how he was transformed from persecutor into preacher. In the second passage, Paul is facing mob violence, and we find an impassioned retelling which highlights his strict Jewish credentials but also leads to an explanation of why he had gone to the Gentiles (see particularly 22.15, 21). The third account, during Paul's hearing before Agrippa II and Berenice, is designed to show that Paul had made a great impression on the king, the most powerful man in the Judaism of his day, who had commented at the close that Paul could have been set free had he not appealed to Caesar (26.32).[48]

Why then has Luke told the story in this way? First, he is deliberately echoing stories of visions and revelations which might be known to some at least of his readers. Second, he is making the point that Paul was truly being authorized by Israel's god to do what he was doing, even if it appeared that he was a rebel against traditional Judaism. There are two well-known parallels to the story, and both are worth glancing at to see why Luke has highlighted things in the way he has.[49]

The most obvious parallel is 2 Maccabees 3, where the Syrian King Seleucus sends his officer Heliodorus to plunder the money stored up in the Temple in Jerusalem:

---

[46] Against e.g. Ashton 2000, 83.

[47] On what follows see e.g. Barrett 1994, 444f.

[48] On the speeches in the setting of formal court hearings in the ancient world see Winter 1993, 327–31. On the role of Berenice during the trial see F. M. Gillman 2002.

[49] Another partial parallel, which is interesting in itself but which would take us too far afield, is Philo *Praem.* 165.

[24]When Heliodorus arrived at the treasury with his bodyguard, then and there the Master of spirits and of all authority created a great revelation (*epiphaneia*), so that all who had been daring enough to go with him were dumbfounded at the power of God and became faint and weak with fear. [25]For there appeared to them (*ophthe*) a horse with magnificent trappings, and a rider of terrifying bearing. It charged fiercely at Heliodorus and struck at him with its front hooves. The one sitting on the horse appeared (*ephaineto*) to have golden armour. [26]Two young men also appeared (*prosephanesan*) to him; they were very strong, wonderfully beautiful and gorgeously dressed. They stood on either side of him and flogged him without stopping, inflicting many wounds on him. [27]Suddenly he fell to the ground and great darkness came over him. His followers picked him up, put him on a stretcher, [28]and carried him away – this man who had shortly before entered into the treasury with a great company and all his guard. He was now powerless to help himself. They clearly acknowledged the mighty power of God.

Now at last we have a horse, but it is more like the visionary horses in Revelation, especially the last great one, than the now riderless horses of Michelangelo and Caravaggio.[50] We should note that, though the language is all about visions and heavenly revelations, the beating Heliodorus received seems real enough. This kind of story makes one wonder again whether the heaven/earth distinction so often assumed in western culture, and so often correlated with the subjective/objective epistemological distinction, corresponds to anything that second-Temple Judaism would have recognized.[51]

If we assume this story or others like it to be well known, it might shed light on Luke's motive for telling the story of Paul's conversion the way he has.[52] The story of Heliodorus is about the sovereign god stopping the marauding and thieving pagan in his tracks just as he was about to plunder the very Temple itself. His pride is humbled before the mighty power of Israel's god. Transpose this to the scene on the Damascus Road, and Luke's point is stunning. Here is Saul of Tarsus, who has just consented to the death of Stephen (Acts 8.1) on a charge, not least, of speaking against the Temple. But the concern of Israel's god is not now for the Jerusalem Temple. The place of the Temple and its treasury is taken by – the disciples of Jesus, whom Saul is persecuting! The almighty divine power is revealed, humbling Saul, knocking him to the ground, plunging him into darkness and making him rely on his companions. The tiny and beleaguered group of disciples is revealed as the true 'Temple'; those who persecute it, however much they may be acting from zeal for Israel's god and his law, are the new pagans.[53]

---

[50] cf. e.g. Rev. 6.2, 3, 5, 8, and esp. 19.11–16, 19, 21. For the background cf. Zech. 1.8; 6.2–8.

[51] A similar story is told, without horse or beating, in 4 Macc. 4.1–14; there the subject is not Heliodorus, but a Syrian provincial governor named Apollonius.

[52] Barrett 1994, 441 belittles the parallel as 'relatively superficial'.

[53] This could fit with of Bowker 1971: Paul's conversion took place through meditation on Ezekiel's throne-chariot, convincing him that the 'rebellious people' of Ezek. 2 were not the Christians but the Jewish leaders who sent him. See Rowland 1982, 374–86; Segal 1990; 1992; Ashton 2000, 95f.; but see the strong caution of Hafemann 2000, 459f.

The second parallel, though not so close, is found in *Joseph and Aseneth*, a romance of the second-Temple period which focuses on the conversion of Aseneth, the daughter of Potiphera, and her marriage to Joseph. After a long prayer of repentance, Aseneth receives a heavenly vision:

> Aseneth kept looking, and behold, close to the morning star, the heaven was torn apart and great and unutterable light appeared. And Aseneth saw it and fell on her face on the ashes. And a man came to her from heaven and stood by Aseneth's head. And he called her and said, 'Aseneth, Aseneth.' And she said, 'Who is he that calls me, because the door of my chamber is closed, and the tower is high, and how then did he come into my chamber?' And the man called her a second time and said, 'Aseneth, Aseneth.' And she said, 'Behold, here I am, Lord. Who are you, tell me.' And the man said, 'I am the chief of the house of the Lord and commander of the whole host of the Most High. Rise and stand on your feet, and I will tell you what I have to say.'[54]

There are of course many differences between this and the stories of Paul in Acts and Heliodorus in 2 Maccabees (and Apollonius in 4 Maccabees). This story is preceded by lengthy repentance, and is followed by marriage and living happily ever after, neither of which feature prominently in Acts or Maccabees. But the parallels are also instructive: the great light, the falling on the face, the repeated call by name, the question as to who is speaking, and the command to get up, to stand up, and receive further instruction. It begins to look, at the very least, as though this format was familiar in the hellenistic Jewish literature of the time, and would be a natural way to cast such a story.

The reason for this may well be that Luke is also evoking biblical stories of the call of the prophets. Ezekiel fell on his face before the glory of the Lord, and was told to stand up and listen.[55] Daniel, after fasting and prayer, sees a man, in circumstances not entirely unlike the story in Acts:

> I looked up and saw a man clothed in linen, with a belt of gold from Uphaz around his waist. His body was like beryl, his face like lightning, his eyes like flaming torches, his arms and legs like the gleam of burnished bronze, and the sound of his words like the roar of a multitude. I Daniel, alone saw the vision; the people who were with me did not see the vision, though a great trembling fell upon them, and they fled and hid themselves. So I was left alone to see this great vision. My strength left me, and my complexion grew deathly pale, and I retained no strength. Then I heard the sound of his words; and when I heard the sound of his words, I fell into a trance, face to the ground. But then a hand touched me and roused me to my hands and knees. He said to me, 'Daniel, greatly beloved, pay attention to the words that I am going to speak to you. Stand on your feet, for I have now been sent to you.' So while he was speaking this word to me, I stood up trembling.[56]

---

[54] *JosAs.* 14.2–8 (tr. C. Burchard in Charlesworth 1985, 224f.).
[55] Ezek. 1.28—2.1. Cf. too e.g. Josh. 5.13–15, which in turn echoes Ex. 3.1–5.
[56] Dan. 10.5–11.

The obvious parallels give further clues about what is going on. This is the kind of narrative Luke wanted his readers to think of as they listened, three times, to the story of what happened to Paul on the road to Damascus.

Luke's underlying aim, and perhaps that of his original sources, seems to have been to tell the story in such a way as to align Paul with the prophets and visionaries of Israel's history, and also (less certainly, but with strong possibility) to place him alongside penitent pagans who turned round and went in a new direction. This serves as both an apologia for Paul's new life and work, a legitimation of him in the eyes of potentially puzzled or hostile readers, and a heightening of the dramatic tension as the story is repeated in a crescendo to accompany Paul's progress, through riots and trials, to his eventual arrival in Rome. Luke, ever the artist, has painted the portrait so as to bring out the features that will speak to his intended audience.

All this provides good historical reason, in addition to the normal rule of privileging Paul as the earlier source, not to force the details of the narratives in Acts over against either Paul's own accounts of his seeing of Jesus or the Easter stories in the canonical gospels (where Luke, famously, depicts a thoroughly embodied risen Jesus). This rules out three common moves that are regularly made by a kind of impressionistic fusion, and confusion, between the two sets of accounts: (a) the move from a vision of heavenly light, as in Acts, to a 'purely subjective experience' (Acts, of course, says no such thing); (b) from this supposedly Pauline 'subjective experience of inner illumination' to the hypothesis that this was the sort of thing all the apostles experienced; and (c) from this universal non-objective experience to a denial of Jesus' bodily resurrection. None of these is legitimate.

This is not to say that we must discount Acts. At a trivial level, its mention of the road to Damascus explains Paul's reference to his going back there later. The accounts dovetail quite well. But the historical conclusion from their juxtaposition cannot be that Paul did not after all see Jesus (which neither of them say), or that he 'saw' Jesus only with his mind or heart (which, again, neither of them say), or that he saw Jesus simply as a 'being of light' (which, once more, neither of them say). You can put apples and pears together and make a fruit salad; you cannot make a pork pie. Paul says that he saw Jesus, and that remains our primary historical datum. Acts tells the story in such a way as to communicate particular interpretations to its own audience. That is the basis on which any historical account of Paul's conversion must proceed.

4. Conversion and Christology

But did not Paul's experience of seeing Jesus in glory lead him directly, without any intermediate stage of 'Messiahship', to a recognition of Jesus' divinity? This has been argued by two recent writers from whom I have learnt much. There is neither need nor space for a full consideration of their theses, but we must note the points at which the question impinges on that of what it was that Paul saw and what conclusions he drew from it.

Seyoon Kim has argued that Paul's seeing of Jesus on the road was part of what Paul took to be a Merkabah-style mystical vision of Jesus as 'the image of God', which he interpreted within a framework of thought in which the other pivotal ideas were 'Adam-Christology' and Daniel's vision of the 'son of man'.[57] For reasons already given, I do not think Kim's pivotal use of 2 Corinthians 4.1–6 within this proposal will work. I am perfectly happy to consider, though, as a hypothesis, that when Paul saw Jesus he interpreted that event within a framework of, among other things, Adam-Christology and 'son of man' ideas, though I remain convinced that the initial primary meaning of the event, for him, lay elsewhere (in the conviction that Jesus was the Messiah). Kim, it seems to me, is always in danger of trying to derive every part of Paul's theology simply from the Damascus Road experience itself, to the exclusion of the second-Temple Jewish context within which it must have made the sense it did.

That is not a problem with Carey Newman, who offers a much fuller account of the Jewish context.[58] But in this respect he is like Kim: he argues that when Paul saw Jesus in glory he interpreted this as an anticipation of the divine glory-revelation which had been promised as part of the restoration of Israel.[59] Like Kim's thesis, this is not intrinsically improbable, and I believe it contains some necessary elements of a complete account. But I remain convinced that it, too, short-circuits the train of thought which actually took place.

The range of data to which Kim and Newman draw attention can indeed come into play, but as a function of an initial belief in Jesus' Messiahship – a category which Kim in particular, like Hengel, seems to me to marginalize completely.[60] From Paul's own references to his coming to faith, and from the way he uses the resurrection of Jesus in relation to Christology, the best understanding we can offer runs like this. Having persecuted Christianity precisely as a false messianic sect, Paul came face to face (so he believed) with living proof that Israel's god had vindicated Jesus against the charge of false messianism. God had declared, in the resurrection, that Jesus really was 'his son' in this essentially *messianic* sense. That is what I take to be the primary import of Romans 1.3–4, with the matching quotation of Isaiah 11.10 in 15.12: the resurrection demonstrates that Jesus is the son of David, the root of Jesse, Israel's Messiah, God's anointed.

---

[57] Kim 1984 [1981]; 2002. Cp. Bowker's theory (above, 391 n. 53).

[58] Newman 1992; 1997.

[59] e.g. Isa. 40.5: the glory of YHWH shall be revealed, and all flesh shall see it together.

[60] See below, 553–63.

If, then, Jesus has been vindicated as Messiah, certain things follow at once. He is to be seen as Israel's true representative; the great turn-around of the eras has already begun; 'the resurrection' has split into two, with Jesus the Messiah as the first-fruits and the Messiah's people following later, when he returns. And if he is Messiah, then it must follow, from those biblical roots we set out earlier (Psalm 2, Daniel 7 and so on), which are reaffirmed in the New Testament as central to the church's developing view of Jesus, that he is *the world's true lord*. He is the *kyrios* at whose name every knee shall bow. He is the 'son of man' exalted over the beasts, Israel's king rising to rule the nations. But every step down this road (I imagine these steps being made extremely quickly in the early church, so that Paul comes into an exegetical tradition already well developed) takes us closer to saying that if Jesus is the *kyrios* now exalted over the world – a deduction, we repeat, from his Messiahship – then the biblical texts which speak in this way are harder and harder to separate from the texts which, when they say *kyrios*, refer to Israel's god, YHWH himself. Jesus, the Messiah, is *kyrios*. Israel's god, believed by Jews and Christians to be God, has exalted him to be the world's true lord; and, with Daniel 7 and Psalm 110 clearly of great significance in the mind of the early church, this seems to mean that the one true God has exalted him to share the divine throne itself. Thus – the move we see perhaps most clearly in Philippians 2.6–11 – if Jesus has now been exalted to share the very throne of God, the God who (as Isaiah 45.23 declares) will not share his glory with another, then this Jesus must have been from all eternity, somehow or other, 'equal with God'.[61]

This belongs more closely than is sometimes realized with the Lukan accounts in Acts of what happened to Paul on the road to Damascus. Luke's interpretation of Paul's conversion is not at all that he saw Jesus and immediately deduced that he was 'divine'. Luke's overall emphasis is on Jesus revealing himself to Saul of Tarsus as 'lord'. But this word, by itself and even in the context of Acts as a whole, has too wide a range of meaning for it to carry, as though in a simple fashion, the meaning of 'divinity'. In fact, after the first account of his conversion, Luke reports that Paul argued powerfully in the synagogues at Damascus that Jesus was 'son of God'.[62] Luke's own immediate explanation of what this means is not 'the divine second person of the Trinity', but, as in Paul's own letters, 'the Messiah'.[63] The only other use of this phrase on Paul's lips in Acts strongly supports this.[64]

At the same time – and integrating these two is perhaps the key move within the study of primitive Christology – we find that Luke's telling of the Damascus Road story is designed in several ways to evoke Old Testament

---

[61] See Wright, *Climax*, ch. 4.
[62] Ac. 9.20 (cf. Gal. 1.16).
[63] Ac. 9.22.
[64] Ac. 13.33, quoting Ps. 2.7. See e.g. Wall 2002, 153.

theophany scenes. The light from heaven, brighter than the noonday sun, has reminded some not only of the most obvious parallel, the vision of Daniel in chapter 10, but also of the revelation on Mount Sinai and the inaugural vision of Ezekiel.[65]

We should not, however, jump too quickly to conclusions. In the closest of these parallels, Daniel 10, the strong implication is that the person Daniel is seeing is not God, but the angel Gabriel.[66] In terms of what Saul is told to do, the nearest parallel seems to be Exodus 3.1–17: Moses sees only a burning bush (no light from heaven, no human-like form), but YHWH speaks to him, revealing himself as the God of Abraham, Isaac and Jacob, the I AM WHO I AM, and commissions him to go to the elders of Israel and announce the long-awaited fulfilment of the promise to rescue them and give them their land. 'Moses, Moses,' calls YHWH, like the 'Saul, Saul,' on the Damascus Road. Instead of I AM WHO I AM, we have 'I am Jesus, whom you are persecuting.'[67] Luke has drawn our attention to parallels, but he still wants to insist on significant differences. He is not portraying Saul/Paul simply as another Moses (a place he reserves principally for Jesus himself) or another Daniel. Paul is like them in some ways, but, just as his commission is not identical to theirs, so his inaugural vision is different. Apart from anything else, in none of the accounts in Acts is the figure seen by Saul actually described. A light shines from heaven,[68] but (despite popular impressions to the contrary, again as with Caravaggio's horse) Luke never says either that Saul sees a figure composed of light or that the light is shining from the figure himself, as opposed to 'from heaven' in a more general sense.

This may seem to be splitting hairs, but it is important not to read into the text, and then to elevate to central status, something which Luke has never said – a fact which, since he tells the story three times, we cannot suppose is an accident. Indeed, it is only in 9.7, out of all three accounts, that there is even the implication that Saul is seeing an actual figure, as opposed to seeing a blinding light and hearing a voice. The light from heaven functions, it seems, more like Moses' burning bush: it forms, within Luke's narrative framing, the dramatic, arresting, illuminating context within which the voice of commission is heard. It is both exegetically and historically risky, to say

[65] There are several parallels between the accounts in Acts and Dan. 10.4–21. Wall 2002, 150 suggests parallels also with Ex. 19.16; Ezek. 1.4, 7, 13, 28; these seem to me not nearly so close, though of course as in many OT revelation-scenes Saul falls to the ground and is told to stand up, listen and obey (Ac. 9.4, 6; cf. e.g. Ezek. 1.28; 2.1; 3.23f.; 43.3; 44.4 with e.g. Gen. 17.3, 17; Lev. 9.24; Josh. 5.14f.; Jdg. 14.20; 1 Kgs. 18.39; Dan. 8.17f.; Tob. 12.16). These almost prove too much, since some of them are revelations of an angel of YHWH, some (such as Elijah's fire) are signs of divine power, and so on.

[66] cf. Ac. 8.16; 9.21.

[67] Ex. 3.4 with Ac. 9.4; Ex. 3.14 with Ac. 9.5; and, for the commission, Ex. 3.10–17 with Ac. 9.15, 20, 22; 22.14f., 21; 26.16–18, 20. See Wall 2002, 150f., noting the parallel between Jesus and Moses in Ac. 7.23–43.

[68] Ac. 9.3; 22.6; 26.13.

the least, to bring together Luke's 'vision of light' story (within which, by a once-stated implication, Paul sees a figure) and Paul's own definite account of 'seeing Jesus', and to identify Jesus as either the light itself or its source.

Huge problems of various sorts thus surround any attempt to mount an overall historical reconstruction of the precise train of thought in the mind of Saul of Tarsus at the moment of his vision. When we face that kind of situation, we do well to go back to safe ground. Luke says that Paul at once preached Jesus as 'son of god' in a messianic sense. Paul says that Jesus was 'designated son of god' in a messianic sense through the resurrection. That is what both of them seem to regard as the vision's primary meaning.

But for both of them, too, the vision took place in a context which gave, and perhaps gave almost instantly, a further dimension to the awareness of Jesus as the messianic 'son of god'. Luke's telling of the story within the framework of prophetic visions corresponds to Paul's hint of a similar framework in Galatians 1.15–16 (where again the centre of the revelation is Jesus as 'son of god'). Here again we are on firm historical ground. Since prophetic calls were perceived as coming from Israel's god, albeit sometimes through intermediaries as in Daniel 10, the revelation of Jesus as the messianic 'son of god' hovers precariously on the edge of the new, previously unthinkable belief: that this messianic title might contain much more than anyone had previously imagined from reading either Psalm 2 or 2 Samuel 7. Paul's own use of Psalm 110 echoes its use in the synoptic tradition: he discovered that David's son was also David's lord.[69]

How did he make this discovery? We should not suppose, I suggest, that Saul of Tarsus, having come instantly to believe that Jesus was the Messiah, then worked out, by a process of logic and biblical reflection alone, that the Messiah was after all divine (though there was both logic and biblical reflection in the process). Rather, we can sketch a sequence something like this (we shall return to the point in chapters 12 and 19).

The context of Saul's coming to believe that Jesus was the Messiah was a vision which seemed to him at the time much like the biblical theophanies. Perhaps, as some have suggested, he was actually meditating on the throne-chariot, and discovered that the figure seated on the throne was Jesus.[70] Then, as he continued to pray to Israel's God day by day as he had always done, but now with the sense that Jesus of Nazareth was the Messiah, the 'son of god' in that sense, he discovered that he needed this phrase 'son of god' to function in a new sense, hidden all along within the original one, and parallel in function to the other notions in which Jews had invoked the presence and activity of the transcendent, hidden God.[71] Logical reasoning

---

[69] 1 Cor. 15.25–8, coupled with an understanding of the risen Jesus as 'the son' who will eventually be subject to 'God'. Cf. Mt. 22.41–5/Mk. 12.35–7/Lk. 20.41–4; cf. *JVG* 507–09, 642f.

[70] Bowker 1971.

[71] See 571–7, 731–6 below.

and biblical reflection took place within the context both of the memory of the original vision (interpreted in relation to biblical models), and of the continuing practice of prayer to, and meditation upon, the one God of Abraham, Isaac and Jacob. Paul had an increasingly clear sense that this God was to be known as the one who sent the son and the Spirit of the son (Galatians 4.4–6); the one who shared his unshareable glory with this new Lord of the world (Philippians 2.9–11); the one in whom the invisible God was reflected (Colossians 1.15); the one whose very Lordship provided, through the multiple possibilities of the word *kyrios*, a way of distinguishing between 'one God, the father' and 'one lord, Jesus Christ', while simultaneously, and with the same words, affirming Jewish monotheism over against pagan polytheism (1 Corinthians 8.6). These breathtaking explorations into the one God of ancestral Jewish belief were not random, undisciplined musings. Every step Paul took he found in scripture; but the reason he took those steps was what he had seen on the road, and what he continued to discover as, in prayer and the fellowship of other believers, he found that Messiah-language, when applied to Jesus, was capable of carrying, seemed indeed designed to carry, a new god-language, to be applied to the same God, the God of Abraham, Isaac and Jacob.

This continuing experience of knowing the one true God in and through Jesus the Messiah, the lord, and of knowing this in the fellowship of the church, was what Paul was talking about in 2 Corinthians 4.1–6. Of course there is theological continuity between what he says there and what can be said (by Paul, by Luke and by us two thousand years later) about the initial event on the road to Damascus, and the meaning that that event seems to have carried. But 2 Corinthians 4 is not describing that event, and we cannot take elements of what it says (e.g. that the light shines 'in our hearts', which is certainly not a description of the Damascus Road event), and read them back into, let alone make them determinative for, Paul's original 'seeing' of Jesus.

5. Conclusion

There is much more to be said about the conversion of Paul and its relation to his wider theology. Some of that will emerge briefly later on. But we have said enough to round off our treatment of Paul with the clear understanding that he believed he had seen the risen Jesus in person, and that his understanding of who this Jesus was included the firm belief that he possessed a transformed but still physical body. Attempts to undermine this conclusion by appeal to 'what really happened' at Paul's conversion, on the basis either of Acts or of other passages in Paul, carry no conviction.

We have now examined our earliest witness. It is time to widen the horizon, and to study the writings of the century and a half that followed.

Part Three

Resurrection in Early Christianity
(Apart from Paul)

Into that strange, unmapped new land,
Round the forbidden corner, through
The locked and bolted door, we grope,
Prisoners released upon a larger world.

from *Easter Oratorio* (see p. xx above)

Chapter Nine

HOPE REFOCUSED (1):
GOSPEL TRADITIONS
OUTSIDE THE EASTER NARRATIVES

1. Introduction

Considering that the canonical gospels undoubtedly reflect the beliefs and hopes of the early Christians, one of the abiding surprises they present is how little they have to say about the topic of resurrection. Of course, they all end with stories of the empty tomb of Jesus, and in all except Mark we find stories of his appearing, alive, to his followers. But we search in vain for extended treatments of the resurrection in the stories that purport to be about the public career of the Jesus whom the early church believed had been raised from the dead.[1]

This, of course, is an obvious sign (one among many such) that the early church was not so quick to invent 'sayings of Jesus' as an earlier generation of scholars liked to suppose.[2] Even if we were to suppose that Paul's high-octane interest in the resurrection was not shared by most of his contemporaries, we must still postulate that resurrection in general, and Jesus' resurrection in particular, would be extremely controversial both in the church's proclamation and self-explanation to outsiders and in the debates that must have marked its internal life. How easy it would have been, on the older assumptions about traditions being generated to serve the needs of the church, to have a few 'words of the Lord' which would explain more precisely what resurrection was and what it meant. According to Mark 9.7–9, the disciples needed an explanation of resurrection, but it wasn't forthcoming. One might even imagine situations being invented that would serve as a showcase for such sayings, and perhaps a parable or two that would turn on the point; but this only goes to show that New Testament scholars are probably more ready to imagine fictional scenarios than the New Testament writers themselves seem to have been. Of one thing we can be sure. Had

---

[1] For the surprise see Evans 1970, 31.
[2] See *NTPG* 421f.

there been any more words of Jesus on the subject of resurrection that anyone could remember, they would have been preserved.[3] The fact that there
are not indicates that this was simply not a major topic of his teaching;
indeed, he hardly addressed it at all, and the one occasion when he seems to
have done so was at someone else's instigation. Jesus certainly believed in
resurrection as the promised future for god's people, but it does not seem to
have played a significantly larger role in his teaching than it did in most of
the Judaism of the time, where, as we have seen, even those who believed it
kept it very much as one topic among others, and not usually a major one.

This apparent reticence on the part of the gospel-writers and the traditions
they collected creates a peculiar structural problem for the present book
which, though not hugely important, had better be noted none the less. Some
of the material in the gospels seems to belong with chapter 3 above, as evidence, primarily, for beliefs held within second-Temple Judaism. That is
notably the case, for instance, with the reported views of Herod Antipas on
the possible identity of Jesus as a resurrected John the Baptist.[4] Other fragments, even if they go back eventually to Jesus, may well be evidence, in
their shaping and wording, for a developed early Christian understanding.
My reason for tackling all this material at this point in the book is partly that
it seemed artificial to divide it up into those passages that seemed simply to
reflect contemporary non-Christian Jewish beliefs, and more particularly
that, since the gospels come to us from the early church, their primary
evidential value is as evidence for the stories early Christians told and the
life and thought that such stories generated and sustained. However true it is,
as I have argued elsewhere, that the gospels do give us much better evidence
about the public career of Jesus than has often been imagined, we still have
to begin by looking at them as evidence for the life, work, thought and particularly story-telling of the church in its first four or five decades.[5]

A particular instance of the apparent peculiarity of this material within
our overall topic is the place, within the resurrection-thinking of early Christianity, of any *teaching* of Jesus on resurrection (either in general or as
applied to himself), as opposed to what was believed about what had happened to him after his death. Paul does not refer to teaching of Jesus on the
subject, but then Paul seldom refers to teaching of Jesus about anything.
Apart from the preservation, and possible adaptation, of the few sayings we
find in the traditions as they stand, and what they tell us about the continuing interest of the early church, almost the only time anyone refers back to
what Jesus had said about resurrection is when the risen Jesus himself
explains that this was what he had been talking about earlier – and when the

---

[3] So, rightly, Perkins, 1984, 74f.
[4] See too the comments in Ac. 23.1–9 about the Sadducees' and Pharisees' views on the
resurrection, which I dealt with at 132–4 above.
[5] On the gospels see esp. *NTPG* chs. 13, 14; *JVG* ch. 4.

chief priests, in Matthew's account, remember that 'that impostor' had predicted that he would rise again from the dead, and so request that the tomb be put under guard.[6]

Having said all that, it is of course important to stress also that the main theme of Jesus' announcement, in word and deed, was the kingdom of god.[7] Granted that not all kingdom-of-god movements at the time were necessarily resurrection-movements as well (i.e. it is perfectly conceivable that some of those who used kingdom-of-god language about their movements distanced themselves from the Pharisaic hope), it is extremely likely that anyone announcing the kingdom of Israel's god in the first half of the first century would be assumed to include resurrection as part of the overall promise. When we find even scattered and oblique references to resurrection within Jesus' teaching and actions, then, we are justified in assuming that he saw resurrection, not as an isolated topic, but as part of the coming kingdom. But the general point stands: resurrection was obviously not one of his central or major themes.

The references to resurrection, or indeed to some kind of new life after death, appear random and unsystematic in the gospel traditions.[8] It would be possible to arrange them in a tidier order; but since the purpose of this Part of the book is to explore early Christianity in general and to see what we can learn about its views on the topic, it seems better to take the passages as they appear within the different layers of gospel tradition normally identified by scholars. I say this without prejudice to specific issues of tradition-history, since I remain sceptical about how much we can know of the ways in which traditions developed prior to their first appearance in our sources, and between then and subsequent appearances.[9] I am not even sure whether to believe in Q or not, and if so in what version of it. The second category below (material in both Matthew and Luke) will of course correspond to it; the first category (material in Mark, all of which is in one or both of the other synoptics) contains material that many regard as reasonably early. That will leave the material unique to Matthew, Luke and John to be dealt with separately.

One final note. Though we must treat this material as at least potentially going back behind the evangelists to earlier tradition, and must in due course

---

[6] Lk. 24.44; Mt. 27.63f. In Lk. 24.25f. Jesus rebukes the two on the road, not for not believing what he had said, but for not believing Moses and the prophets (cp. Lk. 16.31). In the longer ending of Mk. (16.14) he rebukes them simply for not believing the early reports.

[7] See *JVG* Part II (chs. 5–10).

[8] It is noticeable that the non-canonical gospel traditions contain very little parallel material to the canonical gospels on this topic, and such relevant material as they do have is so different as to be best dealt with in a subsequent chapter (ch. 11 below). As a bored American commentator said after yet another goalless draw in a World Cup soccer match: 'Well, folks, I would tell you the score, but there wasn't any.'

[9] cf. *NTPG* ch. 14; and in 'Doing Justice to Jesus', 360–65.

treat the resurrection narratives themselves in the same way, we must always remember that we find these isolated references to resurrection, particularly those in Luke and John, in gospels which contain substantial and detailed accounts of the risen Jesus himself. Unless we are to accuse the evangelists of extreme carelessness, there must always be some sense that they linked Jesus' teaching, such as it was, with what they believed about his own risen state. The most obvious place where this matters is in the triple predictions of the passion and resurrection. We must assume that the evangelists thought the story they told at the end of their books was the fulfilment of these prophecies. But the equivalent point will need to be made in other instances as well.

2. Resurrection in Mark and its Parallels

(i) Healing

The Markan material on resurrection comes in four reasonably obvious categories: healing, challenge, predictions (of future vindication) and puzzles. (I shall treat the debate between Jesus and the Sadducees as a separate section.) The first category contains one story only: the healing of Jairus' daughter.[10]

This story, and the parallel healings unique to Luke and John (see below) inevitably remind us of the resuscitations performed by Elijah and Elisha.[11] The gospels present them as part of Jesus' profile as a prophet, albeit a highly unusual one. Additional internal interpretation is provided by the story of the woman with the issue of blood, which in all three accounts is placed within the larger narrative of the little girl, and which echoes it in certain ways (the woman has been sick for twelve years, the same as the age of the girl; in both cases the importance of faith is stressed).[12]

Within the story, there are a few small but significant points for our investigation. For a start, we note Jesus' comment to the mourners: the girl is not dead, but sleeping.[13] This hardly indicates a language-system in which 'sleep' is a regular and obvious metaphor for death, but it may well indicate, at least in the minds of those who told or heard the story, a hint of Daniel 12.2, where those who 'sleep' will be woken up.[14] The mockery of the bystanders would then echo the disbelief both of the disciples (initially), and then of those who heard the Easter story itself. The mention of 'sleep' leads the mind naturally to the description of the girl's 'awakening'. Jesus' word

---

[10] Mk. 5.21–43/Mt. 9.18–31/Lk. 8.40–56.

[11] 1 Kgs. 17.17–24; 2 Kgs. 4.18–37.

[12] Only Mk. (5.42) and Lk. (8.42) give the girl's age, and at different points of the story; perhaps Lk. wishes to draw attention to the parallelism earlier in the combined narrative.

[13] Mk. 5.39/Mt. 9.24/Lk. 8.52.

[14] See above, 216, on 'sleep' in Paul.

of command (Mark and Luke only) is *egeire*, 'arise', which in Mark translates the Aramaic *talitha koum*.[15] When the girl awakens, the verb used by Mark and Luke is *aneste*, and in Matthew it is *egerthe*.[16] The astonishment of the parents (*exestesan* in both Mark and Luke) mirrors that of the women at Jesus' tomb and the others when they heard the news.[17] Jesus' request that the girl be given something to eat (Mark only) provides a distant echo of his own request for something to eat, in Luke's story of the upper room.[18] An early Christian telling this story in something like this way would almost certainly think of Jesus' own resurrection as a larger and greater instance of the same sort of astonishing power. The evangelists, editing it, would hear, and expect their audiences to hear, an advance statement of the theme which would burst out from the narrative at the end of their books. But there is no indication in the story that anyone, either in the historical world described or the fictive world narrated, looked ahead to a 'resurrection' of a different sort. Jairus' daughter would die again some day. Mark, Matthew and Luke end up telling a story about Jesus going through death and out the other side.

(ii) Challenge

The second category of material in the triple tradition is the challenge of Jesus to his followers, and his predictions of great reversals in the new world. These would almost certainly have been heard as coded warnings about the need to risk all to bring in the kingdom; at that level, they belong with, say, the exhortations of the Maccabaean leaders and others. I quote the Markan version in each case, noting significant variations in the others.

> [8.34]Jesus called the crowd to him with his disciples. 'If anyone wants to come after me,' he said, 'they must deny themselves. They must take up their cross, and follow me. [35]Anyone who wants to save their life (*psyche*), you see, will lose it; and anyone who loses their life for my sake and that of the gospel [Mt. and Lk. omit 'and that of the gospel'] will save it [Mt.: will find it]. [36]For what will it profit you if you gain the whole world and forfeit your life? [37]What will anyone give as a payment in return for that life? [38]For if anyone is ashamed of me and my words in this adulterous and sinful generation, of that person the son of man will be ashamed when he comes in the glory of his father with the holy angels.' [Mt. adds: 'and then he will give to each according to their works.'] [9.1]And he said to them, 'Truly I tell you, there are some standing here who will not taste death until they see that the kingdom of God has come with power.' [Mt.: see the son of man coming in his kingdom; Lk.: see the kingdom of God.][19]

[15] On the significance of the Aramaic see e.g. Guelich 1989, 302f.; Gundry 1993, 274f.

[16] Mk. 5.42/Mt. 9.25/Lk. 8.55. As the refs. throughout Parts II, III and IV of the present book will show, these are the regular 'resurrection' words throughout the NT.

[17] Mk. 5.42/Lk. 8.56; Mk. 16.5, 8; Lk. 24.22.

[18] Mk. 5.43; Lk. 24.40–43.

[19] Mk. 8.34—9.1/Mt. 16.24–8/Lk. 9.23–7; see *JVG* 304. With these passages we may

9.43If your hand causes you to stumble, cut it off. It is better for you to enter into life maimed, than with two hands to go into Gehenna, into the unquenchable fire. 45And if your foot causes you to stumble, cut it off. It is better for you to go into life lame, than with two feet to be thrown into Gehenna. 47And if your eye causes you to stumble, pluck it out. It is better for you to enter into the kingdom of God [Mt.: enter into life] with one eye than with two eyes to be thrown into Gehenna . . .20

10.29Jesus said, 'Truly I tell you, [Mt. adds: you who have followed me, in the regeneration, when the son of man sits on the throne of his glory, you yourselves will also sit on twelve thrones, judging the twelve tribes of Israel. And] there is no one who has left brothers or sisters or mother or father or children or lands for my sake and the gospel's [Mt: for the sake of my name; Lk.: for the sake of God's kingdom] 30who will not receive a hundredfold now in the present time: houses and brothers and sisters and mothers and children and lands, with persecutions, and in the age to come eternal life. 31But many who are first will be last, and the last first.21

Each of these texts in its own way makes promises which, in the light of Josephus and the other second-Temple texts we have studied, could very reasonably be read as a promise of resurrection. At that level, they do not stray outside what would have been normal at the time: follow this path, commit yourself to this teacher, give up these privileges, and in the age to come the true god will give you a new life, a new world, a new family. In the first passage, Mark 8.35 says that those who die in the cause will save their life, which presumably means a new life the other side of death; in context this is of course linked to the specific challenge to follow Jesus, but the promise would make sense within any revolutionary movement of the day. The explicit link in Mark and Luke with the promise of the kingdom, and in Matthew with the son of man and his kingdom, demonstrates what we noted above, that though mention of resurrection is rare in the gospel traditions it would be wrong to forget it when recognizing that the main theme of Jesus' public career was god's kingdom. Certainly the Danielic reference in Matthew would easily be linked in the mind of a second-Temple Jew with the larger Danielic picture in which the victorious kingdom in chapter 2, the vindicated son of man in chapter 7, and the vindicated and resurrected

---

note the very similar tradition in Mt. 10.39 and Lk. 17.33 ('people who seek to keep their life will lose it, and people who lose their life will find it').

20 Mk. 9.43–8. Vv. 44, 46 are later insertions into the text, quoting Isa. 66.24 ('where their worm does not die, and the fire is not quenched'); this itself is of interest, showing that from quite early on scribes were keen to emphasize the link between this passage and the prophetic 'new creation' theme, with its attendant warnings of judgment. The par. is Mt. 18.6–9, with slight variations.

21 Mk. 10.29–31/Mt. 19.28–30/Lk. 18.29f. The question of classification is difficult here; is this really a 'Q' passage, or modifications in triple tradition, or are the differences so great that they have to be classified as Mt. and Lk. special material? Mt. and Lk. both omit the repeated list of what will be gained after having formerly been lost. There are parallels to the challenge to hate father, mother, etc., in *Thom.* 55; 101; but they do not mention the age to come.

martyrs in chapter 12, could be seen as part of a single whole, sharpened up into a challenge by the stories in chapters 1, 3 and 6 of the righteous Jews who were prepared to face danger and death rather than give up their allegiance to Israel's god. Jesus' challenge here, then, is set in classic second-Temple style within a challenge to god's people to risk all for the kingdom, and includes a coded promise (coded, because the word 'resurrection' does not occur here) that those who lose their lives will save them (Mark, Luke), or find them (Matthew). The apocalyptic scenario, with its links to Daniel, also looks on to Jesus' language about his own vindication, to which we shall come in a moment. The promise remains, though, completely at the level of reversal, much like the assurances in 2 Maccabees 7: those who risk all, and even lose all, will simply gain their lives back again. The implication is that the kingdom of god, or of the son of man, will involve the same kind of world as at present, but with god's true people vindicated. There is no suggestion, in other words, of anything like Paul's developed view of resurrection in terms of a transformed world, or transformed embodiment. There is no hint of a post-Easter development or 'Christianization'. This does not of itself prove that Jesus must have said all this. That is not my present purpose. But it does demonstrate, on the one hand, the kind of belief that was current at the time, and the fact that whoever handed on, and then collected and transcribed, such sayings must have considered them compatible with, even if not developed in the same way as, the fuller Christian teaching of his own day.

The second passage speaks of 'entering into life' (changed in the last line into 'in the kingdom of god') at considerable personal cost. This assumes a standard Jewish dichotomy between the present age and the age to come, with a high degree of bodily continuity between the one and the other. Even assuming that Jesus intended the cutting off of feet and hands, and the plucking out of eyes, as vivid metaphors rather than literal advice, the point of the repeated explanation is that, whether the destination is Gehenna or 'life', it is the same person after as before. Though the image is striking,[22] there is nothing about the idea of going forward into god's kingdom or new life, wearing substantially the same body as at present, which could not have been said in the wider world of second-Temple Judaism.[23] Again, though a first-century Christian who read this passage would naturally interpret it in terms of following Jesus into resurrection life (the risen body of Jesus was recognised, according to John at least, by the marks of crucifixion), there is nothing here to suggest that a later theology has been read back.

The third passage draws, like Paul, on Jewish traditions which speak of the covenant people being vindicated in the age to come. The Matthean addition envisages a judgment of Israel, entrusted to the followers of Jesus,

---

[22] For Jewish parallels to the usage see SB 1.779f.
[23] On 'Gehenna' see *JVG* 183 n. 42.

suggesting (as in parts of our next category) a reference to Daniel. The promise of the 'age to come' is explicit, and the life proper to that age (*zoe aionios*, 'life pertaining to the age', usually translated 'eternal life') will be the reward for those who follow Jesus. The main thrust of this passage is, in fact, to assure Jesus' followers of that which was normally assured to 'all Israel'; this is part of the extraordinary redefinition of Israel around Jesus himself which was characteristic of his actions and words at several levels.[24] The passage also promises dramatic reversal, with the 'first' and the 'last' changing places, in line with many other 'reversal' sayings, notably the beatitudes (see below). But the remarkable thing about this passage is that the main reversal is promised, not in the age to come, but within the present age itself. There is no developed theology of the coming age, or of resurrection. Matthew's use of 'regeneration' (*palingenesia*) to denote the coming age is the only New Testament occurrence of the word in this sense.[25] It clearly implies a great change in the world, but says no more about it than could be gleaned from many other second-Temple texts.[26]

Throughout these passages, then, there is a clear sense of a future in which new life will be given to those who follow Jesus faithfully, even if they die or suffer serious maiming in the meantime. If we place these passages on the spectrum of beliefs about life to come, and the age to come, they clearly fit with other Jewish apocalyptic passages, not least those echoing or developing ideas from Daniel. Despite the absence in them of the normal words for 'resurrection', we are safe in saying that the idea is present at least by implication. But there is nothing specifically Christian about them at this point, except in so far as they focus on Jesus as the one around whom the people who cherish these promises are now redefined. Early Christians who passed on, shaped and collected these sayings show no signs of having conformed them to a more nuanced Christian viewpoint, or even to hint that Jesus himself, the speaker, would himself one day be raised from the dead.

(iii) The Future Vindication of Jesus

Three times, famously, the Markan tradition has Jesus predicting not only his death but also his resurrection:

> Jesus began to teach them that the son of man must suffer many things and be rejected by the elders and the chief priests and the scribes, and be killed, and after three days [Mt. and Lk.: on the third day] rise again.[27]

[24] See *JVG passim*, esp. chs. 7, 9.
[25] The one other NT use is Tit. 3.5, where it refers to personal regeneration.
[26] On *palingenesia* cf. *TDNT* 1.686–9; Davies and Allison 1988–97, 3.57f., with bib.
[27] Mk. 8.31/Mt. 16.21/Lk. 9.22. Mk. uses *anastenai* for the final word; Mt. and Lk. both have *egerthenai*.

For he was teaching his disciples, and saying to them that the son of man is to be handed over into the hands of men, and they will kill him, and when they have killed him, after three days [Mt.: on the third day] he will rise again [Lk. omits mention of killing and rising].[28]

We are going up to Jerusalem, and the son of man will be handed over to the chief priests and the scribes, and they will condemn him to death and hand him over to the Gentiles, and they will beat him and spit on him and flog him and kill him, and after three days [Mt. and Lk.: on the third day] he will rise.[29]

I have already argued that, despite widespread scholarly opinion over the last two generations or so, it is highly likely that Jesus went to Jerusalem knowing he would die there and that this was his god-given vocation.[30] I have also argued that it is highly probable that he interpreted his forthcoming death according to various controlling narratives available to him in scripture, in line with other aspects of his vocation and public career; and that, as a second-Temple Jew involved in a kingdom-of-god movement, he would believe, and might well declare, that Israel's god would raise him from the dead, vindicating him after his suffering. That description, of course, would fit the martyrs in 2 Maccabees pretty closely (though the contrasts between their dying threats and the dying words of Jesus then becomes all the more striking).[31] This does not mean, of course, that these predictions are all verbatim reports of things that Jesus said. The shift each time from 'after three days' in Mark to 'on the third day' in Matthew and Luke (with Luke omitting the whole clause on the second occasion) is a clear sign of editorial tidying-up at an early point in the tradition; assuming that Jesus died on a Friday, three full days had not passed before the Sunday morning, but it was 'the third day', and that is what we find in the very early tradition which Paul cites in 1 Corinthians 15.4.

Of especial interest is the reaction of the disciples. After the first prediction, Peter took Jesus and rebuked him; clearly the mention of resurrection did nothing to divert his shock at Jesus talking of his own imminent suffering and death. The second time, Matthew comments that 'they were extremely sad', while Mark and Luke both say that 'they did not understand

---

[28] Mk. 9.31/Mt. 17.22f./Lk. 9.44. Mk. again has *anastesetai*; Mt., *egerthesetai*.

[29] Mk. 10.33f./Mt. 20.18f./Lk. 18.31f. This time Mk. and Lk. have *anastesetai*, while Mt. remains with *egerthesetai*. These two key verbs seem to be spread reasonably evenly between the evangelists, without any having a strong preference for one rather than the other.

[30] *JVG* ch. 12, which stands behind this whole paragraph. Contrast C. F. Evans 1970, 33, who declares that these predictions must be secondary, because otherwise Easter would not have been a surprise to the disciples, as it manifestly was; this kind of comment functions as a blunt instrument to bludgeon the argument into silence, which is a pity, since the situation is far more subtle than that. The question is, how would such comments have been heard? Contrast the recent positive arguments of C. A. Evans 1999a.

[31] cf. the crescendo in 2 Macc. 7.9, 14, 17, 19, 31, 34–7; cp. Lk. 23.34 with e.g. 1 Pet. 2.21–3; 3.18.

the saying, and were afraid to ask him'. Luke speaks of it being deliberately hidden from them, which fits with his theme of the disciples' failure to understand until after Jesus' own resurrection, a theme repeated following the third and final prediction.[32] At no point, in other words, do the disciples show any sign of understanding that Jesus really does seem to mean an almost immediate resurrection. Just as it would have been small comfort in the short term to the followers and associates of the Maccabaean martyrs, or any of those who died in the struggle for YHWH's kingdom during the first centuries BC and AD, to be told that they would rise again on some distant date in the future, so the disciples seem to have been either shocked or saddened by the thought of Jesus contemplating imminent death, or simply unsure what on earth he was talking about.

The traditions themselves, and the evangelists in retelling them, may intend the reader to understand that the disciples were assuming on the one hand that Jesus must be referring to the ultimate future resurrection, and/or, on the other hand, that he was speaking metaphorically of the struggle for Israel's restoration and the need to be prepared to risk all in the process. What they made of 'on the third day' and such phrases is anybody's guess; my guess is that they thought it was a metaphor but had no idea what its concrete referent might be. Thus, though the sayings are striking within the world of second-Temple Judaism, they are at home there, giving solid evidence, like 2 Maccabees, of a belief in bodily resurrection for those who died in obedience to Israel's god. However, apart from the reference to three days (itself, of course, capable of carrying echoes of Hosea 6.2, but there is no sign of anyone in the synoptic gospels drawing attention to this), there is no hint of those innovations from within the Jewish tradition that we find in Paul and elsewhere in early Christianity. Of course, Christians telling the story, and collecting and editing these sayings, would celebrate them in the belief that they had come true, more true than the disciples at the time could have guessed. But, apart from the editing of the three-day saying, they do not seem to have made the passages more explicit.

Along with these predictions of vindication we may note the saying which, echoes Daniel 7 and points to a future vindication:

> '. . . Are you the Messiah, the Son of the Blessed?' 'I am,' replied Jesus, 'and you will see the son of man sitting at the right hand of power, and coming with the clouds of heaven.'[33]

I have argued in *Jesus and the Victory of God* that this saying is about 'vindication' rather than 'return': the 'one like a son of man' in Daniel 7 is

---

[32] Lk. 9.45; 18.34; cp. 24.16, 25, 45. Mk. and Mt. make no comment after the third prediction.

[33] Mk. 14.62/Mt. 26.64/Lk. 22.67–9, with significant variations: see *JVG* 524–8, 550f. for details and discussion.

brought to the Ancient of Days after suffering at the hands of the beasts. By itself, the saying says nothing about resurrection. But anyone who heard it, pondered it and passed it on in the context of an awareness of Daniel as a whole, with its famous prophecy of the kingdom in chapter 2 and its equally famous prophecy of resurrection in chapter 12, would be in a good position to put the references together and to see resurrection as itself constituting the primary vindication. In the light of this we may also include the saying put into the mouth of the false witnesses at the trial, and into Jesus' own mouth by John:

> We heard him saying, 'I will destroy this Temple which is made with hands, and in three days I will build another, not made with hands.'[34]

> Jesus answered them, 'Destroy this Temple, and I will raise it up (*egero auton*) in three days.[35]

Though Mark and Matthew insist that this was said by the *false* witnesses, the Johannine tradition, and the linkage with the other sayings, may well indicate that Jesus had said something like this; after all, the previous chapter in all three synoptics has Jesus making a solemn warning about the destruction of both the Temple and Jerusalem, ending with an assurance of his own vindication and that of his followers.[36] John interprets the saying specifically in relation to Jesus' bodily resurrection. When we glimpse the fuller picture of Jesus' intention I outlined in the previous volume – the picture of Jesus acting symbolically in the Temple and the Upper Room, with the intention of drawing on to himself the long-awaited destiny and vocation of the true Israel – we discover that this makes good historical sense.[37]

(iv) Puzzles

(a) Herod

Of all the unlikely characters from whom we might learn something of first-century Jewish beliefs about the dead and what might happen to them, it falls to Herod Antipas to throw a spanner in the works with his reported

---

[34] Mk. 14.58/Mt. 26.61 (omitting the reference to making/not making with hands). Cf. too Mk. 15.29/Mt. 27.40.

[35] Jn. 2.19.

[36] Other evidence, admittedly again from hostile witnesses and via Acts, is found in Ac. 6.14. There is a half-parallel saying in *Thom.* 71, but it is the exception which proves the rule stated above: 'Jesus said, I shall destroy this house, and no one will be able to rebuild it.' Any hint of resurrection is explicitly ruled out – as is any hint of anything so Jewish as a rebuilt Temple.

[37] Jn. 2.21f. (see below, ch. 17). See again *JVG* ch. 12.

comments about Jesus. Here the accounts in Luke and Mark are significantly different; Matthew is close to Mark, but stops after Mark's verse 14:

> [Mark 6]¹⁴King Herod heard about Jesus, because his name was becoming well known; and he said, 'John the Baptizer has been raised (*egegertai*) from the dead; that is why these powers are at work in him.' ¹⁵Others said, 'It is Elijah.' Others said that 'He is a prophet, like one of the prophets.' ¹⁶When Herod heard it, he said, 'It is John, whom I beheaded; he has been raised (*egerthe*).'³⁸

> [Luke 9]⁷Herod the Tetrarch heard that these things were happening, and he was puzzled because he heard it said by some that John had been raised (*egerthe*) from the dead; ⁸by others, that Elijah had appeared, and by others that one of the old prophets had arisen (*aneste*). ⁹But Herod said, 'John I beheaded; but who is this man about whom I hear these things?' And he sought to see him.³⁹

This little story is interesting at several different levels. We begin with the evangelists: Matthew and Mark use this as the point of entry to their accounts of John's death, whereas Luke, who has no such account, but who has already mentioned Herod's imprisonment of John (3.19–20), contents himself with the reference to the beheading in the final verse, distancing Herod, in 9.9 and 9.7, from the opinion which Matthew and Mark ascribe to him, that Jesus was a resurrected John the Baptist. Not, of course, that either Matthew or Mark think Herod is correct to suggest this. We may guess that the story circulated in earlier tradition, and was included by Mark, partly because it provided a lead in to the story of John's death, but equally because, though Herod was obviously mistaken, it was noteworthy that Jesus had attracted such attention, and that such outlandish explanations were being given for his extraordinary powers. The reports of people thinking that Jesus was Elijah, or another of the old prophets, function in the same way: the early Christians did not identify Jesus in those ways, but preserved the memory of people who did as signposts towards what they believed to be the truth.⁴⁰ When, in fact, we ponder the motives of the evangelists and of those who told the stories before them, it seems highly unlikely that these stories were invented by the early Christians. They would have been unlikely to compromise their belief in the decisive and world-changing nature of Jesus' resurrection by the suggestion that dead prophets might well be raised to life from time to time.⁴¹

---

³⁸ Mk. 6.14–16/Mt. 14.1f. I have quoted the Lk. semi-parallel separately because, as appears immediately below, it is significantly different in several respects.

³⁹ Lk. 9.7–9.

⁴⁰ See too Mk. 8.27f./Mt. 16.13f./Lk. 9.18f.

⁴¹ A suggestion like this is of course made by Jesus himself in e.g. Mt. 11.14; Mt. 17.12f./Mk. 9.13. In what sense Matthew, let alone Jesus, thought that Elijah and John were in any literal sense the same person remains opaque, at least to me; see e.g. Davies and Allison 1988–97, 2.258f.

Working back from the evangelists and their sources to the situation in Jesus' lifetime, it is interesting that the theory about Jesus being a dead prophet raised to life is advanced in Matthew and Mark to explain why he possessed such remarkable powers. This makes obvious sense if Jesus was seen as Elijah *redivivus*, since Elijah had done extraordinary things as well (memories of Elijah's raising of a dead child have just been awakened, not long before in Mark, by the raising of Jairus' daughter). But John the Baptist, unlike Elijah, did not perform healings or other 'mighty works'. To suggest that Jesus was a raised-to-life John was not, then, a way of explaining his remarkable powers by saying he had had them before in a previous life, but rather an indication that being raised from the dead might be supposed to give someone not just a new lease of life but unusual, perhaps superhuman, abilities. There is no other evidence for this belief. No doubt the evangelists might have seen it as a distant and shadowy pointer to their own belief, that when Jesus himself was raised from the dead all sorts of new powers were indeed unleashed into the world.

What does this story tell us about the world of second-Temple Jewish belief? If we assume that Herod and his courtiers really did say something like this, it seems to be an exception to the general rule, that 'the resurrection of the dead' would happen to *all* the righteous dead simultaneously, not to one or two here and there. The mention of Elijah in all these texts may indicate the reason for this exception, in that, as we saw, the story of Elijah ended with him being taken up to heaven without dying in the normal way, and the prophet Malachi promised that he would one day return.[42] We should not, I think, regard Herod and his court as the most accurate indicators of mainstream second-Temple Jewish belief; even if it is true that the Pharisees and Herodians made common cause on a couple of occasions, we may assume that they did not sit down and discuss the finer points of proto-rabbinic theology.[43] However, there are a couple of points worthy of note. First, this is hardly evidence of a belief in 'reincarnation' or 'transmigration', the re-embodiment of a dead soul either immediately upon death or at some time thereafter.[44] That would normally require the soul to pass into a newborn, or newly conceived, child, whereas Jesus was a fully grown man,

---

[42] 2 Kgs. 2.1–18; Mal. 4.5.

[43] Mk. 3.6; 12.13/Mt. 22.15f. Barclay's suggestion that this is evidence of a 'widespread' belief (1996a, 26) is without further support; the parallel with the Nero *redivivus* idea is hardly close.

[44] Against Harvey 1994, 69, 78 n. 1. Harvey suggests that, according to Mark, Herod is not affirming that Jesus is John the Baptist come back to life, 'but that the effect of his "rising from the dead" is that "his powers are at work" in Jesus'. I doubt that Mark would have been happy with this account of what he wrote; certainly it is not what Matthew or Luke made of it. In any case, Harvey's proposed reading would scarcely constitute evidence of 'reincarnation' belief as such. Harvey is right, however (75), to point out that the suggestion that Jesus was John the Baptist come to life again did not entail Herod sending officers to see whether John's tomb was empty.

of about the same age as John. Second, it is of course clear that Jesus was an embodied human being, walking around and saying and doing things. At this point Herod is on target. 'Resurrection' language was not about ghosts, spirits or phantoms; there was plenty of other language for that. It was about bodies. We do not find here any suggestion, apart from the new powers such a being might have, that the body itself had been in any way transformed – or, presumably, that it would not or could not die again.[45] Perhaps the simplest explanation for why Herod said what he did – or why someone said that he said it – is the general idea, current at least since the Maccabees and Daniel, that Israel's god would vindicate a righteous sufferer, and that Herod might well think of John in that way.[46]

(b) The Disciples' Perplexity

If we find first-century language about resurrection sometimes puzzling, it is good to know that the disciples did too:

> [9]As they were coming down the mountain, Jesus told them not to tell anyone what they had seen, except when the son of man would rise from the dead. [10]And they kept the saying (*ton logon ekratesan*) to themselves, questioning what this 'rising from the dead' might mean.[47]

Verse 10 presents translation problems: did they 'keep the word to themselves', or did they 'seize upon it' while 'discussing among themselves'? It is also interesting that some scribes changed the last phrase to something much easier, 'questioning when he would rise from the dead'.[48] This may indeed be in line with Matthew's omission of the disciples' perplexity: surely, a Christian reader might imagine, the disciples would know what 'rising from the dead' was supposed to mean? Does this verse perhaps suggest that, despite all the other signs to the contrary, belief in resurrection was neither widespread nor established as orthodoxy?[49] The question is further complicated, linked to our previous discussion about Herod and John the Baptist, because, in both Matthew and Mark, the disciples continue by asking Jesus about the coming of Elijah, only to receive the reply that Elijah had already been and gone and that they should now be thinking about what

---

[45] So, rightly, Wedderburn 1999, 41. The idea that the resurrected person has special powers is of course related to what we find in Acts (e.g. 2.32f.; 4.10), that healing power is at work by the agency of the risen Jesus through the Spirit.

[46] So Perkins 1995, 598 n. 749, quoting Nickelsburg 1980, 153–84.

[47] Mk. 9.9f.; the par. in Mt. (17.9) only has Jesus' command.

[48] So, rightly, Evans 1970, 31 – though this reading was adopted by e.g. Lagrange and Vincent Taylor.

[49] So e.g. Evans 1970, 30f.

would happen to the son of man.[50] Mark may be hinting that the disciples, faced with the question about resurrection, were casting about for some fixed points and coming up with the same question that Herod's courtiers had faced three chapters earlier.

But the answer to the problem – our problem, wondering what their question was about, as well as theirs, wondering about the resurrection – is not far to seek. Despite what Herod may have imagined, or somebody suggested that he imagined, 'the rising from the dead' (*to ek nekron anastenai*, Mark 9.10) normally referred to the rising of all the righteous at the end of time, not of one righteous person in the middle of time. Harvey puts the point well: Jesus seemed to them to be taking a belief which was about the ultimate future life beyond death, 'and abruptly inserting it into the calendar of imminent events to signal the moment at which they would be free to speak about the transfiguration'.[51]

The passage thus flags up one of the points at which we have seen, in our study of Paul, a significant Christian innovation: the idea that 'the resurrection' has split into two, with Jesus' resurrection coming forwards into the middle of history. Mark, clearly, intends his readers to recognize that they share with hindsight the knowledge that Jesus seemed to have in advance. The reader understands what was, for the disciples at the time, still a puzzle. Mark is thus drawing our attention to the fact that this is precisely an innovation within Jewish thinking. The conversation which follows is, among other things, a way of making sure that we will not agree with the court of Herod and suppose that Jesus is Elijah. Elijah has already come, and they have done what they wanted with him. Now it is time for the son of man to follow in the same path of suffering; but he will be raised from the dead.

(v) The Sadducees' Question

(a) Introduction

Far and away the most important passage about resurrection in the whole gospel tradition is the answer Jesus gives to the Sadducees' question. We know from other sources enough about the Sadducees and their beliefs on this subject, and the kind of question they might put to the Pharisees, for us not to be surprised at what they said to Jesus. The really interesting thing is what he said to them.[52]

---

[50] Mk. 9.11–13/Mt. 17.10–13.

[51] Harvey 1994, 72. Harvey is misleading, though, to speak of resurrection belief at this period as 'a speculative notion about the after-life'; resurrection, as we have repeatedly seen, was not so much about the 'after-life' but about a new life *after* the 'after-life'.

[52] This is the one major synoptic pericope I deliberately left out of *JVG*, with a view to its inclusion here. On the Sadducees and their beliefs see above, 131–40.

[18]Some Sadducees came to him (they say that there is no resurrection), and they put this question to him. [19]'Teacher, Moses wrote for us that if a man's brother dies and leaves a wife but no child, his brother should take the wife and raise up seed for his brother. [20]There were seven brothers. The first took a wife and died without leaving seed. [21]The second took her, and died without leaving seed. And the third likewise. [22]And the seven – without leaving seed. Last of all the woman died also. [23]In the resurrection, when they rise, whose wife will she be? For the seven had her as wife.' [24]Jesus said to them, 'This is why you are wrong, isn't it – that you don't know the scriptures or the power of God! [25]For when they are raised from the dead, they neither marry nor are given in marriage, but are like angels in heaven. [26]But concerning the dead, that they are raised [Mt.: but concerning the resurrection of the dead], did you never read in the book of Moses, in the passage about the bush, how God says to him, "I am the God of Abraham, the God of Isaac and the God of Jacob?" [27]He is not God of the dead, but of the living. You are quite wrong.'[53]

Luke's version of Jesus' answer is significantly different in certain respects:

[34]Jesus said to them, 'The children of this age marry and are given in marriage, [35]but those who are reckoned worthy to take part in that age, and in the resurrection of the dead, neither marry nor are given in marriage. [36]For they cannot die any more, since they are equal to angels, and are children of God, being children of the resurrection. [37]But that the dead are raised, Moses also mentions in the passage about the bush, when he speaks of the Lord as the God of Abraham, the God of Isaac and the God of Jacob. [38]God is not God of the dead but of the living, for all live to him.[54]

This intricate little passage deserves, and has received, far more extensive treatment than present space allows.[55] I hope, however, at least to mark out the path by which we can find our way to a historical understanding of the issues involved.

The passage runs into a classic case of anachronistic reader-assumptions. An illustration may help. I have on my desk a postcard which reproduces Albrecht Dürer's painting of St Jerome. As in many pictures of Jerome, there is a lion sprawled right behind the saint, looking up at his back, while Jerome gazes into the distance, as though seeing a vision. Now supposing I glanced at that picture, knowing nothing of Jerome, but being well versed in the Bible. My first impression might well be that it was a picture of Daniel in the lions' den. (The fact that the painting is set out of doors is irrelevant for the purposes of this illustration; medieval and renaissance artists were quite capable of placing their subjects in new settings.) Here is the holy man in prayer, perhaps seeing an angel. Here is the lion, wanting to attack, but realizing that in the presence of holiness, and perhaps of angels, he must not. Very well, we would conclude: a fine and moving study of Daniel. But in

---

[53] Mk. 12.18–27/Mt. 22.23–33/Lk. 20.27–40. Mt. follows Mk. reasonably closely; for Lk. see below.

[54] Lk. 20.34–8. On the differences from Mk. see e.g. Kilgallen 1986, 481f.

[55] See particularly Schwankl 1987; and other bib. in Davies and Allison 1988–97, 221–34. Juhász 2002, 116–21 provides a fascinating window on the treatment of this passage both by Jerome and in the early English Reformation.

fact the setting, and meaning, are quite different. The reason there is a lion with Jerome is because, according to legend, he, like Androcles, healed it by removing a thorn from its foot, whereupon it became his loyal and devoted companion. The superficial similarity to what an onlooker might imagine would lead in entirely the wrong direction. If anything, the lion is protecting the saint, not contemplating attack.

Something similar happens when the story of Jesus and the Sadducees is read by Christians, and indeed by non-Christians, in the modern western world.[56] For many centuries it has been assumed in western Christendom that the ultimate point of being a Christian was to 'go to heaven when you die'. Though one tradition (that of Rome, different in this respect from both Eastern Orthodoxy and Protestantism) inserted a time-lag into the process ('purgatory') for all except the utterly holy, the picture still remained: a place called 'heaven', where god and the angels lived, into which god's people would be admitted either immediately upon death or at some stage thereafter.[57] This picture was hugely reinforced in the medieval and renaissance periods by such masterpieces as the writings of Dante on the one hand and the paintings of Michelangelo on the other.

When the Protestant reformers challenged Rome on the question of how one might be justified in the first place, and whether one might have to face purgatory on the other, they did not challenge the belief that the ultimate purpose of it all was to end up in 'heaven'. It is by no means clear, in fact, how theologians, let alone ordinary Christians, dealt with the very bodily notion of resurrection within this picture.[58] But since Jesus, after his resurrection, was believed to have 'gone to heaven' anyway, the purpose of Christian life, spirituality and hope was obviously to follow him there. That belief, expressed in a thousand hymns, ten thousand prayers and uncountable sermons, remains the staple diet of most Christians today.[59] Within this context, the word 'resurrection' could be heard, as many still hear it today, simply as a vivid way of saying 'life after death' or 'going to heaven'. And since (a) heaven has always been assumed, within Jewish and Christian tradition, to be populated by angels, and (b) within popular folk-religion there has always been a tendency to suppose that the beloved dead have now *become* angels, the two can easily be combined, and can serve as an interpretative grid for 'understanding' the present passage. 'Resurrection' thus

---

[56] Including Christian scholars: e.g. Evans 1970, 32; Perkins 1984, 74f.

[57] On purgatory, and the remarkable contemporary redefinitions of it within mainstream Roman Catholicism see e.g. Rahner 1961, 32f.; McPartlan 2000, and the full and helpful article in *ODCC*[3] (1349f.).

[58] See esp. Bynum 1995. For the reformation controversies cf. Juhász 2002.

[59] e.g. 'Here for a season, then above,/ O Lamb of God, I come,' the closing lines of Charlotte Elliott's hymn, 'Just as I am, without one plea' (*New English Hymnal* 294). Remarkably few Easter hymns even attempt to express what the first Christians thought Jesus' resurrection was all about: see Wright, 'From Theology to Music'.

comes to mean 'life after death', which (on an optimistic view at least) means 'living in heaven', quite possibly 'becoming an angel'.[60] That, many readers think, is what Jesus is then affirming in his discussion with the Sadducees.[61]

But to approach the present passage with that set of ideas in one's head is like looking at the picture of Jerome while thinking of Daniel in the lions' den. We cannot stress too strongly that this whole complex of ideas, developed so massively and many-sidedly over the years, was simply not in the heads or hearts of either Jesus or the Sadducees, or indeed the Pharisees, or indeed ordinary Jews or pagans in the first century. One might as well assume that when Herod wanted music playing in his court he had to choose between Haydn, Mozart and Beethoven. Within the Jewish tradition, at least, 'heaven' was not, and did not become until some while after the first century, a regular designation for the place where the righteous went either immediately after death or at some stage thereafter. Few supposed, so far as we know, that human beings would *become* angels in that future life. And nobody supposed that the word 'resurrection' meant 'life after death' in general. When the Sadducees engaged in controversies with the Pharisees on the subject, as we saw already in looking at the Sadducees' opinions in chapter 3, there were two levels of the question: first, the ultimate question, whether there would be a final re-embodiment; but second, the penultimate question, what sort of existence those awaiting re-embodiment would have in the meantime.[62] (These were joined with a further question: can you prove this from the Torah?) Since these are not the questions modern westerners have routinely asked (to this day, newspaper surveys tend to ask people simply whether they believe in 'life after death', as though secularist denials of 'survival' and traditionalist affirmations of it were the only options worth considering), it requires a fair amount of historical re-education if we are to get rid of anachronisms in our imaginations and replace them with the appropriate questions and the contexts of meaning those questions would evoke. Unless we are prepared to do this we shall simply end up imagining that Jesus taught something remarkably like Plato – a conclusion which comes all too easily to some theological minds.

---

[60] Out of many works on popular beliefs about life after death see e.g. Barley 1995; Edwards 1999; Jupp and Gittings 1999; Innes 1999; Harrison 2000.

[61] On the question of whether the pericope goes back substantially to Jesus see the *Forschungsberichte* in Schwankl 1987, 46–58. I regard it as coming squarely within the criteria of double similarity and double dissimilarity (see *JVG* 131–3): it is thoroughly at home in Judaism, but the precise point and the way of making it is not otherwise known; it is thoroughly credible as a controversy between the Jesus remembered by the early Christians and the Sadducees, but not as an invention of the early church to back up its own concern with resurrection (they would have done it differently; see the similar argument in ch. 13 below about the resurrection narratives).

[62] Above, 132–5, 194–200.

Fortunately the materials for asking the right questions are ready to hand. We must begin by sketching the context where we find the passage, which in all three synoptics is the long sequence of debates between Jesus and various groups following Jesus' symbolic action in the Temple.[63] Assuming a now-traditional view of synoptic relationships, Mark has placed this story here, flanked on one side by the parable of the wicked tenants and the question about tribute-money and on the other side by the question of the greatest commandment and Jesus' counter-question about David's Lord and David's son. Matthew and Luke have followed this sequence closely.[64] The interesting thing about this is that all the other debates in this sequence, including the extra ones added by Matthew,[65] are themselves framed in a highly polemical and adversarial context, where the issue is emphatically not abstract debates about the finer points of theology or belief about a future life, but the immediate political meaning of what Jesus has just done in the Temple. Mark and Luke speak, just before this sequence, of the conspiracy against Jesus by the chief priests (i.e. the leading Sadducees) and the scribes.[66] They also take us straight on from this sequence into Jesus' 'apocalyptic' denunciation of the city and Temple as a whole; Matthew joins them again here, after a long chapter in which Jesus denounces the scribes and Pharisees. From there, of course, all three synoptists relate the story in swift progression until Jesus stands before the leading Sadducee, the high priest himself, where, in response to a charge about threatening the Temple, he declares, with echoes of Daniel, that god will vindicate him after his suffering. Somehow the evangelists seem to think that the debate about resurrection belongs within this larger complex of thought, within the rich and explosive mixture of politics and theology that forms the climax of the synoptic narrative. We shall conclude that they were probably right.[67]

It is equally interesting, in terms of the evangelists' overall intention, to compare what is said here about the resurrection with what they each say in the extraordinary stories which conclude the gospels. Granted that Mark's own narrative is at this point either deliberately short and uninformative or truncated (I favour the latter, but we do not need to anticipate the argument of chapter 14), Matthew's and Luke's accounts of Jesus' own resurrection do not fit at all with the normal modern western understanding of what the present passage means. We could say, of course, that Matthew and Luke were simply including traditional material in the present passage even though it did not fit with what for both of them was the climax of the story;

---

[63] On the whole sequence cf. *JVG* ch. 11.

[64] Mk. 11.27—12.37/Mt. 21.43—22.46/Lk. 20.1-44.

[65] The parable of the two sons (21.28–32) and of the great supper (22.1–14).

[66] Mk. 11.18f./Lk. 19.47f.

[67] I owe to Dr Andrew Goddard the fascinating point that Jesus, answering this question about men who die childless, stands as himself a celibate, childless man before those who are about to send him to his death.

but that is a fairly desperate measure. Luke, after all, sees fit to edit Mark's version of Jesus' answer quite carefully, and presumably in that process he could have altered it still more had he thought that it conflicted with the picture of Jesus' own resurrection he was planning to offer in chapter 24.[68] The fact that he does not, and that similar points can be made about Matthew, indicates that the matter is not so simple. This is the one time that any of the evangelists have Jesus say anything substantial about what resurrection from the dead actually involves; it strains credulity beyond breaking point to suppose that the evangelists simply turned a blind eye to the fact that this vital piece of teaching contradicted what they were intending to say about Jesus himself. Jesus had not 'gone to heaven' at Easter; when he does (in Luke and Acts) Luke insists that this is a different event to the resurrection. Even if we were to declare that this was an invented distinction, Luke at least does not suppose that Jesus' 'resurrection' consists of him going to heaven and becoming an angel, and there is no reason to think that Matthew did either.

At the same time, it is important to note that Jesus' answer does not function, for the evangelists, as a prediction of the story they will subsequently tell. He does not here say that the Sadducees are wrong and that before too long he will prove the point in person. He does not speak of the third day, of the son of man rising from the dead, of the *palingenesia*. Luke has him speak of the present age and the age to come – using, in other words, the basic categories of Pharisaic eschatology, which Jesus certainly endorsed but which Mark and Matthew do not here have him make explicit. We can read between the lines at this point: Luke at least wants to suggest that, with Jesus' own resurrection, the age to come has actually broken in. For Luke, Jesus' statement points, by implication at any rate, towards the developed theology of Paul. But the main thing in all three writers is that Jesus first rebuts the Sadducees' conclusion by postulating a discontinuity between the present embodiment and the future one, and, second, quotes a passage of scripture which he takes to imply resurrection. Both of these are intricate and easily misunderstood, and we must tackle them one by one.

(b) No Marriage in the Resurrection

The Sadducees' question presupposes one particular command in Torah, namely, the Levirate law of marriage, which is set out in Deuteronomy 25.5–10. According to this, when a man dies childless his brother must marry the widow, and the resulting children will count as though they were those of the original husband. We see the principle applied (or not as the case may be) in passages like Genesis 38 (38.8, 'raise up offspring for your brother', is quoted as part of the Sadducees' question) and the book of Ruth,

---

[68] cf. too the view of resurrection elsewhere in Lk./Ac., e.g. Ac. 2 (below, ch. 10).

and it is frequently discussed in later rabbinic codes.[69] The point, of course, is to avoid families dying out in Israel. This creates a situation where the fact of short life expectancy, with multiple widowhood and remarriage far more common than in the western world today, could, at least in the imagination, be stretched to envisage the folktale-like scenario of all seven brothers in a family marrying the same woman in turn.[70] What is more, Torah itself not only sanctioned but commanded the practice, so that one could not avoid it by suggesting that frequent remarriage was not YHWH's intention.[71] Was Jesus, then, going to be disloyal to Torah, and uphold the illogical and ridiculous Pharisaic notion of resurrection – as might well be implied by the fact that he seemed to be leading a kingdom-of-god pressure group, and had just performed a symbolic act of revolution in the Temple?

Jesus' response in Mark and Matthew begins, as it were, with a headline: the Sadducees show by their question that they are ignorant both of the scriptures and of god's power. This is the more interesting in the light of our reading of Paul, for whom Jesus' own resurrection was of course 'according to the scriptures', and was frequently spoken of as an act of divine power, which refers not least to the power of god as creator. Is Jesus alluding to creation itself, as in Mark 10.2–8, to relativize a later command of Torah?[72]

Yes and no. In Mark 10 Jesus goes back behind the Deuteronomic command (on how to divorce one's wife) to the original command in Genesis 2, taking that command to mean lifelong fidelity. In the present passage he moves, not backwards to original creation, but forwards to new creation. And he states, without explanation in Mark and Matthew, that those who are raised from the dead do not get married, but are like angels in heaven. The latter clause is not merely an explanation of why the resurrected do not marry; had it been, it would have been introduced with *gar*, 'for', not *alla*, 'but'. It adds a new, positive point, which then serves retrospectively as an explanation of the negative: in the resurrection, they are like the angels in heaven.

This last phrase does not mean 'they, like angels, are in heaven'. It does not refer, that is, to the *location* of the resurrected ones, however easy it is for late western minds to assume that it should. After all, had first-century Jews believed that people 'went to heaven when they died', they might well have supposed that marriage continued in that sphere; mentioning the location of the departed would not have made Jesus' point. Rather, as some later

---

[69] See esp. mYeb. *passim*; and e.g. mBekh. 1.7.

[70] The analogy with Tobit 6—8 is obvious. The echoes of 2 Macc. 7 are fascinating (seven brothers and a mother who all die in the hope of resurrection), but not so close in theme. Schwankl 1987, 347–52 argues in detail for actual dependence.

[71] Though cf. Mk. 10.2–12 (opposes a command from Gen. to one from Dt. on divorce). The present passage has some interesting analogies with that one, not least concerning celibacy. Cf. Fletcher-Louis 1997, 78–86, with ref. to the Lukan passage.

[72] cf. *JVG* 284–6.

scribes tried to make clear, it means 'they are like *the angels who are* in heaven',[73] or, if you prefer, 'they are like the angels (who happen to be in heaven)', as I might say to my nephew in London, 'You are just like your cousin (who happens to be in Vancouver).' The 'likeness' in question is meant, not in the *ontological* sense that the resurrected ones are now the same sort of creature as the angels, nor in the *locational* sense that they are sharing the same space, but in the *functional* sense that the angels do not marry. Neither here nor anywhere else in the early Christian literature is it suggested that resurrected people have turned into angels.[74] They are *like* them, as a trombone is like an oboe in that both are wind instruments, though one is made of brass and the other of wood.

Luke, who after all was one of the earliest readers of Mark for whom we have evidence, has taken care to set out this rebuttal of the Sadducees so that it conforms more obviously both to mainstream second-Temple Jewish beliefs and hence to the strand of early Christianity represented by Paul at least. The 'present age' and the 'age to come', as we have seen, were the standard framework within which the Pharisees and their many followers understood cosmology and politics as well as what is sometimes called 'personal eschatology' (i.e. the hope of the individual after death). In Luke's version, Jesus is made to distinguish sharply between these two ages, in the former of which marriage is appropriate and in the latter of which it is not. This, it becomes clear, is not because of anything evil about marriage, still less about sexual identity and behaviour; it is because the 'age to come' will be characterized by immortality. Those who attain it cannot die any more (verse 36). Resurrection will not simply mean resuscitation, like Jairus' daughter or Lazarus. It will not mean starting off again in exactly the same kind of world as at present. It will mean going through death and out the other side into a deathless world. (Already we should note that within the worldview where all this makes sense, that of the resurrection-believing strands of second-Temple Judaism, the phrase 'they cannot die any more' could mean a disembodied immortality. But it could also refer, and when coupled with other language pointing to resurrection certainly would refer, to a resurrected re-embodiment over which death would have no more power – unlike the kind of disembodied state where death does indeed rule, forbidding re-embodiment.)

---

[73] The text is variously expanded in this direction by the MSS A, B, Θ, Γ and several others.

[74] Harvey 1994, 71 is uncharacteristically imprecise when he suggests that Jesus is here distinguishing his own view from that of the Pharisees by describing 'dead persons as (presumably incorporeal) "angels in heaven"'. The point is (a) that they are alive; (b) that they are (not identified as angels, but merely) like angels in one particular respect. For the closest that early Christian writers come to identifying the dead with angels see below, 487, 492, 496, 512. For similar questions in Judaism see e.g. 161 above.

The logic of Luke's version of Jesus' riposte then depends for its force on two unstated assumptions: (a) that marriage is instituted to cope with the problem that people die; (b) angels do not die. The Levirate law, quite explicitly, had to do with continuing the family line when faced with death; Jesus, in Luke's version, not only declares that this law will be redundant in a world without death, but that marriage itself, even with one husband and one wife, will likewise be irrelevant in such a world. A key point, often unnoticed, is that the Sadducees' question is not about the mutual affection and companionship of husband and wife, but about *how to fulfil the command to have a child*, that is, how in the future life the family line will be kept going.[75] This is presumably based on the belief, going back to Genesis 1.28, that the main purpose of marriage was to be fruitful and multiply.

Luke's explanatory phrase about the angels is subtly different to that in Mark and Matthew. Instead of saying that the resurrected are *like* angels, he has Jesus say that they are *equal* to angels, using the rare word *isangeloi*.[76] Once again, though, we must insist that he does not say that they are like, or equal to, angels in all respects; only in this respect (this time it is an ordinary explanation, i.e. with *gar*), that they are immortal.[77] They are 'children of god, being children of the resurrection', and presumably Luke intends that double phrase to carry the same force. God's true children are like their father, and cannot die.[78] Luke has here used more freedom than in some other places, but the basic meaning is the same as in Mark and Matthew: the question about the Levirate law is irrelevant to the question of the resurrection, because in the new world that the creator god will make there will be no death, and hence no need for procreation.[79] Jesus has addressed the question's presupposition, undermining the need to ask it in the first place.[80]

(c) God of the Living

This brings us to the positive proof advanced by Jesus for believing in the resurrection. Luke here rejoins Matthew and Mark, with only one change of wording that has any significance. This is where the normal modern western assumptions let us down most conclusively. What is perceived as the

---

[75] This is the point stressed by Kilgallen 1986, 482–5.

[76] The only other use listed in LSJ is found in Hierocles Platonicus (C5 AD) *in Carmen Aureum* 4. Kittel (in *TDNT* 1.87) lists two other literary uses and one epitaph. The closest other phrase in the NT is at Ac. 6.15 (Stephen's face looking 'like that of an angel').

[77] So e.g. Ellis 1966, 237.

[78] Luke may intend here an echo of Ex. 4.22; see below.

[79] Neither the evangelists, nor Jesus, nor his interlocutors, face the question which occurs to us: if marriage is designed to procreate the species in the face of death, why does Gen. 2 describe it being instituted before the fall? The only answer sees to be that the present question and answer remain limited by the implied scope of the Levirate law.

[80] Kilgallen 1986, 486.

'natural' reading of the passage runs as follows: Abraham, Isaac and Jacob are long since dead; but Moses writes of god speaking of them as still alive; therefore this is what is meant by 'resurrection'. Put this reading together with a too-hasty reading of 'like angels' in the earlier part of the passage, and we end up, as many scholars have done, with the view that this is 'a spiritual resurrection, not a bodily one such as the Sadducees, or Herod, are thinking of';[81] or that 'resurrection, which is here not argued but simply assumed, involves the creative power of god to transform human life into a non-physical form like that of the angels'.[82]

This is to misunderstand the type of argument we are witnessing.[83] Close study of the reported discussions of exactly the same topic in the Talmud will show what is actually going on. To recapitulate what we saw in chapter 4: the Pharisaic, and rabbinic, view of the resurrection always involved two stages: an intermediate stage, in which the dead were in some way or other still alive, and a final stage in which they would be re-embodied. And, since in fact rather few Jews seem to have believed that disembodied immortality was really the final state, into which one passed immediately upon death, the main debate as far as the Pharisees were concerned was between their two-stage view and the Sadducees' no-stage view, in which people ceased to exist altogether after death.[84] What is more, everybody knew that what was normally meant by 'resurrection' had not happened yet. The question 'What do you say about resurrection?' was always a question about the *future*.

If that was the debate, and if both parties knew it, then, as the Talmudic discussions indicate, it was not always necessary to complete the full argument. Like chess players who know perfectly well a dozen moves ahead that the game is won and lost, rabbinic debaters often failed to spell out the closing moves in a discussion; it would almost be like explaining a joke. Thus, for instance, in the Babylonian Talmud, Numbers 18.28 is quoted as proving resurrection because it speaks, after the death of Aaron, of the Israelites paying tithes to him. This is taken to demonstrate, by implication, that he is, after all, still alive, *and will be raised in the future*; but the implication, though vital for the completion of the argument, is not stated.[85] Many political debates, ancient and modern, share this pattern.

This seems to be exactly what we are faced with in the present passage. God introduces himself to Moses as 'the god of Abraham, the god of Isaac, and the god of Jacob' (Exodus 3.6). Jesus draws from this the preliminary conclusion that the patriarchs are still alive, since this god is not god of the

[81] Perkins 1984, 74f.

[82] Evans 1970, 32. Evans says that the quotation from Exodus is added 'somewhat awkwardly', and that the argument 'is not a proof of resurrection in general, but rather its opposite'.

[83] On the underlying logic see esp. Schwankl 1987, 403–06.

[84] See above, ch. 4.

[85] bSanh. 90b.

dead but of the living. But that is not the end of the actual argument. If we place this debate on the template of the equivalent rabbinic ones, it becomes clear that (what we would want to hear as) the real punch-line of the story has been omitted. If they are still alive in YHWH's presence, *they will be raised in the future*. Nobody supposed, after all, that Abraham, Isaac and Jacob had already been raised from the dead. Quoting a text which showed that they were still living on in some non-bodily fashion, if that were the end of the story, would not even be relevant to the discussion. To that extent Evans would be right to say that the quotation from Exodus 3 would seem to prove the opposite of resurrection: that the dead are *not* raised, but only live on in post-mortem disembodiment of whatever sort. That would not be an answer to the Sadducees' question; or rather, it would be a way of saying, 'I actually agree with that young philosopher Philo down in Alexandria, but I want to go on using the word "resurrection", so I intend to use it now, in a whole new way, to denote a view rather like his.' That was such a familiar move in twentieth-century would-be Christian theology that it is fatally easy to assume that Jesus was making it as well.[86] But that is not how the argument works. The patriarchs are still alive, and therefore will be raised in the future. Prove the first, and (within the worldview assumed by both parties in the debate, and any listening Pharisees) you have proved the second.

Luke's minor variation at this point is to add the explanatory clause, 'for all live to him', i.e. to Israel's god. The dead, certainly the dead patriarchs, are thus 'alive to god'. This phrase can, however, be used in two other ways as well, and it should clearly not be taken as a technical term in first-century Judaism for any one particular state. The author of 4 Maccabees consistently changes the clear resurrection teaching of 2 Maccabees into teaching about reason's conquest of the passions, and the promise of a blessed immortality.[87] Those who control fleshly passions (it is a bit of a stretch to speak of the martyrs in this way, but the writer is determined to force his point) believe 'that they do not die to god, just as our patriarchs Abraham, Isaac and Jacob do not, but that they live to god' (4 Maccabees 7.19). The mother of the seven slain brothers encouraged them to die rather than disobey the god-given commands, 'knowing this, that those who die because of god live to god, as do Abraham, Isaac, Jacob and all the patriarchs' (4 Maccabees 16.25). Here the phrase 'live to god' seems to be used to describe a final state of blessed disembodiment. In Romans 6.10–11, however, the same phrase is used to describe the life that Jesus himself now possesses, which we know clearly from elsewhere in Romans is a new bodily existence, and to urge on that basis the 'life to god' of Christian obedience in the present.[88]

---

[86] See the works criticized on this score by Wedderburn 1999, 147–52. Wedderburn himself prefers, as he says, to affirm the alternative belief and drop the word 'resurrection'.

[87] cf. 142f. above.

[88] See 252 above.

These passages indicate that there was no standard meaning for the phrase, which would in any case be unlikely with so general an expression. Luke seems to mean it as referring to the temporary state of disembodiment in which all are 'alive to god' while awaiting their resurrection, and the other two passages cannot be invoked to pull it in another direction.

Jesus' answer to the Sadducees, in fact, does point towards the refocusing of the resurrection hope which was to take place later, not least through the work of Paul. It speaks of a different quality of life, a life which death can no longer touch, and hence a life in which the normal parameters of mortal (i.e. deathbound) life, including procreative marriage, are no longer relevant. It speaks of an intermediate state in which all the righteous dead are held in some kind of ongoing life while waiting for the resurrection which everyone, Pharisee and Sadducee alike, knew perfectly well had not happened yet. It speaks about YHWH's past word to Moses, in order to indicate a present reality (the patriarchs are still alive), in order thereby to affirm the future hope (they will be raised to newly embodied life).

(d) Patriarchs, Exodus and Kingdom

This reading of the text not only has the merit that it places the debate in the world of first-century Judaism rather than in that of late western thought which has taught itself to use the word 'resurrection' as a rough synonym for 'life after death'. It also makes clear that, while the synoptic evangelists have not attempted to use their editing of the passage to highlight specifically Christian points, nor have they passively recorded a discussion in which Jesus affirms something their own later stories about his resurrection will deny (or in which Jesus denies by implication something their later stories will affirm). But there is another dimension yet to be considered which is of weighty significance for understanding the early Christians' view of resurrection. We must not forget the political meaning the doctrine always had for the Pharisees; that was, after all, one of the reasons why the Sadducees opposed it. It seems from this text that the political meaning remained alive and well in early Christianity as well. Perhaps this, after all, and not simply an implicit Humean scepticism, is why late western modernity has had so much trouble with the resurrection.

The passage belongs exactly where Mark has put it, in the middle of a string of tense debates about what Jesus was up to in the Temple, about where his authority came from, about whether his kingdom-movement would abolish taxes to Caesar, and ultimately about whether he really was, as he seemed to be claiming, Israel's Messiah. Mark and the others, in setting these stories in this order and context, seem to be using this particular narrative to point on to the resurrection of Jesus himself. This, they are saying by implication, will be the moment when the Sadducees will be defeated not in debate but in ontological reality. When Jesus is raised from the dead, that event, demonstrating that they are in the wrong, will be tightly linked with the other events, notably the destruction of the Temple, which will have the same practical as well as theological effect. To the extent that we hear the voice of Jesus himself in this story, we should see the entire dialogue as part of a larger one: Jesus' critique of the official rulers of the Judaism of his day. He had his critique of the Pharisees too, but on this point he, like Paul in Acts, could make common cause with them against these particular opponents.

Within this, we should not miss the deliberately subversive implication of the quotation from Exodus 3 which Jesus chooses as the thin end of his pro-resurrection wedge. God appears to Moses in the bush, not simply to tell him that he is the god of Abraham, Isaac and Jacob, but to tell him that he has heard the cry of his people in Egypt, has remembered his covenant with the patriarchs, and has come to set Israel free, taking them off to their own land at last. Exodus 3.6 is not just a potential proof-text about resurrection (which then only works on the assumption that the present tense in the quotation, 'I *am* the god of Abraham . . .' can be invoked to show that Abraham is still alive). It is part of a passage which speaks of YHWH's desire to liberate his people – a desire which formed the backbone of many a Jewish resistance-movement, and which lay at the heart also of Jesus' announcement of the kingdom of god. Jesus' movement was itself a new-exodus movement, a liberation-movement, a return-from-exile movement, in the senses I explored in *Jesus and the Victory of God*. To affirm the resurrection was to affirm the fact that Israel's god was at work in a new way, turning the world upside down, doing (perhaps) to the present Jewish rulers what Jesus had done in the Temple. Put this discussion into this context, and it fits like a glove.

Exodus 3.6 was in fact typical of sayings (about Israel's god as the god of Abraham, Isaac and Jacob) which were quoted not so much to make a point about the patriarchs in question but to make a point about this god: that he is committed to being Israel's saviour, in the present and future as well as the past.[89] YHWH was faithful to the patriarchs; this faithfulness would play itself out in Moses' day (the context of Exodus 3); and it would continue to operate for Israel in subsequent situations.[90] The story of Moses was told and retold, as it still is to this day (at Passover, for instance), to make the

---

[89] For this point see Dreyfus 1959; Janzen 1985; and, within a fuller context, Schwankl 1987, 391–6. None of them, however, see its implications for the political meaning of the discussion with the Sadducees.

[90] So Janzen 47. As he points out, the double quotation with which the Sadducees began linked Moses with the patriarchal generations, and Jesus will now exploit this to answer them; in addition, both quotations use the phrase 'raise up' in the sense of 'beget children', but with the overtone, to the listener/reader, of the sense 'resurrect'.

point that Israel's god, the true god, is the freedom-god. And, as we have seen regularly, the freedom for which Israel longed in the first century could be expressed in terms of new-exodus ideas, which themselves were already firmly linked, as metaphor and metonymy, with belief in resurrection. Ezekiel 37 used the image of resurrection as a metaphor for national liberation; but by Jesus' day resurrection, taken literally, was itself seen as one element in the total freedom-package to which Israel's god was deemed to be committed by covenant.

The reader of the gospel should know by this stage that throughout his public career Jesus had both reaffirmed the hope of Israel and redefined it around himself. His kingdom-message, culminating (thus far) in his powerful symbolic challenge to the Temple, spoke of Israel's god doing that for which, as the Sadducees knew well, 'resurrection' was itself a powerful symbol: overturning the present order and ushering in the kingdom. Thus, when we work our way down through the levels of meaning in this story, we find ourselves not too far from what Paul meant when he spoke of Jesus' resurrection as constituting him as god's son, the Messiah, the lord of the world (Romans 1.3–5), and what he meant when speaking of the resurrection of Jesus' people coming about because Jesus is the lord and saviour who has the power to subject all things to himself (1 Corinthians 15.20–28; Philippians 3.20–21).

This story makes, then, a multi-layered contribution to our investigation of the ways in which the early Christians conceived of resurrection. Jesus' debate with the Sadducees stands at the meeting-point between the debates that were taking place in first-century Judaism and the new view, growing up from within Judaism itself, that quickly took shape in the community that believed he had been raised from the dead. The evangelists, and arguably the sources that they drew on, and certainly Jesus himself, stand at the mainstream Pharisaic point in the spectrum of belief. They believe in a future bodily resurrection, and accept that there will be an intermediate state which precedes it, as at the moment with the patriarchs. What this passage adds is a new note of discontinuity between the present state and the future one, and it corresponds to the discontinuity spoken of by Paul in 1 Corinthians 15: the present body, within the present age, is corruptible and will die, but the new body, inhabiting god's new age, is incorruptible and will not die. That is why sundry other discontinuities can be predicated as well, notably in this case the fact that there will be no need to decide who will be married to whom in the age to come. What is more, the nascent Christian belief in resurrection appears to be every bit as revolutionary, in the political sense, as the Sadducees perceived that of the Pharisees to be. That is why the story belongs where it does in the synoptic narratives. And that is why we should not be surprised, in Paul and on into the second century, to discover that this belief sustains the early church in taking its early steps of giving allegiance to Jesus rather than to Caesar.

None of this tells us much directly, of course, about the resurrection of Jesus, which is the main subject of this book. But it is vital, as we approach the central early Christian statements about that event, to see the way the language and concepts functioned at the time. And it is especially important to note the ways in which, within early Christianity, significant innovations were made from within the Jewish tradition. The present passage has offered us one at least, and there is no good reason to deny that, in principle, it goes back to Jesus himself. But the fact that the story was passed on, was told in this fashion, and in particular that it was collected by Mark as part of a sequence of debates designed to explain what was really going on during that last, fateful exodus-celebration in Jerusalem – this speaks volumes both for the early Christian belief in the resurrection of Jesus and of his people and for their sense that the new age launched at Easter was an age in which the true god would at last fulfil, for the whole world, what had been done for Israel at the exodus. He would judge evil, liberate his people, and bring justice and hope at last.

3. Resurrection in the Matthew/Luke Material (Sometimes Known as 'Q')

No one will doubt that the early Christianity represented by the triple synoptic tradition, and Mark as its normal hypothetical collection-point, believed firmly in the resurrection both of Jesus and, in the future, of all god's people. But many have doubted, at least in recent times, whether the form of early Christianity represented by the double tradition of Matthew and Luke, that is, the passages they have in common with each other but not with Mark, held such a belief. It has even been boldly stated that the 'metaphor' of resurrection 'is fundamentally inappropriate to the genre and theology of Q' – 'Q' being, of course, the label given for over a century now to the material in question.[91] I have argued in a recent article for the opposite possibility: that if 'Q' existed, and if it was indeed the charter document of a community with a recognizable theology, then that theology included the resurrection of both Jesus and believers. We do not need to go over the same ground again.[92] Here, without initial prejudice to the 'Q' hypothesis one way

---

[91] Kloppenborg 1990b, 90. This point is already assumed by e.g. Schillebeeckx 1979 [1974], 409f.

[92] Wright, 'Resurrection in Q?' Cf. too Nickelsburg 1992, 688: 'Q' portrays Jesus as Wisdom's spokesman, standing in the line of the persecuted and vindicated righteous (Mt. 23.34f./Lk. 11.49–51); Q sees Jesus as the coming son of man whose future judicial status is the result of 'the exaltative function of his resurrection'. Also Meadors 1995, 307f. On 'Q' see, in addition to the standard texts (e.g. Kloppenborg 1987; 1990a; Catchpole 1993; Tuckett 1996), the brief treatments in *NTPG* 435–43; *JVG* 35–44. Martin Hengel (2000 ch. 7) has joined the ranks, if not of 'Q sceptics', at least doubters or questioners. For shrewd and sharp remarks from a historian in a neighbouring discipline cf. Akenson 2000, 321–8.

or another, I want simply to glance at the main texts which are more or less parallel in the non-Markan synoptic tradition.

We begin on secure ground. Matthew's Jesus discovers faith in a Roman centurion, and sees it as a sign of a great ingathering, in which some who had thought themselves automatically included will be left out. Luke's Jesus warns, meanwhile, of the danger of presumption. Matthew and Luke overlap at this point:

> [Mt. 8]¹¹I tell you, many will come from east and west and will sit down with Abraham, Isaac and Jacob in the kingdom of heaven. ¹²But the children of the kingdom will be thrown out into outer darkness, where there will be weeping and gnashing of teeth.

> [Lk.13]²⁸There will be weeping and gnashing of teeth, when you see Abraham, Isaac and Jacob and all the prophets in the kingdom of God, and yourselves thrown out. ²⁹And many will come from east and west, and north and south, and sit down in the kingdom of God.

Within the context of second-Temple Judaism, this can only mean one thing: that a great eschatological reversal is on the way, and when it comes the patriarchs will be raised from the dead to share it not only with their descendants, some of whom are in imminent danger of missing the party, but also with a large number from the Gentile world, of whom Matthew's centurion is an early example. This fits, in fact, with several sayings in the double tradition which speak of a coming judgment; in second-Temple Judaism the final judgment was never simply designed to punish evil, but to vindicate and reward the righteous. Acknowledging this saying as 'double tradition' material, despite the superficial differences, it is hard to deny that this strand envisages a future resurrection, even if (like many other second-Temple Jewish works) it only mentions it occasionally.

The same is true of Matthew 19.28/Luke 22.29f.:

> [Mt. 19]²⁸Truly I tell you, you who have followed me, in the regenerated world [*palingenesia*], when the son of man sits on the throne of his glory, you also will sit on twelve thrones judging the twelve tribes of Israel.

> [Lk. 22]²⁸You are those who have continued with me in my trials; ²⁹and I make a covenant with you, as my father covenanted a kingdom to me: ³⁰you will eat and drink at my table in my kingdom, sitting on thrones judging the twelve tribes of Israel.⁹³

The early nature of this saying is indicated not least by the mention of the Twelve, since from early on Judas was of course screened out of the list. The different elements, including Matthew's mention of the newborn world and the son of man on his throne, may of course be later additions to an

---

⁹³ Several MSS add 'twelve' before 'thrones', but this is clearly secondary.

early common tradition, but the core presupposes that there will come a time when the kingdom is well and truly established, when Israel's god is ruling Israel and presumably the world, when the disciples are at table with Jesus and are entrusted – much as Paul had said to the Corinthians! – with dispensing the sovereign rule of the one true god. And for this saying to be circulated at all after Jesus' death, and incorporated into at least two documents and possibly an earlier one which lies behind them, indicates the strong probability that these documents, and those who lived by them, believed both in Jesus' resurrection and also in their own.

The third double-tradition passage which seems to me clearly to speak of resurrection is Jesus' warning and promise about those who kill the body but cannot do any more than that:

> [Mt. 10][28]Do not be afraid of those who can kill the body, but cannot kill the life [*psyche*, 'soul', but within a Jewish context this should not be pressed into hellenistic dualism]. Fear, rather, the one who can destroy both life and body in Gehenna. [29]Are not two sparrows sold for a single coin? And one of them does not fall to the ground without your father. [30]As for you, the very hairs of your head are all numbered. [31]Do not be afraid, then; you are worth more than many sparrows.

> [Lk. 12][4]So I tell you, my friends, do not fear those who kill the body and after that have nothing more they can do. [5]I will show you who to fear. Fear the one who, after killing, has authority to cast into Gehenna. Yes, I tell you, fear him! [6]Are not five sparrows sold for two coins? And not one of them is forgotten before God. [7]But even the hairs of your head are all numbered. Do not be afraid. You are worth more than many sparrows.[94]

The only point in telling people not to be afraid of those who can kill the body is if there is a life to look forward to beyond bodily death. This is, of course, a summons to understand suffering and even martyrdom in the same way as, for instance, 2 Maccabees and the Wisdom of Solomon.[95] The passage that follows immediately in both gospels urges Jesus' followers to confess him without fear, so that he will confess them before god and his angels.[96] This, too, fits comfortably into the spectrum of second-Temple Jewish beliefs about the future, and coheres well with a belief in a future resurrection through which this vindication will take place.

The double tradition, too, has preserved a comment about Jesus' own work of raising the dead. Faced with a question from the imprisoned John the Baptist about whether Jesus really is 'the one who should come', Jesus responds by describing what he is doing:

---

[94] On the meaning of the passage see *JVG* 454f.
[95] See above, 150–53, 162–75. There is a superficial parallel in Mt. 10.28 to the position of 4 Macc. (above, 142f.).
[96] Mt. 10.32f./Lk. 12.8f.

The blind see, the lame walk, lepers are cleansed and the deaf hear, the dead are raised up and the poor have good news announced to them.[97]

As is often noted, this belongs closely with the messianic predictions of 4Q521.[98] The saying refers back, within Matthew, to the raising of Jairus' daughter (9.18–26), and within Luke to the raising of the widow's son at Nain (7.11–17). By itself this simply highlights the raising of the very recently dead as the most dramatic of the healing stories. Taken in conjunction with the other material in the gospels, it must have been heard in the early church not only as a sign within Jesus' ministry that he was indeed the Messiah but also as a pointer to the ultimate resurrection which the other texts had spoken of. With this we should perhaps couple the various texts, not least the beatitudes, that speak of a great reversal: for the hungry to be filled and the persecuted to inherit the kingdom, something dramatic must be about to happen. One might even suggest that, if mourners are to be comforted and weepers to laugh, this might be because the dead were to be given new life.[99]

The most complex and controversial of the relevant double-tradition passages is Jesus' cryptic word about the sign of Jonah:[100]

[Mt. 12][39]A wicked and adulterous generation looks for a sign, and no sign will be given it except the sign of the prophet Jonah. [40]For just as Jonah was in the belly of the monster three days and three nights, even so the son of man will be in the heart of the earth three days and three nights. [41]The men of Nineveh will arise (*anastesontai*) in the judgment with this generation and will condemn it. They repented at the preaching of Jonah, after all, and look, something greater than Jonah is here. [42]The queen of the south will arise (*egerthesetai*) in the judgment with this generation and condemn it; for she came from the ends of the earth to hear the wisdom of Solomon, and see, something greater than Solomon is here.

[Lk. 11][29]This generation is a wicked generation. It looks for a sign, and no sign will be given it except the sign of Jonah. [30]For just as Jonah was a sign to the people of Nineveh, so will the son of man be to this generation. [31]The queen of the south will arise (*egerthesetai*) in the judgment with the men of this generation and condemn them; for she came from the ends of the earth to hear the wisdom of Solomon, and see, something greater than Solomon is here. [32]The men of Nineveh will arise (*anastesontai*) in the judgment with this generation and condemn it; for they repented at the preaching of Jonah, and see, something greater than Jonah is here.

The first thing to notice here is the explicit resurrection-language used of the men of Nineveh and the queen of the south. Both versions underline Jesus' saying that they will 'arise at the judgment', as will the Israelites of Jesus'

---

[97] Mt. 11.5/Lk. 7.22, with virtually identical wording.

[98] See above, 186f.; and *JVG* 531f.

[99] Mt. 5.4; Lk. 6.21.

[100] A further mention of Jonah is found in Matt. 16.4, inserted by Matt. (so it seems) into his version of Mk. 8.11f. See Catchpole 1993, 244.

own generation. Their very presence will show that they are in the right and that Jesus' contemporaries are in the wrong. This, too, belongs firmly on the spectrum of second-Temple Jewish beliefs, with the exception that those Jews who predicted the future resurrection normally envisaged Israel judging the Gentiles, not vice versa. Here we have the same kind of reversal as that spoken of in the passage from Matthew 8 and Luke 13, but set within a classic Jewish scenario of future judgment along the lines of, say, Daniel 7.

This, I think, makes it more likely that Luke as well as Matthew intends 'the sign of Jonah' to be understood as the fact of Jesus' own resurrection. In Matthew it is clear: the only 'sign' that the present generation will receive is the sign which corresponds to that which Jonah embodied. Jonah emerged from the sea-monster after three days and three nights; the son of man will do the same from the heart of the earth, in other words, the grave. Most scholars have supposed, however, that this is Matthew's expansion of the earlier version, with the more cryptic Lukan passage being closer to the original; and that Luke understands the 'sign' being offered by Jesus as either his wisdom and preaching of repentance (as with Solomon and Jonah in Luke 11.31–2) or the fact of being given no sign at all, which in terms of Luke 11.16 may come to the same thing.[101] But it is certainly possible, in the light of the rest of the passage, that Luke, like Matthew, intends the resurrection of Jesus to be the 'sign' in question. I find oblique confirmation of this in the warning of Luke 16.31, which we shall study presently.[102]

The double tradition represented by Matthew and Luke is not, then, out on a limb from the other segments of early Christianity.[103] It is always possible, of course, for scholars carefully to extract a theme from what is already a hypothetical source (i.e. 'Q'), and to announce that they have thereby recovered an earlier version in which this theme was not known. There are, however, strong reasons in the history of early Christianity for doubting such a hypothesis in this case. The enormous pressure in some parts of the New Testament studies guild, particularly in North America, to come up with versions of early Christianity which know little and care less about the death and resurrection of Jesus, in order (dare one say) to legitimate similar movements today, or indeed to discredit movements which emphasize these things, should make us wary of hypotheses according to

---

[101] Catchpole 1993, 245–6, amplified in private correspondence. Catchpole has warned me that the history of interpretation of the present passage should discourage anyone from thinking they had finally unlocked all its secrets.

[102] A fuller argument, taking the 'son of man' material into account, is in Wright, 'Resurrection in Q?', 93–6; see too e.g. Edwards 1971, 56.

[103] More controversial is the saying found variously in e.g. Mt. 5.12/Lk. 6.23, and in some MSS of Lk. 6.35: 'your reward is great in heaven'. This, like Col. 1.5 and 1 Pet. 1.3–5 (see above, 238, and below, 465–7) has normally been taken to mean 'you will be rewarded when you go to heaven', but should, like them, be interpreted as 'God has a great reward in store for you', without prejudice as to the location in which this reward will be given.

which an early version of 'Q' provides evidence for that kind of movement.

It remains the case, of course, that 'Q' has no resurrection narrative, though if the document existed and was intended as a collection of Jesus' sayings there is no reason why it should have done.[104] Whole books exist of the collected wisdom of Abraham Lincoln, say, or Winston Churchill, from which one would glean little or nothing of what those gentlemen did, let alone how they met their respective ends; and while that example is of course manifestly anachronistic, it should alert us to the danger of over-compartmentalizing early Christianity. Matthew, after all, was able to accommodate 'Q' very readily within a theology in which resurrection plays an important part.[105] Not only can the double tradition not be used as evidence for a form of early Christianity which was uninterested in the resurrection; more positively, it provides evidence of early Christian traditions, and of sayings of Jesus himself, which fit firmly on the map of second-Temple Jewish expectations of resurrection. Within that, there is repeated emphasis on the future resurrection of god's people, and perhaps of everybody, in a way which cannot but be taken to designate new bodily life; and there is, in the passage about the sign of Jonah, plausible evidence that the resurrection of Jesus was seen as a new sign, corresponding to that of Jonah but going beyond it, which would retrospectively validate Jesus' prophetic and messianic ministry (that was the point of asking for a sign), and would also look ahead to the final judgment in which the expected roles of Jews and Gentiles might be reversed. If this is anywhere near the right interpretation, we have here evidence for something that points in the direction that Mark 9.9–10 mentioned cryptically and that Paul would later make far more explicit: a general resurrection that has divided into two, with Jesus being raised in advance as a sign of what would later happen to everyone else.

4. Resurrection in Matthew

We have already seen several instances in which Matthew, where he follows Mark or is in parallel with Luke, incorporates small but significant changes to the text. (I say 'incorporates' to leave it open whether Matthew added these or found them in a source now lost to us.) To these we may add the following passages, which complete the picture of 'resurrection' in Matthew (apart, of course, from the events he describes at the end of his gospel).

---

[104] In fact, it is logically possible, even if unlikely, that 'Q' did have a resurrection narrative which corresponds to what we now have in either Mt. or Lk., and that the other evangelist had access to another source which he preferred. We should never forget that 'Q' is simply a construct, and that as soon as we allow for one evangelist modifying it or preferring his own material we have opened a very wide door to all kinds of other possibilities.

[105] I owe this point to David Catchpole in private correspondence.

In Matthew's version of the mission charge to the disciples, Jesus instructs them not only to perform the same kind of healings of sickness that he is doing, but even to raise the dead (10.8). Though this is without parallel, it is of course cognate with the double-tradition passage in 11.5: it denotes the kind of 'raisings' of people recently dead which Jesus is reported to have done, like Elijah and Elisha. It may be a sign pointing to the greater resurrection to come, but at the moment it simply counts as the most remarkable sort of 'healing'.

One of the rare instances of an allusion to Daniel 12.3 (the righteous shining like stars) occurs in Matthew's parable-chapter, at 13.43. At the end of the great apocalyptic scene which constitutes the interpretation of the parable of the weeds of the field, Jesus declares that when the weeds have been thrown into the fire and the wheat gathered into the barn, then 'the righteous will shine like the sun in the kingdom of their father'. It is not an exact reference, since in Daniel the reference is to stars, not to the sun. But it may form a hint, within the complex world of intertextual echo which Matthew certainly knew how to exploit, that the kingdom spoken of in the parables would fulfil, among other promises, that of resurrection. If this is so, it reinforces the point that Matthew, like the other traditions we have studied, belongs at the same place as mainstream Pharisaic theology on the map of second-Temple Jewish belief.[106]

5. Resurrection in Luke

As with Matthew, we have already noted occasions when Luke adds his own slight variations to passages in either the triple or double tradition (recognizing always how difficult it is to be sure at what point variations have come in). But in his case there are several further signs, in addition to the Easter narrative itself, that he intended to weave the theme of resurrection into the fabric of his gospel.

This begins even in the birth and infancy narratives. When Joseph and Mary bring the baby Jesus to the Temple, Simeon first declares that this is the moment he has been waiting for, and then issues a solemn word to Mary in particular:

> [Lk. 2][34]Simeon blessed them, and said to Mary his mother, 'Look! This child is set for the fall and rising (*eis ptosin kai anastasin*) of many in Israel, and for a sign that

---

[106] Another part of the background to the idea of the righteous shining like the sun and exercising judgment is found in 2 Sam. 23.3f., with David's prediction of the righteous ruler, ruling in the fear of God, who is like the morning light at sunrise. See too the judgment which is invoked upon all YHWH's enemies after the defeat of Sisera: 'So let all your enemies perish, YHWH; but let those that love him be like the sun when it rises in strength' (Jdg. 5.31; cf. too Ps. 37.6; Mal. 4.1f.).

is spoken against [35](and a sword shall go through your heart also), so that the thoughts of many hearts may be revealed (*apokalyphthosin*).

This is a miniature judgment scene: the 'revealing' of people's inner thoughts is something that will happen either on the last day or in some great anticipation of it. Luke, knowing where his narrative will end, wants it to be seen that Jesus' death and resurrection will not occur as it were in a private capacity: his fate will determine that of Israel itself. The reader is to understand the growing opposition to Jesus, and Mary's distress at the direction of his life, as a sign that Israel is going through the great metaphorical 'fall and rising', bringing exile to its height and entering the new life beyond. This functions as a re-presentation of the metaphorical sense of 'resurrection' in Ezekiel 37 and elsewhere. Luke does not, of course, reduce the meaning of 'resurrection' to a metaphor for present events, but sees circles of meaning radiating out from the centre which is Jesus' own actual resurrection.

The other hint of resurrection in Luke's first two chapters is found in the story of the twelve-year-old Jesus being left behind in Jerusalem while Joseph and Mary go back to Galilee imagining he is somewhere in the large group of pilgrims.[107] As we shall see later, this superbly crafted story seems designed as a parallel, within the gospel's prologue, to the story of the disciples on the Emmaus road (24.13–35) within its conclusion. Luke intends the reader to understand the whole gospel, not just the final chapter, as the story of resurrection, so that when Easter actually happens there will be a rightness, an appropriateness, about it. It will not simply be a strange 'happy ending' tacked on to the end of a story about something else, but the god-given, scripture-fulfilling completion of what had been true all along.

Within this framework, Luke's gospel contains not only the numerous triple- and double-tradition passages mentioned already, with Luke's own rereading of them frequently prominent, but several passages where we can see the same thing happening as in Luke 2. Resurrection, for Luke, is not only the truth of what happened to Jesus, and the truth of what will happen to the righteous at the end. It is also a truth which comes to birth, anticipating those literal and concrete events, in other events which, though equally concrete, use the language of resurrection metaphorically. Luke has clearly not flattened out the ultimate future promise, as such passages as 14.14 and 18.7–8 indicate: there will be a 'resurrection of the righteous' at which otherwise unrewarded virtue will be repaid, and Israel's god will indeed vindicate his elect who cry to him day and night. But the most striking thing about Luke's special material is the way in which 'resurrection' becomes a metaphor for what is going on in the ministry of Jesus itself.

There is, of course, one example unique to Luke of an actual raising to life: the widow's son at Nain (7.11–17). Luke's interpretation of this is seen

---

[107] Lk. 2.41–52. See 650f. below.

not least in the crowd's reaction (verse 16): 'a great prophet has arisen among us; god has visited his people.' The theme of 'visitation', already occurring in 1.68, reappears in 19.44, where the ambiguity of 2.34 becomes clear: this 'visitation' will result in the fall, as well as the rising again, of many in Israel. This ties in the raising of the young man at Nain with the three parables in which the theme appears. In the parable of the good Samaritan, the Israelite in the ditch is half dead, and the Samaritan restores him; the multiple resonances of the parable within Jesus' ministry are important, but not for our present concern.[108] The parable of the prodigal son emphasizes twice that this is a story of resurrection: 'this my son was dead and is alive again, was lost and is found', followed by 'this your brother was dead and is alive again, was lost and is found'.[109] This *metaphorical* use of resurrection, we note, has in Luke a clear *concrete* referent: Jesus is receiving sinners and eating with them, and, as far as these sinners go, this is a dramatic and vivid form of 'life from the dead', a real return from exile, in the here and now.[110] The future resurrection of Jesus himself, and of all god's people, is coming forwards into the present in the person, and through the public ministry, of Jesus. This metaphorical use, here of all places, is in line with Ezekiel 37, which speaks of that return from exile for which, as I have argued elsewhere, the prodigal son is a vivid image.[111]

This theme becomes most explicit in the striking conclusion of the parable of the rich man and Lazarus. 'If they do not believe Moses and the prophets, neither will they believe even if someone were to rise from the dead' (16.31). This statement looks on to the eventual resurrection of Jesus himself, warning that those who have not believed the scriptures will not be convinced by such an event, and thus foreshadowing the risen Jesus' insistence that the meaning of the resurrection is to be found in the scriptures.[112] It also looks at the present context in the ministry of Jesus, where, as the great parable of the previous chapter had made clear, 'resurrection' was already happening, even if the 'older brothers', the scribes and Pharisees who were looking on as Jesus was welcoming sinners and eating with them, could not see that he was embodying the spectacular welcome of the father for the prodigal son, and was thus celebrating 'resurrection' in something like the metaphorical sense it had had in the scriptures.[113]

I stressed in the earlier volume that the parable of the rich man and Lazarus is to be treated precisely as a parable, not as a literal description of

---

[108] Lk. 10.30–37; cf. *JVG* 305–07.

[109] Lk. 15.24, 32.

[110] Lk. 15.1f.

[111] *JVG* 126–9.

[112] Lk. 24.25–7, 44–7.

[113] Evans 1970, 32f. thus misses the point when he says that the idea of Lazarus going back from the dead to speak to the rich man's brothers is not the kind of thing you find in the normal Jewish view. This is true, but irrelevant to the purposes of the parable.

the afterlife and its possibilities.[114] It is therefore inappropriate to use it as *prima facie* evidence for Jesus' own sketching (or Luke's portrait of Jesus' sketching) of a standard post-mortem scenario. It is, rather, an adaptation of a well-known folk-tale, projecting the rich/poor divide of the present on to the future in order to highlight the present responsibility, and culpability, of the careless rich. However, while the parabolic nature of the story prevents us from treating it as Jesus' own description of how the afterlife is organized, it does not prevent us from saying that for Jesus himself, and/or for those who handed on the tradition, this story indicates, in standard Jewish style, a clear belief in continuity between the present life and the future one. As it stands it is impossible to say whether it belongs with the 'resurrection' strand in second-Temple Judaism, or with a 'disembodied immortality' strand; the possibility is envisaged that Lazarus might return from the dead, but Abraham forbids that it should happen. It does, however, highlight one of the many metaphors current in Judaism for the abode of the blessed, either in perpetuity or prior to their possible rising again: Lazarus has gone to 'Abraham's bosom'.[115] Luke's intention in placing the story here (soon after the 'inaugurated eschatology' of 15.24, 32, and soon before the apocalyptic warnings of 17.22–37) is at least clear: things done and decided in the present are to be seen in the light of the promised future. 'Resurrection' is coming forwards into the present in Jesus' ministry, but those who cannot see it and reorder their lives accordingly are in danger of losing all. Significantly, this message of resurrection is clearly linked to the call for justice, which remains a closely related theme throughout early Christianity. This, we may suppose, was exactly the kind of thing that would put the average Sadducee right off the whole idea.[116]

Luke's distinctive contribution, though striking, does not take him outside the general frame we have seen for the synoptic understanding of the resurrection. All three synoptic evangelists are clear that the forthcoming resurrection of Jesus himself is the critical moment towards which his kingdom-announcement, and its embodiment in the symbolic actions which characterized his ministry, were pointing. They are also clear that his challenge to his followers involved both the call, in the present, to find one's life by losing it, and the promise, for the future, of a new world in which they would have new roles. Future resurrection, in other words, is closely linked to the dying to self which must take place in the present. And they all report occasions when Jesus actually raises to life someone who has very recently died, not only as a dramatic instance of healing power but also as a signpost towards what god will do for Jesus.

---

[114] *JVG* 255f. It is similarly difficult to build much on the famous 23.43; 'Paradise' could well indicate a temporary resting place rather than a permanent destination.

[115] For other occurrences of this theme cf. SB 2.225–7. For the patriarchs welcoming those who have died righteously cf. e.g. 4 Macc. 13.17 (142 above).

[116] See above, 137–40.

The contribution of the synoptic tradition to our present investigation (apart from the resurrection narratives themselves) may therefore be summarized as follows. At one level, it provides significant further evidence for ways in which death, and life beyond it, were being understood within second-Temple Judaism. At another, it provides at least some evidence of what Jesus himself said and thought about the subject. At yet another – and this is the reason for including the material here – it provides evidence for the way in which some strands, probably several different strands, of early Christianity thought about death and life beyond. In other words, it offers a variegated and complex picture of the way in which Christians roughly contemporary with Paul told stories about Jesus and what he had said and done, giving them shape and, ultimately, literary settings in which certain implications could be seen clearly.

Before leaving the synoptic tradition we may draw together its important, though limited, contribution to our wider discussion in terms of the questions we set out earlier. 'Resurrection' here clearly refers to bodily rising again, both of Jesus himself and of his followers. There is the possibility of an intermediate state, but it is not often mentioned. There are signs that this resurrection will be a subtly different sort of thing to that envisaged in mainstream Judaism, in that 'the rising from the dead' seems to be split into two separate events (Jesus first, others later), and in that the resurrection life will be one in which marriage and childbearing will be a thing of the past. 'Resurrection' language functions metaphorically for events within Jesus' ministry, not least his welcome of sinners; this seems to be a refocusing of the Jewish traditions in which 'resurrection' was metaphor, as well as metonymy, for the restoration of Israel.

All this can hardly be explained as a clever set of retrojections from Pauline theology into the traditions of Jesus' teaching and ministry. The relative scarcity of the material, contrasting sharply with the strong and central emphasis on resurrection throughout the early church, makes it look all the more as though the Christians had not, at least in this area, placed on the lips of Jesus material which belonged instead to their own day.[117] The passages in question appear to reflect similar, though not always identical, emphases, which have their own life in the ongoing tradition of the early church. They provide evidence that, across a fair spread of early Christian tradition, belief in resurrection was common Christian coin, belonging (on the spectrum of the history of religions) within Judaism, and (with Judaism itself) as a near neighbour of Pharisaism. There are signs that this Jewish belief, in being thus reinforced, was also being reshaped, just a little, by the *teaching* of Jesus, as well as the events in which he was involved.

---

[117] For other instances of the same phenomenon cf. *NTPG* 421f.

6. Resurrection in John

John's gospel, so very different from the others, resembles them (and also Paul) in this respect: it too bears witness to the centrality and rich variety of 'resurrection' ideas in a separate strand of early Christianity. Like Luke, but in his own distinctive way, John has allowed 'resurrection' themes to be heard at several points in the body of his gospel, and we shall look at them in more detail when considering his Easter stories in chapter 17. The new life which will be consummated in the resurrection itself works backwards into the present, and is already doing so in the ministry of Jesus.[118]

The large-scale outworking of this can be seen in John's deliberate sequence of 'signs'. Though this is controversial, I believe that John intends his readers to follow a sequence of seven signs, with the water-into-wine story at Cana as the first and the crucifixion as the seventh.[119] The resurrection of Jesus takes place, he is careful to tell us twice, 'on the first day of the week', and I believe this is best interpreted as the start of god's new creation. On the Friday, the sixth day of the week, Jesus stands before Pilate, who declares 'behold, the man!' (19.5), echoing the creation of humankind on the sixth day of creation. On the cross Jesus finishes the work the father has given him to do (17.4), ending with the shout of triumph (*tetelestai*, 'it is accomplished', 19.30), corresponding to the completion of creation itself.[120] There follows, as in Genesis, a day of rest, a sabbath day (19.31); and then, while it is yet dark, Mary Magdalene comes to the tomb 'on the first day of the week'. We shall pick up the story at that point in chapter 17 below, but for our present purposes we note the powerful implication for a reading of John's gospel: that Jesus' public career is to be understood as the completion of the original creation, with the resurrection as the start of the new. The whole gospel is a kind of preparation for Easter, with signs of resurrection to be expected at several points.

The first of the signs, indeed, carries its own hint: the wedding at Cana took place 'on the third day', which cannot but have contained powerful echoes for any early Christian reader. Later on in the same chapter John erects another signpost pointing the same way: Jesus explains his dramatic action in the Temple with what the bystanders take to be a prediction of its destruction and rebuilding (a saying that emerges in the night hearing before the Sanhedrin, and in the mocking at the cross, within the synoptic tradition): 'destroy this Temple, and I will raise it up (*egero auton*) in three days.'[121] There then follows what John's readers come to recognize as a typical misunderstanding and interpretation:

[118] For this theme cf. e.g Lincoln 1998, with other bibliog.

[119] See below, ch. 17.

[120] cf. Gen. 2.1–2, where *synteleo* is used twice for the completion of the original creation on the sixth day before God rests on the seventh.

[121] Jn. 2.19; cf. Mk. 14.58/Mt. 26.61/; Mk. 15.29/Mt. 27.40.

[Jn. 2][20]The Judaeans then said to him, 'It has taken forty-six years to build this Temple, and will you raise it up in three days?' [21]But he was speaking of the 'temple' of his body. [22]When therefore Jesus was raised from the dead, his disciples remembered that he had said this, and they believed the scripture and the word which Jesus had spoken.

This should already be enough to scotch the old rumour that John's theology was complete with Jesus' life and death, and did not really need to have Jesus rise bodily from the dead.[122] John's Jesus is here saying that the resurrection will be the ultimate sign that demonstrates both his right to do what he has done and the meaning he gives to it. The present Temple system is corrupt and under divine judgment; Jesus' own death and resurrection will be the means of the true god doing the new thing through which, as much of the gospel will make clear, that which was hitherto accomplished through the Temple would from now on be accomplished through Jesus himself. The resurrection will inaugurate a new world in which Temple-worship will be thrown open in a new way to all and sundry, irrespective of geography and ethnic background.[123] As the chief priests quickly realized after the raising of Lazarus, Jesus' actions were indeed pointing towards a future in which everything would be changed, and in which the Temple in particular would be 'taken away'.[124] John is already indicating to his readers that Jesus' resurrection has indeed opened up the long-promised new world (hence, as in Luke, the importance of 'believing the scripture' as part of appropriating the significance of Easter) in which the long-awaited divine blessing would go out to all peoples. With that, we are not far from the belief of Paul, though to be sure in a very different mood and tone.

Resurrection in John continues to be both present and future, and we should resist attempts to flatten this out by marginalizing the 'future' emphasis or overemphasizing the 'realized eschatology'. It is of course true for John, as for Paul, that 'eternal life' is not simply future, but already to be enjoyed in the present.[125] Some of the most striking statements of this anywhere in early Christianity are found in the discourse about the bread of life; but they are interspersed with, and cannot be separated out from, promises about the ultimate future as well:

---

[122] e.g. Evans 1970, 116 (followed by Selby 1976, 117): 'Strictly speaking, there is no place in the Fourth Gospel for resurrection stories, since the ascent or exaltation has already taken place. Nevertheless, and doubtless in deference to Christian tradition, the evangelist supplies three [resurrection stories] . . . ' Also 120 (the 'massive realism' of the appearances is surprising in contrast to the preceding interpretation of resurrection as 'spiritual ascent to the Father'). Jn. 20.17 offers a fairly conclusive refutation of this line of thought. See too Mencken 2002, 198–204, tracing this view back to Dodd 1953, 441f.

[123] cf. e.g. Jn. 4.19–24; and the fulfilment, in Jn., of the various festivals (Passover: here, in ch. 6, and in chs. 12—19; Tabernacles, in ch. 7; Hanukkah, in ch. 10).

[124] Jn. 11.45–53.

[125] Jn. 3.15f., 36; 4.14, 26; 5.39; 6.27, 40, 47, 54, 68; 10.28; 12.25, 50; 17.2f.

[Jn. 6]³⁹This is the will of the one who sent me, that I should lose nothing of everything that he has given me, but that I should raise it up at the last day. ⁴⁰For this is the will of my father, that everyone who sees the son and believes in him should have eternal life, and I will raise that one up on the last day . . .

⁴⁴No one can come to me unless the father who sent me draws them; and I will raise them up on the last day . . .

⁵⁰This is the bread which comes down from heaven, so that people may eat of it and not die. ⁵¹I am the living bread which came down from heaven; if anyone eats of this bread, they will live for ever (*eis ton aiona*, i.e. into the age to come); and the bread which I shall give is my flesh, for the life of the world . . .

⁵⁴Those who eat my flesh and drink my blood have eternal life, and I will raise them up on the last day.

This effortlessly and seamlessly combines what some scholars have tried to prise apart, namely the future and present meanings of 'resurrection'. In this light it would be wrong to see the famous passage in chapter 5 as an irruption of a different kind of 'resurrection' to what we find elsewhere in John:

[Jn. 5]²⁴Truly, truly, I say to you, those who hear my word and believe in the one who sent me have eternal life; they do not come into judgment but have passed from death to life. ²⁵Truly, truly I say to you, that the hour is coming, and is now here, when the dead will hear the voice of the son of God, and those who hear it will live. ²⁶For just as the father has life in himself, so he has granted to the son that he too should have life in himself. ²⁷And he has given him authority to exercise judgment, because he is the son of man. ²⁸Do not be surprised at this; for the hour is coming in which all who are in the tombs will hear his voice, ²⁹and will come out: those who have done good, to the resurrection of life, and those who have done evil, to the resurrection of judgment.

It is safe to say that if we met this passage in one of the Pseudepigrapha, we should have no trouble lining it up more or less exactly with many other passages which predict the final resurrection, noting as we did so that it belongs with those who see the wicked being raised along with the righteous, so that they may be condemned in their full human existence rather than simply fading away without having to be confronted with their own wickedness.¹²⁶ Here too, however, the note of present, albeit partial, fulfilment is heard: in verse 24, those who believe have already passed from death to life, and in verse 25 the hour is coming 'and now is'.¹²⁷ But this does not permit us to collapse the promise of future resurrection which follows immediately into the metaphorical meaning of the events taking place during Jesus' ministry.

---

¹²⁶ For the resurrection of both righteous and wicked cf. Dan. 12.2; *2 Bar.* 50.2–4; *4 Ezra* 7.32; *1 En.* 51.1f.; mAb. 4.22; in the NT, alongside this passage, Ac. 24.15; Rev. 20.12f. Some cite 2 Cor. 5.10 here as well, but this seems to me rather to refer (like Rom. 2.1–16) to a final judgment, consequent upon which the righteous will be given resurrection life. For resurrection of only the righteous (the view, it seems, of Paul, in the classic passages from Rom., 1 and 2 Cor., Phil. and 1 Thess.) cf. 2 Macc. 7.9; *Ps. Sol.* 3.12; Lk. 14.14; *Did.* 16.7; Ign. *Trall.* 9.2; Pol. *Phil.* 2.2.

¹²⁷ This phrase is missing in Codex Sinaiticus and a couple of early Latin MSS.

Rather, it shows that those still-future events are casting their light before them, so that the reactions of people to Jesus, in belief or unbelief, are true present signs of their future fate. At this point John is very close to Paul. Indeed, the sentence before last, describing John's inaugurated eschatology is very near to Paul's doctrine of justification by faith.

The story of the raising of Lazarus in John 11 is of course one of the most powerful narratives in the canonical portrayals of Jesus.[128] Told with a constant eye on the deep human emotions embedded in the story, it is equally full of theological importance. Lazarus, of course, comes back from death into the sort of life he had before, resuming ordinary activities such as sharing in a dinner party (12.2). He even finds himself facing death threats because of his evidential value in relation to the power of Jesus (12.9–11).

The story opens with a message coming to Jesus about Lazarus being ill, whereupon Jesus deliberately stays where he is rather than coming to help (11.1–6). As later becomes clear (11.41–2), John intends the reader to understand that Jesus knew from the start that Lazarus would die and that, in answer to prayer, he would be able to raise him up again. This then becomes a vivid concretization of the promises in chapters 5 and 6 (with the proviso that Lazarus will remain mortal and will one day die again). When Jesus talks to the disciples about going back to Judaea, and specifically to Bethany, he tells them that Lazarus has 'fallen asleep', but that he is going to 'wake him up'. The disciples' reaction, taking 'sleep' literally, shows that for John at least, as for Mark in the story of Jairus' daughter, this was not so habitual a metaphor for death as to leave no room for explanation.[129]

When Jesus arrives at Bethany, it is already the fourth day that Lazarus has been in the tomb. This is stressed twice (11.17, 39). By all normal expectations, the corpse would by now have begun to decay, and this provides a key dynamic element running through the story. When, despite Martha's warning about the smell (verse 39), the stone is rolled away from the mouth of the tomb (John here points forwards to the final Easter story), Jesus at once offers a prayer of thanksgiving (verse 41). Presumably John wants us to understand that *there was no smell*; Jesus knows his prayer, for Lazarus to remain uncorrupt, has been answered. It is then simply a matter of summoning him out, untying him and releasing him back into normal life. In so far, then, as this points forwards to chapter 20, it does so with significant differences as well as parallels. Nobody needed to untie the graveclothes from Jesus' body, and several other things happen to show that, whatever Jesus' own resurrection means, it is of a very different order from

---

[128] The earlier story of the nobleman's son (Jn. 4.46–54) has some analogies with the synoptic story of Jairus' daughter, and its emphasis on the fact that the boy is about to die but 'will live' (vv. 47, 49, 50, 51, 53) points to the theme of which the Lazarus story is the fullest statement.

[129] Jn. 11.11–16.

that of Lazarus. John intends the reader to see this incident as a signpost, but only a signpost, of what is to come.

This sense of Jesus' action in Bethany pointing ahead, yet also bringing the achievement of the future suddenly into the present, enables us to understand the dialogue upon which the chapter turns:

> [Jn. 11]²¹Martha said to Jesus, 'Lord, if you had been here, my brother would not have died. ²²But even now I know that God will give you whatever you ask him.' ²³'Your brother', said Jesus to her, 'will rise again.' ²⁴'I know he will rise again,' said Martha, 'in the resurrection on the last day.' ²⁵'I am the resurrection and the life,' said Jesus to her. 'The one who believes in me, even if he dies, will live; ²⁶and whoever lives and believes in me, will never, ever die (*eis ton aiona*, i.e. unto the age to come). Do you believe this?' ²⁷'Yes, Lord,' she replied, 'I have believed that you are the Messiah, the son of God, the one who is coming into the world.'

The future resurrection is clearly affirmed; present, undying 'eternal life' is available, anticipating that resurrection, for all who believe. Those who believe are given a real, new identity in the present, a life which now will never die; in other words (drawing on the way John puts it elsewhere), the believer now possesses, already, a divinely given immortal life which will survive death and be re-embodied in the final resurrection. This is John's fullest answer to the set of questions we raised about first-century resurrection beliefs. Though it corresponds in several ways to what we have found in Paul and the synoptics, the way it is expressed remains peculiarly John's. Future resurrection is certain, but the way to it is spelled out more fully, and with different language. 'Resurrection' as a metaphor for something that takes place in the present has to do with the confession of faith in Jesus as the Messiah, the one whom the true god has sent, and with the possession already of the 'life of the age to come' of which that faith is the evidentiary badge. Jesus can thus be spoken of as being himself 'the resurrection', meaning both that through his present work people like Lazarus may be raised to resume normal bodily life, and that those who believe in him already have the life of the age to come, and also that through him, not least through his own forthcoming resurrection, 'the resurrection of the dead', in the sense described in chapter 5, will yet take place.

There then follows, in Jesus' final moment of public ministry in Jerusalem, a saying which resonates both with the synoptic challenges to a discipleship in which life itself is put at risk and with the Pauline analysis of the resurrection body:

> [Jn.12]²³Jesus answered them, 'The hour has come for the son of man to be glorified. ²⁴Truly, truly I tell you, unless a grain of wheat falls into the earth and dies, it remains alone; but if it dies, it bears much fruit. ²⁵Those who love their life will lose it, and those who hate their life in this world will keep it for the life of the age to come (*eis zoen aionion*, 'for eternal life'). ²⁶Whoever serves me must follow me; and where I am, there shall my servant be. Anyone who serves me will be honoured by the father.'

This draws the previous theology into a challenge: to follow Jesus in the path he now must tread, the path for which the best analogy is the death, and fruitbearing new life, of a grain of wheat.[130] This passage looks back to the various previous references in John's gospel to the 'hour' that was to come, which the reader now understands to be arriving in the events of Jesus' death and resurrection; and it looks on to the post-resurrection challenge to Peter to follow Jesus, even though it will mean his own death.[131] There is here that multiple meaning of resurrection which we have seen elsewhere. First, it will mean a transformation, as the seed into the plant. Second, it is something which Jesus must undergo first, and his followers later. Third, through this process not only will the person or people concerned be rescued from death into a new life, but they will 'bear much fruit'. It is significant, and points to another parallel with Pauline thought, that this discourse is given in response to a request from some Greeks to see Jesus (12.20–22). We are not told that Jesus ever spoke to the Greeks in question; rather, he understood their request as a sign that the time was rapidly approaching, and had now arrived, when through his own death and resurrection the whole world, not merely Israel, would come under the saving rule of Israel's god.

This leads us to the Farewell Discourses of chapters 13—17, with all their rich and dense texture of teaching, warning and promise. Jesus is 'going away', he tells them repeatedly; he is now 'going to the father'.[132] It is this that has given rise, it seems, to the widely held view that according to John the death and resurrection of Jesus are simply to be understood as a process of, so to speak, 'going to heaven', and that therefore the rather full and explicitly embodied resurrection appearances are strictly unnecessary.[133] But this misses the point. In John 20 an explicit distinction is drawn between the resurrection life Jesus already possesses and the 'going up to the father' which has not yet happened (20.17). Here the complete sequence is in view, because Jesus is preparing the disciples for the final state in which he will no longer be personally present in the same way as he has been up to now (and will be, fleetingly, after his resurrection). Hence the emphasis on the Spirit who will be sent to make Jesus' presence known in a new way, with all that that will mean in terms of guidance and teaching.

This, I believe, is the best way to understand the passage about the 'dwelling-places' prepared for the disciples:

> [14.2]In my father's house are many dwelling-places. If it were not so, would I have told you that I was going to prepare a place for you? [3]And if I go and prepare a place for you, I will come back and take you to myself, so that you may be where I am.

---

[130] cf. 1 Cor. 15.36f. For the idea of God 'honouring' martyrs cf. 4 Macc. 17.20.

[131] Jn. 21.19, 22. On the 'hour' cf. 2.4; 4.21, 23; 5.25, 28; 7.30; 8.20; and, after the present passage, 12.27; 13.1; 16.32; 17.1.

[132] Jn. 13.1, 3, 33, 36; 14.12, 28; 16.5–7, 16–22, 28; 17.11, 13.

[133] Evans 1970 (see above, 441).

Other references to 'my father's house' clearly refer to the Temple, and it is likely (not least since Jews characteristically thought of the Temple as the place where heaven and earth met) that Jesus is using the image of the many apartments in the large Temple complex as a picture of the many 'rooms' which will be provided in the heavenly world for which the Temple is both the earthly counterpart and the point of intersection.[134] The word here for 'dwelling-place' is *mone*, which is cognate with the word *meno*, 'abide', a frequent and powerful Johannine word which encapsulates the notion of the believer making his or her place of abode in or with Jesus.[135] The normal meaning of *mone*, though, is of the temporary resting-place, or way-station, where a traveller would be refreshed during a journey. Some commentators, trying to bring out that meaning, have suggested that the word here denotes a sense of progress, not merely repose, in the life to come, but without seeing that the natural parallels in Jewish apocalyptic writing are those passages which speak of the chambers in which the souls are kept against the day of eventual resurrection.[136] The 'dwelling-places' of this passage are thus best understood as safe places where those who have died may lodge and rest, like pilgrims in the Temple, not so much in the course of an onward pilgrimage within the life of a disembodied 'heaven', but while awaiting the resurrection which is still to come.

This brings us to the promise which, with hindsight, can be taken as a more specific reference to Easter:

[Jn. 16][20]'Truly, truly I say to you, You will weep and mourn, but the world will rejoice. You will be sorrowful, but your sorrow will turn to joy. [21]A woman has sorrow when she gives birth, because her hour has come; but when the child is born, she no longer remembers the sorrow, for joy that a human being is born into the world. [22]And you therefore now have sorrow; but I shall see you again, and your heart will rejoice, and no one will take your joy from you.'

This seems clearly to be fulfilled in the Easter narratives (20.20). The promise that they will 'see' Jesus again (16.16–19, which this passage explains) is scarcely a reference simply to the coming of the Spirit; nowhere else is that promise spoken of in terms of 'seeing' the Lord. We seem to be hearing two or three things (which John will later separate out) run together into one

---

[134] 'My father's house': cf. Lk. 2.49; Jn. 2.16. Philo *Som.* 1.256 uses 'the father's house' to refer to heaven; 1 Macc. 7.38 refers to a *mone* with apparent reference to a place to live within the Temple (the NRSV 'let them live no longer' is an interpretative paraphrase of the Greek *me dos autois monen*, 'do not give them a dwelling-place').

[135] e.g. 1.38f.; 4.40; 6.56; 8.31, 35; 14.10; 15.4–10.

[136] Progress: e.g. Westcott 1903, 200; denied by e.g. Barrett 1978 [1955], 456f. Barrett notes *1 En.* 39.4 and *2 En.* 61.2 as references to dwelling-places, without seeing that in the passage in *1 En.*, as in e.g. *1 En.* 1.8; 22.1–14; 102.4f.; 4 Ezr. 4.35, 41; 7.32; *2 Bar.* 30.1f. (see above, 154f., 160, 161), the 'chambers' are where the righteous souls are stored until the day of resurrection. For the meaning of *mone* as temporary lodging, cf. e.g. Chariton 1.12.1; Paus. 10.31.7; *OGI* 527.5 (an inscription from Hierapolis).

compact set of promises for the benefit of the disciples. Within John's own theology, it is of course important, as an overarching reality, that Jesus has now gone to the father and has sent the Spirit on his followers, on all who believe in him. But within that it is also important that with the resurrection, and the disciples' seeing of Jesus again after his death, the new creation has dawned, the eighth 'day' of god's creation has arrived, and everything is now to be made new. New creation is, for John, exactly that: new *creation*, the renewal of the 'all things' which were made by the Word in the first place (1.3). Easter is the time when the true light shines in the darkness and cannot be quenched (1.5, cf. 20.1), because 'in him was life' (1.4, cf. 5.26).

From the Prologue onwards, in other words, John has been putting down markers on a road of which Easter, not some 'going to heaven after death', is the intended destination. The life Jesus now has with the father, sending the Spirit to share the inner life of father and son with the disciples (17.20–24), is the life from within which he will in due time accomplish that with which the father has already entrusted him, namely, raising the dead to new life (5.25–9).[137] This, too, is similar to Paul's picture of the future. It is a rich, many-sided set of promises, which cannot be flattened out into a spiritualized 'realized eschatology', or a Platonized expectation of immortality, but remains firmly within the boundaries of Jewish resurrection-theology and within the early Christian parameters of the redefinition of that theology around Jesus himself.

John, in fact, provides a strong and striking further witness, alongside Paul and the synoptic tradition, for the centrality of 'resurrection' within the life and traditions of the early church. Whatever we say about the historical value of his gospel – and that has not been our theme here – we must affirm that the traditions to which John fell heir, and the way in which he shaped and presented them, maintain the position of early Christian resurrection-belief at the Jewish end of the spectrum of beliefs in the ancient world; and, within Judaism, maintain the Pharisaic view of bodily resurrection while giving it considerable nuance and colour. 'Resurrection' is never, for John, simply a metaphor for present spiritual life, though its wider levels of meaning certainly include that. When Jesus says 'I am the resurrection and the life' he opens up several layers of redefinition: a new life through which new possibilities are available in the present. The 'life of the age to come' is brought forward into the present, so that believers can enjoy it already and be assured that it will last through bodily death into god's future; 'eternal life' becomes, as it were, another way of speaking about an intermediate state as well as the final one. The promise of eventual resurrection itself is

---

[137] The idea of Jesus raising the dead is very rare in earliest Christianity. It comes to flower in the long iconographic tradition in which Jesus raises Adam and Eve from the grave. This tradition, mostly associated with the East, nevertheless spread widely enough to include an Anglo-Saxon sculpture in Bristol Cathedral.

reaffirmed. And Jesus is identified as the one around whom all these redefinitions occur. With John, as with Paul and the synoptics, the historian faces the question: why did he put it like this? What belief did he hold that can provide a satisfactory explanation for both his reaffirmation and his reshaping of the Jewish tradition?

7. Resurrection in the Gospels: Conclusion

Bracket out the Easter narratives from the four gospels, then, and what do we find on the subject of resurrection? A wide variety of hints and pointers, spread right across all possible ways of analysing the early traditions, which speak of resurrection – Jesus' own resurrection, and that of all his people – as the promised future. We have looked at the differing emphases and passages in the different writers and traditions, but in summary we can easily put them back together again. When we place the entire gospel tradition on the map of life-after-death beliefs we sketched in chapters 2—4, it is obvious that, as we just said about John, they belong with the Jewish view over against the pagan one; and, within the Jewish view, with the Pharisees (and others who agreed with them) over against the various other options.

However, we not only find a significantly higher incidence of resurrection as a theme, by comparison even with those second-Temple writers who are enthusiasts for it. That would itself call for comment. We also find a development and redefinition of it, not too different (though usually expressed in other ways) from what we found in Paul. 'Resurrection' still means, in the last analysis, god's gift of new bodily life to all his people at the end (and, in the case of John 5, new bodily life even for those who are raised in order to hear their own doom).[138] But it can also be used, in a manner cognate with the development of metaphorical uses in Judaism, to denote the restoration of god's people in the present time, as for instance in the dramatic double summary of the prodigal son's being 'dead and alive again' in Luke 15. This is then dramatically acted out in the 'raisings' of people from death, that of Lazarus being obviously the most striking.

We find, more specifically, the same two features which stood out in Paul. First, there is a repeated sense that 'the resurrection' has split into two, in a way which the disciples found incomprehensible during Jesus' lifetime but which they came to understand thereafter as they reflected on Easter itself not least in the light of the scriptures. Second, we find that, though Jesus did in each of the gospels bring back to life someone who had recently died, 'resurrection' as a notion is continually being stretched so that it does not simply mean a return to the same kind of bodily life that people have had up to now. The final future life will be significantly different; those who

---

[138] See above, 442. This marks a major difference between John and Paul.

share in it will, unlike Lazarus and the others, have left death behind altogether. What sort of body they will have the gospels do not attempt to elucidate. But it is surely significant that the image Paul uses as he begins his answer to that question not only occurs at the point where, in John, Jesus is facing the fact that 'the hour' has now come. It also occurs within the first and most important parable in the synoptic gospels. Though we have not here explored it, the parable of the sower, read in the light of the Easter stories, may turn out, at least for its later hearers, to be a picture not simply of Jesus sowing the word which is the gospel, but of the god of Israel sowing the word which is Jesus.[139]

With Paul and the gospels we may claim to have covered a large part of the early Christian territory that is known to us. But we must now look at two other areas, to complete the picture. First, we must examine the rest of the New Testament. Then we must turn our attention to the vibrant and many-sided witness of those who carried the message forward through the turbulent second century.

---

[139] On the 'sower' (Mt. 13.1–9/Mk. 4.1–9/Lk. 8.4–8/*Thom* 9) cf. *JVG* 230–39.

Chapter Ten

HOPE REFOCUSED (2): OTHER NEW TESTAMENT WRITINGS

1. Introduction

We have now surveyed roughly two-thirds of the material in the New Testament. We have found, representing several significant strands of early Christianity, (1) a belief in the future resurrection which matches that of the Pharisees (and which, like theirs, implies some kind of intermediate state); (2) a much more frequent reference to this than in the surrounding Jewish material; (3) two variations on the Jewish theme, namely the belief that 'the resurrection' had been anticipated in the case of Jesus, and would be completed for all his people, and the belief that this resurrection was not simply a resuscitation into the same kind of life but rather a going through death and out into a new sort of life beyond, into a body that was no longer susceptible to decay and death; (4) a fresh use of 'resurrection' as a metaphor for the restoration of God's people, referring now not to the restoration of Israel after exile, but to the new life, including holiness and worship, which people could enjoy in the present. These striking findings must now be tested against the rest of the New Testament material.

Much of what remains is of course related to what we have already studied. The longest of the books, Acts, is by common consent the work of the same writer as Luke's gospel. The Johannine epistles and Revelation, though presenting all sorts of problems, stand in some kind of family relationship with the fourth gospel. Fortunately the critical problems are not acute for our study, since the main purpose of this chapter is to survey the material not in order to place it in a historical sequence or development but to assess its view on the future hope beyond death (as with the earlier chapters on paganism and Judaism) and the relation of this to what happened to Jesus. From this point of view it does not much matter if the books remaining to be examined were written early or late, by the traditional authors or by someone else. What matters is what they say about resurrection.

We begin with Acts, as being most obviously cognate to the gospel material we have been looking at in the previous chapter; and we omit Acts 1.1–14, since it contains a final resurrection appearance and so must be dealt with alongside the others in chapter 15 below.

2. Acts

Acts offers a rich variety of material on the resurrection.[1] There is never any question what the author believes about the final destiny of God's people: there will be a great day of judgment, at which Jesus, having himself been raised from the dead, will be the judge. At that time, all those who have believed in Jesus will be vindicated:

> [10.40]God raised him on the third day, and permitted him to appear, [41]not to all the people, but to witnesses chosen beforehand by God, namely ourselves, who ate and drank with him after he had been raised from the dead (*meta to anastenai auton ek nekron*). [42]He commanded us to announce to the people, and bear witness, that he is the one marked out by God as judge of the living and the dead. [43]All the prophets bear witness to him, that through his name all who believe in him will receive forgiveness of sins.

> [17.30]God overlooked the times of ignorance, but now he commands everyone everywhere to repent, [31]because he has established a day on which he will judge the world in righteousness by a man whom he has designated; and he has provided assurance of this to everyone, by raising him from the dead.

This 'designation', this 'marking out' of Jesus as the coming judge, is close to what Paul says in Romans 1.4: Jesus is 'marked out' as 'son of God' (i.e. as Messiah, which includes his role of judgment) by the resurrection from the dead.[2] And the judgment which lies in the future is anticipated in the present when people believe in Jesus and so receive, at long last, the promised 'forgiveness of sins'. This, in the following contexts, clearly carries the 'new covenant' overtones we have seen in earlier passages. The 'forgiveness' in question is not just the quieting of individual troubled consciences, but the large-scale 'forgiveness' which Israel had been promised, the moment when the sins which caused the long punishment of exile would be done away:[3]

> [5.31]God exalted him to his right hand as leader and saviour, so that he might give repentance to Israel, and forgiveness of sins.

---

[1] In addition to the commentaries see recently Green 1998. We have of course already studied the narratives of Paul's conversion in ch. 8 above. The probability that Acts, though written quite late, preserves much older tradition is stressed by Michaud 2001, 113, citing other scholars who support this view.

[2] See above, 242f.

[3] See *JVG* 268–74.

^{13.30}But God raised him from the dead, ³¹and he was seen (*ophthe*) for many days by those who had gone up with him from Galilee to Jerusalem. They are now his witnesses to the people. ³²And we bring you the good news of the promise made to the ancestors, ³³that God has fulfilled it for us, their children, in raising Jesus . . .

. . . ³⁸Let it be known to you, men and brethren, that through this man forgiveness of sins is announced to you, and that from everything from which you could not be justified in the law of Moses, ³⁹in him everyone who believes is justified.

A new moment has opened in the divine plan for Israel and the world, because the long-promised, long-awaited event has occurred: 'the resurrection of the dead' has in a sense already happened with the resurrection of Jesus. This is the meaning of the otherwise puzzling passage which speaks of the apostles incurring the wrath of the temple officials and the Sadducees:

^{4.1}While they [i.e. Peter and John] were speaking to the people, the priests and the commander of the Temple and the Sadducees came up to them. ²They were very angry because they were teaching the people and announcing, in Jesus, 'the resurrection from the dead'.

This does not mean simply that they were teaching a particular doctrine (one with which, as we know, the Sadducees disagreed strongly in any case), and doing so on the authority of Jesus, or even with him as an example.[4] It goes further than that. It means that they were announcing (the very word *katangellein* carries the force of an announcement of something that has happened, not simply teaching about a doctrine) that 'the resurrection from the dead' had happened, with this case as its prototype. The Greek is not simply *anastasis nekron*, the resurrection *of* the dead, the great moment which was still awaited when all the dead (or at least all the righteous dead) would be raised. They are teaching *ten anastasin ek nekron*, 'the resurrection "out from among" the dead'. This was, clearly, the dawn of the new day; but it was so in the single, individual case of Jesus himself. He had come 'out from among' the dead bodies. But both halves of this mattered. It was not just that the disciples were saying something outrageous about Jesus. They were saying that in and through him a new era in Israel's history, in world history, had dawned:

^{3.24}All the prophets, from Samuel and those who followed him, all the ones who spoke, also announced these days.

And the resurrection of Jesus had thus opened up the new chance for Israel to find forgiveness at last:

^{3.26}It was to you first that God sent his child, when he raised him up, to bless you, by turning each of you from your wickedness.

---

[4] See Evans 1970, 134. The discussion of this text in Kilgallen 2002 seems to me never quite to reach the point.

If 'the resurrection from the dead' had thus already occurred in Jesus, it would surely occur for all God's people in the future. So central was the resurrection to Paul's preaching among the Gentiles (this is, of course, strongly confirmed from the letters) that the Athenians even misheard Paul and imagined that he was preaching two new divinities, Jesus and 'Anastasis'. The Greek word for 'resurrection' was so frequently on his lips that they thought she was Jesus' consort, a kind of Isis to his Osiris.[5] When Paul makes his defence in Jerusalem and Caesarea, the theme of resurrection is regularly on his lips, beginning with a passage we have already noted:[6]

> [before the Jewish council] 23.6When Paul noticed that some of the council were Sadducees and others were Pharisees, he shouted out in the council, 'Brothers, I am a Pharisee, the son of Pharisees! I am on trial here concerning the hope, and the resurrection of the dead (*anastasis nekron*)!'

> [before Felix] 24.14I confess to you that by the 'way' they refer to as heresy, so I worship the God of my ancestors, believing in all things according to the law and the things written in the prophets, 15having a hope toward God which these men themselves are awaiting, that there will be a resurrection of both the righteous and the unrighteous. 16So I do my best always to maintain a clear conscience before God and all people . . .[7]
> . . . 20Or let them say themselves what crime they found in me when I was standing before the council, 21except concerning this one thing which I shouted out when I was standing there, that 'I am on trial before you today concerning the resurrection of the dead (*anastasis nekron*)!'

> [Felix reporting to Agrippa] 25.18When the accusers stood up to make their case, they brought none of the charges of evildoing that I had been expecting; 19it had to do with disputes about their own systems of piety, and about a dead person called Jesus, whom Paul asserted to be alive.

> [Before Agrippa] 26.6And now I stand here on trial for the hope of the promise which came from God to our ancestors, 7a promise to which our twelve tribes hope to attain as they worship earnestly day and night; and it is because of this hope that I am called to account by the Jews, O King! 8Why should it be judged incredible by you that God should raise the dead (*ei ho theos nekrous egeirei*)?
> . . . 22To this day I have received help from God, and so I stand bearing witness to small and great alike, of nothing other than what the prophets – yes, and Moses too! – said would happen: 23that the Messiah would suffer, and that he would be the first out of the resurrection of the dead (*protos ex anastaseos nekron*) and would announce light to the people and to the nations.

A solid block of evidence thus demonstrates that Acts, whatever earlier traditions it has incorporated, places the resurrection of Jesus at centre stage in its theology. Jesus' own resurrection *from* the dead is the beginning of 'the

---

[5] Ac. 17.18.
[6] Above, 132–4.
[7] For the sequence of thought – living in a certain way in the present because of the future judgment – compare 2 Cor. 5.6–10, 11f.

resurrection *of* the dead'. As in 1 Corinthians 15, 'resurrection' has been divided into two distinct moments. The interval of time thus created is to be understood as the moment for prophecy to be fulfilled, for Israel's consolation to come at last, and for the Gentiles to be brought in:

> [Peter's speech][3.19]Repent then, and turn back to God, so that your sins may be wiped away, [20]and so that times of refreshment may come from the face of the Lord, and that he may send the Messiah he has appointed for you, Jesus. [21]Heaven must receive him until the time of restoration (*apokatastasis*) of all things, which God spoke through the mouth of his holy prophets of old. [22]Moses said that 'The Lord your God will raise up (*anastesei*) a prophet for you . . .

We note here in passing the use of a text from Deuteronomy (18.15) which, containing the word *anastesei* in the LXX, lent itself easily to being a proof of the special resurrection of the prophet-Messiah Jesus.[8] This too appears as an innovation from within the Jewish tradition: the explanation of what had happened to Jesus, and what it all meant, is only comprehensible within Judaism, but nobody had thought of it like this before the early Christians did. And, within the interval between Jesus' resurrection and the *apokatastasis*, a new life was available, with new possibilities of healing, for those who would believe.[9] God's raising of Jesus from the dead is the sign that salvation is found in him alone, which in turn is the explanation for the remarkable healing performed by Peter and John (4.5–12). The whole early Christian message can be summed up in the phrase 'this life' (5.20). When we find, in this context, that Peter raises a widow from the dead, and that Paul likewise restores to life an apparently dead boy, the reader of Acts is bound to feel that such incidents cohere with the underlying theological message – and with events reported in the gospels.[10] This is a time of life, of restoration, of resurrection.

We have already studied two passages in Acts which speak revealingly about the possible intermediate state between bodily death and bodily resurrection.[11] Luke does not give full endorsement to the views of the Pharisees, that people in the intermediate state could be spoken of as either 'angel' or 'spirit', but his almost throwaway mention of their views indicates the world of thought with which the early Christians were engaging, and within which their claims were perceived to make sense.

This entire theology, in which 'the resurrection of the dead' is announced as having already begun in the case of Jesus, is constructed, in Acts, on an extremely important foundation. This foundation consists of a very detailed exposition of Jesus' own resurrection, of the biblical context within which it means what it means, and of the implications that are to be drawn from it.

---

[8] On the use of the LXX in early Christian resurrection-apologetic cf. above, 147–50.
[9] On *apokatastasis* see Barrett 1994, 206f.
[10] Ac. 9.36–42; 20.7–12.
[11] Ac. 23.6–9; 12.15: see above, 132–4.

As we would have expected from all the second-Temple and early Christian material surveyed so far, there is no question of 'resurrection' at any point in Acts referring to anything other than a *bodily* rising from the dead. If this is clear in relation to the future resurrection of both the righteous and the wicked, it is doubly clear when Peter provides, on the day of Pentecost, a scriptural matrix for understanding what has happened in terms of a Psalm which speaks of God not allowing the Messiah to 'see corruption':

> [2.22]Jesus of Nazareth, a man marked out from God to you in powerful deeds, wonders, and signs that God did through him in your midst, as you yourselves know, [23]this man, delivered up by the designated plan and foreknowledge of God, you crucified and killed through the hands of wicked men. [24]God raised him up, having loosed the pains of death; it wasn't possible for him to be kept in their power.
>
> [25]For David says concerning him, 'I saw the Lord always before me; for he is at my right hand, so that I shall not be shaken. [26]Therefore my heart was glad, and my tongue rejoiced, and my flesh too shall dwell in hope; [27]for you will not leave my soul in Hades, nor will you give your holy one to see corruption. [28]You will make known to me the paths of life, you will fill me with gladness by your face.'
>
> [29]Fellow-Israelites, I can speak to you freely about the patriarch David, that he died and was buried, and his tomb is among us to this day. [30]Being then a prophet, and knowing that God had sworn a solemn oath that he would place on his throne one from the fruit of his body, [31]he saw in advance and spoke about the resurrection of the Messiah, that he was not left in Hades, nor did his flesh see corruption. [32]This Jesus God raised up, and all of us are witnesses of it. [33]He has been exalted to God's right hand, and, having received the promise of the Holy Spirit from the father, he has poured it out, as you see and hear.
>
> [34]For David did not ascend into the heavens, but he says, 'The Lord said to my Lord, sit at my right hand, [35]until I place your enemies under your feet.' [36]So let the house of Israel know for certain that God has made him Lord and Messiah, this Jesus whom you crucified.

This long speech is full of interest, but for our present purposes we confine our comments to this: that the only reason for choosing Psalm 16 (LXX 15) as the key text to interpret the extraordinary events of Easter is that Luke at least believed, and the early sources he drew on seem to have believed, that the resurrection of Jesus involved not the corruption of his physical body in the tomb (and his elevation to some non-physical sphere of dignity or Lordship), but its incorruption.[12] The 'exaltation' spoken of in verse 33 is not an alternative interpretation of Easter, but (not least in the light of Acts 1) a reference to a further event. Whoever originally quoted Psalm 16 of Jesus, or edited the source, or put it in its present context, the whole passage only makes the sense it was intended to make if the resurrection is thought of as a bodily event in which Jesus' physical body did not decay as those of the patriarchs had done, but received new life.[13] And from this new life, as we

---

[12] This point seems to be missed by Michaud 2001, 112–15.

[13] It would thus be futile to make anything of the fact that the proclamation in Ac. 10.40f. does not mention the empty tomb. As in 1 Cor. 15.3f., it is clearly assumed.

shall see later, solid conclusions were drawn at once about what God was thereby saying of Jesus.

The same position about Jesus' own resurrection is developed in several subsequent passages, already quoted. Each makes its own contribution to a fuller picture of the early Christian understanding of his resurrection. The summary in 4.33 draws together the impression of the early chapters as a whole: 'With great power the apostles gave their testimony to the resurrection of the Lord Jesus, and great grace was upon them all.' Thus, when we come to Paul's great speeches, we are not surprised (either from what we know of Paul or from what we know of Acts) that the resurrection is prominent and climactic. In Acts 13.30–39, quoted in part above, Paul draws on Psalms 2 and 16 to emphasize that the resurrection declares Jesus to be the Messiah, stressing again the point made in Acts 2 about his body not decomposing. And in Acts 17, at the climax of the speech on the Areopagus, Paul explicitly takes on the whole Homeric and classical tradition we studied in chapter 2:

> [17.31]God has fixed a day on which he will cause the world to be judged by a human being whom he has appointed; and he has given assurance of this to everyone by raising him from the dead.

Not surprisingly, granted their traditions and standard beliefs, some mocked (17.32). But Acts is undeterred, standing foursquare with Paul himself and the other early Christian writers. The resurrection, as an event within recent history, means that the judgment of the world, long awaited within Judaism, is now announced to all. The risen one himself, being thereby marked out as Messiah, will take the role of judge.[14]

The resurrection was thus clearly central to all the strands of early Christianity represented by the traditions in Acts, as well as the viewpoint of the author who drew them together. When we place the resurrection in Acts against the spectrum of views in the ancient world, it belongs, of course, within Judaism, and alongside Pharisaism; but, as in other parts of early Christian thought, it has been drastically modified within that framework. Resurrection is something that has already happened to one man, demonstrating that he is 'prophet', 'lord' and 'Messiah'. But his resurrection *from* the dead is the start of the single event still known as 'the resurrection *of* the dead' or '*out from among* the dead'. It reinforces belief in that future hope, so that announcing Jesus can be presented as loyalty to Judaism's cherished expectation. The new interval of time created by one man rising in advance of the rest can be interpreted as the time for prophecy to be fulfilled, for Israel's long-awaited rescue by God. This itself, though, is also reinterpreted. It is no longer read as political liberation, but as 'forgiveness of sins', not least in the sense of forgiveness for having rejected God's Messiah. And,

---

[14] cf. Rom. 1.3f., 2.16.

though the bodiliness of Jesus' resurrection is affirmed and underlined, he was clearly not simply resuscitated into a life exactly like the present one, since his body seems to have new properties. His body is presently 'in heaven', but will return from there at the time when he appears as judge of all the world, the time when everything will be restored (*apokatastasis*).

Two further interim conclusions may be drawn from this material. First, there are several overlaps between this picture and that of Paul, but Acts does not look like a slavish imitation of Paul on this topic. The closest it comes, interestingly, is the point at which it uses, of God's raising of Jesus, language reminiscent of Romans 1.4. Second, this picture is, as we should expect, fully consonant with what we found in Luke's gospel, but, granted that the same person wrote them both, we must note the commendable restraint in the gospel, in that the author has not introduced, at several points where it would have been possible to do so, the fuller exposition of the meaning of resurrection which is then offered in Acts by Peter and Paul in particular. It is, of course, quite conceivable that this reflects the genuine historical memory of the very early church (Jesus said little on the topic, Peter and Paul said a lot), but it is no part of my present purpose to argue that that is so. What is more important is to note the way in which 'resurrection' was understood, in relation to the future human hope and to Jesus himself, and to observe the way in which, through the various forms of description appearing in the different documents, a many-sided, composite but thoroughly coherent picture emerges which can be placed on the map of first-century views, and which robustly answers our main question: why did they come to hold that kind of hope in that kind of way? Acts, like Paul and the synoptic gospels, answers: because of what happened to Jesus.

3. Hebrews

Hebrews stands out from the rest of the New Testament in many ways, but one of the most obvious is this: it is among the more substantial of the longer early Christian books, yet it hardly mentions the resurrection.[15]

The writer assumes that 'the resurrection of the dead' is among the basic doctrines that new converts would be taught (6.2, along with other things assumed to be rudimentary).[16] But he does not make it a topic of discussion until he produces the long list of the heroes of faith in chapter 11. There we find, as in Paul, Abraham's faith that God could and would give him a child even though he was 'as good as dead' (11.11–12); and, more explicitly than

---

[15] Harvey 1994, 73 overstates in declaring that there is *no* mention; see below. A recent study of resurrection in Hebrews is that of Lane 1998 – all the more moving for those who knew the author to be struggling with terminal illness at the time of writing.

[16] 'The dead' is plural, referring to the future resurrection of the many, not that of Jesus.

in Paul, the use of the story of Abraham and Isaac to show that genuine faith is resurrection faith:

> [17]By faith Abraham, when he was tested, offered up Isaac; he had received the promises, but was ready to sacrifice his only child, [18]about whom it had been said that 'in Isaac shall your seed be called.' [19]He reckoned that God was able (*dynatos*) to raise him even from the dead; and thence, in a manner of speaking, he did receive him back.

The parallels to Romans 4 are obvious, and indicate that at this point the writer of Hebrews is thinking in the same framework as Paul, and indeed as much first-century Judaism.[17] But if this is so, we should probably take most of chapter 11 as pointing in the same direction. The main point of 'faith' in this chapter, as has often been emphasized, is that it looks forward to what has been promised but not yet granted. Noah was warned about things yet to come. Abraham set out for a place he had been promised but had not yet seen. The main antithesis the writer is making is not between an 'upstairs' or 'spiritual' world in the hellenistic sense and a 'downstairs' or 'material' world, but between the present world and the future one, the promised new world which will be God's gift from heaven:

> [13]These all died in faith. They had not received the promises, but they had seen them some distance off, and greeted them, and confessed that they were strangers and pilgrims on the earth. [14]For people who say that sort of thing make it clear that they are seeking a homeland. [15]If they were remembering the country from which they had gone out, they would have had an opportunity to return to it. [16]But now they are aspiring towards a better one, that is a heavenly one (*epouranios*). That is why God is not ashamed to be called 'their God'; for he has prepared a city for them.

But what does this mean? Have we after all stumbled upon an early Christian text which straightforwardly affirms what so many others do not, that the point of faith and hope is, at the end, to 'go to heaven when you die'?

Things are not so simple. If they were, the writer would scarcely have gone on to speak of Abraham's resurrection faith; nor yet of those who looked for 'a better resurrection' than simple resuscitation:

> [35]Women received their dead by resurrection (*ex anastaseos*). Others were tortured, refusing to accept release, so that they might obtain a better resurrection (*hina kreittonos anastaseos tychosin*).

This seems to be an allusion, on the one hand, to the Sidonian widow whose son Elijah restored and the Shunammite woman whose son Elisha restored; and, on the other, to the martyrs in 2 Maccabees.[18] The text thus uses the

---

[17] So, rightly, Koester 2001, 491.

[18] 1 Kgs. 17.17–24; 2 Kgs. 4.18–37; 2 Macc. 7. Koester 2001, 514 points out that, though the biblical stories are resuscitations and the people concerned would die again, they, like Isaac's deliverance, are seen as foreshadowing the final resurrection.

word 'resurrection' in the two senses of 'resuscitation of the very recently dead' and 'resurrection to new bodily life at some stage in the future'. Both are clearly bodily; the reason for distinguishing them, and calling the latter one 'better', is presumably because the writer is aware that in 2 Maccabees the mother was looking not for a short-term resuscitation but a new creation, part of the great new work, ushering in the age of cosmic justice, that the creator god would one day perform.

The 'heavenly country' of which the writer speaks is further identified in chapter 12. This is the heavenly Jerusalem:

> [22]You have come to Mount Sion, to the city of the living God, the heavenly Jerusalem, and to millions of angels gathered in celebration, [23]and to the assembly of the firstborn whose names are written in heaven, and to God the judge of all, and to the spirits of the righteous made perfect, [24]and to Jesus the mediator of the new covenant, and to the sprinkled blood which speaks better things than the blood of Abel.

This, again, looks like a 'spiritual', 'heavenly' and entirely 'other-worldly' goal. So, indeed, it is. The 'spirits of the righteous made perfect' are presumably the saints and martyrs of old awaiting their new bodies in the new creation.[19] Even this, it seems, is an intermediate stage on the way to that new creation, in which both heaven and earth are to be 'shaken', so that what God intends to last for ever may do so:

> [26]Now he has promised, 'Yet once more, I will shake not only the earth but also the heaven' [Haggai 2.6, 21]. [27]This mention of 'once more' indicates the removal of what can be shaken – in other words, things that have been made – so that what cannot be shaken may remain. [28]Therefore, since we are receiving a kingdom that cannot be shaken, let us be thankful . . .

And this future hope, for the world that will last, a world more solid, more real than the present one, is reaffirmed in the final chapter: here we have no lasting city, but we seek that which is to come (13.14), referring to the 'heavenly Jerusalem' of 11.16 and 12.22.[20]

The future hope, which thus emerges at the climax of the book, appears to draw together the belief that God's future world is ready and waiting in heaven and the belief that it will involve the resurrection of the dead. As in the Corinthian correspondence, the two images work together: that which is 'waiting in heaven' is that which is secure in the plan and intention of the

---

[19] Granted the way these concepts work in the Judaism of the time (above, ch. 4), I do not regard this as an unresolved tension in Heb. as Koester 2001, 306 suggests. Koester rightly draws attention (311) to the implicit resurrection teaching in 2.14f.; 12.22–4.

[20] Attridge 1989, 380f., citing other commentators also, sees here the complete destruction of the existing creation rather than its renewal. The poetic language does not, perhaps, permit a firm conclusion on this point, but his suggestion that Heb. is governed here by a popular Platonic dualism, and that the 'things which cannot be shaken' are non-material, seems to me questionable.

creator. And all this is based, throughout the book to this point, on the victory over death that has been won by Jesus, leading him to be installed, in accordance with Psalms 8 and 110, as the Messiah who rules the world in obedience to God. These texts, intriguingly the same ones as we find in 1 Corinthians 15.25–8 and Philippians 3.20–21, are not here explicitly linked to an affirmation of Jesus' resurrection and its results, but rather to Jesus' superiority over the angels (1.13) and his enthronement over 'all things' (2.5–9).

All this does, of course, depend for its logical force on the resurrection. It is hard to see how anyone could have spoken of Jesus 'destroying the one who has the power of death, that is the devil, and freeing those who spent their lives in slavery to the fear of death' (2.14) unless it was presupposed that Jesus has now defeated death through resurrection. The poignant passage about Jesus offering up loud cries and tears to the father who was able to save him from death (5.7) appears at first sight to suggest (as with the Gethsemane narratives in the gospels) that the father did not save him; but when the verse continues that 'he was heard because of his reverent submission', one likely meaning is that the father gave him a life beyond death, a salvation from death which did not consist in avoiding it but in going through it and out into a new, imperishable life beyond. This then becomes the foundation for the superior priesthood which Jesus holds (7.23–5); he has become a priest not through physical descent 'but by the power of an indestructible life' (7.16). It is true that Hebrews focuses its main attention not on the resurrection itself but on the effective sacrifice of the cross which preceded it and the ascension and enthronement which followed.[21] But, as we would guess from chapter 11 in particular, the resurrection is never far away, and becomes explicit in the benediction at the very end of the letter:

> Now may the God of peace, who brought again from the dead our Lord Jesus, that great shepherd of the sheep, by the blood of the eternal covenant, make you perfect in every good work to do his will . . .[22]

The idea of Jesus, the shepherd, being 'brought up' from the dead echoes Isaiah 63.11–14, where YHWH 'brings up' the shepherd, Moses, from Egypt.[23] Moses 'was "led forth", not as an isolated individual, but as the

---

[21] Sacrifice: e.g. Heb. 2.17; 7.27; 10.10; ascension and enthronement: e.g. 10.12f.; both together: e.g. 9.11–28.

[22] Heb. 13.20f. 'Brought again' is *anagagon*, lit. 'led up', as in LXX 1 Kgds. [MT 1 Sam.] 2.6; 28.11; Tob. 13.2; Wisd. 16.13; cf. too Rom. 10.7. Attridge 1989, 406 sees the avoidance of the regular NT 'resurrection' words as part of a consistent ploy of speaking of exaltation rather than resurrection for Jesus, though the actual content of this verse surely calls this into question. Contrast Lane 1991, 561, who sees this verse as making explicit what is implicit elsewhere.

[23] Set out clearly in Lane 1991, 561; cf. too Koester 2001, 573.

shepherd of the flock'; this is true of Jesus as well, the first to rise, anticipating the resurrection of all at the end (6.2).[24]

Here at last the resurrection of both Jesus and his people comes out into the open. For the rest of the book, though, the main emphasis is on Jesus having suffered and having then been exalted into the heavenly realm, whence he will return (as in Philippians 3.20–21) to save those who are waiting for him.[25] The climactic statement of this theme comes in 12.1–2, where the readers are encouraged to keep their eyes on Jesus as they press forward, surrounded by the great cloud of witnesses from past generations. They must continually remind themselves how Jesus 'endured the cross, disregarding its shame, and has taken his seat at the right hand of the throne of God'. The enthronement of Jesus as Messiah and lord is of course integrated, by Paul in particular, with his resurrection. Indeed, for Paul, enthronement presupposes resurrection. But in Hebrews the connection is not made explicit. I am inclined to say, with Lane, Koester and some other commentators, that this is because it is everywhere presupposed; but I recognize that such claims are hard to substantiate, and nothing much in my present argument depends on it. Hebrews cannot be used as a central witness for a redefinition of resurrection, though as we have seen it contains some hints in that direction. It explores one particular vision both of Jesus and of the Christian pilgrimage, which depends on belief both in Jesus' own resurrection and in the future resurrection of believers. But it does not make this in any way a major theme.

4. The General Letters

It is perhaps less surprising that the letter of James has little to say about the resurrection. The closest it comes is in the promise that the prayer of faith will save the sick person, and the Lord will 'raise him up' (*egerei auton*), forgiving him his sins.[26] This combination of prayer, sickness, 'raising up' and forgiveness is familiar from several of the texts we have studied, but the letter of James says nothing more explicit than this about resurrection. It never refers either to the future post-mortem existence of believers, or of all humanity, or to the past event of Jesus' resurrection. As with many other topics, it would be rash to conclude that James did not believe in all this just because the book does not mention it.[27] That is as far as we need to go for our present purposes.

[24] Lane 1991, 561f., stressing the link with Heb.'s theology of covenant renewal.

[25] cf. esp. 4.14; 5.5–10; 6.19f.; 7.16; 7.24; 9.24–8; 10.12–14 (continuing the long-drawn-out exposition of Ps. 110).

[26] Jas. 5.15, keeping the masculine form to emphasize the singular.

[27] Jas. 1.10f. alludes to Isa. 40.6f. (the grass withers, the flower fades), but does not articulate the positive side of the passage, as we find in 1 Pet. 1.23–5.

The same is true for 2 Peter and Jude. This is somewhat more surprising, because with their apocalyptic cast one might have expected some kind of end-time scenario. We do find, in 2 Peter, talk of escaping from the corruption that is in the world because of lust, and of becoming partakers of the divine nature (1.4), but from this passage alone it is not clear what is involved in this 'escaping corruption'. Likewise, the book envisages the goal of Christian living to be 'entry into the eternal kingdom of our lord and saviour Jesus the Messiah' (1.11), but the *aionios basileia* (which might remind us of 1 Corinthians 15.24–8) is not further defined.[28] Though the writer speaks of his forthcoming death, contrasting it as does Paul in Philippians 1 or 2 Corinthians 5 with remaining in the present body as in a 'tent' (*skenoma*), he does not develop a detailed anthropology of what will happen to the present body or its 'inhabitant'.

We do, however, find in 2 Peter a reference to the 'new heavens and new earth' promised by Isaiah.[29] This coheres both with the close of Revelation (see below) and also with Romans 8 and 1 Corinthians 15, which envision a world finally set free from corruption and decay and renewed by the divine power.[30] Though the resurrection itself is not mentioned within this dramatic scenario, the appeal to the creative divine power, and the promise of global renewal, are the same here as in other texts where resurrection is the specifically human hope within this cosmic drama:

> [3.5]They deliberately ignore this, that the heavens existed long ago by God's word, and an earth was made from water and through water, [6]through which the world of those days was destroyed by being flooded with water. [7]The present heavens and earth are being stored up for fire by the same word, for the day of judgment and destruction of wicked people. [8]Do not ignore this one thing, my beloved ones: that one day with the Lord is as a thousand years, and a thousand years as one day. [9]The Lord is not being slow about his promise, as some think slowness to be, but is patient to you, not wanting anyone to perish, but that all should come to repentance.
>
> [10]But the day of the Lord will come like a thief, the day in which the heavens will pass away with a loud noise, the elements will be dissolved by burning, and the earth and the works in it will be found out. [11]Since all these things are to be dissolved in this way, what sort of people ought you to be, in holy pursuits and godliness, [12]as you wait and long for the presence of the day of God, through which the heavens will be dissolved in fire, and the elements will melt with burning? [13]But we wait for new heavens and a new earth, according to the promise, and justice will live there.

The critical moment here, upon which seems to hinge the worldview of the whole, is verse 10. Is the writer saying that creation as a whole is to be thrown away and a new one, freshly made, to take its place? So it would seem if the verse were to end 'will be burned up', as in the AV and RSV.

---

[28] It does, however, anticipate the language of some of the C2 writers; see ch. 11 below.

[29] 3.13; cf. Isa. 65.17; 66.22.

[30] On corruption and escape from it cf. (with 1.4) 2 Pet. 2.19.

That could imply a dualistic worldview in which creation itself was irremediably evil, which seems ruled out by the insistence on its being divinely made, or a Stoic worldview in which the present world would dissolve into fire and be reborn, phoenix-like, from the ashes,[31] which seems ruled out by the fact that the underlying story is not one of an endless cycle, as in Stoicism, but of a linear movement of history, as in Judaism, moving forward towards judgment and new creation.[32] What is going on in this text, and what view of the future world, and humans within it, does it offer?

The translation 'will be burned up' depends in fact on the variant readings of a few manuscripts.[33] Most of the best witnesses have *heurethesetai*, 'will be found'. Until recently it was thought that this was quite unintelligible, but more recently commentators have pointed out the use of 'find' in the sense of 'being found out', in a setting of eschatological judgment, in Jewish texts and elsewhere in the New Testament, including Paul and the gospels.[34] Various possible nuances of meaning emerge from this, of which one in particular stands out: that the writer wishes to stress continuity within discontinuity, a continuity in which the new world, and the new people who are to inhabit it, emerge tested, tried and purified from the crucible of suffering.[35] If something like this is plausible (it is a difficult and obscure text, and likely to remain so) then the worldview we find is not that of the dualist who hopes for creation to be abolished, but of one who, while continuing to believe in the goodness of creation, sees that the only way to the fulfilment of the creator's longing for a justice and goodness which will replace the present evil is for a process of fire, not simply to consume, but also to purge.

The second letter of Peter may thus offer oblique witness to an early Christian eschatology not far removed from that of Paul in 1 Corinthians. The letter of Jude concentrates mostly on fearful warnings of judgment, with a solitary mention, near the close, of the mercy of the Lord Jesus Christ which leads to eternal life (verse 21). The concluding benediction speaks of God 'making you stand without blemish in the presence of his glory with rejoicing' (verse 24). These, again, are too small to build anything upon, but are quite consonant with the larger picture we have observed above.

The letters of John are similarly sparse in mention of the ultimate postmortem future, or of the resurrection of Jesus as its basis. The opening of the first letter, echoing the gospel prologue, is of course all about 'life' – the life that was made manifest in Jesus, the 'eternal life' (1.2) that was with the father and was revealed to us – but the emphasis of the letter is not only on

---

[31] cf. e.g. Cic. *De Nat. Deorum* 2.118.

[32] So, rightly, Duff 2001, 1274.

[33] Notable *katakaesetai* in A (C5) and some other MSS.

[34] See e.g. Bauckham 1983, 303, 316–21; Wenham 1987, pointing out possible roots in Jesus' apocalyptic teaching in the gospels; Wolters 1987; Neyrey 1993, 243f.

[35] So Wolters 1987, 411f., proposing a metallurgical sense connected to the process of smelting.

the future meaning of that phrase, but, as in the gospel, on its present connotations. There are pointers to the future: while the world and its lust are
passing away, anyone who does God's will 'abides for ever' (2.17).

The main mention of the ultimate future, however, is clear, and corresponds quite closely to passages like Colossians 3.1–4. The writer warns
that it is the 'last hour', and looks forward to the day when Jesus, at present
hidden from sight, is 'revealed'. When that happens, his people will be
revealed as well:

> [2.28]And now, little children, abide in him, so that when he is revealed (*ean phaner-
> othe*) we may have confidence and not be put to shame before him at his presence
> (*parousia*). [29]If you know that he is righteous, you know that everyone who does
> righteousness has been born from him.
>   [3.1]See what great love the father has given us, that we should be called God's
> children; and that is what we are. That is why the world does not know us, because it
> did not know him. [2]Beloved, we are now God's children, and it is not yet revealed
> (*oupo phanerothe*) what we shall be. We know that when he appears (*ean phaner-
> othe*), we shall be like him, because we shall see him as he is. [3]And all who have this
> hope within them purify themselves, just as he is pure.

Here the sequence of thought is very close to several passages in Paul. Jesus
is at the moment beyond our sight, and our present lives are bound up with
his, in a way invisible to the world around. But one day Jesus will be
revealed.[36] At that time, the life believers already possess will be revealed.
When it happens, we shall be 'like him', as in Philippians 3.20–21. The
'royal presence' of Jesus (*parousia*) will be the signal for the great transformation in which the hidden reality of present Christian experience will
become the public reality of God's new world, and his renewed people. As
in Paul, this hope gives impetus to the ethical demands made in the present.

The rest of the letter emphasizes what the fourth gospel had stressed: that
there is a passing over from death to life which can occur in the present
time, and that Christians must allow that transition, or transformation, to
have its effect in their thoughts and actions. 'We know that we have passed
from death to life, because we love one another.'[37] This in turn is based on
the incarnation of the divine love in the person of Jesus, now made known
through the Spirit (4.1—5.5). And, as in the gospel, the phrase which carries
the continuity from present Christian experience to future Christian hope is
'eternal life', *zoe aionios*.[38]

This brings us to the first letter of Peter, which contains a couple of sections of more than passing interest. After the initial greeting, the letter opens
with a passage which has regularly been taken to indicate that 'salvation'

---

[36] This is the closest we come in John's letters to the (equally rare) statement of the second coming in the fourth gospel (21.22f.).

[37] 1 Jn. 3.14f.; cf. Jn. 5.24.

[38] 1 Jn. 1.2; 2.25; 3.15; 5.11f., 13, 20.

consists in leaving the present world and going at last to 'heaven':

> [1.3]Blessed be God, the father of our Lord Jesus the Messiah! According to his great mercy he has caused us to be born again to a living hope, through the resurrection of Jesus the Messiah from the dead, [4]to an inheritance which is incorruptible and undefiled and unfading, that is kept in heaven for you, [5]who by God's power are guarded through faith for a salvation ready to be revealed in the last time. [6]In this you rejoice, though for a while you may have to suffer various kinds of testing, [7]so that the genuineness of your faith, more precious than gold which, albeit perishable, is tested by fire, may be found to result in praise and glory and honour at the revelation of Jesus the Messiah. [8]You have not seen him, but you love him; even though you do not see him now you believe in him and you rejoice with an inexpressible and glorified joy, [9]as you receive the goal of your faith, the salvation of your souls (*psychon*).

This, to a modern western reader, seems straightforward enough. The soul (*psyche*, verse 9) is what is saved, and this salvation will take place in heaven (verse 4). But there are three signs that this, though 'obvious' to many today, is not at all what the author intended.

First, the 'salvation' is 'to be revealed in the last time' (verse 5). This sounds more like the picture in Colossians 3 or 1 John 3: at present, the heavenly dimension is unseen, but one day it will be unveiled.[39] If salvation consisted simply of going off to the heavenly dimension and staying there while earth went on its way to destruction, the writer could not have put it like this. The reward of faith and perseverance will be unveiled, not when the recently departed arrive in a disembodied heaven, but 'at the revelation of Jesus the Messiah' (verse 7). This language belongs much more naturally with the idea of 'heaven' as the place where the creator's future purposes are stored up, 'kept safe' (verse 4) until they can be unveiled in the promised new world, than with the dualism which seeks to escape from earth and to arrive, safely disembodied, in 'heaven'.[40]

Second, the salvation in question is spoken of in terms strongly reminiscent of Paul's resurrection-based soteriology. It will be an 'inheritance' (*kleronomia*), using the regular word for the promised land within the exodus-narrative, as in Romans 8 and Galatians 3—4. This inheritance will be 'incorruptible' (*aphtharton*, verse 4). 'Praise and glory and honour' (verse 7) is more or less exactly what Paul promised in Romans.[41] The fact that the writer is drawing, here and elsewhere, on the Pauline tradition is a strong hint that we should take the language in the same way as in Paul.[42]

---

[39] cf. too 1 Pet. 4.13 ('when the Messiah's glory is revealed').

[40] See Achtemeier 1996, 96, demonstrating that the idea of an inheritance currently preserved 'in heaven', i.e. by God, ready to be brought into earthly existence, is familiar both in Judaism and the teaching of Jesus, and coheres well with Paul's sense of 'a totally transformed eschatological reality'.

[41] Rom. 2.7, 10; cf. 249 above.

[42] So, powerfully, Achtemeier 1996, 95f.

Third, the salvation is based on the resurrection of Jesus himself (verse 3). This statement, which takes centre stage in the opening prayer of blessing, must be allowed the full force it would have had in a world innocent of the redefinitions that have gone on in the long tradition of western dualism. If the new birth and new life that belong to the Messiah's people through his resurrection is simply about their leaving their bodies and departing to a non-earthly, non-bodily sphere, is not the resurrection itself a category mistake? We cannot get off this hook by appealing to verse 11 (which speaks of the Spirit of Christ testifying in the prophets 'to the sufferings of the Messiah and the subsequent glory'): this is exactly the language used in Luke 24.26, and the non-mention of resurrection in that specific verse, passing directly from suffering to glory, can hardly be taken as an indication that the writer is downplaying the bodily significance of Easter. In any case, the same passage speaks ten verses later of the one god 'raising him from the dead and giving him glory'. It is always risky to assume that, when writers tell an abbreviated version of a story, they are deliberately intending to downplay, or even deny, the elements that (for the moment) they omit. A comparison of Philippians 2.9–11 and 3.20–21 makes the same point.

Indeed, the new birth spoken of in 1.3, so far from implying that the 'spiritual' life is what really counts, is picked up at the end of the chapter and explained as the birth within the believer of the life which is then 'imperishable', *aphthartos*, the same word that was used of the 'inheritance' in 1.4. 'The living and abiding word of God', as in Isaiah's prophecy of Israel's great restoration (40.6–7), will do its work through the preaching of the gospel, producing the life which will last into the age to come (1 Peter 1.23–5). Though Paul does not use the language of 'new birth' as such, this sequence of thought – the word of the gospel doing its secret work in believers, resulting in their final renewal and resurrection – is very close to his understanding of how people come to faith.

This explains, I think, the use of *psyche*, normally translated 'soul', in 1.9. It is in any case, as we have seen, a multivalent term in the Judaism of the period, and within early Christianity. It cannot be pressed for a Platonic meaning, certainly not when the rest of the passage speaks strongly in the other direction.[43] The most we might say is that it here serves to denote, not indeed an 'immortal' element which all human beings automatically possess, a 'soul' which looks forward to the great day when it will be freed from physicality, but that aspect of the human being, renewed secretly and inwardly (rather like the 'inner human' in 2 Corinthians 4.16), which carries the promise that is to be worked out in the entire human person. This, I suggest, is what the writer means by 'the hope that is in you' (3.15). And this,

---

[43] Achtemeier 1996, 104: the sense of *psyche* here is 'the salvation of the entire person rather than simply the rescue of a higher or spiritual part of a person in contrast to the body'. On resurrection and salvation in 1 Pet. see now Schlosser 2002.

too, is what gives a cross-and-resurrection shape to the frequently repeated appeal, as in Paul, that the readers ought to share the sufferings of the Messiah in order thereby to share his glory.[44] This is all very Pauline.

What then are we to say about the puzzling passage in the middle of the letter? As part of a long exhortation about standing firm under persecution, the author, not for the first time, refers to the example of Jesus. But this time, unlike 2.21–4, he expands the story of Jesus, to include in it a statement of what Jesus did in the time following his death:

> [3.18]For the Messiah suffered once for sins, the just for the unjust, so that he might bring you to God. He was put to death in/by flesh (*sarki*), but made alive in/by spirit (*pneumati*), [19]in which also he went and proclaimed to the spirits in prison, [20]who once were disobedient, when God waited with great patience in the days of Noah, while the ark was being prepared in which a few, namely eight persons, were saved through water. [21]Baptism now saves you on this pattern: not as a putting off of dirt from the body, but as an appeal of a good conscience to God, through the resurrection of Jesus the Messiah, [22]who has gone into heaven at God's right hand, with all angels, authorities and powers subject to him.

The writer returns to his theme of suffering, explaining that 'the Gentiles' will find it inexplicable and offensive that Christians refuse to join them in their lives of dissipation. But, he says, there will come a day of reckoning:

> [4.5]They will have to render an account to the one who is ready to judge the living and the dead. [6]For this reason the gospel was preached to the dead as well, so that, though judged in/by flesh (*sarki*) as humans are, they may live in the spirit as God does.

The two passages are clearly linked, though not necessarily identical in referent. Following the pattern of our enquiry so far, we must ask what is being said, first about human judgment and salvation, and second about Jesus himself.[45]

The writer is quite clear, of course, about final judgment, and about Jesus as its agent (4.5). This is common coin throughout early Christianity. There will come a day when all alike will be judged by the Messiah, and it is important to live in the present in the light of that future (4.1–2). This seems to be the point of the reference to baptism in 3.21–2: baptism, as the symbolic beginning of the Christian life, unites the believer to the risen Messiah where he now is, at the right hand of God, in authority over the world (we may again compare 1 Corinthians 15.25–8 and Philippians 3.20–21). The believer is thus presented before God (3.18), and can stand there with a good

---

[44] 1 Pet. 4.12–19, including a typical warning about the coming judgment; 5.10f., celebrating God's grace, glory and finally power. This whole argument tells strongly against the analysis of Robinson 1982, 19, who suggests that for 1 Pet. the resurrection is mainly a present experience, which merely leaves room 'for lip service to the apocalyptic view of future resurrection as a permanent if relatively passive ingredient in orthodoxy'.

[45] On this passage see recently, in addition to the commentaries, Westfall 1999.

conscience (3.21) because of the vindication of the Messiah who has suffered for his sins (3.18). This is dependent, of course, on maintaining that position, which demands moral effort in the present (4.1–2) to resist the lure of the old life (4.3–4). The overall point of the passage seems to be that as God's judgment comes on the world, so the righteous are brought safely through it. In the case of Christians, baptism functions as a parallel both to the waters which judged the world in the days of Noah and to the death of the Messiah, suffering on behalf of sinners. They must now follow the same pattern through the necessary suffering both of persecution and of vilification for their moral stand. They will thereby maintain their good conscience before God, based on what God himself has done in and through Jesus, and made explicit in the powerful symbolic action of baptism.

What, then, about the spirits in prison? Out of the many interpretations of this passage the overall context seems to me to favour the following train of thought. The writer's main point is that those he is addressing must be prepared to be brought safely through a time of ordeal and judgment. The analogy with Noah implies that the disobedient spirits, either the 'watchers' or simply the careless humans of Noah's day, had not until then been judged as they deserved, but that now they would be. The one true god had been extremely patient in holding back the much-deserved judgment; now, in the flood, it came at last. But what was the end of the time of patience? Was it the flood itself, judging the wicked? Or was it when the Messiah, having suffered for sins, went to announce what he had done to the still-imprisoned spirits? And was that announcement good news for them ('At last, redemption has been found')? Or was it bad news ('At last, your doom is sealed')? If 4.6 addresses the same issue, the implication is that the 'spirits' seem to be the humans of Noah's generation, who, having lost their lives in the flood while only eight people survived in the ark, were then to be saved, so many centuries later, through the Messiah's death. If, however, the 'spirits' are the evil powers awaiting their judgment, as the present passage taken by itself would most probably suggest, then the proclamation would concern their final doom – seen as an encouragement to those who presently suffer the effects of evil. The passage remains one of the hardest in all early Christian literature, and we should not suppose that we have hereby solved its mysteries.[46] If either of the views I have outlined is anything near the truth, however, the passage does not make a substantial contribution to our main enquiry. We do not look here for an early Christian understanding of the afterlife that awaits people in general or Christians in particular.

If one of these options is more or less correct, however, we find ourselves in the same danger of misreading the text as has happened so often with 1

---

[46] See esp. Davids 1990, 138–41; Achtemeier 1996, 252–62, both taking the latter line. Achtemeier also proposes that when v. 19 speaks of Christ 'going' to make his announcement to the 'spirits' this refers, not to a descent to the underworld, but to his ascent into heaven (as in v. 22), from which the announcement of victory would be made.

Corinthians 15, especially verse 50. The 'flesh/spirit' antithesis of 3.18 and 4.6 sounds to modern western ears as though it stands for our 'physical/non-physical' distinction; but this would take us down the wrong path. The writer insists that it is the *resurrection* of Jesus that has accomplished salvation. There is no hint in this text that resurrection is being understood any differently to its standard use across both the pagan and Jewish world and in the rest of early Christianity. When, then, the writer says that the Messiah was 'put to death in/by flesh, but made alive in/by spirit', we should not project on to this text the 'physical/non-physical' antithesis that 'flesh/spirit' conjures up for us today. It is possible, indeed, and I have reflected this in the translation with its two options, that here as in 1 Timothy 3.16 the word 'spirit' should be taken as instrumental, not locative. Perhaps we should understand the word 'flesh' in the previous line in the same way: he was put to death *by* the flesh, and brought to life *by* the Spirit.[47] The link to verse 19 would then not be 'he came to life in the Spirit, and in that mode went to preach to the spirits in prison', but 'he was brought to life by the Spirit, and in the power of, or by means of, that Spirit he went . . .'. Either way, the explicit mention of Jesus' resurrection in 3.21, picking up 1.3, should be recognized as the anchor of the passage. As in Ephesians 1 and Philippians 3, it is the resurrection that qualifies Jesus now to be the lord of angels, authorities and powers. He sits at the right hand of the one true god, as in Romans 8.34, and nothing shall separate his people from his powerful love.

The smaller, general letters in the New Testament thus yield varied results for our enquiry. They do not address the issue in the detail, or the frequency, that we find in Paul, the gospels and Acts. Nevertheless the hope of resurrection remains constant, and the resurrection of Jesus is its basis. If concentration has shifted away from resurrection as a major concern that needed to be hammered out (always assuming that these letters are later than Paul, the gospel traditions and Acts), the subject has not gone away or been subverted or distorted into something else. Resurrection still means what it meant elsewhere in the first century; the early Christians affirmed it as did the Pharisees; the next two or three generations went on doing so, as we shall see in the next chapter. What we find in these letters is a set of partial redefinitions, which fit into the general pattern we observed in Paul and elsewhere, though with local variations.

We must now turn to the book which, arguably, contains the most powerful statement of Christian future hope ever written: the Revelation of St John the Divine.

---

[47] See Achtemeier 1996, 250f. Another more regular solution which likewise rejects any dualism here is that of Davids 1990, 137: Jesus was made alive with respect to the Spirit, leaving behind the sphere of sinful flesh.

5. Revelation

Powerful, perhaps; but of course frequently misunderstood. The picture of
the heavenly city in the last two chapters of Revelation has often been interpreted through the lens of later western piety, imagining that this is simply
the 'heaven' to which Christians will go after their deaths. But that view is
not simply somewhat deficient; it is failing to read the text. In Revelation 21
(and elsewhere; this vision dominates the whole book, not just the ending)
the heavenly city comes down *from* heaven *to* earth. That is what the narrative is all about. As Christopher Rowland has insisted, the end of Revelation
offers an ultimate rejection of a detached, other-worldly spirituality in
favour of an integrated vision of new creation in which 'heaven' and 'earth',
the twin halves of created reality, are at last united. Always intended for one
another, they are by this means to be remade, and to become the place where
the living god will dwell among his people for ever.[48]

That, however, is simply the end of the book. It is important to keep in
mind throughout that that is where the story is going, but we must make our
way there by reading the rest of the book while holding in mind the questions we have been examining throughout.

In the vision of Jesus which forms the climax of the opening chapter, the
risen lord declares that, because of his own victory over death, he now has
the proprietary rights over Death and Hades.[49] One only needs to reflect for
a moment on the material surveyed in chapters 2, 3 and 4 of the present
book, and on the lack of parallel to such a claim in the worlds there
described, to see the enormity, and the precise focus, of what is said:

> [1.17]Do not be afraid. I am the first and the last, [18]and the living one. I was dead, and,
> look! I am alive to the ages of ages (*eis tous aionas ton aionon*), and I have the keys
> of Death and Hades.

This is picked up again in Revelation 2. It clearly forms part of the deliberate framing of the book, since in the penultimate scene Death and Hades
themselves give up all their dead and are thrown into the lake of fire.[50] But
before we can see the whole scene we are taken on a circuitous journey
around the seven churches of Asia Minor, each of which is given a message
containing promise and warning. Many of these echo one of the book's

---

[48] Rowland 1985, 292–4, 310f.; 1998, 720–30. See too O'Donovan 1986, 56.

[49] The vision in 1.13–16 should not be treated as a 'resurrection appearance' (as e.g.
Robinson 1982, 10; so, rightly, McDonald 1989, 19). It is not only Luke, but also Paul and
John, who limit the 'resurrection appearances' to a short, early period. Both form and content proclaim that this is a 'vision', written up with multiple echoes of biblical and post-
biblical tradition (cf. e.g. Rowland 1980; 1998, 561f.; Aune 1997–8, 70–74), so that to treat
it as a straight transcript of 'what the seer saw', as Robinson would require, implies a
literalism – here of all places! – which elsewhere he is the first to discard.

[50] Rev. 2.8; 20.13f.

major themes: the conquest, through suffering, of evil and of the world. This is itself a standard Jewish theme, refined through the Maccabaean period and afterwards, and now given a new focus through the death and resurrection of Jesus. One of the messages in particular, the one to Smyrna, urges the church to be faithful to death, promising that it will be given the crown of life, and that the 'second death' will not harm it. This is the first mention of the 'second death', an important part of the book's climax.[51]

As the book progresses – there is neither space nor need to go into its labyrinthine details – we are offered a glimpse of yet another way of envisaging those who have died in the struggle and are not yet raised. They are waiting and resting 'under the altar', longing for God's eventual victory over evil. They are told to rest a little longer, until the full number of their fellow-Christians have been killed as they were killed.[52] This strange little scene only makes sense if we grant the Jewish, more specifically the Pharisaic, viewpoint that those who have died in the righteous cause *will be* raised in the future, on the day when the creator judges the world at last, but that they *have not been* raised just yet. This is also the right way to read the description of the martyrs in 7.14–17, unless indeed this is an anticipation of the vision in chapters 21 and 22.[53] This, too, is the appropriate explanation for the interjected note in 14.13, where the voice from heaven tells the seer to write this: 'Blessed are the dead who die in the Lord.' The Spirit, he says, affirms this, 'because they rest from their labours, and their deeds follow them'. This should not be taken as a statement of their final destiny (some kind of endless 'rest'), but only of their temporary abode. The same is true for those who are summoned to come up to heaven, and who are taken there on a cloud in full view of their enemies (11.12). We are right to assume that, in the larger drama of the book as a whole, the events of last three chapters will see all these people enter upon a new life.

The strange events narrated in 11.1–13 have been variously understood, and we need not stop to decide on the best interpretation of them. The two witnesses who, like Elijah, have the power to shut up the sky to prevent it raining, are persecuted and killed, but after three and a half days the creator's breath of life enters into them and they stand on their feet. The writer clearly intends us to hear echoes of Genesis 2.7 and Ezekiel 37.5–14. The witnesses are then, like Elijah again, or perhaps like the 'son of man' figure in Daniel 7, caught up to heaven on a cloud. These events, described with the biblical imagery of resurrection, evoke celebration: 'the kingdom of God and the Messiah has come at last' (Revelation 11.15), the nations are to

---

[51] Rev. 2.10f.; cf. 20.6, 14; 21.8.

[52] Rev. 6.9–11. I am not convinced by Beale's attempt (1999, 1010) to suggest that they are in a state of 'spiritual resurrection'; see below on Rev. 20.4–6.

[53] In favour of this being an anticipation of the end: they are guided to springs of living water, with all tears wiped from their eyes (see Rev. 22.1–5; 21.4). Against: they serve the living god in his Temple (7.15), but there is no Temple in the heavenly city (21.22).

be judged, the servants of the true god are to be vindicated, and, significantly, those who destroy the earth will themselves be destroyed (11.18).

All of this is based, of course, on Jesus himself, and his own achievement in death and resurrection. He is the Lion of Judah who has conquered by being also the sacrificial lamb (Revelation 5.5–6, 9–10). As in Colossians 1, he is 'the firstborn of the dead' (Revelation 1.5), who is now 'the ruler of the kings of the earth'.[54] As so often in the New Testament, resurrection retains its strong political emphasis: Easter constitutes Jesus as the world's rightful sovereign in the midst of the warring and raging nations (11.18). The victory which is announced in chapter 11 is then celebrated again in chapter 19, as judgment is proclaimed and executed on Babylon the Whore, the parody of the heavenly city which is the Lamb's true Bride. The constant theme throughout chapters 18—20 is the judgment which is given *against* Babylon, the oppressor of God's people, and *for* the saints, apostles and prophets.[55]

This leads to a differentiated resurrection, the most complex development of resurrection belief in any Jewish or Christian document of the whole period.[56] The beheaded martyrs, who had not worshipped the beast or its image, come to life and reign with the Messiah for a thousand years, being assured in advance that they will escape the 'second death'. The rest of the dead, meanwhile, do not come to life until the thousand years are ended:

> [20.4]And I saw thrones, with people sitting on them; and judgment was given to them. And I saw the souls (*psychas*) of those who had been beheaded for their testimony to Jesus and for God's word, those who did not worship the Beast or his image, and who did not receive the mark on their foreheads or their hands. And they came to life, and reigned with the Messiah for a thousand years. [5]The rest of the dead did not come to life until the thousand years were completed. This is the first resurrection (*he anastasis he prote*). [6]Blessed and holy is the one who has a share in the first resurrection. Over them the second death has no authority, but they will be priests of God and of the Messiah, and they will reign with him for the thousand years.

Endless debates have swirled around the question of what exactly is being described here and when exactly it is supposed to take place. Large and influential schemes of thought about the 'millennium' have characterized different periods of church history from the second century to our own day.[57] What matters for our purposes is that we seem to have here a fresh

---

[54] Some MSS read 'from (*ek*) the dead', bringing the phrase into line with Col. 1.18 (some MSS, however, omit the *ek* there).

[55] Rev. 18.20.

[56] I assume that Revelation is written some time in the last third of the first century, but the precise date does not matter for our purposes. Oegema 2001 provides a history of how the 'double resurrection' in Rev. was treated in the patristic period; Hill 2002 [1992] offers an exegesis of the text and discusses the treatments of it by key early exegetes, including e.g. Origen (181–7) and Cyprian (198–207).

[57] In addition to the commentaries cf. e.g. Clouse 1977; Wright, *Millennium*; Hill 2002 [1992].

and unique mutation of resurrection language and belief, not this time from within Judaism, but from within Christianity itself.

The mutation is not, however, random. It is in line with, though it goes beyond, one of the key developments we have observed in early Christianity, that 'the resurrection' has divided chronologically into two (first Jesus, then all his people).[58] Now the resurrection of Jesus' people is itself split into two: first the martyrs, then, later, everyone else. Nothing is ever simple in Revelation, however, and the word 'resurrection' itself is not actually used either for the subsequent appearing of all the dead in 20.12–13 or for the final state of the blessed in chapters 21 and 22. It is, however, at least clear that the wicked are raised in order to be judged, as in several of the relevant Jewish texts, and as in John 5.28–9; until then, they have been the property of 'Death and Hades', and indeed of the sea (20.13), giving an interesting insight into first-century views of the combined physical and spiritual 'location' of the dead.[59] The wicked, having been raised to hear their own judgment, are then thrown into the lake of fire; so, too, are Death and Hades themselves (20.14–15). The sea is abolished in 21.1, at the same time as the first heaven and earth pass away to make room for the new ones.[60]

The crucial thing for our purposes is the question: what is the first resurrection, spoken of in 20.5–6? It seems to be an initial coming-to-life of some, but not all, the righteous. Not only are martyrs specified rather than ordinary Christians who died in their beds, but one type of martyr is singled

---

[58] The classic statement is 1 Cor. 15.23 (see above, 336f., etc.).

[59] Bauckham 1993a, 56–70 lays out and discusses many Jewish parallels. 'Death' and 'Hades' may be both personifications and places; alternatively, 'Death' may be the ruler of the location called 'Hades'. This, supposedly under the earth, was regarded as a more natural and appropriate place for the dead to be than in the sea; cf. e.g. Achilles Tatius, *Leucippe*, 5.16.2, where Clitophon, supposing that his beloved Leucippe has died at sea, declares that since he and Melite are on board ship at the moment they are sailing over Leucippe's grave, and that perhaps her ghost is circling around the ship at that moment. 'They say', he comments, 'that souls who die in the sea never descend to Hades but wander over the water.' Other refs. in Aune 1997–8, 3.1102f.; further discussion in Chester 2001, 71f. For the variation between a resurrection of all and a resurrection of the righteous only see the note on John 5.28f. at 442 above.

[60] Beale 1999, 1042 lists five possible reasons for the sea's abolition (with further material at 1050f.): it is seen as the origin of cosmic evil, as a picture of the unbelieving nations, as the place of the dead, as the location of idolatrous trade, and as a synechdoche for the entire old creation. The last of these seems unlikely in view of the rest of Rev. 21.1; the fourth is interesting but unlikely to be the primary point; the first three seem, in combination, the best possibilities. Bauckham 1993a, 49f. argues emphatically, on the basis of similar language in other writings, that the 'passing away' of the first heaven and earth 'refers to the eschatological renewal of this creation, not its replacement by another' (see too Chester 2001, 73). Bauckham's discussion of the sea and its abolition (51–3) draws attention to the final fulfilment of God's promise to Noah, never again to flood the world (Gen. 9.11).

out: those who were beheaded.[61] This group appears, then, to be as it were an advance party of the righteous, sharing already in the rule of the Messiah (whether this takes place in a 'millennium' more or less coterminous with the time of the church, or in a literal thousand-year period yet to come, does not at present concern us). When the rest of the dead are raised at last (20.12–13), many of them are found to have their names in the book of life (20.12, 15), and they are brought to life in the new Jerusalem (chapter 21) in which 'death will be no more' (21.4). What exactly does the writer have in mind?

It is conceivable that he thought of this 'first resurrection' in physical terms, locating the righteous in an embodied heavenly world (perhaps in the new Jerusalem which would eventually appear on earth, as in chapter 21), though few modern interpreters have gone this route.[62] Classic 'pre-millennial' interpretation understands the passage in terms of a future period of a literal thousand years in which some or all of the righteous will rise and rule the world with Christ. In an effort to counteract this, it is often proposed that 'the first resurrection' is simply a way of describing the passage through death, into a blessed intermediate state, of all the righteous; but if that was what the writer meant it seems that he has not made it clear (not that that would be unusual in Revelation).[63] Perhaps the most damaging objection to this view arises from the meaning of 'resurrection' throughout the literature we have studied, pagan, Jewish and Christian: however much death itself is to be re-evaluated in the light of Jesus' own death and resurrection, to use the word 'resurrection' to *refer to* death in an attempt to invest it with a new meaning seems to me to strain usage well beyond breaking point. In addition, verse 4 seems to envisage two stages; first, the martyrs are killed; then, at a later stage, they come to life. Collapsing these two into one (though, again, all things are possible with the kind of imagery we find in Revelation) seems implausible.

This does not mean, of course, that we are thereby projected into a pre-millennial literalism. Rather, it seems likely that we are faced here with a radical innovation: a use of the word 'resurrection' to mean a coming-to-life

---

[61] Even if this is figurative and intends to refer to martyrs in general, or even persecuted saints in general, it still leaves many of the righteous out of the category. Beale 1999, 998f. tries to insist that *all* the righteous dead are in fact included here; see below.

[62] cf. however Caird 1966, 253f., who says on the one hand that the martyrs have attained 'a heaven more solid and lasting, and therefore more real, than earth' (but then suggests, puzzlingly, that the resurrections, both first and second, are not 'to earthly, bodily life'). Chester 2001, 73 rightly insists that resurrection here 'is of course a literal, physical resurrection', while also being 'a powerful and evocative symbol for a metaphorical, communal and cosmic resurrection' in the traditions of Ezekiel, Isaiah and Daniel. For the patristic writers who envisaged a literal new Jerusalem, etc., see Hill 2002 [1992] Part I.

[63] For the debates see esp. Beale 1999, 991–1021, taking the view just described; Beale is followed by e.g. Johnson 2001, 290–94.

in a sense other than, and prior to, that of the final bodily raising.[64] For reasons that anyone who has read this far will understand, I regard the use of the word 'spiritual' to mean 'non-bodily' as misleading; and we should note carefully that in 20.4 the souls 'came to life'. This implies that they were formerly 'dead souls' (still existing as souls, but in a state of death), and that they entered a new, second stage of post-mortem existence, a form of new life.[65] For them, it seems, the journey to the ultimate destination is a *three*-step progression after death: first, a state of being 'dead souls'; second, whatever is meant by the 'first resurrection'; third, the implied 'second' or 'final' resurrection described (though not with that phrase) in chapters 21 and 22. Since this corresponds to nothing else in either Jewish or early Christian literature, except for writings dependent on the present passage, it is difficult to get any clearer about what is in mind.

We can, however, suggest that there is some analogy in the concept of an *anticipated* resurrection, as in Romans 6, Colossians 3 and elsewhere. There, as we saw, the baptized believer, whose current life is based on the past event of Jesus' death and resurrection, and whose body will be raised in the future, is in a sense already 'raised with the Messiah'. This metaphorical use of 'resurrection' language to denote the believer's present status seems to me a partial parallel at least to the use in Revelation 20.4 of 'the first resurrection' to denote a new life that these particular 'souls' are given, based on Jesus' resurrection and anticipating the full bodily resurrection still to come. Thus, though the usage is very strange, it can be understood as a bold extension of categories already being tried out within early Christianity, rather than an abandonment of normal Jewish and Christian language.

The judgment scene of chapter 20 gives way to the majestic and moving vision of the heavenly city, coming down out of heaven as a bride ready for her husband, the Messiah himself. Prominent among the descriptions of the city and its life are these: that death will be no more (21.4), and that everything less than the full, rich human life intended by the creator god is banished, cast into the lake of fire (21.8). These two final chapters are, in fact, full of indications of new creation. The key symbols are taken from biblical images of the renewed Jerusalem, which already carried the 'new creation' theme, retaining the outline of earlier pictures though developing many details in fresh ways. The river which flows from the city, like that from Eden only now life-giving in a new sense, supports the tree of life, not

---

[64] Beale 1999, 1008f. attempts to demonstrate a 'spiritual resurrection' in other Jewish and Christian texts. But the passages he cites (apart from 2 Macc. 7, which refers to the ultimate resurrection, not an intermediate state) do not use *anastasis* and its cognates, but rather *zoe* and *zao* ('life', 'live'), which clearly have a much wider referent, regularly including a non-bodily intermediate state.

[65] It is possible that *ezesan* simply means 'they lived', in other words that they 'went on living' after their deaths; but it is much more likely that it means 'they came to life' (so, rightly, Beale 1999, 1000). Cf. the parallel with Jesus' 'coming to life' (*ezesen*) in Rev. 2.8.

now a single tree in the garden, but growing plentifully along both banks of the river.[66] It bears fruit every month, and its leaves are for the healing of the nations. Here and elsewhere we glimpse, not a static picture of bliss, but a new creation bursting with new projects, new goals and new possibilities. The long story of God and the world, of God and Israel, of God and the Messiah, has arrived at its goal. Death always was the ultimate denial of the good creation; now, with its abolition, the creator's new world can proceed.

There is no need to labour the point. Revelation is as resurrection-soaked as any other book in the New Testament, for all that the key words occur only seldom (Revelation is anyway notoriously full of lexical peculiarities). The whole scenario only makes sense within the worldview of second-Temple Judaism, and in particular of that end of the spectrum which, longing for the coming kingdom, saw judgment on the wicked nations and the vindication of God's suffering people as the moment to be longed, prayed and worked for. The message of the crucified and risen Messiah, the Lion who is also the Lamb, has reshaped this worldview, producing several new mutations, not least the splitting of death into two (the 'first death' and the 'second death') and indeed of resurrection itself into three (first the Messiah, then the 'first resurrection' of 20.5, then the final resurrection of 20.12). But, whatever we make of the details, there is no doubt that this book emphatically belongs, with Paul, the gospels and Acts, at the Pharisaic end of the first-century Jewish spectrum of belief about life after death; and that mainstream Pharisaic-style belief in resurrection has here been decisively reshaped around the fundamental belief that Israel's Messiah has himself been raised from the dead, and now has the keys of Death and Hades.

6. Conclusion: Resurrection in the New Testament

The trees are fascinating in themselves, but for my present argument it is the forest that counts. We have not yet examined all the possible early evidence. Our next chapter will look outside the New Testament at several other early texts which indicate a spread of views on our topic. But the New Testament itself speaks, if not with one voice, certainly with a cluster of voices singing in close harmony. All the major books and strands, with the single exception of Hebrews, make resurrection a central and important topic, and set it within a framework of Jewish thought about the one god as creator and judge. This resurrection belief stands firmly over against the entire world of paganism on the one hand. Its reshaping, around the resurrection of Jesus himself, locates it as a dramatic modification within Judaism on the other.[67]

---

[66] Rev. 22.1f.; cf. Ezek. 47.1–12.

[67] This conclusion undermines the extraordinary suggestion of Riley 1995, 66 that physical resurrection 'was (all but) absent at the outset and took generations to develop in the Church'. Even if we were to accept the view that Luke and John were the first to invent

There are five remarkable things about this, each of which calls for historical explanation.

First, even where the resurrection was taught within Judaism, it was seldom the major concern, but in early Christianity it is. It has moved, in Evans's words, from the circumference to the centre.[68]

Second, the Jewish and pagan worlds of late antiquity were, as we have seen, full of speculations about life after death, covering a wide spectrum of opinion inside Judaism as well as outside. Though the early Christians came from many different backgrounds in both Judaism and paganism (and though beliefs about life after death are among the more tenaciously guarded elements of a culture) there is virtually no such spectrum in the New Testament. One might almost say that, from this point of view, Christianity appears as a united sub-branch of Pharisaic Judaism.

Third, however, the Pharisaic view of resurrection has been clearly and consistently modified, right through the texts we have studied, by two things in particular.[69] (1) The resurrection, as the eschatological event, has split into two (first Jesus, then, at his return, all his people – the further subdivision of the latter moment by Revelation 20 does not affect the present point).[70] (2) The nature of the future resurrection body is further clarified: it will be incapable of dying or decaying, thus requiring a transformation not only for those already dead but for those still alive. This new mode of embodiment is hard to describe, but we can at least propose a label for it. The word 'transphysical' seems not to exist, surprisingly enough (one might have thought some enterprising ontologist would have employed it long since), and I proffer it for inclusion between *transphosphorylation* and *transpicuous* in the *Oxford English Dictionary*.[71] The 'trans' is intended as a shortening of 'transformed'. 'Transphysical' is not meant to describe in detail what sort of a body it was that the early Christians supposed Jesus already had, and believed that they themselves would eventually have. Nor indeed does it claim to explain how such a thing can come to be. It merely, but I hope usefully, puts a label on the demonstrable fact that the early

---

stories about Jesus' risen body, that is still only two generations at the outside. Riley's repeated reference to the flesh of a person 'surviving the grave' (8, 66) indicates clearly that he has not begun to come to grips with what the early Christians were talking about.

[68] Evans 1970, 40.

[69] This does not mean that the word 'resurrection' has become a nose of wax, to be moulded into any kind of shape; see the writers reviewed in Wedderburn 1999, 85–95. A sense of the specific meanings in the Jewish context on the one hand, and in the early Christian context on the other, lays most of these cheerful speculations to rest.

[70] This shows how impossible it is to suggest, as does Wiles 1994, 125, that because the hope of resurrection was 'in the air' at the time this somehow made it more likely that people would believe that Jesus had been raised. What the Christians believed was not what was 'in the air' at the time.

[71] Its absence may of course be explained by the curiously Levitical taboo against mixing Latin and Greek roots.

Christians envisaged a body which was still robustly physical but also significantly different from the present one. If anything – since the main difference they seem to have envisaged is that the new body will not be corruptible – we might say not that it will be *less* physical, as though it were some kind of ghost or apparition, but more. 'Not unclothed, but more fully clothed.' As historians we may have difficulty imagining such a thing. But, equally as historians, we should not hold back from affirming that that is what the early Christians were talking about. They were not talking about a non-bodily, 'spiritual' survival. Had they wanted to do so, they had plenty of other language available to them, as indeed we do today. We should not project on to others the limitations of our own imagination.[72]

Fourth, although the early Christians drew on many of the obvious biblical texts to express the meaning of what had happened to Jesus and of what would happen to all Jesus' people, they consistently highlighted some texts and avoided others. There is, for example, virtually no use of Daniel 12.1–3, congenial though we might have supposed it to have been to the early Christians, not least because of its strong affirmation of the vindication of those who had died for their loyalty to God.[73]

Fifth, whereas in Judaism the idea of resurrection was used, at least as early as Ezekiel 37, as a metaphor to give meaning to the concrete events of the expected return from exile, this metaphorical use is totally absent in early Christianity. It is replaced with a metaphorical use of resurrection, and indeed of 'dying and rising', which has different, though equally concrete, referents: baptism, holiness of bodily life, and Christian witness.

The present chapter, along with the preceding one and the earlier Part on Paul, thus pose an enormous question to the historian. How do we account for the sudden rise of a lively and many-sided movement, growing from within a pluriform Judaism and making substantial inroads into a highly pluriform pagan world, within which one strand of belief about what happens to people after death is affirmed exclusively, is made pivotal for several other aspects of the movement, and yet is significantly but consistently modified in specific directions across a wide range of texts?[74]

---

[72] See, rightly, Wedderburn 1999, 150f., with 284 n. 356. Hanging on to 'resurrection' language but using it to mean something quite different is, at best, serving 'to keep up a pretence of orthodox respectability' (151). Küng 1976, 350f. stresses the unimaginability of the resurrection as part of his argument that 'the resurrection of Jesus was not an event in space and time'. Evans 1970, 130 has been widely quoted to the effect that the difficulty lies in 'knowing what it is which offers itself for belief'; this, I trust, is now clarified.

[73] Except for Jn. 5.29; Ac. 24.15 (Dan. 12.2), and Mt. 13.43; Phil. 2.15 (Dan. 12.3). The first two simply make the point that the resurrection will include both righteous and unrighteous (see above, 442). The Mt. and Phil. passages are not early Christian references to the future resurrection; the former is spoken by Jesus prior to Easter, and the latter is used metaphorically of *present* Christian witness.

[74] We have thus returned, though with new content, to the question posed by Moule 1967, 13: 'the birth and rapid rise of the Christian Church . . . *remain an unsolved enigma*

The early Christians, of course, had an answer for this. They did not say that they had seen 'signs of the heavenly presence of Christ'.[75] They said that Jesus of Nazareth had been raised from the dead, and that this event was the necessary and sufficient condition both for their being a 'resurrection' movement and for their being a 'transformed-resurrection' movement. But before we can examine this claim further we must extend our investigation to texts beyond the New Testament. What happened to this early Christian belief in the course of the second century?

---

for any historian who refuses to take seriously the only explanation offered by the Church itself (italics original).

[75] Against e.g. Carnley 1987, 246.

Chapter Eleven

HOPE REFOCUSED (3):
NON-CANONICAL EARLY CHRISTIAN TEXTS

1. Introduction

The remarkable rise of the early church, and its progress through the second century of its existence, is a huge and sprawling story, too vast even to summarize here. Others have laboured and I have entered into their labour.[1] As we should expect, granted its origins and environment, the church developed ways of talking about all kinds of subjects, including life after death, which sometimes reflected the sharp precision of most of the New Testament and sometimes did not. The resurrection of Jesus continued, unsurprisingly, to be central in the church's proclamation, with its meaning being explored from various angles. And, emerging at some point in the first two centuries, we discover 'resurrection' language being used in a quite different metaphorical sense: for the 'spiritual' experience of *gnosis*, or some near equivalent. The question of when and why this happened, and of what this language was taken to mean, must be taken on board in what follows.

The main questions to be addressed all through, however, are the same as those we have put to the New Testament. What view is taken of the future hope beyond death? Where resurrection language occurs, what does it mean? Is there a reference to an intermediate state? What continuity and discontinuity is there between the present body and any future one? How does resurrection, where it occurs, fit within a larger picture? What metaphorical use is made of the language of 'resurrection'? And, last but of course central

---

[1] In particular: Chadwick 1967; Kelly 1977 [1958]; Frend 1984; Stark 1996. On the present topic see esp. Bynum 1995 ch. 1. Unfortunately Bynum assumes (3–6), as a yardstick for measuring later writers, an understanding of Paul which overemphasizes his view of resurrection as transformation and fails to take full measure, as we have tried to do in Part II above, of the importance for him of bodily continuity. An important study of a closely related topic is Hill 2002 [1992]. This entire chapter serves as an outflanking and refutation of Lona 1993, who tries to argue that bodily resurrection was an unimportant theme for the second-century Christian writers.

to the present book, what view is taken of the resurrection of Jesus himself, and how does it relate to the other questions?

We proceed in a fairly standard fashion: first the 'Apostolic Fathers' (with one or two extra works best included there), then the Apologists, then (though not in any great detail, which would require another monograph in itself) the four great writers at the end of the second century and the beginning of the third, Tertullian, Irenaeus, Hippolytus and Origen. All of these we can date with reasonable certainty. Then, after a brief interlude in early Syriac Christianity, we shall examine the writings from Nag Hammadi, which speak of 'resurrection' in a rather different sense.[2] The writings in the last two categories are notoriously difficult to date.

2. Apostolic Fathers

(i) *1 Clement*

The letter now known as *1 Clement* is normally regarded as genuine, being written by the Clement who was bishop of Rome in the mid-90s of the first century. It is therefore very close in date to the New Testament, possibly even earlier than some of the canonical documents. We are not surprised, therefore, to find that Clement articulates a doctrine of resurrection not far removed from that of the New Testament.[3]

To begin with, however, it might have seemed otherwise. In the early chapters Clement speaks of the apostles Peter and Paul having died and gone, in the first case, to 'a place of glory', and in the second to 'the holy place'.[4] He goes on to speak of martyrs who 'received a noble reward', of those who obtain the gift of 'life in immortality', and of presbyters who have finished their course and have obtained 'a fruitful and perfect release (*analysis*)', and who now need have no fear of being moved 'from the place appointed to them'.[5] By themselves these passages could have been taken to indicate a belief in a final disembodied state, capable of being described in shorthand (though Clement does not use this phrase) as 'going to heaven'.[6]

---

[2] If Pelikan 1961 had cited his sources, the book would have been of considerable use for our study; sadly, it remains of interest only at a tertiary level.

[3] Greek texts used: Loeb (1912–13); Lightfoot 1989 [1889]. Translations are my own; see too Lake in Loeb; Holmes 1989. On resurrection and allied ideas in the Apostolic Fathers, see O'Hagan 1968; Van Eijk 1974; Greshake and Kremer 1986, 176–83; Bynum 1995, 22–4; Hill 2002 [1992], 77–101.

[4] *1 Clem.* 5.4, 7.

[5] *1 Clem.* 6.2; 35.1f.; 44.5.

[6] Indeed, into the heavenly sanctuary; cp. Jn. 14.2 (above, 445f.). See Hill 2002 [1992], 80–83, demonstrating that Clement believed in a temporary post-mortem heaven rather than in the righteous going to Hades.

But when Clement expounds his own view of the final state of the blessed departed, he makes it clear that this language about Peter, Paul and the others must refer to their *temporary* abode in a blessed, glorious and holy place. He not only believes in final resurrection; he mounts various arguments to show that it is not as unreasonable a thing to believe as one might suppose. First, the sequence of day and night, and seedtime and harvest, indicates that such a progression is built into the created world. He quotes the opening of the parable of the sower, linking it with an exposition not unlike that in 1 Corinthians 15.36–8:

> 'The sower went forth' and cast each of the seeds into the ground; they fall onto the ground dry and naked, and they dissolve. Then, from their dissolution, the greatness of the foreknowledge of the Master raises them up (*anistesin auta*), and from the one grain more seeds grow, and bear fruit.[7]

Clement then – boldly, we may think – advances the apparent parallel of the phoenix, which rejuvenates itself after dying every 500 years.[8] And he rounds off his exposition with three biblical passages which demonstrate, he says, that 'the creator of all things will create the resurrection of those who have served him in holiness, in the assurance of a good faith.'[9] The passages in question are not exactly those that we might have guessed. The third one is the well-known Job 19.26,[10] but the first two are from the Psalms. The first is a composite quotation from Psalms 41.10, 28.7 and 88.11: 'raise me up, and I shall praise you.'[11] The second is from Psalm 3.5, combined with 23.4: 'I lay down and slept; I arose again (*exegerthen*), for you are with me.'[12] This offers clear evidence of a continuing tradition of exegetical ingenuity, beyond what is already there in the New Testament, in which occurrences of the key Greek 'resurrection' words triggered a reading of a whole passage to demonstrate the truth of what remained, in the wider greco-roman world, an absurd belief. This would not, of course, have been necessary had the assumed final goal been a disembodied immortality. Why would anyone bother to hunt down unlikely texts, and the dubious analogy

---

[7] *1 Clem.* 24.5. Note the echoes, too, of Jn. 12.24.

[8] *1 Clem.* 25.1–5; see the similar accounts in Hdt. 2.73; Pliny *NH* 10.2. In some early Christian circles the analogy was thought to be sanctioned by the LXX of Ps. 92.12 [91.13], where, in the phrase 'the righteous shall flourish like a palm-tree', the word for 'palm-tree' is *phoinix*, the same as the Greek for the legendary bird (so Lake ad loc.). Clement seems aware of the somewhat bizarre nature of the analogy (26.1: the creator shows us this 'even through a bird').

[9] 26.1: the biblical quotations come in 26.2f.

[10] Though with different wording from that of the LXX.

[11] In LXX: Pss. 40.11; 27.7; 87.11; the verb Clement uses, though (*exanistemi*), is not found in the LXX of the Pss.

[12] In LXX: Pss. 3.6; 22.4; the latter is of course appropriate, since it speaks of God's presence even in the shadow of death.

of a fabulous bird, to prove what a good many ancient pagans already believed?

In a subsequent passage Clement sets out more clearly his view of a two-stage post-mortem life: first, a time of rest, and then a 'making manifest' when the kingdom comes:

> Those who were made perfect in love by God's grace have a place among the godly, and they will be made manifest in the visitation of the kingdom of the Messiah. For it is written, 'Enter into your chambers for a very little while, until my anger and wrath have gone away, and I will remember you on a good day, and I will raise you from your graves.'[13]

This too is a creative use of scripture beyond what we find in the New Testament, though drawing on two fairly obvious chapters, Isaiah 26 (quoting verse 20, which is not the most obvious verse from that chapter, but it looks as though the whole passage is in mind) and Ezekiel 37 (quoting verse 12). The 'revealing' (*phaneroo*) of those now dead, at the 'visitation' (*episkope*) of the kingdom, is reminiscent of various biblical passages, notably Colossians 3.4 and Wisdom 3.7. Clement is capable in another passage of describing the intermediate state in terms of 'sleep', though in the light of the other things he says it is likely that for him, as probably for Paul, this is simply a convenient metaphor and should not be taken to indicate unconsciousness.[14]

Clement is quite clear that the future resurrection is based on the resurrection of Jesus himself. This (42.3) was what assured the disciples that it was now time to go out into the world and announce that the kingdom was on the way. Clement thus stands as an early witness to a continuing creative development of the tradition, without in any obvious way deviating from the lines laid down in most of the New Testament.[15]

(ii) *2 Clement*

The so-called *Second Letter of Clement*, long supposed to be by someone else, is a general sermon on Christian living, particularly on repentance. Though shorter than *1 Clement*, it has several passages on the resurrection, including a remarkable one anticipating Tertullian's stress on the resurrection, not simply of the body, but of the *flesh*:

---

[13] *1 Clem.* 50.3f. Is there an echo of the 'chambers of the dead' in *1 En.* and elsewhere?
[14] *1 Clem.* 44.2.
[15] Bynum 1995, 24 is right that Clement draws a very close analogy between natural processes and the resurrection itself. But she goes much too far, in my opinion, in saying that this text and similar ones 'do not mean at all what Paul means'. I suspect that it is her picture of Paul himself (3–6) that is at fault.

None of you should say that this flesh is not judged and does not rise again. Know this: in what were you saved, in what did you see again, if not when you were in this flesh? We must therefore guard the flesh as the Temple of God. For as you were called in the flesh, so you shall also come [i.e. rise again] in the flesh. If the Messiah, the Lord who saved us, though he was spirit at first, became flesh and so called us, in the same way we will receive the reward in this flesh. So let us love one another, so that we may all come into the kingdom of God.[16]

Clearly the author had either not pondered deeply on Paul's subtle distinction between 'flesh' and 'body', or had a polemical axe to grind which made it necessary for him to use 'flesh' and not just 'body'. Equally, there is no question but that he intended to affirm what Paul affirmed in 1 Corinthians 6, namely, that the continuity between the present body and the future one gave substance, via the Temple-image, to ethical endeavour in the present time. Likewise, he stresses that the agency by which the resurrection will happen is the Holy Spirit.[17] Though this writer does not develop the picture further, and, perhaps surprisingly, does not mention the resurrection of Jesus himself, he clearly belongs in the same world of thought here as *1 Clement* and the canonical writers.[18]

(iii) Ignatius of Antioch

Among the many concerns expressed by Ignatius (c.35–107) in his letters, written while on his way to Rome to face martyrdom in the first decade of the second century, the resurrection, of believers and especially of Jesus, is one of the anchor-points to which he repeatedly returns. The docetists, whose theme was that Jesus was not really a genuine human being but only 'seemed' to be, denied that his flesh, passion and resurrection were real; Ignatius affirms robustly that they were. Jesus was truly (*alethos*) raised, and will raise us;[19] the church must be fully assured of his resurrection;[20] the foundation charters of the Christian faith are Jesus Christ, especially his cross, death, and resurrection, and the faith which is through him.[21] Jesus was truly nailed (i.e. to a tree) in the flesh for our sakes, so that he might set up a banner for all ages through his resurrection;[22] he truly raised himself

---

[16] *2 Clem.* 9.1–6. The image of 'entering the kingdom' is found again at 11.7.

[17] 14.3–5, ending with the affirmation (reminiscent of 2 Tim. 1.10) that, if the Spirit is joined to the flesh, the flesh is capable of receiving a great gift of 'life and immortality'. Those who suffer, the writer declares, while obeying the instructions he gives for living as Christians, will 'gather the immortal fruit of the resurrection' (19.3).

[18] So e.g. Hill 2002 [1992], 100.

[19] *Trall.* 9.2.

[20] *Philad.*, introd.

[21] *Philad.* 8.2; similarly, 9.2.

[22] *Smyrn.* 1.2; 'setting up a banner' refers to Isa. 5.26; 11.12.

from death, according to one passage, or, according to another (more in line with the New Testament), the father raised him up by his goodness.[23]

Ignatius's central statement on the subject comes in the letter to Smyrna, where he, like *2 Clement* and Tertullian, insists on the resurrection of the 'flesh':

> For I know and believe that after the resurrection he was in the flesh. And when he came to the people around Peter, he said to them, 'Take, handle me and see, that I am not a bodiless phantom' (*daimonion asomaton*). And at once they touched him and believed, being mixed together with both his flesh and his spirit. For this reason they scorned even death, and were found to be above death. And after his resurrection he ate with them and drank as a fleshly being (*hos sarkikos*), even though he was spiritually united to the father.[24]

On this basis, Ignatius steadily maintains the importance of the future resurrection of believers. The incarnation itself took its significance from the fact that what was being planned was nothing short of the abolition of death.[25] The eucharist is the 'medicine of immortality', because of which, as in John 6, those who eat will not die but live.[26] The reason we keep the Lord's Day rather than the sabbath is that then 'our life sprang up through him and through his death'; he is the one to whom the prophets looked forward, and 'when he arrived, he raised them from the dead' – possibly an allusion to the belief that in his death, descent to Hades, and resurrection he set free the righteous dead.[27] Though Ignatius sees himself at present as a slave (at least compared with the apostles), he goes to his death in the belief that if he suffers and dies he will become Jesus Christ's freedman, and will 'rise free in him'.[28] The real, bodily passion of Jesus is 'our resurrection'.[29]

By contrast, those who do not believe in the reality of Jesus' humanity, both in passion and resurrection, will themselves end up as bodiless phantasms (*asomatois kai daimonikois*). As the rabbis said of the Sadducees, those who don't believe in the resurrection won't attain it.[30] Ignatius belongs at the same point on the scale as the New Testament, even though he, like

---

[23] *Smyrn.* 2.1 (cf. Jn. 2.19; 10.18); 7.1; cf. too 7.2; 12.2; *Rom.* 6.1.

[24] *Smyrn.* 3.1–3. On the traditions underlying this version of Jesus' words see Schoedel 1985, 226–8. The phrase 'mixed together with both flesh and spirit' seems to refer to a fellowship on both levels; cf. *Eph.* 5.1.

[25] *Eph.* 19.3.

[26] *Eph.* 20.1.

[27] *Magn.* 9.1f. Lightfoot (1989 [1889], 2.131f.) gives strong support to this interpretation, seeing it echoed also in *Philad.* 5.2; 9.1, and discussing particularly the supposedly biblical passage quoted by Justin (*Dial.* 72), and also Irenaeus, Tertullian, Clement of Alexandria and Origen. See too Hermas, *Sim.* 9.16 (see below). Lake, ad loc., refers to the later *Gospel of Nicodemus* and *Acts of Pilate* for this theme.

[28] *Rom.* 4.3. I take this as a reference to the final resurrection, not to a 'rising' to heaven; so too *Eph.* 11.2 (against Hill 2002 [1992], 89).

[29] *Smyrn.* 5.3.

[30] *Smyrn.* 2.1. For the rabbis and Sadducees, see above, ch. 4.

Clement, has developed some ideas in new ways and has used different terminology. He does not make the distinction, clear in Paul and implicit elsewhere, between the nature of the crucified body and that of the risen one. His apologetic concern was for continuity, not discontinuity.[31] The closing greeting of the letter to the Smyrneans emphasizes where his heart lay:

> I salute . . . you all, individually and together, in the name of Jesus Christ and in his flesh and blood, by his suffering and resurrection, fleshly and spiritually (*sarkike te kai pneumatike*), in union with God and with you.[32]

(iv) Polycarp: *Letter* and *Martyrdom*

Polycarp (c. 69–155) was bishop of Smyrna, on the western seacoast of Asia Minor. His letter to the Philippians is short, but contains a reasonably full view of our topic. It is completely in line with the New Testament. Jesus himself was raised from the dead by God, and will be the judge of both living and departed. The one who raised him from the dead will also raise up those who do his will.[33] This is expressed in terms of the present age and the age to come:

> For if we please him in the present age, we shall receive also the age to come, just as he promised us that he would raise us from the dead, and that if we conduct ourselves worthily of him we shall also reign with him, if we have faith.[34]

This is very close not only to Paul but to Pharisaic/rabbinic thought – as is the warning that those who deny both resurrection and judgment are among the chief sinners. The passage which makes that declaration (7.1) quotes 1 John 4.2–3, warning against the docetic heresy of supposing that Jesus' humanity was not real. According to Irenaeus, Polycarp later used similar language about Marcion.[35]

Polycarp also, rather after the manner of Clement, speaks of the intermediate state of the martyrs. Believers must be fully persuaded that Ignatius, Zosimus and Rufus, others of their own church, and of course Paul himself and the other apostles, did not 'run in vain' (Polycarp again quotes Paul's letter to the Philippians, here from 2.16), but in faith and righteousness, 'and that they are with the Lord' (*para to kyrio*), with whom they suffered, having now gone to 'the place they have deserved' (*eis ton opheilomenon autois*

---

[31] On Ignatius' apologetic concern in relation to other early writers see Schoedel 1985, 227–9. On whether Lk. 24 was written with the same motive see 659 below.

[32] *Smyrn.* 12.2. We note the use of 'flesh' here, corresponding to Lk. 24.39 over against 1 Cor. 15.50. This anticipates the later usage of e.g. Tertullian.

[33] Pol. *Phil.* 2.1f. On Polycarp cf. Hill 2002 [1992], 91f.

[34] Pol. *Phil.* 5.2. 'If we conduct ourselves worthily' is *ean politeusometha axios*, an echo of Paul's letter to the same church (Phil. 1.27).

[35] Iren. *Adv. Haer.* 3.3.4; cf. Euseb. *HE* 4.14.

topon). We see here the very cautious early Christian attempts to speak of the immediate life after death, in terms similar to Paul's in the first chapter of Philippians, while emphasizing also the importance of the final state, the resurrection life which will be given *after* this state of 'life after death'.

With the letter of Polycarp we may also glance at the account of his martyrdom.[36] Here we find ourselves in a different world of thought. The scene is set by a description of the martyrs of old, who by a single hour of trial have purchased everlasting life. They have compared the short-lived fire they face at the stake with the fire of hell which is everlasting, never to be quenched; they have kept their eyes on the wonderful things promised to those who endure, which have been shown by the Lord 'to those who were no longer men, but already angels'.[37] This identification of the Christian dead as angels is a new idea, though with an echo in Acts 12.15 and 23.9; it is developed in *Hermas*.[38] The writer seems at times unclear whether to emphasize the future resurrection or the present glorious state the martyrs have already attained. Thus we find Polycarp praying as he goes to the fire:

> I bless you, because you have counted me worthy of this day and this hour, that I should have a share in the number of the martyrs, in the cup of your Messiah, for the resurrection of eternal life of both soul and body in the incorruption of the Holy Spirit.[39]

At the same time, the writer – perhaps to encourage potential martyrs of his own day – celebrates the glorious life Polycarp already enjoys:

> By his endurance he overcame the unjust ruler, and so obtained the crown of incorruption. Now, celebrating with the apostles and all the righteous ones, he glorifies God the almighty father, and praises our Lord Jesus the Messiah, the saviour of our souls and guide of our bodies, the shepherd of the universal, worldwide church.[40]

Putting those two together, we may doubt whether the careful distinction between the present state of the dead and their future resurrection was as fully present to the writer's mind as it was to his predecessors, not least Polycarp himself. The account also contains a remarkable description of how, when the fire is not consuming him fast enough, a soldier stabs Polycarp and a dove emerges from his body – an idea with many classical parallels and part-parallels.[41] There is, finally, one of the earliest pieces of evidence for Christian veneration of the tombs of the martyrs. The writer

---

[36] On which see *NTPG* 347f.

[37] *Mt. Pol.* 2.3.

[38] On the Ac. passages see ch. 4 (Sadducee section), and ch. 10 above; on *Hermas* see 491f. below.

[39] *Mt. Pol.* 14.2.

[40] *Mt. Pol.* 19.2.

[41] See Lightfoot 1989 [1889], 3.390–93.

insists, against the charges of Jews and pagans, that there remains a huge distinction between the Christian attitude to Christ himself, whom the Christians worshipped as son of god, and the Christian love for the martyrs as his disciples and imitators.[42] He also makes it clear that there will be regular celebrations at Polycarp's tomb:

> So we finally took up his bones, which are more valuable than precious stones, and more honourable than gold, and placed them where it was appropriate. There the Lord will allow us, as far as we are able, to come together in celebration and joy to perform the ceremonies for the birthday of his martyrdom – both for the memory of those who have already taken part in the contest, and for the training and preparation of those who will do so in the future.[43]

Though the book is thus not completely clear on what exactly happens to the martyrs after death, it provides good evidence of the behaviour of those left behind. This contrasts interestingly with the early Christians' attitude to Jesus' tomb.[44]

(v) The *Didache*

The question of when and where the *Didache* was written is still the subject of considerable debate.[45] From most of its content we would not know that early Christianity was anything other than a life of piety and good works; though the opening indicates the ultimate destination that is in view, speaking of the two ways, the way of life and the way of death.[46] Throughout the detailed ethical exhortations there is no explicit mention of an ultimate sanction or reward beyond death. Only when we reach the instructions relating to the eucharist do we find, in the two prayers, a mention of the eventual goal:

> As this broken bread was scattered over the mountains, and was brought together to become one, even so may your church be gathered together from the ends of the earth into your kingdom; for yours is the glory and the power through Jesus Christ unto the ages.
> Remember, Lord, your church, to rescue it from every evil and make it perfect in your love, and gather it from the four winds, as a sanctified people, into your kingdom, which you have prepared for it; for yours is the power and the glory to the ages.[47]

The notion of a 'kingdom', brought about through the divine power, seems to reflect the early eschatology we have studied. And the eucharist is to be

---

[42] *Mt. Pol.* 17.2f.
[43] *Mt. Pol.* 18.2f.
[44] Below, 701–3.
[45] See e.g. Draper 1996; Niederwimmer 1998 [1989], 52–4.
[46] *Did.* 1.1f.
[47] *Did.* 9.4; 10.5.

held 'on the Lord's day of the Lord' (*kata kyriaken kyriou*), celebrating – not least through this strange repetitive phrase! – the fact that Jesus is the true king.[48]

In the final chapter of the short book, the writer produces a collage of quotations, mostly from Matthew 24, to speak of the coming end. The church must keep awake for the coming of the Lord; false prophets will appear, and ultimately the 'deceiver'; but then will come the signs of the truth:

> First, the sign spread out in heaven; then the sign of the voice of the trumpet; and, as the third sign, the resurrection of the dead. But not of all, rather, as it was said, 'The Lord shall come, and all his saints with him.' Then the world shall see the Lord 'coming on the clouds of heaven'.[49]

This seems to be dependent not only on Matthew's apocalyptic discourse and Old Testament prophecy (here, Zechariah 14.5 and Daniel 7.13), but also on the prediction of the resurrection in 1 Corinthians 15.52 and 1 Thessalonians 4.16.[50] How the *Didache* integrates the future resurrection within a larger eschatological scheme is not our present question.[51] That it affirms the resurrection, as part of a theology of a coming kingdom of god, means that, though the doctrine is not central to the document (it does not integrate it, after the fashion of Paul, with its main concern, which is with small-scale practical details of church life and ethics), it is another witness to the same theology that we find in Clement, Ignatius, Polycarp and of course the New Testament itself.

(vi) *Barnabas*

The *Letter of Barnabas* (which has been variously dated in the last decades of the first century or the first decades of the second) offers an extended exposition of Christian faith largely in terms of the typological fulfilment of Old Testament scripture. Among the central themes it draws out is that of new covenant and new creation. The introduction declares that the first of the three *dogmata* which the writer will expound is *zoes elpis*, 'the hope of life', which, he says, 'is the beginning and ending of our faith.'[52]

---

[48] *Did.* 14.1, 3.

[49] *Did.* 16.6–8.

[50] See e.g. Niederwimmer 1998 [1989], 223–5.

[51] On this question, coupled with the suggestion of a possible lost ending to the work, cf. Aldridge 1999, with Hill 2002 [1992], 77f.

[52] *Barn.* 1.6. The other two *dogmata* are righteousness, the beginning and end of judgment, and a glad and rejoicing love (taking *euphrosynes* and *agalliaseos* as adjectival, not objective as Lake ad loc., Holmes 162), which is the testimony of works of righteousness.

He then argues that the covenant of the Old Testament has been renewed through Jesus, and has been taken away from the Jews; judgment is coming, the judgment spoken of in Daniel and elsewhere, and Christians must hold fast to their faith.[53] Jesus is the truly human one, made in god's image, who suffered and endured at the hands of men 'in order to abolish death and reveal the resurrection from the dead, because he must be made manifest in flesh'.[54] By itself, this might indicate that the writer was taking 1 Timothy 3.16 ('manifest in the flesh') as referring to the resurrection, but the passage which follows indicates that it is an anti-docetic comment about the incarnation.[55] This leads to the promise of new creation, a new land flowing with milk and honey in ultimate fulfilment of the promise of Genesis 1.26–8.[56] The new world will be completed 'when we have been made perfect as heirs of the covenant of the Lord'.[57]

There then follows a long section of typological and allegorical exposition of scripture in relation to Jesus' death and to Christian behaviour, and a further exposition of baptism and the cross (chapters 7—12). This leads the writer to an explicit statement of the promises which indicate that the covenant will be renewed so as to include Gentiles within it (13—14). This is then focused on the sabbath commandment, which (as in Hebrews) is interpreted eschatologically in terms of the 'rest' which is still to come. It points, in fact, to the final new creation, which was inaugurated when Jesus rose from the dead on the first day of the new week:

> The sabbath which I have made [says God], in which I will give rest to all things, is the beginning of an eighth day, that is, the beginning of another world. Therefore we also regard the eighth day as a day of celebration, in which Jesus also rose from the dead and was made manifest, and went up into heaven.[58]

The book closes with an exposition of the 'two ways', and the final summary insists that the path of light makes the sense it does because of what is to come:

> For the one who does these things will be glorified in the kingdom of God, while people who choose the others shall be destroyed along with their works. That is why there is resurrection; that is why there is recompense.[59]

The last paragraph of the book repeats, over and over again, the warning of coming judgment and the promise of final salvation.[60] The present life

---

[53] *Barn.* 4.1–14. Cf. too 19.10.
[54] *Barn.* 5.5f.
[55] *Barn.* 5.9–12; cf. 6.7, 9.
[56] *Barn.* 6.9–19.
[57] *Barn.* 6.19; on 'perfection' here cf. e.g. Phil. 3.12.
[58] *Barn.* 15.8f. For the 'eighth day' scheme in John see 440 above, 669 below.
[59] *Barn.* 21.1.
[60] *Barn.* 21.3, 6, 9.

makes sense in view of that which is to come. Although the exposition is of a very different order to anything we find in the New Testament, this is clearly an attempt to set out, in a different situation (and under pressure from Jewish opposition) the early theology of new creation and new covenant, and we are therefore not surprised to find the resurrection, both of Jesus and of Christians, as an important, though not very developed, strand within it.

(vii) The *Shepherd of Hermas*

The long tripartite work of *Hermas* is now normally dated to the middle of the second century, but was regarded as part of the New Testament by Irenaeus, Clement of Alexandria and (in his early period) Tertullian. The long and winding road of visions, musings, revelations and reflections includes a passage which speaks of new creation in fulfilment of prophecy;[61] but most of the book is about the possibility of repentance following post-baptismal sin, giving lengthy and (to our eyes) tortuous analyses of levels and types of bad and good behaviour. Within this the clear doctrines taught both in the New Testament and in the other Apostolic Fathers are at best muted; this applies (for instance) to Christology as well as life after death.

The only clear statement of resurrection in the whole work comes at the conclusion of the fifth Parable or *Similitude*:

> Guard this flesh of yours pure and undefiled, so that the spirit which dwells in it may bear witness to it, and that your flesh may be justified. Take care lest it come into your heart that this flesh of yours is corruptible, and you misuse it with some defilement or other. If you defile your flesh, you defile also the Holy Spirit. And if you defile the flesh,[62] you shall not live.
>
> [Hermas then asks how a person who defiles the flesh in ignorance of this teaching can still be saved. The teacher continues:] For the former ignorances, it is in God's power alone to give healing, for he has all authority, if, in the future, you do not defile either flesh or spirit. For both are in communion, and it is impossible to defile one without the other. Keep both pure, therefore, and you will live to God.[63]

It remains unclear in this passage precisely what *Hermas* thinks the final state of pure Christians will be. But since he uses the union of flesh and spirit, and the impossibility of defiling one without the other, as the key to his argument, it may be that he intends to affirm the resurrection of both flesh and spirit at the end; and perhaps this is what is meant by 'live to god', a phrase which we have met in other contexts and which recurs three times more in *Hermas*.[64]

---

[61] e.g. *Vis.* 1.3.4, alluding to Isa. 40.4.

[62] Editors sometimes alter this to 'spirit', for obvious reasons of sense, but the MSS clearly represent the harder reading.

[63] *Sim.* 5.7.1–4. Hill 2002 [1992], 94 is clear that *Hermas* takes resurrection for granted.

[64] *Sim.* 8.11.4; 9.22.4; 9.30.5; see above, 252 n. 96; 425.

It is sometimes said that in *Hermas*, as apparently in the *Martyrdom of Polycarp*, the righteous dead become angels.[65] But the relevant passage in *Vision* 2.2.7 simply says 'that your passing (*parodos*) may be with the holy angels'.[66] In *Similitude* 9.27.3 the righteous will be 'sheltered by the Lord'; they are already 'glorious with god', and 'their place is already with the angels, if they continue serving the Lord to the end'. In none of these does the author *identify* the dead with angels; he merely says, as one could say of Lazarus in Luke 16.22, that they are in the company of angels. On another occasion, he refers to the righteous dead 'dwelling with the son of god, having received his spirit'.[67] Frustratingly, the long parable of the willow-tree (*Similitude* 8), having apparently alluded to Ezekiel 37 when asking how these dry things (the sticks in the parable) could live, never develops a full answer which would show what the author believed might be the fulfilment of that particular prophecy.[68] All in all, we have a strong sense that we are asking a question that Hermas was not interested in. We cannot press him one way or the other for the kind of exact answer that so many other early Christian texts were eager to supply.

(viii) Papias

Some fragments survive, in quotations and discussions in later writers, from the teaching and writings of Papias (c. 60–130), who was bishop of Hierapolis around the same time that Polycarp was bishop of Smyrna.[69] Eusebius relates how Papias described 'the resurrection of a dead person' (*nekrou anastasis*) in his own days, and how he believed that there would be a thousand-year period after the resurrection of the dead, when the kingdom of Christ would be set up bodily (*somatikos*) on this earth. Despite the fact that this is obviously based on Revelation 20, Eusebius appears to treat it all as a lapse of taste as well as of theology, and is quick to insist that Papias, 'a man of extremely small intelligence, as the evidence of his writings shows', had misunderstood the apostles, not seeing that they had written 'mystically and symbolically'. He does note, however, that Irenaeus, whom Eusebius would hardly describe in such dismissive tones, followed Papias in this.[70] The same point is made by Jerome, who adds that when Irenaeus and Apollinarius and others follow Papias in his millennial vision they say that, after

---

[65] So Lake on *Vis.* 2.2.7, and *Mart. Pol.* 2.3.

[66] This phrase is repeated almost exactly in *Sim.* 9.25.2.

[67] *Sim.* 9.24.4.

[68] *Sim.* 8.2.6.

[69] The most convenient collection of the fragments is Holmes 1989, 307–29.

[70] *HE* 3.39.9, 12f. A different account of Papias on this point is given by the seventh-century Anastasius of Sinai (Holmes 1989, 321). On the whole question of an earthly paradise (and chiliasm in general) in Papias see above all Hill 2002 [1992], 22f., 63–8.

the resurrection, the Lord will reign in the flesh with the saints.[71] The great seventh-century Maximus the Confessor adds that, according to Papias, food will be among the joys of the resurrection.[72]

Irenaeus' own account of beliefs before his own day, which he had made his own, includes a lavish account of what 'the elders who saw John the disciple of the Lord' used to say about the coming time when vines will grow in abundance, grains of wheat will produce ten thousand heads, and so on. The animals who feed on this wonderful diet will become peaceful and gentle towards one another, and fully subject to human beings (an interesting attempt to explain passages like Isaiah 11.6–9).[73] Irenaeus, aware no doubt of raised eyebrows among his audience, adds firmly that, according to Papias, such things are believable to those who believe. Indeed, he says, Papias reports that Judas had not believed in the coming time of blessing, and that Jesus had responded simply that those who lived until those times would see.[74] Clearly Papias is to be cited as an extra witness, along with Clement and Ignatius, for a robustly physical view of the final time of salvation, for the world as well as for righteous human beings.

(ix) The *Epistle to Diognetus*

The *Epistle to Diognetus*, though normally printed with the other 'Apostolic Fathers', does not really belong with them.[75] It is probably from either the late second century or even the third, and should be classified with the Apologists like Justin and Athenagoras.[76]

Nor does it belong with Clement, Ignatius and Polycarp when it comes to thinking about the Christian hope. At least, it has nothing much to say about it (nor about the resurrection of Jesus), but what it does have to say, about the place of the Christian church within the wider world, inclines one to think that the author held a standard hellenistic view of an immortal soul shut up in a physical body. As the soul dwells in the body, but is not of the body, so Christians dwell in the world, but are not of the world (6.3). The flesh hates the soul, and fights against it, just as the world hates Christians. This is not because it or they have done any wrong but because they oppose

---

[71] Jerome, *Vir. Illustr.* 18, quoted in Holmes 1989, 319; see too the fifth-century Philip of Side (Holmes 318).

[72] Quoted in Holmes 1989, 323.

[73] The text is similar to *2 Bar.* 29.5. Irenaeus implies that this report from 'the elders' was written up by Papias, but does not ascribe it to him directly (as implied by Bynum 1995, 23). See again Hill 2002 [1992], esp. 254–9.

[74] Iren. *Adv. Haer.* 5.33.3f. On Irenaeus, including his insistence that he, unlike the heretics, was following the genuine tradition, see below, 513–7.

[75] So Louth 1987, 140; Holmes 1989, 291f.

[76] Hill 2002 [1992], 102 favours a date around 150.

the pleasures of world and flesh (6.5). The closest we come to a positive view of the body, which could point towards resurrection, is the following:

> The soul loves the flesh which hates it, and the limbs; and Christians love those who hate them. The soul has been shut up in the body, but itself sustains the body; and Christians, shut up in the world as in a prison, themselves sustain the world. The soul is immortal, and lives within a mortal tent; and Christians live for the moment among corruptible things, while they await the incorruptibility in heaven.[77]

This could, at a stretch, be understood to be compatible with, say, 2 Corinthians 4 and 5; but it seems more natural to take it as a moderate Platonic statement, not seeing an incorruptible body as a gift from heaven but seeing the immortal soul awaiting a complete immortality, away from the corruptible material world, as a gift which will be enjoyed in heaven itself. Diognetus thus probably articulates the view of personal eschatology which many western Christians still assume to be that of the New Testament.[78]

The Apostolic Fathers stay quite close to their canonical predecessors. There are new battles to fight, not least against docetism. Some, not least Ignatius, therefore stress the bodily and 'fleshly' resurrection of Jesus without differentiating the risen body from the present corruptible one. They develop new language and imagery to address new situations. As with some of the shorter canonical books, they do not always need to discuss the resurrection, or even affirm it. But in many passages they confirm that, for the vast majority of early Christians known to us, 'resurrection' was the ultimate Christian hope, and was meant in a definitely bodily sense; that this entailed some kind of intermediate state, itself glorious and blissful; and that the future resurrection was dependent on, and modelled on, that of Jesus himself. There was no attempt to use the language of 'resurrection' metaphorically either in the ways developed (alongside the literal use) in the New Testament or in the very different ways developed by, for instance, the *Epistle to Rheginos*. 'Resurrection' remained literal in use, concrete in referent, and foundational to early Christian theology and hope.

3. Early Christian Apocrypha

(i) Introduction

There are certain books normally classified as 'New Testament Apocrypha' which, though their date and circumstances of writing remain controversial, have the potential to reveal a significant amount about the early Christian

---

[77] *Diog.* 6.6–8.
[78] Hill 2002 [1992], 103 suggests, more positively, that though the work does not clearly refer to the resurrection, there is no evidence that the author doubted it.

movement. The texts in question are available in good modern translations.[79] We shall look briefly at four works in particular.

(ii) The *Ascension of Isaiah*

The early Christian work known as the *Ascension of Isaiah* is now found as part of a text surviving only in Ethiopic in a complete form, though with Greek, Latin, Slavonic and Coptic fragments. It has normally been thought that the text is composite, with a Christian second part (chapters 6–11) attached to a pre-Christian Jewish part (chapters 1–5) known as the *Martyrdom of Isaiah*; that is the title under which the work is now often found.[80] Both the composite nature of the text and the date have been controversial; scholars used to favour a cautious placing somewhere in the second century, but the most recent major critical study, which also argues for the essential unity of the work, puts it firmly in the first century, and in the 70s at that.[81] But wherever in this span we date the work, its vision of the resurrection is not gnostic, as has sometimes been maintained.[82] It appears to be more or less in line with the New Testament and the Apostolic Fathers already studied.

There are two key texts for our purposes, one in each part. Those who treat the text as composite explain the first as a Christian interpolation into the supposedly non-Christian, Jewish first part. The first passage speaks of 'the Beloved', that is, the Messiah, who will come from the seventh heaven, adopting the form of a man, and be tormented, crucified and buried, with guards guarding the grave. Then,

> the angel of the Holy Spirit and Michael, the chief of the holy angels, will open his grave on the third day, and that Beloved, sitting on their shoulders, will come forth and send out his twelve disciples, and they will teach all nations and every tongue the resurrection of the Beloved, and those who believe in his cross will be saved, and in his ascension to the seventh heaven from where he came; and that many who believe in him will speak through the Holy Spirit, and there will be many signs and miracles in those days.[83]

This has obvious affinities to elements of the canonical traditions; to the longer ending of Mark (which, if early enough, might be regarded as a

---

[79] See esp. Hennecke 1963, 1965; Elliott 1993.

[80] I have worked from the introduction and text of Knibb in Charlesworth 1985, 143–76.

[81] Bauckham 1998a, 389. See also Hall 1990; Norelli 1994, 1995; Knight 1996; Hill 2002 [1992], 109–16. Full bibliog. in Norelli 1995.

[82] e.g. Helmbold 1972 (more precisely, 'semi-Christian . . . or Christian-Gnostic', 227). That there are many parallels with motifs found in the Nag Hammadi texts is obvious; but what matters is the actual content.

[83] *Asc. Isa.* 3.15–20.

source for it); and also to the story of the two enormous men coming out of the tomb, supporting Jesus, in the *Gospel of Peter*. It is doubtful, though, whether the work is straightforwardly dependent on any of these, or they on it; this is a subject deserving closer study.[84]

The other key text comes in chapter 9, at the climax of the vision of the coming Messiah which is vouchsafed to 'Isaiah' as he ascends through the seven heavens.[85] When he gets to the seventh heaven, he sees Enoch and all who were with him. They are 'stripped of their robes of flesh', and wearing heavenly robes like angels. They are, however, not yet enthroned.[86] For this they must wait until Christ descends to earth in the incarnation, and be killed by 'the god of that world'. After that,

> When he has plundered the angel of death, he will rise on the third day and will remain in that world for five hundred and forty-five days. And then many of the righteous will ascend with him, whose spirits do not receive their robes until the Lord Christ ascends and they ascend with him. Then indeed they will receive their robes and their thrones and their crowns, when he has ascended into the seventh heaven.[87]

This clearly insists both on the resurrection of Jesus and the 'reclothing' of the righteous – and on a temporal sequence in which something new is accomplished, through Jesus' incarnation, death and resurrection, for those already dead. The 'reclothing' with heavenly robes should not be pressed to mean that the new bodies are 'immaterial'; the thought might just as easily be close to that of 2 Corinthians 5.1–5. The plundering of the angel of death is very different to the idea of welcoming death as the shedding of the physical body. The *Ascension of Isaiah*, whether composite or unitary, first or second century, belongs closely with the theology, though not always with the imagery, of the canonical material and the Apostolic Fathers.

(iii) The *Apocalypse of Peter*

The work known as the *Apocalypse of Peter* (unrelated to the Nag Hammadi tractate of the same name, on which see below) is now generally recognized as having been written from within a group of Christians seeking to remain faithful during the Bar-Kochba regime (AD 132–5).[88] The book shows clear

---

[84] See Bauckham 1998a, 389f. On the endings of Mk., see ch. 14 below; on *Gos. Pet.*, ch. 13.

[85] cf. too 4.14–18, which clearly teaches a future resurrection (despite Hill 2002 [1992], 113f., who curiously suggests that the resurrection in 4.18 might be of the wicked only, an idea otherwise unknown in Jewish or Christian sources).

[86] *Asc. Isa.* 9.9–11. For the 'robes' as indicating the transformed state of the righteous cf. also 1.5; 3.25; 4.16f.; 7.22; 8.14, 26; 9.2, 17f., 24–6; 11.40.

[87] *Asc. Isa.* 9.16–18.

[88] Text: Hennecke 1965, 668–83; Elliott 1993, 593–612. On this work, its setting and

dependence on several parts of the New Testament, and on ideas that were current within Jewish apocalyptic writing. The central passage for our present topic comes in chapter 4, where the writer brings together echoes of biblical prophecy, notably Ezekiel 37, with explanations of resurrection that, as with several other second-century writings, draw on the Pauline imagery of seeds and plants:

> Behold now what they shall experience in the last days, when the day of God comes. On the day of the decision of the judgment of God, all the children of men from the east unto the west shall be gathered before my Father who ever liveth, and he will command hell to open its bars of steel and to give up all that is in it. And the beasts and the fowls shall he command to give back all flesh that they have devoured, since he desires that men should appear again; for nothing perishes for God, and nothing is impossible with him, since all things are his. For all things come to pass on the day of decision, on the day of judgment, at the word of God, and as all things came to pass when he created the world and commanded all that is therein, and it was all done – so it says in the Scripture, 'Son of man, prophesy upon the several bones, and say to the bones – bone unto bone in joints, sinews, nerves, flesh and skin and hair thereon.'[89] And soul and spirit shall the great Uriel give at the command of God.[90] For him God has appointed over the resurrection of the dead on the day of judgment. Behold and consider the corns of wheat which are sown in the earth. As something dry and without a soul does a man sow them in the earth; and they live again, bear fruit, and the earth gives them back again as a pledge entrusted to it. And this which dies, which is sown as seed in the earth and shall become alive and be restored to life, is man. How much more shall God raise up on the day of decision those who believe in him and are chosen by him and for whom he made the earth; and all this shall the earth give back on the day of decision, since it shall also be judged with them, and the heaven with it.[91]

This emphatic statement of future judgment, requiring future bodies, is expanded elsewhere in the book, both in terms of the new 'clothes' which the 'elect and righteous' will wear – in other words, the new bodies they will receive – and in terms of the intermediate state, the 'Paradise', which they

---

particular emphases, see above all Buchholz 1988; Bauckham 1998a, ch. 8; and see too Hill 2002 [1992], 116–20. Bauckham (239) specifies the context as a time when 'Christians were suffering for their refusal to accept Bar Kokhba as Messiah and to participate in the revolt', placing this in turn within 'the rabbinic attempt to exclude Jewish Christians from the religious community of Israel'.

[89] Bauckham 1998a, ch. 9 shows in considerable detail that this ref. to Ezek. 37 is dependent on the traditions preserved in 4Q385 (one of the mss. of 4Q *Second Ezekiel*, which may be identical with the otherwise lost 'Apocryphon of Ezekiel'). Similar dependence on these post-biblical traditions are found in e.g. Justin *1 Apol.* 52.5f. and Tert. *De Res.* 32.1.

[90] For Uriel and his role cf. Bauckham 1998a, 221f. In *1 En.* 20.1 Uriel is first in a list of seven angels; elsewhere he is often third behind Michael and Gabriel.

[91] *Ap. Pet.* 4; tr. from Henneke 1963. Bauckham 1998a, ch. 10 locates the notion of the 'giving back' of the dead within the wider world of Jewish and Christian thought about resurrection.

will enjoy.[92] It clearly belongs within the main stream of 'resurrection' ideas we have studied from both Jewish and Christian sources. Though some of the details of its picture appear inconsistent – do the righteous get their new bodies before the last judgment or afterwards? – there is no question about the basic belief. The hope of resurrection, here as elsewhere, is invoked to sustain those who are undergoing persecution.

(iv) 5 Ezra

The work known as 5 Ezra is printed, confusingly, as the first two chapters of the book known as 2 Esdras in the Old Testament Apocrypha.[93] Some still regard it as a Jewish work,[94] but most agree with Graham Stanton, that it is a Christian work written in the aftermath of the Bar-Kochba revolt.[95]

The second chapter of the work, firmly rooted in traditional Jewish themes, promises resurrection for those who have died:

> Call, O call heaven and earth to witness: I set aside evil and created good; for I am the Living One, says the Lord.
> Mother, embrace your children; bring them up with gladness, as does a dove; strengthen their feet, because I have chosen you, says the Lord. And I will raise up the dead from their places, and bring them out from their tombs, because I recognize my name in them . . . I have consecrated and prepared for you twelve trees loaded with various fruits, and the same number of springs flowing with milk and honey, and seven mighty mountains on which roses and lilies grow . . .[96]

The promise of resurrection, with echoes of Ezekiel 37, is thus held within the larger vision of new creation, of Eden restored. The readers are told to do justice in the community, not least burying those who remain unburied. Those who do so are promised 'the first place in my resurrection'.[97] There will come a day of tribulation and anguish, with the nations warring against the chosen people. But they are assured not only of divine protection but also, once more, of resurrection:

> Rejoice, O mother, with your children, because I will deliver you, says the Lord. Remember your children that sleep, because I will bring them out of the hiding places of the earth, and will show mercy to them; for I am merciful, says the Lord Almighty.[98]

---

[92] *Apoc. Pet.* 13.1; 16—17.
[93] 2 Esdr. 3–14 comprises the work more usually known as 4 Ezra; 2 Esdr. 15–16, a further separate work, is better known as 6 Ezra, a Christian work probably from the third century.
[94] cf. e.g. O'Neill 1991.
[95] Stanton 1977.
[96] *5 Ezr.* 2.14–19.
[97] *5 Ezr.* 2.23.
[98] *5 Ezr.* 2.30f.

If this is indeed a Christian work, it shows that at this point the persecuted young church was claiming the same promises (based not least on Daniel 12) as the Jewish martyrs had done in 2 Maccabees and elsewhere.

(v) The *Epistula Apostolorum*

The work under this title was discovered in a Coptic version in the late nineteenth century, and subsequently also in an Ethiopic translation and a few Latin fragments.[99] It purports to be a letter from the eleven surviving apostles to Christians around the world, telling them of the conversations they had had with the risen Jesus after Easter. This fictive setting, familiar from some of the Nag Hammadi and similar writings (see below), is used here to present a theological position very like that of the New Testament, the other Apostolic Fathers and the Apologists. The probable date is around the middle of the second century, or perhaps somewhat earlier.

The work presents, among other things, a robust view of Jesus' bodily resurrection and of the future embodied life of his followers, over against teachers like Cerinthus and Simon Magus. The apostles were able not only to hear but also to feel Jesus after his resurrection.[100] The risen Lord, to convince the disciples (who were even slower to believe, according to this text, than it appears in the canonical stories), invited not only Thomas to touch him, but also Peter and Andrew as well:

> And that you may know that it is I, lay your hand, Peter, and your finger in the nail-print of my hands; and you, Thomas, in my side; and also you, Andrew, see whether my foot steps on the ground and leaves a footprint.[101]

When the risen Jesus promises them that they, too, will be given new and incorruptible bodies as part of the renewal of all creation, he backs up the point by quoting Psalm 3, including the verse: 'I lay down and fell asleep; I rose up, for God raised me up' (the Psalm itself has 'for the Lord sustained me').[102] This is then applied to the disciples themselves; as the father awakened Jesus from the dead, so they too will be raised in the same manner, and will receive 'a garment that will not pass away'.[103] Clearly the early Christian ability to find scriptural passages to buttress resurrection belief was still alive and well, as was the fondness for sayings of the 'I am' type: 'I am the hope of the hopeless,' declares Jesus, 'the helper of those who have

---

[99] Text: Hennecke 1963, 191–227; Elliott 1993, 555–88. See Hill 2002 [1992], 123–5.

[100] *Ep. Ap.* 2.

[101] *Ep. Ap.* 11 (Ethiop.). In the Coptic parallel, Andrew is invited to observe that Jesus' feet really are touching the ground, thus demonstrating that he is not a ghost.

[102] *Ep. Ap.* 19.

[103] *Ep. Ap.* 21.

no helper, the treasure of those in need, the physician of the sick, the resurrection of the dead.'[104]

In company with many second-century writers on the resurrection, this author faces the question of how the resurrection is to be accomplished. How can what is departed and scattered become alive?[105] Jesus explains that the flesh, which has 'fallen away', will arise, just as what is lost will be found and what is weak will recover, and all to the glory of the father.[106] This is nowhere near as full an answer as is provided by the other early Christian writers, not least the one to whom we now turn; but there is no doubt that the *Epistula Apostolorum* had every intention of affirming the bodily resurrection just as clearly as they did.

4. The Apologists

(i) Justin Martyr

Justin (c.100–165), writing in the middle of the second century, is the first Christian thinker to write what we might regard as full-length books.[107] He was a trained and practised philosopher, and following his conversion to Christianity (around AD 130) he continued to teach philosophy, though now expounding the Christian faith. Like the other Apologists, he saw as his principal task the need to rebut charges of immorality, sedition and indeed atheism (a regular accusation against those who denied the propriety of pagan religion).[108] But Justin took it upon himself also to argue that Christianity was actually the truth which made sense of the glimmers of light within paganism. It was not that the rest of the world was simply wrong, and the Christians simply right; the rest of the world was looking at signposts and clues, and the Christians had found the goal to which they led.

Granted the universal pagan disbelief in resurrection, it is not surprising that Justin had to tackle the question on several occasions, including the writing of one entire book. There is no controversy about what his view was, and a brief summary will suffice.

---

[104] *Ep. Ap.* 21; cf. *Ac. Paul & Thecla* 37.

[105] *Ep. Ap.* 24.

[106] *Ep. Ap.* 25 (following the Coptic version).

[107] Since Papias' works have not survived, it is hard to tell how substantial they were. We do know that he composed five *suggramata* (Eus. *HE* 3.39.1) which were probably bigger than *1 Clem.*, though perhaps not on the scale of Justin's works. On Justin the study of Chadwick 1966 is still important. Among other writers of this period we should mention Melito of Sardis; though not much of his work has survived, his treatise *On Pascha* contains a memorable description (102.760–64) of Christ's triumph over death and his carrying of humankind away to heaven; see Hill 2002 [1992], 105f.

[108] cf. *Mt. Poly.* 9.2.

In the *First Apology*, he declares (8) that both the wicked and the righteous will be raised for judgment. Always on the lookout for points of contact in pagan culture from which to mount an argument, he points out (18) that even necromancy provides evidence for the continuing life of the soul after death, and suggests that it is not such a long step from there to the Christian belief.[109] Similarly, pagan beliefs about apotheosis show that within that worldview survival and glorification can be accepted; Justin is not identifying belief in resurrection with this kind of position, merely suggesting it as a stepping-stone towards the truth (21—2). We expect, he says (18), to receive our own bodies again, even though they are dead and cast into the earth; nothing is impossible with god. We know that all sorts of apparently impossible things happen in the physical world. How, for instance, does semen turn into a human being? And yet it happens. So too (19) human bodies, after being dissolved like seeds in the earth (the familiar echo of John 12 and 1 Corinthians 15), will in god's appointed time rise again and 'put on incorruption' (*aphtharsian endysasthai*). Following Paul in 1 Corinthians 15, Justin quotes Psalm 110 as a prophecy that god would first raise Christ from the dead and then bring him to heaven until he had subdued his enemies (45).

Two sections of the *Dialogue with Trypho* deal further with the resurrection. In the first (80), Justin trenchantly expounds his belief in bodily resurrection, over against some who claim to be Christian but disbelieve it, holding instead that their souls simply go to heaven after they die. (He seems unaware of any who take the further drastic step of retaining the language of 'resurrection' while using it to denote a spiritual experience in the present life; for denunciation of that idea we must wait until Irenaeus.) He couples this with an equally clear statement of an earthly paradise, including a rebuilt Jerusalem.[110]

In the other key passage, Justin expounds Psalm 22 to the effect that Christ knew his father would raise him from the dead (106). We can see this also, he says, in the book of Jonah, where the prophet emerges on the third day (107). In 108, Justin comments that the Jews were still saying that the disciples stole the body, and that they were deceiving people in saying Jesus had been raised and then ascended to heaven. He speaks of Joshua giving the people a temporary inheritance, but declares that Christ, 'after the holy resurrection', will give us 'an eternal possession' (113).[111]

---

[109] This can hardly be taken as evidence that he or anyone else would have confused belief in Jesus' resurrection with early necromantic practices (see e.g. Riley 1995, 44–7; see above, 61f.). Had Justin known that such suggestions might be made we may doubt whether he would have regarded this argument as such a useful bridge across which to guide his pagan audience.

[110] On the apparent inconsistencies within Justin's chiliasm cf. Hill 2002 [1992], 25–7.

[111] In the key phrase *meta ten hagian anastasin*, some editors have suggested reading *hagion* for *hagian*, i.e. 'after the resurrection of the holy ones', the full number of God's

There are other fragmentary sayings on the subject which may come from Justin.[112] But it is his treatise on resurrection, itself not preserved complete, which compels attention.[113] After an introduction (1) on the self-evidencing nature of truth, Justin launches into a description (2) of what was by then clearly a common denial of 'the resurrection of the flesh', not, it seems, from paganism (though no doubt that was there too), but from within would-be Christian faith. He mentions the docetists explicitly, who say that Jesus only 'seemed' to have flesh, but was in fact only 'spiritual' (*pneumatikon*); and some who use the saying of Jesus in his response to the Sadducees (Mark 12.25) as evidence that the resurrection there spoken of is not fleshly.

He then takes the relevant topics one by one. It is reasonable to suggest that one may be given back all one's bodily members without them necessarily having to discharge the same function as they do now (3). The fact that one is deformed in the present does not mean that deformity will be retained in the future; the resurrection will itself be an act of healing, 'so that the flesh shall rise perfect and entire' (4). God can do whatever he pleases, as even Homer acknowledges,[114] since he is the creator, which also indicates that he cares for the physical creation, making it not unworthy of a new life (5). What is more (6), there are some aspects at least of the philosophies of Plato, the Stoics and the Epicureans which point in the direction of a 'regeneration of the flesh'.[115] (Justin must have known that there were other aspects which pointed the other way, but he is building bridges between cultures, and is determined to find points of contact wherever he can.) The body is after all valuable in the creator's sight (7), since humans – yes, fleshly humans! – were made in his image. Justin, like the exponents of standard Jewish resurrection theologies, roots himself above all else in a doctrine of creation.

He then turns to the more knotty arguments. The flesh causes the soul to sin, say some; no, he replies (8), they are both responsible, and both will be saved. God made the flesh in the first place and, like an artist restoring spoiled work, will remake it. Even if it is true, as some say (Justin does not deny it) that the soul is incorruptible, being a part of god, that would merely

---

people. Otto (in Migne *PG* 6.736) explains that Justin seems to see a double resurrection, first of the blessed (*hagia*) and then of everybody else. (This may go back to that particular understanding of 1 Cor. 15.23f., or perhaps to Rev. 20, or a combination of both.)

[112] Methodius, as reported in Epiphanius *Haer*. 64 (in Photius *Bib*. 234), reports a saying of Justin that 'that which is mortal is inherited, but that which is immortal inherits; and that the flesh indeed dies, but the kingdom of heaven lives'. This could mean anything or nothing. Similar things could be said about the reported conversation between Justin and the prefect at his final trial (*Martyrdom of Justin* ch. 4).

[113] There is some debate as to whether this actually comes from Justin; a good case for its authenticity is made in Prigent 1964, 28–67; cf. too Bynum 1995, 28f.

[114] *Od*. 2.304.

[115] *he tes sarkos hyparchen palingenesia*, *PG* 6.1581. Cp. above, 34f.

show that god must all the more save the body, since saving is what he certainly does, and on this account it is only the body that needs it.

The next chapter (9), following what appears to be a break in the text, begins from the assumption that god did indeed raise Jesus bodily from the dead. Jesus rose 'in the flesh in which he suffered', and this can only have been to confirm that this is what resurrection is like. Justin refers his readers back to Luke's account of Jesus inviting the disciples to handle him, and of his eating with them. The resurrection cannot therefore be, as some are saying, 'only spiritual'.[116] Such a claim puts one, effectively, alongside the Sadducees. Justin seems again to be echoing Jesus' debate with them, since he cites once more the importance of god's power.

Finally (10), if salvation was only for the soul, what more would this be than what is already said by Pythagoras and Plato? The gospel is 'a new and strange hope', not a slight variation on one already well known. The fragmentary treatise concludes with a passage which belongs exactly with the overall argument of 1 Corinthians: because the flesh rises, its behaviour in the present time matters enormously, whereas if it did not, one might as well indulge its various appetites. In fact,

> if Christ our physician (God having rescued us from our desires) regulates our flesh with his own wise and temperate rule, it is evident that he guards it from sins because it possesses a hope of salvation.

Justin thus stands foursquare with the New Testament, not only on the continuity between the present and future bodies (for which, unlike Paul, he uses the term 'flesh'), but also on the difference between them (the members may not have the same function in the future life as they do now, and deformities will be healed). He offers no theory about an intermediate state, but from his cautious treatment of the question of the soul we may assume he would think in terms of continuity of soul while awaiting renewal of body. He has no doubts that Jesus himself was bodily raised. Like the Apostolic Fathers, he does not use 'resurrection' language in a metaphorical way, though he stresses the continuity between present *ethical* life and the future resurrection. Martyred roughly a hundred years after Paul, he shows every sign of having absorbed essentially the same view of this topic, and of defending it, at more length than Paul had ever done, within the swirling currents of pagan philosophy.

(ii) Athenagoras

Athenagoras was probably a younger contemporary of Justin, and his surviving works cover similar ground to the *Apology* and *Resurrection* of the older

---

[116] *pneumatike mone, PG* 6.1588.

writer. Athenagoras' own *Apology* is a defence of the Christians against what are already standard accusations, and the beginnings of a reasoned explanation of just who is this one god whom Christians worship, over against the follies of paganism. The only part which is relevant for our purposes is where, in rebutting the charge of cannibalism, he points out that it would make no sense for people who believe in resurrection (36). He takes the opportunity to add that even if people suppose this belief to be sheer folly, they can hardly regard it as anti-social; and, on shakier ground, he suggests that one could argue that, according to both Pythagoras and Plato, bodies that have been dissolved may be reconstructed from the same elements.[117] His purpose here is served simply by indicating that resurrection belief makes nonsense of the charges laid against Christians; our purpose in noting this is to point out that when he speaks of resurrection he is of course talking about bodies.

His treatise *On the Resurrection of the Dead*, though similar to Justin's, is fuller; we have it complete, not fragmentary, and he seems to have developed various lines of thought further.[118] He concludes his introduction (chapter 1) with a flourish that, frankly, could be just as well echoed by someone writing today:

> For in regard to this subject also we find some utterly disbelieving, and some others doubting, and even among those who have accepted the first principles some who are as much at a loss what to believe as those who doubt; the most unaccountable thing of all being, that they are in this state of mind without having any ground whatsoever in the matters themselves for their disbelief, or finding it possible to assign any reasonable cause why they disbelieve or experience any perplexity.

He then moves into the more substantive arguments. Resurrection is not impossible for god, who is after all the creator (2); as creator, he is certainly capable of raising the dead (3). It is no objection to point out that some bodies get eaten by animals, and some indeed by other humans; the processes of digestion cope with different types of material, and will eject those that are irrelevant to the body's needs (4–6). (Had Athenagoras known more about how bodies work this argument could have been strengthened, but the issue was clearly important in the second century, as witness Tertullian's efforts on the same topic, to which we shall come presently.) In fact – here he follows Paul more closely than the Apostolic Fathers and Justin had done – the resurrection body will be significantly different from the present one, not least in that it will not be corruptible (7). In any case, god has the power to reassemble human bodies, however much they are dissolved or scattered,

---

[117] This sounds more like the theory ascribed to Democritus by Epicurus and Pliny: see 34f. above.

[118] Grant 1954 disputes Athenagoras' authorship, but he is countered in some degree by Pouderon 1986. Cf. too Bynum 1995, 28f., with extensive bibliog. Athenagoras shows no sign of Justin's chiliasm: see Hill 2002 [1992], 107f.

even if it should be by cannibalism (8).[119] What is impossible for humans is possible for god (9). It cannot be shown that god does not will a resurrection; it is not unworthy of god to raise human bodies (10).

After recapitulating the argument so far (11), Athenagoras goes on to mount a positive argument based on the nature of human beings. When god created humans, he made them creatures with a purpose of their own; and, by analogy, god himself had a purpose in making them. He will not, therefore, allow them to perish, but will ensure that they pass through all the necessary changes appropriate to them (relating to age, appearance or size). The resurrection is the final one in the list of necessary changes, being 'a change for the better of what still remains in existence at that time' (12). The resurrection is thus proved by consideration of the reasons why humankind was made in the first place (13).

Resurrection is closely linked with final judgment, but Athenagoras sees that to argue for resurrection simply on the basis of future judgment will not do (14). In fact, not all will be judged; little children, for instance, will be exempt; but it does not follow that they will not rise. The resurrection is grounded in the nature of humankind itself (15): god has created humans to be composed of body and (immortal) soul together, in harmony, and this unity must be maintained. (The Platonic alternative, that the body is a prison of the soul which the soul would be happy to abandon for ever, is not even considered; Athenagoras is rooted too deeply in a Jewish creation-theology to contemplate such a thing.) The analogy between death and sleep provides an illustration of, and consequently an argument for, the resurrection. The soul goes on, but the body changes, from semen itself to the body of a child, and so through various changes to adulthood, making the further change required for resurrection reasonable and natural (16–17).

Having warned against taking the future judgment as the sole basis for resurrection, Athenagoras now argues that, granted there is to be a future judgment, it must be a judgment of both body and soul; it would be unfair to punish the soul for the misdeeds of the body (18–23). What is more, without resurrection humans would ultimately be worse off than beasts, and it would be better simply to give in and live like animals (19). This, the longest of his arguments, coheres well with that of 1 Corinthians, stressing the continuity between present and future bodily existence as the chief ground for moral living in the present. But Athenagoras saves for last (24–5) what he considers his strongest point. We must enquire what the specific purpose of human beings is. It cannot be the same as that of the beasts; it cannot be simply freedom from pain, or the happiness of a disembodied soul. It must be a goal shared by body and soul alike, reuniting the same soul with the same body (thus incidentally ruling out transmigration and similar theories as well as disembodiment). In this way,

---

[119] On this topic, which became famous in the third century, see Bynum 1995, 32f.

there must by all means be a resurrection of the bodies which are dead, or even entirely dissolved, and the same men must be formed anew, since the law of nature ordains the end not absolutely, nor as the end of any men whatsoever, but of the same men who passed through the previous life; but it is impossible for the same men to be reconstituted unless the same bodies are restored to the same souls. But that the same soul should obtain the same body is impossible in any other way, and possible only by the resurrection; for if this takes place, an end befitting the nature of men follows also. (25)

Athenagoras thus stands with Justin, Ignatius and Clement in articulating a fully embodied resurrection. This, indeed, is what the word always meant in the ancient world; by the second half of the second century the Christian apologists were engaged in debate with people who were starting to use it in a different way, as we saw in Justin and will see in more detail presently, but there is no reason to think that that alternative position was anything except a fresh-minted tactical linguistic innovation. It should not perhaps be necessary to emphasize this, but recent debates indicate that it is worth doing so: none of the arguments used by Justin or Athenagoras make any sense if we suppose that 'resurrection' could mean something other than a bodily return to life (in the case of Jesus, leaving an empty tomb behind him).

Athenagoras, like the others, bases his arguments principally on god as creator. He, unlike most of the other early Christian writers, is comfortable with speaking of a soul which is already immortal, but he never supposes that the soul would be better off without the body. Unlike Justin or Ignatius, he does not speak of the resurrection of the *flesh*, but of the body, finding it appropriate as part of his apologetic to explain (in line with Paul) that resurrection involves change as well as continuity. He does not discuss the intermediate state as such, but his view of the soul indicates that he would see that as the continuity between the present life and the future one. His discussion of death in relation to sleep suggests that he might have been content to use that language as well, probably (as with Paul) metaphorically; in other words, he probably believed in a conscious pre-resurrection post-mortem state. He, like all the others we have surveyed in this chapter, does not use 'resurrection' language as a metaphor for anything else. He keeps his eye on the main purpose, and on the (very Jewish) arguments which support it.

(iii) Theophilus

The sole surviving work of Theophilus, bishop of Antioch in the second half of the second century, is addressed to one Autolycus, who had expressed scepticism about Christianity and its claims. The work shows Theophilus to be an apologist much after the fashion of Justin and Athenagoras.[120]

---

[120] See Bynum 1995, 30f.

As with other writers in this tradition, he has a strong doctrine of god as creator.[121] In the first book he uses this as a basis, in swift strokes, to sketch a doctrine both of new creation and of resurrection, all as part of what today might be called an eschatological verification. When humans are renewed, then they will see the god they at present scorn because they cannot see him:

> When you will have put off mortality, and put on incorruption, then you will see God properly. For God will raise your flesh immortal with your soul; and then, when you have become immortal, you will see the Immortal One, if you believe in him in the present; and then you will know that you have spoken wrongly against him.[122]

Apart from the role given to the soul (which, however, does not seem to possess immortality in advance of god's action), this could have been taken straight from 1 Corinthians 15.[123] So, he goes on, Autolycus may not believe that the dead are raised, he will when the resurrection takes place![124] At the moment it takes faith to see this, but people exercise faith in all sorts of human endeavours, so why not this as well?

This leads Theophilus, after some further denunciations of the pagan gods, to a careful distancing of himself from emperor-worship, and an explanation of the name 'Christian', to a chapter on the resurrection itself.[125] Following Justin in seeking points of contact with his readers' world, he draws attention to the fact that in some versions of pagan mythology Hercules was burned to death but lived on, and Asclepius came back to life after being struck by lightning.[126] Theophilus does not, I think, necessarily say he believes these stories; only that they are part of the stock-in-trade of that paganism of which Autolycus has boasted while dismissing the Christian claims. The argument is at this point *ad hominem*, or at least, so to speak, *ad culturam*. But Theophilus then moves to a more familiar argument: the dying and rising of seasons, of days and nights, and particularly of seeds and plants. His point throughout, also familiar throughout the Jewish and Christian traditions of resurrection-discourse, is the power of god as creator, which, he says, is visible both in the monthly 'resurrection' of the moon and in the recovery of human bodies after sickness. If someone responds that these things happen by 'natural' means, he replies that this, too, is the work of the creator-god:

---

[121] See esp. *Autol.* 2.10–27; also 3.9.

[122] *Autol.* 1.7.

[123] In *Autol.* 2.27 Theophilus insists that humans were created neither mortal nor immortal, but capable of either. Through sinning, humans became mortal, but now have the chance for this to be reversed, since those who are saved will obtain the resurrection and thus inherit incorruption.

[124] *Autol.* 1.8.

[125] *Autol.* 1.13.

[126] See ch. 2 above.

> As you do not know where your flesh went away and disappeared to, so neither do you know whence it grew, or whence it came again. But you will say, 'From meat and drink, changed into blood.' Quite so; but this, too, is the work of God, not of anyone else; that is how he operates.[127]

Still pursuing possible points of contact, Theophilus calls Homer and other poets to witness that there is after all some kind of sensation after death.[128] This does not of itself, of course, prove the truth of future judgment, but it shows that the Jewish and Christian belief in such a thing is not as improbable as it was sometimes made out to be.

Theophilus is thus another witness to the same, essentially Pauline, tradition. We may be surprised that he does not, in this book, speak of the resurrection of Jesus himself. Perhaps he knows only too well the scorn that this would evoke. But he returns, as so many do, to the doctrine of creation, and the analogies to resurrection within the created order, to generate hermeneutical space within which the hope of future incorruptible embodiment might make sense. He also mentions the interim state of the soul, taken care of by the creator in accordance with biblical prophecy.[129] He does not use 'resurrection' language metaphorically, whether with concrete or abstract referent, but always literally, referring concretely to the future embodiment of those who, in the present, believe and follow the way of righteousness.

(iv) Minucius Felix

Minucius Felix is variously regarded as a third-century writer, dependent on Tertullian, or as one of Tertullian's sources, and hence writing in the second half of the second century. His treatise *Octavius* is interesting not least in that, through the dialogue form, it sets out the anti-Christian argument (put into the mouth of one Caecilius), including an attempted *reductio ad absurdum* of the resurrection. We may imagine that this sort of thing was what Paul had in mind, too, when writing 1 Corinthians 15:

> I should be glad to be informed whether or not you rise again with bodies – whether the same, or a renewed body? Without a body? Then, as far as I know, there will neither be mind, nor soul, nor life. With the same body? But this has already been previously destroyed. With another body? Then it is a new man who is born, not the former one restored; and yet so long a time has passed away, innumerable ages have flowed by, and what single individual has returned from the dead either by the fate of Protesilaus, with permission to sojourn even for a few hours, or that we might believe it for an example?[130]

---

[127] *Autocl.* 1.13.

[128] *Autocl.* 2.38.

[129] Ibid., quoting Ps. 51.8; Prov. 3.8. On Theophilus' theory about the 'seven-day week' of world history see Hill 2002 [1992], 162f.; and cp. Plut. *De Isid.* 47.

[130] *Oct.* 11.7f. On Protesilaus see 64f. above.

Minucius Felix's spokesman Octavius works his way round to a response. There will be a future judgment for the world, as the Stoics have said; even the Epicureans, and Plato himself, will be ready to agree with this, at least in part. Pythagoras and Plato, however, are wrong to propose transmigration; they have, says Octavius, 'delivered the doctrine of resurrection with a corrupt and divided faith'. Rather, once again, what matters is that god is the creator. It is harder to create something which has never been than to repeat something that has already been done; resurrection is therefore easier for god than creation itself. We note, however, that Octavius is content to say that after death a human is 'nothing', just as he or she was before conception. He explains that, though Christians are not afraid of other forms of disposal of the body, such as burning, they prefer to follow 'the ancient and better custom of burying in the earth'. He, like many others, offers analogies from creation: in this case, sunrise and sunset, flowers dying and reviving, seeds rotting and so flourishing. Why are you in such a hurry, he asks Caecilius, for the body to revive and return, when it is still winter and the weather is sharp? Better to wait 'for the spring-time of the body'.[131]

The mention of burial customs points to a further argument. Christians do not crown their dead with flowers; there is no need. Their funerals partake of the same tranquillity with which they live:

> We do not bind to ourselves a withering garland, but we wear one living with eternal flowers from God, since we, being both moderate and secure in the liberality of our God, are animated to the hope of future felicity by the confidence of his present majesty. Thus we both rise again in blessedness, and are already living in contemplation of the future.[132]

We find, then, the same simple schema as in the other apologists. There is to be a future resurrection, awaited in conscious rest by those at present dead, and the evidence is not the resurrection of Jesus himself, but the plentiful witness of the natural world. Though some might suppose this a shift away from the secure foundations laid in the New Testament, the motive is not merely the desire to tie the doctrine to things familiar to any reader, but also to demonstrate that Christianity, so far from being a strange superstition, is rooted in the one world made by the creator god.

The Apologists were pioneers. Their arguments may have been fairly simple compared with the New Testament on the one hand and subsequent Christian writers on the other, but there is a certain cheerful boldness about them which compels attention. Working at a time when persecution might break out at any time, and often did, they refused to back off from the extraordinary claims of the gospel, and many of them suffered for it. They thus prepared the way for more sophisticated and thorough writers, among

---

[131] *Octavius* 34.6–12.
[132] *Octavius* 38.3f.

whom we shall look at four, beginning with one of the greatest arguers of them all: the feisty rhetorician-turned-theologian, Tertullian.

5. The Great Early Theologians

(i) Tertullian

The so-called father of Latin theology forms a convenient transition point, indeed overlap, with the Apologists. Whatever his relation to Minucius Felix, he often wrote as an apologist, and certainly his work on the resurrection belongs alongside those we have been examining, however much the range and power of his writing go beyond them. He was younger, too, than all but (perhaps) the last of the other Apologists, being born around 160, converted to Christianity in his 30s in the last years of the second century, and dying around 225. He thus produced his influential books in the first third of the third century, after the death of Irenaeus, whom we shall consider presently. It was around this time that the early creeds for catechumens were being produced, including famously the clause 'the resurrection of the flesh' (*resurrection carnis*), rather than *mortuorum* ('of the dead') or *corporis* ('of the body').[133]

Tertullian's *Apology* is a brilliant, knockabout treatment of most of the controversial matters at issue between Christians and their critics. It contains one short but striking description of the resurrection:

> When this age reaches its full end, [God] will sit as judge, and his worshippers he will repay with life eternal, and the profane he will condemn to fire as perpetual and unceasing; for the dead, every man of them from the beginning, shall be raised, refashioned and reviewed, that their deserts of either kind, good or evil, may be adjudged. Yes! We too in our day laughed at this . . . [134]

But it is Tertullian's book on the resurrection which expounds the subject at full length. It was the most robust treatment of the topic yet written in the early church.[135]

---

[133] See Kelly 1972 [1960], 163–5.

[134] *Apoll.* 18.3f.

[135] *ANF* 3.545–94; for recent discussions, see Bynum 1995, 35; among older works, cf. e.g. Siniscalco 1966, ch. 5. The anti-Marcionite poem on the resurrection (*ANF* 4.145f.), like the collection to which it belongs, was once ascribed to Tertullian but is not now regarded as his. It emphasizes, as did many apologists, the necessity of the restoration of the flesh, as a matter of justice, and the ease of its happening, on the basis (as usual) of God's creative power. Without bodily resurrection, death retains victory over that which God made and already honoured. Tertullian refers to the resurrection elsewhere in his writings, but his treatise directly on the subject is full, and tells us more than enough for our present survey. On Tertullian's strong chiliasm, and his debates with opponents on this subject who nevertheless believed, like him, in a bodily resurrection, see Hill 2002 [1992], 27–32.

The *De Resurrectione* starts right in with an attack on pagan beliefs about the dead. Some say they cease to exist altogether, while others, by 'feeding' the dead in graveside rituals, show that the dead still have an appetite. The theory of transmigration gets halfway there, but not near enough; those who believe it have knocked on the door of truth, but have not entered (*De Resurrectione*, chapter 1). But Tertullian is not only gunning for pagan opponents. He has plenty of scorn reserved for dualists within the church, or on its fringes, who say that Christ did not have real flesh either before or after his death and resurrection (2—4).

Tertullian, like the other Apologists, bases his own argument on the fact that god is the creator of the material world, and that what he made he made as an excellent thing (6). Human flesh, too, is part of god's handiwork; it is the co-heir of the soul (7). Flesh, declares Tertullian, is very important within Christian thinking (8); it received grace, the grace of Christ himself (9), and when St Paul said negative things about 'the flesh', he was referring to its actions, not to the substance itself (10). We see here, as in Irenaeus, that some were starting to quote Paul in a direction that Paul himself rules out.[136] What matters is god's power as creator. What he made, he can remake (11).

We should by now be able to predict where this will lead. Analogies from nature are produced: night and day; the moon; the seasons (12); and, as in Clement, our old friend the phoenix (13), made the object of an impassioned piece of rhetoric. Must men die once for all, while birds in Arabia are sure of a resurrection? The resurrection also fits with a classic Judaeo-Christian view of future judgment: soul and body must be reunited so that judgment can be complete. They have acted together in this life; they will be judged together at the end (14—17).

Tertullian then comes to the point of engagement with the heretics within the church itself. Scripture speaks of the resurrection of the dead, not of the soul (18), while the heretics treat the idea of 'the resurrection of the dead' as referring to a moral change within the present life, or even to the possibility of escaping from the body altogether (19). Tertullian thus faces a *metaphorical* use of 'resurrection' language with an *abstract*, rather than concrete, referent: he admits that there are 'spiritual' senses in which prophecies can be understood, but insists that these are dependent on there being an actual referent within concrete reality (20). 'Resurrection of the dead' is not simply a figure of speech for something else (21). Nor does scripture allow us to say that the resurrection is already past, or that it happens immediately upon death. It takes place, rather, at the end of the world, and this has clearly not happened yet. Thus the heretics who claim that they have already been 'raised' are wrong; they are using the language in a sense which its original

---

[136] cf. 1 Cor. 15.50 ('flesh and blood cannot inherit God's kingdom'), often quoted against the position Paul himself is arguing (above, 358—9).

meaning simply will not bear (22). When Paul speaks of a present resurrection, in passages like Colossians 2 and 3, and when John says something similar in 1 John 3, this refers to something that happens in the mind, which is pointing forward to the bodily resurrection of which Paul also speaks in, for instance, Philippians 3 (23). The two Thessalonian letters speak of a moment still to come, when Christ will come again, and the bodily resurrection will take place (24). So too Revelation speaks of the coming bodily resurrection (25). When scripture uses metaphors, the referent is still the resurrection itself (26—7); Tertullian spends some time explaining the meaning of Ezekiel 37 (28—30) and other related prophetic passages (31). The teaching of Jesus points in the same direction (33—4), indicating the resurrection of the body, not merely a new life for the soul (35). When discussing the debate between Jesus and the Sadducees he insists that the question of marrying or not could only make sense if the subject under discussion was actually the flesh and its restoration (36).

He continues at some length to work through the relevant passages in Acts and Paul (39—55), giving special attention to the key passages in the Corinthian correspondence. It is the *works* of the flesh, not its substance, that Paul condemns (46). The famous saying, 'flesh and blood cannot inherit the kingdom', is not therefore to be seen as a denial of bodily resurrection (48, 50). The fact that Jesus, as a fully human being, is now at god's right hand is a guarantee of bodily resurrection (51). The body will, of course, be changed so as to become incorruptible, but to change like this is not to destroy the substance (55). 'Changes, conversions, and reformations will necessarily take place to bring about the resurrection, but the substance *of the flesh* will still be preserved safe.'[137]

How then can the last judgment take place and be valid? Only through the identity of the risen body with the present one (56). Human bodies will be restored to a state of perfection in which joy and peace will reside for ever (57—8); this will involve changes, but our various characteristics will be preserved, whatever use they may or may not then have (60—1).[138] Thus the risen ones will be 'equal to angels'; not that they will *be* angels, because their humanity will be preserved unimpaired (62). Body and soul are joined together by god and are not designed to be separated (63).

We can thus observe some of the early moves in the long-running chess-match of biblical exposition being played out; and our earlier study of Paul indicates that on these points at least Tertullian had understood what Paul was saying, over against those who were interpreting him in a gnostic direction. In conscious debate with the Valentinians (see below), he sets out a

---

[137] *De Res.* 55 ad fin. (italics in translation: *ANF* 3.589).

[138] Tertullian developed Jewish retellings of the story here: the children of Israel wandering in the wilderness found that their shoes and clothing did not wear out (Dt. 8.4). Nor, he says, did their hair and fingernails grow; this appears to be Tertullian's own expansion of legend, followed by Jerome. On all this see Satran 1989.

doctrine of resurrection, based on that of Jesus himself, expounding the key texts from gospels and epistles and dealing with problems which were arising in the second half of the second century.

He is at this point, in fact, a close ally of one of the great fathers of Greek theology, Irenaeus, bishop of Lyons for the last two decades of the second century. The two of them, in complementary ways, brought together 'an extravagantly materialistic notion of the resurrection body' and an equivalent emphasis, too, on 'radical change'.[139] It is to Irenaeus that we turn for a fuller understanding of the revisionist theses that were current from around the middle of that century, and for the development of the biblical exegesis, and of the arguments of the Apostolic Fathers and Apologists, that were now being shaped in order to meet them.

(ii) Irenaeus

Irenaeus (c.130–200) became bishop of Lyons immediately after the persecution of 177 in which his predecessor was martyred (Irenaeus himself had been in Rome at the time). Thus, when he wrote about the heresies he observed in and alongside the church, not least to do with death and the Christian hope, these were not merely ideas to play with; nor were they, as is sometimes suggested, ideas in the service of a comfortable, bourgeois church existence. For Irenaeus, theology and exegesis were part of the task of equipping the church for its dangerous and difficult witness against both pagan empire and pagan culture. The views he attacked were, in his view, ways of getting off the hook, ways of avoiding the real challenge of the gospel at every level.[140]

Like the other writers we have studied, Irenaeus based his theology on a strong account of god as creator; this is the theme of the opening chapters of *Against Heresies* Book II, following the exposition of the multiple heresies in Book I. This leads to his first exposition of the resurrection, against the Valentinians, who have concocted a complex scheme of what will happen at the end, with a final separation of the 'spiritual' from the 'material'.[141] Like Tertullian, Irenaeus affirms that soul and body belong together, and that when god resuscitates the mortal bodies he will make them incorruptible and immortal.[142] He rejects as absurd the theory of transmigration; once again,

---

[139] Bynum 1995, 38.

[140] On martyrdom as the context for much of the writing about resurrection in this period see Bynum 1995, 43–7. For the significance, for Irenaeus, of the Lyons martyrdoms, see below, 549.

[141] *Haer.* 2.29.1. On the Valentinian movement see e.g. Mirecki 1992b. Valentinus himself was active in the middle of the C2, and his followers remained an identifiable group for several centuries thereafter.

[142] *Haer.* 2.29.2.

god as creator is well capable of conferring its own proper soul on each individual body, which he will do both for the righteous, to be rewarded, and the unrighteous, to be punished.[143] Drawing on Jesus' answer to the Sadducees, he insists that this will be a different sort of life to the present one:

> Both classes shall then cease from any longer begetting and being begotten, from marrying and being given in marriage; so that the number of mankind, corresponding to the fore-ordination of God, being completed, may fully realize the scheme formed by the father.[144]

The intermediate state is the continuing existence of the soul, and such souls are recognizable; here Irenaeus cites Luke 16, the parable of the rich man and Lazarus.[145] But the soul is not possessed of automatic life, nor is it pre-existent; it is held in being by god.[146]

Books III and IV set out at considerable length Irenaeus' arguments against the Valentinians and Marcionites, particularly on the questions of who precisely the true god is, and how the church can be sure that it is faithful to the original message. This is where his famous teaching on the continuity of the church, and the providential ordering of scripture, is to be found. But it is in Book V that he returns, this time at length, to the question of the resurrection. Here his long-running argument for the goodness and god-givenness of human flesh comes into its own. Yes, human flesh is weak, but it is god's power that will raise it from the dead; if the flesh can be thoroughly alive in the present, why should it not be so in the future as well?[147] There is only one god, and the longevity of the ancients is an example of his power to give life against all normal possibility.[148] Humankind consists of a co-mingling and union of soul, spirit and body; this, together, bears the divine image. When Paul calls people 'spiritual' he does not mean that their flesh has been stripped off and taken away, but that they partake of the Spirit.[149] It is this complete human being that becomes a temple of the Spirit; Irenaeus here offers a close exposition of 1 Corinthians 6.[150] The evidence that Jesus himself rose with the same body as before is provided by the mark of the nails; and we shall therefore be raised in the same way, as Paul insists in 1 Corinthians 6 and 15, and in Romans 8, not incorporeally

---

[143] *Haer.* 2.33.1–5. Dr Andrew Goddard suggests to me that the increasing emphasis on the resurrection of righteous and wicked alike may stem from the grounding of resurrection more on the judgment to come than (as with Paul) on the resurrection of Jesus as the Messiah who guarantees the resurrection of his people.

[144] *Haer.* 2.33.5, introducing the idea of a divinely intended fixed number of the saved.

[145] *Haer.* 2.34.1.

[146] *Haer.* 2.34.4.

[147] *Haer.* 5.3.2f.

[148] *Haer.* 5.4f.

[149] *Haer.* 5.6.1.

[150] *Haer.* 5.6.2.

but in bodies.[151] This brings Irenaeus to a more detailed exposition of 1 Corinthians 15.35–49, emphasizing that the phrase 'spiritual body' is not used of either the soul or the spirit alone, but of bodies which possess perpetual life by the agency of the Spirit.[152] This leads to a digression on the work of the Spirit in the present.[153]

Irenaeus then comes face to face with the classic misreading (as we have argued) of 1 Corinthians 15.50, 'flesh and blood cannot inherit god's kingdom.' The heretics, he says, quote this to show that the material creation ('god's handiwork', Irenaeus calls it) is not saved. This, he says, is a wrong understanding: 'flesh and blood' refers to people who do not have the principle of life, that is, the divine Spirit, dwelling within them. They are as good as dead.[154] The Spirit will give life to the flesh, however; and indeed, just as the meek are promised that they will inherit the earth, so the flesh, which is from the earth, can become part of the inheritance of the Spirit, and of those in whom the Spirit works.[155] Just as Paul speaks in Romans 11 of the wild olive that comes to share in the life of the cultivated one, so the flesh will come to share in the life of the Spirit.[156] This means that the present life of god's people must not be lived 'according to the flesh'; they must be led by the Spirit.[157] The flesh is of course capable of death, but it is also and equally capable of being raised to life.[158] The raising of Jairus' daughter, the widow's son at Nain, and Lazarus are clear proof that the Lord was prefiguring the raising of the dead in their own bodies.[159] The heretics are therefore merely 'taking two expressions of Paul's, without having perceived the apostle's meaning, or examining critically the force of the terms, but keeping fast hold of the mere expressions by themselves'.[160] The rest of 1 Corinthians 15, and the ending of Philippians 3, demonstrate the matter clearly, as does the promise in 2 Corinthians 5.4 that what is mortal will be swallowed up with life.[161] The heretics are therefore forced to make Paul contradict with a single phrase what he clearly says everywhere else.[162] What is more, the flesh and blood which Jesus himself shared with the human race is called into question.[163]

---

[151] *Haer.* 5.7.1.
[152] *Haer.* 5.7.2.
[153] *Haer.* 5.8.1–4.
[154] *Haer.* 5.9.1, 4.
[155] *Haer.* 5.9.3f.
[156] *Haer.* 5.10.1f.
[157] *Haer.* 5.10.2—11.2.
[158] *Haer.* 5.12.1–6.
[159] *Haer.* 5.13.1.
[160] *Haer.* 5.13.2.
[161] *Haer.* 5.13.3. Cf. too 3.23.7, which stresses (with 1 Cor. 15.20–28) that death is to be seen as an enemy which will eventually be destroyed completely.
[162] *Haer.* 5.13.1, 5.
[163] *Haer.* 5.14.

Irenaeus then turns from detailed argument to proof from scripture: Isaiah and Ezekiel both declare that the same god who created us will also raise us up.[164] This leads to a consideration of how humans were created, and are healed, showing the creator's concern for the whole person.[165] And this in turn leads Irenaeus away from this particular controversy and back to a larger consideration of god as creator, and, within that, of the appropriateness of the incarnation.[166] He insists that the heretics who have been the object of his critique have arisen much later than the bishops and teachers of the second generation to whom the apostles entrusted their followers.[167]

Moving towards the close of his work, Irenaeus sketches out his view of the future, the final judgment, the appearance of Antichrist, and the victory of the true god.[168] Within this context, he offers a final exposition of the resurrection. He insists, against the heretics, that Jesus did not simply 'die and go to heaven'; he spent three days in the tomb among the dead, in fulfilment of scripture.[169] One cannot conflate resurrection and ascension. The pattern of a two-stage post-mortem existence must then be followed by all the Lord's people: first, a period 'in the invisible places allotted by god', then the final resurrection of the body.[170] The many promises of a new inheritance, of a kingdom in which Jesus will eat and drink with his followers, and the reported teaching of Jesus (via the elders who had heard the apostle John) about the extraordinary fruitfulness of plants in the coming age – all this bears witness to a fulfilment which demands a remade physical universe.[171] These promises cannot be allegorized away (as Eusebius would later attempt to do). They will have their fulfilment, after the coming of Antichrist, in a terrestrial new Jerusalem.[172]

There will thus be a real resurrection within a real renewed world, in which there will be degrees of blessedness. Irenaeus returns once more to 1 Corinthians 15: death itself is to be destroyed; the son will be subject to the father; and the true god will be all in all.[173]

---

[164] *Haer.* 5.15.1.

[165] *Haer.* 5.15.2f.

[166] *Haer.* 5.17f.

[167] *Haer.* 5.20.1f.

[168] *Haer.* 5.25.23–30.

[169] *Haer.* 5.31.1; the heretics say that Jesus, 'immediately upon his expiring on the cross, undoubtedly departed on high, leaving his body to the earth'. Irenaeus quotes, among other biblical proofs, a passage which he also quotes in 4.22.1, where he says it comes from Jeremiah. It is not found in any MSS of the OT known to us; Justin (*Dial.* 72) declares that the Jews had removed it from their texts lest it be used against them. See too *Haer.* 3.20.4 (where Irenaeus says it comes from Isaiah).

[170] *Haer.* 5.31.2.

[171] *Haer.* 5.32–35. See too above, in the section on Papias (492f.).

[172] *Haer.* 5.35. On this theme and its wider role in Irenaeus cf. Hill 2002 [1992], 254–9.

[173] *Haer.* 5.36.2.

This treatment, the longest discussion of the resurrection to this date, shows clearly where the issue was joined. Irenaeus also wrote a separate book on the resurrection, but apart from three very short fragments, preserved in the *Parallela* of John of Damascus (itself only preserved in fragments), it is lost.[174] But there is no question of the position he took, or of the basic position he was most concerned to oppose. The bodily resurrection, both of Jesus and of humans in the future, was not an isolated doctrine for Irenaeus. It was linked in a thousand ways to the doctrines of the good creator, of the Word as truly incarnate, and the church and its canonical scriptures as the repositories of the true teaching of Jesus – in other words, to the central themes of his work.

We must remind ourselves, as well, that it was thereby part of the network, the web of belief, which Irenaeus, like the other writers we have studied, regarded as the strong core of the faith. This strength was needed to maintain the truth of the gospel not only against Jewish unbelief – that was not a particular concern for Irenaeus, but it was for some other second-century writers – but also against pagan hostility; and pagan hostility was far from being merely intellectual. At that level, as we shall see later on, Irenaeus saw the gnostic alternative as a way of escaping from the necessary struggle into a sphere of spirituality which posed no threat to anyone and hence would not incur persecution. The bodily resurrection was one part of the Christian armour, interlocking with all the others, designed to withstand the worst that pagan empire could do.

(iii) Hippolytus

Out of the voluminous work of the early third-century writer Hippolytus (c.170–236), two short passages on the resurrection stand out.[175] The *Treatise on Christ and Antichrist* ends with a catena of quotations on the subject of the resurrection, from both Old and New Testaments. The second chapter of 2 Thessalonians is quoted in full, followed by a collage from Matthew 24 and Luke 21, coupled with passages from Psalms, prophets and Paul.[176] Then, coming specifically to the resurrection, he quotes successively Daniel 12.2; Isaiah 26.19; John 5.25; Ephesians 5.14; Revelation 20.6; Matthew 13.43; Matthew 25.34; Revelation 22.15; Isaiah 66.24; and 1 Thessalonians 4.13–17. The only surprise is what he does *not* quote: where is

---

[174] Iren., *Frags.* 9, 10, 12, the final one expounding the seed-and-plant illustration yet once more. John of Damascus lived in the late C7 and early C8.

[175] On the complex task of discovering which of the works attributed to him Hippolytus actually wrote, and on the integration of his vision of cosmic renewal with individual blessed post-mortem existence in the present and resurrection in the future, see Hill 2002 [1992], 160–69.

[176] *Christ and Antichr.* 63f.

Romans? Where are the Corinthian letters? Was Paul being read in different ways, which made it harder for him to refer to them without more argument? The evidence of Irenaeus, noted above, suggests that this may perhaps have been the case.

The other passage comes in the fragmentary book *Against Plato, on the Cause of the Universe*. Here Hippolytus describes Hades, the place where all the dead currently abide, as a guard-house for souls in which punishments are already being administered in advance of the final judgment. The righteous are also in Hades for the moment, but in a place apart from the wicked, while they await 'the incorruptible and unfading kingdom'.[177] Their present abode is one of light and happy expectation; it is the place referred to as 'Abraham's bosom'. This first chapter seems to be dependent in more ways than one on the parable in Luke 16, read as a description of the after-life, including the great gulf fixed between sinners and righteous.

Then, at the end, god will accomplish the resurrection; not, indeed, by enabling them to transmigrate into another body, but by raising the bodies themselves.[178] Just because the bodies have been dissolved, that does not mean that the creator is unable to bring together the same elements and make the body immortal. The body after death is like seed, sown as bare grain but then to be moulded anew: 'it is not raised the same thing as it is now, but pure and no longer corruptible.' Every one of these bodies will receive the soul proper to it. The unrighteous, however, will receive their bodies in the corrupt, suffering, diseased state they left them in, and in that state they will be judged; this appears to be a new twist in the argument. Hippolytus ends with an exalted passage envisaging the last judgment and the happy state of the righteous thereafter.

(iv) Origen

When we turn to the great Alexandrian writer Origen (c. 185–254) we find ourselves in a different world in several senses. He provides a convenient chronological terminus for our study of early Christianity. His massive learning and speculative theology, much of it sadly lost, gained him a special (though not always favourable) place not only in his lifetime, but also in succeeding centuries, and in theological debates to the present day. He shares with his contemporary Clement of Alexandria the dubious reputation of giving more space to some kind of Platonic philosophy than other theologians had hitherto felt able to do; this is a gross oversimplification in his case, but it makes his views on the resurrection, at least in some of his writings, all the more striking. His doctrine of *apokatastasis*, a restoration or

---

[177] *Ag. Plat.* 1.
[178] *Ag. Plat.* 2.

return of all things to their place of primal origin, was so strong that he even seems to have held that the devil would be saved. For this, following severe attacks by Augustine, he was condemned by the Council of Constantinople in AD 543. He nevertheless emerges as a wonderfully erudite and sensitive exegete and theologian, and represents a special point of interest for our study.[179]

Caroline Bynum, summarizing what seems to be a main stream in the contemporary study of Origen on this point, puts the position thus:

> Origen saw himself as treading a middle way between, on the one hand, Jews, millenarian Christians, and pagans who (he thought) understood bodily resurrection as the reanimation of dead flesh and, on the other hand, Gnostics and Hellenists who (he thought) denied any kind of ultimate reality either to resurrection or to body.[180]

Origen's view seems to have been that the human body is in a continual state of flux. The body is like a river; the actual matter does not remain the same from one day to the next.[181] The thing that stays the same, for Origen, is the *eidos*, a combination of Platonic form and Stoic seminal reason. Bynum suggests that it is 'a bit like a genetic code'.[182] The question is then whether Origen has truly safeguarded the continuity of the body from the present life into the resurrection, or whether he has sacrificed that for the sake of emphasizing (over against a crude getting-the-same-particles-back-again view) the notion of transformation. That was the basis of the attack on him launched by Methodius in the middle of the third century and by the Second Council of Constantinople in the middle of the sixth.[183]

This overview indicates that Origen was indeed wrestling with similar questions to Paul on the one hand (the distinction between the 'flesh and blood' that cannot inherit the kingdom and the 'body' that can and will, and that forms the locus of present worship and obedience) and perhaps the *Gospel of Philip* and even the *Letter to Rheginos* on the other hand (see the next

---

[179] On Origen see Crouzel 1989; on the resurrection, and the subsequent debate, see DeChow 1988, 373–84; Clark 1992; Bynum 1995, 63–71, with full bibliog.; Hill 2002 [1992], 176–89. Among older studies, that of Chadwick 1948 remains seminal, along with Chadwick 1953. See too Perkins 1984, 372–7; Coakley 2002, 136–41.

[180] Bynum 1995, 64. Origen's need to combat chiliasm, and its particular version of bodily resurrection, while defending his own version of the same doctrine, is the particular focus of Hill, loc. cit.

[181] Or. on Ps. 1.5: in Methodius, *De Res.* 1.22f. For the whole question see Clark 1992, 89 n. 31. We may wonder whether C. S. Lewis was aware of the ancestry of his argument in 1960 [1947], 155: 'It is presumably a foolish fancy . . . that each spirit should recover those particular units of matter which he ruled before. For one thing, there would not be enough to go round . . . Nor does the unity of our bodies, even in this present life, consist in retaining the same particles. My form remains one, though the matter in it changes continually. I am, in that respect, like a curve in a waterfall.'

[182] Bynum 1995, 66.

[183] Bynum 1995, 67–9.

section). It would do him no justice to suggest that he represents something of a midway point between Paul and the Nag Hammadi writings, since he is so firmly on Paul's side when it comes to something like a Jewish doctrine of creation. Yet this may also indicate that the two Nag Hammadi texts in question may at least have seen themselves as struggling to remain within some kind of Christian worldview. This is a question to which we must return.

First, though, we must look at more of what Origen himself actually says, in particular at the passages where he wants to affirm bodily resurrection over against gnostics, hellenizers, or no-nonsense pagans like Celsus. Before we turn to his major polemical work against the latter, where the question of the resurrection comes up several times, we glance at his systematic discourse *De Principiis*. Here he twice expounds that most contentious of Pauline terms, the 'spiritual body'.

In the first of these passages Origen finds himself, within the logical order of his exposition, faced with the question of the resurrection, and decides to summarize what he has said more fully elsewhere – usefully from our point of view, since unless this refers to the work against Celsus this 'elsewhere' is lost. He begins by affirming that if it is a body that dies, it will be a body that rises. When Paul speaks of a 'spiritual body', he certainly means a body; Origen here clearly means 'body' in what we would call a physical sense. Bodies will rise, he says, 'in order that we may be clothed with them a second time at the resurrection'.[184] The word 'spiritual' here has to do with the casting off of corruption and mortality. This will involve a transmutation of the earlier, 'animal' body (that is, the *soma psychikon*), but not, it seems, an abandonment of it.

This transformation becomes the key to Origen's view of the resurrection body. It is both the same as and different from the body that died. The key difference – here he is very close to Paul – lies in the incorruptibility of the new, deathless body. Origen sees that problems of envisaging all this will arise not only among pagan critics of Christianity but among less-well-taught Christians themselves. Again he stresses transformation, quoting Paul: 'We shall be changed.'[185]

Origen returns to the point in Book III, where in chapter 6 he addresses the question of the end of the whole world. This time he develops his picture of the new body further, following its transformation in resurrection:

> How pure, how refined, and how glorious are the qualities of that body, if we compare it with those which, although they are celestial bodies, and of most brilliant splendour, were nevertheless made with hands, and are visible to our sight . . . how great are the comeliness, and splendour, and brilliance of a spiritual body.[186]

---

[184] *De Princ.* 2.10.1.

[185] *De Princ.* 2.10.3, quoting 1 Cor. 15.51.

[186] *De Princ.* 23.6.4, having just quoted 2 Cor. 5.1 which speaks of the new body 'not

All this is to happen when everything has returned into one in the final consummation, when death itself, the last enemy, is destroyed.[187]

Origen's main exposition of his views come in reply to the pagan Celsus, whose cynical and many-sided attack on Christianity, *On the True Doctrine*, was almost certainly written in the late 170s.[188] Celsus has plenty of arguments of his own to put, but in some of the work he puts anti-Christian polemic into the mouth of an imaginary Jew, including his first scornful mention of the resurrection: one wonders, he says, why a god should need to resort to the kind of persuasion you [i.e. Jesus] used, even eating a fish after your resurrection.[189] Even if his followers did say Jesus rose from the dead, says Celsus' imaginary Jew, that merely puts him on a level with Samolxis and others in the pagan world, including Orpheus, Protesilaus, Hercules and Theseus. Doubtless, says Celsus, you will admit – as he does himself – that these are simply legends (in any case, as we saw in chapter 2, none of them actually involved 'resurrection' in the strict sense, which ancient paganism routinely denied); but you will go on to claim that your story is believable and noble, despite the awful cry from the cross. I suppose you will say, he continues,

> that the earthquake and the darkness that covered the earth at the time of his death prove him a god, and that even though he did not accept the challenge to remove himself from the cross or to escape his persecutors when he was alive, yet he overcame them all by rising from the dead and showing the marks of his punishment, pierced hands and all, to others. But who really saw this? A hysterical woman, as you admit and perhaps one other person – both deluded by his sorcery, or else so wrenched with grief at his failure that they hallucinated him risen from the dead by a sort of wishful thinking. This mistaking a fantasy for reality is not at all uncommon; indeed, it has happened to thousands. Just as possible, these deluded women wanted to impress the others – who had the good sense to have abandoned him – by spreading their hallucinations about as 'visions'. After getting some few to believe them, it was a small matter for the fire of superstition to spread.[190]

Celsus clearly thinks he is on to a good thing, and turns to mock Jesus himself:

---

made with hands'. Origen seems to assume that the sun, moon etc., being part of the original creation, are in that sense 'made with hands'. It is at points like this that some, in his own day and subsequently, have wondered whether Origen shared to some extent the ancient pagan belief (described in ch. 2 above) in 'astral immortality': see e.g. Scott 1991.

[187] *De Princ.* 3.6.5.

[188] ET Hoffman 1987 (the book is reconstructed from the copious references in Origen's own work; on the problems attending this enterprise the remarks of Chadwick 1953, xxii–xxiv are still salutary). A useful summary of Celsus' objections, tracing them back through Justin's opponent Trypho to first-century themes, is found in Stanton 1994.

[189] Hoffman 1987, 60.

[190] Hoffman 1987, 67f.

If this Jesus were trying to convince anyone of his powers, then surely he ought to have appeared first to the Jews who treated him so badly – and to his accusers – indeed to everyone, everywhere. Or better, he might have saved himself the trouble of getting buried and simply have disappeared from the cross. Has there ever been such an incompetent planner: When he was in the body, he was disbelieved but preached to everyone; after his resurrection, apparently wanting to establish a strong faith, he chooses to show himself to one woman and a few comrades only. When he was punished, everyone saw; yet risen from the tomb, almost no one.[191]

Coming to an end of arguments to put in the mouth of a Jew, Celsus speaks in his own voice. The Christians, he says, ignore the splendid gods available to them in the wider world, and say that people like Hercules, or Castor and Pollux, are not gods because they were humans in the first place:

Yet they profess belief in a phantom god who appeared only to members of his little club, and then, so it seems, merely as a kind of ghost.[192]

By contrast, he says, people who say they see Asclepius going about doing his healings see him not as a phantom but as his true self.[193] There are others, too, in the pagan world of whom strange tales are told; yet the Christians insist on honouring Jesus as if he were the only one. This is the more strange in that Jesus, according to the Christians themselves, shared mortal and weak flesh;

they will have it, however, that he put aside this flesh in favor of another, and so became a god. But if apotheosis is the hallmark of divinity, why not rather Asclepios, Dionysus, or Herakles, whose stories are far more ancient? I have heard a Christian ridicule those in Crete who show tourists the tomb of Zeus, saying that these Cretans have no reason for doing what they do. It may be so; yet the Christians base their faith on one who rose from a tomb.[194]

He is aware of the tensions between, and within, the different resurrection narratives in the gospels: was it one angel or two? Why did the son of god need someone else to roll away the stone on his behalf?[195]

In particular, Celsus attempts to show that the Christian hope, to go to 'another earth, different and better than this one', is simply a variation on Plato's theme of the Elysian fields.[196] It seems, he says, that the Christians have misunderstood Plato's doctrine of reincarnation,

and believe in the absurd theory that the corporeal body will be raised and reconstituted by God, and that somehow they will actually see God with their mortal

---

[191] Hoffman 1987, 68.

[192] Hoffman 1987, 71.

[193] Hoffman 1987, 133 n. 59 (with refs.) points out that this comparison was standard in anti-Christian polemic.

[194] Hoffman 1987, 72.

[195] Hoffman 1987, 90.

[196] Hoffman 1987, 109.

eyes and hear him with their ears and be able to touch him with their hands . . . The Christians are preoccupied with the question of knowing God, and they think one cannot know God except through the senses of the body.[197]

Had they wanted to follow someone who died a hero's death, he says, they would have done better to choose Hercules or Asclepius, Orpheus, Anaxarchus or even Epictetus.[198]

Celsus seems at times to be deliberately obtuse, putting the Christian claims into frameworks of thought that make no sense; but then we do not know which Christians Celsus had met, or read. His polemic is nevertheless valuable in itself for giving us a window on how Christianity was perceived in the pagan world of the late second century, and also, by implication, causing us to reflect on some aspects of the biblical narratives themselves, to which we shall return. But of course the main reason why Celsus features in our present task is because his polemic drew forth from Origen one of his greatest works. It is way beyond our scope to examine it in detail; we simply draw from it Origen's key replies on the subject of the resurrection. Despite what has often enough been thought, Origen remains robustly orthodox on the central points.

He only replies briefly to Celsus' query about the risen Jesus eating fish. This is a trifling point, says Origen; Jesus simply did assume a true body, as one born of a woman.[199] He similarly declares, without argument, that in the interval between Jesus' death and resurrection he went as a bare soul to dwell among the bodiless souls, converting some of them.[200] More seriously, Origen points out that nobody really believes Orpheus, Protesilaus and the others were both really dead and then also truly raised again with a veritable body. The account of Jesus' resurrection simply cannot be put into the same category; the heroes, at best, practised some kind of deception, but the public nature of Jesus' death made that impossible.[201] Nobody could question that Jesus really did die, as people certainly would have done had his death been in private and followed by a claim of resurrection. In particular (an argument beloved by apologists from that day to this):

A clear and unmistakeable proof of the fact I hold to be the undertaking of his disciples, who devoted themselves to the teaching of a doctrine which was attended with danger to human life, a doctrine which they would not have taught with such courage had they invented the resurrection of Jesus from the dead; and who also, at the same time, not only prepared others to despise death, but were themselves the first to manifest their disregard for its terrors.[202]

---

[197] Hoffman 1987, 110.
[198] Hoffman 1987, 112.
[199] *C. Cels*. 1.70.
[200] *C. Cels*. 2.43.
[201] *C. Cels*. 2.55f.
[202] *C. Cels*. 2.56.

Celsus is wrong to allow his fictitious Jew to question whether anyone ever rose with a true body, since scripture itself contains the stories of Elijah and Elisha raising children from the dead.[203] Origen knows perfectly well the difference between myths and historical events, and insists that the resurrection of Jesus is the latter. It is, in fact, of far greater significance than the smaller miracles of the two ancient prophets, and has produced far-reaching effects.[204] And he puts Celsus right about the resurrection narratives; yes, Mary Magdalene did see Jesus, but more than one other person did so as well.[205] Origen also knows about visions, dreams, fantasies and the like, and sees them as evidence of the state of the soul when separated from the body.[206] The recorded appearances of Jesus are not of this type:

> Although Celsus may wish to place what is told of Jesus, and of those who saw him after his resurrection, on the same level with imaginary appearances of a different kind, and those who have invented such, yet to those who institute a candid and intelligent examination, the events will appear only the more miraculous.[207]

Origen then faces what he sees as a more serious question: why did Jesus only appear to his followers, not to those who had ill-treated him? This, he says, opens up deep and wonderful mysteries, beyond the grasp of many even well-taught Christians; but he will make an attempt to explain them.[208] As with the transfiguration, not everyone was yet able to bear the sight; Jesus was sparing them.[209] The risen body is not something that ordinary eyes can see; one needs to receive eyes capable of it; Jesus wished to show his divine power to each one who was capable of seeing it, according to the measure of his capability.[210] As for Celsus' suggestion that Jesus should really have come down from the cross, Origen shows that this misunderstands the whole point of the Jesus' crucifixion and death within the Christian understanding of salvation.[211] Celsus admits that his hypothetical Jew believes in the final resurrection; Origen points out that Christians can and will use the same arguments that a Jew will use to back up this belief.[212]

After dealing with many other problems, Origen returns in Book V to the question of what precisely is meant by the resurrection of the flesh. The first thing he emphasizes, just as in the brief summary in *De Principiis*, is that the future body is not absolutely identical to the present one:

---

[203] *C. Cels.* 2.57.
[204] *C. Cels.* 2.58.
[205] *C. Cels.* 2.59.
[206] *C. Cels.* 2.60f.
[207] *C. Cels.* 2.62.
[208] *C. Cels.* 2.63.
[209] *C. Cels.* 2.64.
[210] *C. Cels.* 2.65, 67. See the similar line of thought in Coakley 2002 ch. 8.
[211] *C. Cels.* 2.69.
[212] *C. Cels.* 2.77.

Neither we, nor the holy scriptures, assert that with the same bodies, without a change to a higher condition, 'shall those who were long dead arise from the earth and live again'.[213]

Origen explains, drawing heavily on 1 Corinthians 15: according to Paul, a change takes place between the seed that is sown and the plant that is reaped, and the central feature of this change is that between corruptibility and incorruptibility. Paul declares it to be a mystery, and so it is; but it is simply a misrepresentation to suggest that the Christian hope is for a body that has seen corruption.[214] Origen then dismisses as ridiculous the cosmological theories of the Stoics and Pythagoreans, which Celsus has advanced as similar, and preferable, to the Christian cosmic hope.[215] And he dismisses, too, those who have the name of Christian but 'who set aside the doctrine of the resurrection as it is taught in scripture'.[216] It is possible that he has in mind here people who teach a 'resurrection' which does not involve a body at all, but the probability is that he has in mind those who teach a simple resuscitation or reconstitution, in which god will find all the bits and pieces of the decomposed body and patch them back together again. This seems to be the force of the following passage:

> We therefore do not maintain that the body which has undergone corruption resumes its original nature, any more than the grain of wheat which has decayed returns to its former condition. But we do maintain, that as above the grain of wheat there arises a stalk, so a certain power (*logos*) is implanted in the body, which is not destroyed, and from which the body is raised up in incorruption.[217]

Origen is careful not simply to claim, in support of this, that god can do anything at all. God cannot do things that are of themselves inconceivable or shameful.[218] At the same time, there may be some things which appear to humans incredible which are in fact not contrary to nature. When it comes to discrepancies between the gospel accounts of Easter, Origen is well aware of the problem, and ready with his answer. Celsus has actually misrepresented the situation: Matthew and Mark speak of one angel (who rolls away the stone), while Luke and John speak of two who appear to the women, or were

---

[213] *C. Cels.* 5.18; the quote is from Celsus.

[214] *C. Cels.* 5.18f.

[215] *C. Cels.* 5.20f.

[216] *C. Cels.* 5.22. For Riley to say that Origen's deduction of bodily resurrection from scripture was simply 'based on his method of interpretation', and that since his opponents had other methods of interpretation their results were just as 'scriptural' as his (1995, 61) is to use the word 'scriptural' in a bizarre sense. We see what Riley means when he declares that Marcion of all people was 'one of the most "scriptural" Christians of his day' (64) – Marcion, who rejected the Old Testament in its entirety and 'edited' the New with a large pair of scissors.

[217] *C. Cels.* 5.23. More or less the same argument is repeated in another context at 6.29.

[218] As Chadwick points out (1953, 281 n. 6) this was an already hackneyed quotation from Euripides (*Frag.* 292).

seen inside the tomb. Each of these occurrences, he says, 'might now be demonstrated to have actually taken place', and to possess a figurative meaning 'to those who were prepared to behold the resurrection of the Word'.[219] What is more, the angel rolled the stone away not to let Jesus out but to let the world see that the tomb was indeed empty.[220]

In Book VII Origen tackles Celsus' suggestion that the Christian doctrine of resurrection is a misunderstanding of Plato's theory of transmigration. Origen admits that resurrection is 'a high and difficult doctrine, and one which more than others requires a high and advanced degree of wisdom to set forth how worthy it is of god'. He then proceeds once more to expound 2 Corinthians 5.1–5 and 1 Corinthians 15 to make the point we have already noted, that the soul must be clothed with a body, but that the body will change from one state to another. Behold then, he says,

> to what a prospect scripture encourages us to look, when it speaks to us of being clothed with incorruption and immortality, which are, as it were, vestments which will not suffer those who are covered with them to come to corruption or death.[221]

We do not simply need a body in order to see god, and seeing god is in any case something that is done with the mind and the heart.[222] The final charge of Celsus on the subject is to imply that the resurrection appearances were like those of a ghost, a spectre flitting before their eyes. But

> how is it possible that a phantom which, as he describes it, flew past to deceive the beholders, could produce such effects after it had passed away, and could so turn the hearts of men as to lead them to regulate their actions according to the will of God, as in view of being hereafter judged by him? And how could a phantom drive away demons, and show other indisputable evidences of power, and that not in any one place, like these so-called gods in human form [whom Celsus has referred to], but making its divine power felt through the whole world, in drawing and congregating together all who are found disposed to lead a good and noble life?[223]

Origen's final answer is thus the evidence of the Christian community itself; this would no doubt leave Celsus with other things to say about the foolishness, bad behaviour, disunity and so on of that community in his own day. But this is another topic; we have now seen what Origen has to say on ours.

---

[219] *C. Cels.* 5.56; further justified in 5.57. Origen says that this question belongs alongside an exposition of the gospel texts themselves.

[220] *C. Cels.* 5.58. Elsewhere Origen was quite ready to let go of the literal meaning: 'If someone carefully studies the Gospels with respect to the incongruities in historical matters . . . he gets dizzy and will either give up any attempt to establish the truth of the Gospels, and – since he does not dare to fully deny his belief with respect to (the story of) our Lord – will at random choose one of them, or will accept that the truth of these four does not lie in the literal text' (*Comm. in Ioannem* 10.3.2).

[221] *C. Cels.* 7.32.

[222] *C. Cels.* 7.33f.

[223] *C. Cels.* 7.35.

He does, in fact, fill out the second-century expositions of resurrection. One would not have known from Clement, Ignatius, Justin or Tertullian that Paul had envisaged the present body being changed; they are so concerned with continuity that they do not mention discontinuity. Origen sees things the other way round. But though he has the reputation of a Platonist, an allegorist more concerned with spiritual meaning than with this-worldly events, he sticks to his guns through all the twists and turns of the argument. Jesus' resurrection was the resurrection, albeit also the transformation, of his actual body. The resurrection of Christians will result in an actual physical body, albeit an incorruptible one.

Origen's answers to our questions (though not necessarily to those of everyone else, then or now) are therefore plain, at least in this central text. When he affirms the resurrection, he means a real body, in both important continuity and important discontinuity with that which went before. He is happy to speak of the intermediate state in terms of the soul, even of the soul of Jesus preaching to the departed in between his death and resurrection. Like the other patristic writers we have surveyed, he places the final resurrection in the context of a larger picture of final judgment, even though he has his own particular views as to its eventual outcome. And the final resurrection is based on that of Jesus himself. What Origen does not have, any more than the other writers we have surveyed, is any metaphorical use of 'resurrection' to denote (as sometimes in the New Testament) the new life which believers have in the present in baptism and holiness.

Nor does he use this language in any way to denote a new spiritual experience in the present which will lead to a final blessed disembodiment in the future (the gnostic option, to be discussed below). We must assume that he knew the texts, opposed by Irenaeus and others, which used 'resurrection' language in this way, but he never commented on them; nor did Celsus make any use of this theme either. Indeed, we have now drawn a line forwards from the New Testament to the early third century, and the only mention we have of such an idea – such a dramatic linguistic innovation within the entire ancient world – is in the more sustained polemic of Irenaeus, who mentions it in order to rule it out. We shall shortly examine such texts as we have which represent the view in question. But first, as a transitional interlude, we must note another set of texts which form something of a halfway house between these different types of early Christianity.

6. Early Syriac Christianity

(i) Introduction

There are three texts which can be considered side by side as representative of early Syriac Christianity. The first and third are of indeterminate date;

that is, they could have been produced at more or less any time between the end of the first and the middle of the third century. They all give evidence of ways in which would-be orthodox Christians were moving, in the Syriac-speaking world, towards a devotion tending to extreme asceticism – not, however, out of a hatred for the body itself, but out of the vocation to follow the poverty and simplicity of Christ.[224] To this extent they need to be placed near some of the gnostic material, though the present bald summary cannot do justice to the subtle similarities and differences between the categories.[225]

(ii) The *Odes of Solomon*

The work now known as the *Odes of Solomon*, written in Syriac, came to light in bits and pieces through several manuscript finds culminating in the early twentieth century. There are forty-two Odes, and both their date and character are still assessed very differently. Some put them as late as the third century, but the clear links to the kind of Jewish thought represented at Qumran, and also to the fourth gospel, have encouraged several writers to hazard a guess at the late first or early second centuries.[226] We place them here, alongside the writers of the late second and early third centuries, not because we can be sure that they belong there chronologically but because they express a theology and spirituality which, although rooted in the Jewish piety represented by the Psalter and the Qumran texts, shows signs (in my judgment) of a more developed theology and range of imagery than we see either in the New Testament or the Apostolic Fathers. Judgments like this are notoriously subjective, however. Nothing in our present argument hangs on a decision about the date or context of this early Christian hymnbook.

The *Odes* offer a warm spirituality, expressed in flowing Syriac poetry. Unlike some later Syrian Christianity, they are firmly rooted in a strong doctrine of creation and incarnation.[227] The believer enjoys a close, intimate and life-giving union with the Messiah, with the Holy Spirit, and with the creator god.[228] Within this, the *Odes* stress the promise of a final 'rest', conceived along the lines of the Old Testament sabbath.[229] In language reminiscent of John's gospel, they speak of the believer being joined to the Messiah, the

---

[224] For a short introduction see e.g. Harvey 2000.

[225] See too below, 537f., on the *Book of Thomas the Contender*.

[226] See e.g. Charlesworth 1992. Text and tr. in Charlesworth 1977 [1973]; tr. updated in Charlesworth 1985, 725–71.

[227] Creation: e.g. *Od. Sol.* 7.9; 16.5–20. Incarnation: e.g. 7.6 and frequently.

[228] For the Spirit, see esp. e.g. *Ode* 36. An early trinitarian formula rounds off *Ode* 23 (23.22).

[229] *Od. Sol.* 3.5; 11.12 (where the rest is 'immortal'); 16.12, etc.; see Charlesworth's note (1977 [1973], 20 n. 7).

immortal one, who has life in himself and gives it to others.[230] Those who belong to the Messiah will receive immortality and incorruption as a gift, rather than possessing it from the start.[231] They are promised paradise, descriptions of which, in the *Odes*, sometimes look remarkably this-worldly.[232]

But do the *Odes* teach resurrection itself? Emphatically yes. The fifteenth *Ode* echoes 1 Corinthians 15:

> I put on incorruption through His name,
> And took off corruption by His grace.
> Death has been destroyed before my face,
> And Sheol has been vanquished by my word.
> And eternal life has arisen in the Lord's land,
> And it has been declared to His faithful ones,
> And been given without limit to all that trust in Him
> Hallelujah.[233]

This statement of Christian hope is reinforced in individual lines here and there, such as when 17.13 speaks of the Messiah giving his resurrection to his followers, and 21.4 speaks of being given new 'members' which will not suffer from sickness, affliction or suffering.[234] *Ode* 29 is reminiscent of Psalm 15 (which, as we saw earlier, was used in Acts as part of the early proclamation of Jesus' resurrection), speaking of the Lord rescuing the believer from Sheol:

> The Lord is my hope,
> I shall not be ashamed of Him . . .
> According to His mercies He exalted me [or: raised me up],
> And according to His great honour He lifted me up.
> And He caused me to ascend from the depths of Sheol,
> And from the mouth of death He drew me.
> And I humbled my enemies,
> And he justified me by His grace.
> For I believed in the Lord's Messiah,
> And considered that He is the Lord.[235]

It has been argued, too, that *Ode* 41 refers to the resurrection:

> For a great day has shined upon us,
> And wonderful is He who has given to us of His glory . . .

---

[230] e.g. *Od. Sol.* 3.8f.; 6.18.

[231] *Od. Sol.* 9.7; 17.2; 28.6f.; 33.9, 12; 40.6.

[232] *Od. Sol.* 11.16, 18, 23, 24; 20.7. It is perhaps surprising that Hill 2002 [1992], 125f. does not explore this further. For the whole theme of immortality in the *Odes*, see Charlesworth 1985, 731.

[233] *Od. Sol.* 15.8–10.

[234] On the translation of *Od. Sol.* 17.13 see Charlesworth 1977 [1973], 77 n. 17. This poem may be an anticipation of the 'harrowing of hell' scene in 42: see below.

[235] *Od. Sol.* 29.1, 3–6.

The Man who humbled Himself,
But was exalted because of His own righteousness.[236]

But the two clearest statements are in *Odes* 22 and 42. In 22, the Messiah himself speaks of the victory that his god has given him over the seven-headed dragon, so that now he has smoothed the 'way' for those who believe. Referring to the divine hand which has done this ('It'), the hymn goes on:

And It chose them from the graves,
And separated them from the dead ones.
It took dead bones
And covered them with flesh.
But they were motionless,
So It gave them energy for life.
Incorruptible was Thy way and Thy face;
Thou hast brought Thy world to corruption,
That everything might be resolved and renewed.
And the foundation of everything is Thy rock.
And upon it Thou hast built Thy kingdom,
And it became the dwelling-place of the holy ones.
Hallelujah.[237]

This is, obviously, a meditation on Ezekiel 37, applying it to the divine act of redeeming a people, bringing the whole world through corruption and decay into a new creation, which is the divine kingdom, the ultimate home of the redeemed. Such sentiments would not be out of place alongside Isaiah, Revelation or Paul. Then, in the final *Ode*, perhaps anticipated in 17 as well, the Messiah speaks, telling the story of his saving accomplishments, including what looks like the harrowing of Hell:

I was not rejected although I was considered to be so,
And I did not perish although they thought it of me.
Sheol saw me and was shattered,
And Death ejected me and many with me.
I have been vinegar and bitterness to it,
And I went down with it as far as its depth.
Then the feet and the head it released,
Because it was not able to endure my face.
And I made a congregation of living among his dead;
And I spoke with them by living lips;
In order that my word may not be unprofitable.
And those who had died ran towards me;
And they cried out and said, Son of God, have pity on us.

---

[236] *Od. Sol.* 41.4, 12; Charlesworth 1977 [1973], 142 n. 7 cites H. Leclercq as taking v. 4 as a reference to the resurrection, though Charlesworth opts for the incarnation. The verb in question (*rûm*), as in 29.3, can be translated either 'exalted' or 'raised', as is reflected in Charlesworth's two translations (1977 [1973], 141 as against 1985, 770; 1992, 114).

[237] *Od. Sol.* 22.8–12.

And deal with us according to Thy kindness,
And bring us out of the bonds of darkness.
And open for us the door
By which we may come to Thee;
For we perceive that our death does not touch Thee.
May we also be saved with Thee,
Because Thou art our Saviour.[238]

It would be easy to misread the opening couplet as a declaration of a docetic or even gnostic position, that the Messiah did not really die.[239] But the real parallel is Wisdom 3.2, 4 and the wider context.[240] The point is not that the righteous (in this case, the Messiah himself) have not suffered physical death, but that the onlookers suppose they, or he, are gone for ever, whereas the living god is looking after them. In the case of the Messiah, he has gone to the world of the dead, in order to rescue those who are there. This has strong echoes of the 'preaching to the spirits in prison' of 1 Peter 3.19, taken in that particular sense.[241] But the main point, a thoroughly Jewish and Pauline one, is that Death and Sheol are enemies of God, the world, and humankind, and that the redeeming work of the Messiah consists of defeating them and releasing those in their grip. This is, of course, a restatement of the mainstream second-Temple Jewish belief, redefined around the Messiah himself. The resurrection of the Messiah is the means, as vividly expressed in this poem as in a gilded icon, whereby he raises from the dead all those who trust him. The *Odes* take their place along with the great theologians of the first two centuries, a living reminder that the church expresses and learns its faith as much by poetry and song as by theological argument.

(iii) Tatian

Roughly contemporary with Athenagoras, and a pupil of Justin though soon going his own way, Tatian is best known for his *Diatessáron*, a harmony of the four canonical gospels.[242] He wrote widely, but, perhaps because he incurred subsequent disapproval, almost all his works are lost. The surviving *Address to the Greeks* is a passionate denunciation of Greek life, philosophy and lifestyle. Not for him the gentle approach to apologetics.

The *Address* includes a short passage (6) on the resurrection. It is based (5) on belief in god as creator; as with Justin, this includes a doctrine of the *logos* as the creator's first-begotten work. There will be a resurrection of bodies after the consummation of all things; this is 'a resurrection once for

---

[238] *Od. Sol.* 42.10–18.
[239] See the note in Charlesworth 1977 [1973], 147 n. 17.
[240] See above, 165–71.
[241] Above, 467–9.
[242] On which see Metzger 1977; Petersen 1994.

all', to be distinguished from a Stoic cyclical sequence. Its purpose is to enable judgment to take place. This is not, as in some pagan beliefs, a matter of coming to stand before Minos or Rhadamanthus;[243] it is the creator himself who will be the judge. Tatian is not as anxious as Athenagoras about what happens to the bits and pieces of human bodies:

> Even though fire destroy all traces of my flesh, the world receives the vaporized matter; and though dispersed through rivers and seas, or torn in pieces by wild beasts, I am laid up in the storehouses of a wealthy Lord. And, although the poor and the godless know not what is stored up, yet God the Sovereign, when he pleases, will restore the substance that is visible to him alone to its pristine condition.

Despite the judgment of later Christian writers on his other opinions (which had more to do with his increasing espousal of the asceticism that characterized Syrian Christianity in this period), on this topic Tatian is firmly in line with the New Testament and the second-century writers studied so far. Indeed, compared with Athenagoras, he is closer to the New Testament in one respect at least: he holds (13) that the soul is not by nature immortal, but mortal.[244] It is possible, however, for it not to die; but if it does not come to know the truth, it will die, be dissolved with the body, and then rise again at the end of time, along with the body, to face punishment. But if it comes to know god during this life, it may be dissolved for a while, but it will not die. Tatian thus holds a form of conditional immortality: the wicked will die, body and soul, but be raised again; righteous souls exist between death and resurrection, separated from the body though held in life. His attempts to explain this, though, seem to rely on an anthropology which he has taken from contemporary philosophy, without fully working out the ways in which it may be suited to express the extraordinary Christian affirmations.[245]

(iv) The *Acts of Thomas*

The *Acts of Thomas,* an originally Syriac work of Manichaean tendency, is the oldest witness for the legend of Thomas's death as a martyr, and the transference of his bones to Edessa.[246] Originating most likely in the early third century, it relates all kinds of exciting episodes in the life of Thomas, which are used as a framework for instruction in an ascetic spirituality. It lacks the developed mythologies of Valentinian gnosticism, but shares in a loosely dualist and encratistic worldview in which the redeemer descends to

---

[243] See above, 43, 45, 50.

[244] For the NT view cf. e.g. 1 Tim. 6.16: Jesus is the only one who possesses immortality as of right. See 269 above.

[245] See Perkins 1984, 351f. For the Jewish background see e.g. Bauckham 1998a, 275f.

[246] See Hennecke 1965, 425–531 (text with full introd.); Attridge 1992 (clear introd. with recent bibliog.); Elliott 1993, 429–511. For discussion, see Riley 1995, 167–75.

earth, reveals to the initiates who he is and thus who they are, and re-ascends to lead the way back to the world of light. The faithful are thus set free from the realm of the material body. This has some analogies with gnosticism, even though the major motifs of the latter are absent.[247]

The theme of revelation and rescue emerges particularly in the remarkable 'Hymn of the Pearl' (chapters 108–13), which is best seen as an allegory of the fate of the soul. The soul, represented in the Hymn by a prince sent to Egypt on a quest for the wonderful pearl which is there, descends into the realm of materiality where he forgets his origin and destiny. Reminded of them by a message from heaven, he accomplishes the quest and sets off with the pearl. The first thing he does as he turns to leave is to take off the dirty, unclean garment he has been wearing in Egypt, and leave it behind. In its place, on the way back home, he is given a royal garment in which he sees himself and realizes who he truly is. Thus, properly clothed once more, he returns with the pearl to the king. In a wide range of other imagery, we note as an example the fourth Act (39–41), in which the colt of an ass offers itself to Thomas, to bear him to the heavenly 'rest', but falls down dead in front of the gate of the city. The ass represents the body, which 'carries' the soul for a while, but cannot be redeemed with it, so is not raised from the dead by the apostle. The watching crowd urge Thomas to raise it, but he says

> I could indeed raise it up through the name of Jesus Christ. But this is not expedient at all. For he who gave it speech that it might speak [like Balaam's ass, this one has had the power of speech] was able also to make it not die. But I do not raise it up, not because I am not able but because this is what is useful and helpful for it.[248]

The great prayer of Thomas in the twelfth Act carries the same message:

> My garment that grows old I have worn out, and the laborious toil that leads to rest I have accomplished . . . I have pulled down the barns and left them desolate on earth, that I may be filled from thy treasures. The abundant spring within me I have dried up, that I may find thy living spring. The prisoner whom thou didst commit to me I have slain, that the freed man in me may not lose his trust. The inside I have made outside, and the outside inside, and thy whole fullness has been fulfilled in me . . . The dead man I have brought to life and the living I have put to death . . . reproach have I received on earth, but give me recompense and requital in heaven.[249]

What matters is the soul, not the body. The latter is cheerfully left behind, not wanted on the final voyage. Here we have truly turned a corner, losing sight of virtually all the texts we have studied in this chapter, never mind the New Testament. We are back once more in the world of ancient Platonism.

---

[247] See Hill 2002 [1992], 126f., referring to other discussions.
[248] *Ac. Thom.* 41; cf. Bornkamm 430f. (in Hennecke 1965).
[249] *Ac. Thom.* 147 (Hennecke 1965, 520f.).

Resurrection is not even reinterpreted, but simply rejected. We are on the threshold of gnosticism.

7. 'Resurrection' as Spirituality? Texts from Nag Hammadi and Elsewhere

(i) Introduction

Placing this material here inevitably lays me open to the charge of erecting an implicit chronological barrier between the Nag Hammadi texts and the New Testament.[250] I plead not guilty. The problem is that we do not know when these documents were written, or what the likely pre-history either of the texts, or the ideas which they contain, may have been. Thus far in the chapter we have followed a reasonably secure historical scheme, with the only exception being the three items from early Syriac Christianity; but at this point we move (perhaps appropriately, given the subject-matter) outside definite space and time, and address the texts both at the level of their view of the body and the resurrection and at the wider level of worldview itself.[251]

(ii) The *Gospel of Thomas*

There is only one place to begin the study of this particular group of texts, and that is with the self-styled *Gospel of Thomas*.[252] The introduction to *Thomas* in the standard texts, by one of the leading scholars in the field (Helmut Koester of Harvard), speaks of the book, its provenance and its basic theology thus:

> The influence of Gnostic theology is clearly present in the *Gospel of Thomas*, though it is not possible to ascribe the work to any particular school or sect . . . According to the *Gospel of Thomas*, the basic religious experience is not only the recognition of one's divine identity, but more specifically the recognition of one's origin (the light) and destiny (the repose). In order to return to one's origin, the disciple is to become separate from the world by 'stripping off' the fleshly garment and 'passing by' the present corruptible existence; then the disciple can experience the new world, the kingdom of light, peace, and life.[253]

[250] cf. Robinson 1982, 6. I include the recently published *Gospel of the Saviour* for reasons that will be obvious (see Hedrick and Mirecki 1999).

[251] On the Nag Hammadi finds, see Robinson 1979; for a review of research on the most important text for our purposes see Fallon and Cameron 1989.

[252] On *Thomas* cf. *NTPG* 435–43; *JVG* 72–4. Many scholars have settled on a mid-second-century date for *Thomas*; but several today, e.g. Koester and Patterson, advocate the middle of the first century. See the summaries in e.g. Elliott 1993, 123–47; and nb. the fresh arguments for the late C2 in Perrin 2002.

[253] Koester, in Robinson 1977, 117. There are many interesting examples of gnostic use of New Testament writings, including several to do with the resurrection, in Pagels 1975.

This viewpoint is clearly embodied (if that is not the wrong term in the circumstances) in the following sayings:

> This heaven will pass away, and the one above it will pass away. The dead are not alive, and the living will not die. (11)

> Mary said to Jesus, 'What are your disciples like?' He said, 'They are like children who have settled in a field which is not theirs. When the owners of the field come, they will say, "Let us have back our field." They will undress in their presence in order to let them have back their field and to give it back to them. Therefore I say to you, if the owner of a house knows that the thief is coming, he will begin his vigil before he comes and will not let him dig through into his house of his domain to carry away his goods. You, then, be on your guard against the world. Arm yourselves with great strength lest the robbers find a way to come to you, for the difficulty which you expect will surely materialize . . .' (21)

> His disciples said, 'When will you become revealed to us and when shall we see you?' Jesus said, 'When you disrobe without being ashamed and take up your garments and place them under your feet like little children and tread on them, then will you see the Son of the Living One, and you will not be afraid.' (37)

> His disciples said to him, 'When will the repose of the dead come about, and when will the new world come?' He said to them, 'What you look forward to has already come, but you do not recognize it.' (51)

> Jesus said, 'I will destroy this house, and no one will be able to rebuild it.' (71)

The two 'undressing' sayings (21, 37) are the most obvious of these: the ordinary physical body constitutes the 'clothes', and the writer urges that one should seek to divest oneself of it, trampling it underfoot as something to be despised.[254] The 'field' in the longer saying is the created world, where we live at present, but which we should be ready to relinquish; as in saying 11, the present order of time, space and matter is essentially transitory.[255]

In the kaleidoscopic imagery of *Gospel of Thomas* 21, the home-owner watching for the thief seems to stand for the initiate who must guard the treasure of spiritual knowledge in case anyone should try to take it away. The world of the flesh is likely to attack the world of the soul, and a prepared defence will be necessary.

The saying about the repose of the dead (51) remains controversial. A recent edition of *Thomas* has suggested that the word 'repose' (*anapausis*) is wrong, and has crept in to this saying by becoming adapted to the end of the

---

[254] See Riley 1995, 130. For other interpretations see Miller 1992 [1991], 309. See *Gos. Thom.* 29; 87; 112. It is possible, though, that the 'undressing' in the Coptic is a mistranslation of a Syriac word meaning 'renounce': see Perrin 2002, 40.

[255] cf. *Gos. Thom.* 56: the person who understands the world has found only a corpse, and the person who has found a corpse (i.e. who realizes that the world is only a lifeless shell), of that person the world is not worthy.

previous saying.[256] Instead, it has been proposed that the real point is not the 'repose' of the dead, but 'resurrection'. This may be an attempt to find 'resurrection' teaching in *Thomas* where it does not occur; but, either way, the point of the saying is that the fate of the departed, however one conceives of it, has already arrived, secretly and without being visible to the naked eye, as in the 'present but invisible kingdom' of saying 113. The saying expressly rejects the early Christian expectation of a final divine act in history producing new heavens and new earth.[257]

The final saying in this group (71) presents an interesting double image: 'I will destroy this house, and no one will be able to rebuild it.' The deviation, and in my view certain derivation, from the well-known canonical saying is clear;[258] the meaning is not so obvious. At one level, it would fit with the rest of *Thomas* to say that the central institution of Judaism, a physical, this-worldly Temple, would be destroyed and not rebuilt; indeed, the deJudaizing that emerges at several points in this document is one of its most striking features. At another level, granted the frequency of 'temple' as an image for the body – already in the Johannine version of the saying, where John says that Jesus was speaking of 'the Temple of his body'[259] – it could well be that the saying is intended, at least at one level, to mean that Jesus will remove the physical body from the initiate and will not replace it. This would then be an explicit denial of bodily resurrection.[260]

The same idea is reflected in three sayings which shudder at the thought of the soul being trapped in its present physical body:

Jesus said, 'If the flesh came into being because of spirit, it is a wonder. But if spirit came into being because of the body, it is a wonder of wonders. Indeed, I am amazed at how this great wealth has made its home in this poverty.'

Jesus said, 'Wretched is the body that is dependent upon a body, and wretched is the soul that is dependent on these two.'

Jesus said, 'Woe to the flesh that depends on the soul; woe to the soul that depends on the flesh.'[261]

---

[256] *Gos. Thom.* 50.3: 'If they ask you, What is the sign of your Father that is in you? say to them, It is movement and repose (*anapausis*).' See Patterson, Robinson and Bethge 1998, ad loc. The idea of 'rest' is also found in the version of saying 2 in *P. Oxy. 654* ('having reigned, they will rest'). Cf. *Rheg.* 43.34f.

[257] Riley 1995, 131.

[258] Mk. 14.58/Mt. 26.61; Mk. 15.29/Mt. 27.40; Jn. 2.19; cf. Mk. 13.2; Ac. 6.14.

[259] Jn. 2.21; cf. 2 Cor. 5.1–5.

[260] This is argued at length by Riley 1995, 133–56, his point being that it provides evidence for a form of early Christianity which specifically denied the bodily resurrection both of Jesus and of his followers. He speculates that an early version of the saying existed which Johannine Christians adjusted one way (so that it spoke of bodily resurrection) and Thomas Christians adjusted in the opposite direction. Other speculative tradition-histories are of course equally possible.

[261] Sayings 29; 87; 112.

Despite the repeated injunction of the text, one does not need ears to hear, or indeed especially sharp eyes to see, what is being said in *Thomas* – and how very different it is from virtually every document we have examined so far, with the only real exception being the Syriac *Acts of Thomas*. It goes beyond that work, though, in being explicitly anti-creational: the world of space, time and matter is the evil creation of a lesser god than that revealed by Jesus.[262] The thing to do is to discover how to escape it, how to return to the disembodied state one had previously enjoyed. This, if not full-blown gnosticism of the Valentinian variety, is certainly well on the way to such a view in its cosmological and anthropological dualism, and the soteriology that goes with it. Though using materials from early Christianity, it has incorporated them within a very different worldview. In that worldview, not accidentally but as a matter of principle, resurrection (in the sense meant by Paul, the gospel traditions, Clement, the *Apocalypse of Peter*, Justin and the rest) is simply ruled out.

(iii) Other Thomas Literature

The *Book of Thomas the Contender* is a dialogue between the risen Jesus and his supposed twin brother, 'Judas Thomas'. It almost certainly comes from Syria in the early third century, and reflects not so much the radical dualism of fully-fledged gnosticism as the extreme asceticism of the Syrian Christianity of which Tatian is a slightly earlier representative.[263] There are, however, overlapping points. Thomas must come to 'know himself' and thus to know 'the depth of the All', that is, the mystery of the place from which Jesus came and to which he will return. Stories about revelations given by Jesus between his resurrection and ascension were frequently part of the gnostic stock-in-trade, enabling them to claim that they had received the true, though secret, wisdom of Jesus over against the standard teachings of the mainstream church. This short work continually stresses how difficult, yet how necessary, it is to understand the secret revelations which are now being given.

The risen saviour first emphasizes that the bodies of humans, like those of beasts, are irrational. They are subject to change, because they eat other created things; they will perish, without hope of life. Bodies are, after all, the result of sexual intercourse; the force of this argument seems to be that intercourse itself is evil and unworthy. The elect must therefore abandon 'bestiality', i.e. the cravings of the flesh.[264] This is a standard theme in

---

[262] Saying 100: 'Give to Caesar what is Caesar's, give to god what is god's, and give to me what is mine.' In other words, Jesus is superior to 'god', as 'god' is to Caesar.

[263] Tr., with short introd., in Robinson 1977, 188–94 (J. D. Turner).

[264] *Thom. Contend.* 138.39—139.30; human intercourse is again denounced in 139.33—140.3; 144.9f.

Syriac Christianity; it does not of itself mean that creation is the work of a lesser god. Its ascetic dualism belongs with some of Tatian's writings, showing signs of encratistic or gnostic tendencies rather than a complete system. Humans come in two kinds, the wise and the foolish; the foolish will arrive at an ordinary human death, whereupon their visible body will dissolve, and

> shapeless shapes will emerge and in the midst of tombs they will forever dwell upon the corpses in pain and corruption of soul.[265]

There follows an extended description of the judgment awaiting those who scorn the truth, and then a list of 'woes' on 'those who hope in the flesh and in the prison that will perish'.[266] The book is more preoccupied with the judgment on those who live in and celebrate ordinary bodily existence than with the hope of the wise who escape it; but it concludes with three beatitudes, echoing the Sermon on the Mount, and a promise of 'rest':

> Watch and pray that you do not come to be in the flesh, but rather that you come forth from the bondage of the bitterness of this life. And as you pray, you will find rest, for you have left behind the suffering and the disgrace. For when you come forth from the sufferings and passion of the body, you will receive rest from the Good One, and you will reign with the King, you joined with him and he with you, from now on, for ever and ever. Amen.[267]

Here again the key to the future is 'rest', in which bodily life is thankfully left behind for ever. The bulk of the book makes clear the prevailing worldview of the writer, a worldview completely at home alongside most of those we studied in chapter 2: the present physical world, with its passions and desires, is a dark and wicked place. The best thing to do is to escape.[268]

(iv) The *Epistle to Rheginos*

An alternative way of dealing with the resurrection while claiming continuity with early Christian tradition was to reinterpret 'resurrection' language so that it now denoted (as it had never done before, in Judaism, paganism or early Christianity) a 'spiritual' resurrection in the present leading to a 'resurrection' of the spirit or soul in the future. This is the line taken

---

[265] *Thom. Contend.* 141.16–19.
[266] *Thom. Contend.* 142.10—143.10; 143.11—144.19.
[267] *Thom. Contend.* 145.8–16.
[268] I am for once in agreement with Riley (1995, 167). I even agree with his description of the worldview in question, in which the soul must remain 'weightless and pure', and must resist being caught and dragged down by being identified with the material realm, as a 'venerable philosophical context'. He does not seem to notice that it is the exact opposite of what all early Christians (and a great many Jews) believed about the created order, the nature of human life, and the ultimate human destiny.

by the *Epistle to Rheginos*, also known as the *Treatise on Resurrection*, the only book in the Nag Hammadi collection to deal directly with our present questions.[269]

The book is generally agreed to be no earlier than the late second century, and to come either from the circle of Valentinus or, just possibly, from a very muddled orthodox believer struggling to hold on to Christian teaching under pressure from other worldviews. The editor and translator in the English edition of the Nag Hammadi documents, who also wrote an entire monograph on the book, introduces it by saying that its most striking feature is the similarity of its teaching to the view condemned in 2 Timothy 2.18, according to which the resurrection has already occurred. Since he also says, however, that the writer's views on several points are closer to those of Paul than to those of Valentinus, our curiosity is aroused further. What does the letter actually say?

As often with the Nag Hammadi texts, the answer is that at some crucial points it is not possible to be exactly sure. But some things are reasonably clear. There are those, says the writer, who have not stood within the word of truth. They are seeking their own 'rest'; we, however, received ours through our saviour, our Lord Christ. We received it when we knew the truth and rested ourselves upon it.[270] This 'rest' may be the same as in *Thomas* 51, a spiritual arrival at a point of repose already in this life.[271] But the writer goes on to speak specifically of resurrection.

He begins by speaking of Jesus, as son of god (by which he means the divine one) living as son of man (by which he means the human one) within the present world, which the writer calls 'death'. Through his divinity he vanquished death (what, we wonder, does this mean?), and through his humanity he restores us to the 'pleroma', the 'fullness' (a familiar term from Valentinian theory), rescuing us from the created world, which is a second-ary and deadly place.[272]

Getting rid of the created world, in fact, is what this writer means by speaking of the saviour 'swallowing up death':

> He put aside the world which is perishing; he transformed himself into an imperish-able Aeon and raised himself up, having swallowed the visible by the invisible, and he gave us the way of our immortality. Then indeed, as the apostle said, 'We suf-fered with him, and we arose with him, and we went to heaven with him.'

The initiates are thus like beams of light in relation to the saviour who is himself the sun, and 'we are enclosed by him until our setting, that is to say,

---

[269] For the text, see Peel in Robinson 1977, 50–53; also in Peel 1969, with full discus-sion; summarized in e.g. Peel 1992, with other more recent bibliog. See too e.g. Perkins 1984, 357–60.

[270] *Rheg.* 43.30—44.4 (the text is numbered according to its place in the NH codex I).

[271] See Peel 1969, 37.

[272] *Rheg.* 44.13–38.

our death in this life.'[273] This will be the 'true resurrection', in which the 'natural' and 'fleshly' are alike done away with:

> We are drawn to heaven by him like the beams by the sun, not being restrained by anything. This is the spiritual resurrection which swallows up the psychic [*psychike*, 'natural', as in 1 Cor. 15] in the same way as the fleshly.[274]

The writer is clearly working with the terminology which Paul uses in 1 Corinthians, but the likeness is superficial. Paul's whole exposition is held in place by a sustained and positive exegesis of Genesis 1 and 2, but the *Treatise on Resurrection* shares with Valentinianism a deep scepticism about the value of the created world. The book does indeed affirm that Jesus 'arose from among the dead', and that he is the one through whom death is destroyed.[275] But this 'rising', when applied to the believer, seems to be a matter of receiving something better than 'flesh' (we recall the emphasis on 'the resurrection of the flesh' by the Apologists of the same period):

> Therefore never doubt concerning the resurrection, my son Rheginos. For if you did not exist in flesh, you received flesh when you entered this world. Why then will you not receive flesh when you ascend into the Aeon? What is better than the flesh is, for it, the cause of life. Is not that which comes into being on your account yours? Does not that which is yours exist with you? Yet, while you are in this world, what is it that you lack? . . . The afterbirth of the body is old age, and you exist in corruption. You have absence as a gain. For you will not give up what is better if you should depart . . . Nothing, therefore, redeems us from this world. But the All which we are – we are saved.[276]

The believer already possesses the better thing in himself, and will not need the flesh where he is going. This develops into what is, in effect, a specific denial of that which Paul (and the later tradition dependent on him) affirms:

> But there are some who wish to understand in the enquiry about those things they are looking into, whether he who is saved, if he leaves behind his body, will be saved immediately? Let no one be given cause to doubt concerning this . . . indeed, the visible members which are dead shall not be saved, only the living members which exist within them would arise. Then, what is the resurrection? *It is always the disclosure of those who have risen.*[277]

Believers, then, 'rise' already in this life; they will leave the body, the 'visible members', behind at death; only the life which is already within them will survive. There will, naturally, be no interim period, no 'sleep', as

---

[273] *Rheg.* 45.32–5.

[274] *Rheg.* 45.36—46.2.

[275] *Rheg.* 46.16–19.

[276] *Rheg.* 47.2–27. Peel 1969, 42 speaks of the believer being given a 'new, transformed flesh upon his ascension to heaven at death'.

[277] *Rheg.* 47.30—48.6 (italics, of course, added).

in Paul and the second-century writers already studied.[278] Think of the transfiguration, says the writer: Elijah and Moses showed that they were alive all the time; this, rather than a future bodily resurrection, is what he means by this language.[279] This 'resurrection' is the reality; the world is an illusion.[280]

The resurrection is thus not a new creation; it reveals what already exists. It does, however, involve a transformation, a 'transition into newness'.[281] By itself this might, again, look almost Pauline; but the writer goes on to insist that anyone who flees from 'the divisions and the fetters' (the divisive views and snares of those who have raised problems with this understanding) already 'has the resurrection'.[282] The believer has therefore already died and been raised, though in a very different sense from that which we saw in Paul.[283] This present resurrection must now determine the direction of present life; again, a potentially Pauline idea but in a very different mode.[284]

The main English-language editor of this text, Malcolm Peel, has pressed the case for seeing it as an odd combination of Valentinian and Pauline ideas.[285] This in turn has been a linchpin in the theory that Paul's views on the resurrection were at least capable of being developed in two different but equally appropriate ways, one to end up with this letter and similar ideas elsewhere in the Nag Hammadi texts, the other to end up with Justin, Tertullian and the rest.[286] But the parallels are strictly superficial. Paul's own treatment of resurrection, particularly in 1 Corinthians but in several other letters, is always part of a theology of new creation, based on the goodness of the original creation in Genesis 1 and 2, and on seeing in Jesus' resurrection the fulfilment, the celebration, the crowning glory, of that first creation. It gave birth to a cosmic eschatology in which the world of space, time and matter would not be thrown away but rather redeemed. Any idea that the present world is an illusion, and that 'resurrection' is to be found by escaping it in the present or the future, is totally foreign to Paul.

(v) The *Gospel of Philip*

One of the 'apocryphal' or non-canonical gospels from Nag Hammadi contains some brief material relating to the resurrection.[287] Three passages in

---

[278] Emphasized by Peel 1969, 43.
[279] *Rheg.* 48.6–11.
[280] *Rheg.* 48.12–16, 27f.
[281] *Rheg.* 48.34–8.
[282] *Rheg.* 49.14–16; cf. Peel 1969, 45f.
[283] *Rheg.* 49.16–24.
[284] *Rheg.* 49.25–36.
[285] See esp. Peel 1969, 139–50.
[286] Robinson 1982; see too Riley 1995, 8f.
[287] It will be more convenient to examine the *Gospel of Peter*, which is not from Nag Hammadi, in ch. 13 below (592–6).

the *Gospel of Philip* stand out, starting with an account of Jesus' resurrection in which his flesh has become 'true flesh'.[288] The text is corrupt, but in the standard reconstruction it reads as follows:

> The [Lord rose] from the dead. [He became as he used] to be, but now [his body] was perfect. [He did indeed possess] flesh, but this [flesh] is true flesh. [Our flesh] is not true, but [we possess] only an image of the true.[289]

This is too short, and indeed fragmentary, for any certainty over what precisely the writer has in mind by 'true flesh'. The second passage, however, speaking of the future hope, seems to indicate a preference for a theology like that of *Rheginos*:

> Those who say they will die first and then rise are in error. If they do not first receive the resurrection while they live, when they die they will receive nothing. So also when speaking about baptism they say, 'Baptism is a great thing,' because if people receive it they will live.[290]

The reference to baptism, coupled with a 'resurrection' in the present, could be taken in the sense of Romans 6 or Colossians 2. But the emphasis seems to be not only on the bodily resurrection which is anticipated by a metaphorical 'resurrection' during this life, marked in baptism, but on a different kind of metaphorical 'resurrection', spelled out in the earliest of the extracts:

> Those who say that the Lord died first and then rose up are in error, for he rose up first and then died. If one does not first attain the resurrection will he not die? As God lives, he would be already dead. No one will hide a large valuable object in something large, but many a time one has tossed countless thousands into a thing worth a penny. Compare the soul. It is a precious thing and it came to be in a contemptible body.
>
> Some are afraid lest they rise naked. Because of this they wish to rise in the flesh, and they do not know that it is those who wear the flesh who are naked. It is those who [. . .] to unclothe themselves who are not naked. 'Flesh and blood shall not be able to inherit the kingdom of God.' What is this which will not inherit? This which is on us. But what is this very thing which will inherit? It is that which belongs to Jesus and his blood. Because of this he said, 'He who shall not eat my flesh and drink my blood has not life in him.' What is it? His flesh is the word, and his blood is the Holy Spirit. He who has received these has food and he has drink and clothing.[291]

This passage thus quotes 1 Corinthians 15.50 in the sense which Irenaeus opposes, and also seems to be criticizing Paul's language about 'not being found naked' in 2 Corinthians 5. But what is this 'nakedness'? One way of

---

[288] cf. Staats in Wissman, Stemberger, Hoffman et al. 1979, 474.

[289] *Gos. Phil.* 68.31–7 (tr. W. W. Isenberg in Robinson 1977, 141).

[290] *Gos. Phil.* 73.1–8.

[291] *Gos. Phil.* 56.15—57.8. The idea that the Lord 'rose up first and then died', and the connection of this with baptism, has an interesting modern parallel in Barker 1997.

interpreting it would be to say that the real 'nakedness' is to have a body at all. In some Syriac Christianity, however, baptism was seen both as a kind of resurrection and as a means of 'reclothing' oneself with the glory lost at the fall. If this is the intended sense, 'nakedness' probably refers to those who did not receive baptism in the proper manner. They should not expect their unbaptized, their (in that sense) unredeemed flesh to enter heaven.[292]

This is immediately followed by what looks like a statement of the opposite point of view:

> I find fault with the others who say that it [the flesh] will not rise. Then both of them are at fault. You say that the flesh will not rise. But tell me what will rise, that we may honour you. You say the spirit in the flesh, and it is also this light in the flesh. But this too is a matter which is in the flesh, for whatever you shall say, you say nothing outside the flesh. It is necessary to rise in this flesh, since everything exists in it. In this world those who put on garments are better than the garments. In the kingdom of heaven the garments are better than those who have put them on.[293]

It is not clear from all this, at least not to me, whether the writer wants to deny future bodily resurrection, and to treat the word 'resurrection' primarily as denoting a spiritual change during this life, as with *Rheginos*, or whether he intends to balance a warning like this with an affirmation of some kind of future 'fleshly' existence. It has been argued that both these texts attempt a synthesis of Jewish-Christian thought (involving actual resurrection) and the hellenistic desire to be rid of physicality and to become a pure spirit.[294] If this is so, we may be able to place these works not too far from the swirling currents of Origen's thought. Some of the language used seems to be attempting to stay with a kind of ultimate 'body', but if it is hard to find words to describe Paul's view of what we have called a 'transphysical' body, and harder again to do justice to Origen, finding the correct terminology for *Rheginos* and *Philip* seems almost impossible. For these writers, there is 'beneath' the corruptible flesh another 'spirit/flesh', or what Menard calls super-terrestrial flesh. It would help to know what position either of these works considers itself to be criticizing; are they anxious about people believing that they will return into an identical body? Are they keen to ward off a view of complete disembodiment?[295]

---

[292] See e.g. Gaffron 1970, citing a parallel from Hippolytus; Van Eijk 1971. This could mean (as some would say for the author of *Rheginos*) that the writer of *Gos. Phil.* was a confused orthodox believer, rather than (as Robinson: see below) a gnostic making a small concession in an orthodox direction.

[293] *Gos. Phil.* 57.9–22.

[294] Menard 1975.

[295] See too Perkins 1984, 360–62. Robinson 1982, 16f. says that *Philip* here represents the furthest point that gnosticism 'could reach out toward orthodoxy without forsaking its basic position of contrast', quoting the *Apocryphon of James* 14.35f. (cited below) in further support. His claim, though, that the position of *Philip* on the future body is the same as that of Paul is frankly absurd.

What is clear, however, is the underlying worldview of both books. Whereas throughout the Jewish and early Christian writings in which resurrection plays a central role we find it correlated closely with belief in the one god as creator, and with the final judgment, neither of these motifs plays any role here. As with *Rheginos* and the other documents in this section, the surrounding worldview of *Philip* is radically different from that of the canonical writings and the early Fathers. It shows no sign of the common strand running from Paul to Tertullian, namely, a strong and repeated affirmation of the goodness of the created world. Rather, it seems to have everything to do with the goodness of the soul over against the contemptible body, and the need of the former to escape from the latter.

(vi) Other Nag Hammadi Treatises

The themes that emerge from these texts can be briefly illustrated from one or two others as well.

The *Apocalypse of Peter* (which bears no relation to the apocryphal book of the same name, noted earlier in this chapter) was written to encourage groups of gnostic believers who were being attacked by the orthodox. It puts into the mouth of Peter a description of spiritual experiences, including a vision of light, which claims Peter's apostolic validation for the experiences of the gnostics.[296] The tractate reinforces a view of Jesus in which the 'real' Jesus was a spiritual being different from his external physical form, so that while the latter was being tortured and killed Jesus was standing by, laughing at their lack of perception. The spiritual substance of Jesus is then released to rejoin the light of the heavenly, 'intellectual' (i.e. non-material) 'pleroma':

> But what they released was my incorporeal body. But I [Jesus] am the intellectual Spirit filled with radiant light. He whom you saw coming to me is our intellectual pleroma, which unites the perfect light with my Holy Spirit.[297]

This then becomes the model for the salvation of those who do not belong to the present world but are already immortal.[298]

The *Apocryphon of James*, described by its editor in the Nag Hammadi collection as coming probably from Egypt in the third century, offers secret revelations vouchsafed to the apostles, particularly James and Peter, by the risen Jesus after a waiting period of 550 days.[299] Jesus tells them that he has

---

[296] *Apoc. Pet.* (NH 7) 72.9–26. Jesus also appears as a great light in the *Letter of Peter to Philip* 134.9–18. See too Mary's vision in *Gos. Mary* 10.10–16 (Robinson 1977, 471–4, here at 472).

[297] *Apoc. Pet.* 83.6–15.

[298] *Apoc. Pet.* 83.15—84.6.

[299] *Apocryph. Jas.* 2.16–28.

been glorified, and that it is only their desire for more teaching which holds him back from going to the father.[300] He describes his going to the father thus:

> But I have said my last word to you, and I shall depart from you, for a chariot of spirit has borne me aloft, and from this moment on I shall strip myself that I may clothe myself.[301]

The ascension is similarly stressed in the *First Apocalypse of James*, where Jesus gives assurance of redemption through suffering. Instead of rising again from the dead, however, creating an interval for teaching, after his suffering Jesus will 'go up to Him who Is'.[302]

The *Letter of Peter to Philip* contains a short scene set on the Mount of Olives, 'the place where they used to gather with the blessed Christ when he was in the body', as it seems he no longer is.[303] The apostles invoke the father and the son to illuminate them:

> Then a great light appeared so that the mountain shone from the sight of him who had appeared. And a voice called out to them, saying, 'Listen to my words that I may speak to you. Why are you asking me? I am Jesus Christ who is with you forever.'[304]

There then follow sundry revelations, including a challenge which seems to belong with the 'undressing' sayings in *Thomas*:

> When you strip off from yourselves what is corrupted, then you will become illuminators in the midst of dead men.[305]

This text is used by Robinson as an example of his 'luminous revelation' hypothesis, though it has to be said that its view of resurrection, and of the present body, seems completely different to that of Paul, where according to Robinson the tradition began.[306] It is, however, a fine example of the tradition which existed by the end of the second century, represented in these Nag Hammadi documents.

Finally, the *Exegesis of the Soul* contains a classic passage for the gnostic redefinition of 'resurrection':

> Now it is fitting that the soul regenerate herself and become again as she formerly was. The soul then moves of her own accord. And she received the divine nature

---

[300] *Apocryph. Jas.* 7.35—8.4.

[301] *Apocryph. Jas.* 14.32–6.

[302] *1 Apoc. Jas.* (NH 5) 29.16–19.

[303] *Let. Pet. Phil.* 133.15–17. Text tr. Wisse in Robinson (ed.), 1977, 395–8, here at 395.

[304] *Let. Pet. Phil.* 134.9–19.

[305] *Let. Pet. Phil.* 137.6–9.

[306] Robinson 1982, 10f.

from the Father for her rejuvenation, so that she might be restored to the place where originally she had been. This is the resurrection from the dead. This is the ransom from captivity. This is the upward journey of ascent to heaven. This is the way of ascent to the Father . . . [there follows a quotation from Psalm 103.1–5] . . . Then when she becomes young again [i.e. when 'her youth is renewed like that of an eagle', as in the Psalm] she will ascend, praising the Father and her brother, by whom she was rescued. Thus it is by being born again that the soul will be saved.[307]

'Resurrection' language is being used, in other words, for a spiritual new birth which leads to escape from the world of 'captivity', i.e. where the soul is in bondage to matter, to the physical body.

(vii) The *Gospel of the Saviour*

In 1967 the Berlin Egyptian Museum purchased a collection of parchment fragments whose Coptic text has now been published.[308] It appears to come from a collection of sayings of Jesus, showing some dependence on at least Matthew and John. Though its original date remains uncertain, it seems clearly to belong with the other material in this section, not least as regards its hints about a reinterpreted 'resurrection'.

The relevant sections are as follows. The disciples ask, like Paul's interlocutors in 1 Corinthians 15.35, 'O Lord, in what form will you reveal yourself to us, or in what kind of body will you come?' John urges the Lord, 'When you come to reveal yourself to us, do not reveal yourself to us in all your glory, but change your glory into [another] glory in order that [we] may be able to bear it, lest we see [you and despair].'[309] One of the most frustratingly fragmentary of the leaves mentions the cross twice, and then, after a gap and with several missing letters, goes on '. . . [in] three days, [and I will] take you to [heaven] with me, and teach you . . .'.[310]

The text is too short, and too fragmentary, for us to be able to say very much about its complete view of the resurrection both of Jesus and of believers. However, it clearly sees Jesus as an exalted and glorious figure, to look at whom would be unbearable unless he were to alter his state somewhat. The 'resurrection', it seems, is not about a renewed life in this world, but about the life of heaven. It is in that sense that 100.7.1–6 speaks of 'spiritual bodies':

. . . and we too became like the spiritual body. Our eyes opened up to every side, and the entire place was revealed before us. We [approached] the heavens, and they

---

[307] *Exeg. Soul* 134.6–29.

[308] Hedrick and Mirecki 1999.

[309] *Gosp. Sav.* 107.12.3f. (lines 4–22).

[310] *Gosp. Sav.* 122 (lines 60–63). There is also a reference to Jesus' descent into Hades 'because of the souls that are bound in that place': 97.2.1 (lines 59–63).

[rose] up against each other. Those who watch the gates were disturbed. The angels were afraid, and they fled to the [. . .] [They] thought [that] they would all be destroyed. We saw our saviour after he pierced [through] all the heavens . . .[311]

This 'body', then, will be like that of Jesus. It will inhabit the uppermost heaven, and will be as terrifying to the residents of heaven as the dazzling body of Jesus himself would be, were we to see it on earth as it really is. This is radically different from the use of 'spiritual body' in Paul – though it is possible that the author thought he was providing an exegesis or at least an outworking of 1 Corinthians 15.

(viii) Nag Hammadi: Conclusion

There are doubtless many other Nag Hammadi and related texts that could be quoted to similar effect. But we have surveyed enough of this material to offer an assessment of its place within the swirling diversities of second- and third-century belief about death and life. The tractates found at Nag Hammadi do not by any means admit of a one-size-fits-all analysis; there are many different views represented, sometimes in the same document. Consistency (even supposing we could tell what would count as consistency in that kind of worldview) was no doubt hard to achieve in the world of Valentinian and similar speculation, and was in any case not likely to be a major priority. But three major points may be made.

First, 'resurrection', in the main sense that we have seen the word and its cognates used in the first two centuries of Christianity, is in these texts either *denied* or *radically reinterpreted*. If 'resurrection' is seen as in any sense a return, at some point after death, to a full bodily life, it is denied. If (as in the *Epistle to Rheginos*) the language of resurrection is retained, it is reinterpreted so that it no longer refers in any sense to the bodily events of either ultimate resurrection or moral obedience in this life, but rather to non-bodily religious experience during the present life and/or non-bodily post-mortem survival and exaltation.

This point can be underlined by observing the difference between the metaphorical meaning of 'resurrection' language in the New Testament (Romans 6, Colossians 2—3, etc.) and the metaphorical meaning in the *Epistle to Rheginos* and elsewhere. The metaphor as Paul uses it, which I argued above was a reinterpretation of the metaphor of 'resurrection' in Ezekiel and elsewhere, has a *concrete* referent, both to baptism and to bodily obedience (actual physical actions). This corresponds, in Paul's thinking about renewed humanity, to the 'return' or 'restoration' of Israel after the exile, which is the referent of the metaphor in the Old Testament. When

---

[311] In the first sentence I have changed 'bodies' in Hedrick and Mirecki 35 to the singular 'body', in accordance with the Coptic *soma*.

Rheginos, the *Exegesis of the Soul*, and other texts use 'resurrection' as a metaphor, they use it to denote a specifically *non-concrete* state of affairs: the abstract (or 'spiritual' in the Platonic sense) elevation of the soul during the present life and/or after death. This is a critical distinction, which demolishes the frequent attempt to suggest that the 'present tense' uses of resurrection language in Paul, and elsewhere in the New Testament, are on a straightforward continuum with this later gnostic language.[312]

Second, we note a complete absence, throughout the Nag Hammadi and related texts, of the three themes which dominate the presentation of the resurrection, both of Jesus and of believers, in the line that stretches from Paul to Tertullian and even to Origen.

(1) There is no emphasis at all on the Jewish and early Christian doctrine of creation, on the goodness of the present created order and on the one true god as having made it and as intending to remake it. Actually, to say there is no emphasis on this is putting it mildly; there is often a sustained and sometimes scornful rejection of it, a complete dismissal of the cosmology and ontology which lies at the heart of all the second-Temple Jewish presentations of resurrection and all the Christian presentations from Paul to Origen.[313] Since the positive doctrine of creation, and of the creator, is central and basic to what the main Jewish and early Christian texts mean by resurrection, the use of resurrection language, visions of light, or whatever, within a completely different worldview is clear evidence, not of a steady development, but of major redefinition.

(2) There is no emphasis on future judgment, a judgment which requires a resurrection if it is to be truly just. This, as we have seen, is a doctrine presented in various ways in Judaism and early Christianity. Sometimes only the righteous are to be raised (and resurrection will itself constitute their vindication; this seems to be the case in 2 Maccabees and Paul); sometimes both righteous and unrighteous will be raised, the latter so that they can be punished for their actions in the body, not just as a shadowy semi-being in Hades or Sheol. None of the Nag Hammadi texts look in this direction at all. What matters for future bliss, as far as they are concerned, is simply discovering the truth about oneself, one's soul, and so forth, in the present life, and abandoning attempts to construe one's identity in terms of the body and the surrounding world. The doctrines of creation and judgment, so central to Jewish and Christian presentations of resurrection, are absent from the gnostic redefinitions.

(3) There is little or no sense that resurrection goes with a stance against the ruling authorities. Sometimes the gnostically redefined 'resurrection',

---

[312] Robinson 1982.

[313] Nothing in the scholarship of the last generation has challenged Moule 1966, 112: 'even the most spiritualized Pauline Pharisaism parts company with the type of gnosticism illustrated by the letter to Rheginos.'

i.e. the ascent of the soul, is spoken of in terms of escaping from present suffering. But we miss entirely the note, which runs from at least Daniel and 2 Maccabees through Paul and John to Ignatius, the *Apocalypse of Peter*, Justin, Tertullian and Irenaeus, that resurrection is a revolutionary doctrine which has to do with the creator's overthrow of the kingdoms of the world and his establishing of a new world altogether. As with the Pharisees facing the Sadducees, so with Paul facing Caesar: it is noticeable that some of the key texts for understanding Paul's subversion of empire are exactly the same as the key texts for understanding Paul's view of both Jesus' resurrection and that of believers (e.g. 1 Corinthians 15.20–28; Philippians 3.19–21). We should not forget that when Irenaeus became bishop of Lyons he was replacing the bishop who had died in a fierce persecution; and that one of the themes of that persecution was the Christians' tenacious hold on the belief in bodily resurrection. Details of the martyrdom are found in the letter from the churches of Vienne and Lyons to those of Asia and Phrygia.[314] The letter describes how in some cases the torturers burnt the bodies and scattered the ashes into the Rhone, so that no relic of the martyrs might still be seen on earth. This they did, says the writer, 'as though they were capable of conquering god, and taking away their rebirth [*palingenesia*]'. He quotes the torturers as saying, not unlike the wicked in Wisdom 2, that the aim is to prevent the Christians from having any hope of resurrection,

> because through trusting in this, they have introduced strange and new worship, and have despised terrors, going to death readily and joyfully. Now let us see if they will rise again, and if their god is powerful enough to help them, and to snatch them out of our hands.[315]

The old slur, that the church quickly settled down and became comfortable and bourgeois, and the suggestion that sometimes accompanies it, that the increasing 'bodiliness' of the doctrine of the resurrection was part of this process, are without foundation.[316] If anything, the boot is firmly on the other foot. Which Roman emperor would persecute anyone for reading the

---

[314] Preserved in Eus. *HE* 5.1.1—2.8.

[315] Eus. *HE* 5.1.63. A further revealing anecdote follows: one of those jailed for professing Christian faith, a certain Alcibiades, was living a life of great austerity in prison, eating only bread and drinking only water. He was persuaded by the other Christians to widen his diet lest any suppose that he had come to believe that material things were evil in themselves.

[316] e.g. Robinson 1982, 6, playing off the 'left-wing' trajectory represented by second-century gnosticism (which, he says, has 'modulated' out of some of the earlier apocalyptic radicalism) against the process whereby 'main-line Christianity . . . standardized, solidified, domesticated itself and moved, as sects are wont to do in the second and third generations, toward the mainstream of the cultural environment.' One only has to imagine what Ignatius, Polycarp or Justin would have said in reply, as they faced martyrdom, to see how totally baseless this picture really is – and to wonder why it has proved so seductive in the scholarship of the last generation.

Gospel of Thomas? Which local officials would feel threatened by someone expounding the *Epistle to Rheginos* or the *Exegesis of the Soul*?[317]

Third, and related to these points, it is noticeable that from Paul to Tertullian the mainstream exponents of bodily resurrection drew repeatedly on the Old Testament scriptures. Not always the same ones; they were well capable of exegetical innovation; but always with the same central belief, that the god revealed in Jesus Christ, the god who had raised him from the dead and would similarly raise all his people, was the god of Abraham, Isaac and Jacob, whose purposes had come to a climax in Jesus' death and resurrection and would now be implemented in the world. It is equally noticeable that, apart from occasional references (not the same ones as in the mainstream texts), the gnostic and similar writings avoid the Old Testament like the plague. Even if they do not explicitly embrace some kind of Marcionism (rejecting entirely the Jews, their god and their tradition), they certainly do not want to give the impression that the spirituality they are talking about, or the Jesus in whom they believe, or any events that may have happened to him, or the future hope they themselves embrace, have anything much to do with Israel, the Jews, the patriarchs and the scriptures.

From all this it should be clear where these documents belong historically as well as theologically. It is impossible to conceive that talk about a 'resurrection', in the sense used by *Rheginos* and the others, should be anything other than a late and drastic modification of Christian language. These documents are attempting to retain a key Christian term while filling it with new content. 'Resurrection' and its cognates never meant, in either pagan or Jewish usage, what these documents make it mean; the only explanation is that they are loath to give up the word, because they want to seem to be some type of Christian, but are using it in a way for which there is no early warrant.

This does not, of course, mean that there is no pre-Christian 'gnosis'. That is another question.[318] What it means is that the bulk of Nag Hammadi and similar documents do not represent a parallel stream, with similarly early sources, to that which we find in the line from Paul to Tertullian.[319]

---

[317] On the non-persecution of gnostics, and its connection with their disbelief in resurrection, see Bremmer 2002, 51f., citing Frend 1954 and Holzhausen 1994. See also Pagels 1980. Irenaeus (*Adv. Haer.* 1.24.6; 3.18.5; 4.33.9) makes the point in various contexts; see too Tert. *Scorp.* 1.6; Eus. *HE* 4.7.7.

[318] See *NTPG* 155f., with other refs.

[319] The grandiose claim of Robinson 1982, 37 that the gnostic vision of 'resurrection' (which he describes thus: 'For Jesus to rise in disembodied radiance, for the initiate to reenact this kind of resurrection in ecstasy, and for this religiosity to mystify the sayings of Jesus by means of hermeneutically loaded dialogues of the resurrected Christ with his gnostic disciples' – a striking summary of these texts) is as *consistent* as that of the orthodox is ambiguous. Internally consistent it may be. But Robinson seems to mean more: that it has as good a claim as, say, Justin or Irenaeus to stand in a direct linear relation to the Easter vision of the first disciples. Our historical study rules this proposal out completely.

They represent a new movement entirely, which has explicitly cut off the roots of the 'resurrection' belief in Judaism, its scriptures, its doctrines of creation and judgment, and its social situation of facing persecution from imperial authority. This is a form of spirituality which, while still claiming the name of Jesus, has left behind the very things that made Jesus who he was, and that made the early Christians what they were.

8. The Second Century: Conclusion

Galen, the great pagan doctor of the second century, provides an interesting comment on the public perception of Christians during this period. In his summary of Plato's *Republic*, he points out that since most people are unable to follow the thread of demonstrative arguments, they need 'allegories' (by which he means particularly tales of rewards and punishments in a future world) if they are to be drawn to higher things. Thus, he says:

> We now see the people called Christians, though they have drawn their faith from mere allegories, sometimes acting like true philosophers. For their lack of fear of death and of what they will meet thereafter is something we can see every day, and likewise their restraint in cohabiting.[320]

This testimony would seem to be amply borne out by the writings we have studied. Just as in the New Testament, belief in the resurrection (the future resurrected life of believers, based foursquare on Jesus' own resurrection) was foundational to early Christianity in all the forms known to us except those we have just studied in section 7, which use 'resurrection' language in a clearly different way, drawing the key term from Christian linguistic usage but setting it within a radically different worldview. Galen had his finger on the central point. Over against the standard pagan view, that death was certainly the end for the body (possibly the end of everything, possibly the gateway to a blissful immortality), Christianity affirmed, alongside a substantial number of non-Christian Jews, the future bodily resurrection of all god's people (and, in the view of many, of all people whether righteous or not). Over against the developed Jewish views of resurrection in 2 Maccabees, the rabbis and elsewhere (many of the rabbis of course being contemporary with the developments we have been studying), Christianity affirmed in great detail the belief that resurrection involved going through death and into a non-corruptible body the other side; that it involved one person, the Messiah, being raised from the dead ahead of everybody else; and that it allowed for an intermediate state which might best be described in terms of the departed person being with the Lord until the resurrection.

---

[320] Text (preserved only in an Arabic paraphrase of Galen's Summary of the *Republic*) tr. in Beard, North and Price 1998, 2.338.

Like the Jews, the Christians based themselves on the doctrines of creation and judgment, and they rooted themselves in a rereading of Jewish scriptures, not simply as prophecies of one-off events but as providing a foundation narrative which they believed had reached its climax in Jesus. They nevertheless developed the notion of resurrection in such a way that, without leaving its literal use and concrete referent, it abandoned the regular Jewish metaphorical use (referring to the concrete events of Israel's national redemption), and they developed instead a different metaphorical use, referring to the concrete events of baptism and holiness of body and behaviour.

It is, then, remarkable that Christianity, apart from the texts studied in section 7, never seems to have developed even the beginnings of a spectrum of belief, either of the pagan variety or of the Jewish variety, but always stuck to one point on the Jewish scale.[321] It is more remarkable that from within this position it then developed, virtually across the board, new ways of speaking about what resurrection involved and how it would come about which could not have been predicted from the Jewish sources but which nevertheless give every appearance of remaining in strong continuity with them. This combination of circumstances now raises, as we draw together the threads of Parts II and III, the question upon which our argument thus far hangs: what caused this remarkable development, which brought resurrection not only from the circumference of belief to the very centre, but also from a semi-formed belief into a very sharply focused one?

The early Christians answered, of course, that this had happened because their movement was decisively launched by, and formed around, the resurrection of Jesus himself. It was because of what they firmly believed had happened to him that they said all these things. We must shortly turn to the texts in which they told these stories, and see how they relate to the mass of material we have studied so far. But before we can do that we must look at early Christianity on a broader front. The developing doctrine of resurrection cries out for historical explanation. So do the early Christian beliefs that Jesus was Israel's Messiah, and that he was the world's rightful lord.

---

[321] Riley 1995, 179 draws the exact opposite conclusion: that 'the early idea of the resurrection of Jesus and the postmortem state of his followers was spiritual, represented in various ways by Paul, the Hellenistic Church to a large extent, and Thomas Christianity'; and that 'the earlier conception' was that 'Jesus had risen alive as a spiritual being, in a spiritual body of light', while for themselves they 'hoped in the promise of a heavenly afterlife, to be free from the body and its sufferings as spiritual beings'. In what way, then, did they differ from the pagans around them? Why were they persecuted?

Chapter Twelve

HOPE IN PERSON:
JESUS AS MESSIAH AND LORD

1. Introduction

The central argument of this Part of the book is now complete. The future hope of the early Christians is focused, in a thoroughly Jewish way, on resurrection; but it has been redefined beyond anything that Judaism had said, or indeed would say later. But it is not only belief in resurrection which has been simultaneously reaffirmed and redefined. Since one of the central redefinitions is that the early Christians believed it had happened to one person in advance of all the rest, we should not be surprised to find that the early Christian belief about that person himself shows signs of a parallel redefinition. This provides in turn, I suggest, powerful supporting evidence for the early Christian belief about what had happened to him.

'God has made this Jesus both "lord" and "Messiah"'. Thus Peter, on the day of Pentecost.[1] Or, as Paul put it, possibly quoting an earlier poem: 'Every tongue shall confess that Jesus, the Messiah, is lord.'[2] *Kyrios* and *Christos* were the key words used by the first Christians to express what they now believed about Jesus. Early Christianity was through and through *messianic*, and, in line with many hints and promises from the biblical and post-biblical literature, the early Christians believed that the Messiah, whose name they now knew, was the true *lord* of the world. Both of these are surprising, not to say shocking, when used of someone recently executed by the Romans. This shock is the pivot for the argument of the present chapter, and will lead us to a final survey of the way in which resurrection functioned within the early Christian worldview. Though the two titles, and the meanings that cluster around them, are closely intertwined, for the sake of clarity we shall take them separately, beginning with the one which seems to me

---

[1] Ac. 2.36. This is, of course, seen from Luke's point of view; see below.
[2] Phil. 2.11.

foundational for everything else. The early Christians believed Jesus was the Messiah; and they believed this because of his resurrection.

2. Jesus as Messiah

(i) Messiahship in Early Christianity

The argument at this point proceeds in three stages. (i) Early Christianity was thoroughly messianic, shaping itself around the belief that Jesus was God's Messiah, Israel's Messiah. (ii) But Messiahship in Judaism, such as it was, never envisaged someone doing the sort of things Jesus had done, let alone suffering the fate he suffered. (iii) The historian must therefore ask why the early Christians made this claim about Jesus, and why they reordered their lives accordingly.

The claim that early Christianity was thoroughly messianic is of course controversial. Those who assiduously promote 'Q' and *Thomas* (or some cleverly shortened versions of them) as the earliest Christian sources conclude from this that there were indeed early Christians who were not interested in Jesus' Messiahship – though whether this is a conclusion from evidence, or the invention of evidence to produce this conclusion, remains a matter of debate. 'Q' itself gives clear signs of messianic belief, as we can see from Matthew 11.2–6 and Luke 7.18–23.[3] But even if we were to allow at least a non-messianic early form of 'Q', we would have to comment that such a strand was quickly swallowed up in the thoroughly messianic movement that emerged almost at once; Messiahship is already so embedded in the thinking of the early Christians that it is taken for granted. Already in Paul the word *Christos* seems to be on its way to becoming simply a proper name, with denotation (referring to Jesus of Nazareth) but no longer with any particular connotation (indicating that he is Israel's Messiah).

Some, indeed, think it has reached that point already. In a famous article Martin Hengel states that the word has become, in Paul, almost entirely a proper name, with only 'a glimmer of its titular use' in a few texts.[4] I have argued exactly the opposite in various places: that Jesus' Messiahship remained central and vital for Paul, closely integrated with the other major themes of his theology.[5] Among other historical and exegetical advantages,

---

[3] On which see *JVG* 495–7.

[4] Hengel 1995, 1; cf. too Hengel 1983 ch. 4. At 1995, 4 n. 3 he admits that the titular sense would work well at Rom. 9.5, but says that since 'Paul nowhere else uses the word as a title' it is better to treat it there as a name as well. This looks suspiciously like the triumph of theory over evidence.

[5] See Wright, *Climax* ch. 3; *Romans* passim, esp. at 1.3f.; 9.5; 15.3, 7, 12. In the present vol. see the treatment of e.g. 1 Cor. 15.20–28 in ch. 7 above.

this brings Paul into line with the Septuagint evidence.[6] But this is not my present point. Even if Hengel is right, and the entire fabric of Paul's messianic belief (which seems to me so clear) is an illusion, that only makes the question more acute: what was it that made early, pre-Pauline Christianity so solidly messianic that within twenty years the word *Christos* had become so familiar as to lose its titular significance and become a name, now with specific denotation but no longer with connotation?

Jesus' Messiahship is not, of course, reduced to the status of a proper name in the multiple traditions represented in the gospels. I have explored the synoptic evidence reasonably fully in chapter 11 of *Jesus and the Victory of God*. Though my main point there was to uncover what Jesus himself believed about his own (often largely hidden) vocation, the range of texts, from different levels within normal synoptic stratigraphy, indicates that Jesus' Messiahship continued to be the central topic in a large number of early Christian traditions.

The same is true in Acts. The early reference in 2.36, which emerges from a long and explicitly Davidic exegesis of Psalm 16, is thematic for the whole book. Just as in Luke 24.26, 46 (see below), the word *Christos* in passages like Acts 3.18, 20 must mean 'Messiah'.[7] The first half of Acts (up to chapter 12) has Herod hovering in the background, eventually dying through divine punishment for pagan-style hubris; part of the point, at the structural level, is that Jesus is the true king of the Jews. The second half of Acts (chapters 13 to the end), as we might expect granted the logic of the Psalms and prophecies which shaped later messianic belief, concentrates on showing how Jesus, now established as king of the Jews, is in fact the true lord of the world. There is indeed 'another king, namely Jesus' (17.7). Acts ends with Paul in Rome, announcing the kingdom of god (the fulfilment of the Jewish hope for the true god to be king, rather than the normal human kings), and teaching about Jesus as lord and Messiah, openly and unhindered (28.31).

Jesus' Messiahship is also a major theme in John. However much John's obviously high Christology dominates the overall movement of the book, Jesus as *Christos* remains a major preoccupation. The first time Jesus is recognized as such, indeed, the word is given in Aramaic: 'We have found the Messiah,' says Andrew to Simon. The evangelist, carefully providing a translation into Greek, indicates that he intends *Christos* to continue to carry this meaning throughout.[8] This is reinforced in the discussion with the woman in Samaria (4.25, 29), the debates among the Jerusalem crowds (7.26f., 31, 41f.; 10.24; 12.34), the decree of the Judaean rulers (9.22), and

---

[6] See Hengel 1995, 1f.

[7] cf. too Ac. 4.26; 9.22; 17.3; 18.5, 28; 26.23.

[8] Jn. 1.41. The theme is already hinted at in the dialogue with John the Baptist, where he denies that he is the *Christos* (1.20, 25; cf. 3.28).

Martha's statement of faith (11.27). On the two occasions where *Iesous Christos* occurs, looking (to the modern eye) like a double name, it is undoubtedly to be read with these messianic overtones (1.17; 17.3). In what was probably the originally intended ending of the gospel, following Jesus' resurrection and Thomas' confession of faith, the writer declares that his purpose in setting all this out is to create and sustain the faith that 'the Messiah, the son of God, is Jesus'.[9] This list of actual occurrences of the word *Christos* hardly does justice to the full range of messianic themes in the gospel; we may note, as one example, the way in which the 'good shepherd' discourse in chapter 10 evokes strongly (among other things) the biblical picture of the king as shepherd.[10]

The Messiahship of Jesus is thus a major theme in the gospels and Acts, and, on one reading at least, in Paul as well (and, on the alternative reading, it is such a major theme prior to Paul's writings that familiarity has flattened the word into a proper name). It continues to be important not only in the rest of the New Testament but also in some other traditions, for instance in the story of the blood-relatives of Jesus who were brought before Domitian on suspicion of being members of a would-be royal family.[11] Among the next generation of writers, Ignatius, the *Didache* and *Barnabas* are all comfortable with the notion of Jesus' Messiahship.[12]

We should therefore not be surprised to find that the early church, as well as being known as followers of 'the Way', were from quite early on known also as 'Christians'.[13] This emerges also from the (admittedly ambiguous) evidence in Suetonius and Tacitus.[14] Josephus, too, in describing Jesus, declares that '"the Messiah" was this man', and, when speaking of the death of James, describes him as 'the brother of the so-called "Messiah"'.[15] The evidence is quite overwhelming: Jesus was firmly known as 'Messiah', right across the board in early Christianity. In view of this it is, of course, far

---

[9] Jn. 20.31: *hoti Iesous estin ho Christos, ho huios tou theou*. The normal translation, 'that Jesus is the Messiah, the son of God', puts the emphasis in the wrong place: the definite article with *Christos*, and the absence of one with *Iesous*, makes this clear, as the grammatical parallel in 5.15 shows. Cf. too 1 Jn. 4.15. I shall argue in ch. 17 below, not least on the basis of the parallels between the prologue (1.1–18) and ch. 20, that ch. 21 was added after the book was basically complete.

[10] e.g. Jer. 23.4f.; Ezek. 34.23f.; 37.24; Mic. 5.4; 7.14; more detail and refs. in *JVG* 533f.

[11] Euseb. *HE* 3.19f. Cf. *NTPG* 351f.

[12] Ign. *Eph.* 18.2 (cp. 20.2); *Trall.* 9.1; *Did.* 9.2; *Barn.* 12.10.

[13] Ac. 11.26; cf. 26.28; 1 Pet. 4.16. For 'the Way' cf. Ac. 9.2; 18.25f.; 19.9, 23; 22.4; 24.14, 22.

[14] Suet. *Claud.* 25.4; Tac. *Ann.* 15.44. Cf. *NTPG* 352–5.

[15] Jos. *Ant.* 18.63f.; 20.200–03 (cf. *NTPG* 353f., where I suggest that the key phrase about Jesus in *Ant.* 18 is neither a Christian interpolation nor a confession that Josephus believes Jesus to be the Messiah, but a way of identifying Jesus: '"The Christos", of whom you have heard, was this man.'). I find it extraordinary that Hengel can claim (1995, 2) that the latter passage 'shows how completely *Christos* had become a proper name'.

easier to accept that this was true for Paul as well than to have him use the word so frequently and yet not understand it as a title. But, as I say, even if this is not so, it merely tightens the screw of the argument even tighter, because clearly it would mean that the very early Christians used the word so frequently for Jesus that it had worn smooth. This in turn prevents any counter-argument to the effect that the evidence of the gospel traditions and Acts is all later. The idea that Christianity began as a non-messianic movement and then, when it went out into the wider world, suddenly developed all kinds of traditions about Jesus as Messiah, ought to be counter-intuitive to anyone thinking historically.

A similar result is reached if we consider one possible reason why Jesus was regarded as Messiah throughout early Christianity: that he had regarded himself in this way, and had said and done things which pointed towards his belief that he had such a vocation. I have argued at some length in the previous volume that this was indeed the case.[16] However, any effect this teaching might have had in convincing his followers during his public career would have been completely undone by his shameful death at the hands of the Roman authorities, for reasons that will shortly become apparent. And, since in any case not everyone will be convinced by my argument about Jesus' understanding of his own vocation, it is important to notice that if Jesus did *not*, in any way, give the impression that he thought he was Israel's Messiah, that merely increases the puzzle still further. Where did this sudden burst of Messiah-belief come from?

(ii) Messiahship in Judaism

The problem is, of course, that the varied pictures of a coming Anointed One in the varied Judaisms of the time do not conform to what Jesus did and said, still less to what happened to him. I have, again, set these out elsewhere and can here simply summarize.[17] In so far as we can generalize about such complex things, three interrelated themes emerge, stressed variously in different sources: the Messiah was supposed to win the decisive victory over the pagans, to rebuild or cleanse the Temple, and in some way or other to bring true, god-given justice and peace to the whole world. What nobody expected the Messiah to do was to die at the hands of the pagans instead of defeating them; to mount a symbolic attack on the Temple, warning it of imminent judgment, instead of rebuilding or cleansing it; and to suffer unjust violence at the hands of the pagans instead of bringing them justice and peace. The crucifixion of Jesus, understood from the point of view of any onlooker, whether sympathetic or not, was bound to have appeared as

---

[16] *JVG* ch. 11. See too e.g. Hengel 1994 chs. 1, 2.
[17] *NTPG* 307–20; *JVG* 481–6.

the complete destruction of any messianic pretensions or possibilities he or his followers might have hinted at. The violent execution of a prophet (which, uncontroversially, was how Jesus was regarded by many), still more of a would-be Messiah, did not say to any Jewish onlooker that he really was the Messiah after all, or that YHWH's kingdom had come through his work. It said, powerfully and irresistibly, that he wasn't and that it hadn't.

We can see this clearly enough if we imagine for a moment the situation after the death of two of the most famous would-be Messiahs of the period, Simon bar-Giora during the first revolt (AD 66–70) and Simeon ben Kosiba (i.e. Bar-Kochba) during the second (AD 132–5).[18] Simon was killed at the climax of Vespasian's triumph in Rome; Simeon, we assume, died as the Romans crushed his movement and with it all prospect of Jewish liberation. We only have to exercise appropriate historical imagination, thinking into the situation a few days after their deaths, to see how it would look.

Take Simon, for example. The year is AD 70. Vespasian has become emperor. Titus, his son and heir, has obliterated the Jewish rebellion, destroying Jerusalem in the process. He returns to Rome to celebrate a magnificent triumph, pictured in stone to this day on Titus' Arch at the east end of the Forum. The bedraggled Jewish prisoners are displayed within the pageant telling the story of the war; the spoils, particularly those from the Temple, are carried through the city. Finally there come the conquering heroes: Vespasian himself, followed by Titus, with Titus' younger brother Domitian riding beside them. But there remains one ceremony:

> The triumphal procession stopped in front of the temple of Jupiter Capitolinus . . . it was an ancient custom to wait there until it was announced that the enemy general had been put to death. This was Simon son of Gioras, who had featured in the pageant among the prisoners, and then, with a halter thrown around him, was dragged to the spot beside the Forum where Roman law requires that criminals under sentence of death should be killed. The people leading him there scourged him as they went. After the announcement of his death, and the universal shouts of rejoicing that followed, the princes began the sacrifices; when they had been duly offered, they went back to the palace . . . The city of Rome held a celebration that day for its victory in the war against its enemies, for the stopping of civil disturbances, and for the beginning of hopes of prosperity.
>
> When the triumphal ceremonies were over, and the empire of the Romans had been established on the firmest possible foundation, Vespasian decided to set up a temple of Peace . . . [19]

Roman victory; Roman justice; Roman empire; Roman peace; all because the Jewish leader had been killed. An interesting parallel to the Christian claim, that salvation had come to the world because of the death of the Messiah; but we will let that pass for the moment. Instead, as our immediate task, imagine two or three of Simon's supporters – if there were any of them

[18] For the details, see *NTPG* 176–8; 165f.
[19] Jos. *War* 7.153–8.

left, hiding in caves or secret cellars – a few days later. Supposing one said to another, 'Actually, I think Simon really was the Messiah.' The kindest view the others might take would be that the speaker had gone mad. Alternatively, the statement might be understood as heavily ironic: he really was our Messiah – in other words, our god has forgotten us, this is the best we can expect, we may as well admit there is no more hope! But if the case were pressed: Simon really was the Messiah, so we should now launch a movement which hails him as such, which declares to our fellow Jews that YHWH's anointed has been in their midst and has established the kingdom (at the very moment when Caesar's kingdom seems more firmly established than ever!), and which may then go out into the world to declare that Simon, as the king of the Jews, is really the lord of the whole world . . . then the verdict of madness, of a kind of criminal lunacy which turns reality upside down and inside out, seems inevitable. And if (to anticipate the sort of theory we shall discuss later) the speaker, realizing his companions' horror at his proposal, were to explain it all by saying that he had received a vision of Simon being with him; that he had a strong sense that Israel's god had forgiven them for their failure to support him properly; that he had enjoyed a wonderful and heartwarming spiritual experience as he thought about the death of Simon; then his companions would have shaken their heads sorrowfully. None of this would remotely mean that Simon was the Messiah after all. None of it would mean that the long-awaited kingdom of Israel's god had come. None of it would mean, either, that Simon had been 'raised from the dead'.[20]

A moment's disciplined historical imagination, then (something 'historical criticism' has often been unwilling to employ), is enough to make the point. Jewish beliefs about a coming Messiah, and about the deeds such a figure would be expected to accomplish, came in various shapes and sizes, but they did not include a shameful death which left the Roman empire celebrating its usual victory. This leads to the third point, the historian's necessary question.

(iii) Why Then Call Jesus Messiah?

Why then did the early Christians acclaim Jesus as Messiah, when he obviously wasn't? He too had been scourged, dragged through the streets and executed. Indeed, his execution was in public, increasing the shame and the sense of utter and devastating victory for the pagans. Faced with his death, why would any of his followers have dreamed of saying that he was

---

[20] This is the basis of the historical answer to theories of the type propounded by e. g. Schillebeeckx 1979 (see ch. 18 below), Marxsen (e.g. 1968a, 1968b), and Wilckens 1968, 68f.

Messiah – and, moreover, as we shall see, of reordering their worldview around this belief, so that Christianity was launched precisely as a messianic movement, albeit with significant differences?

The options before them were clear. If their would-be Messiah had been killed, they could have crept back home, thankful to escape with their lives. They could have done what the post-135 rabbis did, and declared that they were finished with dreams of revolution, and that from henceforth they would find a different way of being loyal to Israel's god. Or they could, of course, *have found another Messiah*.

This was a serious option. That much is clear from several movements in the first century which are linked through a family dynasty. Although not all the details are clear, it seems that for nearly a hundred years, right through the period of Jesus' public career and Paul's travels, a sequence of leaders emerged from within a single family, ending with the Eleazar who led the final, fatal stand on Masada.[21] Since Jesus of Nazareth had blood relatives who were known as such two generations after his death, there would have been no problem in finding some relation on whose shoulders a revived hope might be placed.

There was one relative in particular who might have seemed an ideal candidate. James, 'the brother of the lord', had probably not followed Jesus throughout his public career, but according to the very early tradition he, like the Eleven, had seen the risen Jesus.[22] He had then quickly become one of the central leaders in the Jerusalem church. When Paul first went to Jerusalem after his meeting with Jesus on the road to Damascus, this James was the only one of the 'apostles', other than Peter, whom he met.[23] Acts portrays him as the one who sums up the debate about the conditions for admitting Gentiles to full membership in the community.[24] He was clearly regarded as the, or at least a, central point of authority in the Jerusalem church, and hence in the worldwide church, even though people claiming his authority might be opposed by Paul.[25] Whether or not the letter ascribed to

---

[21] Details in *NTPG* 179f.

[22] 1 Cor. 15.7. On the question of whether, and to what extent, James may have followed Jesus during his lifetime see now Painter 1997, 11–41; Bauckham 2001, 106–09. Bauckham concludes (109) that, 'contrary to the usual view, James was among the disciples who accompanied Jesus and learned his teaching, at least for a significant part of Jesus' ministry.' This remains in apparent tension with Jn. 7.5, and of course James is not mentioned as a follower of Jesus at any point during the gospel narratives.

[23] Gal. 1.19.

[24] Ac. 15.13–21. Cf. too Ac. 12.17; 21.18.

[25] Gal. 2.12. On James and his significance see e.g. Painter 1997; Chilton and Neusner 2001; and other literature there. In view of this it is the more interesting that there is no sign in any of the resurrection stories in the gospels of an attempt to construct a 'resurrection appearance' that would legitimate James as the leader he undoubtedly was; the only relevant reference is of course 1 Cor. 15.7 (until, that is, the much later *Gospel of the Hebrews*, cited by Jerome, *De Vir. Ill.* 2).

him in the New Testament is actually his work (this used to be ruled out automatically in scholarship, but is now much more widely recognized as a distinct possibility), the fact of its being ascribed to him shows something of the status he enjoyed in early Christianity as a wise and reputed teacher.[26] And the account of his death in Hegesippus (preserved in Eusebius) portrays him as James the Just – *dikaios* in Greek, presumably *tzaddik* in Hebrew – on account of his lifelong ascetic piety, constant prayer and effective witness.[27] According to this (seemingly garbled) account of Hegesippus, the Jewish leaders called on James to quell the growing belief in his brother Jesus as Messiah:

> We beseech you to restrain the people since they are straying after Jesus as though he were the Messiah. We beseech you to persuade concerning Jesus all who come for the day of the Passover, for all obey you. For we and the whole people testify to you that you are righteous and do not respect persons. So do you persuade the crowd not to err concerning Jesus, for the whole people and we all obey you.[28]

James, however, did the opposite, proclaiming Jesus as the messianic son of man, and evoking from the crowd shouts of 'Hosanna to the son of David.'[29] The authorities therefore threw him down, stoned him, and finally had him clubbed to death:

> And they buried him on the spot by the temple, and his gravestone still remains by the temple. He became a true witness both to Jews and to Greeks that Jesus is the Messiah. Immediately Vespasian began to besiege them.[30]

The parallel report in Josephus confirms the basic truth: that James was highly regarded by loyal and strict Jews, and that he was known as 'the brother of Jesus the so-called Messiah' (*ton adelphon Iesou tou legomenou Christou*).[31] James was, in other words, a prime candidate to be considered a messianic figure in his own right.

Again, even a small amount of disciplined historical imagination will paint the scene. Jesus of Nazareth had been a great leader. Most considered him a prophet, many the Messiah. But the Romans caught him and killed him, the way they did with so many would-be prophets and Messiahs. Just as John the Baptist's movement faded into comparative obscurity with John's imprisonment and death, with the speculation about John's role within various eschatological scenarios being transferred to his slightly

---

[26] See Chilton and Neusner 2001, esp. the essay of Bauckham.

[27] Euseb. *HE* 2.23.1–7.

[28] *HE* 2.23.10.

[29] *HE* 2.23.13f.

[30] *HE* 2.23.18.

[31] Jos. *Ant.* 20.200. Cf. *NTPG* 353f. At the time of revising this chapter (October 2002), a report has appeared of a first-century ossuary, found near the Mount of Olives, bearing the inscription 'James son of Joseph, brother of Jesus'.

younger cousin, so one can easily imagine Jesus' movement fading into comparative obscurity after his execution, with the spotlight now turning on his somewhat younger brother.[32] The younger brother turns out to be a great leader: devout, a fine teacher, well respected by other devout Jews. What more could one want? *But nobody ever dreamed of saying that James was the Messiah.* He was simply known as the brother of 'Jesus the Messiah'. At this point the argument runs in parallel with the famous Sherlock Holmes story that hinges on the dog doing something remarkable in the night – or rather on the fact that the dog did *not* do anything in the night, though it had every reason to do so, thus revealing the fact that the dog must have recognized the intruder.[33] If we suppose that Jesus of Nazareth had simply been executed as a messianic pretender, and that his younger brother had become a strong and powerful leader among his former followers over the next thirty years, someone would have been bound, given the climate of the times, to suggest that James himself was the Messiah. But nobody ever did.

The historian is therefore faced with the same kind of puzzle as is posed by the striking adoption, but also transformation, of the Jewish belief in resurrection. We are forced to postulate something which will account for the fact that a group of first-century Jews, who had cherished messianic hopes and centred them on Jesus of Nazareth, claimed after his death that he really was the Messiah despite the crushing evidence to the contrary.[34] They did not even consider the possibility that, after his apparent failure, they might find another Messiah from among his own family, even when there was one very obvious candidate.

This historical question is further sharpened by what happened to the portrait of 'Messiah' in early Christianity.[35] Despite what scholars have often said, it was not abandoned, but nor was it simply adopted wholesale from existing Jewish models. It was transformed, redrawn, around Jesus himself. The early Christians maintained, on the one hand, the basic shape of Jewish messianic belief. They reaffirmed its biblical roots in the Psalms, the prophets and the biblical royal narratives; they developed it in biblical ways (such as the belief that Israel's Messiah was the world's true lord; see below). At the same time, on the other hand, they quickly allowed this belief to be transformed in four ways. It lost its ethnic specificity: the Messiah did

---

[32] For the speculation about John, cf. e.g. Lk. 3.15; Jn. 1.24–8; for the transfer to Jesus, cf. Mt. 4.12; Jn. 3.25–30; 4.1–3; Mt. 11.2–15/Lk. 7.18–28.

[33] '"Is there any other point to which you would wish to draw my attention?"
    "To the curious incident of the dog in the night-time."
    "The dog did nothing in the night-time."
    "That was the curious incident," remarked Sherlock Holmes.'
    (Sir Arthur Conan Doyle, *The Memoirs of Sherlock Holmes*, 1894, 'Silver Blaze'.)

[34] So, rightly, Wedderburn 1999, 21.

[35] For this paragraph, which could be considerably expanded, cf. Wright, *Climax* chs. 2, 3; *NTPG* 406–09; *JVG* ch. 11.

not belong only to the Jews. The 'messianic battle' changed its character: the Messiah would not fight a military campaign, but would confront evil itself. The rebuilt Temple would not be a bricks-and-mortar construction in Jerusalem, but the community of Jesus' followers. The justice, peace and salvation which the Messiah would bring to the world would not be a Jewish version of the imperial dream of Rome, but would be God's *dikaiosune*, God's *eirene*, God's *soteria*, poured out upon the world through the renewal of the whole creation. All this is visible in some of the primary documents of early Christianity, such as Romans, 1 Corinthians, Acts and Revelation. Something has happened to belief in a coming Messiah, something which reminds us of what happened to the Jewish belief in a future resurrection. It has neither been abandoned, nor simply reaffirmed wholesale. It has been redefined around Jesus. Why?

To this question, of course, the early Christians reply with one voice: we believe that Jesus was and is the Messiah because he was raised bodily from the dead. Nothing else will do. And to this the historian has to say: yes, this belief would produce that result. If the early Christians believed that Israel's god had raised Jesus from the dead, they would believe that he had been vindicated as Messiah despite his shameful death. But this argument simply takes us to the belief itself. How and why the early Christians arrived at this belief is a further question which we must pursue in due course.

First, though, we must look at the other remarkable thing the early Christians said about Jesus: that he was the *kyrios*, both in the sense of being the world's true lord and in the sense of somehow being identified with the *kyrios* of the Septuagint, where the translators used this word to denote YHWH himself.

3. Jesus, the Messiah, is Lord

(i) Introduction

If Jesus was the Messiah, he was also the lord of the whole world. This early Christian belief is rooted firmly in the Psalms, and cannot be cut off from those roots without losing its particular force. That, of course, is what has happened in a great deal of New Testament scholarship over the last century. The train of thought in scholarly argument seems to have proceeded something like this: (a) Messiahship is of course a Jewish category, so when the gospel went out to the Gentile world it would be meaningless; (b) at that point the early evangelists, particularly Paul, exchanged it for a different category altogether, namely *kyrios*, 'lord', which was already well known in Gentile circles as a title for cultic deities; (c) the 'Lordship' of Jesus in early Christianity is therefore to be understood in terms of hellenistic religion rather than Jewish expectation, and is based on his assumed exaltation to heaven, and on early Christian 'religious experience' of him, rather than on his resurrection from the dead; (d) Jesus' 'Lordship' therefore has little to do with socio-political reality, even less to do with Jewish kingdom-of-god expectation, and nothing whatever to do with anything that might have happened to Jesus immediately after his death.[36]

This analysis of 'Lordship' in early Christianity has been attacked from many sides over recent decades. But even those who have objected to various of its features have regularly missed the point that must be made here: that, from Paul onwards, belief in Jesus as lord was (among other things) a *function of* belief in him as Messiah, not a *move away from* that belief. It was grounded, in fact, in the classic biblical portraits of the Messiah:

I will tell of YHWH's decree:
he said to me, 'You are my son, today I have begotten you.
Ask of me, and I will give you the nations as your heritage,
the ends of the earth as your possession.
You shall break them with a rod of iron,
and dash them in pieces like a potter's vessel.
Now therefore, O kings, be wise;
be warned, you rulers of the earth.
Serve YHWH with fear, rejoice with trembling;
kiss the Son, lest he be angry, and you perish in the way . . .[37]

Give the king your judgments, O God;
and your righteousness to the king's son.
He shall judge your people with righteousness,
and your poor with judgment . . .
He shall have dominion also from one sea to the other,
from the River [Euphrates] to the ends of the earth.
Those who dwell in the wilderness shall bow before him,
and his enemies shall lick the dust.
The kings of Tarshish and of the isles shall bring presents,
the kings of Sheba and Seba offer gifts.
Yes, all kings shall fall down before him,
all nations serve him,
For he shall deliver the needy when they cry,
and the poor, those who have no one to help them . . .
His name shall endure for ever;
his name shall be continued as long as the sun;
And people will be blessed by him;
all nations shall call him blessed.[38]

I have found David my servant; with my holy oil have I anointed him . . .
The enemy shall not harm him; the son of wickedness will not hurt him.

---

[36] This is a highly abbreviated summary of the hypothesis we can trace back to W. Bousset and forward, through Bultmann, to much scholarship between 1950 and 2000.

[37] Ps. 2.7–12. The translation problems in the final phrases do not affect the point.

[38] Ps. 72.1f., 8–12, 17.

I will strike down his enemies before him, and smite those who hate him . . .
I will set his hand also on the sea, and his right hand on the rivers.
He shall cry to me, You are my father, my God and the rock of my salvation;
And I will make him my firstborn, the highest of the kings of the earth.[39]

There shall come forth a shoot from the stock of Jesse,
and a branch shall grow out of his roots . . .
With righteousness he shall judge the poor,
and decide with equity for the meek of the earth;
He shall strike the earth with the rod of his mouth,
and with the breath of his lips he shall kill the wicked . . .
On that day the root of Jesse shall stand as a signal for the peoples;
The nations shall inquire of him, and his dwelling shall be glorious.[40]

Behold my servant, whom I uphold; my chosen, in whom my soul delights;
I have put my spirit upon him; he shall bring forth justice to the Gentiles . . .
He shall not fail, nor be dismayed, until he has established justice in the earth;
And the isles shall wait for his law . . .
I, YHWH, have called you in righteousness,
and will hold your hand, and will keep you;
I will give you for a covenant to the peoples, for a light to the Gentiles . . . [41]

As I watched in the night visions,
I saw one like a son of man, coming with the clouds of heaven.
He came to the Ancient of Days and was presented before him.
To him was given glory and kingship,
so that all peoples, nations and languages should serve him.
His dominion is an everlasting dominion,
and his kingship one that shall never be destroyed.[42]

These passages are all well known, and they need to be read in their larger contexts for their complete impact to be felt. The controversies that surround them, their reuse in second-Temple Judaism, and their fresh use within early Christianity, are too numerous to list, let alone to discuss.[43] But that is not necessary within the present argument. My point is simple, and can be stated in three propositions: (1) these texts all bear witness to a biblically rooted belief in a coming king who would be master not only of Israel but also of the whole world; (2) these are the passages drawn on by the early Christians to speak about Jesus not only as Israel's Messiah (albeit in a redefined sense) but also as the world's true lord, again in a sense which was redefined but never abandoned; (3) we must therefore understand the early Christian belief in Jesus as lord, not as part of an abandonment of Jewish categories and an embracing of Greek ones, nor as part of an abandonment of the hope

---

[39] Ps. 89.20, 22f., 25–7.
[40] Isa. 11.1, 4, 10.
[41] Isa. 42.1, 6; cp. 49.1–6.
[42] Dan. 7.13f.
[43] On 'son of man' cf. *NTPG* 291–7; *JVG* 510–19.

for god's kingdom and a turning instead to 'religious experience', nor yet as an abandonment of the political meaning of this universal sovereignty and a re-expression of it in terms of 'religious' loyalty, but as a fresh statement of the Jewish hope that the one true god, the creator, would become lord of the whole world. The word 'lord', it is true, does not occur in this sense in the passages quoted, but in the first century it was the obvious word to use for one to whom was given sovereignty, mastery, of the kingdoms of the world.

The question of Jesus' Lordship thus opens up into three more specific enquiries: about the inauguration of the 'kingdom of god'; about Jesus as the present world ruler; and about the relationship (a horribly slippery word) between Jesus and YHWH. These are vast topics. For our present purpose we skate lightly over their surface, aware of much cold critical water beneath the ice, but confident that it will bear the weight of the argument.

(ii) Jesus and the Kingdom

Speaking of Jesus as lord became, in early Christianity, a way of speaking also about the fulfilment, at least in anticipation, of the 'kingdom of god'. This, again, is too large to discuss at this point.[44] But here, too, substantial revision has occurred within the Jewish expectation. The kingdom of Israel's god is still spoken of as future, but it is also now spoken of as present. Already by Paul's time the phrase 'kingdom of god' and equivalents were being used, somewhat like 'the Way', as a shorthand for the early Christian movement, its way of life and its *raison d'être*.[45] This stands in apparent tension with other passages which speak of it as still in the future;[46] Paul at least hints at a way of resolving this tension which highlights exactly the point I am making here. The present time, a genuine anticipation of god's kingdom, is the kingdom of the Messiah, who is already ruling the world as its rightful lord. The future kingdom will come when he completes this work and hands over the kingdom to god the father.[47] The two passages where this scheme emerges most prominently (1 Corinthians 15 and Philippians 2—3) are, significantly, passages which also speak of the resurrection.[48]

Nor was this simply a manner of speaking which merely, as it were, highlighted the hope for the coming kingdom somewhat more strongly than it had been before, so much so that people began to speak of it in the present tense – though that by itself would still raise the question of why, granted

[44] See, for a start, *NTPG* 299–307; *JVG passim* (see index s.v.), and esp. chs. 6 and 10.

[45] Rom. 14.17; 1 Cor. 4.20; Col. 1.13; 4.11.

[46] e.g. 1 Cor. 6.9f.; 15.24, 50; Gal. 5.21; Eph. 5.5; 1 Thess. 2.12; 2 Thess. 1.5; 2 Tim. 4.1, 18; and cf. Rom. 5.17, 21 on the future 'reign' of god's people, or of 'grace'.

[47] 1 Cor. 15.24–8; cf. Eph. 5.5 ('the kingdom of the Messiah and of God'). See too e.g. Heb. 2.8f.

[48] For other early Christian texts relevant to this discussion, see *JVG* 663–70.

the continuation of Caesar's kingdom, they would do even that. The early Christians told the story of Jesus as the story of the kingdom arriving – a theme so firmly woven into the gospel traditions that one could only remove it by deconstructing those traditions entirely – and proceeded to reorder their lives on the basis that it had, in one sense, already happened, while knowing that in another sense it was still in the future. This corresponds, of course, to one aspect of the redefinition of 'resurrection' which we have observed: it has happened already in one case, but is still to happen for everybody else. The symbolic universe through which the early Christians constructed their new way of life was the Jewish kingdom-of-god framework redefined around Jesus.

Redefined, but once again not abandoned. They reused the kingdom-themes (Israel's restoration, including the return from exile; the overthrow of pagan empire; and the return of YHWH to Zion), but they reused them in a transferred sense. It would be easy at this point to suppose that this transferred sense was a 'spiritualization', a translation into the categories of private illumination or 'religious experience', but that is precisely what did *not* happen. (When something like this did occur, for instance with *Thomas*, it is noticeable that the specifically Jewish, and this-worldly, referent has disappeared, along with bodily resurrection.) The transferred sense remained a public, this-worldly sense, a sense of the creator god doing something new within creation, not of a god acting to rescue people *from* creation. And the public, this-worldly sense in question included both the common life of the Christian community and, particularly, their claim that Jesus was lord, carrying as it did the meaning, not simply that Jesus was '*their* lord' in a private or strictly personal sense, but that Jesus was already the true sovereign of the world. Thus, although none of the things that second-Temple Jews had hoped for when they used the language of their god becoming king had in fact occurred – Israel had not been rescued from pagan oppression, the Temple was not rebuilt, injustice and wickedness were still rampant in the world – the early Christians declared that in a sense the kingdom had indeed come (while still having a vital future aspect as well), and clearly meant this in a sense which they thought of as the fulfilment, not the abandonment, of Israel's hope. They acted as if they really were the redeemed, new-covenant, returned-from-exile, new-Temple people of the god of Abraham, Isaac and Jacob. Of course, they also believed that they had had a quite new sort of 'religious experience'; but when they spoke of this they did not use the language of 'kingdom of god', but of the Holy Spirit, the renewal of the heart, and so on.

Once again, therefore, as with the redefined resurrection belief which we have examined on a large scale, and the redefined messianic belief which we have sketched much more briefly, we are faced with the question: what would have caused them to do this, to speak and act in this way? Why did they not continue the kind of kingdom-movement that they had had in mind all along, and which they had thought Jesus was leading them into?[49] How do we explain the fact that early Christianity was neither a nationalist Jewish movement nor a private religious experience? How do we explain the fact that they spoke and acted as if the coming denouement, the kingdom-moment, had already arrived, though in another sense it was still awaited; had come, in fact, in a sense which, though continuous with Jewish expectation, had also redefined it? How do we explain the fact that they went out into the Gentile world with the news of something that had happened at the heart of Judaism, in the belief that this was not only relevant but urgent for the whole world?

Their answer, of course, was that Jesus of Nazareth had been bodily raised from the dead. Further (since resurrection was both a metaphorical and metonymic way of referring to the great restoration, to the long-awaited kingdom of the god of Israel), they declared that the kingdom had in fact arrived, even though, like the resurrection itself, it seemed to have as it were split into two: an 'arrival' with Jesus, and a still-awaited 'arrival' which would complete the implementation of what he had already accomplished. This, again, is such a full and complete explanation of the otherwise puzzling data that we should not deny the conclusion: the early Christians, all those for whom we have any actual evidence, really did believe that Jesus was raised from the dead. And, from yet another angle, we are forced to ask: what caused this universal belief, so powerful that it transformed their worldviews, that is, their praxis, symbols, stories, beliefs, aims and motivations?

(iii) Jesus and Caesar

The same conclusion is reached if we consider, even briefly, one of the primary early Christian meanings of Jesus as *kyrios*: the implicit contrast with Caesar. Precisely on the basis of the key texts from the Psalms, Isaiah, Daniel and elsewhere, the early Christians declared that Jesus was lord in such a way as to imply, over and over again, that Caesar was not. I have written about this elsewhere, and here simply summarize what is becoming a major strand in New Testament scholarship.[50]

The theme is strong, though until recently largely unnoticed, in Paul. Romans 1.3–5 declares the 'gospel' that Jesus is the royal and powerful 'son of god' to whom the world owes loyal allegiance; Romans 1.16–17 declares that in this 'gospel' are to be found *soteria* and *dikaiosune*. Every element in

---

[49] cf. the disciples' puzzled question in Ac. 1.6.

[50] See Wright, 'Paul and Caesar'; and e.g Horsley 1997, 2000; Carter 2001; and several works on Revelation, e.g. Rowland 1998.

this double formulation echoes, and parodies, things that were said in the imperial ideology, and the emerging imperial cult, at the time. At the other end of the letter's theological exposition (15.12), Paul quotes Isaiah 11.10: the Davidic Messiah is the world's true lord, and in him the nations will hope. And in the opening and closing passages this belief in Jesus as the royal Messiah, the world's true lord, is founded on the resurrection.[51] Similarly, in Philippians 2.6–11, what is said of Jesus echoes remarkably what was being said, in the imperial ideology of the time, about Caesar.[52] Philippians 3.19–21, in a sudden blaze of christological colour, then builds on this to declare that Jesus is Messiah, saviour and lord; that he now has the power to bring everything in subjection to himself, including the very composition and nature of present human bodies; and that his people are now a 'colony of heaven', an advance guard of the project to bring the whole world under the sovereign and saving rule of Israel's god. First Corinthians 15.20–28 (a central and vital passage for many Pauline themes, not least resurrection itself) speaks of Jesus as Messiah in an explicitly royal sense, with all enemies put under his feet. First Thessalonians 4.15–17 speaks of the 'arrival' of Jesus in language which deliberately echoes the talk of the 'arrival' of the emperor, with his subjects going out to meet him as the citizens would go out to meet Caesar and escort him back into a city. The next chapter then warns (5.3) that those who spoke of 'peace and security' – in other words, the Roman imperial ideology that regularly boasted of just that – would face sudden destruction.

Nor is this confined to Paul. Matthew's risen Jesus declares that all authority in heaven and on earth is now given to him.[53] When the disciples at the start of Acts ask Jesus if this is the time for him to restore the kingdom to Israel, he tells them that they will receive power, and will be his witnesses to the ends of the earth. The answer to their question, in other words, is, 'Yes, but in a redefined sense; and you are to be its agents as well as its beneficiaries.'[54] The gospel of Jesus as king of the Jews is then placed, by implication, in tension with the rule of Herod as king of the Jews, until the latter's sudden death in chapter 12; whereupon the gospel of Jesus as lord of the world is placed in tension with the rule of Caesar as lord of the world, a tension which comes to the surface in 17.7 and smoulders on through to the pregnant but powerful statement of the closing passage, with Paul in Rome speaking of the kingdom of the true god and the Lordship of Jesus himself. Revelation, of course, highlights Jesus as 'the firstborn from the dead, and the ruler of the kings of the earth', and as 'king of kings and lord of lords', and in several passages makes it clear that this is not simply a 'spiritual' or

---

[51] See Wright, *Romans*, on both passages; also Wright, 'Fresh Perspective'.
[52] See esp. Oakes 2001 ch. 5.
[53] Mt. 28.18.
[54] Ac. 1.6–8.

'heavenly' Lordship, but one which is designed to take effect within the created world itself, and ultimately in its great renewal.[55] This entire strand of thought, of the kingdom of Israel's god inaugurated through the Lordship of Jesus and now confronting the kingdoms of the world with a rival call for loyalty, finds classic expression, a century after Paul, in the famous and deliberately subversive statement of Polycarp: 'How can I blaspheme my king who saved me?'[56] Caesar was the king, the saviour, and demanded an oath by his 'genius'; Polycarp declared that to call Caesar these things would be to commit blasphemy against the true, divine king and saviour.

It is important to stress that this does not mean that the early Christians were not prepared to respect legal authorities as constituted by the one true god. The very documents that announce the subversive gospel of Jesus often urge such respect and obedience; a good example is the *Martyrdom of Polycarp*, which in the same short passage, almost the same breath, makes it clear both that Christians owe allegiance to Christ, not Caesar, and that they have been taught to render due honour to the authorities whom God has appointed.[57] Our particular modern and western way of formulating these matters, implying that one must either be a revolutionary or a compromised conservative, has made it harder, not easier, for us to arrive at a historical grasp of how the early Christians saw the matter.[58] The command to respect authorities does not cut the nerve of the gospel's political challenge. It does not mean that the 'Lordship' of Jesus is reduced to a purely 'spiritual' matter. Had that been so, the great persecutions of the first three centuries could largely have been avoided. That, as we saw in the previous chapter, was the road taken by gnosticism.

This subversive belief in Jesus' Lordship, over against that of Caesar, was held in the teeth of the fact that Caesar had demonstrated his superior power in the obvious way, by having Jesus crucified. But the truly extraordinary thing is that this belief was held by a tiny group who, for the first two or three generations at least, could hardly have mounted a riot in a village, let alone a revolution in an empire. And yet they persisted against all the odds, attracting the unwelcome notice of the authorities because of the power of the message and the worldview and lifestyle it generated and sustained. And whenever we go back to the key texts for evidence of why they persisted in such an improbable and dangerous belief they answer: it is because Jesus of Nazareth was raised from the dead. And this provokes us to ask once more: why did they make this claim?

---

[55] Rev. 1.5; 19.16; cf. 5.10; 10.11; 11.15–18; 15.3f.; and the entire sequence of thought of both chs. 13—14 and 21—22.

[56] *Mt. Pol.* 9.3.

[57] *Mt. Pol.* 10.1f.

[58] cf. e.g. Rom. 13.1–7, on which see Wright, *Romans*, 716–23; 1 Pet. 2.13–17; and see above all the analysis of Christian political thought offered by O'Donovan 1996.

(iv) Jesus and YHWH

The third aspect of Jesus' 'Lordship' is closely integrated with both the others, and is not to be separated off as a different subject altogether. It is probably the largest single topic in the study of early Christianity, and yet we cannot devote more than a short sub-section to it as part of our larger argument. It boils down to this: that when the early Christians called Jesus *kyrios*, one of the overtones that word quickly acquired, astonishing and even shocking though this must have been, was that texts in the Greek Bible which used *kyrios* to translate the divine name YHWH were now used to denote Jesus himself, with a subtlety and theological sophistication that seems to go back to the earliest days of the Christian movement. It is already firmly embedded in some of our earliest evidence, looking in some cases as though even there it was already part of traditional formulations. What caused this particular revolution, and how does it relate to the other redefinitions we have been studying?

As usual the primary evidence is in Paul. I have set out the material elsewhere and here simply summarize.[59] In Philippians 2.10 Paul quotes Isaiah 45.23, a fiercely monotheistic text which declares that to YHWH and YHWH only (the Septuagint of course having *kyrios* for YHWH) every knee shall bow and every tongue shall swear; and Paul declares that this will come true when every knee and tongue do homage to Jesus. 'Jesus, Messiah, is *kyrios*', they will declare – to the glory of God the father. In 1 Corinthians 8.6 Paul takes the *Shema* itself, the central Jewish daily prayer and confession of monotheistic faith ('YHWH our God, YHWH is one'), and gives the two words YHWH (*kyrios*) and 'God' (*theos*) different referents, so that *theos* refers to 'the father, from whom are all things and we to him' and *kyrios* refers to 'Jesus the Messiah, through whom are all things and we through him'. In Colossians 1.15–20 the same differentiation is expressed in alternative language, but with the same import. I have attempted a brief explanation of how and why Paul came to this position in chapter 8 above.

What is more, Paul elsewhere takes particular texts which refer to YHWH and uses them, without apology or even much explanation, as texts about Jesus. This occurs in contexts where he clearly has the entire passage in mind; he is not simply grabbing a few words at random without being aware of their full meaning. A good example is Romans 10.13, where Paul quotes Joel 2.32 to the effect that 'all who call on the name of the Lord will be saved'. He is clearly aware that by 'the Lord' (*kyrios*) Joel refers to YHWH; he is, equally clearly, intending *kyrios* to refer to Jesus.[60] Significantly, this passage is part of a sequence of thought in which we also find the resurrection and Lordship of Jesus as the centre of Christian faith and confession

---

[59] Wright, *Climax*, chs. 4–6. On this whole topic see esp. Bauckham 1999.

[60] See Wright, *Romans*, ad loc. Cf. too Ac. 2.20f.

(10.9), and the worldwide spread of the gospel message as the immediate consequence (10.14–19). Likewise, the whole theme of 'the day of YHWH' in the Old Testament has been transposed, in Paul and elsewhere in early Christianity, into 'the day of the *kyrios*', i.e. of Jesus, or into 'the day of the Messiah'.[61]

We do not have to look far in other strands of early Christianity to find similar phenomena. Thomas' great confession of faith in John 20 brings together *kyrios* and *theos*, applying both to Jesus. The evangelist's comment is that the aim of his writing is to produce, or perhaps to sustain, faith that the Messiah is Jesus.[62] The first letter of Peter (2.3) speaks of 'tasting that the Lord is good', quoting, in relation to Jesus, what Psalm 34 had said about YHWH.[63] In 1 Peter 3.15 we find a quotation from Isaiah 8.13 in which 'the Messiah' has been added to 'Lord' to make it clear that what was spoken of YHWH in this Old Testament passage is now to be understood of Jesus the Messiah.[64] This is of course only the tip of the iceberg of the New Testament's remarkably high, early and Jewish Christology, but it is enough to make our present point.

So why did the early Christians not only come to regard Jesus as *kyrios* in the sense of 'the world's true lord, of whom Caesar is a parody', but as somehow identified with, or as, YHWH himself, YHWH in person? Does this, too, have something to do with the resurrection?

Some obvious texts point in this direction. When Thomas bursts through initial doubt to sudden faith in Jesus' bodily resurrection, he exclaims, 'My lord and my God'; and the evangelist clearly intends this as a climactic and decisive concluding statement of what was said in the gospel's prologue.[65] So, too, Paul's statement in Romans 1.4 (if he is quoting an earlier formula, he does so because it says what he wants to say in this highly programmatic opening) is often taken in this sense: Jesus was marked out as 'son of god' as a result of the resurrection of the dead. I have argued elsewhere that 'son of god' in this passage must be taken primarily as meaning 'Messiah', not least because of the explicit Davidic reference in the previous verse.[66] But by Romans 5.10 and 8.3 it is clear that Paul is able to use this messianic title as a way of (so to speak) placing Jesus on the divine side of the equation as well as the human one. Precisely because Romans 1.3–4 is so clearly programmatic this cannot be ruled out here as well.

We must be careful at this point not to short-circuit the developing understanding that seems to have taken place. The story of Thomas is unique in

---

[61] Ac. 2.20; 1 Cor. 1.8; 5.5; 2 Cor. 1.14; Phil. 1.6, 10; 2.16; 1 Thess. 5.2; 2 Pet. 3.10.

[62] Jn. 20.28; 20.30f.

[63] Ps. 34.8 (33.9 LXX).

[64] Isa. 8.13: the Lord, him you shall sanctify (*kyrion auton hagiasate*); 1 Pet. 3.15: the Lord Messiah you shall sanctify (*kyrion de ton Christon hagiasate*).

[65] See esp. Jn. 1.1–5, 14, 18 (see ch. 17 below).

[66] Wright, *Romans*, 416–19.

this respect, as in some others: there is no suggestion in the other resurrection stories, or in the stories of Paul's conversion, that there was an instant deduction that ran 'risen from the dead, therefore in some sense divine'. Hardly surprisingly, there is no sign in second-Temple Judaism of any such link; since no second-Temple Jews known to us were expecting the one god to appear in human form, let alone to suffer physical death, nobody would have thought of resurrection as demonstrating someone's divinity. Equally, such second-Temple Jews as were expecting resurrection were expecting it to happen to everyone – certainly to all the righteous among God's people, and perhaps to all the wicked as well. When the New Testament predicts the resurrection of all who belong to Jesus, there is no suggestion that they will thereby become, or be shown to be, divine. Clearly, therefore, resurrection by itself could not be taken to 'prove' the 'divinity' of Jesus; if it did, it would prove far too much. The over-simple apologetic strategy one sometimes encounters ('he was raised from the dead, therefore he is the second person of the Trinity') makes no sense, from either end, within the historical world of the first century.

In particular, a historical scheme is sometimes proposed which seems to me to get things exactly the wrong way round.[67] According to this view, the *first* thing the disciples came to believe about Jesus after his death was that he had been exalted to heaven, quite possibly in a sort of apotheosis or divinization; then they came to express that belief in terms of his being alive again after his death; then they came to use the language of resurrection to describe this new aliveness; then they made up stories about an empty tomb; and then, finally, they made up further stories about Jesus eating and drinking and inviting them to touch him. The first move in this sequence is striking in that, if true, it would correspond to what was regularly said about greco-roman heroes, especially kings, and particularly the Roman rulers and emperors from Julius Caesar onwards: that they had 'gone to heaven' after their deaths, not in the sense commonly meant today (post-mortem disembodied bliss, or at least rest), but in the sense of joining the pantheon of the gods.[68]

This is where it is vital to keep our feet firmly on the ground of second-Temple Judaism. There is no evidence that Jews in this period would have imagined that any figure of the immediate past could be 'divinized' in this regular pagan fashion. (Of course, this was part of the point within the old history-of-religions model, which argued that at this point Christianity broke away from Judaism and borrowed Gentile ideas; the nemesis of this is when Jewish and agnostic writers criticize the early Christians, not least Paul, for abandoning their Jewish heritage for a mess of pagan speculation.[69]) The

---

[67] See the discussions of the origins of Paul's Christology in ch. 8 above.

[68] See ch. 2 above.

[69] e.g. Maccoby 1986, 1991.

story of Jesus' ascension in Acts 1 has some affinities with tales of imperial apotheosis. That, indeed, may be part of the point of it.[70] But it is hard to see what sort of an event could have convinced second-Temple Jews that someone who had been cruelly executed by the pagan authorities had now been 'exalted to heaven' in the sense of 'divinization' which would be required for this whole train of thought to work. The closest parallels would have to be the deaths of the martyrs, not least the Maccabaean heroes. But, though the martyrs in 2 Maccabees went to their death predicting their future resurrection, there is no suggestion that they had been exalted or glorified, or indeed raised from the dead, still less divinized.

Even if we suppose the very unlikely hypothesis that the early disciples, all of them of course Jewish monotheists, had come to be convinced of Jesus' divinity without any bodily resurrection having taken place, there is no reason to suppose that they would then have begun to think or talk about resurrection itself. If, somehow, they had come to believe that a person like Jesus had been exalted to heaven, that would be quite enough; why add extraneous ideas? What, from the point of view we are hypothesizing, could resurrection have added to exaltation or even divinization? Why would anyone work back by that route, to end up predicating something which nobody was expecting and which everybody knew had not happened? Even supposing that, having come to believe in Jesus' divinity (by what route it is not clear), they then began to pore over the scriptures to find back-up material for the belief to which they had come, and even supposing they pondered Daniel 12, Isaiah 26 or Ezekiel 37 in this context, there is still no reason to suppose that they would have read any of these texts as predicting the resurrection of *one* person out of all Israel, all the righteous – let alone of one who was somehow also the embodiment of Israel's god. Nor is there any reason to suppose that, if they did, they would connect that with the belief in Jesus' divinity to which, on this theory, they had somehow already come. Paul could challenge Agrippa to say whether or not it was incredible that Israel's god would raise the dead. Nobody ever challenged anyone to contemplate the possibility that Israel's god might himself rise from the dead.

What alternative sequence of thought, then, can we propose?

We must begin by distinguishing at least four things: (1) the sequence of thought, starting with Easter, by which the first disciples came to their full view of Jesus' identity; (2) the sequence of thought, following his unique 'seeing' of Jesus, by which Paul came to his full view; (3) the arguments Paul then used to persuade others of his view or to support them in holding it; (4) other early Christian arguments to the same end.[71] And we must frame

---

[70] See ch. 16 below.

[71] For the distinction of the train of thought by which Paul (and others) reached their own conclusions and the (quite possibly very different) arguments they used to convince others of the same point, see Wright, *Climax*, 8–13.

our thinking, if we are to work historically at all, with the worldviews, and networks of aims and beliefs, which we can deduce to have been held by the first disciples, and by Paul, in what we might call Holy Saturday mode, that is, after the crucifixion of Jesus and before any suggestion of Easter. For Paul, this mode lasted longer, of course, and everything we know about him suggests that his head was remarkably well stocked with biblical material and theological understanding long before he rethought it all around Jesus. But we must also suppose that the other disciples knew at least some basic and well-known scriptural texts, and connected them at least loosely with the theological ideas, not least speculations about prophets, Messiahs and the kingdom of god, as would have been readily current at the time.

The account I propose is the mirror-image of the one I have criticized above, and goes in a different direction to those of Kim and Newman which I discussed in chapter 8. It offers a sequence of moves, each step of which is comprehensible within second-Temple Judaism. And, like the other elements of the present chapter, it leaves us once more with the question: what caused the earliest disciples, and then Paul, to hold so clearly the belief which formed the first step in the sequence?

The first disciples had believed Jesus of Nazareth to be 'a prophet mighty in word and deed'.[72] They had come, somewhat more gradually but in the end decisively, to believe that he was Israel's Messiah, the Lord's anointed, the promised redeemer.[73] As I argued at length in *Jesus and the Victory of God*, this was the principal charge against Jesus at his hearings before both the Jewish and the Roman authorities; at least, it was the form in which the Jewish authorities transmitted their charge to the Roman governor, knowing that a would-be rebel king would be of more interest to Pilate than a Jewish blasphemer.[74] The accusatory title on the cross, portraying Jesus as the king of the Jews, drew together several strands of thought, including Jesus' subversive act of prophetic symbolism against the Temple, and his use of cryptic 'royal', i.e. messianic, arguments and texts such as Psalm 110 and Daniel 7.[75] As I argued in the earlier volume, it may well be that Jesus intended these to be a pointer to a deeper vocation and identity than anything previously ascribed to a would-be Messiah, but there is no suggestion that the disciples had picked up this point, or anything like it.[76]

Each step needs to be examined carefully, not taken for granted or short-circuited. Resurrection by itself would not mean that the person who had been raised was Israel's Messiah. Just as there is nothing in pre-Christian Jewish literature to suggest that anyone would connect the fact of someone

---

[72] Lk. 24.19.

[73] Lk. 24.21.

[74] Compare the distinction made by Gallio according to Ac. 18.14f.

[75] On the 'titulus' and its context and meaning within the 'trials' of Jesus, see Hengel 1995, 41–58.

[76] See *JVG* ch. 13.

rising from the dead with their being 'divine', whatever that might mean, so of course there is nothing (or nothing that had been thought of this way before) to connect such an event with that person being Israel's Messiah.[77] The martyrs promise their torturers that they will rise from the dead, but they will not thereby all become Messiahs, any more than they will become 'divine'. Lazarus, Jairus' daughter, and the son of the widow at Nain, were all in a sense 'raised', but nobody imagined that this meant they were messianic figures, let alone 'divine'. If one of the two brigands crucified alongside Jesus had been raised from the dead three days later it would have caused quite a stir, but there is no reason to suppose that people would have concluded that he was Israel's Messiah, the Lord's anointed.

The first and most obvious conclusion which the disciples would have drawn, as soon as they came to believe that Jesus of Nazareth had been bodily raised from the dead, was that he was indeed the prophet mighty in word and deed, and that he was, more particularly, Israel's Messiah. This would *not* be because they had already believed that the Messiah, when he came, would be raised from the dead, but because the Jesus they knew had been tried and executed as Messiah, and this extraordinary and unexpected event (as it seemed to them) had apparently reversed the verdicts of both the Jewish and the Roman courts. We can see at several points in the New Testament, not least in Paul and Acts, the way in which the church scrambled to pull together biblical texts to make the connection between Messiah and resurrection, a connection which nobody had thought necessary before but which suddenly became the key move in early Christology.[78] The texts strongly suggest both that this was a new connection and that it was the first vital link in the chain.

From that point on, our best early evidence is Paul. He had, in the senses we have explored, a different kind of meeting with Jesus, but he quickly came to the conclusion which the others, too, had arrived at: that in this Jesus, now demonstrated to have been Israel's Messiah all along, Israel's one true god had been not merely speaking, as though through an intermediary, but personally present. I have explored in chapter 8 the way in which I envisage Paul coming to that conclusion. It is harder to plot, independently of Paul, the steps by which the other early Christians came to a similar point of view. The synoptic tradition is not much help in such an investigation, not because it reflects a post-Easter situation with a continuing low or non-existent Christology, but because, in this respect at least, those who handed it on were careful not to read back into it the Christology which they themselves were enthusiastically developing.[79] In particular, they came to see Jesus, as I argued in *Jesus and the Victory of God* he saw himself, in terms

---

[77] See above, 24.
[78] cf. e.g. Ac. 2.24–36; 13.32–9, etc., as above, 451–7. Cp. too Lk. 24.26, 46.
[79] See *JVG* ch. 13 for details and arguments.

of new exodus, more particularly, the long-awaited return of YHWH to Zion.[80]

The ways in which Paul explored, developed and explained this new belief would take us a lot longer to unravel, and fortunately there is no need to do so here.[81] The ways in which the other early Christians developed the same insight include the Christology of John, Hebrews and Revelation, for which again there is here neither need nor space. The main point to notice in and through all of this is the way in which the early Christians determinedly spoke of Jesus, alongside the creator god and as his personal self-expression, within categories familiar from the dynamic monotheism of second-Temple Judaism.

As I have shown elsewhere, within second-Temple Judaism there were various strategies for speaking of how Israel's god was God, the one, true and only divine being, who remained the creator, distinct from the world and responsible for it, could nevertheless be present and active within the world. Various writers spoke of God's word, God's wisdom, God's law, God's tabernacling presence (*shekinah*), and God's Spirit, as though these were at one and the same time independent beings and yet were ways in which the one true God could be with his people, with the world, healing, guiding, judging and saving. At a different linguistic level, they spoke of God's glory and God's love, God's wrath and God's power, not least in the eschatological sense that all these would be revealed in the great coming day.[82] The New Testament writers draw on all these to express the point that, I suggest, they had reached by other means: that Jesus was the Messiah; that he was therefore the world's true lord; that the creator God had exalted him as such, sharing with him his own throne and unique sovereignty; and that he was therefore to be seen as *kyrios*. And *kyrios* meant not only 'lord of the world', in the sense that he was the human being now at the helm of the universe, the one to whom every knee, including that of Caesar, must bow, but also 'the one who makes present and visible what the Old Testament said about YHWH himself'. That was why the early Christians ransacked texts about God's presence and activity in the world in order to find appropriate categories to speak of Jesus (and of the Spirit, though that is of course another topic). The high Christology to which they were committed from extremely early on – a belief in Jesus as somehow divine, but firmly within the framework of Jewish monotheism – was not a paganization of Jewish life and thought, but, at least in intention, an exploration of its inner heart.

It all began – this is the point for our present argument – with the belief that Jesus was indeed the Messiah, the 'son of god' in the sense of Psalm 2, Psalm 89 and 2 Samuel 7.14, because the creator god, the covenant god, had

---

[80] See further e.g. Watts 1994; Tan 1997.

[81] See Wright, *Climax* chs. 4, 5, 6; *Romans* on e.g. 9.5, 10.12f.

[82] See Newman 1992, *passim*.

raised him bodily from the dead, after an apparently messianic career and execution.[83] 'As far back as we can go, belief in Jesus' resurrection is the foundation for the Church's speculations and claims about his unique status and role.'[84] If we are to continue to think historically, we can just about account for this dramatic sequence of thought by postulating such a belief in Jesus' resurrection; I can see no way to account for it by any other means. So the question for the historian is, once more: what caused the early Christians to believe, against all expectations, that he had been bodily raised from the dead?

4. Conclusion: Resurrection within the Early Christian Worldview

Before we can begin to answer this question, we must draw together the threads of Parts II and III of this book into a summary statement of the early Christian worldview, highlighting the place of resurrection belief within it. I set out a paradigm for worldview-study in *The New Testament and the People of God* Part II, and (at the conscious risk of over-generalization, which some reviewers were happy to point out) sketched the worldviews of second-Temple Judaism and early Christianity on that template in chapters 8 and 12, with fuller treatments of the early Christian stories in chapters 13 and 14. I then applied the same model to Jesus in *Jesus and the Victory of God* Part II. I assume those studies here, and simply ask: where does the resurrection of Jesus, and of Christians, belong within that picture?

I begin with *praxis*. Where did resurrection show up in what the early Christians habitually did?

Briefly and broadly, they behaved as if they were in some important senses already living in God's new creation. They lived as if the covenant had been renewed, as if the kingdom were in a sense already present, though, to be sure, future as well; often their present-kingdom behaviour (for instance, readiness to forgive persecutors rather than call down curses on them) comes to the fore precisely in contexts where it is all too obvious that the kingdom has not yet been fully realized.[85] The other elements of early Christian praxis, not least baptism, eucharist and martyrdom, point in the same direction.[86] If challenged about their lifestyle, or their existence as

---

[83] cf. e.g. Hengel 1983, 77. For the texts cf. e.g. LXX 2 Sam. 7.12–14: *kai anasteso to sperma sou meta se* ['I will "raise up" your seed after you] . . . *ego esomai auto eis patera, kai autos estai moi eis huion* ['I will be to him a father, and he will be to me a son']. See the discussion at 149 above.

[84] Nickelsburg 1992, 691.

[85] e.g. 1 Pet. 2—3: the difference between this and the solemn curses of e.g. 2 Macc. 7 should be noted carefully (cf. 409 above).

[86] cf. *NTPG* ch. 12.

a community, the early Christians responded by telling stories of Jesus, particularly of his triumph over death.

More specifically, their praxis in relation to Jesus' death, and to the death of members of their own community, is telling. Jews of the period, and some at least of the early Christians, venerated the tombs of prophets and martyrs. People have sometimes suggested that similar things happened in the case of Jesus' tomb, and that the Easter stories gradually grew up from that basis; but there is no evidence whatever that anyone ever went back to Jesus' tomb to pray, to meet friends and family, or to have commemorative meals.[87] There is, however, evidence that the early Christians continued the first-century Jewish practice of secondary burial in caves and catacombs. This, it will be recalled, involved collecting the bones after the flesh had decomposed, and placing them in careful order in an ossuary, which was then stored in a special compartment in a cave-tomb or near equivalent. The practice is usually thought to reflect a belief in resurrection, in that the bones of the individual person continued to matter.[88] Unfortunately we have no evidence of how precisely the early Christians conducted funerals; in the fourth century, the first time such evidence occurs, they were considered an occasion of joy, and those attending wore white.[89] It seems unlikely that this would have been purely a late innovation. The attitude to martyrdom, too, underwent subtle shifts, described in the earlier volume.[90] So far as we can tell, the early Christian praxis in relation to resurrection can be categorized as belonging firmly on the Jewish map, rather than the pagan one, but with signs that from within the Jewish worldview a new clarity and sharpness of belief had come to birth.

This is especially noticeable in the remarkable transfer of the special day of the week from the last day to the first day. 'The Lord's Day', John the seer called it; and there is very early evidence of the Christians meeting on the first day of the week.[91] This is hardly to be explained simply on the grounds that they wanted to distinguish themselves from their Jewish neighbours, or that they believed the new creation had begun; or at least, if either of those explanations is offered, they press us quickly back to the question of why they wanted to do the former, or why they believed the latter. The

---

[87] For Jewish tomb-veneration cf. e.g. Mt. 23.29; on the Antioch martyr-cult see Cummins 2001 ch. 2, esp. 83–6; for Christian martyrs cf. e.g. *Mt. Pol.* 18.2f., and above, 549, with reference to the martyrs of Lyons. For the suggestion that there was a cult at Jesus' tomb see below, 701–3.

[88] On this see e.g. Rutgers and Meyers 1997; McCane 1990, 1997, 2000; and Bynum 1995, 51–8, going beyond our period but with much suggestive material. See above, 90f.

[89] *ODCC*[3] 253. See too Bynum 1995, 55f. for evidence about the rise of eucharistic celebrations in graveyards, and for the link between early eucharistic theology and what was believed about the resurrection.

[90] *NTPG* 364f.

[91] 'Lord's Day': Rev. 1.10; Ign. *Magn.* 9.1; *Did.* 14.1. First day of the week: Ac. 20.7; 1 Cor. 16.2.

early writers face these questions, and give the obvious answers: Ignatius draws attention to the resurrection as the rationale of the new practice, and Justin connects it with the first day of the new creation.[92] Nor should we minimize the significance of the change. The seventh-day sabbath was so firmly rooted in Judaism as a major social, cultural, religious and political landmark that to make any adjustment in it was not like a modern western person deciding to play tennis on Tuesdays instead of Wednesdays, but like persuading the most devout medieval Roman Catholic to fast on Thursdays instead of Fridays, or the most devout member of the Free Church of Scotland to organize worship on Mondays instead of Sundays. It takes a conscious, deliberate and sustained effort to change or adapt one of the most powerful elements of symbolic praxis within a worldview – not least when the sabbath was one of the three things, along with circumcision and the food laws, that marked out Jews from their pagan neighbours.[93] By far the easiest explanation for all this is that all the early Christians believed that something had *happened* on that first Sunday morning.

The *symbolic* world of early Christianity focused upon Jesus himself. The symbolic actions of baptism and eucharist, though of course having Jewish antecedents and pagan analogues, were consciously undertaken with reference to him. His status as Messiah and lord, and the worship accorded him by people determined to remain Jewish-style monotheists rather than pagan polytheists, are everywhere apparent in the early Christian world, generating new symbolic usage; this is particularly noticeable in the case of the cross, which lost its shameful symbolic value as a sign of degrading imperial oppression and became a sign of God's love.[94] The well-known symbol of the fish, which declares its faith in a straightforward but powerful Christology, is first noted in the second century. Whether it was first used because of its acrostic reference to Jesus (*Iesous CHristos THeou (H)Yios Soter*, 'Jesus Christ Son of God Saviour', *ICHTHYS* = 'fish'), or whether the acrostic meaning was exploited after the symbol was already in use, it is still difficult to say.[95] Acrostics were widely used in pagan oracles, and the use of the symbol may have been a way of trying to communicate within a world used to that mode, or may have originated as a secret sign.

---

[92] Ign. *Magn.* 9.1; Justin, *1 Apol.* 67. On the whole question see Rordorf 1968, esp. ch. 4; Polkinghorne 1994; Swinburne 1997, 207–12; Wedderburn 1999, 48–50; Carson 2000.

[93] On the sabbath within second-Temple Judaism see esp. Schürer 2.424–7, 447–54, 467–75; and cf. mShab. *passim*. In the NT see the (admittedly controversial) Rom. 14.5–12 (where the resurrection is given as part of the reason why one must not judge others in such matters); Gal. 4.10; Col. 2.16.

[94] cf. *NTPG* 366f.

[95] The two earliest uses are probably *Sib. Or.* 8.217 (late C2), which launches a whole poem (8.218–50) based on the acrostic, and which adds *stauros* ('cross') at the end; and the inscription of Abercius (in Lightfoot 1989 [1889], 3.496f.), dated c. 200. It is also found in Clement of Alexandria and Tertullian, and in e.g. Aug. *Civ. Dei.* 18.23. Celsus attacks Christians for forging supposedly ancient oracles (Or. *C. Cels.* 7.53).

The *stories* of the early church focus again and again on Jesus and his death and resurrection. We have now studied all but the most central ones, which we reserve for Part IV below, where we shall see that the stories of Jesus' resurrection function, in their present literary contexts, as stories about Israel's and the world's history reaching its divinely ordained climax and new birth, and as stories of the coming of the long-awaited kingdom of Israel's god. But resurrection stories are also told, as we have frequently noted, as ways of speaking of the Christian community itself as resurrection people, as beneficiaries of Jesus' resurrection in both the present and the future. All of these can be plotted on a grid of Jewish-style stories of the vindication of the covenant people after suffering. This itself goes back to the story of the Exodus, and to the many stories, historical and prophetic, of return from exile; and yet the Christian stories have significant differences, characteristics of their own, particularly the suggestion that new creation has already begun. What is more, from Paul onwards Jesus' resurrection was seen as the work of the divine Spirit, and the early Christians claimed, centrally, that the same Spirit was at work within and among them, and would raise them too.[96]

The worldview *questions*, when posed to the early Christians, elicit a set of resurrection-shaped answers.[97] Who are we? Resurrection people: a people, that is, formed within the new world which began at Easter and which has embraced us, in the power of the Spirit, in baptism and faith. Where are we? In God's good creation, which is to be restored; in bodies that will be redeemed, though at present they are prone to suffering and decay and will one day die. What's wrong? The work is incomplete: the project which began at Easter (the defeat of sin and death) has not yet been finished. What's the solution? The full and final redemption of the creation, and ourselves with it; this will be accomplished through a fresh act of creative grace when Jesus reappears, and this in turn is anticipated in the present by the work of the Spirit. What time is it? In the overlap of the ages: the 'age to come', longed for by Israel, has already begun, but the 'present age' still continues. This correlates, obviously, with the redefinition-from-within of resurrection itself which we have already explored.

This worldview finds expression in early Christian beliefs, hopes and aims. The early Christian view of god and the world is, at one level, substantially the same as the second-Temple Jewish view: there is one god, who has made the world, and who remains in an active and powerful relationship with the world, and whose primary response to the problem of evil in the world is the call of Israel, which itself generates a second-order set of problems and questions (why has Israel herself apparently failed? what is the solution to Israel's own problems, and hence to the world's problems?). But

---

[96] Obvious passages include Rom. 8.9–11.

[97] On the nature of the questions see *NTPG* 123f.; *JVG* 137–44, 443–72.

the resurrection of Jesus, and the powerful work of the Spirit which the early Christians saw in that event and in their own lives, has reshaped this view of the one god and the world, by providing the answer, simultaneously, to the problems of Israel and the world: Jesus is shown to be Israel's representative Messiah, and his death and resurrection is the proleptic achievement of Israel's restoration *and hence* of the world's restoration. The first Christians, despite what used to be said in the heyday of existentialist theology, were thereby committed to living and working *within history*, not to living in a fantasy-world where history had in principle already come to a stop and all that remained was for this to be worked out through the imminent end of the space-time universe.[98] The promised future, both for themselves and for the whole cosmos, gave meaning and validity to the present embodied life.

This means, I think, that we can identify clearly the flaw at the heart of much mainstream scholarship over the last century. Ever since Albert Schweitzer, most scholars have done their best to come to terms with an 'eschatological' perspective. That has meant very different things to different people, but at the heart of it lies the recognition that Christianity was born into a world where people were expecting something to *happen*. Because it was assumed by many scholars that nothing much had happened in the world of space-time events – because, in other words, it was taken for granted that the bodily resurrection did not happen – all the weight was put at another point, the imminent 'second coming'. In fact, though the early Christians did indeed hope for a great future event, which might, they thought, happen at any time, they rested the weight of their theology on the event which, they firmly believed, had already happened. It was because of the bodily resurrection that the second coming meant what it did. In that respect, early Christian theology works in the way that a bicycle does: the rear wheel (the past event) supports the rider's weight, the front wheel (the future hope) points in the direction of travel. To ride on the back wheel alone is difficult. To ride on the front wheel alone is downright impossible.

All this means, of course, that the early Christians embraced a completely different view of the world, and of its creator, from that which we find in the Nag Hammadi documents. And it generated a different set of aims: instead of the cultivation of a private spirituality, the resurrection-shaped worldview of the early Christians gave strong impetus to forming communities across traditional barriers, and to a way of life which, both by example and by spoken word, spread quickly, to the alarm of Roman officials, local magistrates and others.[99] In particular, contrary to an often-repeated slur, it encouraged, rather than restrained, a definite confrontation with the Roman empire, which made no sense to those who embraced *gnosis*. If the Christians had believed that Jesus had merely 'gone to heaven', in however

---

[98] On the so-called 'delay of the parousia', see *NTPG* 459–64.
[99] cf. *NTPG* chs. 11, 12, 15.

exalted a capacity, and that their aim should be to join him there in the future, and indeed to experience some anticipations of that blessing in the present, why should the present world be of any concern to them? But if Jesus had been raised from the dead, if the new creation had begun, if they were themselves the citizens of the creator god's new kingdom, then the claims of Jesus to Lordship on earth as well as heaven would ultimately come into conflict with those of Caesar. When we look for the signs of this conflict, and for ways of coming to terms with it within a Christian integrity, we find ourselves looking at the major exponents of the resurrection: Paul, Revelation, Ignatius, Justin, Irenaeus, Tertullian.[100] Just as people used to suppose that the Sadducees were the 'liberals', because they disbelieved the resurrection, not realizing that they opposed it because they were the 'conservatives' of their day, politically as well as theologically, so it has often been supposed that those who embraced a robustly bodily form of resurrection belief, since they happen to correspond to what is thought of as 'conservative' belief today, must have done so in the interests of a 'conservative' or 'status quo' view of the world. Nothing could be further from the truth. Jesus' resurrection, as we have seen earlier in this chapter, vindicated or validated his Messiahship; and if he was Messiah, he was the world's true lord. Resurrection was every bit as radical a belief for the early Christians as it had been for the Pharisees, in fact more so. The Christians believed that 'the resurrection' had already begun, and that the one person to whom it had happened was the lord at whose name every knee would bow.

We have now surveyed the resurrection belief of the early church, including (in the present chapter) the way in which early views of Jesus were themselves shaped by this belief. We are ready at last to embark on the central task of reading the Easter accounts themselves, to see what sense we can make of them as crucial stories told and retold by those who thought and lived in the ways we have described.

---

[100] See above, ch. 11. For the 'political' thought of the early writers see O'Donovan and O'Donovan 1999, 1–29. The book begins (despite its title) not with Irenaeus but with Justin Martyr; it is perhaps a pity that it did not also include e.g. Ignatius or *Mt. Pol.*

Part Four

The Story of Easter

I got me flowers to straw thy way;
I got me boughs off many a tree:
But thou wast up by break of day,
And brought'st thy sweets along with thee.

The Sunne arising in the East,
Though he give light, and th'East perfume;
If they should offer to contest
With thy arising, they presume.

Can there be any day but this,
Though many sunnes to shine endeavour?
We count three hundred, but we misse:
There is but one, and that one ever.

George Herbert, 'Easter'

Chapter Thirteen

GENERAL ISSUES IN THE EASTER STORIES

1. Introduction

The resurrection narratives in the gospels are among the oddest stories ever written. At one level they are simple, brief and clear, at others complex and perplexing. Studying them carefully involves almost all the problems of studying the rest of the gospel narratives, with several extra complications added in for good measure.

I have waited until this point to introduce these stories – rather, one might think, like Beethoven making the choir wait for the first three movements of his ninth symphony before making their entrance – because the history of research shows that if one begins with them it is easy to get bogged down in a mass of detail and never emerge. More particularly, whatever we think of these stories, it is clear that they were told and retold, and finally written down, within the ongoing life of the early church, and it is therefore important that we come to them having already acquired as clear an understanding as possible of what that early church seems to have believed about resurrection in general and that of Jesus in particular. Hence the protracted study involved in Parts II and III above. In terms of our historical enquiry, we have now at last rolled away the heavy stone and can start to peer into the darkness of these most mysterious of all stories.

By the end of the previous Part we have arrived at a point where we can see that the life of early Christianity is inexplicable apart from the assumption that virtually all early Christians – except, of course, the small and late minority represented in the Nag Hammadi texts, in so far as some of them would want to be called Christian – did indeed believe that Jesus of Nazareth had been raised bodily from the dead, but with a transformed embodiment, not simply in a resuscitation to an identical body; and that this event was both the proleptic fulfilment of Israel's great hope and something for which no one at the time had been prepared. This belief is the reason why early Christianity was, to its core, a 'resurrection' movement, with this hope standing at the centre, not the periphery, of its vision. This is the reason why it was a messianic movement, even though its 'Messiah' had died on a cross; why it remained a kingdom-of-god movement, even though the 'kingdom' had not arrived in any of the senses a second-Temple Jew might have hoped for. We have seen that this belief could involve telling, in a longer or shorter version, the basic story of Jesus and his death and resurrection, as in 1 Corinthians 15.3–7 and, more briefly, in 1 Thessalonians 4.14. It would indeed be surprising if we did not have, in early Christian literature, other versions of the same tale.

So, indeed, we do; but the other versions we have – that is, the canonical gospel stories, and one further source (the *Gospel of Peter*) related to them – are themselves almost equally surprising. We have five accounts which, though they converge in some respects, also exhibit striking individual characteristics, not only in the ways the stories diverge in detail, but in the particular emphases they carry. This demands that we ask a string of questions about them: where did the stories come from? were they shaped by particular influences in the community? did the evangelists put their own particular stamp on them, making stories that already existed conform to their particular theology and interest, and if so to what extent and in what ways?

For many years now there has been a broad consensus of answers to these questions among many critical scholars from various backgrounds.[1] There has always been plenty of disagreement, but the following account covers a good many influential writers.

What came first, according to this modern narrative, was a belief in Jesus' exaltation. There then grew up 'Easter legends' about appearances and/or an empty tomb. Mark's account, the first to be written, was short and mysterious, deliberately stopping with the women being so afraid that they said nothing to anyone. There are no actual appearances of the risen Jesus, and no announcement by the women, even to the disciples. All we have is an empty tomb (introduced into the tradition late in the day as an apologetic motif connected with these recently invented 'Easter legends') and an angel who says that Jesus will be seen in Galilee. Matthew's account, written next, has Jesus appearing briefly to the women, and then, at only slightly more length, to the disciples in Galilee, where his closing words serve to round off several themes from earlier in Matthew's gospel.

The modern consensus then continues with a hypothesis about further developments. As the first century winds towards its close, three problems begin to rear their heads. First, the problem which Ignatius addresses: was Jesus really human, or did he only 'seem' (*dokeo*, hence 'docetism') to be a true, flesh-and-blood being? This, it has been assumed, is the setting for Luke's and John's fuller, and more 'bodily', stories of the risen Jesus: breaking bread, expounding scripture, inviting Thomas to touch him, cooking breakfast by the shore. Second, the developed 'Easter legends', including

---

[1] A classic statement may be found in Bultmann 1968 [1931], 290. Modern landmark statements of similar positions are found in e.g. Robinson 1982; Riley 1995.

stories of appearances and the empty tomb, create a problem: how does one relate these stories to the basic belief in Jesus' exaltation? Thus there are invented, around the same time and in the same texts as the anti-docetic material, stories of an 'ascension' which affirms both the initial embodied resurrection and the exaltation, which is now seen as a second stage. Third, some versions of the broad consensus recognize a third problem in the early church: that of rival claims for apostolic authority, dealt with by telling stories which pit one apostle against another (the women against the men, Peter and John against one another, either or both of the latter against Thomas, and so on). Though there is wide disagreement about many details, the consensus that has emerged is that whatever may have happened a few days after Jesus' death, the gospel accounts as we now have them, apart perhaps from Mark, do not take us very far towards a description of the first day of the week following the crucifixion, but rather put us in touch with the theology, exegesis and politics of the early church. Business as usual, in fact, for the modern, and now also the postmodern, critic.

One extra element which has emerged afresh in recent scholarship, and which must be taken into account, is the *Gospel of Peter*. Most scholars have considered it late, derivative and exhibiting quite a different view from the canonical texts; one scholar (J. D. Crossan) has argued, with considerable ingenuity, that it contains elements, including its 'resurrection' story, which go back very early and are in fact the major source for the canonical accounts. This question must now be addressed within a wider consideration of sources.

2. The Origin of the Resurrection Narratives

(i) Sources and Traditions?

Where did the stories come from? Synoptic scholarship, notoriously, has found it difficult to reach any firm conclusions about the interrelationship of the texts at a literary level. It is of course virtually impossible for four sources to tell essentially the same story without using any of the same words. Look at four different accounts of the same football match, and ask yourself whether the word 'goal', common to all of them, indicates collusion among the journalists. But a glance at the Greek synopsis for even the start of the Easter story – Mark 16.1–8 and its parallels – shows that one could be forgiven for thinking that the evangelists had set out to see how *different* from one another they could possibly be.

I regard it as a more or less fixed point of synoptic criticism that Luke used Mark. But at this point he has told the story very much in his own way: a total of only sixteen words out of the 123 in Luke 24.1–9 correspond to equivalents in the 138 words of Mark 16.1–8.[2] Nor are the parallels particu-larly significant: 'on the first day of the week'; 'to the tomb', 'when they arrived', 'you are seeking', 'he is not here, he is risen'.[3] If Luke has 'used' Mark, we must conclude either that he has done so very freely or that he has had another source alongside, which he has almost exclusively preferred. Or maybe 'using' in this case means that he had the scroll of Mark on the table but was so accustomed to telling the story his own way that he glanced at it, decided he could do without it, pushed it to one side and got on without fur-ther reference to it.

The relationship between Mark and Matthew is a little closer. There are moments when it sounds as though we are listening to a version of the same text, though from this passage alone it would be impossible to say which of them has used the other. Even so, out of 136 words in the equivalent Mat-thew passage (28.1–8) there are only thirty-five which are matched in Mark.[4] As for putting Matthew and Luke side by side, there are a bare ten or a dozen matching words, depending what we count as exact parallels.[5] It is, though, worthy of note from this brief glance at the synopsis that there is solid agreement on the words of the angel to the women: he is not here, he is risen (literally, 'he has been raised', *egerthe*). From this point on, of course, Mark stops (we shall discuss the longer endings of Mark in due course), and Matthew and Luke go their separate ways.

John, meanwhile, pursues his own path from the very start, with only the faintest echoes of parallels, after opening words which are more or less identical to a combination of Luke and Matthew ('on the first day of the week Mary Magdalene came to the tomb . . .').[6] His Mary, like Luke's, sees the stone rolled away, but instead of going in she runs off to tell Peter and the beloved disciple. From there on the only overlaps in the whole story are

---

[2] Lk. 24.10 does tell us who the women were, which adds the mention of Mary Mag-dalene and Mary the mother of James (as in Mk. 16.1) to the parallels, though Luke then mentions Joanna while Mark mentions Salome.

[3] Mk. 16.2, 2, 5, 6, 6, 6, parallel to Lk. 24.1, 1, 3, 5, 6, 6. The last phrase is the other way round in Mk. ('he is risen, he is not here').

[4] (In what follows, refs. are to vv. in Mt. 28/Mk. 16): week (1/2); Mary Magdalene, Mary (1/1); white (3/5); you seek Jesus who was crucified (5/6); he is not here, he is risen (6/6, Mark having the phrase the other way round); see the place where (6/6); tell his dis-ciples (7/7), he is going ahead of you to Galilee, there you will see him (7/7), from the tomb (8/8). A few other verbal echoes may indicate that one text has adapted the other, e.g. 'see, I told you' (*idou eipon hymin*, Mt. 28.7) with 'as he told you' (*kathos eipen hymin*, Mk. 16.7).

[5] (Refs. to vv. in Mt. 28/Lk. 24): week (1/1); seek (5/5); he is not here, he is risen (6/6; agreeing against Mark in the order of the phrases, but Luke adds 'but', *alla*, between them); from the tomb (8/9). In Mt.'s ending (8) the women 'ran to tell (*apangeilai*) his disciples'; in Luke's (9), they returned 'and told (*apengeilan*) all these things to the eleven and all the others'. There is, to put it mildly, no 'Q' in sight.

[6] Though with *mnemeion* for tomb rather than Luke's and Mark's *mnema* and Mat-thew's *taphos*.

between the different references to Jesus standing 'in the midst' in the upper room, showing them his hands and side, and making them joyful.[7]

The choice we are faced with, at the level of sources, seems clear. If there is literary dependence, the most likely place to look is between Matthew and Mark. But even there, if one has depended on the other, there has been such substantial rewriting that we might never know. Since the overlaps are either at places where one could hardly avoid it (the name of Mary Magdalene, the mention of the tomb) or, as in the rest of the synoptic tradition, at short, key sentences ('he is not here, he is risen'), it is just as likely that the appearance of literary dependence is an illusion caused by a natural overlap in the swirling, incalculable world of oral tradition. And if that is so, since the hypothesis of at least some literary relationship seems likely for the synoptic gospels as wholes, we must assume that each of the evangelists had access to ways of telling this story which went back via different, though ultimately related, oral and perhaps written traditions.

Might it be possible, then, to trace stages in a pre-literary oral tradition by which these stories arrived at their present shape? Some have attempted to do so, by means of isolating fragments of the stories and arranging them in a hypothetical order of chronological development.[8] But this process, not surprisingly, has produced very little agreement, for the obvious reason that we lack the historical grid against which to plot them. We have no map that would tell us which kinds of moss grew where in early Christianity, so that we could tell which pieces would be picked up by the rolling stone of tradition (always assuming that this rolling stone would disobey the general rule about stones and moss). In particular, the argument of chapter 18 below will lead us to question whether it would have been possible, within early Christianity, for stories of an empty tomb and stories of appearances of Jesus to have circulated in complete independence from one another. Without anticipating that later discussion, we may simply say that historical considerations about the rise of Christianity suggest that such stories must always have at least implied the existence of the other. At the level of method, in the case of the resurrection narratives we cannot use theories about literary units existing before the gospels took their present form as a way of probing the unknown period between Jesus and the evangelists. If we are to peer into that dark tunnel, it will only be when we have borrowed light from either end. There is no light in the tunnel itself that would illuminate, independently, that which lies beyond it.

It is difficult, then, to say very much about either literary sources or oral traditions. The latter certainly existed; Paul tells us as much in 1 Corinthians 15.3, even if we had not guessed. Paul's story, in fact, looks like a brief *summary* of the other stories, including the crucifixion and burial, omitting some

---

[7] Lk. 24.36, 39, 41; Jn. 20.19, 20.
[8] See Alsup 1975; Fuller 1980 [1971]; Lüdemann 1994, ch. 4.

elements (the women) and adding others (the appearance to James, and the 'five hundred at once'). But tracing the relationship between hypothetical sources is like looking for a black cat in a dark room – or, indeed, for a body in a tomb when the stone is still rolled against the door.

(ii) The *Gospel of Peter*

But what if a source should arrive like an unheard-of cousin, make itself at home, and come to be regarded as one of the family? Stringent criteria apply at such a moment. Examples in other fields are rare; one can imagine the searching questions musicologists would ask if a manuscript turned up in a Vienna attic purporting to be the third and fourth movements of Schubert's 'Unfinished' Symphony. Sometimes a work already known turns out to be the missing link in a chain: I remember the excitement I felt when, following a tip-off from scholars working on Thomas More, I was able to publish a work, previously known simply as an anonymous sixteenth-century tract on the eucharist, among the authentic works of the early English reformer John Frith.[9] So when scholars have speculated, as they sometimes have, that behind the canonical narratives of the passion and resurrection there must have been some kind of written source, and when a document describing those events turns up, the question of its origin, and its relation to the documents we already have, must be taken seriously.

The one text that raises these questions is the surviving fragment of the *Gospel of Peter*. This work was mentioned by Origen, Eusebius and Theodoret, but remained otherwise unknown until what seems to be a fragment of it was discovered, along with part of the Book of Enoch in Greek and another fragment now thought to be a separate apocalypse, in a monastic grave at Akhmim in Upper Egypt in the winter of 1886/7. In 1972 two fragments from the Oxyrhynchus Papyri were identified as coming from the same work, providing (together with Eusebius' mention of Serapion in connection with the work) a *terminus ad quem* of the late second century. It has been suggested, not altogether implausibly, that the work was also known by Justin Martyr and Melito of Sardis, pushing the date further back to the middle of the second century at the latest.[10]

---

[9] Wright, *Frith*, 477–84; see the discussion at ibid. 55, 566f. In his second, longer and acknowledged work on the eucharist, Frith refers to an earlier and shorter book. The anonymous tract, known simply by the opening words of its title, *A Christian Sentence*, corresponds closely to the appropriate description; but variations, not least in the proposed consecration prayer, demonstrate that it could not have been the result of someone attempting to produce Frith's 'first treatise' by projecting back from the hints in the later book.

[10] Origen *On Matthew* 10.17; Euseb. *HE* 3.3.2; 6.12.2–6 (noting the doubts about this book held by Serapion, bishop of Antioch in about AD 190); Theod. *Heret. Fables* 2.2. James 1924, 90 says that the discovery was made in 1884; but C. Maurer, in Hennecke

Two different opinions have been canvassed by scholars ever since this text began to be evaluated. Some have argued that the text is dependent upon the canonical gospels (Zahn, Swete and most others); others, that it is independent of them (Harnack, Gardner-Smith). The great majority of scholars continue to follow Zahn and Swete, with increasingly detailed arguments to back up the point. However, in recent years Helmut Koester has argued that this work, though in its present form showing clear signs of dependence on the canonical gospels, must be traced back to an older, less worked-over version, which in its original form was independent of the canonical texts. And J. Dominic Crossan, in a substantial monograph and subsequent works, claims to have identified which parts of the fragment are later additions and hence which parts go back to an original which he dates in the 40s of the first century. He claims, further, that this original work (which he calls 'The Cross Gospel') was the single source for the passion and resurrection stories in the gospels, the rest of the canonical material being explicable in terms of the theological and political interests of the different subsequent authors.[11]

So that we can see what we are talking about, we may quote the relevant texts at some length. There are two segments which offer narratives of Easter day. The first is the one with the famous 'speaking cross':

> Early in the morning, when the Sabbath dawned, there came a crowd from Jerusalem and the country round about to see the sepulchre that had been sealed. Now in the night in which the Lord's day dawned, when the soldiers, two by two in every watch, were keeping guard, there rang out a loud voice in heaven, and they saw the heavens opened and two men come down from there in a great brightness and draw nigh to the sepulchre. That stone which had been laid against the entrance to the sepulchre started of itself to roll and give way to the side, and the sepulchre was opened, and both the young men entered in. When now those soldiers saw this, they awakened the centurion and the elders – for they also were there to assist at the watch. And whilst they were relating what they had seen, they saw again three men come out from the sepulchre, and two of them sustaining the other, and a cross following them, and the heads of the two reaching to heaven, but that of him who was led of them by the hand overpassing the heavens. And they heard a voice out of the

---

1965, 1.179, corrects this to 1886/7. Brief introductions: Maurer loc. cit.; Quasten 1950, 114f.; Mirecki 1992a; Elliott 1993, 150–54; fuller discussions in e.g. Charlesworth and Evans 1994, 503–14; Kirk 1994; Verheyden 2002, 457–65. English text in Hennecke and Schneemelcher 1965 1.183–7; Elliott 1993, 154–8; Greek text in Aland *Synopsis* 479–507, where parallel with the canonical texts.

[11] Crossan 1988, summarized (and with the layered text conveniently displayed) in Crossan 1995, 223–7. See Koester 1982, 163, followed by e.g. Cameron 1982, 78; cf. Koester 1990, 216–40. Koester has not, however, agreed to Crossan's central thesis (1990, 219f.). A different and nuanced view is sketched by Bauckham 1992a, 288 (see too Bauckham 2002, 264): that *Gos. Pet.* was dependent on Mk. and on the 'special material' available to Mt., the latter via oral tradition independent of Mt.'s (different) use of the same material. The fact that several such hypotheses can plausibly be advanced shows how difficult it is to arrive at certainty.

heavens crying, 'Hast thou preached to them that sleep?' and from the cross there was heard the answer, 'Yea.'[12]

This remarkable and dramatic presentation contains several features which seem to me and many others to mark it as a secondary production, dependent on the canonical sources and showing signs of later theological reflection. Despite the characteristic brilliance of his reconstruction, Crossan has won few supporters (an exception being P. A. Mirecki in the *Anchor Bible Dictionary*). Several scholars have rehearsed the arguments for resisting his proposal, both in general and in detail.[13] There are many elements that seem to most readers conclusive evidence for the *Gospel of Peter* being later and more developed than the canonical parallels. I mention only eight. (1) Granted that all the resurrection accounts include exceedingly strange events, nothing in the canonical texts approaches the two enormous angels coming out of the tomb, supporting an even more enormous Jesus between them, and followed by a speaking cross. (2) As I shall argue below, it is far more likely that the almost total lack of explicit biblical reference in the canonical Easter stories, compared both with Paul and the rest of the New Testament on the one hand and with the *Gospel of Peter* on the other, is evidence of their being early rather than of them all having removed, in parallel but independent fashion, the signs of biblical exegesis which, for Crossan and others, 'must have' been there in the earliest accounts. (3) So, too, the strong anti-Jewish bias of the *Gospel of Peter* accords better with a later date. (4) The fact that a crowd of soldiers and Jewish leaders witness the resurrection is very unlikely to have been carefully omitted by all the canonical evangelists in order to make room instead for a few frightened women as the original witnesses. (5) Extra and historically impossible details have been added to the story; in this text, for instance, it is Herod rather than Pilate who sends Jesus to his death. (6) The text speaks of the resurrection happening on 'the Lord's Day', a phrase which is only used in the canonical New Testament at Revelation 1.10.[14] Had it stood in a pre-Markan text, would Mark have suppressed it? (7) If the canonical gospels have used the *Gospel of Peter*, they have all alike omitted several elements: the three men coming out of the tomb, two who had descended from heaven now supporting the third, is without parallel in the New Testament and seems to indicate a resuscitation, or perhaps the rescue of an almost-dead Jesus (if that is what is indicated by having him supported on either side),

---

[12] *Gos. Pet.* 9.34—10.42. The translation follows Maurer (Hennecke 1963, 186) with Crossan's variations (1995, 226).

[13] e.g. D. F. Wright 1984; Green 1987; 1990; Meier 1991, 116–18; Brown 1994, 2.1317–49; Charlesworth and Evans 1994, 506–14; Kirk 1994. Elliott 2001, 1321 says that, with only a very few exceptions, there is a 'general consensus of scholarly opinion' that the work is secondary to, and later than, the canonical accounts. Most recent commentators agree (e.g. Davies and Allison 1988–97, 3.645; Evans 2001, 531). See too *JVG* 59–62.

[14] See too Ign., *Magn.* 9.1; *Did.* 14.1. Contrast 1 Cor. 16.2; Ac. 20.7.

rather than anything like the resurrection narratives in the canonical gospels.[15] And the speaking cross is of course without parallel elsewhere. (8) The meaning of the speaking cross is itself revealing. Crossan ingeniously declares the 'cross' to be a cruciform procession of the redeemed, the great multitude now 'raised' already by the action of Jesus in preaching to the sleepers.[16] But it has to be said that the text itself shows no indication of this, nor is there anything in the other accounts of 'preaching to the dead' (1 Peter 3.19 and the tradition thereafter), or in later resurrection iconography, to suggest that the newly redeemed would form themselves up into a cruciform procession – even supposing such a thing to be thinkable, emerging from a first-century cave-tomb. The presence of this 'harrowing of hell' motif seems, in any case, to be a sign of a theological interpretation for which other early evidence is lacking.[17]

The second passage, in a section which Crossan thinks is later, and derived from the canonical gospels, describes Mary Magdalene and her friends going to the tomb to weep and bring spices. They wondered how they would remove the stone, but they came and found the tomb opened. Then, as they approached,

> they stooped down and saw there a young man sitting in the middle of the sepulchre, handsome, and wearing a brightly shining robe. He said to them, 'Why have you come? Who are you looking for? Surely not him that was crucified? He is risen and gone. But if you don't believe, stoop this way and see the place where he lay, for he is not here. For he is risen and is gone to the place from which he was sent.' Then the women fled in terror.[18]

The main difference between this and the canonical account is that the angels here tell the women that Jesus is not only risen but already ascended. The earlier part of the same passage contains various warnings against the Jews, who are said to be angry.[19]

There is nothing in the *Gospel of Peter* to suggest that it comes from a gnostic setting. It does not seem to belong with the Nag Hammadi documents in tone or content. And, though Serapion had heard that some parts of it were being used in support of a docetic Christology, it does not demand to be read this way. The text does not, then, show too many signs of what the later church came to regard as a heretical standpoint. The problem is more simple. It simply fails to carry conviction, on any theory of Christian origins

---

[15] The closest parallel is with *Asc. Isa.* (possibly late first or early second century) 3.16f.; but which text got the idea from the other, or whether both got it from a lost third, is impossible to judge.

[16] e.g. Crossan 1995, 197.

[17] So e.g. Rebell 1992, 97. The question of whether the awakened 'saints' in Mt. 27 constitute an exception must be dealt with in ch. 15 below.

[18] *Gos. Pet.* 13.55—14.57.

[19] e.g. *Gos. Pet.* 11.50, 12.52.

that will hold water, as coming, in whole or in reconstructed part, from the period before the canonical gospels, let alone Paul.

It is impossible to tell with any precision what precisely the author of the *Gospel of Peter* believed about the nature of Jesus' resurrection body. Was Jesus after all the figure being supported by the two angels? In what sense was he 'risen'? Are the resurrection and ascension regarded as the same thing? There are too many other obvious agendas (not least polemic against 'the Jews', and the careful exoneration of Pilate) for any theory to find sufficient grounding. The *Gospel of Peter* remains an enigma, but an enigma which need not materially affect our assessment of the four major accounts of Jesus' resurrection.

(iii) The Form of the Story

Form-criticism of the gospels has not been anything like as much in vogue in recent decades as it was between roughly 1920 and 1970. One of the reasons for this, I suspect, is that there is tacit recognition among New Testament scholars that the philosophical, hermeneutical and theological agendas of the early form-critics, notably Bultmann himself, were driving the project more than had originally been realized, and that it was time to step back and take a different look. I argued for this point in the first volume, and proposed, not the abolition of form-criticism, but a different way of doing it, working from the likely Jewish story-forms that the earliest followers of Jesus would naturally have adopted and towards the kind of forms that the stories might have taken when retold in an environment more attuned to, say, Cynic aphorisms.[20] Here I presuppose that argument. It may indeed be possible to detect, from the form of a story, what kind of role it played in the early Christian community. But the way in which such attempts have been made in the past is probably not the best way forward now.

The resurrection stories are, in fact, very difficult to classify by the normal canons of form-criticism.[21] They are dense and tight, and do not admit of easy hypotheses, on the basis of form alone, about their use within the community. The opening sequence in Matthew and Mark could conceivably be read as a pronouncement-story, with the punch-line being the word of Jesus (in Matthew) and the angel (in Mark) about going to Galilee.[22] The Johannine story of Jesus' encounter with Thomas reaches a similar climax with Jesus' blessing on those who have not seen and yet have believed.[23] But it would be bold to suggest (as used to be argued about some

---

[20] *NTPG* ch. 14.
[21] The classic argument to this effect was made by Dodd 1967.
[22] Mt. 28.10/Mk. 16.7.
[23] Jn. 20.29.

pronouncement-stories) that the narratives had developed simply as a show-case for these final words. Similarly, there is one miracle-story, the catch of fish in John 21.1–14; but it does not share all the features even of its closest parallel, the fishing story in Luke 5.1–11, and the way the fishing story (21.1–11) runs on smoothly to the breakfast scene (verses 12–14) makes us wonder whether it should be classified that way at all. The disciples' amaze-ment at the huge catch is not the final point of the story, as it would be in a normal miracle-tale. The main points are (1) the strange seeing of Jesus, knowing him yet still wanting to ask 'Who are you?' (verse 12), (2) John's apparently deliberate echo of the much earlier story about Jesus distributing bread and fish, and perhaps (3) the significance John gives to the mention of this being the third resurrection appearance.[24]

The other story elsewhere in the gospels which is sometimes placed alongside the resurrection narratives is of course the transfiguration.[25] Yet at the level of form, as well as of content – and here form and content are closely intertwined – there are significant differences. In the transfiguration story there is preparation for a vision, then the vision itself, and then some closing comments about what it might all mean. It is a reasonably typical vision-story, which the resurrection narratives are not. In particular, though they share some elements with the biblical accounts of visions (the appearance of an angel who tells people not to be afraid, a commission to the visionary to tell other people, and so on), the *form* is again different. Attempts to line up the resurrection narratives with other elements of the gospel tradition, the wider biblical tradition, or indeed the very different stories of empty tombs in the hellenistic novels, all fail.[26] In fact, in terms of their form, these stories become, in themselves, a further element of early Christianity in need of historical explanation. Why did early Christianity not only get under way at all, but tell *this kind of story*, without antecedent or obvious parallel?

(iv) Redaction and Composition?

The more the stories go on, particularly of course in the fuller accounts of Luke and John, the more they reflect the style, and the theological interest, of the particular evangelist. This will emerge over the next four chapters. But even in the early section of the narrative (Mark 16.1–8 and parallels) some unique features appear. Because we cannot tell what literary rela-tionship, if any, there was between the resurrection narratives, it is impossible to say whether, and if so to what extent, any of the gospel writers

[24] Jn. 21.13 with 6.11; 21.14. See ch. 17 below.
[25] Mt. 17.1–9/Mk. 9.2–10/Lk. 9.28–36.
[26] On the latter see above, 68–77.

have consciously modified their sources in the interests of their own theology or other agendas. There are, however, tell-tale signs of the evangelists' particular interests. We shall explore these in more detail in the chapters that follow; but a brief indication here will show what is going on.

The most obvious example is Luke's angel telling the women, as Jesus himself will tell the two on the road and the eleven in the upper room, that the son of man must suffer and be raised (24.7). Another is John's highlighting, even in the opening story, of the role of the beloved disciple. So too, notoriously, Mark's strange comment about the women remaining silent for fear seems to belong with the commands to silence throughout the gospel (though, ironically, this was the moment when silence was no longer appropriate).[27] Each of these we must examine more fully later on. But a more general redaction-critical comment must be made at this point.

Those redaction-critics who have attempted to reconstruct the world, the agenda, and the aims of the different evangelists have increasingly realized that they were, by and large, careful to describe Jesus as they supposed he was in his own day, not simply as though he were a member of their own church.[28] Of course, if this point is taken seriously, it tends to pull the rug out from under a certain amount of form-criticism: if the evangelists are telling the story as though Jesus is talking to someone in a *different* setting to that of their own church, how much value can we place on a theory which depends for its validity on the stories circulating, and perhaps being invented in the first place, in order to address, not a situation in the life of Jesus, but a situation the church was facing at another time or place? Perhaps for this reason, some critics have envisaged the evangelists, sensitive to historical distance between themselves and Jesus, performing a clever 'historicization' upon original material which had no sense of an earlier setting. But this is unwarranted in the present case at least. There is no sign that these stories had a prior life reflecting the situation of a church in, say, the 40s or 50s, but that they have now been faked, like a modern piece of furniture being doctored to look like an antique, to produce a falsely 'historicized' sense.

In these stories above all, in fact, we have a sense that the evangelists are *not* saying 'this is how it is for our own day, our own church'. Nor is there any hint of earlier versions which did intend to say that. Matthew's Jesus will be with his people always, but they do not expect to go to a mountain in Galilee in order to meet him. Mark certainly did not want or expect his readers to 'say nothing to anyone, because they were afraid'. Luke did not suppose that his readers might themselves walk down the road to Emmaus, or anywhere else for that matter, and meet an unrecognized stranger who would expound the scriptures to them and then reveal himself (and then disappear) while breaking bread at the supper table. John writes explicitly for a

---

[27] cf. Mk. 9.9.

[28] See e.g. Lemcio 1991; and the discussion in *NTPG* 142, and chs. 13 and 14.

time when the church will no longer be able to see and touch the risen Jesus, but must believe without having seen. The last great beatitude in the gospel ('Blessed are those who have not seen and yet believe,' 20.29) elevates the difference between the first disciples and the later church into a principle.[29]

It is of course possible for all these stories to be read as 'relevant' to later times and places. Luke has told the Emmaus Road story so that it contains key elements of early church life to which he will then return in, for instance, Acts 2.42. John tells the story of the failed fishing trip, followed by Jesus' command and the miraculous catch, well aware no doubt that Christian readers would take it as a picture of their own failed attempts at working for the kingdom and the remarkable results that might happen if they would only listen more clearly for the Lord's command. The stories can indeed function as allegories or parables of what happens in the church, and the evangelists were certainly aware of that potential. But here again the historian's disciplined imagination must be brought into play. If we start by supposing that the stories are in some way or other based on actual reminiscence of actual events, it is easy to see how they could come to be used in this extended sense. After all, if Jesus' resurrection really was the start of the new covenant, the new creation, the new world in which the early church believed itself to be living, this is the kind of thing one might expect. But if we imagine the movement being made in the other direction we will discover that it is impossible. If the evangelists had started off with a lesson, theological, moral or practical, which they wanted to teach, and had attempted to develop 'historicized' Jesus-stories to serve as allegories of such lessons, they would not have come up with the kind of stories we have here.[30] It is, in other words, easy to see how strange stories about meetings with Jesus, meetings of a sort which everybody in the early church knew did not happen in their own day, could be used for wider purposes. It is impossible to imagine this process happening in the other direction, for four reasons, which we must now examine.

3. The Surprise of the Resurrection Narratives

(i) The Strange Silence of the Bible in the Stories

The first surprise when we read the resurrection stories in the canonical gospels ought to be that they are told with virtually no embroidery from the biblical tradition.[31] This is itself remarkable for two reasons.

---

[29] This is what makes it difficult, simply (for the moment) at the level of paying attention to the texts, to elide the original 'seeings' of Jesus with subsequent Christian experience of the risen lord, as does e.g. Coakley 2002 ch. 8.

[30] So, rightly, Wedderburn 1999, 37.

[31] Noted briefly by Williams 2000, 195.

First, the evangelists have told their stories up to this point not only with a steady crescendo of drama and narrative tension – Jesus' public career, his arrival in Jerusalem, the action in the Temple, the solemn warnings delivered on the Mount of Olives, the final meal, the arrest, the night hearing, the trial before Pilate, the crucifixion itself – but also with a persistent build-up of scriptural quotation, allusion, reference and echo. A glance at the biblical references in the margins of Mark 11—15 will make the point.[32] Even the burial narrative has strong biblical resonances. After this, the resurrection narratives convey the naked feeling of a solo flute piping a new melody after the orchestra has fallen silent. Granted that the evangelists felt so free, as our own scholarly traditions have insisted, to develop, expand, explain, theologize and above all biblicize their sources, why did they refuse to do so, here of all places?

The second reason why this lack of biblical embroidery is remarkable is that, as we saw in 1 Corinthians 15.4 and throughout the subsequent tradition from Paul to Tertullian, from the earliest days of that tradition the resurrection of Jesus was seen as having occurred precisely 'according to the scriptures'. Not only was it seen that way; it mattered vitally to the church that it be seen that way, in its preaching (Acts 2 and 13 are obvious examples), its self-explanation (1 Corinthians 15, 2 Corinthians 4 and 5), its confrontation with critics from outside (the line from Athenagoras to Tertullian), and so on. How easy it would have been, if the stories had developed along the lines the consensus imagined, to have one of the angels at the tomb, or one of the disciples, or even one of the women, or perhaps Jesus himself, give voice to a biblical passage which would do for this story what was done for so many others throughout the gospels! How easy it would have been, for instance, to have the story told in the elevated and dignified language of the fulfilment of prophecy. If we think for a moment of the marvellous passage in 1 Maccabees 14.4–15, which extols the reign of Simon Maccabaeus in high-flown language drawn from various biblical sources, we see how it could be done:

> They tilled their land in peace;
> > the ground gave its increase,
> > and the trees of the plains their fruit . . .
> He established peace in the land
> > and Israel rejoiced with great joy.
> All the people sat under their own vines and fig trees,
> > and there was none to make them afraid.
> No one was left in the land to fight them,
> > and the kings were crushed in those days.
> He gave help to all the humble among his people;

---

[32] In any printing of the NT that carries such references. The Nestle-Aland Greek text provides a good start; the 1898 Oxford edition of the Revised Version has not been superseded in this respect by later English translations.

he sought out the law, and did away with renegades and outcasts.
He made the sanctuary glorious,
    and he added to the vessels of the sanctuary.[33]

This is the kind of thing one might have expected to occur, and quite naturally; but it never does. Matthew, at least, ought to have been capable of outdoing 1 Maccabees, but he never even tries. Not once do we hear his familiar line, 'All this took place so that it might be fulfilled what was spoken by the prophets . . . '. John tells us that the two who ran to the tomb 'did not yet know the scripture, that he must rise again from the dead',[34] but not only does he not tell us which scriptures he has in mind, he does not even hint at them in the story, here or later. Despite the fact that the rest of his book is so full of biblical language and imagery that it takes several books fatter than the original to tease them all out, the last two chapters, containing 56 verses, offer so far as I can see only four biblical allusions, only one of which is of real significance: in 20.22, Jesus breathes on the disciples so that they may receive the Spirit, which looks like a clear echo of Genesis 2.7 and perhaps other passages also.[35] Of course, Luke loses no opportunity to tell us that what has happened to Jesus is what 'must' happen; the angels say it to the women, Jesus himself insists on it while walking to Emmaus, and he repeats the point in the upper room.[36] But these Lukan stories, though in themselves consummate works of art, are not in themselves works of midrash or exegesis.[37]

It is revealing that one critic who has turned the hermeneutic of suspicion into an art form, writing eloquently elsewhere of the way the evangelists and/or their sources have 'historicized prophecy', not least in the crucifixion narratives, cannot even begin to say the same about the resurrection narratives.[38] This, perhaps, is why he falls back on a different kind of suspicion,

---

[33] 1 Macc. 14.8, 11–15. For the echoes, see e.g. Ps. 67.6, and the picture of Solomon's rule in 1 Kgs. 4.20–34, with the prophetic echoes of both passages in e.g. Isa. 17.2; Mic. 4.4; Zech. 3.10. See too the various biblical pictures of the just judge helping the poor, keeping the law, punishing the wicked; and the adornment of the sanctuary, as in the case, once more, of Solomon (1 Kgs. 7.40–51).

[34] Jn. 20.9. See Menken 2002, who offers the very unsatisfactory explanation that John's Christology is complete at the cross and so needs no extra scriptural support thereafter (see below, ch. 17).

[35] cf. too Ps. 104.30; Ezek. 37.9; Wis. 15.11. The other passages are 20.17 with Ps. 22.23 ('I will declare your name to my brethren'); 20.28 with Ps. 35 [34 LXX].23 ('my Lord and my God'); and the various 'shepherd' overtones from Jn. 21.15–19, e.g. 2 Sam. 5.2; Ps. 23.1; 78.71f. (though it would of course be impossible to refer to sheep and shepherds without evoking scripture in the mind of a regular reader).

[36] Lk. 24.7, 26, 46.

[37] See below, ch. 16, for one possible echo; but it remains an echo, not a point which could have generated the whole story.

[38] Crossan 1991 ch. 15. However, Crossan later suggests (1998, 568–73) that an exegetical tradition (which he describes as 'male') was modified by the 'ritual lament' of the 'female lament tradition', and that one crucial modification was the elimination of

claiming that the resurrection stories were told to legitimate different authorities within the early church.[39] But even if that were plausible (we shall see later that, by and large, it is not), this has not begun to explain why stories of this sort, narrating incidents of this sort, would come to be told. From very early on, as we have seen at length, the early Christians developed a sophisticated network of biblical exegesis in order to demonstrate that Jesus' resurrection was exactly what one should have expected, and that it provided both the fulfilment of Israel's hopes and prophecies and the groundwork for their own mission. But, though Matthew, Mark, Luke and John all clearly believe this to be the case, they have not told Easter stories which bring it out. For some reason, the narratives have remained biblically unadorned, and thus distinctly different from a good many of the other stories throughout the gospels, not least the crucifixion narratives which immediately precede them. I think there is an explanation for this; but it must wait until we have examined the other three surprising features of these stories.

(ii) The Strange Absence of Personal Hope in the Stories

The second feature of the resurrection narratives which should cause us considerable surprise is also to do with something they lack. Were this a different sort of book, I would be eager at this point to rub the point into the consciousness of those who organize Easter services, not least those who preach and choose hymns; but that must wait for another occasion. Simply in terms of our attempt to assess, as historians, what these stories think they are about, and where they belong in the early Christian scheme of things, it is extremely strange, and extremely interesting, that at no stage do they mention the future hope of the Christian.

This is, of course, counter-intuitive to most western Christians, Catholic and Protestant, conservative and liberal. A thousand hymns and a million sermons, not to mention poems, icons, liturgies and aids to meditation, have so concentrated on 'life after death' as the central problem, the issue which drives everything else, and have so distorted the Easter stories to feed this concentration, that it has long been assumed that the real point of the Easter story is both to show that there is indeed a 'life after death' and that those who belong to Jesus will eventually share it. As we have seen in reviewing

---

exegesis from the surface of the text. 'There is no evidence for a passion-resurrection *story*', he writes (571) 'that does not presume, absorb, embody and integrate *exegesis* as its hidden substratum and basic content' (italics original). This extraordinary statement invites the counter-assertion: there is no evidence for a later *exegetical* treatment of the resurrection (as in the tradition from Paul to Tertullian) which does not presume, absorb, integrate and embody *history* as its *visible* substratum and basic content.

[39] This is the explanation popularized by e.g. Wilckens 1977; Pagels 1979, 3–27; Gager 1982.

the future hope of the Christian writers of the first two centuries, this is itself far too vague: the hope was, again and again, for bodily resurrection *after* 'life after death'. But the significant thing to notice here is this: neither 'going to heaven when you die', 'life after death', 'eternal life', nor even 'the resurrection of all Christ's people', is so much as mentioned in the four canonical resurrection stories. If Matthew, Mark, Luke and John wanted to tell stories whose import was 'Jesus is risen, therefore you will be too', they have done a remarkably bad job of it.[40]

Instead, we find a sense of open-ended commission *within* the present world: 'Jesus is risen, therefore you have work ahead of you.' This is very clear in Matthew, Luke and John; even in Mark the women have an immediate task (though whether they do it or not we must discuss later), and the angel's message through them to the disciples, especially Peter, implies that they are going to be given things to do as well. This mission coheres closely with the missionary imperative displayed in Paul and Acts.

It does not, however, include any mention of the future resurrection, or of being 'with Jesus' in a post-mortem existence.[41] And the real surprise is that this marks out the resurrection narratives from virtually every mention of resurrection in Paul and the rest of the New Testament outside the gospels and Acts, and virtually every mention of it in the post-canonical literature. When Paul speaks of Jesus' resurrection he connects it again and again with that of his people; his greatest passages on the subject, 1 Corinthians 15 and 2 Corinthians 4 and 5, are focused on that question, and the tight argument of passages like Romans 8.9–11 and 1 Thessalonians 4.14 tie the two beliefs, the resurrection of Jesus and that of his people, tightly together. The first letter of Peter reflects exactly the same sequence of thought: by God's great mercy you have been born again to a living hope, an incorruptible inheritance, through the resurrection of Jesus the Messiah from the dead.[42] Paul is capable of referring to Jesus' resurrection without immediately making the link: as we saw, he declares in opening and closing the theological argument of Romans that the resurrection validates Jesus' Messiahship, his status as 'son of god', and his consequent status as the world's true lord

---

[40] Jn. 20.31 might be thought to be an exception: the resurrection should convince you, John says, that the Messiah is Jesus, and that if you believe this 'you will have life in his name'. But here, as throughout Jn., 'life', though designed to continue beyond bodily death, is something the believer has in the present. Another possible exception is the story in Mt. of the bodies of the saints coming out of the tombs. Among the many puzzling features of that story, however (see ch. 15 below), is the fact that it is not produced as a sign of what will happen to all the righteous in due course. The third possible exception proves the point: in Mk's longer ending, 'those who believe and are baptized will be saved, but those who disbelieve will be condemned' (16.16). There is nothing like this in the genuine narratives.

[41] In the same way, neither of the ascension stories (in Luke and Acts) have anyone say, as I once read in a draft movie script on the life of Jesus, 'He's gone to heaven, and one day we'll be going there too.' As an adviser to the project, I protested; the ending was altered.

[42] 1 Pet. 1.3f.

and ruler.[43] But even there the connection of Jesus' resurrection with that of all his people is implicit. He is marked out as 'son of god' 'on the basis of the resurrection of the dead ones' (*ex anastaseos nekron*, 1.4), which means more or less the same as Colossians 1.18, that Jesus rises as 'the beginning, the first-fruits'. And Romans 15.12 highlights not just the rule of the risen Messiah over the nations, but the fact that 'the nations shall hope in him'.

There are, then, a few places in early Christian literature where the resurrection of Jesus is mentioned without drawing a definite connection to the future hope of the Christian; but the great majority of references make the link explicit. In the gospels, however, it is not just a matter of the balance being the other way round. There is no balance. If all we had was the stories of Jesus' crucifixion and resurrection, we would never know that anyone ever interpreted the resurrection narratives as providing a basis for a future hope beyond the grave. The stories are about something else altogether: the vindication of Jesus, the validation of his messianic claim, and the commissioning of his followers to act as his heralds, announcing to the world its new, surprising, but rightful lord. This, like the first surprising feature, must await an explanation until after we have examined the other two in our list.

(iii) The Strange Portrait of Jesus in the Stories

There is a third feature of the resurrection narratives which should surprise us, especially when we think back to chapter 4 and reflect on the second-Temple Jewish expectation of resurrection. If, as the consensus view has tended to say, these stories developed as the church pondered scripture and expressed and re-expressed its faith, we should have expected the resurrection stories to reflect the kind of things that the favourite 'resurrection' passages in the Old Testament had been saying.

But they do not. To begin with, Jesus is never depicted, in these stories, as a heavenly being, radiant and shining. The brilliant light of the transfiguration is significantly absent, which does rather upset the old theory that it is a misplaced resurrection tale. (So too is the fact that the disciples have no problem recognizing Jesus, despite the radiance.) The sightings of, and meetings with, Jesus are not at all like the heavenly visions, or visions of a figure in blinding light or dazzling radiance, or wreathed in clouds, that one might expect to find in the Jewish apocalyptic tradition, or in connection with Merkabah mysticism.[44] Whatever we say about Paul's conversion (chapter 8 above), these stories are not at all like that.[45] Whatever account we give of the vision of Jesus in Revelation 1, there is nothing in the gospel

---

[43] Rom. 1.3f.; 15.12. See above, 242–5, 266f., 568f.
[44] So, rightly, Dodd 1967, 34.
[45] Perkins 1984, 137: despite apocalyptic imagery elsewhere, here Jesus is still Jesus.

narratives that corresponds to it. They are not, that is, the sort of thing one would expect if the evangelists or their sources had wanted to say that Jesus had been exalted to a position of either divinity or heavenly glory. Nor are they the kind of thing that would have been said if the tradition had begun by wanting to say that Israel's god had approved Jesus' project, that his death was a success not a failure, and that the Bible had now been fulfilled. Jesus appears in the narrative as, in this respect, a human being among human beings.

We can test this out easily enough by thinking of the favourite 'resurrection' texts in second-Temple Judaism. Suppose for a minute that a Christian community, or an individual Christian writer, in the 40s, 50s or 60s of the first century, had been studying the scriptures, and now wanted to tell the story of Jesus' death and of the divine approval of him in terms of a fictitious 'resurrection', and to do so in such a way as to reflect the biblical context. Which scriptural texts would they go to? The one which towers above the rest, in Judaism of both this period and later, is Daniel 12.2–3:

> Many of those who sleep in the dust of the earth shall awake, some to everlasting life, and some to shame and everlasting contempt. Those who are wise shall shine like the brightness of the sky, and those who lead many to righteousness, like the stars for ever and ever.

As we saw earlier, this text was picked up by Jesus' contemporary, the author of the Wisdom of Solomon, when he predicted that the righteous would shine forth and run like sparks through the stubble.[46] But the gospel narratives of Jesus' resurrection are innocent of all this. Why do they not have Jesus shining like a star?

On the other hand, Jesus is almost routinely depicted in these stories as having a human body with properties that are, to say the least, unusual. The same Lukan text that tells us that Jesus ate broiled fish, and invited his followers to touch him and see he was real, also tells us that Jesus appeared and disappeared at will, that at one of these appearances two close friends and colleagues did not recognize him, and that in the end he was taken up into heaven.[47] The same Johannine text that tells us that Jesus invited Thomas to touch him, indeed, to put his finger and hand into the marks of the nails and the spear, is the text that has Jesus twice entering through locked doors, speaking of a 'going up to the father' which he must yet accomplish, and being only half recognized even when in the familiar act of serving food.[48] The same text that has Jesus meeting his followers on the mountain, and commissioning them for worldwide disciple-making, allows that 'some

---

[46] Wis. 3.9; above, 169–71.

[47] Lk. 24.42f., 39, 16, 31, 36, 51. On the non-recognition see Polkinghorne 1994, 114. On the distinction of 'real' and 'visionary' in Luke's thought cf. e.g. Ac. 12.9, 11.

[48] Jn. 20.27, 19, 26, 17; 21.12.

doubted'.[49] It is at this point, as C. S. Lewis once wrote, that awe and trembling should fall on us (not, I grant, a familiar phenomenon among historical critics).[50] What are these stories trying to tell us?

The one thing they can *not* be trying to do, despite a long tradition of scholarship which I have already mentioned, is to disprove docetism.[51] It seems to me totally incredible that stories like these, especially those in Luke and John, represent a late development of the tradition in which for the first time people thought it appropriate or necessary to speak of the risen Jesus being solidly embodied. The idea that traditions developed in the church from a more hellenistic early period (in this case, a more 'non-bodily' view of post-mortem existence) to a more Jewish later period (in this case, a more embodied 'resurrection') is in any case extremely peculiar and, though widely held in the twentieth century, ought now to be abandoned as historically unwarranted and simply against common sense. If there was likely to be development, the model we find in Josephus, for example, suggests that we might expect a hellenistic-style 'spiritualizing' of the tradition, not a re-Judaizing of it. It is far more likely that a very Jewish perception of how things were, in very early Christianity, gave way, under certain circumstances, to a more hellenistic one by the end of the century – though that itself would need careful investigation before we simply assumed it. In the cases before us, it makes no sense to think of Luke sitting down to compose an anti-docetic narrative about the genuine human body of Jesus and allowing himself so far to forget this important purpose as to have Jesus appear and disappear, not be recognized, and finally ascend into heaven. Similar things must be said of John.[52]

Nor, again, are the surprising features of the portrait to be explained as a reading back of theological points from Paul or the later tradition. Paul, too, holds, as we have seen, a view of Jesus in which he is both embodied and somehow different, as the ground of his view that the ultimate redeemed human nature will be both bodily and transformed. But whereas Paul's notion of transformation highlights incorruptibility (the fact that neither the risen Jesus nor his risen and transformed people will ever again face death), nowhere do the pictures of the risen Jesus in the gospels make any mention of this striking fact. It is as though they are talking about 'transphysicality',

---

[49] Mt. 28.16–20.

[50] Lewis 1960 [1947], 152. Coakley 2002, 135, 140f. notes this phenomenon but does not, to my mind, draw exactly the right conclusions from it.

[51] The anti-docetic theory is taken for granted by e.g. Hoffman 1987, 60. Goulder 1996, 56f. makes great play with it. See the summary in Perkins 1984, 110 n. 79. Conversely, Muddiman 1994, 132 is right to reject this as 'most unlikely' (Muddiman 132–4 anticipates in a brief form the whole line of our present section).

[52] For what follows, see Polkinghorne 1994, 115, quoting Baker 1970, 253–5: Jesus is neither dazzling nor a resuscitated corpse.

in the sense I defined it at the end of chapter 10, but have not yet begun to come to terms with it or to figure out its implications.

We are still left with the historical puzzle of accounting for the surprising stories of the risen Jesus which we find in Matthew, Luke and John. There is one more surprise to be noted before we can propose a solution.

(iv) The Strange Presence of the Women in the Stories

One of the most obvious things in common between the four canonical narratives, over against the *Gospel of Peter* and the tradition in 1 Corinthians 15.3–8 (perhaps the only thing those two texts have in common), is that they begin with women. This leads to possibly the most obvious of the four strange things about these stories, which can therefore be stated briefly.

All kinds of questions have been raised about what the women were doing at the tomb, from a historical point of view (were they really going to anoint the body? was this part of a standard lament-process? which women are we talking about, anyway?) and from a literary point of view (the role of the women in the different accounts).[53] A great deal has been said about the role of Mary Magdalene in particular. But there the women are. Granted the very early tradition of 1 Corinthians 15, where did they come from?[54]

It is, frankly, impossible to imagine that they were inserted into the tradition after Paul's day. This is not because of a supposed shift during the first generation from an early period in which women were accepted as full members to a later period when male dominance reasserted itself. We have no evidence to help us plot such a graph. Rather, the tradition which Paul is quoting, precisely for evangelistic and apologetic use, has carefully taken the women out of it so that it can serve that purpose within a suspicious and mocking world. But this only goes round the edge of the issue. The underlying point is more ruthlessly historical.

Even if we suppose that Mark made up most of his material, and did so some time in the late 60s at the earliest, it will not do to have him, or anyone else at that stage, making up a would-be apologetic legend about an empty tomb *and having women be the ones who find it*. The point has been repeated over and over in scholarship, but its full impact has not always been felt: women were simply not acceptable as legal witnesses.[55] We may

---

[53] See e.g. Bode 1970; Osiek 1993; Lieu 1994. See now esp. Bauckham 2002, ch. 8. Bauckham 258f. provides a long list of scholars who support the point I am here summarizing, noting the weakness of opposing arguments.

[54] For a recent survey of the role of women in the stories cf Corley 2002, ch. 5.

[55] cf. e.g. Trites 1977, 54f.; O'Collins 1995, 94; Bauckham 2002, 268–77. For rabbinic evidence cf. e.g. mSheb. 4.1; mRosh haSh. 1.8; bBab. Kam. 88a. Josephus adds the following to the law of witnesses (Dt. 19.15): 'From women let no evidence be accepted, because of the levity and temerity of their sex' (*Ant.* 4.219).

regret it, but this is how the Jewish world (and most others) worked. The debate between Origen and Celsus shows that critics of Christianity could seize on the story of the women in order to scoff at the whole tale; were the legend-writers really so ignorant of the likely reaction? If they could have invented stories of fine, upstanding, reliable male witnesses being first at the tomb, they would have done it.[56] That they did not tells us either that everyone in the early church knew that the women, led by Mary Magdalene, were in fact the first on the scene, or that the early church was not so inventive as critics have routinely imagined, or both. Would the other evangelists have been so slavishly foolish as to copy the story unless they were convinced that, despite being an apologetic liability, it was historically trustworthy?[57]

The argument thus works in the same way as our previous ones. It is easy to imagine that, when a tradition was established for use in preaching to outsiders, stories of women running to the tomb in the half-light would quietly be dropped, and a list produced of solid witnesses who could be called upon to vouch for what they had seen.[58] It is not easy at all – in fact, I suggest, it is virtually impossible – to imagine a solid and well-established tradition, such as that in 1 Corinthians 15, feeling itself in need of some extra stiffening in the first place, or, if such a need was felt (why?), coming up with a scatter of women on a dark spring morning. The stories may all have been written down late in the first century. We do not know (despite repeated scholarly assertions) exactly when the evangelists first put pen to paper. But we must affirm that the story they tell is one which goes back behind Paul, back to the very early period, before anyone had time to think, 'It would be good to tell stories about Jesus rising from the dead; what will best serve our apologetic needs?' It is far, far easier to assume that the women were there at the beginning, just as, three days earlier, they had been there at the end.[59]

4. The Historical Options

There are only two options that will account for these stories being what they are; and I find the first frankly incredible.

We could say, as historically minded readers of these texts, that Matthew, Luke and John (Mark's eight-verse ending does not, of course, bring the risen Jesus on stage) have acquired, from Paul and the other early Christians, a particular theology of resurrected humanity: of human bodies being neither abandoned to rot, nor yet resuscitated into the identical sort of condition

---

[56] Mk.'s highlights Joseph of Arimathea as a 'respected councillor' (15.43; cf. Lk. 23.50, 'good and righteous'). They would have loved to be able to say the same about the people who arrived first at the tomb.

[57] For the different role of women in *Gos. Pet.*, see Verheyden 2002, 466–82.

[58] So e.g. Schweizer 1979, 147.

[59] See Wedderburn 1999, 57–61 (against e.g. Lüdemann).

they were in before, but somehow transformed, so that they are puzzlingly the same and yet different. This 'transphysicality' would represent a theological view of new humanity for which Jewish belief in resurrection had in some ways prepared the ground, but which goes beyond anything we find in non-Christian Jewish texts of the period. As it stands, it is without historical precedent.

We would then have to say, pursuing this line, that the three evangelists who mention Jesus' appearance have turned this theology of transphysicality, the one we find in all the major writers from 1 Corinthians to Origen, into significantly different narratives about Jesus (Matthew's Jesus standing on the mountain, Luke's walking on the road to Emmaus, John's cooking breakfast by the shore) which show no sign of mutual influence, but which all possess this same, strange, like-and-yet-not-quite-like characteristic. We would have to say, in addition, that the evangelists, producing these largely independent and very different stories, have all avoided mentioning the analysis of the like-and-yet-not-quite-like risen humanity which Paul and the others give (that the present body is corruptible, and the risen body will be incorruptible); and that, instead, they all focus on recognition and non-recognition, on the risen body of Jesus doing some things that ordinary bodies do and other things that ordinary bodies never do.

Furthermore, had they been attempting to speak of continuity and discontinuity between the present body and the risen one within the framework of biblical reflection common to mainstream first-century Judaism, they could have reached for an obvious solution, based on Daniel 12: while the present body remains non-luminous, they could have had the risen body shining like a star. Instead, this first option requires that the three evangelists have invented these three quite different stories of a Jesus who is both recognized and not recognized, who comes and goes through locked doors, who is solidly physical, with wounds still visible, and yet who seems to belong in two dimensions at once ('heaven and earth'? – in other words, the human and divine dimensions of reality – though this is never spelled out), so that it appears, to them at least, natural for him, after a while, to leave the ordinary, human dimension of the cosmos ('earth') and to go, still embodied, into the other one ('heaven').[60]

We would have to go further again. We would have to say that Matthew, Luke and John, in writing these very different stories which all, remarkably enough, shared this characteristic, managed at the same time, presumably independently, to abstract from these stories the feature they would surely have had, if they had been invented on the basis of the theology we know from Paul and elsewhere, namely the all-pervasive biblical exegesis, allusion and echo. If, as a first-century Bible-reading writer, you started with

---

[60] I describe the two dimensions thus lest anyone should think that I am attributing to the evangelists a naive belief in a literal three-decker universe.

Paul's theology, or indeed that of Revelation or Ignatius, and tried to turn that theology of resurrection into an artful, just-as-if-it-happened-yesterday sort of narrative, it would be extremely difficult to avoid reference to scripture. If you try to imagine three such people doing it independently and coming up with three different stories which nevertheless all share this remarkable feature, in addition to the others we have noted, I think you will find it incredible. I certainly do.

The same is true in relation to the strange absence of any mention of the future post-mortem hope of Christians. Supposing a Christian group, or several individuals, who had pondered the developing resurrection-belief of the early church, not least as we see it in Paul, were to write a story about 'what really happened' as a way of turning into an aetiological myth the burgeoning belief that Jesus' resurrection was the model and the means for the Christian future hope. By the 50s of the first century, Christians who thought of Jesus' resurrection also thought (among many other things) of their own. The more Christians were persecuted, and the more they began to die in some numbers (the problem addressed directly in 1 Thessalonians 4.13–18, and brought in alongside in 1 Corinthians 15.18), the more this theme of hope beyond the grave, based firmly on Jesus' own resurrection, would have been an inevitable part of any resurrection stories that might be invented. It would have been almost impossible to keep this element out of the new-spun narrative. It is completely unbelievable that four writers would have come up with very different Easter stories and that each one, by a kind of tacit agreement, would have omitted all mention of this increasingly important theme.

Finally, the same is true when we consider the place of the women in the narratives. The point is obvious and often made. Nobody inventing stories after twenty years, let alone thirty or forty, would have done it like that.

There are other similar points as well; indeed, once you begin to reflect on this set of questions all sorts of things come and make themselves at home in the picture. In particular, if it is true that stories of people meeting Jesus were invented in order to legitimate leaders in the early church, it is remarkable that we hear nothing, throughout the gospel stories, of James the brother of Jesus. The only time anyone mentions him as a witness of the resurrection is in 1 Corinthians 15.7. But on the frequently made assumption about the origins of the stories, he should have been here as well. Why does he, too, not run a race against Peter? Would that not have been a convenient fiction to clothe early ecclesial power struggles? The more we try to envisage the first option – the resurrection stories as late inventions – the harder it becomes.

But think of the other option. Try running the movie back to front. Supposing that by Paul's day all early Christians believed that something extremely strange had happened to Jesus, the strangeness consisting not least in this, that though he was bodily alive again, his body was somehow different. Supposing Paul was providing a theoretical, theological and biblical framework for stories which were already well known – stories which, indeed, he is summarizing when he quotes an already official formula at the start of 1 Corinthians 15. Supposing the stories in Matthew, Luke and John – though almost certainly not written down until after Paul had dictated his last letter – were what they were, not because they were a late writing up, or wholesale invention, of what post-Pauline Christians thought ought to have happened, but precisely because they were not. What if they represented, with only light editing, the stories that had been told very early on, without offering theories about what sort of a thing this new, risen body might be, without attempting (except at the level of minor adjustments) to evoke wider theological themes, without adding the element of hope for one's own resurrection, and in particular without the biblical quotations or allusions that might have done for these stories what was done for so many, so recently in the same books. Supposing the reason nobody evoked Daniel 12 in the Easter stories was that everybody knew that the risen body of Jesus had not shone like a star? Supposing, wider, that the reason nobody evoked the Old Testament in the gospel accounts of the resurrection was that there was no immediately apparent point of connection between Jesus' resurrection and the narratives of Jewish tradition? Supposing, in other words, that these stories have the puzzled air of someone saying, 'I didn't understand it at the time, and I'm not sure I do now, but this is more or less how it was.'

I find this second option enormously more probable at the level of sheer history.[61] I can understand, as a historian, how stories like this (and perhaps other similar ones which we do not have) would create a puzzle which the best brains of the next generations would wrestle with, using all their biblical and theological resources. I cannot understand, however, either why anyone would develop that theology and exegesis unless there were stories like this to generate the puzzle, or how that theology and exegesis, formed thus (one would have to suppose) by a kind of intellectual parthenogenesis, would then generate three independent stories from which, in each case, all those developed elements had been carefully removed. The very strong historical probability is that, when Matthew, Luke and John describe the risen Jesus, they are writing down very early oral tradition, representing three different ways in which the original astonished participants told the stories. These traditions have received only minimal development, and most of that probably at the final editorial stage, for the very good reason that stories as earth-shattering as this, stories as community-forming as this, once told, are not easily modified. Too much depends on them.[62]

---

[61] See too J. Barton 1994, 114: 'belief in the resurrection preceded all the interpretations of it.' Contrast e.g. de Jonge 2002, 45–7.

[62] The formulary nature and presumed early dating of 1 Cor. 15.3f. points in the same direction. On the way in which community-shaping traditions like this remain reasonably

This is not an argument for the historical accuracy of the gospel accounts. I have not yet reached the point where we can even contemplate what that might look like. It is an argument for the accounts being chronologically as well as logically prior to the developed discussions of the resurrection which we find in Paul and many subsequent writers. They describe more or less exactly that for which Paul and the others provide a theological and biblical framework and from which they draw further eschatological conclusions: an event involving neither the resuscitation nor the abandonment of a physical body, but its change into a new mode of transformed physicality, what I have called 'transphysicality'; that is, an event for which there was no precedent, for which indeed in very precise terms there was no *prophecy* as such, and of which there remained in their day, and remains still in our own day, no subsequent example. The gospel stories are not dependent on Paul. Nor does he refer to them directly, except in so far as the tradition he quotes in 1 Corinthians 15 is a summary of them, or of others like them. But irrespective of when the gospels reached their final form, the strong probability is that the Easter stories they contain go back to genuinely early oral tradition.

This extremely important conclusion can be supported by a better known argument which, though frequently discounted, should still be allowed some force. We have been pondering the stories of the risen Jesus presented by Matthew, Luke and John. These stories barely overlap at all (Luke and John both have Jesus in the upper room on the first evening; in both, he speaks of the coming of the Spirit to equip the disciples for mission; but the accounts are otherwise completely different). But where the gospels do overlap, as we saw earlier in looking for possible literary relationships between them, they tell the same story in extremely different ways. The surface inconsistencies between Mark 16.1–8 and its parallels, of which so much is made by those eager to see the accounts as careless fiction,[63] is in fact a strong point in favour of their early character. The later we imagine them being written up, let alone edited, the more likely it would be that inconsistencies would be ironed out. The stories exhibit, as has been said repeatedly over the last hundred years or more, exactly that surface tension which we associate, not with tales artfully told by people eager to sustain a fiction and therefore anxious to make everything look right, but with the hurried, puzzled accounts of those who have seen with their own eyes something which took them horribly by surprise and with which they have not yet fully come to terms. This, again, does not prove either that the stories were in fact originally told by eye-witnesses or that everything they say represents a photographic record of what took place. But it strongly supports the idea that they were early,

---

constant, see Bailey 1991. Bailey has been criticized on points of detail, but in my judgment his overall thesis remains sound.

[63] Patterson 1998, 213f. grossly overstates the problem. The more balanced account in e.g. Edwards 2002 is still inclined to conclude that the stories are a hopeless tangle.

that they were not assimilated either to each other or to developed New Testament theology, and that the inconsistencies between them should not be allowed to stand in the way of taking them seriously as historical sources.

In fact, the accounts all tell a story which, in general terms, can be summarized without doing violence to any of them. All four agree that the key events took place early in the morning on the first day of the week on the third day after Jesus' execution. All four agree that Mary Magdalene was at the tomb; Matthew, Mark and Luke agree that another woman was there too, and Mark and Luke add others. All agree that the stone presented an apparent problem, but that the problem was solved without the women having to do anything. All agree that an unusual stranger, an angel or near equivalent, met and spoke to the women. Matthew and John agree that Mary Magdalene then met Jesus (Matthew, of course, has the other Mary there too). All except Mark agree that Mary (and the other women, if they are mentioned) go off to tell the male disciples; Luke and John agree that Peter and another disciple then go to the tomb to see for themselves.

This, by the way, is an interesting point at which a wrong conclusion could easily be drawn. Luke 24.12 has Peter getting up, running to the tomb, stooping down and looking in, seeing the grave-clothes and going away again. This sounds as though only he is involved. But when the two on the road to Emmaus tell the anonymous stranger what had happened that morning, they say (24.24) that 'some of our number' went to the tomb and found it as the women had said. Luke is quite capable of highlighting one person when he knows, and tells us later, that more than one was involved. We might compare Luke's own three different accounts of Paul's conversion; or Josephus' different accounts of events in which he himself was involved, as between the *War* and the *Life*. If Luke can say that there was one person, and then later that there was more than one, the numerical differences between the different accounts of the women and the angels cannot be regarded as serious historical problems.[64]

From that point, of course, the stories diverge more sharply. Mark's angel tells the women that they and the male disciples will see Jesus in Galilee; Matthew's Jesus does indeed appear there (though actually he appears briefly in Jerusalem as well, in 28.9). Luke's Jesus only appears in and near Jerusalem, and never speaks of going to Galilee, but rather of the need for the disciples to stay in Jerusalem itself. John's Jesus appears first in Jerusalem, and then later in Galilee. If John had not existed, and some bright

---

[64] The link between Lk. 24.12 and 24 is complicated because one major MS, the fifth-century western text 'D', omitted v. 12, as did the Old Latin MSS and Marcion. It has sometimes been argued, not unnaturally, that the verse is a compilation of Jn. 20.3, 5, 6 and 10, but if every other MS in the entire tradition contains it, it seems more likely that Luke knew, at this point at least, an abbreviated version of a story like John's. This verse is an example of a wider phenomenon, the so-called 'western non-interpolations', on which see Metzger 1971, 191–3 (on this v., 184).

harmonizer were to declare that the solution to the Mark/Luke divide on this point was that Jesus appeared in both places, such a person would be howled down. The fact that John does it, and that, however fleetingly, Matthew does so too, may, of course, mean that they attract the howls instead, but it might also cause us to pause before making hasty judgments.[65]

I suggest, in fact, that the stories must be regarded as early, certainly well before Paul; and that, when placed side by side, they tell a tale which, despite the multiple surface inconsistencies, succeeds in hanging together. To put it crudely, the fact that they cannot agree over how many women, or angels, were at the tomb, or even on the location of the appearances, does not mean that nothing happened. We should not try to domesticate the stories, either by forcing every last detail into an over-simple harmony,[66] or by forcing them (at least as much violence is required, if not more) into an over-simple hermeneutic of suspicion where they can be explained as the back-projection of later theology or as coded messages in support of the 'political' or 'leadership' claims of the different disciples involved.[67] We should treat them as the key pieces of evidence for answering the question which has built up throughout Parts II and III of this book: why did early Christianity begin in the first place, and why did it take this shape – particularly in relation to its beliefs about resurrection, and also in relation to its beliefs about Jesus? If we had asked that question without knowing of the existence of Matthew 28, Mark 16, Luke 24 and John 20 and 21 (this is the fiction we have tried to maintain until this chapter), and had then come upon these chapters for the first time, we would have known that our question had found its answer.

These stories too, of course, provide evidence not directly for what happened but for what several different people thought had happened. (I do not wish to retreat from the critical realist position advanced in Part II of *The New Testament and the People of God*; I am simply concerned to be absolutely sure, here of all places, that I do not appear to smuggle into my historical argument anything more than it will bear.) The stories are, at this moment in our enquiry, answers to the question: why did early Christianity begin, and why did it take this shape? The answer is: because the early Christians believed that something had happened to Jesus after his death, something to which the stories in the four canonical gospels are as close as

---

[65] On the plausibility of the disciples making various trips to Jerusalem, precisely for festivals such as Pentecost, cf. e.g. Moule 1958.

[66] The harmony offered by Wenham 1984 is hardly over-simple, but not many have found it convincing. The polemic against harmonization by e.g. Carnley 1987, 17–20 is interesting: it is not just that it is difficult to do, but the very attempt 'must be ruled out of court at the outset as a fundamentally mistaken enterprise'. Carnley then, of course, proceeds to mount a lengthy historical reconstruction of what 'must have happened'; why this is not also a mistaken enterprise is not clear.

[67] See the critique of the 'leadership' explanation by Bremmer 2002, 51f.

we are likely to get. I propose, in short, that the four canonical resurrection accounts, granted the presence in all of them of editorial features which we shall examine presently, almost certainly go back to oral traditions which provide the answer to the question of the origin and shaping of Christianity. The question which this then poses is, of course, the crucial one: what caused the earliest Christians to believe that something like this happened, and to tell this sort of story?

That is the question we must address in the final Part of the book. For the remainder of this Part, to fill in details and to make sure we are on firm ground, we must examine each of the four accounts in its own right.

Chapter Fourteen

FEAR AND TREMBLING: MARK

1. Introduction

'They went out and fled from the tomb, for trembling and panic had seized them. They said nothing to anyone, for they were afraid.' Thus Mark (16.8), in what has become one of his most famous lines in modern study. A book of dark mysteries, we are told: secret revelations, flashes of light amid the gloom, the challenge of faith without sight, and finally trembling, panic and silence.[1] A perfect ending for a book like this.

Or is it? I sometimes wonder if the reason scholars have read Mark this way is their boredom with the obvious alternative, for so long a staple diet of biblical teaching in both church and academy: that Mark was the first gospel, the simplest gospel, telling the basic facts about Jesus, leaving it to others to embroider them, to add extra teaching, to turn them into a work of art. This kind of thing has been deeply counter-intuitive to scholars in the second half of the twentieth century, wrestling with faith and doubt amid the storms of secularism and postmodernism, and only too eager to warn against 'happy endings'.[2] Much better – so much more sophisticated, after all – to see Mark as a kind of first-century Kafka, or perhaps R. S. Thomas. Thus, where Mark used to feature on the first-year syllabus because he was easy, straightforward and basic, he now belongs there because he is hard, cryptic and intellectually demanding. This will shock the undergraduates, thinks the teacher, and make them realize that things are harder than they imagined!

The debates about the ending of Mark thus reflect the varied perceptions of conservative modernism and radical postmodernism, with no doubt several stages in between; but that does not mean there are no real arguments to be made. There are historical questions here, and they demand historical discussion, not simply rhetorical position-taking. Did Mark mean to break off at 16.8? Did he really intend his whole gospel, admittedly in rough

[1] For a preliminary discussion of Mark see *NTPG* 390–96.
[2] McDonald 1989, 70.

Greek, to end with *ephobounto gar*, 'for they were afraid'? Where did the two extra endings come from, and what would Mark have thought of them?

I argued briefly in *The New Testament and the People of God* that Mark did indeed write a fuller ending, which is now lost, and for which the two extra endings supplied in some later manuscripts were lame substitutes. Nothing in the overall argument of the present book hangs on this argument; but the fact that the argument can be made, and will be made here slightly more fully, demonstrates an important negative: that Mark cannot be used, as he has often been used, as a sign that the earliest Christians knew nothing more than an empty tomb, trembling and panic. It has been all too easy for scholars in search of a straightforward tradition-history to place the resurrection accounts in a chronological order and produce an apparent QED: first Mark, short, dark and perfectly formed without any resurrection appearances; then Matthew, slightly fuller, with some appearances; then Luke/Acts and John, longer, fuller, with more details about the risen Jesus.[3] The argument of the previous chapter is designed, among other things, to undermine the apparent force of this progression, by showing that even the fuller accounts of Luke and John demonstrate features, positive and negative, for which the best explanation is that they go back to very early oral tradition. The argument of the present chapter is designed, among other things, to undermine the apparent force of the starting-point. If it is at least a serious possibility that Mark really did have a fuller ending which is now lost, it is simply unsafe to proceed as though *ephobounto gar* were his final word to the waiting world. Lovers of dark, mysterious texts need not worry; plenty of hidden secrets remain, in Mark and many another early Christian text. But we must not project our contemporary fondness for certain kinds of narrative on to a historical problem which demands not prejudgment but analysis.

We must therefore begin by examining the question of the ending, before proceeding to ask the other necessary questions: what historical value can be assigned to Mark at this point, and what is he trying to tell us as he lays out his brief narrative?[4]

2. The Ending

The problem is well known. Stated simply (those in search of the full complexity can find it in the critical commentaries and monographs) it appears like this.[5] The earliest manuscripts of the gospel, the great fourth-century codices Sinaiticus and Vaticanus, conclude with 16.8. They are followed by

---

[3] Sometimes we find: first Paul, a kerygma but no empty tomb. See Part II above.

[4] In this chapter and the next three I am writing in parallel with Catchpole 2000. Sadly his book arrived on my desk too late for me to interact with it in the way I might have liked.

[5] For the details see, in addition to critical texts, Metzger 1971, 122–6; and the full bibliographies and discussions in Gundry 1993, 1012–21; Cox 1993; Evans 2001, 540–51.

several later manuscripts, and some of the early Fathers of the church either show no knowledge of the longer ending or show, even while reproducing it, that they know it to be dubious. (Unfortunately, none of the many earlier papyrus fragments of New Testament material contains Mark 16; we can always hope for a providential accident of archaeology.) But the great fifth-century manuscripts, led by Alexandrinus, include the 'longer ending' (verses 9–20), and most subsequent manuscripts follow this lead. In addition, four manuscripts from the seventh, eighth and ninth centuries, and some later ones, insert the so-called 'shorter ending', in effect verse 8b; and all except one of these then continues with the 'longer ending' as well. A good many of the manuscripts that do contain the longer ending, however, have marks in the margin (asterisks or obeli) to indicate that the passage is regarded as of doubtful authenticity.

The apparently independent omission in the two fourth-century manuscripts, coupled with all the other scattered evidence, makes it highly likely that the longer ending is not original. In addition, though the content of verses 9–20 contains some apparently Markan features (e.g. the disciples' lack of faith in 16.11, 13, 14), in other ways it looks suspiciously as though it is derived from elements of the resurrection accounts in the other gospels.[6] Thus, for instance, 16.12–13 is an obvious summary of Luke's Emmaus Road story (24.13–35); the appearance to the disciples as they were eating (verse 14) belongs with Luke 24.36–43; the commission in verse 15 is parallel to Matthew 28.18–20; and the ascension in verse 19 is taken from Luke 24.50 and Acts 1.9–11. And, as is often pointed out, the command about the necessity of baptism for salvation (verse 16) and the the list of wonderful deeds the apostles will do (verses 17–18) look as though they are a summary of some aspects of later church life.[7] All of these have led the great majority of contemporary commentators, of all shades of opinion, to agree that, though the longer and shorter endings are extremely interesting, they are almost certainly not by Mark.

Actually, the 'longer ending' looks, from its opening in verse 9, as if it might even have originally been a separate account altogether, since it begins in *parallel* to Mark 16.1–2/Matthew 28.1/Luke 24.1/John 20.1, not in *sequence* with Mark 16.1–8:

> [9]When he rose early on the first day of the week, he appeared first to Mary Magdalene, from whom he had cast out seven demons. [10]She went out and told the people who had been with him, who were mourning and weeping. [11]But when they heard that he was alive, and that he had been seen by her, they did not believe.

---

[6] See Kelhoffer 2000.

[7] cf. e.g. the parallel between the picking up of snakes in v. 18 and Paul's experience in Malta in Ac. 28.3–6.

This might imply that verses 9–20 were not simply composed by somebody wishing to provide a fuller ending for Mark, but may have originally been a separate summary of Easter events which was then used to plug the gap, even though it actually overlapped with some of the material already present. But this observation, though it opens fascinating possibilities (could it have been originally a separate account? part of a lost gospel?), is not relevant to our present task. There is broad agreement that the author of the gospel did not himself write either verse 8b or verses 9–20.

This is the point at which contemporary criticism has hastened to assure us that we should be content with 16.8 as the proper conclusion. To look for a different ending, perhaps even a 'happy' one, we are told, betokens literary or theological naivety.[8] The book, like its parables, is deliberately open-ended, enticing readers to complete the story for themselves.[9] Similar remarks can be multiplied from recent scholarship, careful to rehabilitate Mark as a grown-up piece of writing, not a naive happy-ever-after book. How much this insistence on ending the book at 16.8 has been motivated by a desire to keep what is normally accepted as the earliest gospel as free as possible from actual resurrection appearances it is difficult to say. Watching the way in which these themes interplay inevitably raises that question.

There are, however, powerful reasons for questioning this theory, and for proposing that Mark did indeed write a fuller ending which is now lost, and for which verses 8b and 9–20 are replacements by later scribes not altogether out of tune with Mark's intentions.[10] We may note, to begin with, that the beginning and ending of a scroll were always vulnerable. A glance at any edition of the Dead Sea Scrolls, in particular at facsimile photographs, will reveal that even the scrolls which are preserved almost in their entirety are in many cases damaged at both ends. One recalls, too, the scroll of Jeremiah's book being steadily whittled away by the king with his penknife.[11] But, while this suggests that lost endings (and beginnings) are very much a physical possibility, it proves nothing.[12] Nor does the fact that it is unusual to end a sentence, let alone a book, with *gar* get us very far.[13]

---

[8] McDonald 1989, 70, quoting Kelber 1983.

[9] e.g. A. Y. Collins 1993, 123.

[10] The strongest recent case for Mark having written an ending which is now lost is that of Gundry 1993, 1009–12, followed by Evans 2001, 539f. Fenton 1994, 6 suggests that the reason such arguments are still made is because of opposition to the regular explanations for the sudden ending. I cannot speak for Gundry or Evans; the reason I make the case for a possible lost ending is because of the exegesis of the rest of the text (below).

[11] Jer. 36.20–26.

[12] On the possibility that the beginning, too, is lost, and that the present opening is a later editorial addition (it is easier to leave a text truncated at the end than at the beginning), see *NTPG* 390 n. 67, with the refs. there to Moule 1982 and Koester 1989.

[13] See Evans 2001, with discussion of various scholarly views: the word *gar* is capable of ending a sentence or even a book, but there is at least as good reason to think that Mark intended to write more as to think that *gar* was intended as his last word. The parallel with

What counts is an understanding of the book Mark was writing, and a sense of what would have been an appropriate ending for this kind of book. Ultimately, of course, making a case on this subject would require a whole commentary; here, inevitably, we can only summarize.

I argued in the earlier volume that Mark is best understood as an 'apocalypse', designed to unveil the truth about who Jesus is through a series of revelatory moments.[14] The famous Markan parables function within this as stories of how Israel's god is fulfilling his strange purposes; one of them uses imagery which, in its Jewish context, might well have been heard as a hint of death and resurrection.[15] Within this apocalyptic scheme, Mark has organized a careful sequence of predictions in which Jesus tells his followers, as they head towards Jerusalem, what is going to happen to him. The son of man must suffer many things, be rejected and killed, and after three days rise again (8.31; 9.31; 10.33–4). The predictions get longer in regard to the suffering, but they all end with 'and after three days he will rise again'. These predictions shape and punctuate the narrative of the second half of the gospel, and belong closely with Mark's telling us that Jesus really is Israel's Messiah (8.29; 14.61–2). Mark's gospel has a stark and simple structure: chapters 1—8 build up to the recognition of Jesus' Messiahship, and chapters 9—15 build up to his death. But always, in looking ahead to his death, they look ahead as well to his resurrection. (Thus, even if the gospel did end at 16.8, there is no doubt that Mark believed that Jesus really had been raised bodily from the dead.) Since part of Mark's point as the story draws to its climax is that Jesus is a true prophet, and that what he has said about the Temple, and about Peter, will come true,[16] the detailed fulfilment in chapters 14—15 of Jesus' earlier prophecies about his rejection, suffering, handing over and death would naturally lead the reader to expect that there would also be a reasonably detailed description of the fulfilment of the other part of the prophecy as well.

Sarah in Gen. 18.15 ('Sarah denied it and said, "I didn't laugh," for she was afraid' (*ephobethe gar*)) remains haunting and suggestive, but proves nothing one way or the other. If anything, it suggests that the story should continue. Sarah, after all, lived to see her sceptical laughter confounded.

[14] *NTPG* 390–96. The moments of revelation come at Mk. 1.10f.; 8.29; 9.7; 14.61; 15.39.

[15] Mk. 4.26–9: the seed grows secretly, while the sower 'goes to sleep and arises' (*katheude kai egeiretai*) night and day; at last he puts in the sickle, because it is time for harvest. The apocalyptic overtones (note the echo of Joel 3.15) reinforce the context of a coming great judgment in which 'many who sleep in the dust shall awake' (Dan. 12.2; the Theodotion version uses the same verbs as Mk. 4.27). For resurrection in the 'sower' parable itself, see McDonald 1989, 55–8, 72.

[16] See Mk. 13.2 with 14.58f. (and the discussion in *JVG* 522f.); 14.30 with 14.66–72, esp. 14.65 (the guards mock Jesus as a false prophet, unable to tell who is hitting him, while out in the courtyard Jesus' earlier prophecy about Peter is coming true).

In particular, the first half of the gospel reaches its climax with Peter's confession in 8.29, which issues in the challenge to follow Jesus to suffering, death and vindication (8.31—9.1). The confession is confirmed by a remarkable event (the transfiguration) in which a voice from heaven declares, in effect, that Peter has been correct in his judgment (9.2—8); but nothing must be said about the event until the son of man is raised from the dead (9.9). This seems to point definitely towards a final account, not just of an empty tomb and frightened women, but of a similar event, following the climactic revelation of Jesus as the suffering, crucified Messiah, within the frame of Caiaphas' ironic statement in 14.61 and the centurion's declaration in 15.39 – a final event in which Israel's god would declare, in effect, that they were right, indeed more right than they had known or intended. There is thus good reason, within the structure of the gospel, to suppose that the author intended to give his work a fuller, more complete ending. He sets up plenty of hints of what is to come. Having explained in such detail how true a prophet Jesus was in relation to his death and the circumstances surrounding it, it is unlikely that he would stop short of explaining the truth of his prophecy about what would happen next.

The same point can be made negatively in terms of the rebuke to Peter in 8.33, and the immediate challenge to follow Jesus, confess him boldly before the watching world, and not be ashamed (8.34–8). This points forward, of course, to a catastrophic moment (14.66–72) in which Peter does exactly the opposite. Is it then likely that the gospel would end with women 'saying nothing to anyone, for they were afraid'? Opinions will differ here, but my opinion is that it is unlikely. The fact that the disciples and others have been afraid on several previous occasions (4.41, after the storm; 5.15, after the healing of the demoniac; 9.32, afraid to ask Jesus about his prediction of suffering; 10.32, afraid as they follow him on the road) does indeed create a context where we are not surprised that the women, too, are afraid at the extraordinary events of the empty tomb. But the point of fear, throughout Mark, is that it should be overcome by faith: 'Why are you afraid? Haven't you got faith yet?' (4.40); 'Cheer up, it's me! Don't be afraid' (6.50).[17]

The closest parallel to the picture of the women running away from the tomb is in 5.33, where the woman who has touched Jesus in the crowd comes 'in fear and trembling' and falls down before Jesus. Her fear had rendered her silent, speechless; but now that power has gone out from Jesus, and he has challenged her, she tells the whole story. He replies, 'Daughter, your faith has saved you; go in peace, and be healed from your illness' (5.34). That story is itself 'sandwiched' within the framing story of Jairus' daughter, who is dead at the moment of this conversation but whom Jesus will shortly raise to life; the parallel between the stories is highlighted by the

---

[17] Mk. 4.40 is followed by a still greater fear, recognizing that Jesus has authority over creation, a pregnant point as we look forward to ch. 16.

fact that the woman has had her ailment for twelve years, the same as the age of the dead girl. Immediately after the healing of the woman, messengers come to tell Jairus that his daughter is dead, and Jesus says to him, as to others, 'Don't be afraid; only believe' (5.36). Mark, it seems, is highlighting precisely the message that will then be needed by the women at the tomb. They may pass from our sight at 16.8, saying nothing to anyone because trembling and panic had seized them; but if the multiple forward references from chapter 5 find any fulfilment at all, we must assume that Mark does not intend to leave them in that condition, any more than Jesus left either the woman or Jairus in their state of fear. True, after the girl had been raised, 'they were amazed with a great amazement' (5.42),[18] and Jesus told Jairus to say nothing to anyone (5.43); but when he gave similar orders to the disciples he made it clear that the command to silence would be rescinded precisely when the son of man was raised from the dead (9.9).

This is not, of course, Mark's only reference to resurrection.[19] We have already examined the strange saying ascribed to Herod Antipas in 6.14–16; in Mark's story, this forms part of the build-up to Peter's confession at Caesarea Philippi (compare 6.14–15 with 8.28). Jesus, Mark is hinting, is not *someone else* raised from the dead; he is *himself* the one who will be raised from the dead (8.31; 9.9). This will demonstrate that he really is the Messiah, the king of Israel, the reality of which Herod is a poor parody.

Just as the larger structure of the gospel, and the hints within it, suggest strongly that Mark intended his gospel to end with an account of the resurrection of Jesus, not merely of the empty tomb, so the build-up towards the crucifixion in chapters 11—14 points in the same direction. Jesus' Temple-action precipitates a sequence of disputes between him and the Jewish leaders, which work steadily towards large, imposing statements that Jesus will be vindicated, that his action in the Temple will be seen to have been justified as a prophetic act by its outworking, and that, whether or not he spoke of the rebuilding of the Temple as well as its destruction, he himself, as John would later interpret that saying, was to be 'destroyed' and 'rebuilt'.[20] In the middle of the sequence of disputes we find the Sadducees' question (12.18–27), which we have discussed in chapter 9 above. Mark, placing it in this sequence of riddles which explain what Jesus had meant by his Temple-action, must have realized that, in the context of several prophecies about Jesus' own resurrection, it too must have functioned to point ahead to a final moment of truth, of Jesus' vindication. Then, within the conversation with the disciples on the way to the garden, Jesus warns that they will all be scattered when, like Zechariah's shepherd, he is struck down; but he declares that 'after I have been raised up, I will go ahead of you to Galilee' (14.28).

---

[18] *exestesan ekstasei megale*; cp. *tromos kai ekstasis* in 16.8.
[19] On this section, cf. Combet-Galland 2001, 106–08.
[20] See Jn. 2.19–22 with Mk. 14.58–62.

This, of course, is picked up in the angel's word at 16.7. It implies that Mark intends to describe, not just a promise that Jesus will meet them there, but the fact of his doing so.

All this suggests that it is highly likely that Mark intended to continue beyond 16.8. What did he intend to say? Something, we may surmise, about Jesus' followers, not least Peter, meeting the risen Lord in Galilee, being commissioned to tell people at last what they had seen earlier (9.9), and to take the gospel to all the nations (13.10; 14.9).

This is not to say, of course, that Mark did write such an ending. Perhaps he died before he could finish the book (as may have happened to John); perhaps he was prevented from completing his task. If that had been the case, however, and if he had been in any way following an account of Jesus' life and death known in the oral tradition of his church, or indeed of the wider church, it is likely that someone else would have finished the job for him soon afterwards (again, as seems to have happened with John). Another option is that, writing at a time when at least some of the 'five hundred at once' (1 Corinthians 15.6) were still alive, he left the ending blank with the intention that, when the text was read out, someone present would tell their own eye-witness story. Neither of these is particularly convincing. The better answer is that Mark did indeed write more, and that what he wrote was lost – by accident most likely, by the fire in Rome possibly, or, just conceivably, by malicious action (perhaps by some early textual critic, bent on causing problems for later readers – or, more seriously, by someone, in the church or outside, who disapproved of what Mark was doing).[21]

So what did this lost ending contain? Here the field is, to say the least, wide open. One can only marvel at the reticence of those who, flushed with the success of reconstructing several different recensions of 'Q', detecting early strata in *Thomas*, 'discovering' a 'Secret Gospel of Mark', and producing a hypothetical and very early version of the *Gospel of Peter*, have not so far given themselves the far more rewarding task of working out what Mark's own ending might have contained.[22] Indeed, so strong has been the fashion for discovering hitherto unknown texts that one might feel quite comfortable about suggesting that Mark had a lost ending – were it not for the fact that that fashion is a sub-branch of a specifically anti-canonical movement within the study of early Christianity, so that this suggestion, probably the most likely of them all, is ruled out before it can start. But if

[21] I find an ally here in Rudolf Bultmann. In his famous *History of the Synoptic Tradition* (1968 [1921], 285 n. 2, with extra material at 441) he has a long note arguing, against E. Meyer in particular, that it is perfectly possible that a further ending was lost, and pointing out that this does not affect the question of whether vv. 1–8 form a complete pericope in themselves. Any who may be anxious about my forming an alliance with Bultmann will find relief in the following section.

[22] Crossan 1991, 415 asks whether 'Secret Mark' concluded with a story about the finding of an empty tomb, and answers 'of course it did'.

others are allowed to invent early Christian texts on the basis of fragments and hints, filling in lacunas and sketching out possibilities, I too may claim the right to do so – while recognizing, like Paul in 2 Corinthians 11, that such foolishness achieves rhetorical effect but little else.

I would not wish to construct an actual text. But since (on the mainstream view of synoptic relations) Matthew has been following Mark reasonably closely up to this point, especially in developing 28.5b–8a out of Mark 16.6–8a, it is not impossible that he continued to do so, and that we have in Matthew 28.9–20 an outline at least of what Mark 16 might have gone on to say.[23] Of course, just as Matthew 28.1–8 displays several major differences from Mark, we would expect the same to be true in the closing passage, and there are several characteristically Matthaean themes which we must assume that Matthew has added, not least the mountain (verse 16), the teaching of commandments (verse 20a), and the final 'I am with you' (20b), which so obviously echoes the Emmanuel prophecy of 1.23 and thus provides a neat Matthaean conclusion. But the outline may well be secure: initial meetings with the women and/or Peter; journeying to Galilee and seeing Jesus again there; final teaching and commissioning for worldwide mission. This shows, in fact, that the existing 'longer ending' may well not be too far, in outline, from what originally stood there, though in quite different language and with emphases for which Mark himself has not prepared us.

Naturally, we cannot know what might have come next. If Luke had broken off at 24.12 we should never have imagined the marvellous Emmaus Road story. If John had stopped with chapter 20 we should never have thought of the scene by the lakeshore. Perhaps Mark had treasures to reveal which are now lost for ever – unless, once more, for a happy archaeological accident. But the main point has been made: not that we know what the real ending of Mark contained, nor that we can be absolutely certain that there was such a thing, but that we can *not* be certain, by any manner of means, that there was *not* such a thing. Nor can we know, if the book really did end with 16.8, whether this was because Mark knew nothing more, or because he knew of stories and wanted to divert attention away from them, or because he knew that someone in the church would at this point tell the story they themselves knew. We must therefore resist the regular argument, all the more powerful for remaining mostly unspoken, to the effect that, since Mark has no 'appearance' stories, they have been made up at a later date. We know from 1 Corinthians 15, of course, that that is not the case. But it is good to be reminded that Mark, as it stands, cannot and must not be used to prove a negative. Mark's gospel and its ending remains an enigma. Part of the enigma is precisely whether he intended it to be as enigmatic as it now appears.

---

[23] If, instead, Mark used Matthew, as e.g. W. R. Farmer continued to argue to his dying day, the same conclusion would naturally follow.

3. From Story to History

So what are we to make of Mark's story? For one of the most influential critics of the twentieth century, the answer is emphatic:

> The story of the empty tomb is completely secondary . . . the point of the story is that the empty tomb proves the Resurrection . . . the story is an apologetic legend . . . Paul knows nothing about the empty tomb, which does not imply that the story was not yet in existence, but most probably that it was a subordinate theme with no significance for the official Kerygma . . . That is finally established by the fact that originally there was no difference between the Resurrection of Jesus and his Ascension; this distinction first arose as a consequence of the Easter legends, which eventually necessitated a special story of an ascension with heaven as an end of the risen Lord's earthly sojourn. But the story of the empty tomb has its place right in the middle of this development, for in it the original idea of exaltation is modified already.[24]

Bultmann has been followed by a host of lesser lights, who have added other points, among them the following. Paul does not mention the women. The original belief in the resurrection was a spiritual, in other words not a bodily, matter; Mark is starting to pull the idea of resurrection away from Daniel 12 (thought to refer to a 'spiritual' and disembodied existence) and towards the more physical interpretation of 2 Maccabees. Q makes no mention of the empty tomb. Nor does Acts. Therefore it is unlikely that the empty tomb has any earlier basis in history.[25]

These points cannot be answered from Mark itself. Mark, at this point, merely provides the playing field for a much larger contest. But the points that have been raised affect how we read Mark, and particularly whether we are likely to dismiss Mark's story of the women at the tomb as a mid-century legend, invented to support a recently invented idea of bodily resurrection, or whether we are prepared to consider that Mark tells us something at least about the historical events which gave rise to the belief of the early Christians. This part of the present chapter thus points beyond the immediate task – to understand the role of Mark in both witnessing to and contributing to the belief of the early Christians – and towards the task of our final Part.

First, the idea that there was originally no difference for the earliest Christians between resurrection and exaltation/ascension is a twentieth-century fiction, based on a misreading of Paul. Actually, Bultmann's account is slippery at the crucial point: though he says there was no difference between resurrection and ascension, what he means is that *there was no early belief in 'resurrection' at all*, since as we have seen the word 'resurrection' and its cognates was not used to denote a non-bodily extension of life in a heavenly realm, however glorious. Plenty of words existed

---

[24] Bultmann 1968 [1921], 290.
[25] e.g. A. Y. Collins 1993, 129–31.

to denote heavenly exaltation; 'resurrection' is never one of them. (One cannot at this point drive a wedge between Daniel 12 and 2 Maccabees 7; in the first century, as the rabbinic evidence bears witness, Daniel 12 was understood to mean bodily resurrection.) Bultmann therefore has to postulate – though he has covered up this large move – that at some point halfway through the first century someone who had previously believed that Jesus had simply 'gone to heaven when he died' began to use, to denote this belief, language which had never meant that before and continued not to mean it in either paganism, Judaism or Christianity thereafter, namely, the language of resurrection; and that, quite soon, other people who knew, as well they might, that resurrection meant bodies, and bodies meant empty tombs, began to invent and then transmit convenient apologetic stories about the empty tomb, of which Mark's is one. What is more, Bultmann has to assume that, though this theory about a risen body was a new thing within the already widely diverse Christian church, it took over almost at once, so that all traces of the original view – that Jesus was not raised from the dead, but simply 'went to heaven', albeit in an exalted capacity – have dropped out of historical sight.[26] Of course, one could easily invent a conspiracy theory to explain this in turn ('The wicked orthodox church suppressed this belief, but it re-emerged in the exciting, radical Nag Hammadi texts'[27]). But at this point the historian must protest. This theory is neither getting in the data, nor doing so with anything like simplicity, nor shedding light on any other areas. Why should we pursue it further? As with many other Bultmannian constructions, the sequence of moves required to support the hypothesis takes far more historical imagination than the thing Bultmann is trying to avoid.

But there is more. Bultmann and his followers are wrong to say that Paul knows nothing of the empty tomb.[28] They are wrong, too, to regard that motif as secondary. As we shall see later, it was always essential. Without it, however many appearances had been witnessed, and however many angels had said remarkable things, there is no chance that even the most devout of Jesus' former followers would have said he had been raised from the dead, or that any of the striking early Christian developments in resurrection belief would have taken place, or that anyone would have thought of Jesus as Messiah. Nor is it significant that Paul does not mention the women.[29] As for Q, since its most skilled and seasoned interpreters believe it had neither a passion narrative nor a resurrection narrative, the absence of an 'empty tomb'

---

[26] The material can be lined up in a different way. According to Perkins 1995, 730 the parallel between the transfiguration story and the Easter story means that the point of the empty tomb is that Jesus has been translated into heaven like Elijah and Moses. I believe this to be a multi-layered misunderstanding.

[27] cf. Robinson 1982.

[28] See 321 above.

[29] See again above, 326.

story is about as significant as the absence of a trombone part in a string quartet. But, as we saw earlier, if Q did exist, one of the things it knew about was a parallel between Jesus and Jonah. And, if I am right about the significance of that parallel, the point is this (more explicit in Matthew than in Luke): Jonah's 'resurrection' from the monster's belly set a pattern which Jesus would follow in his resurrection from 'the heart of the earth'.[30] As for Acts, its resurrection preaching has such a robust and bodily character, emphasizing the Psalms which speak of God's holy one 'not seeing corruption', and making a contrast between Jesus and David, who died and was buried and whose tomb can be checked, that it is hard to think that the empty tomb was not simply taken for granted. And, while on Acts, if Mark 16 is a late, apologetic invention, why does it not feature in the preaching in Acts itself, so often taken to reflect a more developed perspective?[31]

In particular, this theory asks us to believe something more or less impossible as we read Mark 16 and the other accounts which are supposedly derived from it (Bultmann says 'in reality there is but one story').[32] It asks us to swallow the idea that a key story was invented, some time in the 40s, 50s or 60s, whose purpose was apologetic, explaining the new-minted belief in Jesus' bodily resurrection, and that those who invented it for this apologetic purpose decided to call, as the principal witnesses, two or three women, led by Mary Magdalene of all people. I have written about this already in the previous chapter. Gerald O'Collins has pointed out that this theory actually marginalizes the women from the account, since, if it drew attention to them, its own serious weakness would emerge.[33]

The ruling theory, then, is full of improbabilities. However strange a story Mark may be telling, it cannot be explained as a mid-century legend. This does not mean that its every word is automatically proved; merely that the arguments used to suggest that the story is automatically *dis*proved fail at every turn. This conclusion is strongly supported by a study of the central emphases in the way Mark has told the story.

4. Easter Day from Mark's Point of View

There are many small points that could be made about the way Mark has told the story of the first Easter day. Our purpose here is to look at the general thrust of his narrative and highlight certain features which indicate what sort of a story Mark thinks it is.

---

[30] Above, ch. 9. This is of course controversial, but nothing much hinges on it, except for those who go to string concerts and grumble at the absence of wind music.
[31] So, rightly, A. Y. Collins 1993, 114.
[32] Bultmann 1972 [1921], 290 n. 2.
[33] O'Collins 1973, 16.

First, we note that the complete story is told from the perspective of the women. This is so in all the synoptic accounts, and granted the content – where the women are the only, or in Matthew's case the principal, actors – it could hardly be otherwise. But it means that if the story is fiction someone has taken the trouble to think into the situation of the two or three women and describe the whole incident, including their worries about rolling away the stone, from their point of view (had they been three men they would presumably have been strong enough to roll it away; according to 15.46 Joseph of Arimathea rolled it there by himself, and even if somebody helped him it does not sound as though it was too heavy for two or three men at most). Thus the women's reason for going (to anoint the body), their anxieties about the stone, their alarm at seeing the young man in the tomb, and their terror, panic and silent flight – all are narrated from their point of view. We see the whole scene through their eyes. This is sufficiently unusual in the gospel tradition to be considered remarkable.

Second, the emphasis throughout is on the unexpectedness both of the event as a whole and its different segments. Granted the various versions of the 'apologetic legend' theory, it is striking that the story bears no sign of anyone saying, 'Ah yes, we should have expected this.' Just the opposite. This failure to recognize the event as falling into an expected pattern fits with what *we* should expect, granted the Jewish hope of the time (resurrection being something that would happen, if at all, to all the righteous at once). It does not fit with the idea of a story being told as a careful explanation for a belief that has begun to be adopted in some quarters of the church.

Third, the discovery of the empty tomb is not presented as the historicizing 'explanation' of a belief in Jesus' resurrection, but as itself a puzzle in search of a solution. It is not that someone believes in Jesus' resurrection and now finds an empty tomb to confirm that belief; it is, rather, that they have found an empty tomb and are offered the startling and totally unexpected explanation that Jesus has been raised. The resurrection interprets the empty tomb, not vice versa. Nor, in the eight verses that we have (which, in the view of most who have advanced the argument I am opposing, are all we have), does Mark provide any further corroborating evidence. If one were writing this story to convince a sceptic, as the argument requires, not only would one have substituted a well-reputed man for the 'hysterical women' (as Celsus saw them); one would either have removed, or explained more fully, the strange young man in the tomb.

Fourth, the role of this young man is itself striking. Mark does not call him an angel, but Matthew does, and the role he plays in Mark is the equivalent of the role played by angels in apocalyptic visions. Mark, as we have seen, is writing an 'apocalyptic' type of book; but his point is that this is no vision, but startling reality.[34] The angel has come out of the dream and on to

---

[34] See again e.g. Ac. 12.9. On Mark as an 'apocalyptic' book see *NTPG* 390–96.

the stage, or rather into the tomb. To someone used to apocalyptic visions (reading accounts of them, not necessarily experiencing them) this scene has the effect you would get if a man who regularly watches a particular television programme were suddenly to find one of the actors from the programme sitting on the couch beside him. The angel is interpreting the apocalyptic event. But the interpretation, in the verses we have, does not give Jesus the titles 'son of god' and 'Messiah' which he receives in the earlier interpretative moments, at the baptism, Caesarea Philippi, the transfiguration, the trial and the cross. The angel's explanation that he is risen, though, is perhaps meant to tie in with those earlier moments. If Jesus has been raised, as he had said, all those earlier words have been proved true.

Fifth, the story implies that the disciples are to be rehabilitated (16.7). The singling out of Peter for special mention seems obviously designed to go with the tragic story of his denial of Jesus in 14.66–72, not, at the moment at least, to suggest anything about his leadership in the movement that was about to begin in a new way. This mention of Peter, with reference back to his denial, ties in closely with 14.26–31; there as here there is also mention of Jesus going before them to Galilee. At the end of verse 7 the angel declares that 'you will see him, as he told you', but nowhere in Mark's predictions of the resurrection has Jesus said explicitly 'you will see me'. This must be taken to be implied in 14.28 and the other passages; though Mark does not describe the disciples seeing Jesus, he recounts a promise that this will happen. Even within this brief and probably truncated account, then, the two elements emerge (the empty tomb and the seeing of Jesus) which we shall note as the key, non-negotiable historical bedrock required to explain why the early Christians believed what they believed about what had happened to Jesus (chapter 18 below).

Sixth, the narrative grammar of 16.1–8 indicates that it cannot simply have arisen as a separate unit of tradition.[35] It appears to be a separate unit on the surface, because the women's names, noted in 15.47, are repeated in 16.1 – unless indeed the point is that Mary Magdalene was accompanied by one Mary on the Friday night and by a different one, and by Salome as well, on the Sunday morning. But in any case, with the women as the principal 'subjects', the narrative as it stands does not conform to normal story-patterns. The women, we are told, come to the tomb to anoint the body. That, it seems, is the object of the whole action. The problem of which they are aware (the 'opponent' in narrative-analytical language) is how to roll away the stone. This then turns out to be no problem at all, but a different problem presents itself instead: the body has gone. Now we realize that their original intention (to anoint the body) was itself a 'problem', an 'opponent' in the technical sense, within a larger implicit narrative. Jesus' body had, after all, already been anointed for burial (14.8); they did not need to do it

---

[35] For the 'grammar' of stories cf. *NTPG* 69–80.

again.[36] The story we find in these verses only works as part of a different, larger one; the women are summoned to be 'helpers' *in someone else's drama*. Mark 16.1–8, analysed in terms of its narrative grammar, reveals itself not as a free-standing unity, but as part of a larger story. When we enquire what larger story this might be, the answer is obvious: it is the story in which the 'subject' is, at one level, Jesus, and at another level, Israel's god. The women are to be 'helpers' in this drama. It is vital that the male disciples find out quickly both that Jesus has been raised from the dead and that they will see him in Galilee, and they will not find this out unless someone tells them. This confirms what we have been arguing all along, that the story cannot simply have arisen as an apologetic legend to support a newly invented belief in Jesus' resurrection. It also suggests strongly that whoever wrote it down did not intend to leave the readers supposing that the women *never* said anything to anyone. This opens a final possibility.

The implicit story within which 16.1–8 finds its meaning cannot, for these reasons of narrative grammar, be intended to end in failure, in a silence with nobody telling anybody anything. After all, even at a common-sense level, the hearer is bound to ask how, if the women remained silent, anybody ever came to know what happened that morning. Two possible conclusions, which are not mutually exclusive, suggest themselves. Either, as we argued in the first main section of this chapter, the story did indeed carry on, with the women recovering their nerve, telling the disciples, and sending them on their way to Galilee and to a meeting with the risen Jesus. Or the final sentence of 16.8 has been systematically misread. Supposing this is the apologetic point in the story. Supposing Mark is faced with the question, not, 'How do you know Jesus is risen?' (answer: the empty tomb), but 'If the women found the tomb empty, why didn't all Jerusalem hear about it at once? Surely a group of hysterical women rushing about in the early morning would have had the news all over the city within minutes?' This is every bit as likely an apologetic scenario as those envisaged by Bultmann and his followers – in fact, more so. If nobody proclaimed Jesus as risen for a month or two, as Luke suggests, the question might very well arise: why did people not hear about this sooner? And Mark answers: they said nothing to anyone (implying, 'as they were making their way back into the city'), because they were afraid. Afraid, of course, because empty tombs and explanatory angels are enough to scare anyone. Afraid, too, because they had secretly been to the tomb to anoint the body of a condemned would-be Messiah, and they would rather this were not widely known.

Perhaps, after all, Mark is a gospel more of revelation than of concealment; or, at least, of a concealment designed to lead to revelation. But this does not make his story easy, straightforward or basic. There is no need for

---

[36] Matthew has simplified the story by not mentioning anointing or spices. John (19.39f.) has Joseph and Nicodemus anoint the body, so the problem does not arise.

the sophisticated critic to worry that studying the shortest gospel is in danger of becoming boring. Precisely because of what is concealed, and what is then revealed, this remains a dangerous book, revolutionary even, for the philosophies and politics of the twenty-first century as well as those of the first.

Chapter Fifteen

EARTHQUAKES AND ANGELS: MATTHEW

1. Introduction

Matthew goes his own way and poses his own problems. He has two stories, each of them in two parts, which mark him out from the other gospels: a pair of earthquakes, and a guard of soldiers who get bribed to tell tales. In the middle of all this, we have a story of the finding of the empty tomb, quite similar to Mark's though with significant differences. His narrative then concludes with a final commissioning on a mountain in Galilee.

We had better deal with the problems first, since they frame, colour and contextualize the central story. This will open the way for a consideration of Matthew's unique contribution to the early Christian understanding of Easter and its meaning.

2. Ruptured Earth and Rising Corpses

Matthew alone, in his account of Jesus' crucifixion, includes the extra-ordinary tale of an earthquake and what seems to be a localized but quite large-scale rising from the dead. Immediately after Jesus has breathed his last,

> Behold, the veil of the Temple was torn (*eschisthe*) in two, from top to bottom. And the earth shook, and the rocks were torn apart (*eschisthesan*), and the tombs were opened, and many bodies of the sleeping saints were raised, and going out of the tombs after his arising they went into the holy city and appeared to many.
>
> When the centurion and those with him, guarding Jesus, saw the earthquake and the things that happened, they were greatly afraid, and said, 'Truly, this man was God's son!'[1]

---

[1] Mt. 27.51–4.

This account presents all kinds of puzzles, not least at the level of what Matthew actually thinks is going on, and what he thinks it all means.[2] Is the earthquake intended to explain how the Temple veil was torn apart? Does he imply that the centurion and the others saw the tombs opening and corpses getting ready to emerge? Why does he say they only came out after Jesus' resurrection, two days later? What were they doing in between? And what happened to them next? Matthew did not suppose, did he, that they remained alive and resumed some kind of normal life? Did he think, then, that having 'appeared to many', they returned to their tombs, like the ghosts in *Ruddigore*, and lay down again?[3]

I do not think we can find certain answers to any of these questions – which may of course mean that they are, as we say, the wrong questions to be asking. But the obvious starting-point for assessing Matthew's meaning is to examine the biblical echoes which, like the sleepers themselves, are awoken in this account (though not, as we noted in chapter 13, in the Easter narrative itself).

The natural starting-point is Ezekiel 37.12–13, where YHWH declares to Israel in exile that he will 'open your graves and lead you out of your graves' (the wording in the LXX is close to Matthew 27.52–3), and bring Israel back to her own land. As we have seen, what started as metaphor for Ezekiel was already by the first century being understood as literal prediction, though still as part of the expectation of national restoration. Matthew (or his source; but Matthew's use of the Bible elsewhere suggests that this may well be his own work) seems to be echoing this entire tradition.

The two other prominent biblical 'resurrection' passages are also echoed here. Isaiah 26.19 predicts that the dead will arise, 'and those in the tombs shall be aroused', with the LXX again finding an echo in the Greek of Matthew 27.52–3. Daniel 12.2 speaks of 'many of those who sleep' being awoken and raised up, and though Matthew uses a different word for 'sleep' from either the LXX or Theodotion, his description of 'many bodies of the saints that slept' is probably a deliberate allusion to the passage, which he may after all have known best in Hebrew.[4]

What do these allusions tell us about Matthew's intention? There are basically four options.

1. He may know a tradition which speaks of these strange happenings, and is retelling it in such a way as to give a biblically alert reader a sense of

---

[2] On the question, see, in addition to the commentaries, Senior 1976; Wenham 1981; Denaux 2002.

[3] See Davies and Allison 1988–97, 3.634, pointing out that in *Asc. Isa.* 9.17f. they ascend with Jesus; in *Ac. Pil.* 17.1 they return to earthly life and die again subsequently; in Theophylact, writing a thousand years later, some of them are reported to be still alive.

[4] See the analysis of Troxel 2002, who argues that Mt. has composed the scene, on the basis of *1 En.* 93.6, not to signal the dawn of the new age, but to lead to the centurion's confession; Denaux 2002, 133–5, disagrees.

their meaning: this is the real return from exile, the dawn of the new age, and perhaps even the harrowing of hell.

2. This may be Matthew's vivid way of speaking of the crucifixion of Jesus as the apocalyptic act of Israel's god. He may have invented this story with the intention, not that it would be taken as a set of events, but that it would be seen as a dramatic metaphor for what happened at the cross.[5]

3. Matthew may perhaps know the tradition we find in the *Gospel of Peter*, in which three men come out of the tomb, followed by the cross, which answers 'Yes' to the question, 'Have you preached to those who sleep?' His story may be a variation on this: this is the moment when 'the resurrection' happened, at least in principle.[6]

4. Matthew, or his tradition, may simply have invented a story designed to fit with, and 'fulfil', Ezekiel 37, Isaiah 26, Zechariah 14 and Daniel 12, or other subsequent Jewish texts.[7]

We may take these in reverse order. The fourth option is not particularly likely. There are obvious echoes, as we have seen. But it would be strange for a first-century Jew to imply, as these biblical resonances would, that the final national restoration of Israel had occurred, or that the general resurrection had itself happened, when clearly neither of them had. Although Daniel 12.2 speaks of 'many' of the sleepers awakening, allowing at least for the interpretation that this might be a limited number rather than all of the righteous, it would be straining credibility to think of Matthew, or his source, inventing a story about 'many' – presumably a few dozen at most – rising from the dead as though this were to constitute a 'fulfilment' of Daniel or Ezekiel which would somehow supplement the fulfilment which the evangelist, in company with the whole early church, saw in the resurrection of Jesus himself. There is no reason elsewhere in second-Temple Judaism to suppose that anyone imagined that Ezekiel, Isaiah and Daniel would be fulfilled by this kind of event.[8]

The possibility that Matthew knew the *Gospel of Peter* is, in my opinion, remote. Apart from the strenuous advocacy of J. D. Crossan, only a handful of scholars have suggested such a thing.[9] In particular, Crossan's interpretation of the 'cross' that follows the three men out of the tomb as a cruciform procession of the redeemed seems to me to strain the reading of the text quite unbearably; his suggestion that it thus belongs in the same strand of tradition, or indeed theology, as Matthew's multiple raising of dead saints is very far-fetched. It is much easier historically to envisage the *Gospel of*

---

[5] McDonald 1989, 91: the earthquake is 'Matthew's code for an apocalyptic act of God'.

[6] Crossan 1998, 517f.

[7] On Ezek. 37 cf. e.g. Grassi 1965; Cavallin 1974, 110. For Zech. see e.g. Allison 1985, 42–5; Aus 1994, 118–30.

[8] cf. Troxel 2002 for the various possibilities.

[9] See above, 592–6.

Peter as a later text, dependent on both Matthew and 1 Peter as well as other texts, than to see it as a source for them or any other of the canonical writings.[10]

The second option is not particularly likely. There was no reason within pre-Christian Judaism to understand the death of a would-be Messiah as precipitating the general resurrection, or even a small anticipation of it such as this seems to be.[11] Even in a more developed Christian tradition, one might expect such a thing to happen, if at all, as a result of Easter itself, not the crucifixion – though of course Matthew does give us the awkward two-day time-lag between the bodies being aroused and their emerging for a walk around Jerusalem, and this may have been a way of bringing a strange tradition more into line with perceived theological sense.

But this is already pushing us towards the first option: that Matthew knows a story of strange goings-on around the time of the crucifixion, and is struggling to tell it so that (1) it includes the desired biblical allusions, (2) it makes at least some minimal historical sense (the earthquake explains the tearing of the Temple veil, the opening of tombs, and particularly the centurion's comment), and (3) it at least points towards, even if it does not exactly express, the theological meaning Matthew is working towards: that with the combined events of Jesus' death and resurrection the new age, for which Israel had been longing, has begun.[12] There may even be an allusion, here and in 28.2, to the predictions of Jesus in 24.7; but that may just be coincidence.

Matthew knows perfectly well, of course, that the bodies he speaks about were not still walking around, and he makes no attempt to explain what happened to them. He knows equally well that the church is still awaiting the final, complete general resurrection when, again with a sideways glance towards Daniel 12, the righteous will shine like the sun in the kingdom of their father (13.43). In other words, he is not saying that this really was the great general resurrection; it was a strange semi-anticipation of it.

Of one thing we may be sure. This story was not written in order to embody or express the theology of Paul or the other New Testament writers. Though Hebrews speaks of women 'receiving their dead by resurrection', and of others who accepted torture and death because they were 'looking for a better resurrection', neither that writer nor any others referred to such events in connection with Jesus' own death. And Paul is quite clear: 'those

---

[10] See now Troxel 2002, 41. The theme of Jesus raising others – perhaps all the pre-Christian righteous – to new life is developed in several works from the second century onwards: e.g. *Od. Sol.* 42.11; Ign. *Magn.* 9.2; Iren. frag. 26, making the link with the present passage. See further Bauckham 1998, 244.

[11] Senior 1976, 326f. speaks of an 'implicit soteriology'.

[12] Troxel 2002 is right that this is not the immediate meaning in context. Yet, for Matthew, the centurion's confession, which Troxel rightly sees as the main point, is itself related to the inaugurating of the new age.

who belong to the Messiah' will be raised, as a single event, at his *parousia*.[13]

Matthew is very unlikely to have wanted, by telling this story, to upstage his own account of Jesus' resurrection, and of course the picture of the latter event in chapter 28 has several features which distinguish the risen Jesus dramatically from the awakened sleepers of chapter 27. But the accounts have this in common: that on the Sunday morning, as well as the Friday afternoon, there was a great earthquake, which resulted in the opening of a tomb. Actually, the way Matthew has told the latter story it looks as though the arrival of the angel, and the rolling away of the stone, was the *cause* of the second earthquake, rather than, as in 27.51–2, the result of it.[14] Some, of course, have suggested that there was actually one earthquake, not two, but the way Matthew has told the story it looks as though he means the incidents to be separate.[15]

It is impossible, and for our purposes unnecessary, to adjudicate on the question of historicity. Things that we are told by one source only, when in other respects the sources are parallel, may be suspect, especially when events like earthquakes were (as 24.7 makes clear) part of the stock in trade of apocalyptic expectation. But it remains the case that the events Matthew describes in 27.51–3, as well as being without parallel in other early Christian sources, are without precedent in second-Temple expectation, and we may doubt whether stories such as this would have been invented simply to 'fulfil' prophecies that nobody had understood this way before. This is hardly a satisfactory conclusion, but it is better to remain puzzled than to settle for either a difficult argument for probable historicity or a cheap and cheerful rationalistic dismissal of the possibility. Some stories are so odd that they may just have happened. This may be one of them, but in historical terms there is no way of finding out.

3. The Priests, the Guards and the Bribe

The other story which spills over in Matthew's gospel from the crucifixion narrative to the Easter account involves the chief priests getting together with the Pharisees to go to Pilate and request a guard on Jesus' tomb. This is of considerable interest, not so much for its own sake (though that is interesting too) but for the sake of what it tells us about the story-telling motives of the early church.

[13] Heb. 11.35; 1 Cor. 15.23.
[14] Mt. 28.2: 'Behold, there was a great earthquake; *for* an angel of the Lord came down from heaven, and came and rolled back the stone and sat upon it.'
[15] Some (e.g. Troxel 2002, 36, 47, citing others) have suggested that 'after his raising' in Mt. 27.53 must be a later addition, but this is scarcely a satisfactory solution to a problematic passage.

The tale begins on the sabbath itself. Jesus' body has been buried on the Friday afternoon by Joseph of Arimathea, watched by Mary Magdalene 'and the other Mary' (27.61). Then, on the sabbath,

> the chief priests and the Pharisees went together to Pilate and said, 'Sir, we remember that that deceiver, while he was alive, said, "I will be raised after three days." So give orders that the tomb be made safe until the third day, in case his disciples should come and steal him and say to the people, "He has been raised from the dead," and the last deception will be worse than the first.'
> 'You have a guard,' replied Pilate. 'Go and make it as safe as you know how.'
> So off they went and secured the tomb, sealing the stone and posting a guard.[16]

Historically speaking, we raise our eyebrows a bit at the apparently easy collaboration of the Pharisees and chief priests, and of the two together with Pilate, but there is nothing intrinsically implausible about that side of the story. It is perhaps more surprising that all this would be done on a sabbath, but that too is not beyond possibility, especially in an emergency. What is interesting is the description of Jesus in 27.63: 'that deceiver' (*ekeinos ho planos*). This ties in with a regular Jewish charge against Jesus, echoing various biblical warnings about false prophets and teachers who might 'deceive the people'. It is just conceivable that an early Christian, making up this story, would put such a description of Jesus on the lips of the Jewish leaders, since it may well have been quite widely known that this charge was near the heart of the accusation against him. But it seems more likely that it goes back to some kind of well-rooted memory.[17]

The story of the guard continues between the appearance of Jesus to the women in Jerusalem and that to the Eleven in Galilee:

> As the women were going away, behold, some of the guard went into the city and told the chief priests everything that had happened. They got together with the elders and concocted a plan that they would give a large sum of money to the soldiers, telling them, 'Say, "His disciples came by night and stole him while we were asleep"; and if this is overheard by the governor, we will explain things to him and keep you out of trouble.' So they took the money and did as they had been told. And this story is circulated among the Jews to this day.[18]

There is nothing improbable in this narrative; indeed, it makes good sense all round. But when we put the two halves of the story together, the plan to set a guard in case the disciples steal the body, and the tale that, despite the guard, the disciples had managed to do so none the less, some interesting questions emerge about the telling of such an overall account within the early Christian community.

---

[16] Mt. 27.62–6.
[17] For the charge, see Jn. 7.12, 47; cp. Mt. 9.34; Lk. 23.5, 14; more details and discussion in *JVG* 439f.
[18] Mt. 28.11–15.

The story, obviously, is part of an apologia for the bodily resurrection of Jesus. It is an attempt to ward off any suggestion that the disciples had in fact stolen the body, which must have seemed the most natural explanation for the emptiness of the tomb. But, while the historian is always cautious about accepting obviously apologetic tales, there are further considerations which make it very unlikely that this one was actually invented from scratch within the Christian community.

For a start, it is implausible to suppose that the whole story would have been invented in the first place, let alone told and finally written down, unless there was already a rumour going around that the disciples had indeed stolen the body. If nobody had suggested such a thing, it is difficult to imagine the Christians putting the idea into people's heads by making up tales that said they had.

Furthermore, a charge such as this would never have arisen unless it was already well known, or at the very least widely supposed, that there was an empty tomb, and/or a missing body, requiring an explanation. If the empty tomb were itself a late legend, it is unlikely that people would have spread stories about body-stealing, and hence that Christians would have employed the dangerous tactic of reporting such stories in order to refute them.

Third, the story presupposes that for the chief priests, the Pharisees and presumably anyone else involved, the reported prediction that Jesus would 'rise again after three days' must refer to something that would happen to his corpse. If anybody had supposed that 'rising again' meant that Jesus' soul had gone to heaven while his body remained in the tomb, or anything even vaguely like that, there would have been no need for a guard or a stone, or for stories and counter-stories to be circulated.[19]

Finally, the telling of the story indicates well enough that the early Christians knew that the charge of stealing the body was one they were always likely to face – and that it was preferable to tell the story of how the accusation had arisen, even at the risk of putting ideas into people's heads, rather than leave the accusation unanswered.[20]

For our present purposes, the main thing is not to argue that the story, in both its parts, is historically true in all respects, though as we have seen it is unlikely to have been invented as a late legend. The point is that this sort of story could only have any point at all in a community where the empty tomb was an absolute and unquestioned datum. Had there been varieties of Christianity that knew nothing of such a thing – in other words, if Bultmann was right to say that the empty tomb was itself a late apologetic fiction – the rise

---

[19] It will not do to say (Evans 1970, 85) that the story is about a tomb and a body, not about resurrection. As the story makes clear, the reason the tomb and the body matter is because of a reported promise that Jesus would rise again on the third day.

[20] Justin (*Dial.* 108) reports that the story was still being told by anti-Christian Jewish apologists in the mid-second century. A somewhat convoluted account of how the story came into existence is offered by Weren 2002.

both of stories of body-snatching and of counter-stories to explain why such accusations were untrue is simply incredible. In the Bultmannian scheme, by contrast, we are asked to accept a complex theory which makes Matthew's story look extremely simple and obvious: (1) Christianity began without any belief in Jesus' bodily resurrection; (2) early Christians began (unwisely, it seems) to use 'resurrection' language to speak of Jesus' spiritual or heavenly exaltation; (3) other early Christians, misunderstanding this to refer to bodily resurrection, began to tell back-up stories about the discovery of an empty tomb (with scatty women as the principal witnesses); (4) Jewish onlookers, anxious about the rise of Christianity, believed these (fictitious) accounts of the empty tomb and began to circulate the story about the disciples stealing the body; (5) yet other early Christians, discovering that such stories were circulating, made up a convenient tradition which traced them back to the priests, the guard and the bribe; (6) this tradition found its way into Matthew's possession, and he separated it carefully into two fragments and wove it neatly into the closing scenes of his gospel. And all this would have to have happened within sixty years at the outside, dating Matthew around 90, which is as late as most scholars would go; less if the date is earlier, as it might well be.

Of course, we could collapse (4) and (5) into one by having no such Jewish stories existing except ones that early Christians made up in order that, by 'refuting' them, they might ward off a potential accusation. Or we could collapse (4), (5) and (6) into one if we said that Matthew himself was responsible both for the fiction about the Jewish stories and for the fiction about a 'true' version which explained them.

If any historian finds this sequence more probable than the one which Matthew offers, I can only admire their ability to believe such remarkable things. But I suspect that if even Rudolf Bultmann were to find himself as a member of a jury he would be more prepared to believe a story like the one Matthew tells than a story like the five- or six-stage development of tradition that must be told if we are to declare that Matthew's is impossible.

Two final notes about the story of the guard. First, it is noticeable that Matthew's priests have somehow got to know about Jesus' predictions of rising after three days. These were always in private with the disciples (16.21; 17.23; 20.19); unless we are to suppose that Judas revealed this secret as part of his betrayal, the only other hint of such a thing would have to be the accusation that he had spoken of destroying the Temple and rebuilding it in three days (26.61). There is no particular reason for a late apologetic account to accredit the priests with this knowledge; all sides would assume, in any case, that after that period the corpse would begin to putrefy.[21] It looks as though this, too, goes back to an early tradition.

---

[21] Jn. 11.39; cf. mYeb. 16.3; Semahot 8.1.

Second, Matthew's description of the stone and the seal offers another biblical echo, once more from the book of Daniel. In Daniel 6.17 (6.18 LXX) King Darius has a stone laid over the mouth of the lions' den, with Daniel inside it, and he seals it with his own seal and that of his nobles, leaving Daniel, overnight, to an apparently certain fate. In the morning, of course, the king returns and discovers Daniel safe and sound; there is no mention of taking away the stone, let alone of angels and earthquakes. But someone as alert as Matthew was for biblical echoes can surely not have missed the allusion. Jesus goes to his grave as one who, like Daniel, has been faithful to Israel's god despite all the forces ranged against him; and, like Daniel, his god will vindicate him. He is, after all, the true 'son of man' who, as in the next chapter of the book of Daniel, is to be exalted after being apparently prevailed over by the monsters.[22]

4. Tomb, Angels, First Appearance (28.1–10)

Matthew's account of the first Easter may well, as we have seen, be dependent on that of Mark.[23] But it bears all the signs of his own retelling. One of his favourite little words, *idou*,[24] occurs no fewer than six times in the story, four of which come in this first section (verses 2, 7, 7, 9; the remaining two are found in verses 11 and 20).[25] He introduces the story with a formal time-notice, longer than anything in the other three accounts. The women go, not to bring spices but simply 'to see the tomb' (28.1); does he, perhaps, think that they are doing what some rabbinic texts recommend, coming to inspect the tomb after three days to see if the body is truly dead?[26] They do not go into the tomb as they do in Mark; perhaps Matthew was mindful of purity rules according to which entering a tomb with a corpse inside would have rendered them impure.[27] Matthew has the women confronted not simply by

[22] Dan. 7.13f., 17f., 21f., 27. Cf. *JVG* 360–65, 510–19. Kellerman 1991, 184f., in a suggestive meditation on the political significance of Mt.'s story, draws attention to the Dan. parallel (though not with all the meaning I have suggested), and then goes on to point out that, when the guards are bribed, 'now the seal is on their lips. In counterpoint to the Great Commission, they are paid handsomely to advertise a lie . . . to bury again the truth.'

[23] Though hardly 'slavishly', as Evans 1970, 85 suggests; see 589–91 above.

[24] Corresponding to the Hebrew *hinneh*, 'behold'.

[25] Mt. has 62 occurrences of *idou*, as against 8 in Mk. Lk., which is slightly longer than Mt., but similarly fond of biblical language, has 56 occurrences, none of which are parallel to those in Mt. 28. The word is often translated 'suddenly', presumably because 'behold' is archaic and without direct equivalent in contemporary English. But strictly speaking it conveys no temporal sense, but rather introduces an important or striking fact. A colloquial equivalent might be 'Guess what!'

[26] Semahot 8.1.

[27] cf. mOhol. *passim*. As Danby explains (1933, 649 n. 3), this stems from the reading of Num. 19.14 according to which a person or utensil can contract a seven-day corpse-uncleanness by being under the same roof (or 'tent'; *oholoth* means 'tents') as a corpse.

a 'young man' as in Mark, or 'two men in dazzling clothes' as in Luke, but by a palpable angel, looking like lightning, and with clothes white as snow.[28] There is a second earthquake (verse 2, following that in 27.51), perhaps even caused by the angel (see above). We have a long angelic speech, parallel in many ways to those in Mark and Luke but fuller. The women go to tell the disciples, without any suggestion that they say nothing to anyone (Mark) or that their report seems like an idle tale (Luke) – though, to be fair, Matthew fails to mention their actual carrying out of the commission one way or another. On meeting Jesus, the women worship (verse 9, echoing another favourite Matthaean term).[29] Though the angel instructs the women to tell the disciples that they will see Jesus in Galilee, the women themselves (like Mary Magdalene in John) see him then and there, in Jerusalem. Even in so short a story, at almost every point Matthew remains stubbornly independent. Whatever his sources, he has made them his own.

This makes it all the more remarkable that he has not done more. As we pointed out in chapter 13, he has not introduced what we might have expected in terms of biblical and theological allusions and implications. The echoes of the Old Testament continue to the very last verse of chapter 27, but in chapter 28 they are almost non-existent.[30] Instead, we have, as in Mark, two Marys at the tomb; a strange heavenly messenger, explaining why the tomb is empty, and giving the women instructions; and the women going off in haste and fear. And we must ask, with Matthew as with the other accounts: granted that Matthew has felt free to make this his own, and apparently to embroider the angelic and apocalyptic elements, why has he not felt free to make the story more convincing, for instance by having at least one male witness meet Jesus (as in another branch of tradition)?[31]

We have in Matthew 28.1–10, in other words, a story which belongs firmly, in this mode of its telling, within Matthew's gospel. It exhibits many traces of his style. But it is still emphatically the same story, the same *unlikely* story, indeed a story which is so unlikely and improbable that one is astonished yet again at its being told not only as very early tradition but as the climax of a long, complex and artful literary work. The best conclusion we can draw is that, though Matthew felt free to tell the story in his own way, he did not feel free to invent a new one. Precisely because we can see

---

[28] cf. the variant reading in Mt. 17.2, where most MSS read 'white as light'.

[29] 'Worship' of Jesus in Mt.: 2.2, 8, 11; 8.2; 9.18; 14.33; 15.25; 20.20; 28.17. Mk. has two occurrences (5.6; 15.19, the latter being the soldiers' mockery), and Lk. one (24.52), none of which is parallel to anything in Mt.

[30] Unless we count the echoes of Dan. 7.9 (the Ancient of Days, with clothes white as snow), and the more distant ones of 10.6 (the angel whose face is like lightning), in the description of the angel; but these are not strong (snow and lightning are obvious images for whiteness and dazzling brightness), and in any case they cancel one another out (Mt. can scarcely have intended to imply that the angel was simultaneously playing both those roles).

[31] Lk. 24.34.

his hand at work in so much editing, we can also see where he was bound to restrain editorial licence. This was the story all the early Christians knew.[32] Had they been free to make up their own they might have done a superficially better job. They were not, and did not.

5. On the Mountain in Galilee (28.16–20)

Mark's angel reminds the women that Jesus had said the disciples were to go to Galilee (16.7, referring to 14.28). Matthew has a parallel to Mark 14.28 at 26.32, but his angel does not remind the women of this; instead, he simply tells them to instruct the disciples to go to Galilee to see Jesus there (28.7). (Neither he nor Jesus mention a meeting on a mountain, so the comment in verse 16 about Jesus having directed them to go to one remains another unexplained Matthaean puzzle.) This brings us to Matthew's dense closing scene.

Like the earlier one, this paragraph has Matthew's own fingerprints all over it.[33] But the fact that this was also true of 28.1–10, while that passage at the same time told substantially the same story as Mark 16.1–8 and Luke 24.1–12, should make us pause before suggesting, as one might otherwise have done, that this is a free Matthaean composition with no roots in earlier tradition. Some have suggested that this is the time when the 'five hundred at once' of 1 Corinthians 15.6 saw Jesus all together, though it is noticeable that Matthew only mentions 'the Eleven' (28.16). If, then, this is a different event, this is the only mention of it, so we cannot gain historical binocular vision of it. However, as frequently in ancient history, a single source needs to be evaluated on its own merits, not (as often happens in gospel criticism) dismissed because it lacks corroborating parallels.

Like the commissioning scenes in Luke and John, Matthew's final scene concentrates on the instructions the risen Jesus gives to the disciples for their new worldwide mission, which has been in view all along even though the gospel strategy demanded that work be restricted during Jesus' lifetime to 'the lost sheep of the house of Israel'.[34] There is, however, no mention of the

---

[32] Perkins 1984, 135, 137 suggests that the early traditions of the resurrection were auditory, not visionary, and thus that stories such as Mt.'s must have been later. This seems to me without foundation.

[33] Matthaean themes stated one last time include: discipleship, revelation in Galilee, the mountain, worship, authority, teaching, the 'close of the age', and the promise 'I am with you' which evokes the opening angelic promise that Jesus will be the Emmanuel, 'God with us' (1.23). See e.g. McDonald 1989, 93 n. 18. There may be a hint of a 'new Moses' theme, with Jesus on the mountain looking out into the promised land, which is now of course the entire world.

[34] cf. Mt. 10.5f.; 15.24; Evans 1970, 88, 90 is surprised at this widening of the commission, changing the earlier rule. But see too 2.11; 8.11–13, with *JVG* 308–10. On the question of 'all nations' or 'all Gentiles' see Perkins 1984, 134, 147 n. 83.

forgiveness of sins, as in Luke and John, unless it is seen by implication in the command to baptize. Rather, the Eleven are to be teachers, disciple-makers.

But the main emphasis of this closing paragraph is upon who Jesus is now revealed to be, a point which belongs closely with the argument of chapter 12 above. Jesus has been granted 'all authority in heaven and on earth' – virtually identical in phraseology to the kingdom-clause in the Matthaean version of the Lord's Prayer.[35] This, it seems, is how the prayer is being answered; this, in other words, is how the kingdom is coming, how the will of the 'Father' is being done. The significance of the resurrection, as far as Matthew is concerned, is that Jesus now holds the role that had been marked out for the Messiah in Psalms 2, 72 and 89, which became concentrated in such imagery-laden figures as the 'son of man' in Daniel 7 and the texts which developed that line of thought. This scene, in other words, is not an 'exaltation' scene which only becomes a 'resurrection' scene because of its place in the narrative.[36] The worldwide commission Jesus gives the disciples depends directly upon his possessing all authority in heaven and on earth, within the kingdom that is now well and truly inaugurated. The only explanation for this messianic authority on the one hand, and this kingdom-fulfilment on the other, is that Jesus has been raised from the dead.[37]

The strongest mark of authenticity in this paragraph is the jarring note: 'but some doubted' (verse 17). Matthew only has the Eleven there; how many is 'some'? Two or three? Which ones? Were their doubts resolved? What form did their doubts take? We want to know, and again Matthew leaves us in the dark. We can be sure, however, that this strange comment would not have occurred to someone telling the story as a pure fiction, to reinforce faith and mission, some time towards the end of the century. If even some of Jesus' closest disciples had doubts, what hope, a reader might think, would there be for anyone else? Nor will it do to suggest that Matthew is hinting at divisions between different groups of disciples, or different leaders who emerged from the Eleven. If that had been so, we might have

---

[35] Mt. 6.10; cf. too *Did.* 8.2.

[36] Against e.g. Evans 1970, 83. Carnley 1987, 18 takes a similar line: Mt.'s final scene, with Jesus enjoying 'a heavenly status and authority', shows that they simply involve 'the manifestation of the raised and exalted Christ "from heaven", as it were'. The phrase 'as it were' (which Carnley repeats in similar contexts at 25, 143, 199 and 242!) indicates uneasiness, as we might expect granted the implausibility of the argument as a description of what Mt. intended to write about. Carnley has not noticed that Mt.'s Jesus has authority *on earth* as well as in heaven. His theory about heavenly manifestations, however, plays a large part in his own reconstruction (234–42) of a hypothetical early tradition which is (as it were) swallowed up in the gospel resurrection narratives we now have.

[37] Against Evans 1970, 83. On the authority of the 'son of man' in Mt. cf. e.g. 9.6, 8; and cp. 11.27; 21.23–7. The link between the universal Lordship of Jesus and the Gentile mission, both firmly rooted in Jewish messianic expectation, is entirely missed by Bornkamm (see Evans 1970, 89).

expected some names. How else could the story serve to highlight them, and perhaps warn against them? We are given none. This forces us to look for another explanation. One obvious one is that here, as in the other canonical resurrection narratives, the risen Jesus both was and was not 'the same' as he had been before. There was something different about him, something which his closest friends and followers could not put their finger on at the time, something which seemed to enable him to do different things. Matthew's Jesus does not allay their doubts and fears, as do John's Jesus and, still more obviously, Luke's. He allows the tension to remain in the air. This was Jesus all right, but there was a mystery about him which even those who knew him best were now unable to penetrate.

Among the surprises of this paragraph is the trinitarian naming of Israel's god in verse 19. This is by no means the earliest such formula in the New Testament, of course (one thinks of passages like 2 Corinthians 13.13 and Galatians 4.4–7), so it would be illegitimate to argue for a late date on this basis alone.[38] The trinitarian formula has become so entrenched in church tradition and particularly liturgy, largely because of this passage, that the phrase can acquire a 'developed' feel, as though it had taken a large step towards, or had even been generated within, the christological and trinitarian dogmas of the fourth and fifth centuries, a judgment which the parallels in Paul and elsewhere would prove spurious. Once again, as with our discussion in chapter 12, we glimpse in early Christian theology the further dimension of the revelation, through the resurrection, of Jesus as Israel's Messiah: precisely as Messiah, he is the world's true lord, sharing the authority which Israel's god has said he will not share with another. And the mode through which that authority is now to be exercised is the Spirit.

The command to baptize, together with the mention of the Spirit, takes us back to John's baptism, where it was promised that the coming one would baptize with the Spirit. This implies that we are to see the movement initiated with the command of the risen Jesus as the worldwide extension of the movement of covenant renewal that began with John, and is now continuing under the authority of the risen Jesus and in the power of the Spirit – as, in fact, in Acts.[39] In Acts, baptism is normally 'in' or 'into' the name of Jesus;[40] in Paul, it is 'into the Messiah' (*eis Christon*).[41] Just as these are not mutually exclusive, but highlight different features of the same complex event, so we should not suppose that Matthew's trinitarian naming of the true god, and the command to baptize in that name, would be understood by

---

[38] Granted, the father, son and Spirit here are not exactly paralleled in Paul; the two passages quoted give lord–god–Spirit and god–son–Spirit. However, since it is clear that one of Paul's central understandings of Israel's god is that he is the one of whom Jesus is the son, this difference is more apparent than real. Cf. too e.g. 1 Cor. 12.4–6 (Spirit-lord-god).

[39] Mt. 3.11; Ac. 1.5; 11.16.

[40] cf. Ac. 2.38; 8.16; 10.48; 19.3–5.

[41] e.g. Rom. 6.3; Gal. 3.27.

him or other early Christians as being opposed to the practice which Acts describes and Paul reflects. The point is that the risen Jesus is now at the heart of the early Christian picture of the living god. Baptism, with all its exodus-symbolism dating back to John's baptism, is the mode of entry into the family of this god, the family of the renewed covenant. And, as more explicitly in Paul (Romans 6, Colossians 2), baptism is linked in particular to what the living god has accomplished in Jesus' resurrection.

The final promise, that Jesus will be with his people 'until the close of the age' (*heos tes synteleias tou aionos*), belongs closely within the 'two-age' structure of chronology which we have seen to be characteristic of mainstream Pharisaic/rabbinic Judaism, and also of early Christianity, particularly Paul.[42] The point here is that the 'age to come' has now been launched with Jesus' resurrection, and that the risen Jesus represents and embodies this new age, and hence becomes the human bridge between it and the present one. His promise to be 'with you always' is thus at the same time the fulfilment of the Emmanuel promise, and with it of YHWH's promise to be with even a small group of worshippers as though they were actually in the Temple itself.[43] It is also the sign that in him the eschaton has come to birth, so that his people are guaranteed safe passage through the present age and into the long-awaited age to come.

6. Matthew and the Resurrection: Conclusion

Matthew's rich exposition of what he conceives to be the direct outworking of the fact of Jesus' resurrection thus has many points of contact with the various early Christian traditions we studied in Part III. It would be surprising if it were not so. And yet he comes across as his own man. His language and imagery belong with the rest of his gospel. He has not obviously imbibed the resurrection theology of Paul or Revelation. He has not invented resurrection stories from scratch; the arguments mounted in chapter 13 rule that out. He has retold them, shaping and highlighting them so that they belong at the close of the narrative and theological logic of his gospel; but it is impossible that they were simply manufactured out of whole cloth some time in the late first century. Through these retold stories, Matthew gets us to see Jesus fulfilling at last the promises to Abraham and David, the promise of return from exile, the fulfilment of all that Moses had been and said.[44] All of this is present, not as though it were derived from Paul or anyone else, but as though Matthew himself had mulled over the early stories for a long

---

[42] On 'the close of the age' in Mt., cf. 13.39f., 49; 24.3 (where it is linked with the fall of Jerusalem and the *parousia* of Jesus). See too Heb. 9.26; *1 En.* 16.1; 4 Ezra 7.113.

[43] cf. Mt. 1.23; 18.20 with mAb. 3.2, 6 (see *JVG* 297). There are deep biblical roots to the promise of YHWH's being 'with' his people; cf. e.g. Dt. 31.3–6; Hag. 1.12–15.

[44] For these and other Matthaean themes cf. *NTPG* 384–90.

time and retold them in this form while allowing them to remain, essentially, early stories.

Matthew has written, through and through, a book of Jewish history and theology. His whole thesis is that Israel's god has been at work in Jesus, climactically and decisively. As I argued in the first volume, there is no way that we can think of this divine activity, within such a Jewish framework, except in relation to historical events.[45] Matthew believed, every bit as much as did Paul, that Jesus really did rise from the dead, leaving an empty tomb behind him. The stories he tells in chapter 28, though every bit as strange as those told by his fellow gospel-writers, cannot have been intended either by him or his sources to be taken in the sense of 'this is a metaphorical way of speaking of the victory of the cross,' or 'read these tales and you will sense the spiritual presence of Jesus.' These narratives, though heavy with significance at many levels, are not simply built up from that significance to look like history. They are not all icing and no cake. Unless Matthew had believed that there was a real cake, there would have been no significance, nothing to decorate in the first place.

Equally, Matthew, like the others, describes a Jesus who comes and goes, appears and disappears, and is doubted at the very end by some of his close and obedient associates. Matthew never describes a parting moment, but clearly there has been one; as we noted in chapter 13, Matthew's Jesus will be 'with you always', but Matthew does not now expect his readers to meet Jesus on a mountain in Galilee as the Eleven had done. His risen Jesus was sufficiently 'bodily' not only to leave an empty tomb behind him but to generate a complex controversy, between Christians and their opponents, about how such a thing could have come about, which would be inexplicable unless both sides knew that the claim concerned bodily resurrection. (Verses 11–15 are, in other words, incomprehensible except as a reflection of some kind of actual debate; but such a debate is itself incomprehensible except as the result of a claim, not about a disembodied 'life after death', however glorious, but about bodily resurrection.) But Matthew's Jesus is at the same time sufficiently different (words fail us as they did the early Christians; once again we fall back on the word 'transphysical', not to solve the mystery but at least to give it a name) to appear and disappear in unpredictable ways, and to be doubted. As in John, indeed, the fact of doubt becomes in itself a powerful reinforcement of faith.

We shall come to John presently, where we shall find both more explanation and more mystery. But first we turn to Luke, completing the synoptic resurrection accounts with the longest and most artistic of them all.

---

[45] cf. *NTPG* 396–403.

Chapter Sixteen

BURNING HEARTS AND BROKEN BREAD: LUKE

1. Introduction

Luke 24 is a small masterpiece, designed as the closing scene for a large-scale work of art. Whether or not, as tradition fancifully suggested, the author of the third gospel was himself a painter, his skill in sketching verbal pictures is unmatched in the New Testament, and his resurrection chapter displays it in full measure.[1] It is, of course, one of two Lukan descriptions of the risen Jesus, the other being Acts 1; the present chapter will address both.

Luke 24 has three sections and a final conclusion. The central scene, which invites, and has received, subsequent artistic treatment on many a canvas and stained-glass window, is the journey to Emmaus, and the brief meal upon arrival. Much of Luke's gospel, like Acts, has journeying as its underlying motif: the walk to Emmaus becomes the vehicle for the central message Luke wants to convey about Easter and its meaning. This long central story (24.13–35) is flanked by a shorter opening (24.1–12, more or less parallel to the opening Easter scenes in Matthew and Mark) and a closing scene in the upper room where the disciples are gathered (24.36–49). The final four verses (50–53) round off the gospel as a whole, and simultaneously overlap with the opening scene in Acts. The readers are left for the moment where they began, worshipping in the Temple; but Jesus himself ends as the exalted lord of the world, ready now to begin the second phase of his work. (Acts opens by speaking of 'all that Jesus *began to do and teach*' (1.1); it describes his continuing ministry of deed and word.)

Like the other evangelists, Luke is telling the Easter stories in his own way. He feels himself free to shape them and to point up particular lessons, which are fairly obvious since he repeats them in each section of the chapter. But, as we saw in chapter 13, he does not feel free to modify substantially what must be considered very early tradition. His stories share with the other canonical ones the strange features, unique in ancient literature whether

---

[1] J. Gillman 2002, 179–85 offers a recent study of Luke's narrative artistry at this point.

Jewish or pagan, which simultaneously fit with the early Christian reflection on what resurrection actually involved while showing no signs of having borrowed from that reflection the developed theological or exegetical detail which so quickly became bound up with belief in Jesus' resurrection and that of his followers.

There has been no attempt to tidy up details. Luke has followed Mark in many ways throughout his gospel, but he cheerfully departs from him here, with no mention of the disciples being told to go to Galilee, and no hint of resurrection appearances anywhere other than in and near Jerusalem. Luke names three women as the early visitors to the tomb, Mary Magdalene, Joanna, and Mary the mother of James; but he also speaks of 'the others with them' (24.10). Instead of Mark's young man in a white robe, and Matthew's shining angel, there are 'two men in shining clothes' (24.4). There is no mention of the women seeing Jesus, as they do in Matthew, and as Mary Magdalene does in John. Luke agrees with Mark that the women were bringing spices to complete the work of anointing the body, which is not mentioned in Matthew and which in John was done by Joseph and Nicodemus. The women fulfil their commission to tell the disciples, but 'their words seemed to them an idle tale, and they did not believe them' (24.11). As in John, Peter runs to the tomb and sees the grave-clothes. The verse which describes this (24.12) is missing in some manuscripts; but among the reasons for retaining it are the reference back to the incident in verse 24, where Cleopas says that 'some of those with us' went to the tomb.[2] Had verse 12 been a later invention designed to anticipate this, we might have expected it to mention more people than simply Peter. And, most noticeably perhaps among incidental features of the chapter, the entire sequence of resurrection appearances, culminating in the ascension itself, appears to take place on a single day. Within the structural simplicity of the chapter, there are as many loose ends around the place as there are people in a Breughel painting.

The last two features – the appearance to Peter, and the single-day framework – alert us to something which a first-century writer would have taken for granted but which post-Enlightenment critics sometimes forget. In the ancient world, someone who was intending to tell people what actually happened did not feel obliged (any more than a good journalist, or indeed a real practising historian, would today) to mention every single feature of every single incident. Peter went to the tomb; 'some of our number' went to the tomb. If I say 'the bishop went to the party', and if somebody else says 'the bishop and his two daughters went to the party', we have not contradicted one another. When Josephus tells the story of his own participation in the various actions that started the Jewish–Roman war in AD 66, the story he tells in his *Jewish War* and the parallel story he tells in the *Life* do not

---

[2] For the textual problems of this verse cf. 613 above. The parallel passages in Jn. are 20.3, 5, 6 and 10.

always correspond in detail. When Luke fits all the resurrection appearances into a single day in chapter 24, and spreads them over forty days in Acts 1, we should not suppose that we have caught him out in some terrible historical oversight.[3] By the same token, it would be wrong to highlight the small-scale discrepancies between the four canonical narratives as though they constituted evidence that nothing at all actually happened. If anything, the argument should work the other way. If nothing happened, and if someone, years later, invented a story of women discovering an empty tomb, we should expect, not four slightly different stories, but one story. Take a parallel example: we cannot harmonize the different accounts of Peter's denial of Jesus (how many times did the cock crow, and when?), not because Peter did not deny Jesus but because he did.[4]

In Luke's work, as in the other canonical narratives, there is (as we saw) no hint that the primary meaning of Jesus' resurrection has anything to do with anyone else's personal post-mortem future. The conclusion is not 'you too can have a life after death', or anything remotely like it. The conclusion is 'this shows that the divine plan for Israel and the world has come to its unexpected climax, and that you are hereby commissioned to implement it in the world.' Both elements of this – the climax of a long, divinely ordered narrative, the inauguration of a new world mission – are woven into Luke 24 and Acts 1 at several points, and they provide the context for the other feature which must be drawn out, namely the pattern of life to which Jesus' followers are now committed.[5] Easter, for Luke, is about the meaning of history on the one hand (particularly the history of Israel; but that history always was, in his view, designed to benefit the whole world), and the task and shape of the church, flowing directly from that history, on the other.

First, though, we must look at Luke 24 in its context in the gospel as a whole, and at Acts 1 in relation to the book of Acts as a whole. They both have structural roles to play within Luke's overall plan. By observing how they work in this respect we can create a platform from which to view to advantage the detail of Luke's account of the turning-point of history and of the church's task and life.

2. Luke 24 and Acts 1 within Luke's Work as a Whole

If Luke 24 presents us with a well-structured picture, the same is true of the gospel as a whole. The resurrection narrative draws out themes which have

---

[3] See Evans 1970, 98–101.

[4] See Mt. 26.69–75/Mk. 14.66–72/Lk. 22.56–71/Jn. 18.25–7.

[5] Morgan 1994, 13 seems to me wide of the mark when he suggests that Luke/Acts presents Easter more as the reversal of the crucifixion than as 'the inauguration of the new age by an event which anticipates God's final victory'. That last phrase sums up quite a lot both of Luke 24 and of the wider agenda of Acts.

been prominent throughout the gospel, but it seems to have been designed in particular to form a matching pair with the prologue (chapters 1—2), not in slavish parallelism, but through several features which, when placed side by side, appear mutually illuminating.

After the formal opening (1.1–4), Luke introduces us to Zechariah and Elizabeth, who are to be the parents of John the Baptist. Zechariah, working as a priest in the Temple, is confronted with an angel informing him that he will have a son (1.5–23). It could be said of him what was said of the eleven in 24.11: these words seemed to him an idle tale, and he did not believe them. But the power of Israel's god is at work, and the elderly couple are surprised when it all comes true (1.24–5, 57–80) – as, of course, are the characters in Luke 24.

In the centre of the opening chapters is the story of the conception and birth of Jesus, and we must assume that Luke intends this to be seen as in some way parallel to the event of Easter. The story has its own inner logic, and neither it nor Luke 24 have been assimilated towards one another; but we cannot fail to notice the angel, announcing and explaining what is going on, and particularly the emphasis on Jesus as Israel's Messiah (1.32; 2.11, 26; 24.26, 46). This story in turn is the setting for Simeon's comments about Jesus as the bringer of salvation not only for Israel but also for the Gentiles (2.32), which is then repeated as one of the main points at the close of the Easter story (24.47). And, in particular, Simeon speaks fateful words to Mary, in blessing Jesus and speaking of what he will achieve: 'This child', he says, 'is set for the fall and resurrection of many in Israel' (*eis ptosin kai anastasin pollon en to Israel*, 2.34). Israel as a whole is going to 'fall' and 'rise again' in and through him: he will carry Israel's fate as the Exodus people, the enslaved-then-redeemed people, the exiled-then-restored people. He is, as Anna the prophetess declares, the one who will fulfil the hopes of those 'who are looking for the redemption (*lutrosis*) of Jerusalem'. 'We had hoped', says Cleopas on the road to Emmaus, 'that he was the one who would redeem Israel' (*ho mellon lutrousthai ton Israel*, 24.21). These multiple links can hardly be accidental. Luke is telling the Easter story in such a way as to say: all that was promised in the prologue has now come true, though not in the way anyone imagined.

The most spectacular parallel between chapters 1—2 and 24 is between the story of the twelve-year-old Jesus in the Temple (2.41–51) and the Jesus who comes incognito on the road to Emmaus.[6] Another Passover, another Jerusalem visit: a couple beginning their journey away from Jerusalem, discovering (in chapter 2) that Jesus was not with them, or (in chapter 24) that he was, but unrecognized. Mary and Joseph hurry back to the city, like Cleopas and his companion but with a very different mood. They search in

---

[6] I have explored this more fully in *Challenge* ch. 8. On the Emmaus Road story see now Schwemer 2001.

vain for three days (2.46), the parallel to which hardly needs pointing out. When they find the boy Jesus, his quizzical reply echoes down through the gospel story to the response of the unrecognized Jesus to the two on the road. 'Why were you looking for me? Didn't you know that it was necessary for me to be among my father's affairs?' (*hoti en tois tou patros mou dei einai me*, 2.49); and then, at last, 'Foolish ones, slow of heart to believe all that the prophets had spoken! Was it not necessary for the Messiah to suffer these things (*ouchi tauta edei pathein ton Christon*) and enter into his glory?' (24.25–6). The tired, anxious couple in the Temple are matched by the sad, disappointed couple on the road. Mary and Joseph discover Jesus, only to be confronted with a strange word about divine necessity; Cleopas and his companion, hearing the strange word about divine necessity, sit down to eat and discover that it was Jesus all along.

The 'necessity' in both passages – the little Greek verb *dei*, 'it is necessary' – is a recurring theme throughout Luke, and these two occurrences (together with the other two in the final chapter (24.7, 44), which belong very closely with 24.26) serve as a frame for the others, each of which makes its own contribution to the developing story and in particular to the eventual meaning of Easter:

> He was saying that the son of man *must* (*dei*) suffer many things and be rejected by the elders and the chief priests and the scribes and be killed, and be raised on the third day.

> Go and say to that fox [i.e. Herod Antipas], Look, I am casting out demons and performing healings today and tomorrow, and on the third day I shall be finished. But I *must* (*dei*) be on my way today, tomorrow and the following day, because it is impossible for a prophet to die away from Jerusalem.

> Child, you are always with me, and everything that is mine is yours. But *it was necessary* (*edei*) that we celebrate and rejoice, for this your brother was dead and is alive; he was lost and is found.

> But first [the son of man] *must* (*dei*) suffer many things and be rejected by this generation.

> For I tell you, this scripture, 'He was reckoned with the lawless,' *must* (*dei*) find its fulfilment in me.[7]

The significance of Easter, for Luke, is not least that it completes the things that 'must' take place concerning Jesus. In doing so it reveals, to people who had not previously grasped the point, the story that Israel's scriptures had been telling all along.

---

[7] Lk. 9.22; 13.33; 15.32 (the close, of course, of the parable of the prodigal son); 17.25; 22.37. The only other occurrence of the word in Luke is at 21.9 ('wars and revolutions *must* take place').

Not only does Luke tell us that all this 'must' take place, in completion of the as yet unfinished biblical narrative, the story of the creator and covenant god with the world and particularly with Israel. He shows us how it happens, by stitching his account into the biblical one, by his use (especially in chapters 1—2) of Septuagintalisms, by constant reference and implication back to the scriptures. And though, as we remarked earlier, his story like the others is nevertheless remarkably free from direct biblical echoes, there is one, at the heart of the Emmaus story, which surely tells us something about what Luke reckons to be the significance of Easter.

The first meal mentioned in the Bible is the moment when Adam and Eve eat the forbidden fruit. The direct result is new and unwelcome knowledge: 'the eyes of them both were opened, and they knew that they were naked' (*dienoichthesan hoi ophthalmoi ton duo kai egnosan hoti gymnoi esan*, Genesis 3.7).[8] Now this other couple, Cleopas and his companion (most likely his wife, one of the many Marys in the gospel story), are at table, and are confronted with new and deeply welcome knowledge: 'their eyes were opened, and they recognized him' (*auton de dienoichthesan hoi ophthalmoi, kai epegnosan auton*, 24.31). This, Luke is saying, is the ultimate redemption; this is the meal which signifies that the long exile of the human race, not just of Israel, is over at last. This is the start of the new creation. This is why 'repentance and forgiveness of sins are to be announced to all nations' (24.47). If Earle Ellis is right to see the Emmaus scene as the eighth meal in the gospel, there may be a numerical scheme at work to reinforce the same point (which, as we shall see, is highlighted especially by John). This is the first day of the new week.[9]

Luke has not forgotten, in all this, the fact that resurrection in Judaism was always a revolutionary doctrine. It was about the true kingdom of the true god winning the victory over the kingdoms of the world. He introduces the first two chapters of his gospel with reference to the king of the Jews and the (then) king of the world. Chapter 1 opens with Herod, chapter 2 with Caesar Augustus; chapter 3 then brings Augustus' son Tiberius Caesar and Herod's son Antipas into a chronological grid which declares not simply the time when all this took place but the particular form the world's kingdoms had taken at the moment when, unknown to them, the kingdom of the true god, in the person of the true son of this god, was about to be launched.[10] Many readers of the gospels then forget this implicit context, but Luke does not: Herod's puzzlement in 9.7–9, and his threat and Jesus' response in 13.31–3, combine with the threat from the Roman authorities (13.1–3), and when Herod and Pilate finally become friends in 23.12 the reader should

---

[8] cf. too 2 Kgs. 6.17; but that appears to be an accidental parallel.

[9] Ellis 1966, 277 with 192; the other meals are at Lk. 5.29; 7.36; 9.16; 10.39; 11.37; 14.1; and of course 22.14. This depends on not counting the Zacchaeus story (19.8), where the meal is implied but not described.

[10] Lk. 1.5; 2.1; 3.1.

have a sense of the kingdom Jesus has announced finally confronting the combined powers of the world. Luke 24 does not materially add to this picture, but again Luke is not ignoring it. When the message goes out to 'all nations', it offers more than just a new way of being religious. As Acts makes clear, the message is that Jesus is the world's true lord. The creator god is bypassing the networks of imperial power and communication. One central meaning of Easter, as far as Luke is concerned, is that Jesus and his followers are now to confront the kingdoms of the world.

Acts itself, which begins with the brief story of the risen Jesus commissioning the disciples and then ascending, has as its large framework the story of Herod's world and Caesar's world, and of the gospel going out powerfully into both. The first half (Acts 1—12) tells how the Jewish authorities, and especially Herod, do their best to stop Jesus' followers, but overreach themselves, with Herod Agrippa finally giving himself 'divine' airs as though he were a typical hellenistic princeling, and being struck down on the spot (while, Luke notes, 'the word of God continued to advance and gain adherents').[11] The second half (Acts 13—28) has the gospel going out, not least through Paul, into the wider world of the Roman empire, with Paul declaring in Thessalonica that there is 'another king, namely Jesus', and finally arriving in Rome to announce the kingdom of the one true god, and to teach about the lord Jesus, the Messiah, with all boldness and without hindrance.[12] There is, of course, more to Acts than this bald summary indicates, but it shows what is in Luke's mind as the direct result of Jesus being hailed as the risen Messiah and lord.[13]

The role of Acts 1, which completes Luke's account of the risen Jesus with the story of his ascension, can now be understood in a holistic relationship to the rest of Luke's work. It is, of course, a unique account; none of the other gospels attempts such a thing (though the longer ending of Mark refers to it).[14] As in his gospel, Luke insists on Jesus being truly alive: 'he presented himself alive after his suffering in many proofs, appearing to them (*optanomenos autois*) during forty days, and speaking about the things to do with the kingdom of God' (1.3). This, of course, cannot in context be taken as a reference to anything other than Jesus' new bodily life; Luke knows the difference between visions and things that happen in 'real life', and the resurrection is emphatically one of the latter.[15] In particular, Jesus gives the disciples instructions about waiting for the Holy Spirit to be poured out on them (1.4–5), and then about the worldwide mission (1.6–8).

---

[11] Ac. 12.20–23 (cf. the similar story in Jos. *Ant.* 19.343–61); 12.24.

[12] Ac. 17.7; 28.31.

[13] Acts 2.36, etc.; see ch. 10 above. There are of course multiple links forward into Ac. from the thematic moments in Lk. 24: cf. e.g. Ac. 3.18; 17.3; 24.14f.; 26.22f.; 28.23.

[14] Mk. 16.19.

[15] cf. ch. 10: Ac. emphasizes strongly the definite bodiliness of Jesus' resurrection. On the recognition in Ac. of the difference between visions and reality cf. 605 above.

This last point should not be misunderstood. Jesus, faced with the disciples' question, 'Lord, is it at this time that you will restore the kingdom to Israel?' gives an answer which many have taken as a 'no', but which Luke almost certainly intends as a 'yes'. They will not know about particular times, but this is how the kingdom will come: by their Spirit-driven witness to him in Jerusalem, Judaea, Samaria and to the ends of the earth. As has often been pointed out, this sentence is programmatic for the entire book, moving as it does from the initial preaching in Jerusalem and the surrounding area, through a specifically Samaritan mission in chapter 8, on to the worldwide reach of the gospel, begun by Peter's preaching to Cornelius in chapter 10 but carried on particularly through Paul's missionary journeys in chapters 13—28. Though there were Christians in Rome before Paul got there, Luke's final verse, already quoted, is undoubtedly intended to look back to 1.6. This is how the kingdom is to come: not by a national restoration of Israel, as had been hoped (see 24.21), but by the representatives of Israel's Messiah going out into the world to proclaim him as its rightful lord. As we saw in chapter 12, this is a natural result of ancient messianic expectation. It conforms, though in a different way from the mutation urged by Josephus, to what that author describes as a fervent first-century hope.[16]

This theological and political setting is the appropriate context for understanding what Luke intends in his description of the 'ascension' of Jesus in Acts 1.9–11, anticipated in Luke 24.51.[17] Though it is sometimes asserted that this event, and the careful distinction that is drawn between it and the resurrection, is peculiar to Luke, we have already noted that Paul can make the distinction just as well, and we shall see that, again despite repeated claims, John does so too.[18] If Jesus really was alive again in (what we would call) a physical body of some sort, as we have seen that Paul no less than Luke affirms, and if after a short while this physical body ceased to be present (without the body being in a tomb anywhere), then some kind of explanation for the new state of affairs is called for. The real problem, in fact, both for first-century hearers of the story and for their successors in the twenty-first century, is not so much the ascension itself, but the idea of a body which is both physical (in the sense that the tomb was empty after it had gone) and 'transphysical' (in the sense that it can appear and disappear, is not always immediately recognized, and so on). This kind of embodiedness, which involved neither the abandonment of the old body in the tomb nor the mere resuscitation of a corpse, is the difficulty. The ascension is the

---

[16] Jos. *War* 3.399–408; 6.312–15; see *NTPG* 304, 312f.

[17] The phrase 'and was carried up into heaven' in the latter verse is missing in two major MSS. On the ascension and its significance see esp. Farrow 1999.

[18] Jn. 20.17; see below, 666. I do not understand how Perkins 1984, 86 can claim that Lk. 24.51 and Jn. 20.17 'presume that Easter itself is Jesus' ascension into heaven'. That seems to me precisely what both writers insist it is *not*.

solution which Luke and John offer, each in his own way, and which Paul, too, offers in his.

We may remind ourselves at this point of two basic rules for modern readers reading ancient Jewish texts. First, two-decker language about a 'heaven' in the sky above the earth almost certainly did not betoken a two-decker, let alone a three-decker, cosmology. Just as we speak of the sun 'rising', even though we know that the earth is turning in relation to the sun, so ancient Jews were comfortable with the language of heavenly ascent without supposing that their god, and those who shared his habitation, were physically situated a few thousand feet above the surface of the earth. Second, and related to this, the language of 'heaven' and 'earth', though it could be used to denote sky on the one hand and terra firma on the other, was regularly employed in a sophisticated theological manner, to denote the parallel and interlocking universes inhabited by the creator god on the one hand and humans on the other. To speak of someone 'going up to heaven' by no means implied that the person concerned had (a) become a primitive space-traveller and (b) arrived, by that means, at a different location within the present space-time universe. We should not allow the vivid, indeed lurid, language of the Middle Ages, or the many hymns and prayers which use the word 'heaven' to denote, it seems, a far-off location within the cosmos we presently inhabit, to make us imagine that first-century Jews thought literalistically in that way too. Some may indeed have done so; there is no telling what things people will believe; but we should not imagine that the early Christian writers thought like that.

Nor is Luke's story to be assimilated to the strange story of Elijah in the Old Testament.[19] Elijah did not die; he was 'taken up to heaven' directly. The more interesting biblical parallel, which has almost certainly affected the way Luke tells the story, is that of Daniel 7, in which 'one like a son of man' (representing, within the mythological framework of the vision, 'the people of the saints of the most high') is exalted to sit beside 'the ancient of days' after, as it appears, suffering at the hands of the 'beasts', particularly the fourth one.[20] The ascension is not a mere solution to a problem about what happens to a body of this new sort. It is, for Luke as much as for Paul, the vindication of Jesus as Israel's representative, and the divine giving of judgment, at least implicitly, in his favour and against the pagan nations who have oppressed Israel and the current rulers who have corrupted her. It is, in other words, the direct answer to the disciples' question of 1.6. This is how the kingdom is being restored to Israel: by its representative Messiah being enthroned as the world's true lord. This, it turns out, comes by an almost totally different route to the position which Paul expounded in 1 Corinthians

---

[19] 2 Kgs. 2.11f.; see above, 95f.
[20] Dan. 7.9–27; cf. *NTPG* 291–7.

15.20–28, though without, once more, any of the developed exegesis which Paul employs to make the point.

In fact, to any Roman reader of the time, and to plenty of others in the wider pagan world, the story of Jesus' ascension would have had an immediate counter-imperial impact, cognate with what a devout Jew might have picked up from the implicit echoes of Daniel 7. As we saw in chapter 2, by Paul's day the custom was well established of emperors being declared to be divine after their death, with the evidence produced consisting of one or two witnesses who had glimpsed the soul of the dead emperor ascending towards the heavens. Augustus heralded a convenient comet as the soul of his adopted father Julius Caesar; at Titus' funeral, an eagle was released from the pyre to fly aloft. The parallel with the Christian story is not exact, because the point was then that the new emperor was to be hailed as 'son of god' on the basis of the divinization of his predecessor, whereas the early Christians reserved that title for Jesus, now himself raised and exalted. The Christian ascension stories cannot be derived from the pagan ones; but they would certainly have been heard, in the second half of the first century, as counter-imperial. Jesus was lord, and Caesar was not. Not only Jesus' resurrection, but also his ascension, carried inescapable political significance; and that significance corresponded closely to what we discovered when examining Paul. But, once again, Luke has not developed the point in a Pauline way. He simply uses the story, with a minimum of embroidery, as the basis for a book in which he tells of the subversive gospel going out, against fierce opposition, to announce Israel's god and his worldwide kingdom and, in particular, to proclaim Jesus as lord and Messiah.

3. The Unique Event

'Emmaus never happened; Emmaus always happens.' Thus Dominic Crossan, in a typical combination of provocative denial and winsome appeal.[21] He sums up a view which has become so widespread that it is taken for granted in many circles, not only in scholarship but also in many churches: that the resurrection stories in the gospels, not least those of Luke, have nothing to do with things that actually took place in the real world of space and time and everything to do with what goes on in an invisible reality in which, on the one hand, Jesus is 'alive' in some sense which did not involve an empty tomb, and the hearts and minds of believers are strengthened by their experience of him.[22]

---

[21] Crossan 1994, 197. See too Crossan 1995, 216: stories of the empty tomb and the appearances 'are perfectly valid parables expressing [Christian] faith, akin in their own way to the Good Samaritan story'. My point in this section is not so much that I disagree with this interpretation, but that Luke himself would demonstrably have done so.

[22] e.g. Borg, in Borg and Wright 1999, ch. 8.

Whatever we today decide about that matter – which remains to be considered in the final Part of this book – we can be sure that Luke himself would not have agreed with Crossan's judgment. The whole point of his story is that it is about an event which he understands, not as an 'example' of the kind of 'spiritual experience' which people may still have as they ponder strange happenings, meditate on the scriptures and break bread together, but as a shock, a one-off unique moment. Luke presents Jesus' resurrection as a surprise to the women (24.1–8), to the eleven (24.9–11), to Peter (24.12), to the two on the road (24.13–35), and again to the disciples in the upper room (24.37, 41). And the explanation given, over and over again, is not that this simply establishes a pattern which will be repeated in the life and worship of the church (though that also is true, as we shall see in the next section of this chapter), but that it was the single event through which the world, and Israel, were changed for ever. This is what Luke insists upon in both Luke 24 and Acts 1. We cannot take these stories and transform them, without remainder, into pictures of ongoing Christian experience without doing violence, in every line, to Luke's manifest intention. Once more, this is not to say that Luke is unaware of the multiple resonances in Christian experience which the stories set up; only that these are resonances which echo out, as far as he is concerned, from the original event itself.

In particular, Luke insists on the bodiliness of the risen Jesus, describing it indeed so thoroughly that those who have supposed Paul to promote a less-than-fully-embodied risen Jesus have set the two of them in opposition. The tomb, of course, was empty as far as Luke was concerned (verses 1–8); Peter saw the grave-clothes (verse 12); when the stranger at the table suddenly disappeared, he left broken bread behind him (verses 30–31, 35). He presented himself alive by 'many convincing proofs' (Acts 1.4), by which Luke presumably intends to include the scene in the upper room, where he explicitly rebuts any suggestion that this was a phantom, a ghost or a hallucination (all of them, as we have seen, natural ideas to occur to someone in that culture):

24.36As they were saying these things, he himself stood in the midst of them and said to them, Peace be with you. 37They, however, were terrified and alarmed, and thought they were seeing a spirit (*pneuma*). 38And he said to them, 'Why are you troubled? And why do these questionings arise in your heart? 39Look at my hands and my feet: it really is me! Touch me and see; a spirit doesn't have flesh and bones as you see that I have.' 40Saying this, he showed them his hands and his feet. 41While they were still disbelieving from joy, and wondering, he said to them, 'Have you anything here to eat?' 42They gave him a piece of broiled fish, 43and he took it and ate it in front of them.

Every line, almost every word, in this scene demonstrates the point. For Luke, the risen Jesus is firmly and solidly embodied, able to be touched, able to eat. The echoes this awakens in other books show clearly what is meant by this.[23] His hands and feet – Luke does not mention the wounds they still bore, but that seems to be the point, as in John 20.20, 25, 27 – are the same hands and feet as before.[24] He was not a *pneuma*, a 'spirit' or 'ghost'; such a being would not possess the physical accoutrements which he clearly has. 'Flesh and bones' here must not be played off against Paul's phrase 'flesh and blood' in 1 Corinthians 15.50; Luke is not wedded to the special Pauline terminology in which 'flesh' (*sarx*) always designates that which is corruptible, and often that which is rebellious. For him, as later for Tertullian and others, this was simply a way of saying what we today say when we use the word 'physical'.[25] The evidence of Acts, already surveyed, confirms the point vividly with its emphasis on Jesus' body not having decomposed.[26]

What Luke draws in particular from all this is not just the physicality of Jesus' risen body but what that means for an entire view of the world and Israel in the divine purpose: with Easter there has come to birth the new world, the redemption of Israel, the new creation. The thrust of these stories is precisely not that some people began to have a certain type of spiritual experience which they and others can then continue to have thereafter. On the contrary; at no point in Acts, after the ascension in chapter 1, does anyone have an experience remotely like the ones Luke describes in the forty days from Easter onwards. Of course, there are several elements of these experiences which he describes in such a way as to indicate the origin of ongoing Christian communal life. We shall look at these presently. But they grow out of something which, at every point, Luke is at pains to make as discontinuous with subsequent Christian life as he possibly can. Emmaus, he says, *did* happen; and, though partial analogies occur every time hearts burn at biblical exposition and recognizing faith is kindled over broken bread, there is another even more important sense in which Emmaus *will never happen again*.

---

[23] In Tob. 12.19 the angel Raphael, disclosing his identity to Tobit and Tobias, declares that during his time with them he neither ate nor drank; they were seeing a vision (*horasis*). In Ac. 10.41 Peter declares that the disciples ate and drank with Jesus after his resurrection; the strange verb in Ac. 1.4 can be translated 'eating with them' instead of 'staying with them' (on the problem, see Metzger 1971, 278f.; Barrett 1994, 71f.). Segal 1997, 110f., carried away by his interest in Luke's portrait of Jesus' risen embodiedness, has him 'celebrat[ing] the Lord's Supper, eating bread and drinking wine' – something which enthusiasts for sacramental theology would love to have found in Luke's text, but have not, for the very good reason that it is not there.

[24] In John, it is hands and *side* that are mentioned, not feet. Despite popularized accounts of the crucifixion, none of the canonical gospels mentions, in describing the crucifixion, the nailing of Jesus' hands and feet.

[25] See Peters 1993, 67, pointing out (against Cullmann in particular) the danger of getting too tied to particular word-choices.

[26] Ac. 2.27–9, 31; 13.35, 37; see above, 451–7.

At the same time, despite repeated suggestions, it is wrong to suppose that Luke has emphasized the physicality of the risen Jesus in order to combat docetic tendencies within the early church. The parallel at this point between his insistence that Jesus is not a *pneuma* and Ignatius' insistence that the risen Jesus was not a *daimon* might lead us astray.[27] Ignatius did indeed face the problem of a docetic analysis, not just of Jesus' risen body but of his pre-crucifixion humanity too. But if Luke had been writing in order to combat that sort of view, it is unthinkable that he would have included in the same chapter the Emmaus Road story, with its unrecognized and then disappearing Jesus, then the account of Jesus appearing suddenly in the upper room, and finally the ascension itself.

As far as Luke is concerned, then, we need have no doubt: he believed in the one-off, unique event of Jesus' bodily resurrection, and he believed that the entire story of the creator's dealings with the world and with Israel had come into new focus as a result of it. All the scriptural stories pointed this way, not that anyone had read them like that before. Israel's story had reached its climax in its Messiah; with him, the new chapter of world history had opened, a new era characterized by divine forgiveness.[28] Luke's resurrection story is not derived from Paul or other New Testament theologians. It appears to be his own reworking of very early traditions. But by the end he has landed up somewhere very close to all the others.

4. Easter and the Life of the Church

Having said all that, it is important to notice also how Luke has told the story in such a way as to establish or undergird patterns of common life to which he himself later draws attention. The obvious starting-point comes again in the Emmaus Road story, where Luke highlights two features: the fresh exposition of scripture and the breaking of the bread. The hearts of the two on the road are burning within them at the first; their eyes are opened at the second.[29] Then, in the upper room, Jesus 'opened their minds to understand the scriptures'.[30] Bring this forward into Acts, and we find two of the four elements in early church life: the apostles' teaching, the fellowship, the breaking of bread, and the prayers.[31] (We may assume that 'the apostles' teaching' consisted to a large extent of biblical exposition, though no doubt also containing stories about, and teachings of, Jesus himself.) What Luke's whole oeuvre is designed to do at a large scale, to tell the story of Jesus and the early church so that its position at the climax of Israel's scriptural story

[27] Lk. 24.37, 39; Ign. *Smyrn.* 3.1–3. See above, chs. 10, 12, 13.
[28] Lk. 24.47; Ac. 13.38f.
[29] Lk. 24.27, 32, 35.
[30] Lk. 24.45.
[31] Ac. 2.42.

can be fully understood and appropriated, Luke's Jesus enables the disciples to do close up. They are to understand the Bible in a whole new way, in the light of the events that have happened to him. And they are to make this fresh reading of scripture the source of their inner life of burning zeal (24.32) and their framework for understanding who Jesus was and is, who they are in relation to him, and what they must do as a result (24.45–8).

The overtones of the meal at Emmaus, too, cannot be mistaken. Luke describes the four actions of Jesus in taking bread, blessing it, breaking it and giving it in such a way as to echo deliberately the eucharistic action described not only in the Last Supper texts but also by John in the desert feeding and Paul in 1 Corinthians.[32] This is not to deny what was said in the previous section; merely to affirm that Luke has told the one-off story in such a way that it can also be heard as paradigmatic for subsequent worshipping life.

The commissioning, of course, naturally anticipates the later work of the church, both as Luke describes it in Acts and as Paul describes it in his letters. 'Repentance and forgiveness is to be proclaimed in his name to all the nations' (24.47); in addition to the many scenes in Acts which embody this, we might compare 1 Thessalonians 1.9–10, Romans 1.5 and similar passages. It is important to notice that this commission is hardly arbitrary. It is not as though the event of Jesus' resurrection and the detailed things he then tells his followers to do remain unconnected. Because Jesus is risen, he is demonstrated to be Israel's Messiah; because he is Israel's Messiah, he is the true lord of the world and will summon it to allegiance; to this end, he will commission his followers to act on his behalf, in the power of the Spirit which itself is a sign and means of covenant renewal and fresh life. And the key followers, through whom the project will be launched, are the 'witnesses' who have seen for themselves that Jesus really is alive again after his crucifixion.[33]

5. Luke and the Resurrection: Conclusion

This survey of Luke's resurrection narratives confirms what we saw in relation to Mark and Matthew. The individual evangelists have clearly felt free to shape and retell their stories in such a way as to bring out their own particular emphases and theological intentions. Even where Luke overlaps with Mark and Matthew, the story has been substantially rewritten. But the picture of Jesus is the same, and it is a picture which, though deeply puzzling in itself, fits with the more developed theological analysis of resurrection which we find in the theological traditions of which Paul is the earliest

[32] Mt. 26.26/Mk. 14.22/Lk. 22.19; Jn. 6.11; 1 Cor. 11.23f.; cf. Justin *1 Apol.* 1.66.3.
[33] Lk. 24.48; cf. Ac. 1.22; 2.32; 3.15; 10.39, 41; 13.31.

exponent. It is a picture of the risen Jesus as a firmly embodied human being whose body possesses new, unexpected and unexplained characteristics: a picture of what we have called 'transphysicality', or transformed physicality. Luke makes no more effort to explain or justify this extraordinary innovation than do any of the others. He simply hands on, with his own interpretation but without substantially modifying what we must assume to be bedrock early tradition, what it was that all early Christians believed had happened. He takes us one step further along the road, not only to discovering what it was that all early Christians believed, but to asking why it was that they came to believe it.

Chapter Seventeen

NEW DAY, NEW TASKS: JOHN

1. Introduction

John's two Easter chapters rank with Romans 8, not to mention the key passages in the Corinthian correspondence, as among the most glorious pieces of writing on the resurrection. John and Romans are of course utterly different in genre and style. Instead of the tight argument and dense phraseology of Paul, we have John's deceptively simple account of the Easter events, warm with deep and dramatic human characterization, pregnant with new possibilities. Instead of the strong QED, or the bracing 'Therefore . . .' at the end of a long and gritty Pauline argument, we have John's disturbingly open-ended final scene: 'What is that to you? Follow me.' The gospel ends with new-found faith all right, but it is faith that must now go out into a new world, a new day, and attempt new tasks without knowing in advance where it will all lead.[1]

The two final chapters of John's gospel are well known as a problem text. John (I shall refer to him by that name without prejudice as to which of the possible 'Johns', if any, he actually was; likewise, without reaching any conclusion either on the identity of the beloved disciple or on his relation to the actual author of the book) gives every appearance of bringing the book to a close at the end of chapter 20. Verses 30–31 would indeed form a fitting conclusion not only to any story of Jesus but to John's in particular:

> There are many other signs that Jesus did in the presence of his disciples, which have not been written in this book. But these things have been written so that you may believe that the Messiah, the son of God, is Jesus; and that, believing, you may have life in his name.[2]

---

[1] My acknowledgments at this point to the composer Paul Spicer are recorded in the Preface, xx. On the John/Paul divide in the early C20, see my 'Coming Home to St Paul'.

[2] On the translation of v. 31 see 556 above.

But then we have chapter 21; no manuscript gives any hint that there was ever a copy of the gospel circulating without it. Up until the final two verses of the chapter, it looks as though the author is the same as for the rest of the gospel. Indeed, verse 23 looks like a kind of personal signature, perhaps written (if the author of the gospel and the beloved disciple are really the same person) when the author was close to death, or, if the beloved disciple was not the author, by the author around the time of the beloved disciple's death. Certainly this verse warns against supposing that Jesus intended to return before the beloved disciple had died, an idea which had somehow taken root in the church. But then, as though a codicil were added by an editor, the book ends with a kind of affidavit of authorship:

> This [i.e. the beloved disciple, mentioned in the previous verse] is the disciple who is bearing witness to these things, and who wrote these things, and we know that his witness is true.[3]

And the book closes with a final flourish, reminiscent of 20.30, which could have been added by the same editor who added verse 24, or might have been the final words left by the original author, allowed by the editor to stand at the end after his own inserted note:

> There are many other things which Jesus did. If these things were to be written down one by one, I do not think the world would be able to contain the books that would be written.[4]

The question of authorship, never easy in the gospel tradition, is thus made all the more tantalizing: a footnote which tells us who the author is, but which we cannot decode! However, the claim is clear: not only is this witness to be trusted, but he was an eye-witness to it all. Claims like this have of course routinely been discounted by biblical scholarship; indeed, the very fact of such a claim being made has come to be regarded with suspicion, as a sign that someone is trying to smuggle something under our guard. Whether or not that is so in the present case is a topic for another time. The claim must take its place, along with a fresh reading of the passage, as part of our picture of what the author is trying to say.

The basic features of John's Easter story are soon laid out. The initial story of the finding of the empty tomb (20.1–18) overlaps in content with that of the synoptics, but it is the differences that stand out: Mary Magdalene is mentioned alone among the women, and she meets Jesus (as the women do in Matthew). As in Luke 24.12, Peter runs to the tomb on hearing the news; but in this gospel he is accompanied by the beloved disciple, and in a dramatic scene they run together, with the beloved disciple getting to the

---

[3] Jn. 21.24.

[4] Jn. 21.25. The verse is omitted by the first hand in Codex Sinaiticus.

tomb first.[5] There is considerably more detail at every point in this narrative than in the synoptic semi-parallels; the description of the grave-clothes, for example, and the dialogue between Jesus and Mary.[6]

There then follow two stories set in the evening in the upper room, the first on the same day as the events in the garden, the second a week later. The first (20.19–23) seems to correspond, in content though not much in wording, with Luke 24.36–49: Jesus commissions his followers for a mission to the world, and bestows the Spirit on them to equip them for the task. The second presents a scene beloved of artists ancient and modern. Thomas, who was not present that first evening, acquires his now perpetual nickname by declaring his doubt that the Lord had truly risen, and is then confronted by the risen Jesus inviting him to touch and see for himself. Thomas refuses the invitation, coming out instead with the fullest confession of faith anywhere in the whole gospel: 'My lord and my god' (20.28). Jesus makes a wry comment, the scene is over, and so too is (what looks like) the book in its original form.

Chapter 21 is set in Galilee; John, like Matthew, has Jesus appear in both Jerusalem and Galilee, though the appearances are far fuller, and the Galilee appearance is by the lakeshore, not on the mountain. Peter and six others of the disciples (we assume, of the Twelve) go fishing and catch nothing; Jesus, unrecognized, directs operations from the shore, as once before in Luke's gospel, resulting again in a spectacular catch. Coming ashore, they find Jesus already cooking breakfast and inviting them to share it. 'None of them', comments the author in a haunting aside, 'dared ask him, "Who are you?", because they knew that it was the Lord' (21.12). Jesus then takes Simon Peter for a walk along the shore (we discover this later when they find that the beloved disciple is following them), and asks him three times if he loves him, corresponding to Peter's triple denial in chapter 18. Receiving a triple 'Yes' for reply, he commissions him to be a kind of under-shepherd, which will require him, too, to face suffering.[7] Then, seeing the beloved disciple following them, they have the brief exchange about him which leads to the open-ended challenge, 'What is that to you? You must follow me!' This leads straight into the ending, which we have already noted.

As with much of the rest of the fourth gospel, the reader who comes fresh from the synoptic tradition is bound to be struck by one feature in particular, namely, the extended dialogues and the detailed characterization. We learn as much about Mary Magdalene, Thomas and the beloved disciple (whoever he is) in these two chapters as in the other three gospels put together. The

---

[5] As we saw, Lk. 24.24 indicates Lk.'s awareness that more than one male disciple went to the tomb.

[6] It is quite unwarranted to suggest that the story of Peter and John has been inserted or interpolated, at a late stage in the tradition, into an originally independent story of Mary (e.g. Carnley 1987, 19, 45).

[7] Jn. 21.15–19, echoing the 'shepherd' discourse in 10.1–30.

picture of Peter we get from elsewhere is further substantiated. Explanations for this come in three basic kinds: those that see the detailed characterization as evidence of real historical knowledge of actual people, those that see it as a sign of clever novelistic fiction, and those that regard it as, at least in some cases, a political attempt to make a case for the leadership position of one of the apostles against one or more of the others. We do not need to decide this question here; but we must note that, whether through reliance on eye-witnesses or through highly skilled fiction, the writer is certainly attempting to present a coherent and credible portrait of the individuals concerned. They are anything but cardboard cut-outs producing stock responses and questions. The writer intends us to take the story seriously as a narrative which belongs in its own context, not as an obvious allegory of later church experience.

From this brief survey it should already be clear that one common perception of John is significantly flawed. Some have so emphasized John's teaching about 'eternal life' as something available to people within the present life, and at the same time have rightly noted that John sees the crucifixion of Jesus as itself a key moment of glory, of 'lifting up', that they have found no room within his theology for any resurrection, either of Jesus or of his followers. This then, of course, leads not only to a downplaying of the resurrection narratives, but also to the attempt to marginalize the key passage 5.25–9, which we noted in chapter 9 above. It also leads to the suggestion that, for John, crucifixion, resurrection and ascension are all basically the same thing: Jesus is 'going away', and that is that. What matters is his 'exaltation in glory into heaven, not his brief posthumous appearance on earth'.[8]

But the texts themselves are more subtle than this over-realized eschatology warrants. Of course John can see crucifixion, resurrection and ascension as a single event; that makes good sense at one level theologically. But he can also differentiate them carefully. The mere fact of writing resurrection narratives as substantial as these speaks for itself when it comes to the distinction between crucifixion and resurrection; and, as we shall see, the thematic structure of the gospel as a whole tells against collapsing the whole thing into simply a death which is also a moment of glory. (What would that say about Jesus' raising of Lazarus? Would that not also have to be dismissed as a category mistake? But is it not one of the major focal points of the entire narrative?) Further, the key passage in Jesus' exchange with Mary

---

[8] Harvey 1994, 74, summarizing what he takes to be an early Christian view which he then describes as 'good Johannine theology', backing up this claim by suggesting that the resurrection appearances in John are not used as an 'aid to belief'. See too e.g. Macquarrie 1990, 413: though John includes resurrection stories, their significance is reduced. This is a strange comment on the fullest Easter stories in the New Testament. For the theme of Jesus 'going away' cf. e.g. Jn. 13.33; 16.28; and many other passages in the Farewell Discourses (chs. 13—17).

reveals that John is well aware of the distinction between resurrection and ascension, even though elsewhere he has not needed to highlight it:

> Jesus said to Mary, 'Do not touch me, because I have not yet gone up to the father. But go to my brothers and say to them, "I am going up to my father and your father, to my God and your God."'[9]

This famous exchange is worthy of comment in itself. Teresa Okure has plausibly suggested that the command not to touch is part of Mary's commission to go and tell what she has seen rather than stay clinging to Jesus. In addition, if Jesus' command is to be translated as 'Do not cling on to me' or 'Do not grasp me', as may well be the case, John may be intending to contrast the bodiliness of the risen Jesus with the kind of wraith or spirit we met in Homer, which turned out to be precisely the sort of thing one might try to grasp but could not.[10] Putting these suggestions together, John may be saying both that Jesus was indeed, so to speak, graspable, and that Mary was to go and get on with her new task. Thus, though it is obviously true that John does not want to drive a wedge between the different events, it is equally true that he has not collapsed them into one another. It is illegitimate to appeal to John as a witness to a view of Jesus and the resurrection in which Easter stories are simply a dramatic, coded way of saying that his death was somehow victorious, that he was now alive in heaven, and that his followers now experience a new life through him. If that really was what John was trying to say, he went about it in as misleading a fashion as he could.[11]

In fact, the Easter story of chapter 20 in particular can be shown to be, not an addendum which threatens to pull the theology of the rest of the gospel out of shape, but the true completion of the story John has been telling all through, the story that reached its climax in the crucifixion. This can be seen by setting out the ways in which chapter 20 forms a 'frame' at the end of the gospel that corresponds in several ways to the prologue (1.1–18) at the beginning; and by tracing the themes which, important already in the body of the gospel, find their eventual destination in this chapter.

---

[9] Jn. 20.17. See the discussion of Evans 1970, 122f. Brown 1973, 89 suggests that the incident is 'a dramatization of the theological truth that Jesus has not returned to ordinary existence but rather to a glorified existence with his Father'; if that were the truth, the story is surely not a dramatization of it but a falsification. Davies 1999, 15 suggests that 'Do not touch me' is to be explained on the analogy of the pagan belief that until three days were fully past the dead were not fully dead and so were still considered dangerous. This seems to me about as bizarre a misunderstanding of John as one could imagine.

[10] Okure 1992, 181f., highlighting the incident as a kind of apostolic 'sending'. For Homer's wraiths see above, 40–42. See below, 691.

[11] cf. Evans 1970, 116, speaking of a tension between the rest of the gospel and the Easter stories, and suggesting that, strictly speaking, the theology of the gospel leaves no place for resurrection (see above, ch. 9).

2. John 20 within the Gospel as a Whole

I have already commented on the ways in which John's prologue anticipates the themes of chapter 20.[12] The point can be summed up briefly.

John declares from the start, with the obvious allusion to Genesis 1.1, that his book is about the new creation in Jesus. In chapter 20 he makes the same point by stressing that Easter was 'the first day of the week' (20.1, 19; when John underlines things like this he clearly wants us to ponder the point). On the sixth day of the creation narrative, humankind was created in the divine image; on the sixth day of the last week of Jesus' life, John has Pilate declare, 'Behold the man!' The seventh day is the day of rest for the creator; in John, it is the day when Jesus rests in the tomb. Easter is the start of the new creation.

This is reinforced by the themes of light and life. 'In him was life, and the light was the light of human beings,' shining unquenchably in the darkness (1.4–5). Now Mary comes to the tomb while it is still dark, and discovers the new light and life which has defeated the darkness. The prologue continues with the places where there is still darkness: the Word 'came to his own, and his own did not receive him', but those who did receive him were given the right to become children of the creator god. Now, in chapter 20, we find the doors locked for fear of the hostile Judaeans, but the little company of those who 'received him' are told, for the first time, that the creator god is *their* father, *their* god (20.17; up to now Jesus has spoken of 'the father' or 'my father'). They are now children of the father in their own right. Reading chapter 20 in the light of the prologue, we are thus to understand that Jesus' death and resurrection have together effected for the disciples the new birth which was spoken of in 1.13 and 3.1–13. We should not be surprised when Jesus then breathes his own Spirit into them, as YHWH breathed his own Spirit into human nostrils in Genesis 2.7. What happens to Jesus' people is a further indication of who Jesus is: the Word made flesh (1.14). That verse, the climax of the prologue, is hugely important for John: the Word who was with the one god, who was identified with this god, is now also and for ever flesh. There can be no sense that the flesh has been turned back simply into word and spirit. The resurrection matters for John because he is, at his very heart, a theologian of creation. The Word, who was always to be the point at which creator and creation came together in one, is now, in the resurrection, the point at which creator and *new* creation are likewise one.

This highlights the way in which Thomas' confession of faith looks back to 1.18. The explicitly high Christology of the prologue reaches its culmination here: nobody has ever seen the one true god, but 'the only-begotten god' has unveiled and expounded this god, has shown the world who he is.[13]

---

[12] *NTPG* 410–17; and cf. ch. 8 above.

[13] On the textual problems of the verse see Metzger 1971, 198.

We watch in vain, throughout the rest of the gospel, for characters in the story to wake up to what is going on. Jesus 'reveals his glory' to the disciples in various ways, but nobody responds with anything that matches what is said in 1.18.

Until Easter. Rowan Williams has suggested, following Westcott, that the angels at either end of the grave slab function like the cherubim at either end of the mercy-seat of the ark; the true god, John may be suggesting, is to be found in the gap.[14] Whether this is ultimately plausible, by the end of the chapter there is no question what has now been revealed. The so-called 'Doubting Thomas' takes one small verbal step and a giant leap of faith and theology: 'My lord and my god' (20.28). This at last is faith indeed. The disciples, with Thomas (of all people!) as their spokesman, have confessed that the 'flesh' they had known, and now know again in a new way, was also in truth the 'Word' who was one with the father.

All of this underlines the point that *it matters for John that Easter actually happened*. Precisely because he is an incarnational theologian, committed to recognizing, and helping others to recognize, the living god in the human flesh of Jesus, it is vital and non-negotiable for him that when Thomas makes this confession he should be looking at the living god in human form, not simply with the eye of faith (others will come by that road hereafter, as John quickly makes clear), but with ordinary human sight, which could be backed up by ordinary human touch – though Thomas, it seems, remains content with sight. There is, in other words, nothing about John 20, seen in the context of the gospel as a whole and particularly of the prologue which it balances so well, to suggest that these stories originated as, or would have been heard by their first hearers as, an allegory or metaphor of spiritual experience. Of course, like virtually everything in John's gospel, they function at multiple levels of meaning simultaneously; but the meaning which grounds everything else is the Word becoming flesh. To deny that in respect of John 20 is to leave the symphony without its closing coda, its final crashing chords.[15]

In fact, there are several different threads that stitch the resurrection narratives tightly to the rest of the gospel, preventing any possibility that it might be pulled away clean and leave the previous nineteen chapters whole and entire. I here mention seven (curiously enough), each of which deserves fuller treatment.

First, there is the sequence of 'signs' which runs throughout the gospel. John tells us that there were many other signs that could have been mentioned, but that he has arranged these ones so as to bring people to faith in

---

[14] Williams 2000, 186f. His proposal is designed to function more at the level of method and theology: see ch. 19 below.

[15] Against e.g. Evans 1970, 120, who declares himself 'surprised' by the 'massive realism' of these stories.

Jesus as Messiah and thus to the life which is found in his name.[16] Since he has just described Thomas confessing this faith when confronted with the palpably resurrected Jesus, we should clearly take the resurrection itself as the last 'sign' in the sequence. The numbering of the 'signs' in the gospel is endlessly debated, as indeed is the relationship between the hypothetical 'signs source' from which they were taken.[17] But in my judgment the best way of understanding the sequence, which John clearly intends us to follow, is to see them thus:

1. Water into wine (2.1–11)
2. The official's son (4.46–54)
3. The paralysed man at the pool (5.2–9)
4. Multiplication of loaves (6.1–14)
5. The man born blind (9.1–7)
6. The raising of Lazarus (11.1–44)
7. The crucifixion (19.1–37)
8. The resurrection (20.1–29)

The crucifixion is the climax and culmination of the 'signs' which Jesus has given, following the sevenfold sequence of the old creation. (From one point of view, of course, the crucifixion itself, and then the resurrection, are the truths to which the other signs all point; from another, however, they themselves now function as signs to the world, pointers to the divine life and love incarnate in Jesus.[18]) Now, on the eighth day, comes the eighth sign; the sequence was always about the new creation bursting in on the old. The 'signs' performed during the ministry led the disciples to the beginning of faith (2.11), but they made no impact upon most of the onlookers (12.37). Now, with the resurrection itself, the ultimate 'sign' which will explain what Jesus has been doing (2.18–22, on which see below), the new day has opened. People of all sorts are hereby summoned to believe (20.30–31).

Belief, or faith, is the second theme which stitches chapter 20 to the rest of the gospel. Though the noun 'faith' itself (*pistis*) never occurs in John, the cognate verb 'believe' (*pisteuein*) occurs more in this gospel than in Matthew, Mark and Luke put together; and, perhaps even more surprising, more than in all of Paul's letters put together. The concordance lists ninety-nine occurrences, spread over every chapter in the book except 15, 18 and (oddly) 21. This theme comes to fulfilment, not principally with the crucifixion,[19] but in chapter 20. The beloved disciple goes into the tomb, and

[16] Jn. 20.30f.

[17] On the 'signs source' see above all Fortna 1970, 1988, 1992. Recent studies include Köstenberger 1995; Koester 1996.

[18] See the suggestive comments of Barrett 1978 [1955], 78.

[19] There is only one occurrence of *pisteuein* in ch. 19: in v. 35, the writer claims eyewitness knowledge of the blood and water coming from Jesus' side, the evidence that he really is dead, and emphasizes that he says this 'so that you may believe', anticipating 20.31.

sees *and believes* (verse 8). Thomas declares that without sight and touch he will not believe (verse 25); Jesus challenges him to be 'not unbelieving, but believing' (verse 27);[20] Thomas declares that Jesus is his lord and god, and Jesus responds, 'Have you believed because you have seen me? Blessed are those who have not seen and yet believe' (verse 29).[21] The author then moves straight to the conclusion: these things are written so that you may believe, and, in believing, have life (verse 31). There can be no doubt that this theme, which has dominated the entire book, was designed to attain completion in chapter 20.

The third theme running through the gospel, powerfully though less evenly, and also coming to fulfilment in chapter 20, is that of the Spirit. John the Baptist saw the Spirit descend like a dove and remain on Jesus; this was the promised sign that Jesus was the one who would baptize with the Holy Spirit – in other words, that he was the true son of the true god (1.32–4). The Spirit is needed for the promised new birth to take place (1.13; 3.5–8). Jesus is equipped to speak the words the father gives him to speak, by the father's lavish gift of the Spirit (3.34). On the last great day of the feast of Tabernacles, using the water-imagery employed at that festival, Jesus invites anyone who is thirsty to come to him and drink, and thus to have 'rivers of living water' flowing out of them (7.37–8).[22] John's comment is powerful and revealing:

> He said this about the Spirit, which those who believed in him were to receive. For the Spirit was not yet, because Jesus was not yet glorified.[23]

This, of course, prepares us for what is to come, and, like the theme of 'believing' itself with which it is intimately joined, it comes, not immediately at the crucifixion, but on the evening of Easter day (20.21–3). Jesus, in other words, is now 'glorified' – *by both cross and resurrection together*. The Farewell Discourses contribute substantially to this theme as well: Jesus is going away (with the hindsight of chapter 20, we see that this refers to the combined event of death/resurrection/ascension), and will send the Spirit upon his followers, enabling them to bear witness to him, and so bringing

---

[20] These are the only occurrences of *apistos* and *pistos* in the book.

[21] The suggestion of Robinson 1982, 12 that v. 29 moves the thought in a 'gnostic direction' is patently absurd in the light of the new-creation theology that permeates the whole chapter. The possible link between the blessing in v. 29 and the coming to faith of the beloved disciple in 20.8 is explored by e.g. Byrne 1985.

[22] The biblical allusion seems to be to the river that flows from the restored Temple in Ezek. 47.1–12, and behind that to the river that flows, in four branches, from the garden of Eden (Gen. 2.10–14); cf. too Sir. 24.25–7, 30f.; Rev. 22.1f.

[23] Jn. 7.39. The clause 'for the Spirit was not yet' is as stark in Greek (*oupo gar en pneuma*) as it is in that translation. The variations in both the ancient MSS and the modern translations merely highlight this.

divine healing and judgment on the world.[24] When, therefore, we find Jesus in the upper room with the disciples, we have again a sense of a great tune reaching its full and final statement:

> 'Peace be with you,' said Jesus to them once more. 'As the father sent me, so I am sending you.'
> With these words, he breathed on them.
> 'Receive the Holy Spirit,' he said to them. 'Anyone whose sins you forgive, they are forgiven; anyone whose sins you retain, they are retained.'[25]

Like the water flowing from the heart in John 7, this awakens echoes of new creation and new Temple. Jesus breathes on the disciples, as the creator breathed into human nostrils at the beginning; they are equipped to be people through whom forgiveness of sins becomes a reality in the world.[26] They are thereby sent into the world, as the father had sent Jesus to Israel, to implement there, by their witness to him, the unique and decisive events of his ministry, his death, his resurrection.

The fourth theme, which again belongs closely with the others, is that of the restored Temple. John's gospel has Jesus going to and fro to Jerusalem and the Temple for various festivals, framed in chapters 2 and 12 by the opening and closing Passovers. On the first of these occasions, John describes the incident in the Temple which the other gospels place a few days before Jesus' arrest, trial and death.[27] Not surprisingly, Jesus is challenged to explain his actions in overturning tables and driving traders and animals out of the Temple; can he give 'a sign' for doing these things? His response helps us to understand why John has placed this incident here: he intends that we understand the rest of the Temple-scenes in the gospel within the framework provided by this action on the one hand and the resurrection on the other:

> 'Destroy this Temple,' Jesus replied, 'and I will raise it up in three days.'
> 'It's taken forty-six years to build this Temple,' replied the Judaeans, 'and are you going to raise it up in three days?'
> But he was speaking about the 'temple' of his body. When, therefore, he was raised from the dead, his disciples remembered that he had said this, and they believed the scripture and the word which Jesus had spoken.[28]

The sign, the believing, the resurrection, the Temple. Take away chapter 20, and this whole incident, and its explanation, lose their point. Put it back, and the reader will understand that, with Jesus' resurrection, judgment has been passed on the Temple, and that Jesus himself is now the place where, and

---

[24] Jn. 14.16f., 26; 15.26; 16.7–15.
[25] Jn. 20.21–3.
[26] See Gen. 2.7. On 'forgiveness' and the Temple cf. *JVG* 434–7.
[27] Jn. 2.13–22; cf. Mt. 21.12f./Mk. 11.15–17/Lk. 19.45f.
[28] Jn. 2.19–22.

the means by which, the father's presence and forgiving love are to be known. This is the meaning, too, of Jesus' comment to the woman of Samaria, that the hour is coming when true worshippers will not need a particular geographical location, because they will worship the father in spirit and truth (4.20–24).

With this, we arrive at the fifth theme which runs through the gospel to a climax in chapter 20: John's understanding of Jesus himself. 'I know that Messiah is coming,' says the woman of Samaria; and Jesus replies, 'That's me.'[29] This theme, even more than the others, deserves a monograph where space permits only a paragraph or two.

The category of 'Messiahship' is central for John, as I have argued it is for Paul; here, more obviously than in Paul, there is an easy fluidity between this Jewish category, still retaining 'royal' and national overtones, and the title 'son of god' in a fully 'divine' sense. This much is clear from the combination of the obviously high Christology of the prologue (1.1–2, 14, 18) with the words of John the Baptist ('I have seen and testified that this is God's son', 1.34) and the 'discovery of the Messiah' theme in 1.41, 45, and the extraordinary 1.49 ('Rabbi,' exclaims Nathanael, 'you are the son of god! You are the king of Israel!'). The speakers seem to be using 'son of god' in a strictly 'messianic' sense, but John intends his readers to hear it as an incipient confession of the hidden truth he has revealed in the prologue.

The theme then keeps emerging in one story or discourse after another. Jesus is the bridegroom, the one from above, the one the father has sent, and one's eternal fate depends upon one's reaction to him (3.29, 31, 35–6). He is the Messiah, the world's saviour (4.25, 29, 42). He enjoys a unique relationship with the father, who has given him the right to be judge of all, which is of course a messianic role (5.18, 19–47). The crowds recognize him as the prophet who was to come, and they want to go one step further and make him king (6.14–15). The disciples recognize him as 'the holy one of God' (6.69). The crowds and the authorities in Jerusalem are divided as to whether or not he can be the Messiah, or even a prophet (7.25–31, 40–52; 9.22; 12.34). He is the one who has come from Israel's god, the father (8.42–59). He is the shepherd of the sheep – an image which, in the Old Testament, was used mainly of kings but also, on occasion, of YHWH himself (10.11–30). Martha, asked whether she believes that Jesus is 'the resurrection and the life', declares that he is 'the Messiah, the son of god, the one who is coming into the world' (11.27). Those who see Jesus see the father (14.7–11). He is the true vine (15.1–11). The disciples believe that he has come from Israel's god (16.30). The hearing before Pilate turns on whether Jesus is claiming to be Israel's king, and if so what he means by that (18.33–9, 19.12–16, 19–22). Throughout this entire sequence (here abbreviated in breathless fashion) the royal and Davidic meaning of 'Messiah'

[29] Jn. 4.25f.

and hence also of 'son of god' remains active, with the deeper dimension of meaning (as in 1.18) mostly just beneath the surface.

But it is in the resurrection narrative, and once again with Thomas' declaration, that all the threads come together. The disciples' declaration in 6.69, and Martha's in 11.27, point in this direction, but Thomas' words are the most explicit since 1.18: 'My lord and my god!' And John's comment, about the faith he hopes to evoke and sustain through his writing of the gospel, shows that he has seen all along what many characters in his story have not: that 'Messiah, son of god' is to carry *both* the meaning 'Israel's true anointed king' *and* the meaning 'the Word incarnate, the *kyrios*, the human being of whom the word *theos*, God, may be predicated by faithful Jewish monotheists'. Once more, without the resurrection story, this faith has not reached full expression, not least because until Easter the grounds for it are not fully secure.

The last two themes belong closely with Christology. The sixth is the motif, which runs through much of the gospel, of Jesus being 'glorified' and/or 'lifted up', an event through which he will 'return to the father'. These seem to be mutually defining in various passages.[30] The Farewell Discourses are set within the context of the meal in the upper room, which begins with a long and careful statement of the theme:

> Jesus knew that his moment had come to go away out of the world to the father . . .
> he knew that the father had given all things into his hands, and that he had come
> from God and was going to God . . .[31]

The prayer which comes at the end of the Discourses points in the same direction:

> Father, the hour has come. Glorify the son, that the son may glorify you . . . now,
> father, glorify me with the glory I had with you before the world was made . . . I am
> no longer in the world, but they are in the world, and I am coming to you . . . Now I
> am coming to you, and I speak these things in the world so that they may have my
> joy fulfilled in them.[32]

This sometimes becomes bewildering, and commentators have duly been bewildered. If the 'glorification' happens when Jesus is 'lifted up', this clearly refers to the cross. And Jesus' death seems equally clearly to be his 'going away'. Maybe, the reader wonders, the crucifixion is after all the point at which a major theme reaches its goal.

But nothing in the crucifixion narrative itself supports this conclusion. Rather, it is the resurrection narrative that returns to the theme of Jesus going away, going to the father (20.17). Only in the light of Easter does the

[30] e.g. Jn. 3.13–15; 6.62; 12.23, 32–4; 14.12, 28; 16.28.
[31] Jn. 13.1, 3.
[32] Jn. 17.1, 5, 11, 13.

full meaning appear. Just as Jesus had said to Martha that if she believed she would see 'the glory of God' (11.40), so now those who believe, like the beloved disciple in 20.8 and Thomas in 20.28, are seeing 'the glory of God', not by looking simply at the crucifixion, but by looking (whether by faith, as in the first case, or by sight, as in the second) at *the resurrection of the crucified one*. Like the other accounts, John does not have Jesus shining with visible 'glory'; the fact of being raised from the dead is quite sufficient. Easter is where the theme of 'glory', too, finds its proper home. And this shows that for John the events of crucifixion, resurrection and ascension all alike reveal the true cosmology in which 'the world' and 'the father's house' (14.2) are not separated by a great gulf, but are the twin spheres of created reality between which Jesus can and does now pass.

The final theme is one for which John is famous: *agape*, love.[33] 'God so loved the world that he sent his son . . .' (3.16) is one of the most celebrated and often-quoted verses in the whole Bible. But the theme as John presents it is focused not so much on the divine love for the world in general as on Jesus' love for his followers, and on the father's love for the son which sustains him in his own loving work.[34]

The occurrences of the main word-group are only the tip of the iceberg. What we find throughout John's gospel is scene after scene in which Jesus *displays* this love, in his lengthy conversations with one character after another, and finally in his actions in the upper room and on the cross. In particular, the 'good shepherd' discourse in chapter 10 only mentions the word once ('this is why the father loves me', 10.17), but the entire passage is *about* 'love', about the self-giving shepherd who lays down his life for the sheep. Thus, though of course this self-giving love reaches fullest expression in the crucifixion, matchlessly symbolized in advance by the foot-washing scene in 13.1–20, it is in the renewal of the relationships between Jesus and Mary Magdalene, Jesus and the disciples in general ('my brothers', 20.17), Jesus and Thomas, and finally Jesus and Peter (21.15–22) that this theme comes to its final expression. The love which has given itself in death is now renewed with the new life of the resurrection.

Two important conclusions emerge from this brief survey. First, not only does chapter 20 belong firmly as part of the intended 'frame' of the gospel; it is tightly integrated with the entire book, several of whose main themes can only be understood when they are seen to lead the eye not just towards Jesus' crucifixion but also towards his resurrection. John has had the resurrection in mind all along. It has not been added simply in order to conform to tradition, or as a theologically unjustified afterthought.

---

[33] John uses the verb *agapao* 37 times against Paul's 34; he uses the noun *agape* only seven times, against Paul's 76. These statistics of course hide many relevant questions.

[34] cf. e.g. Jn. 3.35; 13.1, 34; 14.21, 31; 15.9; 17.23, 24, 26.

Second, the underlying 'new creation' theology of the whole book, and of these themes within it, indicate that John intends the narratives to be understood realistically and literally. Of course, he also intends that all kinds of echoes and resonances be heard within them; he always does; but these remain echoes and resonances *set off by a literal description of a concrete set of events.* This is not to say, of course, that we as historians can yet pronounce on the likelihood or otherwise of such events having taken place. It is simply to insist that, precisely as historians, in this case readers of ancient texts, we are bound to conclude that this is how John intends us to understand them. Here, as with the synoptic gospels, the ruling hypothesis in much New Testament study, according to which the resurrection narratives were generated and developed as allegories of Christian experience, and then mistakenly read by subsequent generations as literal descriptions of concrete events, fails at the levels of literature, history and theology. The multiple meanings the stories have are multiplications of the basic point, and as with all multiplication you cannot start with zero. The writer believes that these things happened. The indications are that any sources he may have used believed it too.

3. The Contribution of John 21

The material set out in the previous section indicates that chapter 20 was indeed the intended climax of the book as a whole. It forms the outer frame which matches the prologue, and all the major themes we have traced reach their own culmination in it. Strikingly, none of them, except for the last, reappear in chapter 21. It remains, quite clearly, an afterthought.

But an important one. It was not written simply to provide one more resurrection scene, however fascinating. The original writer had already imposed a self-denying ordinance on extra material (20.30), and if he was going to include this there are no doubt many other things he could have added as well. The reason for its inclusion, around the time when the 'beloved disciple' was either facing death or had just died, must have to do with the need within the community to address questions of two sorts, first about the roles of Peter and the beloved disciple, and second about the question of whether the beloved disciple would still be alive at the time when the Lord returned. We may suppose that the story of the fishing trip in 21.1–14 was told primarily to act as a setting for these more pressing concerns, not that it is itself lacking in interest.[35]

---

[35] The suggestion that the disciples' surprise on seeing Jesus indicates that this was the first appearance they had witnessed (Carnley 1987, 17) is purely imaginary. For a recent survey of the chapter cf. Söding 2002.

Of the two main emphases of the chapter, the first is the rehabilitation and commissioning of Peter. This has its own roots earlier in the gospel, though the mention of Peter's blustering declaration of loyalty in 13.38 and then his denial in 18.15–27 would not in themselves have needed a further detailed scene. (As is often noted, the charcoal fire in 21.9 reminds us of the charcoal fire in the high priest's hall in 18.18.) The triple question and response mirror the triple denial with the affirmation of love, the love of disciple for master that was such a major theme in chapter 14.[36] Peter is back on the map of genuine discipleship. This leads to a new commissioning, seen in terms of the shepherd image which dominated chapter 10. The mission of Jesus to Israel has already, in principle, been transformed by the Spirit into the mission of the church to the world (20.21); now, as a sharply focused point within that, Jesus' work as the Good Shepherd is to be carried on by Peter as an under-shepherd, conscious both of his responsibility towards the sheep and of his answerability to the chief Shepherd himself.[37] In all of this, Peter does not move away from the basic call to follow Jesus (21.19), the call which can now be repeated in terms of the need to keep his eyes on the Lord whom he is following, not on those to whom other roles and responsibilities may – or may not – have been assigned (21.22).

The second point is the imminent, or actual, death of the beloved disciple. This is interesting to us for a wholly different reason. The writer assumes that everybody, including readers of his gospel, knows that Jesus is to 'return' at some time in the future, even though there has been no mention of this in the book thus far. Not only must resurrection and ascension be factored in to John's view of Jesus; the second coming needs to be there too. The problem then posed by the death, imminent or actual, of the beloved disciple is that some in the church have believed that Jesus had predicted that he would not die, but would still be alive at the second coming. This, the writer is careful to insist, was not the case. What Jesus had said to Peter was simply, 'What I want for him (even if it should be to wait until I come) is no concern of yours.' The message for the church is then twofold. First, the beloved disciple's death does not constitute a problem; it does not mean that a key saying of Jesus has failed to come true. The writer does not deny or downplay the 'second coming'; he merely insists that the beloved disciple's death does not mean that something has gone wrong with the providential timetable. Second, Christians must learn, like Peter, to regard other people's destiny as of no importance. They must attend to their own discipleship and its responsibilities.

Once again, as with chapter 20, the point of these stories, at the level of apparent authorial intention, is that they intend to refer to incidents that actually took place. If there had not been a firm tradition in the early church

---

[36] Jn. 21.15, 16, 17; 14.15, 21, 23, 28.
[37] cf. 1 Pet. 5.1–4.

about such things having been said, the problem of misunderstanding would never have occurred. This again does not settle the historical question, but sets the literary context within which it may be addressed.

In particular, though, these passages raise the question, about both chapter 21 and chapter 20, as to whether they have been written with at least one eye on questions of comparative authority within the church. Is this story really about 'the primacy of Peter', as the small church at Tabgha (the supposed scene of John 21) has now been renamed by zealous Franciscans? Are there attempts going on in these two chapters to play off Peter and the beloved disciple (and their respective followers) against one another? Is there an attempt to do something similar either with Mary Magdalene in 20.1–18 or with Thomas in 20.24–9?

Arguments like this have often been advanced, but they remain in my judgment unconvincing.[38] Anyone who wanted to use resurrection stories as a way of promoting the primacy of one of Jesus' followers in particular could have done a better job than this. Mary Magdalene is clearly the first one at the tomb and the first one to see the risen Jesus, but we have no reason to suppose either that anyone was hereby making out a case for her primacy or that, facing such a claim, this chapter was written to refute it. Peter and the beloved disciple run together to the tomb; the beloved disciple gets there first, Peter goes inside first and looks around, and the beloved disciple then 'sees and believes' – though still without understanding the scriptures which say he must rise again. If there is a hidden agenda in this breathless description, an attempt to make Peter and the beloved disciple stand for different types of Christianity, it has passed most readers by from that day to this, and in my view rightly so.[39]

What then about Thomas? We could perhaps see his stubborn doubt as a picture of 'Thomas Christians', seen from the point of view of Johannine, Petrine or other Christians – a way of dismissing or sneering at a different movement within the early church.[40] But if that was what the writer had in mind, what would be the point of putting in Thomas' mouth the greatest declaration of Christian faith in the whole gospel (20.28), the one clearly designed to remain in the reader's mind as the paradigm for all subsequent believing? It will hardly do to suggest that in the *Gospel of Thomas* all Christians are equal with Jesus himself, so that by making Thomas confess Jesus as 'lord and god' John is bringing him into line with orthodoxy.[41] This is a spectacular statement of faith, and when we hear it both as the structural

---

[38] e.g. Söding 2002, 231: John 21 is 'ein kirchenpolitisch brisanter Text', 'an explosive church-political text'.

[39] See the judicious comments of Evans 1970, 121 on the theories of Bultmann, Grass and Marxsen.

[40] See Riley 1995, 78–126: the Johannine author and/or community are putting 'Thomas Christians' (i.e. the group who based themselves on *Gos. Thom.*) in their place.

[41] Riley 1995, 123f.; cf. *Gos. Thom.* 13, 108.

end-marker of the book (see above) and as a direct challenge to the rising imperial cult (Domitian at least had himself called 'lord and god') we can hardly imagine it being simultaneously heard by Johannine Christians as saying, 'So that's all right – Thomas did agree with us after all, and those strange Thomas Christians are in the wrong.'[42] Jesus' gentle rebuke in verse 29, implying that Thomas should have believed without seeing, can hardly be read as lessening the force of the declaration. Its real target, we may suppose, is not so much a hypothetical group of Thomas Christians who want to base their faith on the evidence of their senses, but any future reader who might respond by saying, 'It was all very well for Thomas; you can't expect me to imitate that kind of faith unless I have the same evidence.'[43]

Similar points can be made about chapter 21. The wonderfully comic fishing scene has been interpreted – and probably over-interpreted – in numerous ways, but attempts to make it a vehicle for a pro-Peter party surely fail. The conversation between Jesus and Peter is basically about penitence, not primacy; its aim is not to establish or reinforce a particular status, but to effect reconciliation. Giving Peter a fresh task signals the re-establishment of trust, following Peter's own profession of love. Peter must not worry about Jesus' plans for the beloved disciple; but neither he nor anyone else is told that he, Peter, will now hold a position of special honour. Likewise, if the story was told so as to place fresh emphasis on the beloved disciple over against Peter, this too has remained opaque to most readers, and for good reason.

Perhaps the most interesting feature of chapter 21 for our present purposes is the portrait of the risen Jesus that emerges from it. As in the other gospel stories, the Jesus of this one is real, palpable, a physical person capable of performing physical acts including cooking breakfast. Nothing is said about his disappearance at the end of the story; but there is another tell-tale hint that the writer is aware of an oddness, a difference, about him which can hardly be put into words, but only hinted at:

> 'Come and have breakfast,' said Jesus to them.
> But none of the disciples dared to press him with the question, 'Who are you?', since they knew it was the Lord.[44]

The verb I have translated 'to press him with the question' is the rare word *exetazo*.[45] It means more than just 'ask': rather, we should hear something

---

[42] I remember hearing Dominic Crossan say in a lecture that the resurrection narratives 'trivialize Christianity' (by which he meant that they turn it into a power-game). In fact, it is theories like Riley's that trivialize these stories.

[43] It would be a further large jump to link such a hypothetical group of 'Thomas Christians' with *Gos. Thom.* In any case, Thomas' reported desire (in this passage) to base his faith on the evidence of his physical senses hardly corresponds to the theology of that work.

[44] Jn. 21.12.

[45] Elsewhere in the NT only at Mt. 2.8; 10.11.

like 'scrutinize, examine, enquire'.[46] They knew it really was him, says John; but at the same time they wanted to ask, to press him with their question. This makes *us* want to press a question: Why did they want to do that? And, John continues, they were afraid to do so. Again, why? The only possible answer to both questions seems to be that they were aware of Jesus being somehow different, as well as certainly the same. The brief account is heavy with the strangeness of new creation. There is (again) no suggestion that they perceived Jesus as having a body which could neither die nor decay, which is the main point of difference highlighted from Paul onwards between the present body and the risen body. This story does not seem to have been generated, in other words, out of a desire to clothe a developed theology with cunningly devised 'realistic' fiction. It seems to reflect a primal moment of simultaneous recognition and puzzlement, an awareness of something they could hardly put into words except as a question, and a question they dared not ask.

There is, in other words, a sense of discontinuity as well as continuity. But this is not expressed in the language or theology that we find in Paul and beyond. It fits very well with the picture we have discovered across the board in the gospel narratives: something in all the stories which might well generate the kind of developed theology and exegesis we find in Paul and later writers, but which shows no signs of having been projected back as a clever, seemingly 'naively realist' fiction. In terms of a central Johannine image, John's resurrection stories appear more like the root of a vine than its newly grown fruit.

4. The Gospel Easter Stories: Conclusion

The general points common to all four gospel accounts have already been set out in chapter 13. All we need to do at this point is to summarize what we have seen in this more detailed study.

There can be no doubt that each evangelist has told the story in his own way. Even where there is good reason to suppose that one used the other as a source – which I assume for at least Luke with Mark, with Matthew's use of Mark remaining probable and Mark's use of Matthew an outside chance – there is remarkably little verbal overlap. Instead, we find in each of the stories not so much a sign of steady development from a primitive tradition to a form in which the evangelist simply wrote down what the tradition at that point had grown into, but rather a retelling of primitive stories by the evangelist himself in such a way as to form a fitting climax to his particular book. You could not take Luke's ending and substitute it for John's, or John's for Matthew's, without creating an absurdity, like the picture books

---

[46] BDAG 349.

for children in which heads, bodies and legs are swapped around between characters with ludicrous results. The evangelists have exercised considerable freedom in retelling and reshaping the narratives so as to bring out themes and emphases that were important to them throughout their work.

It is therefore all the more remarkable that the basic outline remains so constant, and, in the ways explored in chapter 13, so undeveloped. In particular, though each evangelist has told the story in such a way as to ground a particular understanding of Christian life and particularly Christian mission to the world (Mark of course excepted, though even there the projected journey to Galilee may be seen as a pointer in that direction), the basic stories themselves, of the empty tomb and the appearances of Jesus, show no signs of having been generated at a later stage. There is no reason to imagine that they were generated either by a newly invented apologetic for the fact that the word 'resurrection' was being used of Jesus, or out of a desire to provide legitimation for particular leaders or particular practices. It will of course always remain possible for scholars to think of clever ways in which this might after all have been so, in which the idea of the stories as late apologetic fiction might be rehabilitated; but the main barriers against such a reconstruction are strong and high. If you were a follower of a dead Jesus, in the middle of the first century, wanting to explain why you still thought he was important, and why some of your number had (inexplicably) begun to say that he had been raised from the dead, you would not have told stories like this. You would have done a better job.

We are left with the conclusion that both the evangelists themselves, and the sources to which they had access, whether oral or written, which they have shaped to their own purposes but without destroying the underlying subject-matter, really did intend to refer to actual events which took place on the third day after Jesus' execution. The main conclusion that emerges from these four studies of the canonical evangelists is that each of them, in their very different ways, believed that they were writing about events that actually took place. Their stories can be used to refer metaphorically or allegorically to all sorts of other things, and they probably (certainly in the case of Luke and John) intended it to be so. But the stories they told, and the way they crafted them (each so differently, yet in this respect the same) as the deliberate and climactic rounding-off of their whole accounts, indicates that for reasons of narrative grammar as well as theology they must have intended to convey to their readers the sense that the Easter events were real, not fantasy; historical as well as historic. They believed, of course, that these events were foundational for the very existence of the church, and they naturally told the stories in such a way as to bring this out. But in the worldview to which they all subscribed, the fresh modification-from-within of the Jewish worldview which we can trace throughout earliest Christianity, the whole point was that the renewed people of Israel's god, the creator, had been called into being precisely by events that happened in the world of creation, of space, time and matter. The evangelists, and any sources we may hypothesize behind them, tell a story which offers itself as the explanation for the entire development of 'resurrection' belief, and the other features of early Christianity we have studied in Parts II and III of this book, but which stubbornly resists attempts to turn it into a mere back-projection of those developments and features. Those who told this story, and those who wrote it down, were very interested in the overtones they could hear in it. But you only get overtones when you strike a fundamental.

We have now surveyed the entire corpus of writing about Jesus and his resurrection in the first two centuries, setting it within the framework of beliefs about life after death in the ancient worlds of paganism and Judaism. We have charted the extraordinary range, from Paul to Tertullian and Origen, of Christian writing about the resurrection both of Jesus himself and of his followers (and in some cases of all humankind). We have seen that early Christian resurrection-belief has a remarkable consistency despite varieties of expression, and that this consistency includes both the location of Christianity at one point on the spectrum of Jewish belief (bodily resurrection) and four key modifications from within that point: (1) resurrection has moved from the circumference of belief to the centre; (2) 'the resurrection' is no longer a single event, but has split chronologically into two, the first part of which has already happened; (3) resurrection involves transformation, not mere resuscitation; and (4) when 'resurrection' language is used metaphorically, it no longer refers to the national restoration of Israel, but to baptism and holiness. The exceptions prove the rule: the position ascribed to Hymenaeus and Philetus in 2 Timothy 2, together with the *Letter to Rheginos* and similar texts, were mere innovation, not a natural growth or development. They used the language of resurrection to denote something to which that word-group had never before referred. The only explanation for such usage is that the writers in question were trying to use current Christian language to describe, and perhaps to legitimate, alternative theologies and worldviews. They thereby highlighted, paradoxically, the strength of the position from which they dissented, whose language they found themselves compelled to adopt.

Throughout it all we have seen the obvious but important point, that those who held the complex but remarkably consistent early Christian view gave as their reason that Jesus of Nazareth had himself been raised from the dead. And we have now seen what they meant by this: that on the third day after his execution by the Romans, his tomb was empty, and he was found to be alive, appearing on various occasions and in various places both to his followers and to some who, up to that point, had not been his followers or had not believed, convincing them that he was neither a ghost nor a hallucination but that he was truly and bodily raised from the dead. This belief about Jesus provides a historically complete, thorough and satisfying reason for the rise and development of the belief that he was Israel's Messiah and the world's true lord. It explains the early Christian conviction that the long-awaited new age had been inaugurated, opening new tasks and possibilities. Above all, it explains the belief that the hope for the world in general and for Jesus' followers in particular consisted not in going on and on for ever, not in an endless cycle of death and rebirth as in Stoicism, not in a blessed dis-embodied immortal existence, but in a newly embodied life, a transformed physicality. And we have now seen that the central stories upon which this belief was based, though they have been skillfully shaped and edited by the four evangelists, retain simple and very early features, features which resist the idea that they were made up decades later, but which serve very well to explain the developments from Paul onwards. We are now in a position to face the question: what historical reasons can be given for the rise of this belief?

Part Five

Belief, Event and Meaning

HEROD: He raises the dead?

FIRST NAZARENE: Yea, sire, He raiseth the dead.

HEROD: I do not wish Him to do that. I forbid Him to do that. I allow no man to raise the dead. This Man must be found and told that I forbid Him to raise the dead. Where is this Man at present?

SECOND NAZARENE: He is in every place, my lord, but it is hard to find Him.

Oscar Wilde, *Salomé*
(Wilde 1966, 565)

Let us not mock God with metaphor,
analogy, sidestepping, transcendence;
making of the event a parable, a sign painted in the
      faded credulity of earlier ages;
let us walk through the door.

Let us not seek to make it less monstrous,
for our own convenience, our own sense of beauty,
lest, awakened in one unthinkable hour, we are
      embarrassed by the miracle,
and crushed by remonstrance.

John Updike, from 'Seven Stanzas at Easter'
(Updike 1964, 72f.)

Chapter Eighteen

EASTER AND HISTORY

1. Introduction

The historical datum now before us is a widely held, consistently shaped and highly influential belief: that Jesus of Nazareth was bodily raised from the dead. This belief was held by virtually all the early Christians for whom we have evidence. It was at the centre of their characteristic praxis, narrative, symbol and belief; it was the basis of their recognition of Jesus as Messiah and lord, their insistence that the creator god had inaugurated the long-awaited new age, and above all their hope for their own future bodily resurrection. The question we now face is obvious: what caused this belief in the resurrection of Jesus?

At this point, as the behavioural psychologists used to say, a laboratory rat lay down and cried. The equivalents in my own discipline are clear: hard-headed historians and soft-headed theologians often decide to quit right here. The first say we can go no further, the second that we ought not to try.[1]

Less cautious historians, forgetting that history is the study, not of repeatable events as in physics and chemistry, but of unrepeatable events like Caesar's crossing of the Rubicon, declare that we can indeed go further, and that we can reach a clear negative judgment: we can be quite sure that nothing whatever happened to Jesus' body at Easter, except that it continued to decompose. Dead people don't rise, therefore Jesus didn't either.[2]

Less cautious theologians divide into two camps. Some say it would be wrong of any god to do for Jesus what the resurrection stories claim Israel's god did, or even that it is morally wrong, and socially and psychologically damaging, for people to believe such a thing. Others, however, say that we must believe the stories because the Bible says so, and/or because holding a supernaturalistic worldview is just as valid as holding a naturalistic one, and/or because, if Jesus was 'the son of god', what else would you expect?

---

[1] See ch. 1.
[2] Lüdemann 1994 is a classic example. In public debates following the book's publication, Lüdemann insisted over and over that this conclusion was assured by modern science (as though the ancient world had been ignorant of the fact that dead people stayed dead).

Simply to raise the question, therefore, let alone to address it, demands that we prepare ourselves for criticism on the level of method, before we get anywhere near content. Walking into the middle of this 360-degree barrage of cold epistemological water reminds me of playing golf in the evening and suddenly being bombarded, on the last green, by the automatic sprinkler system. Is there any chance of making the final putt? Or must we retreat, soaked and frustrated?

We must hold our nerve and proceed. Two things can be securely established, and we should not be shy of placing them down as markers. To go beyond that again we must indeed face large issues both of method and of worldview; but we must locate those issues precisely where they belong, and not throw up our hands and give in at the first sign of difficulty.

2. The Tomb and the Meetings

The two things which must be regarded as historically secure when we talk about the first Easter are the emptiness of the tomb and the meetings with the risen Jesus. Once we locate the early Christians within the world of second-Temple Judaism, and grasp what they believed about their own future hope and about Jesus' own resurrection, these two phenomena are firmly warranted. The argument can be set out in seven steps, which I shall state in summary form and then expound at somewhat more length.

1. To sum up where we have got to so far: the world of second-Temple Judaism supplied the concept of resurrection, but the striking and consistent Christian mutations within Jewish resurrection belief rule out any possibility that the belief could have generated spontaneously from within its Jewish context. When we ask the early Christians themselves what had occasioned this belief, their answers home in on two things: stories about Jesus' tomb being empty, and stories about him appearing to people, alive again.

2. Neither the empty tomb by itself, however, nor the appearances by themselves, could have generated the early Christian belief. The empty tomb alone would be a puzzle and a tragedy. Sightings of an apparently alive Jesus, by themselves, would have been classified as visions or hallucinations, which were well enough known in the ancient world.

3. However, an empty tomb and appearances of a living Jesus, taken together, would have presented a powerful reason for the emergence of the belief.

4. The meaning of resurrection within second-Temple Judaism makes it impossible to conceive of this reshaped resurrection belief emerging without it being known that a body had disappeared, and that the person had been discovered to be thoroughly alive again.

5. The other explanations sometimes offered for the emergence of the belief do not possess the same explanatory power.

6. It is therefore historically highly probable that Jesus' tomb was indeed empty on the third day after his execution, and that the disciples did indeed encounter him giving every appearance of being well and truly alive.[3]

7. This leaves us with the last and most important question: what explanation can be given for these two phenomena? Is there an alternative to the explanation given by the early Christians themselves?

The kind of argument I am offering here may be located on the well-known map of theories of explanation, using the tools of *necessary and sufficient conditions*. Most detailed historical enquiry, like the detective work that hunts down criminals, makes at least implicit use of these tools, and I find that making them explicit can bring some clarity in an area where it is often lacking. It is a way of putting the matter under the microscope. There is a substantial literature on the different types, and sub-types, of conditions, and it is impossible and unnecessary to go into the details here.[4] In any case, when dealing with history – not least the history of what people believed and how they came to believe it – we are unlikely to attain the watertight conclusiveness demanded in symbolic logic.

The broad difference between necessary and sufficient conditions is not difficult to grasp. A *necessary* condition is something that has to be the case for the conclusion to follow: it is a necessary condition of my computer working properly that the house be connected to an electricity supply. A *sufficient* condition is something that will certainly and without fail bring about the conclusion: it is a sufficient condition of my having a sleepless night that somebody should practise the bagpipes outside my bedroom window. The difference between the two appears if we consider the alternatives. Connecting the house to the electricity supply may be a necessary condition for my computer to function, but it is certainly not sufficient; any number of things might go wrong with the machine itself. Bagpipes at midnight are sufficient for my sleeplessness, but they are certainly not a necessary condition; a pot of strong coffee, or a pneumatic drill in the street, would have the same effect. The supply of electricity is thus a *necessary but insufficient* condition of the computer functioning; the bagpipes are a *sufficient but unnecessary* condition of my sleepless night.

My argument in the seven steps outlined a moment ago, more precisely in the crucial steps 2, 3, 4 and 5, can be plotted with the same conceptual tools.

---

[3] I use the word 'probable' in the common-sense historians' way, not in the highly problematic philosophers' way (cf. e.g. Lucas 1970); that is to say, as a way of indicating that the historical evidence, while comparatively rarely permitting a conclusion of 'certain', can acknowledge a scale from, say, 'extremely unlikely', through 'possible', 'plausible' and 'probable', to 'highly probable'.

[4] There is a considerable literature devoted to the meaning and use of necessary and sufficient conditions; see e.g. Lowe 1995; Sosa and Tooley 1993. I first met the complexities of necessary and sufficient conditions through the work of J. L. Mackie, now collected in Mackie 1980.

Steps 2 and 3 face the question of whether, and to what extent, the empty tomb and the appearances of Jesus can be seen as *sufficient* conditions for the rise of early Christian belief; steps 4 and 5 raise the question as to whether they should be seen as *necessary* conditions.[5] In both cases the answer needs fine-tuning, but my substantial proposal is that the combination of the empty tomb and the appearances constitute, with qualifications, a sufficient condition for the rise of the early Christian belief (2 and 3), and that, with more substantial qualifications, they also constitute a necessary condition (4 and 5). The qualifications are important, meaning that the argument falls short of anything approaching mathematical proof; but the proposal remains important, advancing well beyond historical possibility to high probability.

The seven steps may now be elaborated as follows.

Step 1 sets the context for the question we face, drawing together the threads of the previous chapters. The early Christian beliefs were conceived and formulated within the context of second-Temple Judaism, and make sense as a mutation from within one well-known position on the Jewish spectrum; but no other second-Temple Jews came up with anything remotely like them. When we ask the early Christians themselves why they held to these beliefs, the answers they give point to the strange stories at the end of the four canonical gospels. The tomb was empty, they say (being careful to let us know that it was certainly the tomb in which the dead Jesus of Nazareth had earlier been buried); and they saw him alive, talked with him, and ate and drank with him.

This brings us to step 2, and to my double argument that neither the empty tomb on the one hand, nor the appearances on the other, constitutes by itself a sufficient condition for the rise of the early Christian belief.[6] Let us examine each in turn.

2a. An empty tomb without any meetings with Jesus would have been a distressing puzzle, but not a long-term problem.[7] It would have proved nothing; it would have *suggested* nothing, except the fairly common practice of grave-robbery. It certainly would not have generated the phenomena we have studied in this book so far. Tombs were often robbed in the ancient world, adding to grief both insult and injury. Nobody in the pagan world would have interpreted an empty tomb as implying resurrection; everyone

---

[5] For a similar way of putting the question, see e.g. Williams 1982, 106.

[6] So, rightly, Stuhlmacher 1993, 48. However Stuhlmacher puzzlingly sees most of the appearances (not that to Mary in Jn. 20) as being 'from heaven'.

[7] Schillebeeckx 1979 [1974], 381: a 'vanished corpse' is not in itself a resurrection. (On Schillebeeckx, however, see further below.) See too McDonald 1989, 140; Macquarrie 1990, 407f.; and cf. Polkinghorne 1994, 116–18. Perkins 1984, 84 is right to say that an empty tomb would not by itself generate belief that someone had been raised, but since she bases this on the belief that the emptiness or otherwise of the tomb is irrelevant for the Christian proclamation her conclusion is worth less than it might have been.

knew such a thing was out of the question. Nobody in the ancient Jewish world would have interpreted it like that either; 'resurrection' was not something anyone expected to happen to a single individual while the world went on as normal.[8] Certainly – a point often ignored by critics – the disciples were not expecting any such thing to happen to Jesus. Had the tomb been empty, with no other unusual occurrences, no one would have said that Jesus was the Messiah or the lord of the world. No one would have imagined that the kingdom had been inaugurated. No one, in particular, would have developed so quickly and consistently a radical and reshaped version of the Jewish hope for the resurrection of the body.[9] The empty tomb is by itself insufficient to account for the subsequent evidence.

An apparent and striking counter-example to this proposal is found in John 20.8. The beloved disciple goes into the empty tomb, sees what Peter had seen a moment before (the grave-clothes lying, separate from the headcloth), and believes. Could it be that in his case, or at least in the mind of the evangelist writing this, the empty tomb by itself was sufficient for the rise of his faith? The answer suggested by the text is 'No'. The grave-clothes seem to be understood as a sign of what had happened to Jesus, a sign which would be the functional equivalent of the actual appearances of Jesus (John 20.19–23). The beloved disciple came to his new belief, the text wants us to understand, not simply on the basis of the emptiness of the tomb (which had been explained by Mary in verse 2 in terms of the removal of the body to an unknown location), but on the basis of what he deduced both from the fact that the grave-clothes had been left behind and from the position in which they were lying. He, like Thomas at the end of the chapter, saw something which elicited faith. The fact that the grave-clothes were left behind showed that the body had not been carried off, whether by foes, friends or indeed a gardener (verse 15). Their positioning, carefully described in verse 7, suggests that they had not been unwrapped, but that the body had somehow passed through them, much as, later on, it would appear and disappear through locked doors (verse 19). The conclusion holds, then: an empty tomb, by itself, could not have functioned as a sufficient condition of early Christian belief in Jesus' resurrection.

2b. 'Meetings' with Jesus, likewise, could by themselves have been interpreted in a variety of ways. Most people in the ancient world (though not so many, it seems, in the modern world) knew that visions and appearances of recently dead people occurred.[10] No doubt there are all kinds of explanations

---

[8] The strange report in Mk. 6.14–16 seems to be the exception that proves the rule; see above, 203, 244.

[9] Wedderburn 1999, 65 rightly concludes that the evidence demands that something must have happened on the first Easter day, then wrongly suggests that the 'something' might simply have been 'a fruitless search for a body'. This would not, I submit, have been sufficient by itself to explain what happened thereafter.

[10] A classic modern study is that of Jaffe 1979. Whatever interpretations are put on such

for things like that. Various theories can be advanced about the psychological state of the person who experiences them, though the evidence seems to suggest that in some cases at least the phenomena are clearly related to actual events (for instance, the recent death, unexpected, otherwise unknown and so far unexplained, of an absent loved one) rather than simply the projection of feelings of guilt or grief.[11] But that such 'seeings', even such 'meetings', occur, and that people have known about them throughout recorded history, there should be no question.

Such things were not, perhaps, quite as frequent as some recent writers have tried to make out.[12] Visions of this sort, in addition, did not normally involve physical contact, let alone watching the recently departed person eating and drinking; indeed, accounts of visions of the dead sometimes made it clear that this is what did *not* happen. But such 'meetings', even if they did seem to involve seeing, touching, or even eating and drinking with the recently dead person, could, at a stretch, have been interpreted as 'angelic' visitations of the kind the disciples thought they were having from Peter in Acts 12. They might have provided a very special case, perhaps even a very encouraging and heart-warming case, of the generally known and widely recognized possibility of short-lived encounters with something that seemed to be the dead person. The response to reported visions of this kind might of course have been, in the ancient as in the modern world, to question the mental balance, or perhaps the recent diet, of the witnesses. As we have remarked more than once, the ancient world as well as the modern knew the difference between visions and things that happen in the 'real' world.[13] But visions did occur.

However, precisely because such encounters were reasonably well known (the apparently strong point of those who have recently tried to insist that this is what 'really happened' at Easter) they *could not possibly*, by themselves, have given rise to the belief that Jesus had been raised from the dead. They are a thoroughly *insufficient* condition for the early Christian belief. The more 'normal' these 'visions' were, the less chance there is that anyone, no matter how cognitively dissonant they may have been feeling, would have said what nobody had ever said about such a dead person before, that they had been *raised from* the dead.[14] Indeed, such visions meant precisely,

---

events (the book is in the 'Jungian Classics Series'), the phenomena which it reports are obviously widespread, though not frequently spoken of in a world where people are afraid of being thought gullible or the victims of fantasies.

[11] Lüdemann 1994, 97–100 makes experiences of this type central to his explanation of the initial 'visions' of Peter and Paul.

[12] cf. Riley 1995, 58–68, followed by e.g. Crossan 1998, xiv–xix.

[13] Ac. 12.9, etc. On the danger of seeing the experience of visionaries as paradigmatic for understanding the 'meetings' with Jesus see e.g. Schneiders 1995, 90f.

[14] Thus, for example, Crossan's insistence that human beings are 'hard-wired' to have this kind of experience (1998, xviii) militates *against* such 'visions' as a way of explaining why the early Christians came to speak of 'resurrection'. His repeated description of the

as people in the ancient and modern worlds have discovered, that the person was dead, not that they were alive.[15] Even if several such experiences had occurred, if the tomb was still occupied by the dead body they would have said to themselves, after the experiences had ceased, 'We have seen exceedingly strange visions, but he is still dead and buried. Our experiences were, after all, no different from the ones we have heard about in the old stories and poems.'[16]

As with the empty tomb, we here face possible counter-arguments. Did not Paul himself come to his belief in Jesus' resurrection on the basis simply of an appearance? Things are again not quite so straightforward. Unless we are to discount entirely the witness of Acts, we must conclude that the empty tomb of Jesus, and the repeated insistence that his body had not decomposed, were of central and foundational importance in the preaching and life of the Christians whom Paul had been persecuting. It is highly likely that he knew at least that the followers of Jesus claimed that his tomb was empty, and that this claim had not been falsified. His seeing of the risen Jesus, therefore, took place in a context where at least the report of an empty tomb may be assumed. In the same way, the story of Mary's meeting with Jesus in John 20.11–18 includes the often puzzling 'do not touch me'; if, as is often suggested, the proper interpretation of this is 'do not cling on to me', the story may be making the point that this was not simply the appearance of a phantom, a bodiless spirit such as Odysseus attempted to cling on to but could not. Though in the longer story Mary had of course seen the empty tomb for herself, someone telling this story in the ancient world would be aware that it contained within itself the sign that the body which was appearing was no mere ghost. The same point is made in Luke, John and Acts by the stories of Jesus eating with the disciples.[17] There seems to be a constant sense that 'appearances' by themselves have to be backed up with evidence that what was seen was a substantial body such as must have left an empty

---

early Christian experience as 'the vision of a dead man' (xiii, xiv, etc.) looks remarkably like deciding the case before examining the evidence. On 'cognitive dissonance' see the discussion of Festinger, below.

[15] See e.g. Chariton, *Call.* 3.7.4f. Jaffe 1979 provides plenty of modern examples, typically of people who suddenly see a friend or family member in the room with them and subsequently discover that they had died at that moment.

[16] The discussion of the empty tomb by Lindars 1993 is full of flaws. Once we read (119) that the narratives were 'rationalisations of the Resurrection faith among people for whom abstract truths tend to be expressed in concrete forms', we no longer expect a serious historical discussion of first-century Jewish belief. O'Collins 1997, 13–17 lists scholars who have been persuaded that the tomb was empty, and argues cogently against the theory that Mark invented the story himself (as held by e.g. A. Y. Collins 1993).

[17] Lk. 24.41–3; Jn. 21.1–14 (the text does not say explicitly that Jesus ate, but it is surely implied in 'come and have breakfast' (21.12; cp. 21.13 with Lk. 24.30); Ac. 10.41. I am grateful to Prof. Charles Talbert of Baylor University for emphasizing this point in private conversation.

tomb behind it. It is thus comparatively straightforward to show that, by themselves, neither an empty tomb nor visual 'appearances' – however we categorize them – would be sufficient to generate the early Christian beliefs we have been studying. This bears importantly on a topic at which we have already glanced: it seems to me unlikely that stories only of an empty tomb or only of 'appearances', without at least some hint of the other, could have been generated, or indeed circulated, independently in early Christianity. The point of the empty tomb stories always was that Jesus was alive again; the point of the appearance stories always was that the Jesus who was appearing was in bodily continuity with the corpse that had occupied the tomb. Neither, without the other, makes the sense that the early Christians believed they made. They are like the two parts of a road sign, the arm which indicates the road and the vertical post which supports it. Without the post, the arm cannot be seen; without the arm, the post cannot say anything. Join them together and they point to the truth.

3. Putting two insufficient conditions together, of course, guarantees nothing. The fact that the house is connected to the main electricity supply, and that the computer is in working order, does not guarantee that the computer will now work. Someone may have taken away the power cable which connects the computer to the supply. Once more, it only takes a little ingenuity to dream up all kinds of twists and turns in such illustrations. But in some cases, two insufficient conditions, put together, will produce a sufficient one. The fact that the plane is in perfect mechanical order does not guarantee a safe landing. Having a well-trained, alert pilot in charge is likewise insufficient. A first-rate plane piloted by a novice, or a poor-quality plane flown by a first-rate pilot, may still crash. But put a first-rate pilot in charge of a first-rate plane, and – granted other things like weather conditions and the state of the runway – the combination produces a sufficient condition of a safe landing.

That is the kind of position we are in, I suggest, with the empty tomb and the appearances. We have seen that they are, by themselves, insufficient to generate early Christian belief. Bring them together, however, and they form, in combination, a sufficient condition.[18] From everything we know both of the second-Temple context and of the beliefs of the disciples about Jesus and his mission, we can be confident that if they discovered on the one hand that his tomb was empty, and found on the other hand that, for a while, they kept meeting him in ways which gave every appearance that he was

---

[18] Against Vermes 2000, 173, who suggests that the empty tomb stories faded as the appearance stories increased. See too the long tradition represented by e.g. Schillebeeckx 1979 [1974], 332f., who suggests that Mt., Lk. and Jn. have combined the originally independent traditions of visions and empty tomb to make it look as though they belonged together as the bases for belief in the resurrection, whereas in fact (he says) the empty tomb stories are later projections and the 'visions' are subjective experiences. See further below.

dead no longer, but actually alive, the belief we have studied throughout the first two centuries of Christianity would certainly emerge.[19]

Once again, a counter-example suggests itself. According to John in the story of Thomas, and to Matthew in the story of the disciples meeting Jesus on the mountain, not everyone did in fact believe, in the first case when reports of the empty tomb were supplemented with reports of appearances, and in the second when, after the discovery of the empty tomb, Jesus was actually appearing at the time.[20] Furthermore, of course, as the gospel message went out into the wider world a great many people refused to believe, even when confronted with enthusiastic eye-witness evidence of both the empty tomb and the appearances. Does this mean that, even in combination, the empty tomb and the appearances did not, after all, constitute a sufficient condition for the rise of the early Christian belief?

This time the counter-example suggests that we introduce a modification into the proposal. The combination of empty tomb and appearances of Jesus was clearly not sufficient for the rise of Christian belief in everyone who heard about it. But we can, I think, propose a nuanced and ultimately stronger case. Granted that those who found the empty tomb and saw the risen Jesus were second-Temple Jews, most of whom had followed Jesus and were hoping he would turn out to be Israel's Messiah, the two pieces of evidence would be sufficient to make most of them conclude that he had been raised from the dead in the sense we have already studied. The doubts of some at the time, and the refusal of others later on to believe the witness of Christian preachers, do not substantially affect this point. (The fact that, because of poor weather or ground conditions, or indeed reckless or hostile action by other parties, not all first-rate planes flown by first-rate pilots make it safely to land does not affect the general point.) The empty tomb and the appearances were sufficient, not for every single person who heard about them to arrive at Christian belief, but for that belief to arise within a community which began with Jesus' followers and spread outwards from there.

4. If the empty tomb and the appearances of Jesus are, in this sense, a *sufficient* condition for the rise of the early Christian belief, we must now ask: are they also a *necessary* one? This is a harder task, since it involves proving a negative. To show that the electricity supply is a necessary condition for the computer to work is one thing. Not only can you experiment with other possibilities and show that nothing else will in fact do; you can examine the computer itself and discover that it is designed to work on electricity and only on electricity. But with history things are seldom that straightforward.

---

[19] At this point I find myself in substantial agreement with Sanders 1993, 276–81, a brief account but one which contains more good historical judgment than many of far greater length.

[20] Jn. 20.25; Mt. 28.17.

Furthermore, when our primary datum is a widely held belief for which we are seeking the causes, matters are even more open-ended. People believe many strange things for many odd reasons. All that is required to demonstrate that the tomb-plus-appearances combination is not a necessary condition for the rise of early Christian belief is the possibility that some other circumstance, or combination of circumstances, was equally capable of generating this belief. If there are two or more quite different sets of possible circumstances, each of which is demonstrably a sufficient condition for the datum we are trying to explain, none of them can be deemed necessary.

This is the point at which we must declare that the matter lies beyond strict historical proof. It will always be possible for ingenious historians to propose yet more variations on the theme of how the early Christian belief could have arisen, and taken the shape it did, without either an empty tomb or appearances of Jesus. However, there are two strong points to be made on the other side as well. First (point 4), the meaning of 'resurrection' within the ancient world in general, and second-Temple Judaism in particular, rules out most of the alternatives. Second (point 5, at more length), the principal theories advanced as alternative explanations turn out, on examination, to be insufficient. Point 4 can be divided, as was point 3, into two, corresponding to the two key elements under discussion, the empty tomb and the appearances.

4a. As we saw in the first Part of the book, the meaning of 'resurrection', both in the Jewish and the non-Jewish world of late antiquity, was never that the person concerned had simply 'gone to heaven', or been 'exalted' in some way which did not involve a new bodily life. Plenty of disembodied post-mortem states were postulated, and there was a rich variety of terminology for denoting them, which did not include 'resurrection'. 'Resurrection' meant embodiment; that was equally so for the pagans, who denied it, as it was for the Jews, at least some of whom hoped for it. This is presumably why some leading non-Christian historians have come to the sober conclusion that, whatever else we say, the tomb must have been empty (in other words, that it is a necessary condition for the subsequent phenomena). Within that world, it is difficult to imagine a 'resurrection' of any other sort:

> When every argument has been considered and weighed, the only conclusion acceptable to the historian must be that the opinions of the orthodox, the liberal sympathizer and the critical agnostic alike – and even perhaps of the disciples themselves – are simply interpretations of the one disconcerting fact: namely that the women who set out to pay their last respects to Jesus found to their consternation, not a body, but an empty tomb.[21]

---

[21] Vermes 1973, 41. In 2000, 170–75, Vermes neither restates nor withdraws this conclusion. Cf. too O'Neill 1972; Rowland 1993, 78. Carnley 1987, 60f. declares that we cannot reach this point 'using only the critical techniques of scientific historiography'; without being sure what presuppositions are thereby being smuggled in, I would nevertheless submit that we have got to this point through step-by-step argument from actual evidence.

We may insist, in fact, that whatever else had happened, if the body of Jesus of Nazareth had remained in the tomb there would have been no early Christian belief of the sort we have discovered. It will not do to suggest, for instance, that because the disciples lived in a world where resurrection was expected, this will explain why they used that language of Jesus. Many other Jewish leaders, heroes and would-be Messiahs died within the same world, but in no case did anyone suggest that they had been raised from the dead. One might imagine other kinds of early faith which could have been generated by events which did not involve an empty tomb. But the specific faith of the earliest Christians could not have been generated by a set of circumstances in which an empty tomb did not play a part. I therefore regard the empty tomb as a *necessary* condition (though by itself, as we have seen, an insufficient one) for the rise of the very specific early Christian belief.

4b. But is the same true of the appearances? Are they, too, necessary conditions of the early Christian belief? I think so, though this is harder to demonstrate. They seem to me to be a kind of *necessary supplement* to the discovery of the empty tomb; they provide the extra element which turns the first insufficient condition (the empty tomb) into a sufficient one. Having a supply of electricity connected to the house is a necessary but insufficient condition for the working of the computer. This condition needs supplementing by other conditions, themselves also necessary but insufficient – a proper connecting cable, and the computer itself being in working order – before the combination of conditions becomes sufficient as well as necessary. So it is, I suggest, with the appearances of Jesus.

This is once more difficult to demonstrate. There is no limit to human ingenuity, and it is always possible that someone might dream up a theory in which some other event or phenomenon could supplement the discovery of the empty tomb and, in combination with it, produce a sufficient condition of the rise of early Christian belief. Dreams, in fact, are the obvious place to look for rival explanations. Perhaps, some might say, the disciples had powerful dreams of Jesus (after all, they had been with him day and night for a long time, and he had made a huge impact on their lives). Perhaps they had such vivid dreams about him that he seemed thoroughly alive, so that they began to speak of him as being alive, not dead at all, and then, bit by bit, to use the language of resurrection . . .

But this could not have generated the actual belief which we have studied. As we saw above, dreams of recently dead people are, and were in the first century, as common as grief itself. Such dreams might be taken to indicate that the dead person had passed into a post-mortem state, and was, in that sense, 'alive'. But that was never, for either pagans or Jews, what the language of 'resurrection' denoted.

In addition, we must also explain one of the striking modifications which we noticed as the Christians picked up the Jewish language of resurrection.

They spoke, in a variety of ways, not only of continuity but of transformation; and we have noted that the Easter stories in the gospels provide a model for this, in their strange portrait of a Jesus who is definitely embodied but whose body has unprecedented, indeed hitherto unimagined, properties. As we saw in chapter 13, it is impossible to explain these pictures as fictional projections from early Christian theology. We must search for an alternative explanation. The best one available is that it was the appearances of Jesus that precipitated this transformation in the understanding of resurrection. The language of 'resurrection', and the specific modifications within Jewish resurrection belief which we have seen in early Christianity, could only have occurred, I suggest, if the early Christians believed they had clear evidence, against all their own and everyone else's expectations, both of continuity between the Jesus who died and the Jesus who was now alive and of a transformation in his mode of embodiment. Appearances of this living Jesus would have provided such evidence. Nothing else could have done.

We are left with the conclusion that the combination of empty tomb and appearances of the living Jesus forms a set of circumstances which is itself *both necessary and sufficient* for the rise of early Christian belief. Without these phenomena, we cannot explain why this belief came into existence, and took the shape it did. With them, we can explain it exactly and precisely.

5. To test this, we must enquire whether in fact anything else could have produced early Christian belief in the same way. Is the combination of tomb plus appearances simply *one* thing that *might have* caused early Christian belief to arise, or is it the *only* thing that could possibly have done so?

A good deal of study has been devoted to the task of proposing alternative explanations for the rise of early Christian belief. Any of these, if sustainable, could challenge the argument of the previous section, leaving the Easter stories to be explained as aetiological or apologetic attempts to flesh out a faith arrived at on other grounds. If, however, it can be shown that the most apparently powerful of these will not do the job, the case for the tomb-and-meetings combination being necessary becomes considerably stronger.

We have already dealt by implication with some of the main alternative proposals. I have shown at various points, for instance, that the early Christians could not have developed beliefs of the type and shape they did if they had simply been working back from first-century readings of the Jewish scriptures and attempting to construct stories about what 'must have' happened to fulfil them.[22] But there are two other types of alternative explanation which need more attention. They warrant a section to themselves, after which we shall return to the sequence of our argument, specifically to steps 6 and 7.

[22] Above, ch. 13.

3. Two Rival Theories

(i) 'Cognitive Dissonance'

The first type of alternative explanation is frequently encountered, though not perhaps quite so often now as a few decades ago. This is the theory that the disciples were suffering from 'cognitive dissonance': the hypothetical state, studied within social psychology, in which individuals or groups fail to come to terms with reality, but live instead in a fantasy which corresponds to their own deep longings. This theory became popular in the 1950s and thereafter through the work of Leon Festinger.[23] Its implicit force in the Easter discussion is obvious: the disciples wanted so badly to believe in Jesus that instead of facing the fact of his death they claimed he was alive.

Much of the material in Festinger's systematic presentation of the theory relates to the dissonance between two different things a person might be said to 'know'. When a smoker faces the medical evidence about health risks;[24] when supporters of two college football teams are asked to evaluate, after a particularly rough game, what had happened, and who started it;[25] or when someone who had chosen a present (from a range including an automatic toaster, a portable radio and an art book) was then presented with more information about the product which cast doubt on the wisdom of the choice;[26] in what sense do they 'know' the evidence which runs so strongly against their prejudices? What happens when, as popular psychology has taught us to say, they 'screen it out'?

These, one may feel, are hardly relevant to the historical study of a group of first-century Jews, and Festinger and his colleagues did not, of course, suggest that they were. But the major study undertaken, with historical analogues such as the Millerite sect in the 1840s, was that of a small flying-saucer cult in mid-western America in the 1950s. In Festinger's systematic analysis of the phenomenon of 'cognitive dissonance', this is placed as the final case study, along with the survey of rumour-mongering following the Indian earthquake of 1934 and the evidence of Japanese people who continued to believe that Japan had won the Second World War. It is clearly intended to be seen as load-bearing for the topic as a whole.[27]

---

[23] See esp. Festinger, Riecken and Schachter 1956; Festinger 1957. See too Jackson 1975. Festinger is often cited as offering an assumed alternative sufficient explanation for the rise of early Christian belief (e.g. C. S. Rodd in his review of *JVG* (*Exp. Times* 108, 1997, 225): 'the challenge which Festinger presented . . . still has to be met').

[24] Festinger 1957, 5f.

[25] Festinger 1957, 149–53.

[26] Festinger 1957, 61–71.

[27] Festinger 1957, 252–9 (Indian earthquake: 236–41; Japan and the war: 244–6; Millerites: 248–51). The full report, upon which the following comments are based, is Festinger, Riecken and Schachter 1956.

From Festinger's summary in his systematic treatment, his main point becomes clear. The small group of flying-saucer devotees centred upon one woman who had convinced them that she was receiving messages from outer space, culminating in the prediction of a massive flood that would engulf America, from which the believers would be rescued in a flying saucer at a given date and time. In the days immediately prior to this date, despite considerable interest in the press, the group seemed anxious to avoid publicity and were not interested in attracting new potential 'believers'. After the crucial hour had come and gone, however (the story is drawn out by various predictable postponements), those who had stayed together in the little group received a message to the effect that 'God . . . had saved the world and stayed the flood because of this group and the light and strength they had spread throughout the world that night.'[28] Immediately the behaviour of the group changed; they avidly sought publicity and attempted to get others to join them in their belief. 'If . . . more and more converts could be found . . . then the dissonance between their belief and the knowledge that the messages had not been correct could be reduced.'[29] The conclusion of Festinger's summary of the study shows clearly what he has in mind as its implication (and what, certainly, many writers on early Christianity have seen as its implication):

> With sufficient social support available so that they could manage to retain the belief to which they were so heavily committed, and with the clear and unequivocal knowledge that the prediction had been false, almost the only avenue for further dissonance reduction was to obtain more cognition consonant with the belief in the form of knowing that more and more people also accepted their beliefs and the messages as valid.[30]

In other words, here is a theory to explain, among other things, why Jesus' followers, having been anxious and secretive before his death, became shortly thereafter enthusiastic and zealous missionaries for the truth of his message, eager to attract more converts in order to sustain their own faith which had been so grievously challenged by the failure of their hopes.[31]

The flaws in this argument are so enormous that it is puzzling to find serious scholars still referring to it in deferential terms – which is, indeed, the only reason for giving space to discussion of it here.[32] The crucial study of the flying-saucer cult was itself riddled with problems. The sociologists

---

[28] Festinger 1957, 258.

[29] Festinger 1957, 259.

[30] Festinger 1957, 259.

[31] A similar proposal is made by Schillebeeckx 1979 [1974], 347, following J. Delorme: that the burial narratives were 'circulated by pious Christians unable to bear the idea of Jesus' being buried dishonourably'.

[32] I was first alerted to the need to deal with this question by the *Exp. Times* review referred to in n. 23 above.

who infiltrated it were obliged to convince the existing members that they, too, were true believers, sitting with them in a suburban house waiting first for more messages from the spacemen and then for the flying saucer itself, and becoming such trusted colleagues that they were not infrequently the ones delegated to answer the door, talk on the phone, or speak to the press. The group was so small that in some meetings the sociologists must have appeared as among the strongest members. If a solitary anthropologist can, by his or her very presence and questions, influence quite seriously both the behaviour and the self-perception of an entire tribe,[33] how much more can three sociologists, forming perhaps a quarter, on some occasions even a third, of a group of flying-saucer believers not only influence but virtually direct proceedings.[34]

In addition, there is no sign that the group maintained its identity or zealous mission for longer than the one month during which the sociologists kept up their study (and, presumably, their apparent bona fide membership). Those who had left jobs and sold possessions had to rebuild their lives. The press lost interest; the sociologists withdrew to their typewriters and tenure applications; the flying-saucer prophecy, having failed, ceased altogether. But none of this, important though it is, gets to the heart of the problem with proposing even the loosest kind of parallel between the material studied by Festinger (including the Indian earthquake rumours and other phenomena) and the rise of early Christianity.

The real problem is something that any first-century historian should recognize: that whatever it was that the early Christians were expecting, wanting, hoping and praying for, this was *not* what they said, after Easter, had happened. This is why (to anticipate a counter-argument) the fact that all the earliest Christians were second-Temple Jews, which needs to be the case for the tomb-and-meetings combination to produce the effect it did, does not mean that these effects can be reduced to terms of 'second-Temple Jews who believed strongly enough in a would-be Messiah were bound to say things like that after his death.' True, their announcement that the kingdom had been fulfilled, and that Jesus really was the Messiah (though not in the sense they had expected) bears a superficial analogy to the drastic modifications of expectations introduced by the fresh 'revelations' vouchsafed after the failure of the spaceship to arrive on time. But the reason the early Christians gave for these modifications was not that they had received a fresh private message which had made them realize their mistake, but that

---

[33] cf. e.g. Barley 1986, 34f.

[34] The flying-saucer group was hardly large enough to warrant inclusion in a chapter whose subtitle was 'Data on Mass Phenomena' (Festinger 1957, viii–ix, acknowledging a need for haste in publication). Festinger, Riecken and Schachter 1956 indicate that they are aware of the serious methodological flaws involved in this project, but one would not guess that from anything in Festinger 1957, the flagship work of the overall hypothesis for which this particular project functioned as the final, and supposedly most telling, example.

something had *happened*, something which was not at all what they expected or hoped for, something around which they had to reconstruct their lives and in relation to which they had to redirect their energies. They were not refusing to come to terms with the fact that they had been wrong all along. On the contrary, they were indeed coming to terms with, and reordering their lives around, dramatic and irrefutable evidence that they had been wrong. They were not so much like confused Japanese citizens refusing to reconcile themselves to the events of 1945, and continuing to cling to their belief that they 'must have' won the war, and that all evidence to the contrary was cunning enemy propaganda. They were more like people who, discovering that they had been fighting for the wrong side, at once changed their allegiance and applied for citizenship in the victorious country. They were more like Herod the Great, who backed Mark Antony in the Roman civil war, and then, after Augustus had won, went at once and offered to back him with the same energy.[35] They were like someone who had been deeply asleep, and would have preferred to stay that way, but who, on hearing the alarm clock, sprang out of bed at once and got on with the business of the day.

Festinger's theory is in any case seriously challenged by the behaviour of other Jewish groups in the second-Temple period. We saw in chapter 12 that many of the messianic movements between roughly 150 BC and AD 150 ended with the violent death of the founder. When this happened, there were two options open to any who escaped death: they could give up the movement, or they could find themselves another Messiah. The followers of a dead prophet could of course go on believing that he was a true prophet; that, indeed, is what happened with some at least of the followers of John the Baptist.[36] But with a would-be Messiah, who was supposed to be inaugurating the kingdom, it was impossible. Nobody, after all, believed that the Messiah would be raised from the dead; nobody was expecting any such thing.[37] Clinging to the belief that the recently executed person was after all the Messiah was simply not an option. We do not find evidence of much 'cognitive dissonance' in the pages of Josephus; first-century Jews seem to have been, in this respect, more hard-headed than twentieth-century flying-saucer devotees. Even if there were anything in Festinger's theory, it is incapable of providing an alternative sufficient explanation for the rise of early Christian belief.

Similar theories continue to crop up from time to time, evidence (it would seem) of the desperation of the critic rather than of serious historical

---

[35] See Richardson 1996, 171–3.

[36] On the continuing followers of John cf. Ac. 18.25; 19.1–7.

[37] This is the flaw in Barr's suggestion (1992, 109: 'the more expectation there was that a great religious leader should come alive again after death, the more that same expectation goes to explain the claims that it had been fulfilled'). Cf. too de Jonge 2002, 47f.

thought.[38] But I turn now to a very different kind of explanation that has been put forward as an alternative sufficient explanation for what the early Christians believed.

(ii) A New Experience of Grace

The Dominican theologian Edward Schillebeeckx wrote one of the largest works on Jesus to appear in the 1970s, and devoted considerable space to the question of Easter. His work received wide notice and has exercised considerable influence.[39] He attempted to distance himself from what he saw as the reductionism of mainstream German Protestantism, as represented by Bultmann and Marxsen; what he means by the rise of Easter faith has nothing to do with the idea that Jesus has risen only 'in the kerygma' or 'in our experience as believers' while he himself lingers on 'in the realm of the dead'.[40] However, this disclaimer seems to me a way of insisting simply that Schillebeeckx is a liberal Catholic rather than a liberal Protestant. His own theory, expounded at length, is essentially very similar to the standard Bultmannian model.

In outline, his view works like this. The first Christians, particularly Peter, had a wonderful experience of grace and forgiveness, of 'seeing' and 'enlightenment', which can be described as 'conversion'.[41] This was not originally anything to do either with an empty tomb or with reports of 'seeing' Jesus in an 'objectivizing' way.[42] At a certain point, however, not least through the cultic practice of visiting Jesus' tomb (see below), stories of an empty tomb began to be told, coupled with the motif 'on the third day', which originally had nothing to do with actual chronology and everything to do with evoking, in a strictly metaphorical sense, an awareness of divine presence and action.[43] Gradually this developing tradition came to include also stories about Jesus being seen; then (at this point Schillebeeckx inverts Bultmann's normal method) sayings of the *earthly* Jesus were put into the mouth of the *risen* lord.[44] This was not, to begin with, anything to do with

---

[38] e.g. Goulder 1996; cf. the comments of O'Collins 1997, 10f., not least his ref. to Pannenberg 1968 [1964], 95–8. Carnley 1987 ch. 4 provides an exposition and critique of several sceptical theories.

[39] Schillebeeckx 1979 [1974] (cf. *JVG* 24f.); the following refs. are to this work unless otherwise noted. A sustained exposition and critique of Schillebeeckx's work on the resurrection, in some ways parallel to my own and in other ways emphatically not, is in Carnley 1987, 199–222. Schillebeeckx, born in Belgium, worked for many years in Holland.

[40] Schillebeeckx, 647.

[41] Schillebeeckx 346f.; 383f.; 387; 390; 397.

[42] Schillebeeckx 352; if this is not an echo of Bultmann, I do not know what is.

[43] Schillebeeckx 329–404, esp. 332; 542; and cf. 725f. n. 33, where Schillebeeckx is careful to justify the literal three days of the liturgical *triduum*.

[44] cf. *JVG* 24.

people supposing that Jesus had actually been physically seen, touched, and so on:

> only we suffer from the crude and naïve realism of what 'appearances of Jesus' came to be in the later tradition, through unfamiliarity with the distinctive character of the Jewish-biblical way of speaking.[45]

Schillebeeckx's appeal to this 'Jewish-biblical way of speaking' needs to be challenged in the light of chapters 3 and 4 above, and we shall return to this presently. But his proposal is at least now clear. What happened, across the first generation of Christianity, was a movement from a basic, early faith and experience, the experience of being 'converted', to an expression of that faith in terms of stories which, through the influence of Jewish ideas, look like naive, literalistic stories of a dead man coming back to life. Schillebeeckx is conscious that with this proposal he is inverting what the New Testament writers actually say.[46] He recognises that some Jews at least thought of resurrection from the dead in a physical sense; but in the full 'eschatological' sense (which Schillebeeckx defines as 'meta-empirical and meta-historical', allowing for plenty of epistemological and hermeneutical elbow room) he says that 'resurrection' has nothing to do with bodies.[47]

Schillebeeckx supports this construction with brief analyses of the gospels and Paul. Mark, he says, develops from the cultic legend associated with pilgrims visiting the holy sepulchre, 'where a religious ceremony then took place and apropos of this visit, in the early morning, the pilgrims were reminded of the apostolic belief in the resurrection'. He follows various scholars who have proposed an early Easter liturgy which then generated empty-tomb stories. This 'aetiological cult-legend', he says, corresponds to something 'deep in human nature'.[48] Matthew, misleadingly, introduces the

---

[45] Schillebeeckx 346.

[46] Schillebeeckx 391. In agreeing with this, we might comment that at 1 Cor. 15.17 Paul ought to have written, 'If your faith is valid, and you are no longer in your sins, then Christ is risen!'

[47] Schillebeeckx 380f.; cf. the wonderfully muddled footnote, 704 n. 45: 'An eschatological, bodily resurrection, theologically speaking, has nothing to do, however, with a corpse.'

[48] Schillebeeckx 331f., 334f., 336, 702f. There are interesting gaps in logic here: (a) however devout the people concerned may have been, visitors to a tomb that contained a body are unlikely to have generated spontaneously a tradition according to which the tomb did *not* contain a body; (b) if the tomb was not empty, why would people start inventing Easter liturgies in the first place? These do not seem to have occurred to Schillebeeckx or those he cites. See the discussions in Perkins 1984, 93f.; Carnley 1987, 50; and cf. e.g. Lindars 1993, 129, citing the Mishnah refs. to the practice of tomb-visits, including the provision of special chambers or booths for visitors (mErub. 5.1; mOhol. 7.1). The *reductio ad absurdum* of the 'tomb-cult' theory is reached in Riley 1995, 67, and in e.g. Williams 1998, 232 (Joseph of Arimathea offered an unused tomb to the early Christians so that they could meet there for symbolic celebrations).

(Jewish) idea that a body has to be involved.[49] Luke, in order to address Greeks, invokes a hellenistic 'rapture' model as part of a *theios aner* ('divine man') Christology, only then to drop it again when he writes some of the speeches in Acts.[50] Paul is first called to a mission to the Gentiles, and this grounds and legitimates his Damascus Road experience, his 'seeing' of Jesus as 'the Christ'. Thus he too has a kind of resurrection experience, though this *follows from the faith he already has*, and does not involve him actually seeing Jesus. Thus

> a Jesus appearance is not the object of neutral observation; it is a faith-motivated experience in response to an eschatological disclosure, expressed in a Christological affirmation of Jesus as the risen One, that is, disclosure of and faith in Jesus in his eschatological, Christological significance. This was again the sole essence of all other Christ manifestations, which have subsequently been filled out either with the theology of the communities represented by Matthew, Luke and John or with the concrete career of the apostle Paul himself.[51]

This view is ingenious and subtle, but demonstrably wrong on almost every count.[52] Schillebeeckx's grasp on the Jewish context is sketchy and misleading. Despite a foray into the history of Jewish views of death and what lies beyond, he never sees that, precisely because there is a spectrum of views, 'resurrection' denotes one point on that spectrum, namely the point to do with dead people stopping being bodily dead and becoming bodily alive again.[53] His invention of a supposed 'Jewish-biblical way of speaking', in comparison with which stories of the risen Jesus appear crude and naively realistic, stands the truth on its head. His picture of the cultic practice of visiting Jesus' tomb, upon which he bases his reading of Mark, is without foundation. He is right to say that Matthew tells stories which assume that 'resurrection' means bodies, but wrong to imply that this is an odd innovation in the tradition. His analysis of a 'rapture' tradition is unwarranted, and does not in any case apply to Luke (when Jesus disappears in Emmaus this hardly constitutes a 'rapture', since he reappears in Jerusalem shortly afterwards).[54] His account of Paul is inaccurate in its reporting both of the Acts stories and of Paul's own evidence.[55]

---

[49] Schillebeeckx 358.

[50] Schillebeeckx 343. Like many writers, Schillebeeckx takes no notice of the striking passages in Ac. about Jesus' body not having decomposed (e.g. Ac. 2.31, quoting Ps. 16.10; see above, 452–7).

[51] Schillebeeckx 378. Similar summaries: 346 (suggesting that modern faith-experience is basically the same sort of thing as that of the early disciples); 384.

[52] The broad viewpoint of which Schillebeeckx is typical is subjected to damaging historical criticism by Stuhlmacher 1993, 47f.

[53] Schillebeeckx 518–23, and frequent refs. to 'Jewish views' etc., e.g. 346.

[54] Schillebeeckx 341.

[55] Schillebeeckx 369, 377f.; in Ac., in fact, Paul sees Jesus while his companions do not; in 1 Cor. 9.1, Paul declares that he has seen Jesus (Schillebeeckx implies he had not).

This alone would be enough to rule out his theory as a historical explanation: he has not done justice to the evidence. But two further features stand out as well. First, he insists repeatedly that experiences of the risen Jesus only happened to people who were already believers. To make this point, as we have seen, he has to manipulate the stories of Paul rather severely; and he never discusses the two other obvious counter-examples. To start with, there is Thomas (who could, we may suppose, be dismissed with a wave of a redaction-critical hand as a figment of the Johannine community's imagination); but there is also James the brother of Jesus, who belongs firmly in the earliest tradition we possess (1 Corinthians 15.7), and stays there, as much a stumbling-block to speculative scholarship as he was to the Jerusalem hierarchy. James may well not have been a follower of Jesus during the latter's public career, but he became a central figure in the early church – the latter indisputable fact undergirding the former, because, if James had been a follower of Jesus, it is very unlikely that the church would make up stories to say, or at least imply, that he had not.[56]

Second, Schillebeeckx admits in a couple of throwaway lines that he cannot in fact explain why the disciples came to faith in the first place. He has simply pushed the historical question one stage further back. The disciples, he says, underwent 'a process of repentance and conversion which it is no longer possible to reconstruct on a historical basis'.[57] The New Testament, he declares, 'nowhere explicitly states' which concrete events it was in which the 'grace and favour', or the 'renewed offer of salvation in Jesus', was manifested. It only speaks, he says, 'of the character of this event as one of amazing grace'. What the disciples experienced, Schillebeeckx proposes, was grace in the form of forgiveness, though this can also be described as 'their concrete experience of forgiveness after Jesus' death, encountered as grace and discussed among themselves' as they mull over the events and sayings of Jesus' life:

> He renews for them the offer of salvation; this they experience in their own conversion; he must therefore be alive . . . A dead man does not proffer forgiveness. A present fellowship with Jesus is thus restored . . . It is the individual's experience of new being that imparts to faith the assurance that Jesus is alive or is the coming judge of the world.[58]

The entire argument of Parts II, III and IV of the present book tell heavily against all this. To deny that the resurrection accounts offer a *prima facie* account of 'concrete events' which manifested the divine grace and favour is

---

[56] cf. e.g. Jn. 7.2–5. On the question about whether, and if so at what stage, James and the other brothers joined the wider group of Jesus' followers see above, 325, 560f. referring also to those who have recently suggested that James did after all follow Jesus during his lifetime.
[57] Schillebeeckx 387.
[58] Schillebeeckx 391f.

bad enough (Schillebeeckx first sweeps all the evidence under the carpet, and then exclaims, 'Look! No evidence!'). To affirm in their place, as a 'concrete experience', the disciples' feeling of forgiveness, which the accounts never actually predicate of the Eleven (except by implication, ironically, in the case of Peter, whom Schillebeeckx is concerned to prioritize[59]) – this is to invent something to do a job which, even if it were there in the texts, it would be incapable of doing. It is like carefully constructing an axe out of plasticine and hoping it will cut down a giant oak. As we noted in chapter 12, if some followers of Bar-Giora or Bar-Kochba had suggested, after their leader's death, that he really was the Messiah, on the grounds that some of them had begun to experience a new sense of forgiveness, the response would have been that Judaism had plenty of categories for talking about divine forgiveness, but that declaring one's recently executed leader to be Messiah (still less 'the Christ' in the sense Schillebeeckx uses the word), or that he had in any sense been raised from the dead, was not one of them. Even granted that Jesus had spoken words of salvation and forgiveness during his public career, and that his followers remembered and cherished those words, and had a strong sense of the divine presence with them in the days that followed, that would not provide grounds for saying that he was 'alive' in a way in which the writers of many much-cherished Jewish texts were not. The Psalms spoke of forgiveness; so did Isaiah. Many Jews lived by those promises while knowing quite well that David and Isaiah were long since dead.

Schillebeeckx's entire construct, in fact, is mistaken and misleading, not so much at the level of Christian theology (that is a whole other question) but at the level of plausible historical reconstruction. It is revealing that when he sums up what he really thinks happened, in perhaps less guarded mode than usual, his position threatens to collapse back into a variation of that of Albert Schweitzer: Jesus was a noble but disastrous failure, but his followers were challenged in a new way by the memory of what he did and said. God must have the last word, despite the 'historical fiasco' of Jesus, and 'this the early Christians try to express with their credal affirmation of Jesus' resurrection' – an affirmation whose wording 'may be subjected to criticism', by which Schillebeeckx seems to mean that it leads one towards a 'crude and naive realism', the unfortunate belief that something actually happened at Easter.[60] But, as we have seen, the historical study of early Christian practice and hope leaves us no choice but to conclude that this unfortunate belief was what all early Christians held. Indeed, they professed that it was the very centre of their life. They would have responded in much the same way as the writer John Updike, in the epigraph to this Part of the

---

[59] Jn. 21.15–19. Perhaps this was an attempt to head off Vatican displeasure at his theories. If so, it failed.

[60] Schillebeeckx 639.

book. Metaphors are important; but they are not to be used for mocking God.

Schillebeeckx is not, of course, the only scholar who has proposed this kind of theory, and there may be other examples which are not subject to all the criticisms I have voiced.[61] But he is one of the fullest exponents of this line of thought, and it is important to show that, in its basic structure as well as in variable details, it simply fails to account for what happened. Like the theory of 'cognitive dissonance', the theory that the early Christians had a profound religious experience which only slowly grew into the (misleading) language of bodily resurrection provides no kind of an explanation for the rise of the early Christian belief.[62]

4. The Necessary Condition

This study of two widely used alternative explanations for the rise of the early Christian belief in Jesus' resurrection leads me back to step 6 in the argument I outlined at the start of this chapter. The empty tomb and the 'meetings' with Jesus, when combined, present us with not only a *sufficient* condition for the rise of early Christian belief, but also, it seems, a *necessary* one. Nothing else historians have been able to come up with has the power to explain the phenomena before us.

This remains, of course, unprovable in logical or mathematical terms. The historian is never in a position to do what Pythagoras did: not content with drawing more and more right-angled triangles and demonstrating that the square on the hypotenuse always does in fact equal the sum of the squares on the other two sides, he constructed a theorem to prove that this *must* always be the case. With history it is not like that. Almost nothing is ever ruled out absolutely; history, after all, is mostly the study of the unusual and unrepeatable. What we are after is high probability; and this is to be attained by examining all the possibilities, all the suggestions, and asking how well they explain the phenomena. It is always possible that in discussing the resurrection someone will come up with the sceptical critic's dream: an explanation which provides a sufficient condition for the rise of early Christian faith but which, by fitting into post-Enlightenment epistemological and ontological categories, or even simply mainstream pagan ones, causes no fluttering in the critical dovecotes. It is worthy of note that, despite the somewhat desperate attempts of many scholars over the last two hundred

---

[61] For a survey of 'naturalistic' theories, and a response, cf. e.g. Habermas 2001.

[62] Goulder 1996 combines a Festinger-like theory about the maintenance of 'collective delusions' with a Schillebeeckx-like theory about the 'conversion visions' of Peter and Paul. Both are thoroughly unconvincing. Davis 1997, 146 puts the point well: 'What they saw was Jesus, not an impostor or a hallucination or a mass of ectoplasm or a sort of interactive hologram.'

years (not to mention critics since at least Celsus), no such explanation has been found. The early Christians did not invent the empty tomb and the 'meetings' or 'sightings' of the risen Jesus in order to explain a faith they already had. They developed that faith because of the occurrence, and convergence, of these two phenomena. Nobody was expecting this kind of thing; no kind of conversion-experience would have generated such ideas; nobody would have invented it, no matter how guilty (or how forgiven) they felt, no matter how many hours they pored over the scriptures. To suggest otherwise is to stop doing history and to enter into a fantasy world of our own, a new cognitive dissonance in which the relentless modernist, desperately worried that the post-Enlightenment worldview seems in imminent danger of collapse, devises strategies for shoring it up nevertheless.[63] In terms of the kind of proof which historians normally accept, the case we have presented, that the tomb-plus-appearances combination is what generated early Christian belief, is as watertight as one is likely to find.

This conclusion provides a solid framework within which some other small but significant pieces of historical evidence must be fitted. These are often noted, and we have described them more fully in chapter 12 above. They do not in themselves compel any particular reading of the evidence; but they strongly support the tomb-plus-appearances hypothesis. First, the early Christians, remarkably soon, began to regard the first day of the week as their special day. Second, there is no evidence whatever that anyone ever venerated Jesus' tomb. Both of these have already been discussed in chapter 12 above.

Third, and related to the point about Jesus' tomb, there was never a question of anyone performing a secondary burial for Jesus. There should have been, of course, in the ordinary way; this is often ignored in historical study, but it is important. The burial so carefully described in the gospels was, as we would expect in first-century Palestinian Judaism, the initial stage of a two-stage burial.[64] The body was wrapped in grave-cloths along with a significant amount of spices, to offset the smell of putrefaction, on the usual assumption that other shelves in the cave would be required soon enough by the same family or group. There would be plenty of coming and going with further bodies; nobody who owned a burial cave would want to leave it with only one body in it. Even Joseph of Arimathea, who according to the story was rich and devoted to Jesus, would have expected to use the cave again.

---

[63] Goulder 1996, 54f. is a good example of this tendency. 'We should', he writes, 'always prefer the natural hypothesis [as opposed to the supernatural one], or we shall fall into supersitition.' The natural/supernatural distinction itself, and the near-equation of 'supernatural' with 'superstition', are scarecrows that Enlightenment thought has erected in its fields to frighten away anyone following the historical argument where it leads. It is high time the birds learned to take no notice. A further example is provided by Williams 1998.

[64] Full details are helpfully available in e.g. Meyers 1971; Longstaff 1981, 279f. The use of stone ossuaries in the Jerusalem area reached a peak in the mid-first century AD.

After a period of between about six months and two years, those coming and going with subsequent primary burials would note that the corpse in question had completely decomposed, leaving only the bare skeleton. They would then collect the bones, fold them reverently and carefully according to a traditional pattern, and place them in an ossuary, which they would store either in a niche within the same cave or in some other location near by. This is what Joseph would have expected to do with the bones of Jesus.

Disciplined historical imagination indicates what would have happened. If Jesus, having been buried in the ordinary way, had remained physically dead, decomposing inside the tomb, so that there never was an empty tomb, let alone 'meetings' between him and his disciples, we must suppose that someone from among his followers or family, or perhaps from the family of Joseph, would sooner or later have returned to perform this final act of respect. And (unless we declare, a priori, that every single scrap of our evidence about early Christianity is a late fiction) we must suppose that this would have happened at precisely the same time that the early church was busily proclaiming him as Messiah and lord on the grounds that he had been raised from the dead – specifically, according to Acts, that his body *had not decomposed*.[65] And we must suppose that this happened around the same time that the zealous Saul of Tarsus, persecuting the church, was confronted by one whom he took to be Jesus, and forthwith declared that he had been raised from the dead. It is because of the impossibility of putting together the story on this basis that scholars have been driven to the desperate expedient of denying everything about Joseph, discounting almost everything about Paul, and offering us instead a narrative of their own, without primary evidence.[66]

A fascinating sidelight on the whole question is provided by an inscription found near Nazareth, probably from the reign of Claudius, forbidding tampering with tombs. Like many pieces of ancient evidence, it may have nothing to do with our question; or it conceivably might. If we suppose that word had got out about a new sect that was hailing a recently executed 'king of the Jews' as Israel's Messiah and the world's true lord, and that rumours such as those in Matthew 28.11–15 had been circulated as an official explanation, it is quite feasible to imagine someone using the emperor's authority to try to lock the door after the horse had bolted:

> Ordinance of Caesar. It is my pleasure that graves and tombs remain undisturbed in perpetuity . . . If any man lay information that another has either demolished them, or has in any other way extracted the buried, or has maliciously transferred them to other places in order to wrong them, or has displaced the sealing or other stones, against such a one I order that a trial be instituted . . . Let it be absolutely forbidden

---

[65] Ac. 2.25–36; see above, 452–6.
[66] e.g. Crossan 1998; see Wright, 'A New Birth?'

for any one to disturb them. In case of contravention I desire that the offender be sentenced to capital punishment on charge of violation of sepulture.[67]

Nothing can be built on this, of course. Like many archaeological finds, it raises questions rather than answering them. But it certainly supplies a bit of teasing embroidery around the edge of the argument.

For all these reasons I conclude that the historian, of whatever persuasion, has no option but to affirm both the empty tomb and the 'meetings' with Jesus as 'historical events' in all the senses we sketched in chapter 1: they took place as real events; they were significant events; they are, in the normal sense required by historians, provable events; historians can and should write about them. We cannot account for early Christianity without them. The tomb-and-meetings scenario is warranted, indeed, by that double similarity and double dissimilarity (to Judaism on the one hand and the early church on the other) for which I argued earlier as a methodological control in the study of Jesus.[68] Stories like these, with the kind of explanation the early Christians offered, make the sense they make within first-century Judaism (similarity), but nobody within first-century Judaism was expecting anything like this (dissimilarity). Stories like these do indeed explain the rise of early Christianity (similarity), but they cannot be explained as the back-projection of early Christian faith, theology and exegesis (dissimilarity).[69]

This conclusion rules out several of the alternative accounts that have been offered from time to time, mostly variations on the theme of mistakes made in the early morning (the women went to the wrong tomb, they mistook someone else for Jesus, and so on). These are in any case trivial when we remember the state of mind of Jesus' followers after his crucifixion and the fact that they were not expecting anything remotely like this to occur. Reports based on misunderstandings would quickly have been sorted out. The hoary old theory that Jesus did not really die on the cross, but revived in the cool of the tomb, has likewise nothing to recommend it, and it is noticeable that even those historians who are passionately committed to denying the resurrection do not attempt to go by this route.[70] Roman soldiers, after all, were rather good at killing people, and when given a rebel leader to practise on they would have had several motives for making sure the job was done properly. A further, more recent suggestion can also be ruled out: that, after his crucifixion, Jesus' body was not buried, but left instead for dogs

---

[67] Barrett 1987 [1956], 15, with other refs.; see too the discussion in Evans 2001, 533.

[68] cf. *JVG* 131–3.

[69] For the latter point, see esp. ch. 13 above.

[70] e.g. Lüdemann 1994. One recent exponent of the idea is Thiering 1992, chs. 25–7, answered in Wright, *Who Was Jesus?*, ch. 2. See too those listed in Theissen and Merz 1998, 476, noting other unlikely theories as well. Moule 1967, 6f. gives a more than adequate response. The only other thing to be said about this theory is its remarkable self-reference: though frequently given the *coup de grâce*, it keeps reviving itself – carrying about as much conviction as a battered but revived Jesus would himself have done.

and vultures to finish off.[71] Had that happened, no matter how many 'visions' they had had, the disciples would not have concluded that he had been raised from the dead. We are left with the secure historical conclusion: the tomb was empty, and various 'meetings' took place not only between Jesus and his followers (including at least one initial sceptic) but also, in at least one case (that of Paul; possibly, too, that of James), between Jesus and people who had not been among his followers. I regard this conclusion as coming in the same sort of category, of historical probability so high as to be virtually certain, as the death of Augustus in AD 14 or the fall of Jerusalem in AD 70.

This brings us to step 7 of the argument I outlined at the start of the chapter. It is important to see that we have got this far by following the historical argument, not by invoking any external a priori beliefs. The widespread belief and practice of the early Christians is only explicable if we assume that they all believed that Jesus was bodily raised, in an Easter event something like the stories the gospels tell; the reason they believed that he was bodily raised is because the tomb was empty and, over a short period thereafter, they encountered Jesus himself, giving every appearance of being bodily alive once more. How then can we explain these two facts, the empty tomb and the 'meetings'?

5. The Historical Challenge of Jesus' Resurrection

The answer is blindingly obvious, as Saul of Tarsus might have said, whether or not he fell off his horse on the road to Damascus. The adverb is important: the obvious answer to the question seems such a bold affront to the principles of post-Enlightenment historical epistemology that it looks as though the only way to affirm it is by shutting both eyes and flailing around in the dark. To say, as the early Christians did, that the tomb was empty, and that the 'meetings' with Jesus took place, because he had indeed been bodily raised from the dead, seems to require the suspension of all our normal language about how we know things about the past.

It is important to stress the word 'obvious', though, as well as 'blinding'. If we were faced with some other historical problem which had brought us to a secure and interrelated pair of conclusions, and if we were looking for a fact or event to explain them both; and if we discovered something which explained them as thoroughly and satisfyingly as the bodily resurrection of Jesus explains the empty tomb and the 'meetings'; then we would accept it without a moment's hesitation. An archaeologist discovers two pillars of an ancient arch. Her colleague, poking about in the long grass nearby, discovers carved stones that complete the top of the same arch. Everyone goes home

---

[71] Crossan 1994 ch. 6.

satisfied; the original has been reconstructed. If I think I see an elephant walking past the Houses of Parliament, I assume either that it is a clever pantomime-like hoax (part of another animal-rights protest, perhaps) or that I must have consumed rather more alcohol last night than I had realized. If I then hear on the news that an elephant has gone missing from a circus in Hyde Park, it will not take me many minutes to come up with a hypothesis to cover both eventualities. If the friend who a short while ago was on the opposite bank of a deep and fast-flowing river is now on the near bank, and I know both that there is no bridge for miles in either direction and that she cannot swim, I assume that she has used some kind of a boat. We make this sort of inference all the time. A good many legal cases depend on it. The murder weapon had the accused's fingerprints all over it; the accused had blood of the right type all over his clothes; however blameless and gentle his previous character, the jury will put two and two together.

Those are all examples of the kind of obvious and satisfying historical explanation which the bodily resurrection of Jesus offers for the data before us. If Jesus was raised, with (as the early Christians in their different ways affirmed) a 'transphysical' body, both the same and yet in some mysterious way transformed, the two key pieces of evidence, the empty tomb and the 'meetings', are explained. The arch fits the pillars exactly.[72]

The problem, of course, is that we know that ancient arches often lie in ruins. We know that elephants exist, and that, given a chance, they might well wander off in search of fresh entertainment. We know that boats will enable people to cross rivers. We know that unlikely people sometimes commit murders. What we do not know – not because we inhabit a modern scientific worldview, but because at this point all human history tells the same story – is that someone who is well and truly dead can become well and truly alive again.

The Christian story about Jesus does not try to suggest otherwise. This point needs to be stressed. The early Christian understanding of Easter was not that this sort of thing was always likely to happen sooner or later, and finally it did. It was not that a particular human being happened to possess even more unusual powers than anyone had imagined before.[73] Nor did they suppose it was a random freak, like a monkey sitting at a typewriter and finally producing *All's Well that Ends Well* (after, we must suppose, several near-misses). When they said that Jesus had been raised from the dead the

---

[72] It will not do to say, with Carnley 1987, 145, that this kind of historical investigation tends to 'naturalize the resurrection' and so approximate it to 'little else than a mundane restoration of a corpse'. Leaving aside the comment that even resuscitation is hardly 'mundane', the historical investigation we have carried out leads us to postulate precisely something which is neither 'naturalizable' nor 'mundane'.

[73] See the extraordinary suggestions in Holt 1999, 11. This is perhaps the logical extension of the famous thesis of de Chardin 1965, seeing Christ as the 'omega-point' in human and cosmic development.

early Christians were not saying, as many critics have supposed, that the god in whom they believed had simply decided to perform a rather more spectacular miracle, an even greater display of 'supernatural' power, than they had expected. This was not a special favour performed for Jesus because his god liked him more than anyone else.[74] *The fact that dead people do not ordinarily rise is itself part of early Christian belief,* not an objection to it. The early Christians insisted that what had happened to Jesus was precisely something new; was, indeed, the start of a whole new mode of existence, a new creation. The fact that Jesus' resurrection was, and remains, without analogy is not an objection to the early Christian claim. It is part of the claim itself.[75]

The challenge for any historian, when faced with the question of the rise of Christianity, is much more sharply focused than is often supposed. It is not simply a matter of whether one believes in 'miracles', or in the supernatural, in general, in which case (it is supposed) the resurrection will be no problem. If anyone ever reaches the stage where the resurrection is in that sense no problem, we can be sure that they have made a mistake somewhere, that they have constructed a world in which this most explosive and subversive of events – supposing it to have occurred – can be domesticated and put on show, like a circus elephant or clever typing monkey, as a key exhibit in the church's collection of supernatural trophies. The resurrection of Jesus then becomes either 'a trip to a garden and a lovely surprise', a happy ending to a fairy story, or a way of legitimating different types of Christianity or different leaders within it.[76] No: the challenge comes down to a much narrower point, not simply to do with worldviews in general, or with 'the supernatural' in particular, but with the direct question of death and life, of the world of space, time and matter and its relation to whatever being there may be for whom the word 'god', or even 'God', might be appropriate. Here there is, of course, no neutrality. Any who pretend to it are merely showing that they have not understood the question.[77]

In particular, any who insist on being post-Enlightenment historians must look in the mirror and ask some hard methodological questions.[78] The

[74] As Crossan frequently hints would follow from resurrection belief: e.g. 1998, 549.

[75] On 'analogy' see the discussion of Troeltsch and Pannenberg at 16–18 above.

[76] See the critiques of Sawicki 1994, 92f.; Riley 1995; Crossan 1995, 202–08; 1998, 550–68; and the way in which e.g. Schillebeeckx's reconstruction is vulnerable to the latter. See also the contrasting 'endings to the story' offered by Macquarrie 1990, 403–14: the 'happy ending' of traditional affirmation contrasted with the 'austere ending' of a post-Kantian Bultmannian viewpoint. See above, 616f.

[77] For an intriguing recent philosophical approach to the problem of how to address the issue, see Gibson 1999.

[78] At this point I am in full agreement, at the general level, with Schillebeeckx's proposal: 'we cannot re-adopt into the present the whole Enlightenment (any more than the larger past). We should update and implement its critical impulse while setting a veto on its uncritical presuppositions' (594). Unfortunately, I do not think Schillebeeckx has carried

underlying rationale of the Enlightenment was, after all, that the grandiose dogmatic claims of the church (and a good deal else besides, but the church was always a key target) needed to be challenged by the fearless, unfettered examination of historical evidence. It will not do, after two hundred years of this, for historians in that tradition to turn round and rule out, a priori, certain types of answer to questions that remain naggingly insistent. The larger dreams of the Enlightenment have, in recent years, been challenged on all kinds of levels. In some cases (colonialism, the global triumph of western capitalism, and so on) they have been shown to be politically, economically and culturally self-serving on a massive scale. What if the moratorium on speaking of Jesus' bodily resurrection, which has been kept in place until recently more by the critics' tone of voice than by sustained historical argument ('surely,' they imply on the edge of every discussion of the subject, 'you cannot be so impossibly naive as to think that something actually *happened*?'), should itself turn out to be part of that intellectual and cultural hegemony against which much of the world is now doing its best to react?[79] What if the resurrection, instead of (as is often imagined) legitimating a cosy, comfortable, socially and culturally conservative form of Christianity, should turn out to be, in the twenty-first century as in the first, the most socially, culturally and politically explosive force imaginable, blasting its way through the sealed tombs and locked doors of modernist epistemology and the (now) deeply conservative social and political culture which it sustains? When I said that there was no neutral ground at this point, I was not only referring to patterns of thought and belief. Indeed, the holding apart of the mental and spiritual on the one hand from the social, cultural and political on the other, one of the most important planks in the Enlightenment platform, is itself challenged by the question of Jesus' resurrection. To address the final historical question is to face, within the worldview model, not only questions of belief but also of praxis, story and symbol.[80]

---

out this agenda. Morgan 1994, 12f. seems to me to have capitulated rather obviously to the Enlightenment's agenda: 'A physical resurrection,' he says, 'looks dangerously like resuscitation, and invites the rationalist explanation that Jesus did not really die on the cross. It is better avoided.' Rationalists, eh? 'There is a lion in the street!' (Prov. 26.13).

[79] For a recent cultural critique along these lines, see e.g. Boyle 1998. Morgan 1994, just referred to, is a good example of the tone of voice I have in mind. Avis 1993b repeats a standard, and very misleading, line: resurrection made sense in the first century because people held an ancient worldview, whereas we hold a modern one. The real distinction is between one kind of Jewish worldview (which then mutated into the Christian worldview) and virtually all other worldviews, ancient and modern alike.

[80] See e.g. the powerful and pertinent remarks of Rowland 1993, 76-9. Rowland is followed and amplified helpfully by Soskice 1997. Williams 1998, 235 is right to say that Jesus' resurrection broke the moulds of our habitual thinking, but his own argument, in which bodily resurrection remains firmly ruled out, carefully protects the most important mould of all from attack.

This is of course what people mean when they say that resurrection faith is 'self-involving'. There are various levels of self-involving statements. If, walking down the street, I say 'I think that was the Number 10 bus', the statement is only minimally self-involving; I do not want to go where the Number 10 bus goes, and anyway I prefer to walk. But if, arriving breathless at the bus-stop on the way to a vital appointment, I look despairingly up the street and say 'I think that was the Number 10 bus', knowing that the next one is not due for another two hours and that there is no other means of arriving on time, the statement not only involves me, it plunges me into gloom. The point is that one cannot say 'Jesus of Nazareth was bodily raised from the dead' with the minimal involvement of the first of those statements. If it happened, it matters. The world is a different place from what it would be if it did not happen. The person who makes the statement is committed to living in this different world, this newly envisioned universe of discourse, imagination and action.

In the same way – this is not so often noticed, but it is just as important – for someone to say 'Jesus of Nazareth was *not* bodily raised from the dead' is equally self-involving. Of course, if the speaker has heard almost nothing about Jesus and has no idea of the central Christian claims, the self-involvement appears minimal. But the more closely the speaker has looked at the question, the deeper the self-involvement becomes. Such a statement then belongs within, and reinforces, the universal ancient pagan worldview, the 'modernist' post-Enlightenment worldview, and (no doubt) many other variations on, or anticipations of, both of them.[81] That is why, ironically, such a denial is usually felt to be unimportant (it merely reinforces a widely held worldview), except when warding off the challenge of mainstream orthodox Christianity. Believing that Jesus did not rise from the dead is not necessarily the central plank of anyone's worldview, as belief in the resurrection is to an orthodox Christian worldview. It is usually a mere corollary, often simply assumed.

How then can we proceed? If there is no neutral 'historiography' that can serve as a tribunal before which one can present such a question and ask for a decision – the point, I take it, which certain theologians have insisted on, anxious lest blind historiography be elevated to a place that belongs only to God, if there be a god – are we condemned to remain for ever in mutually exclusive closed epistemological circles? Is the world to consist only of believers affirming their belief within a context where it makes sense, and unbelievers affirming their unbelief within a context where it makes sense, without either ever having the chance to talk to the other? At this point all kinds of theological, metaphysical, philosophical and cultural issues are raised, and I am well enough aware of them to know that there is no space at

---

[81] cf. Bauckham 1993c, 153: the resurrection 'appears an unacceptable breach of the created order only if creation is deistically left to its own immanent possibilities'.

the end of a book like this to develop them in any detail.[82] I want, instead, to explore a line of thought which seems to me to offer a way forward.[83]

Take, as a model, the scene involving Thomas in John 20. Thomas comes to the question with one particular epistemology uppermost in mind: he wants to touch as well as to see. Indeed, he insists that the data must be caught within his proposed epistemological net or he will not acknowledge it as real data at all. However, when Thomas is confronted by the risen Jesus, and even invited to touch, John does not say (despite, once more, a long and distinguised artistic tradition) that Thomas went ahead and did so.[84] Seeing was enough; and he blurts out the confession which rounds off the theological structure of John's entire gospel. But this, too, evokes a gentle rebuke: blessed are those who have *not* seen, and yet believe.

Enlightenment historiography has often placed itself in the position from which the doubting disciple began. Like Thomas, it protests that it has not shared the deep Christian experience of those who now believe, who look as though they are living in cloud-cuckoo-land. It insists on 'hard evidence', on 'scientific proof'. It maintains a dignified if perhaps brittle scepticism.

Equally, certain branches of theology have stressed the gentle rebuke of Jesus. If you need proof, if you even *want* proof, that seems to show that you have not yet discovered true faith. One should not reply to the Enlightenment in anything like its own terms. As the book of Proverbs warns, answering fools according to their folly is itself a foolish thing to do.[85] And yet the very next verse declares that one *must* answer fools in their own terms, lest they be wise in their own eyes – in other words, lest they imagine they have won their case by default. Far be it from me, of course, to agree with the totally negative view of the Enlightenment implied by that use of Proverbs 26, which is here simply *argumenti causa*. There was much wisdom, as well as much folly, in the eighteenth-century appeal to history against dogma and hierarchy, even if now, with the Enlightenment's own dogma and hierarchy firmly in power, it is time to turn the historical argument against post-Enlightenment scepticism itself.

To return to Thomas: in the story, Jesus welcomes him and invites him to do what he wants, even though there is still a gentle rebuke in store. Neither circle, it seems, is closed. There is enough evidence to lure sceptics forward, even if they still have lessons to learn about how we know things as well as about what there is to be known. And the faith which, in its most mature

---

[82] See ch. 1 above. On the problem of communication between worldviews cf. Coakley 2002, 132.

[83] I proceed in parallel, to some extent, to the very stimulating essay of Watson 1994; and, with some important differences, to Coakley 2002 ch. 8.

[84] Coakley 2002, 134 is misleading to suggest that this artistic tradition stems from 'the already modern Caravaggio'; many medieval icons and wall paintings, including one in the south transept of Westminster Abbey, have Thomas touching the risen Jesus.

[85] Prov. 26.4.

form, might be happy to go forwards without either touch or sight, is after all a belief and trust not simply in otherworldly realities, but (for John of all people!) in the Word made *flesh*, which can be heard, seen and handled.[86] The idea that faith must never have anything to do with history, so popular in certain circles for many years, is long overdue a decent burial.[87]

A challenge must be issued, in any case, not only to misleading ideas of 'faith', but to other assumptions as well. There are plenty of unhelpful ideas still current about what counts as genuine 'scientific' explanation. Not only history, but the physical sciences themselves, often proceed not simply by deduction from hard data, and certainly not always by induction from the particular to the general (particulars are after all the stuff of history), but by *inference to the best explanation*, which is one variety of 'abduction'.[88] In my earlier examples, the best explanation of the old stone columns is that there really was an arch; if we discover one that fits, we should be inclined to conclude the argument. The best explanation of the elephant outside Parliament is something nobody saw: the beast sneaking away from the circus and strolling round the corner. The best explanation of the presence of the friend on this bank of the river is that she has used a boat, even though there is no boat in sight. The best explanation for the fingerprints and the bloodstains (leaving aside the extra circumstances novelists love to invent) is that the accused really did commit the murder, even though there is no other evidence and the character references are impeccable.

In the case of history, these are all inferences to things which are in principle unrepeatable. In the case of the physical sciences, similar inferences are made with the supposition that they would have to be made again on the basis of analogous data.[89] In a recent treatment of 'inference', an example is given which bears some analogy to many debates about the resurrection:

> Do you know that you are looking at a . . . book right now rather than, say, having your brain intricately stimulated by a mad scientist? The sceptic carefully describes this alternative so that no experiment can refute it. The conclusion that you really are looking at a book, however, explains the aggregate of your experiences better than the mad scientist hypothesis or any other competing view. A sceptic who disagrees with this, instead of telling still more stories in which we cannot distinguish radically different situations, needs to address fresh issues about explanation.[90]

The equivalent of the 'mad scientist' hypothesis in the resurrection debate would be the intricately designed hypotheses according to which anything

---

[86] 1 Jn. 1.1.

[87] cf. e.g. Patterson 1998, 238f.

[88] See Wright, 'Dialogue', 249f.

[89] On inference in science, and the parallels and links with theology, cf. e.g. Polkinghorne 1994 ch. 2.

[90] Sanford 1995, 407f., summarizing Harman 1965 and similar work. Cf. too e.g. Thagard 1978.

and everything that pointed towards the resurrection (the gospel accounts, of course, in particular) is to be explained as the work of the early church expounding, legitimating and defending theological, exegetical and church-governmental conclusions reached on quite other grounds. The question which must be faced is whether the explanation of the data which the early Christians themselves gave, that Jesus really was risen from the dead, 'explains the aggregate' of the evidence better than these sophisticated scepticisms. My claim is that it does.

The claim can be stated once more in terms of necessary and sufficient conditions. The actual bodily resurrection of Jesus (not a mere resuscitation, but a transforming revivification) clearly provides a *sufficient* condition of the tomb being empty and the 'meetings' taking place. Nobody is likely to doubt that. Once grant that Jesus really was raised, and all the pieces of the historical jigsaw puzzle of early Christianity fall into place. My claim is stronger: that the bodily resurrection of Jesus provides a *necessary* condition for these things; in other words, that no other explanation could or would do. All the efforts to find alternative explanations fail, and they were bound to do so.

Many will challenge this conclusion, for many different reasons. I do not claim that it constitutes a 'proof' of the resurrection in terms of some neutral standpoint. It is, rather, a historical challenge to other explanations, other worldviews. Precisely because at this point we are faced with worldview-level issues, there is no neutral ground, no island in the middle of the epistemological ocean, as yet uncolonized by any of the warring continents. We cannot simply arrive at a topic and make grand declarations, as in Francis Drake's celebrated annexation of California, and suppose that all the local inhabitants will take them as binding. Saying that 'Jesus of Nazareth was bodily raised from the dead' is not only a self-*involving* statement; it is a self-*committing* statement, going beyond a reordering of one's private world into various levels of commitment to work out the implications. We cannot simply leave a flag stuck on a hill somewhere and sail back home to safety.

As I said in the Preface, this book is in many ways a ground-clearing exercise, hauling away boulders and digging out weeds that have prevented anything useful growing in this patch of soil. But the historical enquiry which we have undertaken, working back from the evidence of early Christianity to the question about its root belief, and back from the stories which encapsulate that root belief to the question of why they came into existence in the first place, ought to raise in the minds of the Thomas-like questioner fresh doubt, doubt about doubt itself, doubt which might pause to consider the difference between inference to the best explanation (that Jesus was indeed raised from the dead) on the one hand and the alternative theories on the other. It is, of course, perfectly possible to say that one cannot decide.

But for those who prefer not to live on such a knife-edge for ever, but who do not want to solve the jigsaw puzzle by putting Jesus' bodily resurrection in the middle of it, the challenge is: what alternative account can be offered which will explain the data just as well, which can provide an alternative *sufficient* explanation for all the evidence and so challenge the right of the bodily resurrection to be regarded as the *necessary* one?

The standard alternative theories have been ruled out, explicitly or implicitly, as we have made our way through this book.[91] The common idea that, when the early Christians said 'Jesus was raised from the dead', they meant something like 'He is alive in a spiritual, non-bodily sense, and we give him our allegiance as our lord' is historically impossible.[92] Not only, as we saw in Part I, did the words simply not mean that; one might as well say that 'Jesus was crucified by the Romans' meant neither more nor less than 'As I think of Jesus, I experience a sense of the crushing power of pagan empire.' If the early Christians *had* meant that, a belief of that kind could not explain, either within the second-Temple Jewish world or that of first-century paganism, why they hailed Jesus as Messiah and lord, or, in particular, why their belief about their own future resurrection took the very precise shape it did (Part III). The suggestion that Paul's view of the resurrection (of Christians, and of Jesus) had nothing to do with what we think of as a 'body' has been shown in Part II to be exegetically unfounded. The idea that there were two parallel streams of 'resurrection' belief in early Christianity, one going from Paul to *Rheginos* and the other going from Luke and John to Tertullian, is ruled out by the evidence surveyed in Parts II and particularly III. The widespread belief that the resurrection accounts in the gospels are back-projections of Christian belief from the middle or late first century simply will not work, as I have argued in Part IV and again, in relation to Schillebeeckx in particular, in the present chapter. These are the major counter-proposals, the main ways in which, over the last century or so, the inference to the best explanation has been avoided. Historical argument alone cannot force anyone to believe that Jesus was raised from the dead; but historical argument is remarkably good at clearing away the undergrowth behind which scepticisms of various sorts have been hiding. The proposal that Jesus was bodily raised from the dead possesses unrivalled power to explain the historical data at the heart of early Christianity.

There remains one final question, which is closely intertwined with the directly historical one. The early Christians declared that because Jesus had been raised from the dead he was 'son of god'. What did they mean by this? What light does this shed both on the historical question and on its meaning and results today?

---

[91] Full surveys of regular arguments are offered in the various works of Gary Habermas, e.g. 2001.

[92] e.g. Borg, in Borg and Wright 1999, ch. 8.

Chapter Nineteen

THE RISEN JESUS AS THE SON OF GOD

1. Worldview, Meaning and Theology

Supposing Jesus was raised from the dead, what would it mean?

The question of meaning is an integral part of the question, whether the resurrection of Jesus is in fact 'the best explanation' for the historical data, both the large-scale data of early Christianity and the specific data, deduced from that, of the empty tomb and the 'meetings'. This is the final question we face in this book.

I pointed out in *The New Testament and the People of God* the ways in which words, sentences and stories 'mean' what they mean because of the place they occupy within a larger whole: words within sentences, sentences within stories, and stories within worldviews.[1] We are now faced with the sentence, 'Jesus was bodily raised from the dead.' What does this *mean*?

We must distinguish two regular meanings of the word 'meaning'. There are several other shades to the word as well, but I shall confine myself to one of the regular ones, and use a different word for the other.[2] The one I shall avoid is 'meaning' as *referent*, as in 'democracy means government by the people'. When I intend that sense, I shall stick to *referent*. The sense I shall intend when I say 'meaning' is 'implication in the wider world within which this notion makes the sense it makes', as in the phrase 'democracy means happiness' (as spoken by a good democrat) or 'democracy means chaos' (as spoken by a disgruntled dictator). This is quite enough for our present purposes.

The question we are now to explore, then, is not the *referent* of 'Jesus was raised from the dead'; we have already established that. Within first-

---

[1] *NTPG* 95f., 115–17.

[2] Those who want to pursue the multiple complexities of 'meaning' might consult e.g. Thiselton 1992, 13 and frequently (the index is helpful in laying out different senses); also e.g. Moore 1993.

century discourse, the sentence referred (whether the speaker believed it or not) to an event which the early Christians claimed took place on the third day after Jesus' execution. (Of course, in the last two centuries plenty of people who have said or written 'Jesus was raised from the dead' have intended to refer, not to something that happened to the body of Jesus, but to events within the minds and hearts of his followers. But we have seen that this referent cannot have been the original one.) I have argued that, though mathematical-style 'proof' is impossible, such an event provides far and away the best explanation for all the other data we have surveyed. The question before us is the *meaning* of this sentence, and (since the sentence intends to refer to an event) the meaning of the event it intends to refer to, within wider worlds of understanding. What larger narrative(s) does the sentence belong in? What worldviews do such narratives embody and reinforce? What are the universes of discourse within which this sentence, and the event it refers to, settle down and make themselves at home – and which, at the same time, they challenge and reshape from within?[3]

It is important not to foreclose on possibilities here. It has too often been assumed that if Jesus was raised from the dead this automatically 'proves' the entire Christian worldview – including the belief that he was and is, in the full Christian sense, not just 'the son of a god', but the Son of God.[4] The fact that the argument can be short-circuited in this way is one reason why those who have wanted to study first-century history without dogmatic constraint have felt obliged to deny the resurrection of Jesus, in order to prevent themselves being (as they would see it) sucked down into the vortex of an all-dominating, heavy-handed orthodoxy.[5] A couple of brief imaginative experiments will show that life is more interesting, and more complicated, than that.

Suppose, to begin with, that a not particularly well-educated Roman soldier, some time in the 70s of the first century, heard people talking about Jesus' resurrection, and became so fascinated with the story that he held in his mind the possibility that it might be true. He might, of course, try to fit it into models where it would not belong, such as apotheosis. But there is at least one model he might be interested in: the myth of 'Nero redivivus', the belief that the maverick emperor, having died in 68, had come back to life again and was even now gathering an army, somewhere in the east, to make a glorious return to Rome.[6] Maybe, our soldier might muse to himself, this Jesus is a bit like that. He had, after all, been condemned as 'king of the

---

[3] It is this challenge and reshaping that Carnley (1987, 93–5) seems not to have allowed for in his attempted critique of Westcott and Pannenberg.

[4] e.g. Schwankl 1987, 631f.

[5] It may well be that the stories of Jesus' resurrection were, from the beginning, deliberately left open-ended in order to stop them from being taken over by this or that party or interest, however important; this is the main point of Williams 2000 ch. 12.

[6] See 68 above.

Jews'. He did indeed die, but perhaps he might be alive again somewhere, and might be gathering some new kind of Jewish resistance movement, ready to march on Jerusalem. Maybe this time he would take the place by storm. There are some interesting parallels between the thoughts in the mind of this hypothetical soldier and the thoughts of some early Christians, as Acts 1.6 indicates. Perhaps that is part of the point Luke is making there. But my present aim is simply to show that by itself the statement 'Jesus has been raised from the dead', referring to an event that happened three days after his execution, could perfectly well acquire 'meaning' by being located within an assumed worldview significantly different from the second-Temple Jewish worldviews which formed the starting-point of all the earliest Christians.

We can go further out again. Imagine someone who assumed a generalized, loose-knit ancient pagan worldview, who believed in all kinds of gods and goddesses. Such a person might well be prepared to think of these divine beings acting within and upon the world of space, time and matter in all sorts of unpredictable ways. Suppose, however, that such a person was not even sufficiently aware of common sense and life in general to know that dead people always stayed dead. Such a person, hearing that Jesus of Nazareth had been raised from the dead, might well shrug their shoulders and conclude that there was yet one more strange thing that happened sometimes in the world, along with all the others – thunder and lightning, eclipses of the sun and moon, fire and laughter and earthquakes and sex. Sometimes dead people came back again! And there it would rest. This, we may suppose, would not be a very stable meaning to latch on to. Most people in the ancient world as in the modern, however uneducated and inexperienced, discovered quite quickly that death was a one-way street. Plenty of people would be on hand to disabuse this easy-going acceptance, to reinforce the normal scepticism about such an event. But we can at least hold in our minds the possibility that the resurrection of Jesus could have had a significantly different 'meaning', within different hypothetical worldviews, to the meaning the first Christians gave it within theirs.

On a more modest scale, we note one contemporary scholar for whom we do not need a thought-experiment. The Jewish writer Pinchas Lapide has declared that he believes Jesus of Nazareth was bodily raised from the dead. Indeed, he believes this far more solidly than many would-be Christian theologians. But this belief does not make him a Christian. For him, the resurrection does not 'mean' that Jesus is in any sense, whether messianic or divine, the 'son of god'. Rather, it means that he was and is a great prophet to whom Israel should have paid attention at the time.[7]

These examples warn us to make sure we get some critical purchase on what the early Christians might have understood the resurrection to 'mean'.

[7] Lapide 1983 [1977].

We must beware of assuming that they automatically took the event, and the language by which they referred to it, to mean what successive generations of Christians have supposed. For many today, living within the assumed long-running war of attrition between secularist denial and obstinate belief, the resurrection validates a 'supernatural' view of the world; it means that there really is a 'life after death', that the destiny of Jesus' followers is 'to go to heaven when they die', and that the true realities in this world are 'eternal' or 'spiritual' rather than 'physical'. For others, the meaning of Easter is the invitation to a Jesus-centred spirituality in the present: 'Jesus is alive today and you can get to know him.'[8] The fact that none of these conclusions (however valid in their own way) is mentioned in any of the gospel resurrection stories, even in Luke and John where post-resurrection teaching is more plentiful, might have provided caution at this point. But in many parts of the church the story people want to hear has drowned out the story which the event, and the writings, actually tell. One might suppose the resurrection itself, both as event and as story, might challenge the semi-platonic worldview within which such things find easy acceptance. But church history, not to mention hymnody, suggests otherwise.

In particular, there has arisen within recent scholarship a view of the bodily resurrection of Jesus according to which its main meaning, had it occurred (which such writers do not believe), would be that whichever god was responsible for such a thing was behaving as an omnipotent tyrant and treating Jesus with an unfair favouritism, 'a miraculous act of intervention, an act which seems not to have been repeated in other apparently deserving cases'. The point seems to be that anyone who believes the early Christian claim is thereby believing in a god who performed a stupendous act to give Jesus a new lease of life without having much apparent relevance to anyone else.[9] I am not sure that any theologian has ever made a case for such a belief, but the vehemence with which this view is attacked makes me suppose that it has been held, at least at a popular level. Not only (this implied view holds) was Jesus the incarnate Son of God; not only was he miraculously preserved from sin; but, after a short and blameless life, he alone was granted the privilege of coming back to life, while everybody else had to stay dead. This is such a caricature of anything any serious Christian would argue that it is hard to know how to approach it. But it seems to correspond to a popular view of what Christians, particularly conservative Christians, are supposed by others to believe – namely that they are the favoured few, sharing Jesus' privileged status, a cut above the rest of humanity. Jesus' resurrection, as we saw in the first chapter, is sometimes seen as an immoral doctrine, because it appears to legitimate Christianity over against all other

---

[8] This argument is sometimes presented the other way round: the fact that you can get to know him means that he is alive and was raised. See e. g. Lampe 1977, 150.

[9] Holt 1999, 10f. Cf. too Crossan 1998, 549; Wedderburn 1999 chs. 9, 10.

religions. It appears to be a triumphalist doctrine, clinging for security to the idea of an omnipotent god who can intervene in the natural world at any point and sort things out, but who apparently chooses not to in most cases. How very undemocratic of god, or God, people think (without realizing that this idea itself is a local, almost tribal, western-Enlightenment view). Surely he, or it, should treat all people just the same. The idea of Jesus as a *representative*, such a key notion in all early Christian expositions of his resurrection, has been screened out both from the 'meaning' which is here under attack and from the critiques which, in demolishing this meaning, have felt obliged to demolish the resurrection along with it.

There seems then to be no necessary compulsion, either for those who believe in Jesus' resurrection or for those who disbelieve it, to interpret it within the framework of thought employed by the early Christians themselves. We can imagine situations in the ancient world where people might try to fit Jesus' resurrection into different worldviews. We have evidence of people doing so in the modern world, often with the best of intentions. But since this has been mainly a historical investigation into what the early Christians believed, and since what they thought the resurrection meant is not as widely known as it should be, and since the point of this whole series is to enquire, not just about the origin of Christianity, but about 'the Question of God' in relation to that origin, it is important in concluding this book to examine what the early Christians meant when they said that the resurrection constituted Jesus as 'son of god' – not least what content this made them give to the word 'god', or 'God', itself. The question of whether anyone today, inside or outside the Christian church, can or should appropriate wholesale the meanings the early Christians had in mind, and if so by what means and to what extent, is a separate one, involving all kinds of other issues of authority and continuity. But at least, when those questions are being faced, let us have a sense of what the early Christians were actually saying and meaning. We must neither project on to them ideas of which they were innocent, nor overlook ideas which they were keen to promote.

2. The Meanings of 'Son of God'

(i) Introduction

We find ourselves faced, from a new angle, with some of the questions we examined in chapters 8 and 12. This time, with passages like Romans 1.3–4 as a key, we take as our starting-point the early Christian belief that the resurrection had demonstrated Jesus to be 'son of god', and enquire what this meant for them as a way of sketching the groundwork for possible meanings today.

'Son of god' is a notoriously fluid title in early Christianity. It is all too easy to jump to conclusions about what it meant to the original writers and their first readers. There were already two worlds of meaning within which the phrase had resonance, and the Christians, addressing both, seem to have consciously transcended both. Within their Jewish world, 'son of god', though not exactly an everyday phrase, had two interlocking meanings in particular: Israel as a whole, and the king (or Messiah) more specifically.[10] Within the pagan world, 'son of god' could refer to various different characters, demigods, heroes and the like. But the referent that would occur easily to many people in Jesus' day, for the good reason that they saw and handled its evidence on a daily basis, was the Roman emperor as 'son of god'. AUGUST. TI. CAESAR DIVI AUG. F., declares the 'tribute penny' shown to Jesus in the well-known incident in Mark 12.13–17: 'Augustus Tiberius Caesar, Son of the Divine Augustus'. From Tiberius onwards, the rule ran like this: get yourself adopted by the emperor, survive plots and intrigues, inherit his throne when he dies, have him divinized in the process, and you will be 'son of a god', and a powerful one at that.[11]

These two worlds of meaning, though impinging on one another in various ways, retained their sharp differences, noticeable not least in the referent, and meaning, of the word 'god/God'. For the Jew there was one god, YHWH, the creator and covenant god; their particular beliefs about this god warrant the capital letter, though when we write 'God' we must always be on our guard against assuming that all those who do so have the same god in mind.[12] When second-Temple Jews thought about their god, prayed to him, sacrificed in his Temple, and longed for him to restore their fortunes, their mental picture of him, formed by Torah, Psalms, Prophets and the rest, was about as unlike the post-Enlightenment sense of 'the divine' as it is possible to be. This god was knowable, albeit mysterious; likely to do things, though one never quite knew what or when; lavish in his promises, but slow (so it seemed) in performance; longing for justice, though not yet putting it into effect; passionate about Israel, but strangely allowing her to suffer; creator of the world, yet ignored or mocked by most non-Jews. He was God, but his right to this position seemed always to be challenged by other powerful gods: the Babylonian ones scorned by Isaiah 40—55, the Greek ones whose culture had spread like a virus across the ancient near east, and now the Roman ones, including the powerful one featured on every coin.

The question of god lay at the heart of second-Temple Jewish life. Each affirmation, each act of worship, contained the question: not Who? (they knew the answer to that), nor yet Why? (again, they knew: because he was

---

[10] Israel: Ex. 4.22; Jer. 31.9; Hos. 11.1; 13.13; Mal. 1.6. The king: 2 Sam. 7.14 (quoted with this sense in 4Q174 10–13; cf. 4Q246 2.1); 1 Chr. 17.13; Pss. 2.7; 89.26f.

[11] On imperial apotheosis and cult cf. 55–7 above. For details on the coin cf. Hart 1984.

[12] This is why, as I explained in *NTPG* xiv–xv, I have regularly used the small 'g', to the alarm of some.

the creator, the covenant god), or particularly Where? (land and Temple remained the focus), but How? What? and, above all, When? How, they wanted to know, would YHWH deliver them? What did he want them to be doing in the meantime? And, *When would it happen*? The resurrection of Jesus of Nazareth provided the early Christians with a new, unexpected and crystal clear answer to these three questions; and, by doing so, it raised the first three in a quite new way.

This was in any case inevitable once Christianity went out into the gentile world, the world of many gods and goddesses. This is not the place to explore the world of ancient paganism in any detail. But, as many scenes in the New Testament indicate, near the surface of early Christian praxis, narrative, symbol and belief stood the question of god: they spoke of the god of Israel, the creator, the one who could be referred to as *ho theos*, God with a capital G, who had made himself known to Israel but also to the whole world in and through Jesus of Nazareth. And the resurrection was the way by which he had done it.[13] They re-employed the standard Jewish critique of pagan divinities and their accompanying ways of life, a critique rooted in Genesis, Deuteronomy, the Psalms, Isaiah and the rest, and expressed in first-century books like the Wisdom of Solomon. They saw the pagan pantheon, and its most powerful current representative, as at best a set of broken signposts to the truth, and at worst a demonic deceit. YHWH is the creator god, said Torah, Psalms and Prophets alike; he is the one who kills and makes alive. When the early Christians declared that the resurrection had marked out Jesus as 'son of god', they were building on the Jewish critique of paganism to make a statement not just about Jesus but also about Israel's god, a statement designed to confront the pagan world with the news of its rightful lord.

This generates three levels of meaning for the phrase 'the resurrection of the son of god', levels which are so closely integrated in some of the earliest Christian writings that to separate them out may seem artificial. It is necessary, however, to prevent the telescoping of the argument which often takes place. Before we can approach the central mystery itself, we must take account of the two levels which were certainly intended and heard by Paul and his successors, and which continued to resonate throughout the period we have studied. It would be possible at this point to begin a whole other book, and we must be content with a brief summary statement of what the resurrection of Jesus of Nazareth meant to the early Christians: what they meant when they said, as Paul does in the opening formula of Romans, that he was and is 'son of god', and indeed Son of God.[14]

---

[13] Obvious examples include Ac. 17.22–31; Rom. 1.3f.; 1 Thess. 1.9f.

[14] See the brief treatments in e.g. Merklein 1981; Perkins 1984. On the background see esp. Hengel 1976.

(ii) Resurrection and Messiahship

Among the first meanings which the resurrection opened up to the surprised disciples was that Israel's hope had been fulfilled. The promised time had come, as Jesus himself had announced during his public career; but it looked very different from what they had imagined. The *eschaton* had arrived. In the sense of 'eschatology' which seems to me to correspond best to what second-Temple Jews were hoping for, the long narrative of Israel's history had reached its climax.[15] 'Resurrection' was a key part of the 'eschaton'; if it had happened to one man whom many had regarded as Israel's Messiah, that meant that it had happened, in principle, to Israel as a whole. The Messiah represented Israel, just as David had represented Israel when he faced Goliath. Jesus had been executed as a messianic pretender, as 'king of the Jews', and Israel's god had vindicated him. This, apparently, was how Israel's god was fulfilling his promises to Israel. Again and again the early Christians emphasized that Jesus was raised from the dead *by god*, and by 'god' they meant Israel's god, YHWH. They saw the resurrection as a life-giving act of the covenant god, the creator who had always had the power to kill and make alive, who indeed was different from the other gods precisely in this respect. The resurrection was the sign to the early Christians that this living god had acted at last in accordance with his ancient promise, and had thereby shown himself to be God, the unique creator and sovereign of the world.

The resurrection therefore constituted Jesus as Messiah, as 'son of god' in the Davidic sense of 2 Samuel 7 or Psalm 2 (texts upon which the early Christians drew, as we might expect within second-Temple Judaism, to explain and expound their belief). 'Davidic' psalms were ransacked for hints about the resurrection of David's coming son. We can watch this process in Acts, with Luke 24 as its programmatic basis; but, in case that should be thought a late development (though it appears early to me), we can see exactly the same in Paul. The entire argument of Romans is framed between two great statements of this theme.[16] In between, at one of the letter's most climactic moments, those who share the 'sonship' of the Messiah will share as well the 'inheritance' that was spoken of also in Psalm 2.[17] The resurrection means that Jesus is the messianic 'son of god'; that Israel's eschatological hope has been fulfilled; that it is time for the nations of the world to be brought into submission to Israel's god.

---

[15] On the meanings of 'eschatology' cf. *JVG* 202–09. Perkins 1984, 95 drives a wedge where the early church would not have done when she says that the disciples' immediate experience of resurrection was 'not that of a "mighty act of God" in the course of history but of the dawn of the new age'.

[16] Rom. 1.3f.; 15.12. See Wright, *Romans*, 416–19, 748f.; and above, 554.

[17] Rom. 8.17; cf. Ps. 2.8.

The resurrection, interpreted in this sense, set the early Christians on a course of confrontation, not to say collision, with other Jewish groups of their day, particularly the authorities. Any claim that Israel's god had acted *here* rather than somewhere else within Judaism (the Temple, for example!) and in *this* way, vindicating a man whose work and teaching had been highly controversial, was bound to create a storm, and soon it did. Hard-line Pharisees like Saul of Tarsus, bent on a very different eschatological and political agenda, were horrified at the talk of *this* man being raised from the dead, with all that it implied. The official hierarchy, mostly Sadducees, were doubly horrified. Resurrection always had been a novel, revolutionary doctrine, and this new movement proved their worst fears about it to be true. 'They were angry that the disciples were announcing, in Jesus, the resurrection from the dead.'[18]

With good reason. The announcement meant the inauguration of the new covenant. Jesus' followers really did believe that Israel was being renewed through Jesus, and that his resurrection, marking him out as Messiah, was a call to Israel to find a new identity in following him and establishing his kingdom. Their belief in the resurrection of the son of god, in this sense, marked out the early Christians from those of their fellow Jews who could not or would not accept such a thing. And it marked them out, of course, not as non-Jews or anti-Jews, not as some kind of pagan group, but precisely as people who claimed that the truest and most central hopes and beliefs of Israel had come true, and that they were living by them. To claim the risen Jesus as 'son of god' in the sense of 'Messiah' was the most deeply Jewish thing the Christians could do, and hence the most deeply suspect in the eyes of those Jews who did not share their convictions.

The 'new covenant' beliefs of the early Christians meant that, in hailing Jesus as 'son of god', they believed that Israel's god had acted in him to fulfil the covenant promises by dealing at last with the problem of evil.[19] One standard Jewish analysis of evil, represented for instance by the Wisdom of Solomon, did not believe that the created order was itself evil, but that human beings, by committing idolatry, distorted their own humanity into sinful behaviour and courted corruption and ultimately death. Death – the unmaking of the creator's image-bearing creatures – was not seen as a good thing, but as an enemy to be defeated. It was the ultimate weapon of destruction: anti-creation, anti-human, anti-god. If the creator god was also the covenant god, and if the covenant was there to deal with the unwelcome problem that had invaded the created order at its heart and corrupted human beings themselves, it was this intruder, death itself, that had to be defeated. To allow death to have its way – to sign up, as it were, to some kind of compromise agreement whereby death took human bodies but the creator was

---

[18] Ac. 4.2 (see above, 452).
[19] On this as the purpose of the covenant see e.g. *NTPG* 259–79.

allowed to keep human souls – was no solution, or not to the problem as it was perceived within most second-Temple Judaism. That is why 'resurrection' was never a *redescription* of death, but always its *defeat*.

Within the New Testament this comes over most clearly in Paul, especially Romans 8 and the Corinthian correspondence, and Revelation. In the most obvious passage, 1 Corinthians 15.20–28, we find an explicitly messianic theology, rooted in messianically read Psalms, in which Jesus, as the 'son of god', is the agent of the creator god in accomplishing precisely this task, of ridding the world of evil and ultimately of death itself. As we saw in chapter 7, this was indeed, so far as Paul was concerned, the defeat of death. The early Christians saw Jesus' resurrection as the act of the covenant god, fulfilling his promises to deal with evil at last. Declaring their faith in his resurrection was a self-involving act in the sense that the world of meaning within which they made sense of Easter was the new world in which sins, their own included, had been forgiven. This did not, of course, reduce the 'meaning' of 'Jesus is risen from the dead' to 'My sins have been forgiven.' It was not simply a way of saying that Jesus' crucifixion had been a victory rather than a defeat. We must not confuse 'meaning' in this wider sense with 'referent'. The statement had a historical *referent* which was perceived to generate and sustain a wider world of *meaning*, but which could not be reduced to terms of that alone.

The first level of a 'son of god' understanding of Jesus' resurrection can therefore be summarized as follows. Jesus is Israel's Messiah. In him, the creator's covenant plan, to deal with the sin and death that has so radically infected his world, has reached its long-awaited and decisive fulfilment.

(iii) Resurrection and World Lordship

If the phrase 'son of god' could mean 'Messiah' to a first-century Jewish ear in the period, there was a significantly different sense, as we saw, which was available in the world of early Christianity. This was the way the title was applied to pagan monarchs, and to Caesar in particular.

The city of Rome itself held back, for much of the first century AD, from explicit worship of emperors during their lifetime. The eastern part of the empire, however, with its long traditions of ruler-worship, had no such scruples. The title 'son of god', officially designating the new emperor as the offspring of the now divinized previous one (a process which began with Augustus' divinization of Julius Caesar), enabled the fiction of renewed republicanism to be maintained in Rome itself while most other parts of Caesar's large empire shrugged their shoulders and accepted this 'son of god' as already virtually divine, if not actually so. At least two of the first-century emperors, Gaius Caligula and Nero, dropped the tactful pseudo-republican reticence and regarded themselves as straightforwardly divine. And they behaved accordingly.[20]

There is no suggestion that the early Christians chose the phrase 'son of god' on the basis of this pagan usage. We must not confuse *derivation* with *confrontation*.[21] The roots of the title as it appears in the New Testament are the firmly Jewish ones noted in the previous sub-section. But there can be no question that the title would have been heard by many in the greco-roman world, from very early on, as a challenge to Caesar. And there is certainly no question that some of the early writers, including Paul, intended it in this way. The long line of Jewish thought that ran from the stories of David and Solomon, through the Psalms, to books like Isaiah and Daniel, and then into the flourishing literature of the later second-Temple period, saw Israel's true king as the world's true lord. The early Christians, precisely because they regarded Jesus as Israel's Messiah, also regarded him (as we have frequently noted) as the true monarch of the gentile world as well. The Christians minted no coins. Had they done so, DIVI F. might well have appeared on them. The fish-symbol, after all, said exactly that in Greek.[22]

Calling Jesus 'son of god' within this wider circle of meaning constituted a refusal to retreat, a determination to stop Christian discipleship turning into a private cult, a sect, a mystery religion. It launched a claim on the world: a claim at once absurd (a tiny group of nobodies cocking a snook at the might of Rome) and very serious, so serious that within a couple of generations the might of Rome was trying, and failing, to stamp it out. It grew from an essentially positive view of the world, of creation. It refused to relinquish the world to the principalities and powers, but claimed even them for allegiance to the Messiah who was now the lord, the *kyrios*.[23]

To use the phrase 'son of god' for Jesus, in a sense which constituted an implicit confrontation with Caesar, was thus part of an affirmation of the goodness of the created order, now claimed powerfully by the creator god as his own. The resurrection of Jesus, in the full bodily sense I have described, supplies the groundwork for this: it is the reaffirmation of the universe of space, time and matter, after not only sin and death but also pagan empire (the institutionalization of sin and death) have done their worst.[24] The early

---

[20] On all this see e.g. the seminal essays in Horsley 2000; and above, 55–8.

[21] See Wright, *What St Paul Really Said*, ch. 5.

[22] See 580 above on the *ICHTHYS* motif. We may suspect that few of those who today attach the fish-symbol to cars, or use it as a lapel badge, are aware of just how explicitly counter-imperial it originally was.

[23] Obvious examples, again from Paul, include Phil. 2.6–11; Col. 1.15–20.

[24] Crossan's attempt (1998, xxvii–xxxi) to retain the words 'bodily' and 'embodied', but to mean by them not that Jesus' body was itself raised from the dead but that his life somehow continues in the embodied communities that work for justice in the world, thus leapfrogs to a kind of postmodern Catholic ecclesiology ('There is only one Jesus, the *historical* Jesus who incarnated the Jewish God of justice for a believing community committed to continuing such incarnation ever afterward' (xxx, italics original)), ignoring the fact that, as

Christians saw Jesus' resurrection as the action of the creator god to reaffirm the essential goodness of creation and, in an initial and representative act of new creation, to establish a bridgehead within the present world of space, time and matter ('the present evil age', as in Galatians 1.4) through which the whole new creation could now come to birth.[25] Calling Jesus 'son of god' within this context of meaning, they constituted themselves by implication as a collection of rebel cells within Caesar's empire, loyal to a different monarch, a different *kyrios*. Saying 'Jesus has been raised from the dead' proved to be self-involving in that it gained its meaning within this counter-imperial worldview. The Sadducees were right to regard the doctrine of resurrection, and especially its announcement in relation to Jesus, as political dynamite.

Once again we must not confuse 'meaning' in this sense with 'referent'. Just as 'Jesus has been raised from the dead' does not *refer to* the fact that 'my sins have been forgiven', even though it *means* that within its wider world of implication, so that same sentence does not *refer to* the fact that the true god disapproves of brutal tyranny, even though it *means* that in the sense of 'meaning' I am using in this chapter. Some recent books, eager to bring out the political implications of the resurrection, have allowed this political 'meaning', in the wide sense, to take over entirely, and have supposed that this argument is strengthened by suggesting that nothing much happened on the third day after Jesus' death.[26] Get rid of the original referent, and (so it appears) you allow the implication to take its place. But this misses the point the early Christians were eager to make, the point that brought them quickly into confrontation with the authorities both Jewish and pagan. To imply that Jesus 'went to heaven when he died', or that he is now simply a spiritual presence, and to suppose that such ideas exhaust the referential meaning of 'Jesus was raised from the dead', is to miss the point, to cut the nerve of the social, cultural and political critique. Death is the ultimate weapon of the tyrant; resurrection does not make a covenant with death, it overthrows it. The resurrection, in the full Jewish and early Christian sense, is the ultimate affirmation that creation matters, that embodied human beings matter.[27] That is why resurrection has always had an inescapable political meaning; that is why the Sadducees in the first century, and the Enlightenment in our own day, have opposed it so strongly. No tyrant is

---

in the present subsection, the very concerns he is stressing are precisely the ones that the actual bodily resurrection of Jesus will ground and sustain.

[25] To follow this theme, see e.g. Gal. 6.15; Rom. 4.13, 18–25; 2 Cor. 2.14—6.10.

[26] e.g. Sawicki 1994. For the substantive point see again Rowland 1993, 76–9.

[27] Morgan 1994, 18f. attempts to arrive at that result despite having denied its premise, like someone trying to sit on the branch through which they have just sawn – a dangerous move, as Thiselton, quoting Wittgenstein, loves to remind us (e.g. 2000, 1216). A more nuanced approach is found in Selby 1976, though I think my present argument grounds his concerns more securely. The way forward is indicated, once more, by Rowland 1993.

threatened by Jesus going to heaven, leaving his body in a tomb. No governments face the authentic Christian challenge when the church's social preaching tries to base itself on Jesus' teaching, detached from the central and energizing fact of his resurrection (or when, for that matter, the resurrection is affirmed simply as an example of a supernatural 'happy ending' which guarantees post-mortem bliss).

This, then, is the second level of meaning. The resurrection constitutes Jesus as the world's true sovereign, the 'son of god' who claims absolute allegiance from everyone and everything within creation. He is the start of the creator's new world: its pilot project, indeed its pilot.

(iv) Resurrection and the Question of God

The third and final 'meaning', in this wider sense, of the resurrection of Jesus has to do with the 'meaning', in the narrower sense of *referent*, of the word 'god' itself. This was, after all, the greatest of the questions which the early Christians posed, not only to their pagan neighbours, but also within the Jewish circles where they began. If there is one true god, as the Jews had always claimed, and if he really is the creator of the world and the covenant god of Israel, then what must now be said of him on the basis of the resurrection of Jesus? How does calling Jesus 'son of god', in this sense, help us to understand not only who Jesus was and is but who the one true god was and is?

As we have seen, the early Christians usually referred to the resurrection of Jesus as the work of this god. 'He has been raised,' they said; 'God raised Jesus from the dead.'[28] The work of this god was, from very early on, part of the interpretation, the grid of meaning through which they viewed this event. And from very early on (it is already taken for granted by Paul), the fact that *this* Jesus had been raised by *this* god, when mulled over and reflected on in the light of all that Jesus had done and said, and all that Israel's scriptures had said about the redeeming and reconciling action of this god, drew from the early Christians the breathtaking belief that Jesus was 'son of god', the *unique* 'Son' of *this* God as opposed to any other. They meant by this not simply that he was Israel's Messiah, though that remained foundational; nor simply that he was the reality of which Caesar and all other such tyrants were the parodies, though that remained a vital implication. They meant it in the sense that he was the personal embodiment and revelation *of* the one true god.[29] Paul's Christology, and perhaps also that which was expressed in

---

[28] e.g. Lk. 24.6; Ac. 4.10; cf. Rom. 4.24f.; 8.11; 10.9. The alternative viewpoint – that Jesus had the power to raise himself – is expressed in Jn. 10.17f.

[29] This whole train of thought shows that it is wrong to play off a truly historical understanding of Jesus and his resurrection against a proper appreciation of Christology, as does Carnley 1987, 75–81 in his comments on Westcott.

credal formulae before he was writing the extant letters, indicates that from very early on in the Christian movement this god and this Jesus were being referred to as 'father' and 'son' *within contexts that clearly put them together on the 'divine' side of the equation.*[30]

The truly remarkable thing about this is that, where we see this happening, the arguments that are being mounted at the time, and even the Old Testament scriptures that are being quoted and expounded, are all of a strongly monotheistic tone. We have already examined the key Pauline texts.[31] In some of them, Paul speaks of Jesus as 'son' in relation to 'God'; in others, of God as 'father' in relation to Jesus. There are, of course, various arguments where, bit by bit, he puts the two together, and not surprisingly the resurrection is never far away when he does so:

> For if, being enemies, we were reconciled to God by the death of his son, how much more, being reconciled, shall we be saved by his life . . .

> For as many as are led by God's Spirit are the children of God. You did not receive a spirit of slavery to go back to fear, but you received the Spirit of sonship, in which we cry, Abba, Father. The Spirit's own self bears witness with our spirit that we are God's children, and, if children, then heirs: heirs of God, and joint heirs with the Messiah, if we suffer with him so that we may also be glorified with him . . .

> For those whom he foreknew, he also predestined to be conformed to the image of his son, so that he might be the firstborn among many brothers and sisters . . .

> He who did not spare his own son, but gave him up for us all, how shall he not also give us all things with him?[32]

These passages only make the sense they do if by 'son of god', when referring to Jesus, Paul means that Jesus is the one sent by God, from God, not only as a messenger but as the very embodiment of his love. To send someone else is hardly an ultimate proof of self-giving love.[33] The same is true in Galatians:

> I am crucified with the Messiah; nevertheless I live; yet not I, but the Messiah lives in me; and the life I now live in the flesh I live by the faith of the son of God, who loved me and gave himself for me.

> As long as the heir is a child . . . he is under guardians and trustees until the time set by the father's will . . . So when the time was fully come, God sent forth his son, born of a woman, born under the law, to redeem those who are under the law, so that we might receive the adoption as sons. And because you are sons, God has sent the

---

[30] For details, see Wright, *Climax*, chs. 4, 5 and 6.

[31] e.g. Phil. 2.10f., using Isa. 45.23; 1 Cor. 8.6, using Dt. 6.4 (where in the LXX 'the Lord' is of course YHWH, translated *kyrios*, the word Paul then uses for 'Lord' in relation to Jesus); 1 Cor. 15.25–8, using Ps. 110.1.

[32] Rom. 5.10; 8.14–17, 29, 32.

[33] cf. too 8.3f. On Paul's high Christology in Romans see Wright, *Romans*, 629f.

Spirit of his son into our hearts, crying, Abba, father. So you are no longer a slave but a son; and if a son, then an heir, through God.[34]

And it is in the light of these rich, multi-layered statements that we can discover the third layer of meaning in the great opening statement of Romans:

> . . . God's gospel concerning his son, who was descended from David's seed according to the flesh, and marked out as son of God in power, according to the Spirit of holiness, by the resurrection of the dead, Jesus the Messiah, our Lord . . . [35]

The resurrection, in other words, declares that Jesus really is God's Son: not only in the sense that he is the Messiah, though Paul certainly intends that here, not only in the sense that he is the world's true lord, though Paul intends that too, but also in the sense that he is the one in whom the living God, Israel's God, has become personally present in the world, has become one of the human creatures that were made from the beginning in the image of this same God.

Does this mean that Jesus only *became* 'Son of God', in this sense or any other, at the resurrection? Certainly not. The whole point of passages like Romans 5.5–11, 8.3–4 and Galatians 2.19–20 and 4.4–7 is that what Jesus did in his public career and supremely in his death was to be understood as the work of 'God's Son' in this sense as well as the others, *and that the resurrection declared that this had been the case.* This is not to say that this conclusion was bound to be drawn by anyone at all hearing about Jesus' resurrection. As we saw earlier in the chapter, that would depend on the worldview within which the resurrection was perceived. The resurrection did not automatically 'prove that Jesus was divine'. However, within the world of meaning the early Christians found themselves exploring, it was clear that the resurrection did not suggest the adoptionist view that Jesus became, at Easter, something or someone he had not been before. It made clear, to those who followed its inner implications, what had always been the case. It declared *that* Jesus always *was* 'God's Son', in this sense as in the others.

This point could be expanded almost indefinitely in a larger treatment of early Christology, but we have neither space nor need for such a thing. Paul is our earliest witness to the theology of the first Christians, and already in his letters, within two or three decades of Jesus' public career, we find it stated firmly and clearly that the resurrection was the act of Israel's God, the world's creator, demonstrating that Jesus of Nazareth always was his 'Son' in this sense and with this meaning. Paul would have agreed with the matchless summary at the end of John's prologue (1.18): nobody has ever seen God, but 'the only-begotten God' has revealed him, has made him known.

---

[34] Gal. 2.19f.; 4.1f., 4–7.
[35] Rom. 1.1, 3f.

And, as we saw in chapter 17, this is designed to match the ultimate confession of faith offered by the ex-doubter, Thomas: the resurrection demonstrates that Jesus is 'my Lord and my God'.

A word is necessary about how such language may best be understood, in full recognition that Christology of this sort is a mystery that has taxed some of the best brains in the last two thousand years. I have explained elsewhere that in second-Temple Judaism there were several quite sophisticated ways of speaking of the one God of Israel, the creator, and his close and complex relation to the world.[36] Maintaining a firm hold on God's transcendence and otherness on the one hand, while simultaneously wanting to express the nearness, love and activity of this God within the world, many Jewish writings spoke of this in various ways which seemed to have been designed to safeguard both the actuality of God's activity and the fact that it was the same God, the creator, the transcendent one, who was acting. What we have in the New Testament, not entirely without precedent in Judaism but nowhere seen with anything like the prominence and emphasis the early Christians gave to it, is the messianic language of the king, seen as YHWH's 'son', taken up and used as a vehicle in exactly the same way.

This is fleetingly and fascinatingly anticipated in Philo.[37] But whereas for the great Alexandrian philosopher such a divine 'son' remained strictly 'incorporeal', the whole point, for Paul and John alike, was that this 'son of God' had not only come in the flesh but had died in the flesh; had not only died and been buried but had been raised three days later; and that this resurrection, this 'rising' in a sense which Philo never imagined, was the public announcement, by the one true God, that this Jesus really was, and had always been, his son in this full, self-revealing, self-embodying sense.

This is the world of meaning which was generated for the early Christians by the resurrection of Jesus. Of course, as with the other meanings of 'son of god', statements about the resurrection, and about Jesus as God's Son, were self-involving. In this case, they indicated a personal faith: a belief *that* God raised Jesus from the dead,[38] and a trust *in* this God, a commitment to discipleship and to the worldwide mission that the resurrection had launched, precisely by inaugurating God's new age. Saying 'Jesus has been raised from the dead' was never simply a dramatic way of saying 'God's cause

---

[36] e.g. *JVG* 629–31; *Challenge*, ch. 5; Wright and Borg, *Meaning*, ch. 10; and cf. above, 577f.

[37] cf. Philo *Conf. Ling.* 62f., quoting Zech. 6.12, which Philo reads as 'the man whose name is Rising [*anatole*]'. 'Strangest of titles,' he comments, 'if you suppose that a being composed of soul and body is here described. But if you suppose that it is that Incorporeal one, who differs not a whit from the divine image, you will agree that the name of "rising" assigned to him quite truly describes him. For that man is the eldest son, whom the Father of all raised up [*aneteile*], and elsewhere calls him His first-born, and indeed the Son thus begotten followed the ways of his Father . . .' (tr. Colson and Whitaker in LCL).

[38] Rom. 4.24; 10.9.

continues!', or (as in the musical *Godspell*), 'Long live God!' That is, once again, to mistake 'referent' and 'implication'. Saying 'God raised Jesus from the dead' *referred to* an event three days after Jesus' crucifixion. But if we allow this event to generate the *world of meaning* most appropriate to it, we shall not be content with reference alone, vital though it is. 'God raised Jesus from the dead' is, after all, the statement which, according to Paul, aligns the believer with Abraham himself. The world of meaning includes the implication that those who believe in Jesus' resurrection form the renewed covenant family. This is part of the meaning of 'justification by faith', a topic for the next volume in this series. Faith in the resurrection power of God, according to Paul, is the alternative to idolatry: it assigns to the creator God the power and glory which are properly his, the very things that idolatry characteristically denies, and, by denying, courts death.[39]

The third sense of 'son of God', then, does not leave the first two behind, but integrates them within a larger picture of who the one true God, Israel's God, actually is. For a fuller picture, we would need to factor in the New Testament's talk of the divine Spirit, the one who, the Christians believed, had been instrumental in God's raising of Jesus from the dead (as we saw frequently in the earlier chapters), and the one who, they believed, lived within them and would raise them too. The New Testament writers resist easy or formulaic systematizing; but in their speech about the creator God, about Jesus of Nazareth, and about the Spirit of the living God, they point towards the later theologies in which these three came to be seen, mysteriously, as differentiated yet interpenetrating revelations of the one God.

The picture of the true God that emerges from all this is totally different from the caricatured 'all-powerful miracle-worker', the 'interventionist' god who has become such an easy target in some recent polemical writing.[40] Theologians today are understandably eager to shed any suggestion of a pompous, omnipotent bully, a triumphalist 'god' in that sense. But it would be a bad mistake to suppose that this is the picture of God offered in the New Testament, or that the resurrection of Jesus lends it any support. Of course there is 'triumph' in the message; where would the power and appeal of the gospel be without Romans 8.31–9 or 1 Corinthians 15.54–7? But we should think again before we accuse the early Christians of 'triumphal*ism*'. Such charges have a habit of rebounding – not least on those who insist on promoting the unstable worldview of late-modern or postmodern western culture to a position of pre-eminence, and then try to climb on top of it, claiming it as high moral ground, and looking down on all who went before them. It is precisely the emerging threefold understanding of Israel's God that prevents a move towards the high-and-dry 'god' of Deism on the one

---

[39] Rom. 4.18–22, forming a deliberate contrast with 1.18–23 (see Wright, *Romans*, 499–501).

[40] cf. e.g. Crossan 1998, 575–86; Wedderburn 1999, 128f., 178–219.

hand, the low-and-wet 'god' of pantheism on the other, together with their respective half-cousins, the 'interventionist God' of dualist supernaturalism, and the 'panentheist' deity of much contemporary speculation. Conversely, where we find resistance to the threefold vision of God offered by the New Testament (a vision which grows precisely from the Easter faith of the early disciples), there is good reason to suppose that the underlying cause of such resistance, in the contemporary world as in the ancient, is to be found in 'the sheer horror that [some] people . . . have for *the being and action of God himself in space and time*'.[41] Once again, questions of worldview have been unearthed, and will not go away.

When the early Christians developed this threefold understanding of Israel's God, they did not abandon their Jewish roots and adopt the language and thought-forms of paganism. They developed their theology by embracing one of the central Jewish beliefs of their day, the resurrection of the dead (which had been the solace of many a righteous Jew when faced with pagan oppression and injustice), and by understanding it all the more deeply in the light of what they believed had happened to Jesus. This was what made them a messianic group within Judaism. This was what made them take on Caesar's world with the news that there was 'another king'. This was what made them not only speak of the one true God, but invoke him, pray to him, love him and serve him in terms of the Father and the lord, of the God who sent the Son and now sends the Spirit of the Son, in terms of the only-begotten God who makes visible the otherwise invisible creator of the world. This is why, when they spoke of the resurrection of Jesus, they spoke of the resurrection of the Son of God.

3. Shooting at the Sun?

I return to the parable with which I began. Have we been shooting arrows at the sun? Have we been trying to prove the unprovable, to reach the unreachable, to unscrew the inscrutable?

No. Of course our arrows of historical enquiry are all earthbound, subject to the epistemological equivalent of the law of gravity. The historian *qua* historian cannot mount an argument from first principles and end up proving God. Christian faith, however, has always declared that earth – gravity and all! – is where the Son of God made his home, pitching his tent, as John puts it, in our midst. And that declaration was the consequence, not the cause, of the belief that on the third day God raised Jesus from the dead. For the earliest Christians, to speak of Jesus' resurrection was to speak of something that, however (in our sense) earth-shattering, however much it drew together things earthly and heavenly, was still an 'earthly' event, and needed to be

---

[41] Torrance 1976, 80 (italics original).

exactly that. It had earthly consequences: an empty tomb, footprints by the shore, and, at Emmaus, a loaf broken but not consumed.

If the sun is truly reflected in the pool, then to shoot at the sun's reflection in the water is not simply a cheat, not simply an avoiding of the real issue, but a way of saying something about the sort of world the creator God has made, and the mode of his presence within it.[42] History matters because human beings matter; human beings matter because creation matters; creation matters because the creator matters. And the creator, according to some of the most ancient Jewish beliefs, grieved so much over creation gone wrong, over humankind in rebellion, over thorns and thistles and dust and death, that he planned from the beginning the way by which he would rescue his world, his creation, his history, from its tragic corruption and decay; the way, therefore, by which he would rescue his image-bearing creatures, the muddled and rebellious human beings, from their doubly tragic fate; the way, therefore, by which he would be most truly himself, would *become* most truly himself. The story of Jesus of Nazareth which we find in the New Testament offers itself, as Jesus himself had offered his public work and words, his body and blood, as the answer to this multiple problem: the arrival of God's kingdom precisely in the world of space, time and matter, the world of injustice and tyranny, of empire and crucifixions. This world is where the kingdom must come, on earth as it is in heaven. What view of creation, what view of justice, would be served by the offer merely of a new spirituality and a one-way ticket out of trouble, an escape from the real world?

No wonder the Herods, the Caesars and the Sadducees of this world, ancient and modern, were and are eager to rule out all possibility of actual resurrection. They are, after all, staking a counter-claim on the real world. It is the real world that the tyrants and bullies (including intellectual and cultural tyrants and bullies) try to rule by force, only to discover that in order to do so they have to quash all rumours of resurrection, rumours that would imply that their greatest weapons, death and deconstruction, are not after all omnipotent. But it is the real world, in Jewish thinking, that the real God made, and still grieves over. It is the real world that, in the earliest stories of Jesus' resurrection, was decisively and for ever reclaimed by that event, an event which demanded to be understood, not as a bizarre miracle, but as the beginning of the new creation. It is the real world that, however complex this may become, historians are committed to studying. And, however dangerous this may turn out to be, it is the real world in and for which Christians are committed to living and, where necessary, dying. Nothing less is demanded by the God of creation, the God of justice, the God revealed in and as the crucified and risen Jesus of Nazareth.

---

[42] Here I am particularly conscious of my debt, implicit throughout the present book, to O'Donovan 1986.

Of course, when we have shot our best and boldest arrows at the target reflected in the pool, the water may be so splashed and stirred that, for a while, we can see the image no longer. Scholarship sometimes has that effect. A voice may whisper that it was no image, but only imagination; it was a mirage, a fantasy. But as the water settles, with gentle ripples still visible where the arrows went in, the image will return. We will gaze at it once more, and know that in the Lord our labour is not in vain.

Bibliography

Abbreviations

1. Stylistic Shorthands

ad fin.	at the end
ad loc.	at the [relevant] place
bib.	bibliography
cf.	confer
com.	commentary
cp.	compare
ed.	edited by
edn.	edition
esp.	especially
frag.	fragment(s)
introd.	introduction/introduced by
MS(S)	manuscript(s)
par(r).	parallel(s) (in the synoptic tradition)
ref(s).	reference(s)
rev.	revision/revised by
subsequ.	subsequent
tr.	translation/translated by

2. Primary Sources

Achill. Tat.	Achilles Tatius
Aelian	Aelian (*Hist. Misc.* = *Historical Miscellany*)
Ael. Arist.	Aelius Aristides (*Orat.* = *Oration*)
Aesch.	Aeschylus (*Ag.* = *Agamemnon*; *Eumen.* = *Eumenides*; *Pers.* = *Persians*)
ANF	*The Ante-Nicene Fathers*, ed. A. Roberts, J. Donaldson et al. 10 vols. Buffalo: The Christian Literature Publishing Company, 1887
Aristoph.	Aristophanes (*Ecclesiaz.* = *Ecclesiazousae*)
Arist.	Aristotle (*De An.* = *De Anima*; *Hist. An.* = *Historia Animalium*; *Nic. Eth.* = *Nichomachean Ethics*)
Aug.	Augustine (*Civ. Dei* = *City of God*)
Caes.	Caesar (*Gall. War* = *Gallic War*)
CAF	*Comicorum Atticorum Fragmenta*, ed. T. Kock. 3 vols. Leipzig: Teubner, 1880–88
Callim.	Callimachus
Catull.	Catullus
Chariton	Chariton (*Call.* = *Callirhoe*)
Cic.	Cicero (*De Nat. Deor.* = *De Natura Deorum*; *De Rep.* = *De Republica*; *Tusc. Disp.* = *Tusculan Disputations*)
Commod.	Commodian (*Inst.* = *Instructions*)
Danby	H. Danby, *The Mishnah, Translated from the Hebrew with Introduction and Brief Explanatory Notes*. Oxford: OUP, 1933

Dio Chrys.   Dio Chrysostom (*Orat.* = *Oration*)
Diod. Sic.   Diodorus Siculus
Diog. Laert. Diogenes Laertius
Epict.   Epictetus (*Disc.* = *Discourses*)
Epicur.   Epicurus (*Ep. ad Men.* = *Epistle to Menoeceus*)
Epiphanius   Epiphanius (*Haer.* = *Against All Heresies*, otherwise known as *Panarion*)
Eurip.   Euripides (*Alcest.* = *Alcestis*; *Hippol.* = *Hippolytus; Madn. Hercl.* = *Madness of Hercules*)
Euseb.   Eusebius (*HE* = *Historia Ecclesiae*; *Life of Const.* = *Life of Constantine*)
EV(V)   English Version(s) of the Bible
FrGrHist. *Die Fragmente der griechischen Historiker,* ed. F. Jacoby. 17 vols. Berlin and Leiden: Weidmannsche Buchhandlung, 1923–58
GM   F. García Martínez, *The Dead Sea Scrolls Translated: The Qumran Texts in English.* Leiden: E. J. Brill, 1994
Herm.   Hermas
Herod.   Herodas (or 'Herondas') (*Mim.* = *Mimiambi*)
Hesiod   Hesiod (*Works* = *Works and Days*)
Hdt.   Herodotus
Hippolytus   Hippolytus (*Ag. Plat.* = *Against Plato*)
Homer   Homer (*Il.* = *Iliad*; *Od.* = *Odyssey*)
Hor.   Horace (*Sat.* = *Satires*)
Hyg.   Hyginus (*Fab.* = *Fables*)
Ign.   Ignatius of Antioch
Iren.   Irenaeus (*Adv. Haer.* = *Adversus Haereseis*)
Jer.   Jerome (*Vir. Illustr.* = *De Viris Illustribus*)
Jos.   Josephus (*Ap.* = *Against Apion*; *War* = *The Jewish War*; *Ant.* = *Jewish Antiquities*)
Juv.   Juvenal (*Sat.* = *Satires*)
Lucian   Lucian (*Adv. Ind.* = *Adversus Indoctum*; *Salt.* = *De Saltatione*; *Pereg.* = *Peregrinus*)
Lucret.   Lucretius (*De Re. Nat.* = *De Rerum Natura*)
LXX   Septuagint version of the Old Testament
MT   Masoretic Text (of the Hebrew Bible)
NH   Nag Hammadi
NPNF   *The Nicene and Post-Nicene Fathers,* ed. P. Schaff et al. 1st series: 14 vols; 2nd series: 13 vols. Buffalo: The Christian Literature Publishing Company, 1886–98
NT   New Testament
NTA   *New Testament Apocrypha,* ed. E. Hennecke and W. Schneemelcher. 2 vols. London: SCM Press, 1963–5 [1959–64]
OGI   *Orientis Graeci Inscriptiones Selectae,* ed. W. Dittenberger. 2 vols. Hildesheims: Olms, 1960 [orig.: Leipzig: Hirzel, 1903–05]
Or.   Origen (*C. Cels.* = *Contra Celsum*; *De Princ.* = *De Principiis*)
OT   Old Testament
Ovid   Ovid (*Her.* = *Heroides*; *Met.* = *Metamorphoses*)
Paus.   Pausanias
Petr.   Petronius (*Sat.* = *Satyricon*)
PG   *Patrologia Graeca,* ed. J.-P. Migne. 162 vols. Paris: Garnier, 1857–86
Philostr.   Philostratus (*Apoll.* = *Life of Apollonius of Tyana*; *Her.* = *Heroikos*)
Photius   Photius (*Bib.* = *Bibliotheca*)
Pind.   Pindar (*Ol.* = *Olympian Odes*; *Pyth.* = *Pythian Odes*)
PL   *Patrologia Latina,* ed. J.-P. Migne. 217 vols. Paris: Garnier, 1844–64

Plato	Plato (*Apol.* = *Apology*; *Cratyl.* = *Cratylus*; *Gorg.* = *Gorgias*; *Phaedr.* = *Phaedrus*; *Rep.* = *Republic*; *Tim.* = *Timaeus*; *Symp.* = *Symposium*)
Pliny	Pliny the Elder (*NH* = *Natural History*)
Plut.	Plutarch (*de Comm. Not.* = *de Communibus Notitiis*; *de Isid.* = *de Iside et Osiride*; *de Ser. Num. Vindic.* = *de Sera Numinis Vindicata*; *de Soll. Anim.* = *de Sollertia Animalium*; *Demetr.* = *Demetrius*; *Mor.* = *Moralia*; *Rom.* = *Romulus*; *Thes.* = *Theseus*)
Polyb.	Polybius (*Hist.* = *Histories*)
PSI	*Papiri greci e latini. Pubblicazioni della Società Italiana.* Florence: Ariani, 1912–35
Ptol.	Ptolemy (*Apotel.* = *Apotelesmatica*)
Sall.	Sallust (*Cat.* = *Catiline*)
SB	H. L. Strack and P. Billerbeck, *Kommentar zum Neuen Testament aus Talmud und Midrasch.* 6 vols. Munich: C. H. Beck, 1926–56
Sen.	Seneca (*Apoc.* = *Apocolocyntosis*; *Ep. Mor.* = *Moral Epistles*; *Herc. Oet.* = *Hercules Oetaeus*)
Soph.	Sophocles (*Antig.* = *Antigone*; *El.* = *Electra*; *Oed. Col.* = *Oedipus Coloneus*; *Trach.* = *Trachiniae*)
Suet.	Suetonius (*Vesp.* = *Vespasian*)
Tac.	Tacitus (*Agr.* = *Agricola*; *Ann.* = *Annals*; *Hist.* = *Histories*)
Tert.	Tertullian (*De Res.* = *On the Resurrection*; *Scorp.* = *Scorpiace*)
Theod.	Theodoret (*Heret. Fab.* = *Compendium of Heretical Fables*)
Val. Max.	Valerius Maximus
Vell. Pat.	Velleius Paterculus
Virg.	Virgil (*Aen.* = *Aeneid*; *Georg.* = *Georgics*)
Xen.	Xenophon (*Mem.* = *Memorabilia*)
Xen. Eph.	Xenophon of Ephesus

3. Secondary Sources, etc.

AB	Anchor Bible
ABD	*Anchor Bible Dictionary*, ed. D. N. Freedman. 6 vols. New York: Doubleday, 1992
ABRL	Anchor Bible Reference Library
AGJU	*Arbeiten zur Geschichte des antiken Judentums und des Urchristentums*
Aland	Aland, K., ed. *Synopsis Quattuor Evangeliorum: Locis Parallelis Evangeliorum Apocryphorum et Patrum Adhibitis.* 2nd edn. Stuttgart: Württembergische Bibelanstalt, 1967 [1963]
AnBib	Analecta Biblica
ANTC	Abingdon New Testament Commentaries
AOAT	Alter Orient und Altes Testament
ATANT	Abhandlungen zur Theologie des Alten und Neuen Testaments
BBB	Bonner Biblische Beiträge
BDAG	*A Greek-English Lexicon of the New Testament and other Early Christian Literature.* 3rd edn., rev. and ed. Frederick W. Danker, based on W. Bauer's *Griechisch-Deutsch Wörterbuch*, 6th edn., and on previous English edns. by W. F. Arndt, F. W. Gingrich, and F. W. Danker. Chicago and London: U. of Chicago Press, 2000 [1957]
BETL	Bibliotheca Ephemeridum Theologicarum Lovaniensium
BNTC	Black's New Testament Commentaries
BZNW	Beihefte zur Zeitschrift für die neutestamentliche Wissenschaft

CBQMS	Catholic Biblical Quarterly Monograph Series
DJG	*Dictionary of Jesus and the Gospels*, ed. J. B. Green, S. McKnight, I. H. Marshall. Downers Grove, Ill. and Leicester: IVP, 1992.
DMOA	Documenta et Monumenta Orientis Antiqui
Exp. Times	*Expository Times*
FAT	Forschungen zum alten Testament
FS	Festschrift
IBC	Interpretation: A Bible Commentary for Teaching and Preaching
ICC	International Critical Commentary
JB	Jerusalem Bible
JSJSup	Journal for the Study of Judaism Supplements
JSNTSup	Journal for the Study of the New Testament Supplements
JSOTSup	Journal for the Study of the Old Testament Supplements
JSPSup	Journal for the the Study of the Pseudepigrapha Supplements
JVG	N. T. Wright, *Jesus and the Victory of God* (vol. 2 of *Christian Origins and the Question of God*). London: SPCK; Minneapolis: Fortress, 1996
KJV	King James ['Authorized'] Version
LCL	Loeb Classical Library (various publishers, currently Cambridge, Mass. and London: Harvard U. P.)
LEC	Library of Early Christianity
LIMC	*Lexicon Iconographicum Mythologiae Classicae*
LS	C. T. Lewis and C. Short, *A Latin Dictionary*. Oxford: Clarendon Press, 1996 [1879]
LSJ	H. G. Liddell and R. Scott, *A Greek-English Lexicon*, 9th edn. by H. S. Jones and R. McKenzie, with suppl. by P. G. W. Glare and A. A. Thompson. Oxford: OUP, 1996 [1843]
NEB	New English Bible
NIB	*The New Interpreter's Bible*. 12 vols. Nashville: Abingdon, 1994–2002
NICNT	New International Commentary on the New Testament
NIDNTT	*The New International Dictionary of New Testament Theology*, ed. Colin Brown. 3 vols. Exeter: Paternoster, 1975–8
NIGTC	New International Greek Testament Commentary
NIV	New International Version
NJB	New Jerusalem Bible
NovTSup	Novum Testamentum Supplements
NRSV	New Revised Standard Version
NTPG	N. T. Wright, *The New Testament and the People of God* (vol. 1 of *Christian Origins and the Question of God*). London: SPCK; Minneapolis: Fortress, 1992
OBC	*The Oxford Bible Commentary*, eds. J. Barton and J. Muddiman. Oxford: OUP, 2001
OCCT	*The Oxford Companion to Christian Thought*, eds. Adrian Hastings, Alistair Mason, and Hugh Pyper. Oxford: OUP
OCD	*The Oxford Classical Dictionary*, eds. S. Hornblower and A. Spawforth. 3rd edn. Oxford: OUP, 1996
ODCC³	*The Oxford Dictionary of the Christian Church*, ed. E. A. Livingstone. 3rd edn. Oxford: OUP, 1997
OED	*The Oxford English Dictionary*, 2nd edn. Prepared by J. A. Simpson and E. S. C. Weiner. Oxford: Clarendon Press, 1989.
OTL	Old Testament Library
PMS	Patristic Monograph Series
QD	Quaestiones Disputatae

REB   Revised English Bible
RSV   Revised Standard Version
SB   H. L. Strack and P. Billerbeck, *Kommentar zum Neuen Testament aus Talmud und Midrasch.* 6 vols. Munich: C. H. Beck, 1926–56
SBL   Society of Biblical Literature
SBLDS   Society of Biblical Literature Dissertation Series
SBT   Studies in Biblical Theology
Schürer   E. Schürer, *The History of the Jewish People in the Age of Jesus Christ (175 B.C.—A.D. 135).* Rev. and ed. M. Black, G. Vermes, F. G. B. Millar. 4 vols. Edinburgh: T. & T. Clark, 1973–87
SNTSMS   Society for New Testament Studies Monograph Series
SP   Sacra Pagina
TDNT   *Theological Dictionary of the New Testament,* ed. G. Kittel and G. Friedrich. 10 vols. Grand Rapids: Eerdmans, 1964–76
TDOT   *Theological Dictionary of the Old Testament,* ed. G. J. Botterweck and H. Ringgren. Grand Rapids: Eerdmans, 1974–
TNTC   Tyndale New Testament Commentaries
VCSup   Vigiliae Christianae Supplements
VTSup   Vetus Testamentum Supplements
WBC   Word Biblical Commentary
WUNT   Wissenschaftliche Untersuchungen zum Neuen Testament

A

Primary Sources

1. Bible

Biblia Hebraica Stuttgartensia, ed. K. Elliger and W. Rudolph. 5th edn. Stuttgart: Deutsche Bibelgesellschaft, 1997 [1967].
Septuaginta: Id est Vetus Testamentum Graece iuxta LXX interpres, ed. A. Rahlfs. 2 vols. in 1. Stuttgart: Deutsche Bibelgesellschaft, 1979 [1935].
Novum Testamentum Graece, ed. B. Aland, K. Aland, J. Karavidopoulos, C. M. Martini, and B. M. Metzger. 27th edn. Stuttgart: Deutsche Bibelgesellschaft, 1993 [1898].
The Holy Bible with the Books called Apocrypha: The Revised Version with the Revised Marginal References. Oxford: OUP, n.d. [1898].
The Holy Bible, Containing the Old and New Testaments with the Apocryphal/Deutero-canonical Books: New Revised Standard Version. New York and Oxford: OUP, 1989.

2. Other Jewish Texts

The Mishnah, Translated from the Hebrew with Introduction and Brief Explanatory Notes, ed. and tr. H. Danby. Oxford: OUP, 1933.
The Babylonian Talmud, ed. I. Epstein. 36 vols. London: Soncino, 1935–8.
The Minor Tractates of the Talmud, ed. A. Cohen. 2 vols. London: Soncino, 1965.
Midrash Rabbah, tr. and ed. H. Freedman and M. Simon. 2nd edn. 10 vols. London: Soncino, 1951 [1939].
Pesikta Rabbati, ed. M. Friedman. Vienna: Kaiser, 1880.
Pirḳê de Rabbi Eliezer, tr. and ed. Gerald Friedlander. New York: Hermon Press, 1965.
(For other rabbinic literature, and details of Targumim, etc., cf. Schürer 1.68–118.)
The Old Testament Pseudepigrapha, ed. J. H. Charlesworth. 2 vols. Garden City, N. Y.: Doubleday, 1983–85.
The Apocryphal Old Testament, ed. H. F. D. Sparks. Oxford: Clarendon Press, 1984.
The Authorised Daily Prayer Book of the United Hebrew Congregations of the British Commonwealth of Nations, tr. S. Singer. New edn. London: Eyre & Spottiswoode, 1962.
Josephus: *Works*, ed. H. St. J. Thackeray, R. Marcus, A. Wikgren and L. H. Feldman. 9 vols. LCL, 1929–65.
Philo: *Works*, ed. F. H. Colson, G. H. Whitaker, J. W. Earp and R. Marcus. 12 vols. LCL, 1929–53.
Qumran: *Discoveries in the Judaean Desert*, ed. D. Barthélemy et al. 39 vols. Oxford: Clarendon Press, 1955–2002.
——, *Die Texte aus Qumran*, ed. E. Lohse. Darmstadt: Wissenschaftliche Buchgesellschaft, 1964.
——, *The Dead Sea Scrolls. Hebrew, Aramaic, and Greek Texts with English Translations*, ed. J. H. Charlesworth. 10 vols. Tübingen: Mohr-Siebeck; Louisville: Westminster, 1994– .

——, tr.: F. García Martínez, *The Dead Sea Scrolls Translated: The Qumran Texts in English*. Leiden: Brill, 1994.

——, tr.: G. Vermes, *The Dead Sea Scrolls in English*. 4th edn. London: Penguin Books, 1995 [1962].

3. Other Early Christian and Related Texts

Apostolic Fathers: *The Apostolic Fathers*, ed. and tr. J. B. Lightfoot. 5 vols. London: Macmillan, 1889–90. Reprint: Peabody, Mass.: Hendrikson, 1989.

——, *The Apostolic Fathers*, ed. and tr. Kirsopp Lake. 2 vols. LCL, 1965.

——, *Early Christian Writings*, tr. Maxwell Staniforth, introd. and ed. by A. Louth. London: Penguin Books, 1968.

——, *The Apostolic Fathers*, 2nd edn, tr. J. B. Lightfoot and J. R. Harmer, ed. and rev. Michael W. Holmes. Leicester: Apollos; Grand Rapids, Mich.: Baker, 1989.

Athenagoras: in *ANF* 2.123–62; *and see under* Justin.

Augustine, *City of God: De Civitate Dei Libri XXII*, ed. B. Dombart and A. Kalb. Stuttgart: Teubner, 1981.

——, tr. in *NPNF*, 1st ser., 2.1–511.

——, *City of God*, tr. H. Bettenson. Harmondsworth: Penguin, 1972.

Commodian: in *ANF* 4.199–219.

Epiphanius, *Panarion*, tr. and ed. F. Williams. Nag Hammadi Studies 35 and 36. Leiden: Brill, 1987–94.

Eusebius: *Eusebius. The Ecclesiastical History*, ed. and tr. Kirsopp Lake, H. J. Lawlor and J. E. L. Oulton. 2 vols. LCL, 1973–5.

——, *Life of Constantine*, in *NPNF* 2nd series, 1.481–559.

Gospel of the Savior: *The Gospel of the Savior: A New Ancient Gospel*, ed. Charles W. Hedrick and Paul A. Mirecki. Santa Rosa, Ca.: Polebridge, 1999.

Hippolytus: in *ANF* 5.9–259.

Irenaeus: in *ANF* 1.309–578.

Jerome, *Liber de Viris Illustribus*, in *PL* 23.602–719.

Justin: in *ANF* 1.159–306.

——, *The Writings of Justin Martyr and Athenagoras*, tr. M. Dods, G. Reith and B. P. Pratten. Edinburgh: T. & T. Clark, 1870.

——, *St. Justin Martyr: The First and Second Apologies*, tr. and introd. L. W. Barnard. New York and Mahwah, N. J.: Paulist Press.

Melito of Sardis: *On Pascha and Fragments: Melito of Sardis*, ed. and tr. S. G. Hall. Oxford: Clarendon Press, 1979.

Methodius: in *PG* 18.9–408.

Minucius Felix: in *ANF* 4.169–98; *and see under* Tertullian.

Nag Hammadi texts: *The Nag Hammadi Library in English*, ed. J. M. Robinson. Leiden: Brill; San Francisco: Harper & Row, 1977.

New Testament Apocrypha, ed. E. Hennecke and W. Schneemelcher. 2 vols. London: SCM Press; Philadelphia: Westminster, 1963–5 [1959–64].

——, *The Apocryphal New Testament: Being the Apocryphal Gospels, Acts, Epistles, and Apocalypses*, tr. M. R. James. Oxford: Clarendon Press, 1924.

——, in *The Other Gospels: Non-Canonical Gospel Texts*, ed. Ronald D. Cameron. Philadelphia: Westminster, 1987.

——, in *The Complete Gospels: Annotated Scholars Version*, ed. R. J. Miller. Sonoma, Ca.: Polebridge, 1992.

——, *The Apocryphal New Testament: A Collection of Apocryphal Christian Literature in an English Translation based on M. R. James*, ed. J. K. Elliott. Oxford: Clarendon

Press, 1993.

Odes of Solomon: *The Odes of Solomon*, ed. and tr. J. H. Charlesworth. Oxford: Clarendon Press, 1973.

——, *The Odes of Solomon: The Syriac Texts*, ed. J. H. Charlesworth. Chico, Ca.: Scholars Press, 1977.

Origen: in *ANF* 4.223–669.

——, *Origen: Contra Celsum. Translated with an Introduction and Notes*, ed. H. Chadwick. Cambridge: CUP, 1953.

Photius: *Bibliothèque*, ed. R. Henry. 9 vols. Paris: Les Belles Lettres, 1959–91; ref. by page, col. and line in *Photii Bibliotheca*, ed. I. Bekker. Berlin: Reimeri, 1824.

Rheginos: *The Epistle to Rheginos: A Valentinian Letter on the Resurrection*, introd., tr., etc. Malcolm L. Peel. London: SCM Press, 1969.

Tatian: in *ANF* 2.59–83.

Tertullian: in *ANF* 3.1—4.166.

——, *Apology & De Spectaculis*, tr. T. R. Glover, with Minucius Felix, *Octavius*, tr. G. H. Rendall. LCL, 1931.

Theodoret: in *NPNF*, 2nd. ser., vol. 3; *PG* 80–84.

Theophilus: in *ANF* 2.85–121.

Thomas: *The Gospel According to Thomas*, ed. A. Guillaumont et al. Leiden: Brill; London: Collins, 1959.

——, in several *New Testament Apocrypha* collections (above).

4. Pagan Texts

Achilles Tatius: in *Collected Ancient Greek Novels*, ed. B. P. Reardon. Berkeley: U. of California Press, 1989, 170–284.

Aelian, *Historical Miscellany*, tr. N. G. Wilson. LCL, 1997.

Aelius Aristides, *Panathenaic Oration*, etc., ed. C. A. Behr. 4 vols. LCL, 1973–86.

Aeneas of Gaza: *Epistole/Enea di Gaza*, ed. L. M. Positano. 2nd edn. Naples: Libreria scientifica editrice, 1962 [1950].

Aeschylus, tr. and ed. H. Weir Smyth and H. Lloyd-Jones. 2 vols. LCL, 1956–7 [1922–6].

Alcaeus: *Alcée: Fragments*, tr. Gauthier Liberman. 2 vols. Paris: Les Belles Lettres, 1999.

Antiphanes, *Aphrodisias*, ed. T. Kock. *CAF* 2.31–3.

Antonius Diogenes: in *Ancient Greek Novels: The Fragments. Introduction, Text, Translation, and Commentary*, S. A. Stephens and J. J. Winkler, eds. Princeton, N. J.: Princeton U. P, 1995, 101–57.

Apollodorus, *The Library*, tr. J. G. Frazer. 2 vols. LCL, 1921.

Apuleius: *Apuleius, the Golden Ass, or Metamorphoses*, tr. and ed. E. J. Kenney. London: Penguin, 1998.

Aristophanes, ed. J. Henderson. 4 vols. LCL, 1998–2002.

——, *Fragments*: in *Poetae Comici Graeci*, ed. R. Kassel and C. Austin. 2 vols. 1983–91.

Aristotle, *De Anima: On the Soul*, ed. W. S. Hett. LCL, 1936.

——, *Nicomachean Ethics*, ed. H. Rackham. LCL, 1926.

——, *The Ethics of Aristotle*, tr. J. A. K. Thomson. Harmondsworth: Penguin, 1955.

——, *Historia Animalium*, ed. A. L. Peck and D. M. Balme. 3 vols. LCL, 1965–91.

Arrian, *Anabasis Alexandri*, tr. P. A. Brunt. 2 vols. LCL, 1976–83.

Artemidorus, *The Interpretation of Dreams* (*Oneirocritica*), tr. and com. Robert J. White. Park Ridge, N. J.: Noyes Press, 1975.

Augustus, *see under* Velleius Paterculus.

Caesar, *The Conquest of Gaul*, tr. S. A. Haniford, rev. J. F. Gardner. London: Penguin, 1982 [1951].

——, *The Gallic War*, ed. H. J. Edwards. LCL, 1917.
Callimachus, *Hymns and Epigrams*, tr. G. R. Mair. LCL, 1921.
Cassius Dio: see Dio Cassius.
Catullus: *The Poems of Catullus*, ed. and tr. Guy Lee. Oxford: Clarendon Press, 1990.
——, *Catullus*, ed. and tr. G. P. Goold. London: Duckworth, 1983.
——, *Catullus, Tibullus and Pervigilium Veneris*, tr. F. W. Cornish et al. LCL, 1962.
Celsus: *Celsus on the True Doctrine: A Discourse Against the Christians*, tr. and introd. R. J. Hoffmann. New York/Oxford: OUP, 1987.
——, *see also under* Origen.
Chariton, *Callirhoe*, ed. G. P. Goold. LCL, 1995.
Cicero, *De Finibus Bonorum et Malorum*, tr. H. Rackham. LCL, 1914.
——, *De Natura Deorum: Cicero: The Nature of the Gods*, tr. H. C. P. McGregor. London: Penguin, 1972.
——, *De Natura Deorum* and *Academica*, ed. H. Rackham. LCL, 1933.
——, *De Re Publica, De Legibus*, tr. C. W. Keyes. LCL, 1928.
——, *Tusculan Disputations*, tr. J. E. King. LCL, 1927.
Dio: *Dio Chrysostom*, ed. and tr. J. W. Cohoon and H. L. Crosbie. 5 vols. LCL, 1932–51.
Dio Cassius: *Dio's Roman History*, tr. H. B. Foster and E. Cary. 9 vols. LCL, 1914–27.
Diodorus Siculus, tr. C. H. Oldfather et al. 10 vols. LCL, 1933–67.
Diogenes Laertius, *Lives of Eminent Philosophers*, tr. R. D. Hicks. 2 vols. LCL, 1925.
Dionysius of Halicarnassus, *Roman Antiquities*, tr. E. Spelman and E. Cary. 7 vols. LCL, 1937–50.
The Egyptian Book of the Dead: The Book of Going Forth Day by Day, tr. R. Faulkner, introd. O. Goelet. San Francisco: Chronicle Books, 1994.
Epictetus: *The Discourses as reported by Arrian, the Manual, and Fragments*, ed. and tr. W. A. Oldfather. 2 vols. LCL, 1978–9.
Epicurus: *Epicurea*, ed. H. Usener. Dubuque, Iowa: Reprint Library, n.d. [1887].
——, *Letters, Principal Doctrines, and Vatican Sayings*, tr. and ed. R. M. Geer. Indianapolis: Bobbs-Merrill, 1964.
Euripides: *Euripides*, tr. and ed. D. Kovacs. 5 vols. LCL, 1994–2002.
Galen, *On the Natural Faculties*, tr. A. J. Brock. LCL, 1952.
Heliodorus: *Heliodori Aethiopica*, ed. A. Colonna. Rome: Typis Regiae Officinae Polygraphicae, 1938.
Hellanicus: in *FrGrHist*. 1.104–52.
Herodas, *Herodae Mimiambi: Cum Appendice Fragmentorum Mimorum Papyraceorum*, ed. I. C. Cunningham. Leipzig: Teubner, 1987.
Herodotus, *History of Greece*, tr. A. D. Godley. 4 vols. LCL, 1921–5.
——, *Herodoti Historiae*, ed. C. Hude. 2 vols. Oxford: Clarendon Press, n.d.
——, *Herodotus: The Histories*, tr. A. de Sélincourt. Harmondsworth: Penguin, 1954.
Hesiod, *Works and Days*, ed. with Prolegomena and Commentary by M. L. West. Oxford: Clarendon Press, 1978.
Hierocles Platonicus (C5 AD), *In Carmen Aureum*: in *Fragmenta Philosophorum Graecorum*, ed. F. W. A. Mullach, 1.416–84. Paris: Didot, 1860–81.
Homer, *The Iliad*, tr. A. T. Murray, rev. W. F. Wyatt. 2 vols. LCL, 1999 [1924–5].
——, *The Odyssey*, tr. A. T. Murray, rev. G. E. Dimock, 2 vols. LCL, 1995 [1919].
Horace: *The Satires of Horace*, ed. A. Palmer. London: Macmillan, 1885.
——, *Horace: Satires and Epistles; Perseus: Satires*, tr. and ed. N. Rudd. Rev. edn. London: Penguin, 1987 [1973].
Hyginus: *Fables*, ed. and tr. J.-Y. Boriaud. Paris: Les Belles Lettres, 1997.
Juvenal: *Juvenal and Persius*, tr. G. G. Ramsay. LCL, 1920.
——, *Juvenal. The Sixteen Satires*, tr. and introd. P. Green. London: Penguin Books, 1974 [1967].

Livy, *History of Rome*, tr. A. C. Schlesinger et al. 14 vols. LCL, 1919–59.
Lucian: *Lucian of Samosata*, ed. and tr. A. M. Harmon et al. 8 vols. LCL, 1921–67.
Lucretius, *De Rerum Natura*, tr. W. H. D. Rouse, rev. M. F. Smith. LCL, 1992 [1975].
Marcus Aurelius: *Marcus Aurelius*, ed. and tr. C. R. Haines. LCL, rev. edn. 1930 [1916]
Menander: *Menandri Reliquae Selectae*, ed. F. H. Sandbach. 1990.
——, *Menander*, tr. F. G. Allinson. LCL, 1964.
Ovid, *Fasti*, tr. J. G. Frazer. LCL, 1931.
——, *Heroides and Amores*, tr. G. Showerman, 1914; 2nd edn., ed. G. P. Goold. LCL, 1977.
——, *Metamorphoses*, tr. F. J. Miller. 2 vols. LCL, 1916.
Pausanias, *Description of Greece*, tr. and ed. W. Jones. 5 vols. LCL, 1918–35.
Petronius, *see* Seneca
Pherecydes of Athens: in *FrGrHist.* 1.58–104.
Philostratus, *Heroikos*, ed. L. de Lannoy. Leipzig: Teubner, 1977 (retaining the pagination of the 1870–71 edn. of Kayser).
——, *The Life of Apollonius of Tyana*, tr. F. C. Conybeare. 2 vols. LCL, 1912.
Pindar, *Odes*, etc. tr. J. Sandys. LCL, 1938.
Plato, *Cratylus, Parmenides, Greater Hippias, Lesser Hippias*, ed. H. N. Fowler. LCL, 1926.
——, *Euthyphro, Apology, Crito, Phaedo, Phaedrus*, tr. H. N. Fowler. LCL, 1914.
——, *Laches, Protagoras, Meno, Euthydemus*, ed. W. R. M. Lamb. LCL, 1924.
——, *Laws*, tr. R. G. Bury. 2 vols. LCL, 1926.
——, *Lysis, Symposium, Gorgias*, tr. W. R. M. Lamb. LCL, 1925.
——, *Politicus, Philebus, Ion*, tr. H. N. Fowler and W. R. M. Lamb. LCL, 1925.
——, *Platonis Res Publica*, tr. J. Burnet. Oxford: Clarendon Press, 1902.
——, *The Republic*, tr. P. Shorey. LCL, 1935.
——, *Timaeus, Critias, Cleitophon, Menexenus, Epistles*, tr. R. G. Bury. LCL, 1929.
——, *The Collected Dialogues, Including the Letters*, ed. E. Hamilton and H. Cairns. Princeton, N. J.: Princeton U. P. , 1963 [1961].
Pliny the Elder, *Natural History*, tr. H. Rackham et al. 10 vols. LCL, 1938–62.
Pliny the Younger: *C. Plini Caecili Secundi Epistularum Libri Decem*, ed. R. A. B. Mynors. Oxford: OUP, 1963.
——, *The Letters of the Younger Pliny*, tr. and introd. B. Radice. London: Penguin Books, 1963.
Plotinus, tr. A. H. Armstrong. 7 vols. LCL, 1966–88.
Plutarch, *Lives*, tr. B. Perrin. 11 vols. LCL, 1914–26.
——, *Moralia*, tr. F. C. Babbitt et al. 16 vols. LCL, 1927–69.
Polybius, *Histories*, tr. W. R. Paton. 6 vols. LCL, 1922–7
Ptolemy, *Apotelesmatica*, ed. F. Boll and E. Boer. Leipzig: Teubner, 1940
Sallust, *Catiline*, tr. J. C. Rolfe. LCL, 1921.
Seneca, *Tragedies*, tr. F. J. Miller. 2 vols. LCL, 1917.
——, *Apocolocyntosis* (with Petronius, *Satyricon*), tr. W. H. D. Rouse and E. H. Warmington. LCL, 1969 [1913].
——, *Apocolocyntosis*, ed. P. T. Eden. Cambridge: CUP, 1984.
——, *Moral Essays*, tr. J. W. Basore. 3 vols. LCL, 1928–35.
——, *Epistulae Morales*, tr. R. M. Gummere. 3 vols. LCL, 1917–25.
——, *L. Annaei Senecae Tragoediae. Incertum Auctorum: Hercules [Oetaeus]; Octavia*, ed. O. Zwierlin. Oxford: Clarendon Press, 1986.
Servius: *Servianorum in Vergilii Carmina Commentarium*, ed. A. F. Stocker, A. H. Travis, et al. 3 vols. Oxford: OUP, 1965.
Sophocles, ed. H. Lloyd Jones. 2 vols. LCL, 1994.
Strabo, *The Geography of Strabo*, tr. H. L. Jones. 8 vols. LCL, 1917–32.

Suetonius: *C. Suetoni Tranquili Opera*, vol. 1. *De Vita Caesarum Libri VIII*. Ed. M. Ihm. Stuttgart: Teubner, 1978 [1908].

——, *Suetonius*, tr. J. C. Rolfe. 2nd edn. 2 vols. LCL, 1997–8 [1913-14].

——, *Suetonius. The Twelve Caesars*, tr. R. Graves. London: Penguin Books, 1957.

Tacitus, *Annals*: *Cornelii Taciti Annalium ab Excessu Divi Augusti Libri*, ed. C. D. Fisher. Oxford: Clarendon Press, 1906.

——, *Tacitus. The Annals of Imperial Rome*, tr. M. Grant. London: Penguin Books, 1956.

——, *Histories*: *Cornelii Taciti Historiarum Libri*, ed. C. D. Fisher. Oxford: Clarendon Press, n.d.

——, *Tacitus. The Histories*, tr. K. Wellesley. London: Penguin Books, 1964.

——, *Agricola, Germania, Dialogus*, tr. M. Hutton and W. Peterson; rev. by R. M. Ogilvie, E. H. Warmington, and M. Winterbottom. LCL, 1970 [1914].

——, *Histories and Annals*, tr. C. H. Moore and J. Jackson. 4 vols. LCL, 1925–37.

Themistius: *Themistii Orationes*, ed. G. Downey and A. F. Norman. 3 vols. Leipzig: Teubner, 1965–74.

Thucydides: *Thucydidis Historiae*, ed. H. S. Jones. 2 vols. Oxford: OUP, 1898.

——, *Thucydides: History of the Peloponnesian War*, tr. R. Warner. London: Penguin Books, 1954.

Valerius Maximus, *Memorable Doings and Sayings*, tr. D. R. Shackleton Bailey. LCL, 2000.

Velleius Paterculus, *Compendium of Roman History*, and the *Res Gestae Divi Augusti*, tr. F. W. Shipley. LCL, 1924.

Virgil, *Eclogues, Georgics, Aeneid and the Minor Poems*, tr. H. R. Fairclough, rev. G. P. Goold. 2 vols. LCL, 1999 [1916–18].

Vitruvius, *On Architecture*, tr. F. Granger. 2 vols. LCL, 1931–4.

Xenophanes: *Senofane: Testimonianze e Frammenti*, ed. M. Untersteiner. Florence: 'La Nuova Italia' Editrice, 1956.

Xenophon, *Memorabilia* and *Oeconomicus*, tr. E. C. Marchant. LCL, 1923.

——, *Symposium* and *Apology*, tr. O. J. Todd. LCL, 1922.

Xenophon of Ephesus: in *Collected Ancient Greek Novels*, ed. B. P. Reardon. Berkeley: U. of California Press, 1989, 125–69.

B

Secondary Literature

Achtemeier, Paul J. 1996. *1 Peter: A Commentary on First Peter*. Hermeneia. Minneapolis: Fortress.

Ackroyd, P. R., and C. F. Evans, eds. 1975 [1970]. *The Cambridge History of the Bible*. Vol. 1, *From the Beginnings to Jerome*. Cambridge: CUP.

Akenson, Donald H. 2000. *Saint Saul: A Skeleton Key to the Historical Jesus*. Oxford: OUP.

Aldridge, R. E. 1999. 'The Lost Ending of the *Didache*.' *Vigiliae Christianae* 53:1–15.

Alexander, Loveday. 2001. 'Acts.' In *OBC* 1028–61.

Allison, Dale C. 1985. *The End of the Ages Has Come: An Early Interpretation of the Passion and Resurrection of Jesus*. Philadelphia: Fortress.

Alston, William P. 1997. 'Biblical Criticism and the Resurrection.' In *The Resurrection: An Interdisciplinary Symposium on the Resurrection of Jesus*, eds. Stephen T. Davis, Daniel Kendall and Gerald O'Collins, 148–83. Oxford: OUP.

Alsup, John E. 1975. *The Post-Resurrection Appearance Stories of the Gospel Tradition*. Stuttgart: Calwer.

Alves, M. I. 1989. 'Ressurreição e Fé pascal.' *Didaskalia* 19:277–541.

Andersen, F. I., and David N. Freedman. 1980. *Hosea*. AB 24. Garden City, N.Y.: Doubleday.

Anderson, Graham. 1986. *Philostratus: Biography and Belles Lettres in the Third Century A. D.* London: Croom Helm.

Ashton, J. 2000. *The Religion of Paul the Apostle*. New Haven/London: Yale U. P.

Attridge, Harold W. 1989. *The Epistle to the Hebrews*. Hermeneia. Philadelphia: Fortress.

———. 1992. 'Thomas, Acts Of.' In *ABD* 6:531–4.

Aune, David E. 1997–8. *Revelation*. 3 vols. WBC 52. Dallas: Word Books.

Aus, Roger A. 1994. *Samuel, Saul and Jesus*. Atlanta, Ga.: Scholars Press.

Avemarie, Friedrich, and Hermann Lichtenberger, eds. 2001. *Auferstehung – Resurrection*. WUNT 135. Tübingen: Mohr-Siebeck.

Avis, Paul, ed. 1993a. *The Resurrection of Jesus Christ*. London: Darton, Longman & Todd.

———. 1993b. 'The Resurrection of Jesus: Asking the Right Questions.' In *The Resurrection of Jesus Christ*, ed. Paul Avis, 1–22. London: Darton, Longman & Todd.

Badham, Paul. 1993. 'The Meaning of the Resurrection of Jesus.' In *The Resurrection of Jesus Christ*, ed. Paul Avis, 23–38. London: Darton, Longman & Todd.

Bailey, Cyril. 1964. *The Greek Atomists and Epicurus*. New York: Russell & Russell.

Bailey, Kenneth E. 1991. 'Informal Controlled Oral Tradition and the Synoptic Gospels.' *Asia Journal of Theology* 5:34–54.

Baird, W. 1985. 'Visions, Revelation, and Ministry: Reflections on 2 Cor 12:1–5 and Gal 1:11–17.' *Journal of Biblical Literature* 104:651–62.

Baker, John Austin. 1970. *The Foolishness of God*. London: Darton, Longman & Todd.

Balzer, K. 2001. *Deutero-Isaiah: A Commentary on Isaiah 40—55*. Hermeneia. Minneapolis: Fortress.

Barclay, John M. G. 1996a. 'The Resurrection in Contemporary New Testament Scholarship.' In *Resurrection Reconsidered*, ed. Gavin D'Costa, 13–30. Oxford: Oneworld.

——. 1996b. *Jews in the Mediterranean Diaspora: From Alexander to Trajan (323 BCE – 117 CE)*. Edinburgh: T. & T. Clark.

Barker, Margaret. 1997. *The Risen Lord: The Jesus of History as the Christ of Faith*. Valley Forge, Pa.: TPI.

Barley, Nigel. 1986. *A Plague of Caterpillars: A Return to the African Bush*. London: Penguin.

——. 1997. *Grave Matters: A Lively History of Death Around the World*. New York: Holt.

Barr, James. 1985. 'The Question of Religious Influence: The Case of Zoroastrianism, Judaism, and Christianity.' *Journal of the American Academy of Religion* 53:201–35.

——. 1992. *The Garden of Eden and the Hope of Immortality*. London: SCM Press.

Barrett, C. K. 1973. *A Commentary on the Second Epistle to the Corinthians*. BNTC. London: A. & C. Black.

——. 1978 [1955]. *The Gospel According to St John. An Introduction with Commentary and Notes on the Greek Text*. London: SPCK.

——, ed. 1987 [1956]. *The New Testament Background: Selected Documents*. Rev. edn. London: SPCK; New York: Harper & Row.

——. 1994. *A Critical and Exegetical Commentary on the Acts of the Apostles*. Vol. 1. ICC. Edinburgh: T. & T. Clark.

Barton, John. 1994. 'Why Does the Resurrection of Christ Matter?' In *Resurrection: Essays in Honour of Leslie Houlden*, eds. Stephen Barton and Graham Stanton, 108–115. London: SPCK.

Barton, Stephen. 1994. 'The Hermeneutics of the Gospel Resurrection Narratives.' In *Resurrection: Essays in Honour of Leslie Houlden*, eds. Stephen Barton and Graham Stanton, 45–57. London: SPCK.

——, and Graham Stanton, eds. 1994. *Resurrection: Essays in Honour of Leslie Houlden*. London: SPCK.

Bartsch, H.-W., ed. 1962. *Kerygma and Myth*. London: SPCK.

——. 1962–64. *Kerygma and Myth*. London: SPCK.

Baslez, Marie-Françoise. 2001. 'Le corps, l'âme et la survie: anthropologie et croyances dans les religions du monde gréco-romain.' In *Résurrection: L'après-mort dans le monde ancien et le Nouveau Testament*, eds. Odette Mainville and Daniel Marguerat, 73–89. Geneva: Labor et Fides; Montreal: Médiaspaul.

Bauckham, Richard J. 1983. *Jude, 2 Peter*. WBC 50. Waco, Tex.: Word Books.

——. 1992a. 'Gospels, Apocryphal.' In *DJG* 286–91.

——. 1992b. 'Jesus, Worship of.' In *ABD* 3:812–19.

——. 1993a. *The Climax of Prophecy: Studies on the Book of Revelation*. Edinburgh: T. & T. Clark.

——. 1993b. *The Theology of the Book of Revelation*. Cambridge: CUP.

——. 1993c. 'The God Who Raises the Dead: The Resurrection of Jesus and Early Christian Faith in God.' In *The Resurrection of Jesus Christ*, ed. Paul Avis, 136–54. London: Darton, Longman & Todd.

——. 1995. 'James and the Jerusalem Church.' In *The Book of Acts in Its First Century Setting*, eds. Richard J. Bauckham and Bruce W. Winter, 415–80. Carlisle: Paternoster; Grand Rapids: Eerdmans.

——. 1998a. *The Fate of the Dead: Studies on the Jewish and Christian Apocalypses*. Leiden: Brill.

——. 1998b. 'Life, Death, and the Afterlife in Second Temple Judaism.' In *Life in the Face of Death: The Resurrection Message of the New Testament*, ed. Richard N.

Longenecker, 80–95. Grand Rapids: Eerdmans.

——. 1999. *God Crucified: Monotheism and Christology in the New Testament*. Grand Rapids: Eerdmans.

——. 2001. 'James and Jesus.' In *The Brother of Jesus: James the Just and His Mission*, eds. Bruce Chilton and Jacob Neusner, 100–35. Louisville: Westminster John Knox.

——. 2002. *Gospel Women: Studies of the Named Women in the Gospels*. Grand Rapids: Eerdmans.

Beale, Gregory K. 1999. *The Book of Revelation: A Commentary on the Greek Text*. NIGTC. Grand Rapids: Eerdmans; Carlisle: Paternoster.

Beard, Mary, John North, and Simon Price. 1998. *Religions of Rome*. 2 vols. Cambridge: CUP.

Beauchamp, P. 1964. 'Le Salut Corporel dans le Livre de la Sagesse.' *Biblica* 45:491–526.

Beckwith, Roger T. 1980. 'The Significance of the Calendar for Interpreting Essene Chronology and Eschatology.' *Revue de Qumran* 38:167–202.

——. 1981. 'Daniel 9 and the Date of Messiah's Coming in Essene, Hellenistic, Pharisaic, Zealot and Early Christian Computation.' *Revue de Qumran* 40:521–42.

——. 1996. *Calendar and Chronology, Jewish and Christian: Biblical, Intertestamental and Patristic Studies*. AGJU 33. Leiden: Brill.

Begbie, Jeremy, ed. 2002. *Sounding the Depths: Theology Through the Arts*. London: SCM Press.

Benoit, P. 1960. 'Marie Madeleine et les Disciples au Tombeau Selon Jean 20,1–18.' In *Judentum, Urchristentum, Kirche* (FS J. Jeremias), ed. M. Eltester, 143–52. Berlin: Töpelmann.

Bieringer, R., V. Koperski and B. Lataire, eds. 2002. *Resurrection in the New Testament*. FS J. Lambrecht. BETL 165. Leuven: Peeters.

Black, Matthew. 1964 [1954]. 'The Account of the Essenes in Hippolytus and Josephus.' In *The Background of the New Testament and its Eschatology. Studies In Honour of Charles Harold Dodd*, eds. W. D. Davies and D. Daube, 172–5. Cambridge: CUP.

Bloch-Smith, Elizabeth. 1992. 'Burials, Israelite.' In *ABD* 2:785–9.

Boardman, John. 1993. *The Oxford History of Classical Art*. Oxford: OUP.

Bode, E. L. 1970. *The First Easter Morning: The Gospel Accounts of the Women's Visit to the Tomb of Jesus*. AnBib 45. Rome: Pontifical Biblical Institute Press.

Boismard, Marie-Emile. 1999. *Our Victory Over Death: Resurrection?* Collegeville, Minn.: Liturgical Press.

Bolt, Peter G. 1998. 'Life, Death and the Afterlife in the Greco-Roman World.' In *Life in the Face of Death: The Resurrection Message of the New Testament*, ed. Richard N. Longenecker, 51–79. Grand Rapids: Eerdmans.

Borg, Marcus J. 1999. 'The Irrelevancy of the Empty Tomb.' In *Will the Real Jesus Please Stand up: A Debate Between William Lane Craig and John Dominic Crossan*, ed. Paul Copan, 117–28. Grand Rapids: Baker.

——, and N. T. Wright. 1999. *The Meaning of Jesus*. London: SPCK.

Borgen, Peder. 1984. 'Philo of Alexandria.' In *Compendia Rerum Iudaicarum ad Novum Testamentum, Section Two: The Literature of the Jewish People in the Period of the Second Temple and the Talmud*. Vol. 2, *Jewish Writings of the Second Temple Period: Apocrypha, Pseudepigrapha, Qumran Sectarian Writings, Philo, Josephus*, ed. Michael E. Stone, 233—82. Assen: Van Gorcum; Philadelphia: Fortress.

Bostock, D. Gerald. 2001. 'Osiris and the Resurrection of Christ.' *Expository Times* 112:265–71.

Bovon, F. 1995. *New Testament Traditions and Apocryphal Narratives*. Allison Park, Pa.: Pickwick Publications.

Bowersock, G. W. 1982. 'The Imperial Cult: Perceptions and Persistence.' In *Jewish and Christian Self-Definition.* Vol. 3, *Self-Definition in the Greco-Roman World*, eds. Ben F. Meyer and E. P. Sanders, 171–82. Philadelphia: Fortress.

——. 1994. *Fiction as History: Nero to Julian.* Sather Classical Lectures, vol. 58. Berkeley: University of California Press.

Bowker, John W. 1971. '"Merkabah" Visions and the Visions of Paul.' *Journal of Semitic Studies* 16:157–73.

Boyce, Mary. 1975–91. *A History of Zoroastrianism.* 3 vols. Handbuch der Orientalistik. Leiden: Brill.

——. 1992. 'Zoraster, Zoroastrianism.' In *ABD* 6:1168–74.

Boyle, Nicholas. 1998. *Who Are We Now? Christian Humanism and the Global Market from Hegel to Heaney.* Notre Dame/London: U. of Notre Dame Press.

Bream, Howard N. 1974. 'Life Without Resurrection: Two Perspectives from Qoheleth', in *A Light Unto My Path: Old Testament Studies in Honor of Jacob M. Myers*, ed. H. N. Bream, R. D. Heim and C. A. Moore. Philadelphia: Temple U. P., 49–65.

Bremmer, Jan N. 1996. 'The Resurrection Between Zarathustra and Jonathan Z. Smith.' *Nederlands Theologisch Tijdschrift* 50:89–107.

——. 2002. *The Rise and Fall of the Afterlife: The 1995 Reed-Tucker Lectures at the University of Bristol.* London: Routledge.

Brown, Raymond E. 1973. *The Virginal Conception and Bodily Resurrection of Jesus.* New York: Paulist Press.

——. 1994. *The Death of the Messiah: From Gethsemane to the Grave. A Commentary on the Passion Narratives in the Four Gospels.* New York: Doubleday; London: Geoffrey Chapman.

Brueggemann, Walter. 1997. *Theology of the Old Testament: Testimony, Dispute, Advocacy.* Minneapolis: Fortress.

Brunschwig, J., and Martha C. Nussbaum, eds. 1993. *Passions and Perceptions: Studies in Hellenistic Philosophy of Mind. Proceedings of the Fifth Symposium Hellenisticum.* Cambridge/New York: CUP.

Buchholz, D. D. 1988. *Your Eyes Will be Opened: A Study of the Greek (Ethiopic) Apocalypse of Peter.* SBLDS, vol. 97. Atlanta, Ga.: Scholars Press.

Bultmann, Rudolf. 1968 [1931]. *The History of the Synoptic Tradition.* 2nd ed. Oxford: Blackwell.

——. 1969. *Faith and Understanding.* New York: Harper & Row.

Burkert, W. 1985. *Greek Religion.* Cambridge, Mass.: Harvard U. P.

——. 1987. *Ancient Mystery Cults.* Cambridge, Mass.: Harvard U. P.

Bynum, Caroline Walker. 1995. *The Resurrection of the Body in Western Christianity, 200–1336.* New York: Columbia U. P.

Byrne, Brendan. 1985. 'The Faith of the Beloved Disciple and the Community in John 20.' *Journal for the Study of the New Testament* 23:83–97.

Caird, G. B. 1966. *The Revelation of Saint John.* London: A. & C. Black.

——. 1997 [1980]. *The Language and Imagery of the Bible.* Grand Rapids: Eerdmans.

Cameron, Ronald D., ed. 1987. *The Other Gospels: Non-Canonical Gospel Texts.* Philadelphia: Westminster.

Carnley, Peter. 1987. *The Structure of Resurrection Belief.* Oxford/New York: OUP.

——. 1997. 'Response.' In *The Resurrection: An Interdisciplinary Symposium on the Resurrection of Jesus*, eds. Stephen T. Davis, Daniel Kendall and Gerald O'Collins, 29–40. Oxford: OUP.

Carson, D. A. 2000 [1982]. *From Sabbath to Lord's Day: A Biblical, Historical and Theological Investigation.* Rev. ed. New York: Wipf & Stock.

Carter, Warren. 2001. *Matthew and Empire: Initial Explorations.* Harrisburg, Pa.: TPI.

Catchpole, David R. 1992. 'The Beginning of Q: A Proposal.' *New Testament Studies* 38:205–21.

——. 1993. *The Quest for Q.* Edinburgh: T. & T. Clark.

——. 2000. *Resurrection People: Studies in the Resurrection Narratives of the Gospels.* London: Darton, Longman & Todd.

Cavallin, Hans Clemens Caesarius. 1972/3. 'De visa lärarnas död och uppstandelse.' *Svensk exegetisk årsbok* 37–38:47–61.

——. 1974. *Life After Death: Paul's Argument for the Resurrection of the Dead in 1 Cor 15, Part I. An Enquiry Into the Jewish Background.* Lund: CWK Gleerup.

Chadwick, Henry. 1948. 'Origen, Celsus and the Resurrection of the Body.' *Harvard Theological Review* 41:83–102.

——. 1953. *Origen: Contra Celsum. Translated with an Introduction and Notes.* Cambridge: CUP.

——. 1966. *Early Christian Thought and the Classical Tradition: Studies in Justin, Clement, and Origen.* Oxford: OUP.

——. 1967. *The Pelican History of the Church.* Vol. 1, *The Early Church.* Middlesex: Penguin.

Charlesworth, James H., ed. 1973. *The Odes of Solomon.* Oxford: Clarendon Press Press.

——, ed. 1977. *The Odes of Solomon: The Syriac Texts.* Chico, Ca.: Scholars Press.

——, ed. 1983. *The Old Testament Pseudepigrapha.* Vol. 1, *Apocalyptic Literature and Testaments.* Garden City, N. Y.: Doubleday.

——, ed. 1985. *The Old Testament Pseudepigrapha.* Vol. 2, *Expansions of the 'Old Testament' and Legends, Wisdom and Philosophical Literature, Prayers, Psalms and Odes, Fragments of Lost Judaeo-Hellenistic Works.* Garden City, N. Y.: Doubleday.

——. 1992. 'Solomon, Odes of.' In *ABD* 6:114–15.

——, and Craig A. Evans. 1994. 'Jesus in the Agrapha and Apocryphal Gospels.' In *Studying the Historical Jesus: Evaluations of the State of Current Research*, eds. Bruce D. Chilton and Craig A. Evans, 479–533. Leiden: Brill.

Chester, A. 2001. 'Resurrection and Transformation.' In *Auferstehung – Resurrection*, eds. Friedrich Avemarie and Hermann Lichtenberger, 47–77. Tübingen: Mohr-Siebeck.

Childs, Brevard S. 2001. *Isaiah.* OTL. Louisville: Westminster John Knox.

Chilton, Bruce, and James H. Charlesworth. 1994. 'Jesus in the Agrapha and the Apocryphal Gospels.' In *Studying the Historical Jesus*, eds. Bruce Chilton and James H. Charlesworth, 479–533. Leiden: Brill.

——, and Craig A. Evans. 1994. *Studying the Historical Jesus: Evaluations of the State of Current Research.* New Testament Tools and Studies. Leiden: Brill.

——, and Jacob Neusner, eds. 2001. *The Brother of Jesus: James the Just and His Mission.* Louisville: Westminster John Knox.

Clark, Elizabeth A. 1992. *The Origenist Controversy: The Cultural Construction of an Early Christian Debate.* Princeton, N. J.: Princeton U. P.

Clavier, H. 1964. 'Breves Remarques sur la Notion de σῶμα πνευματικόν.' In *The Background of the New Testament and Its Eschatology: Studies in Honour of C. H. Dodd*, eds. W. D. Davies and D. Daube, 342–62. Cambridge: CUP.

Clouse, R. G., ed. 1977. *The Meaning of the Millennium: Four Views.* Downers Grove, Ill.: IVP.

Coakley, Sarah. 1993 'Is the Resurrection a "Historical" Event? Some Muddles and Mysteries.' In *The Resurrection of Jesus Christ*, edited by Paul Avis, 85–115. London: Darton, Longman & Todd.

——. 2002. *Powers and Submissions: Spirituality, Philosophy and Gender.* Oxford: Blackwell.

Cohen, Shaye J. D. 1987. *From the Maccabees to the Mishnah*. LEC 7. Philadelphia: Westminster.

Cohn, N. 1993. *Cosmos, Chaos, and the World to Come*. New Haven/London: Yale U. P.

Collart, P. 1937. *Philippes, ville de Macédonie depuis ses origines jusqu'à la fin de l'époque romaine*. Paris: Boccard.

Collins, Adela Yarboro. 1993. 'The Empty Tomb in the Gospel According to Mark.' In *Hermes and Athena: Biblical Exegesis and Philosophical Theology*, eds. Eleonore Stump and Thomas P. Flint, 107–140. Notre Dame, Ind.: U. of Notre Dame Press.

———. 1999. 'The Worship of Jesus and the Imperial Cult.' In *The Jewish Roots of Christological Monotheism. Papers from the St. Andrews Conference on the Historical Origins of the Worship of Jesus*, eds. Carey C. Newman, James R. Davila and Gladys S. Lewis. JSJSup, vol. 63, 234–57. Leiden: Brill.

Collins, John J. 1974. 'The Place of the Fourth Sibyl in the Development of the Jewish Sibyllines.' *Journal of Jewish Studies* 25:365–87.

———. 1978. 'The Root of Immortality: Death in the Context of Jewish Wisdom.' *Harvard Theological Review* 71:177–92.

———. 1993. *Daniel: A Commentary on the Book of Daniel*. Hermeneia. Minneapolis: Fortress.

———. 1995. *The Scepter and the Star: The Messiahs of the Dead Sea Scrolls and Other Ancient Literature*. ABRL. New York: Doubleday.

———. 1998. *Jewish Wisdom in the Hellenistic Age*. OTL. Louisville: Westminster; Edinburgh: T. & T. Clark.

Collins, R. F. 2002. 'What Happened to Jesus' Resurrection from the Dead? A Reflection on Paul and the Pastoral Epistles'. In *Resurrection in the New Testament* (FS J. Lambrecht), eds. R. Bieringer, V. Koperski and B. Lataire, 423–40. Leuven: Peeters.

Combet-Galland, Corina. 2001. 'L'Évangile de Marc et la pierre qu'il a déjà roulée.' In *Résurrection: L'après-mort dans le monde ancien et le Nouveau Testament*, eds. Odette Mainville and Daniel Marguerat, 93–109. Geneva: Labor et Fides; Montreal: Médiaspaul.

Conzelmann, Hans. 1975. *1 Corinthians: A Commentary on the First Epistle to the Corinthians*. Hermeneia. Philadelphia: Fortress.

Cooley, R. E. 1983. 'Gathered to His People: A Study of a Dothan Family Tomb.' In *The Living and Active Word of God* (FS S. J. Schultz), eds. M. Inch and R. Youngblood, 47–58. Winona Lake, Ind.: Eisenbrauns.

Corley, Kathleen E. 2002. *Women and the Historical Jesus: Feminist Myths of Christian Origins*. Santa Rosa, Ca.: Polebridge Press.

Cox, S. L. 1993. *A History and Critique of Scholarship Concerning the Markan Endings*. Lewiston/Queenston: Edwin Mellon Press.

Cross, F. M. 1983. 'A Note on a Burial Inscription from Mount Scopus.' *Israel Exploration Journal* 33:245–6.

Crossan, J. Dominic. 1988. *The Cross That Spoke: The Origins of the Passion Narrative*. San Francisco: Harper & Row.

———. 1991. *The Historical Jesus: The Life of a Mediterranean Jewish Peasant*. Edinburgh: T. & T. Clark; San Francisco: HarperSanFrancisco.

———. 1994. *Jesus: A Revolutionary Biography*. San Francisco: HarperSanFrancisco.

———. 1995. *Who Killed Jesus? Exposing the Roots of Anti-Semitism in the Gospel Story of the Death of Jesus*. San Francisco: HarperSanFrancisco.

———. 1997. 'What Victory? What God? A Review Debate with N. T. Wright on *Jesus and the Victory of God*.' *Scottish Journal of Theology* 50:345–58.

———. 1998. *The Birth of Christianity: Discovering What Happened in the Years Immediately After the Execution of Jesus*. San Francisco: HarperSanFrancisco.

——. 2000. 'Blessed Plot: A Reply to N. T. Wright.' *Scottish Journal of Theology* 53:92–112.

Crouzel, Henri. 1989. *Origen: The Life and Thought of the First Great Theologian.* San Francisco: Harper.

Cummins, S. A. 2001. *Paul and the Crucified Christ in Antioch: Maccabean Martyrdom and Galatians 1 and 2.* SNTSMS 114. Cambridge: CUP.

Cumont, Franz V. M. 1923. *After Life in Roman Paganism.* New Haven: Yale U. P.

——. 1949. *Lux Perpetua.* Paris: Librarie Orientaliste Paul Guethner.

Dahl, M. E. 1962. *The Resurrection of the Body: A Study of I Corinthians 15.* London: SCM Press.

Dahood, M. J. 1966–70. *Psalms.* AB 16, 17, 17a. 3 vols. Garden City, NY: Doubleday.

Danby, Herbert. 1933. *The Mishnah, Translated from the Hebrew with Introduction and Brief Explanatory Notes.* Oxford: OUP.

Daube, David. 1990. 'On Acts 23: Sadducees and Angels.' *Journal of Biblical Literature* 109:493–7.

Davids, Peter H. 1990. *The First Epistle of Peter.* NICNT. Grand Rapids: Eerdmans.

Davie, Martin. 1998. 'The Resurrection of Jesus Christ in the Theology of Karl Barth.' *Proclaiming the Resurrection: Papers from the First Oak Hill College Annual School of Theology*, ed. Peter M. Head, 107–30. Carlisle: Paternoster Press.

Davies, J. 1999. *Death, Burial and Rebirth in the Religions of Antiquity.* London: Routledge.

Davies, W. D., and Dale C. Allison. 1988. *A Critical and Exegetical Commentary on the Gospel According to Saint Matthew.* ICC (New Series). 3 vols. Edinburgh: T. & T. Clark, 1988–97.

Davis, Stephen T. 1997. '"Seeing" the Risen Jesus.' In *The Resurrection: An Interdisciplinary Symposium on the Resurrection of Jesus*, eds. Stephen T. Davis, Daniel Kendall and Gerald O'Collins, 126–47.

——, Daniel Kendall and Gerald O'Collins, eds. 1997. *The Resurrection: An Interdisciplinary Symposium on the Resurrection of Jesus.* Oxford: OUP.

Day, John. 1980. 'A Case of Inner Scriptural Interpretation: The Dependence of Isaiah xxvi.13—xxvii.11 on Hosea xiii.4—xiv.10 (Eng. 9) and Its Relevance to Some Theories of the Redaction of the "Isaiah Apocalypse".' *Journal of Theological Studies* 31:309–19.

——. 1996. 'The Development of Belief in Life After Death in Ancient Israel.' In *After the Exile: Essays in Honour of Rex Mason*, eds. J. Barton and D. J. Reimer, 231–57. Macon, Ga.: Mercer U. P.

——. 1997. 'Resurrection Imagery from Baal to the Book of Daniel.' In *Congress Volume, Cambridge 1995*, ed. J. A. Emerton. VTSup 66, 125–33. Leiden: Brill.

D'Costa, Gavin, ed. 1996. *Resurrection Reconsidered.* Oxford: Oneworld.

de Boer, M. C. 1988. *The Defeat of Death: Apocalyptic Eschatology in 1 Corinthians 15 and Romans 5.* JSNTSup 22. Sheffield: JSOT Press.

de Chardin, Pierre Teilhard. 1965. *The Phenomenon of Man.* 2nd ed. New York: Harper & Row, Harper Torchbooks/Cathedral Library.

DeChow, Jon F. 1988. *Dogma and Mysticism in Early Christianity: Epiphanius of Cyprus and the Legacy of Origen.* PMS 13. Macon, Ga.: Mercer U. P.

De Jonge, H. J. 2002. 'Visionary Experience and the Historical Origins of Christianity'. In *Resurrection in the New Testament* (FS J. Lambrecht), eds. R. Bieringer, V. Koperski and B. Lataire, 35–53. Leuven: Peeters.

Delobel, J. 2002. 'The Corinthians' (Un-)belief in the Resurrection'. In *Resurrection in the New Testament* (FS J. Lambrecht), eds. R. Bieringer, V. Koperski and B. Lataire, 343–55. Leuven: Peeters.

Demson, David E. 1997. *Hans Frei and Karl Barth: Different Ways of Reading Scripture.* Grand Rapids: Eerdmans.

Denaux, A. 2002. 'Matthew's Story of Jesus' Burial and Resurrection (Mt. 27,57—28,20)'. In *Resurrection in the New Testament* (FS J. Lambrecht), eds. R. Bieringer, V. Koperski and B. Lataire, 123–45. Leuven: Peeters.

de Sola, D. A. 1962. *The Complete Festival Prayers*, Vol. 2: *Service for the Day of Atonement.* London: Shapiro, Vallentine & Co.

Dillon, John. 1996 [1977]. *The Middle Platonists: A Study of Platonism 80 B.C. to A.D. 220.* 2nd edn. London: Duckworth, 1996.

Dodd, C. H. 1953. *The Interpretation of the Fourth Gospel.* Cambridge: CUP.

——. 1959. *The Epistle of Paul to the Romans.* London: Collins-Fontana.

——. 1967. 'The Appearances of the Risen Christ: An Essay in Form-Criticism of the Gospels.' In *Studies in the Gospels: Essays in Memory of R. H. Lightfoot*, ed. D. E. Nineham, 9–35. Oxford: Blackwell.

Dodds, E. R. 1965. *Pagan and Christian in an Age of Anxiety: Some Aspects of Religious Experience From Marcus Aurelius to Constantine.* Cambridge: CUP.

Draper, Jonathan A. 1996. *The Didache in Modern Research.* Leiden: Brill.

Dreyfus, F. 1959. 'L'argument scriptuaire de Jésus en faveur de la résurrection des morts (Marc XII, vv. 26–7).' *Revue Biblique* 66:213–24.

Duff, Jeremy. 2001. '2 Peter.' In *OBC* 1270–74.

Dunn, James D. G. 1990. *Jesus, Paul and the Law: Studies in Mark and Galatians.* London: SPCK.

——. 1991. 'Once More, Pistis Christou.' *SBL Seminar Papers* 30:730–44. Reprinted, with an additional note, in Hays 2002, 249–71.

——. 1996. *The Acts of the Apostles.* Epworth Commentaries. Peterborough: Epworth Press.

——. 1998. *The Theology of Paul the Apostle.* Grand Rapids: Eerdmans.

Dupont-Sommer, A. 1949. 'De l'immortalité astrale dans la "Sagesse de Salomon" (III 7)'. *Revue des Études Grecques* 62:80–87.

Edwards, David L. 1999. *After Death? Past Beliefs and Real Possibilities.* London: Cassell.

——. 2002. *The Church That Could Be.* London: SPCK.

Edwards, Richard A. 1971. *The Sign of Jonah in the Theology of the Evangelists and Q.* Naperville, Ill.: Allenson.

Eichrodt, Walther. 1961. *Theology of the Old Testament.* 2 vols. OTL. London: SCM Press; Philadelphia:Westminster.

——. 1970. *Ezekiel: A Commentary.* London: SCM Press.

Elliott, J. K. 1993. *The Apocryphal New Testament: A Collection of Apocryphal Christian Literature in an English Translation based on M. R. James.* Oxford: Clarendon Press Press.

——. 2001. 'Extra-Canonical Early Christian Literature.' In *OBC* 1306–30.

Ellis, E. Earle. 1966. *The Gospel of Luke.* New Century Bible. London: Nelson.

Evans, Craig A. 1999a. 'Did Jesus Predict His Death and Resurrection?' In *Resurrection*, eds. Stanley E. Porter, Michael A. Hayes and David Tombs, 82–97. Sheffield: Sheffield Academic Press.

——. 1999b. 'Jesus and the Continuing Exile of Israel.' In *Jesus and the Restoration of Israel*, ed. Carey C. Newman, 77–100. Downers Grove, Ill.: IVP.

——. 2001. *Mark 8:27—16:20.* WBC 34b. Nashville: Nelson.

Evans, C. F. 1970. *Resurrection and the New Testament.* London: SCM Press.

Evans, C. S. 1999. 'Methodological Naturalism in Historical Biblical Scholarship.' In *Jesus and the Restoration of Israel*, ed. Carey C. Newman, 180–205. Downers Grove, Ill.: IVP.

Fallon, Francis T., and Ron Cameron. 1989. 'The Gospel of Thomas: A Forschungsbericht and Analysis.' In *Aufstieg und Niedergang der Römischen Welt*. Vol. 2.25.6, eds. Wolfgang Haase and Hildegard Temporini, 4195–251. Berlin/New York: De Gruyter.

Farrow, Douglas. 1999. *Ascension and Ecclesia: On the Significance of the Doctrine of the Ascension for Ecclesiology and Christian Cosmology*. Grand Rapids: Eerdmans.

Fee, Gordon D. 1987. *The First Epistle to the Corinthians*. ed. F. F. Bruce. NICNT. Grand Rapids: Eerdmans.

Fenton, John. 1994. 'The Ending of Mark's Gospel.' In *Resurrection: Essays in Honour of Leslie Houlden*, eds. Stephen Barton and Graham Stanton, 1–7. London: SPCK.

Ferguson, Everett. 1987. *Backgrounds of Early Christianity*. Grand Rapids: Eerdmans.

Festinger, Leon. 1957. *A Theory of Cognitive Dissonance*. Stanford, Ca.: Stanford U. P.

——, H. Riecken, and S. Schachter. 1956. *When Prophecy Fails*. Minneapolis: U. of Minnesota Press.

Figueras, Pau. 1974. 'Jewish and Christian Beliefs on Life After Death in the Light of the Ossuary Decoration.' Ph.D. diss., Hebrew University, Jerusalem.

——. 1983. *Decorated Jewish Ossuaries*. DMOA 20. Leiden: Brill.

Finkelstein, Louis. 1962 [1938]. *The Pharisees: The Sociological Background of their Faith*. 2 vols. 3rd edn. Philadelphia: The Jewish Publication Society of America.

Fischer, Ulrich. 1978. *Eschatologie und Jenseitserwartung im hellenistischen Diasporajudentum*. BZNW 44. Berlin: De Gruyter.

Fletcher-Louis, C. H. T. 1997. *Luke-Acts: Angels, Christology and Soteriology*. WUNT 2.47. Tübingen: Mohr.

Fortna, Robert T. 1970. *The Gospel of Signs*. SNTSMS 11. Cambridge: CUP.

——. 1988. *The Fourth Gospel and Its Predecessor*. Philadelphia: Fortress.

——. 1992. 'Signs/Semeia Source.' In *ABD* 6:18–22.

Fraser, P. M. 1972. *Ptolemaic Alexandria*. Oxford: OUP.

Frazer, Sir James George. 1951 [1922]. *The Golden Bough: A Study in Magic and Religion*. Abridged edn. New York: Macmillan. (Full edn. 1911–15)

Frei, Hans W. 1975. *The Identity of Jesus Christ, the Hermeneutical Bases of Dogmatic Theology*. 1967. Philadelphia: Fortress.

——. 1993. *Theology and Narrative: Selected Essays*. New York: OUP.

Frend, W. H. C. 1954. 'The Gnostic Sects and the Roman Empire.' *Journal of Ecclesiastical History* 5:25–37.

——. 1984. *The Rise of Christianity*. Philadelphia: Fortress.

Fuller, Reginald. *The Formation of the Resurrection Narratives*. New York: Macmillan, 1971.

Furnish, Victor P. 1984. *II Corinthians*. AB 32a. New York: Doubleday.

Fyall, Robert S. 2002. *Now My Eyes Have Seen You: Images of Creation and Evil in the Book of Job*. Downers Grove, Ill.: IVP.

Gaffron, H. G. 1970. 'Eine gnostische Apologia des Auferstehungsglaubens: Bemerkungen zur "Epistula Ad Rheginum".' In *Die Zeit Jesus*. FS für Heinrich Schlier, 218–27. Freiburg/Basel/Wien: Herder.

Gager, J. 1982. 'Body-Symbols and Social Reality: Resurrection, Incarnation, and Asceticism in Early Christianity.' *Religion* 12:345–64.

Garland, R. 1985. *The Greek Way of Death*. Ithaca, N.Y.: Cornell U. P.

Gathercole, S. J. 2002. 'A Law Unto Themselves: The Gentiles in Romans 2.14–15 Revisited.' *Journal for the Study of the New Testament* 85:27–49.

Gaventa, Beverley R. 1987. 'The Rhetoric of Death in the Wisdom of Solomon and the Letters of Paul.' In *The Listening Heart: Essays in Wisdom and the Psalms in Honor of Roland E. Murphy, O. Carm.*, eds. K. G. Hoglund, E. F. Huweiler, J. T. Glass, and R. W. Lee, 127–45. Sheffield: JSOT Press.

Ghiberti, G., and G. Borgonovo. 1993. 'Bibliografia sulla resurrezione di Gesù (1973–92).' *La Scuola Cattolica* 121:171–287.

Gibson, Arthur. 1999. 'Logic of the Resurrection.' In *Resurrection*, eds. Stanley E. Porter, Michael A. Hayes and David Tombs, 166–94. Sheffield: Sheffield Academic Press.

Gilbert, Maurice. 1999. 'Immortalité? Résurrection? Faut-il choisir?' In *Le Judaïsme à l'aube de l'ère chrétienne: XVIIIᵉ congrès de l'association catholique française pour l'étude de la bible (Lyon, Septembre 1999)*, 271–97. Paris: Cerf.

Gillman, F. M. 2002. 'Berenice as Paul's Witness to the Resurrection (Acts 25—26)'. In *Resurrection in the New Testament* (FS J. Lambrecht), eds. R. Bieringer, V. Koperski and B. Lataire, 249–64. Leuven: Peeters.

Gillman, John. 1982. 'Transformation in 1 Cor 15, 50–53.' *Ephemerides Theologicae Louvaniensis* 58:309–33.

——. 2002. 'The Emmaus Story in Luke-Acts Revisited'. In *Resurrection in the New Testament* (FS J. Lambrecht), eds. R. Bieringer, V. Koperski and B. Lataire, 165–88. Leuven: Peeters.

Gillman, N. 1997. *The Death of Death: Resurrection and Immortality in Jewish Thought*. Woodstock, Vt.: Jewish Lights Publishing.

Gilmour, S. M. 1961. 'The Christophany to More Than Five Hundred Brethren.' *Journal of Biblical Literature* 80:248–52.

——. 1962. 'Easter and Pentecost.' *Journal of Biblical Literature* 81:62–6.

Ginzberg, Louis. 1998 [1909–38]. *The Legends of the Jews*. 7 vols. Baltimore, Md.: Johns Hopkins U. P.

Glasson, T. F. 1961. *Greek Influence on Jewish Eschatology: with Special Reference to the Apocalypses and Pseudepigraphs*. London: SPCK.

Goldin, Judah. 1987. 'The Death of Moses: An Exercise in Midrashic Transposition.' In *Love and Death in the Ancient Near East: Essays in Honor of Marvin H. Pope*, eds. John H. Marks, Robert M. Good, 219–25. Guildford, Ct.: Four Quarters Publishing.

Goldingay, John E. 1989. *Daniel*. WBC 30. Dallas, Tex.: Word Books.

Goodenough, Erwin R. 1967 [1938]. *The Politics of Philo Judaeus: Practice and Theory*. Hildesheim: Georg Olms.

Goulder, Michael. 1996. 'The Baseless Fabric of a Vision.' In *Resurrection Reconsidered*, ed. Gavin D'Costa, 48–61. Oxford: Oneworld.

——. 2000. 'The Explanatory Power of Conversion-Visions.' In *Jesus' Resurrection: Fact or Figment: A Debate Between William Lane Craig and Gerd Lüdemann*, eds Paul Copan and Ronald K. Tacelli, 86–103. Downers Grove, Ill.: IVP.

Grabar, André. 1968. *Christian Iconography: A Study of Its Origins*. Princeton, N.J: Princeton U. P.

Grabbe, Lester L. 1997. *Wisdom of Solomon*. Sheffield: Sheffield Academic Press.

Grant, R. M. 1954. 'Athenagoras or Pseudo-Athenagoras.' *Harvard Theological Review* 47:121–9.

Grappe, Christian. 2001. 'Naissance de l'idée de résurrection dans le Judaïsme.' In *Résurrection: L'après-mort dans le monde ancien et le Nouveau Testament*, eds. Odette Mainville and Daniel Marguerat, 45–72. Geneva: Labor et Fides; Montreal: Médiaspaul.

Grassi, J. 1965. 'Ezekiel XXXVII.1–14 and the New Testament.' *New Testament Studies* 11:162–4.

Green, Joel B. 1987. 'The Gospel of Peter: Source for a Pre-Canonical Passion Narrative?' *Zeitschrift für die neutestamentliche Wissenschaft* 78:293–301.

——. 1990. Review of Crossan 1988. *Journal of Biblical Literature* 109:356–8.

——. 1998. '"Witnesses of His Resurrection": Resurrection, Salvation, Discipleship, and Mission in the Acts of the Apostles.' In *Life in the Face of Death: The Resurrection Message of the New Testament*, ed. Richard N. Longenecker, 227–46. Grand Rapids: Eerdmans.

Greenspoon, Leonard J. 1981. 'The Origin of the Idea of Resurrection.' In *Traditions in Transformation: Turning Points in Biblical Faith*, eds. Baruch Halpern and Jon D. Levenson, 247–321. Winona Lake, Ind.: Eisenbrauns.

Greshake, Gisbert, and Jacob Kremer. 1986. *Resurrectio Mortuorum: Zum theologischen Verständnis der leiblichen Auferstehung*. Darmstadt: Wissenschaftliche Buchgesellschaft.

Griffiths, J. G. 1999. 'The Legacy of Egypt in Judaism.' In *The Cambridge History of Judaism*. eds. William Horbury, W. D. Davies and John Sturdy. Vol. 3, *The Roman Period*, 1025–51. Cambridge: CUP.

Gruen, E. S. 1998. 'Rome and the Myth of Alexander.' In *Ancient History in a Modern University*. Vol. 1, *The Ancient Near East, Greece and Rome*, eds. T. W. Hillard, R. A. Kearsley, C. E. V. Nixon, and A. M. Nobbs, 178–91. Grand Rapids: Eerdmans.

Guelich, Robert A. 1989. *Mark 1—8:26*. WBC 34a. Dallas, Tex.: Word.

Gundry, Robert H. 1976. *SOMA in Biblical Theology with Emphasis on Pauline Anthropology*. SNTSMS 29. Cambridge: CUP.

——. 1993. *Mark: A Commentary on His Apology for the Cross*. Grand Rapids: Eerdmans.

Guthrie, W. K. C. 1962–81. *A History of Greek Philosophy*. 6 vols. Cambridge: CUP.

Habermas, Gary R. 1989. 'Resurrection Claims in Non-Christian Religions.' *Religious Studies* 25:167–77.

——. 2001. 'The Late Twentieth-Century Resurgence of Naturalistic Responses to Jesus' Resurrection.' *Trinity Journal* n.s. 22:179–96.

Hachlili, Rachel. 1992. 'Burials, Ancient Jewish.' In *ABD*, 1:789–94.

Hafemann, Scott J. 1995. *Paul, Moses, and the History of Israel*. Tübingen: Mohr-Siebeck.

——. 2000. *2 Corinthians*. The NIV Application Commentary. Grand Rapids: Zondervan.

Hall, R. G. 1990. 'The *Ascension of Isaiah*: Community Situation, Date, and Place in Early Christianity.' *Journal of Biblical Literature* 109:289–306.

Hamilton, Edith, and Huntingdon Cairns, eds. 1961. *The Collected Dialogues of Plato, Including the Letters*. Princeton: Princeton U. P.

Handy, Lowell K. 1992. 'Tammuz.' In *ABD* 6:318.

Harman, Gilbert H. 1965. 'The Inference to the Best Explanation.' *Philosophical Review* 74:88–95.

Harrington, D. J. 2002. 'Afterlife Expectations in Pseudo-Philo, 4 Ezra, and 2 Baruch, and their Implications for the New Testament.' In *Resurrection in the New Testament* (FS J. Lambrecht), eds. R. Bieringer, V. Koperski and B. Lataire, 21–34. Leuven: Peeters.

Harrison, Ted. 2000. *Beyond Dying: The Mystery of Eternity*. Oxford: Lion.

Hart, H. StJ. 1984. 'The Coin of "Render Unto Caesar . . ." (A Note on Some Aspects of Mark 12:13–17; Matt. 22:15–22; Luke 20:20–26).' In *Jesus and the Politics of His Day*, eds. Ernst Bammel and C. F. D. Moule, 241–8. Cambridge: CUP.

Hartley, John E. 1988. *The Book of Job*. Grand Rapids: Eerdmans.

Harvey, Anthony E. 1982. *Jesus and the Constraints of History: The Bampton Lectures, 1980*. London: Duckworth.

——. 1994. '"They Discussed Among Themselves What This 'Rising from the Dead' Could Mean" (Mark 9.10).' In *Resurrection: Essays in Honour of Leslie Houlden*, eds. Stephen Barton and Graham Stanton, 69–78. London: SPCK.

Harvey, Susan Ashbrook. 2000. 'Syriac Christian Thought.' In *OCCT* 692–3.

Hays, Richard B. 1997. *First Corinthians*. IBC. Nashville: Abingdon.

——. 1999. 'The Conversion of the Imagination: Scripture and Eschatology in 1 Corinthians.' *New Testament Studies* 45:391–412.

—— 2000. *The Letter to the Galatians: Introduction, Commentary, and Reflections.* In *NIB* 11.181–348.

——. 2002 [1983] *The Faith of Jesus Christ: An Investigation of the Narrative Substructure of Galatians 3:1—4:11.* 2nd ed. Grand Rapids: Eerdmans; Dearborn, Mich.: Dove Booksellers.

Hedrick, Charles W., and Paul A. Mirecki. 1999. *Gospel of the Saviour: A New Ancient Gospel.* Santa Rosa, Ca.: Polebridge Press.

Helmbold, A. K. 1972. 'Gnostic Elements in the "Ascension of Isaiah".' *New Testament Studies* 18:222–7.

Hemer, Colin J. 1989. *The Book of Acts in the Setting of Hellenistic History.* Tübingen: Mohr-Siebeck.

Hengel, Martin. 1963. 'Maria Magdalene und die Frauen als Zeugen.' In *Abraham Unser Vater* (FS O. Michel), eds. O. Betz et al., 243–56. Leiden: Brill.

——. 1974. *Judaism and Hellenism: Studies in Their Encounter in Palestine During the Early Hellenistic Period.* London: SCM Press.

——. 1976. *The Son of God: The Origin of Christology and the History of Jewish-Hellenistic Religion.* Philadelphia: Fortress.

——. 1983. *Between Jesus and Paul: Studies in the Earliest History of Christianity.* London: SCM Press.

——. 1995. *Studies in Early Christology.* Edinburgh: T. & T. Clark.

——. 2001. 'Das Begräbnis Jesu bei Paulus und die leibliche Auferstehung aus dem Grabe.' In *Auferstehung – Resurrection*, eds. Friedrich Avemarie and Hermann Lichtenberger, 120–83. Tübingen: Mohr-Siebeck.

Hennecke, Edgar, and W. Schneemelcher, eds. 1963–5 [1959–64]. *New Testament Apocrypha.* 2 vols. Philadelphia:Westminster.

Hill, Charles E. 2002 [1992]. *Regnum Caelorum: Patterns of Millennial Thought in Early Christianity.* 2nd edn. Grand Rapids: Eerdmans.

Hillard, T., A. Nobbs and B. Winter. 1993. 'Acts and the Pauline Corpus I: Ancient Literary Parallels'. In *The Book of Acts in its Ancient Literary Setting*, ed. B. W. Winter and A. D. Clarke, 183–213. Vol. 1 of *The Book of Acts in its First Century Setting*, ed. B. W. Winter. Grand Rapids: Eerdmans; Carlisle: Paternoster.

Hoffman, R. Joseph, ed. 1987. *Celsus on the True Doctrine: A Discourse Against the Christians.* New York/Oxford: OUP.

Hofius, O. 2002.'"Am dritten Tage auferstanden von den Toten": Erwägungen zum passiv ΕΓΕΙΡΕΣΘΑΙ in christologischen Aussagen des Neuen Testaments'. In *Resurrection in the New Testament* (FS J. Lambrecht), eds. R. Bieringer, V. Koperski and B. Lataire, 93–106. Leuven: Peeters.

Holmes, Michael W, ed. 1989. *The Apostolic Fathers.* 2nd edn. Rapids, Mich.: Baker; Leicester: Apollos.

Holt, Stephen. 1999. 'Foreword.' In *Resurrection*, eds. Stanley E. Porter, Michael A. Hayes and David Tombs, 9–11. Sheffield: Sheffield Academic Press.

Holzhausen, J. 1994. 'Gnosis und Martyrium. Zu Valentins viertem Fragment.' *Zeitschrift für die neutestamentliche Wissenschaft* 85:116–31.

Hooker, M. D. 1989. 'ΠΙΣΤΙΣ ΧΡΙΣΤΟΥ.' *New Testament Studies* 35:321–42.

——. 1990. *From Adam to Christ: Essays on Paul.* Cambridge: CUP.

——. 2002. 'Raised for our Acquittal (Rom 4,25).' In *Resurrection in the New Testament* (FS J. Lambrecht), eds. R. Bieringer, V. Koperski and B. Lataire, 321–41. Leuven: Peeters.

Horbury, William. 2001. 'The Wisdom of Solomon.' In *OBC* 650–67.

Horsley, Richard A., ed. 1997. *Paul and Empire: Religion and Power in Roman Imperial Society*. Harrisburg, Pa.: TPI.

———. 1998. *1 Corinthians*. ANTC. Nashville: Abingdon.

———, ed. 2000. *Paul and Politics: Ekklesia, Israel, Imperium, Interpretation. Essays in Honor of Krister Stendahl*. Harrisburg, Pa.: TPI.

Horst, Friedrich. 1960. *Hiob*. Neukirchen: Neukirchener Verlag.

Horst, P. W. van der. *See* van der Horst, P. W.

Hume, David. 1975 [1777]. *Enquiries: Concerning Human Understanding and Concerning the Principles of Morals*. ed. L. A. Selby-Bigge. 3rd edn. Oxford: OUP.

Innes, Brian. 1999. *Death and the Afterlife*. New York: St Martin's Press.

Isser, Stanley. 1999. 'The Samaritans and Their Sects.' In *The Cambridge History of Judaism*. eds. William Horbury, W. D. Davies and John Sturdy. Vol. 3, *The Roman Period*, 569–95. Cambridge: CUP.

Jackson, Hugh. 1975. 'Resurrection Belief of the Earliest Church: a Response to the Failure of Prophecy?' *Journal of Religion* 55:415–25.

Jaffe, Aniela. 1979. *Apparitions: An Archetypal Approach to Death, Dreams, and Ghosts*. Irving, Tex.: Spring.

James, M. R. 1924. *The Apocryphal New Testament, Being the Apocryphal Gospels, Acts, Epistles, and Apocalypses, with Other Narratives and Fragments*. Oxford: Clarendon Press.

Janzen, J. Gerald. 1985. 'Resurrection and Hermeneutics: On Exodus 3.6 in Mark 12.26.' *Journal for the Study of the New Testament* 23:43–58.

Jarick, John. 1999. 'Questioning Sheol.' In *Resurrection*, eds. Stanley E. Porter, Michael A. Hayes and David Tombs, 22–32. Sheffield: Sheffield Academic Press.

Jeremias, Joachim. 1955. '"Flesh and Blood Cannot Inherit the Kingdom of God" (1 Cor. XV. 50).' *New Testament Studies* 2:152–9.

Johnson, Dennis E. 2001. *Triumph of the Lamb: A Commentary on Revelation*. Phillipsburg, N.J.: P. & R. Publishing.

Johnson, Luke T. 1995. *The Real Jesus*. San Francisco: HarperSanFrancisco.

———. 1999. *Living Jesus: Learning the Heart of the Gospel*. San Francisco: HarperSanFrancisco.

Johnston, P. S. 2002. *Shades of Sheol: Death and Afterlife in the Old Testament*. Leicester: Apollos.

Johnston, Sarah Iles. 1999. *Restless Dead: Encounters Between the Living and the Dead in Ancient Greece*. Berkeley, Ca.: U. of California Press.

Judge, Edwin A. 1960. *The Social Pattern of Christian Groups in the First Century*. London: Tyndale.

———. 1968. 'Paul's Boasting in Relation to Contemporary Professional Practice.' *Australian Biblical Review* 16:37–50.

Juhász, G. 2002. 'Translating Resurrection: the Importance of the Sadducees' Belief in the Tyndale-Joye Controversy'. In *Resurrection in the New Testament* (FS J. Lambrecht), eds. R. Bieringer, V. Koperski and B. Lataire, 107–21. Leuven: Peeters.

Jupp, Peter C., and Clare Gittings, eds. 1999. *Death in England: An Illustrated History*. New Brunswick, N.J.: Rutgers U. P.

Kaiser, Otto. 1973. *Isaiah 1—39: A Commentary*. London: SCM Press.

Kákosy, Lászlo. 1969. 'Probleme der aegyptischen Jenseitsvorstellungen in der Ptolomaeer- und Kaiserzeit.' In *Religions en Egypte hellenistique et romaine. Colloque de Strasbourg, 16–18 Mai 1967*, 59–68. Paris: Presses universitaire de France.

Keesmaat, Sylvia C. 1999. *Paul and His Story: (Re)Interpreting the Exodus Tradition*. JSNTSup. Sheffield: Sheffield Academic Press.

Kelhoffer, James A. 2000. *Miracle and Mission: The Authentication of Missionaries and Their Message in the Longer Ending of Mark.* WUNT 2.112. Tübingen: Mohr-Siebeck.

Kellerman, Bill W. 1991. *Seasons of Faith and Conscience: Kairos, Confession, Liturgy.* Maryknoll, N.Y.: Orbis Books, 1991.

Kellermann, Ulrich. 1979. *Auferstanden in Den Himmel: 2 Makkabäer 7 und die Auferstehung der Märtyrer.* Stuttgarter Bibelstudien 95. Stuttgart: Katholisches Bibelwerk.

——. 1989. 'Das Danielbuch und die Märtyrertheologie der Auferstehung.' In *Die Entstehung der Jüdischen Martyrologie*, ed. W. van Henten, 51–75. Leiden: Brill.

Kelly, J. N. D. 1977. *Early Christian Doctrines.* 5th edn. London: A. & C. Black.

Kendall, D., and Gerald O'Collins. 1992. 'The Uniqueness of the Easter Appearances.' *Catholic Biblical Quarterly* 54:287–307.

Kenney, E. J. 1998. *Apuleius, the Golden Ass, or Metamorphoses: Translated with an Introduction and Notes.* London: Penguin.

Kilgallen, John J. 1986. 'The Sadducees and Resurrection from the Dead.' *Biblica* 67:478–95.

——. 2002. 'What the Apostles Proclaimed at Acts 4,2'. In *Resurrection in the New Testament* (FS J. Lambrecht), eds. R. Bieringer, V. Koperski and B. Lataire, 233–48. Leuven: Peeters.

Kim, Seyoon. 1984. *The Origin of Paul's Gospel.* 2nd edn. WUNT 2.5. Tübingen: Mohr-Siebeck; Grand Rapids: Eerdmans.

——. 2002. *Paul and the New Perspective: Second Thoughts on The Origin of Paul's Gospel.* Grand Rapids, Mich.: Eerdmans.

Kirk, Alan. 1994. 'Examining Properties: Another Look at the Gospel of Peter's Relationship to the New Testament Gospels.' *New Testament Studies* 40:572–95.

Klauck, Hans-Josef. 2000. *The Religious Context of Early Christianity: A Guide to Graeco-Roman Religions.* Edinburgh: T. & T. Clark.

Kloppenborg, John S. 1987. *The Formation of Q: Trajectories in Ancient Wisdom Collections.* Studies in Antiquity and Christianity. Philadelphia: Fortress.

——. 1990a. *Q Parallels: Synopsis, Critical Notes, & Concordance.* Sonoma, Ca.: Polebridge Press.

——. 1990b. '"Easter Faith" and the Sayings Gospel Q.' *Semeia* 49:71–100.

Knight, J. M. 1996. 'Disciples of the Beloved One: The Christology, Social Setting and Theological Context of the Ascension of Isaiah.' JSPSup, vol. 18. Sheffield: Sheffield Academic Press.

Koenig, Jean, 1983. 'La vision des ossements chez Ézéchiel et l'origine de la croyance a la résurrection dans le Judaïsme.' In *Vie et service dans les civilisations orientales*, eds. A. Thésdoridès, P. Naster and J. Riez. Acta Orientalia Belgica 3. Leuven: Peeters, 159–79.

Koester, Craig R. 1996. *Symbolism in the Fourth Gospel: Meaning, Mystery, Community.* Minneapolis: Fortress.

——. 2001. *Hebrews: A New Translation with Introduction and Commentary.* AB 36. New York: Doubleday.

Koester, Helmut. 1982a. *Introduction to the New Testament.* Vol. 1, *History, Culture and Religion of the Hellenistic Age.* Hermeneia: Foundations and Facets. Philadelphia: Fortress; Berlin/New York: De Gruyter.

——. 1982b. *Introduction to the New Testament.* Vol. 2, *History and Literature of Early Christianity.* Hermeneia: Foundations and Facets. Philadelphia: Fortress; Berlin/New York: De Gruyter.

——. 1990. *Ancient Christian Gospels: Their History and Development.* London: SCM Press; Philadelphia: TPI.

Kolarcik, Michael. 1991. *The Ambiguity of Death in the Book of Wisdom 1—6: A Study of Literary Structure and Interpretation.* AnBib 127. Rome: Pontifical Biblical Institute Press.

König, Jason. 2003. 'The Cynic and Christian Lives of Lucian's Peregrinus.' In *The Limits of Biography*, eds. Judith Mossman and Brian McGing, [forthcoming]. Swansea: Classical Press of Wales.

Koperski, V. 2002. 'Resurrection Terminology in Paul'. In *Resurrection in the New Testament* (FS J. Lambrecht), eds. R. Bieringer, V. Koperski and B. Lataire, 265–81. Leuven: Peeters.

Köstenberger, A. J. 1995. 'The Seventh Johannine Sign: a Study in John's Christology.' *Bulletin of Biblical Research* 5:87–103.

Krieg, Matthias. 1988. *Todesbilder im Alten Testament, oder, Wie die Alten den Tod Gebildet.* ATANT, vol. 73. Zürich: Theologische Verlag.

Küng, Hans. 1976. *On Being a Christian.* Garden City, N. Y.: Doubleday.

Künneth, Walter. 1965. *The Theology of the Resurrection.* London: SCM Press.

Lacocque, André. 1979. *The Book of Daniel.* London: SPCK; Atlanta, Ga.: John Knox.

Lambrecht, Jan. 1982. 'Paul's Christological Use of Scripture in 1 Cor. 15.20–28.' *New Testament Studies* 28: 502–07.

Lampe, G. W. H. 1977. *God as Spirit.* Oxford: Clarendon Press Press.

Lane, William L. 1991. *Hebrews.* WBC 47. 2 vols. Dallas, Tex.: Word Books.

——. 1998. 'Living a Life of Faith in the Face of Death: The Witness of Hebrews.' In *Life in the Face of Death: The Resurrection Message of the New Testament*, ed. Richard N. Longenecker, 247–69. Grand Rapids: Eerdmans.

Laperrousaz, E.-M. 1970. *Le Testament de Moïse.* Paris: Librarie d'Amérique et d'Orient Adrien-Maisonneuve.

Lapide, Pinchas. 1983. *The Resurrection of Jesus: A Jewish Perspective.* Minneapolis: Augsburg.

Larcher, C. 1969. *Études sur le Livre de la Sagesse.* Études Bibliques. Paris: Gabalda.

——. 1983. *Le Livre de la Sagesse ou la Sagesse de Salomon.* Paris: Gabalda.

Lattimore, Richard. 1942. *Themes in Greek and Latin Epitaphs.* Illinois Studies in Language and Literature 28. Urbana, Ill.: University of Illinois Press.

Lemcio, Eugene E. 1991. *The Past of Jesus in the Gospels.* SNTSMS 68. Cambridge: CUP.

Le Moyne, S. 1972. *Les Sadducceens.* Paris: Cerf.

Lewis, C. S. 1960. *Miracles: A Preliminary Study.* London: Collins-Fontana.

Lewis, Theodore J. 1989. *Cults of the Dead in Ancient Israel and Ugarit.* Harvard Semitic Monographs, vol. 39. Atlanta, Ga.: Scholars Press.

Lichtenberger, Hermann. 2001. 'Auferstehung in den Qumranfunden.' In *Auferstehung – Resurrection*, eds. Friedrich Avemarie and Hermann Lichtenberger, 79–91. Tübingen: Mohr-Siebeck.

Lieu, Judith. 1994. 'The Women's Resurrection Testimony.' In *Resurrection: Essays in Honour of Leslie Houlden*, eds. Stephen Barton and Graham Stanton, 34–44. London: SPCK.

Lightfoot, J. B. 1989 [1889], ed. and tr. *The Apostolic Fathers.* 5 vols. London: Macmillan. Reprint: Peabody, Mass.: Hendriksen.

Lincoln, Andrew T. 1981. *Paradise Now and not Yet: Studies in the Role of the Heavenly Dimension in Paul's Thought with Special Reference to His Eschatology.* SNTSMS 43. Cambridge: CUP.

——. 1998. '"I Am the Resurrection and the Life": The Resurrection Message of the Fourth Gospel.' In *Life in the Face of Death: The Resurrection Message of the New Testament*, ed. Richard N. Longnecker, 122–44. Grand Rapids: Eerdmans.

Lindars, Barnabas. 1993. 'The Resurrection and the Empty Tomb.' In *The Resurrection of Jesus Christ*, ed. Paul Avis, 116–35. London: Darton, Longman & Todd.

Lohfink, Gerhard. 1980. 'Der Ablauf der Osterereignisse und die Anfänge der Urgemeinde.' *Theologische Quartalschrift* 160:162–76.

Lohfink, N. 1990. 'Das Deuteronomische Gesetz in der Endgestalt – Entwurf einer Gesellschaft ohne marginale Gruppen.' *Biblische Notizen* 51:25–40.

Lohse, E. 2002. 'Der Wandel der Christen im Zeichen der Auferstehung: zur Begründung christlicher Ethik im Römerbrief'. In *Resurrection in the New Testament* (FS J. Lambrecht), eds. R. Bieringer, V. Koperski and B. Lataire, 315–22. Leuven: Peeters.

Lona, Horacio E. 1993. *Über der Auferstehung des Fleisches: Studien zur frühchristlichen Eschatologie*. BZNW 66. Berlin and New York: De Gruyter.

Longenecker, Bruce W. 1991. *Eschatology and the Covenant: A Comparison of 4 Ezra and Romans 1–11*. JSNTSup 57. Sheffield: JSOT Press.

Longenecker, Richard N., ed. 1997. *The Road from Damascus: The Impact of Paul's Conversion on His Life, Thought and Ministry*. Grand Rapids/Cambridge: Eerdmans.

———. 1998a. 'Is There Development in Paul's Resurrection Thought?' In *Life in the Face of Death: The Resurrection Message of the New Testament*, ed. Richard N. Longenecker, 171–202. Grand Rapids/Cambridge: Eerdmans.

———, ed. 1998b. *Life in the Face of Death: The Resurrection Message of the New Testament*. Grand Rapids/Cambridge: Eerdmans.

Longstaff, Thomas R. W. 1981. 'The Women at the Tomb: Matthew 28:1 Re-Examined.' *New Testament Studies* 27:277–82.

Lowe, E. J. 1995. 'Necessary and Sufficient Conditions.' In *The Oxford Companion to Philosophy*, ed. T. Honderich, 608. Oxford: OUP.

Lüdemann, Gerd. 1994. *The Resurrection of Jesus: History, Experience, Theology*. London: SCM Press.

Maccoby, Hyam Z. 1980. *Revolution in Judea. Jesus and the Jewish Resistance*. New York: Taplinger.

———. 1986. *The Mythmaker: Paul and the Invention of Christianity*. London: Weidenfeld & Nicolson.

———. 1991. *Paul and Hellenism*. London: SCM Press; Philadelphia: TPI.

Mackie, J. L. 1980 [1974]. *The Cement of the Universe: A Study of Causation*. Oxford: Clarendon Press Press.

MacMullen, Ramsey. 1984. *Christianizing the Roman Empire (A.D. 100—400)*. New Haven/London: Yale U. P.

Macquarrie, John. 1990. *Jesus Christ in Modern Thought*. London: SCM Press; Philadelphia: TPI.

Malherbe, Abraham J. 1968. 'The Beasts at Ephesus.' *Journal of Biblical Literature* 87:71–80.

———. 1989. *Paul and the Popular Philosophers*. Minneapolis: Fortress.

Marcus, Joel. 1989. 'Jane Austen's *Pride and Prejudice*: A Theological Reflection.' *Theology Today* 46:288–98.

———. 2001. 'The Once and Future Messiah in Early Christianity and Chabad.' *New Testament Studies* 47:381–401.

Martin, Dale B. 1995. *The Corinthian Body*. New Haven: Yale U. P.

Martin, Luther H. 1987. *Hellenistic Religions: An Introduction*. Oxford/New York: OUP.

Martin-Achard, R. 1960. *From Death to Life: A Study of the Development of the Doctrine of the Resurrection in the Old Testament*. Edinburgh/London: Oliver and Boyd.

Martyn, J. Louis. 1997a. *Galatians: A New Translation with Introduction and Commentary*. AB 33a. New York: Doubleday.

———. 1997b. *Theological Issues in the Letters of Paul*. Nashville: Abingdon.

Marxsen, Willi. 1968. 'The Resurrection of Jesus as a Historical and Theological Problem.' In *The Significance of the Message of the Resurrection for Faith in Jesus Christ*, ed. C. F. D. Moule, 15–50. London: SCM Press.

Mason, Steve N. 1991. *Flavius Josephus on the Pharisees: A Composition-Critical Study*. Studia Post-Biblica 39. Leiden: Brill.

Matera, F. J. 2002. 'Apostolic Suffering and Resurrection Faith: Distinguishing between Appearance and Reality (2 Cor 4,7—5,10)'. In *Resurrection in the New Testament* (FS J. Lambrecht), eds. R. Bieringer, V. Koperski and B. Lataire, 387–405. Leuven: Peeters.

Mays, James L. 1994. Psalms. IBC. Louisville: John Knox.

McAlpine, Thomas H. 1987. *Sleep, Divine and Human, in the Old Testament*. Sheffield: JSOT Press.

McArthur, H. K. 1971. 'On the Third Day.' *New Testament Studies* 18:81–6.

McCane, Byron R. 1990. 'Let the Dead Bury Their Own Dead: Secondary Burial and Matthew 8.21–22.' *Harvard Theological Review* 83:31–43.

——. 1997. 'Burial Techniques.' In *The Oxford Encyclopaedia of Archaeology in the Near East*, ed. Eric M. Meyers, 1.386–7. New York/Oxford: OUP.

——. 2000. 'Burial Practices, Jewish.' In *Dictionary of New Testament Background*, Craig A. Evans and Stanley E. Porter, 173–5. Downers Grove, Ill.: IVP.

McCaughey, J. Davis. 1974. 'The Death of Death (I Cor. 15:26).' In *Reconciliation and Hope: New Testament Essays on Atonement and Eschatology Presented. to L. L. Morris on His 60th Birthday*, ed. R. Banks, 246–61. Grand Rapids: Eerdmans.

McDannell, Colleen, and Bernhard Lang. 2001 [1988]. *Heaven: A History*. 2nd edn. New Haven: Yale U. P.

McDonald, J. I. H. 1989. *The Resurrection: Narrative and Belief*. London: SPCK.

McDowell, Josh. 1981. *The Resurrection Factor*. Nashville: Thomas Nelson.

McKenzie, Leon. 1997. *Pagan Resurrection Myths and the Resurrection of Jesus*. Charlottesville, Va.: Bookwrights Press.

McPartlan, Paul. 2000. 'Purgatory.' In *OCCT* 582–3.

Meadors, E. P. 1995. *Jesus the Messianic Herald of Salvation*. WUNT 2.72. Tübingen: Mohr-Siebeck.

Meier, John P. 1991. *A Marginal Jew: Rethinking the Historical Jesus*. Vol. 1, *The Roots of the Problem and the Person*. New York: Doubleday.

Menard, J.-E. 1975. 'La notion de résurrection dans l'épître à Rheginos.' In *Essays on the Nag Hammadi Texts in Honor of Pahor Labib*, ed. M Krause, 110–24. Leiden: Brill.

Menken, M. J. J. 2002. 'Interpretation of the Old Testament and the Resurrection of Jesus in John's Gospel'. In *Resurrection in the New Testament* (FS J. Lambrecht), eds. R. Bieringer, V. Koperski and B. Lataire, 189–205. Leuven: Peeters.

Merklein, H. 1981. 'Die Auferweckung Jesu und die Anfänge der Christologie (Messias bzw. Sohn Gottes und Menschensohn).' *Zeitschrift für die neutestamentliche Wissenschaft* 72:1–16.

Mettinger, T. N. D. 2001. *The Riddle of Resurrection: 'Dying and Rising Gods' in the Ancient Near East*. Lund: Almqvist and Wicksell International.

Metzger, Bruce M. 1957. 'A Suggestion concerning the Meaning of 1 Corinthians XV.4b.' *Journal of Theological Studies* 8:118–23.

——. 1971. *A Textual Commentary on the Greek New Testament*. London/New York: United Bible Societies.

——. 1977. *The Early Versions of the New Testament: Their Origin, Transmission and Limitations*. Oxford: Clarendon Press.

Meyer, Marvin W., ed. 1987. *The Ancient Mysteries: A Sourcebook*. Philadelphia: U. of Pennsylvania Press.

Meyers, Eric M. 1970. 'Secondary Burials in Palestine.' *The Biblical Archaeologist* 33:2–29.

768 *Bibliography*

——. 1971. *Jewish Ossuaries: Reburial and Rebirth. Secondary Burials in Their Ancient Near Eastern Setting*. Biblica et Orientalia, vol. 24. Rome: Pontifical Biblical Institute Press.

Michaud, Jean-Paul. 2001. 'La résurrection dans le langage des premiers chrétiens.' In *Résurrection: L'après-mort dans le monde ancien et le Nouveau Testament*, eds. Odette Mainville and Daniel Marguerat, 111–28. Geneva: Labor et Fides; Montreal: Médiaspaul.

Miller, Robert J., ed. 1992. *The Complete Gospels: Annotated Scholars Version*. Sonoma, Ca.: Polebridge Press.

Mirecki, Paul A. 1992a. 'Peter, Gospel Of.' In *ABD* 5:278–81.

——. 1992b. 'Valentinus.' In *ABD* 6:783–4.

Mitchell, Margaret M. 1991. *Paul and the Rhetoric of Reconciliation: An Exegetical Investigation of the Language and Composition of 1 Corinthians*. Tübingen: Mohr-Siebeck.

Mondésert, C. 1999. 'Philo of Alexandria.' In *The Cambridge History of Judaism*. eds. William Horbury, W. D. Davies and John Sturdy. Vol. 3, *The Roman Period*, 877–900. Cambridge: CUP.

Moore, A. W., ed. 1993. *Meaning and Reference*. Oxford: OUP.

Moore, George Foot. 1927. *Judaism in the First Centuries of the Christian Era: The Age of the Tannaim*. 3 vols. Cambridge, Mass.: Harvard U. P.

Morgan, Robert. 1994. 'Flesh is Precious: The Significance of Luke 24:36–43.' In *Resurrection: Essays in Honour of Leslie Houlden*, eds. Stephen Barton and Graham Stanton, 8–20. London: SPCK.

Morris, Jenny. 1993. 'The Jewish Philosopher Philo.' In Schürer 3.2.809–89.

Motyer, J. Alec. 1993. *The Prophecy of Isaiah*. Leicester: IVP.

Moule, C. F. D. 1958a. 'Once More, Who Were the Hellenists?' *Expository Times* 70:100–02.

——. 1958b. 'The Post-Resurrection Appearances in the Light of the Festival Pilgrimages.' *New Testament Studies* 4:58–61.

——. 1966. 'St Paul and Dualism: The Pauline Conception of Resurrection.' *New Testament Studies* 12:106–23.

——. 1967. *The Phenomenon of the New Testament: An Inquiry Into the Implications of Certain Features of the New Testament*. SBT 2nd Series, vol. 1. London: SCM Press.

——, ed. 1968. *The Significance of the Message of the Resurrection for Faith in Jesus Christ*. London: SCM Press.

——, and Don Cupitt. 1972. 'The Resurrection: A Disagreement.' *Theology* 75:507–19.

Moulton, James H. 1908–76. *A Grammar of New Testament Greek*. 4 vols, completed by Nigel Turner. Edinburgh: T. & T. Clark.

Muddiman, John. 1994. '"I Believe in the Resurrection of the Body".' In *Resurrection: Essays in Honour of Leslie Houlden*, eds. Stephen Barton and Graham Stanton, 128–38. London: SPCK.

Müller, U. B. 1998. *Die Entstehung des Glaubens an die Auferstehung Jesu*. Stuttgart: Katholisches Bibelwerk.

Murphy-O'Connor, Jerome. 1996. *Paul: A Critical Life*. Oxford: Clarendon Press Press.

——. 1998 [1980]. *The Holy Land: An Oxford Archaeological Guide from Earliest Times to 1700*. 4th edn. Oxford: OUP.

Neufeldt, R. W., ed. 1986. *Karma and Rebirth: Post-Classical Developments*. Albany, N.Y.: State University of New York Press, 1986.

Neusner, Jacob. 1971. *The Rabbinic Traditions about the Pharisees Before 70*. Leiden: Brill.

——, W.S. Green, and E. Frerichs, eds. 1987. *Judaisms and Their Messiahs at the Turn of the Christian Era*. Cambridge: CUP.

Newman, Carey C. 1992. *Paul's Glory-Christology: Tradition and Rhetoric*. NovTSup 69. Leiden: Brill.

——, ed. 1999. *Jesus and the Restoration of Israel: A Critical Assessment of N. T. Wright's Jesus and the Victory of God*. Downers Grove, Ill.: IVP.

——, James R. Davila and Gladys S. Lewis, eds. 1999. *The Jewish Roots of Christological Monotheism. Papers from the St. Andrews Conference on the Historical Origins of the Worship of Jesus*. JSJSup 63. Leiden: Brill.

Neyrey, Jerome H. 1993. *2 Peter, Jude*. AB 37C. New York: Doubleday.

Nickelsburg, George W. E. 1972. *Resurrection, Immortality and Eternal Life in Intertestamental Judaism*. Harvard Theological Studies 26. Cambridge, Mass.: Harvard U. P.

——. 1980. 'The Genre and Function of the Markan Passion Narrative.' *Harvard Theological Review* 73:153–84.

——. 1984. 'The Bible Rewritten and Expanded.' In *Compendia Rerum Iudaicarum Ad Novum Testamentum, Section Two: The Literature of the Jewish People in the Period of the Second Temple and the Talmud*. Vol. 2, *Jewish Writings of the Second Temple Period*, ed. Michael E. Stone, eds. W. J. Burgers, H. Sysling, and P. J. Tomson, 89–156. Assen: Van Gorcum; Philadelphia: Fortress.

——. 1986. 'An *ektrōma*, Though Appointed from the Womb: Paul's Apostolic Self-Description in 1 Cor 15 and Gal 1'. *Harvard Theological Review* 79:198–205.

——. 1992. 'Resurrection: Early Judaism and Christianity.' In *ABD* 5:684–91.

Niederwimmer, Kurt. 1998. *The Didache: A Commentary on the Didache*. Hermeneia. Minneapolis: Fortress.

Nigosian, S. A. 1993. *The Zoroastrian Faith: Tradition and Modern Research*. Montreal: McGill-Queen's U. P.

Nineham, Dennis. 1965. *Historicity and Chronology in the New Testament*. London: SPCK.

Nodet, Étienne, and Justin Taylor. 1998. *The Origins of Christianity: An Exploration*. Collegeville, Minn.: Liturgical Press.

Norelli, E. 1994. *L'Ascensione di Isaia: Studi su un apocrifo al crocevia dei cristianesimi*. Origini n.s., vol. 1. Bologna: Centro editoriale dehoniano.

Nussbaum, Martha C., and Amelie O. Rorty, ed., 1992. *Essays on Aristotle's De Anima*. Oxford: Clarendon Press Press.

Oakes, Peter. 2001. *Philippians: From People to Letter*. SNTSMS 110. Cambridge: CUP.

Oberlinner, L., ed. 2002. *Auferstehung Jesu – Auferstehung der Christen*. QD 105. Freiburg/Basel/Wien: Herder.

O'Collins, Gerald. 1973. *The Resurrection of Jesus Christ*. Valley Forge, Pa.: Judson Press.

——. 1973. 'Karl Barth on Christ's Resurrection.' *Scottish Journal of Theology* 26:85–99.

——. 1987. *Jesus Risen*. London: Darton, Longman & Todd.

——. 1988. *Interpreting the Resurrection: Examining the Major Problems in the Stories of Jesus' Resurrection*. New York: Paulist Press.

——. 1993. *The Resurrection of Jesus: Some Contemporary Issues*. Milwaukee: Marquette U. P.

——. 1995. *Christology: A Biblical, Historical, and Systematic Study of Jesus*. Oxford: OUP.

——. 1997. 'The Resurrection: The State of the Questions.' In *The Resurrection: An Interdisciplinary Symposium on the Resurrection of Jesus*, eds. Stephen T. Davis, Daniel Kendall and Gerald O'Collins, 5–28.

——. 1999. 'The Risen Jesus: Analogies and Presence.' In *Resurrection*, edited by Stanley E. Porter, Michael A. Hayes and David Tombs, 195–217. Sheffield: Sheffield Academic Press.

O'Donnell, Matthew Brook. 1999. 'Some New Testament Words for Resurrection and the Company They Keep.' In *Resurrection*, edited by Stanley E. Porter, Michael A. Hayes and David Tombs, 136–63. Sheffield: Sheffield Academic Press.

O'Donovan, Oliver M.T. 1986. *Resurrection and Moral Order: An Outline for Evangelical Ethics*. Leicester: IVP; Grand Rapids: Eerdmans

——. 1996. *The Desire of the Nations: Rediscovering the Roots of Political Theology*. Cambridge: CUP.

——. 2002. *Common Objects of Love: Moral Reflection as the Shaping of Community*. Grand Rapids: Eerdmans; Cambridge: CUP.

——, and Joan Lockwood O'Donovan, eds. 1999. *From Irenaeus to Grotius: A Sourcebook in Christian Political Thought*. Grand Rapids: Eerdmans.

Oegema, Gerbern S. 2001. 'Auferstehung in der Johannesoffenbarung: Eine Rezeptions-geschichtliche Untersuchung zu der Vorstellung zweier Auferstehungen in der Offenbarung des Johannes.' In *Auferstehung – Resurrection*, eds. Friedrich Avemarie and Hermann Lichtenberger, 205–27. Tübingen: Mohr-Siebeck.

O'Flaherty, W. D., ed. 1980. *Karma and Rebirth in Classical Indian Traditions*. Berkeley, Ca.: U. of California Press.

O'Hagan, Angelo P. 1968. *Material Re-Creation in the Apostolic Fathers*. Berlin: Akademie-Verlag.

Okure, Teresa. 1992. 'The Significance Today of Jesus' Commission to Mary Magdalene.' *International Review of Missions* 81:177–88.

Ollenburger, Ben C. 1993. 'If Mortals Die, Will They Live Again? The Old Testament and Resurrection.' *Ex Auditu* 9:29–44.

O'Neill, J. C. 1972. 'On the Resurrection as an Historical Question.' In *Christ Faith and History*, eds. S. W. Sykes and J. P. Clayton, 205–19. Cambridge: CUP.

——. 1991. 'The Desolate House and the New Kingdom of Israel: Jewish Oracles of Ezra in 2 Esdras 1—2.' In *Templum Amicitiae: Essays on the Second Temple Presented. to Ernst Bammel*, ed. W. Horbury, 226–36. Sheffield: Sheffield Academic Press.

Osborne, G. R. 2000. 'Resurrection.' In *Dictionary of New Testament Background*, eds. Craig A. Evans and Stanley E. Porter, 931–6. Downers Grove, Ill.: IVP.

Osiek, Carolyn. 1993. 'The Women at the Tomb: What Are They Doing There?' *Ex Auditu* 9:97–107.

Pagels, Elaine. 1975. *The Gnostic Paul: Gnostic Exegesis of the Pauline Letters*. Philadelphia: Fortress.

——. 1979. *The Gnostic Gospels*. New York: Weidenfeld & Nicolson.

——. 1980. 'Gnostic and Orthodox Views of Christ's Passion: Paradigms for the Christian's Response to Persecution?' In *The Rediscovery of Gnosticism: Proceedings of the International Conference on Gnosticism at Yale, New Haven, Connecticut, March 28–31, 1978*, ed. Bentley Layton, 262–88. Leiden: Brill.

Painter, John. 1997. *Just James: The Brother of Jesus in History and Tradition*. Columbia, S. C.: U. of South Carolina Press.

Pannenberg, Wolfhart. 1968. *Jesus: God and Man*. Philadelphia: Westminster.

——. 1970. *Basic Questions in Theology: Collected Essays*. Philadelphia: Westminster; London: SCM Press.

——. 1991-8 [1988–93]. *Systematic Theology*. 3 vols. Grand Rapids: Eerdmans; Edinburgh: T. & T. Clark.

Park, Joseph S. 2000. *Conceptions of Afterlife in Jewish Inscriptions with Special Reference to Pauline Literature*. WUNT 2.121. Tübingen: Mohr-Siebeck.

Parsons, Mikeal C. 1988. 'ΣΑΡΚΙΝΟΣ, ΣΑΡΚΙΚΟΣ In Codices F and G: A Text-Critical Note.' *New Testament Studies* 34:151–5.

Patterson, Stephen J. 1998. *The God of Jesus: The Historical Jesus and the Search for Meaning*. Harrisburg, Pa.: TPI.

——, James Robinson, and Hans-Gebhard Bethge. 1998. *The Fifth Gospel : The Gospel of Thomas Comes of Age.* Harrisburg, Pa.: TPI.

Peel, Malcolm Lee. 1992. 'Resurrection, Treatise on the.' In *ABD* 5:691–2.

——. 1969. *The Epistle to Rheginos: A Valentinian Letter on the Resurrection. Introduction, Translation, Analysis and Exposition.* London: SCM Press.

Pelikan, J. 1961. *The Shape of Death: Life, Death, and Immortality in the Early Fathers.* Nashville: Abingdon Press.

Perkins, Pheme. 1984. *Resurrection: New Testament Witness and Contemporary Reflection.* London: Geoffrey Chapman.

——. 1995. *The Gospel of Mark: Introduction, Commentary, and Reflections.* In *NIB*, 8.507–733.

Perrin, Nicholas. 2002. *Thomas and Tatian: The Relationship Between the Gospel of Thomas and Tatian's Diatessaron.* Academia Biblica 5. Leiden: Brill; Atlanta, Ga.: Scholars Press.

Pesch, R. 1999. *Biblischer Osterglaube.* Neukirchen–Vluyn: Neukirchener Verlag.

Peters, Melvin K. H. 1992. 'Septuagint.' In *ABD* 5:1093–1104.

Peters, Ted. 1993. 'Resurrection: What Kind of Body?' *Ex Auditu* 9:57–76.

Petersen, William L. 1994. *The Diatessaron: Its Creation, Dissemination, Significance, and History in Scholarship.* VCSup 25. Leiden: Brill.

Pfeiffer, R. H. 1949. *History of New Testament Times, with an Introduction to the Apocrypha.* New York: Harper.

Pinnock, Clark H. 1993. 'Salvation by Resurrection.' *Ex Auditu* 9:1–11

Plass, P. 1995. *The Game of Death in Ancient Rome: Arena Sport and Political Suicide.* Madison, Wisc.: University of Wisconsin Press.

Plevnik, Joseph. 1984. 'The Taking up of the Faithful and the Resurrection of the Dead in 1 Thessalonians 4:13–18.' *Catholic Biblical Quarterly* 46:274–83.

Polkinghorne, John. 1994. *Science and Christian Belief: Theological Reflections of a Bottom-up Thinker.* London: SPCK.

Porter, Stanley E. 1999a. 'Resurrection, the Greeks and the New Testament.' In *Resurrection*, eds. Stanley E. Porter, Michael A. Hayes and David Tombs, 52–81. Sheffield: Sheffield Academic Press.

——, Michael A. Hayes, and David Tombs, eds. 1999b. *Resurrection.* JSNTSup 186. Sheffield: Sheffield Academic Press.

Porton, Gary G. 1992. 'Sadducees.' In *ABD* 5:892–5.

Pouderon, B. 1986. 'L'authenticité du traité sur la résurrection attribué à l'apologiste Athénagore.' *Vigilae Christianae* 40:226–44.

Price, Simon R. F. 1984. *Rituals and Power: The Roman Imperial Cult in Asia Minor.* Cambridge: CUP.

——. 1999. *Religions of the Ancient Greeks.* Cambridge: CUP.

Priest, J. 1977. 'Some Reflections on the Assumption of Moses.' *Perspectives in Religious Studies* 4:92–111.

Prigent, Pierre. 1964. *Justin et l'ancien testament: L'argumentation scripturaire du traité de Justin contre toutes les hérésies comme source principale du Dialogue avec Trypho et de la Première Apologie.* Paris: Librarie Lecoffre.

Puech, É. 1990. 'Ben Sira 48:11 et la Résurrection.' In *Of Scribes and Scrolls. Studies on the Hebrew Bible, Intertestamental Judaism, and Christian Origins Presented. to John Strugnell on the Occasion of His Sixtieth Birthday*, eds. H. Attridge, J. J. Collins and T. H. Tobin, 81–9. Lanham, Md.: U. P. of America.

——. 1993. *La croyance des Esséniens en la vie future: immortalité, résurrection, vie éternelle? Histoire d'une croyance dans le Judaïsme ancien.* 2 vols. Paris: Cerf.

Quasten, J. 1950. *Patrology.* Vol. 1, *The Beginnings of Patristic Literature.* Utrecht: Spectrum, 1950.

Rahmani, L. Y. 1981/2. 'Ancient Jerusalem's Funerary Customs and Tombs.' *Biblical Archaeologist* 44, 45:171–7; 229–35; 43–53; 107–119.

Rahner, Karl. 1961. *Theological Investigations*. Vol. 1, *God, Christ, Mary and Grace*. Baltimore: Helicon Press.

Reardon, B. P., ed. 1989. *Collected Ancient Greek Novels*. Berkeley: U. of California Press.

———. 1991. *The Form of the Greek Romance*. Princeton, N. J.: Princeton U. P.

Rebell, Walter. 1992. *Neutestamentliche Apokryphen und apostolischen Väter*. Munich: Chr. Kaiser.

Reese, James M. 1970. *Hellenistic Influence on the Book of Wisdom and Its Consequences*. AnBib 41. Rome: Biblical Institute Press.

Rese, M. 2002. 'Exegetische Anmerkungern zu G. Lüdemanns Deutung der Auferstehung Jesu'. In *Resurrection in the New Testament* (FS J. Lambrecht), eds. R. Bieringer, V. Koperski and B. Lataire, 55–71. Leuven: Peeters.

Reumann, J. 2002. 'Resurrection in Philippi and Paul's Letter(s) to the Philippians'. In *Resurrection in the New Testament* (FS J. Lambrecht), eds. R. Bieringer, V. Koperski and B. Lataire, 407–22. Leuven: Peeters.

Richard, Earl J. 1981. 'Polemics, Old Testament, and Theology: A Study of II Cor., III, 1—IV, 6.' *Revue Biblique* 88:340–67.

———. 1995. *First and Second Thessalonians*. SP. Collegeville, Minn.: Liturgical Press.

Richardson, Peter. 1996. *Herod: King of the Jews and Friend of the Romans*. Columbia, S. C.: U. of South Carolina Press.

Riesenfeld, H. 1948. *The Resurrection in Ezekiel XXXVII and in the Dura-Europos Paintings*. Uppsala: Uppsala U. P.

Riley, Gregory. 1995. *Resurrection Reconsidered: Thomas and John in Controversy*. Minneapolis: Fortress.

Robertson, Archibald, and Alfred Plummer. 1914. *A Critical and Exegetical Commentary on the First Epistle of St Paul to the Corinthians*. ICC. Edinburgh: T. & T. Clark.

Robinson, James M., gen. ed. 1977. *The Nag Hammadi Library in English*. San Francisco: Harper & Row.

———. 1979. 'The Discovery of the Nag Hammadi Codices.' *Biblical Archaeologist* 42:206–24.

———. 1982. 'Jesus from Easter to Valentinus (or to the Apostles' Creed).' *Journal of Biblical Literature* 101:5–37.

Robinson, John A. T. 1952. *The Body: A Study in Pauline Theology*. Philadelphia: Westminster.

———. 1979. *Jesus and His Coming: The Emergence of a Doctrine*. London: SCM Press.

Rohde, E. 1925. *Psyche: The Cult of Souls and Belief in Immortality Among the Greeks*. New York, N.Y.: Harcourt Brace.

Rordorf, Willy. 1968. *Sunday: The History of the Day of Rest and Worship in the Earliest Centuries of the Christian Church*. London: SCM Press.

Rowland, Christopher C. 1980. 'The Vision of the Risen Christ in Rev i.13 ff.: The Debt of an Early Christology to an Aspect of Jewish Angelology.' *Journal of Theological Studies* 31:1–11.

———. 1982. *The Open Heaven: A Study of Apocalyptic in Judaism and Early Christianity*. New York: Crossroad.

———. 1985. *Christian Origins: From Messianic Movement to Christian Religion*. London: SPCK; Minneapolis: Augsburg.

———. 1993. 'Interpreting the Resurrection.' In *The Resurrection of Jesus Christ*, ed. P. Avis, 68–84. London: Darton, Longman & Todd.

———. 1998. *The Book of Revelation: Introduction, Commentary, and Reflections*. In *NIB*, 12.501–743.

Rowley, H. H. 1963. *The Relevance of Apocalyptic*. London: Lutterworth.

Rutgers, Leonard V., and Eric M. Meyers, eds. 1997. 'Catacombs.' In *The Oxford Encyclopaedia of Archaeology in the Near East*, 1:434–8. New York/Oxford: OUP.

Saldarini, Anthony J. 1988. *Pharisees, Scribes and Sadducees in Palestinian Society*. Wilmington, Del.: Michael Glazier; Edinburgh: T. & T. Clark.

Sampley, J. P. 2000. *The Second Letter to the Corinthians: Introduction, Commentary, and Reflections*. In *NIB* 11.1–180.

Sanders, E. P. 1977. *Paul and Palestinian Judaism: A Comparison of Patterns of Religion*. Philadelphia: Fortress; London: SCM Press.

——. 1983. 'Jesus and the Sinners.' *Journal for the Study of the New Testament* 19:5–36.

——. 1991. *Paul*. Past Masters. Oxford: OUP.

——. 1992. *Judaism: Practice and Belief, 63 BCE — 66 CE*. London: SCM Press.

——. 1993. *The Historical Figure of Jesus*. London: Penguin.

Sandnes, Olav. 1991. *Paul – One of the Prophets?* WUNT 2.43. Tübingen: Mohr.

Sanford, D. H. 1995. 'Inference to the Best Explanation.' In *Oxford Companion to Philosophy*, 407–08. Oxford: OUP.

Satran, D. 1989. 'Fingernails and Hair: Anatomy and Exegesis in Tertullian.' *Journal of Theological Studies* 40:116–20.

Sawicki, Marianne. 1994. *Seeing the Lord: Resurrection and Early Christian Practices*. Minneapolis: Fortress.

Sawyer, John F. A. 1973. 'Hebrew Words for the Ressurection [*sic*] of the Dead.' *Vetus Testamentum* 23:218–34.

Schillebeeckx, Edward. 1979. *Jesus: An Experiment in Christology*. New York: Seabury Press.

Schlosser, Jacques. 2001. 'Vision, extase et apparition du ressuscité.' In *Résurrection: L'après-mort dans le monde ancien et le Nouveau Testament*, eds. Odette Mainville and Daniel Marguerat, 129–59. Geneva: Labor et Fides; Montreal: Médiaspaul.

——. 2002. 'La résurrection de Jésus d'après la *Prima Petri*'. In *Resurrection in the New Testament* (FS J. Lambrecht), eds. R. Bieringer, V. Koperski and B. Lataire, 441–56. Leuven: Peeters.

Schmidt, B. B. 1994. *Israel's Beneficent Dead: Ancestor Cult and Necromancy in Ancient Israelite Religion and Tradition*. FAT 11. Tübingen: Mohr-Siebeck.

Schneiders, S. 1995. 'The Resurrection of Jesus and Christian Spirituality.' In *Christian Resources of Hope*, ed. M. Junker-Kenny, 81–114. Dublin: Columbia.

Schoedel, William R. 1985. *Ignatius of Antioch. A Commentary on the Letters of Ignatius of Antioch*. Hermeneia. Philadelphia: Fortress.

Schürer, E. 1973–87.*The History of the Jewish People in the Age of Jesus Christ (175 B.C.—A.D. 135)*. Rev. and ed. M. Black, G. Vermes, F. G. B. Millar. 4 vols. Edinburgh: T. & T. Clark.

Schüssler Fiorenza, E. 1993. *Discipleship of Equals*. New York; London: Crossroad; SCM Press.

Schwankl, Otto. 1987. *Die Sadduzäerfrage (Mk 12,18–27 Parr): Eine Exegetisch-Theologische Studie zur Auferstehungserwartung*. BBB 66. Bonn: Athenäum.

Schweizer, E. 1979. 'Resurrection — Fact or Illusion?' *Horizons in Biblical Theology* 1:137–59.

Schwemer, Anna Maria. 2001. 'Der Auferstandene und die Emmausjünger.' In *Auferstehung – Resurrection*, eds. Friedrich Avemarie and Hermann Lichtenberger, 496–117.

Scott, Alan. 1991. *Origen and the Life of the Stars*. Oxford: Clarendon Press.

Scroggs, R. 1966. *The Last Adam*. Oxford: Blackwell.

Segal, Alan F. 1990. *Paul the Convert: The Apostolate and Apostasy of Saul the Pharisee*. New Haven and London: Yale U. P.

——. 1991. 'Jesus, the Revolutionary.' In *Jesus' Jewishness: Exploring the Place of Jesus Within Early Judaism*, ed. James H. Charlesworth, 199–225. New York: Crossroad.

——. 1992. 'Conversion and Messianism: Outline for a New Approach.' In *The Messiah: Developments in Earliest Judaism and Christianity*, ed. James H. Charlesworth, 296–340. Minneapolis: Fortress.

——. 1997. 'Life After Death: The Social Sources.' In *The Resurrection: An Interdisciplinary Symposium on the Resurrection of Jesus*, eds. Stephen T. Davis, Daniel Kendall and Gerald O'Collins, 90–125. Oxford: OUP.

Seitz, Christopher R. 1993. *Isaiah 1—39*. IBC. Louisville: John Knox.

Selby, Peter. 1976. *Look for the Living: The Corporate Nature of Resurrection Faith*. London: SCM Press.

Senior, Donald. 1976. 'The Death of Jesus and the Resurrection of the Holy Ones (Mt 27:51– 53).' *Catholic Biblical Quarterly* 38:312–29.

Singer, S. 1962. *The Authorised Daily Prayer Book of the United Hebrew Congregations of the British Commonwealth of Nations*. London: Eyre and Spottiswood.

Siniscalco, Paolo. 1966. *Ricerche sul "De Resurrectione" di Tertulliano*. Rome: Editrice Studium.

Sleeper, C. E. 1965. 'Pentecost and Resurrection.' *Journal of Biblical Literature* 84:389–99.

Smith, Jonathan Z. 1990. *Drudgery Divine: On the Comparison of Early Christianities and the Religions of Late Antiquity*. London: School of Oriental and African Studies; Chicago: Chicago U. P.

Smith, Morton. 1958. 'The Description of the Essenes in Josephus and the Philosophumena.' *Hebrew Union College Annual* 29:273–313.

——. 1999. 'The Troublemakers.' In *The Cambridge History of Judaism*. eds. William Horbury, W. D. Davies and John Sturdy. Vol. 3, *The Roman Period*, 501–68. Cambridge: CUP.

Söding, T. 2002. 'Erscheinung, Vergebung und Sendung: Joh 21 als Zeugnis entwickelten Osterglaubens'. In *Resurrection in the New Testament* (FS J. Lambrecht), eds. R. Bieringer, V. Koperski and B. Lataire, 207–32. Leuven: Peeters.

Sosa, E., and M. Tooley, eds. 1993. *Causation*. Oxford: OUP.

Soskice, J. M. 1997. 'Resurrection and the New Jerusalem.' In *The Resurrection: An Interdisciplinary Symposium on the Resurrection of Jesus*, eds. Stephen T. Davis, Daniel Kendall and Gerald O'Collins, 41–58. Oxford: OUP.

Sparks, H. F. D., ed. 1984. *The Apocryphal Old Testament*. Oxford: Clarendon Press Press.

Spicer, Paul. 2002. '*Easter Oratorio*: The Composer's Perspective'. In *Sounding the Depths: Theology Through the Arts*, ed. Jeremy Begbie, 179–92. London: SCM Press.

Spronk, Klaus. 1986. *Beatific Afterlife in Ancient Israel and in the Ancient Near East*. AOAT 219. Kevelaer: Butzon & Berker; Neukirchen-Vluyn: Neukirchener Verlag.

Stanley, D. M. 1961. *Christ's Resurrection in Pauline Soteriology*. Rome: Pontifical Biblical Institute Press, 1961.

Stanton, Graham. 1977. '5 Ezra and Matthaean Christianity in the Second Century.' *Journal of Theological Studies* 28:67–83.

——. 1994. 'Early Objections to the Resurrection of Jesus.' In *Resurrection: Essays in Honour of Leslie Houlden*, eds. Stephen Barton and Graham Stanton, 79–94. London: SPCK.

Stark, Rodney. 1996. *The Rise of Christianity: A Sociologist Reconsiders History*. Princeton, N.J.: Princeton U. P.

Stemberger, Günter. 1972. *Der Leib der Auferstehung. Studien zur Anthropologie und Eschatologie des palästinischen Judentums im neutestamentlichen Zeitalter (Ca. 170 v. Chr.–100 n. Chr.).* AnBib 56. Rome: Biblical Institute Press.

——. 1999. 'The Sadducees – Their History and Doctrines.' In *The Cambridge History of Judaism.* eds. William Horbury, W. D. Davies and John Sturdy. Vol. 3, *The Roman Period,* 428–43. Cambridge: CUP.

Stendahl, Krister. 1976. *Paul Among Jews and Gentiles.* Philadelphia: Fortress.

——. 1995. *Final Account: Paul's Letter to the Romans.* Minneapolis: Fortress.

Stephens, Susan A., and John J. Winkler, eds. 1995. *Ancient Greek Novels: The Fragments. Introduction, Text, Translation, and Commentary.* Princeton, N.J.: Princeton U. P.

Strack, H. L., and G. Stemberger. 1991 [1982]. *Introduction to the Talmud and Midrash.* Edinburgh: T. & T. Clark.

Stroumsa, G. G. 1981. 'Le couple de l'ange et de l'esprit: Traditions juives et chrétiennes.' *Revue Biblique* 88:42–61.

Strugnell, J. 1958. 'Flavius Josephus and the Essenes: *Antiquities* xviii.18–22.' *Journal of Biblical Literature* 77:106–15.

Stuhlmacher, Peter. 1993. 'The Resurrection of Jesus and the Resurrection of the Dead.' *Ex Auditu* 9:45–56.

Swinburne, Richard. 1997. 'Evidence for the Resurrection.' In *The Resurrection: An Interdisciplinary Symposium on the Resurrection of Jesus,* eds. Stephen T. Davis, Daniel Kendall and Gerald O'Colllins, 191–212. Oxford: OUP.

Tabor, James D. 1989. '"Returning to Divinity": Josephus's Portrayal of the Disappearences of Enoch, Elijah, and Moses.' *Journal of Biblical Literature* 108:225–38.

Tan, Kim Huat. 1997. *The Zion Traditions and the Aims of Jesus.* SNTSMS 91. Cambridge: CUP.

Tavard, George H. 2000. *The Starting Point of Calvin's Theology.* Grand Rapids: Eerdmans.

Thagard, P. 1978. 'The Best Explanation: Criterion for Theory Choice.' *Journal of Philosophy* 75:76–92.

Theissen, Gerd, and Annette Merz. 1998. *The Historical Jesus: A Comprehensive Guide.* London: SCM Press.

——. 1999. *A Theory of Primitive Christian Religion.* London: SCM Press.

Thielman, Frank. 1989. *From Plight to Solution: A Jewish Framework for Understanding Paul's View of the Law in Galatians and Romans.* NovTSup, vol. 61. Leiden: Brill.

Thiering, Barbara. 1992. *Jesus the Man: A New Interpretation from the Dead Sea Scrolls.* New York: Doubleday.

Thiselton, Anthony C. 1978. 'Realized Eschatology at Corinth.' *New Testament Studies* 24:510–26.

——. 1992. *New Horizons in Hermeneutics: The Theory and Practice of Transforming Biblical Reading.* London/New York: Harper Collins.

——. 2000. *The First Epistle to the Corinthians: A Commentary on the Greek Text.* NIGTC. Grand Rapids: Eerdmans.

Thrall, Margaret E. 1994–2000. *A Critical and Exegetical Commentary on the Second Epistle to the Corinthians.* 2 vols. ICC. Edinburgh: T. & T. Clark.

——. 2002. 'Paul's Understanding of Continuity between the Present Life and the Life of the Resurrection.' In *Resurrection in the New Testament* (FS J. Lambrecht), eds. R. Bieringer, V. Koperski and B. Lataire, 283–300. Leuven: Peeters.

Tomson, P. J. 2002. '"Death, Where is thy Victory?" Paul's Theology in the Twinkling of an Eye.' In *Resurrection in the New Testament* (FS J. Lambrecht), eds. R. Bieringer, V. Koperski and B. Lataire, 357–86. Leuven: Peeters.

Torrance, Thomas F. 1976. *Space, Time and Resurrection*. Edinburgh: Handsel Press.
Toynbee, J. M. C. 1971. *Death and Burial in the Roman World*. Baltimore: Johns Hopkins U. P.
Trites, A. A. 1977. *The New Testament Concept of Witness*. Cambridge: CUP.
Troeltsch, Ernst. 1912–25. *Gesammelte Schriften*. 4 vols. Tübingen: Mohr.
Tromp, Nicholas J. 1969. *Primitive Conceptions of Death and the Nether World in the Old Testament*. Biblica et Orientalia 21. Rome: Pontifical Biblical Institute Press.
Troxel, Ronald L. 2002. 'Matt 27.51–4 Reconsidered: Its Role in the Passion Narrative, Meaning and Origin.' *New Testament Studies* 48:30–47.
Tuckett, C. M. 1996. *Q and the History of Early Christianity: Studies on Q*. Edinburgh: T. & T. Clark.
Updike, John. 1964. *Telephone Poles and Other Poems*. New York: Alfred A. Knopf.
Urbach, E. E. 1987. *The Sages: Their Concepts and Beliefs*. Cambridge, Mass./London: Harvard U. P.
van der Horst, P. W. 1992. *Ancient Jewish Epitaphs*. Kampen: Kok Pharos.
VanderKam, James C. 1984. *Enoch and the Growth of an Apocalyptic Tradition*. CBQMS 16. Washington, D.C.: Catholic Biblical Association of America.
——. 1995. *Enoch: A Man for All Generations*. Columbia, S.C.: U. of South Carolina Press.
——. 2001. *An Introduction to Early Judaism*. Grand Rapids: Eerdmans.
Van Eijk, A. H. C. 1971. 'The Gospel of Philip and Clement of Alexandria: Gnostic and Ecclesiastical Theology on the Resurrection and the Eucharist.' *Vigiliae Christianae* 25:94–120.
——. 1974. *La résurrection des morts chez les pères apostoliques*. Paris: Beauchesne, 1974.
Verheyden, J. 2002. 'Silent Witnesses: Mary Magdalene and the Women at the Tomb in the Gospel of Peter'. In *Resurrection in the New Testament* (FS J. Lambrecht), eds. R. Bieringer, V. Koperski and B. Lataire, 457–82. Leuven: Peeters.
Vermes, Geza. 1973. *Jesus the Jew: A Historian's Reading of the Gospels*. London: Collins.
——. 2000. *The Changing Faces of Jesus*. London: Penguin.
Vermeule, C. C. 1979. *Aspects of Death in Early Greek Art and Pottery*. Berkeley, Ca.: U. of California Press.
Via, Dan O. 2002. *What is New Testament Theology?* Minneapolis: Fortress.
Viviano, Benedict, and Justin Taylor. 1992. 'Sadducees, Angels, and Resurrection (Acts 23:8–9).' *Journal of Biblical Literature* 111:496–8.
von Rad, Gerhard. 1962–5. *Old Testament Theology*. 2 vols. New York: Harper & Row; Edinburgh: Oliver and Boyd.
Vos, J. S. 1999. 'Argumentation und Situation in 1Kor. 15.' *Novum Testamentum* 41:313–33.
——. 2002. 'Die Schattenseite der Auferstehung im Evangelium des Paulus'. In *Resurrection in the New Testament* (FS J. Lambrecht), eds. R. Bieringer, V. Koperski and B. Lataire, 301–13. Leuven: Peeters.
Walker, P. W. L. 1999. *The Weekend That Changed the World: The Mystery of Jerusalem's Empty Tomb*. London: Marshall Pickering.
Wall, Robert W. 2002. *The Acts of the Apostles. Introduction, Commentary, and Reflections*. In *NIB* 10:1–368.
Warmington, B. H. 1969. *Nero: Reality and Legend*. London: Chatto & Windus.
Warnock, G. J. 1995. 'Berkeley, George.' In *The Oxford Companion to Philosophy*, ed. Ted Honderich, 89–92. Oxford: OUP.
Wartofsky, M. 1977. *Feuerbach*. Cambridge: CUP.

Watson, Francis. 1994. '"He is not Here": Towards a Theology of the Empty Tomb.' In *Resurrection: Essays in Honour of Leslie Houlden*, eds. Stephen Barton and Graham Stanton, 95–107. London: SPCK.

Watts, Rikki E. 1997. *Isaiah's New Exodus and Mark*. WUNT 2.88. Tübingen: Mohr-Siebeck.

Wedderburn, A. J. M. 1999. *Beyond Resurrection*. London: SCM Press.

Weiser, Artur. 1962. *The Psalms*. OTL. London: SCM Press.

Weitzmann, K., ed. 1979. *Age of Spirituality: Late Antique and Early Christian Art, Third to Seventh Century. Catalogue of the Exhibition at the Museum of Art, November 13, 1977 through February 12, 1978*. New York: Metropolitan Museum of Art and Princeton U. P.

Wenham, David. 1987. 'Being "Found" on the Last Day: New Light on 2 Peter 3.10 and 2 Corinthians 5.3.' *New Testament Studies* 33:477–9.

Wenham, John W. 1981. 'When Were the Saints Raised?' *Journal of Theological Studies* 32:150–52.

——. 1984. *Easter Enigma*. Exeter: Paternoster.

Weren, W. J. C. 2002. '"His Disciples Stole Him Away" (Mt 28, 13): A Rival Interpretation of Jesus' Resurrection'. In *Resurrection in the New Testament* (FS J. Lambrecht), eds. R. Bieringer, V. Koperski and B. Lataire, 147–63. Leuven: Peeters.

West, M. L. 1971. *Early Greek Philosophy and the Orient*. Oxford: OUP.

Westcott, B. F. 1903. *The Gospel According to St. John*. London: John Murray.

Westfall, Cynthia Long. 1999. 'The Relationship Between the Resurrection, the Proclamation to the Spirits in Prison and Baptismal Regeneration: 1 Peter 3.19–22.' In *Resurrection*, ed. Stanley E. Porter, Michael A. Hayms and David Tombs, 106–35. Sheffield: Sheffield Academic Press.

Whanger, Mary, and Alan Whanger. 1998. *The Shroud of Turin: An Adventure of Discovery*. Franklin, Tenn.: Providence House Publishers.

Wiesner, J. 1938. *Grab und Jenseits: Untersuchungen im ägäischen Raum zur Bronzezeit und frühen Eisenzeit*. Berlin: Töpelmann.

Wilckens, Ulrich. 1968. 'The Tradition-History of the Resurrection of Jesus.' In *The Significance of the Message of the Resurrection for Faith in Jesus Christ*, ed. C. F. D. Moule, 51–76. London: SCM Press.

——. 1977. *Resurrection: Biblical Testimony to the Resurrection: An Historical Examination and Explanation*. Edinburgh: The Saint Andrew Press.

Wilde, Oscar. 1966 [1948]. *Complete Works of Oscar Wilde*. Introd. V. Holland. London and Glasgow: Collins.

Wiles, Maurice. 1994. 'A Naked Pillar of Rock.' In *Resurrection. Essays in Honour of Leslie Houlden*, eds. Stephen Barton and Graham Stanton, 116–27. London: SPCK.

Williams, Bernard A. O. 2002. *Truth and Truthfulness: An Essay in Genealogy*. Princeton, N. J. and Oxford: Princeton U. P.

Williams, Margaret. 1999. 'The Contribution of Jewish Inscriptions to the Study of Judaism.' In *The Cambridge History of Judaism*. eds. William Horbury, W. D. Davies and John Sturdy. Vol. 3, *The Roman Period*, Cambridge: CUP.

Williams, Michael A. 1996. *Rethinking 'Gnosticism': An Argument for Dismantling a Dubious Category*. Princeton, N.J.: Princeton U. P.

Williams, Rowan D. 1982. *Resurrection: Interpreting the Easter Gospel*. London: Darton, Longman & Todd.

——. 2000. *On Christian Theology*. Oxford: Blackwell.

Williams, Trevor S. M. 1998. 'The Trouble with the Resurrection.' In *Understanding, Studying and Reading: New Testament Essays in Honour of John Ashton*, eds. Christoper Rowland and Crispin H. T. Fletcher-Louis, 219–35. Sheffield: Sheffield Academic Press.

Williamson, H. G. M. 1998. *Variations on a Theme: King, Messiah and Servant in the Book of Isaiah*. Carlisle: Paternoster Press.

Winkler, J. J. 1980. 'Lollianos and the Desperadoes.' *Journal of Hellenic Studies* 100:155–81.

Winston, David. 1979. *The Wisdom of Solomon*. AB 43. New York: Doubleday.

Winter, Bruce W. 1993. 'Official Proceedings and the Forensic Speeches in Acts 24—26.' In *The Book of Acts in Its First Century Setting*. Vol. 1, *The Book of Acts in Its Ancient Literary Setting*, eds. Bruce W. Winter and Andrew D. Clarke, 305–36. Grand Rapids: Eerdmans; Carlisle: Paternoster.

———. 2001. *After Paul Left Corinth: The Influence of Secular Ethics and Social Change*. Grand Rapids: Eeerdmans.

Wise, Michael O. 1999. *The First Messiah: Investigating the Savior Before Christ*. San Francisco: HarperSanFrancisco.

Wissman, H., G. Stemberger, P. Hoffman, et al. 1979. 'Auferstehung.' In *Theologische Realenzyklopädie*, 4:442–575. Berlin: De Gruyter.

Witherington III, Ben. 1995. *Conflict and Community in Corinth: A Socio-Rhetorical Commentary on 1 and 2 Corinthians*. Grand Rapids: Eerdmans.

———. 1998a. *The Acts of the Apostles: A Socio-Rhetorical Commentary*. Grand Rapids; Carlisle: Paternoster.

———. 1998b. *Grace in Galatia: A Commentary on St Paul's Letter to the Galatians*. Edinburgh: T. & T. Clark.

Wolff, H. W. 1974. *Hosea*. Philadelphia: Fortress.

Wolters, Al. 1987. 'Worldview and Textual Criticism in 2 Peter 3:10.' *Westminster Theological Journal* 49:405–13.

Wright, David F. 1984. 'Apocryphal Gospels: The "Unknown Gospel" (Pap. Egerton 2) and the *Gospel of Peter*.' In *Gospel Perspectives*. Vol. 5, *The Jesus Tradition Outside the Gospels*, ed. D. Wenham. 207–32. Sheffield: JSOT Press.

———. 1986. 'Apologetic and Apocalyptic: The Miraculous in the Gospel of Peter.' In *Gospel Perspectives*. Vol 6, *The Miracles of Jesus*, 401–18. Sheffield: JSOT Press.

Wright, N. T. 1986. *The Epistles of Paul to the Colossians and to Philemon* (= *Colossians*). TNTC. Leicester: IVP; Grand Rapids: Eerdmans.

———. 1991. *The Climax of the Covenant: Christ and the Law in Pauline Theology* (= *Climax*). Edinburgh: T. & T. Clark; Minneapolis: Fortress.

———. 1992. *The New Testament and the People of God* (*Christian Origins and the Question of God* vol. 1) (= *NTPG*). London: SPCK; Minneapolis: Fortress.

———. 1993. 'On Becoming the Righteousness of God: 2 Corinthians 5:21' (= 'Becoming the Righteousness'). In *Pauline Theology*. Volume 2, *1 & 2 Corinthians*, ed. David M. Hay, 200–08. Minneapolis: Fortress.

———. 1994. 'Gospel and Theology in Galatians' (= 'Gospel and Theology'). In *Gospel in Paul: Studies on Corinthians, Galatians and Romans for Richard N. Longenecker*, eds. L. Ann Jervis and Peter Richardson, 222–39. Sheffield: Sheffield Academic Press.

———. 1996a. *Jesus and the Victory of God* (*Christian Origins and the Question of God* vol. 2) (= *JVG*). London: SPCK; Minneapolis: Fortress.

———. 1996. 'The Law in Romans 2' (= 'Law'). In *Paul and the Mosaic Law*, ed. J. D. G. Dunn, 131–50. Tübingen: Mohr.

———. 1997. *For All God's Worth* (= *God's Worth*). London: SPCK; Grand Rapids: Eerdmans.

———. 1999. 'In Grateful Dialogue: A Response' (= 'Grateful Response'). In *Jesus and the Restoration of Israel: A Critical Assessment of N. T. Wright's* Jesus and the Victory of God, ed. Carey C. Newman, 244–77. Downers Grove, Ill.: IVP.

——. 1999. 'New Exodus, New Inheritance: the Narrative Substructure of Romans 3—8' (= 'Exodus'), in *Romans and the People of God: Essays in Honor of Gordon D. Fee on the Occasion of his 65th Birthday*, ed. S. K. Soderlund and N. T. Wright (Grand Rapids: Eerdmans, 1999), 26–35.

——. 1999. *The Millennium Myth*. Louisville: Westminster; London: SPCK.

——. 2000. 'Paul's Gospel and Caesar's Empire' (= 'Paul's Gospel'). In *Paul and Politics: Ekklesia, Israel, Imperium, Interpretation. Essays in Honor of Krister Stendahl*, ed. Richard A. Horsley, 160–83. Harrisburg, Pa.: TPI.

——. 2000. 'A New Birth?' review article of J. D. Crossan's *The Birth of Christianity*. In *Scottish Journal of Theology* 53:72–91

——. 2000. 'Resurrection in Q?'. In *Christology, Controversy and Community: New Testament Essays in Honour of David R. Catchpole*, ed. D. G. Horrell and C. M. Tuckett, 85–97. Leiden: Brill.

——. 2002. *The Letter to the Romans: Introduction, Commentary and Reflections* (= *Romans*). In *NIB* 10.393–770.

——. 2002. 'Resurrection: From Theology to Music and Back Again,' (= 'From Theology to Music'). In *Sounding the Depths: Theology Through the Arts*, ed. J. Begbie, 193–202. London: SCM Press.

——. 2002. 'Paul and Caesar: A New Reading of Romans' (= 'Paul and Caesar'). In *A Royal Priesthood. The Use of the Bible Ethically and Politically*, ed. C. Bartholemew, 173–93. Carlisle: Paternoster.

——. 2002. 'Jesus' Resurrection and Christian Origins,' in *Gregorianum* 83/4:615–635.

——. 2002. 'Coming Home to St Paul? Reading Romans a Hundred Years after Charles Gore'. *Scottish Journal of Theology* 55:392–407

Xella, P. 1995. 'Death and the Afterlife in Canaanite and Hebrew Thought.' In *Civilisations of the Ancient Near East*, eds. J. M. Sasson, J. Baines, G. Beckman, and K. S. Rubinson, 2059–70. New York: Macmillan.

Yamauchi, E. M. 1965. 'Tammuz and the Bible.' *Journal of Biblical Literature* 84:283–90.

——. 1998. 'Life, Death and the Afterlife in the Ancient Near East.' In *Life in the Face of Death: The Resurrection Message of the New Testament*, ed. Richard N. Longenecker, 21–50. Grand Rapids: Eerdmans.

Zanker, Paul. 1988. *The Power of Images in the Age of Augustus*. Ann Arbor, Mich.: U. of Michigan Press.

Zeller, D. 2002. 'Erscheinungen Verstorbener im griechisch-römischen Bereich'. In *Resurrection in the New Testament* (FS J. Lambrecht), eds. R. Bieringer, V. Koperski and B. Lataire, 1–19. Leuven: Peeters.

Zimmerli, Walther. 1971 [1968]. *Man and His Hope in the Old Testament*. Naperville, Ill.: Allenson.

INDEX OF ANCIENT SOURCES

major discussions are highlighted in **bold type**

2. Apocrypha

4. Qumran

11. Persian Texts

12. Egyptian Texts

INDEX OF MODERN AUTHORS

INDEX OF SELECTED TOPICS

Nb. since much of the book is expository,
many topics are best tracked through their occurrences in key texts,
for which see the Index of biblical and other references above

Abraham, 100, 145, 230, 255, 424f., 427, 430,
    438, 457; covenant with, 246; family of,
    246; faith in life-giving God, 246f., 457f.
'Abduction' (inference to the best explana-
    tion), 716
Achilles, 39f., 44f., 53, 55, 67, 71
Acts, motives for writing, 653
Adam, 228, 250, 254, 333f.; 'final Adam',
    341; Adam-Christology, 394
Aeneas, 43
Agrippa II, 390
Akiba, 192, 197
Alcestis, 65–8, 82
Alexander the Great, 228
Analogy, principle of in history, 16–18;
Ananias, sent to Saul, 389f.
Ancient Mariner, The Rime of the, 298
Andrew, 499
Angel, in Mark's empty tomb story, 628f.
Angels, Sadducean denial of, 132f., dead
    become equal to, 145, 421f., 492; at the
    tomb in John, 668
Antigonus of Soko, 192
Apocalyptic, as context for resurrection,
    153–62, 333–8; but not in 2 Pet. and
    Jude, 462
apokatastasis, in Origen, 518f.
Apollo, 33, 66–8
Apollonius, 74–6
Apollos, 284, 286
Apologists, task of, 500
'Appearing', *see* Parousia
Arabia, Paul's visit to, 377
Aristotle, 53
Aseneth, 392
Ascension, in NH texts, 545; in Ac. 1, 653,
    654–6; problems of understanding
    within modernism, 655f.; political sig-
    nificance of, 656
Asclepius, 55, 507, 522f.
Astrabacus, as phantom, 63
'Astral Immortality', 50, 57–60, 110–12,
    344–6

Augustus, 700, 710
Awe and trembling, not familiar among histor-
    ical critics, 606

Baal, 126f.
Babel, tower of, 230
Bach, J. S., 255
Baptism, 251, 467; for the dead, 338f.; in *Gos.
    Phil.*, 542f.; in Mt., 644f.
Bar-Giora, death of, 558, 705; possible Mes-
    siahship of, 559
Bar-Kochba: revolt and death, 558, 705; set-
    ting for *Apoc. Pet.*, 497
Barnabas, 389
Beethoven, L. van, 418
Beloved Disciple, 663f.; race with Peter, 663f.;
    significance, 675f.
Berenice, 390
Body, importance of in Paul, 287–90; con-
    tinuity of, 288–90, 293, 370; discounted
    in gnostic texts, 535–51
Brutus, 170
Burial customs, ancient Jewish, 90f.; sec-
    ondary burials, 90f.; no question of sec-
    ondary burial for Jesus, 707f.; burial
    pref. to cremation by early church, 509,
    579; non-use of flowers, 509
Burial of Jesus, 321

Caecilius, 508
Caesar, divinization of, *see* Emperor; lord and
    saviour, 569f.; clash of Christ and,
    225–36, 568–70, 728f., 731f.; taxes for,
    426; avoidance of conflict with in
    gnostic texts, 549f.
Cambyses, son of Cyrus, 33
Canaanite worship, 126
Cannibalism, Apologists rebut charge of, 504
Canterbury, Archbishop of, xxi
Caravaggio, 375f., 391, 396
Celsus, 521–7
Cerinthus, 499
Charon, underworld ferryman, 38

Scipio's dream, 59f.
Scriptures, 'in accordance with', 320f.; use of in *1 Clem*, 482f.
Sea, abolished, 473
'Second death', 471
'Secret Mark', 623
Seleucus, King of Syria, 390f.
Seneca, 54f., 57, 82; lampooning Claudius, 57
Septuagint, and resurrection, 147–50; as read by Christians, 149
Servant of YHWH, in Isaiah, 116; in Paul, 234
Sexual ethics and resurrection, in Paul, 286–90
Shakespeare, W., 63, 66, 96
Shammaites, 195f.
Shekinah, in Paul, 256
Sheol, 87–90, and ch. 3 *passim*; deliverance from? 103f., 108, 118, 156; 548
Shooting at the sun, 11f., 736–8
Sicarii, 179f.
Signs, in John, 440f., 668f.
Simeon, 435
Simon Magus, 499
'Sleep', as metaphor for death, 108f.
Socrates, 51–3, 55, 82
Solomon, 433
soma/sema pun, 145
'Son of god', meanings of, 719–23, 723–31
Soul, in Plato, 48–52; compared with Homer, 48f.; in Judaism, 140–2; in Wis., 172f.; in Paul, 282–4, 346; in popular philosophy, 314f.; in 1 Pet., 465f.; opposed to body in *Diognetus*, 493; in Athenagoras, 505f.; in Tertullian, 514
Spirit, Sadducean denial of, 132; *see also* Holy Spirit
'Spiritual body' in Paul, 161, 277, 282, 346, 347–56 *passim*; in Origen, 520f.; in *Gos. Sav*., 546f.
Spiritual gifts, 295f.
Stephen, stoning of, 391
Stoicism, 52, 54, 177, 463, 502, 525
Stories in early Christianity, 581
Suffering, 300, 305–7, 339f., 361f.
Suicide, ancient attitudes towards, 46

Temple, as theme in John, 671f.; water flowing from, 671
Theseus, 69, 69, 521
'The Way' as title for early Christianity, 556

'Third day', on the, 321f., 409, 440,
Thomas, 499, 532, 572, 605f., 663f., 662f., 677, 715; point of confession, 677f., relation to hypothetical 'Thomas Christians', 678; medieval painting of T. in Westminster Abbey, 715
Thomas, R. S., 616
Tiberius, 724
Timothy, 228f.; *see also* in Biblical Index
Titus, sharing Vespasian's triumph, 558
Titus' Arch, 558
Tombs, veneration of, 487f.; hypothetical but unlikely veneration of Jesus' tomb, 701–3
Transfiguration, 414f., 524; reinterpr. in gnosticism, 540f.; story not like Easter stories, 604
Transformation of body, in Paul, 264f., 273, 356f., 477; in Origen, 519, 524f.; in gospels, 696
Transmigration of souls, 77–9; in Josephus? 176–8; half right, half wrong, in Tertull., 511; Origin against Celsus on, 526
'Transphysicality', 477, 606f., 612, 678f.
Tribute penny, 724
Turin Shroud, xvii

Valentinians, 512, 532, 539–41, 547
Vespasian, 55; triumph in Rome, 558
Visions, 323

Water of life, 475
Weakness, Paul's theology of, 307–9
Wicked, resurrection of?, 194, 442, 478
Witnesses of resurrection, 317f., 322–6
Women at tomb, 607f.; not legal witnesses, 607f.
Worldview, early Christian, 582; different from NH, 582f.; as generating meaning, 719–23

YHWH, Day of, 102; faithfulness of, 103; as basis of hope, 107f., 117; justice of as basis for resurrection, 195, 198; attributes of when active in world, 577

Zeus, tomb of (in Crete), 522
Zion-oracles, 100–02
Zoroastrianism, 124f., 127